THE COOKBOOK AMERICA HAS TURNED TO FOR NEARLY A CENTURY

Since 1896, when Fannie Merritt Farmer published the first *Boston Cooking School Cook Book*, it has been the culinary bible for generations of American cooks. Over the years, *The Fannie Farmer Cookbook*, as it came to be called, has been periodically updated and has become a perennial classic.

Gifted chef, food columnist, and author Marion Cunningham edited the first complete revision of this wonderful cookbook in the 1980s. Now she brings a lifetime of skill and her expert knowledge of American tastes in the 1990s to this expanded edition of *The Fannie Farmer Cookbook*.

Its impressive 1,990 recipes include not only Old-Fashioned Beef Stew, New England Clam Chowder, Chicken Jambalaya, Gingerbread, and Apple Pie but Crudités with Aïoli, Enchiladas with Chicken and Green Sauce, Springtime Shrimp with Cashews, Crusty French Bread, Tuscan Bean and Tuna Salad, Turkey Breast with Sage Stuffing, and hundreds of other luscious desserts, warm breakfast rolls, innovative appetizers, and irresistible entrées you and your family will savor for years to come.

BANTAM LIBRARY OF CULINARY ARTS by Jill Norman
BETTER HOMES & GARDENS NEW COOKBOOK
BETTY CROCKER'S COOKBOOK (revised 6th edition)
THE BRILLIANT BEAN by Sally Stone and Martin Stone
THE COMPLEAT I HATE TO COOK BOOK by Peg Bracken
COOKING WITHOUT A GRAIN OF SALT by Elma W. Bagg
CROCKERY COOKERY by Mable Hoffman
FIELDS OF GREENS by Annie Somerville
THE FRENCH CHEF COOKBOOK by Julia Child
THE GOURMET GAZELLE COOKBOOK by Ellen Brown
THE GREENS COOKBOOK by Edward Espe Brown and Deborah
    Madison
THE JOSLIN DIABETES GOURMET COOKBOOK by Bonnie
    Saunders Polin and Frances Towner Giedt
MEDITERRANEAN LIGHT by Martha Rose Shulman
MOMMY MADE by Martha and David Kimmel
RECIPES FOR DIABETICS (revised and updated edition) by Billie
    Little
THE SAVORY WAY by Deborah Madison
SPLENDID SOUPS by James Peterson

THE
FANNIE FARMER
COOKBOOK

Thirteenth Edition

by Marion Cunningham

Illustrated by Lauren Jarrett

BANTAM BOOKS

NEW YORK · TORONTO · LONDON · SYDNEY · AUCKLAND

*This edition contains the complete text
of the original hardcover edition.*
NOT ONE WORD HAS BEEN OMITTED.

THE FANNIE FARMER COOKBOOK: REVISED 13TH EDITION
*A Bantam Book / published by arrangement with
Alfred A. Knopf, Inc.*

PUBLISHING HISTORY
Published originally in 1896 under the title The Boston Cooking-
School Cook Book *by Fannie Merritt Farmer.*
FANNIE FARMER *is a registered trademark owned by Fanny Farmer
Candy Shops, Inc., and used by Alfred A. Knopf, Inc., under license
from Fanny Farmer Candy Shops, Inc.
Knopf edition published September 1979
A Special Fall 1979 offering (Alternate) and a Main Selection
of Book-of-the-Month Club.
A Main Selection of Horchow Book Society and Meredith Book Club.
An Alternate Selection of Nostalgia Book Club; Readers' Subscription Book
Club; Scholastic Book Club; and Times Mirror "Woman's How-To"
Book Club.
Serialized in* Woman's Day *October 1979 and January 1980;* Cuisine;
Family Circle; Self *magazine; and* Vogue.
*Bantam edition / September 1983.
Bantam revised edition / August 1994*

*All rights reserved under International and Pan-American
Copyright Conventions.
Copyright 1906, 1912, 1914 by Fannie Merritt Farmer. Copyright 1915,
1918, 1923 by Cora D. Perkins. Copyright 1930, 1933, 1934, 1936,
1940, 1941, 1942, 1943, 1946, 1951, © 1959, 1962, 1964, 1965 by
Dexter Perkins Corp.
Copyright © 1979, 1990 by Fannie Farmer Cookbook Corporation.
Cover art by Lauren Jarrett, courtesy of Alfred A. Knopf, Inc.
No part of this book may be reproduced or transmitted
in any form or by any means, electronic or mechanical,
including photocopying, recording, or by any information
storage and retrieval system, without permission in writing
from the publisher.
For information address: Alfred A. Knopf, Inc.,
201 East 50th Street, New York, N.Y. 10022.*

ISBN 0-553-56881-7

Published simultaneously in the United States and Canada

*Bantam Books are published by Bantam Books, a division of Bantam
Doubleday Dell Publishing Group, Inc. Its trademark, consisting of the
words "Bantam Books" and the portrayal of a rooster, is Registered in U.S.
Patent and Trademark Office and in other countries. Marca Registrada.
Bantam Books, 1540 Broadway, New York, New York 10036.*

PRINTED IN THE UNITED STATES OF AMERICA

OPM 10 9

To the home cooks of America,

young and old

CONTENTS

PREFACE TO
THE THIRTEENTH EDITION

Today, more than ever, I sense a hankering for home cooking, for a personal connection to our food, despite all the statistics thrown at us that no one is cooking at home anymore. What with our busy, complicated, high-tech lives, there seems to be a yearning to be in closer touch with a simpler, more natural world. Why else would there be such a warm and enthusiastic response to the hundreds of farmers' markets that have sprung up all over the country? People are discovering the pleasures of touching and smelling and even tasting the fresh produce as they shop. We are enjoying the opportunity to talk to the farmers who grow the food and to share recipes with one another. We are reminded of a world we have almost lost. And the recognition makes us realize how precious it is.

Part of that yearning is an unconscious sense of the loss of a family center. Too many families seldom sit down together; it's gobble and go, eating food on the run, reheating it in relays in the microwave as one dashes off to a committee meeting, another to basketball practice. As a result, we are losing an important value. Food is more than fodder. It is an act of giving and receiving because the experience at table is a communal sharing; talk begins to flow, feelings are expressed, and a sense of well-being takes over.

Because so many young people have never been exposed to cooking, they imagine it to be more difficult and intimidating than it really is. The truth is it's far harder to learn to drive a car than it is to cook. What I hope to do is to lure you into the kitchen and show you how easy it is to make a simple meal—and how exciting the results can be. It's contagious. The more you accomplish, the more you'll want to do. Right away you'll instinctively realize that part of the pleasure is in pleasing others.

For a long time now we have been given a heavy dose of propaganda from the food industry that the working woman (and, of course, man) hasn't got time to cook anymore. But what are we saving all the time for? Another half-hour of television? If you come to enjoy cooking, that half-hour of cooking will become the high point of your day, as relaxing as swinging in a hammock, after long hours at work.

In addition, in the last decade particularly, we have been made increasingly aware of the hazards to our health in our daily diet. Much of this awareness has had a positive influence—and Fannie Farmer herself, who was extremely concerned and knowledgeable for her time about nutrition, would approve. We are cutting down on fats, we are eating more fresh vegetables, we are exercising more, and we are becoming more alert to the potentially harmful chemicals in our foods. But in concentrating so much on the negative aspects of eating, we are making ourselves overly fearful and we are missing the pleasure that a good meal provides. Instead of stringent diets, eliminating almost all fats, all salt, all sugar from our diets, and bloating ourselves with high-fiber products, I believe that the best possible approach for the average person is to eat a wide variety of foods and to eat sensibly, in moderation. That is what the Fannie Farmer for the nineties is all about.

I have gone through every recipe in the last edition, which was a major overhauling and updating of the preceding volumes, and I have often reduced the amount of fat called for in a recipe, giving the option of using vegetable oil only where the quality of a dish isn't compromised. For the most part, I have left the amount of salt up to personal tastes. I have eliminated some old recipes that seemed a bit stodgy for today's tastes. And I have added some 325 new recipes that reflect some of the new ethnic flavors that have become a part of American cooking—such as some lively risottos, polentas, and pastas, and stir-frys. Of course, I can't resist tempting you with some luscious new desserts and several warm-from-the-oven breakfast treats. In addition, I have introduced three new chapters: one on outdoor grilling, with a lot of useful information—and some dandy sauces to boot; one providing an interesting range of vegetarian dishes, for those of us who are eating less meat as well as those who are faced with feeding vegetarian family members and friends; and a chapter on my personal assessment of the pros and cons of the microwave, with about fifty recipes that I have worked out which do particularly well in the microwave (you'll find, as well, notes and comments in every chapter on my experiences with the microwave).

A word about metrics. Since the last edition, when we introduced the metric system as an alternative method of measurement, the U.S. government has abandoned their target date for imposing the system on Americans. Because most cooks in this country simply don't want to adapt to the metric system, which involves weighing ingredients rather than using the familiar cups-and-spoons way of measuring, we have dropped the metric alternative in this edition. It seems merely cumbersome if it's not going to be used.

I hope that these improvements and new recipes will make this thirteenth edition of *The Fannie Farmer Cookbook* even more enticing than its predecessors. Above all, instead of letting strangers cook your food at some quick stop or take-out place, I hope it will persuade you to go into your own kitchen and enjoy the satisfaction of preparing a simple, good meal that you can take the time to savor at your own table.

Marion Cunningham

ACKNOWLEDGMENTS

My great appreciation to:

Joyce McGillis for her discriminating palate, cooking skills, organization, and enthusiasm—her contribution was enormous to this revision, Berkeley, California

John Phillip Carroll, cookbook author, for his expertise on grilling and good grilling recipes, San Francisco, California

Bill Hughes for his helpful ideas and recipe testing, Walnut Creek, California

Marilyn Hanscom for her all-around ability and spirit, Concord, California

Michael Bauer, San Francisco *Chronicle* Food Editor, for his keen advice and help whenever needed, San Francisco, California

Merle Ellis, cookbook author and columnist, for all his expertise, Tiburon, California

Marian Burros, food columnist for *The New York Times*, for her good-sense advice on the impossible subject of food safety.

Sharon Kramis, restaurant consultant and cookbook author, for her great homecooking influence.

Sibella Kraus, produce consultant, San Francisco, California

Jerry DiVecchio, *Sunset* magazine Food Editor, Menlo Park, California

Chris Moore, nutritionist, Eisenhower Memorial Hospital, Rancho Mirage, California

Regina Blancett, master food preserver, University of California Cooperative Extension, Solano County, California

Catherine Boor, staff research associate, University of California, Davis, California

Mary Jo Feeney, director of education for the California Beef Council, Foster City, California

Tony Aiello, butcher for the California Beef Council, Foster City, California

Stephanie Turner, registered dietician

Dr. Jack Sheneman, Food & Drug branch of California Department of Health Services

My deep appreciation to Bill Jorgenson, whose interest and support in my work, and ever-generous friendship, have meant so much.

My deepest respect and appreciation to Judith Jones, my editor, a wonderful teacher and friend.

THE
FANNIE FARMER
COOKBOOK

ও indicates a vegetarian recipe (Note that baked
    goods and desserts have not been flagged).

M≋ denotes microwave information.

*   means that the recipe is a family favorite: ei-
    ther an old one or a new one.

ABOUT THE KITCHEN

What Is Good Everyday Cooking?

Every meal should be a small celebration. If you acknowledge so joyous a fact of life, the pride you take in your efforts in the kitchen won't be confined to company occasions. You'll find it rewarding every day to see that the table is nicely set so that you won't have to jump up all the time to fetch things and disrupt the conversation. Butter should be in a butter dish with its own knife; milk in a pitcher; bottled sauces and condiments, unless the jar is particularly pretty, should be removed from their commercial containers and placed in small bowls with spoons. If your table looks like a hash-house counter, you encourage people to eat accordingly.

The prime attraction, of course, of any meal will always be what you serve, and no amount of table dressing will make up for food that is tasteless and monotonous. But don't let that intimidate you if you are new to cooking. Fortunately, experience is the greatest teacher. The more you cook, the more facile you become—and the more you enjoy it.

There is a tendency nowadays to make a separation between an everyday cook and a so-called gourmet cook. And the simpler cooks seem to stand in awe. Unfortunately *gourmet* has become synonymous with *fancy* and it conjures up the kind of cook who **NOTE** gussies up dishes with rich sauces and goes in for fussy, overworked dishes. We'd all be better off today if we admitted that there is really no such thing as gourmet cooking—there is simply good cooking. It takes more sophistication to know when to serve something simply in its own good juices and more cooking sense—born out of experience—to get perfect results. You get there by trial and error. Experiment when you have the time and inclination but evaluate your own performance critically. Do only what you have the time for, but do it well. And always shop carefully and respect the materials you work with. In other words, care. That is the path to good cooking and we should forget about "gourmet." Above all, don't get

1

discouraged if something doesn't turn out perfectly the first time; too many fledgling cooks give up too easily, failing to realize that there are so many small unpredictable elements that confound even the most experienced cook, such as the variables in flour in different parts of the country, which can affect the outcome of a loaf of bread. So try to be resilient in the face of the unpredictable. Think of cooking as more of an art than a science. You'll have much more fun that way and you'll develop far more confidence than if you just rely on formulas.

Developing Good Cooking Habits

As a first good cooking habit, learn to read recipes through. Think about what you're supposed to be doing and why. Consider the time it will take and give yourself leeway so you don't get flustered. When you're making a complete meal, see if there is anything you can do ahead, like preparing your dessert ahead. Then figure out what parts of the dinner are going to take longest and decide when you should

---

TASTE

The only way to get the most from a recipe is to taste while you are making a dish—that is, taste critically and taste often, at different stages of the cooking. Recipe instructions frequently say "correct seasonings," a most important piece of advice that is usually ignored. What you want to achieve is a balance of flavors. Actually there are only four possible tastes: sweet, sour, salty, and bitter (coffee, for example, is bitter), and you won't encounter all of them necessarily at once. To understand, think of making a glass of lemonade, where the balance between sour (acid lemon juice) and sweet (sugar) is critical. If the balance is right, the drink is pleasing. Of course, other factors are also important: the use of good, fresh lemon juice, a clean glass, and just the right amount of ice so the lemonade is chilled but not diluted.

When you are first learning to cook it is hard to know what ingredients integrate harmoniously and how to balance taste. You learn by doing; practice is the only way to develop that taste judgment. A fledgling artist expects to ruin some canvases in the learning process and knows that not every picture will be a museum piece. The same applies to cooking, so be prepared to have less than perfect results at first. And never stop tasting, no matter how experienced you think you have become. When tasting food, move it around your mouth rather than just tasting with the tip of your tongue so that all your taste buds are working to make the proper evaluation.

start their preparation. If there are unfamiliar techniques involved in a recipe that is new to you, immerse yourself in all the general introductory material first so that you'll understand the principles underlying what you're about to attempt.

A second and almost equally important habit—one that develops with experience—is to start thinking in the market, especially when you're planning dishes that depend on specific fresh produce, like a particular cut of meat, or a kind of fish, certain vegetables and fruits. You will not only cook more economically if you look for what's "on special" or what's in season, but the end result will taste much better when you use ingredients that are at their peak of flavor. Try not to have your heart set on certain items and then pay an exorbitant price for hothouse versions that lack the quality of the real thing. Be flexible in choosing recipes, and be open to alternatives.

It's intelligent and creative to think ahead, both when you're in the market and in your own kitchen. Shop for several interrelated meals at a time and do the more time-consuming preparation when you know you're going to be around the house. For working people, as well as other cooks, it may be easiest to cook a big roast and a large stew on the weekend and then use the cooked meat in various ways on week nights when time is more limited. If you know you are having people for the weekend, pick a few hours earlier in the week to do a lot of the initial cooking so you'll be freer when your guests are around.

Don't let your family be scornful of the word "leftover"—a cook who plans two or three meals at a time deserves an Oscar for efficiency, economy, and imagination. By deliberately planning for leftovers, you'll find that you spend less time and money than if you always shop at the last minute for fresh hamburger, steak, chops. You will also have far more variety in your menus. For instance, even if your family is small, buy a pot roast at least twice the size you think you need for one meal. The next day, using some of the pot roast ground up, you could have a main course of stuffed vegetables such as Green Peppers or Eggplant or Cabbage Leaves, depending on what's in season. And there would undoubtedly be enough left for a Beef-Noodle Casserole at another meal. Leftover meat or poultry is always good in someone's sandwich, particularly if there's a little gravy to drizzle over a crusty roll, or they could go into a taco filling, where a little goes far. Again, if you're planning to roast chicken for Sunday dinner or to sauté some cut-up chicken, get twice what you need. The carcasses and gizzards and necks will go into the soup pot. Later in the week you can have chicken hash, chicken salad, stuffed crêpes with mushrooms, a chicken gumbo, or chicken tetrazzini—any number of imaginative dishes.

By the same token, store away in small containers all the extra bits of vegetables, cooked rice, a little sauce, even pan scrapings. You'll be surprised how useful they can be in soups, omelets, salads, and baked dishes. Think ahead when you're making those crêpes, or a pie dough, or bread, and make a double batch so that you have some ready in the freezer for an impromptu meal.

If you have a well-stocked freezer there is no need to buy a lot of "convenience" foods, which are expensive and usually not very satisfying. What you're doing is furnishing your own kinds of convenience supplies. If, in addition, you keep a well-stocked pantry and freezer, you'll feel a great sense of well-being with everything at your fingertips.

Menu Planning for Family and Friends

Eating is much more a matter of individual taste today, and menus are more flexible. We are less rigidly a meat-and-potatoes society, although there are still plenty of Americans who feel they haven't eaten if that isn't the mainstay of the meal. But whether because of travel, economic necessity, ecological awareness, or vegetarian persuasion, more and more Americans are kicking over old traditions, borrowing from the European pattern of dividing the meal into more than one main course, putting less stress on the size of the meat portion and making it go farther in all sorts of inventive ways. Sometimes you'll find a hearty soup as the centerpiece of a dinner. Or a platter of vegetables when they're at their summer best, accompanied by good wholegrain bread. Pasta dishes can be either a first or a main course; the same goes for salads, fish and seafood, eggs.

A well-planned meal should maintain a pleasing balance between contrasting textures, colors, and tastes. But don't make a fetish of it; just use common sense. If, for example, Smothered Chicken is to be your *pièce de résistance*, you won't want to precede it with a cream soup or an appetizer bathed in a cream sauce; nor would you want a creamy dessert. A white piece of fish with mashed potatoes and white onions, turnips, celery, or cauliflower would be depressingly colorless on the plate and cries out for an accent of fresh green beans or blanched broccoli, or at least some parsley and a few cherry tomatoes to relieve the monotony. If your main course is a stew full of sauce, soup is not your best bet as a starter; choose something with a contrasting texture—a cold vegetable or salad.

A very spicy dish, in general, is best with something soothing; that is why hot curries are traditionally served with small side dishes of cooling cucumbers or bananas, and Mexican tacos, stuffed with peppery meat and sauce, have crisp lettuce, bland avocado, and chill sour cream to quench the fire. Dominant tastes like garlic, tomato sauces, and cabbagy flavors shouldn't be repeated. And watch out for heaviness—again, the tendency today is to want to leave the table pleasingly full but not glutted. Don't try to cap a triumphant rich dinner with an even richer dessert; if that torte or cake is to have star billing, plan accordingly so that it can be genuinely appreciated.

If you serve a vegetable as a first course—sliced tomatoes, for example, or an artichoke, or cold beans vinaigrette—you may not necessarily need a vegetable with your main dish. If you have a lot of gravy with your meat, you'll want something to sop it all up. That something doesn't always have to be potatoes, however; try rice, noodles, pasta, a grain like barley or cracked wheat, or a good homemade bread. If you follow the principle of good texture-color-and-taste contrast, you are very likely to end up with a good nutritional balance, too.

Lunches are generally lighter, of course, as are suppers when you have had dinner in the middle of the day—see menu suggestions at the back of the book. Lunch is always a pleasant, relaxed time to entertain, to set the table prettily, and to make a dish that is a little different. And brunch, that flexible meal that combines breakfast and lunch, is a grand time to indulge with family and friends in all those good old-fashioned breakfast delights like pancakes and sausages, kippered herring, corned beef hash with poached eggs, popovers, and bacon—things we so seldom have time for in the morning during the week.

ENTERTAINING

If you try to please your guests as you would your family, you'll realize that it is not necessary to do something extravagant to impress. Simplicity, using good ingredients well, is usually more impressive than a lot of fancy cooking that is sometimes too much to handle when you are doing everything yourself. Serve dishes that you know you can manage, and plan ahead so that you can enjoy your own company.

Dinner Parties

In planning what to have for a sit-down dinner, much depends on the guests. If you don't know them very well and suspect they may be fairly conservative in their eating habits, stick to a traditional menu: a first course of soup or an appetizer, a meat course (probably a roast) with vegetables and potatoes, and a dessert. If you know your guests love good food, be more experimental. Try special treats on those you know will appreciate them—a dish made with duck or crab or maybe game. Celebrate the seasons with their special bounty. Think seasonally, too—what tastes particularly good in certain kinds of weather, on a stormy winter night or a humid summer evening. If the dinner includes many young people, they may have vegetarian leanings and you will find ideas in our new chapter of non-meat dishes.

NOTE Remember that today many people are less meat-and-potatoes oriented. There is nothing wrong with making a hearty soup with crusty bread the centerpiece of the meal or a kedgeree or a pasta with a platter of cold dressed vegetables (it doesn't always have to be tossed salad).

It is a good idea to plan dishes that don't require too much last-minute attention that will keep you in the kitchen away from your guests. Get as much cooking as possible done before the guests arrive. Decide when you will eat and figure out exactly when each dish should be put in the oven or heated on the stove.

"Complicated" dishes will seem easy if some of the component parts of a recipe are cooked well ahead, such as the making of a sauce, browning the meats, making stuffings. For instance, if you were making Cannelloni, a splendid party dish, you could do the crêpes well ahead (have them with your family the night you make them, stuffed a different way, and freeze an extra batch of crêpes). Have something that requires Tomato Sauce another night—a big bowl of spaghetti and meatballs, perhaps—and make lots of sauce, setting aside the 1½ cups required for the cannelloni (it freezes beautifully). You might even do a double batch of spinach for supper the night before, so that that would be ready, too, or something that requires cream sauce. What you'll have left to do the day of your party then is primarily an assembly job.

Always count on making a little more for guests than you would ordinarily. Offering seconds is a part of hospitality, and a dinner party is an occasion when people may want to indulge more than usual, particularly if your food is good—and it will be. If there are leftovers to be frozen, you'll welcome them eaten some evening when you'd rather not cook.

If you are serving more than nibbles with predinner drinks, choose your appetizers in relation to the rest of the meal; they should fit in with it appropriately and not be so overwhelming that they sate the appetite. Sometimes it's pleasant at a dinner party to serve a real first course in the living room with drinks—a portion of pâté on a plate, for instance, or a small hot tart, or a cup of soup; if your main dish does demand some finishing, having appetizers in this way provides a natural break for you (moreover, you won't have to clear off a course and be away from the table).

While too many different courses may lead to a lot of scurrying and plate clearing, it *is* nice to stretch out a company meal with a pause for a separate salad with a little cheese. There is nothing like lingering at the table when the conversation is good and everyone is enjoying the food and the slow rhythm of eating.

Cocktail Parties and Receptions

See also Appetizers and First Courses (p. 63).

Serve food that you can eat with your fingers at cocktail parties and receptions, so you don't have to bother with plates. The food should be substantial enough to fortify the stomach, especially when cocktails are being served. See suggested foods for cocktail parties and receptions (p. 63).

Since there are usually a few guests who stay on after a cocktail party is over, it's nice to plan for them by having one hot buffet dish, like Lentils and Lamb (p. 451) or Cheese-stuffed Manicotti (p. 467), that you can pop into the oven and bring out for the late stayers-on.

Buffet Dinners

A buffet dinner is the simplest way to entertain a large group of people. Everything *must* be ready ahead of time, whether it is set out hot in a chafing dish or on a hot tray or is served cold or at room temperature.

Buffets present the interesting challenge of combining a number of dishes in a creative way. It is important that they look inviting on the table and that the dishes complement each other. (See suggestions for buffet dinners, p. 66.) Choose foods that can be cut with a fork; it's a lot easier than trying to handle a knife while you're balancing a plate on your lap. Don't serve dishes that are too soupy or everything will slop together on the plate.

Plan to serve at least one hot thing; there are always a few people who don't think they've had a real meal unless it includes something hot.

If you have a very large crowd, you can avoid long lines by setting the table up so guests may help themselves from either end.

Picnics and Barbecues

A picnic, or just eating out of doors, is a holiday from our daily table. Whether we are sitting in a meadow, on a mountaintop, by the shore, or in our own garden, nature creates a casual mood and whets our appetite. Prepare food that is easy to serve and easy to eat, tucking in extra just in case. If you are barbecuing, get your fire started well ahead. (See p. 361.)

An outdoor barbecue offers such a tempting way to get out of the kitchen on a warm evening that it is no wonder it has become a fixture in American life. It's also a means of getting everyone in the family into the act of cooking, if they aren't already, and provides a simple answer to feeding a number of people, yet making a party of it as good cooking smells waft across the backyard. One is apt to get into a rut, however, and fall back too often on hamburgers or steaks as the standard barbecue fare. Don't let that happen. There are so many things that can be barbecued deliciously. Consult the fish chapter, for instance; any fish or seafood that broils successfully can be done as well on an open fire. The same goes for meats—Butterflied

Lamb, for instance, or skewered chicken livers, or Shish Kebab—and chicken. If you have a spit, then try doing roast meats that way—duck is particularly delicious. Vegetables and potatoes can be wrapped in foil and tucked in among the coals, once your fire is going well, or some, like eggplant, can be grilled at the last minute after the meat is done.

A picnic basket could contain the welcome sight of something like cold vegetables, fresh scallions, small tomatoes, hearts of celery, avocado, slices of cold meat loaf, fried chicken, perhaps, ham on buttered homemade bread, cooked shrimp—the possibilities are endless. Think ahead so that you will have the cooked foods ready; fill small containers with pickles or preserves and olives; and don't forget the mustard. If something hot is deemed necessary, fill a thermos with soup. Wine, coffee, or lemonade can tend to the thirst. Cheese is simple to pack, and it's nice to have a variety. Cookies or a coarse, moist carrot cake would make the meal complete, with fresh fruit as the snack before starting home. As well as the necessary plates and cups and cutlery, the basket must have lots of paper napkins so crumbs and grease on fingers can be wiped away.

Communal and Pot-Luck Dinners

Like old-fashioned church suppers, communal dinners are coming into their own again. Whether they are planned as a family undertaking or a cooperative venture with friends, they are usually fun and full of surprises, everyone putting his or her best foot forward. It's a good way for working people, who might not otherwise have the time, to put together a festive dinner. And if everyone chips in, the financial burden is shared.

Sometimes friends like to cook all together, particularly if they love cooking and like to experiment with new dishes. If it's your first attempt at puff pastry, for instance, it is reassuring to make it with someone who has done it before; we learn a lot from each other in the kitchen. But more often for a communal dinner each member of the party prepares something at home and brings it. It is always wise to have someone coordinate the meal so that everything goes together well.

WINES

What to Serve with Meals

More and more often today, mineral waters are being served with dinner. If you choose to serve wine, you can be more casual about your choices today. There is less emphasis on what wine is correct with a particular food. But if you're not a wine buff, there's nothing wrong with following the old guidelines.

The general rule of thumb is that white wines—that is dry white wines—go with fish and poultry, and red wines with meats and usually cheese. Rosés are generally served with cold summer dishes, and are fine with poultry or ham. Sweet white wines are reserved for dessert, while champagne, which is particularly delightful with some sweet dishes, can be served also throughout a meal.

White and rosé wines should be served chilled. An hour or so in the refrigerator is sufficient; you don't want them numbingly cold so you kill their flavor. Red wines should be served at room temperature. And champagne should be chilled; it really calls for an ice bucket.

Wines are always much more pleasant if they are served in stem glasses—clear, not colored. Don't settle for those that hold only tiny amounts. A wineglass should be ample enough so that you can swirl the wine around to appreciate its bouquet—seven ounces is right for an all-purpose glass—and it should be filled only about one-third to one-half full.

Storing Wines

Wines should be kept in a relatively cool dry place.

If you have some wine left over in an open bottle, store it in the refrigerator and use it for cooking. Thus kept cool, it will last about a week and contribute flavor to many dishes; after that it turns vinegary. There are gadgets which you can buy in wine and department stores that draw the air from a partially consumed bottle of wine, leaving a vacuum. This will extend the life of an opened bottle of wine and better preserve its quality for drinking.

STAPLES

BAKING POWDER.　See also Leavening Agents (p. 17).

Baking powder, which comes in small, sturdy, airtight containers, is an early-nineteenth-century invention that changed the course of American cooking, making the art of baking much more predictable. It is used in making cakes, quick breads, muffins, cookies, and the like—the mysterious leavening agent that makes them rise. Recipes in this book call for *double-acting baking powder*, which is the most readily available everywhere today. Old-fashioned single-acting baking powder, technically *tartrate* or *phosphate baking powder*, goes to work as soon as it is mixed with liquid, thus demanding that the batter be baked immediately. Double-acting baking powder, on the other hand, acts twice—both when it is first mixed and again when the heat of the oven releases the full force of the leavening gases, so there is less urgency about baking your mixture. Both are equally effective in the long run, but it is important to note if you're using single-acting that you must double the amount called for in recipes because it is that much less potent.

There are those who prefer the old-fashioned baking powder, claiming that they can detect a chemical taste in double-acting. If you wish to make your own baking powder, combine ¼ teaspoon of baking soda with ½ teaspoon of cream of tartar and you will have the equivalent of 1 teaspoon of tartrate or phosphate baking powder. Do not store homemade baking powder; it will not keep well.

NOTE | *Store commercial baking powder* in its own airtight container. For best results, replace it every six months.

BAKING SODA.   See also Leavening Agents (p. 17).
Baking soda is also a form of leavening, but it must be mixed with something acid like sour milk, sour cream, buttermilk, yogurt, molasses, or citrus juice to produce the gases that make a batter rise. About 1 teaspoon of soda is used for every cup of liquid, but the soda should be combined first with the dry ingredients. As soon as the batter is mixed it should be set to bake.

Many recipes using baking soda call for sour milk as the acid activator. *To "sour" pasteurized milk,* add 1 tablespoon of white vinegar or lemon juice to 1 cup of milk and let it stand at room temperature for 10 to 15 minutes: Or use buttermilk, a good substitute for sour milk in any bread or cake recipe.

Baking soda is also used *to destroy odors.* A large box left open in the refrigerator is surprisingly effective in absorbing odors and a tablespoon in a couple of cups of warm water is a refreshing cleanser.

BEANS.   For variety, preparation, cooking, and recipes, see Beans (p. 445).
Dried beans keep well in covered containers. Don't hold them for more than a year, though; eventually they will become stale.

BOUILLON CUBES AND MEAT CONCENTRATES.   You'll get a better flavor from pure canned bouillon (not consommé), but cubes are all right in a pinch providing you adjust the seasoning accordingly; they are apt to be salty (unless, of course, you buy the unsalted kind).

BOUQUET GARNI.   *Bouquet garni* means a bouquet for garnish—parsley, thyme, and bay leaf being the traditional ingredients; sometimes celery and other aromatic seasonings are added. Make a bundle of the herbs and tie with a piece of string or put the herbs in a cheesecloth bag so that it can be easily removed from the casserole or stewpot.

BREAD CRUMBS. It's easy—and economical—to make bread crumbs at home, and it's a good way to use up bits and ends of bread. Both *fresh and dry bread crumbs* are most easily made by pulverizing bread in a blender or food processor or by tearing up by hand; dry crumbs can also be made with a rolling pin. Use unsweetened white bread without crusts for fresh crumbs (sweetened bread crumbs are all right in a dessert). For dry crumbs dry out the bread first in a 250°F oven, and use some of the crust, if you wish. Whole-wheat or rye-bread crumbs add a robust touch to less delicate dishes. Do not use bread that is stale or the crumbs will have a stale taste.

If you store bread crumbs in the refrigerator for more than a short period of time, they may become moldy. It's best to put them in the freezer, wrapped tightly in a plastic bag, where they will keep and taste fresh for several weeks.

If you buy packaged bread crumbs, avoid the seasoned variety.

To make cracker crumbs, use unsweetened, unsalted soda crackers or common crackers. Never pulverize cracker crumbs completely: it's best to crush them with a rolling pin or whirl them quickly in a food processor.

BUTTER.   See also Fats (p. 15); Oils (p. 19); Herb Butters (p. 24).

Butter has its own lovely flavor; there's nothing like it on vegetables, in sauces, and for certain kinds of cooking and baking. All the recipes will indicate when butter is preferred—no substitute will taste the same.

Whether you use *sweet (unsalted) butter* or *"lightly salted" butter* is a matter of personal preference. Sweet butter is preferred by many, especially in pastrymaking, but we don't feel it's crucial.

To store butter, when refrigerating, make sure it's covered or well wrapped so that it doesn't absorb food flavors. Butter can be left out for a limited period if the kitchen is cool. Sweet butter will keep refrigerated for about a week; salted butter for about ten days. Butter freezes very well; it will hold for many months and can be defrosted and refrozen.

Measuring butter is easy when you buy it in ¼-pound sticks; there are 8 tablespoons or ½ cup to a stick. If you buy your butter in bulk, there's a cold-water trick for measuring it: to measure ½ cup of bulk butter, for example, fill a 1-cup measure with ½ cup of cold water, then add enough butter to bring the water level to 1 cup.

Creaming butter requires butter that is at room temperature. Do not try to force cold butter by heating; break it into bits instead and let it stand a while or massage it with your fingers.

Butter will burn at a lower temperature than other fats, and for this reason it is often mixed with oil or shortening for frying. If you clarify butter, however, by removing the milk solids, it will not burn and will keep almost indefinitely in a covered container in the refrigerator. *To clarify butter*, put it in a large glass measuring cup in a warm (225°F) oven and let it stand until it melts and the milky substance settles at the bottom. You can strain the clear liquid at the top into a container through damp cheesecloth or just put the melted butter in the refrigerator to harden and then scrape off the milky residue.

When *serving butter*, it's nice sometimes to use a butter mold to make a pretty pattern. You can also use a butter curler or two chilled wooden paddles to make butter balls, but that may take a bit of practice.

CEREALS. Cereals keep well and are always good to have on hand (if you eat cereal). For varieties, cooking instructions, and recipes, see Cereals (p. 425).

CHESTNUTS. Chestnuts are most generally available around the Christmas holidays. Buy them fresh (they should feel absolutely firm when you press them, with no shrinkage of the meat from the shell) and freeze them for long-term storage. Actually, chestnuts will peel a little more easily when they have been frozen. *To shell chestnuts*, see p. 560.

CHOCOLATE. Chocolate for baking is available *unsweetened*, *semi-sweet*, and *sweet*, and comes divided into squares, usually weighing 1 ounce each. You may substitute chocolate bits or chips for semi-sweet chocolate, using the same number of ounces.

Storing chocolate is no problem; it keeps well, wrapped and in a cool place, not the refrigerator. When chocolate is exposed to air over a long period of time, it sometimes takes on a harmless white discoloration and becomes crumbly; this does not mean that it is stale, and it is perfectly usable.

To melt chocolate, put it in a pan over barely simmering water until the chocolate has melted. Chocolate when melting sometimes "tightens"; if that happens, add 1 teaspoon of solid vegetable shortening per ounce of chocolate and it will smooth out again.

COCOA. *To substitute cocoa for chocolate*, use 3 tablespoons of un-sweetened cocoa for each ounce of unsweetened chocolate and add 1 tablespoon of shortening.

COCONUT. *Commercial flaked coconut* comes in cans or packages and is usually sweetened, unless you buy it in a natural-foods store. It's marvelous for cakes and fine in other sweet baked products. *Fresh unsweetened coconut* is best for nonsweet main-course dishes like salads, curries, and soups.

To open a fresh coconut, pierce the "eyes" of the coconut with a screwdriver and drain off the liquid. Put the coconut in a 400°F oven for 20 minutes. Tap it all over with a hammer to loosen the shell, then split it with a heavy knife or with a mallet or hammer. Pry out the white meat with a sharp knife, then pare off the dark skin.

NOTE | The easiest way to open a fresh coconut is to fling it onto a cement or rock surface (not the kitchen floor). This is the way the monkeys do it, and they are professionals. Don't worry about losing the liquid—it's not the "coconut milk" called for in recipes.

To grate fresh coconut, put the white meat in a rotary grater, a blender, or a food processor. A medium-size coconut will produce 3 to 4 cups of grated coconut.

Coconut liquid has few uses and is usually discarded; despite a common misconception, it is not "coconut milk." *To make coconut milk,* steep the freshly grated coconut in boiling water to cover for 30 minutes. Then strain out the coconut, extracting all the flavorful juices by squeezing them through a towel back into the steeping liquid.

To toast fresh, grated coconut, spread it in a shallow pan in a 350°F oven for about 20 minutes, stirring frequently and watching carefully, until delicately brown.

Store fresh, grated coconut in the refrigerator for no more than four or five days or it will turn moldy. To keep longer, toast it and put it in a sealed jar; don't refrigerate.

CREAM. For whipped cream recipes, see Dessert Sauces (p. 993); for freezing cream, see Frozen Foods (p. 1120).

Half-and-half is more like milk than cream, but can be used instead of light cream; it will not whip, unless specially treated (see p. 994).

Light cream, also called "coffee cream," has a relatively low butterfat content and will not whip (see above). Use when you want a very light cream.

Heavy cream, also called "whipping cream," is the best for making whipped cream and is the richest cream you get commercially today. Depending on how fresh it is when purchased, it will last refrigerated anywhere from a few days to a week. Check the expiration date on the carton. The only test for sourness is to taste it.

To whip cream, use a whisk or an electric beater. Be careful to whip just until soft peaks form: cream that is beaten too long will begin to turn to butter, often quite suddenly, especially when electric beaters are used. It really doesn't matter when sugar or other flavorings are added.

To stabilize whipped cream (to use as frosting) add 2 tablespoons of nonfat dry milk to each liquid cup of heavy cream before whipping.

Commercial whipped cream substitutes bear little resemblance in taste or texture to freshly whipped cream.

Ultrapasteurized (or sterilized) heavy cream has been sterilized at high temperatures so that it will keep for several weeks in the refrigerator. It is as thick as old-fashioned heavy cream and whips well. It's good for desserts that must be held for a long time; sweetening will mask its slightly "boiled" taste.

Sour cream is thick with a slightly sour flavor. It is often used as a garnish, to flavor, and sometimes to thicken. *To avoid curdling* when adding sour cream to a hot sauce, have it at room temperature and stir it well before adding; do not let it boil.

Crème fraîche is what the French call their own fresh cream, which is thicker than ours and has a fine, tart edge. *For a homemade version*, add 1 teaspoon of buttermilk or 2 teaspoons of sour cream to 1 cup of heavy cream, put the mixture in a jar, shake it, and let it stand at room temperature, uncovered, for one or more days until it is thick, then cover. Refrigerate; it will keep for several weeks. Ultrapasteurized (sterilized) cream takes longer to thicken than regular, old-fashioned cream.

To reduce cream, boil it until it becomes thick and almost pale gold in color.

CREAM OF TARTAR. See Baking Powder (p. 9).

CROUTONS. Croutons are small cubes of bread that have been dried out in the oven or fried, then seasoned. They are used as a garnish. When made at home (p. 768), they have a fresh flavor, far preferable to the packaged variety.

EGGS. Unless otherwise indicated, all eggs used in these recipes should be "large" in size.

For buying, storing, measuring and separating eggs, for beating and *folding egg whites*, for *tempering egg yolks* and for *cooking eggs*, see Eggs (p. 471). For *freezing leftover egg whites and egg yolks*, see Frozen Foods (p. 1122).

If you have an excessive number of *leftover egg whites*, you might think of making meringues, an angel cake, or a dessert soufflé (check through the recipes). And don't forget that egg whites are essential for clarifying stocks and for certain bread glazes. If you have a lot of *leftover egg yolks*, maybe it's time for a hollandaise sauce, a custard, some mayonnaise. And remember how often you'll use yolks as a thickener in a sauce.

FATS. See Butter (p. 11); see Oils (p. 19).

Margarine. Margarine is a vegetable fat which is used as a substitute for butter. It does not have as fine a taste and texture as butter and does not hold up in cooking. Since margarine is no longer especially economical in comparison with butter, butter is always preferable, unless you have been told to avoid animal fats.

Solid vegetable shortening comes in cans and keeps indefinitely. It is usually white and has no taste. While its appearance is not exactly enticing, this vegetable fat has many uses; it tolerates high heat in frying, and it provides moisture and tenderness in baking, making a particularly flaky piecrust.

Lard is rendered pork fat. In its pure form, it's considered the best of all cooking fats. Commercial lards, however, are not always as dependable. Pick your brand carefully because some taste slightly "barny"; lard should have no taste. Refrigerate, well wrapped, and it will keep a long time.

Bacon fat has its own character and flavor. It's good for frying things like corn cakes and potatoes when you want a little of that flavor, and in the South it is often used in cooking field greens. After frying bacon, pour off the fat into a crock or coffee can and keep in a cool place.

Salt pork is cured pork fat. The crisp fried bits of salt pork that remain after the fat has been rendered are delicious in chowders, with greens, and mixed into biscuits. The fat itself is very salty, so salt judiciously.

Rendered chicken and goose fat have distinctive flavors and are marvelous for frying potatoes, onions, and root vegetables. Properly rendered fat will keep indefinitely. For rendering instructions, see p. 305.

Suet is beef fat; the best suet is the fat from around the kidney. It imparts a wonderful flavor—try it sometime for fried potatoes. It is particularly valued for steamed puddings and mincemeat, adding moisture as it melts in the cooking.

FLOUR. See also Thickening Agents (p. 22).
When recipes call for flour, unless otherwise noted, all-purpose white flour is to be used (unbleached or not, as you prefer).

For information about bread flour and meals, see Yeast Breads (p. 713).

For information about cake flours and about sifting and measuring flour, see Cakes (p. 784).

GARLIC. Buy garlic that is firm and heavy to the touch, with no soft spots. Store it in an airy place, not in the refrigerator. A clove of garlic is one section of the bulb.

Always peel garlic unless otherwise directed. If you smash the unpeeled garlic clove lightly with the flat blade of a knife, you'll find it easy to peel.

Garlic is not always the highly aggressive seasoner that many people think it is. To understand the full range of its seductive power, you must sample it in its different stages.

Raw garlic is particularly assertive and its taste lingers long. Don't inflict chunks of it on a salad or in a sandwich, for instance. Use it sparingly—unless you deliberately want that dominant flavor—and always very finely minced. For a salad, if you don't know the tastes of your fellow diners, better just rub the bowl with a cut clove. (Sprinkling ½ teaspoon of salt over a clove or two of garlic and finely mincing will add a full, robust flavor of garlic to a dressing.)

Chopped garlic cooked in hot fat will give a very pronounced garlicky flavor to a dish. Be careful not to let it brown or the flavor becomes bitter. If you add chopped raw garlic to something you are baking or broiling, it will have a dominant taste, too.

Garlic cloves, whole or crushed, cooked moist for a long time in a soup or stew or braised dish, for instance, impart a richness and an ineffable flavor to the sauce that never overwhelms.

Whole cloves of garlic, uncrushed, cooked slowly, either a whole head baked or the bulbs just separated and scattered around meat or poultry in a tightly covered baked dish, will surprise you the most with their mildness. When you crush the cooked cloves, the inside will be delicate and buttery, delicious to mop up with crusty bread.

A garlic *press* releases garlic oils in the most volatile way, leaving you with little but the juice. *Mincing* and/or *chopping* gives you more pulp with the juice and is more satisfactory, particularly if you sauté the pieces. When you *smash* or *crush* a whole clove of garlic, it releases its flavor but remains whole and can be removed from the cooking pot if desired.

GARLIC OIL. Garlic oil is used as a flavoring in salad dressings, in cooked vegetables, as well as for frying. To make your own put a couple of crushed cloves in a cup of olive oil. But be sure to keep the jar uncovered. Botulism, which is cultivated in an oxygen-free environment, could develop.

GELATIN. For recipes using gelatin, see Molded Salads (p. 693); Gelatin Desserts (p. 959). For molding and unmolding, see Desserts (p. 936).

True gelatin is pure and unsweetened and will solidify any liquid. Don't use too much, however, or you will get a solid, rubbery block: 1 tablespoon of gelatin is enough to gel 2 cups of liquid mixed with 1 to 2 cups of solid ingredients (depending on water content of solids—see p. 693).

Gelatin *must* be softened for about 5 minutes in a cold liquid before it is dissolved in something hot. If the broth or juice that you wish to gel is cold, you can sprinkle the gelatin right onto it and then, when it is soft, heat the liquid until the gelatin dissolves. If the liquid is already hot—a freshly made chicken stock, for example— soften the gelatin in ¼ cup of cold water and then dissolve it in the hot stock.

Do not let gelatin mixtures boil; the gelatin will lose its vigor. Allow at least a few hours for a gelatin mixture to solidify, overnight if the mold is very large.

LEAVENING AGENTS. See also Yeast (p. 23); Baking Powder (p. 9); Baking Soda (p. 10).

Leavening agents are used to lighten a batter or dough by creating carbon dioxide gas, air, or steam that will make it rise.

Beaten eggs or *egg whites* (p. 473) are often used to leaven; they enclose air which is forced to expand in a hot oven.

MARROW. The soft interior of bones. It has a delicate taste and an almost gelatinous texture when poached, and it is highly prized for use in soups, sauces, as a garnish, and on toast.

MILK. To "sour" milk, see Baking Soda (p. 10).

To scald milk, heat it slowly in a small pan until tiny bubbles appear around the edges, but before the milk boils up.

Homogenized milk is whole milk that has been mechanically treated so that the globules of cream will not separate from the rest of the milk.

Skim milk is milk from which the cream has been removed.

Low-fat milk is skim milk which still retains a little of the cream. It tastes more like whole milk and looks less anemic than skim milk, although it's not rich.

Buttermilk is the product that remains after sweet or sour milk has been churned and the fat removed. *Cultured buttermilk* is the soured product after pasteurized skimmed milk is treated with a suitable lactic acid bacteria culture.

Evaporated milk is the whole cow's milk from which 60 percent of the water has been removed. It is homogenized and sealed in cans.

Sweetened condensed milk is made by evaporating half the water from whole milk and adding enough cane or corn sugar to preserve it. It is then heated, cooled, and canned.

Dry whole milk solids are what remain after all the water has been removed from whole milk. They can be reconstituted with water or another liquid.

Yogurt is fermented milk—delicious on its own, plain or mixed with fresh fruit. It can be used in salad dressings and is a good lower-calorie substitute for sour cream. It's simple and economical to make yogurt and you don't need a special yogurt maker, if you follow the simple method below.

To make yogurt

Heat 1 quart of milk to the boiling point for just 1 minute. Cool to 115°F. Gently mix in 2 tablespoons of fresh plain yogurt (the starter), pour into a crockery bowl or several small bowls, even custard cups, if that is more convenient. Cover tight with plastic wrap and set in a warm place, preferably an oven with just a pilot light burning, or place in a warm kitchen corner and drape a blanket over the bowls to prevent drafts. An ideal temperature of about 110°F will hasten the incubation. The yogurt should be ready in about five to eight hours: tilt the bowl to see if it holds together. It should then be chilled for at least three hours and it will firm up even more. If the yogurt sets for too long a time or if you use too much starter, it will be watery; the longer you incubate the more sour it will be.

NUTS. Almonds, walnuts, peanuts, pecans, hazelnuts (or filberts), and pistachios are the nuts most frequently used in cooking. Shelled and unshelled nuts keep well in the freezer.

To blanch (i.e., remove the inner skins of) almonds or *pistachios,* put them in a bowl, pour boiling water over them, and let them sit for just a minute. Drain, and then rub off the skins.

To blanch filberts, drop in boiling water for a minute, drain, then rub while still warm between Turkish towels to remove the skin. If any don't skin easily, return them to the boiling water for another minute. Don't try to remove every little bit—it's impossible; actually, peeling filberts is a refinement and for most cakes and cookies, you don't need to bother.

To roast nuts, spread them in a single layer on a cookie sheet and toast them for about 5 minutes in a 375°F oven. Shake the pan once or twice and watch them—they can burn suddenly. Blanched nuts should be roasted to restore their crispness in a 325°F oven for 10–15 minutes, watching carefully.

To grind nuts, a hand grinder is preferable to a food processor or a blender. Electric machines bring out the oils in nuts; if you use one, grind the nuts quickly, turning the machine on and off, and do only ½ cup at a time. Don't pack them down when measuring.

To shell chestnuts, see p. 560.

OILS. Don't refrigerate oils. If they are pure, they will keep a long time.

NOTE | **OLIVE OIL.** The best way to buy olive oil that pleases you is to taste and decide. Money does not always buy the best and I have found the terms "virgin" and "extra virgin" not very meaningful. Olive oil should taste of the olive, and some are more robust than others. Don't use olive oil for deep-frying or even browning. Use it when the flavor counts—to toss with cooked vegetables or pasta or to use in a salad dressing. The terms virgin or extra virgin don't necessarily insure a flavor that will please you. Flavor is a personal choice, and delicate foods call for a more subtle olive flavor whereas rustic foods bloom with gutsy, full-flavored olive oil.

Vegetable oil is a good, all-purpose cooking oil. Corn oil and peanut oil are heavier than vegetable oil, excellent for frying and sautéing because they can be brought to a high temperature without burning.

Walnut oil, an expensive delicacy, makes an unusual salad dressing. Buy it in small quantities; it is perishable.

ONIONS. Onions should be peeled except when you deliberately leave the skin on to deepen the color of a stock. With a largish onion just strip off the skin and outer layer. (Incidentally, if you are prone to tears when peeling and cutting onions, chill them in the refrigerator first; the coldness will retard the volatile juices.) To peel small onions, drop them first in boiling water for a minute; the skins will then slip off easily. To keep them intact, don't trim the root end; but you can pierce the root for even cooking.

PASTA. Dried pastas—i.e., spaghetti, macaroni, noodles, etc.—keep well and are a staple one should always have on hand. For information and recipes, see Pasta (p. 452).

PRESERVES. For information about preserves of all kinds—Jams, Jellies, etc.—see p. 1077.

RICE. Basic food for a large part of the world, rice belongs in every larder. For information and recipes, see Rice (p. 436).

SOUR CREAM. See Cream (p. 13).

SOYBEAN CURD. As the name indicates, a bland cheeselike curd made from soybeans. Also known as tofu, it comes in white, square cakes and should be kept in cold water in the refrigerator; if the water is changed daily, it will keep up to a week. It is especially high in protein and is used a lot in Oriental cooking.

SPROUTS. Alfalfa and mung bean sprouts, crunchy and healthful, have become staples these days in many supermarkets. Americans use them primarily in salads and sandwiches, sometimes in an omelet.

STOCKS OR BROTHS. A stock is a result of mingling the bones and flesh of meat, poultry, or fish, as the case may be, with vegetable aromatics and herbs, cooking slowly until the essence of flavor is extracted. For cooking, cooling, reducing, storing, freezing, and clarifying the different stocks and for substitutes, see About Stocks and Broths (p. 104).

SUGAR

Granulated sugar is the sugar most commonly used. It's what is called for in these recipes, unless otherwise indicated.

Superfine sugar is finely pulverized granulated sugar. You can buy it that way or pulverize it yourself in a blender. It's good to use in meringues and other delicate desserts and for sprinkling over fruit.

Confectioners' sugar is powdered granulated sugar with a small amount of cornstarch added to prevent caking.

Raw sugar is less refined than regular sugars and has a coarse texture. It's nice in beverages and for sprinkling when a coarse, less dissolvable texture is desired.

Brown sugar comes in a light and a dark form. The dark has a deeper, more intense flavor; light-brown sugar is more commonly used in baking. Recipes will specify which to use when it makes a difference; otherwise feel free to use either light or dark.

Brown sugar should be stored in an airtight container in a cool spot or in the refrigerator. Add to the container a small slice of apple in an open plastic bag; it will keep the sugar soft. If your brown sugar becomes hard, soften it by putting it in a covered bowl with a few drops of water in a warm (200°F) oven for about 20 minutes. Don't put hard brown sugar in the blender or food processor; it may damage the blades. Pack brown sugar firmly when you are measuring it.

Granulated brown sugar doesn't cake because much of its moisture has been removed. It's useful to have around if you like brown sugar on cereals and fruits and pancakes. But don't substitute it in baking for regular brown sugar—you won't get about the same results.

Maple sugar has a wonderful, rich flavor and is very expensive. Don't waste it in cooking. Use it as a delicious topping for desserts and cakes.

Caramelized sugar is sugar that has been cooked long enough to liquefy and turn a caramel color, and in the process it takes on a new flavor. To prepare for use in desserts, see p. 973. Caramel is also used to flavor and color gravy and sauces. To make it for this purpose and to store in liquid form, melt 1 cup of sugar over medium heat in a heavy-bottomed pan, stirring often until the sugar is a rich, golden color, about 5 or 6 minutes. Take care that the sugar doesn't burn. Remove from the heat and be sure to let it cool a little. Add 1 cup of hot water, stirring briskly; if it is partly thick and tacky at this stage, don't worry—it will always melt. Put the mixture back over medium heat until blended. Cool, pour into a container, cover, and store; it will keep indefinitely. (To clean the pot, soak it in hot water, or fill it with water and return to the heat to dissolve the bits of hard sugar syrup that cling to the pan.)

SYRUPS. *Molasses* is what remains after the granulated sugar has been removed from sugarcane. It comes in a light and in a dark form and should be stored in a tightly closed jar in a cool place. Unsulfured molasses is preserved, but is a purer, unrefined molasses. Blackstrap is also unrefined but to some it has an unpleasant bitter taste.

Corn syrup is available light and dark, and the difference is an intensity in flavor. Used exclusively in desserts—the recipes will indicate which kind is called for.

Honey has different flavors, depending on the kinds of flowers the bees have frequented. It comes in three forms: strained and clear; unstrained and thick; and in the edible comb. Thick honey is grand to spread on toast.

Maple syrup is boiled-down maple sap. Keep it in the refrigerator. It will turn dark after a while, but this will not affect its flavor.

Pure maple syrup is expensive. If you read the labels carefully of less expensive syrups, you'll see that they are usually a mixture of syrups with some maple added in.

THICKENING AGENTS. See also Eggs (p. 14); Cream (p. 13).

Flour, to be properly used as a thickener, is blended into melted butter or other fat over low heat, stirred constantly, and cooked for 2–3 minutes. This is called making a *roux*. When liquid is stirred into the roux and cooked to the boiling point, the roux will thicken the liquid. Incidentally, if the liquid is hot when you add it your sauce will not lump on you.

Beurre manié is French for "handled butter." To thicken a soup or sauce that is already cooked, make a beurre manié by blending equal amounts of flour and soft butter, working them together quickly with your fingers. Add the mixture, bit by bit, to a hot sauce, stirring after each addition, until it is absorbed and you have the thickness you want.

Instant-blending flour is expensive. It dissolves in hot liquid without lumping and may be added directly to a gravy or pan drippings, or to a sauce. Do not use it in bread, cakes, or cookies.

Cornstarch must be dissolved in cold water before it is added to a hot mixture or it will lump. It's used frequently in Oriental cooking and produces the glazy, translucent sheen so often associated with Chinese food.

Arrowroot is very expensive and not always easy to find. It must be dissolved in water first. It is clear and almost tasteless and gives a nice gleam to food.

Potato flour cooks quickly and smoothly in liquid, is transparent, and leaves no raw taste. It's nice in fruit and egg sauces, but it cannot be heated to more than 176°F without thinning out.

VINEGAR. Vinegar is the result of the acetic fermentation of an alcoholic liquid and has an acid taste. There are four basic, common vinegars: white, all-purpose vinegar, which is very sharp; cider vinegar, which is strong and often used in pickling; gentler red and white wine vinegars, particularly nice in salads; and herb vinegars, available commercially but also easy to make yourself. Japanese rice vinegar, generally available, is lovely and mild on fruit salad and tender-tasting vegetables. In addition to being essential in the kitchen as a seasoning, vinegar acts as a preservative and is also useful in marinades to break down tough tissues.

To make wine vinegar, put red or white wine in a large-mouthed bottle and let it stand, uncovered, in a warm, dark place for several months. Don't use a wine that has turned sour: it takes good wine to produce a good wine vinegar. If you add a "mother"—the thick glob of skin that forms in the bottom of a vinegar bottle—the wine vinegar will be ready much sooner, a matter of weeks.

WINES AND LIQUORS. The reason for cooking with wines and liquors is that they impart an incomparable flavor and bouquet. Use the same quality wines and liquors in cooking that you would want to drink. Sweet wine should be used primarily with desserts, but sometimes the sweet cooked wines are used to flavor a savory sauce.

Alcohol evaporates during cooking: when you cook with wine, the finished dish will not be "alcoholic." The longer it cooks, the deeper and richer a wine sauce will be. Avoid special "cooking wines"; they are not the real thing and often give a harsh flavor.

YEAST. Yeast is a form of leavening that comes in dry, granular form, which can be stored simply in the cupboard, or in compressed cakes, which are more perishable and should be kept in the refrigerator or freezer. Both are equally satisfactory. For information about using yeast, see p. 714.

YOGURT. See Milk, p. 17.

HERBS, SPICES, AND SEASONINGS

Herbs should never overwhelm a dish. The purpose of any seasoning is to provide an accent that enhances natural flavors, and it is important in using *dried herbs* that they be as fresh-tasting and fragrant as possible. Colors should be bright, not faded, and a good sniff will tell you about pungency. Store dried herbs in a cool place away from strong light—the refrigerator is excellent, if you have room there.

NOTE You'll be wise to buy in small quantities, because most herbs do turn stale quickly—some more than others. And even though it may hurt, throw out stale jars.

Fresh herbs are a great treat, and if you are fortunate enough to come by them, by all means use them in place of dried. The flavor is invariably more seductive and their fresh-cut look is so appealing in any dish, particularly as a final garnish. Increasingly farmers' markets and even supermarkets are carrying more common herbs like dill, basil, chives, and, of course, fresh parsley is now a standard fixture. If you have a kitchen garden, plant a small bed of your favorite herbs. Some herb-lovers manage to grow plants of basil, chives, rosemary, tarragon, and thyme on a sunny window sill or under plant lights, but indoor herb gardening under lights can be tricky so consult a good guide.

In *cooking with fresh herbs,* you will always need to use at least twice the quantity of dried herbs. In many cases it will be even more than that and your only gauge is to taste and make your own adjustments.

Should you have an overabundance of fresh herbs, try storing them by making *herb butters* which can be frozen and used during winter months on homemade bread, with vegetables, or swirled into a simple sauce to provide a lovely burst of summer flavor. To make herb butters, chop a cup or more of fresh herbs with a stick of butter and blend until smooth, adding a few drops of lemon juice (this can be done in a blender or food processor if you have one).

Spices are usually dried, either whole or ground. If you don't use a spice very often, it's a good idea to buy it whole and grind or grate it according to need.

In addition to the *seasonings* listed below, sauces, marinades, barbecue sauces, relishes, and stuffings are also used to enhance the flavor of foods. For recipes see Sauces, Marinades, and Stuffings (p. 378).

ALLSPICE. Allspice comes whole or ground and it is a separate spice, not a collection of spices as the name might lead one to believe. Use it in baking and in pâtés and terrines.

ANISE. Anise is a spice, usually bought ground. It has a strong licorice flavor and is good in cookies.

AROMATICS. Aromatics are vegetables like onions, shallots, leeks, garlic, carrots, and celery used primarily to give off their flavor and aroma to foods they are cooked with. Sometimes they are simply dropped into the cooking pot or sometimes a combination of chopped aromatics will provide a bed on which meats, fish, and poultry are braised. A good kitchen is never without at least onions, carrots, garlic, and celery.

BASIL. Basil has a robust flavor and lovely pungent smell. It's particularly good in tomato dishes and delicious fresh with salads and sliced tomatoes.

BAY LEAF. Bay leaf is very pungent and keeps its flavor well. The imported variety is far preferable, but if you have California bay use with great care: it's very strong. Bay leaf is essential in a bouquet garni, and something seems missing if a pot roast or pâté isn't cooked with a bay leaf.

CAPERS. Capers are the small buds of a shrub grown in the Mediterranean. They are pickled in vinegar or dried and salted. The salted should be washed before they are used. Capers are particularly good with seafood, in sauces and salads, and as a garnish.

CARAWAY SEED. A spiky seed, caraway is a flavor commonly associated with rye bread, but it also has other interesting uses—

tossed with noodles, for instance, or embedded in sauerkraut and cole slaw.

CARDAMOM. Cardamom is a spice that is bought whole or ground and is used in baking.

CELERY LEAVES. Chopped, fresh celery leaves are apt to be on hand if you keep a fresh bunch of celery in the refrigerator (as you should). Finely chopped, the leaves are good added to soups, to a vegetable salad, and sometimes to the juices around a roast, rounding out the balance of flavors. Dried leaves are strong, so use only in soups, sparingly.

CELERY SEED. Celery seed is not called for often but it is used sometimes in a potato salad and in aromatic vegetables. It is strong and should be used judiciously.

CHERVIL. Chervil, fresh or dried, has a delicate flavor, and the fresh leaves look a bit like parsley. It's lovely when subtle seasoning is desired—with fish, eggs, and delicate cream sauces.

CHILI POWDER. Made from chilies that have been dried, commercial chili powder is only mildly hot. *Ground chili* is usually labeled hot; use with more caution.

CHIVES. Chives belong to the onion family. Fresh are preferable when available; when they're not, use freeze-dried chives, rather than frozen, and be sure that they are very green. Chives have many uses—in soups, eggs, salads, with sour cream and cream cheese, and in simple sauces.

CINNAMON. Ground cinnamon is used in desserts and occasionally in main dishes and drinks. Mixed with sugar, it's wonderful on French toast or pancakes or sprinkled on a crisp slice of apple. Stick cinnamon is used primarily in mulled winter drinks and in sugar syrups for preserving.

CLOVES. Ground cloves are used in baking while a few whole cloves, stuck into an onion or tied in a cheesecloth bag, often lend flavor to soups or stews; press them into a scored ham to bake, the more the merrier.

CORIANDER OR CILANTRO (CHINESE PARSLEY). There are the seeds and there are the leaves, used quite differently. The ground coriander seeds are sometimes used in baking; the whole seeds are essential in pickling and making aromatic vegetables. The leaf, also known as Chinese parsley and cilantro, has a surprising, unfamiliar taste, one which must be acquired. But it is much appreciated by connoisseurs and used frequently in Mexican, Indian, and Chinese cooking.

CURRY. Curry is not a single spice but a blend including turmeric, cumin, coriander, fenugreek, red peppers, and other strong spices. It's derived from the cooking of India and used in what we call curry dishes or to give a slight accent to a sauce or eggs. Since it varies in composition, buy a good, reliable blend of excellent quality.

DILL. Fresh dill is increasingly easy to find in the market in the right season and is better than the dried, which is sometimes called dillweed. Dill seed is often used in pickling. Dill is good with fish and with cucumbers and is basic to Scandinavian and Russian cooking. Although its flavor is lovely and mild, it should not be used with a heavy hand.

DUXELLES. Minced mushrooms that have been sautéed in butter (p. 578) until all their liquid has evaporated, thus preserving them and condensing their flavor. They may be refrigerated or frozen in a tightly closed container and used, as needed, for seasoning.

FENNEL. Fennel seed has a licoricelike flavor; use it judiciously or it can taste bitter. It is essential in aromatic vegetables. The fennel bulb, like celery, is used both as a vegetable and chopped raw in salads.

GINGER. Ground ginger is used primarily in baking. Candied ginger is used in desserts. Fresh ginger root, used especially in Chinese cooking, has become a staple in many markets. It will keep in the refrigerator for a week or so, but if you want to store longer, freeze and then just hack off a piece as you need it.

HORSERADISH. Horseradish is usually bought in a jar—the white or red variety being equally good—and it should be stored in the refrigerator. If you have a chance to buy fresh horseradish, grate it and use just as is—it's delicious. To keep, put it in a bottle with white vinegar to cover and add a little salt.

JUNIPER BERRIES. The berries are from a wild European shrub. Their aromatic flavor gives gin its characteristic taste, and they are used sometimes in meat marinades and sauces, providing a particularly good foil for game.

LEMON JUICE. A few drops of lemon juice are often what's needed to properly sharpen the flavor of a great variety of dishes. Use fresh-squeezed lemon juice whenever possible. While frozen juice may do in a pinch, bottled lemon juice with its strong, medicinal taste is a poor substitute.

It's hard to say how much juice one lemon gives; some lemons are juicier than others; some have thicker skins. The best way to be accurate is to measure the juice.

LEMON PEEL, GRATED. See Zest, p. 32.

MACE. Mace comes dried and ground. It is the outer covering of nutmeg, but has a lighter, milder flavor than the nutmeg it conceals. Classic with pound cake, it is used mainly in baking and in desserts.

MARINADES. Marinades are used both to tenderize and to add flavor. They usually contain an acid liquid like lemon juice, vinegar, or wine, which helps to break down tough tissues, and they always have a variety of seasonings, sometimes with a liaison of oil. For recipes, see Marinades (p. 397).

MARJORAM. Marjoram is a very pungent herb—even more so, surprisingly, when it is fresh. It requires discretion and is particularly good with grilled fish and with egg dishes. Dried, it loses its flavor quite quickly.

MINT. Dried mint is good; fresh mint is better. Iced tea is not its only use—it's good especially with fruit, in mint sauce for lamb, in peas, and in certain cold soups.

MONOSODIUM GLUTAMATE. Known also as MSG and produced under several brand names, this chemical product has been used and overused to bring out the flavors in food. If food is well seasoned, there's no need for it, especially since many people have a bad physical reaction to it and it is now considered unhealthful.

MUSTARD. Dry ground mustard is made of finely ground mustard seeds; it's very strong, so use in small quantities as directed. There are many kinds of prepared mustards, from ballpark to the imported French Dijon, and when a particular kind is called for, the recipe will specify.

NUTMEG. Ground nutmeg loses its flavor quickly when it sits around in a tin. Buy whole nutmeg instead and grate it fresh, using the small holes of your regular grater (or there are special small graters just for nutmeg). A few gratings give a wonderfully fragrant taste to certain vegetables and sauces, but nutmeg is used mostly in desserts.

OREGANO. Dried oregano is much more pungent than fresh oregano. Don't keep it too long; it changes color and character as it gets stale.

PAPRIKA. It pays to buy a good variety of Hungarian paprika; too many ordinary paprikas are more color than flavor. Recipes in this book call for sweet, not hot, paprika, so be sure to.ask for the sweet if you are buying it imported. In making a stew or a sauce, if you cook paprika first in the fat, it helps to blossom the flavor.

PARSLEY. There is no excuse for using anything other than fresh parsley, particularly since it is so readily available today. The dried flakes are tasteless. Fresh parsley does much more than decorate a dish, although it is always a welcome garnish; like a drop of lemon, parsley is a seasoning that brings out other flavors in a dish. Curly parsley is tasty and decorative; Italian parsley has a flat leaf and a more pronounced flavor. When fresh chopped parsley is rubbed with dried herbs it is surprising how the herbs seem to come to life.

PEPPER. For the brightest, most vivacious taste, buy *whole black peppercorns* and use them freshly ground: it really does make a difference. Experiment with different kinds of peppercorns. When whole peppercorns are called for be sure to crush them slightly first or they won't release any flavor.

White pepper has less flavor than black pepper. It's used in light-colored sauces because it doesn't show, but do a few black specks really matter very much?

Cayenne pepper is hot red pepper, dried and ground. It adds a lot of fire to a dish, so use it sparingly, respecting the palates of family and guests. Be sure it's fresh: it dies quickly.

Green peppercorns are the berries of a special species found primarily in Madagascar. They are preserved fresh in water or vinegar, water being preferable, even though the peppercorns won't last as long. Not as sharp as dried pepper, this relatively new seasoning is an exciting one, and adds zest to meats and poultry. Available in specialty stores.

Hot dried red pepper flakes are very hot and add verve to things like pasta and eggs. Again, use sparingly.

Tiny dried hot peppers, both red and green, should be seeded and chopped and used very sparingly in cooking. Be careful to wash your hands and not to rub your eyes when handling hot peppers.

Hot red pepper sauce is a liquid which mixes hot red pepper with vinegar, salt, and seasonings. It has its place, and not only in barbecue sauces or chili; a few drops added at the end to certain dishes bring out their flavors.

1. basil; 2. bay; 3. chervil; 4. chives; 5. dill; 6. mint; 7. coriander, also known as cilantro and Chinese parsley; 8. marjoram; 9. curly parsley; 10. oregano; 11. Italian parsley; 12. rosemary; 13. summer savory; 14. tarragon; 15. sage; 16. thyme.

Pimientos are sweet red peppers that have been preserved in oil. Use
them whole or chopped in salads, but always buy them whole, for
the chopped pieces absorb too much water.

For information about pimientos and red and green peppers,
both hot and sweet, see p. 588.

PICKLING SPICE. This mixture of whole spices—such as coriander,
mustard seed, cinnamon, bay leaves, allspice, dill seed, ginger,
cloves, and peppers—is used primarily for pickling.

POPPY SEEDS. Used on rolls and in other baked products, poppy
seeds are also good tossed with noodles and in an American favorite, poppy-seed salad dressing.

ROSEMARY. Rosemary has a strong, pungent flavor in both its fresh
and its dried forms. It's good with pork, lamb, and beans, and in
stuffings.

ROSEWATER. Made of roses distilled with water, rosewater is a
distinctive, delicate flavoring, often used in Middle Eastern cooking.

SAFFRON. Saffron is the stamen from the crocus. It gives a beautiful
yellow color and lovely flavor to rice and other dishes; but never
use more than is called for. Although good saffron is very expensive, don't settle for the cheaper varieties. Buy it in threads, rather
than ground, for fresher flavor. Before using it, saffron *must* be
steeped in hot liquid to bring out its flavor.

SAGE. Sage is very pungent—even fresh (if using fresh try the
pineapple sage for a fruity aromatic flavor). In the American
kitchen it is used primarily in stuffings, in sausages, and with pork.

SALT. There's no substitute for salt. It adds its own flavor and also
helps bring out the other flavors in food.

The effect of salt is quite variable, depending on whether it is
added during cooking or after a dish is done. Because *the amount of
salt* is very much a matter of personal taste, we have tried to avoid
prescribing an exact amount when your own palate should be the
guide: a good cook always tastes a dish as he goes along and ad-
justs the salt and other seasonings again at the end, if necessary.
However, one must be precise when salt is mixed into raw ingredients before cooking, such as when baking, and in these instances
the recipes will call for a precise amount. But whenever possible in
these recipes we are asking you to use your own critical palate. Inexperienced cooks are often too timid using salt; there must be

enough to develop the natural flavors of foods, so keep adding and sampling until the taste blossoms and pleases. There are times, however, when you must consider that those you are serving cannot tolerate much salt, and in that case try to use lots of fresh herbs instead.

Table salt is the fine-textured salt commonly used and therefore what is generally called for in these recipes; it has been dissolved, purified, and then recrystallized and is either iodized or uniodized. A little rice in your salt shaker helps to keep salt from getting too damp in humid weather.

Kosher salt is used by many good cooks and particularly by those who observe Jewish dietary laws. It has an even, coarse texture and measure for measure is not as strong as table salt.

Sea salt has a coarse texture and fresh flavor. It's often ground in a salt grinder when adding salt to cooked dishes. *Rock salt* is also used freshly ground.

Seasoned salt tends to taste dehydrated and is undesirable in cooking.

SAVORY. *Winter savory* is a perennial, strong in flavor with limited uses. *Summer savory* is a very versatile, all-purpose herb, used frequently in early American recipes.

SESAME OIL. Sesame oil is used to give a distinctive nutty flavor to foods and should be added in small quantities at the end of cooking. It's a very familiar taste in Chinese cooking.

SESAME SEED (BENNE SEED). This seed, brought over from Africa by the slaves, has an especially good flavor. The flavor intensifies when the seeds are dry-roasted in a skillet.

SORREL. Sorrel is sour grass, an easy-to-grow perennial that also grows wild in many parts of the United States. It's a wonderful, slightly sour addition to soups and sauces; cut in strips, it adds a tart taste to salads.

SOY SAUCE. Soy sauce is made from soybeans, salt, yeast, wheat, and sugar. Used primarily as a seasoning in Oriental cooking, soy sauce has been adopted by Western cooks increasingly in the last few decades. It is particularly good for marinating meats, since it tenderizes them, and it adds flavor and color to sauces. It is apt to be salty so be careful about adding salt when using it.

TABASCO. Tabasco is a liquid pepper seasoning. It is hot, so use judiciously; a few drops go a long way.

TARRAGON. Tarragon is a beautiful herb with a delicate, subtle, lemon-and-licorice flavor. It's especially good in dishes where flavors do not compete, like eggs, chicken, fish, veal, and certain sauces.

THYME. Thyme is very strong and good, essential to a bouquet garni and to many soups and stews.

TOMATO. Tomatoes in various forms are used frequently as a seasoning.

Tomato paste is made of puréed tomatoes that have been reduced at least by half. Because it is so concentrated, a spoonful of tomato paste is sometimes called for where a hint of tomato flavor is desired, but use judiciously to intensify a tomato sauce or perhaps to flavor a stew. You can freeze leftover tomato paste, either in its own small can or spooned into a plastic bag. It will be soft enough to spoon out in small quantities as you need it, and you can leave the remainder in the freezer for future use.

Tomato purée is unseasoned tomato pulp with some tomato juice. It is quite bland in taste.

Tomato sauce is made from tomatoes, salt, peppers, and spices. Make your own or choose from a variety of different brands, basically the same but seasoned differently. Taste and remember that you can add flavors to your own liking. Prepared sauces can be useful at certain times.

Solid-packed tomatoes are peeled whole unseasoned tomatoes in their own juice. They are the best substitute for fresh tomatoes, sometimes better to use when fresh tomatoes have little flavor.

TURMERIC. Turmeric is an Indian spice made from a ground root that gives a yellow color and an exotic flavor to foods.

WORCESTERSHIRE SAUCE. This spicy sauce, based on a recipe from India, was first manufactured in Worcestershire, England—hence the name. It is good with meats and in some sauces, but use it sparingly so that it doesn't overwhelm natural flavors.

ZEST, LEMON, LIME, ORANGE, OR GRAPEFRUIT. The rind of citrus fruit should be pared away, leaving behind the bitter white. You can grate it, or strip it off with a vegetable parer, or use a special "zester." The peel or zest gives a concentrated but beautifully refreshing flavor to desserts, main courses, and other dishes.

EQUIPMENT

For Food Preparation

MEASURING CUPS.   It is important to have one set for dry measure and one for wet measure. For *dry measure* a graduated set of four cups: ¼ cup, ⅓ cup, ½ cup, and 1 cup, which can be filled to the brim and then leveled off at the top with the flat edge of a knife, are the only kind that provide an accurate measure of flour and other dry ingredients. For *wet measure* use cups with a spout and made of see-through material so that the measure can be read at eye level. There is a little leeway at the top which is necessary as liquids are bound to spill over when carried. One-cup and 2-cup sizes are essential; a 4-cup measure is also very useful.

MEASURING SPOONS.   A set of measuring spoons, shaped so that they can easily be leveled off with a knife, is a must; ¼ teaspoon, ½ teaspoon, 1 teaspoon, and 1 tablespoon are the standard sizes.

RULER.   A ruler is necessary for taking the size of pastry shapes, for measuring pans, and for other kitchen needs.

THERMOMETERS.   The most common and least expensive *meat thermometer* is one that you insert in meat or poultry at the start and leave in throughout the cooking process. Far more accurate and convenient, however, are the smaller *instant thermometers*. These are not left in the oven: take the temperature at intervals by inserting the thermometer into whatever part of the flesh you want to test—such as the breast meat and the thigh meat of a chicken or a turkey. Furthermore, they can be slipped into the side of a steak, chops, or hamburgers to test for doneness. They are more expensive, but well worth the investment.

A *candy/frying thermometer* is important for measuring how hot the syrup or fat may be. For checking the accuracy of a candy thermometer, see p. 1045.

A *freezer thermometer* is good if you wish to be sure that your freezer is cold enough for proper storage. See p. 1116.

An *oven thermometer*, which you set on a rack in your oven, is a valuable tool to tell you how accurate your oven temperature is. If it is slightly off you can make allowances when baking, but if it is badly off have your oven recalibrated.

TIMER.   A timer is absolutely necessary in the kitchen. If your stove doesn't have one built into it, get a freestanding one.

BOWLS. You will need mixing bowls in at least three different sizes. Stainless steel, glass, plastic, and earthenware are all fine; it's a matter of personal preference. A very large bowl is handy if you cook in large quantities or do a lot of entertaining.

CHOPPING BOARD. Your chopping board should be thick, solid, and large. A built-in chopping board is a wonderful convenience. Acrylic, hard rubber, and wood are good choices. A nonporous surface is easiest to clean and best for cutting up raw meat, fish, or poultry. Some like to have more than one board and reserve it only for that task. Always wash a cutting board with soap and hot water after cutting up raw meat, fish, or poultry. To remove odors and flavors try a baking soda solution or lemon juice.

KNIVES. Whether you use stainless steel or carbon steel is a matter of personal preference. Stainless knives will not rust and are easy to keep shiny; many of the newer ones seem to hold an edge as fine as carbon steel knives. But there are still many traditional cooks who prefer good-quality carbon steel knives, which can be sharpened so easily after each use. You will need an 8- or 9-inch chef's knife, a paring knife or two, a bread knife with a serrated edge, and a carving knife. Knives should never be kept in a drawer unless the blades are protected by sheaths. It is really better to keep them on magnets attached to the wall or to slip them into slots, if you have that kind of knife holder.

KNIFE SHARPENER. Of the numerous knife sharpeners available, an ordinary whetting stone or sharpening steel does a good job. To

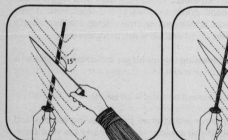 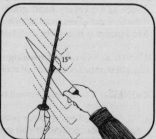

sharpen, draw the blade across the stone at an angle of no more than 15 degrees (about 1 o'clock), repeating until you get a good edge. There are electric knife sharpeners available. They are costly but efficient. Be sure to follow the manufacturer's directions for use.

KITCHEN SHEARS. You'll need a large pair of scissors in the kitchen for a number of jobs.

VEGETABLE PARER. Essential for peeling fruits and vegetables.

OPENERS. You will need a bottle opener, corkscrew, and beer opener for cans. A jar opener that works for different sizes is also very handy. A substantial, heavy-duty *can opener* will make life easy. Electric ones are good, but keep a hand model around for when the power fails, and be sure to wipe off the blade occasionally, which can build up a residue.

PEPPER GRINDER. Essential for grinding fresh pepper. See Pepper (p. 28). It pays to spend more for a very good grinder; it will last for years.

ROTARY EGG BEATER. Important even if you have an electric hand beater (p. 49) and, again, for emergencies or just to save power, or to grab and smooth out a batter, or to quickly whip a little cream.

NUTCRACKER. Get the sturdy, old-fashioned kind (see illustration, p. 36).

FUNNEL. Both a small and a large one are useful.

GRATER. Use either a four-sided, standing grater or a single-sided grater and a rotary hand grater for nuts and cheese. Even if you have a food processor, which grates most things successfully, a hand grater is less violent and will be wanted occasionally.

COLANDER. Good for draining many things, including pasta. Get a big, substantial one made of metal.

STRAINER. You'll need a small one and a large one.

JUICER. A small hand juicer is necessary for squeezing lemons and other fruit for cooking. If you squeeze juice regularly for your family's breakfast, it's wonderful to have an electric juicer.

SALAD SPINNER. A wire basket for drying greens is attractive and useful. The newer plastic salad spinners that will catch the water and whirl with great force are exceptionally efficient, particularly if

1. *glass measuring cups for liquids;* 2. *measuring spoons;* 3. *measuring cups for dry ingredients (fill to top and level off with a knife);* 4. *scale;* 5. *can/bottle opener;* 6. *and* 7. *corkscrews;* 8. *manual can opener;* 9. *jar opener;* 10. *kitchen scissors;* 11. *ruler;* 12. *wall can opener;* 13. *garlic press;* 14. *juicer;* 15. *funnels;* 16. *nutcracker;* 17. *nut grinder;* 18. *and* 19. *pepper grinders;* 20. *nutmeg grater;* 21. *grater (with different size holes on its four sides);* 22. *cheese grater;* 23. *food mill;* 24. *rotary beater;* 25. *ricer.*

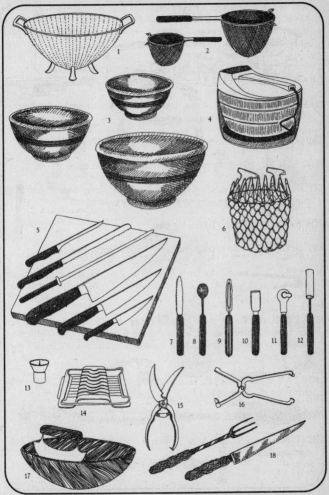

1. colander; 2. strainers; 3. bowls; 4. salad spinner; 5. cutting board with (from top to bottom): boning knife, bread knife, knife sharpener, chef's knife, medium-size knife, paring knife; 6. salad basket; 7. grapefruit knife; 8. melon baller; 9. vegetable parer; 10. zester (for narrow strips of orange and lemon peel); 11. stripper (for wider strips); 12. apple corer; 13. egg piercer; 14. egg slicer; 15. poultry shears; 16. pitter; 17. wooden bowl and chopper; 18. carving knife and fork.

you are an apartment dweller and don't have a backyard in which to swing a wet basket. You can also put washed greens loosely in a large clean dish towel and swing it—outside of course. This works quite well if you don't have a spinner.

GRAPEFRUIT KNIFE.   To loosen segments from a halved grapefruit.

MELON BALLER.   To scoop out perfect balls of melon and other fruit. It can also be used for potatoes.

ZESTER.   To extract in thin strips the yellow rind of a lemon.

EGG SLICER.   To cut perfect slices of hard-boiled eggs.

CHOPPING BOWL AND CHOPPER.   Particularly useful for chopping items that are going to jump around on a board.

POULTRY SHEARS.   To cut up poultry.

APPLE CORER.   To extract the core from an apple neatly.

SCALES.   It is useful to have kitchen scales. As you begin to use scales, you may find out how convenient it is to weigh rather than measure by cups.

MEAT GRINDER.   A meat grinder is not absolutely necessary if you have a food processor (p. 49), although for tough meats it still does a better job, particularly if your food processor does not have a very strong motor.

MORTAR AND PESTLE.   For crushing and pulverizing and sometimes for mashing.

TRUSSING NEEDLE.   For sewing up meat, fish, and poultry.

MEAT POUNDER.   To help tenderize and thin out pieces of meat and poultry.

For Cooking

POTS, SKILLETS, AND PANS.   Use good-quality heavy *saucepans* of various sizes. They will last longer than pans of flimsy material, which burn easily and don't distribute the heat evenly. Some useful basic sizes are 1–2 cups, 1 quart, 2 quarts, and 8 quarts.

You'll need 7-inch and 12-inch *skillets* or *frying pans* (they mean the same thing); a 10-inch is also very handy. Skillets should have covers, or get a flat, "pigtail" lid which works for many sizes. Nonstick surfaces, the kind that are bonded to the metal, are excellent for skillets, but not necessary for saucepans; it's helpful to have a 7-inch nonstick pan to make crêpes and omelets. Heavy enamel-coated frying pans are good for long, slow cooking, but they don't give a brown crust; the old-fashioned black cast-iron skillet is the best for that.

It is very useful to have a *flameproof casserole* or *Dutch oven* of heavy porcelain-coated iron or attractive stainless steel or lined copper which can be used on top of the stove, then go into the oven, and be presentable at the table. Three quart is a basic size; 4–6 quart is good for a party or a large family.

There are many kinds of *casseroles* and *baking dishes*—glass, porcelain, earthenware—and you may want a variety, but most of them cannot be used on top of the stove, only for baking.

A shallow *roasting pan* for the oven, fitted with a V-shaped rack, is essential for roasts and can double as a baking dish or basin to hold smaller baking dishes that must be surrounded with boiling water.

A *double boiler* is not a necessity because you can always improvise by placing a heatproof mixing bowl over a larger pot filled with water. A glass *double boiler*, however, is useful because you can see the water level in the bottom and keep a check on it.

A *steamer* with a perforated top that sits above the water is very handy. An inexpensive, collapsible trivet made for steaming is equally satisfactory. A steamer can also be improvised by resting a heatproof plate on an empty tuna can in a large pot with a cover.

KETTLE. The term today is usually applied to a tea kettle for boiling water. Ones with a whistle are nice so you'll be warned when the water has come to a boil. A large pot with a lid for boiling or stewing is also often referred to as a kettle.

COFFEE POT. The type of coffee pot you use is a matter of personal preference; but a metal pot is apt to retain a stale coffee taste and it must always be carefully cleaned.

METAL RING MOLD. It would be good to have these in 1- and 2-quart sizes. Useful for gelatin salads and desserts, they are also used for cakes and molded rice dishes.

WOODEN SPOONS. There's a quiet, nice feeling about wooden cooking utensils: they don't conduct heat and/or scrape against the sides of the pan. Have several, one of them with a flat bottom that will scrape the bottom of the pan and get into the inside edges.

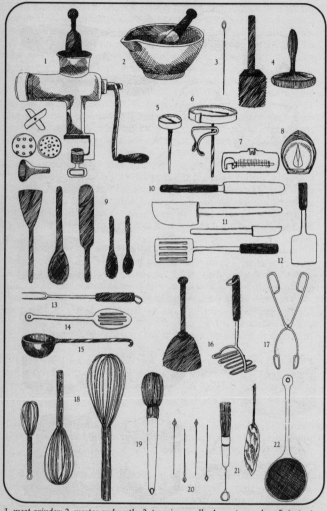

1. meat grinder; 2. mortar and pestle; 3. trussing needle; 4. meat pounders; 5. instant thermometer; 6. candy/frying thermometer; 7. oven thermometer; 8. timer; 9. wooden spoons; 10. spatula for cake frosting; 11. rubber spatulas; 12. cooking spatulas; 13. kitchen fork; 14. slotted spoon; 15. ladle; 16. potato mashers; 17. tongs; 18. wire whisks; 19. bulb baster; 20. skewers; 21. pastry brushes; 22. skimmer.

1. saucepans; 2. skillets, with pigtail lid; 3. steamer basket; 4. Dutch oven; 5. wok;
6. double boiler; 7. frying basket; 8. pressure cooker; 9. tea kettle; 10. large cooking pot;
11. fish steamer; 12. stockpot; 13. roasting pan and rack.

RUBBER SPATULA. Almost better than the human hand, a rubber spatula scrapes absolutely clean so there's no waste. One or two are a must in any kitchen.

METAL UTENSILS. Metal utensils should have plastic handles that won't heat up. Every kitchen needs a *metal spatula*, a *pancake turner*, a *slotted spoon*, a *cooking fork*, a *ladle*, and a *potato masher*. The best kind of potato masher is one with a spiral bottom. Plastic or coated utensils should be used in nonstick pots and pans to avoid scratching the surface.

TONGS. Tongs are particularly useful for turning something you don't want to risk piercing with a fork or in extracting something from a pot of boiling water.

WHISK. The whisk is designed so that its many strands of looped wire make it particularly effective for beating. A medium-size balloon whisk is a good size to start with.

SKEWERS. You will need both large and small depending on what you are skewering: the small ones are particularly useful for keeping stuffing from spilling out.

BULB BASTER. A marvelous kitchen invention for sucking up the juices from the pan in order to baste. It also works quite well for drawing off fat. The glass basters are apt to break; plastic melts if left carelessly near a heated surface; so metal is probably your best bet.

BRUSH. Good for basting and glazing.

USEFUL BUT NOT ESSENTIAL

GRIDDLE. A flat metal surface for dry top-of-the-stove baking. You can get one with a nonstick surface.

OLD-FASHIONED BEAN POT. The old-fashioned bean pot is a high-sided pot with a narrow neck usually made of earthenware with a tight-fitting top.

WOK. This round-bottomed Oriental cooking pot set on a collar is particularly good for stir-frying. Woks work only on a gas stove, however. There is an electric plug-in model available, but it doesn't respond very well to rapid temperature changes.

SKIMMER. A flat, very fine mesh strainer, excellent for removing scum and particles from the surface of liquids.

FOOD MILL. A hand-operated food mill is especially useful if you don't have a food processor. It also does certain things a food processor can't do, like straining out the skins and seeds as you mash certain fruits and vegetables.

RICER. Excellent for making mashed potatoes without any lumps.

DEEP-FAT FRYER WITH A BASKET. See Fry (p. 57).

PUDDING MOLD WITH A LID THAT SEALS. Necessary for steamed puddings (p. 934).

ESPRESSO POT AND ESPRESSO MAKERS. One way to make strong Italian espresso coffee is to use an espresso pot. Electric espresso coffee makers are generally available today too, with cappucino-making attachments.

SCALLOP SHELLS. Nice for baking and serving seafood and other fishy appetizers.

FISH POACHER. A great convenience if you are apt to poach a whole fish quite often.

STOCKPOT. Tall, narrow, and straight-sided, designed for the slow cooking-down of a stock, a stockpot is useful but not essential; any large pot will do.

GRATIN PAN. An attractive, party-size gratin pan is useful to have; you can run it under the broiler, then bring it directly to the table. As an alternative, wrap a napkin or two around whatever baking pan you've used to present it at the table.

PRESSURE COOKER. A specially manufactured heavy pot with a lid that seals tightly, in which foods can be cooked rapidly under pressure. Useful when time is short, and many cooks swear by them. In my opinion, as with the microwave, the intense heat of the pressure cooker does not integrate and mellow the flavors of the ingredients you are cooking. A stew, for instance, tends to be watery; all the liquid has been extracted from the meat and the meat seems shredded. There are new models on the market now with improved safety devices and they are easier to handle. Check your instruction book for what pressure-cooks successfully. You must time very accurately (see pressure-cooking charts, pp. 530–32).

CLAY COOKER. Cooking in a covered clay pot, which seals in the juices so beautifully, is particularly satisfactory for lean, slightly tough meats and birds. The pots must always be soaked in water well before using and no cooking fat is necessary. If you turn the oven temperature up high at the end, the food inside will brown nicely, still covered.

CHAFING DISH. The sauté pan usually sits over another pan of hot water warmed by canned heat, so the average chafing dish permits only relatively slow cooking. But it is fine for dishes that require just that, and, of course, it can all be done at the table. It is also useful for keeping foods warm on a buffet table.

For Baking

PASTRY BLENDER. The several wire strands cut shortening or butter into flour quickly and efficiently—sometimes better than you can do with your fingers.

ROLLING PIN. Don't get a dinky rolling pin. A large heavy one is essential for rolling out dough successfully. For a *surface* you can use anything from a Formica counter top, a board at least 24 × 18 inches, or a marble slab. A lot of beginning cooks find a *pastry cloth* helpful.

SIFTER. For sifting flour and sugar. The spring action kind that you squeeze with one hand is simplest to use and most readily available. Don't wash it every time you use it: just knock it and shake out any residue.

CAKE PANS. If you do a fair amount of baking, you'll need two sizes of cake pans—a pair of 8-inch and a pair of 9-inch 1½ inches deep. Removable bottoms are not necessary. You'll also need an *8- or 9-inch square cake pan* and a *9 × 12-inch rectangular pan*. Nonstick surfaces are a welcome feature, although we still recommend buttering them. A *10-inch tube pan* (p. 45) is also useful, as are other specialized sizes.

LOAF PANS. For breads, quick breads, and loaf cakes. These come in two standard sizes: 9 × 5 × 3 inches and 8½ × 4½ × 2½ inches. The smaller size is preferable for the bread recipes in this book.

NOTE ▌**COOKIE SHEETS.** You need at least two cookie sheets, as cookies take up a lot of space and must usually be baked in batches; the nonstick surfaces are good. There is a line of bakeware which contains a layer of air between two pieces of metal. This serves the same purpose of insulation as double-panning (see p. 855). You will have to bake everything an

1. *sifter;* 2. *pie dough/pastry blender;* 3. *pastry-pizza cutter;* 4. *rolling pin;* 5. *biscuit cutter;* 6. *doughnut cutter;* 7. *cookie cutters;* 8. *pastry bag and tips;* 9. *cookie press;* 10. *pastry scraper;* 11. *pie pan;* 12. *quiche pan;* 13. *cake pans;* 14. *square cake pan;* 15. *small tart tins;* 16. *ring mold;* 17. *springform pan;* 18. *tube pan;* 19. *bread pans;* 20. *cake rack;* 21. *muffin tin;* 22. *cookie sheet;* 23. *jelly-roll pan.*

1. *clay cooker*; 2. *bean pot*; 3. *chafing dish*; 4. *gratin dish*; 5. *soufflé dish*; 6. *casserole*; 7. *pudding mold*; 8. *custard cups*; 9. *scallop shells*; 10. *hand electric mixer*; 11. *electric juicer*; 12. *food processor*; 13. *standing electric mixer*; 14. *blender*.

additional 2 to 3 minutes if you use it, but the results are well worth the added time. You'll find you will use cookie sheets for other purposes as well, like toasting nuts and crackers and catching drippings.

JELLY-ROLL PAN. Jelly-roll pans have a little edge around them; the standard size is 10½ × 15½ × 1 inch. They're used for classic jelly rolls, of course, and can also be used for cookies and other baked goods; they are particularly useful in making candy in case of too much spreading.

MUFFIN TINS. Muffin tins come in several sizes. The standard-size cups hold about ½ cup when full. Muffin tins with a nonstick surface are especially convenient.

PIE PANS. Some recipes call for an 8-inch pan, others for 9-inch, so get both of these standard sizes. A 10-inch pan is wonderful to have for entertaining. Glass is nice because you can see the color of the crust, but it cooks faster so you must lower your oven temperature by 25 degrees.

TART PAN. A 10-inch tart pan with a removable rim is the right thing for tarts and quiches.

SOUFFLÉ DISH. A 2-quart soufflé dish with straight sides will fill most needs, though for a small family a 1-quart or 1½-quart is convenient. Porcelain and glass are both fine.

CUSTARD CUPS. Either glass or earthenware will do. Use them for custard, small soufflés, baked desserts, and popovers.

CAKE RACK. Designed so that there is air space below, racks are necessary for cooling cakes, breads, and cookies.

Useful But Not Essential

DOUGH SCRAPER. A flat-edged device for scraping dough from counter tops and boards. Good for cleanup, too. Plastic ones that bend are great for getting every bit of dough or batter out of the bowl easily.

PASTRY-PIZZA CUTTER. For cutting various pastry shapes.

BISCUIT CUTTERS. The rim of a glass will also do.

DOUGHNUT CUTTERS. Necessary if you make doughnuts.

COOKIE CUTTERS. They come in three standard sizes and in many fanciful shapes.

SPRINGFORM PANS. A round tin with a removable rim, used particularly for cheesecakes.

SMALL TART TINS. Good for making appetizers and desserts. Fit leftover pieces of pie dough into them and freeze (see Savory Tarts, p. 95).

PASTRY BAG. The best kind is made of lightweight material that is washable with a set of standard-size nozzles. To make your own, see p. 835.

COOKIE PRESS. For pressed cookies, see p. 856.

Appliances

In buying *large appliances*, ask a lot of questions, compare models, and consider not only what something costs but how much energy it is going to use.

For small electric appliances start out with only those that you need the most. Exciting as the food processor is, for instance, if you can learn to chop and slice and mix and knead with your hands first, you will understand food better and appreciate what any machine can and cannot do.

Space is also a consideration. If you haven't enough room for an appliance and have to store it somewhere, you tend not to use it. So consider your space before buying.

REFRIGERATOR AND FREEZER. For owning and maintaining a freezer, see Frozen Foods, p. 1115.

Select a refrigerator according to the way you live and how much cooking you do.

Self-defrosting refrigerators and freezers use more energy but are a wonderful convenience. Since there is a constant evaporation in a frost-free refrigerator, foods dry out more rapidly and should always be tightly covered.

If you do a lot of freezing, you will probably need a separate freestanding freezer.

RANGES. If you have the opportunity to choose between a gas stove and an electric range, consider the advantages and drawbacks of each. Gas ranges respond more immediately when you turn up or lower the heat, which can be very important in certain kinds of cooking—making omelets, for instance, or quick browning followed by a slow braise. Electric ovens, however, are apt to be more dependable than gas. And the electric broiler goes on with the turn of a switch while all too often the pilot light on a gas broiler is knocked out by the heat of the oven and can be very difficult to relight. Many custom-designed kitchens feature gas burners and wall-hung electric ovens.

Both gas and electric ovens come with an optional self-cleaning feature. It's expensive and energy-consuming, but a great boon.

MICROWAVE OVENS. Cooking with a microwave oven is an entirely different kind of cooking. For details, see p. 626.

STANDING ELECTRIC MIXER. One of the most useful kitchen appliances, especially if you do a lot of baking. Select a heavy-duty model with a rounded bowl for even beating, and a dough hook for making bread.

HAND ELECTRIC MIXER. A relatively inexpensive appliance, an electric hand mixer is useful, whether or not you have a freestanding mixer. You can use it on the stove, to beat up sauces and frostings while they are heating.

FOOD PROCESSOR. The food processor is certainly the most exciting new appliance to appear on the market in many years. But although it has revolutionized many people's cooking habits, it does *not* do everything. It's particularly good for chopping, slicing, grating, grinding, and puréeing (without overblending) and for the ntedious shredding of things like carrots and cabbage, and it is excellent for chopping meat.

There are some tricks for using a fod processor properly. Feed it a little at a time, rather then filling up the entire bowl. Learn to turn the machine on and off again in rapid succession (to pulse) or use the pulse button: this will chop food more evenly rather than puréeing some of the pieces while leaving others in larger hunks.

The food processor is all right for making tart pastry but not for basic pastry (see p. 895). It can knead dough but only enough for one loaf at a time. Don't try to whip potatoes in it: they will turn gluey. Liquids that need to be aerated as they are beaten, such as egg whites and whipped cream, cannot be done in a food processor.

That food processor tends to extract liquid from raw vegetables such as onions and peppers while it is chopping them. Turning the machine on and off helps somewhat, but does not eliminate juiciness entirely. This is a problem, since you can't possibly brown a chopped vegetable that has been somewhat liquidized—it will simply steam in its own juice. The best solution is to pour off any liquid that has accumulated before attempting to brown (the juice can always be added later or used in a soup).

The new mini-choppers are a great help in mincing small amounts of foods.

BLENDER. A blender does not chop, although it will pulverize a few absolutely dry ingredients like nuts and coffee beans—more satisfactorily than a food processor, incidentally. It's also better than a food processor if you want a very fine purée. But most owners of food processors find they can do without a separate blender.

TOASTER. An "old-fashioned" toaster is still the best way of toasting bread, but it does not offer the other features of the dual-purpose toaster oven (see below).

TOASTER OVEN. For quick-grilled cheese sandwiches, baked potatoes, and small casseroles, it is more efficient and energy-saving to use a toaster oven rather than a large oven. It's not good for meat, however, which spatters—and the fat can not only catch fire but it makes it difficult to clean.

WAFFLE IRON AND GRIDDLE. Great for waffle lovers; the griddle will also make good grilled cheese sandwiches.

ELECTRIC STEAMER. A useful piece of equipment if you do a lot of steaming. It is also convenient for heating up foods—and you won't burn the bottom of the pot since it turns off automatically when the water has boiled away.

ELECTRIC SKILLET. An electric skillet is an auxiliary appliance that is helpful if your range has a limited number of burners. It is useful for outdoor patio cooking, too. You can also use it covered as an oven to heat small baked dishes.

ELECTRIC ROTISSERIE. Miraculously there is no spattering or smoking with the new electric rotisseries, so they can be used indoors. For spit-roasting meats and poultry they are great—the exterior becomes beautifully browned and the inside remains juicy and the house is filled with a wonderful fragrance as the spit turns. Many ovens are furnished with a rotisserie attachment which does almost as good a job and, of course, takes up less room.

ELECTRIC DEEP-FAT FRYER. This appliance holds oil at an even temperature for deep frying. It is not always easy to pour off the oil from an electric fryer after using, and they are awkward to clean. A heavy pot with a strainer used on top of the stove with a thermometer to check the oil does just as well.

ELECTRIC JUICER. A great convenience if you make fresh juice regularly.

ELECTRIC ICE CREAM MAKER. The old-fashioned hand-cranked type of ice cream maker and its electric counterpart, both of which must be packed with ice and salt, still make very good ice cream, whether turned by hand or by electricity. The still more advanced, totally electric ice cream makers both freeze and churn automatically. More expensive than the old-fashioned version, these countertop units will churn up to a quart of ice cream in about 20 minutes. Also available are the canister-type units. You must put the canister insert, which is filled with a liquid, in your freezer until frozen. Then fit the frozen canister into the ice cream unit and fill it with your ice cream mixture. Turn the crank only a few times, just enough to allow the paddle to scrape the frozen mixture from the sides of the canister and the ice cream to freeze evenly. These Donvier ice makers come in several sizes, and are easy to operate. For ice creams, sherbets, and ices, see Desserts and Dessert Sauces (p. 933).

CROCK-POT. These slow cookers are very popular, especially with working families. They require special recipes adapted to the Crock-Pot. A crock pot can also be improvised: an earthenware pot set over a hot tray or in a very slow oven will accomplish practically the same thing.

ELECTRIC COFFEE GRINDER. More and more people are grinding their own coffee; you can blend your own beans and the coffee tastes so good. Beans kept in the freezer stay freshest and you grind only the amount you need, still frozen. The simplest types of electric coffee grinders are the best. You can also use a blender.

ELECTRIC COFFEE POT. Electric coffee pots are available in drip and percolator models in a variety of makes and sizes. Be sure to clean the interior and the parts carefully because they retain a stale coffee flavor. A very large electric percolator is good if you do a lot of entertaining; the big pots taking up to a full pound of coffee usually make a surprisingly good cup.

Other Things

CANISTERS. Canisters, containers for keeping flour, sugar, rice, tea, and other dry things, should be easy to wash and have wide tops so that you can get into them with a scoop. Square canisters are better for storage, since they use space more efficiently. But it is also nice to have glass jars so that you can see at a glance what you have on hand. All canisters should have tight-fitting lids.

PLASTIC CONTAINERS. See also Frozen Foods (p. 1115). Plastic containers for refrigerator and freezer storage should vary in size. There's no reason why you can't use supermarket containers that you've saved, although they won't hold up as well as the sturdier kind you buy specifically for the refrigerator and freezer.

ALUMINUM FOIL. Foil is a blessing in the kitchen. It can serve as a broiler lining, a drip catcher, a lid fitted snugly over an oven dish, and like old-fashioned parchment can be wrapped around foods which are to be baked. In addition it's an excellent, durable wrap, molding naturally to odd-shaped items, and it seals itself.

PLASTIC WRAP. Transparent plastic wrap tends to hold moisture and is excellent for wrapping because it clings tightly. It also makes a good covering for bowls. It's less good in the freezer, where it often doesn't stick well and should be used with ties or bindings of some kind.

PLASTIC BAGS. Plastic bags with ties are excellent for freezing and refrigerator storage.

WAX PAPER. Wax paper for spreading out on your working surface when measuring dry ingredients is very useful. It is also good for covering a sauce so that it won't form a skin and for wrapping things when you don't want the moisture that plastic wrap gives.

PARCHMENT. Parchment paper is very handy in baking.

PAPER TOWELS. Paper towels are essential in the kitchen these days for drying everything from hands to greens, from draining fried foods to sopping up fats from the surface of a broth.

CHEESECLOTH. It is always necessary to use fine-mesh cheesecloth when you want to strain out the residue to get a clear broth. It is also useful for binding something, for poaching, and for making a bouquet garni or herb bags.

STRING. You'll find you can't do without a ball of good strong kitchen twine.

COOKING TERMS AND PROCEDURES

AU JUS. A French expression meaning "with the juice" (pronounced "oh zhu"), it is a term applied to meat, usually roast beef, which is served in its own juices.

BAKE. To cook by dry heat. Do not crowd things in the oven; the free circulation of air is important. Always preheat the oven 10–15 minutes, unless otherwise indicated, and use an oven thermometer to check the temperature.

Oven Temperatures

250°F	Very slow
300°F	Slow
325°F	Moderately slow
350°F	Moderate
375°F	Moderately hot
400°F	Hot
450–500°F	Very hot

BARBECUE. As commonly used, to cook on a grill over intense heat, usually a live fire made with charcoal or wood, sometimes called "grilling" or "charcoal broiling."
To build an outdoor fire. See p. 361.

BARD. To cover meats with a thin layer of fat before roasting them, usually done with very lean meats to keep them from drying out.

BASTE. To moisten while cooking in order to add flavor and keep things from drying out. Use a bulb baster, a spoon, or a brush.

BATTER. A mixture containing flour and liquid, thin enough to pour.

BEAT. To mix rapidly in order to make a mixture smooth and light by incorporating as much air as possible. If you're beating by hand, use a whisk, a fork, or a wooden spoon in a rhythmic, circular motion, lifting and plopping; beat from the wrist without using your whole arm and you won't get tired. Rotary egg beaters and electric beaters are a great convenience. If you use an electric mixer it is better to have one with a rounded bowl for proper beating. For *beating egg whites,* see Eggs (p. 473); for *whipping cream,* see Cream (p. 13).

BEURRE MANIÉ.   A mixture of butter and flour added at the last to thicken a hot sauce or soup. *To make a beurre manié,* mix equal amounts of flour and soft butter, working them together quickly with your fingers. Add small bits to a hot liquid, stirring and cooking after each addition until they are absorbed and you can determine the desired thickness. Use only as much as is needed.

BLANCH.   To boil rapidly in lots of water briefly, sometimes for just an instant. Blanching is done for various purposes: as a preliminary cooking process; as a way of setting color, sealing in juices, or sometimes removing strong flavors; as an aid in removing peels or shells; and as a way of destroying harmful enzymes when canning or freezing.

BLEND.   To incorporate two or more ingredients thoroughly. When the term is used in a recipe, it means to blend by hand or with an electric beater.

BOIL.   To heat a liquid until bubbles break continually on the surface. Boiling temperature at sea level is 212°F. At a high altitude it is much lower.

BRAISE.   To cook slowly, usually covered, in a little liquid or fat, often on a bed of aromatics.

BROIL.   To cook on a grill under strong, direct heat. The term "broiling" is sometimes used loosely; "charcoal broiling" is really barbecuing or grilling, and "pan broiling" is closer to frying, although usually done with little or no fat.

BROWN.   Browning may be done under a broiler, in fat in a skillet, or in the oven. The purpose is to sear, to seal in juices, and to give good color. When browning meat for a stew, make sure it is absolutely dry, turn so all sides are seared, and when doing cut-up pieces, do not crowd the pan or they will steam rather than brown.

BRUISE.   To crush partially in order to release flavor, as with peppercorns and garlic cloves.

CARAMELIZE.   To heat sugar in order to turn it brown and give it a special taste.

CHOP.   To cut solids into pieces with a sharp knife or other chopping device. It is worth learning the right chopping techniques for different ingredients, because once you are proficient, you'll save your-

self a lot of time—to say nothing of deriving satisfaction
from your skill. To chop: Holding the blade at both ends,
bring a large knife up and
down firmly all over the material to be chopped.

CLARIFY. To separate and remove solids from a liquid, thus making
it clear. *To clarify butter*, see p. 12; *to clarify stock*, see p. 107.

CODDLE. To poach gently in barely simmering water.

CREAM. To work one or more foods together until soft and blended.
To cream butter, see Butter (p. 11).

CRIMP. To seal together by pinching at intervals the edges of a two-
crust pie, making a decorative edge (see illustration p. 892).

CURDLE. Certain foods curdle—or separate—when too much heat is
applied too quickly. Sometimes you can correct this; other times
you have to start all over again, but you can incorporate the curdled mixture into the new one. Cream and custard sauces with a little flour in them will not curdle, even over high heat. See also Eggs
(p. 14); Sour Cream (p. 14).

CURE. To preserve meats by drying and salting and/or smoking.

CUT IN SHORTENING. To incorporate shortening into flour until it
resembles coarse crumbs, uneven in size and texture. Use your fingers, two knives, or a pastry blender. It is better if the shortening is
chilled.

DEGLAZE. To remove and preserve the natural glaze that accumulates in a cooking pan by adding liquid to the pan in which meat (or
fish or poultry) has been cooked, scraping up any remaining bits.
Sometimes the liquid is boiled down to a more concentrated form
and sometimes additional butter is swirled in. Deglazing makes a
small amount of natural sauce that can be poured over the meat or
used as an enrichment for a more elaborate sauce.

DEGREASE. To remove grease from a soup, stock, gravy, or sauce.
Skim the fat off the top with a spoon or skimmer, blotting out what

remains with paper towels. It is difficult to degrease thoroughly when something is hot; the simplest way, whenever time permits, is to chill until the fat solidifies at the top and can be easily lifted off.

DICE. To dice: Remove, if necessary, a small slice from the bottom of the onion, or whatever you want to chop, so that it lies flat on the board.

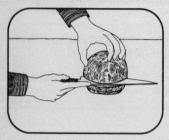

a) Using one hand to hold it steady, first make horizontal cuts at even intervals, slicing not quite through to the root end (at the back).

b) Repeat with evenly spaced vertical cuts.

c) Slice straight down, making sure that the fingers at the edge are tucked under, and move them back with each slice. The chopped pieces will fall in uniform dice.

DOUGH. A mixture of flour, liquid, and other ingredients, stiff enough to shape and knead with your hands.

DREDGE. To cover a solid food with sugar, flour, or other dry ingredients. Dredging can be done by dragging the solid food through the powdery substance, by shaking the two together in a bag, or by using a strainer or sifter.

DRIPPINGS. The juices, fats, and browned bits that collect in the pan after meat or poultry has been roasted. Unless burned or very greasy (and excess fat can be removed), the drippings are valuable for a little sauce (see Deglaze, p. 55) and for gravy.

DRIZZLE. To sprinkle drops of liquid lightly over food in a casual manner.

DUST. To sprinkle food with dry ingredients. Use a strainer or a jar with a perforated cover, or try the good, old-fashioned way of shaking things together in a paper bag.

EVISCERATE. To remove the entrails of a fish, fowl, or animal in preparation for cooking.

FILLET. As a verb, to remove the bones from meat or fish. A fillet (or filet) is the piece of flesh after it has been boned.

FLAMBÉ. To flame foods by dousing in some form of potable alcohol and setting alight. It's fun to do at the table, and if the alcohol is warmed beforehand, it will be sure to catch fire. Flambéing is enjoyed for the taste as much as for the spectacle.

FLUTE. To make a decorative scalloped or undulating edge on a piecrust or other pastry (see illustration p. 891).

FOLD. To incorporate an aerated substance like whipped cream or beaten egg whites with what is usually a heavier substance. The purpose of folding is to retain volume and lightness by taking care not to deflate the pockets of air. Use your hands or a rubber spatula for folding. Cut through and turn over, rotating the bowl. For folding egg whites, see p. 474.

FRICASSEE. To stew gently in liquid and aromatic vegetables. It is usually done with poultry; a white sauce is then made from the broth. But today the term is used more loosely and a fricassee of vegetables or seafood could be made by stewing in butter and oil and natural juices.

FRITTER. A food that is coated in a batter, then fried in deep fat. Fritters should be crispy on the outside, moist and succulent within.

FRY. Frying is cooking in a skillet with fat. *Pan frying* is done in a skillet. It can be a light sauté in a very small amount of butter, a quick browning in a layer of hot fat, or "pan broiling" over high heat of meats just in their own fat. *Deep-fat frying* requires a deep heavy pan with 3 or 4 cups or at least 1½ inches of hot fat into which the food is lowered. Anything to be deep-fried should be thoroughly dried first or the fat will splatter.

Sometimes foods are batter-coated first, sometimes just floured, according to the recipe. The frying temperature varies slightly according to the food (recipes will indicate). If you have no deep-fat thermometer, drop a 1-inch bread cube into the hot fat and count slowly to sixty; if the bread browns in just one minute, the fat should be around 365°F—the average deep-frying temperature. It is important that the fat be hot enough so that foods you are cooking will not absorb it and become greasy. Fry in batches, if necessary, so the pan is never crowded, and don't have the food ice-cold when it goes in. Do not let the fat smoke or you'll frizzle things too quickly on the outside, leaving an uncooked interior.

Vegetable or peanut oil or solid shortening is recommended for deep-fat frying. Do not use butter or olive oil. A deep-fat fryer is not essential, but a wire basket in which food can be lowered into the hot fat is a great convenience.

If you plan to reuse the oil, clarify it by adding a few slices of peeled potatoes to the hot oil to absorb flavors. Remove the potato, let the oil cool a bit, then strain it through cheesecloth. Store it in the refrigerator and taste it before reusing it to be sure it's still good. It will darken with each use.

GARNISH. To decorate a dish both to enhance its appearance and to provide a flavorful foil. Parsley, lemon slices, raw vegetables, chopped chives, and other herbs are all forms of garnishes. See also Quick Relishes (p. 1102).

GLAZE. To apply a thickish liquid over the surface to give a final sheen. One refers also to meat glaze, which is reduced, highly concentrated stock, as well as the glaze left in the pan after cooking meat.

GRATE. To break up a solid into small particles, usually by rubbing against a metal object or disk with sharp-edged holes.

GRATIN. A shallow baking dish, usually round or oval, that can be slipped under the broiler. In common parlance the food baked and/or broiled in this kind of dish is called a gratin. Gratinéing is the browning process of the topping of crumbs or cheese.

GRILL. To cook on a grill over intense heat.

GRIND. To process solids by hand or mechanically to reduce them to tiny particles.

JULIENNE. To cut into thin strips. A julienne of vegetables would be a mixture of vegetables that have been so cut. To julienne: Make a stack of ⅛-inch slices (p. 61) and then cut downward at ⅛-inch intervals to make matchstick pieces.

KNEAD. To manipulate dough, with one's hands or mechanically, to develop the gluten in the flour.

LARD. To insert into a piece of meat strips of fat or sometimes other meat in order to tenderize, to give texture, and to add flavor.

LUKEWARM. Neither cool nor warm, lukewarm means approximately body temperature.

MACERATE. To toss fruits in sugar and lemon, wine, or a liqueur, and let them stand to absorb the flavors.

MARINATE. To cover foods in seasoned liquid, always containing some acid, such as lemon, vinegar, or wine, to tenderize and to infuse flavor.

MASK. To improve the appearance or flavor of a food with a sauce or a seasoning.

MEASURE. When measuring, use accurate measuring cups and spoons (see p. 33); fill, then level. Do not pack ingredients except for brown sugar.

MINCE. To chop very fine. To mince: After chopping roughly, with one hand on the tip of the blade and the other on the handle, rock the blade back and forth, marching from one end of the pile to the other; then repeat crosswise.

MIX. To combine two or more ingredients.

MOLD. To form into an attractive shape by filling a decorative container (termed a mold) and steaming or baking or chilling, as the case may be.

PAN BROIL. See Fry (p. 57). Sometimes the skillet is salted first; sometimes a piece of fat from the meat you are pan broiling is rubbed over the warm skillet.

PARBOIL. To precook in boiling water; see also Blanch (p. 54).

PARE. To finely shave away the skins of fruits.

PÂTÉ. A baked, well-seasoned loaf of various meats, most of which are ground, sometimes studded with strips of other meats, well lubricated with fat. To be served cold.

PEEL. To remove the peels from vegetables or fruits. The swivel-bladed vegetable peeler is a great tool.

PICKLE. To preserve meats, vegetables, and fruits in brine.

PINCH. A pinch is the trifling amount you can hold between your thumb and forefinger.

PIPE. To squeeze a soft (but not runny) smooth food through a pastry tube in order to make decorative shapes or a border.

PLANKED. Cooked on a thick hardwood plank.

PLUMP. To soak dried fruits in liquid until they swell.

POACH. To simmer very gently.

PROOF. To test yeast for potency.

PURÉE. To mash to a smooth blend. The result—the mashed substance—is also referred to as a purée.

REDUCE. To boil down to reduce the volume.

REFRESH. To run cold water over something that has been boiled.

RENDER. To make solid fat into liquid by melting it slowly.

ROAST. To cook by dry heat in an oven. See also Bake (p. 53).

ROUX. A mixture of melted fat and flour (see p. 378).

SAUTÉ. A gentle cooking on top of the stove, less violent and requiring less fat than frying. Often one browns the food first, tossing to seal all sides, and then continues with a gentle sauté, covered or uncovered; at other times one does just a quick sauté.

SCALD. To scald milk is to bring it just to the boil. To scald a solid food means to drop it in boiling water for a second.

SCALLOP. A word that has several meanings. The verb means to bake with a sauce or cream, or to make a decorative piecrust edge. The noun *scallop* can mean either a small, thin slice of meat or the bivalve scallops (see Fish and Shellfish chapter).

SCORE. To make shallow cuts in meat or fish both to tenderize and to help keep the shape.

SEAR. To subject meat to very high heat in order to seal in the juices.

SHRED. To cut or grate into shreds. To shred cabbage or lettuce: First cut the head in quarters. Place one flat side down on the board and cut against the perpendicular side, shaving as close to the edge as possible.

SIFT. To remove possible lumps and to lighten the dry ingredients of a batter by putting them through a strainer or a sifter.

SIMMER. To boil so gently that the liquid barely bubbles.

SLICE. To slice: Holding the potato, or whatever, with fingers tucked under, bring the knife down firmly to make slices (⅛-inch thick if you are going to julienne).

SPIN A THREAD. When sugar syrup is cooked to the point that it reaches the softball stage (238°F), it will spin a thread. Dip a spoon into the boiling syrup, then remove and hold it at a tilt above the pan, and it will spin a thread.

STEAM. To cook or heat a food over boiling water without touching the water and allowing the steam to circulate (see illustration of steamer basket, p. 41). Sometimes foods are put into an airtight mold, as in steamed puddings, in which case they are simply lowered into gently boiling water to cook. Also when a food is enfolded in foil, sealed tightly, and then baked, the result is very much the same as steaming.

STEEP. To pour boiling water over something and let it sit.

STEW. Long slow cooking in liquid.

STIR. To rotate ingredients in a bowl or in a pan, using a spoon or whisk, in order to mix, or to insure even cooking and prevent sticking.

SUGAR POACHING SYRUP
Thin syrup, 3 cups water combined with 1 cup sugar makes 3 cups.
Medium syrup, 2 cups water combined with 2 cups sugar makes 2 cups.
Heavy syrup, 1 cup water combined with 1 cup sugar makes 1 cup.
Put the sugar and water in a small pan and bring to a boil. Boil for about 2 minutes or until the sugar has dissolved. Cool. Put in a container and cover. Store indefinitely.

TEMPER. To prepare eggs for a hot liquid (see p. 474).

TOAST. To broil or grill to crisp on the outside.

TRUSS. To bind a bird so that it will keep its shape during cooking (see p. 309).

UNMOLD. To turn out of a mold so that the interior keeps its shape.

WHIP. To lighten and increase the volume by beating.

WHISK. To beat with a whisk or whip until well mixed.

APPETIZERS & FIRST COURSES

One of the first changes that seemed necessary in this chapter was to eliminate so many dips and dunks. But I have kept the good basic ones. A few things, such as Meatballs Rémoulade and Rissolettes, seemed more trouble to make than they were worth for today's busy cooks. Simpler, more straightforward appetizers have become popular, such as the Stuffed Cherry Tomatoes (they taste just like a BLT sandwich without bread) and the Swiss Cheese Spread that everyone asks for; the New Red Potatoes with Rosemary are wonderful—tiny, hot, and easy to eat—and they seem to go with drinks of all kinds.

Keep your appetizers and first courses simple. Don't serve dinner so late that everyone has become sated before they are seated at the table. Appetizers are intended only to stave off acute hunger pangs and temper drinking on an empty stomach.

ABOUT FOOD TO SERVE WITH DRINKS AND TO START OFF A MEAL

An appetizer should make an immediate appeal to the eye and the palate, stimulating without satisfying the appetite. You want such foods to demand attention with their bright colors and appealing arrangement; the hot dishes are served bubbling hot, and cold dishes well chilled. When served with drinks, salty or piquant tastes will encourage thirst while at the same time tempering the effects of alcohol; as an opener at dinner, their purpose is to awaken and stimulate the appetite. Portions are small: when passed with drinks, they are bite-size; when served on a plate either in the living room before dinner or at the table, a small plateful attractively arranged will suffice.

You are likely to serve different kinds of appetizers in different circumstances, so let's look at several typical occasions and consider which foods seem appropriate.

For a Large Cocktail Party or Reception

At this kind of affair you will want to concentrate on foods which can be eaten with the fingers—a combination of cold appetizers and some hot ones. Most of these should be passed on trays; with a big crowd people cannot always make their way easily to a buffet table. It's nice to have placed strategically around the room some bowls of things to nibble, like nut mixtures, olives, freshly roasted popcorn, or potato chips, as well as some dips that can be scooped up with raw vegetables or crackers. Lots of small napkins for sticky fingers are a must; as for the appetizers passed on trays, avoid messy foods that are apt to drip before they can be popped into the mouth. Near the drinks, a buffet table might hold a pâté or something hot in a chafing dish, but this is the kind of cocktail party or reception where guests are expected to go on to their own dinners, so you need give them only enough for the road and to take away with them a lingering taste of your delicious tidbits. Count on about four appetizers per person, with the buffet offering and the snacks and dips as extra.

For a Stay-on Cocktail Party

This, too, could be a large party that dwindles down to a manageable number of more intimate friends you've asked to stay on. Or it could be a smaller gathering at which you really want your guests to hang around and talk, so you plan to feed them handsomely enough to sustain them for the whole evening. In either case have some nibbles and dips and a few simple appetizers available at the beginning of the party; at a smaller gathering it is easier for people to spread their own crackers. Then offer a satisfying spread of hot and cold dishes with small plates, forks, and napkins so that guests will help themselves as they feel the proddings of hunger (see ideas for the hot and cold buffet on the next page and also Buffet Dinners in Menu Suggestions at the back of the book). Everyone serves himself and eats perched on the edge of a chair or leaning against the dining-room wall. Eventually, the coffee urn and maybe even little cakes or cookies will be welcome.

First Courses

Here your appetizers are usually more selective, very often just one delicious, tempting creation on a plate that fits in with the meal to come (see Menu Planning, pp. 4–8) and can be served either in the living room or at table. There are such a lot of possibilities. For guidance in selection to determine what goes well with what, consult the sample menus in Menu Suggestions at the back of the book; a first course could be anything from hot stuffed clams to oysters Rockefeller, for particularly elegant occasions, or stuffed avocados, individual molds of a chilled mousse, a slice of quiche, and so on. If it's to be a salad, somehow that's more fitting when you're sitting down at the table. It is also splendid sometimes to have a large, colorful platter of mixed hors d'oeuvre, like an Italian antipasto, which can be passed around the table so everyone takes what he wants; make it a gorgeous arrangement with portions of homemade pâté, piles of aromatic vegetables, some shrimp or crabmeat with mustardy mayonnaise, thin slices of country ham or dry sausage, celery, olives, and sliced tomatoes.

Types of Appetizers

Dips and Spreads: These are more or less interchangeable: the same mixture that can be scooped up on the end of a carrot stick can be spread on a round of Melba toast. They are easy to prepare ahead of time, and have the advantage of allowing everyone to help himself. Surround the dip or the crock of spread with interesting crackers, potato chips, corn chips, fried tortillas, or toasted pita; set out some cold shrimp, scallops, cocktail sausages, or spears of ham; or present a colorful arrangement of raw vegetables.

Cold Appetizers: These can be made by piping different spreads onto crackers or thin slices of good bread cut into decorative shapes or into cornucopias of ham and salami. Such canapés can be made in the morning and refrigerated, covered with foil, plastic wrap, or a damp towel. For *stuffed vegetables* use the same spreads and savory butters to fill mushroom caps, hollowed-out cherry tomatoes, cucumber boats, or celery ribs. If it's a very warm evening, keep cold dishes chilled by presenting them on beds of chipped ice.

Hot Appetizers: All those piping hot, tempting morsels like cheese and crab puffs, cocktail sausages in pastry, tiny filled savory tarts, skewers of chicken livers and bacon, hot biscuits, fritters, and so on are included here. One can never get enough of them, but remember that if you are both host and cook, you'll have to keep your eye on the stove and replenish the platters, so don't attempt more than you can manage comfortably.

DIPS AND SPREADS

CRUDITÉS ଛୈ

A welcome offering with drinks is a plate of icy-crisp raw vegetables. They spoil neither the appetite nor the waistline, and are usually presented with a variety of sauces and dips. Look in other chapters for more ideas for dips to serve with raw vegetables: you might try Aïoli (p. 389) for garlic lovers, flavored Mayonnaises (p. 707), and Yogurt Green Sauce (p. 395) to start.

The culinary name *crudités* means raw, and the vegetables must be garden-fresh, crisp, and well washed. Sometimes it helps to scrub and scrape early in the day; keep certain vegetables (not tomatoes or mushrooms) in bowls of ice water in the refrigerator to crisp them. Choose one or many for your arrangement: cherry tomatoes, orange carrot sticks, snow-white cauliflower flowerets, jade-green broccoli, zucchini rounds or spears, peppery rounds of radish, sticks of turnip or kohlrabi, bland cucumber slices, green and red pepper chunks, and whole mushrooms. On the West Coast they serve jicama, a plain brown root vegetable that is sweet and crisp when it is peeled and sliced. The ultimate alternative to potato chips for dips is a trayful of chilled cooked artichoke leaves.

HOT AND COLD BUFFET: The buffet table might include a handsome pâté on a platter surrounded by tiny pickles or in a crock, accompanied by Melba toast, thin slices of French bread or of dark rye; a decorative ball of cheese or a mound of paprika-dusted Liptauer; aromatic vegetables; stuffed eggs; meatballs in a chafing dish, or a cheese fondue. Even though guests use their fingers, these things are easier to manage if they are laid out on a buffet table than from a passing tray. The food can be prepared well ahead, and it's the kind that always looks enticing on the table.

NIBBLES: These are the seductive snacks that dare you to eat only one—popcorn, pretzels, salted nuts, and nut mixtures with dried fruit, pickled vegetables, olives. Most snacks are ready to serve when purchased and need only to be set out.

(2 CUPS)   ঽ‍‍‍‍‍ **SPICY CHOPPED EGGPLANT**

Serve with crackers or corn crisps.

1 medium eggplant	2 cloves garlic, minced
4 scallions, minced	3 tablespoons vinegar
3 tablespoons minced parsley	4 tablespoons olive oil
½ teaspoon freshly ground pepper	Salt

Preheat the oven to 350°F. Bake the eggplant for 1 hour. When it is cool enough to handle, peel and chop coarsely. Blend the scallions, parsley, pepper, garlic, vinegar, and olive oil in a blender or food processor. Put the mixture in a bowl and add the coarsely chopped eggplant and salt to taste. Serve chilled or at room temperature.

(2 CUPS)   ঽ‍‍‍‍‍ **GUACAMOLE**

Don't purée the avocados; an authentic guacamole contains small chunks of avocado. Serve with tortilla chips.

2 large ripe avocados	3 tablespoons lemon juice or lime juice
4 canned, peeled green chili peppers, chopped fine	¼ teaspoon freshly ground pepper
1 clove garlic, minced	Salt to taste
2 tablespoons finely chopped cilantro (optional)	

Peel and seed the avocados. Mash one avocado in a bowl, and finely chop the other. Mix the two with remaining ingredients. Cover and refrigerate for several hours before serving.

EGGPLANT-ZUCCHINI APPETIZER ❧   (10 CUPS)

This is good served with small slices of thin French bread or in a crisp lettuce leaf.

1 eggplant, stem removed, in ½-inch cubes

4 zucchini, stem end removed, sliced ½ inch thick, then quartered

2 green peppers, stem and seeds removed, cut in ½-inch squares

1 bunch scallions, stem ends removed, chopped

4 cloves garlic, chopped fine

¼ cup chopped parsley

4 tomatoes, stem removed and chopped, or a 1-pound 12-ounce can Italian plum tomatoes

½ cup olive oil

Hot red pepper to taste

4 tablespoons lemon juice

Salt and freshly ground pepper to taste

Combine all the ingredients in a large saucepan and simmer over very low heat for at least 1 hour, checking frequently to make sure the bottom isn't burning; add a little water or tomato juice if too dry. It is done when the vegetables are soft and the flavors have blended. Taste and correct seasonings during the cooking process.

BAKED EGGPLANT APPETIZER

Mix all the ingredients in a baking dish and bake, covered, at 300°F for 2 hours, stirring occasionally.

YOGURT DIP ❧   (2 CUPS)

2 cups yogurt

1 clove garlic, minced

½ cucumber, seeded and chopped fine

½ teaspoon dried mint, crumbled, or 1 teaspoon fresh, chopped

Mix all the ingredients and chill thoroughly to let the flavors develop.

(2½ CUPS)   ६◆ **GREEN DIP**

          1 cup parsley   ¼ teaspoon Tabasco
          5 scallions, chopped   1 teaspoon curry powder
          1¼ cups mayonnaise   Salt
          1 cup sour cream
          1 tablespoon chopped fresh
              dill, or 1¼ teaspoons dried,
              crumbled

Liquefy the parsley, scallions, and ½ cup of the mayonnaise in a
blender or food processor. Add the remaining ¾ cup mayonnaise, the
sour cream, dill, Tabasco, curry powder, and salt to taste, and chill.

(2½ CUPS)   ६◆ **SOUR-CREAM DIP**

Garden-fresh with raw vegetables in summer.

          2 cups sour cream   2 tablespoons grated onion
          ¼ cup mayonnaise   2 tablespoons chopped chives
          2 tablespoons chopped fresh   1 tablespoon chopped parsley
              dill, or 1 tablespoon dried,   Salt
              crumbled   Freshly ground pepper

Mix the sour cream, mayonnaise, dill, onion, chives, and parsley. Season to taste with salt and pepper, and chill.

(2 CUPS)   ६◆ **BASIL COTTAGE CHEESE DIP**

For the proper creamy texture you must use a blender or food processor.

          2 cups cottage cheese   6–8 fresh basil leaves, or 1
          2 tablespoons vinegar   teaspoon dried, crumbled
          ¼ cup chopped scallions   Salt to taste
          2 tablespoons chopped   Freshly ground pepper to
              parsley   taste

Purée all the ingredients in a blender or food processor, and chill.

FRESH SALSA ఇ≫

(3 CUPS)

This is a cold Mexican-style tomato salsa, good with tortillas or tortilla chips. Also, serve on tacos or fajitas. It is best eaten within a few hours but will keep in the refrigerator for a few days. If fresh cilantro is not available, just leave it out.

1 pound fresh ripe tomatoes, seeded and chopped
1 onion, chopped
2 cloves garlic, minced
4-ounce can green chilies, chopped
1 jalapeño pepper, seeded, deveined, and minced, or ¼ to ½ teaspoon cayenne pepper

Juice of 1 lime
2 tablespoons red wine or cider vinegar
1 tablespoon olive oil
1 teaspoon salt
⅓ cup chopped fresh cilantro (optional)
½ teaspoon ground or dried and crushed oregano

Combine all the ingredients in a large bowl and mix until well blended. Refrigerate until used.

About Caviar

Little jars of "caviar" found in supermarkets are disappointing. If, for a special occasion, you want caviar, make sure you get real sturgeon-egg caviar. It should be eaten simply, by itself, with toast and maybe sweet butter, sour cream, or chopped onion or hard-boiled egg.

Salmon eggs—roe which is often called caviar—are far less expensive and can be a very good substitute for the real thing in recipes calling for caviar.

RED CAVIAR DIP

(2½ CUPS)

8 ounces cream cheese, softened
1 cup sour cream

4 ounces red caviar (salmon roe)
2 teaspoons Worcestershire sauce

Mix all the ingredients, and chill.

RED CAVIAR SPREAD

Use only 2 tablespoons of sour cream and substitute *1 tablespoon grated onion* for the Worcestershire sauce, seasoning to taste with *salt* and *freshly ground pepper*. Spread on crackers or dark bread squares.

(2½ CUPS) ## CLAM DIP

8 ounces cream cheese, softened
½ cup sour cream
6½-ounce can minced clams

1 tablespoon Worcestershire sauce
1 teaspoon grated onion

Mix all the ingredients, and chill.

(2½ CUPS) ## HOT CLAM SPREAD

This can also be good made with cold shrimp or scallops.

Two 6½-ounce cans minced clams
¼ pound butter
1½ cups cracker crumbs

1 medium onion, chopped fine
1 tablespoon lemon juice

Preheat the oven to 350°F. Drain the juice from one can of clams (use it for another purpose). Melt the butter and add the drained clams, the other can of clams with juice, the crumbs, onion, and lemon juice. Pour into a shallow baking dish, bake for 30 minutes, and serve immediately.

(1 CUP) ## ⪫ ROQUEFORT DIP

4 ounces Roquefort cheese
3 ounces cream cheese, softened

⅓ cup light cream
Dash of cayenne pepper

Mix the Roquefort, cream cheese, and cream. Season to taste with cayenne, and chill.

ROQUEFORT SPREAD

Omit the cream. Serve with crackers or toasted rounds of French bread.

HAM SPREAD   (1 CUP)

A good way to use up leftover bits from a baked ham.

1 cup chopped cooked ham	1 tablespoon chutney
1 tablespoon grated onion	4 tablespoons mayonnaise
2 teaspoons prepared mustard	

Cut the ham into small pieces and purée in a blender or food processor. Add the rest of the ingredients, put into a crock, and chill.

CORNED BEEF SPREAD

Substitute *1 cup chopped cooked corned beef* for the ham.

TUNA SPREAD   (1¼ CUPS)

7-ounce can tuna	¼ teaspoon green peppercorns
1½ tablespoons mayonnaise	

Purée all the ingredients in a blender or food processor. Put into a crock and chill.

SALMON SPREAD   (2 CUPS)

7¾-ounce can salmon	2 teaspoons lemon juice
¾ cup unsalted butter	1 teaspoon Worcestershire sauce
1 tablespoon anchovy paste	

Mix all ingredients, put into a crock, and chill.

(2 CUPS) **SARDINE-PARSLEY SPREAD**

Two 4⅜-ounce cans sardines, mashed
8 ounces cream cheese, softened

2 tablespoons chopped parsley
1 tablespoon lemon juice

Mix all ingredients, put into a crock, and chill.

SARDINE-OLIVE SPREAD

Omit the parsley and add *2 tablespoons chopped green olives* and *1 teaspoon grated onion*.

(BETWEEN ¾ AND 2 CUPS) **FLAVORED BUTTERS**

These butters are always good to have on hand and keep well frozen if tightly sealed. Make them when you have some of the following flavoring ingredients on hand and then they'll be ready to take out and use as spreads at a moment's notice. Or you can scoop out just a little bit to toss with fresh cooked vegetables or to use to round out the flavor of vegetables, meats, poultry, and fish.

To ¼ **pound butter** add any of the following ingredients, blending in a bowl or food processor until smooth. Put in a crock and chill (or freeze for later use).

For **Chive Butter:** *2 tablespoons minced chives* and *2 tablespoons minced parsley.*

For **Shrimp Butter:** *½ cup finely chopped shrimp* and *1 tablespoon lemon juice.*

For **Herb Butter:** *3–4 tablespoons finely chopped fresh herbs.*

For **Anchovy Butter:** *1 tablespoon anchovy paste.*

For **Horseradish Butter:** *1 tablespoon freshly grated or prepared horseradish.*

For **Watercress Butter:** *2 tablespoons chopped watercress.*

For **Blue Cheese Butter:** *1⅓ cups blue cheese* and, if desired, *⅛ teaspoon finely chopped garlic.*

CRAB AND CUCUMBER ROLLS ✳ (18–20 ROLLS)

2–3 cucumbers, peeled
Salt
1½ cups cooked fresh
  crabmeat, shredded
⅔ cup yogurt
2–3 tablespoons fresh lemon
  juice

Cut the cucumbers into 1-inch lengths. Using a small, sharp knife, shave around and around the cucumber until you have a continuous thin strip about 8 to 10 inches long, or use the method described on p. 77 for Cucumber Sushi. Discard the soft centers and seeds. Lay strips out flat and sprinkle with salt. Place a small mound of crabmeat at one end of a cucumber strip and roll up. Secure with a wooden toothpick. Arrange rolls on a serving dish and chill until served. Mix the yogurt and lemon juice until blended and chill. Serve the dipping sauce with the rolls.

BELGIAN ENDIVE APPETIZER (12 PIECES)

Tidy to eat and very elegant.

½ cup cooked crabmeat or 6
  crab legs, smoked oysters,
  or mussels
2 tablespoons mayonnaise
12 Belgian endive leaves

Put a piece of crabmeat or a crab leg, oyster, or mussel and ½ teaspoon mayonnaise on the wide white end of each endive leaf.

CUCUMBER SANDWICHES ぐ (8 SMALL SANDWICHES)

These used to be called tea sandwiches, but there's no reason why they shouldn't appear with cocktails as well.

4 thin slices fresh white bread
4 tablespoons butter, softened
1 large cucumber
Salt
¼ cup mayonnaise
¼ teaspoon dried tarragon,
  crumbled
Freshly ground pepper

Cut the crusts from the bread and spread slices with butter. Peel and seed the cucumber, finely chop or thinly slice, and sprinkle with salt. Let stand in a colander for 10 minutes. Pat dry, mix with the mayonnaise and tarragon, season to taste, and spread on the bread. Cover with the second slices, cut into quarters, and arrange on a plate.

WATERCRESS SANDWICHES

Substitute ½ *cup chopped watercress* for the cucumber, and omit the salting and draining.

(10 SANDWICHES) ñ* **ONION SANDWICHES**

These are wonderfully simple, simply wonderful little sandwiches which may be served as a cold appetizer. James Beard used to make them with a rich brioche dough, and this is a variation of his recipe. Try them with sweet red onions when in season. Sweet butter may be used in place of the mayonnaise.

10 slices white bread	1 large onion, sliced thin
¾ cup mayonnaise, preferably homemade	Salt
	½ cup finely chopped parsley

Cut 2 rounds from each slice of white bread, using a canapé cutter or small biscuit cutter. Spread the rounds with mayonnaise. On half of the rounds place a very thin slice of raw onion, just the size of the round, and sprinkle with salt. Place another bread round on top; roll the edges first in mayonnaise and then in the finely chopped parsley.

(16 PIECES) ñ **RADISH BITES**

4 slices thin black bread	6–8 large radishes
¼ pound butter or ripe Camembert or Brie cheese	

Spread each slice of bread thickly with butter, or cheese, and cut each into 4 square pieces. Thinly slice the radishes and press into the butter or cheese.

PROSCIUTTO AND MELON   (24 PIECES)

This is quick and simple and brings together the sweet fruity melon flavor and the salty contrast of the ham. Be sure to use ripe melons.

    1½- to 2-pound melon   Lemon or lime wedges, for
        (cantaloupe, honeydew, or   garnish
        cranshaw)
    12 paper-thin slices prosciutto
        or Smithfield-type ham

Cut the melon in half and then quarters so that it is easy to handle. Remove the rind from the melon pieces and cut into small wedges so that you have about 24 pieces. Cut each prosciutto or ham slice in half lengthwise. Wrap each melon wedge with a piece of ham. Arrange on a serving platter. Refrigerate to chill until served.

PROSCIUTTO AND FIGS

Use *12 ripe figs* in place of the melon. Remove stems and cut each fig in half. Wrap each half with prosciutto or ham.

PROSCIUTTO AND PEAR

Use *4 firm but ripe winter pears*, such as Bosc or d'Anjou, in place of the melon. Peel, core, and slice into wedges. Wrap each wedge with the prosciutto or ham. Pear may darken, so assemble these just before serving.

DEVILED EGGS   (SERVES 4)

If you want the eggs to look elegant, use a pastry tube to pipe the creamy yolk mixture into the white. Imaginative garnishes such as a fat caper on top or a cross of slivers of green or red pepper, a slice of olive or pickle, a sprinkling of fresh herbs or watercress, makes stuffed eggs particularly lovely.

    4 hard-boiled eggs (p. 476)   Freshly ground pepper
    3 tablespoons mayonnaise   1 tablespoon minced parsley
    1 teaspoon Dijon mustard   or fresh herbs (optional)
    Salt

Shell the eggs and slice them in half lengthwise. Remove the yolks and mash them with the mayonnaise, mustard, and salt and pepper to taste until it is smoothly blended and creamy. Stuff equal amounts into the hollow of each egg white. Sprinkle parsley or fresh herbs on top, if desired.

ANCHOVY-STUFFED EGGS

Omit the mustard and add *1–1½ teaspoons anchovy paste*, to taste.

HAM-STUFFED EGGS

Add *1 heaping tablespoon finely chopped ham* to the filling.

CHEESE-STUFFED EGGS

Use *2 tablespoons freshly grated Parmesan cheese* instead of the mustard.

CURRIED-STUFFED EGGS

Add *2 teaspoons curry powder* to the filling.

(ABOUT 48 ROLLS) &? * **CUCUMBER SUSHI**

"Sushi" is a culinary term that has recently been absorbed into our language. The Japanese mean by the term molded vinegared rice, and although we usually associate it with a topping of raw fish, it can be molded with vegetables.

Make most of this recipe the day before, then assemble an hour or so before serving.

2 cups water
1 cup medium- or short-grain white rice
1 tablespoon sugar
2 tablespoons rice wine vinegar

1 teaspoon salt
½ cup chopped carrot
½ cup chopped scallions
2 teaspoons finely chopped fresh ginger
2 cucumbers

In a saucepan, bring the water to a boil. Add the rice, sugar, vinegar, and salt, cover, and simmer for 15–20 minutes, or until the rice is tender and the water is absorbed. Let cool a little and stir in the carrot, scallions, and ginger. Taste the rice mixture and correct the seasonings. The rice should be very sticky. Divide the mixture in half and turn out onto two large pieces of wax paper. Dampen your fingers and form the rice into a long roll or log about 1 inch across, compressing the rice firmly. Roll up in the wax paper and refrigerate for at least 6 hours or overnight. Peel the cucumbers and cut off the ends. Then using a vegetable peeler, peel strips of cucumber the entire length. Continue making strips in the same place on the cucumber until you reach the seeds at the center. (You will have about 12 strips, each a little more than ½ inch wide.) Then turn the cucumber one quarter-turn and repeat the process. Lay the strips out on paper towels two at a time, overlapping slightly on the long side in order to make a strip 1 inch wide. Roll up, and refrigerate several hours or overnight. To assemble the sushi, unroll a strip of the cucumber and lay it out on a flat surface. Cut a piece of the firmed rice mixture about the same width—1 inch—as the cucumber, lay it at one end of the strip, and roll up. Secure with a toothpick if you wish, although it is not necessary, and place on a serving dish. Refrigerate if not served immediately.

(1½ CUPS)   **SALMON BALL**

7¾-ounce can salmon, drained   1 tablespoon grated onion
3 ounces cream cheese,   Salt to taste
    softened   ¼ cup minced parsley
1 tablespoon lemon juice   ¼ cup finely chopped pecans
1 teaspoon prepared
    horseradish

Mix the salmon, cream cheese, lemon juice, horseradish, onion, and
salt. Refrigerate until firm enough to handle. Form into a ball, and roll
in a mixture of parsley and pecans.

(8 ROLLS)   **SMOKED SALMON ROLLS**

Serve whole or cut in bite-size pieces.

3 ounces cream cheese,   2 teaspoons minced onion
    softened   1 teaspoon minced parsley
2 tablespoons lemon juice   2 tablespoons mayonnaise
1 tablespoon capers, drained   8 slices smoked salmon

Beat the cream cheese, lemon juice, capers, onion, parsley, and mayonnaise until smooth and well blended. Spread some of the mixture on
each slice of smoked salmon. Roll up, cover, and refrigerate.

                                              HAM ROLLS

Use *8 slices good smoked ham* in place of salmon.

A Warning About Raw Fish

There is considerable concern today about eating raw fish. To
kill possible bacteria and parasites, freeze fillets at 10°F or below for 3 days and whole fish or large pieces for 5 days before
curing. Freezing fish does diminish some of the fresh flavor that
is so enticing about cured, raw fish. When frozen fish is
thawed, lots of liquid is lost, some of which are the fish juices.

GRAVLAX   (SERVES 20)

This is a delicate cured salmon appetizer which is best made with the freshest salmon available. The salt and sugar marinade cures and firms the fillets. Serve with fresh lemon, capers, and a light rye or French bread and sweet butter.

2 fresh salmon fillets, center cut with skin attached (about 3 pounds)	¼ cup coarse or kosher salt
	¼ cup sugar
	2 tablespoons white or black peppercorns, crushed
1 large bunch fresh dill	

Pat the salmon fillets dry and cut away or tweeze out any small bones. Place one fillet, skin side down, in a deep, flat-bottomed glass baking dish. Spread the dill evenly over the fish. Mix together the salt, sugar, and crushed peppercorns and sprinkle this mixture evenly over the dill. Top with the other salmon fillet. Place a piece of plastic wrap over the salmon, then put a dish over the salmon and weight with heavy cans of food or bricks, making sure the weight is evenly distributed. Refrigerate for 48 hours, turning the fish over every 12 hours and basting with the marinade that accumulates, letting it flow between the fillets. When the gravlax is finished, remove the fillets from the dish, separate the halves, and scrape off the dill and seasonings. Pat dry with paper towels. Refrigerate until served. To serve, place fillets skin side down on a cutting board and slice thinly on the diagonal and off the skin.

LIPTAUER CHEESE ক্ষ   (2 CUPS)

Very popular on the American cocktail scene, Liptauer is really an adaptation of a Hungarian recipe. The original uses a native, soft sheep's cheese called Liptó. Pile in a mound and serve surrounded with crackers.

8 ounces cream cheese, softened	2 teaspoons minced anchovies
4 tablespoons sour cream	2 shallots or scallions, minced
4 tablespoons butter, softened	1 tablespoon paprika
2 teaspoons drained capers	1 teaspoon caraway seed
	Salt to taste

Blend all the ingredients in a food processor, blender, or bowl. Press into a small bowl and chill.

16–20 PIECES)   **STUFFED CHERRY TOMATOES**

These little appetizers taste like a BLT—and you're not eating any bread.

> 1 pound cherry tomatoes   ½ cup mayonnaise
> (preferably small), stems   4 strips cooked bacon,
> removed   crumbled

Wash and dry tomatoes. Cut a thin slice from the stem end of each tomato. Using a small spoon, scoop out most of the juice and seeds from the inside and discard. In a small bowl, combine the mayonnaise and the crumbled bacon and mix well. Fill each tomato cavity with some of the mayonnaise mixture. The yield in this recipe may vary greatly depending on the size of the tomatoes.

ABOUT 4 CUPS)   ?❧ **AROMATIC VEGETABLES**

Vegetables cut in bite sizes and cooked in a broth of olive oil and Middle Eastern seasonings are unusual and delightfully refreshing with drinks. The vegetables should be firm enough so they can be speared with toothpicks. Each must be cooked separately, but sometimes it is nice to serve several kinds arranged colorfully on a platter.

> 1 pound mushrooms, small   ¼ teaspoon fennel seed
> onions, and/or zucchini,   Pinch of celery seed
> in 1-inch pieces, and/or   Pinch of salt
> cauliflower in small   8–10 peppercorns, lightly
> flowerets, and/or 1   crushed
> package frozen artichoke   2–6 scallions, in ½-inch pieces,
> hearts   using some green, or 5–6
> ⅓ cup olive oil   shallots, peeled and sliced
> 2 tablespoons lemon juice   2 tablespoons chopped
> ¼ teaspoon coriander seed   parsley

Place the mushrooms (quartered if large; halved if medium; left whole if small), onions, zucchini, cauliflower flowerets, and artichoke hearts (thawed) in a heavy saucepan and cover with the remaining ingredients, except the scallions and parsley. Add indicated amount of water, salt liberally, and boil for the number of minutes recommended, adding the scallions for the last 30 seconds.

Mushrooms: ¼ cup water. Boil 5 minutes, uncovered, over medium-high heat, shaking pan frequently.

Onions: ¾ cup water and 2 tablespoons red wine vinegar (instead of
lemon juice). Cook, covered, over medium-high heat 10 minutes,
then remove cover and cook down 2 minutes, letting onions darken
slightly.

Zucchini: ⅓ cup water. Cook, covered, 4 minutes, shaking the pan once
or twice.

Cauliflower: ½ cup water. Cook, covered, 5 minutes, shaking pan once
or twice.

Artichoke Hearts: ½ cup water. Boil rapidly, covered, 6 minutes, shaking
once or twice.

Toss each vegetable with parsley, taste and correct seasoning. Chill
several hours in its sauce. Bring to room temperature before serving so
the oil is not congealed.

CHEESE BALL ﻩ   (2 CUPS)

8 ounces cream cheese,   1 clove garlic, minced
   softened   Dash of Tabasco
1 ounce blue cheese, softened   ¼ cup finely chopped
¼ pound sharp Cheddar   almonds, toasted
   cheese, grated   ¼ cup finely chopped parsley

Combine the cream cheese, blue cheese, and Cheddar cheese in a bowl.
Add the garlic and Tabasco and blend until well mixed. Chill 2–3
hours. Form into a ball. Roll the ball in the almonds and then in the
parsley, patting the coating in firmly. Chill; remove from the refrigerator 30 minutes before serving.

SWISS CHEESE SPREAD ﻩ   (2½ CUPS)

Whenever I make this, everyone clamors for the recipe.

½ cup mayonnaise   Crackers
2 cups grated Swiss cheese
2 tablespoons finely chopped
   parsley

Mix the mayonnaise thoroughly with the Swiss cheese, using enough
mayonnaise to make it spreadable. Put in a bowl just large enough to
hold it, cover with plastic wrap and refrigerate. When ready to serve,
turn out onto a platter and mold into a mound using your hands.
Sprinkle with the parsley and place crackers around mold.

(ABOUT 44 PIECES)   • **CHEESE TRUFFLES**

Not what they seem sitting in little candy papers, these are a creamy, smooth cheese "truffle" rolled in dark rye crumbs.

4–5 slices dark Russian rye
  bread (no seeds)
8 ounces Brie, at room
  temperature
8 ounces cream cheese, at
  room temperature

¼ pound butter, softened
44 candy papers,
  approximately

Remove the crusts from the bread and tear bread into pieces. Place in a food processor and process into fine bread crumbs. In a mixing bowl, put the Brie, cream cheese, and butter and mix well to thoroughly blend. Cover bowl with plastic wrap and refrigerate for 1 to 2 hours, until the cheese mixture has chilled and become firm enough to handle. Place some of the bread crumbs on a piece of wax paper or a large plate. Using a teaspoon, scoop up some of the cheese mixture and place on the bread crumbs and roll into a ball, slightly smaller than a walnut. Press enough bread crumbs onto the ball to completely cover it. Place each in a candy paper. Refrigerate until served.

(ONE 2-QUART CASSEROLE)   **CHICKEN AND PORK PÂTÉ**

A pâté is not unlike a meat loaf—and really not that much more difficult to prepare. But because pâtés are served cold as a tasty appetizer (and one slice goes a long way), they must be full of flavor, rich, and moist. Almost one-third of the mixture should consist of good pork fat because it is the fat that keeps the meat moist during the cooking. After the pâté has been baked, it should be weighted so that some of the fat runs out and the loaf is compressed, thus giving you dense slices that hold together when cut. This particular pâté uses a ground meat base of chicken, pork, and pork fat interlarded with strips of marinated chicken breast, which gives the finished slice a lovely marbled look. The most economical approach would be to buy a whole chicken, 3½–4 pounds, and bone it yourself using the dark meat in the ground mixture known as the forcemeat (and reserving all the meaty bones and carcass for a soup); but for those who don't have the time, buy instead the easily available chicken parts as recommended below. Pâtés are good served with thinly sliced sour pickles, mustard, and French or dark rye bread.

1 whole chicken breast,
    skinned and boned
1¾–2 pounds chicken thighs
1¾ pounds pork, with some
    fat on
1 pound solid pork fat
3 eggs
¾ cup Madeira wine

1 tablespoon salt
1 cup minced shallots
½ teaspoon ground allspice
½ teaspoon ground cloves
Freshly ground pepper
½ teaspoon ground thyme
¾ pound bacon

Cut the chicken breast lengthwise into ½-inch strips. Remove the skin
and cut away the meat from the chicken thighs (if using a whole
chicken, use all the meat you can cut off the bones); you should have
about 1 pound dark chicken. Grind this along with the pork and the
pork fat by either running through the food processor or putting
through a meat grinder twice. Add the eggs, Madeira, salt, shallots, allspice, cloves, a generous amount of pepper, and thyme. Beat the mixture until smooth and well blended. If you want to taste to check the
seasonings, fry a small amount of this forcemeat and taste when
cooked through; it should be highly seasoned, so adjust seasonings if
necessary, remembering that flavors are dulled when chilled. Preheat
the oven to 325°F. Bring a large pot of water to a boil and drop the
strips of bacon in; let them cook 2–3 minutes, just enough to reduce
their saltiness, then drain, rinse, and pat dry. Line a 2-quart casserole

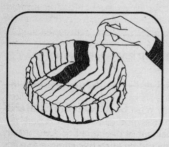

with the bacon, as illustrated,
leaving overhanging pieces to
cover the top. Pat in a layer of
the forcemeat, then lay strips of
chicken breast over in a neat line,
about ½ inch apart. Add another
lay of forcemeat, then chicken
strips, ending with a final layer
of forcemeat. Pull the bacon
strips over to cover the top of the
meat, trimming off excess to

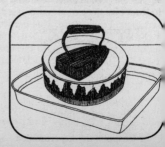

avoid a double layer anywhere. Cover with foil and with a snug-fitting lid. Place the casserole in a pan of hot water that comes halfway up the sides. Bake for 1–1½ hours, or until the fat runs clear and the internal temperature reads 150°F on a meat thermometer. Remove from the oven, uncover, and weight down with a plate that just fits inside the casserole, on which you place heavy cans, or any solid object like an old iron. Let cool completely. Refrigerate, preferably 24 hours, then serve cool, but not ice cold.

CHICKEN LIVER PÂTÉ

(3 CUPS)

¼ pound butter
1 onion, minced
1 pound chicken livers
4 tablespoons brandy
1 teaspoon dry mustard
¼ teaspoon mace

¼ teaspoon powdered cloves
½ teaspoon freshly ground pepper
Pinch of cayenne pepper
Salt to taste

Melt the butter in a skillet. Add the onions and sauté until soft. Stir in the livers and cook 2–3 minutes over medium-high heat, stirring, until they are just cooked but still rosy inside. Purée the onions and livers in a food processor or blender, or put through a food mill. Over medium heat, pour the brandy into the skillet and scrape up the bits from the bottom of the pan. Add to the liver mixture along with remaining ingredients, and blend until smooth. Pack into a mold and refrigerate until chilled and set. Serve unmolded with thin toast or crackers.

COUNTRY TERRINE

(ABOUT 10 CUPS)

A terrine is the dish in which a meat loaf or pâté is baked. One usually serves the pâté in its terrine so it should be attractive enough to come to the table.

1½ pounds ground pork, approximately ⅓ fat
1 pound ground veal
1 pound fresh spinach, blanched, drained, and chopped
1 large onion, chopped fine
2 cloves garlic, minced
2 eggs, beaten
1 teaspoon thyme, crumbled

1 teaspoon dried basil, crumbled
¼ teaspoon nutmeg
¼ teaspoon mace
¼ teaspoon allspice
1½ teaspoons salt
1 teaspoon freshly ground pepper
10 slices bacon

Preheat the oven to 325°F. Put a shallow baking dish in the oven with 1 inch of hot water. Grease a 2½-quart terrine. Combine all ingredients except bacon. Use your hands to mix and blend well. Fry a spoonful of the mixture until no longer pink; taste and correct the seasoning. Lay 6 or 7 bacon strips crosswise over the bottom and sides of the terrine. Pack the meat mixture into the lined dish; fold the loose ends of bacon over the top and cover any blank spaces with the extra bacon strips. Cover the dish with foil, place in the pan of water, and bake 1–1½ hours. The meat is done when the juices are clear and the internal temperature reads 150°F on a meat thermometer. Remove from the oven, cover with a plate, and weight down with a heavy can to remove the fat and press out air pockets. Cool, drain off the fat, and refrigerate.

SMOKED SALMON TARTARE (ABOUT 1 CUP)

This is from a dear friend of mine. It is wonderful spread thin on a slice of cucumber or on a piece of good light rye or French bread.

½ pound smoked salmon, chopped
2 stalks celery, minced
2 tablespoons minced red onion

1 tablespoon chopped capers
Salt, if necessary

In a mixing bowl, mix the smoked salmon, celery, red onion, and capers until well blended. Taste and add salt if necessary. Keep covered in the refrigerator until served.

Other Suggestions for Appetizers

Consult the sandwich chapter for sandwiches that could be made on thin slices of bread with crusts removed and cut into triangles or finger shapes. In the Fish and Shellfish chapter you'll find Cold Mussels and also shrimp and lobster that can be skewered with a toothpick. For a buffet table try some of the mousses and aspics. Many smoked meats, poultry, and fish are often available in supermarkets today. Thinly sliced and served with rye bread or crackers, they make a simple and tasty appetizer.

HOT APPETIZERS

(48 PUFFS) **CRAB PUFFS**

Miniature crab soufflés: luscious, hot, and puffy.

¾ cup mayonnaise
1 cup flaked cooked crabmeat
1 tablespoon finely chopped
  scallions
⅛ teaspoon cayenne pepper

2½ tablespoons lemon juice
Salt
2 egg whites
48 1½-inch rounds of bread

NOTE
see p. 471

Preheat the broiler. Combine the mayonnaise, crabmeat, scallions, cayenne, lemon juice, and salt to taste. Beat the egg whites until stiff and gently fold in the crab mixture. Spoon a mound of mixture on each of the bread rounds. Place on cookie sheets and put under the broiler until lightly browned. Serve immediately.

SHRIMP PUFFS

Substitute *1 cup finely chopped cooked shrimp* for the crabmeat.

(SERVES FOUR) **CHICKEN LIVERS EN BROCHETTE**

1 pound chicken livers
¼ pound bacon slices, in 1-
  inch pieces

20 whole mushrooms

Preheat the broiler. Thread chicken livers, bacon, and mushrooms on skewers. Place them on a broiler rack 3 inches beneath the broiler element. Broil 3–5 minutes on each side.

(2 CUPS OR 24 PIECES) **HOT SEAFOOD WITH MAYONNAISE**

Serve these hot from the oven. Crabmeat, tiny shrimp, chopped steamed mussels, tuna, or leftover cooked fish can be used, or combinations thereof.

1½ cups cooked shellfish or
  boned and flaked fish
¾ cup mayonnaise
3–4 tablespoons lemon juice
1 teaspoon minced onion

2 teaspoons minced parsley
Salt
Freshly ground pepper
24 small bread rounds

Preheat the oven to 400°F. Combine the seafood and/or fish and the seasonings, and add salt and pepper to taste. Spread on bread rounds and bake 7–8 minutes.

COLD SEAFOOD WITH MAYONNAISE

Instead of baking the fish mixture, mound it in a bowl and serve cold, surrounded with crackers.

CLAM FRITTERS   (30 FRITTERS)

Spear with toothpicks to serve.

Two 6½-ounce cans minced
  clams, or 1 cup chopped
  clams
1 egg, beaten
⅔ cup flour

1 teaspoon baking powder
½ teaspoon salt
⅛ teaspoon freshly ground
  pepper
Vegetable oil for frying

Preheat the oven to 250°F and put in an ovenproof platter. Drain the clams and reserve the liquid; if necessary, add milk or bottled clam juice to make ⅓ cup of liquid. Combine the liquid, egg, flour, baking powder, salt, and pepper, and beat until well blended. Stir in the clams. Heat 1 inch of oil in a skillet. When it is very hot, drop in the clam batter by teaspoonfuls. Fry until brown on each side. Don't crowd the skillet; do a few at a time until all are fried. Remove with a slotted spoon, drain on paper towels, and transfer to the warm platter.

BAKED CHEESE WITH
TOMATO SAUCE * ࣾ   (SERVES EIGHT)

Scoop up the hot cheese and sauce with the bread slices. This is a sit-down appetizer for a small group, or a great first course.

3 tablespoons olive oil
½ small onion, chopped fine
15 ounces canned peeled
    tomatoes, crushed
½ cup water
1 teaspoon salt
1 teaspoon sugar
12 ounces cream cheese, at
    room temperature

4 ounces goat cheese, at room
    temperature
Salt
Freshly ground pepper
2 tablespoons chopped basil
1 long, thin loaf French bread,
    sliced thin

Put the olive oil and the onion in a saucepan, and cook over medium heat for about 3 minutes, until the onion is soft but not browned. Add the tomatoes, water, salt, and sugar and simmer for 15 to 20 minutes, stirring occasionally. Preheat the oven to 350°F. In a mixing bowl, combine the cream cheese and goat cheese until smooth. You will need eight 6-inch shallow baking dishes. (Placing them on two baking sheets will make it easier to put them in and remove them from the oven.) When you are ready to serve, place a scoop of cheese in the center of each baking dish. Bake in the oven for about 5 minutes, until the cheese is just lightly browned but not melted. Remove from the oven and carefully pour some of the tomato sauce around the cheese. Sprinkle with salt and pepper to taste and garnish the top with the chopped basil. Serve at once with the French bread on the side.

(36 STRAWS)   ॐ **CHEESE STRAWS**

¼ pound butter
2 cups flour
¼ teaspoon cayenne pepper

1 pound sharp Cheddar
    cheese, grated
Salt to taste

Preheat the oven to 400°F. Cream the butter until light; add the flour, cayenne, cheese, and salt. Knead until dough forms a ball, then roll out on a floured board or pastry cloth. Cut into strips 5 inches long and ⅜ inch wide. Place on a greased cookie sheet and bake 6 minutes, until golden.

(48 PUFFS)   ॐ **CHEESE PUFFS**

To freeze these unbaked, allow an extra 3–5 minutes of baking time.

2 cups grated sharp cheese
¼ pound butter
1 cup flour

Salt to taste
48 pimiento-stuffed green
    olives

Preheat oven to 400°F. Put the cheese and butter in a mixing bowl or food processor, and blend until smooth. Add the flour and salt and mix well. Roll out to ¼-inch thickness. Cut the dough into 2-inch squares and wrap a square around each olive, sealing the seams. Place on a cookie sheet and bake 15 minutes. Check after the first 10 minutes to see puffs don't burn.

FRIED CHEESE BALLS ﻩ   (15 SMALL BALLS)

Serve hot or cold, with a salad or with pre-dinner drinks.

1 cup grated mild cheese	2 egg whites, stiffly beaten
2 teaspoons flour	¾ cup fine cracker crumbs
¼ teaspoon salt	½ cup vegetable oil
⅛ teaspoon cayenne pepper	

Combine the cheese, flour, salt, and cayenne pepper. Using your hands, gently stir in the egg whites. Pat the mixture into small balls and roll them in cracker crumbs until thoroughly coated. Heat the oil in a skillet. When it is hot, put the balls in the pan without crowding them. Cook over medium-high heat, turning so all sides become golden brown. Drain on paper towels.

CHEESE WAFERS ﻩ   (ABOUT FIVE DOZEN)

Good to have on hand in the freezer: just cut slices from the frozen tube of dough.

½ pound butter, softened	1 cup chopped pecans
1 cup flour	2 cups grated cheese
¼ teaspoon cayenne pepper	Salt to taste

Combine all ingredients. Make two rolls about 1½ inches in diameter. Wrap in foil and refrigerate at least 8 hours. Preheat the oven to 375°F. Slice the dough into thin wafers and bake 6–10 minutes, depending on the thickness of the wafers. Watch closely to see that they don't burn.

(ABOUT 40 PIECES)   **MUSHROOM-STUFFED
                                        ↬ MUSHROOMS**

1 pound mushrooms (with   Freshly ground pepper to
    caps about 1½ inches   taste
    across)   1 teaspoon dried thyme
3 tablespoons butter or oil   ¼ cup cream
½ cup chopped onion   2 tablespoons chopped
¾ cup bread crumbs   parsley, for garnish
½ teaspoon salt, or to taste

Wipe the mushrooms clean and gently pull the stem from the cap. Set
the caps aside. Chop the mushroom stems and set aside. Heat the butter or oil in a skillet over medium-high heat. Add the onion and cook
for about a minute. Add the chopped stems and cook for 2–3 minutes.
Stir in the bread crumbs, salt, pepper, and thyme and continue to cook
for about a minute more. Remove from the heat and stir in the cream.
Using a small spoon, fill the cavity of each mushroom cap with some
of the mushroom mixture. Place the filled mushrooms on a jelly-
roll pan and put under the broiler for 5–7 minutes, or until the tops
are lightly browned and the caps have softened slightly and give off
just a little juice. Sprinkle the tops with the parsley and serve hot or
warm.

(16 PIECES)   ↬   **TOASTED MUSHROOM SANDWICHES**

2 tablespoons butter   ½ cup milk or half-and-half
½ pound mushrooms,   Salt and freshly ground
    cleaned, stemmed, and   pepper
    chopped fine   16 thin slices dense white
2 tablespoons flour   bread, crusts removed
Pinch of curry powder   Melted butter

Melt the 2 tablespoons butter in a sauté pan, add the mushrooms
and cook rapidly over moderately high heat, stirring, until lightly
browned, about 3 minutes. Sprinkle with the flour and curry powder
and continue to cook, stirring, for about 2 more minutes. Add the milk
and cook, stirring, until the mixture is very thick. Season to taste with
salt and pepper. Spread the filling generously on one slice of bread, top
with another slice, and cut in half so that you have an oblong or finger
sandwich. Brush each side with melted butter. Place on a cookie sheet.
Turn on oven to broil. Place the rack about 5 inches from the broiler.
Broil, watching constantly, as sandwiches will brown rapidly. When

one side is golden, turn with a pancake turner and toast the other side. Serve immediately.

ANCHOVY, TOMATO, AND BASIL TOASTS

(24 TOASTS)

2 cloves garlic, chopped fine
2-ounce can anchovy fillets, drained
⅓ cup Niçoise olives, pitted
2 to 4 tablespoons olive oil
1 hard-boiled egg yolk
24 thin slices long, thin French bread, toasted

4 medium tomatoes, halved, then sliced
½ cup freshly grated Parmesan cheese
3 tablespoons dried basil, or ½ cup fresh basil leaves, chopped

Put the garlic, anchovy fillets, olives, 2 tablespoons of the olive oil, and the egg yolk in a food processor or blender and process to a thick paste. Add the 1 or 2 remaining tablespoons of olive oil to make the mixture spreadable but not runny. Spread each of the toast slices with about ½ tablespoon of the mixture, covering to the edges. Top each with a half slice of tomato and sprinkle with Parmesan cheese. Place under a broiler for a minute or two, watching closely, to melt cheese. Sprinkle with dried or fresh basil and serve at once.

HOT CREAM CHEESE CANAPÉS ও্ও

(30 CANAPÉS)

Light and puffy, always popular.

8 ounces cream cheese, softened
1 egg, lightly beaten
½ onion, minced

Freshly ground pepper
Salt
30 small bread squares, toasted

Preheat the broiler. Mix the cream cheese, egg, onion, and pepper together, mashing them well with a fork. Add salt to taste. Spread generously on toasted bread and run under the broiler until puffed and lightly browned. Serve at once.

๛ NACHOS

5-ounce bag tortilla chips
1 pound Monterey Jack or
   Cheddar cheese, grated

⅓ cup chopped canned peeled
   green chilies
½ cup chopped onion

Preheat the oven to 400°F. Lay the tortilla chips on a cookie sheet. Toss together the cheese, chilies, and onion, and sprinkle over the tortilla chips. Bake for about 5 minutes, until the cheese has melted. Serve hot.

(SERVES EIGHT)   ## ๛ FRIED CHEESE

This is good served with sliced tomatoes or a fresh tomato sauce (p. 387) or a marinara sauce.

¾ cup flour
2 eggs, beaten
3 cups dried bread crumbs
1 pound Italian Fontina,
   Danish Fontina, or
   Mozzarella cheese

Vegetable oil for frying
Salt and pepper to taste
8 sprigs parsley, preferably
   Italian flatleaf
2 lemons, sliced or cut into
   wedges

Put the flour, beaten eggs, and dried bread crumbs into three separate shallow dishes. Cut the cheese into eight even slices about ½ inch thick. Dip the cheese slices, one at a time, into the flour (shaking off any excess), then into the beaten egg (letting the excess drip off). Then coat with the bread crumbs, patting the crumbs onto the surface until the cheese slice is completely covered. Place the slices on a dish in a single layer. Heat 1 inch oil in a large deep frypan over medium-high heat. When it is hot, put four of the slices in the pan without crowding them and fry until golden, about 2 minutes. Turn over carefully and brown on the other side. Remove and drain on paper towels and keep warm. Fry the remaining slices. Season with salt and pepper to taste. Serve garnished with the parsley and lemon.

(MAKES 30)   ## ๛ SESAME SEED OR BENNE PASTRIES

½ cup sesame seeds
1 cup flour
½ teaspoon salt

2½ tablespoons shortening
2½ tablespoons butter

Put the sesame seeds in a skillet and toast over medium heat, shaking the pan often, until golden brown. Set aside. Place the flour and salt in a bowl and cut in the shortening and butter, using a pastry cutter or two knives, until it resembles coarse meal. Add the toasted sesame seeds. Beginning with 1 tablespoon, sprinkle on not more than 2½ tablespoons of ice water. Stir with a fork, using only enough water to allow the dough to stick together. Pat into a ball, cover, and chill. Preheat the oven to 400°F. Roll out the dough ¼ inch thick and cut into rounds or diamonds. Place on a cookie sheet and bake 7–8 minutes.

SAVORY CREAM PUFFS ?☙   (ABOUT 30 PUFFS)

Look to the section on spreads for filling suggestions; but don't forget Creamed or Curried Chicken, Mushroom Duxelles, Seafood Mayonnaise, or Creamed Chipped Beef.

1 recipe Cream Puffs (p. 926)   1 cup filling (see above)

Preheat the oven to 375°F. Make the cream puff dough and drop by rounded teaspoonfuls onto an ungreased cookie sheet. Bake 1½ inches apart for 25 minutes. Remove to racks, cut nearly in half, and let cool. Using a small spoon, push through the slice just enough filling to fill the puffs. Heat for a few minutes more before serving. The puffs can be made ahead of time, and even frozen, but they should be filled just before the final reheating or they will become soggy.

SMALL BISCUITS AND HAM   (25–30 BISCUITS)

1 recipe Baking Powder   ½ pound cooked ham, sliced
    Biscuits (p. 764)   thin
¼ pound unsalted butter,   3 tablespoons prepared
    softened   mustard

Preheat the oven to 450°F. Roll out the biscuit dough a little thinner than usual, and cut into rounds the size of a half-dollar. Place 1 inch apart on buttered cookie sheets and bake 8–10 minutes until golden. While still warm, split and generously butter the insides of the biscuits. Cut the ham to size and place two slices, with a dab of mustard, between the halves. Close the sandwiches and serve warm.

(12 MUFFIN-SIZE SHELLS,
OR 24 SMALLER SHELLS)   ಶಿ **SAVORY TARTS**

Make tart shells on the back of 1¾-inch muffin tins or in special small tartlet tins.

1 recipe Tart Pastry (p. 897),   About 1½ cups filling (see
    using 2 cups flour   following recipes)

Preheat the oven to 425°F. Roll out the dough. For muffin tins, cut circles 3 inches in diameter and drape the dough circle on the greased outside of each muffin tin, pleating and pinching the edges and pressing tightly onto the tin. For tartlet tins, cut circles of dough just larger than the diameter and press them into the tins, trimming off the excess to make a neat edge. For partially baked shells, bake 8 minutes. For fully baked shells, bake 15 minutes for small tarts, 18–20 minutes for the muffin-size tarts.

FILLINGS FOR PARTIALLY BAKED TART SHELLS

These fillings are the right amount to fill one recipe of tart shells (see preceding recipe). Preheat the oven to 375°F.

Ham and Cheese

2 teaspoons sharp prepared   ½ cup cream
    mustard   Salt to taste
2 ounces cooked ham, minced   Freshly ground pepper to
¾ cup grated Swiss cheese   taste
2 eggs, lightly beaten

Paint the bottom of the shells with mustard and distribute the ham evenly over them. Mix the rest of the ingredients, pour into the shells, and bake 20 minutes.

Blue Cheese

½ pound blue cheese,   2 eggs, lightly beaten
    crumbled   ⅛ teaspoon cayenne pepper
½ cup heavy cream

Mix the ingredients, pour into the shells, and bake 20 minutes.

Spinach and Ricotta

1 cup chopped spinach,
  cooked and drained
½ cup ricotta cheese
2 eggs plus one egg yolk,
  lightly beaten

Salt to taste
Freshly ground pepper to
  taste
⅛ teaspoon nutmeg

Mix all the ingredients, pour into the shells, and bake 20 minutes.

Cheddar, Onion, and Bacon

6 strips bacon, cooked,
  drained, and crumbled
½ cup finely chopped onion
1 tablespoon butter

½ cup light cream
1¼ cups grated sharp
  Cheddar cheese

Distribute the crumbled bacon over the shells. Sauté the onion in the butter for 5 minutes. Remove from the heat, add the rest of the ingredients, pour into the shells, and bake 20 minutes.

FILLINGS FOR FULLY BAKED SHELLS

Preheat the oven to 450°F and fill the baked shells straight from the freezer, if you like. These fillings are enough for one recipe of tart shells (p. 95).

Tomato and Mozzarella

1½ cups seeded, peeled,
  chopped tomatoes
1 tablespoon olive oil
2 anchovies
1 clove garlic, minced
½ teaspoon dried basil,
  crumbled

Freshly ground pepper
¾ cup coarsely grated
  mozzarella cheese
6 black olives, pitted and
  halved
2 tablespoons grated
  Parmesan cheese

Cook the tomatoes in the oil until they are just soft and the liquid has evaporated. Mash the anchovies with the garlic and add to the tomatoes. Add basil and pepper to taste. Mix with the mozzarella and pour into fully baked tart shells. Top each with one half of a black olive and a sprinkle of Parmesan and bake 5 minutes, until bubbly.

Mushroom and Cream Cheese

1 cup Mushroom Duxelles (p. 578)

6 ounces cream cheese

About ¼ cup heavy cream

1 tablespoon grated Parmesan cheese

Mix the mushrooms, cream cheese, and enough of the cream so that it spreads easily. Pour into fully baked tart shells, dust the top with Parmesan, and bake 5 minutes.

(24 PIECES)   **"BARBECUED" CHICKEN WINGS**

12 chicken wings

½ cup honey

2 tablespoons Worcestershire sauce

⅓ cup soy sauce

Juice of 2 lemons

1 clove garlic, minced

Few drops Tabasco sauce

Preheat the oven to 325°F. Remove the wing tips and break each wing into two pieces. Place in a shallow baking dish. Mix the remaining ingredients and pour over the wings. Bake for 1 hour and serve in the baking dish.

NEW RED POTATOES

(30 SMALL POTATOES)   ‍‍ ❧ ✳ **WITH ROSEMARY**

These are as good as potato chips—and better for you. They can also be baked alongside a roast or fish in the oven after you've tossed them with the oil and rosemary.

2 pounds small new red potatoes, about 1½ inches in diameter (approximately 30 potatoes)

2 tablespoons olive oil

1 teaspoon salt

2 tablespoons fresh rosemary leaves

Cook the new potatoes in boiling water for about 12–15 minutes, until just done in the center when pierced with a fork. Drain and let cool slightly. Slice in half while still warm, place the potatoes in a large bowl, and toss with the olive oil, salt, and rosemary leaves. Transfer to a serving platter and serve warm.

Other Suggestions for Appetizers

In the Fish & Shellfish chapter, there are Baked or Broiled Clams, which, if done in small shells, can be passed and eaten with the fingers; fried oysters, tiny fish croquettes, and small codfish cakes or balls also make good hot appetizers. In the Meat chapter, you'll find other kinds of meatballs that could be made into smaller balls and served from a chafing dish with toothpicks alongside. The Chicken chapter will give you ideas for Deviled Chicken-on-the-Bone, or try Delmonico's Deviled Chicken, using just wings; bite-size chicken croquettes are delicious. In Eggs & Cheese, try Cheese Toast cut into bite-size pieces and quiches, which can always be made in small tart tins or served in a big one and cut into bite-size pieces. You can do the same with pizza.

NIBBLES

CURRIED PEANUTS ?❧   (2 CUPS)

2 cups salted peanuts   2 teaspoons curry powder

Preheat the oven to 300°F. Combine the peanuts and curry powder in a paper bag and shake well. Spread the coated peanuts in a single layer on a cookie sheet and bake 20 minutes, shaking once or twice during that time.

RAISIN-NUT MIX ?❧   (ABOUT 3 CUPS)

Begin this recipe a week ahead by drying the orange rind. The mixed seeds are the kind one buys in a health food store.

2 oranges   ½ cup raisins
1 pound salted mixed nuts   ½ cup mixed seeds

A week before you plan to serve the mix, remove thin strips of orange peel, taking only the colored part, the "zest." Cut it into julienne strips and air-dry on a pie plate or a sheet of wax paper. When thoroughly dried, toss with the nuts, raisins, and seeds and store in an airtight container until ready to serve.

(3½ CUPS) &ev **TRAIL MIX OR GORP**

Created to provide energy for hikers, trail mix or "gorp" has become an all-purpose snack.

2 cups raisins
¾ cup chocolate chips
½ cup walnut pieces

¼ cup cashew pieces
½ cup dried or grated coconut
   shavings

Toss all the ingredients together. Store in an airtight jar.

(ABOUT 2 CUPS) &ev **SUGARED NUTS**

Traditionally served with dessert, but irresistible as an appetizer.

1 egg white
1 pound pecan or walnut
   halves

½ cup sugar
½ teaspoon salt
½ teaspoon cinnamon

Preheat the oven to 225°F. Beat the egg white with 1 tablespoon water, and dip the nuts into it. Roll them in the mixed sugar, salt, and cinnamon, spread on a cookie sheet, and bake 1 hour, stirring every 15 minutes. Let cool; store in the refrigerator.

(3 QUARTS) &ev **POPCORN**

Popcorn kernels should be plump and fresh to pop up well. They keep well in a screwtop jar, even better in the freezer. For long storage, keep them in the refrigerator. If the kernels start to dry out, add a tablespoon or two of water for each two cups of kernels and shake together in the jar.

3 tablespoons vegetable oil
½ cup popcorn kernels

3–4 tablespoons melted butter
   (optional)
Salt

Put the oil (butter would burn) in a 4-quart heavy pot and let it heat over medium heat for 30 seconds. Stir in the kernels, turning with a spoon so that they are evenly covered with oil, then spread them in one layer on the bottom of the pot. Put on the cover, leaving a small air space at the edge for escaping steam. As soon as the first kernel pops, move the pot gently and continuously back and forth over medium-high heat until the popping stops. Turn into a warm bowl. If you like, toss with melted butter and salt to taste.

CORN CRISPS &

(ABOUT 30 CORN CRISPS)

Crisp, coarse, and salty.

¾ cup water
2 tablespoons butter

½ cup yellow cornmeal
¼–½ teaspoon salt

Preheat the oven to 425°F. Butter a cookie sheet. Bring the water and butter to a boil in a small pan. Quickly stir in the cornmeal and salt and mix well. Drop by teaspoonfuls onto the cookie sheet and bake for 10–15 minutes.

SOUPS

You will find here some new soups that you may never have tasted before, such as Oatmeal Soup, Chinese Winter Soup, and Tomato Bread Soup, all worth your trying. There are also soups that have become part of the American scene in the last decade, such as Gazpacho and Fish Soup Marseilles. A lot of these are good cold and you'll find a list of them in the index under cold soups.

About making soups in the microwave: yes, you can do it in small quantities, but the intense heat and very brief cooking time do not allow the flavors to integrate. However, there are some exceptions, particularly single-ingredient soups, so take a look at the soups in the Microwave chapter.

ABOUT SOUP

Soup may be thick or thin, hot or cold, subtle or spicy, jellied, puréed, or creamed. It may be as clear as glass or full of chunky bits of vegetables and meats. Some soups derive their essential flavor from a rich stock; others depend upon water or milk to capture the pure taste of the ingredients. Certain soups can be cooked in thirty minutes (some do not even take cooking), but others require hours of slow simmering and taste better when they've been left to mellow in the refrigerator for several days.

When to Serve Soup

There used to be an obligatory "soup course" in every formal meal. Today we use soup less conventionally: soup and a sandwich often constitute lunch; a really hearty soup can be the whole supper; a good soup can be the centerpiece of a meal with deliberately light dishes surrounding it—a salad, cheese, and dessert. When soup does preside as the first course, it is usually a clear, delicate soup to stimulate the appetite, unless the courses to follow are light and demand a rich or heavy soup at the outset.

Because the size of the portion you serve will vary considerably, depending upon the kind of soup and when you're having it, we have used the 8-ounce cup as the basic measure of yield per recipe, instead of the number of servings. Allow up to 1 cup of soup per person if the soup is a first course and as much as 2 cups if it is the main course. The quantity of soup that a recipe produces may vary a bit each time you make it, depending upon the proportion of liquid in the ingredients and how long and briskly it has been cooked.

Using Leftovers in Soup

Fortunately, soup recipes do not have to be precise: a little more or less of the ingredients prescribed, or the addition of something new, can often be an improvement. This flexibility presents the cook with a thrifty way to use leftovers: the contents of the refrigerator shelves may even dictate what kind of soup to make. But a potpourri of tired, tasteless food that would otherwise be thrown away will not be transformed, nor will it improve the soup. Moreover, any leftovers you use must seem agreeable with the distinctive flavors of the soup. An equal amount of experience and good judgment is required to decide both what *should* and what *should not* go into the soup.

Seasoning Soup

Most soups should be cooked in a covered pot to retain flavor and nutrients, although you may want to cover the pot only partially to reduce the liquid a bit and to intensify its taste.

It is better to season a soup when it is nearly done because, as it simmers, it cooks down, so any salt you may have put in is intensified. Also, if it is a stock-based soup you are making, the salt content of the stock, particularly if it is a canned or dehydrated variety, is apt to vary greatly. For these reasons we have not given precise amounts of either salt or pepper in the recipes that follow. It is so much better to taste a soup toward the end of its cooking and let your palate be your guide. But don't be timid about seasoning; it may surprise you to discover how much salt is needed to bring out the good flavor of a soup. Nothing is less appealing than a bland soup.

Cold Soups

Many soups are equally good hot or cold. You can sometimes make one soup serve as two by offering it hot one day and cold the next.

Soups thicken as they cool, and chilled soup may need to be thinned with extra broth or cream. If the stock base is rich and meaty, it may gel when refrigerated, in which case beat well with a wire whisk. Cold soups, like all cold foods, require more seasoning than hot.

Storing and Freezing Soup

Almost all soups can be made in advance. Many, in fact, are better on the second or third day, after the flavors have mingled. To keep refrigerated soups from spoiling, reheat them to the boiling point every third day.

Soup freezes very well, so it's good to make a lot and freeze what you do not use. Be sure to divide the soup into quantities that will be useful later: a portion which is enough to serve your family, for example, or another which may be added as a supplement for a few unexpected guests. Soups that have been held in the refrigerator for a while or frozen may need diluting and may also need reseasoning before they are served.

Binding and Thickening Soup

Flour is used with certain soups to add body and as a binder to inhibit separation and curdling. One tablespoon of butter to 1 of flour is the right proportion for every 2 cups of soup. Stir the flour into the melted butter and cook it for about 3 minutes over low heat; then stir in a little of the hot soup, whisk well, cook until thick, then add to the remaining soup; heat and stir until smooth.

Some soups are thickened with egg yolks: 1 egg yolk beaten with 1 teaspoon of milk or cream to each cup of soup shortly before serving. To prevent curdling, drizzle a little hot soup slowly into the egg yolks, whisking briskly, then pour into the pot of soup, reheating slowly and stirring until it thickens. Do not boil, or the eggs will curdle.

Cooked vegetables and rice can be puréed and used to thicken soup.

Canned Soups

Canned soups are unquestionably a convenience, and they can often be improved by the addition of fresh ingredients (see p. 693 for refreshing canned stocks, for instance). Sometimes several compatible kinds of canned soups are mixed together successfully, but there are no particular formulas so we are not including them here; follow your own instincts. It is really so very easy and economical to make wholesome, full-bodied soups from scratch, which have their own individual flavors, that you are urged to try some of the recipes that follow and discover for yourself the difference.

Soup Garnishes

The trend today is toward simple garnishes rather than the more elaborate garnishes that accompanied soups in our grandmothers' day. Small touches are all you need to enhance the appearance and flavor of a soup—a sprinkling of chopped parsley, chives, dill, or other fresh herbs, for instance, or a bundle of quickly blanched vegetables such as carrots, turnips, broccoli stems, or a scattering of raw ones like scallions and mushrooms; a dusting of freshly grated Parmesan cheese, chopped eggs, or nuts; a little rice or pasta for body; a hint of sherry or wine for accent; a dollop of sour cream, a slice of lemon, some chopped, cooked chicken, or a few crisp pork scraps added to each bowl at the last minute—these are all fine finishing touches and are suggested in specific recipes when they seem appropriate.

There are recipes for croutons, bread sticks, rolls and biscuits, garlic bread, cream bread fingers, and corn crisps, all of which are especially good with soup, as is almost any homemade bread, particularly when the soup is to be a full meal (see chapters on Yeast Breads and Quick Breads for ideas).

ABOUT STOCKS AND BROTHS

Stock or broth is water enriched by the good things that have been cooked in it: various combinations of meat, poultry, fish, vegetables, bones, and scraps. Full of flavor and nutritional value, it is the essential ingredient in many classic soups and sauces. Although commercially produced substitutes are often used, sometimes quite acceptably, there is no *true* replacement for the full-bodied flavor of good homemade stock or broth.

Any strained stock can be served as a soup. The terms stock and broth are used interchangeably in American cooking, although broth is apt to be thinner and milder in flavor. Chicken soup is nothing more than chicken stock, seasoned to taste; beef bouillon is beef stock; clam broth and mushroom broth are also stocks. Since stock is almost always made in quantity, you can serve some as soup for dinner and freeze the rest for use later in soups and sauces.

Don't be intimidated by the common notion that stock is difficult to make. Although many stocks may take a long time to cook, they don't entail much work. The ingredients can be assembled quickly in the stockpot and left to simmer very slowly, requiring no attention other than a check from time to time to see that they are not cooking too briskly; broths do not need to cook as long.

Keeping your own stock or broth on hand can easily become a simple kitchen routine. And it makes you feel so provident to use up all those scraps and juices and carcasses that would otherwise go in the garbage. Once it becomes a habit, you'll find you may plan a boiled dinner or a stewed chicken just to replenish your stock when you see it running low. Blessed as we are with freezers today, it is always possible to have an adequate supply at the ready for an impromptu meal for your family on a stormy night or for unexpected guests.

Ingredients for Stock or Broth

The ingredients for stock or broth should always be fresh and flavorful: don't use the stockpot for foods that have been refrigerated too long and have lost their flavor.

Most ingredients for stock or broth are readily found in a well-tended kitchen. In addition to staples like onions, celery, bay leaves, peppercorns, and cloves, most scraps and leftovers should be saved to use in stocks. Scallion, leek, and celery tops; stems from mushrooms, parsley, and dill; cooked carcasses; meat bones; chicken bones, skin, necks, and giblets; leftover gravies, sauces, and meat and vegetable juices—all of these add value to the stockpot and can be refrigerated or frozen until their moment arrives. There's no need to buy bones especially for stock if you remember to ask the butcher to save them for you when he is boning your meat. Fish heads and skeletons can be had for the asking at many fish markets.

Smoked and corned meats, strongly flavored vegetables like cabbage and turnips, and dark, oily fish like mackerel may make the stock salty, bitter, or too overpowering and should be avoided.

Cooking Stock or Broth

Brown stocks are made by browning the ingredients in fat or roasting them in a very hot oven or under the broiler before they are put in the stockpot. Cold water is added so that the juices of the meat are drawn out into the soup as it is brought to a boil.

All stocks and broths should be gently simmered—just a bubble or two breaking the surface is ideal. During the first half-hour of cooking, skim off any scum that rises to the surface. When the scum changes from a yellowish brown foam to a white froth, you may stop skimming; the foam that remains will disappear by itself.

If you keep the stockpot partially covered, the stock will be more easily maintained at a slight simmer and the liquid will be reduced a bit without any loss of flavor or vitamins.

If fish or vegetable broths are allowed to cook for more than about 30 minutes, they may become bitter. Meat and poultry stocks, on the other hand, should be simmered as long as possible—all day when convenient.

If you want to cook some meat or poultry in the stock or broth as it is simmering, both the stock and the meat will benefit from this exchange of flavors. Add the meat or chicken when the broth has begun to develop body, let it cook until it is tender enough to eat, then remove it and serve. Return to the stockpot any bones, skin, or leftover juices to cook longer and deepen the flavor of the soup.

Seasoning Stock or Broth

Always taste any juices or cooking liquids before they are added to the stockpot. Season toward the end of the cooking and take into account any salty ingredients that you may be adding as a garnish or when the stock or broth serves as a base for a soup. It is really better to hold back on the salting of a stock if you are storing it for later use because at that point you do not know how you will be using it; you may want to reduce it further, for instance, to add intense flavor to a sauce, but if you have already salted it, it will not stand the further reduction.

Cooling Stock or Broth

When the stock or broth has finished cooking, strain it through a colander and let it cool, uncovered, as quickly as possible, in a cold place or the refrigerator. If stock is covered tightly while cooling, it may turn sour. Stock or broth made with bones will gel when it is cold.

Removing Fat

The easiest way to remove fat from a stock or broth is by chilling in the refrigerator until the fat congeals on the surface; it can then be lifted or spooned off.

If you do not have time to chill the soup, patiently spoon off the clear fat that will rise to the top. Run a paper towel over the surface to absorb the residue that you have not been able to trap in a spoon.

If you need to remove fat from just a small amount of stock—a cup or two for a sauce perhaps—pour it into a small metal bowl and put it in the freezer until the fat congeals.

Do not remove the fat until you are ready to use the stock. A layer of fat will serve as a seal which helps preserve the stock.

Reducing Stock or Broth

Strained stock, free of fat, can be evaporated to about half its volume by cooking it slowly, uncovered. The flavor will intensify as the stock becomes more concentrated, and the reduced stock will take less space in your freezer. You can later expand it with water if you need a larger quantity or if the flavor is too strong. This is another reason not to finish salting until serving: should you wish to reduce, any salt flavor will become greatly intensified.

A heavily reduced stock will ultimately become syrupy. When cool you will have the thick, jellylike substance that the French call *glace de viande,* meat glaze.

Storing and Freezing Stock or Broth

To keep stock from spoiling when it is being stored in the refrigerator for some time, reheat every three days and let it boil for about 2 minutes. The refrigerated stock should also be boiled whenever you add gravy or juice to it.

Stock freezes well. Freeze it in quantities calculated for use in soups and sauces. If you freeze the stock in clean tins or in heavy-duty plastic containers, you can take the container directly from the freezer and heat it in a pan of simmering water when you want to defrost the contents in a hurry. It's also convenient to freeze stock in ice-cube trays, then store the cubes in the freezer in plastic bags from which you can remove a few when you need a small quantity for a sauce.

Clarifying Stock or Broth

If you plan to use stock as a clear broth or in an aspic, you'll want it sparkling and crystal-clear. Start with a stock that is seasoned and fat-free and follow this procedure carefully.

To Clarify Stock or Broth

| 8 cups cold stock or broth, strained through a coffee filter | 3 egg whites |

Combine 2 cups of the stock in a large bowl with the egg whites, and beat well. Bring the remaining 6 cups of stock to a boil and slowly pour over the egg-white mixture, whisking constantly. Return everything to the pan and heat over medium-low heat, whisking slowly, but continually, until a simmer is reached. Then stop whisking and turn the heat as low as possible, just so there is a bubble or two on the surface,

barely quivering; keep the stock on this very low heat for 15 minutes, then turn off the heat and let rest 10 minutes. Carefully ladle or pour the liquid slowly through a colander lined with a clean napkin or dishcloth. (Don't use the commercial cheesecloth generally available today; it is coarse and made of harsh threads so that it does not do a good job of filtering.)

Stock or Broth Substitutes

You can substitute beef stock or broth for chicken in many of these recipes—or chicken for beef, if you wish. Vegetable broths can be used instead of water in making beef stock, or instead of beef stock in making soups. Fish stock should be saved for fish soups and chowders or for sauces to be used with seafood.

Commercial products may be used, of course, as substitutes for stock (see pp. 693–94 for suggestions on enriching their flavor). When the soup is very simple, that is when a high-quality stock makes the difference.

Canned beef and chicken broths are the most common commercial substitutes for beef or chicken stock. Some brands are better than others for this purpose. Try to find a canned broth that is not condensed and has good, but not overpowering, flavor. Do not use canned consommé as a stock substitute; it is too sweet. Bouillon cubes or powdered mixes, dissolved in water, may also be substituted if necessary, but they do not have as much body. All canned broths, bouillon cubes, or powdered mixes are apt to be very salty, so watch your seasoning accordingly.

STOCKS, BROTHS, AND CLEAR SOUPS

BEEF STOCK (ABOUT 12 CUPS)

Beef stock made from bones alone will be rich in gelatin but will lack flavor unless some lean meat is included. One of the best cuts to use for stock is beef shank because it provides the shin bone with its marrow plus a solid piece of shank meat surrounding it. Have the shank cut up into 2-inch pieces. If you can't get that cut, use whatever bones are available (have them cracked if they are solid pieces like knuckle) and add an equal amount of lean stewing beef. Browning the meat, bones, and vegetables at the beginning will add color and flavor to the finished stock. If you want to be more provident and use the meat for a meal of sliced boiled beef, or in hash or a filling, remove it from the stockpot after 2½ hours, returning the bones to finish cooking.

2 tablespoons shortening, cooking oil, or marrow	1 cup boiling water
4–5 pounds beef shank or 2½ pounds beef bones and 2½ pounds stew meat	1 teaspoon dried thyme
	1 bay leaf
	2 sprigs parsley
3 carrots, sliced	6 crushed peppercorns
3 onions, sliced	4 quarts cold water
3 stalks celery, sliced	Salt

Preheat oven to 450°F. Heat the shortening, oil, or marrow in a large roasting pan, add the pieces of shank (or the bones and stewing beef, cut into chunks) and brown them in the oven, stirring, turning, moving them about frequently. After about 10 minutes, add the carrots, onions, and celery to the roasting pan and let them brown, taking care that they do not scorch. When everything has browned, transfer it all to a stockpot or large cooking pot. Pour off the fat in the roasting pan, add a cup or so of boiling water, and scrape up all the browned bits in the pan, then pour into the stockpot. Add the thyme, bay leaf, parsley, and peppercorns, and cover with the 4 quarts cold water. Bring the water slowly to a boil, then reduce the heat and simmer very gently, partially covered, for at least 4 or 5 hours, skimming off any scum that rises to the surface during the first 30 minutes or so. Salt carefully to taste. Strain and cool, uncovered. (See About Stocks and Broths, p. 104, for general information about seasoning, cooling, removing fat, reducing, storing, and clarifying stocks and about substitutes for beef stock.)

BEEF BOUILLON

Beef bouillon is a strong Beef Stock, reduced slightly if necessary to intensify the flavor, and seasoned to taste with *salt* and *freshly ground pepper*. It may be clarified and served as a consommé (see p. 110). Sprinkle each serving of bouillon with *finely chopped parsley, chives,* or *celery*.

BEEF BOUILLON WITH NOODLES

Add ¼–½ cup *cooked egg noodles* or *broken-up vermicelli* for each 2 cups Beef Bouillon.

BEEF BOUILLON WITH
MARROW BALLS
(16 MARROW BALLS)

Using a wooden spoon, a blender, or a food processor, blend to a smooth paste *2 tablespoons marrow (from marrow bones)*, *4 tablespoons fine cracker crumbs*, *1 egg*, *1 teaspoon finely chopped parsley*, *¼ teaspoon salt*, *⅛ teaspoon freshly ground pepper*, and *⅛ teaspoon nutmeg*. Shape into ½-inch balls and chill in the refrigerator until ready to use. Drop into simmering 1 quart Beef Bouillon and cook for 5 minutes, then turn each ball with a spoon and cook for another 5 minutes. Taste one to see if it is cooked through.

CONSOMMÉ

"Consommé" is generally used these days to describe any clear soup. In the earliest editions of *Fannie Farmer*, the definition was more specific: consommé then was described as a highly seasoned, clarified soup made from a combination of two or three different kinds of meat, usually beef, veal, and fowl.

You can make an excellent, old-fashioned consommé by substituting Chicken Broth (below) for water in the recipe for Beef Stock (p. 108) or by adding 1–2 pounds chicken backs and necks to the beef stock ingredients. The finished stock should be cooled, degreased, seasoned well with salt and pepper, and then clarified (p. 107).

Serve consommé hot with a spoonful or two of mixed vegetables in each bowl: finely diced carrots, celery, green pepper, and scallions, which have been sautéed together in a little butter. Or serve consommé jellied, and flavored with a little lemon juice or sherry.

CHICKEN BROTH
(ABOUT 7 CUPS)

Simmering 1 to 1½ hours enriches a broth, but longer than that isn't necessary. A fine broth is good in sauces. Do not use the liver and heart because they detract from the clear chicken flavor.

2 pounds chicken backs,   1 bay leaf
   wings, necks, bones   6 crushed peppercorns
8 cups cold water   1 teaspoon dried thyme
1 onion, cut in half   Salt
2 carrots, cut in thirds
3 stalks celery with leaves, cut
   in half

Wash the chicken parts and put them in a large soup pot. Add the cold water and remaining ingredients, except salt. Bring to a boil, reduce heat, and simmer, skimming off the scum during the first 30 minutes. Simmer, partially covered, for 4 or 5 hours, longer if possible. Salt carefully to taste. Strain and cool quickly, uncovered. (See About Stocks and Broths, p. 104, for general information about seasoning, cooling, removing fat, reducing, storing, and clarifying stocks and about substitutes for chicken stock.)

CHICKEN STOCK WITH COOKED CARCASS

A pleasant light broth can be made of cooked carcasses. Or they may be added to the above soup. For 1 carcass use 5 cups water, 1 chopped onion, and ¼ teaspoon salt. Simmer 1 hour and correct seasoning.

CHICKEN RICE SOUP

Add ¼ cup *cooked rice* for each 2 cups of well-seasoned Chicken Broth. Or add 1½ tablespoons *uncooked rice* for each 2 cups and cook in the soup until done.

RICH CHICKEN STOCK
(7–8 CUPS)

Chicken stock can be made from the water in which a chicken is cooked, and you will have both stock and cooked chicken as the end result. To keep the chicken from being tough, stop cooking it when it is tender, remove the meat, and use just the bones and skin to complete the stock.

4-pound chicken or 4 pounds chicken parts (not backs, wings, and necks)	3 stalks celery with leaves, cut in half
8 cups cold water	1 bay leaf
1 onion, cut in half	6 crushed peppercorns
2 carrots, cut in thirds	1 teaspoon dried thyme
	Salt

Put chicken or chicken parts in a soup pot with the water, vegetables, and seasonings, and simmer for about 25 minutes. Turn off the heat and remove all the chicken from the pot. When the chicken is cool enough to handle, separate the meat from the skin and bones and return the skin and bones to the pot. Continue to simmer, 4 or 5 hours in all. Strain and cool the stock, uncovered. Use the cooked chicken in soups, salads, sandwiches, crêpe fillings, or other dishes calling for cooked chicken.

TURKEY SOUP   (7–8 CUPS)

Serve turkey soup as a clear broth, or add some cooked noodles, rice, or barley. It can also be used as a base in many vegetable soups.

1 turkey carcass plus giblets, if available	1 carrot, sliced
	2 stalks celery, cut up
8 cups water	6 crushed peppercorns
1 onion, sliced	Salt

Break the turkey carcass into pieces and put them in a soup pot with any small pieces of turkey meat and giblets that you can spare. Add the water, onion, carrot, celery, and peppercorns. Bring to a boil, lower the heat, cover partially, and simmer for 3 or 4 hours. Strain the broth and cool it quickly, uncovered. Chill it and remove the fat when it solidifies, or scoop any fat off the surface with a spoon. Add salt to taste before serving.

MUSHROOM BROTH ಈ   (4 CUPS)

Especially good when you're feeling frail.

½ pound mushrooms, chopped	4 cups cold water
½ teaspoon grated onion	Salt

Put the mushrooms, onion, and cold water in a saucepan and simmer, partially covered, for about 1 hour. Remove from heat and let stand for at least 4 hours, overnight if possible. Strain and reheat, adding salt to taste. Mushroom broth can also be used as stock in vegetable soups or in place of water in making meat stocks. For a more intense flavor, cook 5 or 6 boletus mushrooms with the broth.

FISH STOCK OR COURT
BOUILLON   (ABOUT 7 CUPS)

Use only white fish to make fish stock. If you use dark, oily fish like mackerel or if you cook a fish stock more than about 30 minutes, the stock will be too strong. Always save liquid in which fish has been cooked (it may be frozen) and add it to the fish stock. Clam Broth diluted half and half with water may be used instead of fish stock in many recipes.

1½–2 pounds fish skeleton, with heads if available	½ bay leaf
	6 crushed peppercorns
1 carrot, sliced	2 cups dry white wine
1 onion, sliced	(optional)
2 stalks celery, sliced	6–8 cups cold water
2 cloves	Salt

Wash the fish trimmings. Combine them with the other ingredients except salt in a soup pot and simmer, uncovered, for about 30 minutes, skimming any scum from the surface. Season carefully to taste with salt. Strain and cool, uncovered. (See About Stocks and Broths, p. 104, for general information about seasoning, cooling, removing fat, reducing, storing, and clarifying stocks and about substitutes for fish stock.)

(6 CUPS)   ဆ**VEGETABLE BROTH**

Vegetable broth is the liquid in which vegetables have been cooked. It contains many valuable vitamins and minerals. Use broths from highly flavored vegetables like cabbage, turnips, and carrots sparingly, and do not cook vegetable broths for more than about 30 minutes or they may become bitter. You may use vegetable broths instead of water in making Beef Stock (p. 108) or instead of water or meat stock in many soups.

2 leeks, sliced thin	1 teaspoon dried thyme
2 stalks celery with leaves, sliced or chopped	1 bay leaf
	¼ teaspoon salt
2 onions, sliced or chopped	6 cups water
4 carrots, chopped	
4 sprigs parsley with stems, chopped	

Put all of the ingredients into a large soup pot. Bring slowly to a boil, then reduce the heat and simmer very gently for about 30 minutes, skimming off any scum that rises to the surface at first. Strain and cool uncovered.

CLAM BROTH   (ABOUT 2 CUPS)

Do not overcook clams or they will be tough. If you are cooking soft-shelled "steamers," eat them as soon as the shells open, dipping each clam first in melted butter. If you are using hard-shelled clams, chop, mince, or freeze the clams to use in chowders, spreads, or other seafood dishes. The strained broth, seasoned to taste with salt and pepper, makes a fine soup, or it can be used instead of fish stock in chowders, soups, and sauces.

1 quart clams in shell	½ cup water
1 stalk celery, cut up	Salt
Small piece of bay leaf	Freshly ground pepper

Wash the clams in the shell, scrubbing them with a brush and changing the water several times. Put them in a kettle with the celery, bay leaf, and water. Cover and steam until the shells open wide, 10–30 minutes, depending on the clams. Remove the clams from the broth. Let the broth stand for 15 minutes before straining so that the sediment will settle, or strain it through several layers of wet cheesecloth. Season to taste with salt (judiciously—clams can be very salty) and pepper before serving.

CHICKEN NOODLE SOUP   (6 CUPS)

Not only is this one of the most popular soups; it can be made easily in about 20 minutes. It is hearty, satisfying, and low in calories.

6 cups chicken broth	Salt and freshly ground
1 stalk celery, chopped fine	pepper
2 (dry) ounces flat egg	2 teaspoons chopped parsley
noodles	
½ cup raw chicken meat, cut	
into bite-size pieces	

Simmer the chicken broth and celery about 5 minutes. Add the noodles and cook until tender. Add the chicken pieces and cook about 2 minutes, or until done. Add salt and pepper to taste and garnish with the parsley.

SOUPS WITH STOCK OR BROTH

(4 CUPS)   **CREAM OF ASPARAGUS SOUP**

An appealing-looking soup with a pleasing asparagus taste.

1 pound fresh asparagus, or 1 package frozen	2 tablespoons chopped onion
1½ cups Chicken Broth (p. 110) or canned broth	1 cup milk or cream
	Salt
	Freshly ground pepper

If using fresh asparagus, wash stalks and cut off the coarse ends. Cook the asparagus in 2 cups boiling water until tender. Drain, reserving 1 cup of the water. Cut off the asparagus tips, chop them, and reserve. Put the chicken stock, onion, and reserved water in a pan and bring to a boil. Add the asparagus and simmer for 5 minutes. Put through a strainer or vegetable mill or purée in a food processor or an electric blender. Return to the pot and add the milk or cream and salt and pepper to taste. Reheat and adjust the seasonings. Before serving, sprinkle with chopped asparagus tips.

THICK CREAM OF ASPARAGUS SOUP

Before adding the milk, melt *2 tablespoons butter* in a large pot, stir in *2 tablespoons flour*, and cook for a few minutes until smooth. Slowly add the milk or cream and salt and pepper. Then add the asparagus purée and reheat until thickened.

(8 CUPS)   **CABBAGE AND BEET SOUP**

A coarse peasant soup that stirs up memories of farms and fields.

1 quart Beef Stock (p. 108) or beef bouillon	Freshly ground pepper
2 cups peeled and diced raw beets	2 tablespoons cider vinegar
1 onion, chopped	Salt
2 cups coarsely chopped cabbage	½ cup sour cream (optional)

Put the stock or bouillon, beets, onion, and cabbage in a soup pot. Bring to a boil, lower heat, and simmer, partially covered, replacing any liquid that evaporates with additional stock or water. Simmer for about 30 minutes or until the beets are tender. Season with pepper and vinegar, adding salt to taste. Serve hot or cold with a tablespoon of sour cream floating on top of each bowlful.

CHEESE SOUP
(4 CUPS)

This is a very nice change from meat and vegetable soups.

1 tablespoon butter
1 tablespoon finely chopped onion
1 tablespoon flour

1 cup well-seasoned Beef Stock (p. 108) or bouillon
2 cups milk
¾ cup grated Cheddar cheese

Melt the butter in a pot, add the onion, and cook slowly until limp. Stir in the flour and continue to cook for 3 minutes, stirring. Slowly add the seasoned stock and milk, and heat to the boiling point, stirring frequently. Stir in the cheese and whisk until it has melted and the soup is very hot.

PUMPKIN SOUP
(8 CUPS)

2 medium onions, chopped
2 tablespoons butter
1 tablespoon flour
4 cups Chicken Broth (p. 110)
3 cups pumpkin purée (see p. 604)

Salt
Freshly ground pepper
½ cup cream, whipped
Dusting of nutmeg
3 tablespoons toasted pumpkin seed (optional)

Over low heat, sauté the onions with the butter in the bottom of a heavy, large saucepan until soft. Sprinkle in the flour; stir and cook 2 or 3 minutes. Gradually add the chicken broth, whisking thoroughly, then the pumpkin purée, and cook gently about 15 minutes. Salt and pepper to taste. Pour into warm bowls and top with a dollop of whipped cream, a dusting of nutmeg, and, if you like, a scattering of toasted pumpkin seeds.

CREAM OF ALMOND SOUP
(4 CUPS)

A delicate soup to serve hot or cold. Use a mild chicken broth so that the almond flavor is not overwhelmed.

½ cup blanched almonds,
  ground (p. 18)
2 cups Chicken Broth (p. 110)
  or canned broth

¼ teaspoon almond extract
2 tablespoons cold water
2 cups cream
Salt to taste

Put the almonds and chicken broth in a soup pot, bring to a boil, then simmer, partially covered, for 20 minutes. Mix the almond extract with the cold water, add it to the pot, and simmer 10 minutes more. Slowly stir in the cream, add salt if necessary, and heat without allowing to boil. Serve hot or cold.

(7 CUPS)   **CREAM OF CARROT SOUP**

4 tablespoons butter
1 onion, chopped
6 carrots, sliced
1 stalk celery with leaves,
  chopped
2 medium potatoes, peeled
  and diced

2 sprigs parsley
5 cups Chicken Broth (p. 110)
  or canned broth
1 cup heavy cream
Salt
Freshly ground pepper

Melt the butter in a large pot, add the onion, carrots, and celery, and cook for 10–15 minutes, stirring from time to time. Add the potatoes and parsley and stir until coated. Stir in the stock and cook, partially covered, until the potatoes are tender, about 20 minutes. Put through a strainer or vegetable mill or purée in a blender or food processor. Return to the pot, stir in the cream, add salt and pepper to taste, and reheat without boiling. Serve hot or cold.

(6 CUPS)   **CREAM OF CHESTNUT SOUP**

This soup has a good winter taste. It's worth the bother of shelling the chestnuts, a job for which there is no shortcut. To shell chestnuts, cut a slit on the flat side of each nut and drop several at a time into a pan of boiling water. Boil for a couple of minutes, remove from pot, and cut away the shell with a small knife. Peel off the dark skin. If the skin is stubborn, drop the chestnut back into boiling water for another minute or two; the heat will usually loosen the skin. Discard any chestnuts that are very hard and shriveled, and cut away any possible moldy spots.

1 quart Chicken Broth (p. 110)
  or canned broth
1 cup chestnuts, shelled (see
  above)

1 cup cream or milk
Salt to taste
1 teaspoon paprika

Put the stock and chestnuts in a large pot, heat to the boiling point, and simmer until the chestnuts are soft. Put through a strainer or vegetable mill or purée in a food processor or an electric blender. Return to the pot, stir in the cream or milk, and season with the salt and paprika. Reheat before serving.

CREAM OF WATERCRESS SOUP   (6 CUPS)

Cream of Watercress Soup is also good cold, as are the Spinach and Sorrel variations. Simply chill thoroughly, add ½ cup more cream, and adjust the salt. Wash the watercress, if necessary (you can always tell if it is gritty by tasting it), by submerging it in several changes of cold water. Pat it barely dry, and keep in the refrigerator until ready to use.

2 bunches watercress, coarsely chopped	2 tablespoons flour
4 cups Chicken Broth (p. 110) or canned broth	1 tablespoon lemon juice
	1 cup cream
4 tablespoons butter	Salt
	Freshly ground pepper

Put the watercress and the chicken stock in a pot and simmer for 10 minutes. Purée in a blender or food processor. Melt the butter in a large pot, stir in the flour, and cook slowly, stirring, for several minutes. Stir in a little of the purée and then add the rest. Bring the soup to the boiling point, stirring constantly. Stir in the lemon juice, cream, and salt and pepper to taste.

CREAM OF SPINACH SOUP   (6 CUPS)

Substitute ¾ *pound spinach* for the watercress.

CREAM OF SORREL SOUP   (6 CUPS)

Substitute ¾ *pound sorrel* for the watercress and omit the lemon juice.

FRESH CORN SOUP

(12 CUPS)

Fresh white corn if available is very good in this soup.

1 large onion, chopped
4 tablespoons butter
6 cups fresh corn, cut off the cob
5 cups chicken broth

1 cup heavy cream
Salt and freshly ground pepper to taste
Chopped green chilies and cilantro, for garnish

In a large pot, cook the onion in the butter for about 5 minutes, until it is soft and translucent. Add the corn and 3 cups of the chicken broth and simmer for about 10 minutes. Remove about 4 cups of the cooked corn and some of the broth to a food processor or blender, in batches if necessary, and process to a coarse purée. Return the purée to the pot, add the remaining chicken broth, cream, salt, and pepper, and bring to a simmer, stirring to blend. Serve in warmed soup bowls garnished with the chopped green chilies and cilantro.

CREAM OF CELERY SOUP

(4 CUPS)

Don't use the dark-green outer stalks of the celery; the tender, inner stalks have a better consistency and flavor for this soup. This soup may be served cold on a warm summer day.

6 stalks celery, chopped (about 2 cups)
1 small onion, chopped

3 cups Chicken Broth (p. 110)
1½ cups light cream
Salt to taste

Put the celery, onion, and chicken broth in a soup pot, bring to a boil, reduce heat, and simmer, partially covered, for 30 minutes or until the celery is tender. Put through a strainer or vegetable mill or purée in a blender or food processor. Return to pot. Add the cream and salt and reheat slowly.

CREAM OF MUSHROOM SOUP

(3 CUPS)

4 tablespoons butter
¼ cup finely chopped onion
½ pound mushrooms, chopped fine
1 tablespoon flour

2 cups Chicken Broth (p. 110) or canned broth
½ cup cream
Salt
Freshly ground pepper

Melt the butter in a pot and add the onion and mushrooms. Cook over low heat for 15 minutes, stirring occasionally. Sprinkle with the flour and cook for a few minutes more. Slowly add the stock, and heat, stirring, until it reaches the boiling point. Reduce heat and simmer for 20 minutes. Stir in the cream, add salt and pepper to taste, and reheat before serving.

COLD MUSHROOM SOUP

Use an additional ¼ cup cream and chill. Adjust salt. Serve in cold soup bowls with *chives* sprinkled on top.

PHILADELPHIA PEPPER POT (8 CUPS)

3 tablespoons butter
1 small onion, chopped
1 stalk celery, chopped
1 green pepper, chopped
1 large potato, peeled and diced
3 tablespoons flour

5 cups Chicken Broth (p. 110)
1 pound honeycomb tripe, cooked (p. 296) and diced
Pinch of cayenne pepper
Salt to taste
½ cup heavy cream
Freshly ground pepper

Melt the butter in a large pot, add the onion, celery, and green pepper, and cook slowly for about 15 minutes. Stir in the potato and flour, and cook, stirring, for about 2 minutes. Add the broth, tripe, cayenne, and salt, simmer, partially covered, until the potato is just tender, about 15–20 minutes. Before serving, stir in the cream, add pepper to taste, and reheat slowly.

NEW CHICKEN GUMBO SOUP (6 CUPS)

2 tablespoons butter
1 onion, chopped fine
2 stalks celery, chopped fine
4 cups chicken broth
½ green pepper, chopped fine
2 cups sliced okra
2 cloves garlic, minced

1½ cups canned tomatoes, with juice
Salt
Pinch of cayenne pepper, or to taste
1 cup diced raw chicken meat
1 cup cooked rice

Melt the butter in a large soup pot, add the onion and celery, and cook, stirring, for about 5 minutes, until golden. Stir in the broth, green pepper, okra, garlic, and tomatoes. Bring to a boil, then simmer for about 30 minutes. Add salt to taste, the cayenne pepper, chicken meat, and rice, and cook for 2 more minutes. Taste and correct seasonings.

VEGETABLE SOUP
(6 CUPS)

Other vegetables—tomatoes, shredded cabbage, green beans, corn—may be added to this soup, if you wish.

4 tablespoons butter
2 carrots, diced
2 stalks celery with leaves, diced
½ onion, chopped
1 small turnip, peeled and diced
1 medium potato, peeled and diced

5 cups Chicken Broth (p. 110)
1 tablespoon butter
1 tablespoon finely chopped parsley
Salt
Freshly ground pepper

Melt the butter in a soup pot, then add the carrots, celery, onion, turnip, and potato. Cook over low heat, stirring, for about 10 minutes. Add the broth, partially cover, and simmer for about 30 minutes or until the vegetables are tender. Before serving, add butter, parsley, and salt and pepper to taste.

COLD CUCUMBER OR AVOCADO SOUP
(4 CUPS)

These soups are very refreshing on a summer evening. They'll have a more interesting texture if you don't overblend them, and hold back enough cucumber to add a slice or two to each soup bowl or enough avocado to dice so you can add about two tablespoonsful to each serving.

2 peeled and seeded cucumbers or avocados
2 tablespoons lemon juice
1 cup Chicken Broth (p. 110)

1 cup heavy cream
Salt to taste
4 tablespoons minced chives or scallion greens

If you have a blender or food processor, simply chop the cucumbers or avocados in rough pieces, leaving out enough for the garnish as suggested on p. 134, and whirl with all the other ingredients in the machine until just blended. Otherwise, grate the cucumbers or avocados and blend with the other ingredients by hand. Add salt and chill. Serve in bowls with their garnish, and chives or scallions scattered on top.

QUEEN VICTORIA SOUP   (6 CUPS)

Adapted from an old English recipe.

2 tablespoons butter
1 small onion, chopped fine
½ cup chopped mushrooms
3 stalks celery, diced
Pinch of nutmeg
4 cups Chicken Broth (p. 110)
    or canned broth
1 tablespoon quick tapioca

½ cup diced cooked chicken
½ cup diced cooked ham
2 hard-boiled eggs, chopped
    fine
1 cup cream
Salt
Freshly ground pepper

Melt the butter in a large saucepan, add the onion, and cook slowly until golden. Add the mushrooms, celery, and nutmeg, and cook for 10 minutes. Stir in the stock, tapioca, chicken, and ham and simmer for 20 minutes. Before serving, add the eggs and cream, season to taste, and reheat slowly, without boiling.

SIMPLE SUMMER VEGETABLE SOUP   (8 CUPS)

2 tablespoons butter
1 onion, chopped
2 carrots, scraped, quartered
    and sliced
2 stalks celery, sliced
8 cups Chicken Broth (p. 110)
2 tomatoes, peeled and
    chopped

2 zucchini, quartered and
    sliced
½ cup string beans or peas
1 cup fresh spinach, washed
    and cut into strips
Salt and freshly ground
    pepper to taste

Melt the butter in a soup pot; add the onion, carrots and celery. Cook over medium heat, stirring often, for 5 minutes. Add the broth and tomatoes and simmer another 10 minutes. Stir in the zucchini and beans and cook 2 minutes. Add the spinach and cook 1 minute more. Season with salt and pepper to taste.

VICHYSSOISE   (6 CUPS)

This splendid chilled soup was devised on American soil by a French chef, Louis Diat. It is also good served hot.

4 tablespoons butter
1 onion, chopped
4 leeks, white part only, sliced
    fine
2 stalks celery, chopped
2 medium potatoes, peeled
    and sliced
2 sprigs parsley

4 cups Chicken Broth (p. 110)
    or canned broth
1 cup heavy cream
1 tablespoon finely chopped
    chives
Salt
Freshly ground pepper

Melt the butter in a large pot, add the onion, leeks, and celery, and cook over low heat, stirring often, for 10–15 minutes or until limp but not brown. Stir in the potatoes, parsley, and stock. Cook, partially covered, until the potatoes are tender, about 20 minutes. Put through a strainer or vegetable mill or purée in a blender or food processor. Pour into a bowl, stir in the cream and chives, and chill in the refrigerator. Add salt and pepper to taste before serving.

(ABOUT 12 CUPS)   ✳ **MINESTRONE SOUP**

This is a hearty bean and vegetable soup of Italian origin.

1½ cups Great Northern white
    beans
3 quarts water
2 teaspoons salt
½ cup olive oil
½ pound salt pork, diced fine
⅓ cup finely chopped parsley
2 large onions, chopped fine
Leaves from 3 stalks celery,
    chopped fine
1 teaspoon dried thyme,
    crumbled
4 tomatoes, peeled and
    coarsely chopped

2 carrots, diced
3 stalks celery, diced
3 or more cups beef broth
2 cups chopped cabbage
2 cups chopped zucchini
4 Swiss chard leaves, sliced
2 teaspoons dried basil,
    crumbled, or 1 tablespoon
    fresh, chopped
2 cups grated Parmesan
    cheese

Soak the beans overnight in water to cover. Drain and simmer the beans in 3 quarts of water with the salt. Cook until tender, about 1 to 1½ hours. Purée beans and cooking liquid in a blender or food processor. Heat the olive oil in a large soup or stockpot over medium heat— take care that the olive oil does not get too hot. Add the salt pork, parsley, onions, celery leaves, and thyme, and cook, stirring constantly, for 1 to 2 minutes. Add the tomatoes, carrots, celery, beef broth, and bean purée. Cover and simmer gently for 15 minutes. Add the cabbage, zucchini, and Swiss chard. Add more broth if necessary. Simmer another 20 minutes. Stir in the basil and taste to correct seasonings. Serve with the Parmesan cheese.

OXTAIL SOUP   (9 CUPS)

3 pounds oxtail, in 2-inch pieces
2 tablespoons flour
2 tablespoons cooking oil
8 cups Beef Stock (p. 108) or bouillon
2 carrots, diced
2 stalks celery, diced

½ cup diced turnip
1 medium onion, diced
1 tablespoon lemon juice
2 teaspoons Worcestershire sauce
Salt
Freshly ground pepper

Dust the oxtail pieces with flour. Heat the oil in a soup pot, add the oxtail, and brown slowly on all sides. Drain the oil from the pot, remove the meat, and slowly add the stock, scraping the bottom of the pot to deglaze it. Return the meat to the pot, partially cover, and simmer for 2½ hours or until the meat is tender, adding more water to replace any that evaporates. Strain the soup and allow the meat and bones to cool enough to be handled. Remove the meat from the bones and return it to the soup. Add the carrots, celery, turnip, and onion to the soup and simmer for another 30 minutes or until tender. Stir in the lemon juice, Worcestershire, and salt and pepper to taste; serve very hot.

OATMEAL SOUP ✻   (SERVES FOUR)

This recipe was published in my *San Francisco Chronicle* food column and I had an amazing number of enthusiastic responses. Try it!

3 tablespoons butter
1 onion, chopped fine (about ¾ cup)
½ cup uncooked oatmeal
6 cups Chicken Broth (p. 110)

Salt and freshly ground pepper to taste
1 cup cooked oatmeal
3 tablespoons finely chopped parsley

Melt the butter in a large sauté pan over medium-low heat. Stir in the onion and cook, stirring often, just until the onion is soft. Add the raw oatmeal and stir constantly over medium-high heat (add a little more butter if needed), until the oatmeal is slightly golden. Stir in the chicken broth and mix well. Bring the broth to a simmer and add the cooked oatmeal, stirring until it is well mixed. Season with salt and pepper, and cook at a simmer for 5 minutes. Add the parsley and serve.

(6 CUPS)   ✳ **CHINESE WINTER SOUP**

4 cups Chicken Broth (p. 110)
1 cup sliced mushrooms, wiped clean
1 cup fresh raw spinach (use young small leaves), washed
2 tablespoons light or mild soy sauce
2 tablespoons cider vinegar
½ teaspoon freshly ground pepper
1½ tablespoons dark sesame oil

¼–½ teaspoon hot pepper oil or Tabasco (use carefully)
½ pound tofu (soybean cake), cut into small dice
2 tablespoons cornstarch dissolved in 3 tablespoons water
½ egg, beaten
2 tablespoons finely chopped cilantro
1 scallion, chopped fine

Put the broth in a saucepan, add the mushrooms and spinach, and simmer for 3 or 4 minutes. Combine the soy sauce, vinegar, pepper, sesame oil, and hot pepper oil or Tabasco together in a small bowl; stir to blend, and add to the broth. Taste and correct seasonings. Add the tofu and the cornstarch and water, stirring constantly, and continue to cook until thickened. Pour the egg into the broth, stirring constantly until it forms bits of ribbons. Sprinkle some of the cilantro and scallion on each serving. Serve hot.

(16 CUPS)   ✳ **TOMATO BREAD SOUP**

Don't be put off by the humble ingredients. This Tuscan soup is full of good Italian flavors.

5 tablespoons olive oil
1 onion, sliced thin
1½–2 cups peeled and chopped tomatoes
6-ounce can tomato paste
7 cups water
4 cups Chicken Broth (p. 110)
1 loaf Italian bread (not sourdough), torn in pieces
3 large cloves garlic, chopped fine

2 teaspoons kosher or coarse salt
2 tablespoons dried basil, or ¼ cup chopped fresh basil
Salt and freshly ground pepper to taste
Olive oil, to drizzle over top of soup when serving
Grated Parmesan cheese, to sprinkle on top when serving

Put the olive oil in a skillet and add the onion. Cook over medium heat, stirring often, until soft. Add the tomatoes and tomato paste and continue to cook over low heat, stirring often, for about 15 minutes. Combine and heat the water and the chicken broth; add the bits of bread, garlic, salt, and basil. Bring to a simmer and cook for about 5 minutes. Combine the tomato mixture and the bread mixture and stir off heat until blended. Put the soup through a food processor. Season with salt and freshly ground pepper to taste. Serve hot with the olive oil and Parmesan.

SOUPS WITHOUT STOCK

BAKED BEAN SOUP ह्ळ   (8 CUPS)

It is worth making extra Baked Beans in order to have some leftovers to make this delicious soup.

4 cups Baked Beans (p. 448)	1½ teaspoons chili powder
1 onion, chopped	6 cups water
3 stalks celery, chopped	Salt
1½ cups canned tomatoes	Freshly ground pepper

Put 3 cups of the baked beans, the onion, celery, tomatoes, and chili powder in a large pot with the water. Bring to a boil, reduce heat, and simmer, partially covered, for 30 minutes. Mash and beat until smooth or purée in a blender or food processor. Return to the pot, and add the reserved 1 cup of baked beans. Reheat, adding salt and pepper to taste.

NEW MULLIGATAWNY SOUP   (8 CUPS)

This soup from India found its way into American cookery long before the Civil War. A recipe for it appeared in the original *Fannie Farmer Cook Book* of 1896. I have added a little sparkle to the original and you'll discover how surprisingly good bananas are with the soup.

6 tablespoons butter	1 apple, peeled and diced
1 onion, diced	1½ cups raw chicken or beef
1 carrot, peeled and diced	(about 1 pound) (optional)
2 stalks celery with leaves, diced	⅓ cup flour
	1 tablespoon curry powder
1 green pepper, seeded and diced	½ teaspoon nutmeg
	6 cups chicken or beef broth

2 cloves, crushed
1 cup peeled and chopped
    tomatoes
Salt to taste
⅛ teaspoon cayenne pepper,
    or ½ teaspoon freshly
    ground black pepper

3–4 cups hot cooked white
    rice
1 cup toasted, sliced almonds,
    for garnish
4 ice-cold bananas, sliced, as
    side dish (optional)

Melt 4 tablespoons of the butter in a large soup pot. Add the onion, carrot, celery, green pepper, apple, and optional chicken or beef, and simmer, stirring frequently, for about 15 minutes. Add the remaining 2 tablespoons of butter to the pot. Mix the flour with the curry and nutmeg, add it to the pot, and cook over low heat for about 5 minutes, stirring occasionally. Stir in the broth, cloves, tomatoes, salt, and cayenne or black pepper. Partially cover and simmer for 30 to 40 minutes. Taste and correct seasonings. To serve, place a mound of rice in each warmed soup bowl, ladle the soup into the bowl, and garnish with the toasted almonds. Pass the bananas separately.

BLACK BEAN SOUP

(8–10 CUPS)

Black bean soup has a distinct personality. Robust and nourishing, it can be a complete meal in itself.

2 cups dried black beans
Water
1 onion, sliced
2 stalks celery, chopped
1 ham bone

1½ cups cooked ham chunks
1½ teaspoons dry mustard
2 tablespoons lemon juice
Salt to taste
Freshly ground pepper

Soak the beans, if necessary, overnight in water to cover (or see p. 447). Drain the beans, reserving the soaking liquid, and add enough cold water to the soaking liquid to make 2 quarts. Put the beans and water in a soup pot and add the onion, celery, and ham bone. Bring to a boil, then lower the heat and simmer, partially covered, for 3–4 hours or until the beans are soft, adding more water to replace any that evaporates. Remove the ham bone. Purée in a blender or food processor, or beat by hand. Add the cooked ham and reheat, seasoning with mustard, lemon juice, salt, and a generous amount of pepper.

BLACK BEAN SOUP WITH SHERRY

Omit the lemon juice and add *sherry to taste* during the final seasoning.

BLACK BEAN SOUP WITH RICE

Top each serving with a tablespoonful of *hot cooked rice* and a sprinkling of *chopped onion*.

BLACK BEAN SOUP WITH LEMON AND EGG

Top with a thin slice of *lemon* and a slice or two of *hard-boiled egg*.

CREAM OF JERUSALEM ARTICHOKE SOUP ?~   (4–5 CUPS)

This soup has the delicate, unusual flavor of the Jerusalem artichoke, a root vegetable, sometimes called sunchoke, that was once very common in this country (see p. 535).

1 pound Jerusalem artichokes (about 4 large)	Dash of cayenne pepper
	Dash of nutmeg
4 cups water	1 cup cream
2 tablespoons butter	½ cup milk
2 tablespoons flour	Salt to taste

Peel the Jerusalem artichokes with a potato peeler and drop them into cold acidulated water—a few drops of lemon juice will suffice. Save ⅓ of a large raw artichoke to dice fine just before serving and use as a garnish. Bring the water to a boil and add the remaining artichokes, cut in half. Cook them briskly, in a partially covered pot, for about 30 minutes or until they are just soft. Put the artichokes and the cooking liquid through a strainer or food mill or purée them in an electric blender or food processor. Melt the butter in a large pot, stir in the flour, cayenne, and nutmeg, and cook, stirring, for 3 or 4 minutes. Gradually stir in the puréed artichoke mixture and bring to a boil, stirring until smooth and thick. Just before serving, add cream, milk, and salt and reheat. Put a little of the reserved diced artichoke in each bowl of soup.

(4 CUPS)   ❧ **CREAM OF PEA SOUP**

A fresh pea flavor with just a hint of sweetness.

2 tablespoons butter
1 tablespoon chopped onion
2 cups fresh or frozen peas
½ teaspoon sugar

2 cups water
1 cup milk or cream
Salt to taste

Melt the butter in a pot, add the onion, and cook, stirring, until translucent. Add the peas, sugar, and water, cover, and cook until the peas are tender. Put through a strainer or vegetable mill or purée in a food processor or electric blender. Return to the pot, add the milk or cream and salt, and reheat before serving.

(5 CUPS)   ❧ **SPICY CLEAR TOMATO SOUP**

Make this when you have an abundance of summer tomatoes. Serve hot or cold.

2½ pounds fresh ripe
   tomatoes (about 10
   medium-size)
1½ cups water
4 stalks celery, chopped
2 carrots, sliced
1 onion, chopped
1 green pepper, seeded and
   chopped

5 cloves
Salt and freshly ground
   pepper to taste
2 teaspoons sugar
2 tablespoons fresh lemon
   juice

Cut up the tomatoes and put them with the water into a soup pot. Add the celery, carrots, onion, green pepper, and cloves. Bring the soup to the boiling point, reduce the heat, and add the salt, pepper, and sugar. Simmer, partially covered, for 15 minutes. Remove from the heat and stir in the lemon juice. Strain (I drain the soup into a bowl, and put the vegetables through the food processor; then I strain them again, pushing all the juice into the bowl with the back of a spoon). Correct the seasonings and serve hot or cold.

LEEK AND POTATO SOUP ૐ   (8 CUPS)

Leeks tend to be gritty and need careful cleaning: cut off the roots and
the coarse green tops, cut lengthwise through the remaining green tops
starting within an inch of the white bottom, gently separate the stiff
leaves, and rinse well under cold, running water.

3 tablespoons butter	2 medium potatoes, peeled
6 leeks, sliced very thin	and diced
3 stalks celery with leaves,	3 cups milk
sliced very thin (about 6	Salt
cups)	Freshly ground pepper
3 cups water	

Melt the butter in a large pot and add the leeks and celery. Cook for
about 10 minutes over moderate heat, stirring often. Stir in 1 cup of the
water, cover, and cook 10 minutes more. Add the potatoes and 2 more
cups water, cover, and cook 10 minutes. Stir in the milk, cover, and
cook until the potatoes are just tender, about 10 minutes more. Add
salt and pepper to taste.

COLD CREAMY LEEK AND POTATO SOUP

Purée the soup when done and stir in *1 cup heavy cream.* Serve well
chilled.

PURE CREAM OF TOMATO SOUP ૐ   (7 CUPS)

Cream of tomato soup should be gentle and soothing. This is a perfect
example. Adding baking soda to the tomatoes keeps the milk from curdling.

5 tablespoons butter	1½ teaspoons sugar
½ cup chopped onion	1½ teaspoons salt
4 tablespoons flour	½ teaspoon baking soda
4 cups milk	3 cups tomatoes, chopped
½ bay leaf	(fresh or canned)

Melt the butter in a soup pot. Add the onion and cook over medium
heat, stirring, until the onion is softened but not browned. Sprinkle the
flour over the butter mixture and continue to stir and cook for 1 to 2
minutes. Slowly add the milk, bay leaf, sugar, and salt and continue to

cook and stir until slightly thickened. Stir the baking soda into the tomatoes. Add the tomatoes to the milk, and bring just to a simmer. Remove from the heat and put through a strainer. Taste and correct seasonings. Reheat before serving.

(10 CUPS)   **CORN CHOWDER**

You can use commercially frozen corn in this soup, but fresh summer corn is better. Cut the kernels from leftover ears of corn, cooked or uncooked. You can freeze them, if necessary, until you're ready to make this chowder.

2-inch cube salt pork, diced small	2 cups corn kernels
1 onion, chopped fine	3 cups milk
4 medium potatoes, peeled and diced	3 tablespoons butter
3 cups water	Salt
	Freshly ground pepper

Cook the salt pork slowly in a deep pan until the fat has melted and the pieces are brown. Pour off all but 2 tablespoons of the fat, add the onion, and cook for 5 minutes. Add the potatoes and water, cover, and cook until the potatoes are just tender. Add the corn and milk and cook 5 minutes more. Before serving, add the butter and salt and pepper to taste, and reheat.

(8 CUPS)   **PARSNIP SOUP**

Parsnips are of the carrot family and have a faint sweetness. This soup has a nice, old-fashioned character.

1½-inch cube salt pork, diced fine	Salt to taste
4 medium parsnips, scraped and diced	1½ cups water
2 medium potatoes, peeled and diced	4 cups milk
	Freshly ground pepper

Cook the salt pork slowly in a soup pot until the fat has melted and the pieces are crisp and lightly browned. Pour off all but 1 tablespoon of fat, add the parsnips, potatoes, and salt, and cook, turning frequently, for 5 minutes. Add the water, cover, and simmer for about 15 minutes, until the vegetables are tender. Stir with a fork to mash some of the vegetables slightly. Stir in the milk and cook over low heat for about 10 minutes, until thick and hot. Add more salt, if needed, and pepper to taste.

ONION SOUP ಕ್ತಿ   (4 CUPS)

Allow about 45 minutes to cook the onions. Very slow cooking will give them a deep golden color and release their full flavor.

3 tablespoons butter	Freshly ground pepper
4 cups thinly sliced onions	4 slices dried or toasted
½ teaspoon sugar	French bread
1 tablespoon flour	½ cup freshly grated
4 cups water	Parmesan cheese
Salt	

Melt the butter in a large pot, add the onions, and cook them very slowly over low heat, stirring often. Stir in the sugar and flour and cook for 3 minutes. Add the water and simmer, partially covered, for 30 minutes. Add salt and pepper to taste. Serve with a slice of French bread in each bowl. Pass the Parmesan cheese separately.

ONION SOUP WITH MELTED PARMESAN CHEESE

Before serving, sprinkle each filled bowl generously with grated Parmesan cheese and set the bowls in a 400°F oven until the cheese is melted and brown.

SCOTCH BROTH   (8 CUPS)

Inexpensive cuts of lamb will give this soup the best flavor. Be patient and try to trim off as much of the fat as possible.

3 pounds lamb breast or neck	1 small white turnip, peeled
8 cups cold water	and diced
½ cup barley	1 medium onion, diced fine
2 tablespoons butter	Salt
2 carrots, diced fine	Freshly ground pepper
2 stalks celery, diced fine	

Remove most of the fat from the meat and cut meat into small pieces. Put it in a pot with the cold water. Bring to a boil and stir in the barley. Simmer, partially covered, for 1½ hours, or until the meat and barley are tender, adding more water if any evaporates. Remove the meat from the bones. Cool the soup and skim off the fat. Melt the butter in a skillet and add the carrots, celery, turnip, and onion. Cook over low heat, stirring often, for 10 minutes. Add to the soup. Season with salt and pepper to taste, and cook for another 10 minutes or until the vegetables are tender. Serve piping hot.

(5 CUPS)   🍃 **WINTER SQUASH SOUP**

2 cups cooked winter squash, put through a strainer	½ teaspoon grated fresh ginger
3 cups milk	Salt to taste
3 tablespoons grated onion	3 tablespoons butter

Mix the squash, milk, onion, and ginger in a pot and cook over moderate heat for about 10 minutes. Season with salt. (You may thin the soup with more milk, water, or stock.) Stir in the butter just before serving.

(7 CUPS)   **SPLIT PEA SOUP WITH HAM BONE**

2 cups dried split peas	7 cups water
3 tablespoons butter	1½ teaspoons salt
1 onion, chopped (about 1 cup)	Freshly ground pepper
1 ham bone plus about ½–¾ cup ham scraps, scraped from bone	

Soak peas overnight in water to cover or use a quick method (see p. 447). Drain. Melt the butter in a soup pot, add the chopped onion and the ham bone and cook, stirring often, for about 5 minutes. Add the water, peas, and salt, and simmer for about an hour, or until the peas are mushy. Add pepper to taste and correct seasoning. Remove the ham bone, and put the soup through a sieve or food mill. Return to the pot, add the ham scraps, and reheat over low heat, stirring frequently, before serving.

(4 CUPS)   🍃 **YOGURT SOUPS**

These are much lighter than the usual cold soups with a cream base and the yogurt gives a pleasant tangy taste. They're easy to make in a blender or food processor.

2 peeled and seeded
   cucumbers, or 2 avocados,
   or 2 cups cooked beets
3 cups yogurt

2 scallions, or 1 tablespoon
   chopped onion
Salt

Garnishes

8 thin slices cucumber and 1
   tablespoon dill (for the
   cucumber)
4 slices lime (for the avocado)

4 tablespoons shredded beets,
   raw or cooked
Additional dollop yogurt or
   sour cream (optional)

Spin the cucumbers, avocados, or beets in a blender or food processor
with the yogurt and scallions or onion until just smooth. Salt to taste
and chill. Serve in chilled bowls with the suggested garnishes.

GAZPACHO ?➤   (6 CUPS)

Spanish in origin, this is a cold vegetable soup, light and refreshing.

5 ripe tomatoes, peeled and
   chopped
2 cucumbers, peeled, seeded,
   and coarsely chopped
1 large onion, chopped
1 green pepper, seeded and
   chopped
3 cloves garlic, chopped fine
   (about 2 teaspoons)

4 cups torn-up crustless
   French bread
¼ cup olive oil
1 tablespoon tomato paste
4 cups cold water
¼ cup red wine vinegar
1 teaspoon salt, or to taste

In a large bowl combine the tomatoes, cucumbers, onion, green pepper, garlic, and French bread, mixing thoroughly. Stir in the olive oil,
tomato paste, water, vinegar, and salt. Process in batches in a food
processor or blender. Leave a little texture—don't blend until smooth.
Return the soup to the bowl, cover, and refrigerate for at least 2 hours.
Correct seasoning and serve ice cold.

COLD CUCUMBER SOUP   (7 CUPS)

This soup is like a Gazpacho; you can add any number of different garnishes to the finished soup when serving.

2 pounds cucumbers (about 4 medium), peeled and seeded
2 cloves garlic
½ small onion
3 cups chicken broth

1 cup sour cream
3 tablespoons white wine vinegar
1 teaspoon salt, or to taste
Dash of Tabasco or cayenne pepper

Garnishes

1 tomato, chopped
1 small bunch scallions, trimmed and sliced thin

¼ cup chopped parsley
¼ cup toasted sliced almonds

Using a food processor and working in two or three batches, process the cucumbers, garlic, onion, and 1 cup of the chicken broth, until you have a purée. Pour all of the cucumber mixture into a large mixing bowl and add the remaining broth, sour cream, vinegar, salt, and Tabasco or cayenne and whisk together until thoroughly blended and smooth. Taste and correct seasonings. Chill in the refrigerator for 4 to 6 hours. Stir well before serving. Pass the garnishes of tomato, scallion, parsley, and almonds in separate bowls or spoon some of each into the soup bowls before serving.

FISH SOUPS

(SERVES SIX)

FISH SOUP MARSEILLES

This is like a bouillabaisse. Use a variety of fish for flavor and interest. It is served with a rouille or red pepper sauce.

¼ cup olive oil
2 medium onions, chopped
2 leeks, chopped
2 tomatoes, chopped fine
3 cloves garlic, chopped fine
bouquet garni (bay leaf, oregano, and parsley)
3 quarts water
2 pounds white fish bones, with heads if available

½ pound very small pasta, such as orzo or pastina
Pinch of saffron (optional)
Salt and freshly ground pepper to taste
2 pounds fillet of bass, red snapper, cod, haddock, or any firm white fish, cut into chunks

Rouille

4 cloves garlic	1 tablespoon tomato paste
2 small sweet red peppers	Croutons
2 tablespoons bread crumbs	½ cup grated Parmesan cheese
2 tablespoons olive oil	

In a large kettle, heat the oil and sauté the onions and leeks over low heat for about 5 minutes, or until limp but not browned. Add the tomatoes, garlic, bouquet garni, water, and fish bones, and simmer 30 minutes. Strain, return the liquid to the kettle and simmer 30 minutes to reduce. Add the pasta, optional saffron, and salt and pepper. Cook 10 minutes, then add the fish and cook only until it flakes easily with a fork—about 5 minutes. While the soup is cooking, make the sauce. In a food processor or blender put the garlic cloves, red peppers, bread crumbs, oil, and tomato paste and process until puréed. Add a little broth from the soup to thin if necessary. Serve the soup with croutons, grated cheese, and rouille.

OLD-FASHIONED FISH CHOWDER (10 CUPS)

Use the head and bones from the filleted fish to make a rich fish stock for this chowder. If you can, let the chowder mellow in the refrigerator for a day before you eat it. Serve it with common crackers.

2-inch cube salt pork, diced fine	2 pounds fillet of cod, haddock, or any firm white fish
2 onions, sliced thin	
3 medium potatoes, peeled and diced	2 cups cream or milk
	2 tablespoons butter
4 cups Fish Stock (p. 112) or Clam Broth (p. 114) or juice	Salt
	Freshly ground pepper

Cook the salt pork very slowly in a small skillet until the fat has melted and the scraps are brown. Strain, setting aside the crisp scraps, and put 2 tablespoons of the fat in a soup pot. Heat the fat, add the onions, and cook over low heat until golden. Stir in the potatoes and toss until well coated. Add the fish or clam liquid and simmer for about 5 minutes. Cut the fish in chunks, add it to the pot, and simmer, partially covered, for about 10 minutes, or until the fish is cooked through and the potatoes are tender. Stir in the cream or milk and heat slowly, without boiling. Add the pork scraps. Just before serving, stir in the butter, add salt and pepper to taste, and heat until butter melts.

(11 CUPS) CONNECTICUT FISH CHOWDER

Omit the cream and substitute *4 cups undrained canned tomatoes*. If you wish, you may add *½ teaspoon dried marjoram* or *thyme* along with the tomatoes.

(5 CUPS) CRAB BISQUE

A creamy texture and delicate taste. The faint flavor of onion or shallot and chicken broth does not overpower the crab.

2 tablespoons butter
1 teaspoon finely chopped
    onion or shallot
1 tablespoon finely chopped
    parsley
1½ cups chopped crabmeat
    (fresh-cooked, canned, or
    frozen)

2 tablespoons flour
2 cups Chicken Broth (p. 110)
    or canned broth
2 cups light cream
Pinch of cayenne pepper
Salt

Melt the butter in a saucepan, add the onion or shallot, and cook slowly until golden. Add the parsley and crabmeat and cook over low heat, stirring often, for 5 minutes. Add the flour, stir to blend, and cook 3 minutes. Stir in the chicken broth and simmer, partially covered, for 20 minutes. Add the cream and cayenne pepper. Heat and add salt to taste before serving.

(8 CUPS) LOBSTER BISQUE

A splendid soup with an excellent bouquet of flavors. Have the lobster killed and split at the market, if you can then cook it promptly. Or follow the directions on p. 181.

2 cups Beef Stock (p. 108) or
    bouillon
¼ cup rice
3 tablespoons butter
1 carrot, sliced
1 onion, chopped
¼ bay leaf
½ teaspoon dried thyme
1½ pounds lobster, killed and
    split

1 cup dry white wine
4 cups Chicken Stock (p. 110)
    or canned broth
1 tablespoon tomato paste
Lobster liver, if any
Lobster coral, if any
1 cup cream
Salt
Freshly ground pepper

Put the beef stock and rice in a saucepan, cover, and cook over moderate heat until the rice is done, about 15 minutes. Set aside. Melt 2 tablespoons of the butter in a large pot, add the carrot and onion, and cook slowly for 5 minutes. Add the bay leaf, thyme, and lobster, cover, and cook until the lobster shells are red, about 10 minutes. Add the wine and chicken stock, and simmer, partially covered, for another 15 minutes. Remove the lobster and strain the broth. Add the undrained cooked rice to the broth. Remove the lobster meat from the shell and cut it into bite-size pieces. Add it to the broth. Melt the remaining tablespoon of butter in a small pan and stir in the tomato paste and any lobster liver or coral. Cook until smooth, then add to the soup. Stir in the cream, add salt and pepper to taste, and heat to serving temperature without allowing the soup to boil.

SHRIMP BISQUE (4 CUPS)

Shrimp vary in size: small or medium-size ones are best in this soup.

1¼ pounds fresh shrimp, or 1 cup shelled or cooked	Pinch of marjoram
	Pinch of nutmeg
3 tablespoons butter	1 tablespoon lemon juice
2 tablespoons finely chopped celery	2 cups Chicken Broth (p. 110) or canned broth
¼ onion, chopped fine	1 cup cream or milk
¼ carrot, chopped fine	Salt
¼ bay leaf	

Wash the shrimp, remove the shells, and devein them. If they are large, cut them in small pieces. Set aside. Melt the butter in a pot and add the celery, onion, carrot, bay leaf, marjoram, and nutmeg. Cook slowly, stirring occasionally, for 10 minutes. Add the lemon juice and chicken stock, cover partially, and simmer for 15 minutes. Add the shrimp and simmer for about 5 minutes, until they are cooked and pink. Add the cream or milk and heat, but do not allow to boil. Add salt to taste.

(3 CUPS)   **CLAM AND TOMATO BISQUE**

1 cup Clam Broth (p. 114)   Pinch of nutmeg
1 cup peeled and stewed   1 stalk celery, coarsely
   tomatoes or chopped   chopped
   canned tomatoes   Parsley sprig
1 cup milk or cream   Small piece of bay leaf
3 tablespoons finely chopped   Salt
   onion

Simmer the clam broth and tomatoes together for 10–15 minutes. Stir in the milk or cream, nutmeg, celery, parsley, bay leaf, and onion. Heat slowly, without boiling. Strain and reheat, adding salt to taste before serving.

(6 CUPS)   **OYSTER SOUP**

4 cups milk   2 cups shucked or canned
1 thick slice onion   oysters and their juice
2 stalks celery with leaves   3 tablespoons butter
¼ teaspoon nutmeg   3 tablespoons flour
2 parsley sprigs   Salt
Small piece of bay leaf   Pinch of cayenne pepper

Put the milk, onion, celery, nutmeg, parsley, and bay leaf in a pot, together with any oyster juice. Simmer for 15 minutes, then strain. Add the oysters and simmer for 10 minutes more. Melt the butter in a small pan, stir in the flour, and cook, stirring, for 3 minutes. Slowly add about 1 cup of the oyster mixture, stirring constantly, and cook until smooth and thick. Stir the thickened mixture into the remaining milk and oyster soup. Add salt to taste and the cayenne pepper and stir until smooth. Serve hot with oyster crackers, if you wish.

(6 CUPS)   **MILDRED'S OYSTER STEW**

Very fresh butter, milk, and cream will give this stew a pure, wonderful flavor.

2 cups milk   Salt
2 cups light cream   3 tablespoons butter
2 cups shucked or canned
   oysters and their juice

Heat the milk and cream in a pot; do not boil. Add the oysters and any oyster juice and simmer for 5 minutes. Season to taste with salt. Add the butter, heat until it melts, and serve very hot.

NEW ENGLAND CLAM CHOWDER   (9 CUPS)

Raw, shucked clams and their undiluted juices are best for chowder; brief cooking in the chowder will keep the juice full of flavor and the clams very tender. Since it takes some skill and practice to shuck them easily, see if you can have this done for you at the fish store. Or steam the clams in a little water (see p. 176) until they open, and use them and the broth for the chowder. Clams are also available in cans and clam juice in bottles; these products will produce an acceptable chowder.

3–4 cups shucked or steamed chowder clams, with their juice or broth
1½-inch cube salt pork, diced small
1 onion, chopped fine
2 tablespoons flour

3 medium potatoes, peeled and diced
3 cups milk
3 tablespoons butter
Salt
Freshly ground pepper

Measure the clam juice or broth from the shucked or steamed clams and add water, if necessary, to make 2½ cups. Cut the clams in small pieces and set aside. Cook the salt pork slowly in a small skillet until the fat has melted and the scraps are brown. Strain, set aside the scraps, and put 2 tablespoons of the fat in a large pot. Heat the fat, add the onion, and cook slowly until golden. Sprinkle the flour over the onion and cook, stirring, for 3 minutes. Add the potatoes and clam juice or broth. Cover and simmer 10 minutes. Add the clams and simmer 10 minutes more, or until the clams are cooked and the potatoes are tender. Add the milk, butter, and salt and pepper to taste, and heat until the butter has melted. Serve with a few crisp pork bits in each bowl.

MANHATTAN CLAM CHOWDER   (6 CUPS)

To prepare clams for chowder, see preceding recipe for New England Clam Chowder.

2 cups shucked or steamed chowder clams, with their juice or broth
1½-inch cube salt pork, diced fine
1 onion, chopped fine
1 medium potato, peeled and diced

2 cups stewed peeled tomatoes or chopped canned tomatoes
¼ teaspoon thyme
Salt
Freshly ground pepper

Measure the clam juice or broth from the shucked or steamed clams and add water, if necessary, to make 2½ cups. Cut the clams in small pieces and set aside. Cook the salt pork slowly in a small skillet until the fat melts and the scraps are brown. Strain, set aside the scraps, and put 2 tablespoons of the fat in a large pot. Heat the fat, add the onion, and cook until limp. Stir in the potatoes and clam juice. Cover and simmer 10 minutes. Add the tomatoes and simmer 10 minutes more. Stir in the clams and thyme, and cook for another 5–10 minutes, until the clams and the potatoes are done. Add salt and pepper to taste. Serve with a few crisp pork bits in each bowl.

(SERVES SIX)   ✳ **CIOPPINO**

From Fisherman's Wharf, San Francisco: half Italian, all-American. This is really more of a stew than a soup and is usually served as a main course.

2 large onions, chopped
3 carrots, chopped
3 cloves garlic, mashed
½ cup olive oil
1 cup chopped parsley
4 cups tomato sauce
2 cups water
1½ teaspoons thyme, crumbled

1 tablespoon basil, crumbled
3 pounds clams in shell, scrubbed
2 pounds white fish fillets
2 crabs, cooked and cracked
¼ cup dry white wine
Pinch of cayenne pepper
Salt

In a large kettle, sauté the onions, carrots, and garlic in olive oil until the onions are soft. Add the parsley, tomato sauce, water, thyme, and basil. Partially cover and simmer 45 minutes. If the soup gets too thick, add a little water. Add the clams and simmer 10 minutes. Add the white fish and crab, and simmer 5 minutes. Stir in the wine, cayenne pepper, and salt to taste, and simmer 10 minutes more. Ladle some of each variety of fish and shellfish into each bowl with a generous helping of broth.

CREAM OF SCALLOP SOUP WITH DILL   (6 CUPS)

5 tablespoons butter
2 tablespoons onion, chopped
    fine
5 tablespoons flour
4 cups milk
½ bay leaf

4 cups cut-up scallops, in ¼-
    inch pieces
2 teaspoons chopped fresh
    dill, or 1 teaspoon dried
Salt and freshly ground
    pepper to taste

Melt the butter in a soup pot over medium heat. Add the onion and cook for about 5 minutes, until soft and translucent. Stir in the flour and cook over low heat for 2 minutes. Stir in the milk, bay leaf, and 1 cup of the scallops and simmer for 5 minutes. Remove the bay leaf. Add the remaining scallops, dill, and salt and pepper to taste and heat thoroughly.

FISH & SHELLFISH

In the past decade, with the public's increasing health consciousness, fish has gained great popularity among Americans. Fish is expensive, but many underutilized types are coming into our markets and there is considerable fish farming being developed throughout the country. So try unfamiliar varieties. You will note that I have grouped recipes for fish fillets together because you can use various kinds interchangeably and you'll find a lot of new combinations of flavors there.

ABOUT FISH AND SHELLFISH

America's coastal waters are rich with bounty—cod, swordfish, bass, various kinds of sole, bluefish, red snapper, pompano, mackerel, and others—and the fish lover has a wide variety to choose from. Inland the catch is more limited—trout, bass, perch, pickerel, catfish, and the like—and they are more often caught by sportsmen, and so are not readily available in supermarkets. But a good deal of coastal fish is shipped now all around the country and it is worth finding a market that handles it so that you can enjoy the delicious flavor of fresh fish at least once in a while.

Too many people have been put off by fish either because they *had* to eat it or because they have been subjected to it when it has been poorly prepared. The greatest enemy of fish is overcooking. Respect fish by giving it only the briefest cooking in a minimum of fat and by flavoring it delicately—as in the recipes that follow—and you will have the finest example of a perfect food. Fish has been recognized for its high-protein, low-calorie nutritional value, and thus it is not only a joy to the palate but eminently good for you. Try to make it a regular part of your diet.

Americans seem to have a more instinctive love of shellfish. A lobster or a shore dinner is considered a great treat. And look at how much shrimp we consume. Perhaps this is because shellfish are now considered a luxury, though that was certainly not the case in the nineteenth century, when oysters, lobsters, and crab were so abundant that they were used almost profligately in American cooking. Many an old recipe, for instance, calls for oysters in a stuffing or to fill out a pie—a luxury today (but one that's still fun to indulge in for the superb taste they give).

Unlike fish, which have scales and fins and an interior skeleton, shellfish are either mollusks or crustaceans. Mollusks are shellfish without legs, such as oysters and scallops; some have one shell, while others have two. Crustaceans are shellfish that move about by means of claws and a tail.

Buying Fresh Fish and Shellfish

Buy the freshest fish you can get. Fresh fish has the clean scent of the sea; fresh-water fish should have barely any smell at all. Never buy fish that has a strong fishy odor. The eyes and skin should be shiny and bright, the scales tight to the skin, and the gills clear red; you may have to pull back the covering flap to check on this. The flesh should be firm to the touch, springing back when it is pressed. If fish looks dull, if its eyes are sunken, if it is soft to the touch or has a strong fishy odor, don't buy it. You won't be able to fix it up or to disguise the off-taste.

Allow ¾ pound of fish with bone per serving, and ⅓ to ½ pound of boneless steaks or fillets. Fish is sold whole; drawn (that is, gutted); dressed (drawn, with scales and fins removed); split (dressed and cut in half, with the backbone removed); and cut up into steaks, chunks, fillets, or sticks.

Boned fish is easier to eat than unboned, but is less flavorful. If you are going to cook a whole fish, leave on the head and tail. If you can't stand having the head looking up at you, at least don't let the fishmonger throw it away; save it for making fish stock and enriching a sauce.

Like fish, shellfish should always be bought impeccably fresh. As a matter of fact, much seafood is alive when purchased—lobsters, clams, oysters, mussels, soft-shell crabs. Shrimp today has usually traveled from its source frozen, unfortunately, so what you're buying has probably been thawed. It deteriorates quickly, so smell it for freshness and feel whether it has gone soft; this is difficult with a plastic, sealed wrap, so try to avoid buying shrimp that way.

Buying Frozen Fish and Shellfish

Fresh fish is always preferable to frozen or canned. However, for many people in inland areas of the country, frozen fish is what is primarily available, and if you shop carefully, you will get quite a variety now that has been flash-frozen (rapidly at a very low temperature) successfully. If it is handled well by the various purveyors, there is no reason why it shouldn't be fine. Select only solidly frozen packages; if there is ice on the outside of the box, it may have been thawed and then refrozen, and this can ruin fish. If there is any odor at all, don't buy it. Take frozen fish home and put it in your freezer immediately. Defrost it slowly, preferably in the refrigerator. It is best prepared with a sauce or lively seasoning, since it does not have quite the lovely pure taste of fresh fish.

Buying Surimi Seafood

Fresh seafoods are expensive and few of us can afford them on a regular basis. Yet our demand is increasing and the general availability of surimi-based seafood is filling this need. Surimi is the 1000-year-old Japanese method for processing underutilized fish to simulate the taste, texture, and look of crab, shrimp, lobster, and scallops. The fish undergoes several washings and is then stabilized, flavored, and colored, and you'll find it packaged in supermarkets labeled "imitation," or "blend," or some such euphemism. Some surimi-processing plants do a better job than others, so the taste and texture of surimi varies depending on which plant supplies your market. Obviously, surimi does not have the nutritive value or the flavor of the real product.

Storing Fish and Shellfish

Do not keep any fish longer than two days without freezing it. When you bring it home, rinse it thoroughly under cold running water and pat it dry with paper towels. Cover loosely with wax paper so that the air can circulate around it, and store in the coldest part of the refrigerator, preferably on a bed of ice.

Shellfish is very perishable and should be used as quickly as possible. Fresh crab and shrimp can be frozen, but they will lose something in taste and texture. Hardshell seafood, like oysters, clams, and mussels, can't be frozen, but they will keep several days, if you store them on ice in the refrigerator, pouring off water as it accumulates.

Scaling Fish and Removing Fins

Cover a table or counter top with newspaper. Take hold of the fish tail with a clean cloth, and scrape off the scales, using a fish scaler or a straight sharp knife. Scrape from the tail toward the head, slanting the knife slightly to keep the scales from flying. Turn the fish over and repeat on the other side.

To remove the fins, insert the tip of the knife at one end of the fin.

1. *bluefish;* 2. *catfish;* 3. *cod;* 4. *halibut;* 5. *flounder;* 6. *mackerel;* 7. *pompano;* 8. *porgy;*
9. *red snapper;* 10. *salmon;* 11. *shad and roe;* 12. *blowfish and meat (sea squab);*
13. *smelts;* 14. *swordfish and steak;* 15. *striped bass;* 16. *sole;* 17. *trout;* 18. *tuna;*
19. *whiting;* 20. *whitefish. Note: fish are not drawn to scale.*

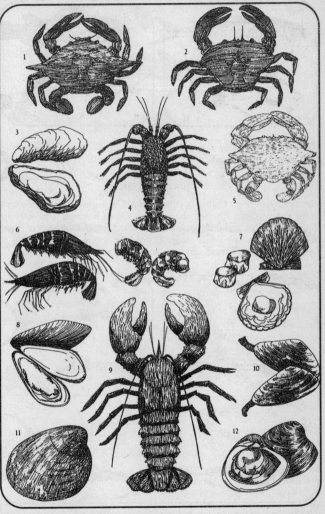

1. *blue crab;* 2. *rock crab;* 3. *oyster;* 4. *crayfish;* 5. *soft-shell crab;* 6. *shrimp (whole and shelled);* 7. *scallops;* 8. *mussels;* 9. *lobster;* 10. *soft-shell clam;* 11. *abalone;* 12. *hard-shell clam.*

Run the blade up one side of the fin and then down the other, tilting the blade so that the cuts meet. Lift out the fin with a tug.

Cleaning Fish

Lay newspapers on a table or counter top. Cut a gash in the underside of the fish with scissors or a sharp knife, slitting from the anal opening to the head. Cut at the throat where attached and remove the entrails; rinse under running water to get rid of any clotted blood clinging to the backbone. Wipe inside and out with a paper towel or a damp cloth.

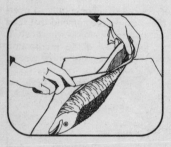
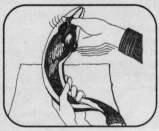

Skinning Fish

Cut off a narrow strip of skin along the entire length of the backbone. Loosen the skin on one side from the bony part of the gills. If the flesh is very firm, the skin will peel off easily. If it is soft, you will have to work slowly and carefully, pushing the flesh away from the skin with the back of the knife. Turn over and skin the other side.

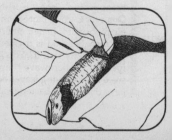

Boning Fish

Lay the fish on newspapers on a table or counter top. Beginning at the tail, run a long sharp knife under the flesh close to the backbone. Follow the bone for its entire length, making as clean a cut as possible. Cut away the flesh, laying the knife flat, and lift it off in one piece. Turn over and repeat, cutting off the flesh from the other side. Pick out any small bones that remain.

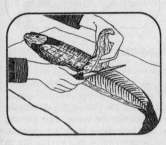 

Cooking Fish

Fish should be moist when it is served, but it is commonly so over-cooked that it is dry and tasteless. Many books recommend that it be cooked until it is flaky, a measurement that results in overdone fish. If the fish is cooked whole, probe with a fork to look at the flesh around the bone. When this is opaque (usually white, or pink in the case of salmon) and no longer raw-looking, and when it pulls away easily from the bone, the fish is done. Fillets are done when the flesh has turned opaque at the thickest part.

Microwaving Fish

NOTE

The microwave can cook fish successfully; much as when steaming, you must watch constantly and check for doneness because in a flash the fish can become dry and overdone. Don't try to cook more than a pound at a time, and if it's a single piece, cut it in half and turn the fat centers to the outside of the dish. Seafood is trickier as it can "turn"—since it's so expensive, why risk it? You'll find several microwave fish recipes in the Microwave chapter. A word of warning, however: since microwaving leaves hot and cold spots, some experts believe that not all bacteria is killed in the unevenly cooked fish.

Using Leftover Fish and Shellfish

Leftover fish and shellfish will last two or three days if it is well chilled and covered. Too often, little bits are thrown away that could be used to good advantage in a salad, a crêpe, or an omelet. Larger pieces can be stretched by garnishing with quartered hard-boiled eggs, tomato wedges, and black olives, and serving with homemade mayonnaise with herbs or a yogurt dressing. Save fish heads and skeletons to use in a court bouillon or a fish soup, lobster shells and shrimp peelings for seafood bisques.

Using Canned Fish

The familiar small flat can of tuna delivers honest value and has aided many a fledgling cook in preparing a tasty dish for little money. Canned salmon is also a provider of good and thrifty meals. Canned shrimp, clams, and mackerel have their uses, too. There is a difference among brands; experiment until you discover the brand that pleases you. Use canned and leftover cooked fish interchangeably in recipes.

BROILED BLUEFISH   (SERVES TWO)

A dark-fleshed fish with a distinctive flavor, young bluefish is delicate and makes superb eating when simply broiled.

1 lemon	2 teaspoons butter
1½-pound bluefish, split and boned	Salt
	Sprinkling of fresh herbs

Preheat the broiler. Squeeze half the lemon over the fish and let it sit while the broiler heats. Smear a little butter on the broiler rack. Place the fish, skin side down, on the rack, sprinkle with salt, and dot with remaining butter. Broil close to the broiling element about 6 minutes. Do not turn. Serve with a sprinkling of herbs and the remaining half of the lemon, cut in wedges.

BLUEFISH BAKED WITH
AROMATIC VEGETABLES   (SERVES FOUR)

A particularly good way to cook larger bluefish fillets. They are also tasty when baked like mackerel over potatoes with bacon, tomatoes, and peppers (p. 163).

4 tablespoons butter
1 onion, chopped
1 carrot, chopped
1 stalk celery, chopped
¼ cup dry white wine
3–4-pound bluefish, split and boned

¼ pound mushrooms, chopped
2 tablespoons chopped parsley
Salt
⅛ teaspoon paprika

Preheat the oven to 425°F. Heat the butter in a flameproof baking dish large enough to accommodate the fish. Add the onion, carrot, celery, mushrooms, and parsley, and cook, stirring often, for about 5 minutes. Add the wine and cook 3–4 minutes more. Remove half the vegetables, lay the fish on top. Cover with the remaining vegetables, and sprinkle with salt and paprika. Cover loosely with foil, and bake 20 minutes.

(SERVES SIX)   **STUFFED BAKED WHOLE FISH**

1 whole fish (such as ling cod or red snapper), about 4 pounds, dressed
½ recipe Celery Stuffing (p. 403)

5 tablespoons butter
Salt
Lemon wedges

Preheat the oven to 450°F. Cover the bottom of a baking dish with heavy-duty foil and butter the foil. Rinse the fish inside and out under cold running water; pat dry with paper towels. Fill with the stuffing and close with skewers. Rub the outside of the fish with 2 tablespoons butter and sprinkle with salt. Melt the remaining butter with 3 tablespoons water. Place the fish on the foil and bake 30–40 minutes, basting every 10 minutes with the melted butter. The fish is done when the flesh around the bone is opaque. To serve, make a deep cut along the backbone, then cut into pieces at right angles to the backbone. Serve with lemon wedges.

(SERVES SIX)   **BROILED MARINATED CARP**

Carp has firm, rather tasteless flesh, and is particularly good when it is marinated and then broiled.

3–4-pound carp, dressed and split
⅓ cup oil
½ cup thin onion rings
2 tablespoons lemon juice

1½ teaspoons salt
½ teaspoon freshly ground pepper
1½ teaspoons basil, crumbled

Rinse the carp with cold water and pat dry with paper towels. Combine the oil, onions, lemon juice, salt, pepper, basil, and 3 tablespoons water in a jar. Cover tightly and shake until well blended. Put the fish in a shallow baking dish, cover with the marinade, and let stand at room temperature for 1 hour. Preheat the broiler. Place the fish skin side down on a heavily buttered piece of foil in the broiler pan. Spoon on the marinade. Place the pan 4 inches beneath the broiler element and cook 10 minutes, until the meat is opaque throughout.

PAN-FRIED CATFISH (SERVES THREE)

A firm-flesh fish popular all over the southern United States, catfish is sold whole or in fillets. It can be fried, baked, or broiled. Pan fry whole catfish according to the recipe for Pan-fried Porgy (p. 169).

1½ pounds catfish fillets	2 eggs, slightly beaten
⅓ cup flour	1 cup cornmeal
1½ teaspoons salt	Oil for frying
½ teaspoon freshly ground pepper	Lemon wedges

Rinse the fish under cold water and pat dry with paper towels. Mix the flour with salt and pepper, and spread it on a piece of wax paper. Put the eggs in a shallow bowl and the cornmeal on another piece of wax paper. Lightly dust each fillet in the seasoned flour and shake off the excess. Dip the fillet into the egg. Hold over the bowl to let excess egg drip off. Dip into the cornmeal. Warm a platter in a 250°F oven. In a large skillet, heat ¼ inch of oil. Put your hand over the oil in the skillet, and when you can feel a good amount of heat rising, put in the fish and brown on each side. This should take 1½–2 minutes on each side. Don't crowd the skillet; do only a few at a time. Remove to a paper towel to drain, transfer to the warmed platter, and continue frying the fillets. Serve with lemon wedges.

FOIL-STEAMED COD STEAKS (SERVES FOUR)

Heavy foil, securely sealed around a piece of fish, serves much the same purpose as steaming: it locks in the juices so that the flavors are beautifully preserved. This process works on an outdoor grill as well, and is a clean and easy method of cooking. The package is brought right to the table, and the taste of a bland fish like cod, tilefish, halibut, or flounder is greatly enhanced.

6 tablespoons butter
Four ½-pound cod steaks
Salt
Freshly ground pepper
Juice of 1 lemon

2 tablespoons chopped
  parsley, chives and fresh
  basil, tarragon, chervil, or
  dill (or 1 teaspoon dried)
Lemon wedges

Preheat the oven to 425°F. Liberally butter four pieces of aluminum foil large enough to enclose the fish steaks generously. Sprinkle the fish with salt, pepper, lemon juice, and herbs. Dot with remaining butter and wrap the foil around the fish, folding the edges to seal well. Place on a baking sheet and bake 15 minutes for fillets, 20 minutes for steaks 1 inch thick or more. Serve with lemon wedges.

FOIL-STEAMED COD WITH MUSHROOMS

Thinly slice ¼ pound of mushrooms and scatter over the pieces of fish along with the lemon juice and herbs.

FOIL-STEAMED COD WITH AROMATIC VEGETABLES

Sauté 1 carrot, chopped, 1 stalk celery, chopped, and 1 onion, chopped, in 2 tablespoons butter for 5 minutes, then spread over the pieces of fish along with the lemon juice and herbs.

(SERVES FOUR)   **COD WITH MUSTARD SAUCE**

White vinegar is a clean, sharp complement to fish.

2 tablespoons olive oil
2 tablespoons Dijon mustard
1 tablespoon chopped parsley
¼ cup white vinegar
¼ cup water
¼ teaspoon salt, or to taste
Flour

1¾–2 pounds cod fillets (or
  bass or red snapper)
Freshly ground pepper to
  taste
3 tablespoons butter or
  vegetable oil

In a small bowl, mix together the olive oil, mustard, parsley, vinegar, water, and salt, and stir well to blend. Set aside. Lightly flour the fish fillets and season with salt and pepper. In a skillet, melt the butter or vegetable oil over medium-high heat and fry the fillets about 3–4 minutes on each side, or until the fish is golden and flakes easily with a fork. When fish is done, remove it to a serving dish and keep warm. Pour the mustard sauce into the skillet and cook for only about 30 seconds, until it is hot and bubbly. Pour over the fish or return the fish to the skillet and coat with the sauce. Serve at once.

About Fish Fillets

These recipes for fish fillets are grouped together because you can use any fish fillet available. There are many underutilized fish coming into the market—sea trout, pollack, ocean perch, hake. Many of these are found frozen. Defrost slowly in the refrigerator.

BRAISED FISH FILLETS (SERVES FOUR)

Pleasing and mild-tasting. Serve with spoon bread.

4 tablespoons butter
⅓ cup chopped shallots, or scallions (white part)
¼ cup dry white wine or water

1 tablespoon chopped parsley
1½–2 pounds white-fleshed fish fillets (see Box above), bass, orange roughy, or snapper

Heat 2 tablespoons of the butter in a sauté pan with the shallots and cook over a moderate heat for 5–7 minutes, or until the shallots are soft. Stir in the wine or water and parsley. When it is simmering, add the fish fillets, cover, and cook about 3 minutes. Turn the fish and continue to cook for 3–4 more minutes, until fish flakes with a fork. Remove fish to serving dishes and keep hot. Whisk the remaining 2 tablespoons butter into pan juices and pour over fish.

FISH FILLETS WITH GRAPES AND CELERY (SERVES FOUR)

This is a light, summer dish. Slightly sweet Thompson seedless grapes and crisp celery are very nice with white fish fillets.

2 cups water
1 tablespoon white vinegar
2 teaspoons lemon juice
Salt to taste
2 teaspoons chopped fresh
  thyme, or 1 teaspoon
  dried, crumbled
½ cup chopped celery (stalks
  and leaves)
1 cup Thompson seedless
  grapes

1 bay leaf
2 pounds white-fleshed
  fish fillets, such as
  sole, flounder, or
  halibut
3 tablespoons butter
¼ cup flour
¾ cup poaching liquid
1 cup chicken broth
1 cup small slices celery,
  barely cooked

Put the water, vinegar, lemon juice, salt, thyme, chopped celery, and
bay leaf into a sauté pan large enough to hold the fish in a single layer.
Bring the poaching liquid to a boil, reduce the heat, and simmer for 3–4
minutes. Put the fish into the simmering liquid and poach for 2–3 minutes, depending on how thick the fillets are. Check for doneness by
carefully cutting with a small knife into the thickest part of the fish. If it
looks opaque, it is done. Gently remove and keep warm on a serving
platter. Melt the butter in a small saucepan. Strain the poaching liquid,
reserving ¾ cup, and set aside. Stir the flour into the melted butter and
stir constantly for a minute or two, then slowly stir in the poaching liquid and the chicken broth, stirring constantly over medium heat, until
it is thickened and smooth. Taste and add more salt to taste. Stir in the
grapes and celery and heat briefly. Spoon the sauce over the fish and
serve.

(SERVES FOUR)   **STEAMED FILLETS WITH FENNEL**

Make this from fall through early spring, when fennel is available.

Salt to taste
1 large fennel bulb, trimmed,
  halved, and sliced
1½ pounds fish fillets, cut in 4
  pieces

4 tablespoons butter
1 tablespoon chopped parsley

Put 1 inch of water in the bottom of a large deep skillet and fit a
steamer rack in the bottom. Cover and bring the water to a boil. Salt
the fennel, put it on the rack, and steam for 5 minutes. Add the fish fillets and steam for 5–7 minutes more, or until the fish flakes with a fork.
Remove the fish to a platter. Melt the butter and parsley together and
pour over the fish.

SKILLET FISH SUPPER   (SERVES FOUR)

This is a fish chowder without the broth. Use one or several kinds of
fish.

5 tablespoons butter or vegetable oil	1 cup corn kernels
1 cup chopped onion	1 pound fish fillets (cod, bass, snapper, or halibut), in 1-inch chunks
1½ cups diced potato	
Salt and freshly ground pepper	⅓ cup chopped parsley

Heat 4 tablespoons of the butter or oil in a large skillet over medium-
high heat, then add the onion and potato and cook slowly until tender.
Stir in the corn kernels and the remaining tablespoon of butter. Add
the fish chunks and salt and pepper to taste, and continue cooking,
stirring occasionally, until the fish is cooked through, about 5 minutes.
Be careful not to break up the fish while stirring. Sprinkle the parsley
over and serve.

FISH FILLETS WITH ANCHOVY AND
GREEN PEPPERCORNS   (SERVES FOUR)

Even though you think you don't like anchovies, you will like them in
this recipe.

3 tablespoons green peppercorns, drained, or ½ teaspoon Tabasco	Lemon juice to taste
1 tablespoon anchovy paste	2½–3 pounds firm white-fleshed fish fillets
¼ pound unsalted butter, softened	

Preheat the oven to 400°F. In a bowl, crush or mash the peppercorns. If
you cannot find green peppercorns, use about ½ teaspoon of Tabasco in
their place. Stir in the anchovy paste, butter, and lemon juice. Mix until
well blended. Be sure to taste the mixture and adjust the seasonings.
Butter an ovenproof dish and place fish in the dish. Bake about 10 minutes, or until flesh separates when gently probed with a fork. Spread
the seasoned butter mixture over the fish and let it briefly melt. Serve
at once.

FILLETS OF SOLE WITH BUTTER, LEMON, AND PARSLEY

(SERVES FOUR)

All species of sole are members of the flounder family: the most common are Dover, grey, lemon, rex, and petrale. Sole is a lean fish, usually sold in fillets, whose white delicate meat lends itself to all kinds of adornment.

⅓ cup flour
1¼ teaspoons salt
¼ teaspoon freshly ground
  pepper
1½ pounds sole fillets

6 tablespoons butter
1 tablespoon oil
2 tablespoons lemon juice
1½ tablespoons minced
  parsley

Preheat the oven to 225°F. Put in an ovenproof platter. Combine the flour, salt, and pepper, spread it on wax paper, and drag each of the fillets through it so they are well coated. Shake off excess flour. In a large skillet, heat 3 tablespoons of the butter with the oil. Without crowding, put some of the fillets in the skillet and pan fry over medium heat until golden. Unless they are unusually thick, this should take 1–2 minutes on each side. Transfer to the warm platter and cook the rest of the fillets, adding the remaining butter as needed. When all the fish is cooked, turn the heat to high, stir in the lemon juice, and cook for a few seconds. Add the parsley, stir, and drizzle over the fillets.

SOLE WITH ALMONDS

Omit the parsley and, after the fillets are done, sauté ½ cup sliced almonds in 2 tablespoons butter until they are golden. Distribute over the fish before serving.

FILLETS OF SOLE BAKED IN HERBED CREAM

(SERVES FOUR)

Most any white-fleshed fish fillets can be used here.

1 teaspoon salt
¼ teaspoon freshly ground
  pepper
1½ pounds sole fillets
¼ teaspoon tarragon,
  crumbled

2 tablespoons finely chopped
  chives
2 tablespoons minced parsley
3 tablespoons lemon juice
¾ cup heavy cream

Preheat the oven to 450°F. Butter a shallow baking dish large enough to hold the fillets in a single layer, slightly overlapping. Salt and pepper the fish. Lay the fillets in the baking dish and sprinkle with the tarragon, chives, parsley, and lemon juice. Pour on the cream and bake about 15 minutes.

SOLE BAKED WITH WINE, GRAPES, AND CREAM

Omit the tarragon, chives, parsley, and lemon juice. Add *1½ cups seedless green grapes* to the baking dish, and pour *½ cup dry white wine* over the fillets and grapes before baking for 12–15 minutes. Heat *1 cup heavy cream* in a saucepan. When the fillets are done, spoon 6 tablespoons of the baking liquid into the hot cream and whisk for a few seconds until blended. Transfer the fish to a warm platter and pour on the cream sauce; when serving, give everyone a few grapes.

SOLE BAKED WITH CREAM AND MUSHROOMS

Sauté *3 cups sliced mushrooms* in *5 tablespoons butter*, just before serving, and pour over the fish.

BAKED FISH FILLETS WITH CAPER AND BLACK OLIVES   (SERVES FOUR)

Capers and black olives taste surprisingly good with fish.

4 tablespoons butter
3 tablespoons capers, rinsed of brine and drained
⅛ cup pitted black olives, cut lengthwise into eighths
3 tablespoons olive oil
2 teaspoons chopped oregano, or 1 teaspoon dried, crumbled

Salt and freshly ground pepper to taste
2 pounds bass or halibut fillets
2 tablespoons lemon juice
2 tablespoons finely chopped parsley

Melt the butter in a small saucepan over medium heat until it turns light brown. Remove from the heat and stir in the capers and black olives. Set aside. In a skillet, heat the olive oil and stir in the oregano, salt, and pepper. Put the fish in the pan, then move the fillets around and turn them over so they are coated with the seasoned olive oil. Cook over medium heat for about 2 minutes on each side, depending on the thickness of the fillets. Check for doneness by cutting into the thickest part with a small knife; if the center looks opaque they are done. Remove to a platter and reheat the caper-olive-butter mixture. When it is hot, remove from the heat and stir in the lemon juice and parsley. Spoon the sauce over the fish fillets and serve hot.

(SERVES FOUR) **FISH FILLETS BAKED IN PACKETS**

Here the fish is baked in parchment packets known as "papillottes," which you lightly oil on the inside, fill with fish, then seal. This makes a nice presentation at the table; each person opens his or her own packet of steaming fish. Aluminum foil can be used, but the look will not be the same.

4 pieces of parchment paper
    or aluminum foil about
    12 × 18 inches
Vegetable oil or butter for the
    paper
½ cup grated carrot
½ cup finely chopped celery

¼ cup grated onion
Salt and freshly ground
    pepper to taste
Four 4–5-ounce fish fillets,
    such as cod, bass, red
    snapper, or sole
4 lemon wedges

Preheat the oven to 425°F. Fold each piece of parchment or foil in half, then open and lay flat. Oil or butter both sides of the inside surface of each piece. Set aside. Combine the carrot, celery, and onion. Using

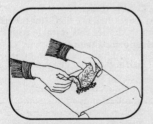

about half of the carrot mixture, place some over the bottom of each of the pieces of paper or foil. Salt and pepper the fish fillets and put one on each bed of vegetables. Top each fillet with some of the remaining carrot mixture. Fold the paper or foil over and seal by rolling the edges of each

packet tightly. The finished packet will be about 6 × 9 inches. Place on a large baking sheet and bake for 10–15 minutes, depending on the thickness of the fillet. Serve, sealed, with a lemon wedge.

OCEAN PERCH FILLETS, FILLED AND BAKED
(SERVES FOUR)

Ocean perch is the most common of the frozen fish fillets in our supermarkets. This easy cooking method lends tastiness to the rather bland, lean fish cut from a variety of large ocean fish: to be distinguished, incidentally, from small fresh lake perch, which should be cooked the way you would trout (p. 166). For this recipe you may substitute any other fillet, such as halibut, flounder, or sole.

1¾–2 pounds ocean perch or other fillets	2 tablespoons butter, melted
Salt	2 tablespoons lemon juice or dry vermouth
Freshly ground pepper	2 tablespoons heavy cream

Fillings

½ cup Bread Stuffing (p. 400), or ⅓ cup Mushroom Duxelles (p. 578)	½ cup finely chopped cooked seafood

Preheat the oven to 425°F. Butter a shallow casserole large enough to hold half the fillets in one layer. Lay down half the fish, and sprinkle with salt and pepper. Brush with half the butter and sprinkle with the lemon juice or vermouth. Spread with one of the fillings, and cover with the remaining fillets. Season again with salt, pepper, and remaining butter, and pour on the cream. Cover loosely with foil and bake 20–30 minutes, depending on the thickness of the fillets.

STEAMED HALIBUT
(SERVES FOUR)

This old Chinese technique makes a sensational dish.

½ pound carrots, peeled and julienned	Salt and freshly ground pepper to taste
¼ pound snow peas, cut into ¼-inch strips	6 tablespoons butter, melted
8 scallions, halved, then cut into slices lengthwise	2 teaspoons fresh thyme, or 1 teaspoon dry
1½ pounds halibut steaks	Lemon wedges

Bring some water to a boil in a pan or steamer with a rack and lid. Layer the carrots, snow peas, and scallions evenly on the rack. Place the halibut steaks, in a single layer, on top of the vegetables. Sprinkle with salt and pepper. Cover and steam for about 5–7 minutes, or until fish is opaque and flakes easily with a fork. While the fish is cooking, mix the butter and thyme together and set aside. When done, transfer the vegetables and fish to a warmed platter or serving dishes and pour the butter-thyme mixture over. Garnish with the lemon wedges.

(SERVES FOUR)   **HALIBUT CREOLE**

In this recipe, as in many others, cod and halibut may be used interchangeably.

1¾–2 pounds halibut steaks	½ cup finely chopped onion
Salt	6 tablespoons butter
Freshly ground pepper	3 tablespoons lemon juice
3 large tomatoes, peeled, seeded, and chopped	⅛ teaspoon Tabasco
½ cup finely chopped green pepper	

Preheat the oven to 400°F. Butter a shallow baking dish large enough to hold the fish in one layer, and place the fish in it. Season with salt and pepper to taste and spread the tomatoes, green pepper, and onion over the top. Melt the butter with the lemon juice and Tabasco and drizzle it over the fish and vegetables. Bake about 25 minutes, basting with pan juices every 10 minutes.

(SERVES FOUR)   **HOLLENDON HALIBUT**

The salt pork melts into the fish, making it moist and delicious.

⅛ pound salt pork, sliced thin	4 tablespoons butter, softened
1 onion, sliced thin	3 tablespoons flour
2 bay leaves	½ cup fresh bread crumbs
Two 1-pound halibut steaks	¼ teaspoon paprika
Salt	Chopped parsley
Freshly ground pepper	Lemon slices

Preheat the oven to 350°F. Place all but three or four slices of salt pork in the bottom of a shallow baking dish. Cover with onion and bay leaves and place halibut steaks on top. Season with salt lightly, pepper liberally. Cream together 3 tablespoons of the butter and the flour, and smear it over the fish. Cover with remaining salt pork slices, top with the bread crumbs, and dot with the remaining 1 tablespoon butter. Cover with foil and bake 40 minutes; remove foil and bake another 10 minutes to brown. Serve sprinkled with paprika and parsley and surrounded with lemon slices.

STEAMED LING COD WITH SOY
AND GINGER   (SERVES FOUR)

In spite of its name, ling cod is not a member of the cod family. It is sold whole or in fillets, fresh or frozen. It is excellent roasted, like pompano (p. 163), broiled, like shad (p. 174), or steamed Chinese-style with delicate seasonings.

3-pound ling cod, dressed	¼ cup vegetable oil
6 scallions, in 1-inch pieces	½ teaspoon sesame oil
4 slices fresh ginger root, in ½-inch slices	1 teaspoon soy sauce
	3 tablespoons dry sherry

Rinse the fish under cold water and pat dry. Make four or five 1½-inch incisions to the bone on each side of the fish. Put the scallions and ginger inside the cavity. If you don't have a steamer, use a roasting pan with a heatproof platter or rack to support the fish above the boiling water (p. 38). Place the fish on the steamer, cover, and cook 20–25 minutes, until the meat is opaque. In a small saucepan, whisk together the vegetable oil, sesame oil, soy sauce, and sherry. Heat and spoon over each portion of fish.

MACKEREL BROILED IN MILK   (SERVES FOUR)

Small mackerel are good filleted and simply broiled with lemon, like bluefish (p. 150). Oily fish, they also take well to being grilled with milk. Whole fillets from a larger mackerel are delicious baked on a bed of potatoes with pungent flavorings to balance the richness of the fish, as in the recipe that follows this one.

¾ cup milk	1 tablespoon chopped fresh dill, or 1 teaspoon dried, crumbled
1¼–2 pounds mackerel fillets	
Salt	
Freshly ground pepper	
2 tablespoons chopped parsley	

Preheat the broiler. Pour the milk in a baking dish large enough to hold the mackerel in one layer. Season the fillets with salt and pepper. Lay them in the dish and broil about 6 inches below the heat for 10 minutes, basting twice. Sprinkle with herbs and broil 5 minutes more.

(SERVES SIX)   **BAKED MACKEREL HUNGARIAN**

6 medium potatoes	¼ pound bacon, in 1-inch
2½ pounds large mackerel	slices
fillets	1 teaspoon paprika
1 green pepper, sliced	1 cup sour cream, at room
2 tomatoes, sliced	temperature

Preheat the oven to 400°F. Peel and cut the potatoes into ¼-inch slices. Boil them in salted water for 5 minutes; drain and scatter over the bottom of a large buttered baking dish. Make slashes in the mackerel about ¾ inch apart and insert in each one a slice of green pepper, tomato, and bacon. Place the fish over the potatoes, sprinkle with paprika, and bake for 20 minutes. Spread with sour cream and bake 5 minutes more.

(SERVES TWO)   **WHOLE ROASTED POMPANO**

Serve these superb silvery fish from the Gulf of Mexico by roasting them simply, one to a person.

2 whole pompano, about ¾	Salt
pound each	Freshly ground pepper
1 tablespoon oil	Lemon wedges

Preheat the oven to 400°F. Rub the fish with oil. Season lightly inside and out with salt and pepper. Bake in a shallow pan 25–30 minutes or until you see the skin bubbling slightly and swelling from the flesh— the sign that it is done. Serve with lemon wedges.

(SERVES TWO)   **SAUTÉ OF SHAD ROE**

The roe of the shad, sold in pairs, is one of our finest culinary treasures. It is often broiled with bacon, which tends to dry and toughen it. It is much more delicate and tender cooked this way, either done at the table in a chafing dish or in a kitchen skillet.

2 pairs shad roe	1 lemon
6 tablespoons butter	2 tablespoons chopped
Salt	parsley
Freshly ground pepper	4 slices bacon, fried

Sauté the shad roe in the butter in a chafing dish or skillet. Using moderate heat, cover and cook for 15 minutes, turning several times. Season with salt and pepper and squeeze on the juice of half the lemon, slicing the other half to use as garnish. Sprinkle with parsley and serve with crisp bacon.

SHAD STUFFED WITH ROE   (SERVES SIX)

2 pairs shad roe	2 sides of large shad, boned,
2 tablespoons butter	about 3 pounds
2 tablespoons minced	1 teaspoon cornstarch
scallions	dissolved in 2 tablespoons
½ cup dry vermouth or dry	water
white wine or water	1 cup heavy cream
¼ cup water	1 teaspoon tarragon,
Salt	crumbled
Freshly ground pepper	

Preheat the oven to 350°F. Sauté the roe in the butter with the scallions for 1–2 minutes. Add the vermouth and the water and simmer 10 minutes. Remove the roe, mash and season with salt and pepper, and stuff into the two sides of the shad. There are natural flaps to tuck the roe under. Put the stuffed fish in a pan, cover with foil, and bake 30 minutes. Meanwhile, boil down the roe poaching liquid to about ¼ cup. Add the cornstarch to the roe liquid along with the cream. Blend well, cook until thickened, add the tarragon, and adjust the seasoning. Pour this sauce over the baked fish.

PAN-FRIED SMELTS WITH SPINACH   (SERVES FOUR)

Small bony fish that are wonderful fried crisp and eaten with the fingers. Nibble the flesh off the larger bones; the smaller ones are tender enough to eat.

2 pounds smelts	¼ pound butter
⅓ cup flour	2 tablespoons oil
1½ teaspoons salt	1 pound fresh spinach,
¼ teaspoon freshly ground	washed and stemmed
pepper	3 tablespoons lemon juice

Preheat the oven to 225°F and put in an ovenproof platter. Rinse the smelts under cold water and pat dry. Mix the flour with 1 teaspoon of salt and the pepper, put it on a piece of wax paper, and drag each smelt through it so each side is coated. Melt the butter and oil in a large skillet. When it is hot, put in as many smelts as you can without crowding the skillet. Fry 1–1½ minutes on each side over high heat. Transfer to a warm platter and continue until all are fried. Put the spinach in the skillet, sprinkle with the remaining ½ teaspoon salt, and stir in the lemon juice. Cover and cook 3 minutes, until just wilted. Serve covered with the smelts.

SMELTS WITH BROWN BUTTER

Omit the spinach. Remove the fried fish to a platter. Add another *4 tablespoons butter* to the pan and heat until it turns brown. Mix in *2 tablespoons capers* with a little of their juice. Pour over the smelts and sprinkle with *chopped parsley*.

SMELTS WITH ANCHOVY BUTTER

Omit the spinach. Remove the fried fish to a platter. Stir *1 tablespoon anchovy paste* into the pan juices with *several squirts of lemon*. Pour over the smelts and sprinkle with *chopped parsley*. Serve with *lemon wedges*.

(SERVES FOUR)   ## BROILED SWORDFISH

Even people who don't like fish like swordfish, because its firm, oily flesh so resembles meat. Swordfish steaks should be cut about 1 inch thick for broiling. Thicker than that, the outside is apt to get too dry while the inside is undercooked; thinner than that, the steaks dry out completely and are better pan-fried. Swordfish is also very good cooked on an outdoor grill.

2-pound swordfish steak	½ teaspoon anchovy paste
4 tablespoons butter, melted	(optional)
Salt	Lemon wedges
Freshly ground pepper	

Preheat the broiler. Brush both sides of the swordfish with some of the melted butter, and season with salt and pepper. Broil on the highest level for 5 minutes; then turn, pour on a tablespoon of butter, and broil another 4–5 minutes. Mix the remaining butter with the anchovy paste, if you like a sharper accent, and pour it over the fish. Surround with lemon wedges.

BROILED SHARK

Similar to swordfish in texture, *shark* can be used instead.

PAN-FRIED BROOK TROUT   (SERVES FOUR)

Fresh-water trout is unequaled when cooked straight from the stream, but it is beautiful eating anytime.

4 brook trout, cleaned, with head and tail left on	7 tablespoons butter
2 tablespoons flour	3 tablespoons oil
Salt	2 tablespoons lemon juice
	2 tablespoons minced chives

Rinse the fish under cold running water and pat dry with paper towels. Dust lightly with flour, and sprinkle with salt. In a large skillet, melt 3 tablespoons of the butter and the oil. When it is hot, put in the trout and fry over medium-high heat. When browned, turn and brown the other side: each side will take about 3 minutes. Melt the remaining 4 tablespoons butter with lemon juice and chives in a small saucepan. When the trout is done, transfer to a warm platter and pour on the sauce.

BROILED RAINBOW (OR SPECKLED OR BROWN) TROUT   (SERVES FOUR)

4 rainbow trout, cleaned, with head and tail left on	Freshly ground pepper
Salt	Oil
	Lemon wedges

Preheat the broiler. Sprinkle the cavity of the fish with salt and pepper. Rub the outside with oil. Place on an oiled rack 5 inches beneath the broiler (at the second level) and broil for 5 minutes on each side. The skin will just be spottily charred and the flesh moist and tender. Serve with lemon wedges.

BROILED TROUT WITH ROSEMARY

Place a *sprig of fresh rosemary* in the cavity of each trout before cooking.

BROILED TROUT WITH CREAM

Use a shallow pan instead of the broiler rack. After broiling 2–3 minutes on the second side, pour *¼ cup heavy cream* over the trout and broil another 5 minutes, basting a couple of times. Omit lemon wedges and sprinkle with *1 tablespoon chopped parsley* and *1 tablespoon chopped fresh tarragon*, or *1 teaspoon dried, crumbled*.

TILEFISH WITH TOMATOES AND RIPE OLIVES

(SERVES FOUR)

A large, moist, fairly bland fish that has recently returned to Atlantic waters, tile is best cut into thick steaks and cooked bathed in a tasty sauce. Steaks from a large bass, or cod, could be done the same way.

3 tablespoons oil	1-pound 12-ounce can whole
2 cloves garlic	tomatoes
1 medium onion, sliced	8–10 large pitted ripe olives,
4 tilefish steaks, ⅓–½ pound	sliced
each	2 tablespoons chopped
Salt	parsley
Freshly ground pepper	

Heat the oil in a large skillet. Sauté the garlic cloves until they begin to turn color. Remove, and cook the onion in the oil about 3 minutes. Push to the side and add the fish, browning lightly on one side for 1 minute before turning. Season with salt and pepper. Drain the tomatoes, chop the pulp roughly, and add to the skillet with 2–3 tablespoons of the juice. Cover and cook over medium heat 12–15 minutes. Remove the fish to a warm platter. Boil down the tomatoes if too liquid, add the olives until warmed through, spoon over the fish, and sprinkle with parsley.

BAKED FRESH TUNA   (SERVES FOUR)

Once in a while, fish markets will advertise fresh tuna, and it is well worth experimenting with the red-fleshed steaks and tasting the difference between them and the canned version. Swordfish and kingfish are both good prepared this way.

1¾ pounds fresh tuna steaks
2 tablespoons olive oil
Salt
Freshly ground pepper
1 large red onion, sliced thin

4 medium tomatoes, peeled,
    seeded, and chopped
½ cup dry vermouth
1 teaspoon basil, crumbled

Preheat the oven to 425°F. Rub the tuna steaks with 1 tablespoon olive oil and season lightly with salt and pepper. In a skillet, sauté the onion in the remaining oil until it is limp. Add the tomatoes and vermouth and cook briefly. Place the steaks in a shallow baking dish, pour on the onion-tomato mixture, and bake 12–15 minutes, depending on their thickness. Sprinkle with basil.

WHITEFISH BROILED WITH SESAME SEEDS
                                       (SERVES FOUR)

This tasty fish from the Great Lakes and other northern inland waters can also be pan-sautéed, particularly if you have fillets, but do run the pan under the broiler if you sprinkle the fish with sesame seeds—just long enough to toast them as here.

1 whole whitefish, about 2½
    pounds
Salt
2 tablespoons melted butter
    with ½ teaspoon lemon
    juice

3 tablespoons sesame seeds
Lemon wedges

Preheat the broiler. Rub the fish inside and out with a little salt and melted butter with lemon juice. Broil 5 inches from the heat 5 minutes, basting once or twice, then turn and broil 4 minutes, brush well with butter, and coat with sesame seeds. Broil another minute or so until seeds are golden brown. Serve with lemon wedges.

(SERVES FOUR)   **PAN-SAUTÉED WHITING**

Whiting is an Atlantic fish with a mild flavor. People who think they
object to fishy flavors, often favor a whiting. It is usually served whole,
one to a person.

4 whole whitings, about ¾ pound each	¼ teaspoon paprika
Salt	3 tablespoons butter
Freshly ground pepper	2 tablespoons oil
½ cup flour	1 lemon
	1 tablespoon chopped parsley

Rinse the whitings inside and out, pat dry, and sprinkle with salt and
pepper. Mix the flour and paprika, dust the fish with it, and shake off
excess. In a large skillet heat 2 tablespoons of butter and the oil until
the foam subsides. Add the fish and brown on both sides. Lower the
heat and cover, cooking about 12 minutes or until the flesh is opaque
around the rib cage. Remove to a warm platter. Squeeze half the lemon
into the pan, add the remaining butter, and cook 1 minute more, scraping up the bits from the pan. Pour over the fish and garnish with parsley and the remaining lemon cut in wedges.

(SERVES FOUR)   **PAN-FRIED PORGY**

A popular game fish in Atlantic waters, porgy is usually sold whole.

4 porgies, ½–¾ pound each	1 clove garlic, minced
½ cup cornmeal	(optional)
½ teaspoon salt	½ teaspoon marjoram or basil
Freshly ground pepper	1 lemon
4 tablespoons oil	1 tablespoon butter

Wash the porgies and pat dry. Season the cornmeal with salt and pepper, and dredge the fish. Heat the oil in a large skillet, and brown the
fish quickly on both sides. Turn the heat to medium, add the garlic (if
desired) and herbs, and cook 10–15 minutes. Remove to a warm platter. Squeeze half a lemon into the pan with the butter, scrape up the
browned bits, and pour the juices over the fish. Cut the other half of
the lemon into slices and garnish the fish with them.

RED SNAPPER, STUFFED AND BAKED   (SERVES FOUR)

One of our finest fish from the Gulf Coast, so handsome on the platter
when served whole with its glistening silver and pinkish red skin.

6 tablespoons butter	½ teaspoon salt
¼ pound mushrooms, chopped fine	Freshly ground pepper
4 scallions, chopped	1 whole red snapper, about 2½ pounds
1 stalk celery, chopped	2–3 tablespoons dry white wine
½ cup bread crumbs	
½ teaspoon rosemary	

Preheat the oven to 400°F. Melt 5 tablespoons of the butter, add the
mushrooms, scallions, and celery, and sauté about 10 minutes. Mix in
the bread crumbs, rosemary, salt, and pepper to taste. Fill the cavity of
the fish with the stuffing and skewer or sew up the opening. Brush the
fish with some of the remaining butter and bake for 30 minutes, basting with what's left of the butter and a little wine twice during the
cooking.

STUFFED BLACK BASS OR ROCK BASS, SALMON, WHITEFISH, MACKEREL, OR BLUEFISH

Any of these fish, if available at 2½ pounds, can be stuffed in the same
manner.

RED SNAPPER FILLETS, FLORIDA STYLE   (SERVES FOUR)

1½ pounds red snapper fillets	1 teaspoon grated grapefruit rind, or a combination of lemon and lime
Salt	
Freshly ground pepper	
A few gratings of nutmeg	
1½ teaspoons grated orange rind	

Preheat the oven to 400°F. Put the fillets in a lightly buttered baking
dish. Sprinkle them lightly with salt and pepper and nutmeg and distribute the grated rinds on top. Cover with foil and bake 15 minutes.

SNAPPER BAKED IN TOMATILLO SAUCE

(SERVES FOUR)

This is good served on Polenta (p. 432) or on warm tortillas.

3 cloves garlic	½ teaspoon salt
½ medium onion	1½ pounds red snapper fillets
18-ounce can tomatillo, drained (see p. 616)	4 corn tortillas, warmed (optional)
¼ cup cilantro leaves	

Preheat the oven to 400°F. Put the garlic in a food processor and process until finely chopped. Scrape down sides of bowl. Cut the onion into quarters, add to the bowl, and process until coarsely chopped. Add the tomatillo, cilantro, and salt, and process until all is finely chopped and you have a coarse purée. (Or you may chop the garlic, onions, tomatillo, and cilantro by hand and mix together in a bowl.) Grease a baking dish. Lay the fish fillets in a single layer and spread the sauce over. Cover with foil and bake 12–15 minutes. Serve with tortillas, if you wish.

BROILED ROCKBASS WITH FENNEL SEED

(SERVES FOUR)

Rockbass is from the bass family, a lean fish found in the Midwest and South. Sold whole or in fillets, it benefits from added seasonings and sauces.

3-pound rockbass, split, with backbone removed	Freshly ground pepper
4 tablespoons butter	1 large tomato, peeled, seeded, and chopped
¾ cup dry white wine	1 tablespoon finely chopped parsley
2 teaspoons fennel seed	
Salt	

Rinse the fish and pat dry. Place it, skin side down, on a well-oiled broiler pan. Melt the butter with the wine and fennel. Let simmer 2 minutes, remove from the heat, and let steep 15 minutes. Preheat the broiler. Sprinkle the fish with salt and pepper, and pour on the butter mixture. Place 4 inches beneath the broiler element and cook 6–8 minutes, depending on the thickness of the fish. Remove to a warm platter. Mix the tomato with parsley and spoon it on the fish.

POACHED SALMON   (SERVES EIGHT TO TEN)

Salmon is one of the most flavorful fish. It weighs between 5 and 10 pounds when whole; larger salmon are generally cut into steaks or sections. The meat is pink, tender, and firm, the flavor mild and delicious. It lends itself to poaching whole, baking split, or broiling (planked or not, as you wish). It is equally delicious cold, and makes a splendid buffet dish.

6-pound whole dressed salmon	4 bay leaves, in pieces
4 quarts water	12 sprigs parsley
2 cups dry white wine	1 teaspoon freshly ground pepper
1½ tablespoons salt	1 recipe Hollandaise Sauce (p. 388)
4 carrots, sliced	
3 onions, sliced thin	

Rinse the salmon under cold running water. In a fish poacher or a large roasting pan with a lid and rack to hold the fish, combine the water with the wine, salt, carrots, onions, bay leaves, parsley, and pepper. Bring to a boil and simmer 15 minutes. If you want to make sure that the salmon remains in one piece, wrap it in a cheesecloth sling before placing it in the broth; it will be easy to lift out later. Lay the fish on the rack; if there is not enough broth to cover it, add some more water. Put on the lid and simmer 25–30 minutes or until meat loses its deep pink color around the backbone. A thermometer will register 140°F when the fish is done. Remove the pan from the heat and let the fish remain in the broth until you are ready to serve it, up to 45 minutes. Serve with hollandaise.

COLD POACHED SALMON

Follow the recipe for Poached Salmon, but remove the fish from the broth and refrigerate until it is cool. Place on a platter and decorate with *tomato wedges, cucumber slices, black olives,* and *watercress.* Serve with *Mayonnaise* (p. 708), *Green Mayonnaise* (p. 708), or *Cucumber Sauce* (p. 395).

(SERVES FOUR)   **BROILED SALMON**

6 tablespoons butter, melted
4 salmon steaks, about ¾ inch
   thick
Salt to taste
Freshly ground pepper to
   taste

1 tablespoon mixed chopped
   parsley, chives, and dill
Juice of 1 lemon
Lemon wedges

Preheat the broiler. Brush 2 tablespoons of the butter over the salmon
steaks. Mix remaining butter with salt, pepper, herbs, and lemon juice.
Place salmon steaks on the broiler pan and put it on the highest level
under the broiling element. Cook 5 minutes each side. For the last minutes of cooking, pour on the butter mixture. Serve with accumulated
pan juices and surround with lemon wedges.

(SERVES FOUR)   **SALMON WITH ASPARAGUS**

This is a harbinger of springtime in Scandinavia. Serve with small
boiled new potatoes.

1 pound fresh asparagus,
   washed and trimmed
4 tablespoons butter
Salt to taste
4 salmon steaks, about ¾ inch
   thick

1 teaspoon sesame oil
   (optional)
Lemon wedges

Cut the asparagus on the diagonal into ¼–½-inch-thick slices. Bring a
pot of water to a boil, add the asparagus, and blanch for 1 minute.
Drain and set aside. Put 2 tablespoons butter in a skillet over a
medium-high heat. (I find a nonstick pan is foolproof.) Salt the salmon
and sauté in the butter for about 2–3 minutes; turn and cook another
2–3 minutes, or until the fish is opaque and flakes easily with a fork.
Remove the fish to a dish and keep warm. Add the remaining 2 tablespoons of butter and the optional sesame oil to the skillet, reduce the
heat to medium, and add the asparagus. Cook for about 3–4 minutes,
until crisp-tender. Serve the salmon and asparagus with the lemon
wedges.

BROILED SCROD   (SERVES FOUR)

Scrod is young cod. It is most delicious when very fresh, split down
the back, and broiled quickly with a crusty topping to contrast with the
tender flesh.

Four ½-pound pieces split scrod	Salt
½ cup fresh bread crumbs	Freshly ground pepper
¼ cup grated Swiss cheese	Lemon wedges
6 tablespoons butter, melted	

Preheat the broiler. Oil the broiler pan, and place the scrod on it. Mix
together the bread crumbs and cheese. Sprinkle the fish with half the
melted butter, salt, and pepper, and place beneath the broiling element. Cook 6 minutes on one side. Turn, cook 4 minutes, and then
sprinkle on the bread crumbs and cheese. Pour over the remaining butter and broil another minute or two until nicely browned. Garnish with
lemon wedges.

BROILED SHAD   (SERVES FOUR)

Like asparagus, fresh broiled shad is one of the pleasures of spring—
that is, for those lucky enough to live in parts of America where the
shad run. It used to be an onerous task to pull out all the small bones,
but now one can buy fillets impeccably boned. If you should be con-
fronted with an unboned shad, try the next recipe, in which the fish is
cooked so long that the bones melt away.

2 tablespoons butter	Salt
2 sides of shad, boned, about 2 pounds	Freshly ground pepper
	Lemon wedges

Preheat the broiler. Rub a little butter on the rack and place the shad on
it, skin side down. Season with salt and pepper and dot with remaining butter. Broil at highest level for 8 minutes, without turning. Serve
garnished with lemon wedges.

FISH STEAKS BAKED WITH VEGETABLES

(SERVES FOUR)

Cod, halibut, tilefish, and kingfish steaks can all be cooked this way.

2 tablespoons oil
1 large onion, chopped
1 clove garlic, chopped
2 large tomatoes, peeled, seeded, and chopped, or ¾ cup canned tomatoes, drained and chopped
1 green pepper, chopped
Cayenne pepper to taste

¼ teaspoon oregano
4 fish steaks
½ teaspoon salt
Freshly ground pepper to taste
2 tablespoons lemon juice
¼ cup fresh bread crumbs
2 tablespoons butter

Preheat the oven to 375°F. In a skillet, heat the oil and sauté the onion, garlic, tomatoes, and green pepper over low heat for 10 minutes. Add the cayenne and oregano and spread half the mixture in a shallow baking dish large enough to hold the fish in one layer. Season the fish steaks with salt and pepper, place them on the vegetables, and cover with the remaining vegetable mixture. Sprinkle with lemon juice and bread crumbs and dot with butter. Bake for 25 minutes.

SHELLFISH

PAN-FRIED ABALONE

(SERVES TWO)

Abalone is a large single-shelled mollusk that is found along the California coast. It is in short supply, and cannot be canned or shipped fresh or frozen out of California. Preserved abalone from Japan is sometimes available. Should you be so lucky as to obtain abalone steaks, tenderize them by pounding with a wooden mallet. Use persistent, firm strokes, and flatten them to quarter-inch thickness. Do not overcook, or the abalone will be tough and rubbery. Thirty seconds to a side is enough; less is better.

2 abalone steaks, tenderized
3 tablespoons butter
1 tablespoon oil
Salt

Freshly ground pepper
1 tablespoon lemon juice
2 parsley sprigs

Pat the abalone dry with paper towels. Melt the butter with the oil in a large skillet. When the butter foams and is very hot, add the steaks.

Season with salt and pepper and fry 30 seconds on each side. Transfer to a warm platter, drizzle with lemon juice, and garnish with parsley.

STEAMED CLAMS   (1 QUART PER SERVING)

Clams are a bivalve, or two-shelled, mollusk. There are three principal varieties, soft-shelled, hard-shelled, and razor clams from the Pacific. The so-called soft-shelled are oval and come from northern New England. The hard-shelled are round and come in small littlenecks, medium cherrystones, and large quahogs or chowder clams. Small clams are eaten raw, steamed, or on the half-shell; quahogs are good minced and in soups. When buying clams, be sure the shells are clamped tightly together; this indicates that the clam is alive. Discard broken or cracked shells. To get rid of all the sand, scrub under running water and then soak in a salt-water brine for about ½ hour.

1 quart clams per serving   Lemon juice or vinegar
¼ cup butter, melted, per
    serving

Scrub the shells with a brush, changing the water until there is no trace of sand. Put the clams in a deep kettle with 2 tablespoons water for each quart of clams. Cover tightly and cook over low heat until the shells open, about 15 minutes. Don't overcook. Using a slotted spoon, remove the clams to large soup plates. Strain the broth into small glasses and serve with the clams. Set out individual dishes of melted butter, to which you may add a little lemon juice or vinegar, and a small amount of boiling water which will make the butter float to the top and stay hot. To eat, lift the clam from the shell by the black neck. Dip in the clam broth, then in the butter, and eat; some like the neck, some don't.

BAKED OR BROILED CLAMS   (SERVES FOUR)

To open clams for serving on the half-shell, insert a knife between the shells near the muscle. Cut through the muscle and twist the knife a little to pry the shells apart. Drain the juice into a bowl.

24 medium-size clams   1 lemon, quartered
¼ pound butter, melted

Preheat the oven to 400°F or preheat the broiler. Remove the top shell from hard-shelled clams. Spoon a teaspoon of melted butter on each clam and bake for 6 minutes or broil 3–4 minutes. Serve hot with lemon quarters.

SEASHORE CLAMBAKE

1 quart clams per person   1–2 ears corn per person
1 small lobster per person

Dig a pit in the sand about 1 foot deep. Put down a layer of stones and build a wood fire on the stones. Burn until the fire dies down and the stones are white-hot, about 1 hour. Meanwhile, scrub the clams in sea water, kill the lobsters (p. 181), and dip the corn in sea water. Rake off the ashes and spread a thin layer of seaweed on the stones. Put a piece of chicken wire over the seaweed and pile on the clams, lobsters, and corn. Cover with more seaweed and a piece of canvas to keep in the steam, working quickly so that the rocks do not cool. Steam about 1 hour.

FRICASSEE OF CLAMS

(SERVES FOUR AS FIRST COURSE)

2 tablespoons butter   Pinch of cayenne pepper
2 tablespoons flour   2 tablespoons dry sherry
¾ cup milk or heavy cream   1 pint chopped clams
Salt

Melt the butter in a saucepan. Stir in the flour and cook over medium heat until smooth and blended. Slowly add the cream, stirring constantly, until the sauce is smooth. Stir in the salt, cayenne pepper, sherry, and clams, and cook over low heat for 3 minutes, stirring constantly. Serve on toast.

STUFFED CLAMS UNION LEAGUE

(SERVES FOUR)

8 tablespoons butter   5–6 drops Tabasco
1 tablespoon finely chopped   2 teaspoons finely chopped
   shallot or onion   parsley
36 small clams in the shell   1 cup freshly made bread
1 cup dry white wine   crumbs
3 tablespoons flour   ½ cup freshly grated
½ cup heavy cream   Parmesan cheese

Melt 5 tablespoons of the butter in a large saucepan. Add the shallot or onion and stir over low heat for 5 minutes. Add the clams and wine, cover, and cook until the shells open, 12–15 minutes. Remove the clams from the shells and chop them. Save the shells. Preheat the oven to 400°F. Melt the remaining 3 tablespoons butter in a saucepan. Blend in the flour and cook 1 minute. Slowly add ½ cup of the clam liquid and the cream, and stir until the sauce is smooth. Add the clams and Tabasco and stir constantly until the sauce is thickened. Remove from the heat, add the parsley, and spoon the clams and sauce back into the shells. Mix the bread crumbs and cheese and sprinkle on each clam. Bake for 15 minutes or until the crumbs are lightly browned.

BROILED CRABS   (SERVES FOUR)

There are three types of crab on the market: blue crabs from the At-lantic and Gulf coasts, Dungeness crabs from the Pacific, and king crab from North Pacific waters. Crab is sold alive, frozen, or cleaned and packed in refrigerated tins. Canned crab is good, but lacks the delicate flavor of fresh. The best way to learn to eat a hard-shelled crab is to go to a Baltimore crab house and ask a waiter to show you. Failing that, we offer instructions below. Choose lively crabs.

Salt   6 live blue crabs

Bring a large kettle of salted water to the boil. Drop in the crabs and boil 15 minutes; they will turn pink. Drain and run them under cold water to make them cool enough to handle. Twist off the large legs and crack with a nutcracker or pliers. Pull and break off the apron. Remove the gills, intestine, and the rest of the innards. Reserve the roe, which is orange, and the tomalley, which is pale green—both are delicious. Dig out the small amount of precious meat, to be found beneath the gills. If the shell is to be stuffed, remove the stomach sac, rinse the shell well, and dry.

STEAMED CRABS

Set the crabs on a steamer over boiling water. Sprinkle them with *Tabasco* and *vinegar*, cover the pot, and steam about 10 minutes.

(SERVES THREE)   **SOFT-SHELL CRABS, SAUTÉED**

Soft-shell crabs are a seasonal delicacy. All crabs have hard shells, which they shed as they outgrow them. It is at the time of molting, in late spring and summer, that they are caught and sold as soft-shell crabs. Buy them alive, whole, and have them killed and cleaned just before you bring them home.

¼ cup flour	6 tablespoons butter
Salt	1 tablespoon oil
Freshly ground pepper	Juice of 1 lemon
6 soft-shell crabs	

Season the flour with salt and pepper, dust the crabs with it, and shake off excess. In a large skillet, heat the butter and oil. Toss in the crabs and cook over moderately high heat about 3 minutes each side. Remove to a warm platter. Squeeze in the lemon juice and stir, scraping up all the brown bits. Pour over the crabs.

SOFT-SHELL CRABS AMANDINE

Before adding the lemon juice, sauté ⅓ cup *slivered almonds* in the pan, adding additional *butter* if necessary. When the nuts are golden, scatter them over the crabs, and finish with the lemon juice.

(SERVES FOUR)   **✳ CRAB CAKES**

It is critical in making crab cakes that they be moist—use only enough cracker or bread crumbs to coat. The flavoring should be mild so you can taste the fresh crab. A wedge of chilled, crisp iceberg lettuce with tartar sauce (p. 394) is very good with them.

1 pound crabmeat	2 tablespoons fresh lemon juice
1 egg, lightly beaten	
1½ teaspoons Dijon mustard	1½ cups freshly made bread crumbs (or cracker crumbs)
Cayenne pepper to taste	
2 tablespoons minced scallions	
2 tablespoons minced parsley	¼ pound butter
6 tablespoons mayonnaise	¼ cup vegetable oil

In a large mixing bowl mix together the crab, egg, mustard, cayenne, scallions, parsley, mayonnaise, and lemon juice. Mix well, using your hands, and taste and correct seasonings as you are mixing the cakes. The mixture should have a little bite and sparkle of flavor to round out the crab. Pat the crab mixture into about 12 small cakes. Spread the crumbs on a piece of wax paper. Heat the butter and oil in a large skillet over medium-high heat. Coat the cakes in crumbs on all sides, then put them in the hot fat and fry until golden, turning so all sides are crisp and brown—2–3 minutes on each side. Serve hot.

DEVILED CRAB   (SERVES FOUR)

Be bold with the Tabasco sauce and mustard so that the crab is really deviled. Serve with a salad of grapefruit and lettuce.

5 tablespoons butter, melted	1 teaspoon Worcestershire
½ cup thinly sliced celery	sauce
2 tablespoons chopped	2 teaspoons lemon juice
scallion	¼–½ teaspoon Tabasco
1 tablespoon flour	2 cups flaked fresh cooked
½ teaspoon dry mustard	crabmeat
½ teaspoon salt	¾ cup bread crumbs
½ cup cream	1 tablespoon chopped parsley
½ cup milk	

Preheat the oven to 400°F. Put 2 tablespoons of the butter in a saucepan with the celery, and cook over low heat until the celery is softened. Add the scallions and cook about 30 seconds more. Stir in the flour, mustard, and salt, and cook until it froths. Then slowly add the cream and milk, and continue cooking, stirring constantly, until slightly thickened. Add the Worcestershire sauce, lemon juice, and Tabasco, and stir to blend. Remove from the heat and stir in the crabmeat. Place in four buttered ramekins or baking dishes. Toss the bread crumbs with the remaining 3 tablespoons of butter and the parsley and cover each of the ramekins with the crumbs. Bake for 20 minutes, until slightly browned and heated through.

CRABMEAT INDIENNE   (SERVES FOUR)

This is good on rice.

3 tablespoons butter	2 teaspoons curry powder
1 tablespoon finely chopped	2 cups chicken broth
onion	1½ cups crabmeat
4 tablespoons flour	

Melt the butter in a saucepan. Add the onion and cook over low heat for 3 minutes, stirring often. Stir the flour and curry powder into the skillet and cook 2 minutes more. Add the chicken broth slowly and cook and stir for 5 minutes. Add the crabmeat and cook only until heated through.

BROILED LOBSTER

Lobster   Melted butter

Preheat the broiler. Kill the lobster by inserting a sharp knife where the head meets the shell. Turn on its back and make a deep cut through the length of the body with a heavy sharp-pointed knife. Spread the halves apart and remove the black line and the stomach. Leave the tomalley (the green-black soft matter) and the orange roe—both are delicious. Crack the claw shells with a hammer. Drizzle melted butter over the body. Place on rack in the broiler, meat side up, and broil for about 15 minutes without turning. Serve with more melted butter.

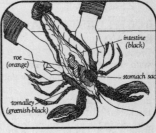

BOILED LIVE LOBSTER

Lobsters are found in waters all over the world. They range from one to thirty pounds. The commercial grading is: "chicken," 1 pound; "quarters," under 1½ pounds; "large," 1½–2½ pounds; and "jumbo," over 2½ pounds. When buying a live lobster, look for one that is active and lively and heavy for its size. Killed lobsters should be cooked as soon as possible after purchase. The meat of the claws, body, and tail are wonderful to eat. The green liver or tomalley is a choice morsel, as is the roe or "coral" of the female lobster.

Salt   Lobsters

Fill a kettle with plenty of water to cover the lobsters. Add 2 teaspoons salt for each quart of water used. Bring to a rolling boil and put the lobsters in the pot. Allow 10 minutes cooking time for small lobsters, 15 minutes for medium, and as much as 25 minutes for large. Using tongs, lift from the water and cool just enough to handle. To prepare a boiled lobster to be eaten, first twist off the claws. Break the claws with a hammer or nutcracker so the meat is easily removed. Gently pull apart the tail from the body. Holding the tail with the hard shell down, cut the length of the cartilaginous tail with scissors. Bend it apart so the meat comes loose. Insert a small knife down the center and remove the dark line of intestine. Take the body and carefully remove the meat, discarding the lungs and stomach. Pick carefully for any small shell-like particles.

CORAL BUTTER

Put the lobster coral into a blender or food processor and slowly add *4 tablespoons butter, softened.* Spread on toast or use in a sauce.

ROCK LOBSTER TAILS, BOILED
(½ POUND PER SERVING)

Rock lobster tails are imported frozen from South Africa, New Zealand, and Australia. They vary in size from 4 ounces to 1½ pounds.

Salt   Melted butter
Rock lobster tails

Bring a large pot of salted water to a boil. Drop in the frozen lobster tails and boil 3 minutes for small and 5 minutes for large tails. Drain until just cool enough to handle. With a knife, remove the shell-like covering on the underside of the tail. Cut down the center of the flesh deeply enough to remove the dark vein. Serve with melted butter.

ROCK LOBSTER TAILS BROILED

Drizzle lobster tails with melted butter and put them on a baking sheet, shell side down. Broil in a preheated oven 3–4 minutes.

(SERVES EIGHT)   **LOBSTER THERMIDOR**

Serve this with steamed rice.

8 tablespoons butter	4 cups cooked lobster meat
½ pound mushrooms, sliced	Salt
3 tablespoons flour	⅓ cup freshly grated
2 cups heavy cream or milk	Parmesan cheese
¼ cup dry sherry	

Preheat the oven to 450°F. Butter a shallow baking dish. Melt 5 tablespoons of the butter in a saucepan. Add the mushrooms and cook until they are softened. Remove and set aside. Melt the remaining 3 tablespoons of butter, stir in the flour, and cook until smooth and blended. Slowly stir in the cream or milk and cook over low heat, stirring until the sauce is smooth and thickened. Add the sherry and cook 1 minute more. Remove from the heat and add the lobster and salt to taste. Spoon into the baking dish, sprinkle with cheese, and bake about 10 minutes, until the cheese is melted and lightly browned.

(SERVES FOUR)   **LOBSTER À L'AMÉRICAINE**

2 large lobsters, about 1½ pounds each	1 teaspoon thyme, crumbled
4 tablespoons oil	¼ cup finely chopped shallots
6 tablespoons butter	⅛ teaspoon cayenne pepper
1 bay leaf, crumbled	2 tablespoons tomato paste
	⅓ cup dry white wine

Kill and split the live lobsters (p. 181). Cut in 8 pieces, remove any liver and coral, and set aside. In a large skillet, heat the oil and butter. When they are hot, add the lobster pieces, bay leaf, thyme, and shallots. Lower the heat, cover, and simmer 5 minutes. Mix the cayenne pepper, tomato paste, and wine in a small bowl. Add to the lobster, stirring with the juices in the skillet. Cover and simmer another 10–15 minutes, until the shells are red. Take out the lobster and remove the meat. Strain the liquid and return it to the pan with the liver and coral. Blend, add the lobster meat, and heat through.

(SERVES FOUR)   **LOBSTER NEWBURG**

In spite of changing food trends, this dish deserves to be made as it was created, if only on special occasions. Serve with steamed rice or crisp buttered toast.

1½ cups cream
3 egg yolks, well beaten
Salt and freshly ground
  pepper to taste

3 cups cooked lobster meat
1 tablespoon butter
1 tablespoon sherry

Heat the cream in a heavy-bottomed saucepan over medium-high heat until hot but not boiling. Remove from the heat. Stir a little of the hot cream into the egg yolks, then pour the egg yolk mixture back into the hot cream, stirring constantly. Return the pan to medium heat and cook and stir until the mixture thickens enough to coat a spoon. Add salt and pepper and lobster meat, and cook until heated through. Add the butter and sherry and cook 1 minute more.

STEAMED MUSSELS IN WHITE WINE   (SERVES FIVE)

A bivalve mollusk like the clam, the mussel in its blue-black oval shell is a great delicacy as well as one of the most abundant of seafoods. Mussels must be very well scrubbed, have their beards scraped away, and any open raw mussels should be discarded. Also, try to move the halves of the shell. If they slide, discard the mussel, for it may be full of mud.

2 cups dry white wine, or 1½
  cups dry vermouth mixed
  with ½ cup water
¼ cup finely chopped shallots
  or scallions

Pinch of thyme
1 bay leaf
4 pounds mussels, scrubbed
  and scraped
⅓ cup chopped parsley

Put the wine, shallots or scallions, thyme, and bay leaf in a large pot and boil briskly for 10 minutes. Add the mussels, cover tightly, and boil 3–5 minutes, giving the pot a shake once or twice. If the mussels have opened, they are done; if not, cover and cook 1–2 minutes longer until all are opened. Spoon into large soup plates with a portion of broth. Sprinkle with parsley and serve with crusty bread.

COLD MUSSELS ON THE HALF-SHELL
                                          (SERVES FOUR)

2½ dozen steamed mussels
  (see preceding recipe)
Juice of 1 lemon
½ cup Mustard Sauce (p. 391)
  or Green Mayonnaise (p.
  708)

3 tablespoons mixed chopped
  parsley and chives
Lemon slices

Loosen each cooked mussel from its shell, break the shells apart. Then place a mussel on each half. Squeeze a drop or two of lemon juice on each, cover with the sauce or mayonnaise, and sprinkle generously with parsley and chives. Chill, then serve with lemon slices.

(SERVES FOUR) **OYSTERS ON THE HALF-SHELL**

Oysters have a long history on this continent; ancient Indian settlements have been located because their inhabitants left heaps of empty oyster shells. Oysters are two-shelled mollusks, having one half of the shell flatter than the other. When they are served "on the half-shell," the deep half is always used. They vary in size from the tiny western Olympias to the huge Japanese variety. On the East Coast, Maryland's Chincoteagues are famous. Buy oysters with shells tightly clamped together, indicating they are still alive. The pure and perfect way to eat an oyster is to have it fresh, raw, and alive with, at most, a few drops of lemon juice. Clean, briny, and tender, they are the perfect first course, preparing the palate for the meal to follow.

24 oysters in the shell	Lemon wedges

Use a blunt-ended oyster knife to shuck the oysters. Insert the end of the knife between the shells near the hinge; work it until you cut through the muscle that holds the shells together. Catch the oyster liquor in a bowl. When the oysters are all shucked, strain the liquor through muslin before setting aside to use in sauces. Place an oyster in the deep half of each shell; serve with lemon wedges.

(SERVES FOUR) **OYSTERS CASINO**

Clams are delicious prepared this way, too.

24 oysters on the half-shell (see preceding recipe)	2 tablespoons minced parsley
	Salt
2 tablespoons lemon juice	Freshly ground pepper
3 tablespoons minced green pepper	6 strips bacon

Preheat the broiler. Spread 1 inch of rock salt in a shallow baking dish large enough to hold the oyster shells, or use crumpled foil—anything to hold the oysters steady. Arrange the oysters on the salt. Sprinkle each with a few drops of lemon juice. Mix the green pepper, parsley, and salt and pepper to taste, and sprinkle over each oyster. Cut the bacon into 1½-inch lengths and put one piece on each oyster. Broil until the bacon is slightly brown.

OYSTERS ROCKEFELLER   (SERVES FOUR)

3 scallions, including 1 inch of green tops
¼ cup chopped celery
2 tablespoons chopped parsley
½ cup chopped spinach
2 tablespoons freshly made bread crumbs

Dash of Tabasco
¼ teaspoon Worcestershire sauce
½ pound butter, softened
Salt
24 large oysters on the half-shell (p. 185)

Preheat the oven to 450°F. Combine the scallions, celery, parsley, and spinach and mince them with a knife or chop in a blender or food processor. Put the mixture into a bowl with the bread crumbs, Tabasco, and Worcestershire sauce. Add the butter and salt to taste, and cream all together into a smooth paste. Spread 1 inch of rock salt over a pan or baking dish large enough to hold the oyster shells or use crumpled foil. Arrange the oysters on top. Put 1 tablespoon of butter mixture on each oyster and bake 10 minutes or until the mixture has melted.

OYSTER FRICASSEE   (SERVES FOUR)

Spoon over toast or patty shells.

2 tablespoons butter
2 tablespoons flour
1 pint shucked oysters, with their liquor
Milk

1½ tablespoons dry white wine
2 teaspoons minced parsley
Salt
Freshly ground pepper

Melt the butter in a saucepan. Stir in the flour and blend until smooth. Measure oyster liquor, add enough milk to make 1 cup, and slowly stir mixture into saucepan. Cook, stirring constantly, until the sauce is smooth and thickened. Stir in the wine and oysters and cook 1 minute. Add parsley and salt and pepper to taste, and simmer 2 minutes more.

(SERVES FOUR)   **PANNED OYSTERS**

6 slices bread	24 medium oysters, shucked
¼ pound butter, softened	Salt
2 tablespoons lemon juice	Freshly ground pepper

Preheat the oven to 400°F. Toast the bread. Cream the butter with lemon juice and spread it on the toast. Cut each slice of toast into four squares. Place an oyster on each square and sprinkle lightly with salt and pepper. Place the squares on a flat baking sheet and bake 5–6 minutes: only long enough to plump up oysters. The bread soaks up the lovely oyster liquor.

(SERVES FOUR)   **DEVILED OYSTERS**

Try making clams this way, too.

1 pint shucked oysters	1 teaspoon dry mustard
2 tablespoons butter	2 teaspoons Worcestershire
3 shallots, chopped fine	sauce
2 tablespoons flour	2 tablespoons minced parsley
1 cup light cream	1 cup freshly made bread
⅛ teaspoon nutmeg	crumbs, buttered
Pinch of cayenne pepper	

Preheat the oven to 400°F. Have on hand 6–8 deep halves of oyster shells or 4–6 scallop shells. Chop the oysters coarsely and set aside. Melt the butter in a saucepan and add the shallots, cooking until soft. Stir in the flour, cook for 2 minutes, and slowly add the cream, nutmeg, cayenne, mustard, and Worcestershire sauce. Cook over medium-low heat, stirring constantly, for 4–5 minutes, until the sauce is smooth and thickened. Stir in the oysters and 1 tablespoon of the parsley. Remove from the heat and spoon into the shells. Place the shells on a baking sheet. Mix the remaining parsley and bread crumbs and sprinkle evenly over the oyster mixture. Bake 15–20 minutes.

SCALLOPED OYSTERS   (SERVES FOUR)

¼ pound butter
½ cup freshly made bread
    crumbs
1 cup freshly made cracker
    crumbs

1 pint shucked oysters, with
    their liquor
Salt
Dash of Tabasco
1 tablespoon cream

Preheat the oven to 425°F. Melt the butter in a skillet and toss in the
bread and cracker crumbs, coating with the butter. Spread half the
crumbs over the bottom of a shallow baking dish. Drain the oysters, reserving liquor, and arrange them in a single layer over the crumbs, and
sprinkle with salt. Mix a healthy dash of Tabasco with the cream and 2
tablespoons oyster liquor, and dribble over oysters. Cover with remaining crumbs and bake 25 minutes.

FRIED OYSTERS   (SERVES FOUR)

1 quart shucked oysters
3 eggs
Salt
Freshly ground pepper

1½ cups freshly made fine
    cracker crumbs
Oil for frying

Preheat the oven to 225°F and warm an ovenproof platter. Pat the oysters dry on paper towels. Beat the eggs with a sprinkle of salt and pepper. Dip each oyster in egg, letting the excess drip back into the bowl,
then dip in the cracker crumbs. Shake so that the excess falls off. Each
oyster should be well covered with crumbs. In a heavy skillet, heat 1
inch of oil. When the oil is hot enough to brown a cube of bread in 30
seconds or registers 360°F on a fat thermometer, add the oysters. Don't
crowd the skillet: do a few at a time. Drain on paper towels and keep
warm in the oven.

SAUTÉED SCALLOPS   (SERVES FOUR)

Scallops, like oysters and clams, are bivalve mollusks. The part of the
scallop we eat is the muscle that opens and closes the shell. Buy tiny
bay scallops or larger sea scallops; they should have a shiny moist look
and a faint fresh scent of the sea. Scallops, even more than other
seafood, tend to toughen and lose their fine character when they are
overcooked. Clean by rinsing under cold water; pat dry with paper

towels, and then cook them briefly, just until they lose their translucency and become creamy-white.

1½ pounds scallops	1 tablespoon minced parsley
¼ pound butter	Salt to taste
1½ tablespoons lemon juice	

Rinse the scallops and pat dry with paper towels. Melt the butter in a large skillet and, when it foams, add the scallops. Cook over high heat about 1 minute each side. Be careful not to let the butter burn. Reduce the heat or lift the skillet if necessary. Remove to a warm platter and sprinkle with lemon juice, parsley, and salt.

(SERVES FOUR)   **FRIED SCALLOPS**

1½ pounds scallops	Oil for frying
1¼ cups freshly made dry bread crumbs	Salt to taste
	Lemon wedges
2 eggs, well beaten	Watercress sprigs

Preheat the oven to 225°F and warm an ovenproof platter. Rinse the scallops, shake off excess water, and roll in the bread crumbs. Dip into the beaten eggs and again in the crumbs. Heat ½ inch of oil in a heavy skillet. When it is very hot, put in the scallops without crowding the pan. Do only a few at a time, and fry until the crumbs are nicely browned. Turn and brown the other side. Drain on paper towels and place on the warm platter. Season with salt and garnish with lemon wedges and watercress.

(SERVES FOUR)   **SCALLOPS WITH CITRUS SAUCE**

The orange and lemon here make a sparkling sauce. Serve with a butter lettuce and avocado salad.

¼ cup chopped scallions	1 tablespoon lemon juice
¼ cup olive oil or vegetable oil	1 teaspoon prepared mustard
⅓ cup orange juice	Salt and freshly ground pepper to taste
1 teaspoon grated or minced orange zest	1½ pounds scallops

In a bowl, mix together the scallions, olive or vegetable oil, orange juice, orange zest, lemon juice, mustard, and salt and pepper. Stir well to blend. Set aside. Bring a pot of salted water to a boil. Put the scallops in the pot and simmer only 1–2 minutes, depending on the size of the scallops. Test for doneness by cutting one in half. They should have lost their translucency and be creamy white but still soft. Drain at once. If serving cold, plunge into cold water. Toss with the citrus sauce and serve.

DEVILED SCALLOPS   (SERVES THREE)

1 pound scallops	Dash of cayenne pepper
4 tablespoons butter, softened	1 cup freshly made buttered
½ teaspoon dry mustard	bread crumbs

Preheat the oven to 375°F. Butter a small baking dish or three scallop shells. Rinse the scallops and pat dry with paper towels. Cream the butter, mustard, and cayenne in a small bowl. Put the scallops in the baking dish or shells, dot with the creamed butter, and cover with buttered crumbs. Bake for 20 minutes.

DEVILED SCALLOPS WITH A CHINESE ACCENT

Instead of using mustard and cayenne as seasonings, toss the scallops with ¼ cup chopped scallions and 2 teaspoons minced ginger before baking.

SCALLOPS WITH MUSHROOMS   (SERVES FOUR)

The mushrooms should stay firm. Serve with spinach and buttered toast.

4 tablespoons butter or ¼ cup vegetable oil	1½ pounds scallops
½ cup chopped shallots or scallions (white part only)	Salt and freshly ground pepper to taste
1 pound small fresh button-size mushrooms	¼ cup freshly grated Parmesan cheese
	4 lemon wedges

Heat butter or oil in a large skillet over medium-high heat. Add the shallots and mushrooms and cook about 2–3 minutes, stirring frequently. Add the scallops and salt and pepper, and cook only 1–2 minutes more, until the scallops are creamy white and have lost their translucency. Remove to a warmed platter and sprinkle with the Parmesan cheese. Garnish with lemon wedges.

(SERVES FOUR)   **NEW ENGLAND SCALLOPS**

2 tablespoons butter
¾ cup chopped onion
¾ cup chopped green pepper
1 pound corn kernels (about 4
    cups)

1 cup chicken broth
1 pound scallops

Put the butter in a skillet over medium heat. Add the onion, green pepper, and corn, and cook for about 5 minutes, until the onion and pepper are soft but not browned. Add the chicken broth and heat just to boiling. Stir in the scallops and cook only 1–2 minutes, until they are opaque and just cooked through. Serve with rice.

(SERVES TWO TO SIX)   **BOILED SHRIMP**

Shrimp are bright in texture and flavor, full of protein and low in calories. Americans buy more shrimp than any other shellfish: fresh, canned, and frozen, raw and cooked, shelled and unshelled. Two pounds of shrimp yield slightly more than a pound after shelling; depending on the recipe and appetites, that pound serves two people or six. If you shell shrimp before cooking, add the shells to the cooking liquid to give extra flavor. Shrimp should be cooked only until they turn pink: 3 to 5 minutes at most. If they are going into a sauce or casserole they should not be cooked first or they will become rubbery.

Salt
4 quarts water

2 pounds raw unshelled
    shrimp

Salt the water and bring to a boil. Add the shrimp, and turn the heat down so the water is boiling gently. Cook the shrimp until they turn pink, 3–5 minutes. Drain. When cool enough to handle, shell and devein the shrimp: gently pull the shells apart, and with the tip of a knife, remove the black vein that runs down the center of the back. Don't be too fussy about this: some people mangle the shrimp getting out the last unappetizing but harmless speck.

SHRIMP WIGGLE   (SERVES SIX)

Serve on buttered toast for lunch or supper.

4 tablespoons butter	2 cups small cooked shrimp,
4 tablespoons flour	shelled (p. 191)
1 cup milk	1 cup peas, cooked
1 cup light cream	Salt to taste

Melt the butter in a saucepan and stir in the flour. Stir constantly over low heat until smooth and blended. Slowly add the milk and cream, and cook over medium-low heat for 5 minutes, until smooth and thickened. Add the shrimp, peas, and salt, and cook only long enough to heat through.

SHRIMP JAMBALAYA   (SERVES SIX)

One version of a fine Cajun dish of Spanish origin.

3 slices bacon, diced	1 teaspoon chili powder
½ cup chopped celery	¼ teaspoon thyme, crumbled
½ cup chopped onion	2 pounds shrimp, cooked,
½ cup chopped green pepper	shelled, and deveined
1 tablespoon minced garlic	(p. 191)
4 cups canned tomatoes with	¼ cup finely chopped parsley
liquid	Salt to taste
⅛ teaspoon cayenne pepper	4 cups hot cooked rice

Fry the bacon in a skillet and, when it is crisp, drain on paper towels. If the skillet is very hot, let it cool down a bit. Put it over medium heat and cook the celery, onion, and green pepper in the bacon fat until the onion is soft. Add the garlic, tomatoes, cayenne pepper, chili powder, and thyme. Lower the heat and simmer 20 minutes. Add the shrimp, parsley, and salt to the tomato sauce and cook for a few minutes until the shrimp is hot. Mound the rice on a platter, spoon the shrimp and tomato sauce over it, and garnish with bits of crisp bacon.

SAUTÉED SHRIMP   (SERVES FOUR)

2 pounds raw shrimp	2 teaspoons minced parsley
4 tablespoons butter	Lemon wedges

Shell and devein the shrimp (p. 191), leaving the tails on. Melt the butter in a skillet and, when it foams, add the shrimp. Cook over high heat, shaking the pan and turning the shrimp once or twice, until they turn pink. This should take about 5 minutes, depending on size. Remove from the heat, sprinkle with parsley, and serve with lemon wedges.

SPRINGTIME SHRIMP
* WITH CASHEWS

(SERVES FOUR)

Cashews make this dish; don't substitute.

1 teaspoon cornstarch	1 pound raw shrimp, shelled
4 tablespoons water	and deveined
2 tablespoons sherry	12 scallions (about 2
½ teaspoon dark sesame oil	bunches), in 2-inch slices
1 teaspoon sugar	1 cup cashews
½ teaspoon salt, or to taste	
2 tablespoons corn, peanut, or	
vegetable oil	

In a bowl, mix the cornstarch and water together, stirring until dissolved. Stir in the sherry, sesame oil, sugar, and salt. Set aside. Heat the oil in a skillet over medium-high heat. Add the shrimp and scallions and sauté for about 2 minutes, stirring and tossing. Stir in the cashews and the cornstarch mixture; cook and continue stirring for about 1 minute, until slightly thickened.

BATTER FRIED SHRIMP

(SERVES SIX)

Serve with Chili Sauce (p. 1107) or Tartar Sauce (p. 394).

1 cup flour	2 tablespoons oil
½ teaspoon salt	1 cup ice water
½ teaspoon sugar	2½ pounds raw shrimp
1 egg	Oil for frying

Preheat the oven to 225°F and warm an ovenproof platter. Beat the flour, salt, sugar, egg, 2 tablespoons oil, and 1 cup ice water in a bowl and refrigerate. Shell and devein the shrimp (p. 191). Pat the shrimp dry with paper towels. Heat 3 inches of oil to 365°F in a heavy pot or skillet. Dip each shrimp into the batter and drop into the hot oil. Don't crowd the pot. Do a few at a time, frying for about 1 minute or until golden. Proceed until all the shrimp are fried, draining each batch and keeping warm on the platter in the oven.

BROILED SHRIMP   (SERVES FOUR)

If you can find large shrimp, broil them this Italian way. And serve lots of crusty Italian bread to mop up the sauce.

1½ pounds large shrimp	1 teaspoon minced garlic
½ cup olive oil	1 teaspoon oregano, crushed
1 tablespoon lemon juice	1 tablespoon finely chopped
½ teaspoon salt	parsley
Freshly ground pepper to taste	

Remove the shell from the shrimp, except around the tail; leave that intact. If there is a dark vein running just under the surface on the outside, scrape it out. Mix all the rest of the ingredients in a large bowl and add the shrimp to marinate for at least 1 hour, turning once or twice. Preheat the broiler. Place the shrimp in a large shallow pan with their marinade and broil close to the heat, about 3–4 minutes each side.

SHRIMP WITH GREEN PEPPERS   (SERVES FOUR)

Adapted from a Mandarin classic, this is a skillet stir-fry.

2 tablespoons vegetable or peanut oil	1 pound raw shrimp, cleaned and deveined
Salt to taste	1 recipe All-Purpose Sweet-and-Sour Sauce (p. 393)
2 green peppers, in 1½-inch squares	8 sprigs cilantro
1 medium onion, halved and cut in ¼-inch slices	

Place a sauté pan or skillet over high heat. When hot, add the oil and let it get hot. Lightly salt the peppers and onion, then add to the skillet and cook, stirring and tossing constantly, for 2 minutes. Add the shrimp and continue to cook, stirring and tossing, for about 1½ minutes, until the shrimp are pink. Remove from the heat and stir in the sauce. Garnish with cilantro.

(SERVES SIX)   **SHRIMP AND CORN PIE**

This old classic dish still has the best flavors to show off shrimp.

6 tablespoons butter
2 cups fine saltine cracker
    crumbs
2 eggs
2 cups milk, scalded
2 teaspoons prepared
    mustard
½ cup finely chopped celery

¼ cup finely chopped green
    pepper
1 cup corn kernels
1 pound raw shrimp, shelled
    and deveined
Salt and freshly ground
    pepper to taste

Preheat the oven to 325°F. Melt 4 tablespoons of the butter and blend
into the cracker crumbs, tossing and lightly stirring until all the crumbs
are coated. Reserve ½ cup of the buttered crumbs and pat the remaining crumbs into the bottom and sides of a 3-quart baking dish. In a
bowl, beat the eggs slightly. Add the remaining 2 tablespoons of butter
to the hot milk, then add the eggs and mustard, stirring briskly. Stir in
the celery, green pepper, corn, shrimp, and salt and pepper. Pour into
the crumb-lined baking dish and sprinkle the reserved crumbs evenly
over the top. Bake for 30–40 minutes, or until the custard has set. Serve
hot.

(SERVES SIX)   **SAN FRANCISCO CIOPPINO**

Originally from Italy, this dish was made from what fish was left over
from the day's catch. I have prepared this many times over the years.
The only thing you need serve with this is a good loaf of bread. I've
called for prawns here but large shrimp will do.

½ cup olive oil
3 cloves garlic, minced
1 pound raw prawns, shelled
    and deveined
1 pound scallops
12 clams (optional)
1 cup white wine

2 cups Italian tomatoes
1 teaspoon oregano
1 teaspoon sugar
2 bay leaves
Salt and freshly ground
    pepper to taste
1 cup chopped parsley

Heat the oil in a large sauté pan over moderate heat. Add the garlic
and cook about 1 minute. Roughly chop enough prawns, scallops, and
clams (if used) to make ½ cup, then add with the wine, tomatoes,
oregano, sugar, bay leaves, and salt and pepper. Bring to a simmer,
cover, and cook for 5 minutes. Add the remaining seafood and cook
2–3 minutes more. Sprinkle with parsley and serve.

To clean squid, if it has not been done when purchased:

(1) Above is a whole squid. (2) Holding the squid in one hand, with the other hand pull the tentacles and insides out of the sac in one piece.

(3) Cut off the tentacles just above the eyes; discard the insides. (4) There is a hard knot just within the cut side of the tentacles; squeeze it out and discard.

(5) Remove the cartilage from the sac (it looks like cellophane). (6) Under running water, peel off the outer skin of the sac. Rinse both the sac and the tentacles thoroughly. Pat dry, and they are ready to cook. (The tentacles are usually cut into lengths of about ¼ inch.)

QUICK-FRIED SQUID

I like this best with Tartar Sauce (p. 394) and Cole Slaw (p. 669).

1 pound squid bodies, cleaned and cut in ¼-inch rings Flour for dredging Salt	1–2 tablespoons corn or vegetable oil, approximately Lemon wedges

Preheat the oven to 225°F and warm an ovenproof platter. Put the squid in a plastic bag with some flour and salt, and shake well to lightly coat all the pieces. Use a nonstick frypan or skillet, if you have one, and only enough oil to coat the bottom of the pan. Place the pan over high heat, swirling to spread the oil. When the oil is hot, toss in about a quarter of the squid and cook for only 1–2 minutes, until lightly golden. Stir and shake the pan as they cook so they will brown evenly. Remove to paper towels and keep hot on the platter in the oven. Repeat in batches. Serve with lemon wedges.

SQUID SAUTÉED WITH ASPARAGUS

The tentacles are a very tender part of the squid. Be adventurous, and chop them and add them to the sauté.

2 tablespoons corn or vegetable oil ½ pound asparagus, washed, trimmed, and sliced diagonally in 1-inch pieces 1 cup chicken broth	2 shallots or scallions, chopped 1 pound squid, cleaned and cut in ¼-inch rings 1 teaspoon sesame oil

Place a skillet or sauté pan over high heat and add the oil. When the oil is hot, add the asparagus and cook about 1 minute, stirring and tossing constantly. Pour in the broth, stir, cover, and cook for about 2–3 minutes. Remove the lid and add the shallots or scallions and the squid, toss, and cook for about 1 minute, tossing occasionally until the squid turns white and opaque. It won't take long. Do not overcook or the squid will be rubbery. Remove from the heat and stir in the sesame oil. Serve at once.

CREAMED FISH   (SERVES FOUR)

Many recipes for cooked fish can be made with canned fish as well.
Serve this over toast or rice, or use it in an omelet or crêpe.

3 tablespoons butter
3 tablespoons flour
2 cups milk
1 tablespoon lemon juice
1–1½ cups cooked or canned
   fish

Salt
Freshly ground pepper
1 tablespoon minced parsley,
   chives, or dill

Heat the butter in a heavy-bottomed saucepan. Stir in the flour and
cook until smooth, about 2 minutes. Slowly add the milk, continuing to
stir. Simmer for 2 minutes. Mix the lemon juice into the fish and add to
the cream sauce. Add salt and pepper to taste. Heat thoroughly, remove from the heat, and sprinkle with parsley.

CREAMED FISH WITH MUSHROOMS

Add ½ *cup mushrooms*, sautéed in *2 tablespoons butter*, to the sauce.

CREAMED FISH WITH TARRAGON

Add ¼ *teaspoon dried tarragon, crumbled*, with the milk.

CREAMED FISH FLORENTINE

Cook 1½ *pounds of spinach* in boiling salted water. Drain well and spoon
the creamed fish over the spinach.

KEDGEREE   (SERVES SIX)

A popular breakfast dish in England.

4 tablespoons butter
2 cups cooked rice
2 cups cooked smoked fish
3 tablespoons raisins
¾ cup heavy cream
1 teaspoon curry powder

Salt to taste
4 hard-boiled eggs, chopped
3 tablespoons finely chopped
   parsley
Lemon wedges

Melt the butter in a heavy-bottomed pan. Stir in the rice, fish, raisins, cream, curry powder, and salt. Mix well and cook only until heated through. Arrange on a warm platter and garnish with chopped egg, parsley, and lemon wedges.

(12 CROQUETTES)   **FISH CROQUETTES**

Golden, crisp, and delightful.

2 cups chopped cooked fish
½ teaspoon salt
½ teaspoon dry mustard
Pinch of cayenne pepper
1½ tablespoons lemon juice

1 cup Thick Cream Sauce (p. 380)
1½ cups freshly made bread crumbs
Oil for frying

Warm a platter in a 250°F oven. Combine the fish, salt, mustard, cayenne pepper, lemon juice, and sauce. Refrigerate at least 1 hour, until the mixture is well chilled. Make small conelike shapes and roll in the bread crumbs. Heat 1 inch of oil in a heavy-bottomed pan to 360°F. Without crowding, fry a few croquettes at a time until they are golden. Don't fry too quickly, or the insides will be cold. Drain on paper towels and keep warm in the oven until all are done.

(SERVES FOUR)   **FISH HASH**

You may use a vegetable oil in place of the salt pork, but the flavor will not be quite the same. Serve with thick slices of fresh tomatoes.

¼ pound salt pork or bacon, diced small
1 onion, chopped
1½ cups diced boiled potatoes

1½ cups flaked or chopped cooked fish
Salt
Freshly ground pepper

In a hot skillet, cook the salt pork until the fat is rendered and the bits of pork are brown and crisp. Remove, drain on paper towels, and set aside. Toss together the onion, potatoes, fish, and salt and pepper to taste—take care not to oversalt: the salt pork may supply enough. Stir into the fat in the skillet and cook over medium heat. Press down with a spatula and cook about 5 minutes, until the bottom is brown. Turn the hash over and cook until the underside is nicely browned. Tip out onto a warm platter and sprinkle with the crisp bits of salt pork.

SCALLOPED FISH   (SERVES FOUR)

5 tablespoons butter
2 tablespoons finely chopped
    shallots or scallions
1 cup toasted bread crumbs
2 tablespoons flour

1¼ cups milk
1 cup cooked fish, flaked
2 tablespoons dry sherry
Salt
Freshly ground pepper

Preheat the oven to 425°F. Butter a shallow baking dish. Melt 3 table-spoons of the butter in a saucepan and sauté the shallots or scallions until soft. Stir in the bread crumbs and toss. Remove and set aside. Melt the remaining 2 tablespoons of butter in the skillet. Stir in the flour and cook for 2 minutes, until smooth. Slowly add the milk, and cook, stirring constantly, until thickened, about 3 minutes. Add the fish, sherry, and salt and pepper to taste. Spread half the fish mixture in the baking dish and cover with half the bread crumbs; repeat the two layers. Bake 20 minutes, until the sauce bubbles.

SEAFOOD CRÊPES   (SERVES SIX)

Different varieties or combinations of seafood may be used: chopped shrimp, clams, mussels, scallops, or crabmeat, cooked lean fish, salmon, cod, or sole.

3 tablespoons minced shallots
    or scallions
5 tablespoons butter
4 tablespoons flour
1 cup hot chicken broth or
    fish stock
½ cup light cream
3 tablespoons dry sherry
2 cups flaked cooked shellfish
    and/or fish

Tabasco to taste
Salt to taste
1 recipe Crêpes or French
    Pancakes (p. 778)
½ cup heavy cream
¼ teaspoon nutmeg
2 tablespoons minced parsley
Lemon slices

Preheat the oven to 350°F. Butter a baking dish measuring approximately 15 × 9 × 2 inches. Sauté the shallots or scallions in the butter for 2 minutes. Sprinkle on the flour, stir, and cook for 2 minutes. Slowly add the hot broth or stock. Stir until thick and smooth, then add the cream and sherry. Cook for 5 minutes, stirring constantly, until sauce is smooth and thickened. Add the shellfish and/or fish, taste and season with Tabasco and salt. Stir a minute and remove from the heat. Fill each crêpe with 3 tablespoons of filling. Roll and place seam side down

in the baking dish. Spoon any extra filling around the edges and between the crêpes. Lightly whip the heavy cream, add the nutmeg, and
spread over the crêpes. Bake for 20–25 minutes or just until the sauce
bubbles. Sprinkle the parsley on top and serve garnished with lemon
slices.

(SERVES FOUR)   **FISH MOUSSE**

Try making this with leftover or canned salmon.

2 cups cooked fish	3 egg whites
Dash of cayenne pepper	⅓ cup heavy cream, whipped
1 tablespoon lemon juice	1 recipe Hollandaise Sauce (p.
Salt	388)

Preheat the oven to 350°F. Butter a 1½-quart mold or baking dish. Put 1
inch of hot water in a pan larger than the mold, and place it in the
oven. Combine the fish, cayenne pepper, lemon juice, and salt to taste.
Add ¼ teaspoon of salt to the egg whites, and beat until stiff. Fold the
whipped cream and the whites gently into the fish mixture. Spoon into
the buttered mold, place in the oven in the pan of water, and bake
about 20 minutes, until firm. Remove, unmold on a warm platter, and
serve with Hollandaise.

(SERVES FOUR)   **FISH SOUFFLÉ**

2 cups well-drained cooked or	½ cup milk
canned fish	2 egg yolks, beaten
Pinch of cayenne pepper	Salt
3 tablespoons lemon juice	3 egg whites, beaten stiff but
½ cup freshly made bread	not dry
crumbs	1 recipe Lemon Sauce (p. 382)

Preheat the oven to 325°F. Butter a 1½-quart mold or baking dish. Toss
together the fish, cayenne pepper, and lemon juice. In a saucepan, heat
the bread crumbs and milk and stir in the fish mixture. Beat a little of
the hot mixture into the egg yolks and return the yolk-crumb mixture
to the fish blend. Add salt to taste. Cook over low heat, stirring, for 1
minute. Remove from the heat and gently fold in the egg whites.
Spoon into the buttered dish and bake until firm, about 25 minutes.
Serve with the sauce.

SALMON OR TUNA LOAF   (SERVES SIX)

2 cups well-drained cooked or
    canned salmon or tuna
½ cup freshly made bread
    crumbs
4 tablespoons butter, melted
2 eggs, well beaten
1½ tablespoons minced onion
2 teaspoons minced parsley

1 tablespoon minced green
    pepper
¼ teaspoon Worcestershire
    sauce
Dash of Tabasco
Salt to taste
1 recipe Mustard Sauce (p.
    391)

Preheat the oven to 350°F. Butter a 1-quart loaf pan. Combine the fish, bread crumbs, butter, eggs, onion, parsley, green pepper, Worcestershire, Tabasco, and salt. Mix well, press into the loaf pan, and bake about 35 minutes. Serve with the sauce.

TUNA-NOODLE CASSEROLE   (SERVES FOUR)

7-ounce can tuna, well
    drained
2 cups cooked narrow
    noodles
3 hard-boiled eggs
2 cups White Sauce (p. 379)

1 cup sliced mushrooms,
    sautéed
1 tablespoon minced onion
4 tablespoons butter
1 cup freshly made bread
    crumbs

Preheat the oven to 350°F. Butter a 1½-quart baking dish. Combine the tuna, noodles, eggs, sauce, mushrooms, and onion, mix carefully, and put into the baking dish. Melt the butter in a skillet and toss the bread crumbs until they are coated and lightly browned. Sprinkle evenly over the tuna mixture and bake 20 minutes, until very hot.

TUNA AND RICE   (SERVES FOUR)

3 tablespoons butter
¼ cup finely chopped onion
¼ cup finely chopped celery
7-ounce can tuna, drained
    and flaked

2 cups cooked rice
¼ cup minced parsley
Salt to taste
½ cup chopped cashews

Melt the butter in a saucepan. Add the onion and celery and cook over medium heat, stirring often, until the onion is soft. Stir in the tuna, rice, parsley, and salt and heat through. Sprinkle with cashews and serve hot.

(SERVES FOUR)   **FINNAN HADDIE BAKED IN MILK**

Finnan haddie is smoked haddock. It is usually sold in fillets, but occasionally sold whole.

1½–2 pounds smoked haddock	1 cup milk
4 tablespoons butter	1 bay leaf
1 medium onion, sliced thin	⅛ teaspoon nutmeg
½ teaspoon freshly ground pepper	Dash of cayenne pepper

Soak the haddock in warm water for 1 hour. Butter a shallow baking dish. Drain and place the haddock in the baking dish. Preheat the oven to 375°F. Melt the butter in a skillet and cook the onion over medium heat until soft. Stir in remaining ingredients, and pour mixture over the haddock. Bake for 45 minutes.

(SERVES FOUR)   **FINNAN HADDIE WITH POTATOES**

1 pound smoked haddock	1 cup sliced scallions
3 tablespoons vegetable or olive oil	Freshly ground pepper to taste
3 unpeeled potatoes, quartered and sliced	Salt, if needed

Cut the haddock into strips. Put in a pan, cover with water, bring to a boil, and simmer 20 minutes. Drain and rinse thoroughly with cold water. Press dry and separate into flakes. Set aside. Heat the oil in a skillet over medium-high heat and cook the potatoes until golden brown and tender. Add the flaked fish and scallions and toss over medium heat for only a minute until fish is heated through. Season with pepper and taste for salt.

(SERVES FOUR)   **SKILLET SARDINE SUPPER**

I think sardines are best eaten on a soda cracker. However, this makes a quick and flavorful meal.

2 tablespoons olive oil
2 cups chopped onions
3 cups chopped tomatoes
½ cup dry white wine
½ teaspoon dried thyme

¼ teaspoon dried tarragon,
    crumbled
2 teaspoons chopped parsley
Salt to taste
2 cans sardines, drained

Heat the oil in a skillet over medium-high heat. Add the onions and cook for 3–4 minutes, or until the onions are soft but not browned. Add the tomatoes, wine, and herbs, reduce the heat, and simmer for about 5 minutes. Taste for salt. Using a fork, gently separate the sardines and lay them in the skillet on top of the onion-tomato mixture. Cover and let simmer 2–3 minutes more, or until the sardines are heated through.

BAKED KIPPERED HERRING   (SERVES FOUR)

Try an adventurous English breakfast and make this dish.

1 pound kippered herring
Juice of 1 lemon
2 tablespoons butter, melted
Freshly ground pepper to
    taste

1 tablespoon chopped parsley
4 lemon slices

Preheat the oven to 350°F. Put the herring in a baking dish and pour the lemon juice and butter over them. Grind pepper on top and heat in the oven for about 10–15 minutes. Garnish with parsley and lemon slices.

CREAMED CODFISH   (SERVES FOUR)

Serve on toast or mashed potatoes for a wholesome family supper.

1 pound salt cod
4 tablespoons butter
2 tablespoons flour
2 cups milk

Dash of Tabasco
1 tablespoon minced parsley
2 teaspoons chopped chives
2 hard-boiled eggs, chopped

Freshen the salt cod as directed in Codfish Cakes recipe (p. 205), then simmer it for 10 minutes in a pan with water to cover. Drain, and shred or chop in a food processor. Melt the butter in a heavy-bottomed pan. Stir in the flour and cook until smooth. Slowly add the milk and cook, stirring constantly, until smooth and thickened. Add the Tabasco, parsley, chives, and cod, and cook, stirring, until heated through. Add the eggs and cook 1 minute more.

(15 CAKES)   **CODFISH CAKES**

Salt-cured codfish is available in a few markets and Italian delicatessens. It is generally packaged in small wooden 1-pound boxes or
1-pound packages in the refrigerated section. It must be freshened before use to get rid of excess saltiness; this is done by soaking overnight
or at least 6 hours in several changes of cold water.

1 pound salt cod, freshened (see above)	½ teaspoon freshly ground pepper
3 cups mashed potatoes	5 tablespoons shortening
⅓ cup light cream	2 tablespoons minced parsley
4 tablespoons butter, softened	

When you have freshened the salt cod, simmer it for 10 minutes in a
pan with water to cover. Drain, and flake the fish or chop it in a food
processor. Add the potatoes, cream, butter, and pepper and blend well.
Pat into cakes about 2½ inches in diameter. Melt half the shortening in
a large skillet over medium-high heat. When it is hot, put in as many
cakes as possible without having them touch. Fry quickly on each side
until golden-brown, then remove. Add remaining shortening and fry
rest of cakes. Sprinkle cakes with parsley and serve immediately on a
warm platter.

SALT CODFISH HASH WITH TOMATOES AND GARLIC
(SERVES FOUR)

1 pound salt cod	3 cups cooked potatoes in small dice or mashed
5 tablespoons oil	
1 cup finely chopped onion	¾ teaspoon freshly ground pepper
2 cloves garlic, chopped fine	
3 tomatoes, peeled, seeded, and chopped	

Freshen the salt cod as directed in Codfish Cakes recipe, then simmer it
for 10 minutes in a pan with water to cover. Drain, and flake or chop in
a food processor. Heat 2 tablespoons of the oil in a large skillet. Add
the onion and garlic and sauté over medium heat until the onion is
soft. Toss together the onion, garlic, tomatoes, potatoes, cod, and pepper in a bowl. Heat the remaining 3 tablespoons oil in the skillet, and
when it is hot, spread the hash over the bottom. Fry over medium-high
heat until it is brown on the bottom. Turn over and brown the other
side.

Other Suggestions for Using Leftover Cooked Fish and Seafood

Cooked fish, boned and flaked, as well as seafood of all kinds, can be used effectively in appetizers; try the Hot Seafood with Mayonnaise, improvise with the recipe for Salmon Spread, or make fillings for Savory Cream Puffs, tarts, and rissolettes. For an entrée, substitute cooked fish or seafood, or a combination thereof, for chicken in Chicken Soufflé, Chicken Divan, and Chicken Croquettes; try also Fish Timbales. See also the Egg chapter for using as a filling for omelets and frittatas. There are a number of seafood recipes in the Salad chapter and a lovely Seafood Aspic using both cooked fish and shellfish.

MEAT

In the past, Americans have been big meat eaters. What with our rich farms and vast grazing lands, the supply of good meat has seemed inexhaustible and the American table has been notoriously generous with its home-cured hams and thick slabs of beef (often served for breakfast, too). But today Americans seem to be eating less meat or are more conscious of the fat in their diet. Often now, meat is the accent rather than the largest portion on a plate.

Moreover, there has been a dramatic change in the raising of meats to reduce the fat content (see specific types, such as beef, pork, etc., for more details). Many of the recipes in the previous edition have been adjusted because of this difference. Many of the variety meats have been eliminated because innards are generally less available. With the interest in Southwestern foods I've given you a Chili Con Carne with much more spirit, an excellent Tamale Pie, and an interesting Mandarin Barbecue Pork.

BUYING MEAT

The United States Department of Agriculture inspects all the beef, veal, and lamb sold in interstate commerce, marking it with a purple vegetable dye according to grade. "Prime," the highest grade, is generally sold only to fancy butchers and restaurants. Supermarkets carry both "choice" and "select": while "choice" is more tender and juicy, "select" is quite adequate for cuts of meat that require long, slow cooking. Few of the many lower grades of meat are offered for retail sale. All of the meat has been cut and packaged at a central packing plant and is distributed to the supermarkets. The old-fashioned family butcher who would cut meat to order is almost nonexistent. Most meat has been precut into the uniform nine primal cuts, and packaged in heavy-duty plastic wrap. What this means to the consumer is that personal cuts and special cuts are not available the way they used to be. Beef suet, bones, and less-known cuts of meat are hard to find today, and variety meats are often not available. There are, however, a sprinkling of small old-fashioned butcher shops around.

Each section of this chapter—beef, veal, lamb, and pork—is introduced by an illustration pointing out the tender cuts that can be broiled, pan-fried, or roasted, and the tougher cuts that need long, slow braising or stewing. Notice on the beef one, p. 217, for instance: the most heavily exercised parts of the animal produce meat with the toughest muscle fibers, while the least-used parts are the most tender. If you compare this chart with the others, you will see that the rear portion of the steer that produces tender sirloin and rump is the same as the part of the lamb that produces leg of lamb; also, from the rear portion of a calf we get the leg and scallops, and from the pig we get the ham. In a similar way, there is a relationship between beef rib steaks, lamb and veal rib chops, and the tender meat on pork spareribs. And the shoulder of all these animals produces a tough but flavorful cut, delicious when cooked gently.

To determine how much meat to buy, take into account the amount of fat and bone in a particular cut, as well as individual appetites. A quarter-pound of meat with no bone and little fat—lean hamburger, for instance—may make an adequate serving for a nonravenous eater, but meat with even a little bone, such as a chop or steak, will provide only two servings per pound. With short ribs and breast veal, which have an even greater proportion of bone, you allow a pound per person.

Storing Meat

As soon as you bring meat home, either open the wrappings or rewrap the meat loosely. This allows air to circulate freely, drying the surface of the meat and retarding the growth of moisture-loving bacteria. Store in the coldest part of the refrigerator. Variety meats will keep for a day, chopped meat for two, and roasts for as much as four or five days. Beef usually keeps longer than other meats, larger cuts better than small pieces. Smoked and cured meats are good for at least several weeks, sometimes much longer depending on how they have been cured. Tenderized hams are all right for about ten days, but bacon, once the package has been opened, tastes fresher if used within a week.

To store a cooked roast, let it cool thoroughly before putting it in the refrigerator; if you don't, when the hot meat encounters the cool refrigerator air a steamy cloud will form that will encourage the growth of bacteria. Cover cooked meats loosely to permit air circulation.

For freezing meat, see p. 1122.

Salmonella

Salmonella, a bacterium that causes food poisoning, is a growing concern each year. Salmonella is found in raw meats, poultry, eggs, milk, fish, and products made from all of them. There are several simple rules, easy to follow, that will help protect you from the danger of cross-contamination and of food poisoning.

1. Reserve one cutting board exclusively for cutting raw meats and poultry. Use a different cutting board for work with fruits and vegetables.
2. Scrub the cutting board and utensils and your hands with hot, soapy water after working with raw meat and poultry. Leave the board out to dry.
3. Thoroughly cook all foods derived from animals or poultry to 160°F. Keep hot food hot and cold food cold (45 degrees or less).

Cooking Meat

SALTING. NOTE The question of whether to salt meat before or after cooking is often asked. Always salt before cooking. It does not draw out juices, as we used to think, to any degree that matters. Salting before cooking develops a flavor that salting at the table cannot achieve. All chopped meats should always have salt and other seasonings mixed in before cooking.

ROASTING. Always preheat the oven. Some cooks prefer to start roasting at 500°F, then to reduce the heat to 325°F after the meat is seared and has browned. We prefer a consistent temperature of 325°F (or 350° for pork), having found that this steady temperature seems to reduce shrinkage. Either way, place your roast on a rack in a shallow pan, with the fat top side up, so that it seeps down and bastes the meat as it cooks.

Be sure to remove roasts from the oven when the thermometer reads 5°F below the desired doneness, cover loosely with foil, and let stand for 15–30 minutes, depending on the size of the roast. Less of the juice will be lost and the meat will be easier to carve.

TESTING FOR DONENESS.　Recipe directions and charts for roast-ing meat can give only approximations about doneness of meat. Cooking times will vary not only according to weight but also shape (a long-and-thin roast cooks more quickly than a short, fat roast), the amount of marbling fat, and whether or not it has been boned. Always have meat at room temperature before cooking, and preheat the oven or broiler.

When the recommended time is almost up, start testing with an instant meat thermometer—by far the most accurate kind (see p 33). Stick it into the center of the meat, avoiding any bone, and you'll get an immediate reading. For rare meat you want 130°F, 140° for medium, and 160° for well done. Pork should always be cooked to 160°F; any longer will make it dry. Don't follow the rec-ommended temperatures on old-style meat thermometers; they are almost always invariably too high.

Here are some good old-fashioned methods for testing meat. (1) Prod it with your finger. If the meat feels soft, it is rare; if it is hard it is well done. Medium falls somewhere in between. (2) A more persistent nudge will make juices flow: if they are red, the meat is still bloody-rare; if they are pink, it is medium; if they run clear, it is well done. Pork juices, of course, should always run clear—and to be safe, test with a meat thermometer.

BROILING.　Remove the broiler rack and preheat the broiler. If the meat is very lean, grease the rack with some fat cut from the meat or with vegetable oil. If your steak is not very thick and you like it rare in the center but well browned on the outside, freeze it, then broil or pan-fry quickly over high heat on both sides. The center will thaw and be perfectly rare. Score the edges of the meat by mak-ing shallow cuts in the outside every 2 inches to prevent curling while it cooks. In general, set the rack 3 inches below the broiler el-ement (usually the highest rung); very thick cuts of steak should be placed lower down.

Cook on one side until nicely brown—the cooking time will de-pend on the thickness of the meat—then turn and cook on the other side. Test with a meat thermometer or your forefinger. When the meat is nearly done, remove it from the rack, season with salt and pepper, and place, loosely covered with foil, on a carving board. I will finish cooking in its own heat.

CHARCOAL GRILLING.　Any meat that can be broiled can also be grilled over charcoal. See the Outdoor Cooking chapter for details.

PAN BROILING.　Use a heavy skillet that heats evenly and will no scorch. If the meat is lean, brush the surface of the pan with oil. Heat, and when the surface looks wavy, add the meat. Brown i quickly until the blood rises to the top surface, then turn and sear the other side. Pour off any fat that accumulates.

Remove to a hot platter as soon as the meat is done: it will toughen if it overcooks. You can add broth, cream, or wine to deglaze the pan (p. 55), and pour over the pan-broiled meat.

SAUTÉING AND FRYING.   Sautéed and fried meats are cooked in hot fat, such as butter, lard, or vegetable oil or a combination. Butter, which gives the most delicate flavor, burns easily; it helps to add a tablespoon of oil for every 2 or 3 tablespoons of butter.

In a skillet, heat the amount of fat called for in the recipe, then add the meat, a few pieces at a time. Do not crowd the pan, or the temperature of the fat will be lowered and the frying process will stop. Cook the meat in shifts, removing the cooked pieces to a warm platter as they are done.

For deep-fat frying, see p. 57.

STEWING AND BRAISING.   Some of the world's great dishes are made by stewing or braising tougher cuts of meat slowly and gently in aromatic liquid until they are tender, thus making a virtue of necessity. Usually the meat is first browned in fat to produce good color, then a well-seasoned liquid, such as wine, broth, the juice of tomatoes, water, or a combination thereof, is added, and the pot, tightly covered, is set in a slow oven or over a gentle burner for several hours. The trick is to keep the liquid just at a simmer—not over 185°F—for the entire cooking time; any more strenuous boiling toughens the meat fibers.

The resulting gravy is apt to have a considerable amount of fat, which you should skim off with a spoon; let it rest a moment and the fat will rise to the top. If you wish to remove every last bit of fat (and if you allow enough time) it will be simpler to remove if you let it chill and solidify; just put the pot in the refrigerator, or pour the juices into a separate, metal bowl, then refrigerate or set in the freezer or cool quickly over ice.

NOTE

MICROWAVING MEAT.   Microwaving meat seems to draw the juices out and it steams rather than roasts. The color of the meat is pallid and the texture is not as appealing. Moreover, you can microwave successfully only in small amounts—about two servings—and the flavors of the meat don't integrate well. I do not recommend it.

TENDERIZING.   In addition to stewing and braising, there are other ways to deal with tough cuts of meat. Grinding is one way; most of our hamburger meat comes from less tender cuts of meat. Tough fibers are also broken down and tenderized by pounding with a meat mallet or with the edge of a saucer. Some steaks, such as flank or round, can be scored in a diamond pattern, the cuts running through some of the tough fibers.

Tough roasts and steaks may be tenderized by soaking them in flavorful marinades that contain an acid liquid such as wine or vinegar. There are also chemical meat tenderizers, usually papaya derivatives. When too heavily applied, they produce an unpleasant, pulpy piece of meat, but, used judiciously, they will help make a piece of braising steak more tender.

LEFTOVER MEAT. If you feel that leftover meat reheated loses some of its original sparkle, try serving it cold. When food is cold the flavor is diminished, so the added accent of a sauce or condiment will perk it up and provide new interest. See the Sauce chapter for ideas as well as the Preserves chapter for quick relishes. Refer to the end of each meat-variety section for ideas on using leftover meat.

BEEF

About Beef

The quality of beef depends on the feeding of the animal, the age at which it is slaughtered, and the handling of the meat. Although the

---

Today's Beef

Today's beef is vastly different from the beef of yesteryear. Over the last dozen or more years, beef has been bred and fed in new ways which produce younger and leaner meat. Our old-fashioned beef was fed a high-protein diet, raised for about 3½ years before slaughtering, and yielded approximately a 900-pound carcass. It was big and "blocky" and had a square conformation.

Today our beef is "slim and trim," range-fed on grass, and slaughtered at 12 to 18 months, yielding about a 600-pound carcass. This young, lean beef has very little marbling of fat, and the butchers in our supermarkets are trimming the outside fat on steaks and roasts to a thin ¼ inch to ⅛ inch. The new look in beef is a striking reflection of our national interest in health. The Beef Council recommends that we cook beef more quickly and at a higher heat. The reduction of fat in our meat, however, has resulted in less flavorful beef, and it is not as tender.

very best beef goes to restaurants and fancy butchers, it is possible to choose intelligently in a supermarket. In *color*, look for bright pink-red flesh, light-colored bones, and creamy-white fat. In *texture*, look for fine flesh, soft-looking bones, and crumbly suet or exterior fat. The best beef—the sort that is served at top-notch steak houses—has a delicate network of fat running through the flesh. This is the "marbling," which dissolves during cooking, providing automatic internal basting.

Since tender and less tender cuts have practically the same food values, it is good to be able to recognize and use a variety of beef cuts. Then you can experiment with unfamiliar recipes and take advantage of sales and specials. Tender beef, like the tenderloin roast and steak, is cooked dry for short periods of time, while tougher cuts, like the chuck, round, and brisket, need slow moist cooking, as in Pot Roast (p. 221). Stew beef is cut from small pieces and ends of the less tender roasts. The best stew beef has some bone in it to add to the flavor. For some reason, it is seldom packaged this way. Simply combine two packages of supermarket "stewing beef" with one package of soup bones, and you will make an Old-fashioned Beef Stew (p. 226) of surprising quality.

As for the great American hamburger, it is in fact made from almost any part of the steer. Our grandmothers used to buy their steaks whole and watch suspiciously while the butcher ground them to order. If you have a food processor, it is simple to buy labeled cuts such as chuck or skirt and grind your own; that way you know exactly what your hamburger consists of. Except for people on special diets, some fat is needed in the meat to give it flavor and hold it together: 20 percent of the hamburger should be fat. Too much fat, on the other hand, simply melts away in the broiler, wasting flavor and money.

Retail Beef Cuts
How to Cook Them
ROAST = dry heat and longer cooking
BRAISE OR STEW = moist heat and longer cooking
BROIL, PAN BROIL, OR PAN FRY = dry heat and quick cooking

Where They Come From	*Cooking Method*
ROUND	
Round steak	Braise, pan fry
Top round roast	Roast
Top round steak	Broil, pan broil, pan fry
Boneless rump roast	Roast, braise or stew
Bottom round roast	Braise or stew, roast
Tip roast, cap off	Roast, braise or stew
Eye round roast	Braise or stew, roast
Tip steak	Broil, pan broil, pan fry

SIRLOIN

Sirloin steak, flat bone	Broil, pan broil, pan fry
Sirloin steak, round bone	Broil, pan broil, pan fry
Top sirloin steak	Broil, pan broil, pan fry

SHORT LOIN

T-bone steak	Broil, pan broil, pan fry
Boneless top loin steak	Broil, pan broil, pan fry
Porterhouse steak	Broil, pan broil, pan fry
Tenderloin roast	Roast, broil
Tenderloin steak	Broil, pan broil, pan fry

RIB

Rib roast, large end	Roast
Rib roast, small end	Roast
Rib steak, small end	Broil, pan broil, pan fry
Rib eye roast	Roast
Rib eye steak	Broil, pan broil, pan fry
Back ribs	Braise or stew, roast

CHUCK

Chuck eye roast	Braise or stew, roast
Boneless top blade steak	Braise or stew, pan fry
Arm pot roast	Braise or stew
Boneless shoulder pot roast	Braise or stew
Cross rib pot roast	Braise or stew
Mock tender	Braise or stew
Blade roast	Braise or stew
Upper blade pot roast	Braise or stew, roast
7-bone pot roast	Braise or stew
Short ribs	Braise or stew
Flanken style ribs	Braise or stew

FLANK AND SHORT PLATE

Flank steak	Broil, pan broil, pan fry
Flank steak rolls	Broil, pan broil, pan fry
Skirt steak	Braise or stew, broil, pan broil, pan fry

FORESHANK AND BRISKET

Shank, cross cut	Braise or stew
Brisket, whole	Braise or stew
Corned brisket, point half	Braise or stew
Brisket, flat half	Braise or stew

OTHER CUTS

Ground beef	Broil, pan broil, pan fry
Cubed steak	Pan fry, braise or stew
Beef for stew	Braise or stew
Cubes for kabobs	Broil, braise or stew

Use the meat thermometer to test the doneness of beef.

RARE 130°F   MEDIUM 140°F   WELL DONE 160°F

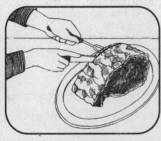 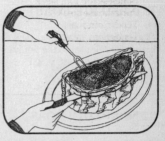

To carve a rib roast: 1. The old-fashioned way has always been to stand the roast on its ribs and carve downward in slices as thin as you wish.

2. The more professional method, particularly for a many-ribbed roast and thicker slices, is to lay the roast on its side. First cut along the rib to loosen the meat from the bone, then make horizontal slices.

(ALLOW ½–1 POUND PER SERVING)   **STANDING RIB ROAST**

Cooking time varies widely, depending on the shape of the roast and internal temperature. You'll need a meat thermometer. For Yorkshire Pudding, traditionally served with Roast Beef, see p. 769.

> 1 standing rib roast, at least 4 pounds
> ¼ cup beef broth or water
>
> Salt
> Freshly ground pepper

Preheat the oven to 325°F. Place the meat, fat side up, in a shallow open pan and allow it to come to room temperature. Roast for approximately 20 minutes to the pound. Insert a meat thermometer toward the end of the estimated cooking time: the meat is rare at 130°F, medium at 140°F, and well done at 160°F. Remove from the oven when the thermometer registers 5 degrees lower than the desired temperature, and let the roast sit on a carving board while the Yorkshire pudding bakes, if you are making it, and while you make a simple gravy: the roast will continue to cook and become easier to carve. Drain off most of the fat and place the roasting pan over a burner. Add the broth or simply ¼ cup water, and stir and scrape with a large kitchen spoon, loosening the brown glaze on the bottom of the pan. Add more liquid if you wish and salt and pepper to taste, and cook over low heat until well blended, about 2 minutes. Spoon over slices of carved beef.

ROLLED RIB ROAST

Place meat in a V-shaped rack and increase cooking time to approximately 30 minutes to the pound. Allow ⅓ pound per serving. Carve as you would Pot Roast, p. 221.

TENDERLOIN ROAST   (ALLOW ⅓ POUND PER SERVING)

The tenderloin or fillet of beef is very costly because it is the tenderest part of the steer, but you are buying 4–6 pounds of pure meat with no bones and fat to discard.

  1 whole tenderloin
  ¼ cup vegetable oil or butter;
      or thin strips beef fat or
      blanched salt pork

Preheat the oven to 450°F. Have the meat at room temperature and place it on a rack in an open shallow pan, tucking the thin end under to make it as thick as the rest of the roast. Brush the meat with vegetable oil, dot with butter, or lay strips of fat over the top. Roast for about 30–35 minutes. A meat thermometer will show 130°F for rare, 140°F for medium, and 160°F for well done. Take the roast from the oven when the thermometer reads 5 degrees short of the desired temperature. Place the meat on a warm platter, cover loosely with a towel or foil, and let sit for 15 minutes. It will be fork-tender and easy to slice.

PAN-BROILED STEAK   (ALLOW ⅓–½ POUND PER SERVING)

The term "broiling" is used because here thin slices of tender steak are done in a pan with almost no fat, so the effect is much the same. A heavy frypan, such as one made of cast iron, is necessary for this method. When you plan to cook a *very* thin steak rare, freeze it first then fry in a very hot skillet while still frozen.

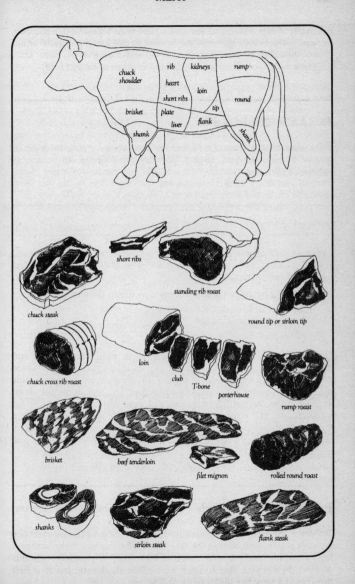

1 thin steak, such as	Freshly ground pepper
tenderloin or minute steak	¼ cup beef broth, red wine, or
1 tablespoon oil	sherry (optional)
Salt	

Allow the meat to come to room temperature. Heat the oven to 225°F and warm an ovenproof serving platter. Rub the pan with fat cut from the meat or with a paper towel lightly dipped in oil: just slick the surface. When the pan is searing hot and the fat looks wavy, add the steak. Cook on one side until brown, then turn and brown the other side. If necessary, turn the heat down and cook longer, but pour off any accumulated liquid, so that the meat will cook by dry heat. Cook as little as 2–3 minutes on each side and remove to the warm platter. Season and serve as is, or return any cooking juices to the pan along with the broth, red wine, or sherry. Cook down, scraping the bottom of the pan, adjust the seasoning, and pour the sauce over the steaks.

BROILED STEAK   (ALLOW ½ POUND PER SERVING)

For broiling, select a steak that is at least 1 inch thick. Trim its excess fat and slash the edges of the steak every 2 inches to prevent curling.

1 steak, such as sirloin,	Salt
porterhouse, club, rib	Freshly ground pepper
1 tablespoon oil	

Allow the meat to come to room temperature. Preheat the broiler. Rub oil on a broiler rack set in a drip pan, and place the meat on the rack. Cook it 2 inches beneath the broiler if it is thin or as much as 4 inches beneath the broiler if it is thick. Broil for at least 4 minutes per side for rare, depending on the thickness and temperature of the meat and the heat of the oven. Cut into the steak to see if it is done; eventually you will be able to test this by pressing the surface of the meat with a forefinger protected by a paper towel: rare steak feels soft, well done feels hard, and medium is somewhere in between. Remove from the broiler when slightly underdone, sprinkle liberally with salt and pepper, slice, and serve.

CARPETBAG STEAK   (ONE STEAK PER SERVING)

Oyster and steak was a familiar combination in the improvident days of the nineteenth century, but it is a rare and delicious treat today. Multiply the ingredients to serve as many as you like.

Tenderloin steaks, 2 inches   4–5 oysters per steak
   thick   Salt
3 tablespoons butter per steak   Freshly ground pepper

Allow ½–¾ pound of meat for each person. With a sharp knife, cut a slit on the side of each steak and make a deep pocket nearly all the way through. Preheat the broiler. For each serving, melt 2 tablespoons of the butter in a skillet, and sauté the oysters for 2–3 minutes. Drain the oysters and stuff 4–5 into the pocket of each steak. Skewer or sew up the opening. Rub the steaks with the remaining butter and broil them on a rack placed 3 inches beneath the broiling element. Cook 5–7 minutes on each side for rare and season with salt and pepper before serving.

(SERVES FOUR)   **LONDON BROIL**

A chewy, flavorful cut of meat that becomes tender when it is carved diagonally across the grain into thin slices. A hearty marinade aids the tenderizing process.

  1 clove garlic, peeled   1½ tablespoons vegetable oil
    (optional)   Salt
  1½ pounds flank steak   Freshly ground pepper

Preheat the broiler. If you want a garlic flavor, rub the clove of garlic vigorously on both sides of the steak. Rub with oil and place the meat on a rack over a drip pan. Broil 1½ inches beneath the broiling element 4–5 minutes each side for medium, 3–4 for medium-rare. Remove, sprinkle with salt and pepper, and slice as directed above.

MARINATED LONDON BROIL

Early in the day, mix ¾ cup red wine, ¼ cup oil, 1 small onion, chopped, 1 tablespoon oregano, crumbled, and 1 teaspoon salt. Marinate the steak in this mixture until ready to cook. Remove, pat dry with paper towels, and follow the recipe, eliminating the salt, pepper, and garlic.

(SERVES FOUR)   **PEPPER STEAK**

A lively way to serve tender steaks, and an exception to the rule against seasoning before cooking.

4 shell or fillet steaks, about ½ pound each	3 tablespoons butter
1 teaspoon salt	1 tablespoon oil
3 tablespoons peppercorns, coarsely crushed	4 tablespoons bourbon, beef broth, or water
	2 tablespoons water

Heat the oven to 225°F and warm an ovenproof platter. Rub the steaks with salt. Sprinkle with the peppercorns and use a meat pounder or the bottom of a pot to pound the pepper into the steak. Turn the meat over, and repeat the seasoning on the other side. Heat the butter and oil in a heavy skillet and sauté the steaks about 4 minutes on each side. Transfer to the warm platter. Add the bourbon and 2 tablespoons water to the skillet and cook rapidly, stirring and scraping, to incorporate the bits of meat and fat in the pan. Boil down for 1 minute and spoon the sauce over the steaks.

QUICK THEATER STEAK ✳ (SERVES FOUR)

This is a snappy supper dish which will enable you to get to the theater on time. It can also be quickly made for supper or after the theater.

½ cup butter or vegetable oil	1 cup water
2 large onions, in thin rings	4 slices good fresh white bread
½ pound fresh mushrooms, sliced	2 bunches fresh watercress, stemmed, washed, and dried
Salt and freshly ground pepper to taste	
Two ½-pound beef fillets, cut in half lengthwise	

Melt the butter in a large skillet, and when butter is hot, stir in the onions and mushrooms. Add salt and pepper and sauté over medium-high heat, stirring constantly, until the vegetables are just soft. Remove the vegetables from the skillet and keep warm on a plate.

Salt and pepper the steak amply. Turn the heat to high, and fry the steak quickly, turning over as soon as the steak is well browned. Remove to a plate and keep warm. Over high heat, stir in the water and deglaze the skillet (scraping and stirring the remaining bits from the bottom of the pan) for a minute. Quickly dip one side of each of the slices of bread into the drippings in the skillet and place each on the serving plate.

Assemble by placing some of the watercress on each slice of bread. (Reserve a little of the watercress and onion for garnish.) Add the onions and mushrooms, then add any remaining juices from the skillet and place the steak on top. Press the steak gently down so a little of the juices flow into the watercress and bread. Garnish with the watercress and onion and serve.

(SERVES EIGHT TO TEN) **POT ROAST**

The secret of tender pot roasts lies in keeping the heat below the boil. Violent boiling toughens meat fibers. Cooking ahead allows you to chill the meat and remove the fat on the surface; chilled meat is also easy to slice.

2 tablespoons flour
1½ teaspoons salt
½ teaspoon freshly ground
  pepper
4–5 pounds boneless chuck or
  rump roast

3 tablespoons shortening or
  vegetable oil
1 onion, sliced
2 teaspoons thyme, crumbled
1 cup tomato juice
¼–½ teaspoon Tabasco

Combine the flour, salt, and pepper. Rub it all over the roast. Melt the shortening in a heavy casserole with a lid or in a Dutch oven. When

the shortening is hot, add the roast and brown it to a deep rich color on all sides. Lower the heat and add the onion, thyme, tomato juice, and Tabasco. Cover and simmer for 3–3½ hours, turning once or twice during the cooking. When fork-tender, cool. Remove the fat, slice the meat, and reheat in the degreased sauce, or skim off the fat, reheat, and bring to the table to carve.

(SERVES TEN) **BEEF À LA MODE**

Call it pot roast, braised beef, or beef à la mode, but the process is the same: long, slow cooking in liquid tenderizes and flavors a tough cut of meat. The savory sauce is the bonus.

4 tablespoons shortening,
  vegetable oil, or salt pork
2 tablespoons flour
4 pounds boneless round or
  chuck roast
⅓ cup diced carrot
⅓ cup diced turnip

⅓ cup diced celery
Salt
Freshly ground pepper
3 sprigs parsley
1 bay leaf
2 cups water

Place a Dutch oven or heavy pot with a lid over medium-high heat. Add the shortening. Flour the beef on all sides and brown in the melted fat. Remove and set aside. Spread the diced vegetables on the bottom of the pot. Place the beef on top and sprinkle with salt and pepper to taste. Add the parsley, bay leaf, and water. Cover closely and simmer for 3 hours. Remove the meat and slice it. Strain the juices, spoon some over the meat, and serve the rest as a sauce.

CHICKEN FRIED STEAK   (SERVES FOUR TO SIX)

Next to Sunday chicken dinners, Chicken Fried Steak was the family favorite during the forties and fifties. Tougher cuts of steak that are pounded into tenderness, floured, and quickly fried bring forth a rich good flavor, especially with onions and milk gravy.

1½ pounds top round steak
¼ cup plus 3 tablespoons flour
Salt and freshly ground
   pepper
3 tablespoons vegetable
   shortening

1 large onion, coarsely
   chopped
1½ cups milk

Cut the steak into 4 to 6 serving pieces. Pound ¼ cup flour into the steaks using a meat pounder or the rim of a sturdy plate. Pound in as much flour as you can until the steaks are saturated and quite thin. Sprinkle generously with salt and pepper. Heat the shortening in a large skillet over high heat. Cook the steaks very quickly, about 2–3 minutes on each side, until golden brown. Remove to a platter and keep warm. Remove all but 2 tablespoons of fat. Add the onion and sauté, over medium heat, for about 2 minutes, or until soft. Stir the remaining flour into the onion, continuing to stir, and let it cook for 2 or 3 minutes. Slowly add the milk, constantly stirring, and cook until the gravy is thickened. Serve with mashed potatoes and pass the gravy.

NEW ENGLAND BOILED DINNER   (SERVES SIX TO EIGHT)

Serve this American classic with Mustard Sauce (p. 391), Horseradish Cream (p. 390), corn muffins, and unsalted butter. Plan for some leftovers for corned beef hash.

4–5 pounds corned beef brisket

6 carrots, scrubbed and scraped

4 medium onions, outer skins removed

6 small turnips, scrubbed

6 medium potatoes, peeled

1 medium head green cabbage, quartered and cored

8 small young beets

Rinse the corned beef under cold running water to remove the brine. Place in a large pot, cover with cold water, and bring to a boil, skimming off the scum that rises to the surface during the first 10 minutes. Cover and simmer for 2 hours. Then add the onions and potatoes, and continue to simmer. Meanwhile, bring a quantity of water to boil in another saucepan and add the beets. Boil them for 30–40 minutes, or until they are barely tender when pierced with a knife. Drain and put them in a 250°F oven to keep warm. When the onions and potatoes have cooked for 15 minutes, add the carrots and turnips to the pot and simmer for 30 minutes more. Remove and slice the meat and arrange, surrounded by vegetables, on an ovenproof platter. Place in the warm oven, along with the dish of beets. Turn up the heat under the broth and, when it boils, add the cabbage. Boil for 3 minutes, drain, and place in a separate serving bowl. Serve the beef surrounded by carrots, turnips, onions, and potatoes, with the beets and cabbage in separate bowls.

(SERVES SIX)   **✳ BEEF STROGANOFF**

Tender beef in a lightly tangy sauce with the flavor of mushrooms: good over brown rice. If your pocketbook can't manage tenderloin, try making it with thin slices of flank steak, cut diagonally across the grain. Incidentally, if you freeze the meat for an hour or so—just enough for it to firm up—it will be easier to slice thin. This dish is outstandingly good to eat and also quick to make.

6 tablespoons butter or vegetable oil

Salt to taste

2 tablespoons minced onion

Freshly ground pepper to taste

2 pounds beef tenderloin, cut thin in 1 × 1½-inch strips

⅛ teaspoon nutmeg

½ pound mushrooms, sliced

1 cup sour cream, at room temperature

Melt 3 tablespoons of the butter in a heavy skillet. Add the onion and cook slowly until transparent. Remove and set aside. Turn the heat to medium-high, add the beef, and cook briefly, turning to brown on all sides. Remove the beef and set aside with the onions. Add the remaining 3 tablespoons butter to the skillet. Stir in the mushrooms, cover, and cook 3 minutes. Season with salt, pepper, and nutmeg. Whisk the sour cream and add to the pan, but do not allow it to boil. Return the beef and onion to the pan and just heat through.

SAUERBRATEN (SERVES TEN)

Long a standby in German-American households, sauerbraten displays the thrift and foresight of the cook. A less than tender cut of meat is placed in a marinade for two days. It is slow-cooked, then sliced, and its piquant sweet-and-sour sauce is complemented by bland potatoes, thin slices of dark bread, and butter.

4-pound top or bottom round roast	2 tablespoons pickling spices
1 cup dry red wine	2 cups water
1½ teaspoons salt	3 tablespoons shortening
10 peppercorns, crushed	½ cup gingersnaps, crushed fine
1 onion, sliced thin	½ cup sour cream
2 bay leaves	

Two days before you plan to use it, put the beef in a deep glass or pottery bowl. In a saucepan, mix the wine, salt, peppercorns, onion slices, bay leaves, and pickling spices with 2 cups water and bring to a boil. Remove from the heat. When it is cool, pour over the beef. Cover the bowl tightly with foil and refrigerate for at least two days, turning the meat in the marinade twice a day. Preheat the oven to 350°F. Melt the shortening in a covered roasting pan or casserole. Remove the meat from the marinade, pat it dry with paper towels, and brown it well on all sides in the hot shortening. Drain off the fat, strain the marinade, and pour it over the meat. Cover and cook in the oven for 2–2½ hours, or until tender. Remove the meat and keep warm on a platter. Put the roasting pan on a burner and add the gingersnap crumbs, stirring until the gravy is smooth and thickened. Stir in the sour cream, letting it get hot but not allowing it to boil, lest it curdle. Slice the meat, pour the gravy into a sauce bowl, and serve with the sauerbraten.

SWISS STEAK (SERVES FOUR)

Midway between pot roast and stew, this is a fine way to use a less than tender steak. Lots of gravy to go over mashed potatoes or noodles.

1½ pounds rump, round, or
  chuck steak
2 tablespoons flour
¾ teaspoon salt
½ teaspoon freshly ground
  pepper

3 tablespoons shortening
1½ cups canned stewed
  tomatoes
1 onion, sliced

Preheat the oven to 325°F. Trim excess fat from the steak. Combine the flour, salt, and pepper. Sprinkle half the flour mixture on one side of the meat and pound it in with a meat-tenderizing mallet or the rim of a saucer. Turn the meat over and repeat the flouring and pounding. Melt the shortening in a covered pan or Dutch oven. When it is hot, add the meat and brown over medium heat until both sides are well colored. Add the tomatoes and onion, cover, and place in the oven for about 2 hours or until tender.

(SERVES FOUR)   **HUNGARIAN GOULASH**

Goulash can resemble stew or soup: this one must be eaten in bowls with a spoon to manage its abundant paprika and onion sauce.

3 tablespoons butter
1 onion, chopped
2 tablespoons sweet
  Hungarian paprika
2 pounds beef round, in 1½-
  inch cubes
2 tablespoons flour

Salt
¾ teaspoon marjoram,
  crumbled
4 cups beef broth
1½ cups potato cubes
1½ tablespoons lemon juice

Melt the butter in a covered casserole. Add the onion, stir, and cook until soft. Stir in the paprika and cook slowly 1–2 minutes. Roll the meat in flour and add to the onion, cooking only long enough to brown lightly. Sprinkle with a little salt, and add marjoram. Pour in broth and bring to a boil. Cover and simmer for about 1 hour, or until tender. Add the potato cubes and cook 15–20 minutes, until done. Remove from heat, stir in the lemon juice, and add more salt if necessary.

(SERVES FOUR)   **GOULASH STEW**

A drier goulash than the previous one, this is good served over broad noodles.

3 tablespoons butter	2 pounds beef round
2 large onions, sliced thin	2 cups drained canned
2 tablespoons paprika	tomatoes
½ teaspoon salt	¼ cup sour cream, at room
1 clove garlic, minced	temperature

Melt the butter in a casserole with cover. Add the onion slices and cook gently for 10 minutes. Stir in the paprika, salt, and garlic, and cook 2 minutes more. Remove the onions with a slotted spoon and set aside. Turn up the heat and brown the beef, a few pieces at a time, in the pan oils. Return the onions to the pot with all the meat and the tomatoes. Cover and simmer for 2½ hours. When it is done, remove the pot from the burner and briskly stir in the sour cream.

CREAMED DRIED BEEF   (SERVES FOUR)

An old-fashioned and simple-to-fix supper. Dried or chipped beef, once a kitchen staple, is paper-thin dried beef. It is best if you use a good sliced dried beef from a deli or meat market—not the ground, rolled, and pressed products found in jars and plastic bags today. The salty taste is soothed by a rich cream sauce and the small amount of beef goes far; serve on a base of buttered toast or mealy baked potatoes, split open.

¼ pound dried beef	1 cup light cream
4 tablespoons butter	¼ teaspoon freshly ground
3 tablespoons flour	pepper
1 cup hot milk	

Separate the slices of beef and set aside. In a saucepan, melt the butter, and when it foams, sprinkle on the flour and stir until well blended. Add the milk and cook over low heat, stirring. Add the cream slowly, continuing to stir constantly until the cream sauce is thickened. Add the pepper and the dried beef and mix well until heated through.

OLD-FASHIONED BEEF STEW   ✳   (SERVES SIX)

A stew you will serve in soupbowls: dark-brown beef and vegetables in lots of rich gravy.

⅓ cup flour
1 teaspoon salt
¼ teaspoon freshly ground
    pepper
2 pounds stewing beef plus
    bones (see p. 213)
4 tablespoons shortening
4 cups boiling water
1 tablespoon lemon juice
1 tablespoon Worcestershire
    sauce

1 teaspoon sugar
1 large onion, sliced
2 bay leaves
¼ teaspoon allspice
12 small carrots, trimmed and
    scraped
12 small white onions,
    trimmed
8 small new potatoes, peeled

Mix the flour, salt, and pepper and roll the beef cubes in the mixture. Shake off excess. Melt the shortening over high heat in a Dutch oven or heavy-bottomed pot with a cover. When the fat is very hot add the beef, about 5 or 6 pieces at a time so as not to crowd them, brown on all sides, and remove. When the last batch of meat is a richly dark color, return all to the pot and pour on the boiling water. Stand back when you do it, because it will spit and sputter. Stir and add the lemon juice, Worcestershire sauce, sugar, onion, bay leaves, and allspice. Lower the heat, cover, and simmer for 1½–2 hours, or until the meat is tender. Add the carrots, onions, and potatoes and cook another 20–25 minutes or until they can be pierced easily with a fork.

(SERVES FOUR)   **BURGUNDY BEEF**

Beef and red wine just seem to go together. Steamed potatoes, salad, and crusty bread finish off the meal.

4 tablespoons shortening or
    vegetable oil
1 large onion, chopped
3 tablespoons flour
½ teaspoon salt
¼ teaspoon freshly ground
    pepper
2 pounds stewing beef plus
    bones (see p. 213)

½ teaspoon marjoram,
    crumbled
1 teaspoon thyme, crumbled
1 cup Burgundy or other red
    wine
1 cup beef broth
12 small white onions,
    trimmed and peeled
½ pound mushrooms

Melt the shortening over medium heat in a heavy Dutch oven or covered casserole. Add the chopped onion to the melted fat in the pan, slowly cook to a light golden brown, remove, and set aside. Mix the flour, salt, and pepper on a dinner plate and roll the meat in the mixture. Brown the beef, a few pieces at a time, and add the marjoram, thyme, wine, and beef broth. Return the onion to the pot, cover, and simmer for 1½ hours. Add the small onions and cook 20 minutes, then add the mushrooms and cook 10 minutes more. Correct seasoning. When the onions are fork-tender, the stew is done.

BRAISED OXTAIL   (SERVES FOUR)

When your supermarket features oxtail, don't pass it up. Try this simple recipe for hearty beef in dark-brown sauce, but plan to cook ahead so that you can cool it and remove the fat easily.

3 tablespoons shortening	2 onions, sliced thin
3 tablespoons flour	1½ cups beef broth
½ teaspoon salt	1½ cups canned tomatoes
Freshly ground pepper	1 cup water
3–4 pounds oxtail, in 2-inch pieces	2 bay leaves

Preheat the oven to 300°F. Melt the shortening in a heavy skillet. Mix the flour, salt, and pepper, and roll the oxtail pieces in it. Brown the meat in the shortening, turning so that all sides are colored. Transfer to a covered casserole and cook the onions in the fat remaining in the skillet. When they are lightly brown, add them to the meat in the casserole. Pour on the beef broth, tomatoes, and the water. Stir, add the bay leaves, cover, and bake for 3 hours. Remove the bay leaves, cool the whole dish, and remove the fat. Reheat and serve.

BEEFSTEAK AND KIDNEY PIE   (SERVES EIGHT)

The essence of winter goodness, this traditional favorite mingles tender steak and pieces of kidney under a flaky crust or baking-powder biscuits. Because kidneys are not always readily available, buy them when you can, and freeze the extras. They will keep well in your freezer for two months.

1 beef kidney	½ teaspoon freshly ground pepper
4 tablespoons shortening	
2 onions, chopped	2 tablespoons butter, softened
2 pounds round steak, in 1-inch cubes	2 tablespoons flour
2 cups boiling water	2 tablespoons minced parsley
1½ tablespoons Worcestershire sauce	1 recipe Basic Pastry for 9-inch shell (p. 895), or 1 recipe Baking Powder Biscuits (p. 764)
½ teaspoon salt	

Wash the kidney, remove membranes and fat, and cut kidney in 1-inch cubes. Melt the shortening in a heavy pot. Add the onions and cook, stirring often, until well browned. Add the steak and kidneys. When the meat is browned on all sides, pour on the boiling water, Worcestershire, salt, and pepper. Cover and cook over very low heat for 1½ hours, or until the steak is tender. Preheat the oven to 400°F. Blend the butter with the flour to make a beurre manié. Drop small pellets of this paste into the sauce and stir to thicken it. Put meat and sauce into a deep pie plate and sprinkle with parsley. If you wish to use a pastry topping, roll out the dough and cover the pie plate. Slash the top, crimp the edges, and bake about 30 minutes, or until well browned. Or form enough baking powder biscuits to cover the meat and bake 20–25 minutes until done.

(SERVES FOUR) **BRAISED SHORT RIBS**

Meat with lots of bone makes an especially tasty and juicy stew, and you have the fun of nibbling at the bones! Serve with big napkins.

3 tablespoons flour	2 large onions, peeled and
1½ teaspoons salt	quartered
½ teaspoon freshly ground	1 cup sliced celery
pepper	4 parsley sprigs
4 pounds beef short ribs	2 bay leaves
4 tablespoons shortening	1 teaspoon marjoram,
1 cup water	crumbled
8 small carrots, scraped	1 cup red wine

Preheat the oven to 350°F. Combine the flour, salt, and pepper in a brown paper bag. Shake the short ribs in the bag with the flour, coating it on all sides. Melt the shortening in a heavy casserole or Dutch oven. When it is hot, add the meat and brown to a rich dark color. Pour off the fat in the pan, reduce the heat, and add 1 cup water and remaining ingredients. Cover and cook in the oven for 1½–2 hours. Since this is very fatty meat, it is good to chill it and remove the fat if there is time. Then reheat to serve.

(SERVES EIGHT) **MEAT LOAF**

A hearty family meal, susceptible to many variations. The second day, slice it thin and make sandwiches on rye bread with sweet pickles.

2 cups freshly made bread
   crumbs
1 onion, chopped fine
2 eggs, slightly beaten
2 pounds ground beef
2 tablespoons Worcestershire
   sauce

1½ teaspoons dry mustard
1½ teaspoons salt
½ teaspoon freshly ground
   pepper
¾ cup milk

Preheat the oven to 350°F. Butter a loaf pan. Combine all the ingredients in a large bowl; your freshly washed hands are the best tools for the job. Pat into the loaf pan and bake for 45 minutes.

MEAT LOAF WITH PARSLEY AND TOMATO

Omit the Worcestershire sauce and mustard; in place of the milk, use ¾ *cup of juice from a can of tomatoes* and add *¼ cup minced parsley* plus ½ *teaspoon basil, crumbled.* Pat into pan and cover with ¾ *cup of the tomatoes from the can, roughly chopped,* or ¾ *cup tomato sauce.*

MEAT LOAF WITH CHEESE

Omit the Worcestershire sauce and add *½ cup grated cheese.*

MEAT LOAF WITH BACON

After patting the loaf into the pan, cover with *4 strips uncooked bacon.*

MEAT LOAF WITH THREE MEATS

Instead of 2 pounds ground beef, use *1 pound ground beef* mixed with *⅔ pound ground veal* and *⅓ pound ground pork. Red wine* may be used instead of milk if desired. Bake 1 hour.

MEAT LOAF WITH LEMON AND MUSHROOM SAUCE

Omit the Worcestershire sauce and dry mustard and add 1 *tablespoon grated lemon rind*, 2 *tablespoons minced parsley*, and 1 *teaspoon nutmeg*. Serve with 1 recipe Mushroom Sauce (p. 386).

INDIVIDUAL MUFFIN-SIZE MEAT LOAVES

Instead of using a loaf pan, pack the meat into muffin tins or Pyrex baking cups, top each with a square of *bacon*, and bake for only 25 minutes at 400°F. Turn out and serve with *tomato sauce*.

(SERVES FOUR)   **HAMBURGERS**

The secret of first-rate hamburgers is to use medium-lean meat. Chuck is about the best, or grind your own from the skirt, particularly if you have a food processor, which does a good job. The more you handle or grind hamburger the more compact and dry it becomes. Divide and shape the patties as lightly as possible and don't press down on them when cooking or you'll squeeze all the juice out. For hamburger patties in buns with various trimmings, see p. 364.

Salt	1 tablespoon butter
Freshly ground pepper	1 tablespoon cooking oil
1½ pounds medium-lean ground beef	

Salt and pepper the meat and mix with a light hand. Shape into four patties about ¾ inch thick. Melt the butter and oil in a skillet until bubbling, then add the hamburgers. Fry 2–3 minutes on each side for rare; 4–5 minutes each side for medium; 6 minutes each side for well done. Pour pan drippings over and serve.

BROILED HAMBURGERS

Put the patties on a lightly oiled broiler rack and place 4 inches below a preheated broiler. Broil 4–5 minutes on each side for medium-rare; 5–6 for well done.

HAMBURGERS WITH RED WINE SAUCE

After removing the hamburgers from the pan sauté *2 tablespoons minced shallots* or *scallions* for 1 minute, then add *⅓ cup red wine*. Cook down rapidly to half, swirl in *2 tablespoons butter,* and pour over the hamburgers.

HAMBURGER STROGANOFF

Keep the cooked hamburgers warm while you prepare the stroganoff sauce: melt *2 tablespoons butter* in the same skillet, add *1 onion, finely chopped,* and sauté until translucent. Add *¼ pound sliced mushrooms* and cook 5 minutes, then stir in *¾ cup sour cream*. When warm through, return the hamburgers to the skillet and spoon sauce over them to heat. Serve dusted with *paprika*.

SALISBURY STEAK   (SERVES FOUR)

2 slices white bread	1 teaspoon Worcestershire
¼ cup milk	sauce
1¾ pounds medium lean	4 strips bacon, cooked and
ground beef	crumbled
1 teaspoon salt	⅓ cup bread crumbs
Freshly ground pepper	

Remove the crusts from the bread and soak bread in the milk until soft. Squeeze out excess milk, then lightly mix the moist bread with the ground beef until thoroughly absorbed. Add the seasonings and shape into a large round about 1 inch thick. Preheat the broiler. Place meat on an oiled broiler rack and cook 4 inches from heat on one side for 5 minutes, then turn and sprinkle the bacon and the bread crumbs over the top and broil another 4–5 minutes for medium-rare; add another minute each side for better done.

(SERVES SIX)   **CORN PONE PIE**

3 tablespoons vegetable oil
1 onion, chopped
1 pound lean ground beef
3 cloves garlic, chopped
1½ cups cooked pinto beans
2 cups stewed or canned
    tomatoes

2–3 tablespoons chili powder
1 teaspoon diced jalapeño
    pepper
Salt
1 recipe Corn Bread batter
    (p. 769)

Melt the oil in a large skillet, add the onion, and cook over medium heat until it is soft. Add the beef, breaking it up into small bits. Stir and mix with the onion, and cook until the beef loses its redness. Stir in the garlic, pinto beans, tomatoes, chili powder, and jalapeño pepper. Mix well and add salt to taste. Simmer for 45 minutes, stirring often. Preheat the oven to 400°F. Spread the chili mixture into a shallow 2- or 2½-quart baking dish. Spread the corn bread batter over the top and bake about 20 minutes.

(SERVES SIX)   **CHILI CON CARNE**

There are probably more chili recipes than chocolate chip cookie recipes. This is a good one. In Texas, where the dish originated, strong men have been known to do battle over the proper way to cook chili con carne. This recipe can be made with ground beef, but cubed beef has more character. Serve in the traditional manner, with red pinto beans and fluffy rice.

4 tablespoons shortening or
    vegetable oil
2 onions, chopped
6 cloves garlic, minced
3 pounds beef chuck, in 1-
    inch cubes

1 teaspoon salt
4–6 tablespoons chili powder
1 tablespoon ground cumin
1 tablespoon dried oregano
Cayenne pepper to taste
4 cups beef broth

Heat the shortening in a large skillet. Stir in the onions and garlic and cook until they are soft. Add the beef and salt and cook until the meat loses its pink color. Add the chili powder, cumin, oregano, and cayenne and continue to cook for about 5 minutes. Add the beef broth and simmer, partially covered, for about 2 hours, stirring occasionally. Serve in large bowls.

REVOLTILLOS *   (SERVES EIGHT)

An unusual dish with a strong flavor of bay and the contrasting tastes
of sweet raisins and salty olives.

¼ cup oil	¾ cup raisins
3 green peppers, chopped	¾ cup ripe olives
3 onions, chopped	5 bay leaves
2 cloves garlic, minced	2 cups beef broth
2 pounds chopped beef	1 cup rice

Heat the oil in a large skillet with a lid. Stir in the peppers, onions, and
garlic. Cook, stirring, until they are soft. Add the beef and break it up
with a fork, cooking until it loses its pink color. Add the raisins, olives,
and bay leaves, cover, and simmer for 30 minutes. Remove the bay
leaves. Meanwhile, bring the beef broth to a boil in a saucepan and
slowly add the rice. Shake the pan so the rice will level and cook
evenly. Cover and cook 20 minutes. When the liquid is absorbed, toss
the rice with a fork, add to the meat mixture, and serve.

LITTLE JOE'S   (SERVES SIX)

This is a version of a very popular San Francisco dish.

3 tablespoons oil	Salt
1 onion, chopped	Tabasco
1 pound lean ground beef	4 eggs, slightly beaten
1 pound spinach, blanched,	¼ cup freshly grated
well drained, and chopped	Parmesan cheese

Heat the oil in a large skillet, add the onion, and cook over medium
heat until soft. Add the beef, mixing with the onion and breaking it up
into small bits with a fork; cook until the redness is gone. Add the
spinach and mix well. Stir and cook for 3–4 minutes, then salt to taste.
Mix a dash or so of Tabasco with the eggs, then pour them over the
beef mixture and stir until the eggs are set. Remove from heat and put
on a warm platter. Sprinkle the Parmesan cheese over.

(SERVES SIX)   **BEEF AND CORN CASSEROLE**

2 tablespoons oil
1 green pepper, chopped
1 onion, chopped
1 pound lean ground beef
2 cups corn kernels

Salt
2 firm ripe tomatoes, peeled
   and sliced
1 cup buttered bread crumbs

Preheat oven to 350°F. Heat the oil in a skillet, add the pepper and onion, and cook, stirring often, until the onion is soft. Add the ground beef, breaking it up into small bits, and cook until it loses its redness. Stir in the corn and salt to taste. Mix well. Place in a baking dish, cover with tomato slices, and sprinkle the crumbs over the top. Bake 25 minutes, or until the crumbs are brown.

(SERVES SIX)   **BEEF À LA LINDSTROM**

A spicy mix of beef, potatoes, beets, and capers. Fry it in patties, bake in a loaf, or fashion a crisp hashlike pancake.

2 potatoes, boiled and
   mashed, or about 1¼ cups
   mashed potatoes
1½ pounds ground beef
2 egg yolks, lightly beaten
½ cup milk
½ cup finely diced pickle
   beets

2 tablespoons minced onion
3 tablespoons capers
¾ teaspoon salt
½ teaspoon freshly ground
   pepper
2 tablespoons butter
   (optional)
1 tablespoon oil (optional)

If you are going to make a meat loaf, preheat the oven to 350°F. Mix the mashed potatoes, beef, egg yolks, milk, beets, onion, capers, salt, and pepper. Shape to fit a loaf pan, and bake 45 minutes. Or, shape the mixture into six patties. Melt the butter and oil in a skillet and fry the patties over medium heat, turning as they brown. Or, preheat the broiler. Melt the butter and oil in a skillet and press the mixture flat with a spatula. When it has formed a crust on the bottom, place under the broiler to brown the top. Serve in pie-shaped wedges.

(20 MEATBALLS)   **SWEDISH MEATBALLS**

These small meatballs, faintly flavored with allspice and nutmeg in a creamy sauce, would be good at a cocktail buffet speared with toothpicks. They are equally good served six to a person over noodles for dinner.

1¼ pounds ground beef
2½ cups whole-wheat bread crumbs
1 egg, lightly beaten
1 teaspoon sugar
¾ teaspoon allspice
¾ teaspoon nutmeg
½ teaspoon salt
¼ teaspoon freshly ground pepper
2 tablespoons shortening
½ cup beef broth
½ cup heavy cream

Preheat the oven to 325°F. Combine the ground beef, bread crumbs, egg, sugar, allspice, nutmeg, salt, and pepper. Shape into 1½-inch balls. Melt the shortening in a skillet and brown the meatballs. Transfer to a shallow casserole, pour on the beef broth, cover with foil, and bake for 25 minutes. Add the cream and cook without a cover for 15 minutes more.

TAMALE PIE

(SERVES SIX)

This is adapted from James Beard's great Tamale Pie recipe. It looks splendid cooked and brought to the table in a colorful casserole.

4 cups water
1½ cups yellow cornmeal
2 cups cold water
3 teaspoons salt
¼–½ cup butter or lard
½ pound bulk sausage
2 tablespoons chili powder
¾ teaspoon ground cumin
1 clove garlic, minced
1–1½ cups finely chopped onions
1 small green pepper, seeded and chopped
1 cup finely chopped celery
1½ pounds ground beef
3 cups canned Italian plum tomatoes, or 4 cups peeled and seeded fresh tomatoes
2 cups fresh, frozen, or canned corn kernels
4 ounces canned, mild green chilies, diced
1 teaspoon minced jalapeño pepper (optional)
1 cup pitted ripe olives
2 cups grated medium or sharp Cheddar cheese

Bring the water to a boil in a 3-quart saucepan. Meanwhile, stir the cornmeal into the 2 cups of cold water (this helps prevent lumping) and then stir this into the boiling water. Continue to stir while the water returns to a boil. Turn the heat to low, stir in 1½ teaspoons of the salt and the butter, cover, and simmer 30 to 40 minutes, stirring often.

In a large frying pan, mash the sausage and cook over medium heat until it begins to lose color. Add the chili powder and cumin, stir, and cook about 5 minutes. Add the garlic, onions, green pepper, celery, and remaining salt. Stir and cook until the vegetables are limp. Crumble the beef into the pan and mash and cook until the raw color disappears. Add the tomatoes, corn, and green chilies (and jalapeño pepper, if used), and let the mixture simmer for 15 to 20 minutes. Grease or oil a large baking pan at least 10 × 14 × 2 inches. Spread two-thirds of the cornmeal mixture on the bottom and sides of the pan. Spoon in the filling and distribute the olives evenly over. Spoon the remaining cornmeal over the top and sprinkle with the cheese. Bake in a 350°F oven for about 1 hour.

MEATBALLS IN SAUCE FOR SPAGHETTI

(SERVES FOUR TO SIX)

This family favorite is particularly good made from scratch with your own homemade tomato sauce, prepared only yesterday or frozen months earlier when tomatoes were ripe and plentiful.

1 pound ground beef	1 egg, lightly beaten
½ cup dried bread crumbs	½ teaspoon salt
1 clove garlic, minced	2 tablespoons oil
2 tablespoons minced parsley	4 cups Tomato Sauce (p. 387)
¼ teaspoon freshly ground pepper	½ pound Parmesan cheese, grated
1 tablespoon basil, crumbled	

Combine the beef, bread crumbs, garlic, parsley, basil, egg, salt, and pepper. Mix thoroughly and shape into balls 1½ inches in diameter. Melt the oil in a saucepan. Brown the meatballs lightly on all sides; drain off the fat. Add the tomato sauce, cover, and simmer 25 minutes. Serve over spaghetti, and pass the grated cheese.

DISHES USING LEFTOVER BEEF

ROAST BEEF HASH

(SERVES FOUR)

The secret to good roast beef hash is the gravy. If you have not saved enough from your leftover roast you will have to improvise (see p. 384). Be sure to include any beef juice or drippings to add flavor.

4 tablespoons shortening	1 onion, chopped
3 cups finely chopped cooked roast beef	1 cup gravy, leftover or improvised (p. 384)
3 medium potatoes, cooked, peeled, and chopped	Salt
	Freshly ground pepper

Heat the shortening in a sauté pan and when it is hot add the beef, potatoes, onion, and gravy. Cook over high heat, stirring and turning often, until brown underneath. Add salt and pepper to taste. Turn over and cook on the other side—about 10–15 minutes in all.

CORNED BEEF HASH   (SERVES FOUR)

The chopped corned beef is mixed with potato and onion, doused with rich cream, and fried to form a crust top and bottom. Thick slices of fresh tomatoes, warm bread, and butter go well with it. So does a poached egg on each serving.

2 cups chopped cooked corned beef	Freshly ground pepper
2 cups chopped boiled potatoes	Salt
1 small onion, chopped fine	4 tablespoons butter
	5 tablespoons heavy cream

Mix the beef, potatoes, onion, and pepper and salt to taste (be careful: the beef is salty!). Melt the butter in a 10-inch skillet: iron is best, if you have one. Spread the beef mixture over the bottom and press down with a spatula. Fry over medium-low heat for 15–20 minutes. Use the spatula and take a peek at the underside. If it is nicely browned, turn the hash over. Slide it out onto a dinner plate, and invert the plate over the skillet. Pour the cream evenly over the meat and cook another 15–20 minutes, until the second side is nicely brown.

RED FLANNEL HASH

Mix *1 cup finely diced cooked beets* with the hash and fry.

BEEF, BROWN RICE, AND FETA CASSEROLE

(SERVES FOUR)

6 large dried mushrooms, or
  ¼ cup pieces
1 onion, chopped
1 tablespoon oil
1½ cups canned tomatoes
1 clove garlic, minced
Salt
Freshly ground pepper
2 cups cooked brown rice

1½ cups cooked beef in
  medium chunks
3 ounces feta cheese,
  crumbled
6 black olives, pitted and
  sliced
2 tablespoons grated
  Parmesan cheese

Put the dried mushrooms in ½ cup hot water and let stand 20 minutes. Sauté the onion in the oil slowly for 5 minutes, then add the tomatoes and garlic, and let cook gently, uncovered, about 10 minutes. Salt and pepper to taste, then add the dried mushrooms, cut in quarters if large, with any tough stems removed, and the mushroom soaking liquid. Cook another 5 minutes. Preheat oven to 400°F. Line the bottom of 1½-quart casserole with 1 cup of the rice, add the cooked beef, and strew over the top the feta cheese, the olives, and half the sauce. Add the remaining rice and the rest of the sauce, and sprinkle with Parmesan. Bake 20 minutes.

BEEF POT PIE

(SERVES FOUR)

Serve with thick slices of fresh tomato and Bermuda onion.

4 slices bacon
1 onion, chopped
1 pound cooked beef, in bite-
  size pieces
1½ cups gravy, leftover or
  improvised (p. 384)
4 carrots, cooked and sliced

3 potatoes, cooked, peeled,
  and diced
½ teaspoon cinnamon
Salt
Freshly ground pepper
1 recipe Basic Pastry for 9-
  inch shell (p. 895)

Fry the bacon until soft but cooked and drain on paper towels. Discard all but 3 tablespoons of the bacon fat in the skillet, add the onion, and cook until soft. Add the beef, gravy, carrots, potatoes, and cinnamon, stirring constantly until bubbling. Salt and pepper to taste. Put beef mixture into a deep pie dish or shallow casserole. Preheat the oven to 425°F. Roll out the pastry and place on top; crimp the edges and cut a small vent on top. Bake about 20 minutes, or until bubbling and top is golden.

BEEF AND SCALLIONS, MUSHROOM SAUCE

(SERVES SIX)

¼ pound butter
1 pound mushrooms, wiped clean and cut in half
1 cup chopped scallions
2 teaspoons minced garlic
2 tablespoons tomato paste
½ teaspoon thyme, crumbled
2 bay leaves

1½ cups beef broth
¼ cup Burgundy wine
1 cup tomato purée
Salt to taste
½ teaspoon freshly ground pepper
1½–2 pounds cooked beef, in bite-size pieces

Melt the butter in a large sauté pan, add the mushrooms, and cook, stirring often, until they are soft. Add the scallions, garlic, tomato paste, thyme, bay leaves, broth, wine, tomato purée, salt, and pepper. Mix well, turn the heat to low, and simmer for 1 hour. Stir in the beef and cook until just hot through.

Other Suggestions for Using Leftover Beef

For an appetizer, try using a mixture of cooked beef and mushroom duxelles in savory tarts or rissolettes. And any scraps are always good in the soup pot. Cooked beef can be substituted for raw in many of the recipes in this chapter—Beef and Corn Casserole, Beef à la Lindstrom, Beefsteak and Kidney Pie, and Beef Stroganoff, provided you have some rare leftover pieces; also, beef can be used in place of lamb in a Shepherd's Pie. Ground-up leftover beef makes good stuffings; check the pastas, enchiladas, and stuffed vegetable recipes. Leftover beef is good in sandwiches and salads. There is also a fine Aspic of Cold Beef and Vegetables in the Salad chapter.

VEAL

About Veal

The finest and most expensive veal comes from calves that were slaughtered when they were less than six months old, so young that the animal was not yet weaned. This "milk-fed" or "dairy" veal is white and tender, but, although widely enjoyed in Europe, it is hardly ever found in American markets. Recently many states have been sponsoring the careful raising and milk-feeding of calves up to about twelve weeks, which produces much more tender veal than has been available in the past in this country. Usually here the animals have been allowed to graze, and the iron in the grass gives the flesh a pinkish red color, more like the color of young beef.

Veal has little fat and no visible marbling. It should, therefore, be cooked slowly and gently, preferably by moist heat (except when you are quickly sautéing thin slices). A very good leg or loin of veal can be oven-roasted, but care must be taken to add fat to the meat and to baste it frequently while it is cooking. Veal roasts from the breast or shoulder are gently braised in a flavorful liquid.

Veal cutlets are steaks cut from the leg of the calf. Trimmed and pounded thin, they become scallops, the most tender, delicate morsels imaginable. Because veal is scarce and costly, many of the recipes that specify veal scallops can be made instead with pounded slices of boned chicken or turkey breast. These are a reasonable alternative to the more expensive meat, although they lack the succulence and special flavor of veal scallops.

Since its delicate taste and texture are perfect foils for cooking embellishments, veal is usually presented with a little sauce.

Use the meat thermometer to test the doneness of veal.
It should read 160°F.

VEAL BRAISED WITH VEGETABLES

(SERVES SIX TO EIGHT)

If you have your butcher remove the bone, you can fill the cavity with any desired stuffing, such as Bread Stuffing (p. 400). A 6-pound roast will then serve eight to ten hungry people.

4–6-pound veal roast, leg or loin	12 carrots, peeled and cut in 1-inch pieces
¼ cup oil	2 onions, peeled and sliced or quartered
4 turnips, peeled and quartered	1½ cups chicken broth

Preheat the oven to 325°F. Place the meat in a roasting pan and rub it with the oil. Roast 30 minutes per pound, until the veal registers 160°F on a meat thermometer. One hour before the end of the roasting time, scatter the vegetables around the roast in the pan and add the chicken broth. When the roast is done the pan juices may be thickened and used as a sauce (see Brown Gravy, p. 385).

POT-ROASTED VEAL (SERVES SIX TO EIGHT)

¼ cup oil
4–6-pound veal roast,
  shoulder or breast
½ cup chicken broth

½ cup white wine
2 tablespoons butter, softened
2 tablespoons flour
Salt

Preheat the oven to 325°F. Heat the oil in a Dutch oven and brown the roast on all sides. Pour the chicken broth and wine over the meat. Cover and cook until tender, about 2 hours. Remove the meat and keep warm. Work the butter and flour together with your fingers into a smooth paste. Set the Dutch oven over a medium flame and drop pellets of this paste into the broth, stirring constantly, until thickened to your liking. Add salt to taste. Slice the meat and serve with the sauce.

BRAISED LEG OF VEAL (SERVES SIX)

2 tablespoons shortening
1 clove garlic, minced
1 teaspoon salt
1 teaspoon sage, crumbled
½ teaspoon freshly ground
  pepper
5-pound leg of veal
6 tablespoons butter

2 tablespoons oil
2 onions, sliced
2 stalks celery, with leaves
1½ cups water
1 tablespoon cornstarch
¼ cup dry sherry or white
  wine

Preheat the oven to 350°F. Cream together the shortening, garlic, salt, sage, and pepper. Spread mixture over the leg of veal. Melt the butter and oil in a Dutch oven or casserole with a lid. Add the meat, onions, celery, and water. Cover and cook in the oven until tender, 1½–2 hours. Remove the veal from the pot and keep warm in the oven. Strain the broth and return to the pot. Mix the cornstarch and sherry or wine, and stir into the broth over medium heat, beating with a whisk until smooth, thickened, and slightly clear. Slice the veal and serve with the sauce.

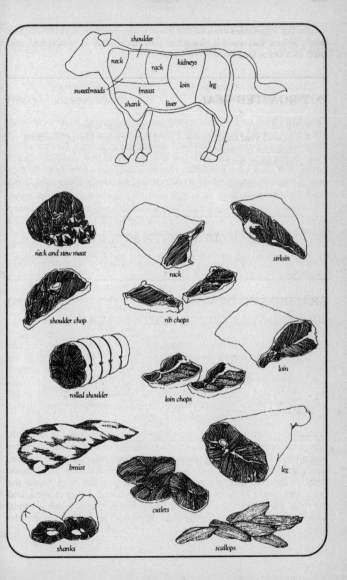

neck and stew meat

rack

sirloin

shoulder chop

rib chops

rolled shoulder

loin chops

loin

breast

leg

cutlets

shanks

scallops

BRAISED VEAL CHOPS   (SERVES SIX)

2 tablespoons butter	Salt
2 tablespoons vegetable oil	Freshly ground pepper
6¾-inch-thick veal chops	¾ cup cream

Heat the butter and oil in a frying pan large enough to accommodate the chops. Brown the meat 2–3 minutes on each side; if this cannot be done without crowding, brown a few chops at a time. Return all the meat to the pan. Season with salt and pepper to taste, add the cream, cover, and cook over low heat. This will take anywhere from 20 minutes for tender young chops to 40 minutes for tough older ones. Serve with pan juices.

BRAISED VEAL CHOPS WITH MUSHROOMS

Before adding the cream, toss in *¾ pound quartered mushrooms*. Sauté briefly, then add the cream.

BRAISED VEAL CHOPS WITH VEGETABLES

Parboil *16 small white onions*. When the chops are brown, remove and set aside. Pat the onions dry and brown lightly in the pan. Return the chops, omitting the cream and adding instead *½ cup chicken broth*. Cover and cook until tender, adding up to *¼ cup chicken broth* if needed. Serve, sprinkled with *1 tablespoon grated lemon peel*. Or, instead of the onions, cut *1 fennel bulb* into julienne strips (these will not require parboiling). Toss into the pan and cook gently.

BRAISED VEAL CHOPS WITH ARTICHOKE HEARTS

Parboil *1 package frozen artichoke hearts*, drain, and pat dry. Add to the pan along with *¾ cup diced carrots* and *½ cup chopped scallions* and cook for 1 minute. Omit the cream and add *½ cup chicken broth* and *2 tablespoons butter*. Cover and cook until tender, adding up to *¼ cup chicken broth* if needed. Serve, sprinkled with *¼ cup chopped parsley*.

(SERVES FOUR)   **BREADED VEAL CUTLETS**

3 tablespoons flour
2 eggs, lightly beaten
1½ cups bread crumbs
1 teaspoon salt
½ teaspoon freshly ground
   pepper

1 pound veal cutlets (about
   ¼–⅓ inch thick), pounded
1½ tablespoons butter
1½ tablespoons oil
1 tablespoon finely chopped
   parsley
1 lemon, in 4 wedges

Put the flour, eggs, and crumbs in three separate shallow dishes. Mix
the salt and pepper into the crumbs. Dip the cutlets one at a time into
the flour, shaking off any excess, then into the beaten eggs, letting any
excess drip off. Then drag the cutlet lightly through the seasoned
crumbs. Set aside for 15 minutes so that the coating can dry. Heat the
butter and oil in a skillet, and fry the cutlets over medium heat, 3–5
minutes on each side, or until brown and cooked through. Sprinkle
with parsley and serve with lemon wedges.

(SERVES THREE)   **SAUTÉED VEAL CUTLETS**

A cutlet is a ½-inch cut from the leg. When it is neatly trimmed of bone,
gristle, and fat and pounded very thin, it is also called a scallop.

1 pound veal cutlets, trimmed
   and pounded thin
Salt
Freshly ground pepper
2 tablespoons butter

2 tablespoons oil
¼ cup dry white wine
1 teaspoon finely chopped
   parsley

Sprinkle the cutlets with salt and pepper. Heat the butter and oil in a
skillet, add the cutlets, and cook over medium heat for 1–2 minutes on
each side. Remove the veal to a warm platter. Pour in the wine and
turn the heat up high, letting the wine and pan juices bubble for another 1–2 minutes. Pour over the veal, sprinkle with the parsley, and
serve.

VEAL CUTLETS WITH MUSHROOMS

Sauté ½ pound sliced mushrooms in 4 tablespoons butter for 3–4 minutes.
Sprinkle with salt and set aside. Follow the recipe for Sautéed Veal
Cutlets, omitting the wine, and serve the veal with the mushrooms.

VEAL CUTLETS AUX FINES HERBES

Omit the wine and sprinkle *3 tablespoons minced parsley*, *1 tablespoon minced chives*, and the *juice of 1 lemon* over the veal just before serving.

VEAL CUTLETS PICCATA

After removing the veal, add *4 tablespoons fresh lemon juice*, *½ lemon* cut into very thin slices, and *1 tablespoon capers* to the pan with the wine.

VEAL PAPRIKA   (SERVES SIX)

A good-quality Hungarian paprika makes all the difference in this dish.

2 pounds veal cutlets, trimmed and pounded thin	2 onions, sliced thin
	1½ tablespoons paprika
	1½ cups chicken broth
2 tablespoons butter	1 cup sour cream
1 tablespoon oil	Salt

Cut the veal into 2-inch squares. Melt the butter and oil in a skillet, add the onions, and cook, stirring, until golden brown. Push the onions to the side of the pan, add the veal, and brown lightly. Stir in the paprika and then the chicken broth. Simmer, uncovered, until most of the liquid has evaporated. Before serving, turn down the heat, whisk in the sour cream, add salt to taste, and heat through without boiling.

SCALOPPINE OF VEAL MARSALA   (SERVES THREE)

1 pound veal cutlets, trimmed and pounded thin	1 tablespoon oil
	1 clove garlic, peeled
⅓ cup freshly grated Parmesan cheese	¼ cup beef broth
	¼ cup Marsala wine
3 tablespoons butter	

Cut the veal into 2-inch pieces. Dip in Parmesan cheese to coat both sides. Melt the butter and oil in a skillet, add the garlic and the veal, and cook until lightly browned on both sides. Discard the garlic. Remove the veal to a warm platter. Turn the heat up and add the beef broth, stirring and scraping the bits of meat clinging to the bottom of the skillet. Cook 1 minute over high heat, then add the wine and cook 1 minute more. Pour over the veal and serve.

(SERVES FOUR)   **VEAL BIRDS**

Thin slices of boneless veal wrapped around succulent stuffing. Nice with hot tart applesauce.

1½ pounds veal cutlets, trimmed	1 tablespoon oil
	Salt
1½ cups Celery Stuffing (p. 403)	Freshly ground pepper
	1½ cups chicken broth
2 tablespoons butter	½ cup heavy cream

Preheat the oven to 350°F. Pound the veal with a meat mallet or the edge of a saucer until ¼ inch thick. Cut into 4 × 6-inch pieces. Spread some stuffing down the middle of each piece and roll lengthwise. Tie securely with string. Melt the butter and oil in a pan and brown the veal birds on all sides, a few at a time. Transfer to a casserole, sprinkle with salt and pepper, and pour the chicken broth over them. Cover and cook in the oven 45 minutes. Stir in the cream and cook, uncovered, for 20–30 minutes more.

(SERVES SIX)   **BLANQUETTE OF VEAL**

Serve gently sautéed spring vegetables and fried bread triangles or rice with this creamy veal stew.

2 pounds stewing veal, in 2-inch pieces	3 tablespoons butter
	3 tablespoons flour
6 small white onions	3 egg yolks
1 medium onion, stuck with 2 cloves	Juice of 1 lemon
	¼ teaspoon nutmeg
2 carrots, in thick slices	Salt
1 bay leaf	Freshly ground pepper
2 teaspoons thyme, crumbled	

Put the veal into a pot and cover with cold water. Add the small onions, onion with cloves, carrots, bay leaf, and thyme. Bring to a boil, then simmer, covered, for 1½ hours or until tender. Skim off the scum as it rises. Remove the meat and keep warm. Strain the broth. Melt the butter in a saucepan. Stir in the flour and cook over medium heat for a few minutes, then slowly add 3 cups of the veal broth. Stir constantly over medium heat until well blended, smooth, and thick. In a separate bowl, beat the egg yolks with the lemon juice. Pour a spoonful or two of the hot sauce into the egg mixture, then remove the sauce from the heat and briskly stir the egg mixture into the remaining sauce. Add nutmeg, salt and pepper to taste, put the meat in a serving dish, and pour the sauce over it.

OSSOBUCO (SERVES FOUR)

This braised veal shank dish is Italian in origin. It is finished off with a lively mixture of parsley, garlic, and lemon rind called gremolata. Serve with noodles, steamed rice, or risotto (p. 441).

4 tablespoons butter	Salt
¼ cup olive oil	Freshly ground pepper
4 large onions (about 2 pounds), peeled and sliced	3 bay leaves
	3 cloves garlic, minced
4 pounds veal shank, in 1½-inch slices, with bone and marrow	3 whole cloves
	3 cups chicken broth, approximately
½ cup flour, approximately	

Gremolata

Rind of 1 lemon, minced	¼ cup minced parsley
2 teaspoons minced garlic	

In a large skillet, heat 2 tablespoons of the butter and 1 tablespoon of the olive oil. Add the onions and cook over medium-high heat 10–12 minutes, or until very soft and lightly colored. Stir frequently to keep from sticking. Remove onions to a roasting pan or large casserole and set aside. Preheat the oven to 400°F. Flour the veal shanks and season with salt and pepper. Put remaining butter and oil in the skillet over medium-high heat and sauté the meat until golden brown on both sides. Arrange the meat in a single layer over the onions. Add the bay leaves, garlic, cloves, and 2½ cups of the chicken broth. Mix gently with a spoon and taste for salt and pepper. Cover with a lid or aluminum foil and bake for about 1½ hours. At the end of 1 hour remove the cover and test for moisture and doneness. Add the remaining ½ cup of chicken broth if most of the liquid has evaporated, re-cover, and continue to cook for the remaining half-hour. In a small bowl mix together the lemon rind, minced garlic and parsley. Serve the Ossobuco with some of the onion-gravy mixture and sprinkle with a spoonful of gremolata.

(SERVES SIX)   **VEAL LOAF**

This makes a lighter loaf than the beef version. Expensive milk-fed veal is not necessary for this dish.

2 pounds ground veal
½ pound ground pork
½ green pepper, chopped fine
1 onion, chopped fine
1 tablespoon lemon juice
1 teaspoon salt

½ cup cracker crumbs
1 egg
½ cup milk
2 teaspoons Worcestershire
  sauce

Preheat the oven to 325°F. Combine all ingredients and mix until well blended, using a large spoon or your hands. Press into a loaf pan. Cover with foil and bake for 40 minutes. Uncover and bake 20 minutes more to brown the top.

(SERVES SIX)   **PRESSED VEAL**

A jellied veal loaf with the subtle flavor of tarragon. Serve it cold, sliced thin, with Horseradish Cream (p. 390).

1½ pounds veal, in cubes
1 stalk celery with leaves,
  chopped
1 small onion, stuck with 1
  clove
Salt
Freshly ground pepper

½ teaspoon tarragon,
  crumbled
1 envelope gelatin
3 tablespoons cider vinegar
1 tablespoon finely chopped
  parsley

Put the veal, celery, onion with clove, salt, and pepper in a pot. Cover with 3 cups water, bring to a boil, and simmer for 30 minutes, or until very tender. Strain and reserve 2 cups of the broth. Put the veal and tarragon through a meat grinder or food processor. Soften the gelatin in ¼ cup cold water. Stir the gelatin into the hot liquid until dissolved and clear, then add the vinegar and parsley. Blend in the veal and tarragon. Add salt and pepper to taste, remembering that when the loaf is chilled the flavors will be less intense. Pour into a mold and chill until firm, at least 6 hours. Unmold before serving.

VITELLO TONNATO * (SERVES SIX)

This Italian favorite (it means "veal tuna") makes a marvelous summer dish, lovely with an accompanying platter of fresh tomatoes, cucumbers, and blanched green beans. You can substitute an equal amount of skinned cooked turkey breast for the veal.

3-pound boneless veal roast
4 cups chicken broth
2 cups water
2 cups white wine
2 onions, quartered
2 carrots, in 1-inch pieces

3 stalks celery, in 1-inch
    pieces
2 bay leaves
10 whole peppercorns
6 sprigs parsley

Sauce

½ cup olive oil
3½-ounce can tuna, drained
1 egg yolk
2 tablespoons lemon juice
Salt and freshly ground
    pepper to taste
2 flat anchovy fillets, drained
    and soaked in water for 10
    minutes, then cut in small
    pieces

4 tablespoons heavy cream
2 tablespoons capers,
    thoroughly washed and
    drained
2 sprigs parsley, for garnish

Blanch the veal by putting it in a large pot, covering with water, and boiling over high heat for 1 minute. Pour off water and rinse meat of any scum. Return the veal to the pot and add the chicken broth, water, wine, onions, carrots, celery, bay leaves, peppercorns, and parsley. Add more stock or water if necessary to cover veal. Bring to a boil, then simmer for about 1½ hours, or until veal is tender. Let the veal cool in the broth, then strain and set aside. To make the sauce, place the olive oil, tuna, egg yolk, lemon juice, salt and pepper, and anchovies in a blender or bowl of a food processor and blend about 10 seconds. Transfer to a small bowl and slowly stir in the heavy cream. Stir in the capers. To assemble the dish, thinly slice the veal and arrange on a serving dish. Spoon the sauce over and chill at least 2 hours. Garnish with parsley.

(SERVES FOUR) ## QUICK VITELLO TONNATO

⅔ cup mayonnaise
½ cup drained tuna
2 anchovy fillets
2 teaspoons capers

Salt to taste
Freshly ground pepper
8–10 slices cooked veal

Spin the mayonnaise, tuna, anchovies, and all but 8 capers in the blender or food processor or beat well together until blended. Salt and pepper to taste. Spread over the veal and chill for several hours. Dot the remaining capers on top.

DISHES USING LEFTOVER VEAL

(SERVES FOUR) ## MINCED VEAL IN CREAM WITH MUSHROOMS

Serve on toast or nestled in rice.

2 tablespoons butter
1 cup minced mushrooms
1 tablespoon minced scallions
   or shallots
2 cups minced cooked veal

1 cup heavy cream
Salt
Freshly ground pepper
½ teaspoon tarragon

Melt the butter in a skillet and add the mushrooms and scallions or shallots. Cook slowly for 5 minutes. Add the veal, cream, salt and pepper to taste, and tarragon, and cook over medium heat, stirring often, for about 5 minutes, until the cream has reduced and thickened somewhat.

Other Suggestions for Using Leftover Veal

Cooked veal could be used perfectly well to make the Blanquette in this chapter, provided you simmer the stew for only about a half-hour and substitute chicken broth if you don't have any veal stock. Try leftover veal instead of lamb in Shepherd's Pie and Lamb Curry. In recipes in the Poultry chapter, veal could be used in place of chicken in Creamed Chicken, or any of the variations, like Creamed Chicken with Vegetables, as well as in Chicken à la King, Chicken Tetrazzini, Chicken Divan, and Chicken Croquettes. Cold veal is good sliced in a sandwich. Look at recipes for stuffed vegetables and crêpes for ways of using ground veal as a filling.

LAMB

About Lamb

Lamb is the meat from sheep that were less than a year old when they were slaughtered. Older sheep give us mutton, long popular in England, but rarely seen in American markets.

The choicest, most tender lamb, called "spring lamb," was once available only between March and September, making it a traditional Easter dish. Its mild flavor came from the kind of feed available in the spring. Now that sheep are imported from all over the world, we can get Australian or New Zealand "spring lamb" even in January. A spring leg of lamb will weigh between 4 and 7 pounds, while a winter leg may weigh as much as 9 pounds and is generally considered less desirable since it is older. When choosing lamb, look for bright pink flesh, pink bones, and white fat. Older lamb has dark-red meat and bones.

A leg of lamb makes a meaty, tender roast. You can buy half the leg for a small family, but it is most economical to buy the whole joint, and there are many good ways to use leftover lamb. Choicer, but far less economical, is the rack, consisting of a series of rib chops, and the crown roast, made by tying two racks back to back in a circle. Other cuts, such as the shank, breast, and flank, are flavorful but not so tender and require gentle, moist braising. Chops cut from the rib or loin are broiled or pan-fried.

Europeans eat only very pink lamb and think it a desecration to cook it beyond an internal temperature of 140°F. Pink lamb is very tender and gives off delicious juices. As with roast beef, the degree to which it is cooked is ultimately a matter of personal preference. Lamb will be medium-rare when the meat thermometer registers 145°F, and will be well done at 165°. Allow the meat to set, lightly covered with a towel or foil, for 15 minutes before you carve and serve it.

Use the meat thermometer to test the doneness of lamb.
RARE 140°F   MEDIUM-RARE 145°F   MEDIUM 155°F
WELL DONE 165°F

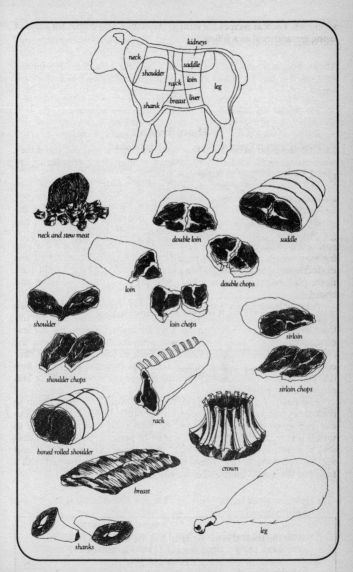

neck and stew meat

double loin

saddle

loin

double chops

shoulder

loin chops

sirloin

shoulder chops

sirloin chops

boned rolled shoulder

rack

crown

breast

shanks

leg

ROAST LEG OF LAMB

(SERVES SIX)

Allow about a pound per person when cooking a leg of lamb with the bone in; if it has no bone, a 4-pound roast will serve twice as many people.

5–6-pound leg of lamb
Oil
Salt
Freshly ground pepper

½ teaspoon rosemary,
    crumbled
2 cloves garlic, in slivers
    (optional)

Preheat the oven to 350°F. Have the meat at room temperature. Place the lamb, fat side up, in a shallow open roasting pan. Rub with oil, salt, pepper, and the rosemary. If using garlic (and it's delicious with lamb) make 8–10 slits in the meat with the point of a paring knife, and tuck a sliver of garlic into each slit. Roast for about 1½ hours, or until meat is done the way you like it (see chart, p. 252). Let the roast rest for 5–10 minutes, then carve at the table as illustrated.

CROWN ROAST OF LAMB

(SERVES SIX)

A crown roast of lamb is an expensive delicacy: two racks of lamb set upright and tied back to back to form a circle. Have the butcher prepare it and ask him to crack the chine bone between each rib so it will be easy to carve. Because there are only small morsels of meat on each rib, it's a good idea to stuff the inside of the crown. If you want to be very elegant, serve with paper frills, but add only at the last; when cooking, protect the ends of the rib bones by wrapping them in foil.

1 crown roast of lamb,
    approximately 12 ribs
Oil
½ teaspoon rosemary,
    crumbled
2 cloves garlic, in slivers
    (optional)

1 recipe Bread Stuffing (p. 400)
¼ pound mushrooms,
    chopped, or ¼ pound
    lightly browned sausage
    meat

Preheat the oven to 350°F. Have the roast at room temperature. Place it in a shallow open roasting pan. Rub all over with oil and then with the rosemary. If using garlic, make 8–10 slits in the meat with the point of a paring knife, and tuck a sliver of garlic into each slit. Prepare the stuffing, adding the mushrooms or sausage meat. Fill the cavity of the roast with stuffing. Roast for 1¼ hours, or until meat is done the way you like it (see chart, p. 252). Let rest 5–10 minutes before carving.

(SERVES FOUR)   **PAN-BROILED CHOPS**

Pan broiling works best on chops that are less than 1 inch thick. Serve two to each hungry eater.

  8 thin loin or rib lamb chops   Freshly ground pepper
  Salt

Trim excess fat from the chops, and rub a hissing-hot heavy skillet with a piece of the fat. Brown the chops quickly on each side, reduce the heat, and finish cooking, allowing 3 minutes on each side for 1-inch chops. Pour off any excess fat during the cooking. Salt and pepper to taste.

(SERVES SIX)   **BROILED LAMB CHOPS**

A loin or rib chop cut 1½ inches thick makes an ample serving for one moderate eater.

  6 loin or rib lamb chops   Freshly ground pepper
  Salt

Trim excess fat from the chops. Preheat the broiler and place the meat 3 inches below the heat. Broil 1-inch chops 3–4 minutes on each side for medium-rare; broil 1½-inch chops 5–6 minutes each side. Salt and pepper to taste.

BROILED CHOPS WITH BACON

Follow the recipe for Broiled Lamb Chops, but have the butcher bone the chops and wrap each one in *1 strip bacon*.

MIXED GRILL   (SERVES FOUR)

Potatoes fried with lots of onion and parsley go well with this dish.

3 tablespoons vegetable oil
4 lamb kidneys, cut in half
   lengthwise, cleaned, and
   trimmed (see p. 291)
4 tomatoes, cut in half
8 large mushrooms, stems
   removed

Salt
Freshly ground pepper
4 lamb chops, about 1 inch
   thick
8 breakfast sausages,
   parboiled 3 minutes

Preheat the broiler. Rub oil over the kidneys, tomatoes, and mushrooms. Sprinkle salt and pepper over the chops, kidneys, tomatoes, and mushrooms. Place the chops and kidneys on a rack 3 inches beneath the broiler, cook for 3 minutes, then turn them over. Add the sausages, tomatoes (cut side up), and mushrooms (top side up) to the rack. Broil 3–4 minutes more, or until the chops are browned. The tomatoes and mushrooms should just be heated through.

SHISH KEBAB   (SERVES EIGHT)

Start your marinade early in the day or the night before. Shish kebab is at its best if it can be cooked over coals, but if that isn't possible, broiling works very well. You cannot, incidentally, use cheaper cuts because they'll be too tough cooked this way. Be sure to push the cubes of meat together on the skewer, so they do not dry out while they cook. Try separate skewers of vegetables—the cooking time will be different from the lamb (see page 366). Serve with rice.

1 leg of lamb, boned, in 1½-
   inch cubes
2 medium onions, sliced
2 teaspoons salt
½ teaspoon freshly ground
   pepper

½ cup dry sherry
1 tablespoon vegetable oil
⅛ teaspoon oregano,
   crumbled

Trim most of the fat from the meat. Mix remaining ingredients in a small bowl and blend well. Spread the meat in a shallow dish and cover with the marinade, tossing so meat is well coated. Cover the dish with foil and refrigerate several hours or overnight. When you are ready to cook, place the lamb on skewers, pushing the pieces snugly together. Cook over charcoal or place on a rack 3 inches under the broiler and broil 4–5 minutes on each side. Serve either on the skewers or pushed off on a plate.

VARIATION ON SHISH KEBAB

See Outdoor Cooking chapter, p. 366.

(SERVES SIX) ## FILLETS OF LAMB

Mix your marinade early in the day or the night before you make these tender lamb fillets.

2 pounds lamb steak cut from
    the leg, in strips ¾ inch
    thick and about 2½ inches
    long
¼ cup olive oil
3 tablespoons vinegar

½ teaspoon salt
½ onion, chopped fine
1 tablespoon finely chopped
    parsley
2 tablespoons butter

Pound the strips of lamb with the edge of a saucer to break down the fibers. Mix 3 tablespoons of the olive oil, vinegar, salt, onion, and parsley together and pour over the lamb strips in a shallow dish. Cover with aluminum foil and refrigerate at least 6 hours, turning the meat once or twice in the marinade. When you are ready to cook, remove the lamb from the marinade and pat dry with paper towels. Heat the butter and remaining tablespoon of oil in a skillet. When the foam begins to subside, add the lamb and cook quickly over high heat, about 2 minutes on each side.

(SERVES SIX) ## ROAST LEG OF LAMB WITH ORZO

Orzo, a tiny rice-shaped pasta, absorbs the good juices and rounds out the flavors.

Juice of 1 lemon
3 cloves garlic, sliced
½ teaspoon dry mint
½ teaspoon (or more) dried
    basil
Pinch of oregano
Salt and freshly ground
    pepper to taste

5-pound leg of lamb or
    shoulder of lamb
2 onions, chopped
3-pound can plum tomatoes
7 cups chicken broth
2 cups orzo
¼ cup grated Parmesan cheese

Preheat the oven to 450°F. Combine the lemon juice, garlic, mint, basil, oregano, and salt and pepper in a small bowl and mix well. Rub the lamb all over with the mixture. Place in a roasting pan, adding the onion around the lamb, and roast for 20 minutes. Spread the tomatoes around the meat and stir in 2 cups of the chicken broth. Return to the oven, lower the heat to 350°F, and roast for 40 minutes more. Remove the pan from the oven and lightly cover with a towel to keep warm.

Bring 4 cups of the chicken broth to a boil and slowly add the orzo. Stir, lower heat, and cover. Simmer until tender, about 8 to 10 minutes. Remove the lamb from the roasting pan to a warm platter, then scrape to deglaze the pan, adding the remaining 1 cup of broth. Stir in the orzo, place the lamb back in the pan, and cook 15 minutes more in a 350°F oven.

Stir the pan juices and the orzo together again to mix well. Serve the lamb on a warm platter surrounded with the orzo. Sprinkle the Parmesan cheese over the orzo.

BRAISED BREAST OF LAMB   (SERVES FOUR)

A thrifty family dish, good with fresh green beans and corn bread. There is excess fat on lamb breast, so trim away all you can before you cook it, and remove the fat when the dish is finished.

1 tablespoon shortening	½ onion, stuck with 3 cloves
3 pounds lamb breast	½ cup cubed turnip
1 tablespoon thyme, crumbled	½ teaspoon freshly ground pepper
1 carrot, chopped	Salt

Melt the shortening in a heavy pot with a cover or a Dutch oven. Add the lamb breast and brown lightly on both sides. Sprinkle with thyme and pour 2 cups of boiling water over it. Add carrot, onion stuck with cloves, turnip, and pepper. Lower the heat, cover, and simmer for 1½ hours. Salt to taste. Remove as much fat as possible with a spoon. Cut the ribs apart before serving.

GRILLED BUTTERFLIED LEG OF LAMB   (SERVES SIX)

A tender lamb steak that may be cooked over coals or in the broiler, offering both a crisp well-done exterior and succulent rare insides. Start to marinate in the afternoon.

4 tablespoons olive oil
2 cloves garlic, minced
1 teaspoon rosemary,
    crumbled
1 teaspoon salt

1 teaspoon freshly ground
    pepper
5-pound leg of lamb, split
    open and bone removed

Put the olive oil in a small bowl and add the garlic, rosemary, salt, and pepper. Mix well, and rub mixture all over the lamb. Put the meat on a broiler rack and cover it lightly with wax paper. Let stand for 2–3 hours before broiling. Preheat the broiler. Remove the wax paper and place the lamb on the rack 4 inches below the broiler. Cook 15 minutes on each side. Test by cutting a small slit in the thickest part. It should be slightly pink inside and nicely browned on top. Slice across the grain on the diagonal, and serve with natural juices or spicy Dried Fruit Sauce (p. 394).

(SERVES SIX) ## FRICASSEE OF LAMB

A succulent dish to serve with parslied boiled potatoes. For garlic lovers, add lots of garlic.

2 pounds boneless shoulder
    of lamb, in 1½-inch cubes
2 tablespoons flour
2 tablespoons vegetable
    shortening
2 cups boiling tomato juice
1 medium onion, chopped
6–8 cloves garlic, minced
    (optional)

2 carrots, chopped
4 parsley sprigs, chopped
1 bay leaf
4 cloves
Salt
Freshly ground pepper

Trim off most of the lamb fat. Dust the lamb cubes with the flour. Melt the shortening in a heavy pot with a cover or a Dutch oven. Brown the lamb pieces on all sides. Pour the boiling tomato juice over the meat, then add the onion, optional garlic, carrots, parsley, bay leaf, and cloves. Lower the heat, cover, and simmer for 1½–2 hours, or until lamb is very tender. Salt and pepper to taste. Remove the bay leaf and serve.

IRISH STEW   (SERVES SIX)

The simple goodness of lamb and roast vegetables tasting of themselves. Try that fine old-fashioned twosome—Irish Stew and Dumplings (p. 329, for Feather Dumplings).

2 pounds boneless shoulder of lamb, in 1½-inch cubes	1 cup cubed white turnip
2 tablespoons shortening	1 potato, peeled and cubed
2 cups boiling water	1 onion, sliced
1 cup ½-inch carrot slices	Salt and freshly ground pepper

Take care to trim off most of the lamb fat. Melt the shortening in a heavy pot, add the lamb cubes, and brown them well on all sides. Stand back while you pour the boiling water over the lamb—it will sizzle and sputter. Cover and simmer for 1 hour. Add the carrot, turnip, potato, onion, and salt and pepper to taste. Cover and simmer 30 minutes more. Taste, correct for seasoning, and serve.

SAVORY LAMB PATTIES   (SERVES FOUR)

1 pound lean ground lamb	½ teaspoon rosemary, crumbled
1 cup freshly made dry bread crumbs	2 tomatoes, peeled, seeded, and chopped fine
¾ teaspoon salt	1 egg, slightly beaten
¼ teaspoon freshly ground pepper	2 tablespoons shortening
½ cup finely chopped celery	
2 teaspoons Worcestershire sauce	

Combine the lamb, bread crumbs, salt, pepper, celery, Worcestershire sauce, rosemary, tomatoes, and egg in a large bowl. Mix together and shape into six patties. Melt the shortening in a skillet and fry the patties over medium heat for 5 minutes on each side or until brown and cooked as desired.

BRAISED LAMB SHANKS   (SERVES FOUR)

The meat on lamb shanks is particularly succulent. You will need one per person because there is not actually much meat on them.

4 lamb shanks
2 fat cloves garlic, each in 8
   slivers
2 tablespoons flour
3 tablespoons shortening
1 bay leaf
1 tablespoon grated lemon
   rind

⅓ cup lemon juice
¼ cup water
Salt and freshly ground
   pepper
4 carrots, in ½-inch pieces
8 small onions, peeled

Cut four slits in the flesh of each lamb shank; insert a sliver of garlic in each slit. Lightly dust the shanks with flour. Heat the shortening in a Dutch oven or a heavy pot with a lid. Put the shanks in and brown on all sides. Remove all but 1 tablespoon fat. Add the bay leaf, lemon rind, lemon juice, and water, and sprinkle salt and pepper to taste over all. Lower the heat, cover, and simmer for 1½–2 hours, depending on the tenderness of the shanks. Add the carrots and onions for the last 40 minutes of cooking. Remove shanks and vegetables to a platter and keep warm. Serve with the pot juices or make a gravy following the recipe for Brown Gravy (p. 385).

(SERVES SIX) **LAMB CURRY**

This dish produces a flavorful curry sauce; serve it with plenty of hot rice.

4 tablespoons butter or
   vegetable oil
2 pounds boned lean lamb, in
   1½-inch cubes
½ cup flour
2 onions, chopped
2 cloves garlic, minced
2 chili peppers, seeded and
   chopped fine (use jalapeño
   or serrano chilies)

2 apples, unpeeled and
   chopped fine
2 cups chicken broth
1–2 tablespoons curry
   powder, or more to taste
1 teaspoon salt
1 teaspoon grated fresh
   ginger
½ cup coconut milk (see p. 12)

Melt the butter in a large skillet. Dust the lamb cubes with the flour. Sauté the lamb over medium-high heat until lightly golden. Add the onions and garlic, and continue to cook over moderate heat until the onions are soft. Add the chili peppers, apples, and chicken broth, and simmer, covered, for about 40 minutes. Add the curry powder, salt, ginger, and coconut milk, and continue to cook for another 10 minutes, or until the lamb is tender.

DISHES USING LEFTOVER LAMB

SHEPHERD'S PIE (SERVES SIX)

Not really a pie, but a fragrant dish of lamb (or beef), onion, rosemary, and garlic, under a "crust" of browned mashed potatoes. Use any kind of cooked lamb.

3 cups chopped cooked lamb or beef	2 tablespoons flour
1 large clove garlic, peeled	¾ cup beef broth
1 medium onion	Salt
1 teaspoon rosemary or savory, crumbled	Freshly ground pepper
4 tablespoons butter	4 medium potatoes, cooked and mashed (about 3 cups)

Preheat the oven to 375°F. Combine the lamb or beef, garlic, onion, and rosemary or savory. Put through a meat grinder twice, or chop until fine in a food processor. Melt the butter in a skillet and stir in the flour. Cook for a few minutes until smooth and blended. Slowly add the beef broth. Stir and cook until the gravy is thickened, cooking at least 5 minutes to get rid of the raw flour taste. Add the meat mixture, stir to blend, and add salt and pepper to taste. Spoon into a 1½-quart casserole or deep pie dish. Spread the mashed potatoes on top and cover evenly to the edge of the casserole. Make a crisscross design with a fork. Bake for 35–40 minutes, or until the meat is bubbling hot and the potatoes are browned.

MOUSSAKA (SERVES SIX TO EIGHT)

Pronounced "*moo*-sah-kah," this is a traditional Greek dish. Make it with either uncooked or leftover lamb. For best results when frying eggplant, see p. 568.

6 tablespoons vegetable oil	1 cup tomato sauce
¼ cup chopped onion	3 eggplants
1 pound fresh or cooked ground lamb	3 eggs, lightly beaten
½ teaspoon allspice	2 cups light cream
½ teaspoon salt	2 tablespoons minced parsley
½ teaspoon freshly ground pepper	1 cup freshly made dry bread crumbs
	4 tablespoons butter, melted

Preheat the oven to 350°F. Grease a 2½-quart baking dish. Heat 2 tablespoons of the oil in a skillet, add the onion, and cook, stirring, until soft. If using fresh lamb, add to the onion and cook, stirring, until most of the pinkness disappears. Add the allspice, salt, pepper, and tomato sauce to the skillet, along with the cooked lamb if you are using it. Cover and simmer for 30 minutes. Heat the remaining 4 tablespoons of oil in a skillet. Cut the eggplants into ¼-inch slices. Have the oil very hot, and quickly brown each side of the eggplant slices, then pat them dry of excess oil. Mix the eggs, cream, parsley, and ½ cup of the bread crumbs. Put a layer of eggplant on the bottom of the casserole and spread a layer of the lamb mixture over it. Continue layering, ending with eggplant on top. Pour the egg mixture over all, sprinkle the remaining ½ cup of crumbs on top, and drizzle the butter over. Bake 40 minutes, or until the egg custard is set.

(SERVES FOUR) **QUICK LAMB CURRY**

This is a quick curry dish.

2 onions, coarsely chopped	1 tablespoon curry powder
2 tablespoons butter	2 tart apples, peeled and cut
2 cups cooked lamb in	in wedges
medium pieces	1 tablespoon raisins
2 tablespoons flour	Salt and freshly ground
1¼ cups hot beef or chicken	pepper
broth	

In a large heavy skillet, sauté the onions in the butter slowly until they are translucent. Add the lamb and when warm through sprinkle on the flour. Stir into the meat and onions to blend thoroughly, then add the hot broth, stirring constantly until thick. Add the curry, apples, raisins, and salt and pepper to taste, and simmer, covered, for 5 to 10 minutes, until the apples are just cooked but still hold their shape. Serve with rice.

(SERVES FOUR) **STUFFED EGGPLANT**

Eggplant and lamb always seem to marry well. This is a good dish to make when you have some leftover roast lamb or stew with some juice; if the lamb is dry and no gravy or juice is left, use canned tomatoes to moisten the filling.

1 medium or 2 small eggplants	1½ cups cooked rice
Salt	¾ cup lamb gravy, drippings,
4–5 tablespoons olive oil	or stew liquid, or 1 cup
1 onion, chopped	canned tomatoes,
1 garlic clove, minced (optional)	chopped, with juice
2 cups minced or ground cooked lamb	Freshly ground pepper
	¼ cup chopped parsley

Cut the eggplant(s) in half lengthwise. Leaving the shell intact, about ¼ inch thick, carefully scoop out the flesh and chop into rough pieces. Place in colander, sprinkle liberally with salt, and drain for at least 30 minutes. Salt the empty shells and turn upside down to drain. Heat the oven to 350°F. Rinse off the eggplant pieces, pat dry, and sauté in hot olive oil in a large skillet until browned on all sides. Add the onion and a little more oil if necessary and cook until almost soft. Add the garlic (if you wish), the lamb, rice, and lamb sauce or tomatoes. Mix well, cook a few minutes, add pepper and salt to taste, then pile into the drained eggplant shells. Bake 50 minutes. Sprinkle parsley over the tops before serving.

Other Suggestions for Using Leftover Lamb

Cooked lamb could be used in the Fricassee of Lamb in this chapter, but cook the stew only ½ hour, and also in the Savory Lamb Patties. Lamb croquettes are particularly delicious—just follow the recipe for Chicken Croquettes and add a touch of dill. Use lamb instead of veal in Blanquette of Veal. Leftover lamb makes a good sandwich, particularly nice when stuffed into pita bread—and try Lentils and Lamb, a fine main-course bean dish.

PORK

About Pork

Fresh pork is flavorful, high in protein and in vitamin B_1. Unfortunately, it is too often served tasteless and dry, overcooked in an effort to make it safe to eat. It is true that pork should be cooked enough to destroy any trichinae, but an internal temperature of 140°F is considered safe, and you can be absolutely sure when a thermometer registers 160°F, well before the pork loses its wonderful succulence.

Nearly every part of the pig is edible and delicious, from the costly tenderloin to the lowly pig's feet. In general, allow ⅓ pound of meat for a serving. Look for light pink to white meat, pink bones, and white fat. The graining in pork is not fat, but muscle, which is why it is sometimes dry. Contrary to our preconceptions, some cuts of pork, such as the tenderloin, are so lacking in fat that they need some added fat in cooking.

For roasting, choose the loin, shoulder, or leg, or, for a very special occasion, a whole suckling pig. Chops, too, are cut from the loin, rib, and shoulder; although they are tender, they dry out quickly when they are broiled, and are usually baked or braised instead. Wonderful meals can be made from the spareribs, the feet, or salt pork. Cured in salt or in brine, salt pork is used to add flavor to many complicated stews.

Use the meat thermometer to test the doneness of pork.
It should read 160°F.

(SERVES FOUR)   **ROAST PORK**

Ask the butcher to cut through the chine bone, and the roast will be easy to carve. If you want to do a 5- to 7-pound roast, it will need three or more hours of cooking time. Serve with hot applesauce and horse-radish.

4-pound loin of pork	Freshly ground pepper
Salt	½ teaspoon thyme, crumbled

Preheat the oven to 350°F. Put the roast, fat side up, on a rack in a shallow open pan. Rub lightly with salt, pepper, and thyme. Roast 1¾–2 hours, or until the internal temperature is 160°F. Remove from the oven and let rest for 15 minutes for easy carving.

(SERVES SIX)   **BROILED PORK TENDERLOIN**

2 pork tenderloins, about ¾ pound each	1 tablespoon mixed dried herbs, such as thyme,
2 tablespoons olive or vegetable oil	sage, rosemary, and/or oregano, crumbled

Preheat the broiler. Brush the meat on all sides with oil. Then roll each in half of the crushed dried herbs. Place the meat on a rack over a shal-

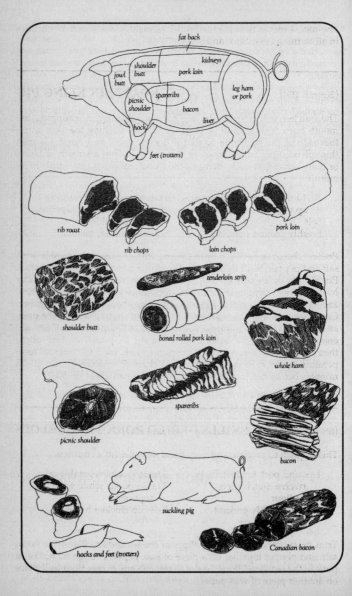

rib roast

rib chops

loin chops

pork loin

shoulder butt

tenderloin strip

boned rolled pork loin

whole ham

picnic shoulder

spareribs

bacon

suckling pig

hocks and feet (trotters)

Canadian bacon

low pan, 4 inches beneath the broiler element. Cook about 12 minutes in all, turning once. Slice and serve.

(SERVES TEN)   **ROAST SUCKLING PIG**

The butcher will prepare the pig for you, cleaning it, propping the mouth open with a small piece of wood, and slashing the skin on either side of the backbone so that it doesn't swell and burst. Garnish this splendid pig with parsley or watercress, or put a wreath of laurel or holly around its neck. Remove the wood and put a rosy apple in its mouth.

10–15-pound suckling pig	Two recipes Bread Stuffing
½ cup vegetable oil	(p. 400), plus 2 teaspoons
Salt	sage, crumbled
Freshly ground pepper	¼ pound butter, melted

Preheat the oven to 350°F. Rub the pig with the oil and sprinkle with salt and pepper. Stuff lightly with the stuffing and sew the cavity shut. Put the pig on its side on a rack in a shallow roasting pan or, if your oven is large enough, lay it on its stomach, with its front knees bent and tied to the rack and its hind legs stretched backward, tied together. Cover the ears and tail with foil so they don't burn. Place in the oven and baste every 20 minutes with the melted butter until there are enough pan juices for basting. Roast about 2½ hours, basting often, then remove foil. Roast about 30 minutes more, until the internal temperature is 165°F. Remove and let rest at room temperature for 10–15 minutes before carving. Make sauce from the pan juices (p. 383).

(SERVES FOUR)   **SKILLET-FRIED PORK TENDERLOIN**

This is quick to prepare and very good served with a chutney.

1-pound pork tenderloin, in	3 tablespoons vegetable oil
twelve ¾-inch slices	2 tablespoons white wine
½ cup flour	(optional)
Salt and freshly ground	⅓–½ cup chicken broth
pepper to taste	

Trim most of the fat from the edges of the tenderloin. Blend the flour, salt, and pepper together on a piece of wax paper. Dredge each slice of pork in the seasoned flour. Shake to remove any excess flour and place on another piece of wax paper.

Heat the oil in a 10-inch skillet. When the oil is hot, place the pork pieces in a single layer in the skillet. Brown quickly on each side, lower heat, and let the pork cook gently for about 5 minutes, or until cooked through. Remove and keep warm while you add optional wine and chicken broth to the skillet. Cook down rapidly, scraping up any browned bits, until almost syrupy. Serve 3 slices tenderloin per serving with a spoonful of pan sauce poured over.

SKILLET-FRIED PORK CHOPS   (SERVES SIX)

Fried pork chops retain their tenderness and moisture when they aren't cooked to death. Cook ½-inch chops 5 minutes each side; ¾-inch chops only 8 minutes; 1-inch chops 10 minutes a side. Anything thicker should be lightly browned and then braised in liquid. All are especially nice served with a snowdrift of mashed potatoes.

6 pork chops, cut ½–¾ inch thick	Freshly ground pepper
2 tablespoons flour	3 tablespoons shortening
Salt	½ cup apple cider or chicken broth

Lightly dust the pork chops with flour, shaking off the excess. Sprinkle with salt and pepper. Heat the shortening in the skillet and brown the chops over medium heat for 10–12 minutes, as directed above. Remove to a warm platter. Pour off all but 2 tablespoons of fat. Splash in the apple cider or broth, cook down 1 minute, and spoon over the chops.

BRAISED PORK CHOPS WITH SWEET POTATOES   (SERVES SIX)

4 sweet potatoes	Salt
6 pork chops, cut 1½ inches thick	Freshly ground pepper
2 tablespoons flour	3 tablespoons shortening

Parboil the sweet potatoes for 20 minutes in boiling water. Peel, cut into ½-inch slices, and set aside. Lightly dust the chops with flour, shaking off the excess. Sprinkle with salt and pepper. Melt the shortening in the skillet and brown the chops over medium-high heat for 1 minute on each side. Add the sweet potatoes to the pan, cover, and cook over medium heat for 30 minutes.

BRAISED PORK CHOPS WITH APPLES

Omit the sweet potatoes and add *4 apples, peeled, cored, and sliced*, to the chops in the skillet.

BRAISED PORK CHOPS WITH CABBAGE

Omit the sweet potatoes and add *4 cups finely shredded cabbage* and *½ teaspoon caraway seeds* to the chops in the skillet.

BRAISED PORK CHOPS WITH SAUERKRAUT

Omit the sweet potatoes and add *2 cups sauerkraut* and *6 juniper berries* to the chops in the skillet.

(SERVES SIX TO EIGHT)   ❋   MANDARIN BARBECUE PORK

Steamed white rice and spinach are exceptionally good with this dish.

5-pound pork butt, trimmed of most excess fat and cut in 1 × 2-inch pieces	½ cup dry sherry
	4 tablespoons soy sauce
	2 teaspoons salt
¼ cup hoisin sauce	Freshly ground pepper
5 tablespoons catsup	¼ cup honey, warmed
1 cup sugar	

Put the pork pieces in a shallow dish. Mix together the hoisin sauce, catsup, sugar, sherry, soy sauce, salt, and pepper to taste, and pour over the pork pieces. Marinate for 8 hours, turning the pieces over in the sauce several times. Preheat the oven to 450°F. Roast the meat for 30 minutes, turning the pieces over once, then lower the heat to 375°F and roast for 15 minutes more. Remove the pork from the oven and pour the warmed honey over the meat, turning to coat on all sides. Serve.

PORK CHOPS AND APPLES
IN MUSTARD SAUCE   (SERVES FOUR)

This is a dish I make year after year. The flavors bring out the best in the pork chops.

2 pounds green apples,
   peeled, cored, and sliced
   thin
Salt and freshly ground
   pepper to taste
4 thick pork loin chops,
   trimmed of excess fat

1 tablespoon butter or oil
¼ cup chicken broth
1 cup heavy cream
⅓ cup Dijon mustard

Preheat the oven to 400°F. Butter a baking dish. Spread the apples over the bottom and bake for 15 minutes. Remove from the oven and set aside. Salt and pepper the pork chops. Melt the butter in a skillet and slowly brown the pork chops on each side. Remove the pork chops and place them over the apples. Heat the skillet over medium heat, add the broth, and scrape the bottom, loosening and mixing the bits and juices remaining from the pork chops. Continue to stir, letting the mixture boil for a minute. Put the cream and mustard in a small bowl and whisk until smooth. Add to the skillet with the broth mixture and bring just to a boil, stirring to blend. Pour over the top of the pork chops. Cover and bake 20 minutes.

CASSEROLE OF PORK CHOPS,
SWEET POTATOES, AND APPLES   (SERVES SIX)

4 large sweet potatoes
3 tablespoons shortening
6 pork chops, cut 1½ inches
   thick, and trimmed
Salt

Freshly ground pepper
½ recipe Onion Stuffing (p.
   401)
3 large tart apples
½ cup raisins

Preheat the oven to 400°F. Peel the sweet potatoes and cut into thirds. Put the pieces into a pan, cover with water, bring to a boil, and cook about 10 minutes or until barely tender when pierced with a fork; drain and set aside. Melt the shortening in a large skillet. Add the chops and brown quickly on both sides. Sprinkle with salt and pepper, remove, and set aside to cool. Cut a slit in the side of each chop, deep enough to make a pocket. Fill each pocket with stuffing. Arrange the chops in a shallow baking dish and place the sweet potatoes around them. Peel, halve, and core the apples. Fill the cores with most of the raisins, and place the apples around the chops. Sprinkle remaining raisins on top. Cover snugly with foil, and bake for 45–60 minutes, or until the chops and apples are tender.

RIB CHOPS WITH CELERY STUFFING AND APPLES

(SERVES SIX)

Apples and meat juices add flavor to the stuffing.

2 tablespoons shortening
6 thick rib pork chops, trimmed
Salt
Freshly ground pepper

1 recipe Celery Stuffing (p. 403)
3 firm red apples, cored and halved

Preheat the oven to 350°F. Grease a 1½-quart covered casserole. Melt the shortening in a skillet and brown the chops on each side. Sprinkle with salt and pepper to taste. Spread the stuffing on the bottom of the casserole and place the browned pork chops over it. Put one half-apple, cut side down, on top of each pork chop. Cover snugly and bake about 45 minutes.

SIMPLE OVEN-ROASTED ✳ SPARERIBS

(SERVES FOUR)

These are better than anything you can imagine. Serve with cole slaw and oven-browned new potatoes.

4 pounds spareribs, in whole racks

Salt and freshly ground pepper to taste

Preheat oven to 425°F. Season the spareribs with salt and pepper generously on both sides. Place on a roasting rack in a pan and roast for 30 minutes. Turn the spareribs over and continue to roast for another 30 minutes.

OVEN-BARBECUED SPARERIBS   (SERVES SIX)

Marinate these ribs for several hours before cooking.

    6 pounds spareribs in 1 or 2   1½ recipes Barbecue Sauce (p.
       pieces or racks   398)

Place the spareribs in a large shallow baking pan and cover them with
the sauce. Cover with aluminum foil and marinate at room temperature for several hours. Preheat the oven to 350°F. Leave the foil in place
and bake for 45 minutes; uncover and bake another 30–40 minutes.
Serve, cut in portions of 2–3 ribs.

SPARERIBS AND SAUERKRAUT   (SERVES FOUR)

    4 cups sauerkraut, drained   1 teaspoon salt
    3 tart apples, peeled, cored,   ½ teaspoon freshly ground
      and sliced thin   pepper
    1 onion, cut in thin rings   1 cup dry white wine
    2 bay leaves   4 pounds spareribs, trimmed

Preheat the oven to 350°F. Spread the sauerkraut over the bottom of a
shallow baking dish. Cover with the apples, onion rings, bay leaves,
salt, and pepper. Drizzle the wine over and lay the spareribs on top.
Cover snugly with foil and bake for 1 hour. Uncover, and bake another
20 minutes. Cut the ribs into 3-rib portions and serve each over a
spoonful of apples, onions, and sauerkraut.

STUFFED SPARERIBS   (SERVES SIX)

    5 pounds spareribs, in racks
    2 recipes Celery Stuffing (p.
      403)

Preheat the oven to 350°F. Place half the spareribs on the bottom of a
shallow baking pan. Spread the stuffing over them, and cover with the
remaining spareribs. Bake for 1½ hours. Divide the ribs and serve with
the stuffing.

(SERVES FOUR) **CITY CHICKEN**

A favorite recipe from Depression days, when chicken was more expensive than pork.

1 pound pork, trimmed, in 1-inch cubes
1 pound lean veal or skinned, boned chicken, in 1-inch cubes
1 egg, slightly beaten
1½ cups freshly made bread crumbs

Salt
Freshly ground pepper
4 tablespoons butter
2 tablespoons oil
1 cup chicken broth
1 tablespoon cornstarch

Place alternating cubes of pork and veal or chicken on eight wooden skewers. Push the meat cubes together snugly. Mix the egg with 1 tablespoon water and dip the skewered meat in it. Roll meat in the crumbs and sprinkle with salt and pepper. Heat the butter and oil in a large skillet and brown the meat lightly. Add ½ cup of the chicken broth, cover, and simmer for 20–30 minutes. Dissolve the cornstarch in the remaining ½ cup of chicken broth and add it to the pan juices, cooking and stirring until clear and thickened. Serve the skewers with sauce poured over them.

(SERVES SIX) **PIG'S FEET (HOCKS)**

Allow one or two hocks per person. Serve with a pot of Great Northern white beans.

8 pig's feet or hocks
1 onion, sliced
1 carrot, sliced
3 parsley sprigs

1 teaspoon peppercorns, crushed
2 bay leaves
1½ teaspoons salt

Wash the pig's feet and tie individually in cheesecloth so they will hold their shape. Put into a deep pot and cover with cold water. Add the remaining ingredients. Bring to a boil, skim the scum from the top, reduce the heat to simmer, cover, and cook gently for about 1½ hours, or until the meat is tender. Remove from the liquid, discard the cheesecloth, and serve.

BROILED PIG'S FEET

Remove the cheesecloth when the pig's feet are cooked. Rub *1 table-spoon butter* all over each foot and roll in about *2 cups freshly made bread crumbs* mixed with *2 tablespoons minced parsley*, *1 teaspoon salt*, and *½ teaspoon freshly ground pepper*. Place the hocks 6 inches below the broiling element and cook until golden, turning once. Serve with mustard.

PICKLED PIG'S FEET

Add *1 cup cider vinegar* for each 3 cups of water in the pot.

JELLIED PIG'S FEET

Strain the broth and remove the meat, discarding the skin and bones. Adjust the seasonings in the broth and replace the meat. Pour into a mold and chill until firm.

SCRAPPLE   (SERVES SIX)

A fine old Philadelphia tradition, served at breakfast or Sunday supper. Homemade takes some time, but it is much better than the canned product.

1 pound pork, with bones	⅔ cup cornmeal
2 pig's feet	2 tablespoons chopped onion
Salt	Freshly ground pepper

Place the pork, pig's feet, and a sprinkle of salt in a large pot and cover with 1 quart of water. Bring to a boil, cover, and simmer until the meat falls from the bones, at least 1½ hours. Remove the meat and reserve the broth. Discard the bones and grind the meat in a meat grinder or food processor. Add cornmeal to the broth, and cook, stirring, for 5 minutes. Add the ground meat and onion. Place in the top of a double boiler, and cook over simmering water for an hour. Add salt and pepper to taste. Pack into a small loaf pan that has been rinsed with cold water and chill until set. To serve, cut into ½-inch slices and pan-fry until crisp and brown.

DISHES USING LEFTOVER PORK

PORK BAKED WITH CABBAGE AND CREAM

(SERVES FOUR)

You could use any kind of leftover cooked pork to make this delicious dish—slices or chops from a roast—or even cook up extra chops when next you are frying some so you'll have them handy.

1 small cabbage or ½ large (about 1½ pounds)	½ teaspoon caraway seeds
½ cup heavy cream	½ teaspoon paprika
Salt	4 thick slices cooked pork or leftover chops
Freshly ground pepper	½ cup grated Swiss cheese

Preheat oven to 350°F. Shred the cabbage, discarding the core. Boil in several quarts of salted water for 5 minutes. Drain. Bring the cream to a boil, then add the well-drained cabbage, salt and pepper to taste, caraway, and paprika, and cook briskly, stirring occasionally, for 5 minutes. Distribute half the cabbage and cream over the bottom of a baking dish, place the pork on top, seasoning it well to taste and adding any drippings that may be left over from cooking; add the rest of the cabbage, and top with the cheese. Bake for 40 minutes.

PORK SWEET AND SOUR

(SERVES SIX)

1½ pounds cooked pork	1 onion, cut in narrow strips
¾ cup soy sauce	1-pound 4-ounce can pineapple tidbits
3 tablespoons oil	
3 green peppers, cut in narrow strips	

Sauce

3 tablespoons cornstarch	⅓ cup sugar
1 tablespoon soy sauce	⅓ cup water
3 tablespoons vinegar	

Trim the pork of excess fat and slice. Put the pork in a shallow dish and cover with the ¾ cup soy sauce. Let stand for 1 hour, turning the meat often so it thoroughly marinates. Heat the oil in a sauté pan, add the peppers and onion, and cook over high heat for just a minute, stirring constantly. Remove from the pan and set aside. Drain the pork, add to the skillet along with the juice from the pineapple tidbits, and

bring to a boil. Lower the heat and simmer for 5 minutes. Add the
pineapple, peppers, and onion, stir to mix and simmer a minute. Combine thoroughly the sauce ingredients and add to the pork mixture
stirring constantly. Cook until sauce thickens.

Other Suggestions for Using Leftover Pork

Use pork instead of beef in Beef and Corn Casserole; Beef and Scallions, Mushroom Sauce; and Beef Pot Pie, and instead of lamb in
Lentils and Lamb, Shepherd's Pie, Fricassee of Lamb, Moussaka, and
Lamb Curry. Pork is good instead of ham in Ham and Noodle Casserole. Chopped cooked pork can be used to make Fried Rice, and
ground up it can serve you well for fillings for savory tarts, stuffed
pasta, and vegetables.

HAM

About Ham

A ham is, correctly, a leg of pork, but that meaning has faded, and the
word "ham" (unless labeled "fresh ham") is now used to describe any
cut of pork that has been through a preserving process. Although refrigeration has made it unnecessary to preserve pork this way, our
palates have learned to enjoy the salty, smoked flavor of ham.
    Salt curing destroys the organisms that cause meat to spoil. There
are two methods of salt curing: salt brining and dry curing. Brined
pork is soaked in or, more often, injected with a brine solution. Dry-
cured pork is rubbed all over with salt and then aged in a cool place.
The most famous hams are dry-cured, such as our own Smithfield and
Virginia hams and imported Parma ham or prosciutto. Different pack-
ers have their own recipes, which often include sugar, spices, and pepper. These recipes are closely kept secrets.
    Smoking is the next step in curing, although not all ham is smoked.
Smoked ham has a robust, country character, and many people prefer
the milder flavor of salt curing. Smoking is done over wood in airtight
containers or rooms, where a low fire of beechwood or hickory provides a constant cloud of aromatic smoke.
    Country-style hams, usually ordered by mail or bought in specialty
shops, have been dry-salted and rubbed with black pepper, then
smoked and aged for about a year. Most of them arrive with detailed
directions for their preparation, which involves soaking, blanching,
boiling, scrubbing, peeling, glazing, and baking.
    Among the many cuts of ham that are available in supermarkets,
the best are those that have the bone left in. Water is sometimes in-

jected into these hams, but it must be noted on the label and cannot exceed 10 percent of the fresh meat weight. A whole ham is usually 10–14 pounds in weight, but you can also buy the meaty butt end or the flavorful shank end of the ham. The loin of pork—not, strictly speaking, ham—has an excellent flavor. Picnic ham is the smoked pork shoulder, which has very good flavor but a great deal of waste, and the smoked or Boston butt is also good but extremely fatty. Boned hams are less flavorful, but have little waste and are easy to carve.

Most of these hams are available either partially or fully cooked. If they are fully cooked, they have been kept at an internal temperature of 160°F for at least half an hour, destroying any possibility of trichinosis. But almost all hams on the market today have been held at 137°F for half an hour, and need only heating through to be safe. Canned hams tend to be bland and dull and coated with gelatin.

Be sure to read the label on the ham: some are precooked, some partially cooked. If the ham has not been precooked at all, allow 20 minutes per pound in a 350°F oven, then use a meat thermometer to be sure that the internal temperature is 160°F. If the ham is precooked, you must still allow 10 minutes per pound to warm the meat and melt the glaze.

(ALLOW ½ POUND PER SERVING)   **BAKED HAM**

Baked ham is an ideal main dish for beginning cooks and the best answer for the harried cook. It requires only that you put it into the oven and set the timer. It suffers no ill effects being reheated as a leftover and is also good cold. (See above for information about ham.)

1 ham	2 teaspoons dry mustard
1 cup brown sugar	15 or more cloves
¼ cup honey, maple syrup, or cider vinegar	1 can pineapple rings (optional)

Basting Sauce (optional)

1 cup brown sugar	1 cup orange juice
1 teaspoon dry mustard	

Preheat the oven to 350°F. Place the ham on a rack in a shallow roasting pan, fat side up. Bake the ham unglazed until the thermometer reads 130°F, or until 1 hour before the ham is done. Prepare for glazing

by scoring the outside fat in a diamond pattern, cutting ¼ inch deep with a sharp knife. Combine the brown sugar with the honey, syrup, or vinegar and the mustard. Mix well and spread over the outside of the ham. Stud with whole cloves set decoratively in the center of each diamond. Or if you like pineapple rings, set them in place with toothpicks, putting the cloves in the holes. Return to the oven for 1 hour to finish baking, brushing, if you wish, every 15 minutes with basting sauce. Let it rest and carve at the table as illustrated.

PICNIC HAM   (ALLOW 1 POUND PER SERVING)

A picnic ham is a pork shoulder that has been cured and smoked. Its waste in bone and fat (thus you need more per person) is made up for by its flavor.

    5–8-pound picnic ham

Put the ham into a large pot and cover it with cold water. Bring to a boil and reduce the heat. Simmer for 1½–2 hours, depending on the size. A 5-pound ham cooks in 1½ hours, an 8-pound ham in 2 hours. Add more water as it cooks away. When it is done, drain and remove the rind. Preheat the oven to 325°F. Place the ham on a rack in a shallow pan and bake for 2 hours.

BOILED COUNTRY HAM   (ALLOW ½ POUND PER SERVING)

Begin preparing home-cured ham the day before you serve it. Long soaking and cooking make country ham a special treat.

1 home-cured Smithfield or	1 cup dark-brown sugar
Virginia ham	8 cloves

Soak the ham overnight in cold water to cover. Drain, scrub with a stiff brush, and place in a large pot. Cover with water, heat, and simmer for 25 minutes per pound, or until an instant meat thermometer shows an internal temperature of 150°F. Add more water as it cooks away. Allow the ham to cool in the water in which it cooked, then remove it and peel or cut off the tough outer skin and most of the fat. The ham is now ready to eat, but a brief glazing and baking will make it even better. Preheat the oven to 350°F. Place the ham on a rack in a shallow roasting pan, and rub it all over with the brown sugar. Stud with cloves and bake for 10 minutes per pound, until the meat is heated through and the glaze is melted and shining.

SLICE OF HAM BAKED IN MILK

(SERVES FOUR)

2 pounds ham, in a 1½-inch slice
1 tablespoon prepared mustard

1 tablespoon brown sugar
2 cups milk

Preheat oven to 300°F. Put the ham in a shallow baking dish. Paint the top with the mustard and sprinkle the brown sugar over. Pour the milk around the ham and bake for 2 to 2½ hours. Serve with a little of the clotted milk spooned over the top.

THIN SLICES OF HAM IN MILK

A good way to use leftover baked ham, particularly when it is salty. Cut serving slices of ham, paint lightly with mustard, and sprinkle with brown sugar. Arrange in a baking dish and cover with milk. Bake about ½ hour.

HAM WITH RED-EYE GRAVY

(ALLOW ⅓ POUND PER SERVING)

In this regional southern dish, the fried ham lends a slightly reddish tint to pan gravy. Often a few drops of coffee are added for a richer color. Serve with grits or hot biscuits.

⅓-pound slice of ham
1 tablespoon flour

Salt
1½ tablespoons coffee

Cut a piece of fat from the ham and melt it in a skillet. Add the ham and fry over medium heat until the edges are slightly brown. Remove and keep warm. Turn the heat to high and stir in the flour. Cook flour slowly until golden, then add 1 cup water, stirring constantly. Sprinkle in salt and the coffee. Turn the heat to medium-low and cook 5–7 minutes, stirring often to keep the gravy smooth. Return meat to the gravy to heat through.

HAM LOAF (SERVES SIX)

This is tasty hot or cold and dandy for picnics.

3 cups ground ham	1 whole bay leaf
3 cups ground pork	1 cup fresh bread crumbs,
½ teaspoon freshly ground	preferably dark rye
pepper	1 egg, lightly beaten
2 teaspoons finely chopped	½ cup milk
fresh thyme, or 1 teaspoon	
dried, crumbled	

Preheat the oven to 350°F. Butter a medium-size loaf pan.

Mix all ingredients together in a bowl, tossing until well combined. Lightly pack into the loaf pan. Bake for 40 to 50 minutes, or until the fat is bubbling around the edges. Remove and pour off any excess fat. Allow to set for 10 to 15 minutes in the pan before turning out. Serve hot or cold.

HAM CASSEROLE COUNTRY STYLE (SERVES FOUR)

2 cups potatoes, sliced thin	2 teaspoons thyme, crumbled
Salt	1 thick slice ham, trimmed
Freshly ground pepper	(1½–2 pounds)
1 large onion, sliced thin	2 cups milk

Preheat the oven to 350°F. Butter a 1½-quart covered casserole. Cover the bottom of the casserole with the potatoes and sprinkle with salt and pepper to taste. Spread the onions on top and scatter with thyme. Lay the ham slice over the onions, pour on the milk, cover, and bake for about 1 hour, or until the potatoes are tender.

TOMATO-HAM CASSEROLE COUNTRY STYLE

Omit the milk and substitute *2 cups chopped tomatoes and juice.*

DISHES USING LEFTOVER HAM

(SERVES SIX)   **NANCY'S HAM LOAF**

Buy ground meat, or do it yourself in a meat grinder or food processor. Use a brave hand with the Tabasco.

1 pound ground ham	¼ teaspoon Tabasco
½ pound ground beef	¾ cup instant dry milk
½ pound ground pork	1 onion, chopped fine
1 cup freshly made bread crumbs	1 egg, lightly beaten
	1 cup tomato juice

Preheat the oven to 325°F. Butter a 1½-quart casserole. Lightly mix all the ingredients in a large bowl. Pack into the buttered casserole and bake for 50–60 minutes.

(SERVES FOUR)   **HAM AND SPINACH SOUFFLÉ**

A soufflé must go right from the oven to the table, or it will fall. The extra egg whites make this soufflé extra light!

3 tablespoons butter	2 teaspoons dry mustard
3 tablespoons minced onion	3 egg yolks, lightly beaten
3 tablespoons flour	1 cup cooked or defrosted
¾ cup milk	spinach, squeezed dry
½ teaspoon salt	¾ cup diced cooked ham
¼ teaspoon freshly ground pepper	6 egg whites

Preheat the oven to 350°F. Grease the bottom and sides of a 2-quart soufflé mold. Melt the butter in a saucepan, add the onion, and cook over low heat until the onion is limp. Stir in the flour and cook for 2 minutes. Slowly pour in the milk, stir, and cook for 1 minute. Add the salt, pepper, and dry mustard and cook for 3–4 minutes, stirring, while the sauce boils. Remove from the heat and vigorously stir in the egg yolks. Put back on the heat and cook, stirring constantly, for another minute, no more. Remove from the heat and add the spinach and ham. Mix thoroughly and set aside to cool to lukewarm. Beat the egg whites until they are stiff but moist, then stir a large spoonful into the ham mixture. Fold the mixture gently into the remaining egg whites. Gently spoon into buttered soufflé mold. Bake for 30–40 minutes, or until just set, and serve immediately.

HAM MOUSSE ALEXANDRIA   (SERVES FOUR)

The Russian Sauce is a necessary complement to the taste and texture of this mousse.

½ pound cooked ham, ground fine
4 egg whites
¼ teaspoon nutmeg
⅛ teaspoon freshly ground pepper

½ cup heavy cream
2 tablespoons chopped parsley
1 recipe Russian Sauce (p. 382)

Preheat the oven to 350°F. Butter four custard cups or molds with a ¾-cup capacity. Blend the ham and egg whites until smoothly puréed by whirring them through a blender or food processor or rubbing them through a sieve. Add the nutmeg and pepper, stir in the cream very slowly until blended, and spoon into the cups or molds. Set them in a shallow pan containing 1 inch of hot water and bake until firm, 25–35 minutes. A knife stuck in the center should come out clean. Turn out onto a platter or individual plates, sprinkle with parsley, and serve hot with the sauce.

HAM PATTIES   (SERVES FOUR)

Ham sharpened with dry mustard. A salad of chilled cucumbers in a sugar and vinegar dressing makes a good accompaniment.

2 cups ground cooked ham
1 egg, slightly beaten
½ cup freshly made bread crumbs

1 tablespoon dry mustard
3 tablespoons heavy cream
2 tablespoons bacon fat or shortening

Mix the ham, egg, crumbs, mustard, and cream until thoroughly combined. Shape the mixture into four equal patties. Melt the bacon fat or shortening in a large skillet, and sauté the patties until well browned on each side.

(ABOUT 15 CROQUETTES)   **HAM CROQUETTES**

3½ cups ground cooked ham
2 cups Thick White Sauce (p. 380)
1 tablespoon minced parsley
1 tablespoon Dijon mustard
3 tablespoons minced onion

¼ teaspoon freshly ground pepper
1½ cups freshly made bread crumbs
1 egg
Vegetable oil

Combine the ham, sauce, parsley, mustard, onion, and pepper in a bowl and blend well. If mixture is slightly warm, chill in the refrigerator until firm. Put the bread crumbs in a shallow dish, and in another dish beat the egg with 1 tablespoon water. Shape the meat into 1½-inch balls or cylinders. Roll them in the crumbs, then dip into the egg, and again roll in the crumbs. Let the croquettes dry in the refrigerator for at least 30 minutes to set the coating. Fill a skillet halfway with vegetable oil and heat to about 360°F. Fry a few croquettes at a time to golden brown, turning to brown on all sides. Remove with a slotted spoon and dry on paper towels.

(SERVES FOUR)   **✳ STUFFED CABBAGE LEAVES**

A wonderful way to transform cooked beef or pork, particularly if you save some sauce—meat juices, drippings, or leftover gravy—to add flavor and moisture to the filling. If you use ham or corned beef, add 1 teaspoon mustard in place of leftover gravy. The inner part of the cabbage, chopped and sautéed with a little butter and cream, makes a vegetable course for another meal.

1 head cabbage
2 onions, chopped
4 tablespoons butter
1 teaspoon sweet paprika
2 cups minced cooked beef or pork
2 cups cooked rice
¼ cup chopped parsley

½ teaspoon rosemary, crumbled
Salt
Freshly ground pepper
¾ cup meat sauce (gravy, juice, or strong bouillon)
16-ounce can tomatoes

Preheat the oven to 350°F. Cut a circle around the core of the cabbage to loosen the leaves, then drop them into a large pot of boiling, salted water. Lift out after 3–4 minutes. Carefully select 8 of the large outer leaves. Lay them out flat, and cut out a small V from the root end to remove the hard spine. Sauté the onions in the butter with paprika until soft. Leaving 2 tablespoons of the onion in the pan, spoon the rest into a bowl and add the meat, rice, parsley, most of the rosemary, some salt and pepper, and ½ cup of the meat sauce or other liquid. Place one-eighth of the filling in the center of each leaf. Fold in the sides, then roll to make a neat sausage-shaped package. Place the rolls, seam side down, in a shallow baking dish that holds them snugly. Add the tomatoes and their juice to the onions remaining in the skillet, breaking them up roughly. Add the remaining ¼ cup meat sauce and boil hard for 5 minutes until the liquid is somewhat reduced. Season to taste with salt, pepper, and a pinch more rosemary, and pour around the stuffed cabbage leaves. Cover loosely with foil and bake for 50 minutes.

STUFFED ONIONS (SERVES FOUR)

Large round Spanish onions that range in color from yellow to red are ideal for this dish. You could use tongue or corned beef instead of ham—any tasty cooked meat.

4 large onions	⅓ cup freshly made bread
6 tablespoons butter, melted	crumbs
Salt	1½ teaspoons finely chopped
Freshly ground pepper	parsley
½ cup coarsely chopped	¼ teaspoon nutmeg
cooked ham	2 tablespoons dry sherry

Preheat the oven to 300°F. Butter a casserole or baking dish large enough to hold the onions. Put the onions in a pan of boiling water to cover, and parboil for 10 minutes. Drain and refresh under cold water. Scoop out the centers, but leave a sturdy shell. Brush the insides with a little of the melted butter, and sprinkle with salt and pepper. Set aside. Combine the ham, crumbs, parsley, and nutmeg in a small bowl, add salt and pepper to taste, and toss until mixed well. Divide the ham filling and stuff the four onions. Add the sherry to the remaining melted butter, and pour over each of the onions. Cover and bake for about 1 hour or until tender.

Other Suggestions for Using Leftover Ham

It seems almost superfluous to make suggestions for using leftover ham, it has so many uses. In fact, ham is something you never want to be without. As a Virginia-born friend, Edna Lewis, said of her childhood: "Ham held the same rating as the basic black dress. If you had a ham in the meat house any situation could be faced. On short notice it would be sliced and fried with special red gravy. . . . The smoked shoulder was indispensable as a seasoning for other meat dishes; a slice would be added in to fried chicken, guinea fowl, rabbit, squirrel, or quail. It was used also in boiled pots of cabbage, beans, watercress, and green black-eyed peas." Today, ham is as indispensable as ever. In Appetizers you'll find ham used as spreads, in pâtés, on small hot biscuits, and in savory tarts; thin slices of smoked country ham are good with slices of melon as a starter. It is the leftover ham bone that makes Split Pea Soup special and gives that authentic taste to Mixed-Greens Southern Style. You can always whip up an omelet or a frittata or a quiche if you have some scraps of ham on hand, to say nothing of fried or shirred eggs and ham. Soufflés, croquettes, timbales, bean dishes, pumpkin, and macaroni casseroles all make hearty main-course dishes when you have some ham. And what would we do without ham for ham and cheese sandwiches and chef's salad?

SAUSAGE AND FRANKFURTERS

About Sausage and Frankfurters

Sausage meat is nothing more than ground pork and fat with seasonings. The simplest "fresh" or "country" sausages are made by combining newly ground pork with such seasonings as thyme, basil, salt, and pepper. You can make sausages yourself; season the meat lightly, fry a tablespoonful to kill any trichinae, and then taste. Add more seasoning to the raw mixture if it is needed. You will find the results quite an improvement on commercial sausage meat. Commercial brands of sausage meat are bought either loose or in casings, and many brands are advertised as precooked: that is, they have been kept at 160°F for half an hour and need only to be heated through for palatability.

Smoking, another form of precooking, is the method that produces the familiar taste in hot dogs. Frankfurters can be all-beef, all-meat, or a blend of meat with soy and milk fillers. Although they, too, are perfectly safe to eat raw, we'd as soon eat them uncooked as without mustard and relish!

Finally there are dry sausages, the group that includes salami, bologna, pepperoni. Like dried hams, they are highly seasoned, unparalleled in flavor and keeping power, and delicious to eat without further cooking. Leftover sausages are best used in stuffings or omelets or to top the filling of a quiche or pizza.

SAUSAGE MEAT

(ABOUT 3 CUPS; SERVES FOUR)

Many people are going back to making their own sausage meat: it's easy, fresh, and preservative-free. You need to use proportions of 2 parts lean meat to 1 part fat in order to have a moist sausage (much of the fat will cook out). Remember to fry a tablespoonful of the mixture before you taste it to adjust the seasonings.

1 pound pork, ground	½ teaspoon freshly ground
½ pound fresh pork fat,	pepper
ground	½ teaspoon sage, crumbled
1 teaspoon salt	

Mix all the ingredients. Use in recipes requiring sausage meat, or shape into patties and cook in a skillet about 8 minutes a side, pouring off the fat as it accumulates.

HERBED AND SPICED SAUSAGE MEAT

Instead of the sage, use ¾ *teaspoon ground* herbs and spices combined: *allspice, paprika, bay leaf, and thyme.*

ITALIAN SAUSAGE MEAT

Omit the sage and add ½ *teaspoon each fennel seed and anise seed* and 1 *teaspoon dried basil, crumbled.*

BUBBLE-AND-SQUEAK

(SERVES FOUR)

An old-fashioned English dish.

1 pound sausage meat	Salt to taste
½ onion, chopped	2 cups White Sauce (p. 379)
2 cups cooked chopped	
cabbage	

Preheat the oven to 350°F. Butter a 1½-quart casserole. Cook the sausage meat in a skillet, breaking it up with a fork as it cooks. When no pink shows, transfer it to a bowl. Add the chopped onion to the sausage drippings in the skillet and cook until limp. Add to the meat and mix well. Spread the meat in the bottom of the casserole. Cover with the cabbage, add salt to taste, then cover with the sauce, and bake 30–40 minutes, or until bubbling hot.

COOKED FRANKFURTERS, KIELBASA, BRATWURST, KNOCKWURST

The simplest and most effective way to cook all of these sausages is to simmer in water to cover until heated through (see page 411 for Frankfurters or Hot Dogs). Kielbasa, Bratwurst, and Knockwurst should be pricked in several places and will take 10–15 minutes to cook. Count on 1 pound of sausage serving 2–3 people.

Another method is to partially cover with simmering water, turn often as they are cooking, then turn up the heat the last few minutes to boil off the water. Let the sausages brown finally in a little of their own fat. Serve with mustard and pickles and hash brown potatoes.

(SERVES FOUR) **PAN-FRIED FRANKFURTERS**

Cooked this way, frankfurters taste like the ones we get at ball games. Serve with mustard and, if you like, sauerkraut.

8 frankfurters

Heat a skillet with barely enough oil to film the bottom of the pan. Slice the frankfurters in half lengthwise; don't cut through entirely, but leave a "hinge" of skin. Put them, cut side down, in the hot skillet and fry until nicely browned around the edges. Turn and cook until lightly browned on both sides.

VARIETY MEATS

About Variety Meats

In America, we call them variety meats, innards, organs, or glands. In England, they call them "offal," which many Americans think is a pun for "awful." Whatever we call them, we mean certain organ and muscle meats such as tongue, heart, kidney, liver, tripe, sweetbreads, and brains.

Colonial Americans enjoyed variety meats: old cookbooks are studded with instructions for preparing sweetbreads and brains. But today,

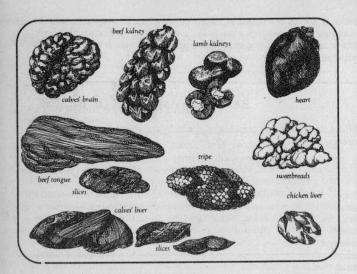

beef kidney

lamb kidneys

calves' brain

heart

beef tongue

slices

tripe

sweetbreads

chicken liver

calves' liver

slices

some of us feel a certain distaste for innards, reflecting a cultural attitude that makes no sense. On the other hand, many fine cooks consider them a treat and a delicacy. Aside from the fact that variety meats are high in protein, minerals, and iron, we also have an obligation to make good use of all our resources.

Variety meats are very perishable and require careful purchasing and storage. They should be stored, loosely wrapped, in the refrigerator, and cooked within 24 hours. Loose wrapping will allow air to circulate around the meat, drying its surface and retarding the growth of bacteria. Most variety meats freeze very well. Often you will find them frozen in the meat counter, and most are perfectly satisfactory bought that way.

Pay careful attention to the directions here for cleaning and precooking. It can make all the difference between a clumsy dish and one that is done with finesse.

About Brains

Brains should have a shiny moist surface, pinkish color, and full plump consistency. This delicate and tender meat must be bought only when it is absolutely fresh. The ease with which the outer membrane can be removed in the basic preparation is a good indication of the freshness. Although calves' brains are generally considered to be the most choice, beef, pork, and lamb brains are also excellent. Allow about ¼ pound per serving: lamb and pork brains are the smallest, weighing only ¼ pound; veal brains weigh about ½ pound; and beef brains are around ¾ pound. The recipes can be used interchangeably with the different varieties of brains.

BASIC PREPARATION OF BRAINS

After this preliminary soaking and blanching, brains may be covered loosely and stored in the refrigerator for a day before final preparation.

1½ pounds brains	Salt
Lemon juice	Vinegar

Put the brains in a bowl and cover with cold water. Add 2 tablespoons lemon juice for each quart of water. Let soak for 30 minutes. Drain and rinse under cold running water. Working carefully, remove the outer membrane with a sharp knife and wash off any traces of blood. Put the brains in a saucepan. Cover with water and add 1 teaspoon salt and 1 teaspoon vinegar for every quart of water. Bring to a boil and simmer, uncovered, for 15 minutes. Drain. Cover with cold water again and let stand 15 minutes more to keep the brains firm, or, better yet, refrigerate a few hours with a plate on top.

(SERVES FOUR)   ## BRAINS WITH BROWN BUTTER

Serve with triangles of warm dry toast.

1½ pounds brains	2 tablespoons vinegar
¼ pound butter	1 tablespoon minced parsley
2 tablespoons lemon juice	1 tablespoon capers

Prepare the brains as directed (in Basic Preparation). Cut them into thick slices. Melt 4 tablespoons of the butter in a skillet. Sauté the brains quickly and place them on a warm plate. Add the remaining 4 tablespoons of butter to the skillet, turn the heat to high, and heat until butter turns brown. Stir in the lemon juice and vinegar, and let them bubble together for about 30 seconds. Remove from heat, then add parsley and capers and pour over the brains.

BRAINS SAUTÉED WITH BACON   (SERVES FOUR)

1½ pounds brains   Freshly ground pepper
8 slices bacon   1 bunch watercress

Prepare the brains as directed (in Basic Preparation). Fry the bacon until crisp; drain on paper towels and keep warm in the oven. Remove all
but 4 tablespoons of bacon fat from the skillet. Keep the skillet medium
hot. Cut the brains into thick slices and brown them lightly on each
side in the bacon fat. Sprinkle with pepper and arrange on a platter,
surrounded by bacon and garnished with watercress.

SCRAMBLED EGGS AND BRAINS   (SERVES FOUR)

½ pound brains   1 teaspoon salt
6 eggs, lightly beaten   5 tablespoons butter
¼ teaspoon Tabasco
2 tablespoons minced
    scallions

NOTE
see page 471

Prepare the brains as directed (in Basic Preparation). Cut
them into ½-inch cubes and add to the eggs. Stir in the
Tabasco, scallions, and salt. Melt the butter over medium
heat. When it foams, pour in the egg and brain mixture.
Cook over low heat, stirring and scraping the bottom of the pan so the
eggs don't dry out and stick to the bottom; don't overcook. Remove
when partially set, but still very moist.

About Heart

Heart has a mild flavor, similar to that of liver, although not as pronounced in taste. The texture is firm and dense. Like all variety meats,
it is perishable and should be used within a day or two of purchase.
Parboiling helps to prevent rapid spoilage, but is not necessary if the
heart will be used soon or undergo long cooking. A lamb heart weighs
¼ pound, a pork heart about ½ pound, a veal heart about 1 pound, and
a beef heart 3–4 pounds. Allow ⅛ pound for each serving.

BASIC PREPARATION OF HEART

Wash the heart thoroughly under cold water, cutting away any arteries, fat, or connective tissue. Heart is tender, and so it must be either sautéed quickly, in which case it should be served slightly pink in the center, or braised slowly as in Stuffed Hearts with Vegetables.

(SERVES FOUR)   ## SAUTÉED HEART

1 pound veal heart   Salt
3 tablespoons butter   Freshly ground pepper
1 tablespoon oil   1 cup freshly made bread
½ teaspoon rosemary,   crumbs
   crumbled

Prepare the hearts as directed above. Slice them in half lengthwise and then into ½-inch slices crosswise. Heat the butter and oil in a skillet, add the heart slices, and sprinkle with rosemary, salt, and pepper to taste. Cook slowly, turning and stirring until the heart slices are done—about 5 minutes. Meanwhile, brown the bread crumbs on a cookie sheet in a 350°F oven for about 5 minutes. Put the heart slices on a serving dish and sprinkle with crisply brown bread crumbs.

About Kidneys

Kidneys taste something like liver and, like liver, tend to toughen quickly when overcooked. Choose kidneys that have a bright, shiny appearance. Like the other variety meats, they are very perishable and should be cooked within a day of purchase or defrosting. Veal kidneys are especially highly prized; pork kidneys are scarce because they are used for commercial preparations and pâtés.

A beef kidney serves four; a veal kidney, three; and a pork kidney, one. Two or three lamb kidneys are required for one serving.

BASIC PREPARATION OF KIDNEYS

Remove the outside membrane from the kidneys. If you are preparing large beef or pork kidneys, cut them in half lengthwise and remove the white core and fat from the center. The fat around the outside of a pork kidney is called "leaf lard" and is considered the purest fat for cooking and baking.

Don't soak veal or lamb kidneys; they need only to be rinsed and
dried off. Beef and pork kidneys, however, must be soaked for 1 hou
in acidulated water. Use 2 tablespoons vinegar or lemon juice for every
quart of water. Soak, rinse, and pat dry. Then plunge the kidneys into
boiling water for a minute to refresh. Drain, rinse quickly under cold
running water, and pat dry. If any unpleasant odor lingers, rub the
kidneys with a little baking soda and rinse again.

BROILED KIDNEYS   (SERVES FOUR

1 pound veal or lamb kidneys	½ teaspoon thyme, crumbled
⅓ cup olive oil	½ teaspoon salt
3 tablespoons red wine	¼ teaspoon freshly ground
¼ teaspoon oregano, crumbled	pepper

Prepare the kidneys as directed (in Basic Preparation). Mix remaining
ingredients in a jar, cover closely, and shake. Slice the kidneys cross
wise in 3 slices for lamb kidneys, about 5 for veal. Place them in a shal
low dish, pour on the marinade, and marinate for 1 hour. Preheat the
broiler. Thread the kidneys on skewers and place 3 inches beneath the
broiler element. Cook 1–2 minutes on each side or until lightly
browned.

SAUTÉED KIDNEYS   (SERVES FOUR

1 pound veal or lamb kidneys	1 cup sliced mushrooms
3 tablespoons butter	4 tablespoons red wine
1 tablespoon oil	Salt
¼ cup finely chopped onion	Toast

Prepare the kidneys as directed (in Basic Preparation). Melt the butter
and oil in a skillet. Quickly brown the kidneys, cooking for just a
minute before removing to a warm plate. Add the onion and mush
rooms to the pan and cook, stirring, until the onion is soft. Pour in the
wine and cook a minute; then return the kidneys to the pan, add salt to
taste, and heat through. Serve on toast.

About Sweetbreads

Sweetbreads, with brains, are the most delicate of all variety meats, the
lightest in taste, and the most expensive. They are also among the most
perishable, and should be used on the day they are purchased. If this is
not possible, they can be frozen with good results.

A sweetbread is the thymus gland of an animal. This gland has two lobes. One lobe, called the "throat," is uneven and veiny, and disappears almost completely as the animal matures. The other, the "heart" or "belly" lobe of the thymus, grows larger in the maturing animal. It is smooth and round and, when it comes from a calf, is considered the choicest piece of sweetbread available.

When shopping for sweetbreads, look for moisture and freshness. They should be rosy-colored if they come from steer and whitish if they come from calves or lamb. A pound of sweetbreads serves four people.

BASIC PREPARATION OF SWEETBREADS

After the preliminary soaking and blanching, the sweetbreads may be covered loosely and stored in the refrigerator for a day before final preparation.

Sweetbreads	Salt
Lemon juice or vinegar	

Soak the sweetbreads in cold water for 1 hour. Bring to a boil a pot full of acidulated water: for every quart of water, add 2 tablespoons lemon juice or vinegar and ½ teaspoon salt. Add the sweetbreads and boil gently for 15 minutes. Drain, then plunge immediately into cold water. Allow the cold water to run over the sweetbreads to cool them rapidly. Working gently with a sharp knife, trim away the membranes and connecting tubes. Pat dry.

(SERVES FOUR)   **BROILED SWEETBREADS**

Serve on toast triangles.

1 pound veal sweetbreads	Juice of 1 lemon
Salt	4 tablespoons butter, melted

Prepare the sweetbreads as directed (in Basic Preparation). Preheat the broiler. Split the sweetbreads crosswise, sprinkle with salt, place 3 inches under the broiler element, and cook 2–3 minutes on each side. Put on a platter and pour lemon juice and butter on top.

SAUTÉED SWEETBREADS

(SERVES FOUR)

1 pound sweetbreads
3 tablespoons butter
1 tablespoon oil
Salt

½ cup white wine or dry
  sherry
1 tablespoon minced parsley

Prepare the sweetbreads as directed (in Basic Preparation). Slice them. Melt the butter and oil in a skillet, and brown the sweetbreads quickly over high heat. Sprinkle with salt and transfer to a warm plate. With heat kept high, pour the sherry into the skillet and let it boil for 1 minute. Pour over sweetbreads and sprinkle with parsley.

SWEETBREADS À LA NAPOLI

(SERVES FOUR)

1½ cups heavy cream
1 pound sweetbreads
6 tablespoons butter
2 tablespoons beef broth
Salt

1 cup grated Parmesan cheese
8 pieces of toast, in 3½-inch
  rounds
8 mushroom caps

Preheat the oven to 350°F. Prepare four individual baking dishes by putting 2 tablespoons of cream in each. Prepare the sweetbreads as directed (in Basic Preparation). Cut them into eight pieces. Melt 2 tablespoons of the butter in a skillet and sauté the sweetbreads quickly. When they are lightly brown, add the beef broth, stirring to blend, until glazed; salt lightly, remove and set aside. Mix the remaining cream with the cheese. Spread it on the toast rounds. Melt the remaining 4 tablespoons butter in the skillet. Sauté the mushroom caps until they darken slightly but are still firm; set aside. Put two toast rounds in each dish. On each piece of toast, place a slice of sweetbread and then a mushroom cap. Bake, covered with foil, for 8 minutes.

About Tongue

Tongue is available pickled, smoked, and fresh. Fresh tongue has the most delicate flavor, but the others are equally good; and canned tongue is convenient to have in the pantry. Although pickled and smoked tongues have been partially preserved, they need the same scrubbing and long simmering as fresh tongue, and may be used interchangeably in the recipes.

We are most familiar with the 4–6 pound beef tongue and the 1½-pound calves' tongue. Lamb and pork tongues are scarce, tiny, and delicious. For fine texture, choose a tongue that is 3 pounds or less in weight. With little waste, it will easily provide three servings per pound. Remember to allow for leftovers, since this is one meat that is just as good cold as hot.

BASIC PREPARATION OF TONGUE

After it is cooked and trimmed, this is ready to serve with Mustard Sauce (p. 391). Tongue is particularly good cold.

1 tongue, fresh, pickled, or smoked	2 bay leaves
	2 teaspoons salt
½ lemon, sliced	8 peppercorns, crushed
1 onion, sliced	6 cloves

Scrub the tongue with a vegetable brush in warm running water. Soak for 1 hour in cold water. Put into a pot of boiling water along with remaining ingredients. Partially cover and simmer gently until tender: a beef tongue takes 3–4 hours, veal 1½–2 hours, pork 1–1½ hours, and lamb about 1 hour. Let the tongue cool in the broth. Split the skin and peel it off. Trim away all the small bones and gristle at the root end. To serve, slice thin on a slight angle.

FRESH TONGUE WITH VEGETABLES

(SERVES EIGHT, WITH LEFTOVERS)

If the onions are larger than ½ inch in diameter, cut them in half before using.

4–6-pound fresh beef tongue	3 potatoes, peeled and diced
4 carrots, in ¼-inch slices	1 pound onions, peeled
2 turnips, in small dice	3 tablespoons butter, softened
4 ribs celery, in ¼-inch slices	3 tablespoons flour
1 pound green beans, in ½-inch lengths	Salt
	Freshly ground pepper

Prepare the tongue as directed (in Basic Preparation). Drain and reserve the liquid. Preheat the oven to 300°F. Spread the carrots, turnips, celery, green beans, potatoes, and onions over the bottom of a roasting pan. Place the tongue on the vegetables. Add 3 cups of the reserved liquid, cover snugly with foil, and bake for 2 hours. Remove the meat and vegetables and keep warm. Blend the soft butter and flour into a smooth paste. Drop pellets of this paste into the simmering pan liquid, whisking it briskly until it is properly thickened. Add salt and pepper to taste, and cook, stirring, for 5 minutes. Cut the tongue into thin, slanted slices, and serve on a platter surrounded by the vegetables. Pass the gravy separately.

About Tripe

Tripe is the gastronomic name for part of the stomach of an animal that chews its cud. In this country, only beef tripe is generally available, and of the four kinds of beef tripe, we can usually find only two: smooth and honeycomb. The honeycomb is considered the more desirable.

Before it is offered for sale, tripe is processed by soaking in lime, brining, and boiling. The preparation of tripe used to be long and arduous before this process became common: some old recipes call for more than 24 hours of cooking time.

BASIC PREPARATION OF TRIPE

Tripe is tough, with a texture like that of gristle, and if it has not been precooked, it requires long cooking to be edible. The only way to tell is to taste—it is cooked when the meat still has some resistance; a slight chewiness, before it has become completely soft.

Tripe	½ cup chopped celery with
Salt	leaves
1 onion, stuck with 3 cloves	6 peppercorns, crushed
1 bay leaf	

Scrub the tripe with a vegetable brush. Blanch it by covering with cold water and bringing to a boil. Drain, and plunge it into a bowl of cold water. Fill the saucepan with water again, adding 2 teaspoons salt for every quart of water. Add the tripe and simmer until it is tender: anywhere from 1 to 2 hours, depending on how much previous tenderizing was done. After it has simmered for 20 minutes, add the onion, bay leaf, celery, and peppercorns. The tripe is now ready to use in one of the following recipes.

BAKED TRIPE WITH TOMATOES AND ONIONS
(SERVES SIX)

This dish is really better the next day. Serve it with boiled or baked potatoes, lots of crusty bread, and a crisp green salad.

2 pounds tripe
¼ cup olive or vegetable oil
4 onions, peeled and sliced
3 cloves garlic, minced
1 pound tomatoes, peeled,
    seeded, and chopped
½ teaspoon dried rosemary

1 teaspoon dried thyme
1 teaspoon salt
Freshly ground black pepper
2 cups chicken or beef broth
2 tablespoons red wine
    vinegar

Prepare the tripe as directed (in Basic Preparation) and cut into strips 1 × 3 inches. (This can be done the day before.) Preheat the oven to 325°F. Heat the oil in a skillet. Add the onions and garlic and cook over moderate heat until the onions are soft. Add the tomatoes, rosemary, thyme, salt, and pepper to taste, and simmer for about 5 minutes more. Add the broth, vinegar, and the tripe pieces, and mix well with the tomato mixture. Pour into a casserole, cover, and bake for 3 hours.

(SERVES FOUR) **TRIPE IN BATTER**

Serve with Chili Sauce (p. 1107).

1 pound tripe
1 cup flour
½ teaspoon salt
1 teaspoon baking powder

1 egg, beaten
⅓ cup milk
1 cup plus 1 teaspoon
    vegetable oil

Prepare the tripe as directed (in Basic Preparation) and cut into serving-size pieces. Make a batter by combining the flour, salt, baking powder, egg, milk, and 1 teaspoon oil in a bowl. Beat until well blended. Dip pieces of tripe in the batter. Heat the remaining cup of oil in a large skillet. When it is very hot, fry the battered tripe until brown on both sides. Don't crowd the pan: do a few pieces at a time and keep those that are done warm in the oven.

(SERVES FOUR) **LEMON-PARSLEY TRIPE**

1 pound tripe
2 tablespoons butter
2 tablespoons finely chopped
    onion
Salt to taste

Freshly ground pepper to
    taste
3 tablespoons lemon juice
1 tablespoon minced parsley

Prepare the tripe as directed (in Basic Preparation) and cut it into ½ × 2-inch pieces. Melt the butter in a skillet and add the onion. Cook over moderate heat, stirring often, until onion is soft. Add the pieces of tripe and cook 4 minutes. Sprinkle with salt, pepper, and lemon juice; arrange on a platter and garnish with parsley.

About Liver

Liver is unquestionably the most generally used variety meat in America. With no waste, it provides four highly nutritious servings a pound. Look for a bright, shiny surface when you buy it; avoid liver that is dull-colored. The butcher will probably not have removed the outer membrane for you. Scrape and peel it off, then wipe the liver clean with a paper towel. Keep it loosely wrapped in the refrigerator, and plan to use it within 24 hours. If that is not possible, freeze it; like all variety meats, liver freezes well.

The best quality, flavor, and tenderness are found in calves' liver. Beef liver is tougher and stronger in flavor, though still very good, while pork liver has a stronger odor and flavor but is very nutritious. Pork and goose livers are both widely used for making pâtés. Chicken, duck, turkey, and goose livers are all tender, flavorful, and highly perishable.

Even the most tender piece of calves' liver, if overcooked, will tighten and toughen. Never overcook it: either sauté it quickly over high heat, a minute on each side, or cook it gently over medium heat only to the point of tenderness.

LIVER SAUTÉED IN BUTTER   (SERVES FOUR)

1 pound liver, in ⅛–¼-inch slices	1 tablespoon oil
3 tablespoons flour	Salt
3 tablespoons butter	Freshly ground pepper

Dip the liver in flour and shake off any excess. Heat the butter and oil in a skillet until foaming, then add the liver. Cook about 1 minute—or less for very thin pieces—on each side or until the red color is gone. Sprinkle with salt and pepper.

LIVER AND BACON

Fry *8 slices of bacon*, drain on paper towels, and keep warm. Remove all but 3 tablespoons bacon fat from the skillet, and use this instead of butter and oil to sauté the liver. Serve with the cooked bacon.

LIVER AND ONIONS

Slice 2 *large onions* thin, and separate the rings. Melt 2 *tablespoons butter* in a skillet over medium heat, and cook the onions until light golden. Remove and keep warm. In sautéing the liver, omit the oil. Serve covered with onions.

(SERVES FOUR) ## LIVER VENETIAN STYLE

1 pound liver, in ⅛-inch-thick slices	4 onions, sliced thin
4 tablespoons vegetable oil	Salt
	Freshly ground pepper

Cut the liver into ½-inch-wide strips, using scissors or a sharp knife. Heat the oil in a large skillet. Add the onions and cook, stirring often, over medium heat until soft and lightly browned. Push the onions to the side of the pan, turn the heat up, and sauté the liver for about 1 minute, until it turns from red to brown. Sprinkle with salt and pepper to taste.

RABBIT

About Rabbit

The rabbit we get in this country has been raised domestically, so we cannot consider rabbit as game. The meat tastes very much like chicken, a little more dense and dry, and it would be worthwhile experimenting by substituting rabbit in some of the chicken recipes. Rabbit usually comes packaged, cut up in pieces, more often than not frozen. Defrost slowly in the refrigerator.

(SERVES FOUR OR FIVE) ## FRIED RABBIT

Like fried chicken, this tastes good served hot or cold.

4-pound domestic rabbit, in serving pieces	Salt
¼ cup flour	Freshly ground pepper
	3 tablespoons shortening

Wipe the rabbit pieces with a damp towel and pat dry. Lightly dust each piece with flour and sprinkle with salt and pepper to taste. Heat the shortening in a large skillet, then add the rabbit and brown. Lower the heat and fry, turning often, for 25 minutes, or until the juices run clear when a small slit is made in the thick part of the thigh.

RABBIT WITH CREAM GRAVY

Remove rabbit from pan and keep warm. Add 2 *tablespoons flour* to the pan drippings. Stir in 1½ *cups light cream* and simmer, stirring until thickened. Pour over rabbit.

BRAISED RABBIT   (SERVES SIX)

Serve with spoon bread, garnished with fresh rosemary.

2 tablespoons butter	1 bay leaf, crumbled
2 tablespoons vegetable oil	1 tablespoon chopped fresh
Two 3-pound rabbits, each	rosemary, or 1 teaspoon
cut into 6 pieces	dried
4 medium onions, sliced	Salt
4 cloves garlic, chopped fine	Freshly ground pepper
2 cups chicken broth	2 tablespoons cornstarch
¼ cup fresh lemon juice	2 tablespoons water

Heat the butter and oil in a large heavy-bottomed skillet. Add the rabbit pieces, a few at a time, to the skillet and brown on all sides. Remove the browned pieces and place on paper towels. Add the onions to the skillet and cook about 5 minutes or until soft. Return the rabbit to the skillet and add the garlic, chicken broth, lemon juice, bay leaf, rosemary, and salt and pepper to taste. Cover and simmer for about 20 to 25 minutes, until the juices run clear when a small slit is made in the thickest part of a thigh. When the rabbit is done, remove it to a serving platter and keep warm. In a small bowl mix the cornstarch with the water until smooth. Slowly add the cornstarch mixture to the hot liquid in the pan, stirring, and simmer gently until well blended and thickened. Taste for seasonings. Pour the hot sauce over the rabbit and serve.

VENISON

About Venison

Venison is seldom available in our markets, so you have to know a hunter to enjoy this treat. Also, only he will know the approximate age of the deer when killed, which is important because that is your guide to how to cook the meat. Tender young venison will need no marinating and can be cooked very briefly, as in Broiled Venison Steak, or you may use some of the recipes for lamb—chops or roasts. Older venison should always be marinated before cooking.

VENISON STEAK AND CHESTNUT SAUCE

(SERVES FOUR)

3 tablespoons butter
½ onion, chopped
½ carrot, chopped
3 tablespoons flour
1½ cups beef broth
½ bay leaf, crumbled
1 teaspoon freshly ground
    pepper

1 teaspoon salt
¼ cup Madeira
1 cup cooked chopped
    chestnuts
1 or 2 1¼-inch-thick venison
    steaks

Melt the butter in a skillet. Add the onion and carrot and cook until lightly browned, about 5 minutes. Stir in the flour and cook until brown. Add the beef broth, bay leaf, pepper, and salt, and simmer for 10–15 minutes. Strain, then add the Madeira and chestnuts and set aside. Preheat the broiler. Place the venison steaks on a rack 5 inches beneath the broiler element. Cook 5 minutes on each side. Remove to a hot platter and cover with the hot chestnut sauce.

BROILED VENISON STEAK

(SERVES TWO)

¾–1-inch-thick venison steak
4 tablespoons butter, softened
Salt
Freshly ground pepper

1 cup dry red wine
¼ teaspoon allspice
½ cup currant jelly

Preheat the broiler. Rub the venison steak with butter and sprinkle liberally with salt and pepper. Place the steak 4 inches beneath the broiling element on a rack in a shallow pan. Broil 4 minutes each side.

Remove the steak to a warm platter and set the pan over a burner. Add the wine, allspice, and jelly to the pan drippings. Bring to a boil and stir until smooth and blended. Spoon a little sauce over the steak and pass the rest in a bowl.

MARINATED LEG OF VENISON   (SERVES EIGHT TO TEN)

Start to marinate the meat two days before you plan to cook it.

5-pound leg of venison	1 teaspoon salt
2 cups dry red wine	1 teaspoon freshly ground
½ cup olive oil	pepper
2 bay leaves	4 slices bacon
4 cloves garlic, chopped	3 tablespoons flour
2 teaspoons dry mustard	½ cup red currant jelly
1 teaspoon rosemary, crumbled	

Place the leg of venison in a deep bowl. Combine the wine, oil, bay leaves, garlic, mustard, rosemary, salt, and pepper, and pour over the venison. Cover with foil and refrigerate two days, turning the meat several times. Preheat the oven to 450°F. Drain the venison and reserve the marinade. Place the meat on a rack in a shallow pan and cover with the bacon strips. Roast for 30 minutes, basting several times with the marinade, then reduce the heat to 350°F and continue to roast another 40–60 minutes (to an interior temperature of 130°F for rare; 140°F for medium). Put the venison on a platter and keep warm. Set the roasting pan over a burner, add the flour to the pan drippings, and cook until it is browned. Strain the reserved marinade and stir into the pan, cooking until smooth and thickened. Add the currant jelly; cook only until the jelly is melted and blended with the sauce. Carve at the table the way you would a roast of lamb, with the gravy in a sauceboat.

POULTRY & GAME BIRDS

While Americans have been eating chicken even more abundantly, there has been considerable concern in the last several years about salmonella. It is important to handle raw chicken carefully (see p. 209 for details) and to cook it sufficiently so that the bacteria are killed, and we have adjusted some of the cooking times accordingly. As well as a dozen or so new recipes that have made their way into this chapter (I am particularly fond of Smothered Chicken with Mushrooms, on p. 325), you'll find chicken strips in a pasta recipe and some new ideas for chicken salads.

Microwaving Poultry

The only part of the chicken that microwaves successfully, I find, is the breast with the skin removed. It must be done very carefully—see instructions in the Microwave chapter. The flavor of the dark meat in chicken is impaired by microwaving and the skin is like steamed skin, unpleasant in taste and texture. Turkey is equally disappointing, except for the breast meat.

I have tried poaching in the microwave a whole chicken in broth and aromatics, and while it turned out reasonably well, it is easier and just about as quick to poach it on top of the stove.

ABOUT POULTRY

The dream of the good life in America is embodied in the promise of "a chicken in every pot." Domestic and wild fowl have always been abundant and popular, and each wave of immigrants has brought along favorite dishes—such as paella and chicken cacciatore—which have soon become naturalized citizens.

Thanks to modern scientific techniques, the birds we buy today are rich in nutrition, low in fat, and reasonable in price. Whereas once we had to wait for spring broilers, summer fryers, fall roasters, and the stewing hens of deep winter, we now have an endless supply of tender wholesome poultry all year round.

Types of Poultry

By "poultry" we mean all the domestic birds that are raised for food: chicken, turkey, duck, goose, Cornish game hen, and squab or pigeon.

CHICKEN.   Chicken is classified by its age and weight and sold with names that are suggestions rather than prescriptions for cooking. The differences among fryers, broilers, roasters, stewing hens, and Cornish hens relate primarily to age. The terms fryer and broiler are used interchangeably, and apply to young birds between 49 and 56 days old, which may weigh from 2½ to 4½ pounds. Roasters are two to six weeks older than fryers and are consequently larger birds in the 5- to 6-pound range. The stewing hens are spent breeders, and are the most mature chickens commonly sold. Because they are more mature they require slow cooking with moist heat to develop tenderness and full flavor. Today's commonly grown chickens are of mixed breeds; those which contain a strain of Cornish hen may be so labeled and are generally processed for this use when the packaged bird is in the 1- to 1½-pound size range.

TURKEY.   Turkey also comes in various weights. There are fryer-roasters at 4 to 8 pounds and young hens weighing 7 to 15 pounds. Fully mature hens or tom turkeys—both have their enthusiasts— weigh up to 30 pounds and are splendid for holiday feasts. Their appearance is generous, and they are more economical than smaller birds, costing less per pound and having a higher ratio of meat to bone than less imposing fowl.

OTHER POULTRY.   Domestic ducklings, only 3 to 4 pounds in weight, are tender and delicate when fried or broiled; mature ducks at 5 to 6 pounds should be roasted or braised. Goose is still larger, ranging from 8 to 16 pounds.

Buying Poultry

All the poultry offered for sale in this country has been inspected by the United States Department of Agriculture, and the clip, tag, or stamp on each bird certifies its freshness. A flexible breastbone is a good sign of youth; if it is stiff and unyielding, try some long slow cooking.

The color of the chicken does not indicate its quality: in the midwestern and eastern states white-skinned chicken is preferred, while corn-feeding produces yellow skin in chickens, considered desirable in the West.

About 1 pound of chicken or turkey with bones makes a serving, but allow at least 1½ pounds of raw duck or goose for each person, for they have a large amount of body fat that melts away during cooking, making their raw weight misleading. Buy more rather than less: using up leftover poultry is no problem.

If your family strongly prefers white or dark meat, you may decide to buy cut-up poultry in packages containing only the parts that you want. Resist the temptation to buy either prebasted or frozen stuffed turkeys; you will be paying someone else to do jobs that are simple and so much better done at home.

Storing Poultry

Poultry is among the most perishable of meats. Take it straight home from the market and remove it from its wrappings. Thoroughly rinse in cold water and rewrap it loosely and refrigerate it immediately, keeping it no more than a day or two. Chicken parts are even more perishable than whole chickens. For freezing poultry, see p. 1122.

Preparing Poultry for Cooking

Today's poultry is usually ready to cook; all you need do is to wipe it with a damp paper towel or rinse it quickly under cold running water, patting it dry so that it will brown nicely. Remove any lumps of fat around the cavities, particularly the tail. Save chicken and goose fat and render it so that it can be used in cooking.

Be careful. Keep poultry refrigerated until cooking. If frozen, thaw only in the refrigerator or microwave. Cook all poultry thoroughly. Wash hands, utensils, and work surfaces with hot soapy water after contact with any uncooked poultry.

Don't use the same utensil, cutting board, or surface for cutting up raw poultry, meat, or fish that you do for vegetables or salad fixings that may not be cooked. Cutting surfaces should be nonporous and easy to wash.

To render chicken fat. Pick the yellow fat off each chicken you cook; you'll find most of it around the tail. Collect raw chicken fat in the freezer until you have enough to render, about ½ to 1 cup. One pound of raw chicken fat will produce about 2 cups of rendered fat.

Cut the fat into very small pieces and put them in a large skillet over very low heat until the fat has melted and the small pieces are crisp and brown. Remove them from the pan and drain on paper towels. If you wish, flavor the rendered fat in the pan by browning a diced onion or two in it. Strain the fat into a jar or container, cover tight, and refrigerate. It will keep almost indefinitely.

The browned bits of fat and onions are traditionally mixed into chopped liver or mashed potatoes or sprinkled with salt and served as a snack.

To melt chicken fat. This is a simple way to render chicken fat. The fat will be pure and unflavored and will keep indefinitely.

Pick fat off the chicken. Preheat the oven to 275°F. Put the chicken fat in a heatproof cup or bowl and fill two-thirds full with water. Place in the oven and let the fat melt slowly; this will take an hour or more, depending on the amount of fat. Remove and cool. The fat will rise to the top and should then be carefully spooned into a container, covered, and stored in the refrigerator.

Cutting Up a Whole Chicken

You not only save money by cutting up your own chicken but, when you do it yourself, it is neater, with none of the little splintered bones that the electric saw sometimes produces. See p. 209 for sanitary rules.

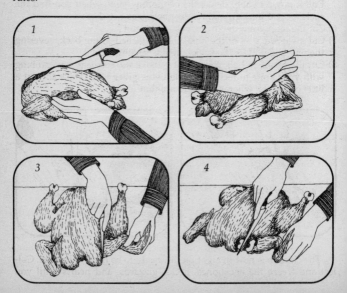

1) Place the chicken breast side down on a nonporous work surface (not wood). Using a very sharp knife, cut through the backbone along the spinal column.
2) Turn the chicken over and break both sides of the breastbone by pushing down on it with the heel of your hand. Firmly flatten the chicken as much as possible.
3) Wiggle the wing joint at the shoulder, poking around with the tip of your knife until you feel the connecting tissue.
4) Cut through to remove the wing. Repeat with the other wing.

5) Wiggle the leg back and forth to see where it connects to the body. Pull it down to help detect the connecting joint; when you find the socket, cut through it and remove both legs.
6) Cut the thigh from the drumstick at the joint.
7) Cut away the side of the breast, still attached to the back, severing the tiny bones. (Use the back bone for making stock.)
8) Cut the breast in half, starting just above the cartilage and probing with your knife to feel where the tissue gives way. Make the cut a little off-center, where the bones are thin.

The chicken is now in eight pieces, ready to be fried or broiled. Collect and freeze the backbones, necks, gizzards, and hearts until you have enough to make a rich chicken stock or soup. Freeze the liver separately to use in liver dishes.

Boning chicken breasts
Chicken breasts, skinned, boned, and pounded thin, are the basis for

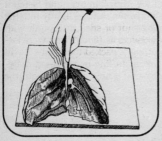

many interesting, delicate dishes and, like turkey, make a delicious and thrifty substitute in recipes calling for veal cutlets. Save money by boning them yourself, using a sharp knife: following the breastbone cut the meat in half lengthwise, then scrape it away from the breastbone as you gently tug it. The bones should go into the stockpot. Three pounds of chicken breasts will weigh about 2¼ pounds after boning.

A boned breast will be about ½ inch thick. To make a cutlet, place it between two sheets of wax paper and pound it with a mallet or rolling pin until it is only ¼ inch thick. Cooked for 10 minutes or less, it should be tender, moist, and delicately flavored.

Stuffing Poultry

For stuffings, see p. 399.

To stuff a bird, wash it briefly and pat it dry with paper towels. Season it inside and out. You can prepare the stuffing ahead of time, but don't put it into the bird more than a few hours before you cook it and be sure to refrigerate. Even after it has been cooked, stuffing

should not sit around too long in the bird. It's a good idea to store it separately in the refrigerator if you are going to keep it several days.

Prepare about ¾ cup of stuffing for each pound of poultry; 9 cups of stuffing for a 12-pound turkey, for example. Pack a little stuffing loosely into the neck cavity, then pull the neck skin over and fasten it to the back with a skewer. Spoon the rest of the stuffing lightly into the body cavity and either sew the opening shut or stick it through with skewers, wrapping string around the skewers as though you were lacing a boot. Leave some space: if the stuffing is packed too firmly, it will burst the skin as it expands. Put any extra stuffing in a greased casserole and bake it along with the bird, basting it now and then with the pan drippings.

Trussing Poultry

Stuffed or unstuffed, a whole bird should be trussed before it is roasted or braised to keep it from drying out during cooking, to ensure an attractive presentation, and to add ease to carving.

1) Place the bird, breast side up, on a counter top. Bend the second joints of the wings back. 2) Place the middle of a long piece of string underneath the tail, bring the ends over the tail, and cross them over

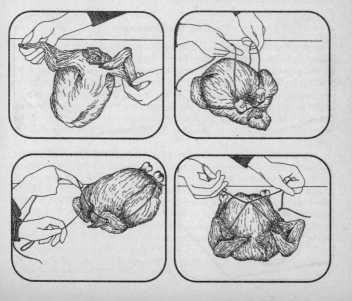

the body, looping around the ends of the drumsticks. 3) Run the string snugly across the sides of the body, pulling it through the holes made by the folded wings. 4) Turn the bird, breast side down, and tie the string in a knot in the back. One snip before carving will remove the string, while the bird stays neatly in shape.

Cooking Poultry

Poultry may be roasted, broiled, fried, stewed, braised, or poached. Steaming is used primarily in Chinese cooking and for special fat-free diets.

When you are roasting or broiling, basting helps to keep the skin from drying out. Birds can be roasted stuffed or unstuffed; stuffed poultry requires extra cooking time. If you don't want to bother with a stuffing, season the cavity with salt and pepper and put in a whole onion, a handful of fresh herbs, or perhaps a half a lemon, for flavor. Roasting times vary considerably: tiny game hens take less than an hour, but a stuffed goose weighing 12 or more pounds will take nearly 4 hours to become succulent and brown.

When you fry small, tender chickens, they will become crisp and brown in a very short time. Less tender birds should be browned in butter and then gently simmered in liquid, as in Chicken Fricassee. Older chickens when gently cooked in lots of liquid will produce a rich broth, as in chicken and dumplings.

Testing for Doneness

The poultry we get today has been fed scientifically; it's tender and moist, and the cooking time is shorter than it was some years ago. Test to see if poultry is done by cutting a deep slit in the flesh between leg and body: if the juices run clear the bird is done; pink blood indicates that more cooking is required. The old test of "shaking hands with the bird" is unreliable, for if the leg moves easily in its socket, the dark meat is probably overdone. With experience you will be able to feel when the meat is done by pressing the thigh and breast with your finger.

An instant meat thermometer provides real assurance, of course. When the approximate cooking time is coming to an end, insert the tip of the thermometer into the breast meat or the thickest part of the thigh, being careful not to touch the tip of the thermometer to a bone. The bird is done when the temperature of the breast meat reads 170°F and that of the thigh meat is at 185°F. This slight disparity in required cooking time makes it advisable, if you are cooking poultry cut up into parts, to start dark meat cooking a few minutes before white meat when possible; it also explains why roast turkeys sometimes have dried-out white meat while their dark meat is still succulent and flavorful.

Carving Cooked Poultry

Carving will be easier if you let the bird rest at room temperature for 15 minutes after it is cooked. Use a freshly sharpened carving knife. Place the cooked chicken or turkey on a platter breast side up, with the legs to your right. (Reverse this position, of course, if you are left-handed.) Holding a large fork in your fist, stick it firmly into the fleshy part of the drumstick near you. Cut through the skin that joins the leg to the body. Pull the leg away from the body, finding the connecting joint with the tip of your knife so you can sever it. Once removed, detach the drumstick from the second joint. Next, cut off the wing, again probing with the tip of your knife to find the socket before you cut. Then carve the breast meat into thin slices, sticking the fork into the meat above. Repeat on the other side as more meat is needed.

Using Leftovers

For specific dishes using leftover chicken, turkey, and other poultry, see p. 342.

Poultry Livers

Liver, with its pronounced flavor, should never go into a stock. Save the livers for another use; even if there's just one liver, save it and freeze it until you have enough to make a dish. Or if you are roasting the poultry, add the liver to the pan during the last 5 minutes (10 minutes for a large turkey liver). The liver will absorb a little of the pan drippings and turn brown while retaining its rosy center, and is delicious chopped and added to your gravy (or just eaten whole).

Chicken, turkey, duck, and goose livers should be cooked only long enough to brown them, leaving them lightly pink inside. Overcooking makes them tough and rubbery and destroys the good, creamy texture.

TURKEY

ROAST STUFFED TURKEY   (1 POUND PER SERVING)

Before you place the turkey on its **V**-shaped rack, cover the rack with heavily greased parchment, foil, or brown paper to keep the skin from tearing when you turn the turkey. Check p. 308 to determine the amount of stuffing per pound of turkey you will need.

1 turkey	Salt
Stuffing (pp. 399–405)	Freshly ground pepper
¼–½ pound butter, depending on size of turkey	

Preheat the oven to 325°F. Rinse the turkey and pat it dry. Stuff the body and neck cavities before trussing (p. 309). Soften ⅛–¼ pound butter and rub all over the turkey, depending on its size—it should be thoroughly buttered. Sprinkle with salt and pepper and place, breast down, on the paper-covered rack in a roasting pan. Put in the oven. Melt the remaining butter (about ¼ pound) with ¼ cup water and baste the turkey every 20 minutes with this mixture until enough pan drippings for basting have accumulated in the bottom of the roasting pan. Cook 15 minutes per pound if the turkey weighs less than 16 pounds; 12 minutes per pound if it is heavier. Turn breast up after 1 hour if the turkey weighs less than 12 pounds; after 1½ hours if it weighs more. When a meat thermometer registers 170°F in the breast meat and 185°F in the thigh meat, remove the turkey to a warm platter and cover loosely with a towel or foil. Let rest 15 minutes before carving.

UNSTUFFED ROAST TURKEY

Omit the stuffing. Sprinkle the body cavity with *1 teaspoon salt* and *½ teaspoon poultry seasoning*, then place in the cavity *5 sprigs parsley, 4 stalks celery*, and *3 onions, peeled and quartered*.

Basic Chicken or Turkey Gravy   (2 CUPS)

Two factors help make a lovely deep-brown gravy: the drippings on the bottom of the roasting pan and the slow browning of the flour in the fat.

4 tablespoons fat from poultry pan drippings	Freshly ground pepper
3 tablespoons flour	2 cups liquid: stock, giblet broth, water, or milk
Salt	

When the bird has been removed from the roasting pan, skim off all but 4 tablespoons of fat in the pan. If there is not enough fat in the drippings, add butter. Place the pan over a burner and heat it, scraping the bottom of the pan to loosen all the browned bits. (If the roasting pan is clumsy to handle, scrape and pour the drippings into a saucepan.) Stir in the flour and blend well over medium heat for 3 minutes or more, until lightly browned. Add salt and pepper to taste, and slowly pour in the liquid, stirring constantly, until smooth. Simmer for 10 minutes to develop the flavor.

Giblet Broth

NOTE

In general "giblets" refers to all the loose parts—the neck, heart, liver, and gizzard of poultry. A broth made of giblets and vegetables will add richness to gravy, as will the chopped giblets themselves. Because of its strong flavor, the liver should not be cooked in the broth, but separately.

Giblets	Salt
1 teaspoon thyme, crumbled	Freshly ground pepper
1 thick slice onion	Butter (optional)
1 stalk celery with leaves, sliced	

Rinse the gizzard, heart, and neck, and trim all fat, membranes, and blood. Put the giblets in a saucepan, cover with cold water, and add the thyme, onion, celery, and a sprinkle of salt and pepper. Bring to a boil and simmer 45 minutes, or until the gizzard is tender. Meanwhile, cook the liver under the roasting bird 5–10 minutes or sauté lightly in some butter. Strain the giblets, reserve the broth, and finely dice the gizzard, liver, and heart. Using this broth, make the gravy following Basic Chicken or Turkey Gravy (preceding recipe) and add the giblets at the end.

MAKING GRAVY AHEAD

A great help in reducing the frantic hassle of last-minute preparations is to make the turkey gravy a day ahead. Buy one or two inexpensive packages of turkey parts such as wings. Put them in a roasting pan and roast to a dark mahogany color. Use the drippings and pan juices from this to make the gravy, using the recipe above. (You can always use the browned wings for broth.) Refrigerate, then reheat when needed.

GROUND TURKEY PATTIES   (SERVES FOUR)

This happens to be healthful, in addition to tasting very good!

1 pound ground turkey	½ teaspoon poultry seasoning
1 cup grated zucchini	Freshly ground pepper to
1 cup finely chopped onion	taste
1 cup fresh bread crumbs	1 tablespoon vegetable oil
½ teaspoon salt	

In a large bowl put the turkey, zucchini, onion, bread crumbs, salt,
poultry seasoning, and pepper, and lightly toss with a fork until well
mixed. Form the turkey mixture into 4 or 6 patties. Heat the oil in a
skillet over medium heat and cook the patties about 3–4 minutes on
each side, or until done and the meat in the center has turned opaque
and is no longer pink. Do not overcook or they will be dry.

ROAST TURKEY BREAST   (1 POUND SERVES THREE)

To bone a turkey breast, slip a knife between the bone and the meat
and separate the two, using a sawing motion. Tie the two halves together to make a cylindrical roll.

1 whole boned turkey breast	Salt
4 tablespoons butter	Freshly ground pepper

Preheat the oven to 325°F. Rub the turkey breast liberally with butter
and sprinkle with salt and pepper. Place in a shallow pan and roast for
25 minutes per pound or until the meat thermometer registers 170°F.

TURKEY BREAST WITH RED CURRANT SAUCE

Mix ½ cup red currant jelly, ¼ cup port wine, 3 tablespoons butter, and 1½
teaspoons Worcestershire sauce in a small saucepan. Stir over low heat
until melted and simmering, then brush on the roasting turkey breast
every 15 minutes. Spoon some of the sauce over the sliced meat.

CHICKEN

ROAST CHICKEN

Although a 3–5-pound chicken is called a roaster, small broiler-fryers can also be cooked this way. Use a roasting pan that accommodates the bird comfortably; if the pan is too big, the good pan drippings will spread out and cook away.

2½–5-pound chicken	¼–⅓ pound butter
Stuffing (pp. 399–405; optional)	Salt
	Freshly ground pepper

Preheat the oven to 325°F. Rinse the chicken and pat it dry. Stuff the body and neck cavities, if desired, before trussing (p. 309). Soften 3–4 tablespoons of the butter and rub it all over the chicken. Sprinkle with salt and pepper and place the chicken in the oven, breast up, on a **V**-shaped rack in a roasting pan. Melt the remaining butter in a saucepan. Baste every 15 minutes with the melted butter until enough pan drippings for basting have accumulated in the bottom of the roasting pan. Cook about 25 minutes a pound, or until a meat thermometer registers 170°F in the breast meat and 185°F in the thigh meat. A stuffed chicken will take longer to cook. Remove the chicken to a warm platter and cover loosely with a towel or foil. Let rest 10 minutes to distribute the juices and settle the meat for carving.

THYME-ROASTED CHICKEN

Omit the stuffing and rub *½ teaspoon salt* in the body cavity before inserting *1 carrot, sliced*, and *1 stalk celery with leaves, sliced*. Add *1 teaspoon thyme, crumbled*, to the butter rubbed on the chicken. Make basic gravy (p. 312), using *1 cup chicken broth* and *1 cup water* and adding the *juice of 1 lemon* before serving.

OVEN-BROILED CHICKEN

Unlike real broiled chicken, fowl cooked by this simple method does not require careful watching. The plainness of this preparation proves again that simple is often best. It is good when hot, and unequaled later in salads or sandwiches.

3 tablespoons oil   Salt
2½–3-pound chicken, in   Freshly ground pepper
    halves or quarters or
    chicken parts

Preheat the oven to 400°F. Lightly oil a shallow pan. Coat the chicken with oil and season to taste with salt and pepper. Place skin side up in the pan. Bake for 30–45 minutes, or until a meat thermometer reads 170°F in the breast meat, 185°F in the dark meat.

BROILED CHICKEN   (SERVES FOUR)

Quick and juicy, but requiring careful watching.

Salt   4 tablespoons butter, melted
Freshly ground pepper
2½–3-pound chicken, in
    halves or quarters

Preheat the broiler. Sprinkle salt and pepper on the chicken and place it on the broiler pan, skin side down. Brush with the melted butter. Place the pan 5 inches beneath the broiling element and cook 10 minutes. Turn the chicken, brush with melted butter, and broil 10 minutes more. Turn and brush with melted butter again. Check with a meat thermometer (see p. 33) or cut a slit in the thickest part of the thigh and see if the juices run clear. Turn and cook longer if necessary.

ORANGE-BROILED CHICKEN

Baste with a mixture of ½ cup orange juice, ¼ cup oil, 2 tablespoons grated orange rind, ½ teaspoon dry mustard, ¼ teaspoon salt, and a dash of Tabasco instead of the melted butter.

BARBECUE-ROASTED CHICKEN   (SERVES FOUR)

This may be done on an indoor rotisserie as well as over hot coals.

2½–3-pound chicken   Freshly ground pepper
¼ cup oil   1 recipe Light Barbecue Sauce
Salt   (p. 377)

Light the coals. Truss the chicken (p. 309), rub it with oil, and sprinkle it with salt and pepper to taste. Arrange on a spit. When the fire is ready, place the spitted chicken on the rotisserie and cook for 1–1½ hours, or until a meat thermometer registers 170°F in the breast meat and 185°F in the thigh meat, basting every 15 minutes with the sauce.

BARBECUE-BROILED CHICKEN

Cut the chicken into halves or quarters. (Smaller pieces tend to dry out and overdarken.) Place on the grill, skin side up, and cook 10 minutes. Turn and baste every 10 minutes until done, about 40 minutes in all.

(SERVES FOUR) ## PAN-FRIED CHICKEN

Remember all the nice things that go with this: biscuits with butter and maybe honey, cream gravy—and mustard greens cooked with salt pork for a real southern dinner.

2½–3-pound chicken, in 8 pieces	½ teaspoon freshly ground pepper
Milk	Oil for frying
¾ cup flour	Cream Gravy (p. 318)
1 teaspoon salt	

Wash and dry the chicken pieces. Place them snugly together in one layer in a shallow dish. Pour on milk to cover, and soak 1 hour, turning once. Mix the flour, salt, and pepper on a piece of wax paper or in a paper bag. Remove chicken from the milk and roll it in the seasoned flour or shake vigorously in the paper bag. Pour oil into a large skillet to a depth of ½ inch. Heat until a small cube of bread browns in 60 seconds or a frying thermometer registers 365°F. Put the dark meat into the pan first, adding the white meat 5 minutes later. Do not crowd the chicken; if necessary, cook in two batches. Fry about 20–30 minutes, turning often with a pair of tongs. Remove, drain on paper towels, and keep warm while you make the gravy. Serve hot with the gravy.

VARIATION

If you cover the skillet after the first 10 minutes of cooking and then uncover for the last 10 minutes, you will have a southern-style fried chicken, which is a chicken that is moist and only slightly crisp on the outside.

Cream Gravy (1¾ CUPS)

A must with all types of fried chicken!

3 tablespoons pan drippings and butter	Salt
3 tablespoons flour	¼ teaspoon freshly ground pepper
1½ cups cream	

Heat the pan drippings in the skillet, adding butter, if necessary, and scraping up any brown bits in the pan. Stir in the flour and blend, cooking over low heat until lightly browned. Slowly add the cream, stirring constantly until smooth. Season with salt to taste and pepper, and cook for about 7 minutes.

BATTER-FRIED CHICKEN (SERVES FOUR)

The batter coating makes a crunchy crust. An electric deep-fat fryer with automatic temperature controls is good for this, but you can use an ordinary heavy-bottomed pan.

2½–3-pound chicken, in 8 pieces	Oil for deep frying
1 recipe Beer Fritter Batter (p. 533)	

Wash and dry the pieces of chicken. Prepare the fritter batter. Heat at least 3 inches of oil until a small cube of bread browns in 60 seconds or a frying thermometer registers 365°F. Dip the chicken pieces into the batter and submerge them carefully in the oil. Use tongs to move the pieces about so they don't stick together. Fry 15 minutes or until done, and drain on paper towels.

MARYLAND FRIED CHICKEN (SERVES FOUR)

In Maryland, they dip their chicken in flour, egg, and soft bread crumbs before frying it.

½ cup flour	1 egg
1 teaspoon salt	2½–3-pound chicken, in 8 pieces
½ teaspoon freshly ground pepper	Oil for frying
2 cups freshly made bread crumbs	Cream Gravy (see above)

Mix the flour with the salt and pepper on wax paper. Spread the bread crumbs on another piece of wax paper. Lightly beat the egg in a shallow bowl with 2 tablespoons of water. Wash and dry the chicken pieces. Coat them with flour, dip in the egg, then roll them in the bread crumbs. Heat ½ inch of oil until a small cube of bread browns in 60 seconds or a frying thermometer registers 365°F. Using tongs, put the chicken in the hot oil and fry for about 20 minutes, turning often, until brown and done. Drain on paper towels and keep warm while you make the gravy.

(SERVES FOUR) **DELMONICO'S DEVILED CHICKEN**

"Deviled" here means that the chicken is seasoned with spices and then sprinkled with crumbs.

2½–3-pound chicken, in quarters
4 tablespoons butter, softened
1 tablespoon prepared mustard
1 tablespoon vinegar
½ teaspoon salt
¼ teaspoon cayenne, or to taste
1 cup freshly made bread crumbs

Preheat the oven to 375°F. Wipe the chicken with a paper towel. Mix the butter, mustard, vinegar, salt, and cayenne, and rub the mixture all over the skin side of the chicken. Place the quarters, skin side up, in a shallow roasting pan. Sprinkle evenly with the crumbs and bake for about 40 minutes, or until a meat thermometer registers 170°F in the breast meat, 185°F in the dark meat.

(SERVES FOUR) **CHICKEN PROVENÇAL**

This may not be a spa recipe, but if you can be indulgent, it is worth the calories. It is equally good served cold.

¼ cup olive oil
1 head garlic, cloves separated and peeled
3 slices crustless bread, torn in small pieces (about ¾ cup)
¼ cup red wine vinegar
Salt and freshly ground pepper to taste
½ cup whole almonds
1 bay leaf
4–6 chicken breasts
1 cup chicken broth
½ cup mayonnaise
3 tablespoons fresh lemon juice

Heat 2 tablespoons of the oil in a skillet over medium-high heat. Add the garlic and toss for about 1 minute, then remove and reserve. Soak the bread in the vinegar and season with salt and pepper. Lightly brown the bread in the skillet for 2–3 minutes, then remove and reserve. Put the garlic, bread, almonds, and bay leaf in a blender or food processor, and process until you have a paste. Add the remaining 2 tablespoons olive oil to the same skillet and brown the chicken pieces on both sides. Mix the garlic paste with the chicken broth, and add it to the pan with the chicken. Cover, and simmer about 20 minutes, or until chicken is done. Remove the chicken to a serving dish and keep warm, leaving the sauce in the pan. Skim off and remove any excess fat with a spoon. Mix the mayonnaise and lemon juice together and gradually add to the pan, stirring it into the sauce. Pour the finished sauce over the chicken and serve.

SAVORY CASSEROLE OF CHICKEN   (SERVES FOUR)

2½–3-pound chicken, in 8 pieces
4 tablespoons flour
¼ cup oil
¼ cup finely chopped onion
¼ cup finely chopped celery
1 tablespoon finely chopped green pepper

1½ cups chopped canned or fresh tomatoes
¾ teaspoon oregano, crumbled
1¼ teaspoons salt
½ teaspoon freshly ground pepper

Preheat the oven to 325°F. Wash and dry the chicken pieces and lightly dust with flour. Heat the oil in a skillet and quickly brown the chicken pieces. Put the chicken into a casserole with a lid. Add the remaining ingredients, cover, and bake 1 hour.

CHICKEN CACCIATORE   (SERVES FOUR)

An Italian dish—*cacciatore* meaning "hunter's"—which has a good earthy taste. The final garnish adds wonderful zest to the finished dish—and those shy of garlic *can* always leave the garlic out.

1 ounce dried mushrooms
¼ cup olive oil
1 medium chicken, in 8 pieces
1 large onion, chopped
½ cup dry white wine
1 clove garlic, minced
1 tablespoon tomato paste

2 cups fresh tomatoes, peeled, seeded, and chopped, or canned drained
½ teaspoon allspice
Freshly ground pepper
2 bay leaves
½ teaspoon thyme, crumbled
Salt to taste

Garnish

Grated rind of 1 lemon   3 tablespoons minced parsley
½ clove garlic, minced

Put the mushrooms to soak for a half-hour in a cup with just enough warm water to cover. Heat the oil in a large skillet and cook the chicken until lightly browned on all sides. Add the onion and sauté a minute or two, then splash in the wine and let it boil up. Lower the heat and add the garlic, paste, and tomatoes, the soaked mushrooms and their liquid, carefully strained, and the seasonings. Cover and cook slowly for about 40 minutes, or until done. Remove bay leaves, taste and correct the salt. Mix together the lemon rind, minced garlic, and parsley and scatter over the top.

(SERVES SIX)   **CHICKEN JAMBALAYA**

From the South: chicken, ham, and vegetables in tomato-flavored rice.

4–5-pound chicken, in   1 large onion, chopped
    quarters   4 cloves garlic, minced
2 tablespoons oil   5 cups chicken broth
2 tablespoons bacon fat   ¼ cup minced parsley
Salt   1 bay leaf
Freshly ground pepper   1½ teaspoons thyme,
⅛ teaspoon cayenne pepper   crumbled
1 cup diced ham   1 cup chopped canned or
1 cup chopped green or red   fresh tomatoes
    pepper   2 cups rice
1 cup chopped celery

Preheat the oven to 325°F. Rinse the chicken pieces and wipe dry. Heat the oil and bacon fat in a large skillet. Brown the chicken pieces and sprinkle them with salt, pepper, and cayenne pepper. Remove from the pan and set aside. Add the ham, green pepper, celery, onion, and garlic to the pan and cook until the vegetables are soft. Add the chicken broth, parsley, bay leaf, and thyme; bring to a boil and cook, uncovered, until the broth is reduced to 4 cups. Remove the chicken meat from the bones in large pieces. Put the chicken meat, the unstrained broth, the tomatoes, and rice in a casserole. Stir, cover, and bake for 1 hour, checking every 20 minutes and adding more hot broth or water if it dries out. Remove the bay leaf before serving.

HUNTER'S CHICKEN

(SERVES FOUR)

18¾-ounce can solid pack
   tomatoes
1 large onion, chopped (about
   1 cup)
4 cloves garlic, minced
2 bay leaves
2 teaspoons ground cumin

1½ teaspoons dried oregano,
   crumbled
2 tablespoons wine vinegar
Salt and freshly ground
   pepper
2½–3-pound chicken, in 8
   pieces

Drain the tomatoes, reserving the juice. Put them in a large pot and break them in bits. Add the onion, garlic, bay leaves, cumin, oregano, and vinegar and about half of the reserved tomato juice. Stir and heat, adding salt and pepper to taste. Let the sauce simmer, stirring occasionally, for 30 minutes. If the sauce becomes very thick, add the remaining tomato juice. Add the chicken parts and let simmer 20–30 minutes more. Test for doneness at 20 minutes by piercing a thigh with a knife tip. If still pink continue to cook. This dish is good served hot or cold.

COUNTRY CAPTAIN CHICKEN

(SERVES FOUR)

Early Americans adopted this English classic, which originated in the East Indies. With its many flavors and textures it is still a great-tasting dish. This version has been our family favorite.

4 slices bacon
2–3-pound chicken, in 8
   pieces
1 green pepper, seeded and
   chopped
1 onion, chopped
2 cloves garlic, minced
¾ cup celery chopped into
   small pieces

6 canned tomatoes with juice
1 cup orange juice
2 tablespoons curry powder
½ teaspoon dried thyme
½ cup raisins
½ cup almonds, toasted
¼ cup minced parsley
About 4 cups cooked rice

In a skillet, sauté the bacon until crisp. Then remove, and pat dry on paper towels. Have the bacon fat hot in the pan and brown the chicken pieces quickly, a few at a time, turning and allowing room between the pieces. Set the browned pieces aside and continue until all are browned. Drain all but 2 tablespoons of fat from the pan. Add the pepper, onion, garlic, and celery, and sauté for 5 minutes. Coarsely chop the tomatoes and add to the pan with a little of their juice and the orange juice. Season with curry powder and thyme. Bring to a boil, reduce the heat, and simmer for 5 minutes. Put the chicken pieces back into the pan and spoon the sauce over them. Cover and simmer for 30 minutes. Serve with rice and garnish with the raisins, almonds, and parsley.

(SERVES EIGHT)   **CHICKEN CURRY**

This is an old-fashioned, smooth, mild curry that even a child would like. It is served with rice and a variety of condiments, such as toasted coconut, sliced banana, chutney, chopped peanuts, fried bacon bits, snipped chives or scallions—much like the spicier Indian versions, but the mildness of this dish makes it strictly American.

1 cup water
1 cup milk
2 cups freshly grated coconut
  (see p. 12)
5 tablespoons butter
1 onion, chopped
¼ cup flour
2 cups warm chicken broth

1½–2 tablespoons curry
  powder, or to taste
Salt
2 tablespoons lemon juice
Two 2½–3-pound chickens,
  cooked and boned
About 8 cups cooked rice

Heat the water and milk until bubbles form a ring around the edge of the pan. Remove from heat and stir in the coconut. Let steep for 1 hour. Drain, squeezing the coconut to extract all the "milk," and reserve this liquid. Save the squeezed coconut to add to sauce. Spread 1 cup of the coconut over a baking sheet and toast, under the broiler or in a 350°F oven, until lightly golden. Melt the butter in a sauté pan, stir in the onion, and cook only until the onion is soft. Add the flour and stir until smooth and thick. Cook for 2 to 3 minutes over medium-low heat. Don't brown. Slowly add the warm chicken broth, stirring constantly. Add the curry powder and salt to taste. Cook, stirring often, until the sauce is smooth and thickened. Slowly add the water that the coconut was soaked in, known as the "coconut milk," and soaked coconut until the sauce is the desired consistency. (Use any leftover coconut milk, plus water, to cook the rice.) Stir in the lemon juice, and taste and correct seasonings. Add the chicken meat, and stir until heated through. Serve with rice and the condiments—toasted coconut, sliced banana, chutney, peanuts, or your favorites.

MEXICAN CHICKEN
(SERVES SIX)

2 small chickens, each in 8
    pieces
¼ cup oil
Salt
Freshly ground pepper
1½ cups chopped onion
2 cloves garlic, minced
1 green pepper, chopped
½ teaspoon cumin

¼ teaspoon ground cloves
2 teaspoons chili powder
1½ cups chopped canned or
    fresh tomatoes
⅓ cup raisins
4 tablespoons dry sherry
6 sprigs fresh cilantro, or
    Chinese parsley

Rinse the chicken and pat dry. Heat the oil in a heavy pan with a lid. Sprinkle the chicken with salt and pepper and brown in the hot oil. Remove the chicken and set aside. Add the onion, garlic, and green pepper to the pan and cook until soft. Stir in the cumin, cloves, chili powder, tomatoes, raisins, and browned chicken. Pour on the sherry, cover the pan, and simmer 30–40 minutes. Garnish with cilantro just before serving.

CHICKEN PAPRIKA
(SERVES FOUR)

A Hungarian dish that is good served with wide noodles.

3-pound chicken, in quarters
4 tablespoons butter
½ cup chopped onion
Salt
2 tablespoons sweet
    Hungarian paprika

1 tomato, peeled and chopped
½–1 cup chicken broth
3 tablespoons flour
¼ cup heavy cream
½ cup sour cream, at room
    temperature

Rinse the chicken and pat it dry. Melt the butter in a heavy pan. Cook the onion until lightly browned, then add the chicken and sprinkle with salt. When the chicken pieces are browned, remove them from the pan and set aside. Mix in the paprika and cook for 1 minute; add the tomato and ½ cup chicken broth, lower the heat, and simmer for 7 minutes. Return the chicken to the pan, cover, and cook 30–40 minutes. Remove the chicken to a warm platter. Sprinkle the flour over the pan drippings, stirring briskly to smooth and blend, and cook for 3 minutes. Gradually add enough chicken broth to make 1 cup of liquid, then stir in the heavy cream. When it is heated through, turn off the heat, whisk the sour cream in a small bowl, and add it to the sauce, blending it quickly without letting it boil. Spoon over the chicken pieces to serve.

SMOTHERED CHICKEN
(SERVES FOUR) **✳ WITH MUSHROOMS**

The old-fashioned version of this dish called for heavy cream at
the end of cooking. I have found the dish does not need the extra calories.

3-pound frying chicken, in serving pieces	1½ cups chopped onions
	¼ cup flour
Salt and freshly ground pepper	2 cups chicken broth
	1 pound mushrooms, sliced
¼ cup olive or vegetable oil	¼ cup chopped parsley

Preheat the oven to 400°F. Wash the chicken pieces and pat dry. Season
to taste with salt and pepper. In a large heavy-bottomed skillet, heat
the oil over high heat and brown the chicken pieces, turning when necessary. Adjust the heat so that the chicken browns quickly but does not
burn. Transfer the chicken to a shallow casserole large enough to hold
the chicken in one layer. Add the onions to the skillet and cook, stirring frequently, for about 5 minutes, or until they are soft and lightly
colored. Stir in the flour and mix it in well with a spoon. Pour in the
chicken broth and, stirring constantly, bring to a boil. Reduce the heat
and let it simmer for 2–3 minutes. Pour the sauce over the chicken in
the casserole, cover tightly, and cook in the oven for about 20 minutes.
Scatter the mushrooms over the chicken, re-cover, and bake for another 10 minutes, or until the chicken is tender. Sprinkle the parsley
over the top and serve.

(SERVES FOUR) **SPICED CHICKEN WITH DRIED FRUIT**

This is a tantalizing mixture of spiciness, and of sweet and tart flavors;
a fine dish for winter, particularly when served with steamed brown
rice. You can use 1 cup of only dried prunes or apricots rather than a
combination, if you prefer.

½ cup dried prunes, in large pieces	½–1 teaspoon ground mace
	6 tablespoons flour
½ cup dried apricots, in large pieces	Salt and freshly ground pepper to taste
1 cup orange juice	2½–3-pound chicken, in 8 pieces
2 tablespoons brown sugar	
2 tablespoons cider vinegar	4 tablespoons butter

Combine the prunes, apricots, orange juice, sugar, vinegar, and mace in a saucepan, and cook, simmering, for 10 minutes. Remove from heat and set aside. Lightly flour, salt, and pepper the chicken pieces. Melt the butter in a sauté pan. Brown the chicken pieces on all sides. Remove any fat from the pan, lower the heat, and pour the dried-fruit sauce over the chicken. Cover and let simmer for about 20 minutes, or until done.

CHICKEN FRICASSEE (SERVES SIX)

A great old-fashioned dish, the essence of chicken in a creamy sauce.

5-pound chicken, in large pieces	1 carrot, sliced
	1 bay leaf
¼ pound butter	4 tablespoons flour
2 tablespoons oil	1 cup heavy cream
1 small onion, sliced	2 tablespoons lemon juice
2 stalks celery with leaves, in pieces	Salt
	Freshly ground pepper

Rinse the chicken and pat it dry. Heat 4 tablespoons of the butter with the oil in a Dutch oven, and brown the chicken on all sides. Lower the heat, pour on boiling water to cover the chicken, and add the onion, celery, carrot, and bay leaf. Cover and simmer 40–45 minutes. Remove the chicken to a platter and keep warm. Strain the broth and remove any surface fat. Bring the broth to a boil and reduce to 1½ cups. Melt the remaining 4 tablespoons of butter in a saucepan. Stir in the flour and cook for 2–3 minutes. Slowly add the cream and broth, continuing to stir and simmer for 4–5 minutes until thickened and smooth. Add the lemon juice and salt and pepper to taste, spoon over the chicken, and serve.

CHICKEN FRICASSEE WITH MUSHROOMS

Add *1 cup mushrooms* sautéed in *2 tablespoons butter* to the sauce just before adding the lemon juice.

CHICKEN GUMBO

Gumbo seems to appeal to most everyone. Serve it in bowls with steamed white rice and crusty bread to soak up the broth.

¼ cup olive oil
1 pound Louisiana-style sausage, mild or hot or a combination, or other spicy sausage
Two 2–3-pound chickens, each in 8 pieces
2 large onions, sliced
6 cloves garlic, minced
3 red peppers, seeded and sliced
3 green chilies (mild Anaheim variety), seeded and sliced
2 pounds tomatoes, sliced (Italian plum tomatoes preferred)

1 pound okra, washed, trimmed, and sliced
2 lemons, sliced
2 bay leaves
1 tablespoon chopped fresh thyme, or 1 teaspoon dried
1 teaspoon chopped fresh savory, or ½ teaspoon dried
Salt and freshly ground pepper to taste
2 quarts water
2 tablespoons filé powder (see Note)

Note: Filé powder is found in the spice section of most supermarkets. It is an herb ground from young leaves of sassafras. It has a distinctive flavor and is the classic thickener for Creole dishes.

Heat the oil in a large skillet over medium-high heat. Brown the sausages on all sides, then remove and set aside. When the sausages are cool, slice into 1-inch pieces and reserve. Add the chicken pieces in batches and brown on all sides. Remove and set aside. Add the onions, garlic, red peppers, and chili peppers, and cook until soft, stirring frequently, about 7–8 minutes. Add the tomatoes, okra, lemons, bay leaves, thyme, savory, salt and pepper, water, and the chicken pieces, and simmer for about 30 minutes, or until chicken is done. Add the sausage and simmer until heated through, about 5 minutes more. Remove the skillet from the heat and stir in the filé powder. Serve at once over hot rice.

PAELLA   (SERVES EIGHT)

You can do your own improvisation in this saffron-colored Spanish dish.

Pinch of saffron (about ⅛ teaspoon)
4 cups chicken broth
4–5-pound chicken, in 8 pieces
Salt
Freshly ground pepper
4 tablespoons olive oil
1 teaspoon oregano, crumbled
12 thin slices spicy Spanish sausage (chorizo)

2 cups chopped onion
4 cloves garlic, sliced
4 tablespoons butter
2 cups short-grain rice
1 pound shrimp, cooked, shelled, and deveined
1½ dozen clams in the shell
1 package frozen tiny peas, or 1½ cups fresh
½ cup chopped parsley
1 teaspoon salt

Preheat the oven to 350°F. Put the saffron to soak in 2 tablespoons of the chicken broth. Rinse the chicken, pat it dry, and sprinkle liberally with salt and pepper. Heat the olive oil in a large skillet, add the chicken, and brown well on all sides. Add 4 tablespoons water and the oregano. Cover and cook over low heat for 20 minutes or until the chicken is done. Remove the chicken and set aside. Lightly brown the sausage slices; remove and set aside. Add the onion and garlic to the pan and cook, stirring, for 5 minutes. Melt the butter in the pan and stir in the rice, saffron, and about a teaspoon of salt, cooking for 5 minutes. Add the remaining chicken broth, bring to a boil, cover, and simmer 20 minutes. In a shallow 4-quart casserole, arrange the rice, chicken, shrimp, sausage, and clams so that some of each shows on the top. Heat in the oven until the clams open, about 15–20 minutes. Meanwhile either pour boiling water over frozen peas or blanch fresh peas 2 minutes. Scatter over the casserole, sprinkle with parsley, and serve.

PAELLA IMPROVISATIONS

2 cups green and red pepper strips, added with clams
1 cup black olives, pitted, scattered over the top for the last 5 minutes in the oven
1 package artichoke hearts, cooked, and added at the last
1 cup ham in strips, added during the last 5 minutes of cooking

(SERVES FOUR)   **POACHED CHICKEN**

Chicken prepared this way stays juicy and moist for salads and sandwiches. The broth may be saved and used for stock, for boiling noodles or rice, or for poaching another chicken.

    3-pound chicken, whole   Salt

Wash the chicken with cold water. Truss (p. 309) and place in a large saucepan. Add water halfway up the chicken, with ½ teaspoon salt for every quart of water used. Cover and simmer over medium-low heat for 1 hour, turning the chicken over once or twice during the cooking. Cool the chicken in the broth and refrigerate until needed.

(SERVES FOUR)   **RHODE ISLAND CHICKEN**

3-pound chicken, whole	1 bay leaf
1 stalk celery with leaves, in 4 pieces	1 carrot, sliced
½ onion, sliced	3 tablespoons butter
1 teaspoon thyme, crumbled	3 tablespoons flour
½ teaspoon freshly ground pepper	2 egg yolks, lightly beaten
3 parsley sprigs	2 tablespoons lemon juice
	Salt

Wash and truss the chicken (p. 309). Place it in a large saucepan and add water halfway up the chicken. Add the celery, onion, thyme, pepper, parsley, bay leaf, and carrot. Partially cover and simmer for 1 hour. Remove the chicken and keep it warm in the oven. Strain the broth, return it to the pan, and boil until reduced to 2 cups. Melt the butter in a second saucepan. Stir in the flour and cook, stirring 2–3 minutes until smooth. Slowly add the reduced broth, stirring over low heat for 3–4 minutes more. Little by little, add ½ cup of simmering sauce to the egg yolks, beating constantly. Return the sauce-egg mixture to the sauce remaining in the pan, and cook 1 minute more. Remove from the heat, stir in the lemon juice, then add salt to taste. Serve the sauce alongside the chicken.

(SERVES SIX)   **❋ CHICKEN WITH DUMPLINGS**

Serve in soupbowls: pieces of chicken in broth with a dumpling floating on top.

4–5-pound chicken, in 8
  pieces
2 carrots, sliced thin
2 stalks celery with leaves,
  sliced thin
1 large onion, chopped
1½ teaspoons thyme,
  crumbled

½ teaspoon rosemary,
  crumbled
2 teaspoons salt
½ teaspoon freshly ground
  pepper

Feather Dumplings

1 cup flour
½ cup fresh bread crumbs
2 teaspoons baking powder
¾ teaspoon salt
1 egg, well beaten
2 tablespoons butter, melted

¼ cup finely chopped onion
⅓ cup milk
1 tablespoon finely minced
  parsley
Freshly ground pepper to
  taste

Rinse the chicken pieces, put them in a large pot with a cover, and cover with water. Add the carrots, celery, onion, thyme, rosemary, salt, and pepper. Bring to a boil and reduce to a simmer. Combine the flour, bread crumbs, baking powder, and salt in a mixing bowl, and stir to mix. In another bowl lightly beat the egg, melted butter, onion, and milk together. Stir into the dry ingredients to make a stiff batter. Stir in the parsley and pepper. When the chicken has simmered for 20 minutes, drop spoonfuls of dough on top of the bubbling broth. Cover and steam for 20 minutes without lifting the cover.

BRUNSWICK STEW   (SERVES SIX)

A southern stew, originally made with squirrel or rabbit, that is traditionally long-cooked so that the vegetables become soft and the potatoes are cooked to a thickening paste.

4–5-pound chicken, in
  quarters
Salt
1 cup chopped canned or
  fresh tomatoes
2 onions, sliced thin

1 cup green lima beans
3 potatoes, peeled and diced
1 cup whole-kernel corn
1 teaspoon sugar
⅛–¼ teaspoon cayenne pepper

Rinse the pieces of chicken and put them into a large pot with 2 teaspoons salt and water to cover. Bring to a boil and simmer for 40 minutes. Remove the chicken from the broth, take the meat off the bones, and set aside. Put the tomatoes, onions, lima beans, potatoes, corn, sugar, and cayenne pepper into the broth and boil gently for 30 minutes, covered. Add the pieces of chicken and simmer for 10 minutes more, uncovered. Taste and add cayenne pepper and more salt if needed.

(SERVES FOUR) **CHICKEN VINEGAR SAUTÉ**

The simple addition of vinegar makes this a splendid dish. Vinegar and lemon juice both give the same sharp sparkle to many foods that are delicate in flavor.

2–3-pound frying chicken, in 8 pieces	½ cup red wine vinegar
Salt to taste	¼ cup water
Freshly ground pepper	1 teaspoon minced garlic
6 tablespoons butter or vegetable oil or combination	1 tablespoon minced parsley
	1 teaspoon minced fresh tarragon, or ½ teaspoon dried

Sprinkle the chicken pieces with salt and pepper to taste. Heat 4 tablespoons of the butter in a skillet over medium-high heat. Add the chicken, skin side down, and brown on all sides for about 8–10 minutes. Pour ¼ cup of the vinegar and the water over the chicken, cover the pan, and reduce the heat to low. Cook for about 15 more minutes, or until done. Remove the chicken to a serving dish and keep warm. Add the garlic to the skillet and cook for about 1 minute. Add the remaining ¼ cup vinegar to the skillet and boil for another minute. Toss the parsley and tarragon together and set aside. Season to taste with salt and pepper, then add the remaining 2 tablespoons of butter to the skillet and stir to blend. Pour the sauce over the chicken on the serving dish and sprinkle with the parsley and tarragon. Serve at once.

(SERVES FOUR) **SAUTÉED CHICKEN BREASTS**

Buy 3 pounds of unboned chicken breasts if you are boning them yourself. This is equally good made with thin slices of turkey breast.

⅓ cup flour	2 tablespoons oil
1½ pounds skinned and boned chicken breasts (p. 308)	Juice of 1 lemon
	Salt
4 tablespoons butter	Freshly ground pepper
	1 tablespoon minced parsley

Spread the flour on a piece of wax paper and dredge each chicken breast. Melt the butter and oil in a skillet. When it foams, add the chicken, and cook over medium-high heat for about 3 minutes on each side. Remove to a warm platter. Pour off all but 2 tablespoons of fat from the pan, and stir in the lemon juice and salt and pepper to taste. When it is very hot, spoon this sauce over the chicken and sprinkle with parsley.

BAKED CHICKEN BREASTS

Omit the flour. Season each breast with salt and pepper, place in a shallow pan, and dot with *4 tablespoons butter*. Cover with foil and bake in a preheated 375°F oven for 20 minutes or until done. Remove the foil, drizzle on the lemon juice, and sprinkle with the parsley.

MUSHROOM-STUFFED
CHICKEN BREASTS

(SERVES FOUR TO SIX)

5 tablespoons butter
½ pound mushrooms, chopped fine
½ teaspoon salt
¼ teaspoon freshly ground pepper
1½ cups freshly made bread crumbs

¼ teaspoon nutmeg (optional)
4 chicken breasts, boned, halved, and pounded flat (p. 308)
½ cup heavy cream
½ cup chicken broth

Preheat the oven to 350°F. Melt 4 tablespoons of the butter in a skillet. Add the mushrooms, salt, and pepper, and cook, stirring often, until the mushrooms turn very dark and absorb all the butter. Remove from the heat and stir in ¾ cup of the bread crumbs and the nutmeg. Divide the mushroom stuffing into 8 portions and place a portion in the center of each piece of chicken. Fold the chicken around the stuffing, and place, seam side down, in a buttered shallow casserole or baking dish. Melt the remaining tablespoon of butter and brush over the chicken. Sprinkle with the remaining ¾ cup of bread crumbs. Pour on cream and broth. Bake for 30 minutes, until lightly brown.

(SERVES FOUR)   **CHICKEN PARMESAN**

Also good made with thin slices of turkey breast.

1 egg, lightly beaten	Freshly ground pepper
1 cup freshly made bread crumbs	2 tablespoons lemon juice
½ cup freshly grated Parmesan cheese	¼ teaspoon nutmeg
1½ pounds skinned and boned chicken breasts (p. 308)	1½ cups chopped cooked spinach, or 1 package frozen chopped spinach, cooked
⅓ cup flour	4 tablespoons butter
Salt	2 tablespoons oil
	1 cup heavy cream

Mix the egg with 2 tablespoons water in a shallow bowl. Combine the bread crumbs and cheese on a piece of wax paper. Coat the chicken breasts with flour, and sprinkle with salt and pepper. Dip them into the egg and then into the bread crumb–cheese mixture; set aside. Add the lemon juice and nutmeg to the spinach and stir over low heat until it is warm. Melt the butter and oil in a large skillet. When it foams, add the chicken and sauté over medium-high heat for 2–3 minutes on each side, or until just done. Spread the spinach on a warm platter, place the chicken on top, and keep warm. Remove all but 3 tablespoons of fat from the skillet. Place it over high heat and add the cream. Stir, scraping the bottom of the pan, until the cream comes to a boil. Spoon a little of this sauce over the chicken and spinach, and pour the rest into a serving bowl.

(SERVES FOUR)   **CHICKEN LEGS WITH FRESH GINGER**

This is a simple Cantonese-type dish, full of good flavors and textures. Serve with steaming bowls of rice, and spoon some of the lively ginger sauce over. You may use chicken thighs or breasts or a cut-up whole chicken; however, it will take longer to cook. I like it best with the dark meat of the chicken.

¼ cup peanut oil	⅓ cup soy sauce
8 chicken legs	⅓ cup dry sherry
1 cup peeled fresh ginger, in ¼-inch slices	⅓ cup sugar
	½ cup sliced scallions

Put the peanut oil in a large sauté pan over medium-high heat. When hot, add the chicken and ginger slices and brown the chicken on all sides. (It is important to use a deep skillet as the chicken tends to spatter while browning and the sauce will foam up during cooking.) Reduce the heat if necessary to keep the chicken and ginger from burning. Mix together the soy sauce, sherry, and sugar, and pour the mixture over the chicken. Cover and cook for about 7–8 minutes. Lower the heat a little as necessary so that the sauce continues to foam during cooking but does not bubble over. Remove to a serving dish and garnish with the scallions.

CHINESE CHICKEN IN LETTUCE LEAVES ✳

(SERVES FOUR)

This is a variation on one of the all-time favorite recipes at San Francisco's Mandarin Restaurant. The filling goes into a crisp lettuce leaf, is rolled up, and is eaten with your hands, like a sandwich. It is a great party dish.

3 tablespoons vegetable oil
1⅓ cups skinned, boned, and finely chopped chicken breast meat
1 cup seeded and finely chopped green or red pepper
½ tablespoon sugar
½ tablespoon salt

Freshly ground pepper to taste
2½ tablespoons minced fresh ginger
1½ tablespoons soy sauce
3 tablespoons water
1 tablespoon lemon juice
1 large scallion, sliced
½ cup walnuts, chopped

Sauce

½ cup rice wine vinegar
1½ tablespoons soy sauce
1 teaspoon sesame oil

Dash hot sauce or chili oil
8–12 iceberg lettuce leaves, washed, dried, and chilled

Heat the oil in a skillet over medium-high heat. Add the chicken, chopped pepper, sugar, salt, and pepper, and cook, stirring constantly, until the peppers turn a deeper color and the chicken is cooked, about 3 to 5 minutes. Add the ginger, soy sauce, water, and lemon juice to the chicken mixture, stirring well, and cook for 1 more minute. Remove the chicken from the heat. Sprinkle with the scallion and walnuts. For the sauce, mix the vinegar, soy sauce, sesame oil, and hot sauce in a small bowl until well blended. To serve, place 2 or 3 tablespoons of the chicken mixture on a lettuce leaf, roll up, and place on a serving dish. Pass the sauce separately for dipping.

CHICKEN SAUSAGE PATTIES

These are good for breakfast, lunch, or anytime.

3 chicken breast halves, skinned and boned	1 teaspoon salt
6 chicken thighs, skinned and boned but with bits of solid yellow chicken fat attached	Freshly ground pepper to taste
	½ teaspoon poultry seasoning
	¼ teaspoon sage
	2 tablespoons vegetable oil

Cut the chicken meat into chunks and chop in a food processor or put through a meat grinder. It should resemble coarse ground meat. Put in a mixing bowl and add the salt, pepper, poultry seasoning, and sage, and mix well. Form into 6 small patties. The meat is sticky to handle so dampen your hands with water. Heat the oil in a skillet and cook the patties over medium-high heat, turning once, about 3 to 4 minutes on each side, or until browned and done in the center.

CHICKEN LIVERS

SAUTÉED CHICKEN LIVERS WITH MADEIRA

Serve the livers and sauce spooned over toast with broiled tomato halves.

2 tablespoons butter	4 tablespoons Madeira
2 tablespoons oil	Salt
1 pound chicken livers	Freshly ground pepper

Heat the butter and oil in a skillet, toss in the chicken livers, and cook very quickly, shoving them about in the pan, until dark brown; remove to a warm platter. Turn the heat up very high and add the Madeira. Let it come to a boil as you scrape up the pan juices. Add salt and pepper to taste.

CHICKEN LIVERS WITH MUSHROOMS

(SERVES FOUR)

1 pound chicken livers	1½ tablespoons lemon juice
5 tablespoons butter	¾ cup beef broth
2 cups sliced mushrooms	Freshly ground pepper
3 shallots or scallions, minced	1 tablespoon minced parsley

Trim the chicken livers of any discolored membranes or tough connective tissue, and wipe with a paper towel. Melt the butter in a skillet. Add the mushrooms and cook, stirring, over medium heat for 1½ minutes. Add the livers, shallots or scallions, lemon juice, broth, and salt and pepper to taste. Turn the heat to high and cook, stirring, for another 1½ minutes. Serve, sprinkled with the parsley.

CURRIED CHICKEN LIVERS

(SERVES FOUR)

This is very nice served with a chutney (pp. 1098–99).

4 tablespoons butter	½ cup golden raisins
½ cup finely chopped onion	½ cup chopped apple
1 pound chicken livers, trimmed and cleaned	Salt to taste
	4 cups hot cooked rice
2 teaspoons curry powder	1 cup peanuts, chopped
1 cup chicken broth	(optional)

Melt the butter in a skillet. Stir in the onion and cook for 5 minutes over low heat. Turn the heat to medium, add the chicken livers, and cook until brown, about 2 minutes on each side. Remove livers to a warm plate. Add the curry powder to the skillet and stir to blend with the onion and pan juices. Add the chicken broth, raisins, and apple, bring to a boil, and reduce to about ¾ cup. Taste, and add salt. Put the hot rice on a platter with the chicken livers on top, and pour the curried sauce over it. Sprinkle with the peanuts, if you wish.

OTHER POULTRY

(SERVES FOUR)   **ROAST DUCK**

For a crisp brown duck, try this recipe: the secret is basting it with water.

    5-pound duck   Freshly ground pepper
    Salt

Preheat the oven to 450°F. Rub the inside of the duck with salt and pepper. Prick the skin all over, especially along the sides under the breast, to allow the fat to run out while the duck roasts. Place the duck breast up on a rack in a shallow roasting pan. Baste every 15 minutes, pouring off the fat from the pan as it accumulates. Turn the duck breast down after the first 30 minutes of roasting. Turn it breast up again and roast another 30 minutes, then baste it with 3–4 tablespoons of ice water and roast another 15 minutes—1¼ hours altogether or until a meat thermometer reads 170°F in the thigh. If you like your duck very well done, roast it another 15 minutes, but be forewarned, the meat is going to be dry. Remove from the oven and let rest for 15 minutes before carving.

(SERVES TWO)   **EVERYONE'S ROAST DUCK**

Crisp and brown on the outside, moist and tender on the inside, this alternate way to roast a duck and render most of the fat before roasting is always a sure-fire method.

    5-pound duck
    Salt and freshly ground
        pepper to taste

Place the duck in a large pot, cover with cold water, and bring to a boil. Reduce the heat and simmer for 35 minutes. Drain and pat dry with paper towels. Preheat the oven to 400°F. Salt and pepper the duck and place it on a roasting rack in a shallow roasting pan. Roast the duck for about 45 minutes, until nicely browned and a meat thermometer reads 180°F in the thigh. Remove from the oven and let rest for about 15 minutes before carving.

DUCK À L'ORANGE

(SERVES FOUR)

5-pound duck	3 tablespoons wine vinegar
Salt	2 cups beef broth
Freshly ground pepper	1 tablespoon cornstarch
5 oranges	2 tablespoons red currant jelly
2 lemons	¼ cup dry white wine
3 tablespoons sugar	

Preheat the oven to 350°F. Prick the duck skin all over and rub the cavity with salt and pepper. Roast for 1¾ hours (or until interior temperature is 180°F in the thigh) on a rack in a shallow roasting pan, pouring off the fat every 20 minutes. Using a vegetable peeler, remove the colored part, or "zest," of the skins of 2 of the oranges and 1 of the lemons. Cut the zest into thin strips. Squeeze the juice from the peeled fruit and set aside. Bring a pan of water to a boil and add the strips. Steep them 5 minutes, drain, and set aside. Cut the pieces of fruit free from the membranes of the remaining 3 oranges and 1 lemon. Put the sections in a bowl and set aside. In a small heavy-bottomed pan, cook the sugar over medium-high heat. Caramelize it by moving the pan over the heat so that the sugar turns golden, taking care that it does not burn. Add the vinegar, orange juice, and lemon juice, and boil rapidly until the liquid is reduced by half. Stir in the broth and simmer for 5 minutes more. In a small bowl, dissolve the cornstarch in 2 tablespoons water. Add it to the caramelized sauce with the currant jelly, stirring until the sauce is clear and thickened. When the duck is roasted, put it on a warm platter. Pour off the fat from the roasting pan and place it over a burner. Add the wine, scrape up the bits from the bottom of the pan, and boil rapidly for 1 minute. Strain into the sauce. Sprinkle the duck with the fruit rind strips, surround with fruit sections, and pour enough of the rich brown sauce over to glaze the duck, serving the rest in a sauceboat.

BRAISED DUCK

(SERVES FOUR)

This would surprise you with the good complementary flavors that bring out the best in the duck.

2 tablespoons butter	1 stalk celery with leaves, chopped
5-pound duck	2 teaspoons thyme, crumbled
½ cup Port wine	Salt
1½ cups chicken broth	Freshly ground pepper
1 bay leaf	
4 parsley sprigs	

Melt the butter in a heavy pot. Prick the duck all over and brown it on all sides. Drain the fat from the pot and stir in the wine, chicken broth, bay leaf, parsley, celery, and thyme. Cover and simmer 45 minutes–1 hour. Remove the duck to a warm platter and skim off all the fat from the liquid. Strain the liquid, return it to the pan, and boil rapidly until reduced by one-third. Add salt and pepper to taste. Carve the duck, and spoon the concentrated broth over.

(SERVES FOUR)   **SALMI OF DUCK**

A salmi is a dish made from cooked game. If you should have some leftover duck, you could use it this way, adjusting the proportions of the other ingredients according to the amount of duck you have.

5-pound duck, roasted (opposite)	4 tablespoons flour
4 tablespoons butter	2 cups beef broth
1 tablespoon finely chopped onion	½ bay leaf
1 stalk celery, chopped fine	2 parsley sprigs
1 small carrot, chopped fine	¼ teaspoon mace
3 tablespoons finely chopped ham	Pinch of cloves
	3 tablespoons dry sherry
	12 black olives, pitted
	Salt to taste

Carve the duck into serving pieces. Melt the butter in a saucepan and add the onion, celery, carrot, and ham. Cook, stirring often, until the vegetables are browned. Stir in the flour; when it is nicely browned, slowly add the broth, bay leaf, parsley, mace, and cloves. Cook, stirring constantly, for 5 minutes. Strain the sauce and return to the saucepan. Add the duck, sherry, olives, and salt, and heat through. Arrange the duck on a warm platter surrounded with the olives and covered with a glaze of sauce.

ROCK CORNISH GAME HENS WITH
(SERVES SIX)   **✳ WILD RICE STUFFING**

Serve one hen to a person, garnished with watercress.

¼ pound butter	Salt
½ onion, chopped fine	Freshly ground pepper
1 cup chopped mushrooms	6 Rock Cornish game hens
1½ cups cooked wild rice	1½ cups chicken broth
½ teaspoon thyme, crumbled	
½ teaspoon marjoram, crumbled	

Preheat the oven to 400°F. Melt 4 tablespoons of the butter in a saucepan. Add the onion and mushrooms and cook over medium heat until soft. Mix in the rice, thyme, and marjoram. Stuff loosely into the cavities of the hens. Rub them all over with the remaining butter and sprinkle with salt and pepper to taste. Place the hens, not touching, in a shallow pan and roast, basting every 10–15 minutes with the chicken broth. After 15 minutes, reduce the heat to 300°F and cook another 30–40 minutes, or until the juices run clear when a small slit is made in the upper thigh. Serve with pan juices as a natural sauce.

ROCK CORNISH GAME HENS WITH RICE-RAISIN STUFFING
(SERVES SIX)

12 tablespoons butter	½ cup raisins
½ onion, chopped fine	3 cups chicken broth
1½ cups rice	12 juniper berries
Salt	6 Rock Cornish game hens
Freshly ground pepper	1 cup red wine

Preheat the oven to 325°F. Melt 4 tablespoons of the butter in a saucepan. Add the onion and cook over medium heat until soft. Add the rice, a sprinkle of salt and pepper, and the raisins. Slowly stir in the chicken broth. Cover and simmer for 20 minutes, until the rice is tender. Put 2 juniper berries in each hen's cavity, stuff with the rice, and skewer closed. Rub the hens with 4 tablespoons of the butter and sprinkle with salt and pepper to taste. Place hens in a shallow pan, not touching. Melt the remaining 4 tablespoons butter and mix with the wine. Brush hens with this mixture, and roast 50–60 minutes, basting with the wine-butter marinade every 10 minutes. Serve with pan juices as a natural sauce.

ROAST GOOSE WITH APPLES AND PRUNES
(SERVES SIX)

2 dozen prunes, pitted	Freshly ground pepper to taste
1 cup red wine	2 tablespoons flour
5 tart green apples	1½ cups chicken or goose broth
8–10-pound goose	
Salt to taste	

Note: If the neck and gizzards come with the goose, simmer them with a small carrot and onion in about 4 cups water for 1½–2 hours; the broth will reduce to about 1½ cups.

Soak the prunes in wine for 30 minutes. Peel, core, and quarter the apples. Preheat the oven to 325°F. Rub the goose inside and out with salt and pepper. Drain the prunes, toss with the apple sections, and stuff into the goose cavity. Sew up or skewer the opening. Place the goose on a rack in a shallow pan, pricking the skin all over to release the fat as the bird roasts. Cook 3–3½ hours, until the juices run clear when the skin is cut at the upper thigh or a meat thermometer registers 185°F. During the roasting, pour off the fat every 20 minutes, using a bulb baster or spoon. Save and process the fat (see below). Remove the goose to a platter and keep warm. Remove all but 1 tablespoon fat from the roasting pan. Set it over a burner, stir in the flour, and brown it lightly. Slowly add the broth, stirring until thickened. Season the gravy with salt and pepper, strain it, and pass with the goose.

ROAST GOOSE WITH POTATO STUFFING

(SERVES SIX)

4 medium potatoes	8–10-pound goose
4 tablespoons butter	3–4 tablespoons ice water
2 onions, chopped	2 tablespoons flour
½–¾ cup heavy cream	1½ cups chicken or goose
Salt	broth
Freshly ground pepper	

Peel, quarter, and boil the potatoes until tender. Melt the butter in a skillet and cook the onions until soft. Mash the potatoes with enough cream to make a fluffy mixture. Add the onions and salt and pepper to taste, and stuff into the cavity of the goose. Sew up or skewer it closed. Rub the outside of the goose with more salt and pepper and prick the skin all over to release the fat as it melts during roasting. Preheat the oven to 325°F. Place the goose on a rack in a shallow roasting pan and roast 3–3½ hours. Pour off the fat every 20 minutes, saving it as directed below. Spoon 3–4 tablespoons ice water over the goose during the last 15 minutes of roasting in order to crisp the skin. Prepare gravy as in the preceding recipe.

Rendered Goose Fat

Goose fat is a kitchen treasure. Use it to fry golden-brown potatoes or to season a bowl of freshly cooked vegetables.

Fat from an 8–10-pound goose

Cut raw goose fat into small dice. Place in a deep saucepan over very low heat, adding ¼ cup water for every pound of fat. When it is melted, pour the fat through a fine strainer or cheesecloth. If you are roasting the goose, remove the fat every 20 minutes with a bulb baster or spoon. Strain it through a fine strainer or cheesecloth and set aside. When it congeals, it will separate from the liquid. Remove it and preserve by placing it in a covered jar in the refrigerator. Goose fat must be free of liquid and clean of all residue or it will spoil; cleaned and chilled, it will keep for months—up to a year, in fact, if well refrigerated.

Recipes for Cooked Chicken, Turkey, and/or Other Poultry

There are so many good ways of using cooked turkey and chicken. In recipes calling for one or the other, feel free to use them interchangeably, or to substitute any other leftover poultry meat for that matter; there may be a little difference in flavor, but that lends variety to any dish. Cool cooked poultry that you plan to use again, then scrape and save the bones, skins, bits of gristle—they will go into the soup pot, and the jellied juices that accumulate can go into whatever sauce you may be making for the poultry leftovers. If you are not going to use the meat within a few days, freeze it.

CHICKEN PIE

(SERVES SIX)

6 tablespoons butter	12 small white onions, cooked
6 tablespoons flour	¼ cup peas, cooked
2 cups chicken broth	¼ cup carrots, cooked
1 cup heavy cream	¼ cup celery, cooked
½ teaspoon freshly ground pepper	1·recipe Basic Pastry for 9-inch shell (p. 895)
Salt	
4 cups large chunks of cooked chicken	

Preheat the oven to 425°F. Melt the butter in a saucepan, stir in the flour, and cook, stirring, for 2 minutes. Slowly add the broth, cream, pepper, and salt to taste. Cook for 5 minutes, until thickened and smooth. Put the chicken pieces in a deep pie plate or casserole, cover with sauce, and stir in the small onions, peas, carrots, and celery. Place the prepared piecrust over the casserole, allowing enough overhang so that the edges can be crimped. Cut vents in the crust to allow the steam to escape. Bake for 25–30 minutes, or until the crust is nicely browned.

CHICKEN PIE COUNTRY STYLE

Use *1 recipe Baking Powder Biscuits* (p. 764) instead of Basic Pastry. Roll out the biscuit dough ½ inch thick, cut in 2-inch rounds, and place them, edges touching, all over the top of the pie. Bake at 450°F for 15–20 minutes, until browned.

(SERVES FOUR) **DEVILED CHICKEN-ON-THE-BONE**

"Deviled" here means a spicy sauce with mustard and cayenne.

2 tablespoons butter	⅛ teaspoon cayenne pepper
2 tablespoons chili sauce	8 pieces cooked chicken, on
2 tablespoons Worcestershire	the bone
sauce	1 cup chicken broth
2 teaspoons prepared	Salt
mustard	Freshly ground pepper

Heat the butter, chili sauce, Worcestershire sauce, mustard, and cayenne pepper in a saucepan. Add the chicken pieces, turning them in the sauce so they are coated, and cook, stirring often, for 4–5 minutes. Add the chicken broth and salt and pepper to taste, and simmer 3 minutes more.

(SERVES TWO) **CREAMED CHICKEN**

Serve this slightly lemony creamed chicken over toast or biscuits.

2 tablespoons butter	1½ cups cubed cooked
3 tablespoons flour	chicken
1 cup milk	2½ tablespoons lemon juice
⅓ cup heavy cream	1 teaspoon grated lemon zest
⅛ teaspoon freshly ground	Salt
pepper	

Melt the butter in a saucepan and stir in the flour. Cook for 2–3 minutes over medium heat, stirring constantly, until well blended. Gradually add the milk and cream and stir for 5 minutes until thickened and smooth. Add the pepper, chicken, lemon juice, lemon zest, and salt to taste. Simmer 5 minutes more.

CREAMED CHICKEN WITH VEGETABLES

Add to the cream sauce 2 *hard-boiled eggs, chopped,* ¼ *cup finely sliced cooked celery,* ½ *cup cooked peas,* and ½ *cup sliced cooked mushrooms.*

BLANQUETTE OF CHICKEN

Stir ½ cup of the finished sauce into *1 egg yolk, lightly beaten.* Return to the creamed chicken in the pan, stirring constantly. Sprinkle with *2 tablespoons minced parsley.*

CHICKEN CURRY

Stir in *2 teaspoons curry powder* and ¼ *cup raisins* after adding the milk and cream.

CREAMED CHICKEN WITH MUSHROOMS

After melting the butter in a saucepan, add ½ *pound sliced mushrooms* and cook for about 3–5 minutes before adding the flour. Omit the lemon juice and zest and add ½ *cup dry sherry.*

CHICKEN OR TURKEY AND NOODLES   (SERVES FOUR)

This comforting casserole with a golden sauce can be assembled ahead.

¼ pound broad egg noodles or green noodles	1 cup heavy cream
¾ cup freshly grated Parmesan cheese	1 cup chicken broth
	2 cups cubed cooked chicken or turkey
2 tablespoons butter	2 egg yolks, lightly beaten
2 tablespoons flour	Salt

Preheat the oven to 375°F. Butter a 2-quart baking dish. Cook the noodles until just done. Drain them, and, while they are still hot, stir in all but 2 tablespoons of the cheese. Melt the butter in a saucepan, add the flour, and cook for 2–3 minutes. Gradually stir in the cream and broth. Cook over low heat, stirring often, for 5 minutes. Add the chicken or turkey and cook another minute. Beat ¼ cup of the hot sauce into the egg yolks, then return the yolk-sauce mixture to the chicken mixture. Stir briskly for 1 minute, remove from the heat, and add salt to taste. Place the chicken mixture over the noodles. Sprinkle with the reserved 2 tablespoons of cheese, and bake 20–30 minutes, until golden.

(FILLING FOR 12 CRÊPES) **CHICKEN OR TURKEY CRÊPES**

4 tablespoons butter
2 tablespoons finely chopped
  shallots or scallions
¼ cup flour
1¼ cups light cream
¾ cup chicken broth
¼ cup dry white wine
¼ teaspoon tarragon,
  crumbled

2 egg yolks, lightly beaten
2 cups diced cooked chicken
  or turkey
Salt
1 recipe Crêpes or French
  Pancakes (p. 778)

Melt the butter in a saucepan, add the shallots or scallions, and cook, stirring, for 2 minutes. Add the flour, stir to blend, and slowly add 1 cup of the cream, stirring constantly. Add the broth, wine, and tarragon, and stir over medium-low heat until the sauce thickens. Cook for 5 minutes. Beat 3 tablespoons of hot sauce into the yolks, and then return the yolk-sauce mixture to the saucepan, stirring briskly. Cook 1 minute more, and remove from the heat. Mix half the sauce with the chicken or turkey and add salt to taste. Preheat the oven to 350°F. Fill each crêpe with 3 tablespoons of the filling. Roll and place seam side down in a baking dish approximately 13 × 9 × 2 inches. Thin the rest of the sauce with the remaining ¼ cup cream and spread it over the crêpes. Bake for 25 minutes, or until the sauce begins to bubble.

CHICKEN AND MUSHROOM FILLING

Omit the shallots or scallions and the tarragon. Sauté *2 cups sliced mushrooms* in the melted butter. Toast *1 cup slivered almonds* and add half of it to the sauce with the chicken. Sprinkle the rest over the crêpes just before serving.

CHICKEN À LA KING

(SERVES TWO TO THREE)

Serve in flaky patty shells.

½ cup sliced mushrooms
3 tablespoons red bell pepper, finely chopped
2 tablespoons butter
1½ cups Velouté Sauce (p. 381)

1 cup cubed cooked chicken
1 egg yolk, lightly beaten
2 tablespoons dry sherry
2 tablespoons fresh chopped parsley
Salt to taste

Sauté the mushrooms and pepper in butter. In a saucepan over low heat, mix them into the sauce together with the chicken. When it is hot, add ¼ cup of this mixture to the egg yolk, beating constantly. Return the yolk-sauce mixture to the saucepan with the sherry, parsley, and salt, and blend well.

CHICKEN SOUFFLÉ

(SERVES FOUR)

Mild and light, good for a gentle lunch or supper.

2 tablespoons butter
1 tablespoon finely chopped onion
2 tablespoons flour
1 cup chicken broth
1 cup heavy cream
½ cup soft bread crumbs
½ teaspoon salt
Pinch of cayenne pepper
2 teaspoons Worcestershire sauce

2 cups finely chopped cooked chicken
3 eggs, separated
2 tablespoons chopped parsley
1 teaspoon fresh chopped tarragon or ½ teaspoon dry

Preheat the oven to 325°F. Butter a 2-quart soufflé dish. Melt the butter in a saucepan and add the onion. Cook for 2 minutes and stir in the flour, cooking for another 2–3 minutes. Slowly add the chicken broth and cream, stirring until smooth and thickened. Add the crumbs, salt, cayenne, and Worcestershire sauce. Cook for another minute and add the chicken. Beat the egg yolks lightly, add ¼ cup of the hot sauce, mix well, then return the mixture to the saucepan. Add the parsley and tarragon, and remove from the heat. Let cool slightly. Beat the egg whites until stiff but not dry, stir a third of them into the chicken sauce, then gently fold in the remaining whites. Spoon into the soufflé dish and bake in the bottom half of the oven 30–35 minutes, or until high and set.

(SERVES FOUR)   **CHICKEN OR TURKEY TETRAZZINI**

4 cups cooked spaghetti
    (about ½ pound)
¼ teaspoon nutmeg
3 tablespoons dry sherry
Salt to taste
1 recipe Velouté Sauce (p.
    381)

2 tablespoons butter
1 cup sliced mushrooms
8 or more slices cooked
    chicken or turkey
½ cup freshly grated Romano
    or Parmesan cheese

Preheat the oven to 400°F. Butter a 2-quart shallow baking dish, and
spread the cooked spaghetti in it. Stir the nutmeg, sherry, and salt into
the warm velouté sauce and set aside. Melt the butter in a skillet, add
the mushrooms, and cook, stirring, until soft. Spoon half the sauce
over the spaghetti. Place the chicken or turkey slices and mushrooms
on top, and spoon on the remaining sauce. Sprinkle with the grated
cheese and bake for 30 minutes.

(SERVES FOUR)   **CHICKEN DIVAN**

3 cups cooked broccoli
8 or more slices cooked
    chicken
¼ cup dry sherry

2 cups White Sauce (p. 379)
Salt to taste
½ cup freshly grated Romano
    or Parmesan cheese

Preheat the oven to 375°F. Butter a shallow baking dish and lay the
broccoli over the bottom. Put the chicken over the broccoli. Add sherry
to the white sauce and heat. Add salt to taste. Spoon evenly over the
chicken, sprinkle with cheese, and bake 15–20 minutes, until very
hot.

CHICKEN-ASPARAGUS DIVAN.

Use *1 pound asparagus, cooked,* instead of broccoli.

(SERVES THREE)   **✳ CHICKEN MOCK HOLLANDAISE**

Wonderfully crunchy, with a touch of lemon. Serve on whole-wheat
toast.

3 tablespoons butter
1 tablespoon minced onion
¼ cup cornstarch
2 cups chicken broth
½ cup chopped celery

1 tablespoon lemon juice
2 cups cubed cooked chicken
2 egg yolks, lightly beaten
Salt
Pinch of cayenne pepper

Melt the butter in a saucepan and add the onion. Cook, stirring, until soft. Stir in the cornstarch and cook over medium-low heat until smooth and blended. Slowly add the chicken broth, celery, lemon juice, and chicken. Cook, stirring, for 3–4 minutes. Beat ¼ cup of the hot sauce into the yolks and then return the yolk-sauce mixture to the saucepan. Cook for 1 minute more, and add salt and cayenne to taste.

CHICKEN OR TURKEY HASH   (SERVES FOUR)

3 tablespoons butter
½ cup chopped onion
1 teaspoon rosemary
2 cups cubed cooked chicken
    or turkey
2 cups cubed cooked potatoes
1 cup chicken or turkey gravy
    or heavy cream or mixture
    of both

Salt
Freshly ground pepper
1 tablespoon finely chopped
    parsley

Heat the butter in a large skillet until foaming. Add the onion and rosemary and cook until the onion is soft. Add the chicken or turkey and potatoes, stir well, and cook for 3–4 minutes, pressing down with a spatula to form a flat cake. Lower the heat to medium low and pour in the gravy and/or cream. Sprinkle with salt and pepper and cook for 5 minutes more. Turn out onto a serving platter and sprinkle with parsley.

ENCHILADAS WITH CHICKEN AND GREEN SAUCE

(SERVES SIX)

½ cup peanut oil
12 flour tortillas
3 cups shredded cooked chicken
1 pound Monterey Jack cheese, grated
¼ cup heavy cream
½ cup finely chopped scallions
Salt

1½ cups chopped Mexican green tomatoes or tomatillos verdes, fresh or canned (drained, if canned)
1 cup chopped cilantro
4-ounce can peeled green chilies, drained and chopped
1½ cups sour cream

Heat the oil in a skillet. Put each tortilla into the hot oil for a few seconds, turning it over so it softens. Stack the tortillas in a pan. Preheat the oven to 375°F. Oil a baking dish about 14 × 9 × 2 inches. Put some chicken, cheese, 1 teaspoon of the cream, a sprinkling of scallions, and salt to taste down the center of each tortilla. Roll them loosely and set side by side in the baking dish, with ends overlapping. Cover the dish snugly with foil and bake 30 minutes, until the cheese melts and bubbles a little. Meanwhile, prepare the sauce. Finely chop the tomatoes, cilantro, and green chilies. These can be run through the food processor very briefly so that the texture is in chunks instead of puréed. Stir in the sour cream until it is well blended. Remove the enchiladas from the oven, spoon a little of the green sauce over the top, and pass the rest of the sauce in a bowl.

CHICKEN CROQUETTES

(6–8 CROQUETTES)

A firm, creamy blend of chicken and crisp brown crumbs. Tradition dictates that they be shaped like small upside-down ice cream cones, but other shapes taste just as good.

2 cups finely diced cooked chicken
½ teaspoon salt
¼ cup minced celery with leaves
Pinch of cayenne pepper
2 teaspoons lemon juice
¼ cup minced onion

1 tablespoon minced parsley
1 cup Thick Cream Sauce (p. 380)
2 eggs, lightly beaten
2 cups freshly made bread crumbs
Oil for frying

Mix the chicken, salt, celery, cayenne pepper, lemon juice, onion, parsley, and cream sauce until well blended. Cover with foil, refrigerate until chilled, then form into small cones, 1½ inches at the base and about 2 inches high. Dip them into the beaten eggs, then roll them in the crumbs. Set them to dry on a piece of wax paper. Heat 3 inches of oil in a heavy pot, until medium hot—360°F. Add the croquettes, let them brown, turn, and brown on the other side. Don't crowd the pot; do in two batches, if necessary. Drain on paper towels. Place on a warm platter and serve with White Sauce.

CHICKEN AND ALMOND CROQUETTES

Add ½ cup blanched, chopped almonds to the mixture. Serve with Brown Sauce (p. 385).

CHICKEN AND MUSHROOM CROQUETTES

Sauté 1 cup chopped mushrooms in 2 tablespoons butter and add to the chicken mixture. Serve with White Sauce.

CHICKEN AND HAM CROQUETTES (SERVES SIX)

3 tablespoons butter
1 tablespoon finely chopped shallot or onion
¼ cup flour
½ teaspoon salt
¼ teaspoon paprika
⅛ teaspoon nutmeg
1 cup chicken broth
3 egg yolks, lightly beaten

1 cup finely diced cooked chicken
½ cup finely diced cooked ham
1 large egg, lightly beaten
2 cups freshly made bread crumbs
Oil for frying
White Sauce (p. 379)

Melt the butter in a saucepan and stir in the shallot or onion. Cook, stirring, over medium heat until soft. Stir in the flour, salt, paprika, and nutmeg, and cook 2–3 minutes more. Gradually add the chicken broth and bring to the boiling point. Stir ¼ cup of the sauce into the egg yolks, and then return the yolk-sauce mixture to the hot sauce. Add the chicken and ham, and cook over low heat, stirring constantly, for 4–5 minutes. Pour into a shallow bowl and refrigerate until chilled. Shape into small cones, 1½ inches at the base and about 2 inches high. Dip into the beaten egg and roll gently in the bread crumbs. Set to dry on a rack or a piece of wax paper. Heat 3 inches of oil in a heavy pot, until medium hot—360°F. Add the croquettes, and let them brown, turning them, on all sides. Drain on paper towels and place on a warm platter and serve with the sauce.

(SERVES SIX)
CHICKEN AND OYSTERS FOR A CHAFING DISH

One thing I've found is that the cook who is the host hates to be away from the table, yet has to be for last-minute cooking. The chafing dish, which is too rarely used today, should be dusted off and reinstated for just this purpose.

6 tablespoons butter
½ pound mushrooms, sliced
4 tablespoons flour
2 cups cream
2 cups diced cooked chicken
2 cups oysters, drained and in ½-inch pieces (or use tiny Olympias)

3 tablespoons dry sherry
Salt to taste
Toast

Melt the butter in the chafing dish. Add the mushrooms and cook for 5 minutes, stirring often. Stir in the flour and cook 2–3 minutes. Slowly pour in the cream and cook until thick and smooth. Add the chicken, oysters, sherry, and salt, and spoon over toast.

(SERVES THREE)
SCALLOPED TURKEY

2 cups minced cooked turkey
About 1½ cups turkey gravy
1½ cups cracker crumbs
Salt

¼ teaspoon freshly ground pepper
4 tablespoons butter

Preheat the oven to 350°F. Butter a 1½-quart casserole. Combine the turkey, the gravy, and ¾ cup of the cracker crumbs. Mix well, and season with salt and pepper to taste. Melt the butter in a skillet and lightly brown the remaining ¾ cup cracker crumbs. Spoon the turkey mixture into the casserole, sprinkle the buttered crumbs on top, and bake for 25–35 minutes, or until bubbling hot.

Other Suggestions for Using Leftover Chicken and Turkey

Use thin strips of cooked poultry to garnish a clear broth or a cold soup like Avocado. Chicken or turkey could be used in place of lamb to make a curry, and in place of veal to make a Veal Loaf. Cooked chicken is called for in Pilaf with Chicken, Chicken-Noodle Casserole, Chicken-stuffed Manicotti, and it would be good in a Wild Rice Casserole. And there are always omelets, crêpes, stuffed vegetables, sandwiches, and all those delicious ways to use chicken and turkey in salads.

ABOUT GAME BIRDS

Wild birds, lacking the fat that comes from an easy domestic life, tend to be tough, especially as they grow older. Fat is often added by basting or by barding, that is, by placing thin sheets of pork fat over the fowl while it is cooking.

The flavor we call "gamy" develops when a bird is hung properly. Also, the flesh tends to be richer and tastier because the bird has fed on wild hings. This special flavor, which gives game its character, is often complemented by tart currant jelly or sour applesauce, and as an accompaniment wild rice and a robust vegetable, preferably of the cabbage family.

Game birds such as wild duck, Canada goose, guinea hen, partridge, pheasant, quail, and grouse make festive eating. Very small birds can be prepared the same way quail is done on pages 354–55; pheasant and partridge should be cooked the same as guinea hen; wild goose is similar to wild duck but takes longer. You'll need to buy these birds in a special market, unless you have a hunter in the family. Be fastidious about cleaning and cooking wild game birds: wash them thoroughly in cold water, inside and out; dry them well; and don't overcook them!

ROAST GUINEA HEN   (SERVES FOUR)

Because guinea hen is naturally dry, it should be covered with sheets of barding fat during roasting.

2 young guinea hens	¼ pound salt pork, in thin
Salt	sheets
Freshly ground pepper	

Preheat the oven to 350°F. Rub the guinea hens liberally inside and out with salt and pepper. Place them on a rack in a shallow roasting pan and lay sheets of salt pork over the breasts. Roast for 45–60 minutes.

GUINEA HEN BRAISED IN CREAM

(SERVES FOUR)

¼ pound butter
2 guinea hens, in quarters
Salt
Freshly ground pepper

12 small white onions
1½ cups heavy cream
3 tablespoons lemon juice
2 tablespoons cranberry jelly

Melt the butter in a large skillet over medium heat. Lightly brown the guinea hens in the butter, sprinkle them with salt and pepper to taste, remove from the pan, and set aside. Brown the onions in the fat remaining in the pan. Return the guinea hens to the pan and pour the cream over them. Cover and simmer for 40 minutes, basting with the cream every 10 minutes. When done, remove the guinea hens to a warm platter. Add the lemon juice and cranberry jelly to the cream and pan drippings and simmer, stirring, for 2–3 minutes. Spoon over the guinea hens before serving.

BROILED WILD DUCK

(ALLOW ONE-HALF DUCK PER SERVING UNLESS VERY SMALL)

2 wild ducks
4 tablespoons olive oil
Salt
Freshly ground pepper

¼ pound butter
¼ cup lemon juice
2 tablespoons minced parsley

Preheat the broiler and place the rack 5 inches beneath it. Split the ducks down the back and flatten them by pressing the breastbone with the heel of your hand. Rub both sides with olive oil and sprinkle with salt and pepper. Place the ducks, skin side down, on the broiler rack and cook 5–7 minutes on each side for rare, 10–12 for medium. In a small saucepan melt the butter and add the lemon juice and parsley. Put the ducks on a warm platter and pour the butter sauce over them.

ROAST WILD DUCK

(ALLOW ONE-HALF DUCK PER PERSON)

A hunter with thirty years of duck-shooting experience claims this is the best way to cook a wild duck. He serves it with an extravagant amount of wild rice and currant jelly, and a wedge or two of lemon alongside each serving. If anyone finds the duck too rare, a hearty squeeze of lemon juice will turn the rosy meat instantly brown.

1 wild duck   Lemon wedges

Preheat the oven to 500°F. Rinse the duck inside and out with cold water and dry thoroughly. Place on a rack in a shallow pan and roast for 18 minutes for very rare, 25–30 minutes for pink duck.

WILD DUCK WITH PEANUT STUFFING

(ONE-HALF DUCK PER SERVING UNLESS VERY SMALL)

The peanuts add a congenial taste and a nice crunch to the meat.

¾ cup cracker crumbs
½ cup chopped dry-roasted peanuts
½ cup or more heavy cream
2 tablespoons butter, melted
2 teaspoons grated onion

Pinch of cayenne pepper
1 wild duck
Salt
Freshly ground black pepper
2 slices salt pork

Combine the crumbs, peanuts, cream, butter, grated onion, and cayenne. If the stuffing seems too dry, add a little more cream. Preheat the oven to 450°F. Rinse the duck inside and out with cold water; dry thoroughly. Stuff and skewer shut, then truss by winding string twice around one leg, then leaving an inch of slack and winding it around the other leg. Place the duck breast up on a rack in a shallow pan. Sprinkle with salt and pepper to taste and cover the breast with the salt pork. Roast for 20–30 minutes, basting every 5 minutes with the melted fat.

BROILED QUAIL

(SERVES ONE)

Place a tiny bird on a piece of toast, with currant jelly, watercress, and thin slices of lemon on the side.

2 quail   4 tablespoons butter, melted

Preheat the broiler. Split each bird in two pieces down the center. Brush with melted butter and place, skin side down, on a rack in a shallow pan, about 5 inches below the broiler element. Baste frequently with melted butter. Turn the birds once, broiling about 5 minutes on each side until well done.

(SERVES ONE OR TWO)   **ROAST QUAIL**

The one absolute must about roasting quail is that the skin become dark brown and crisp. It is this darkened, crisp skin that is delicious and converts people into quail lovers. It seems to me that a slightly sweet coating brings out the best in quail, so I'm adding a favorite baste of butter and honey. Serve the quail with Basic Polenta (p. 432) or Spoon Bread (p. 431) and some bitter greens.

2 quail	Salt to taste
¼ pound butter	Freshly ground pepper
2 tablespoons honey	

Preheat the oven to 450°F. Rinse the quail under cold water and pat dry. Put the butter and honey in a small pan and melt over low heat until the basting sauce is blended. Dip each quail and turn on all sides to coat with butter mixture. Salt and pepper all over. Place on a rack in a shallow pan. Roast for about 20 to 30 minutes, basting the quail twice with the butter mixture. Roast until the skin is dark brown. Remove from the oven, split the quail down the back, and serve.

OUTDOOR COOKING

ABOUT OUTDOOR COOKING

No wonder outdoor cooking is still so popular. We all love the aromas of fire, smoke, herbs, sauces, and the flavors of grilled food. The use of charcoal goes back to Neanderthal man, who discovered that a burning log, extinguished and relit later on, would burn hotter and longer than raw wood. Caribbean Indians used long, slow cooking, a precursor of modern-day smoking, as a means of preserving meat and fish. Today we barbecue for the fun of it, and for the wonderful flavors in everything from old-fashioned pit cooking to inventive restaurant grilling.

The word "barbecue" has become generic, and means many things. To be more precise, *grilling* is cooking food uncovered on a wire rack, directly above hot coals. *Barbecuing*, in many parts of the country, means long, slow cooking in a pit or on a turning spit. Most of what is discussed in this chapter is simple grilling, and the cooking equipment is called "the barbecue," since that's how most of us know it.

EQUIPMENT

Barbecues come in a variety of shapes and sizes, and many enthusiasts have two or three. Most people can get by with just one. Here are the most common types.

Round, portable braziers are the simplest and least expensive uncovered barbecues, with a shallow metal pan for the fire, and a wire grilling rack, sometimes adjustable with a hand crank, above. They come in many sizes, and are suitable for cooking hamburgers, steaks, chops, fish, and chicken parts, but are not very good for roasts and whole birds, unless you have an electric spit attachment.

Brazier

Covered kettle

Water smoker

Hibachi

Covered kettle barbecues enable you to turn an open barbecue into an oven, so you can maintain the lower temperature and smokiness needed for cooking large roasts and whole birds. A spit attachment is unnecessary, and the temperature is controlled by adjusting the vents in the top and bottom. The grilling rack, which is not adjustable, is set 4 to 6 inches above the fire pan. Without the cover, the kettle barbecue can be used just like the brazier. Some manufacturers suggest doing all your cooking—even hamburgers, steaks, and fish—with the cover on at least part of the time. If you do this, keep in mind that foods will cook a little faster with the cover on.

Hibachis are small, sturdy, and easy to move. They seem to last for years in backyards and on patios, and have the same uses as a brazier, though their small grilling area makes them particularly suitable for one or two people, especially apartment dwellers.

Kamados, heavy, oval-shaped covered clay cookers which originated in Japan, are not very common here. They are porous and hold the heat, making them ideal for long, slow cooking and smoking.

Water smokers, which resemble a tall, skinny, covered kettle barbecue, are the most widely available of smokers. Most of them use charcoal for heat, but there are also gas and electric models. A large water smoker, like a stackable Chinese steamer, makes efficient use of cooking space. They consist of one or two wire racks for the food, with a dome-shaped cover, and below is one pan to hold water or other aromatic liquid, with a fire pan underneath for the charcoal. It is possible to smoke large turkeys and huge roasts, and the flavors are wonderful. The smoker is also versatile, and without the water pan it can double as a covered kettle barbecue.

Gas barbecues are a popular alternative, especially if you like to keep your hands out of the charcoal sack. It is difficult to tell the difference between food cooked over charcoal and that from a gas-fired barbecue, although there are devoted outdoor cooks who claim that with gas you really can't attain the woodsy, outdoor flavor of a real fire. On the plus side, they are easy to light and ready in minutes, and if you want speed and convenience, they can't be beat. Most models have a hinged cover, and can be used like a covered kettle barbecue.

It is dangerous to cook in your fireplace, or over any indoor fire, unless it is properly designed and ventilated for cooking.

TIPS

- Prepare your fire about 30 minutes before you plan to cook—see p. 361.
- Watch food closely when cooking on an open grill, and have a sprayer of water handy to douse flare-ups.
- Bring large pieces of meat and poultry to room temperature before cooking; they will cook a little faster.
- Use long tools, with insulated handles, and have two pairs of tongs; one for turning food, the other for moving hot coals.
- Fruit juice, water, wine, or beer may be used in the water pan of a smoker.
- Use most basting sauces only during the last 10 or 15 minutes of cooking, so they form a light glaze. Almost all of them contain sugar or oil, or both, and make the fire flare up if they drip on hot coals. Pass any remaining sauce at the table.

Grilling Fish

- Fish is more fragile than meat and poultry, so fish steaks and fillets for the barbecue should be at least 1 inch thick. Lightly rub the fish, or the grilling rack, with oil, to help prevent sticking.

- As a rule of thumb, cook all fish approximately 10 minutes per inch, measured at the thickest part. For example, a piece of fish 1½ inches thick needs about 15 minutes on the grill, while a ¼-inch piece will take about 7 minutes.
- Any firm-fleshed fish is good for grilling. Salmon, tuna, swordfish, sturgeon, and shark are especially appropriate choices.
- Delicate white fish fillets, like sole and flounder, are best cooked in the kitchen; they fall apart on the grill.

Grilling Birds

- Game birds, like quail and squab, are ideal for butterflying, marinating, and grilling, and they cook in minutes. They are also a nice appetizer, and their size makes them just right for cooking on small hibachis and braziers.

Grilling Meats

- Disregard the prohibition against turning steaks and burgers more than once on the grill. They actually retain their juices better if turned 4 or 5 times.
- Use tongs for turning meat; forks puncture, and the juices drip out.
- Remove large pieces of meat from the barbecue about 10 degrees below the desired temperature of doneness; the temperature will continue to rise as the meat stands.

Grilling Vegetables

- Soft vegetables, like large mushroom caps, and zucchini and eggplant slices, may be grilled as is. Very firm vegetables, like potato and carrot slices, should first be blanched in boiling water.

Other tools you will need include at least 1 spatula, 1 basting brush, and 2 pairs of tongs (one for turning food, and another for moving hot coals). Get them all with extra-long handles. Have a spray bottle of water, to stop flare-ups, and a couple of heavy potholders reserved just for the barbecue.

FUELS

Fuel is a basic barbecue necessity. Here are the most common types.

Lump charcoal is made by burning hard wood until it is charred, then extinguishing it. When relit later on it burns slower and hotter than raw wood. Mesquite is the most common lump charcoal, though depending on where you live you might find oak, hickory, apple, pecan, or cherry.

Lump charcoal is a natural fuel with no additives. When first lit, it throws a lot of sparks that are hard to contain—so be forewarned if you live around wood-frame houses and dry grass. It also comes in large, irregular chunks, which should be broken into more uniform pieces with a hammer. Once lit, it makes a good, hot fire that remains hot for several minutes longer than a briquet fire.

Briquets, which are made from pulverized charcoal combined with a lighting additive, are easier to use than lump charcoal, and they make a safer fire since they don't spark nearly as much. Price usually indicates quality, and discount brands don't often burn as long or as hot as the more expensive ones. I find that there is no difference in flavor between meat grilled over mesquite and that grilled over briquets.

Lump charcoal and briquets can absorb moisture, making them difficult to light, so store them in a dry place with the sack closed.

Small, dry *sticks and logs* can also be used in your barbecue. They burn quite hot at first, but they quickly die down to a smolder, and the heat is not as intense as a charcoal fire. If the pieces are too small, they are apt to burn out before you finish cooking. Look for pieces of wood about 2 inches in diameter, which will remain hot long enough for cooking chicken pieces and thick steaks.

Don't use soft woods such as pine, spruce, and fir, which give off a tar-like pitch and lots of black smoke.

AROMATICS

Small chips and chunks of aromatic wood, especially hickory and oak, can be soaked in water for about 30 minutes, then tossed on the fire during cooking, so they smolder and impart their smokiness to the food. Chunks burn slowly, so you should drop them on at the start. Chips burn quickly, so add them at intervals during cooking. Hickory and oak are the easiest to find, and they are strongly flavored, so be careful not to overdo it. You will need about ¼ pound for an average fire, and about twice that amount for a large turkey or roast.

Fruitwoods, nutwoods, grapevine twigs, and sprigs of fresh herbs are so mild they impart little if any flavor when tossed on a fire.

STARTING THE FIRE

Before using your barbecue, or any package of charcoal or briquets, read the instructions.

The average barbecue fire takes about 40 briquets, more or less, and igniting them is easy and safe using one of the following methods. Never use gasoline, paint thinner, or anything not especially made for fire starting.

The *chimney starter* is a metal cylinder into which you stuff a couple sheets of crumpled newspaper, pile on the briquets or charcoal, then light the paper. It is a method I prefer because it is fast—the fire is ready in about 20 minutes—and requires no electricity or lighter fluid, which makes it practical for camping or the beach.

The *electric starter*, which is buried in the mound of charcoal or briquets and quickly gets red hot, works very well, but you must be near an electrical outlet. Never leave the starter in the fire for more than about 15 minutes after plugging it in, or the coil will melt.

Liquid starter fluids do their job, although they are petroleum-based and when lit give off a foul odor. This aroma does not penetrate the food, though, since by the time you start cooking, the starter has burned away.

Instant-lighting briquets are already impregnated with starter. Depending on brands and where you shop, they can cost up to twice as much as regular briquets. The advantage is that they light quickly and easily with a match, without the need for other starters, so their convenience may justify the price.

Paraffin-saturated blocks and sticks, which you place among the stack of charcoal or briquets and light with a match, are not the best choice. They tend to light only the area around them, and the fire is slow to spread.

No matter how you light the fire, it takes about 20 to 30 minutes for the coals to be ready for cooking, and temperature is important. During the day, coals will look gray-white all over; at night, they will glow red. At this point, spread them out. Coals pushed close together will burn hotter than if they are spread out with some space between them. If in doubt, it's better to have a fire a little too hot than too cool.

COOKING METHODS

There are two ways of cooking over an outdoor fire, *direct* and *indirect*. Which to use depends on the food you are cooking.

The direct method—cooking on the grilling rack 4 to 6 inches directly above the hot coals—is for hamburgers, steaks, chops, and most fish. This is fast cooking, and requires constant watching, with a spray bottle of water handy to stop flare-ups. Don't wander from the barbecue even for a minute; you'd be surprised how fast things can burn.

Indirect cooking is more leisurely; it's like using your oven. You need to be there, but you're not watching it continuously. The hot coals are spread around the perimeter of the fire pan, so the food on the grilling rack above is surrounded by radiant heat, but not directly over it. This method is generally used with covered kettle barbecues for long, slow cooking. It is the best way to cook large roasts, whole chickens and turkeys, and fatty foods, like spareribs, because grease is not dripping directly on hot coals and flare-ups are minimized.

With the indirect method, some cooks like to place a foil drip pan in the fire pit, directly underneath whatever is cooking above, to catch the fat and juices. This is especially useful if you are cooking something very fatty, like a whole goose or duck, since it keeps the bottom of the barbecue clean. Whatever juice you catch in the drip pan is likely to be burned and flecked with ashes, and is not usually pleasant to eat.

ADDING FUEL TO THE FIRE

If your cooking is going to take more than about 45 minutes to an hour, you'll have to replenish the coals to maintain a constant temperature. Though many people do it with success, adding unlit briquets or charcoal to an existing fire can be unpredictable, because they may ignite very slowly, and can even lower the temperature of the fire. As an alternative, if you plan to do a lot of long, slow cooking, purchase a small, inexpensive hibachi or brazier for lighting additional coals, so you have them in reserve to transfer—with tongs—to the fire.

Don't add instant-lighting briquets or briquets that have been sprayed with starter fluid to a hot fire; they will flare up.

CLEANUP

It is not necessary to wash the grilling rack. Before each use, let it heat over the fire for a few minutes, which sterilizes it, then clean it with a stiff wire brush before putting the food on. Don't put it in the dishwasher; it is difficult to remove the gritty residue it leaves.

WHAT TO GRILL OR BARBECUE

There are more variables in barbecuing and grilling than in stove-top cooking, since you have less control over the heat.

Almost any cut of beef or chicken works well on the barbecue, and they are good with many sauces and marinades. Marinating will not tenderize a tough cut of meat; only long, slow cooking will do that. But marinating will add flavor to steaks, chicken parts, chops, and fish.

Don't get into a rut, cooking only hamburgers and hot dogs. Try lamb or pork, which can be very good grilled. Pork is nice with spicy sauces, like Basic Barbecue Sauce (p. 377), and also tastes good if you toss damp hickory or oak chips on the fire during cooking.

Remember that just about anything cooked in the kitchen can also be done over an open fire, so there is no need to limit your choices.

(SERVES 4) **GRILLED T-BONE STEAKS**

A pat of flavored butter, placed on each hot steak just before serving, melts slowly and makes a delicious bit of sauce.

Tarragon Butter

4 tablespoons butter
1 teaspoon dried tarragon, crumbled
2 tablespoons chopped parsley

¼ teaspoon salt
¼ teaspoon freshly ground pepper

Steaks

4 T-bone steaks, about 1 inch thick

Salt
Freshly ground pepper

To make the herb butter, beat the butter, tarragon, parsley, salt, and pepper together until blended. Form into a rough log, wrap in wax paper, and chill. Have a barbecue fire ready. Sprinkle the steaks with salt and pepper to taste and grill them, turning every minute or two, about 8 minutes total for rare, 10 minutes for medium, and 12 minutes for well-done. Top each steak with a slice of the herb butter before serving.

PEPPER STEAK

Sprinkle the steaks lightly with salt, and rub about ½ *tablespoon coarsely crushed peppercorns* into each side. Press firmly into the meat and grill as directed.

BASIC HAMBURGERS   (SERVES FOUR TO EIGHT)

Handle the meat as lightly as possible when shaping the hamburgers. A chip of ice placed in the center of each patty before grilling helps keep it rare and moist. Set the condiments out, so people can have their hamburgers as plain or as dressed up as they like.

2 pounds ground beef	Mustard
1½ teaspoons salt	Mayonnaise
½ teaspoon freshly ground	Raw or grilled onion slices
pepper	Tomato slices
8 hamburger buns, split	Iceberg lettuce leaves
Catsup	Dill pickle slices

Have a barbecue fire ready. Combine the beef, salt, and pepper and mix gently. Shape into 8 patties about 3½ inches across; don't worry about getting them perfectly round. Grill over hot coals, turning every minute or so, 6 to 8 minutes total for rare, 10 minutes for medium, and 12 minutes for well-done. Place the buns on the grill, cut side down, for 1–2 minutes, just until lightly toasted, then place the hamburgers on the buns and serve with the garnishes above.

CHEESEBURGERS

About 1 minute before removing from the grill, place a slice of *Cheddar, Swiss,* or *American cheese* on each patty.

TERIYAKI FLANK STEAK   (SERVES FOUR TO SIX)

Soy sauce and ginger are good on thin steaks because their flavor penetrates the meat all the way through. This is also a favorite with chicken, but chicken should be refrigerated while marinating.

¼ cup oil	2 teaspoons powdered ginger,
¼ cup red wine or sherry	or 1 tablespoon grated
¼ cup soy sauce	fresh
2 tablespoons sugar	1½ pounds flank steak
1 clove garlic, minced	

Early in the day combine the oil, wine, soy sauce, sugar, garlic, and ginger. Marinate the steak in this mixture for at least 3 hours, turning it occasionally. Have a barbecue fire ready. Remove the steak from the marinade and pat it dry. Grill 4–6 inches from hot coals, turning every minute or so, for about 6–8 minutes total for rare, 10 minutes for medium, and about 12 minutes for well-done. Carve across the grain, into thin diagonal slices.

TERIYAKI SKIRT STEAK

Substitute 1½ *pounds skirt steak* for the flank steak.

TERIYAKI CHICKEN

Double the marinade ingredients, and substitute *2 chickens, halved*, for the flank steak. Grill for about 25 to 30 minutes, turning frequently.

(SERVES SIX TO EIGHT) ❋ BUTTERFLIED LEG OF LAMB

A boned and butterflied leg of lamb is a fairly large, flat piece of meat. It cooks more evenly and is easier to carve than a whole leg.

1 cup dry red wine	Grated rind of 1 lemon
¼ cup olive oil	1 teaspoon salt
1 onion, chopped	½ teaspoon freshly ground
2 cloves garlic, minced	pepper
2 tablespoons chopped fresh rosemary, or 2 teaspoons dried, crumbled	6-pound leg of lamb, butterflied and trimmed of fat

Combine the wine, oil, onion, garlic, rosemary, lemon rind, salt, and pepper, and mix well. Pour over the lamb and let marinate for at least 3 hours, turning occasionally. (Or place the lamb in a large plastic bag, pour in the marinade and seal tightly. Rub gently to distribute the marinade around the meat and marinate as directed, rubbing occasionally.) Have a barbecue fire ready. Remove the lamb from the marinade and pat it dry with paper towels; reserve the marinade. Grill for 35 to 45 minutes, turning frequently and brushing with the reserved marinade. Test for doneness by cutting a small slit in the thickest part; it should be pink inside. Carve across the grain into thin diagonal slices.

LAMB SKEWERS OR KABOBS   (SERVES SIX)

Use only tender cubes of lamb cut from the leg; other cuts of lamb are too tough.

½ cup dry red wine
¼ cup oil
2 cloves garlic, minced
½ teaspoon rosemary
½ teaspoon thyme

½ teaspoon salt
½ teaspoon freshly ground
   pepper
2½ pounds lean boneless leg
   of lamb, in 1½-inch cubes

In a large bowl combine the wine, oil, garlic, rosemary, thyme, salt, and pepper. Add the lamb, toss to coat, and let marinate for at least 1 hour, tossing occasionally. Have a barbecue fire ready. Place the lamb on skewers, pushing the pieces together snugly. Grill for 8 to 10 minutes, turning frequently, until lightly browned.

LAMB CHOPS WITH MINT SAUCE   (SERVES FOUR)

Rib or loin lamb chops about 1 inch thick are the best choice for grilling. Part of the mint mixture in this recipe flavors the chops as they cook, and the remainder can be served at the table.

Mint sauce

½ cup cider vinegar
¼ cup sugar
½ cup chopped fresh mint
   leaves

2 tablespoons oil

Chops

8 rib or loin lamb chops,
   trimmed of excess fat

Salt
Freshly ground pepper

To make the mint sauce, boil the vinegar and sugar together, remove from heat, add the mint, and let sit for 30 minutes. Remove 3 tablespoons of the mixture and combine it with the oil, to brush on the chops as they cook. Serve the remaining mint mixture at the table. Have a barbecue fire ready. Sprinkle the chops with salt and pepper to taste. Grill for about 8 minutes, turning three or four times and brushing occasionally with the oil-mint mixture.

(SERVES EIGHT) **MUSTARD-GLAZED PORK LOIN**

The orange-mustard mixture gives the roast a dark, sweet glaze.

½ cup orange marmalade
½ cup prepared mustard
1 tablespoon grated fresh
    ginger
1 tablespoon soy sauce

¼ teaspoon salt
¼ teaspoon freshly ground
    pepper
3½–4-pound boneless pork
    loin, tied for roasting

Combine the marmalade, mustard, ginger, soy sauce, salt, and pepper, and blend well. Have a barbecue fire ready for indirect cooking (p. 362). Place the pork on the grilling rack, cover the barbecue, and open the vents halfway. Cook for 45 minutes, then turn the roast over. You will need to add more briquets to maintain a constant temperature. Cook covered for 45 minutes longer, brushing with the orange mixture every 10 minutes. Total cooking time is about 1½ hours, or to an internal temperature of 160°F. Let rest for 10 minutes before carving into thin slices.

(SERVES TEN TO TWELVE) **HERBED LEG OF PORK**

A salty "dry marinade" rubbed into the meat sharpens the natural flavor, and forms a crisp coating. Leg of pork is sometimes called "fresh ham," and it makes splendid sandwiches.

1 tablespoon salt
2 teaspoons freshly ground
    pepper
2 teaspoons thyme

2 teaspoons sage
3 cloves garlic, minced
2 tablespoons oil
6–8-pound leg of pork

Stir together the salt, pepper, thyme, sage, and garlic. Rub the oil over the pork, then coat it evenly with the herb mixture. Soak a couple of large handfuls (about ¼ pound) hickory chips in water. Have a barbecue fire ready for indirect cooking (p. 362). Drop some of the damp wood chips on the fire and set the meat on the grilling rack. Cover the barbecue and open vents halfway. Cook for about 2½ hours, turning the meat once. Every 45 minutes, sprinkle more wood chips on the fire and add more briquets as necessary to maintain a constant temperature. Pork is done at an internal temperature of 160°F. Let rest for about 15 minutes before carving.

PORK CHOPS AND APPLE RINGS   (SERVES FOUR)

An old-fashioned combination that works well on the barbecue. If you haven't room for both the pork and apples on the grill together, do the chops first, and keep them warm in a low oven or on a cooler part of the grill while you cook the apples.

3 large apples	Four 1-inch-thick pork chops
6 tablespoons butter, melted	Salt
2 tablespoons sugar	Freshly ground pepper
½ teaspoon cinnamon	

Core the apples, but do not peel them, and slice into ½-inch rings. Stir together the butter, sugar, and cinnamon. Have a barbecue fire ready. Sprinkle the chops with salt and pepper. Grill for 15 to 20 minutes, turning occasionally, until no longer pink inside. Place the apple rings on the grill the last 10 minutes, also turning them occasionally and brushing two or three times with the butter-sugar mixture. Arrange the chops and apple rings together on a warm platter.

BARBECUED SPARERIBS   (SERVES FOUR TO SIX)

Sticky and delicious, and an easy recipe to make. To add a smoky flavor, toss a couple of handfuls of dampened hickory or oak chips on the fire.

Salt	1 recipe Basic Barbecue Sauce
Freshly ground pepper	(p. 377)
6 pounds pork spareribs, in 2	
slabs	

Have a barbecue fire ready for indirect cooking (p. 362). Generously salt and pepper the ribs on both sides. Place them on the grilling rack, cover the barbecue, and open the vents halfway. Cook for 50 minutes, turning once. Brush the tops of the ribs with sauce and cook, covered, for 10 minutes more. Turn them over, brush with more sauce, then cover and cook for a final 10 minutes. Cut into single-rib pieces, and serve with the remaining sauce at the table.

SAUSAGES

There are a variety of sausages suitable for grilling. Frankfurters, knockwurst, bratwurst, chorizo, and German, Italian, and Polish sausages are among those you're most likely to find. Fully cooked and ready-to-eat sausages need only be placed over hot coals and turned frequently until heated and browned.

Fresh sausages, especially those with pork, must be cooked through. A raw sausage about 1 inch in diameter takes about 15 minutes to cook fully. Turn them frequently, and have a spray bottle of water handy to douse flare-ups.

You may remove some of the fat from fresh sausages before grilling by pricking them several times with a fork, and blanching for 5–10 minutes in simmering water. Then grill for about 10 minutes, until browned. The result will be sausage that is slightly drier, but lower in fat.

(SERVES FOUR TO SIX) **BARBECUED CHICKEN**

For perfect barbecued chicken, use a combination of direct and indirect cooking, and brush on the sauce just the last few minutes of grilling, so it doesn't get too dark.

5–6 pounds assorted frying chicken pieces	Freshly ground pepper
Salt	1 recipe Basic Barbecue Sauce (p. 377)

Have a barbecue fire ready for indirect cooking (p. 362), so the hot coals are around the perimeter of the fire pan. Sprinkle the chicken pieces with salt and pepper and place them, skin side down, around the edge of the grilling rack, so they are directly over the hot coals. Turn frequently for about 10 minutes, until well browned. Watch the chicken carefully; it burns easily. Have a spray bottle of water handy to stop flare-ups. Move the browned chicken pieces to the center of the grilling rack—they may overlap slightly—so they are no longer directly over the fire. Cover the barbecue, open the vents halfway, and cook for 10 minutes. Turn the chicken and cook covered for 5 minutes more. Brush generously with the sauce, cover, and cook a final 5 minutes. Pass the remaining sauce at the table.

LEMON-BASTED CHICKEN
BREASTS   (SERVES SIX TO EIGHT)

Skinned breast of chicken is low in calories and grills quickly.

½ cup fresh lemon juice
½ cup fresh orange juice
1 tablespoon grated lemon
    rind
1 clove garlic, minced
1½ teaspoons tarragon

½ teaspoon salt
½ teaspoon freshly ground
    pepper
10 chicken breast halves, skin
    removed

Combine the lemon juice, orange juice, lemon rind, garlic, tarragon, salt, and pepper. Place the chicken pieces in a baking pan big enough to hold them in a single layer, and pour in the juice mixture. Let marinate for about 3 hours in the refrigerator, turning occasionally. Have a barbecue fire ready. Remove the chicken, reserving the marinade. Grill 4–6 inches from hot coals for about 20 minutes, turning three or four times and brushing with the reserved marinade, until browned, and the chicken is no longer pink when cut at the bone.

MARINATED GRILLED CHICKEN
HALVES   (SERVES TWO TO FOUR)

Thyme, garlic, and lemon juice give a clean, pleasing flavor to chicken.

⅓ cup olive or vegetable oil
3 tablespoons lemon juice
1 clove garlic, minced
1 teaspoon thyme
½ teaspoon salt

½ teaspoon freshly ground
    pepper
2½–3-pound broiler chicken,
    split

Blend together the oil, lemon juice, garlic, thyme, salt, and pepper. Place the chicken in a large plastic bag, pour in the lemon mixture, and seal the bag tightly. Rub gently to distribute the marinade. Marinate for at least 2 hours in the refrigerator, or all day if you wish, turning and rubbing the bag once or twice. Have a barbecue fire ready. Remove the chicken and pat it dry with paper towels; reserve the marinade. Cook 4–6 inches from hot coals for about 30–35 minutes, turning frequently. The last 10 minutes, brush two or three times with the marinade. If the chicken starts to get too dark, turn skin side up, and cover the barbecue (which will cool the fire a little) for the last 10 or 15 minutes, or move the chicken to a cooler part of the grill. Brush with the marinade as directed during last 10 minutes of cooking.

(SERVES FOUR) **HICKORY-SMOKED CHICKEN**

The hickory smoke penetrates throughout, making the whole chicken flavorful.

4–5-pound chicken
1 lemon
Sprigs of fresh parsley,
 tarragon, or rosemary

Salt to taste
Freshly ground pepper to
 taste
2 tablespoons butter

Soak a couple of large handfuls (about ¼ pound) of hickory chips in water. Rinse the chicken and pat it dry. Prick the lemon several times and place it inside the body cavity, along with a few sprigs of fresh herbs and a sprinkling of salt and pepper. Rub the chicken skin all over with butter, sprinkle with salt and pepper, and truss. Have a barbecue fire ready for indirect cooking (p. 362). Drop half the damp wood chips on the fire and place the chicken, breast-down, on the grilling rack. Cover the barbecue. After 30 minutes, turn breast-up, sprinkle the remaining wood chips on the fire, then cover and cook 45 minutes to 1 hour longer. You will need to add more briquets to maintain a constant temperature. The chicken is done when a meat thermometer registers 170°F in the breast or 185°F in the thigh. Let rest for 10 minutes before carving.

HICKORY-SMOKED TURKEY

For a *10–12-pound turkey*, stuff the cavity with 2 *pricked lemons*, a large handful of fresh herbs, and sprinkle with salt and pepper. Rub the skin with *4 tablespoons butter*, truss, and sprinkle with salt and pepper. Cook as directed above, breast-down for 1 hour, then breast-up for about 1½ hours longer, to the recommended temperatures. Use about ½ pound hickory chips.

GRILLED HALIBUT WITH
(SERVES FOUR) **OLIVE-CHILI SAUCE**

Firm-textured fish is good for grilling. Thin, delicate fillets, such as sole and flounder, tend to fall apart on the grill and are better pan-fried. The olive-chili sauce livens up the mild fish. It is nice served with warm tortillas.

Olive-Chili Sauce

4-ounce can diced green chilies	2 tablespoons wine vinegar or lemon juice
4-ounce can chopped ripe olives, drained	¼ teaspoon salt
⅓ cup olive oil	¼ teaspoon freshly ground pepper

Fish

2 pounds fish steaks (halibut, snapper, sea bass, or tuna), about 1 inch thick	Olive oil Salt Freshly ground pepper

To make the sauce, combine the chilies, olives, oil, vinegar or lemon juice, salt, and pepper, and stir until blended. Have a barbecue fire ready. Rub the fish lightly with oil and sprinkle with salt and pepper to taste. Grill 4–6 inches from hot coals for about 10 minutes, turning once. The fish is done when it has turned from translucent to opaque at the thickest part and no longer looks raw; make a small cut with a knife to check. Transfer to a warm platter, spoon some of the sauce over the fish, and pass the remainder at the table.

GRILLED SALMON WITH FENNEL   (SERVES FOUR)

Grill salmon over a hot fire so it cooks quickly and stays moist. Fennel is very firm, and must be blanched before grilling.

2 large fennel bulbs	4 salmon steaks, about 1 inch thick
¼ cup olive oil	
2 tablespoons lemon juice	4 tablespoons butter, melted
½ teaspoon salt	Lemon wedges

Chop enough of the feathery fennel tops to make ¼ cup and combine with the oil, lemon juice, and salt. Pour over the fish steaks on a large platter, turn to coat both sides, and let sit for about 30 minutes, turning once. Trim off and discard the remaining fennel tops, as well as any discolored outer stalks. Cut each bulb in half and blanch in boiling salted water for about 7 minutes, just until tender. Have a barbecue fire ready. Remove the fish from the marinade. Place on the grilling rack 4–6 inches from hot coals. Place the fennel, cut side down, on the grilling rack also. Grill both fish and fennel for 8 to 10 minutes, turning the fish once and the fennel three or four times, brushing it with the melted butter. Place on a warm platter and garnish with lemon wedges.

(SERVES SIX)   ✻   **GRILLED WHOLE TROUT**

A good way to prepare fresh-caught trout for breakfast. Even with store-bought fish, this simple recipe makes good eating.

6 cleaned whole trout, about 8 ounces each	Freshly ground pepper
Oil	¼ pound butter, melted
Salt	Lemon wedges

Have a barbecue fire ready. Rub the outside of each fish with oil and sprinkle the cavities with salt and pepper to taste. Grill 4–6 inches from hot coals for 10–12 minutes, turning carefully three or four times with a spatula, and brushing lightly with melted butter. The skin will darken and blister in spots, but the fish stays moist. Serve with lemon wedges.

(SERVES FOUR TO SIX)   **GINGERED SCALLOPS**

Grill scallops quickly, just until nicely browned. When overcooked they toughen and lose their delicate character.

¼ cup olive oil	2 pounds sea scallops
2 tablespoons lemon juice	¼ pound butter, melted
2 tablespoons chopped cilantro	1 tablespoon grated fresh ginger
½ teaspoon salt	1 clove garlic, minced
¼ teaspoon freshly ground pepper	

Blend together the oil, lemon juice, cilantro, salt, and pepper in a large bowl. Add the scallops, toss to coat, then let sit for 30 minutes, tossing occasionally. Have a barbecue fire ready. Combine the melted butter with the ginger and garlic. Remove the scallops from the marinade and push them on metal skewers so they touch. Grill over hot coals for about 6–8 minutes, turning frequently and brushing two or three times with the ginger-butter mixture. Serve immediately.

GINGERED PRAWNS

Substitute 2 *pounds shelled large or jumbo shrimp*, deveined, for the scallops. To skewer, bend them almost in half, so the large end nearly touches the smaller tail end, then insert the skewer just above the tail, passing it through the body twice. Cook and baste as directed above for 6–8 minutes, until they turn pink.

GRILLED ZUCCHINI, EGGPLANT, AND PEPPERS ⤳ (SERVES SIX)

These take only minutes to cook, and are delicious right off the grill or at room temperature.

1 large eggplant	½ cup olive oil
Salt	¼ cup lemon juice or wine
1 pound small zucchini or	vinegar
crookneck squash, or a	1 clove garlic, minced
mixture	1 teaspoon basil
1 green pepper	¼ teaspoon freshly ground
1 red pepper, or another	black pepper
green pepper	

Cut the eggplant into slices about ½ inch thick. Sprinkle both sides lightly with salt and let drain on paper towels for about 1 hour. Meanwhile, cut the squash in half lengthwise; set aside. With a vegetable peeler, peel the peppers—do the best you can, but don't worry about removing every bit of skin. Quarter the peppers and remove the ribs and seeds. Flatten each quarter slightly. Pat the eggplant slices dry. In a jar with a tight lid shake together the oil, lemon juice or vinegar, garlic, basil, black pepper, and ½ teaspoon salt. Have a barbecue fire ready. Grill all the prepared vegetables 4 inches from the coals for about 7–10 minutes, until tender and lightly browned, turning two or three times with a spatula and brushing with the oil mixture.

VEGETABLE BROCHETTES ⤳ (SERVES FOUR)

These look appealing served on a platter with steaks or lamb chops. The vegetables are blanched first so they grill more evenly.

½ pound zucchini, in 1-inch	2 tablespoons wine vinegar
pieces	1 clove garlic, minced
½ pound crookneck squash, in	½ teaspoon thyme
1-inch pieces	½ teaspoon salt
12 large mushroom caps	¼ teaspoon freshly ground
¼ cup oil	pepper

Drop the pieces of zucchini and crookneck squash into a large pot of boiling salted water, and boil 2 minutes. Drain, rinse with cold water, then drain again and pat dry. In a large bowl combine the oil, vinegar, garlic, thyme, salt, and pepper. Add all the vegetables and toss well. Let sit 30 minutes, tossing occasionally. Have a barbecue fire ready. Remove the vegetables from the marinade (save the marinade), and thread them alternately on long metal skewers. Grill 4–6 inches from the coals for about 10 minutes, turning occasionally and brushing with the reserved marinade, until lightly browned in spots.

(SERVES FOUR)   ∾ **CORN IN THE HUSKS**

The husks blacken and burn, but the kernels remain moist and sweet, with just a hint of smokiness.

8 ears of corn	Salt
Butter, softened	Freshly ground pepper

Peel back the corn husks without removing them, and pull off the silky threads. Rub each ear of corn with ½ tablespoon of butter and sprinkle to taste with salt and pepper. Bring the husks back up around the corn. Have a barbecue fire ready. Cook 4–6 inches from hot coals for 10–12 minutes, turning frequently, until the husks are darkened. Remove the husks and serve the corn with more butter, salt, and pepper.

CORN IN FOIL

Remove the husks and pull off the silky threads. Rub with butter and sprinkle with salt and pepper. Wrap in foil and cook over the coals as directed.

(SERVES FOUR TO SIX)   ∾ **MUSTARD ONIONS**

Red onion slices are quite sweet and mild when grilled, and go well with barbecued steaks and hamburgers.

6 tablespoons butter, melted	2 large red onions, peeled and
2 tablespoons prepared	sliced ½ inch thick
mustard (regular or Dijon-	Salt
type)	Freshly ground pepper

Have a barbecue fire ready. Stir together the butter and mustard. Sprinkle the onion slices with salt and pepper to taste. Grill them 4–6 inches from hot coals for about 10 minutes, turning two or three times with a spatula and brushing with the mustard mixture, until lightly browned and tender.

GARLIC CHEESE BREAD   👝   (SERVES EIGHT TO TEN)

Warm and crusty—if you like garlic, you know how good this is.

1 loaf French bread	¼ teaspoon salt
½ cup butter	¼ teaspoon freshly ground
1 cup grated Parmesan cheese	pepper
2 cloves garlic, minced	Dash of Tabasco

Slice the bread at 1-inch intervals, cutting not quite all the way through, so the slices remain attached at the bottom. Beat together the butter, cheese, garlic, salt, pepper, and Tabasco until smooth and blended. Gently open the bread slices and between each slice spread a scant tablespoon of the cheese mixture. Wrap the bread tightly in a double thickness of foil. Set on the grilling rack 4–6 inches from hot coals and heat for about 15 minutes, turning frequently.

HERBED BAKED POTATOES   👝   (SERVES FOUR)

These baked potatoes come from the grill buttery and soft with a good herb flavor. They're great with chicken.

4 large baking potatoes	½ teaspoon salt
6 tablespoons butter, softened	¼ teaspoon freshly ground
2 tablespoons chopped	pepper
parsley, thyme, and/or	
rosemary	

Slice each potato at ½-inch intervals, cutting not quite all the way through, so the slices remain attached at the bottom. Beat together the butter, herbs, salt, and pepper. Gently open the potato slices a little, and between each slice use a small knife to spread about ½ teaspoon of the butter mixture. Have a barbecue fire ready. Wrap individually in foil, and place on the grilling rack 4–6 inches above hot coals. Cover the barbecue and cook for 1¼–1½ hours, turning occasionally. To check for doneness, squeeze to see if the potato feels soft.

(ABOUT 2½ CUPS)   ❧ **BASIC BARBECUE SAUCE**

A traditional American sauce that has a nice balance of sweet, tart, and spicy. Because the sauce contains sugar, it burns easily, and is best brushed on food just during the last 5 or 10 minutes of cooking. Pass the remaining sauce at the table.

3 tablespoons vegetable oil	⅓ cup Worcestershire sauce
1 onion, chopped	⅓ cup brown sugar
2 cloves garlic, minced	2 teaspoons chili powder
1¼ cups catsup	¼ teaspoon cayenne pepper
⅓ cup cider vinegar	

Heat the oil in a medium saucepan and cook the onion and garlic gently for 10 minutes. Add the catsup, vinegar, Worcestershire, brown sugar, chili powder, and cayenne, and mix well. Let simmer for about 20 minutes, stirring occasionally, until slightly thickened.

(ABOUT 2 CUPS)   ❧ **LIGHT BARBECUE SAUCE**

Lighter and less spicy than Basic Barbecue Sauce. This sauce doesn't burn easily, and can be brushed on beef, pork, or chicken every 20 or 30 minutes throughout cooking.

1 cup dry white wine	1 onion, chopped fine
½ cup cider vinegar	2 tablespoons sugar
¼ cup olive oil	1 tablespoon grated lemon
3 tablespoons Worcestershire	peel
sauce	Drops Tabasco

Combine all the ingredients in a saucepan and bring to a boil. Reduce the heat and simmer, partially covered, for 20 minutes.

SAUCES, MARINADES & STUFFINGS

The new sauces here have a much fresher taste and reflect the use of a variety of fresh ingredients that are not cooked to death. For example, the new Green Sauce has an abundance of scallions and parsley that round out the tastes of the foods they are served with—cold meats, poultry, and fish. Spicy Peanut Sauce is particularly good over pork, fish, and steamed vegetables, and there is an All-Purpose Sweet-and-Sour Sauce that makes a whole new dish out of leftovers.

ABOUT SAUCES AND GRAVIES

Today there seems to be a movement toward serving foods more naturally, and thick gravies and rich cream and egg sauces are not as prevalent on the American table as they once were. Still, no cook should be without the basic skills of saucemaking. There are times when a well-made sauce or gravy is the very thing that is needed to complement a roast, to stretch leftovers, to elevate a modest dish, or simply to provide variety and please the palate. A scant spoonful of hollandaise makes it pleasurable for the dieter to fill up on quantities of blanched broccoli.

The simplest gravies or sauces can be made from pan juices, adding perhaps a dollop of cream or a little broth and/or wine, boiling up and blending well to incorporate all the tasty browned bits in the pan. But you can produce only a little bit of sauce this way. When a gravy is wanted, you must add flour to the pan drippings and then liquid to increase the volume (see p. 384). The basic fat (whether it be drippings, butter, or other fat) and flour mixture is called a roux, and it is the beginning of many sauces. It is always important to cook the flour in the fat for several minutes to remove its raw pasty taste. Sometimes a roux is cooked longer until it turns a nut-brown color, which then gives a definite flavor to the finished dish, a taste that is very characteristic of New Orleans cooking. But for most delicate sauces, the roux is cooked so briefly that it does not take on color. Two tablespoons of flour will thicken a cup of liquid; one tablespoon makes a thin sauce; three tablespoons a thick sauce. If you have the liquid hot when you add it, and you stir well, you will never have trouble with lumping.

Egg yolks are the thickening agent in sauces like hollandaise and mayonnaise (to be found in the Salad chapter, p. 707), a pair that is intimidating to many cooks. The trick is to whisk rapidly, adding oil or butter to the egg yolks slowly, either by hand, or in the blender or food processor. And, if the sauce *should* curdle or separate, there are reliable techniques for rescuing it.

Thickening for sauces is also provided by crumbs, or by a cornstarch and water mixture, the latter giving the sauce a somewhat translucent look. A tablespoon of cornstarch will thicken lightly 2 cups of liquid. Rapid boiling down will also thicken a sauce and intensify its flavor.

In general, a sauce should be thick enough to flow from a spoon and should be smooth and well flavored. All of these recipes should be seasoned to taste at the end. The effort spent in learning to make sauces will be well repaid. After all, who wants to live on broiled meat and steamed vegetables alone?

(1 CUP)   ❧ **WHITE SAUCE OR BÉCHAMEL SAUCE**

This used to be one of the first lessons in home economics classes; invariably white and pasty, it coated many a bland dish. When well made, however, it has a proper place in homey, creamed dishes, often making leftovers stretch or giving cooked foods new life. And it is important as a base for soufflés. The French term for this medium-thick white sauce is *béchamel*. The foolproof way to attain a perfectly smooth sauce is to have the milk hot when added to the butter and flour. It uses an extra pot, but as you become more proficient, this cautionary measure may not be necessary.

2 tablespoons butter	Salt
2 tablespoons flour	Freshly ground pepper
1¼ cups milk, heated	

Melt the butter in a heavy-bottomed saucepan. Stir in the flour and cook, stirring constantly, until the paste cooks and bubbles a bit, but don't let it brown—about 2 minutes. Add the hot milk, continuing to stir as the sauce thickens. Bring to a boil. Add salt and pepper to taste, lower the heat, and cook, stirring, for 2–3 minutes more. Remove from the heat. To cool this sauce for later use, cover it with wax paper or pour a film of milk over it to prevent a skin from forming.

THICK CREAM SAUCE

Use 3 tablespoons flour to 1 cup milk. This is the consistency needed as a base for croquettes and for soufflés.

CURRY CREAM SAUCE

Add 1 teaspoon curry powder and ¼ teaspoon ground ginger.

LEMON CREAM SAUCE

Just before serving, beat in 2 egg yolks, 6 tablespoons butter (1 tablespoon at a time), and 1 tablespoon lemon juice.

CHEESE SAUCE

Stir in ½ cup grated Cheddar cheese during the last 2 minutes of cooking, along with a pinch of cayenne pepper.

MORNAY SAUCE

Add 2 tablespoons grated Parmesan cheese and 2 tablespoons grated Swiss cheese during the last 2 minutes of cooking. Stir until blended. Just before removing from the heat, beat 2 tablespoons of the sauce into 1 lightly beaten egg yolk. Stir the sauce-yolk mixture back into the sauce and add 2 tablespoons butter. Cook, stirring, 1 minute more.

EGG SAUCE

Add 2 hard-boiled eggs in ¼-inch slices and thin sauce with 4 tablespoons additional milk, or chicken or fish stock, depending on what it is served with.

ONION SAUCE

Increase butter to 3 tablespoons. Before adding the flour, add *1 cup finely chopped onions* and *¼ teaspoon nutmeg*, and cook until onions are soft.

(1½ CUPS)   **VELOUTÉ SAUCE**

Another basic sauce: creamy with a background taste of well-flavored broth.

2 tablespoons butter   ⅓ cup heavy cream
3 tablespoons flour   Salt to taste
1 cup hot chicken broth

Melt the butter in a heavy-bottomed pan. Stir in the flour and blend over moderate heat until smooth. Continue to cook, stirring constantly, for 2 minutes. Add the chicken broth, continuing to stir as the sauce thickens. Bring to a boil, lower the heat, and cook 2 minutes more. Pour in the cream, add salt, and heat thoroughly.

SUPREME SAUCE

Just before serving, lightly beat *2 egg yolks* in a small bowl. Beat 2 tablespoons of the sauce into the yolks, then stir the sauce-yolk mixture back into the sauce with *¼ teaspoon nutmeg* and the *juice of ½ lemon*.

SEAFOOD VELOUTÉ SAUCE

Cover the *shells of 1 (pound or more) lobster or shrimp* with water and simmer for 1 hour. Strain the broth and return to the boil, reducing to 1 cup. Omit the chicken broth and use the lobster or shrimp broth instead. If a richer sauce is desired, beat *2 egg yolks* in a small bowl. Beat 2 tablespoons of the sauce into the yolks, then stir the sauce-yolk mixture back into the sauce. Add *1 tablespoon lemon juice*. Stir to blend.

RUSSIAN SAUCE

Before adding cream, add 1 *teaspoon finely chopped chives*, ½ *teaspoon prepared Dijon mustard*, 1 *teaspoon grated horseradish* (or *prepared horseradish*). Cook 2 minutes, then add the cream and 1 *teaspoon lemon juice*.

SHALLOT SAUCE   (1 CUP)

Creamy yellow, with the flavor of shallots. A good sauce for heating leftover chicken or veal; also good on fish.

3 tablespoons butter	1 cup hot chicken broth
2 tablespoons minced shallots	Salt
2 tablespoons flour	

Melt 1 tablespoon of the butter in a small pan. Add the shallots and cook, stirring, for 2–3 minutes. Add the flour, blend well, and cook, stirring for 2 minutes more. Slowly pour in the chicken broth, stir until smooth, and simmer for 15 minutes. Strain the sauce through cheesecloth or a fine sieve, and add the remaining 2 tablespoons of butter and salt to taste.

LEMON SAUCE   ✳   (1½ CUPS)

Pale yellow, with a nice lemony bite. Good over cauliflower, spinach, or broccoli.

1 cup chicken broth	2 egg yolks, lightly beaten
1 tablespoon butter	2–3 tablespoons lemon juice
2 tablespoons cornstarch	Grated rind of 1 lemon
¼ cup cold water	

Heat the chicken broth and butter in a heavy-bottomed pan. In a small dish, blend the cornstarch with the cold water until smooth; slowly stir the mixture into the chicken broth. Cook over low heat for 5 minutes, stirring constantly, until thickened and smooth. Beat 2 tablespoons of the thickened broth into the yolks, then stir the broth-yolk mixture back into the broth. Add the lemon juice and rind and cook 1 minute more. Do not boil. This sauce will keep for a couple of days if it is well covered in the refrigerator. It can be reheated by stirring over low heat.

NOTE
see page 471

(½ CUP)   ‌‌&ᴗ **PARSLEY BUTTER**

Good on steaks, chops, broiled fish, as well as vegetables. For other variations on the flavored butter theme, see p. 73, and try to marry compatible flavors.

¼ pound butter, softened   1 tablespoon lemon juice
⅛ teaspoon freshly ground   Salt
   pepper
2 tablespoons finely chopped
   parsley

Put the butter into a bowl with the pepper and parsley and blend with the back of a spoon. Or spin the ingredients in a food processor. Slowly add the lemon juice, a few drops at a time, then salt to taste. Form into a cylinder, wrap in wax paper or foil, and chill in the refrigerator. Once it is chilled, cut it into slices and place a slice or two to melt on each serving of meat or fish.

HERB BUTTER

Omit the parsley. Substitute a combination of herbs, making approximately *1 tablespoon fresh herbs* or *1–1½ teaspoons dry herbs*. For example, use *1½ teaspoons chopped chives*, *½ teaspoon dried thyme or tarragon*, and *½ teaspoon chopped parsley*.

(5 TABLESPOONS)   ‌&ᴗ **BROWN BUTTER**

A dark-brown sauce with a nutty, tart taste. Traditional with sweetbreads, brains, white fish.

5 tablespoons butter   2 teaspoons vinegar

Melt the butter over low heat. Stir and cook until the butter turns dark brown. Add the vinegar and blend well.

(½ CUP)   **PAN SAUCE**

The simplest, purest gravy imaginable.

2 tablespoons melted fat from   Salt
   cooked meat   Freshly ground pepper
½ cup boiling water or broth

Spoon off all but 2 tablespoons of fat from the roasting pan or from a skillet in which you have cooked chops, steaks, hamburger, or liver. Using a spatula or a wooden spoon, stir and scrape the bits from the bottom of the pan over low heat. Deglaze by pouring ½ cup boiling water or broth (beef or chicken depending on the meat) into the pan. Season with salt and pepper to taste, and cook for 1 minute.

PAN SAUCE WITH CREAM

Instead of using water or broth, add *½ cup cream* and cook down rapidly for a minute or two.

PAN SAUCE WITH WINE

Instead of using water or broth, add *½ cup red or white dry wine* and cook down rapidly; you could also use a combination of broth and wine.

IMPROVISED GRAVY   (ABOUT 1½ CUPS)

When you don't have enough natural pan juices and drippings to make a gravy or need a gravy to create a tasty dish out of leftover meat, here is a basic recipe that will serve well. You can add compatible seasonings like fresh herbs or a little duxelles. Use beef bouillon for red meat and chicken for poultry.

2 tablespoons minced shallots, scallions, or onion	1½ cups beef or chicken broth
3 tablespoons butter	Leftover drippings or additional tablespoon butter
3 tablespoons flour	
¼ cup red wine or dry vermouth (optional)	Salt
	Freshly ground pepper

Sauté the minced shallots or other kind of onion in the butter until translucent. Stir in the flour and, cooking slowly, stir until it turns light brown. Remove the pan from the fire, add the wine, if you are using it, and an equal amount of broth. Stir until smooth, return to the fire, and slowly add the remaining broth, stirring constantly. Continue to cook, stirring often, for another 5 minutes. Swirl in leftover drippings or butter, salt and pepper to taste.

(2 CUPS)   **BROWN GRAVY**

2 tablespoons fat from a roast   Salt
2 tablespoons flour   Freshly ground pepper
1½ cups liquid: pan juices,
    water, broth, wine, or a
    combination

Remove the meat from the roasting pan. Pour all the pan juices into a
measuring cup. When the fat rises to the top, spoon off 2 tablespoons
and return them to the pan. Discard the excess fat but save whatever
juices are left in the cup. Put the pan over a burner and heat gently. Stir
in the flour. Cook it thoroughly for several minutes, stirring to keep it
smooth. Add enough additional liquid to the juices in the cup to make
1½ cups in all. Slowly stir the liquid into the roasting pan and cook for
5–6 minutes. If the gravy is too thick to flow easily from a spoon, add
more liquid and cook for 1 minute. Season with salt and pepper to
taste.

CLEAR OR TRANSPARENT GRAVY

Omit the flour. Dissolve *1 tablespoon cornstarch* in *½ cup cold stock, wine,
or water*. Pour the pan juices into the pan. Heat gently, and stir in the
cornstarch mixture until the gravy is clear and thickened.

(1 CUP)   **BROWN SAUCE**

2 tablespoons butter   2 tablespoons flour
1 slice onion, about ½ inch   1¼ cups beef broth
    thick   Salt to taste
⅛ teaspoon freshly ground
    pepper

Melt the butter in a saucepan and add the onion. When the butter is
barely brown, stir in the pepper and flour, and cook slowly until the
flour is brown. Gradually add the broth, stirring, and boil gently for 1
minute. Remove the onion, add salt, turn the heat to simmer, and cook
15 minutes. Add more liquid if the sauce is too thick.

ONION-BROWN SAUCE

Omit the onion slice. Cook 4 *tablespoons finely chopped onion* in the butter, and do not remove.

WINE SAUCE

Omit the onion slice. Add ¾ *cup red wine* and ½ *cup beef broth*, then stir in 2 *green onions, minced*, 2 *sprigs parsley*, ½ *bay leaf*, 1 *whole clove*, and 1½ *teaspoons Worcestershire sauce*. After cooking 15 minutes, remove bay leaf and clove.

SAUCE PIQUANTE

Omit the onion slice. After adding the broth, stir in 1 *tablespoon vinegar*, 2 *teaspoons minced scallions*, 2 *teaspoons capers*, 1 *tablespoon minced dill pickle*, and a *dash of cayenne pepper*.

MUSHROOM SAUCE ࢧ   (1½ CUPS)

As well as its use as a sauce, this is very good over buttered toast. Unless mushrooms are very dirty, trim off the hard end of the stems and just wipe them clean with a damp cloth or paper towel.

5 tablespoons butter	1 cup heavy cream
½ pound mushrooms, sliced	Salt to taste
2 tablespoons flour	
2 tablespoons fresh lemon juice	

Melt the butter in a large skillet. Stir in the mushrooms and cook for 2–3 minutes, until they darken a little. Stir in the flour, blend to smooth, and cook 2 minutes. Slowly stir in the lemon juice, cream, and salt, and cook only until hot.

(5 CUPS)   ج& **FRESH TOMATO SAUCE**

2 tablespoons olive oil
1 medium onion, chopped
  fine
1½ teaspoons thyme,
  crumbled
½ teaspoon oregano
5 large fresh tomatoes, peeled,
  seeded, and chopped

1 teaspoon sugar
½ teaspoon freshly ground
  pepper
½ cup chopped parsley
Salt to taste

Heat the oil in a sauté pan and add the onions. Cook, stirring, for 1 minute. Add the thyme, oregano, tomatoes, sugar, and pepper. Simmer for 20 minutes. Add parsley and salt.

(4 CUPS)   ج& **TOMATO SAUCE**

This is a simple sauce with no onions or garlic; the grated carrot adds a little sweetness, but if you prefer, use a little sugar to counter the acidity of the tomatoes. For a more robust flavor, try one of the variations.

2 tablespoons olive oil
¾ cup tomato paste
2½ cups peeled and chopped
  fresh or canned tomatoes
1 carrot, grated, or 1 teaspoon
  sugar

½ teaspoon freshly ground
  pepper
1 tablespoon basil, crumbled
5 tablespoons butter
Salt to taste

Heat the oil in a heavy-bottomed saucepan. Stir in the tomato paste, tomatoes, carrot, pepper, and basil. Simmer for 30 minutes. If the sauce becomes too thick, add a little water. Cook 15 minutes more, then stir in the butter and salt. Serve with cooked pasta.

I ITALIAN TOMATO SAUCE WITH GROUND BEEF

Add *1 pound ground beef* to the heated oil. Cook, stirring and breaking the beef into tiny pieces, until the meat loses its pinkness. If the beef is fat, spoon off all but 3 tablespoons of fat and proceed as directed.

II ITALIAN TOMATO SAUCE WITH GARLIC AND ONIONS

Cook 1 *onion, chopped,* and 2 *cloves garlic, minced,* in the heated oil for 3 minutes before adding the remaining ingredients.

SALSA VERDE 🐦   (ABOUT 1 CUP)

Fresh tomatillos (see p. 616) give this sauce a peppy flavor.

3 large cloves garlic	½ medium onion
2 tablespoons cilantro, or Chinese parsley (coriander), approximately	6 tomatillos
	½ teaspoon salt
1 small jalapeño pepper, seeded	

Finely chop by hand the garlic, cilantro, jalapeño pepper, onion, and tomatillos. Mix them together in a bowl with the salt. Or put all of the ingredients in a food processor and process until coarsely chopped. This sauce will keep in the refrigerator for 3 or 4 days.

HOLLANDAISE SAUCE 🐦   (1 CUP)

There's no reason to fear this classic sauce, yellow with butter and egg and tart with lemon juice. Made the traditional way, or whirred in the blender (following recipe), it should cause no problems for the careful cook. And if it does, there are two sure-fire ways to fix it (see below).

3 egg yolks	2 tablespoons hot water
1 tablespoon lemon juice	Dash of cayenne pepper
¼ pound butter, melted	Salt to taste

Use a double boiler or a metal bowl placed over hot, but not simmering, water. Put the egg yolks in the boiler top, and beat with a wire whisk until smooth. Add the lemon juice and gradually whisk in the melted butter, pouring in a thin stream. Slowly stir in 2 tablespoons hot water, the cayenne, and salt. Continue to mix for 1 minute. The sauce should be thickened. Serve immediately, or hold over warm water for an hour or two, but don't try to keep it too long without refrigerating.

NOTE *see page 471*

To correct a curdled or "broken" hollandaise or mayonnaise sauce, whisk in a teaspoon or two of boiling water, a drop at a time. If that doesn't work, put an egg yolk in a bowl and add the "broken" sauce very slowly, beating with a whisk. Be patient and take lots of time; eventually you will have a smooth sauce.

BÉARNAISE SAUCE

Cook *1 tablespoon minced shallots* or *white ends of scallions* with *2 tablespoons vinegar* and *½ teaspoon dried tarragon* until reduced to 1 tablespoon; then strain. Use this in place of the lemon juice. Add *1 teaspoon minced parsley* and, if available, *1 teaspoon minced fresh tarragon* to the sauce when thickened.

SAUCE MOUSSELINE

Fold in *⅓ cup heavy cream, whipped,* just before serving. This is a good way to stretch the sauce.

BLENDER OR FOOD PROCESSOR ৯ HOLLANDAISE

(1¼ CUPS)

Smooth, buttery, tart, and easy. Fish, broccoli, asparagus, and eggs all benefit from a cover of hollandaise. The same variations as in the preceding recipe can be made with this Hollandaise and the same rules about storage apply.

3 egg yolks	1 tablespoon lemon juice
2 tablespoons boiling water	Dash of cayenne pepper
½ pound butter, melted	Salt to taste

NOTE
see page 471

Put the egg yolks in the electric blender or food processor. If using the blender, turn to low speed. Slowly add the boiling water, and then add the butter very slowly in a thin stream. Add the lemon juice, cayenne, and salt. Taste and correct the seasonings.

(1½ CUPS)

৯ AÏOLI

Pronounce it "i-oh-lee." It is robust with garlic, adds zest to fish, especially cod, and boiled new potatoes, hard-boiled eggs, or green beans.

3 egg yolks
½ teaspoon salt
4–6 cloves garlic, peeled

1 cup olive oil
½ cup vegetable oil
1 tablespoon lemon juice

NOTE
see page 471

Put the yolks in a bowl. Put the salt on a cutting board with the garlic on top. Mince the garlic, incorporating the salt as you chop. At the end, use the flat edge of the knife blade to mash and crush the garlic and salt into a paste. Add this to the yolks. Mix the olive and vegetable oils together. Blend in the oils, drop by drop, whisking or stirring briskly with a fork. Be patient. When the sauce has thickened a little, increase the speed of the oil to a thin slow stream. When all the oil is incorporated, add the lemon juice, blend well, and correct the seasoning.

HORSERADISH CREAM 🍃 (1 CUP)

A creamy, sharp accompaniment to roast beef.

¾ cup heavy cream
4 tablespoons prepared
horseradish

2 tablespoons vinegar
Salt to taste

Beat the cream until stiff. Gently stir in the horseradish, vinegar, and salt. Refrigerate until needed.

SPINACH SAUCE 🍃 (ABOUT 1 CUP)

I originally used this sauce on simply cooked fish, but it is equally good on roast leg of lamb.

1 large bunch fresh spinach
(about 1 pound)
1 tablespoon olive oil
2 cloves garlic, minced

2 tablespoons heavy cream
¼ cup mayonnaise
Salt

Wash the spinach thoroughly and place in a pot or skillet with the water that clings to the leaves; cover, and cook on medium-high heat for about 2 minutes, until all the leaves have wilted. Add the olive oil and garlic to the pan and sauté for about 1 minute. Purée the spinach mixture in a food processor or blender until you have a smooth purée. Add the cream and mayonnaise and process until blended. Taste for seasoning and add salt to taste. Return mixture to the pot and reheat gently.

(1 CUP) **CREAMY MUSTARD SAUCE** ‿

This is a cold sauce, good on fish, chicken, or cold meats. It can also be used as a dipping sauce for fresh or cooked vegetables.

1 cup sour cream
1 tablespoon prepared
  mustard

1 tablespoon minced onion
¼ teaspoon salt
¼ teaspoon pepper

Put all the ingredients in a small bowl and mix well to blend. Store in the refrigerator up to 1 week until used.

(ABOUT ¾ CUP) ‿ ✱ **EMALEE'S MUSTARD SAUCE**

This sauce is compatible with salads, fish, and chicken.

2 tablespoons olive oil
2 tablespoons Dijon mustard
¼ cup white vinegar
¼ cup water

½ teaspoon salt, or to taste
2 tablespoons chopped
  parsley

In a mixing bowl, whisk together the olive oil, mustard, vinegar, water, and salt. Stir in the parsley.

(ABOUT ⅔ CUP) ‿ **WARM MUSTARD SAUCE**

This is good as a sauce or as a basting for chicken or pork loin roast. Coat the meat while roasting and serve the rest as a sauce on the side.

⅓ cup prepared mustard
3 tablespoons honey
2 tablespoons olive or
  vegetable oil
1 tablespoon red wine or
  balsamic vinegar

1 teaspoon ground sage
½ teaspoon salt
½ teaspoon freshly ground
  pepper

Combine all of the ingredients in a small saucepan and mix well to blend. Place over a medium-low heat and heat until very warm, but do not boil.

RAISIN SAUCE ≥∾   (2 CUPS)

Raisin sauce is a traditional American sauce that makes a thick slice of
country ham or a piece of good simmered tongue better than you can
believe.

1 tablespoon plus 1 teaspoon flour	¼ cup fresh lemon juice
1 tablespoon dry mustard	1½ cups unsweetened apple juice
4 tablespoons light-brown sugar	¼ teaspoon salt, or to taste
	½ cup raisins

Put the flour, mustard, brown sugar, lemon juice, and ½ cup of the apple juice in a small saucepan. Stir until the mixture is smooth and
blended. Turn the heat to medium and add the remaining cup of apple
juice, the salt, and the raisins. Cook, stirring, for about 5 minutes. Remove from the heat and serve hot. This keeps very well stored in the
refrigerator.

SPICY PEANUT SAUCE ≥∾   (1 CUP)

This sauce adds a liveliness to cooked chicken, pork, or fish—or you
may serve it with steamed vegetables.

5 ounces chunky peanut butter	6 cloves garlic, minced
2 tablespoons soy sauce	⅓ cup chopped cilantro, or Chinese parsley
⅓ cup water	1 tablespoon plus 1 teaspoon hot chili oil
3 tablespoons sugar	
1 tablespoon sesame oil	
1½ tablespoons rice wine vinegar	

Beat all the ingredients together in an electric mixer. (Do not use a food
processor as it may distort the texture and color of this sauce.) Store in
the refrigerator in a covered container. This sauce will keep for weeks.

GREEN SAUCE ≥∾ ✳   (ABOUT 2 CUPS)

A sauce with many purposes, Green Sauce can be served with thinly
sliced roast beef, with hard-boiled eggs, escarole, watercress, fish, and
boiled beets. Or mix it into mayonnaise for a salad dressing, sauce al-

most any cold vegetable with a spoonful or two, excellent over pasta . . .

1 cup olive oil	2 teaspoons Dijon mustard
⅓ cup water	1 rounded tablespoon cream-style horseradish sauce
3 tablespoons cider vinegar	4 large cloves garlic
1 teaspoon kosher or coarse salt	¾ cup chopped parsley
Freshly ground pepper	3 scallions, green part only

Combine the olive oil, water, vinegar, salt, and pepper to taste in a food processor and process until well blended. Add the mustard, horseradish, garlic, parsley, and scallions, and blend well. Store in an airtight jar in the refrigerator until needed.

(ABOUT 1½ CUPS)   ⇜ **SWEET CIDER SAUCE**

A nice complement to baked ham or a slice of pan-fried ham.

2 tablespoons butter	juice concentrate, defrosted
2 tablespoons brown sugar	1–2 tablespoons lemon juice (optional)
1 tablespoon flour	Pinch of cloves (optional)
12-ounce can frozen apple cider concentrate or apple	

Melt the butter and brown sugar together in a saucepan over moderate heat. Put the flour and ⅓ cup of the apple cider concentrate in a container with a lid. Shake well, until blended and smooth. Add the rest of the apple cider concentrate to the saucepan and stir to blend. Then add the flour mixture and bring it to a boil, stirring constantly. Cook until slightly thickened. Add the optional lemon juice and cloves.

ALL-PURPOSE SWEET-AND-

(ABOUT 1 CUP)   ⇜ **SOUR SAUCE**

This is very good on pan-fried or steamed fish and is a good sauce to mix into a stir-fry dish of shrimp, pork, or chicken.

¼ cup catsup	2 teaspoons soy sauce
½ cup sugar	1 tablespoon cornstarch mixed with 2 tablespoons cold water
¼ cup water	
¼ cup vinegar	
2 tablespoons lemon juice	

In a small saucepan, put the catsup, sugar, water, vinegar, lemon juice, and soy sauce. Stir to blend and place over high heat. Just before the sauce comes to a boil, slowly add the cornstarch mixture, stirring constantly, and continue to heat until thickened. Remove from the heat.

DRIED FRUIT SAUCE ❧ (ABOUT 2 CUPS)

This is a tantalizing mixture of spicy, sweet, and tart flavors—a sauce that goes well on lamb or chicken.

½ cup dried prunes, in large pieces
½ cup dried apricots, in large pieces

1 cup orange juice
2 tablespoons brown sugar
2 tablespoons cider vinegar
1 teaspoon mace

In a saucepan, combine the prunes, apricots, orange juice, brown sugar, vinegar, and mace, and simmer over low heat for 10 minutes. Serve hot.

CHINESE SWEET-AND-SOUR SAUCE (ABOUT 1 CUP)

This is good with fish, poultry, or pork. Use some during the cooking and pass the remaining at the table.

1 tablespoon sesame oil
2 tablespoons chopped cilantro, or Chinese parsley

2 tablespoons soy sauce
3 tablespoons white vinegar
4 tablespoons chicken broth
¼ cup sugar

Place the oil, cilantro, soy sauce, vinegar, chicken broth, and sugar in a small saucepan, and stir to blend. Place over a medium heat and bring to a boil. Remove from the heat.

TARTAR SAUCE ❧ (1½ CUPS)

A homemade tartar sauce is much better than the store-bought versions and well worth the time to make.

1 cup mayonnaise
2 tablespoons minced scallions, white part and 2 inches of green tops

½ cup finely chopped "old-fashioned" dill pickles
1½ teaspoons chopped capers
⅛ teaspoon cayenne pepper

Combine the mayonnaise, scallions, dill pickles, capers, and cayenne pepper in a bowl and stir until well mixed. Refrigerate until ready to use.

(1¼ CUPS)   ⊱ **CUCUMBER CREAM**

More a relish than a proper sauce, this is lovely and fresh-tasting with fish.

1 cucumber	2 tablespoons vinegar
½ cup sour cream	Salt to taste

Peel and finely chop the cucumber. Pat dry of excess liquid, put in a bowl, and stir in the sour cream, vinegar, and salt.

(ABOUT ¾ CUP)   ⊱ **CUCUMBER SAUCE**

Another fresh cucumber relish to serve with fish.

1 medium cucumber	1 tablespoon white vinegar
⅛ teaspoon freshly ground pepper	Salt to taste

Pare the cucumber. Grate it by hand or in a food processor, and squeeze out most of the juice. Mix with the pepper, vinegar, and salt.

(1 CUP)   ⊱ **YOGURT GREEN SAUCE**

The tartness of the yogurt makes this a particularly good foil for cold fish or chicken. When you have some homemade green mayonnaise on hand in the refrigerator, try this interesting sauce. It is easy enough to increase or decrease the ingredients according to your needs.

½ cup Green Mayonnaise (p. 708)	Fresh lemon juice
	Salt to taste
½ cup yogurt	Freshly ground pepper
1 tablespoon capers, drained	1 tablespoon chopped parsley

Beat the mayonnaise and yogurt together. Add the capers and a few drops of lemon juice to taste, and salt and pepper. Sprinkle on fresh parsley.

ORANGE SAUCE ❧   (1 CUP)

A dark, sweet-orange flavor. Pleasing with lamb, duck, or cold meats.

⅓ cup currant jelly	2 tablespoons orange juice
3 tablespoons sugar	2 tablespoons lemon juice
Grated rind of 2 oranges	⅛ teaspoon cayenne pepper
2 tablespoons Port wine	Salt

In a saucepan, combine the jelly, sugar, and grated orange rind and beat until smoothly blended. Stir in the wine, orange juice, lemon juice, and cayenne pepper. Heat through to melt the jelly. Add salt to taste.

OYSTER SAUCE   (2 CUPS)

A creamy sauce for fish.

1½ cups shucked oysters and their liquor	1¼ cups milk
4 tablespoons butter	Salt to taste
2 tablespoons flour	¼ teaspoon freshly ground pepper

If the oysters are very large, cut into pieces about the size of a grape. Put the oysters and oyster liquor in a pan and cook over low heat for about 3 minutes, or until the oysters look plump. Remove the oysters and pour the liquor into a cup. Melt the butter in a pan and, when it foams, stir in the flour. Cook and stir for 2 minutes. Slowly add the oyster liquor and milk, stirring constantly. Add the salt and pepper and cook another 5 minutes over low heat. The sauce should flow easily from a spoon; if it becomes too thick, add more milk. Stir in the oysters and cook only until they are heated through.

MINT SAUCE   (½ CUP)

A thin, slightly sweet sauce of fresh mint in tart vinegar: so much better than the bright-green commercial mint jelly. It is very good made with fresh spearmint.

½ cup white vinegar	½ cup minced mint leaves
¼ cup sugar	

Put the vinegar and sugar in a small pan. Heat until it boils and the sugar dissolves. Pour the hot sauce over the mint and let stand at least 1 hour.

(ABOUT 1 CUP)   **LEMON MINT CREAM SAUCE**

A cold creamy sauce, good on hot or cold fish, fresh fruit, or ham with melon or figs.

¼ cup fresh lemon juice   Grated or minced zest of 1
4–6 large mint leaves   lemon
1 cup heavy cream

Put the lemon juice and mint leaves in a mixing bowl and bruise the leaves with a spoon against the bottom of the bowl. Set aside for about 15 minutes to allow the flavor of the mint to infuse the lemon juice. Remove the mint leaves. Pour the cream in a thin stream into the lemon-mint mixture, whisking until all the cream is incorporated and the cream has thickened. Continue to stir the sauce with a spoon and it will thicken more. Stir in the lemon zest. Cover and refrigerate until needed, or up to two days.

ABOUT MARINADES AND BARBECUE SAUCES

Marinades and barbecue sauces are similar in composition but are used differently. Each usually contains oil, seasoning, and an acid liquid such as wine, vinegar, tomatoes, or lemon juice. Meat is soaked in a marinade so that the seasonings can add flavor while the acid in the liquid softens tough fibers. A plastic bag, sealed tightly, can be used instead of a bowl, thus making it easy to turn the meat. Then the meat is patted dry and cooked in one of several ways; often the marinade is used in the cooking. A barbecue sauce sometimes serves as a marinade as well, seasoning and softening meat put to soak in it, but ordinarily it is brushed over food as it is baked or grilled, imparting a surface flavor.

(2 CUPS)   ❧ **WINE MARINADE**

Red wine is good with beef and lamb. Use a white wine for chicken or pork. Let the meat marinate for at least 3 hours before cooking, turning it several times in the marinade.

1 cup red wine   ½ teaspoon rosemary,
1 cup olive oil   crumbled
3 cloves garlic   1 teaspoon thyme, crumbled
1 teaspoon salt   4 tablespoons minced parsley
½ teaspoon marjoram,   1 teaspoon freshly ground
   crumbled   pepper

Mix the wine and oil together in a jar with a tight-fitting lid. Crush and chop the garlic with the salt until almost a paste. Add to the wine and oil, along with remaining ingredients. Cover tightly and shake until all ingredients are well blended.

BARBECUE SAUCE & (ABOUT 2 CUPS)

A basic barbecue sauce with a peppy taste; good on pork chops, spareribs, and hamburgers.

2 tablespoons butter	4 tablespoons brown sugar
1 onion, chopped fine	4 tablespoons vinegar
2 cloves garlic, minced	4 tablespoons Worcestershire
2 cups water	sauce
¼ teaspoon salt	1 cup catsup
1 tablespoon chili powder	1 teaspoon Tabasco

Melt the butter in a saucepan and cook the onion and garlic until soft. Add the water and remaining ingredients. Stir until well mixed. Place over medium-low heat and simmer for 30 minutes. Cook longer for a thicker sauce.

SIMPLE BARBECUE SAUCE & (ABOUT 1¼ CUPS)

¼ cup Worcestershire sauce	¼ cup brown sugar
¼ cup vinegar	¼ cup catsup
¼ cup water	

Combine all of the ingredients in a small saucepan and stir until well mixed. Place over a medium-low heat and simmer for about 10 minutes.

GINGER-SOY MARINADE
OR SAUCE & (ABOUT 1½ CUPS)

This is good on chicken and pork, especially spareribs.

4 cloves garlic, minced or crushed	½ teaspoon freshly ground pepper
1 cup soy sauce	1-inch piece fresh ginger, grated or minced
½ cup brown sugar	2 tablespoons Worcestershire
¼ cup olive oil	sauce

Combine all of the ingredients above in a container with a cover. Shake to mix well and let it mellow for at least 1 hour.

LEMON-PEPPER SAUCE
(ABOUT 2 CUPS)   〜 OR BASTE

1 cup vegetable oil
⅓ cup vinegar
½ cup lemon juice
¼ cup brown sugar

2½ teaspoons salt
2 tablespoons freshly ground
    pepper

Combine all ingredients in a jar. Shake well and let stand for a while before using.

ABOUT STUFFINGS

Use day-old bread for stuffing or let fresh bread dry out slightly in the oven. Don't economize by using old, stale bread: its tired flavor will haunt the stuffing unless the seasoning is very strong. You don't always have to use bread crumbs—try croutons, cracker crumbs, crumbled corn bread, wild rice, white rice, and barley, or kasha.

Always taste and correct the seasoning before you use the stuffing. Fry a tablespoonful in a small skillet before tasting it, and bear in mind that the stuffing will absorb additional flavor and moisture as it cooks from the juices of the meat, poultry, or vegetable in which it is encased.

The amount of liquid in stuffing is a matter of personal taste; some people prefer a steaming, porridgy stuffing, while others like the crunch of croutons or dry buttery crumbs. Stuffing expands as it cooks: handle it lightly, tossing rather than beating it, and pack it gently to allow plenty of room for expansion. (For stuffing poultry, see p. 308.)

To store leftovers, remove the stuffing from the cavity, put it in a casserole, and refrigerate. To reheat, place the casserole in a 325°F oven for half an hour, or toss the stuffing in a skillet in a few tablespoons of melted butter.

Suggested Uses for Stuffings

These are only suggestions, not inflexible rules, in an area in which cooks should use their imaginations. Vegetables such as tomatoes, peppers, eggplants, onions, zucchini, and mushrooms are all delicious when baked with stuffings, and there is no reason why a number of the stuffings below could not also be used to stuff such vegetables.

Bread Stuffing	
Savory Bread Stuffing	Chicken, Turkey, Fish
Raisin-Nut Stuffing	Chicken, Turkey, Pork
Corn Bread Stuffing	Turkey, Pork, Ham
Corn Stuffing	Turkey, Ham
Giblet Stuffing	Chicken, Turkey
Herb Stuffing	Chicken, Turkey, Fish
Mushroom Stuffing	Chicken, Turkey, Cornish Game Hens, Fish
Onion Stuffing	Chicken, Veal, Ham
Oyster Stuffing	Chicken, Turkey, Fish
Apple Stuffing	Duck, Goose, Pork, Veal
Celery Stuffing	Chicken, Duck, Fish
Mint Stuffing	Lamb, Chicken, Cornish Game Hens
Orange Stuffing	Duck
Lemon Stuffing	Chicken, Fish, Veal
Prune and Apple Stuffing	Duck, Goose, Pork, Veal
Wild Rice and Mushroom Stuffing	Cornish Game Hens, Goose, Turkey, Chicken
Sausage Stuffing	Turkey
Sausage and Chestnut Stuffing	Turkey, Squabs, Chicken

BREAD STUFFING ૨≈   (ABOUT 3 CUPS)

A pleasant basic stuffing. For a moister stuffing, add ¼ cup chicken broth.

¼ pound butter	4 cups dry bread crumbs
4 tablespoons finely chopped onion	¼ teaspoon freshly ground pepper
4 tablespoons finely chopped celery	Salt to taste

Melt the butter in a skillet and stir in the onion and celery. Cook over low heat until the onion is soft. Add this mixture to the crumbs and toss lightly with plenty of pepper and salt.

SAVORY BREAD STUFFING

Add 1 *teaspoon sage, crumbled,* or 1 *teaspoon poultry seasoning.*

RAISIN-NUT STUFFING

Add *½ cup raisins* and *½ cup walnuts.*

GIBLET STUFFING

Cover the *giblets* with 1 quart cold water in a saucepan. Bring to a boil and simmer. When the liver is tender, remove it. Continue to cook the gizzard until it is tender, about 45 minutes. Drain the giblets and chop into small bits, and add to the stuffing. Save the liquid for soup.

HERB STUFFING

Add 1 *teaspoon thyme, crumbled,* 1 *teaspoon basil, crumbled,* and *½ teaspoon marjoram, crumbled.*

MUSHROOM STUFFING

Omit the celery and cook 2 *cups chopped mushrooms* with the onions. Add *½ teaspoon nutmeg.*

ONION STUFFING

Add 6 *onions,* boiled until barely tender, drained, and chopped.

OYSTER STUFFING

Add 2 cups oysters, in bite-size pieces, and use about ¼ cup of oyster liquor for moistening the crumbs.

CORN BREAD STUFFING

Substitute 2 cups corn bread crumbs for 2 cups of the bread crumbs. For Corn Stuffing, add 1 cup cooked whole-kernel corn.

APPLE STUFFING   (2½ CUPS)

The apples, which turn lightly brown and tender, are mixed with spices and crumbs to make a fine Christmas stuffing.

4 tablespoons bacon fat
2 cups diced unpeeled tart
    apples
2 teaspoons sugar

½ cup dry bread crumbs
¼ teaspoon nutmeg
¼ teaspoon cinnamon

Melt the bacon fat in a skillet. Add the apples and sugar and cook over medium-low heat, stirring, for 5 minutes. Remove from the heat and toss in the crumbs, nutmeg, and cinnamon.

PRUNE AND APPLE STUFFING ❧   (2 CUPS)

1 cup dried prunes, pitted
2 tablespoons raisins
1½ cups boiling water
2 tablespoons fine cracker
    crumbs

2 teaspoons sugar
1 large apple, peeled, cored,
    and diced fine
Salt to taste

Put the prunes and raisins in a bowl and pour on the boiling water. Let stand 5 minutes. Drain and cut the prunes into pieces. Add remaining ingredients, and toss.

WILD RICE AND MUSHROOM

STUFFING

(3 CUPS)

1 cup wild rice	¼ teaspoon freshly ground
4 tablespoons butter	pepper
2 cups chopped mushrooms	¼–½ teaspoon ground nutmeg
1 small onion, chopped fine	Salt to taste

Steam the rice (p. 437). Melt the butter in a saucepan, add the mushrooms and onion, and cook over low heat until soft. Toss in the rice with the pepper, nutmeg, and salt.

(6 CUPS)   **CELERY STUFFING**

This is a nice moist stuffing.

4 tablespoons butter	4 cups dry bread crumbs
1 cup chopped celery	¼ teaspoon freshly ground
4 tablespoons finely chopped	pepper
onion	¼ cup chicken broth
4 tablespoons minced parsley	Salt to taste

Melt the butter in a skillet. Stir in the celery and onion and cook over low heat for 3–4 minutes. Remove from the heat and blend in the parsley, crumbs, pepper, chicken broth, and salt.

(3½ CUPS)   **MINT STUFFING**

Dry, crisp, with lots of fresh mint flavor; a natural kin to lamb.

6 tablespoons butter	½ cup finely cut fresh mint
2 tablespoons minced onion	leaves
3 tablespoons finely chopped	3 cups fine dry bread crumbs
celery	Salt to taste

Melt 3 tablespoons of the butter in a skillet. Add the onion and celery and cook for 3 minutes. Add the mint leaves and cook until most of the liquid has evaporated. Remove from the heat and toss with the remaining 3 tablespoons of butter, the crumbs, and salt.

ORANGE STUFFING ễ≫   (4 CUPS)

3 cups croutons (p. 768)
¼ cup orange juice
2 teaspoons grated orange
    rind
⅔ cup orange sections, with
    membranes removed

2 cups finely chopped celery
5 tablespoons butter, melted
Salt to taste

Put the croutons in a bowl and stir in the orange juice. Let stand 15 minutes. Mix in remaining ingredients.

LEMON STUFFING

Use *2 tablespoons lemon juice* and *2 teaspoons lemon rind* instead of the orange juice and rind. This is particularly nice with chicken, fish, and veal.

SAUSAGE STUFFING   (8 CUPS)

1 pound sausage meat
4 tablespoons minced onion
8 cups freshly made dry
    bread crumbs

1 teaspoon freshly ground
    pepper
2 tablespoons minced parsley
Salt to taste

Heat a skillet and add the sausage, crumbling it into small bits as it cooks. Brown lightly and remove to a bowl, leaving the drippings in the skillet. Add the onion and cook, stirring, for 2 minutes. Add the crumbs, pepper, and parsley, and cook 1 minute more, stirring to mix well. Toss with the sausage meat and salt.

SAUSAGE AND CHESTNUT STUFFING   (5 CUPS)

2 cups braised chestnuts (p.
    561)
4 tablespoons butter
1 small onion, chopped
1 pound sausage meat
1 teaspoon thyme, crumbled

½ teaspoon freshly ground
    pepper
1 tablespoon minced parsley
2 cups freshly made bread
    crumbs
Salt to taste

Cut the chestnuts into quarters. Melt the butter in a skillet, add the onion, and cook, stirring often, over medium heat until soft. Scrape into a bowl and mix with the chestnuts. Cook the sausage in the skillet, crumbling it into tiny bits until it is brown. Add the sausage, with some of its fat, to the chestnut mixture with the thyme, pepper, parsley, bread crumbs, and salt.

(8 CUPS)   **✳ FRESH SAGE STUFFING**

¼ pound butter, melted
1½ cups finely chopped
   onions
1½ cups finely chopped celery
8 cups bread, dried and
   broken into small pieces
3 tablespoons or more finely
   chopped sage

½ cup finely chopped parsley
1 teaspoon salt, or to taste
½ teaspoon freshly ground
   pepper
½–1 cup turkey or chicken
   broth

Put 2 tablespoons of the butter in a skillet over medium heat. Add the onions and celery and cook, stirring often, until the vegetables are soft but not browned. In a large bowl place the bread, sage, parsley, salt, and pepper. Add the onion mixture and the remaining melted butter and toss well. Slowly add the broth, a little at a time, tossing the mixture. Add only enough broth to moisten; too much will make the stuffing sodden. To test the stuffing to see if the moisture and seasonings are correct, melt a little butter in a skillet, add a rounded tablespoon of the stuffing, and stir until lightly golden. Taste, and if livelier flavor is needed, add more sage, onion, and/or pepper.

SANDWICHES, PIZZA & TACOS

In the last edition, the chapter called Filled Things included stuffed pastas, crêpes, and vegetables, but readers had a hard time locating those recipes, so they now appear where you would expect them to. And this chapter is confined to sandwiches, plus pizzas and tacos, both of which have now become an all-American form of sandwich. I have included a new recipe for the folded-over pizza sandwiches known as calzones, which are sold all over now in take-outs and street fairs but which are so much better made at home.

ABOUT SANDWICHES, PIZZAS, AND TACOS

Hamburgers, hot dogs, and sandwiches make up our great movable feast, the foods that can be eaten with the fingers and on the run: at the desk, in the lunchroom, at ball games, and at picnics. While there is no need to decry the fast-food vendors, it's far better to prepare these foods yourself from the highest-quality ingredients. Since portable foods constitute about one-third of the American diet, they should be prepared with great care, and attention should be paid to both their taste and their nutritional quality.

Sandwiches

What makes a good sandwich? Good bread, generous filling, contrasting textures, and the mysterious mating of the right filling with the right bread. There was a time when you couldn't get a sandwich in this country on anything but soft white bread: the choice was to have it plain or toasted. Now Americans have not only adopted French, Italian, and Portuguese breads, Greek pitas and Scandinavian flatbreads and ryes, but revived whole-grain breads to the great enrichment of the noonday meal.

What makes a bad sandwich? Dryness, a poor proportion of filling to bread, staleness, incompatible combinations, and wet greens that make everything soggy or undrained tomatoes that sit too long on the bread. Firm, tastily ripe tomatoes are wonderful in sandwiches, adding moisture and goodness.

Unless you must, don't make sandwiches until just before they are to be eaten. When they have to be made in advance for picnics or lunchboxes, wrap each sandwich individually, making an airtight package with plastic wrap or foil. A good idea is to put the lettuce and sliced tomato in a separate plastic bag, to be tucked into the sandwich just before eating.

Pizzas

And then there is pizza, once Italian, now the quintessential American meal. Far more nutritious than our children imagine, pizza is a worthwhile combination of bread, cheese, and tomatoes. In addition to the familiar garnishes of sausage, anchovy, and mushrooms, pizza can serve as a delicious base for chopped leftover meat and vegetables. Even people who hate leftovers will eat them spread over a bed of yeasty dough and tomato sauce, covered with a blanket of bubbling mozzarella cheese.

Tacos

Tacos are fried tortillas, the Mexican pancakes made of a flour ground of cooked corn grain, called *masa harina*. You can make them yourself if you have either a tortilla press or a lot of experience: they are tricky. Luckily, many markets now carry tortillas in the frozen food section and some markets even have them fresh, so it isn't necessary to create your own. Tacos are usually made very crisp. They are folded in half while they are being fried and are then removed, filled, and served.

SANDWICHES

SANDWICHES WITH MEAT
OR FISH FILLINGS   (SERVES ONE)

Sliced Chicken or Turkey
Season at least 3 or 4 slices of the white meat with salt and pepper. Because they're apt to be dry, top the slices with a good tablespoon of mayonnaise, preferably homemade. Pile on buttered white or whole-wheat bread and add 2 or 3 generous sprigs of watercress or a crisp lettuce leaf.

Ham
Use 3 thin slices of ham, preferably good baked ham, on buttered rye bread with 1 tablespoon of mayonnaise on one side, and 1 teaspoon of mustard on the other—mild or Dijon according to preference.

Ham and Cheese: Eliminate the mayonnaise and add a slice or two of Swiss or other mild cheese.

Roast Beef
Use beef that is somewhat rare, or else it will be dry. Pile a generous 2 or 3 slices on buttered white or rye bread. Add salt and pepper, a teaspoon of mustard, and a crisp lettuce leaf. Serve with dill pickle.

Hot Roast Beef
Hot roast beef is particularly good on a hard roll, such as kaiser, onion, or sesame seed, with the juices poured over. Salt and pepper to taste and pass the mustard.

Corned Beef or Tongue
Most aficionados like 4 or 5 generous slices with mustard only on buttered rye bread. Serve with dill pickle.

Meat Loaf
Place two slices of meat loaf (p. 229) on buttered rye or white bread with 1 tablespoon of mayonnaise or catsup or both. Add a leaf of crisp iceberg lettuce and serve with sweet pickles.

Hot Pastrami
This spicy cousin of corned beef must always be served warm, 4 or 5 slices on buttered pumpernickel or rye with a good teaspoon of mustard.

Cold Sliced Pork, Veal, or Lamb

These meats are apt to be a little dry when cold, so serve 3 or 4 slices with a generous tablespoon of mayonnaise, and watercress or crisp lettuce, on well-buttered bread. A relish such as chutney or bread-and-butter pickle can be good on the meat, especially the pork.

Bologna, Liverwurst, or Salami

Place 3 or 4 good slices of bologna, liverwurst, or salami on dark buttered rye or whole-wheat bread, with 1 teaspoon prepared horseradish or 2 teaspoons peppery mustard, or 2 teaspoons mayonnaise. Serve with dill pickle.

Sardine

Place a row of well-drained sardines on a thin slice of buttered rye bread. Squeeze 1 teaspoon of lemon juice on top, sprinkle with ½ teaspoon chopped dill, and cover with buttered slice of rye.

(SERVES ONE)   **SANDWICHES WITH SALAD FILLINGS**

Chicken or Turkey Salad

Mix ¼ cup chopped cooked chicken with 1 tablespoon finely chopped celery, ½ hard-boiled egg, chopped, 2 tablespoons mayonnaise, salt, and freshly ground pepper. Spread the chicken mixture between 2 slices of buttered fresh white bread, and add a crisp lettuce leaf or sprigs of watercress.

Curried Chicken or Turkey Salad

Follow the directions for Chicken Salad, but add ¼ teaspoon curry powder and 1 teaspoon chutney. Omit the lettuce or watercress and use whole-wheat bread instead of white.

Tuna or Salmon Salad

Mix ¼ cup drained flaked tuna with ½ hard-boiled egg, chopped, 1 teaspoon sweet relish (optional), 2 teaspoons chopped celery, 1½ tablespoons mayonnaise, and ½ teaspoon lemon juice. Spread between 2 slices buttered white or whole-wheat bread and cover with a crisp lettuce leaf.

Shrimp, Crab, or Lobster Salad

Mix ⅓ cup cooked shrimp, crab, or lobster with 2 tablespoons mayonnaise, 1 teaspoon lemon juice, 4 drops Tabasco, and salt to taste. Butter two slices of fresh French bread, preferably sourdough, sliced ⅜ inch thick. Spread the seafood salad over the bread, and cover with other slice.

Shrimp-Cucumber Salad
Follow the recipe for Shrimp Salad using ¼ cup, and add about 2 table-spoons chopped, seeded cucumber.

Lobster Roll
Follow the recipe for Lobster Salad, and serve on a toasted hot-dog roll.

Egg Salad
Mash 1 hard-boiled egg with 1 tablespoon mayonnaise. Scrape the cut side of an onion and add ½ teaspoon of the juicy purée to the egg. Spread between 2 buttered slices of fresh white bread or a whole-grain bread, adding a crisp lettuce leaf.

Ham, Tongue, or Corned Beef Salad
Coarsely chop cooked ham, tongue, or corned beef to make ¼ cup. Add 2 teaspoons mayonnaise, 1 teaspoon prepared horseradish, and 1 tea-spoon prepared mustard. Spread between 2 slices of rye bread, either light or dark.

HAMBURGER   (1 HAMBURGER)

One pound of ground beef makes four ample patties. Use medium-lean beef, since a little fat is needed for moistness. The more you handle or grind hamburger the more compact and dry it becomes. Try to divide and shape each patty as lightly as possible, and don't press down on it when it is cooking, since that pushes out the juice. Have the hamburger roll hot or toast it lightly. Some like a hamburger plain; some prefer it dressed up in one or more of the following garnishes: *catsup, prepared mustard, sliced raw onion,* a mixture of *mayonnaise* and finely chopped *onion* or *scallions, sweet pickle relish,* slices of *dill pickle,* thin slices of *tomato,* a slice of *Cheddar, Monterey Jack,* or *Swiss cheese, chili sauce,* and either a crisp dry leaf or a small mound of shredded ice-berg *lettuce.*

Salt	1 teaspoon shortening
Freshly ground pepper	
¼ pound medium-lean ground beef	

Salt and pepper the ground beef as liberally as you like it, then, lightly, handling as little as possible, shape it into a patty about 3½ inches in di-ameter, about the size of a hamburger bun. To fry, melt the shortening in a skillet. When it is hot, add the patty and fry a few minutes on each side, 2 for rare, 3 for medium, 4 or more for well done. To broil, place patty on a rack 2 inches beneath a preheated broiler, and broil a minute longer for each side than you would for frying. Serve garnished with any of the above suggestions according to your taste on buttered hot hamburger rolls, or on toasted English muffins, kaiser rolls, or just toast, as you wish.

HOT DOGS

Hot dogs or frankfurters are ready-to-eat when bought, but their flavor and texture are improved with heating. Again, some like their frankfurters plain, some like them with all the trimmings, which can include one or more of the following: prepared *mustard, chopped onions,* some *chili beans, sweet pickle relish,* slices of *dill pickle, chopped tomato,* or *sauerkraut.* Have your hot-dog rolls warm or toasted. The different methods of cooking are:

BOILING

Bring a pan of water to boil, lower the heat so water is simmering, and add the hot dogs. Cook, keeping at a simmer, for 5 minutes; if the water boils too hard, the frankfurters will break out of their casings.

FRYING

Heat a teaspoon of fat in skillet. Cut the hot dogs lengthwise down the middle, but not completely through; or cut diagonal slashes. Place cut side down in the hot fat and fry for 2 minutes over medium heat on each side.

GRILLING

Place the hot dogs over glowing coals (or under a preheated broiler, as close to the heat as possible) and grill, turning until all sides are well browned.

BACON, LETTUCE, AND TOMATO SANDWICH (BLT)

(1 SANDWICH)

Don't be skimpy with the bacon: use at least three strips. The authentic bacon, lettuce, and tomato sandwich is on toasted white bread.

3 strips bacon
2 slices white bread
2 tablespoons mayonnaise

4 slices tomato
Salt
Leaf of crisp iceberg lettuce

Fry the bacon crisp and drain on paper towels. Toast the bread, and spread mayonnaise on each slice. Pile the tomatoes on one slice, salt to taste, and top with bacon, lettuce, and the second slice of bread. Cut in half.

AVOCADO, LETTUCE, AND TOMATO SANDWICH

For the bacon, substitute *one-quarter of an avocado*, peeled and sliced.

DENVER SANDWICH

(2 SANDWICHES)

This is also known as a Western Omelet Sandwich. Part of the delight is having the egg soak into the soft bread.

3 tablespoons butter
⅓ cup finely chopped onion
⅓ cup finely chopped green
  pepper
2 slices ham, chopped

3 eggs, slightly beaten
Salt to taste
Cayenne pepper to taste
4 slices buttered bread
Prepared mustard

Melt the butter in a skillet. Add the onion, green pepper, and ham, and cook until the onion is soft. Pour the beaten eggs over the ham and vegetables, and add salt and cayenne pepper. Cook over low heat until lightly golden. Turn over with a spatula and quickly brown only lightly the other side (the center should remain moist). Divide the omelet in half and place each half on a piece of buttered bread. Spread with mustard and close with the other slice of bread. Serve warm.

(1 SANDWICH)   **REUBEN SANDWICH**

2 slices corned beef
1 slice Swiss cheese
2 slices dark rye or
    pumpernickel bread

4 tablespoons sauerkraut
1½ tablespoons Russian
    Dressing (p. 708)
3 tablespoons butter

Put 1 slice corned beef and 1 slice Swiss cheese on a piece of bread.
Heap on sauerkraut and spread the dressing over it. Put on the second
slice of corned beef and second slice of bread. Melt the butter in a skillet over medium-low heat. Put in the sandwich and grill on each side
until the cheese melts, or grill in a sandwich toaster. Serve warm.

(1 SANDWICH)   **✳ CLUB SANDWICH**

Quite a perfect sandwich, particularly made of newly baked bread
freshly toasted with ample slices of breast of chicken and thin slices of
tomatoes. (The faint of heart *can* use only two slices of bread—but then
it hardly qualifies as a genuine lofty club sandwich.)

Butter
2 tablespoons mayonnaise
3 slices fresh bread, toasted
    crisp
4 thin slices cooked chicken
    breast
Salt

Freshly ground pepper
3 thin slices ripe, firm tomato
3 slices bacon, fried crisp and
    drained
Green olives
Sweet pickles

Spread butter and mayonnaise on one side of each slice of toast, cover
with chicken, sprinkle with salt and pepper, and cover with a slice of
toast. Place the tomatoes and bacon on it, and season with salt and
pepper. Cover with the last slice of toast. Cut in quarters, diagonally,
and serve with olives and pickles.

(4 SANDWICHES)   **BARBECUED PORK SANDWICH**

Serve with pickles and/or cole slaw.

4 French rolls, split and
    buttered
8 slices roast pork

1½ cups Basic Barbecue Sauce
    (p. 377)

Put the rolls under the broiler and toast only on the buttered side. Put the pork slices in a skillet with the barbecue sauce, and heat gently. Put the pork on the toasted rolls and spoon sauce over the top.

GRILLED CHEESE SANDWICH ॐ   (1 SANDWICH)

A perennial favorite: soft melted cheese and pressed, buttery toast.

    2 slices Cheddar, American,   2 slices white bread
        or Swiss cheese   2 tablespoons butter

Put the cheese between the slices of bread. Heat 1 tablespoon of the butter in a skillet or grill and when it is melted add the sandwich. Gently press down with a spatula once or twice during the grilling. When one side is golden, add the remaining tablespoon of butter, turn the sandwich over, and brown.

GRILLED CHEESE WITH BACON

Fry *3 slices bacon* until cooked but not crisp. Pat dry of excess fat, add on top of the cheese, and grill as directed.

GRILLED CHEESE WITH HAM

Put *2 thin slices ham* on the cheese and grill as directed. Serve with sweet pickle.

ONION-CHEESE SANDWICH

Follow the recipe for Grilled Cheese Sandwich, but lightly coat 1 slice of bread with *Dijon mustard*. Sauté *3–4 slices onion* in *butter* and put on top of the cheese. Cover and grill.

TOMATO-CHEESE SANDWICH

Follow the recipe for Grilled Cheese Sandwich, but add *2 thin slices tomato* to the sandwich before grilling.

(SERVES TWO OR THREE)   **POOR-BOY SANDWICH**

In New Orleans they make poor-boy sandwiches with fillings that start with fried potatoes and ascend to crabmeat. The classic is this hot sandwich made with leftover roast beef and gravy; if you don't have enough leftover gravy, use the improvised recipe, p. 384.

12-inch loaf French bread
½ cup mayonnaise
1 cup shredded lettuce
6 thin slices cooked beef

About ½ cup beef gravy, warmed
2 tomatoes, sliced thin

Split the bread lengthwise and warm it in the oven. Spread the bottom half with mayonnaise. Pile on shredded lettuce and top with overlapping slices of beef. Spoon warm gravy over the meat, top with tomato slices, and add the top half of the bread. Cut in 2–3 pieces and serve warm.

(1 SANDWICH)   **HERO SANDWICH**

Depending on where you live, you may call it a hero, hoagie, submarine, or grinder. Make it in individual 6-inch rolls as below, in loaves of French bread cut in 4-inch wedges, or, heroically, for a party in a special 2-foot-long loaf—increasing amounts of filling proportionately.

6-inch French roll
4 tablespoons butter
¼ cup mayonnaise
2½ tablespoons prepared mustard
4 slices cheese: Cheddar, Swiss, Fontina, or others

4 slices salami, bologna, mortadella, ham, or other cooked meat
Tomato slices
Onion rings
Pickle slices
Shredded lettuce

Split the roll lengthwise. Butter each half and spread with mayonnaise and mustard. Place the cheese and meat, overlapping, along the length. Add any of the remaining ingredients you like: the more, the better. If you want to serve it warm, omit the lettuce and tomato, wrap snugly in foil, and cook in a 350°F oven for 30 minutes.

MEXICAN HERO SANDWICH

Add 2½ *tablespoons chopped, canned green chili to 6 ounces softened butter*. Omit the mustard and mayonnaise. Spread chili butter on the loaf, and use *salami* and *Monterey Jack cheese*. Wrap in foil and heat in a 350°F oven for 30 minutes.

ITALIAN HERO SANDWICH

Omit the mustard. Use sliced *prosciutto ham* and *Genoa salami* and *Fontina, Romano,* or *Parmesan cheese*. Top with *onion* and *green pepper* slices and *olive relish*. Serve cold.

MEATBALL HERO   (SERVES FOUR)

Two 12-inch loaves French   1 cup grated Parmesan cheese
  bread
1 recipe Meatballs in Sauce
  (p. 237)

Preheat the oven to 300°F. Split the bread lengthwise. Spoon some tomato sauce on the bottom half. Cut the meatballs in half and lay them along the length. Cover with more sauce and with a good sprinkling of Parmesan cheese. Cover with top half of bread, wrap in foil, and warm 20 minutes.

LUNCHBASKET PITA   (1 SANDWICH)

Flatbreads, commonly known as pita, can be found in most supermarkets today. The smaller size is often labeled pocket bread and makes a lovely sandwich when stuffed. Plain white pita is the most readily available but sometimes you can find whole wheat and the kind baked with sesame seeds (which can be improvised in this recipe; if sesame seed pita is available, skip the next to last step). Pita is also delicious cold with fillings of cheese and bean sprouts and other vegetables.

1 small pita   Several thin slices sweet
Butter, softened   pickle
3 thin slices ham   1 egg yolk beaten with 1
2 slices mozzarella, Fontina,   teaspoon water (optional)
  or other melting cheese   Sesame seeds (optional)

Slit open the side of the pita and spread the interior with soft butter. Stuff in slices of ham, alternating with cheese, and distribute the pickle inside evenly. Place under the broiler and toast one side until warm. Then turn and brush the top with a little egg glaze and sprinkle sesame seeds over. Toast until just light brown.

LAMB-FILLED PITA

A traditional filling. Be sure to save some lamb and a little juice from your next roast. Stuff pita with *3–4 slices of warm cooked lamb*, moistened with juices or gravy.

CORNED BEEF PITA

Use *3–5 slices cooked corned beef brushed with mustard*. Toast or not, as you wish. Particularly good with whole-wheat pita.

(1 SANDWICH)   ટ્ટ **HEALTH SANDWICH**

Nutritionally this is just about everything you need in a sandwich: vary the ingredients with fresh things in season, such as tomatoes or other raw vegetables.

¼ cup shredded lettuce
¼ cup fresh bean sprouts
¼ cup grated Cheddar cheese
3 tablespoons grated carrot
2 tablespoons raisins
2 tablespoons chopped walnuts

1 slice good whole-grain bread
2 teaspoons honey
2 teaspoons lemon juice
4 tablespoons yogurt
2 tablespoons alfalfa sprouts

Toss the lettuce, bean sprouts, cheese, carrot, raisins, and walnuts together, and place on the bread. Combine the honey, lemon juice, and yogurt and blend until smooth. Spoon the dressing over the vegetables and sprinkle alfalfa sprouts on top.

(1 SANDWICH) ✱ **OPEN-FACED SWEDISH SANDWICH**

There are two requirements: dark bread and sweet butter. After that, the possibilities are endless.

1 slice thin dark bread	1 slice smoked salmon
1–2 tablespoons unsalted butter	Capers
	Dill sprigs

Spread the bread thickly with the butter. Arrange the salmon over it, and garnish with capers and dill.

MEATBALL SANDWICH

Top the buttered bread instead with *sliced Swedish Meatballs* (p. 235), *pickled onions*, and *parsley*.

TONGUE SANDWICH

Lay over the buttered bread 2 *slices tongue*, 4 *slices cucumber*, and a *dab of red currant jelly*.

EGG SANDWICH

Lay over the buttered bread 1 *hard-boiled egg, sliced*, and 2 *anchovies*.

SILVER DOLLAR   (4 SANDWICHES)

An extravaganza from the silver mine area of the Rockies, where sandwiches are big, open, and healthful. Vary it as you like, but keep in mind contrasts of texture and flavor.

8 broccoli spears	8 generous slices cooked
1 recipe Welsh Rabbit (p. 497)	turkey breast
4 large slices whole-grain bread, buttered	2 tablespoons sesame seeds
8 slices Canadian bacon, fried in butter	

Drop the broccoli spears into a large pot of salted boiling water and cook 5 minutes, then drain well. Meanwhile, make the rabbit. On each buttered bread slice, pile the bacon, turkey, and broccoli. Spoon on a generous portion of sauce and sprinkle with sesame seeds.

GOLDEN EAGLE

Use *8 slices cooked ham* instead of Canadian bacon, *8 asparagus spears* instead of broccoli, and top with *Cheese Sauce* (p. 380).

HAM AND CREAM CHEESE
(2 SANDWICHES)   **BUTTER-FRIED SANDWICHES** ✱

Here nourishing ingredients are brought together in a simple form that appeals especially to children. This is a good breakfast sandwich.

> 4 slices fresh whole-wheat or
>   white bread
> 3 ounces cream cheese,
>   softened

> 4 thin slices ham
> 4 tablespoons butter

Lay the 4 slices of bread on a surface and spread each slice on one side with a rounded tablespoon of cream cheese. Place 2 ham slices on top of 2 of the slices and cover with the remaining slices of bread. Melt the butter over medium-low heat. Place the sandwiches in the pan and fry gently until the bottom is golden, pressing down on each sandwich occasionally with a spatula—this will help to melt the cheese. Turn and fry the other side. Serve warm.

CRABMEAT SPECIAL ON
(SERVES TWO)   **ENGLISH MUFFINS**

> 2 English muffins
> Butter
> 6 ounces crabmeat, canned or
>   fresh
> 3 tablespoons mayonnaise

> Fresh lemon juice
> Salt
> Freshly ground pepper
> 1 large tomato, sliced thin
> 4 slices Swiss cheese

Split and toast the muffins and butter them while they are warm. Drain the crabmeat and toss with mayonnaise and a few drops of lemon juice, and salt and pepper to taste. Spread evenly over the muffin halves, cover with tomato slices, and top with cheese. Slip under the broiler until the cheese melts and is bubbly.

About Pizzas

Homemade pizza is fun to make—the dough is no harder to put together than a bread dough and while the stretching may take a little practice you can always roll out the dough instead. And they taste so good fresh from the oven. Try other fillings, using the same proportions as those in the variations that follow this basic recipe.

PIZZA ❧   (THREE 14-INCH PIZZAS)

1⅓ cups warm water
1 package dry yeast
3–4 cups flour, approximately
Olive oil
2 teaspoons salt

3 cups Tomato Sauce (p. 387)
3 cups grated mozzarella
   cheese
3 teaspoons oregano, crushed

In ⅓ cup warm water dissolve the yeast, and let stand for 5 minutes. Add about 2 cups of the flour, 2 tablespoons oil, 1 cup warm water, and the salt, and beat. Add more flour, mixing well, until the dough holds together in a rough mass. Lightly flour a board or work surface and knead the dough for 10 minutes, or until it is smooth and elastic. Put in an oiled bowl to rise, covered with plastic wrap. When the dough has doubled in bulk, about 2 hours, punch it down and divide in thirds. Let rest for 5 minutes. Preheat the oven to 450°F. Roll the dough with a rolling pin or stretch it over your fists until you have three 14-inch circles. Place on pizza pans or cookie sheets and prick all over. On each circle, spoon 1 cup tomato sauce; sprinkle with 1 cup mozzarella and 1 teaspoon oregano. Drizzle with about 2 tablespoons olive oil. Let rest another 10 minutes and then bake for about 18–20 minutes, until lightly browned. To test for doneness, lift an edge—if the bottom has turned golden, it is probably done.

✳ FRESH TOMATO BASIL FILLING

Add 3 *tomatoes,* sliced, to the pizzas during the last 5 minutes of cooking, and add ⅓ *cup sliced basil leaves* just before serving.

WHITE FILLING

Omit the tomato sauce and brush the pizza dough with olive oil. For each pizza, add 2 *cloves garlic, minced,* 2 *cups thinly sliced onions,* and substitute 2 *cups Fontina cheese* for the mozzarella.

PIZZA WITH TOMATO-MUSHROOM FILLING

Add to the filling 3 *cups sliced mushrooms* sautéed 3 minutes in 3 *tablespoons olive oil* and sprinkle 3 *tablespoons capers* on top.

PIZZA WITH ANCHOVY FILLING

Arrange over the tomato filling 24 *anchovy fillets* like the spokes of a wheel and decorate each pizza with ¾ *cup black olives.*

PIZZA WITH SAUSAGE

Distribute over the tomato filling 1 *pound pepperoni* cut in thin slices, or 1¼ *pounds other cooked sausage,* sliced.

(1 CALZONE)   ટ✎ **CALZONE**

Calzone is much like a pizza, except that it is made like a turnover, with the filling enclosed. This is a simple version, but you can add almost anything to this basic mixture, such as chopped prosciutto or ham or crumbled cooked sausage.

4 ounces cream cheese	¼ teaspoon dry marjoram, or
4 ounces mozzarella, grated	½ teaspoon fresh
¼ cup chopped scallions	½ teaspoon salt, or to taste
2 tablespoons chopped	Freshly ground pepper to
parsley	taste
2 cloves garlic, minced	14-inch disk of rolled-out,
¼ teaspoon dry thyme, or ½	uncooked pizza dough
teaspoon fresh	Olive oil

Preheat the oven to 500°F. Put the cream cheese and mozzarella in a bowl and mix until blended. Stir in the scallions, parsley, garlic, thyme, marjoram, salt, and pepper. Place the prepared pizza dough on a pizza pan or cookie sheet. Put the filling on one half of the dough, leaving a 1-inch margin at the edge. Moisten the edge with water. Fold the dough over the filling to meet the edges. Seal the edges by rolling up ½ inch of dough and crimping it to form a tight seal. Bake for about 15–18 minutes, until it is brown on both the top and bottom. Remove from the oven and brush the top with olive oil. Serve it whole.

About Tacos

TACO FILLING   (FILLING FOR 8 TACOS)

A taco is a tortilla fried crisp, then folded with the sauce and filling tucked inside. Crisp tacos may be filled with many different things, such as cold cooked meats or poultry or vegetables. This is a general outline of a typical taco filling. The sauce will keep for a few days, but it is at its best if used as soon after making as possible, since the cilantro tends to fade quickly. If you can't find cilantro, try flat-leaved Italian parsley. Add more fresh cilantro if possible just before using.

1 cup shredded or chopped	1 cup chopped tomato
cooked meat or poultry	Taco Sauce (following recipe),
8 fried tacos	or approximately 2 cups
1¼ cups shredded iceberg	sour cream
lettuce	1 cup grated Cheddar or
½ cup finely chopped onion	Monterey Jack cheese

OPTIONAL ADDITIONS TO TACOS

Sliced avocado, Salsa Verde (p. 388), sliced or chopped green chilies, sliced black olives, cilantro leaves, or refried beans.

To Make Fried Tacos

In a skillet, heat ⅓ inch of oil, preferably peanut oil, to 360°F. Then slip a tortilla into the hot fat. After just one second, take a spatula and fold the tortilla in half. Insert the spatula between the folds and press down and fry for about 30 seconds to 1 minute until golden, then turn it over and repeat. Drain on paper towels, standing it curved side down like a rocking horse so the oil will drip off. Keep warm while you fry others.

Spread the meat or poultry across the bottom of the taco. Add the lettuce, and sprinkle with the onion and tomato. Spoon the sauce or sour cream on top, and evenly sprinkle with cheese. Serve.

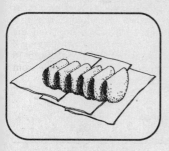 

(ABOUT 2 CUPS)   **Taco Sauce**

3 fresh tomatoes, chopped, or
  1½ cups canned tomatoes
  with juice, chopped
½ cup chopped onion
2 cloves garlic, chopped fine
¾ teaspoon salt
½ cup cilantro, washed, dried,
  and chopped

2 ounces canned peeled green
  chilies, drained and
  chopped
Pinch of sugar
4 tablespoons water

Combine all ingredients in a bowl. Beat until well blended.

(FILLS 10 TO 12 TACOS)   **BEEF FILLING FOR TACOS**

3 tablespoons vegetable oil
1 onion, chopped fine
2 cloves garlic, chopped fine
2 teaspoons chili powder

1 pound lean ground beef, or
  2 cups chopped leftover
  beef
Salt to taste

Heat the oil in a large skillet, add the onion, and stir often until the onion is soft. Add the garlic and cook, stirring for 2 minutes; add the chili powder, beef, and salt. Mix and cook, stirring, breaking the meat into tiny bits, until the meat loses its pinkness. If using leftover beef, simply heat through. With a slotted spoon, leaving the fat behind in the skillet, remove the meat mixture to a bowl. Use about 2 tablespoons per taco or enchilada when filling.

CEREALS, RICE, BEANS & PASTA

In the last decade Americans have become more and more health-conscious, and fiber is the latest cure-all. If you're looking for a source of natural fiber, this chapter is full of things that contain fiber, particularly beans. There are some new ideas here for Italian polenta and risotto—both popular dishes today—and a number of new pasta recipes, several using fresh vegetables, and some with buttered bread crumbs instead of the usual Parmesan cheese.

Cereals, rice, beans, and pasta: these are wholesome foods that fill the stomach and warm the heart, that provide energy for a snowy morning and restore courage at the end of a long day. Basic foods for the world's poorer nations, they often replace meat on the American table as well, for, in the right combinations, they provide a valuable source of low-fat protein.

ABOUT CEREALS

Grains are the dried seeds of grass plants; those that are used for food are called cereals. About one-quarter of our diet is made up of grains such as wheat, rice, corn, oats, barley, and rye.

All cereals contain a high percentage of carbohydrate, with varying amounts of protein, minerals, and vitamins. Although they don't provide complete protein by themselves, they become highly valuable foods when they are mixed with milk products, eggs, dried beans, or animal proteins. In many parts of the world where meat is scarce, people live largely on grains.

Breakfast Cereals

Be careful when you are buying cold cereals for your family that you
get ones that supply real food value. Many whole-grain or enriched
cold cereals are available now. Read the list of contents on cereal boxes
carefully: sugar appears under many guises, and "refining" often
means the removal of nutritional value. If you want real value and
goodness, try making your own granola (p. 428).

Consider sometimes starting the day with an "old-fashioned" hot
cereal! A steaming bowl of whole-grain cereal is a complete meal.
"Real meal" cereals like Wheatena, hominy grits, cornmeal, and oatmeal will increase in bulk as they are cooked in liquid. Add more liquid for a thinner cereal; add more cooking time for a smoother cereal.
Use skim milk instead of water for extra nutrition, and cover the pot at
the end of the cooking time to prevent a crust from forming. Stir in
some applesauce, nuts, or chopped dried fruits and top with a big
spoonful of yogurt, honey, brown sugar, or maple syrup—a good way
to start the day.

Lunch and Dinner Cereals

Cereals often take the place of potatoes at lunch or dinner. They are
low in fat, high in vitamins, and, combined with a little cheese or
served with meat, are a good source of protein. Cereals are also inexpensive and satisfying.

Turkey is well served by a casserole of buckwheat and onions;
hominy grits are delicious with fried ham; bland cornmeal is a natural
background for spicy sausages. A new dinner can be created when leftover meat and pan drippings are mixed into rice or barley. And, if
calories are a concern, it's comforting to know that it takes 1½ cups of
rice or 2⅔ cups of cooked cornmeal to equal the calories in one small,
unadorned hamburger!

Kinds of Cereals

Barley. Barley was probably the first cereal cultivated by man. In Scotland it is exceedingly popular, used in soups as a thickener, as a
porridge, in cake, and in the distillation of Scotch whisky. Pot or
hulled barley has had the outer hull removed; pearled barley has
been processed to remove both hull and germ, leaving small,
cream-colored balls that look like pearls. Cooked barley has a mild
flavor and chewy texture; it is very good steamed and buttered,
particularly delicious served with lamb. Pot or hulled barley has a
very earthy flavor, which makes it very different from pearl barley.
Hulled barley makes a splendid pilaf or breakfast cereal. It takes
longer to cook than pearl barley.

Wheat Berries. The health-food movement is responsible for the popularity of this delicious, chewy grain, made from whole-wheat ker-

nels with only the outer layer removed. Without the strawlike chaff or husk, wheat berries have a nutlike taste and are bursting with nutrients. They are very good mixed with hot rice, or chilled and added to salads.

Bulgur Wheat. Bulgur is made by boiling, drying, and cooking whole-wheat grains. It resembles brown rice in its chewy texture, hearty flavor, and nutritional makeup. Because bulgur is dehydrated, it must be reconstituted by soaking in liquid for an hour if you are using it raw, as in a salad, but not when it is cooked. Use a ratio of one part bulgur to two parts water, broth, tomato juice, or other liquid, depending on the flavor you wish to add. Long popular in the Middle East, bulgur is increasingly familiar here, used in soups, stuffings, breakfast cereals, salads, and with meat and poultry.

Cornmeal. The only native American grain, corn was used by the Indians before Columbus and was introduced to Europe by the early explorers of this continent. Cornmeal is made of ground corn kernels. Water-ground meal retains the vitamin-rich germ, while commercially ground meal is made from only the starchy part of the kernel. As with all ground kernels, the texture of the meal can range from coarse to fine, depending on the dish being prepared. A coarse grind is ideal for Italian polenta, while finer grinds are usually used for American southern favorites such as spoon bread, muffins, and mush, although some prefer a coarser texture in these dishes as well. Cornmeal dishes are traditionally cooked in heavy iron pans to encourage the formation of a thick, dark crust. Both yellow and white cornmeal are available. The difference is really only in the color, but there are strong partisans of each kind in different regions of the country.

Hominy. Hominy is a staple in the American South: dried corn that has had its hull and germ removed with lye or soda. Hominy grits are ground hominy grains. They are white, about the size of toast crumbs. Cooked, their texture is thick and chewy and their flavor rather mild. You can stir in a keen-flavored cheese, spread the grits in a casserole with more cheese on top, and bake until the cheese melts. Serve grits with fish, ham, or sausage, or make them into a breakfast cereal with raisins, butter, and brown sugar. The unflavored porridge is delicious cooled, sliced, and fried in butter.

Buckwheat. Buckwheat has nothing to do with wheat: wheat is a grass, whereas buckwheat is a low, shrublike plant producing a seed that is often ground into flour, used in pancakes and in Asian and Russian cooking. When the seed is parboiled, dried, and coarsely ground, it is called buckwheat groats or kasha. Groats make wonderfully hearty side dishes for turkey, duck, venison, and other game.

For general information about Rice, see page 436; about Beans, page 445; and about Pasta, page 452.

CEREALS

GRANOLA   ೩ (10 CUPS)

Here is a basic formula for granola. Vary it as you wish—with different varieties of nuts, dried fruits, etc.

1 cup water	1 cup honey
¾ cup peanut oil	1 teaspoon vanilla
4 cups rolled oats	¾ cup sunflower seeds
½ cup sesame seeds	1 cup roasted unsalted
½ cup wheat germ	peanuts
1 cup soy grits	1 cup raisins
1 cup shredded coconut	Salt

Preheat the oven to 350°F. Bring the water to a boil, and mix it with the oil. In a large heavy pot combine the oats, sesame seeds, wheat germ, soy grits, and coconut. Combine the honey with the oil and water and vanilla, stirring well, and mix into the dry ingredients a little at a time; when all the particles are covered with the honey mixture, put the pot in the oven and toast for 15 minutes. Stir well. Reduce the heat to 275°F and repeat the process, stirring every 10 to 15 minutes for 1½–2 hours, until the granola is thoroughly toasted. Let the granola cool, then stir in the sunflower seeds, peanuts, raisins, and salt to taste. To store, refrigerate in a tightly closed jar.

BARLEY   ೩ (SERVES FOUR)

3 cups water	1½ cups pearl barley
Salt	

Bring the water to a boil with about 1 teaspoon salt. Stir in the barley, cover, and simmer for 25 minutes.

BARLEY IN BROTH

Substitute 3 *cups chicken or beef broth* for the water.

BARLEY AND RICE

Substitute *½ cup white rice* for ½ cup of the barley.

BARLEY AND WALNUTS

Add *½ cup chopped walnuts* just before serving.

CURRIED BARLEY

Add *1 teaspoon curry powder* and *¼ cup raisins* to the water before adding the barley.

(SERVES FOUR)   ## BARLEY CASSEROLE

Serve by itself or with cold sliced beef or chicken. Try this with hulled or pearl barley.

3 tablespoons butter	½ cup cashews, chopped
1 cup barley	3 cups chicken broth, boiling
1 small onion, chopped	Salt
¼ cup finely chopped green pepper	Freshly ground pepper

Melt the butter in a saucepan. Add the barley and onion, and cook, stirring often, until the onion is slightly cooked and the grains of barley are coated. Add the green pepper and cook 2 minutes more. Add the cashews, boiling chicken broth, and salt and pepper to taste. Cover and simmer 25 minutes; or bake for 1 hour at 350°F in a covered casserole.

(SERVES SIX)   ## ?❧ WHEAT BERRIES

1 cup wheat berries	4 tablespoons butter
4 cups water	Salt to taste

Combine the wheat berries with the water in a saucepan. Bring to a boil and cook gently for 2 minutes. Remove from the heat, cover, and soak for 1 hour. Return to the heat and simmer 1 hour more. Stir in the butter and salt.

BULGUR ?❧ (SERVES FOUR)

One cup of dry bulgur becomes three when it is cooked. Vary by using different liquids in place of water, such as beef or chicken broth, tomato juice, orange juice, or milk.

2 tablespoons butter
1 cup bulgur
Salt

Freshly ground pepper
2 cups water

Melt the butter in a saucepan. Stir in the bulgur and cook, stirring, for 2 minutes. Add salt and pepper to taste, pour in the water, cover, and simmer 15 minutes.

BULGUR PILAF

Cook ¼ teaspoon *turmeric* in the butter. Use *beef broth* instead of water, and add *½ cup frozen peas* and *1 small onion, chopped and sautéed*.

BULGUR STUFFING

Use *chicken broth* instead of water and add *½ cup chopped celery, ½ cup chopped onion*, and *½ teaspoon sage, crumbled*.

CORNMEAL MUSH ?❧ (SERVES SIX)

Good with fried chicken and cream gravy or with fried pork.

1 cup cornmeal
4 cups water

1½ teaspoons salt

Mix the cornmeal with 1 cup cold water. In a saucepan, bring 3 cups water and the salt to a boil. Add the cornmeal mixture to the boiling water and cook, stirring often, over medium heat for 7 minutes or until thick.

(SERVES SIX) **FRIED CORNMEAL MUSH**

Good both as an accompaniment to meats and for breakfast with butter, honey, or maple syrup.

   1 cup cornmeal
   4 cups water
   1½ teaspoons salt

   6 tablespoons bacon fat, or 4
      tablespoons butter plus 2
      tablespoons oil

Follow the directions for Cornmeal Mush (preceding recipe). Spread the mush in a loaf pan and refrigerate. When it is thoroughly chilled, cut in ½-inch slices. Melt the fat or butter and oil in a skillet and fry the slices until golden on both sides.

(SERVES SIX) ཞ **SPOON BREAD**

This is one of the best dishes I know to keep company with roast pork, chicken, pot roast. Light, moist, with a good coarse texture, it can't be beat served piping hot with butter melted on top.

   2½ cups water
   1 cup yellow cornmeal
   1 teaspoon salt

   2 tablespoons butter
   4 eggs, well beaten
   1 cup milk or buttermilk

Preheat the oven to 400°F. Butter a 1½-quart casserole. Stir ½ cup of cold water into the cornmeal. (This prevents lumping when cornmeal is added to boiling water.) Bring 2 cups of water to a boil. Add the salt, then the cornmeal slowly, stirring constantly, and cook for 1 minute. Beat in the butter, eggs, and milk until smooth. Pour into the casserole and bake for about 40 minutes, until a straw in the center comes out clean.

(SERVES SIX) ཞ ✱ **LIGHT SPOON BREAD**

This is different from Spoon Bread because it is soufflé-like with the beaten egg whites folded into the batter. It can be served by itself; it is also good with a light main course, such as fish.

   1½ cups water
   1 cup white cornmeal
   1 tablespoon butter, melted
   3 eggs, separated
   1 cup buttermilk

   1 teaspoon salt
   1 teaspoon sugar
   1 teaspoon baking powder
   ¼ teaspoon baking soda

Preheat the oven to 375°F. Butter a 2-quart casserole. Bring the water to a boil, and pour it over the cornmeal in a bowl, briskly stirring so no lumps form. Add the butter, egg yolks, buttermilk, salt, sugar, baking powder, and baking soda. Stir until well blended. Beat the egg whites until stiff but not dry. Gently stir a fourth of the whites into the cornmeal mixture, then fold in the remaining whites. Spoon into the casserole. Bake about 45 minutes or until the center is dry when a straw is inserted.

BASIC POLENTA   ❦   (SERVES SIX)

A recent import from northern Italy, polenta is not unlike the old southern standby cornmeal mush. Buy coarsely ground cornmeal at an Italian delicatessen or a health-food store. Polenta can be baked and served with a sauce such as this one, chunky with mushrooms, sausages, and cheese.

4 cups water	1 teaspoon salt
1 cup coarsely ground cornmeal	4 tablespoons butter

Bring 3 cups of water to a boil in a heavy-bottomed saucepan. In a small bowl stir the cornmeal into 1 cup cold water, then pour the mixture into the boiling water, stirring constantly. Add the salt and continue to stir, letting the polenta return to a boil. Reduce the heat to low and let simmer, stirring constantly, until the mixture becomes very thick, about 10 to 15 minutes. Stir in the butter until well blended. Serve immediately.

POLENTA WITH CHEESE

You will need 2 *cups cubed Fontina, Monterey Jack,* or *semi-soft white cheese,* and 3 *tablespoons chopped parsley.* Put ⅓ cup of the cheese cubes in each of six serving bowls. Spoon the hot polenta over the cheese and garnish with the chopped parsley.

(SERVES SIX)   ✳ **POLENTA WITH SAUSAGE**

7 cups water
Salt
2 cups coarsely ground
    cornmeal
6 tablespoons olive oil
1 large onion, chopped
2 Italian sausages, in ½-inch
    slices

½ pound mushrooms, sliced
2 cups Italian Tomato Sauce II
    (p. 388)
1 tablespoon basil, crumbled
½ pound Cheddar or
    Monterey Jack cheese,
    cubed

Bring the water to a boil with 1 tablespoon salt, and slowly stir in the
cornmeal in a thin, steady stream. Cook, stirring occasionally, for 20
minutes, until the polenta is stiff and leaves the sides of the pan.
Spread in a baking dish to a depth of 1½ to 2 inches. Cover, refrigerate,
and use later, or keep warm in a 250°F oven while making the sauce.
For the sauce, heat 3 tablespoons of the oil in a saucepan, add the
onion, and cook over medium heat until soft. Add the sausages and
cook another 3–4 minutes; stir in the mushrooms and cook 2 minutes
more. Add the tomato sauce, basil, and salt to taste. Cover and simmer
for 30 minutes. If the sauce becomes too thick, add ½ cup water, stir,
and continue to cook. Add the remaining 3 tablespoons oil and cook 10
minutes more. Remove the polenta from the oven and dot with cubes
of cheese. Turn the oven up to 350°F and bake the polenta and cheese
until it is hot and the cheese is melted. Cut in squares and spoon the
sauce over the top.

                              POLENTA WITH SPINACH AND
(SERVES FOUR)   ઙ✐ ✳ **FISH**

A hearty dish with a layer of cornmeal, a layer of spinach, and topped
with a layer of fish fillets. It is plain and good and can be served with a
plate of sliced tomatoes and onions for a complete meal.

¾ cup cornmeal or polenta
3 cups water
1½ tablespoons white vinegar
Salt

1 pound spinach, cooked and
    chopped
2 pounds fish fillets
Freshly ground pepper

Put the cornmeal in a bowl with 1 cup of the water. Bring the remaining 2 cups of water to a boil, then stir in the cornmeal. Stir often for
about 7 minutes, until the cornmeal mush is thick and smooth. Preheat
the oven to 400°F. Grease an 8 × 8 × 2-inch baking dish. Spread the
cornmeal in the baking dish. Stir the vinegar and 1 teaspoon salt into

the chopped spinach. Spread the spinach over the cornmeal and put the fish in a layer on top. Salt and liberally pepper the fish. Bake in the oven for about 10 minutes, or until the center of the thickest part of the fish is opaque like the outside. Serve hot.

HOMINY GRITS 🥢 (SERVES FOUR)

4 cups water
1 cup hominy grits

1 teaspoon salt

Bring the water to boil in a saucepan. Slowly stir in the grits and salt and cook 3–5 minutes (for quick-cooking grits; otherwise 15–20 minutes), stirring occasionally, until thick.

FRIED GRITS (SERVES SIX)

Good as a meat accompaniment and with eggs, sausage, and maple syrup for breakfast.

1 cup hominy grits
6 tablespoons bacon fat, oil,
   butter, or combination

2 eggs, beaten
1½ cups freshly made bread
   crumbs

Cook the grits as directed (preceding recipe). Spread in a loaf pan, refrigerate until thoroughly chilled, then cut into ½-inch slices. Melt the bacon fat or butter and oil in a large skillet. Dip the slices into the egg and then into the crumbs, coating both sides completely. Place in the skillet and cook for 3 minutes on each side or until hot and golden brown.

HOMINY GRITS CASSEROLE 🥢 (SERVES SIX)

1 cup hominy grits
3 cups milk
1 teaspoon salt
2 eggs, lightly beaten
1 cup water

6 tablespoons butter
1 cup grated Cheddar or
   Monterey Jack cheese
½ cup canned green chilies,
   rinsed and chopped

Preheat the oven to 350°F. Stir the hominy grits into the milk in a saucepan, add the salt, and cook over medium heat, stirring often so the mixture doesn't scorch. When it is thick, remove from the heat and add the eggs and water, stirring vigorously. Return to the burner and cook until thickened again. Stir in the butter, cheese, and chilies. Spread in a casserole and bake for 30 minutes.

(SERVES FOUR)   &e   **ALACE'S GRITS SPOON BREAD**

The surprising texture of canned whole hominy mixed with hominy grits in a baked pudding.

2 eggs, well beaten
1 cup milk
½ cup hominy grits
½ cup canned hominy,
    drained

1 teaspoon baking powder
3 tablespoons butter, softened
½ teaspoon salt

Preheat the oven to 375°F. Butter a 1½-quart casserole. Combine all ingredients, and beat until well blended. Pour into the casserole and bake 50–60 minutes, or until a straw inserted in the center comes out clean.

(SERVES FOUR)   &e   **BUCKWHEAT GROATS OR KASHA**

1 egg, slightly beaten
1 cup buckwheat groats
2 cups water, boiling

2 tablespoons butter
Salt to taste

Put the egg and groats in a bowl and mix well. Put the mixture in a dry skillet and cook over medium-high heat, stirring constantly, until each grain is separate and dry; set aside. Heat a saucepan, add the egg-groats mixture, and quickly pour in the boiling water. Cover and simmer for 15 minutes. Add the butter and salt; stir, cover, and cook 5 minutes more.

KASHA IN BROTH

Substitute 2 *cups chicken or beef broth* for the water.

KASHA WITH ONION

Sauté 1 *large onion, chopped*, in 2 *tablespoons oil* and add to the saucepan with the boiling water.

KASHA WITH MUSHROOMS

Sauté *1 cup sliced mushrooms* in *2 tablespoons butter*, and add to the saucepan with the boiling water. Just before serving, stir in *½ cup yogurt*.

RICE

Rice is the staple food for most of the world's population. Although it comes in many forms, we know only a few in this country.

Kinds of Rice

White Rice. White rice has had its outer covering removed by a process called "polishing" that takes away many of the B vitamins as well; nonetheless, it remains more popular than unpolished rice. *Long-grain white rice*, when it is cooked, tends to separate nicely into individual fluffy grains. Kernels of *short-grain or medium-grain white rice* cook up tender and moist, clinging together; they are best used in croquettes, puddings, and rice rings.

Converted Rice. Converted rice is hulled under moist conditions, steamed, and dried so that all the nutrients are incorporated back into the grain and not lost. It always tastes a little pasty and doesn't have the same good texture as plain long-grain rice.

Brown Rice. Brown rice is superior to white rice in nutrients because it retains its outer coating. Although it takes longer to cook than white rice, its good, nutty flavor and high food value are making it ever more popular.

Dehydrated, Precooked Rice, usually known as Instant or Minute Rice. Dehydrated, precooked rice, the sort you rehydrate by covering with boiling water and soaking for five minutes, is the least desirable kind of rice. The exterior has an unnatural fluffiness when cooked and the center seems raw. It is at best a convenience food to be used when in a hurry.

Wild Rice. Wild rice, also known as Indian rice or water oats, is not a rice at all, but the seed from a grass that grows wild along the edges of lakes in Minnesota, Wisconsin, and southern Canada and is cultivated elsewhere. There it is harvested in the old-time way by Indians who paddle along the water's edge, bending the grasses and beating the seeds into their boats. It is expensive, dark in color, strong, and intriguing in taste, well worth an occasional indulgence.

Basmati. Basmati is long-grain rice from India that has a unique nutty taste and an aroma reminiscent of popcorn.

Arborio. Arborio is a short-grain rice from Italy. It is used to make risotto and cooks up creamy.

(3½ CUPS WHITE RICE AND 3½ CUPS BROWN RICE)

≈ **BOILED RICE**

There is no reason to worry about failures if you cook rice like pasta in lots of boiling salted water and watch the timing. White rice will be done in 15–18 minutes; brown rice will be done in 35–40 minutes.

3 quarts water
1 teaspoon salt

1 cup rice

Bring the water and salt to a boil in a deep pot. Trickle the rice slowly into the water so that it doesn't stop boiling. Don't stir, but give the pan a shake so the rice levels. Keep the water boiling over medium-high heat. Test at the minimum time by removing a few grains with a slotted spoon; bite into the kernel—it should be firm, not mushy and splayed out at the ends. If in doubt, it is better to undercook rice slightly and steam it longer at the end, particularly if you are planning to hold the rice 10 or 15 minutes before serving. Drain the rice in a colander. Keep warm by placing the colander over gently boiling water, covering the rice with a dishtowel.

(3 CUPS WHITE RICE OR 2 CUPS BROWN RICE)

≈ **STEAMED RICE**

Steamed white rice will cook in 20 minutes; brown rice in 40 minutes.

2 cups water
¾ teaspoon salt

1 teaspoon butter (optional)
1 cup rice

Using a deep, heavy-bottomed pot, bring to a boil the water, the salt, and the butter, if desired. Add the rice slowly so that the boiling doesn't stop. Cover and simmer without stirring and don't remove the cover for 20 minutes. Then check: the rice should be just soft and the water absorbed. Fluff up with a fork before serving.

RICE WITH PEANUTS

Add *1 cup finely chopped celery* and *½ cup chopped salted peanuts* to the rice before cooking.

MUSHROOM RICE

Just before serving add *¼ teaspoon nutmeg* and *1 cup chopped mushrooms*, sautéed in *2 tablespoons butter*.

BAKED RICE &   (SERVES FOUR)

A nice way to serve rice when the meat is rather plain and the casserole, popped in the oven about a half an hour before serving, is all ready to come to the table.

⅓ cup chopped onion	2 cups water
2 tablespoons butter	2 chicken or beef bouillon
1 cup rice	cubes

Preheat the oven to 375°F. Sauté the onion in the butter about 3 minutes. Add the rice and stir, cooking just long enough to coat it, 2 or 3 minutes. Pour in the water, bring to a boil, stir in the bouillon cubes, dissolve, and mix well. Turn into a 1-quart casserole, cover, and bake for 30 minutes.

BAKED RICE WITH PEPPER AND HAM

Add *½ cup chopped green* or *red pepper* along with the onion. After the rice has been coated, add up to *1 cup chopped ham*. Sprinkle the top with *2–3 tablespoons Swiss* or *Parmesan cheese* and remove the cover for the last 5 minutes of baking.

SAFFRON RICE WITH RAISINS AND PINE NUTS

Before turning the mixture into the casserole, remove 4 tablespoons of the hot liquid and pour over *⅛ teaspoon crumbled saffron;* let steep 5 minutes. Remove to the casserole and stir in *½ cup raisins* and *2 tablespoons pine nuts.*

(SERVES FOUR)   ‿♥ ✻ **FEATHERED RICE**

Unlike ordinary cooked rice this puffs up, becomes light and fluffy, and has a slightly toasted flavor. Brown rice may be cooked the same way.

1 cup white rice   2½ cups water, boiling
1 teaspoon salt

Preheat the oven to 400°F. Spread the rice out in a shallow baking pan, place in the oven, and bake, stirring occasionally, until golden brown. Put the rice into a casserole, add the salt and boiling water, cover with a tight-fitting lid, and bake for 20 minutes. If using brown rice, allow 30 to 40 minutes. A pound or so of rice may be browned at one time and then stored in an airtight container until ready to bake.

(SERVES FOUR)   ‿♥ **RICE WITH CHEESE**

If you use brown rice and mix wheat germ with the cracker crumbs, you'll have a fine vegetarian dish.

4 cups cooked rice, slightly   4 tablespoons butter
    underdone   1 cup milk
1 cup grated Cheddar cheese   1 cup buttered cracker
Pinch of cayenne pepper   crumbs
Salt to taste

Preheat the oven to 350°F. Butter a 1½-quart baking dish. Spread half the rice on the bottom of the baking dish, sprinkle with half the cheese, cayenne pepper, and salt, and dot with 2 tablespoons of the butter. Repeat. Finish by pouring the milk evenly over all and sprinkling the top with buttered crumbs. Bake for 30 minutes.

(SERVES FOUR)   ‿♥ **GREEN RICE**

A creamy, green-flecked dish to go with tuna, chicken, or chipped beef.

1½ cups cooked rice, slightly   ½ cup finely chopped parsley,
    underdone   spinach, watercress, or
1 cup milk   dandelion greens
4 tablespoons butter, melted   1 egg, well beaten
½ cup grated Swiss cheese   Salt to taste
½ onion, chopped fine

Preheat the oven to 350°F. Butter a 1½-quart casserole or ring mold. Combine all ingredients. Pour into the casserole or mold and bake, uncovered, for 40 minutes or until set.

RICE WITH FRESH VEGETABLES (SERVES SIX)

This can be served hot as a side dish or cold as a salad.

1 cup brown rice
4 cups chicken broth
1 tablespoon soy sauce
1 cup white rice
1 red onion, chopped
1 bunch scallions, sliced,
    including tender greens
2 sweet peppers (preferably 1
    red and 1 green), chopped
1 cucumber, peeled (if waxed)
    and chopped
3 tablespoons vinegar
¾ cup olive oil
Salt and freshly ground
    pepper to taste

Put the brown rice, chicken broth, and soy sauce in a large pot, and bring to a boil. Reduce the heat to low and cook for about 10 minutes. Add the white rice and continue to cook for about 15 minutes, or until tender. Remove from the heat and add the onion, scallions, peppers, and cucumber, and toss to mix. Mix together the vinegar, olive oil, and salt and pepper, pour over the rice mixture, and toss to mix well.

PILAF (SERVES FOUR)

Pilaf is a seasoned rice dish common to many Eastern countries. It can be a whole meal made with fish, poultry, or meat, or a simple side dish made with herbs, spices, nuts, or raisins.

3 tablespoons olive oil
3 tablespoons finely chopped
    onion
1 cup long-grain rice
½ teaspoon salt
¼ teaspoon freshly ground
    pepper
2 cups beef broth

Heat the oil in a saucepan. Add the onion and cook, stirring often, until soft. Add the rice and cook over low heat, stirring constantly, for 3 minutes. Add the salt, pepper, and beef broth. Cover and simmer 20 minutes or transfer to a covered casserole and bake in a 350°F oven for 1 hour.

MUSHROOM PILAF

Add the broth to *1 cup chopped mushrooms* that have been sautéed in *2 tablespoons butter.*

CHICKEN PILAF

Substitute *2 cups chicken broth* for the beef broth, and with the broth add *1 cup diced cooked chicken* and *½ teaspoon tarragon, crumbled.*

(SERVES FOUR)   ✱ **BAKED SPANISH RICE**

A pleasant side dish to serve with sausages or ham.

¼ cup olive oil	2 large tomatoes, peeled and
1 onion, chopped	chopped
1 small green pepper,	1 cup long-grain rice
chopped	½ teaspoon salt
2 cloves garlic, minced	¼ teaspoon freshly ground
1 stalk celery, diced	pepper
1 cup chopped mushrooms	2 cups chicken broth

Preheat the oven to 375°F. Lightly oil a 2-quart casserole. Heat the olive oil in a skillet and add the onion, green pepper, garlic, celery, and mushrooms. Cook over medium-low heat, stirring often, for 5 minutes. Transfer to a casserole and add the tomatoes, rice, salt, and pepper. Pour in the broth, stir, cover, and bake 30 minutes. Stir again and bake for another 30 minutes.

(SERVES FOUR)   **RISOTTO**

This is a creamy rice dish made by gradually adding liquid to the rice as it cooks. It is Italian in origin and is made with arborio rice, a high-starch medium- to short-grain white rice unique to Italy. Medium-grain white rice, grown in this country, is a perfectly good substitute.

1 tablespoon butter
1 tablespoon olive oil
1 onion, chopped
1 cup Arborio or medium-grain white rice
2 cups (or more) hot chicken broth

1 cup (or more) hot water
½ cup freshly grated Parmesan cheese
½ cup chopped parsley
Salt and freshly ground pepper to taste

In a large, heavy-bottomed pot or deep skillet, heat the butter and oil. Add the onion and cook over moderate heat for 2 to 3 minutes, until the onion is just soft but not browned. Stir in the rice and cook another minute, until the rice is heated and coated with the fat. Stir in 1 cup of the hot broth and let simmer until the liquid is mostly absorbed, stirring frequently to prevent sticking. Add the other cup of hot broth and continue simmering and stirring until absorbed. Stir in the cup of hot water and continue to simmer and stir. The total cooking time will be approximately 20 minutes. Taste for doneness. The rice should be very creamy and slightly chewy in the center; not dry. Add more hot liquid if longer cooking is necessary. Stir in the Parmesan cheese and parsley. Taste and add salt, if necessary, and pepper to taste.

RISOTTO WITH PEAS AND PROSCIUTTO

Add *1 cup cooked peas* and *½ cup chopped prosciutto* with the Parmesan cheese.

RISOTTO WITH MUSHROOMS

Stir in *1 recipe Sautéed Mushrooms* (p. 576) when adding the Parmesan cheese.

SAUTERNES RICE   (SERVES EIGHT)

An elegant side dish for game hens, chicken, or veal.

1 cup water, boiling
½ cup currants
5 tablespoons butter
2 cloves garlic, halved
2 cups long-grain rice
4 cups chicken broth
½ cup dry white wine

1½ teaspoons salt
¼ teaspoon freshly ground pepper
¼ teaspoon nutmeg
¼ teaspoon allspice
2 teaspoons sugar

Pour the water over the currants. Soak for 10 minutes, drain, and set aside. Melt the butter in a skillet. Add the garlic and mash with the back of a fork. Cook for 1 minute to flavor the butter and then remove the garlic. Add the rice and cook, stirring, for 2 minutes. Bring the broth to a boil with the wine in a deep pot. Add the buttered rice with remaining ingredients. Cover and simmer 25 minutes. Add the plumped currants, toss with a fork, and serve.

(SERVES FOUR)   ❧ ❊ **RICE CAKES**

Delicate golden patties, especially good with poached fish.

½ cup short-grain rice
½ teaspoon salt
½ cup water, boiling
1 cup milk
2 eggs

6 tablespoons butter
1½ cups freshly made bread
    crumbs
2 tablespoons oil

Sprinkle the rice and salt into the boiling water. Cover and cook slowly until the water is absorbed, 7–10 minutes. Add the milk, stir, cover, and cook 10–12 minutes more, or until the rice is tender. Stir in 1 egg and 2 tablespoons of the butter. Spread the mixture on a shallow plate, cover with plastic wrap, and refrigerate. Beat the remaining egg in a shallow dish and put the crumbs on a piece of wax paper. Shape the well-chilled rice mixture into 6 conical or patty shapes, pressing firmly together. Carefully dip each cake into the egg and then cover with crumbs. Melt the remaining 4 tablespoons of butter in a skillet with the oil. When hot, fry the cakes until golden brown; don't cook them too quickly or the insides will remain cold.

(SERVES FOUR)   **CURRIED RICE**

3 tablespoons oil
1 onion, chopped fine
1 cup long-grain rice
2 teaspoons curry powder

½ teaspoon salt
2 tablespoons butter
½ cup raisins
2 cups chicken broth

Preheat the oven to 375°F. Butter a 1½-quart casserole. Heat the oil in a skillet, add the onion, and cook until it is soft. Stir in the rice and cook, stirring, for 3 minutes. Add the curry powder, salt, butter, and raisins, and cook 1 minute more. Transfer to a casserole, pour in the chicken broth, stir, cover, and bake for 1 hour.

FRIED RICE & (SERVES FOUR)

Add cooked diced shrimp, pork, or chicken, if you wish, and serve as a supper dish.

4 tablespoons oil
4 cups cooked rice
¼ cup chopped scallions
1½ tablespoons soy sauce

¼ teaspoon freshly ground
    pepper
2 eggs, slightly beaten

Heat the oil in a large skillet, and add the rice, scallions, soy sauce, and pepper. Cook over medium-high heat, stirring often, for 6 minutes. Add the eggs and stir briskly so they cook and break into small bits throughout the rice. As soon as the egg is set, remove and serve.

PARCHED RICE WITH TOMATO SAUCE
AND CHEESE * & (SERVES SIX)

A unique rice dish. The rice kernels are crisp and crunchy, and will have you reaching for seconds. Dandy for a meal when you don't want to fuss—be sure to use freshly grated cheese.

6 tablespoons butter
6 cups cooked white rice
2 cups Tomato Sauce (p. 387)

1¼ cups freshly grated
    Parmesan cheese

Melt the butter in a skillet. Add the rice and cook, stirring, until heated through and lightly browned. Put into a warm serving bowl, heat the tomato sauce, and cover the rice; then sprinkle with the cheese. Lift and toss the rice with a fork so that every kernel is coated.

WILD RICE & (3 CUPS)

Wild rice is expensive and special. Cook it simply to enjoy its distinctive flavor and texture.

1 cup wild rice
3 cups water

1 teaspoon salt
4 tablespoons butter

Rinse the rice several times in cold water and remove any foreign particles. Boil the water with the salt and slowly add the rice. Simmer for 45–50 minutes or until the grain is tender and has absorbed all the water. Stir in the butter, toss with a fork, and serve.

(SERVES FOUR)   ❧ **WILD RICE CASSEROLE**

Wild rice needs little adornment; serve this casserole with duck or game. You could even tuck pieces of leftover duck or game into the casserole as it bakes and serve as a main course.

¼ pound butter	3 cups chicken broth
½ cup finely chopped onion	1 teaspoon salt
2 cups sliced mushrooms	½ teaspoon freshly ground
1 cup wild rice	pepper

Preheat the oven to 325°F. Butter a 1½-quart casserole. Melt the butter in a skillet, add the onion, and cook until soft. Add the mushrooms and cook, stirring, until they darken. Put the onion and mushrooms into the casserole with remaining ingredients. Cover and bake for 1 hour or until the broth is absorbed and the rice is tender.

DRIED BEANS

About Dried Beans

NOTE
Dried beans are full of fiber, wholesome, filling, and inexpensive. When cooked with rice, as in the traditional black beans and rice combination, they provide a complete protein. They are splendid in casseroles, robust and satisfying in soups and salads, and, on a hike, a cold bean sandwich has no peers.

Kinds of Dried Beans

Of the many varieties of dried beans available in our markets, some are more familiar than others.

Kidney Beans and Red Beans. Kidney beans and red beans are used in chili, casseroles, and pork dishes. *Cannellini*, a white kidney bean, is a great favorite in Italian cooking and is available both dried and canned in Italian markets.

Black Beans. Black beans are a national winner in South America and the Caribbean. They make a wonderful soup, flavored with lemon, sherry, or rum, and are excellent boiled, mashed, and served with melting squares of cheese.

Chickpeas or Garbanzo Beans. A roundish, wrinkled bean used a great deal in Mexican cooking. They take a lot of cooking to soften; add ½ teaspoon of baking soda to the water when boiling. They are delicious puréed and particularly good in salads.

Pinto Beans and Pink Beans. These are the beans used in Mexican dishes such as refried beans. They provide a good base for intense spices.

Lima Beans and Baby Lima Beans. Limas are good in lamb, pork, or ham casseroles and as a side dish with barbecued meats.

Great Northern Beans and Navy Beans (Small White Beans). These are the beans used to make Boston baked beans and in minestrone-type soups. They also make a fine meal when simmered with a ham bone, celery leaves, and onions.

Lentils. Lentils, traditional with lamb at Easter time, are served year-round in hearty soups and robust sausage and vegetable casseroles.

Black-eyed Peas. Black-eyed peas are as common in the South as the navy bean is in the Northeast. Cook them with molasses or with chili; serve them in soups or with ham or rice. They are particularly high in fiber.

Split Peas. Split peas and ham are a classic combination. Both green and yellow make satisfying winter soups.

Amount of Dried Beans to Cook

A cup of cooked beans will provide two servings, but different varieties of dried beans will produce different amounts of cooked beans, as the following chart shows. The time represents the amount of time for cooking *after* soaking.

COOK 1 CUP:	IN:	FOR:	YIELD:
Baby Lima Beans	4 cups water	1 hour	3½ cups
Black Beans	8 cups water	1½ hours	4 cups
Black-eyed Peas	6 cups water	1 hour	4 cups
Chickpeas or Garbanzo Beans	8 cups water (plus ½ teaspoon baking soda)	2½–3 hours or more	4 cups
Great Northern Beans	7 cups water	1 hour	4 cups
Kidney Beans	6 cups water	¾–1 hour	4 cups
Lentils	6 cups water	35 minutes	4½ cups
Lima Beans	6 cups water	1½ hours	2½ cups
Pink Beans	6 cups water	1 hour	4 cups
Pinto Beans	6 cups water	1½ hours	4 cups
Red Beans	6 cups water	2 hours	4 cups
Small White Beans or Navy Beans	6 cups water	¾–1 hour	4 cups
Split Peas	6 cups water	45 minutes	4½ cups

Pressure-Cooking Chart for Dried Vegetables

Dried vegetables can be cooked very successfully in the pressure cooker, and it will save you a good deal of time and energy. Vegetables should be presoaked, even lentils and those labeled "no soaking necessary," because of their tendency to foam and clog the vent. Cover with cold water in the pressure-cooker pot, add 2 tablespoons of cooking oil for every cup of dried vegetables, and soak overnight; or bring to a boil, cook 2 minutes, and let soak 1 hour (lentils and others marked "no soaking" need only be brought just to the boil and then soaked 20 minutes). When you are ready to proceed with the pressure cooking, add 1 teaspoon salt to every cup of dried beans, use the same water they have soaked in, and follow the recommended cooking times. Make sure the vent pipe is open and don't fill the pressure cooker more than half full (no rack is needed). After cooking, let the pressure drop of its own accord before removing the cover.

Vegetable	Time
Black Beans	35 minutes
Black-eyed Peas	20 minutes
Chickpeas or Garbanzo Beans	45 minutes
Great Northern Beans	30 minutes
Kidney Beans	25 minutes
Lentils	15 minutes
Lima Beans	25 minutes
Navy Beans or Small White Beans	25 minutes
Pink Beans	30 minutes
Pinto Beans	25 minutes
Red Beans	35 minutes
Split Peas (green or yellow)	5 minutes

Preparing Dried Beans for Cooking

Wash beans by covering them with cold water and picking out any pebbles or floating particles. Soak them overnight to reduce the cooking time, or, if you forget to do this or are short of time, use the following short method: put 2 cups of beans in a pot, cover with 6 cups of water, bring to a boil, and cook for 2 minutes; remove from the heat, cover the pot, and let stand for 1 hour before cooking.

Black beans will triple in size when soaked overnight. 1 cup of dried beans becomes 3 cups after soaking overnight.

Lentils do not have to be soaked before cooking, nor do those beans with package directions that say "no soaking necessary."

Cooking Dried Beans

To preserve food values, don't drain off the soaking liquid before proceeding with the cooking: just add enough additional liquid to cover the beans. Add about ½ teaspoon of salt for every cup of dried beans, cover, and simmer until the beans are tender. The amount of liquid does not have to be exact; just keep the beans covered with water while they are cooking.

An old-fashioned bean pot is usually tall and made of clay. Heated in a slow oven, it's ideal for keeping beans and liquid at a slow simmer. If you don't have a bean pot, use a good, heavy casserole.

To use a pressure cooker for dried beans or peas see chart p. 447.

BOSTON BAKED BEANS   (SERVES EIGHT)

2 cups navy beans, small white beans, or Great Northern beans
Water for soaking
1 teaspoon salt, approximately

¼ pound salt pork
2 teaspoons dry mustard
5 tablespoons dark-brown sugar
4 tablespoons molasses

Wash the beans. Soak overnight or use the short method (p. 447). Add salt, stir, and drain, reserving the liquid. Preheat the oven to 300°F. Cut off a third of the salt pork and place the piece on the bottom of a bean pot. Add the beans to the pot. Blend the mustard, brown sugar, and molasses with the reserved bean liquid and pour over the beans. Cut several gashes in the remaining piece of salt pork and place on top of the beans. Cover and bake for about 6 hours, adding water as needed. Uncover for the final hour of cooking so the pork will become brown and crisp. Taste and correct seasoning.

CHILI BEANS   (SERVES EIGHT)

A touch of cayenne pepper heightens the taste of this old favorite.

2 cups red, pink, or pinto beans
¼ pound salt pork, diced small
2 large onions, chopped
2 cloves garlic, chopped
2 tablespoons vegetable oil or bacon fat, if needed
1 teaspoon freshly ground pepper
1 teaspoon salt, approximately

2 teaspoons oregano, crumbled
1 teaspoon sage, crumbled
2 teaspoons cumin
2 tablespoons chili powder
¼ teaspoon cayenne pepper (optional)
2 tablespoons cornmeal
1 cup peeled and chopped fresh or canned tomatoes

Wash the beans. Soak overnight. Or use the short method (p. 447). In either case do not drain. Sauté the salt pork; after 5 minutes, add the onions and garlic and cook until the onions are golden. If the pork does not render enough fat, add 2 tablespoons vegetable oil or bacon fat. Add black pepper, salt, oregano, sage, cumin, chili powder, cayenne pepper (if you wish), cornmeal, tomatoes, and 1 cup of the bean liquid. Cook, stirring constantly, for 5 minutes and add to the pot of beans and liquid. Stir to blend, and simmer for 2 hours, checking frequently to see if the liquid needs replenishing. Taste, and correct seasoning.

(SERVES SIX) **BEANS BRETONNE**

1½ cups navy beans, small
    white beans, or Great
    Northern beans
Water for soaking
1 cup stewed tomatoes,
    drained
1 cup chicken broth
1 onion, chopped fine

4-ounce can whole pimientos,
    puréed
2 cloves garlic, minced
4 tablespoons butter
1 teaspoon salt,
    approximately
Freshly ground pepper to
    taste

Wash the beans. Soak overnight or use the short method (p. 447). Preheat the oven to 300°F. Drain the beans and place in a bean pot with remaining ingredients. Stir, cover, and bake until the liquid is nearly absorbed, about 2 hours. Correct seasoning.

(SERVES EIGHT) **REFRIED BEANS WITH CHEESE**

A classic dish south-of-the-border. "Refried" means that they are first simmered and then fried.

2 cups pink or pinto beans
Water for soaking
1½ teaspoons salt,
    approximately
½ teaspoon freshly ground
    pepper

5 tablespoons bacon fat
1½ cups cubed Cheddar or
    Monterey Jack cheese

Wash the beans. Soak overnight or use the short method (p. 447). Return to the heat and simmer about 1½ hours, or until tender. Add salt and pepper. Heat the bacon fat in a skillet. Drain 1 cup of beans and put in the skillet. Mash thoroughly, adding ½ cup of the reserved liquid. Stir and cook for 1–2 minutes. Add and mash more beans with more of the reserved liquid. Repeat until all the beans and liquid have been used and the mixture is creamy. Add the cheese, blend, and cook until the cheese is melted.

CHICKPEA PURÉE 🍃   (SERVES SIX)

Particularly delicious mingling with the meat juices from a roast of lamb or of pork. You can use canned chickpeas or garbanzo beans.

3 cups cooked chickpeas	Freshly ground pepper
1 clove garlic, minced	2 tablespoons butter
Salt	1 tablespoon chopped parsley

Purée the chickpeas in a food mill, a blender, or a food processor. Add the minced garlic and a little of the cooking liquid to make a smooth purée, and season to taste with salt and pepper. Heat and add the butter. Sprinkle parsley on top.

FARMERS-STYLE LIMA BEANS   (SERVES SIX)

2 cups dried lima beans	¼ pound salt pork, diced
Water for soaking	1 onion, chopped
1 teaspoon salt	1 cup finely diced carrot
¼ teaspoon freshly ground pepper	2 tablespoons butter

Wash the lima beans. Soak overnight or use the short method (p. 447). Drain the beans and put in a casserole, reserving the liquid. Stir in the salt and pepper. Preheat the oven to 300°F. Cook the salt pork in a skillet until it is golden brown. Add the onion and carrot, and cook, stirring, until the vegetables are golden. Mix the vegetables and butter into the casserole with the lima beans. Pour in 1 cup reserved bean liquid, cover, and bake for 2 hours, adding more bean liquid as needed.

(SERVES FOUR)   ## LENTILS WITH SAUSAGE

Good served with sliced tomatoes or a cucumber salad.

1¼ cups dried lentils
2½ cups water
2 onions, chopped
2 cloves garlic, minced
1 bay leaf

2 potatoes, peeled and
    quartered
½ pound spicy sausage (such
    as chorizo, Italian, or
    Linguica), cooked and in
    2-inch pieces

Put the lentils and water in a pot. Add the onions, garlic, and bay leaf, and bring to a simmer. Add the potatoes and sausage, cover, and simmer for about 20–30 minutes, until the lentils are done and most of the liquid has been absorbed. Serve in bowls.

(SERVES SIX)   ## LENTILS AND LAMB

This classic combination is a harbinger of spring.

1 cup dried lentils
5 cups water
1 onion, chopped
2 tablespoons finely chopped
    parsley
2 cloves garlic, minced
½ cup chopped celery

¼ teaspoon freshly ground
    pepper
1 teaspoon salt
2 tomatoes, peeled, seeded,
    and chopped
2 cups cooked lamb, in bite-
    size pieces

Wash the lentils and put in a large pot. Add the water, onion, parsley, garlic, celery, pepper, salt, and tomatoes. Bring to a boil and simmer 30 minutes, or until the lentils are tender. Drain, reserving the liquid, and put the lentils into a casserole. Preheat the oven to 350°F. Put 2½ cups of liquid into a saucepan and boil briskly until it is reduced by half, about 15 minutes. Pour over the lentils, stir in the lamb, cover, and bake 1 hour.

LENTILS AND HAM

Omit the lamb and salt and add 2 *cups chopped cooked ham.*

PASTA

About Pasta

Pasta Shapes. Pasta is the general name for the many variously shaped flour-and-water-dough products that we sometimes call "macaroni." For a long time it was the generic term for dried pasta. But tubular *macaroni* is only one member of the pasta family, which ranges from broad *lasagna* to tiny *pastini,* from simple *tagliatelle* to intricate *tortellini*—names that mean things like "angel hair," "badly cut," and "little hat." Pasta may be white, or egg-enriched yellow, or spinach-touched green.

The real difference among pastas, however, lies not in their shapes but in their origins—domestic, imported, or homemade.

Domestic Pasta. Unfortunately, because of the kind of flour used, American-made pastas tend to become gummy when cooked, and it is often hard to separate the strands. Adding a little oil to the cooking water, as is often recommended, does not really help much. It *does* help if you are careful not to overcook the pasta; if pasta sticks, pour boiling water over it after draining it and separate the strands with a fork.

Imported Pasta. If you have an Italian grocery nearby, you may be able to buy imported, factory-made dry pasta. More expensive than local brands, it is still well worth trying if you care about the texture. Italian pasta, made with flour ground from the heart of hard durum wheat, is firm and chewy without a trace of gumminess.

Homemade Pasta. If you live near an Italian neighborhood you can sometimes find a shop that sells its own fresh, homemade pasta; made with flour, eggs, and sometimes a little water, it is both tender and firm, with a roughish surface that catches the sauce, and it takes less than a minute to cook. To make your own takes some skill, but if you have a hand-cranked pasta machine, the task becomes really simple and it is fun to do, particularly when children join in to catch the strands as they roll out and to lay them across a broomstick. There is another recipe for an American-style egg noodle and these are simpler to do with a rolling pin, partially because you don't need to get them so thin.

Cooking Pasta

Bring a large amount of salted water to a boil, using at least 8 quarts for 1 pound of pasta. When the water is boiling violently, add the noodles gradually so as not to slow the boiling. Stir gently to separate the strands. Put your serving bowl or platter into a 250°F oven so that it will be warm and ready when the pasta is done. (If you are cooking fresh pasta, begin heating the bowl 5 minutes before the noodles go into the water, since they cook so quickly.)

Underdone pasta has a core of uncooked dough, while overcooked pasta is mushy and unappetizing. Italians cook spaghetti until it is *al dente*, that is, resistant to the bite. Since cooking times vary considerably, begin testing before you expect the noodles to be ready, and disregard the cooking times recommended on the box—they are almost always too long. Use a fork to remove a strand of pasta from the boiling water, run the pasta under cold water, and bite into it. Or pinch it in two with your fingernail and look at the center of one end of the pasta. If it still has a core of white, it needs further cooking. It should be tender, but quite firm, with no hard core. Test every minute until the pasta is ready. When draining the cooked pasta, allow some water—as much as ¼ cup per pound of pasta—to remain in order to toss the pasta in. If you should drain away all the water, just add some hot water and toss.

Serving Pasta

Pour the cooked pasta into a colander, letting most of the water run out. Leave a little water on the pasta. Transfer the noodles immediately to a heated bowl and stir in the sauce. A 1-pound box of pasta makes 8 cups of cooked noodles, enough to serve four as a main course, six as a first course.

Cooked pasta is delicious simply served, tossed with only a little olive oil, garlic, chopped parsley, salt, and pepper. Top, if you wish, with some bread crumbs which have been lightly browned in a skillet with a little olive oil or butter (1 tablespoon of oil to 1 cup of bread crumbs will do the job). A good way to use up already cooked vegetables such as spinach, zucchini, broccoli, green beans, or peas is to cut them into bite-size pieces and toss with the pasta. Or try serving cooked pasta with the uncooked tomato sauce on page 387, as well, of course, as with one of the traditional Italian tomato sauces on pages 387–388.

Garnishes: Garnishes for pasta can be other than the old favorite, Parmesan cheese. Try a grated Romano, Asiago, or dry aged Monterey Jack or Cheddar. Or leave out cheese altogether and top pasta with chopped fresh parsley or basil, toasted or fried bread crumbs seasoned with a dried herb such as sage or oregano, a squeeze of lemon juice, fresh cracked or coarsely ground black pepper, or chopped black olives.

HOMEMADE ITALIAN NOODLES 🐝 (MAKES ABOUT 1 POUND, TO SERVE FOUR)

This recipe calls for a hand-cranked Italian pasta machine. If you don't have one, you can try rolling the dough out by hand, following the instructions in the recipe that follows for American-style noodles, but it won't be an easy job.

2 cups flour   3 eggs

Put the flour in a heap on a clean counter or pastry board. Make a hole in the center and crack the 3 eggs and drop them in. Add 2 tablespoons water and break up gently with a fork, continuing to beat until frothy and gradually incorporating a little of the flour around the sides. Continue beating and incorporating the flour until it is all used up. If the dough gets too dry, add a little bit more water until you have a manageable ball of dough with no dry pieces that aren't absorbed. Scrape and clean the counter and then start kneading with the palm of your hand as you would bread, until the dough holds together and becomes flexible. If you have a food processor, it can do the kneading: add a little more water and process until the dough forms a mass. Divide the dough in half and start feeding one half into the machine rollers opened to their largest opening, usually number 8. Using the hand crank, roll the dough through. Then fold and roll again at the next setting. Repeat until it has gone through the narrowest setting, at which point it will look like a long, smooth stocking. Do the same with the other half of the dough. For broad noodles, put the smooth pieces of dough through the wider cutters, catching them as they come out and spreading them over a broomstick or on large cookie sheets. For thinner noodles, use the narrower cutters. They need to dry long enough to remove surface moisture. To cook, plunge into a large pot of boiling salted water and start tasting 30 seconds after it has returned to the boil; the noodles are usually done in less than a minute. Drain and toss with butter and lots of freshly grated Parmesan cheese.

 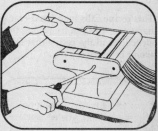

Pasta for Ravioli. After you have rolled out each half of dough into a long, smooth piece, place one on a lightly floured surface and distribute filling over it as directed on p. 469, using the other half to cover.

Pasta for Cannelloni. After you have rolled out each half, cut squares roughly 4 × 4 inches and cook them in rapidly boiling salted water until just tender, a minute or two. Drain, separate, and pat off excess water before filling. Use instead of the crêpes to make Cannelloni, p. 465.

HOMEMADE AMERICAN-STYLE NOODLES
(1 POUND)

Noodles freeze very well placed uncooked in a plastic bag or container.

3 egg yolks	1 tablespoon salt
1 egg	2 cups flour

Beat the yolks and egg until they are light. Beat in the salt and 3 tablespoons cold water. Using your hands, work the flour into this mixture to make a stiff dough. Cut into three equal parts. Cover with plastic wrap and let rest a few minutes. Dust a board or pastry cloth with flour and roll out one part of the dough as thin as possible. Cover with a dishcloth and let rest for 10 minutes. Repeat with the other two pieces. Sprinkle one sheet of dough very lightly with flour and roll up like a jelly roll. With a sharp knife, cut across the roll into ⅛-inch-wide strips for fine noodles and ½-inch-wide strips for broad noodles. Open out the strips and hang over a broomstick or chair back to dry.

They will be ready to cook when they have lost their surface dampness. About ten minutes should be enough. Bring a large pot of boiling salted water to a rolling boil and drop the noodles in. Boil vigorously until just tender—between 5 and 10 minutes, depending on how thin you have succeeded in rolling them; fork out one and taste to determine doneness.

ALFREDO'S NOODLES ⮞   (SERVES THREE)

You may know this creamy, delicate dish as Fettucine Alfredo. As a first course, which is the way Italians would serve it, this recipe makes enough for four.

½ pound noodles, ¼ inch wide   Salt to taste
¼ pound unsalted butter,   ¼ teaspoon freshly ground
   melted   pepper
1 cup heavy cream, warmed
¾ cup freshly grated
   Parmesan cheese

Have a large bowl warmed and ready before you cook the noodles. Drain the cooked noodles and put them into the bowl. Quickly add remaining ingredients, tossing briskly to coat all the noodles, and serve at once.

NOODLES WITH POPPY SEEDS

Omit the Parmesan cheese and add 3 *tablespoons poppy seeds*.

SOUR-CREAM BAKED
(SERVES FOUR) &ะ * **NOODLES**

This recipe has infinite variations. Use the butter to sauté any one or more of the following, then add to the noodles: *¼ cup chopped onion, ¼ cup chopped green pepper, ½ cup chopped celery, 1 cup sliced mushrooms, 1 cup well-drained flaked tuna, or 1½–2 cups diced cooked poultry.*

> ¼ pound noodles, ¼ inch wide or wider, cooked
> 1 cup cottage cheese
> 1 cup sour cream
> 1 egg, slightly beaten

> ½ teaspoon salt
> ⅛ teaspoon freshly ground pepper
> 4 tablespoons butter, melted

Preheat the oven to 375°F. Butter a 1½-quart casserole. Put the cooked noodles into a bowl and toss with the remaining ingredients. Put into the casserole and bake 50–60 minutes, or until bubbling and set.

NOODLE PUDDING

Add *1 cup finely chopped ham* and *½ cup raisins* to the mixture before baking.

(SERVES SIX) HAM AND NOODLE CASSEROLE

> 4 tablespoons butter
> 1 small onion, chopped fine
> 2 eggs, slightly beaten
> 1 cup sour cream
> ½ cup grated Gruyère or Swiss cheese

> 1½ cups finely chopped cooked ham
> Salt
> ½ pound noodles, ¼ inch wide, cooked

Preheat the oven to 350°F. Butter a 2-quart casserole. Melt the butter in a skillet and cook the onion over medium heat until soft. In a small bowl, mix the eggs and sour cream, then add the onion, cheese, and ham. Add salt to taste. Put the noodles in the casserole, then add the sauce and toss gently. Bake for 45 minutes or until a straw inserted in the middle comes out clean.

BEEF-NOODLE CASSEROLE

Substitute *1½ cups diced cooked beef*. If the beef is left over from a pot roast or stew and you have some gravy, add it to the casserole, adjusting the amount of sour cream accordingly.

CHICKEN-NOODLE CASSEROLE

Substitute *1½ cups finely chopped cooked chicken or turkey* for the ham.

FETTUCINE WITH EGGPLANT AND TOMATO SAUCE ?✒   (SERVES FOUR)

1 small eggplant, cubed or
   coarsely chopped
½ pound fettucine
½ recipe Tomato Sauce (p.
   387)

½ cup freshly grated
   Parmesan cheese

Steam the eggplant for 5–7 minutes, or until soft. Set aside and keep warm. Cook the pasta in a very large pot of boiling salted water until just tender, about 8–10 minutes. While the pasta is cooking, heat the tomato sauce in a saucepan over low heat. Drain the pasta, leaving a little bit of the water, and place in a large serving bowl. Add about 1½ cups of the hot tomato sauce and the eggplant and toss to coat all strands. You need only enough sauce to coat the pasta; it should not be swimming in sauce. Freeze any extra or pass it at the table. Serve on warmed plates or in bowls topped with the Parmesan cheese.

SPAGHETTI WITH WHITE CLAM SAUCE

(SERVES FOUR)

This sauce has the same homey flavor as a good clam chowder.

4 tablespoons butter	1 cup minced fresh or canned
⅓ cup flour	clams
2 teaspoons minced garlic	Salt
2 cups clam juice	1 pound spaghetti
⅔ cup milk	½ cup Parmesan cheese
¼ cup finely chopped parsley	(optional)

Melt the butter in a heavy-bottomed saucepan. Stir in the flour and blend over moderate heat until smooth. Continue to cook, stirring constantly, for 2 minutes. Add the garlic and clam juice, continuing to stir as the sauce thickens. Bring to a boil, lower the heat, and cook 2 minutes more. Pour in the milk, add the parsley and clams, stirring to blend, and heat thoroughly. Add salt to taste. Set aside and keep warm. Warm a large bowl while you cook the spaghetti. Drain the spaghetti, put it into the bowl, and add the clam sauce. Toss to mix. Serve immediately and pass the cheese at the table.

(SERVES THREE OR FOUR) ❧ PASTA WITH PESTO SAUCE

This sauce is quite good over chicken or stirred into corn meal or rice. Make it when fresh basil is available and freeze it.

½ cup fresh basil leaves	¾ pound dried pasta, such as
2 cloves garlic	spaghetti, spaghettini,
¼ cup walnuts or pine	capellini, fettucine or
nuts	vermicelli
½ cup olive oil, approximately	Grated Parmesan cheese, for
Salt to taste	garnish

Put the basil, garlic, and nuts in a food processor or blender and blend until finely chopped. Add the oil and process until smooth. If the mixture is too thick (this is not a sauce that flows; it is more of a paste), thin it out with a little more olive oil. Salt to taste. Refrigerate or freeze any unused sauce. Cook the pasta in a very large pot of boiling water, until just tender, 8–10 minutes depending on the size of the pasta used. Drain and toss with the pesto sauce. Serve at once.

JAMES BEARD'S PLEASANT PASTA   (SERVES FOUR)

This was one of James Beard's favorite pasta dishes. He described it as "amusing-looking, delicious-tasting and a worthy pasta."

1 pound pasta, such as
 spaghetti or fettucine
1 pound sugar snap peas or
 snow peas
4 tablespoons butter
1 cup finely cut prosciutto or
 good-quality ham

⅔ cup cream
Salt and freshly ground
 pepper to taste
Freshly grated Parmesan or
 Romano cheese

Cook the pasta in a large pot of boiling salted water until just tender. While the pasta is cooking, cook the peas in boiling water for only a minute or two. Drain and set aside. Drain the pasta, return it to the pot, and toss it with the butter. Add the peas, prosciutto or ham, and the cream, and toss. Add salt and pepper to taste. Serve piping hot with the grated cheese.

PASTA WITH ZUCCHINI ご   (SERVES THREE OR FOUR)

¾ pound dried thin pasta,
 such as spaghetti,
 spaghettini, or capellini
3 tablespoons olive oil
2 cloves garlic, chopped fine
 or put through a press

4 cups grated zucchini
3 ounces cream cheese
½ cup cream or milk
Salt and freshly ground
 pepper to taste
½ cup chopped basil

Cook the pasta in a very large pot of boiling water, until just tender. Timing will vary with the size of the pasta. While the pasta is cooking, make the sauce. Put the oil and garlic in a large saucepan and cook over medium-high heat for a minute. Add the zucchini and cook for another 2–3 minutes. Stir in the cream cheese and cream or milk and cook just till it bubbles and the cream cheese has melted. Season with salt and pepper. Stir in the basil. Drain the pasta and toss with the sauce.

CAPELLINI WITH SHRIMP, LEMON,
(SERVES THREE)   ✳   AND PARSLEY

This dish has good, clear flavors.

Grated or minced zest of 2
    lemons
½ cup chopped parsley
1 tablespoon minced garlic
½ pound capellini or other
    very thin pasta
1½ cups chicken broth

1 pound raw shrimp, shelled
    and deveined
Salt and freshly ground
    pepper to taste
1 cup bread crumbs tossed
    with 3 tablespoons melted
    butter

In a small bowl, mix together the lemon zest, parsley, and garlic. Set aside. Bring a large pot of salted water to a boil. Add the capellini and cook for about 4–5 minutes, or until tender. Drain, leaving about 4 tablespoons water in the pot. Return pasta to the pot, cover, and keep warm. Put the chicken broth in a saucepan and bring to a boil. Add the shrimp, lower the heat, and simmer 1–2 minutes, depending on the size of the shrimp. Pour the shrimp and broth over the pasta, add the lemon-parsley mixture and salt and pepper, and toss to mix well and coat the pasta. Transfer to a warm serving bowl and top with the bread crumbs, or serve in individual bowls, adding bread crumbs at last minute before serving.

(SERVES FOUR TO SIX)   ❧ GUIDO'S SPAGHETTI

This goes together in a flash. The simple flavors go well with cold chicken.

1 pound spaghetti or
    spaghettini
6 tablespoons butter
¼ cup olive oil
4 cloves garlic, minced

½ cup chopped parsley
Salt to taste
½ cup freshly grated
    Parmesan cheese

Bring a pot of salted water to a boil and cook the spaghetti until just tender, about 8–10 minutes. Put the butter, oil, and garlic in a small saucepan and cook over medium heat until the butter is melted and the mixture is hot. Remove from the heat and stir in the parsley. Drain the spaghetti, leaving about ⅓ cup of the pasta water in the pot. Return the spaghetti to the pot, toss with the butter mixture, and add salt. Serve hot, topped with the Parmesan cheese.

SPAGHETTI WITH CHICKEN AND
FRESH TOMATOES   (SERVES FOUR)

12 ounces spaghetti	3 cups fresh tomatoes, in
2 tablespoons olive oil	chunks
4 cloves garlic	1 cup medium pitted black
¼ cup chopped onion	olives
1 pound chicken breast	1 cup chicken broth
halves, in 1-inch pieces	½ cup basil leaves, chopped

Bring a pot of salted water to a boil and cook the spaghetti until just tender, about 8–10 minutes. While the spaghetti is cooking make the sauce. Put the oil, garlic, and onion in a skillet over medium-high heat and sauté until the onion is soft, but not browned. Add the chicken meat and cook 3–4 minutes, stirring often. Add the tomatoes, olives, and chicken broth and simmer for 3 minutes, then add the basil. Drain the spaghetti, return to the pot, and toss with the chicken mixture.

SPAGHETTI CARBONARA   (SERVES SIX)

Eggs make the strands of pasta glisten; cheese adds sharpness; lots of coarse black pepper heightens the spiciness.

1 pound bacon	3 tablespoons butter
1 pound spaghetti	Freshly ground pepper
¼ cup freshly grated	2 eggs, slightly beaten
Parmesan cheese	

Fry the bacon until it is just crisp, drain on paper towels, chop into bite-size pieces. Cook the spaghetti in a very large pot of boiling salted water, until just tender, about 8–10 minutes. Meanwhile warm a serving bowl. Drain the spaghetti well and toss in the bowl with the bacon, cheese, butter, and lots of freshly ground pepper—as much as a teaspoonful—for a few seconds, allowing to cool slightly. NOTE ▌Add the eggs and stir vigorously to coat all the strands.
see page 471 ▌Serve immediately.

SPAGHETTI WITH LIMA BEANS   (SERVES FOUR)

I like lima beans in this dish; however, you may substitute red kidney or Great Northern beans.

1 pound spaghetti
¼ pound bacon, in ½-inch slices
1 cup chopped onion
¾ cup chopped green pepper
1 cup chopped celery
2 cloves garlic, minced
10 ounces fresh or frozen lima beans, cooked until tender

1 cup chicken broth
½ teaspoon salt or to taste
Freshly ground pepper to taste
1 cup bread crumbs
2 tablespoons butter, melted

Put the spaghetti in a large pot of salted boiling water. Cook until just tender. While the spaghetti is cooking, cook the bacon in a frying pan until almost crisp. Remove the bacon, drain on paper towel, and crumble. Drain all but 1 tablespoon of the fat from the pan and sauté the onion, green pepper, celery, and garlic until the vegetables are soft. Drain the spaghetti when cooked, and toss with the bacon, lima beans, chicken broth, salt, and pepper, until mixed together. Place on a heated serving platter. Combine the bread crumbs and butter and distribute over the top.

VERMICELLI IN FRESH ❧ TOMATO SAUCE

(SERVES SIX)

6 vine-ripened tomatoes, peeled and chopped
1 tablespoon lemon juice
2 tablespoons basil, chopped fresh, or 1 tablespoon dried
¼ teaspoon freshly ground pepper

4 tablespoons finely chopped parsley
½ cup olive oil
3 cloves garlic, minced
½ cup sliced scallions
Salt to taste
1 pound vermicelli

Mix the tomatoes, lemon juice, basil, pepper, and parsley in a bowl. Heat the olive oil in a saucepan. Add the garlic and cook, stirring, for 2 minutes; add the scallions and continue to cook and stir for 1 minute more. Add the tomato mixture and salt, and simmer for 10 minutes as you cook the vermicelli. Drain the pasta, place in a large warm bowl, add the tomato mixture, and mix well.

CHINESE NOODLES ∂❧ (SERVES FOUR)

1 cup grated carrots
1 cup grated zucchini
1 cup grated turnip
½ cup sliced scallions
¼ cup olive oil
3 tablespoons rice vinegar
1½ tablespoons soy sauce

1 teaspoon sesame oil
1 teaspoon chili oil or chili flakes
2 teaspoons minced garlic
14 ounces fresh Chinese noodles, approximately

In a large bowl, toss the carrots, zucchini, turnip, and scallions. Set aside. In a small bowl, mix together the olive oil, vinegar, soy sauce, sesame oil, chili oil or flakes, and garlic. Stir well to blend. Set aside. Bring a large pot of salted water to a boil. Add the fresh noodles and cook for only about 2–3 minutes. Drain, and turn into the bowl with the vegetables. Add the oil mixture and toss well to mix and coat the noodles. Serve at once.

MACARONI AND CHEESE ∂❧ (SERVES FOUR)

It is so easy and inexpensive to make this favorite dish from scratch.

½ pound macaroni, cooked
2 cups Cheese Sauce (p. 380)
½ cup grated sharp Cheddar cheese

½ cup freshly made buttered bread crumbs

Preheat the oven to 375°F. Butter a 1½-quart casserole. Put the cooked macaroni into the casserole, pour the cheese sauce over it, and mix gently with a fork. Sprinkle the grated cheese evenly over the top and spread the crumbs over the cheese. Bake, uncovered, until the top is golden and the sauce is bubbling, about 30 minutes.

(SERVES SIX)   **LASAGNE**

3 tablespoons olive oil
½ cup chopped onion
⅓ cup chopped carrot
3 cloves garlic, minced
1 pound lean ground beef
3 cups canned Italian plum
   tomatoes
3 tablespoons butter, melted
1 teaspoon oregano, crumbled
1 tablespoon basil, crumbled

1 teaspoon salt
½ teaspoon freshly ground
   pepper
½ pound lasagna noodles,
   cooked
½ pound mozzarella cheese,
   grated
2 cups ricotta cheese
¼ pound freshly grated
   Parmesan cheese

Heat the oil in a skillet. Add the onion, carrot, and garlic, and cook, stirring, until they are lightly browned. Push to the side of the pan and add the beef. Break it up into bits, cooking until it loses its pink color. Purée the tomatoes in a blender or food processor, add to the meat, and simmer 15 minutes. Add the butter, oregano, basil, salt, and pepper, partially cover, and simmer 30 minutes. Preheat the oven to 375°F. Assemble the lasagne by drizzling some sauce over the bottom of a shallow rectangular baking dish. Put in a layer of noodles, sprinkle with some of the mozzarella, and spread on a layer of ricotta. Make another layer of noodles, sauce, mozzarella, and ricotta. Finish with noodles and sauce. Sprinkle Parmesan cheese evenly over the top and bake 20 minutes, or until hot and bubbling.

(SERVES EIGHT)   ❊ **CANNELLONI**

This cannelloni is made with crêpes, which gives the finished dish a delightful texture. It can also be made with the pasta that is sold as cannelloni, if you can find it; or make your own (p. 455). The same filling could go into manicotti and ravioli.

1 recipe Crêpes or French
   Pancakes (p. 778)

Filling

1 onion, chopped fine
3 tablespoons olive oil
1 clove garlic, minced
1 pound lean ground beef
2 tablespoons cream
1 teaspoon oregano, crumbled
2 eggs

1½ pounds fresh spinach,
   cooked, drained, and
   chopped; or one 10-ounce
   package frozen spinach,
   thawed and drained
Salt to taste
Freshly ground pepper

Sauté the onion in the olive oil until just soft, then add the garlic and cook, stirring, a minute more. Remove to a bowl. Add the beef to the skillet, breaking it up, and cook until it loses its pinkness. Scrape into the onion and garlic, then add the cream, oregano, eggs, spinach, salt, and pepper. Mix vigorously with a wooden spoon or with your hands until the ingredients are well blended. Set aside.

Sauce I

6 tablespoons butter	¼ teaspoon nutmeg
6 tablespoons flour	Salt and freshly ground
1 cup hot milk	pepper
1 cup heavy cream	

Melt the butter in a saucepan, add the flour, and cook, stirring constantly, over medium heat 3–4 minutes. Add the milk, stirring until the sauce is smooth and thick, then add the cream and continue to cook gently a few minutes. Sprinkle in the nutmeg, and salt and pepper to taste. Set aside.

Sauce II

1½ cups Tomato Sauce (p. 387)

To Assemble the Cannelloni: Preheat the oven to 375°F. Film the bottom of a shallow baking dish, about 13 × 9 × 2 inches, with tomato sauce. Fill each crêpe with 4 tablespoons of the filling. Roll up and place each crêpe seam side down in the baking dish. Proceed until the crêpes are filled and in a single layer. Spoon the white sauce, Sauce I, over the top and drizzle the remaining tomato sauce lengthwise in two rivulets over the white sauce. Bake for 40 minutes or until the sauce bubbles around the edges.

CHICKEN-STUFFED MANICOTTI

Manicotti are large tubular pasta shapes, about 4 inches long and 1½ inches in diameter. Here are three fillings for manicotti: a mild cheese filling, a heartier meat filling (for which you could use cooked beef if you have some leftovers), and a subtle chicken or turkey filling. All are quite rich and the dish will serve eight as a first course or lunch dish, but for a main dinner dish, count on its serving only four with just a green salad.

Stuffing

2 cups finely chopped cooked
  chicken
4 tablespoons minced parsley
1 teaspoon thyme, crumbled
½ cup finely chopped celery
1 cup grated Monterey Jack
  cheese

3 tablespoons dry white wine
½ teaspoon salt
8 manicotti, cooked (slightly
  underdone) and drained

Combine the chicken with remaining ingredients. Divide the stuffing
into 8 parts and stuff the manicotti.

Sauce

6 tablespoons butter
6 tablespoons flour
3 cups chicken broth
1 teaspoon tarragon,
  crumbled

1 cup grated Monterey Jack
  cheese
Salt to taste

Melt the butter in a saucepan and slowly stir in the flour, cooking 3
minutes. Slowly add the chicken broth, cooking 3 minutes more, until
the sauce is smooth and thickened. Add the tarragon, cheese, and salt,
and cook until the cheese is melted. Preheat the oven to 350°F. Spoon a
light film of the sauce over the bottom of an 11¾ × 7½ × 1¾-inch baking
dish. Make a single layer of manicotti, leaving room for expansion, and
spread the remaining sauce over it. Cover with foil and bake 40 minutes.

(SERVES FOUR OR EIGHT)   **CHEESE-STUFFED MANICOTTI**

8 manicotti, cooked, slightly
  underdone, and drained

Stuffing

2 cups ricotta or small-curd
  cottage cheese
1 egg, slightly beaten
2 tablespoons minced parsley
4 tablespoons freshly grated
  Parmesan cheese

1 teaspoon basil, crumbled
¼ teaspoon nutmeg
½ teaspoon salt
¼ teaspoon freshly ground
  pepper

Combine the ricotta or cottage cheese with remaining ingredients. Mix
well and use it to stuff the manicotti.

Sauce

¼ pound butter	2 cups grated Monterey Jack
7 tablespoons flour	cheese
3 cups chicken broth	¼ teaspoon Tabasco
1 cup heavy cream	Salt to taste

Melt the butter in a saucepan. Stir in the flour and cook, stirring constantly, for 3 minutes. Slowly stir in the broth and cream and cook 3 minutes more, until sauce is smooth and thickened. Add the cheese, Tabasco, and salt and cook until the cheese melts.

To Assemble the Manicotti: Preheat the oven to 375°F. Film the bottom of an 11¾ × 7½ × 1¾-inch baking pan with the sauce. Make a single layer of the stuffed manicotti. Cover with the remaining sauce, cover with foil, and bake 1 hour.

BEEF-SPINACH STUFFED MANICOTTI

(SERVES FOUR OR EIGHT)

3 tablespoons olive oil	½ teaspoon salt
½ pound lean ground beef	¼ teaspoon freshly ground
½ cup minced onion	pepper
1 cup freshly made bread	8 manicotti, cooked (slightly
crumbs	underdone) and
3 tablespoons freshly grated	drained
Parmesan cheese	2 cups Tomato Sauce (p. 387)
3 eggs, slightly beaten	
1½ pounds fresh spinach,	
cooked, drained, and	
chopped, or 10-ounce	
package frozen spinach,	
thawed, drained, and	
chopped	

Preheat the oven to 375°F. Heat the olive oil in a skillet and add the beef and onion. Cook, breaking the meat into tiny bits with a fork, until it has lost its pinkness. Put the meat and onion in a bowl and mix with the bread crumbs, cheese, eggs, spinach, salt, and pepper. Stuff the cooked manicotti with the mixture and make a single layer in an 11¾ × 7½ × 1¾-inch baking dish, allowing space between the manicotti for expansion. Spoon the tomato sauce on top, cover with foil, and bake 45 minutes.

(ABOUT 24 RAVIOLI)   **RAVIOLI**

1 recipe Homemade Italian
   Noodles (p. 454)

Filling for Ravioli

½ cup finely chopped cooked   ¼ teaspoon salt
   meat or chicken   ¼ teaspoon freshly ground
½ cup finely chopped cooked   pepper
   spinach   ⅛ teaspoon nutmeg
1 egg   ½ teaspoon oregano,
2 tablespoons freshly grated   crumbled
   Parmesan cheese

Combine all the filling ingredients in a bowl. Mix until well blended
and set aside.

Cut the pasta dough into two even pieces and roll paper-thin into
rectangular sheets. Put teaspoonfuls of filling on half the strips, dotting
them 2 inches apart. Using a narrow brush, or your finger, moisten
with water a rectangle around each mound of filling. Cover with the
other sheet. Seal between the mounds of filling by pressing with your
thumbs. Cut apart and let dry 2 hours before cooking.

Cooking Ravioli

Bring 6 quarts salted water to boil in a large pot. Drop in the ravioli
and boil for 5–6 minutes. Stir gently with a wooden spoon to keep
them from sticking to one another. Lift them out with a skimmer or
strainer and place on a warmed platter.

Assembly of Ravioli

> 1 cup Tomato Sauce (p. 387)
> ½ cup freshly grated
>   Parmesan cheese

Drizzle the sauce over the platter of ravioli and sprinkle with the cheese.

GNOCCHI ALLA ROMANA ह≈   (SERVES SIX)

The good graininess of gnocchi comes from semolina, coarsely ground durum wheat that is available in Italian markets and health-food stores.

3 cups milk	1 cup semolina
1 teaspoon salt	3 eggs, slightly beaten
¼ teaspoon nutmeg	1 cup freshly grated
¼ teaspoon freshly ground	Parmesan cheese
pepper	6 tablespoons butter, melted

Butter a jelly-roll pan (18 × 13 × 1 inch). Combine the milk, salt, nutmeg, and pepper in a heavy-bottomed pan, bring to a boil, and slowly drizzle in the semolina, stirring constantly with a wooden spoon. Cook for about 2 minutes or until thick enough so that the spoon will stand up in the mixture. Cool slightly, beat in the eggs vigorously, and add the cheese and half the butter. Beat until well blended. Spread the rest of the mixture in the buttered pan and chill for 2 hours or longer. Preheat the oven to 400°F. Cut the dough into 1½- or 2-inch squares, triangles, or circles. Arrange the pieces in a buttered baking dish, spoon the butter over the top, and bake for 20–25 minutes, or until piping hot and lightly golden.

Other Suggestions for Pasta Dishes

For a fine dish of spaghetti and meatballs, see Meatballs in Sauce, p. 237. Leftover pasta is always good in soup, and cold pasta can be used in salad, although I find it loses its flavor.

EGGS & CHEESE

There is an ever-growing concern about the threat of salmonella, bacteria that contaminate eggs, poultry, and meat. Because we often eat eggs lightly cooked and even raw (in sauces like mayonnaise, for instance), they pose a greater threat (see rules for handling meat and poultry, pp. 209 and 303). In trying to assess the seriousness of the problem, I have consulted government agencies—the Food and Drug Administration, the Agricultural Department, and the Centers for Disease Control—and many other food safety experts. The findings are frustrating because there seems to be no collective information as to how many eggs are infected, and how many people have been stricken with salmonella in this country, so there is no way of knowing the degree of risk one is taking when eating raw or lightly cooked eggs, which are used in many recipes (see alert Note in the margin alongside the recipes). Government officials recommend that immuno-compromised patients, the very young and the elderly, all of whom are the most severely affected when stricken, should not eat raw or lightly cooked eggs. Until the problem has been licked, the rest of us are consuming eggs that have not been cooked to 165° at our own risk. Incidentally, eggs in cakes, cookies, and breads have been sufficiently cooked to be safe.

EGGS

Buying Eggs

It's heaven when you are in the country to enjoy the taste of a newly laid farm egg for breakfast. But supermarket eggs are reliable and certainly fresh enough for general purposes. Commercial eggs are graded A, AA, or B, depending on their quality. Grades of eggs are called AA, A, B. There is no difference in nutritive value among the different grades.

Because production and marketing methods have become very efficient, eggs move so rapidly from laying house to market that you will find very little difference in quality between grades AA and A. Although grade B eggs are just as wholesome to eat, almost no grade Bs find their way to the retail supermarket: some go to institutional egg-users, such as bakeries and food-service operations, and most go to processors who use them in egg products.

An old-fashioned method for determining whether an egg is really stale is to see if it floats in a bowl of water; if it does, or tips noticeably upward, it means an air sac has formed as the interior has shrunk away from the shell and the egg is definitely old. However, it would take at least three weeks for eggs left at room temperature to reach this state so it is not likely to occur with modern methods of fast distribution and refrigeration.

If an egg is fresh, the white and yolk will cling together tightly when you crack it open. The older it gets, the flatter the yolk becomes and the runnier the white. You don't have to throw the eggs out at that stage, but where flavor counts, they certainly won't have a pleasant fresh taste; however, the eggs would still retain their rising power.

The color of an egg's shell has nothing to do with its quality or taste, despite local prejudices. Buy whichever is least expensive. Yolks also vary in color, from pale yellow to nearly orange. This comes from variations in the chicken's feed and makes little difference in taste. A speck of blood in a yolk is not harmful.

Storing Eggs

Today eggs are more widely available and cheaper than ever before. And the eggs from our big supermarkets have been stored carefully and are fresher than you probably think. Once you get the eggs home, refrigerate them immediately. Eggs can deteriorate as much in one day at room temperature as they would in a week in the refrigerator. If you have any cracked or broken eggs, use them only in baked goods.

If you use several whites in a meringue or a cake, you can keep the uncooked yolks for two or three days in the refrigerator, using them to enrich scrambled eggs or to thicken a sauce. Cover them with a film of cold water and some plastic wrap to prevent a skin from forming. For freezing egg yolks, see p. 1122.

If you are going to use leftover egg whites within a few days, store them in a covered container in the refrigerator. For freezing egg whites, see p. 1122.

Measuring Eggs

Egg size is standardized by the government. The recipes in this book call for "large" eggs, weighing 2 ounces each or 24 ounces a dozen. A dozen "small" eggs weigh 18 ounces, "medium" weigh 21, and "extra large" weigh 27 ounces. To make 1 cup of eggs requires 7 "smalls," 6 "mediums," 5 "large," or 4 "extra large." It's easy enough to adapt egg sizes in recipes where it matters, like cakes, custards, and soufflés.

An egg is one-third yolk, two-thirds white. A cup of egg whites contains 10 "small," 8 "medium," 7 "large," or 6 "extra large" egg whites, while a cup of yolks uses 18 "small," 16 "medium," 14 "large," or 12 "extra large" yolks.

If, on doubling or halving a recipe, you wind up needing to use half an egg, just break it, beat it, and measure off half: about 1½ tablespoons.

Separating Eggs

To separate an egg, crack it with a knife or against the edge of a bowl and split the shell into two parts. Pass the yolk back and forth between the halves of the shell, letting the white fall into a cup underneath. Or pass the shelled egg from one hand to the other, letting the white fall through your fingers. Play safe: drop each white into a cup before adding it to the other egg whites in the bowl. In that way, if some yolk breaks into the white, it will not ruin the whole bowl.

Beating Egg Whites

When beating egg whites, aim for as much volume as possible. Start with whites that are at room temperature. Make sure that the bowl and beater are absolutely grease-free: you can remove unwanted bits of broken egg yolk by using the shell or the corner of a paper towel. Beat with a whisk or a mechanical beater. Some believe that an unlined copper bowl produces the greatest volume, but actually that is not so. Beating in a copper bowl produces a finer, stronger network of air pockets—an advantage if you are making meringue and want it fine

and delicate. However, glass, earthenware, or stainless steel is also fine for beating egg whites. Aluminum and plastic are less than satisfactory. If you are using an electric beater, start out on slow speed until whites are foamy, then increase to medium; if it is a hand-held beater, circulate it around the bowl. Many recipes instruct you to beat egg whites until they are "stiff but not dry." This is a way of describing the point at which the beaten whites have achieved their greatest degree of elasticity. That point is reached when a whisk or beater removed from the mixture pulls with it stiff peaks of egg white that have a shiny, glossy surface.

Folding Egg Whites

Properly beaten, egg whites will grow to as much as six times their original volume. See p. 788 for the remedy for overbeating egg whites. Use beaten whites immediately, before they begin to shrink and separate, and always fold the light whites into the heavier mixture. Start by spooning the egg whites on top of the heavier batter, using a rubber spatula. Cut down into the batter and back up again in a circular motion, using the spatula or your hands and turning the bowl as you fold. Your aim is to incorporate the air captured in the beaten egg whites; if you overfold, the tiny air pockets will be flattened.

Tempering Egg Yolks

Egg yolks are frequently added to hot mixtures, often to sauces, so that as the heat works on the yolks, it will cause them to thicken the sauce. Yolks must be tempered first so that they do not cook too quickly and wind up floating, scrambled, in the sauce. To temper them, gently beat the yolks with a fork in a separate bowl, then add a bit of the hot sauce to them in a thin stream, beating constantly until the mixture is blended. When this mixture has become warm and thick, you can stir it into the whole potful of simmering liquid. Keep it below the boiling point unless the sauce is bound by flour, which prevents curdling.

Cooking Eggs

There are about ten basic ways to cook an egg, and a nearly infinite number of variations. *Soft-boiled eggs* are simmered in the shell for 3–4 minutes until the whites are opaque but still soft. *Medium-boiled eggs* are cooked in the shell for 4–5 minutes until the white is solid, but the yolk still liquid. They are also called *coddled eggs* or *eggs mollet* and, when peeled, they may be substituted for poached eggs. *Hard-boiled eggs* are simmered for 15 minutes, until both white and yolk are solid.

Poached eggs are turned out of their shells and cooked in simmering liquid until the whites become opaque. *Fried eggs* are broken into hot butter or oil and cooked in a skillet to the same point. *Scrambled eggs* are mixed in a bowl with a tablespoonful of liquid, then dropped into a buttered pan and stirred lightly over heat until curds form.

Shirred eggs are dropped into a flat dish and baked in the oven, while *eggs en cocotte* are placed in covered porcelain cups that are then immersed in simmering water. Finally, there are *omelets* and *soufflés*, perhaps the most elegant of ways to present eggs.

No matter what the technique, it is essential to use low, gentle heat when cooking eggs: egg protein begins to thicken at only 144°F, and toughens rapidly. The only exception is omelets; there the bottom is cooked quickly over medium-high heat, but the surface remains slightly runny, making for a soft interior when folded. Serve cooked eggs on warm, not sizzling hot, plates or they will continue to cook after they are removed from the pan.

❧ SOFT-BOILED EGGS

Soft-boiled eggs have softly set whites and runny yolks.

NOTE
see page 471

Fill a saucepan with enough water to cover the egg, and heat to a gentle boil. Pierce the large end of the egg with an egg piercer (see illustration p. 37) or a needle; this will release the pressure that often cracks the shell.

When the water is gently simmering, lower the egg on a tablespoon. Set the timer; it will take 3–4 minutes for a "large" egg to be soft-boiled. If you are cooking many eggs at the same time, it is helpful to lower them into the water in a wire basket such as those used for deep frying.

❧ MEDIUM-BOILED EGGS

Coddled or medium-boiled eggs have firm opaque whites and soft yolks. They can be shelled and used in place of poached eggs.

NOTE
see page 471

Fill a saucepan with enough water to cover the egg, and heat to a gentle boil. Pierce the large end of the egg with an egg piercer or with a needle; this releases the pressure that often cracks the shell.

When the water is gently boiling, lower the egg on a tablespoon. Cover the pan, remove from the heat, and let the egg stand for 4–5 minutes, depending on how firm you want it to be.

HARD-BOILED EGGS ౭∾

Hard-boiled eggs have firm whites and yolks.

Pierce the large end of the egg with an egg piercer or a needle; this will release the pressure that often cracks the shell. Put the egg in a pan and fill it with water. Bring it to a boil, and simmer for 15 minutes.

Remove from the heat and place the egg in cold water immediately. An overcooked egg develops a harmless dark ring that isn't as appetizing as the bright-yellow yolk.

POACHED EGGS ౭∾   (SERVES TWO TO FOUR)

A poached egg is cooked out of its shell in simmering liquid until its white is opaque and firm and its yolk is still runny. Delicious on toast, on hash, or on English muffins.

    2 teaspoons vinegar   ½ teaspoon salt
    4 eggs, at room temperature

NOTE
see page 471

Fill a nonstick 10–12-inch skillet two-thirds full of water. Add the vinegar, to help coagulate the egg white. Bring the water to a simmer, break each egg, one by one, into a saucer, and slide it tenderly into the water. Slip each additional egg into a different place in the skillet. Add salt. Spoon the simmering water over the eggs for about 3 minutes until they are set; or turn off the heat, cover the pan, and let the eggs stand in the water for about 5 minutes. The eggs are done when the whites become opaque and the yolks lose their shine. Remove one by one with a slotted spoon. If you prepare the eggs ahead of time, place the poached eggs in a bowl of cold water and refrigerate until needed. Just before serving, place them in a bowl of very hot water for a few minutes to warm them or slide them into a skillet full of simmering water and cook for 1 minute.

For a single poached egg, simply use a smaller skillet. Until you get the knack of poaching eggs, you may find it easier to do one at a time.

FRIED EGG ౭∾

Use a heavy skillet or nonstick pan, and don't cook over high heat or the white will become tough and rubbery.

    2 teaspoons butter, oil, or   1 egg
        bacon fat

NOTE
see page 471

Melt the fat in a skillet. Break the egg into a saucer. When the fat is hot, slide in the egg and reduce the heat. If the eggs are to be cooked "sunny side up"—that is, not turned over—spoon the hot fat over them until the white is set and the yolk loses its shine, or else cover the skillet and let the eggs cook for 2–3 minutes. If they are to be turned over, use a spatula to lift each egg gently. Turn and cook for 30 seconds more until white is set over yolk. Remove to a warm plate.

(SERVES ONE)   ⊱ **SHIRRED EGGS**

Shirred eggs are baked with butter in a shallow dish until they are barely set. A wonderful way for an inexperienced cook to fix eggs, particularly since you can add garnishes to make a delicious and satisfying dish.

1½ teaspoons butter	Salt
2 eggs	Freshly ground pepper

NOTE
see page 471

Preheat the oven to 325°F. Use baking dishes that accommodate no more than two eggs, such as gratin dishes. Put the butter in the dish and place it in the oven until the butter melts. Swirl it to coat the bottom and sides. Crack the eggs, put them in the dish, and cover snugly with foil. Bake for 12 minutes. Uncover, and season to taste.

SHIRRED EGGS WITH CRUMBS

Sprinkle 2 *tablespoons freshly made bread crumbs* over the buttered bottom of the baking dish. Add the eggs, and sprinkle with another 2 *tablespoons bread crumbs*.

SHIRRED EGGS IN CREAM

For each egg add 1½ *tablespoons heavy cream* to the bottom of the baking dish and spoon another 1½ *tablespoons heavy cream* over the eggs.

SHIRRED EGGS WITH SAUSAGE

For each 2 eggs cook 4 *small sausages* until done. Drain and place the sausages around the eggs in the baking dish.

SHIRRED EGGS WITH CHICKEN LIVERS

For each 2 eggs add *2 or 3 chicken livers*, sautéed first in *1 tablespoon butter* for 2 or 3 minutes. Add *1 teaspoon sherry*, scrape up the livers and butter and browned bits from the sauté pan, and place around the eggs in the baking dish.

SHIRRED EGGS WITH HAM

For each 2 eggs add *2–3 tablespoons diced cooked ham* or other tasty meat such as *corned beef, tongue, chipped beef* to the baking dish.

SHIRRED EGGS MORNAY

Make a *Mornay Sauce* (p. 380); one recipe will be enough for 6 eggs. Divide the sauce in thirds and spoon each third over 2 eggs. Cover the dish and bake for 5 minutes; uncover and slip under the broiler for 1 minute more to brown lightly.

SHIRRED EGGS FLORENTINE

Spread *1 tablespoon chopped cooked spinach* for each egg on the bottom of the baking dish. Put the egg on top and sprinkle with *1 tablespoon freshly grated Parmesan cheese*.

SHIRRED EGGS LORRAINE

Butter a baking dish. Line with *thin slices of cooked bacon* and *slivers of Gruyère or Swiss cheese*. Break eggs on top. Pour a *ring of cream* around yolks, cover, and bake as for shirred eggs.

SCRAMBLED EGGS ❧   (SERVES THREE)

Some like their scrambled eggs moist and some like them rather dry. The longer they cook, the drier they become. Either way, use low heat so the texture remains soft and creamy.

4 tablespoons butter	⅛ teaspoon freshly ground
5 eggs	pepper
¼ teaspoon salt	2 tablespoons water

NOTE
see page 471

Melt the butter in a heavy skillet or nonstick pan. Combine the eggs, salt, pepper, and 2 tablespoons water in a bowl. Briskly whisk, pour into the skillet, and turn the heat very low. Gently stir the egg mixture, lifting it up and over from the bottom as it thickens. Continue to stir until the desired texture is achieved. They thicken and dry out very quickly toward the end, so if you like them soft and moist, remove them from the heat a little before they reach the desired texture; they will continue to cook after being removed from the pan.

SCRAMBLED EGGS WITH HAM

Add *½ cup finely chopped cooked ham* to the egg mixture.

SCRAMBLED EGGS WITH CREAM CHEESE

Cut *4 ounces cream cheese* into small cubes and add to the eggs after they begin to thicken in the skillet.

SCRAMBLED EGGS WITH CHIVES

Add *1 tablespoon chopped chives* and *1 tablespoon chopped parsley* to the egg mixture, and substitute *2 tablespoons cream* for the water.

SCRAMBLED EGGS WITH LOX

Fry *½ onion, sliced*, and *2 slices lox* in the butter before adding the eggs, and eliminate the salt from the mixture.

SCRAMBLED EGGS WITH CHICKEN LIVERS

Fry *2 chicken livers, diced*, in the butter before adding the egg mixture.

SCRAMBLED EGGS WITH ASPARAGUS

Add ⅔ *cup crisp-cooked asparagus*, in 2-inch pieces, to the eggs just after they begin to thicken in the skillet.

SCRAMBLED EGGS WITH PEPPERS AND ONIONS

Fry ½ *red pepper, diced*, and ¼ *onion, chopped*, in the butter for about 5 minutes before adding the egg mixture.

SCRAMBLED EGGS WITH MUSHROOMS

Melt the butter in a heavy skillet. Sauté *1½ cups sliced mushrooms* with *4 tablespoons finely chopped onion* over medium-high heat for 4–5 minutes. Lower the heat before adding the egg mixture.

SCRAMBLED EGGS BOURGET ❧ (SERVES SIX)

Anne Bourget, who has a cooking school in Sacramento, California, shared with me her wonderful recipe for scrambling eggs: they can be held in a warm oven, or a chafing dish, for up to an hour. This way they can be made ahead of time for parties or large groups.

2 tablespoons butter	1 recipe White Sauce (p. 379)
12 eggs	2 tablespoons chopped chives
2 tablespoons cold water	or basil (optional)
Salt and freshly ground	
pepper to taste	

NOTE
see page 471

Melt the butter in a heavy skillet or nonstick pan over medium-low heat. Combine the eggs, water, and salt and pepper in a bowl. Briskly whisk, pour into the skillet, and turn the heat very low. Gently stir the egg mixture, lifting it up and over from the bottom as it thickens. Continue to stir until the desired texture is achieved. Remove from the heat and gently fold the white sauce into the cooked eggs. Add the fresh herbs if desired. At this point the eggs may be served or placed in a buttered casserole and held in a warm, 150°F–200°F oven for up to an hour until ready to serve.

(SERVES ONE)   ೋ **FRENCH OMELET**

Read this recipe from beginning to end before starting to cook. A perfectly made omelet is a mass of creamy scrambled eggs enclosed in an envelope of coagulated egg. The keys to making a good omelet are quickness and proper heat. Almost any leftover food makes a good filling, as long as it isn't too liquid. It is always better to make omelets one at a time. You cannot achieve the same result working with more than two or three eggs and a larger pan.

2 "large" eggs	3–4 tablespoons filling
Salt	(optional: see following)
Freshly ground pepper	1 tablespoon butter
Tabasco (optional)	

NOTE
see page 471

Beat the eggs in a bowl only until they are just blended. Add a pinch of salt and pepper or a dash of Tabasco. If a filling is to be used, have it prepared and warm, if necessary. Heat a 7- or 8-inch nonstick skillet until hot. Add butter. When it foams and sizzles, quickly pour in the eggs. Shake the skillet with a short forward and backward motion. Using a fork, pull back a little of the edge of the egg that will have started to curl up and, by tipping the skillet, allow the liquid egg in the center of the pan to run over. Continue to shake and fork around the edges, but work quickly: it should take only 15 seconds from the time the eggs are poured into the skillet until the filling (if you are using one) is added. Spread the filling across the center of the omelet. Have a warm plate ready. Use a spatula or the fork and roll one-third of the omelet over onto itself, then out of the skillet onto the plate, encouraging it to make the second fold as it falls. Don't cook the omelet dry; the center of a finished omelet should be moist, which means that you start to roll it when the surface is still a little runny.

HERB OMELET

Add 1 *teaspoon minced parsley,* 1 *tablespoon minced chives,* and *⅛ teaspoon tarragon, crumbled,* to the egg mixture.

CROUTON OMELET

Lay *¼ cup buttered croutons* over the omelet just before folding.

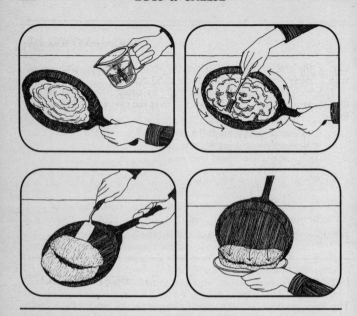

CHEESE OMELET

Sprinkle ¼ cup *fresh grated Gruyère or Swiss cheese* over the omelet just before folding.

MUSHROOM OMELET

Spread ½ cup *sliced mushrooms*, first sautéed in a little butter, over the center of the omelet just before folding.

BACON OMELET

Fry 2 *slices bacon*. Drain, break into small pieces, and sprinkle over the omelet just before folding.

AVOCADO OMELET

Lay on the omelet ¼ *avocado, peeled and sliced* lengthwise, and spread with *3 tablespoons sour cream* just before folding.

Other excellent omelets can be made by using ¼–½ cup of any of the following fillings. Heat and spread over the omelet just before you fold it.

> Chicken or turkey, cooked and creamed
> Chicken livers, chopped and sautéed
> Fish, cooked and flaked or creamed
> Ham, cooked and chopped
> Tomato, chopped with onions, peppers, or canned green chilies
> Cooked vegetables, diced and heated in butter
> Lobster, shrimp, tuna, or crabmeat, cooked and creamed or heated in butter

For a special dessert, follow the recipe for Sweet Omelet (p. 948).

(SERVES TWO)   ⪜ **PUFFY OMELET**

This is a light dish akin to a soufflé. Any of the fillings for the French Omelet (preceding recipe) may be used for the Puffy Omelet. If you use a filling, have it warm and spread it over the top when the omelet is done.

2 teaspoons butter	¼ teaspoon salt
4 eggs, separated	⅛ teaspoon freshly ground
¼ cup hot water	pepper

Preheat the oven to 400°F. Spread the butter around the sides and bottom of a 10-inch skillet. Beat the egg yolks, hot water, salt, and pepper until thick and lemon-colored. In another bowl beat the egg whites until stiff but not dry. Gently stir a fourth of the whites into the yolk mixture and then fold the yolk mixture into the remaining whites. Heat the buttered skillet over low heat. Spoon the omelet mixture into the pan and spread it evenly. Cook very slowly over low heat. When the omelet is nicely puffed, transfer the skillet to the oven and bake it 3–4 minutes, or until it is lightly browned. Or, if a moist interior is desired, slip the pan under the broiler to brown the top instead of cooking it longer in the oven.

POTATO AND LEEK FRITTATA ୧ଈ   (SERVES FOUR)

A frittata is the flat omelet served in Mediterranean countries that is often a background for spicy vegetables. It is easier to make (than separate omelets) for four or more.

4 tablespoons butter	5 eggs
1 tablespoon oil	½ cup heavy cream
1 cup ½-inch cubes peeled	¼ teaspoon salt
potato	⅛ teaspoon freshly ground
1 cup sliced leeks	pepper
1 tablespoon minced parsley	
¼ cup freshly grated	
Parmesan cheese	

Heat 2 tablespoons of the butter and the oil in a skillet. Add the potatoes and leeks and cook until the potatoes are cooked and lightly browned. Put into a bowl, toss in the parsley and cheese, and set aside. Combine the eggs, cream, salt, and pepper, and add to the potatoes and leeks. Melt the remaining 2 tablespoons of butter in the skillet. Pour in the egg mixture and cook very slowly over low heat, pricking the top with a fork and lifting the bottom gently. Cover and cook 2–3 minutes until the bottom is brown and set. Slide out onto a dinner plate and invert into the pan. Or else place the frittata under a preheated broiler until the top is brown.

SPINACH-CHEESE FRITTATA

Eliminate the potatoes and leeks. Sauté *½ cup chopped spinach* and *½ onion, chopped,* in the butter and add *¼ cup freshly grated Parmesan cheese* to the egg mixture.

FRITTATA WITH CHEESE AND VEGETABLES ୧ଈ   (SERVES FOUR)

Makes a fine hot lunch or may be cut into wedges and served cold as a summer appetizer.

3 tablespoons olive oil	spinach, green beans,
2 cloves garlic, minced	eggplant, artichoke hearts,
1 small onion, chopped	tomatoes
6 eggs	½ cup freshly grated
3 tablespoons finely chopped	Parmesan cheese
parsley	½ teaspoon thyme, crumbled
¼ cup drained and diced	Salt to taste
cooked vegetables, a	¼ teaspoon freshly ground
combination of 2 or more:	pepper
zucchini, asparagus,	

Preheat the broiler. Heat the oil in a heavy skillet. Add the garlic and onion and cook until soft. Remove the skillet from the heat. In a bowl, mix the eggs with the remaining ingredients. Put the skillet back on very low heat. Pour in the egg mixture, stirring to incorporate the garlic and onions. Cover and cook 2–3 minutes, until the edges shrink a little. Slip under the broiler to brown lightly.

SAUSAGE AND PEPPER FRITTATA

Instead of using the ¾ cup cooked vegetables, sauté with the onion and garlic *½ green pepper, in ½-inch squares*, and *8 thin slices pepperoni sausage* in the oil before adding the eggs.

MUSHROOMS, HAM, AND RED (OR GREEN) PEPPER FRITTATA

Instead of using ¾ cup cooked vegetables, sauté with the onion and garlic *¼ pound small mushrooms (or large ones cut in quarters)*, about *⅓ cup diced ham*, and *½ red or green pepper, diced*.

QUICHES

About Quiches

A quiche is a custard cooked in a tart shell. Learning to make quiches is a very useful addition to your cooking knowledge because you can use so many different things in the custard filling to vary it. Follow this first basic recipe and improvise with your fillings. Try 1½ cups of cooked vegetables, or different cheeses, or slices of sausage or ham. For other ideas see fillings of Savory Tarts on p. 95.

CHEESE AND BACON QUICHE   (SERVES SIX)

10 slices bacon, fried crisp and crumbled	2 cups light cream
1 partially baked Tart Pastry (p. 897), without sugar	½ teaspoon salt
	⅛ teaspoon nutmeg
4 eggs	Pinch of cayenne pepper
	1¼ cups grated Swiss cheese

Preheat the oven to 425°F. Sprinkle the crumbled bacon over the bottom of the tart shell. Combine the eggs, cream, salt, nutmeg, and cayenne pepper in a bowl and beat to mix thoroughly. Sprinkle the cheese over the bacon and ladle the custard over all. Bake for 15 minutes at 425°F; then lower the heat to 350°F and bake for 30 minutes more, or until a knife inserted in the center comes out clean. Serve in wedges, hot or cold.

SPINACH QUICHE

Omit the bacon and use only ½ cup grated Swiss cheese. Add *1 cup cooked, chopped spinach, well drained,* and *2 tablespoons minced onion* sautéed in *1 tablespoon butter* to the custard mixture.

ONION QUICHE

Omit the bacon and add to the custard mixture *2 onions, thinly sliced* and sautéed in *3 tablespoons butter.*

EGGPLANT QUICHE WITH TOMATOES AND OLIVES ≥   (SERVES SIX)

This is a particularly tasty filling for a quiche.

1 small eggplant
2 tomatoes, peeled, seeded,
    chopped, and drained
½ cup chopped onion
¼ cup olive oil
1 clove garlic, minced
¼ cup sliced black olives
Salt
¼ teaspoon freshly ground
    pepper

½ teaspoon oregano,
    crumbled
4 eggs
1½ cups heavy cream
1 unbaked Tart Pastry (p.
    897), without sugar
½ cup freshly grated
    Parmesan cheese

Preheat the oven to 350°F. Put the eggplant on an oiled pie plate and bake in the oven for 45 minutes to 1 hour or until tender when pierced with a fork. Turn up the oven to 425°F. When the eggplant is cool enough to handle, peel it and coarsely chop the pulp. Put in a colander with the tomatoes, press once gently to drain, and let stand for 15 minutes. Heat skillet and sauté the onions in the oil slowly until soft; add the garlic, eggplant and tomatoes, sauté 2 minutes, then add the olives, salt, pepper, and oregano. Cook 2 minutes more. Remove from the heat. Put the eggplant mixture in the colander and drain 2–3 minutes. Beat the eggs and cream in a bowl until mixed. Spread the eggplant mixture over the bottom of the tart shell. Pour the egg mixture over the eggplant and sprinkle with the cheese. Bake for 15 minutes, lower the heat to 300°F, and bake for 30 minutes more, or until a knife inserted in the center comes out clean. Serve in wedges, hot or cold.

(SERVES FOUR)   ౼ **FLUFFY EGG NEST**

One golden yolk nestled in a tender nest of egg white. This is a cheerful supper dish.

4 eggs
½ teaspoon salt
4 slices toast

4 teaspoons butter
4 teaspoons heavy cream

NOTE
see page 471

Preheat the oven to 375°F. Separate the eggs and beat the whites with the salt until they are stiff but not dry. Put the toast on a cookie sheet. Mound a fourth of the whites on each piece of toast. Using the back of a teaspoon, make a dent or nest in the center of each mound. Put 1 teaspoon of butter and 1 egg yolk in each nest. Spoon 1 teaspoon of cream over each yolk. Bake for 10–12 minutes, or until the whites are golden and the yolk is slightly set.

CREAMED EGGS ❧ (SERVES FOUR)

8 hard-boiled eggs (p. 476)
3 cups Thick Cream Sauce (p. 380)
8 slices toast

Dusting of paprika
2 tablespoons minced parsley and chives or other fresh herbs (optional)

Chop the eggs into small dice. Stir them into the warm sauce and cook until very hot. Spoon over the toast and dust with paprika and/or fresh parsley and herbs.

CURRIED EGGS

Add *1 tablespoon curry powder* and, if you like, *½ cup peanuts* to the egg sauce. Serve with *chutney or raisins*. Omit the paprika and parsley.

GOLDENROD EGGS

Sieve and set aside the egg yolks. Chop and add only the whites to the sauce. To serve, spoon the sauce over toast and garnish with sieved yolks. Omit paprika and use parsley and herbs if you wish.

EGGS BENEDICT ❧ (SERVES ONE)

Multiply this recipe according to the number of persons being served, and encourage heartier appetites to have two.

⅓ cup Hollandaise Sauce (p. 388)
1 ⅜-inch-thick slice cooked ham, the size of the muffin, or 1 slice Canadian bacon

½ English muffin
Butter
1 egg

NOTE
see page 471

Prepare the hollandaise and keep it warm. Put the ham in a small skillet and heat thoroughly or fry the Canadian bacon. Spread the English muffin with butter, and toast under the broiler. Poach the egg (p. 476). To assemble, put the English muffin on a plate, place the ham or bacon on the muffin, carefully place the egg on the ham, and cover with hollandaise sauce.

(SERVES FOUR)   **EGGS BEATRICE**

Eggs Beatrice are a lighter and more delicate version of Eggs Benedict.
1 recipe Blender or Food Processor Hollandaise (p. 389)

    8 poached eggs   Butter
    8 thin slices ham
    8 slices thin-sliced white
        bread (dense, rather than
        airy bread)

NOTE
see page 471

Make hollandaise sauce as directed. Be sure to thin the sauce with a little hot water to the point where it flows readily from a spoon. Hollandaise that is too thick will coarsen the dish. Set aside while you are poaching the eggs. You may keep it warm over warm water or use it at room temperature. To assemble, put the ham in a small skillet, cover, and place over the lowest possible heat while you make the toast. Put a piece of lightly buttered toast on each warmed plate, cover with 2 slices of ham, then place 2 eggs on the ham. Spoon 3–4 tablespoons of hollandaise on top of each serving. Lightly butter the remaining 4 slices of toast, cut in half and serve on the side. Serve the remaining hollandaise sauce in a small bowl.

(SERVES FOUR)   ॐ **LUNCHEON CUSTARD**

Serve with a tomato or mushroom sauce to add distinction to this mild custard.

    4 eggs, slightly beaten   Pinch of cayenne pepper
    1 cup milk   1 tablespoon minced onion
    ½ teaspoon salt   1 cup Tomato Sauce (p. 387)
    ⅛ teaspoon freshly ground   or Mushroom Sauce (p.
        pepper   386)

Preheat the oven to 350°F. Butter four 1-cup molds or ramekins and place them in the oven in a shallow pan with 1 inch of hot water. Combine the eggs, milk, salt, pepper, cayenne pepper, and onion. Divide the mixture among the molds and bake 25–30 minutes until set. Serve with a sauce.

HUEVOS RANCHEROS ও   (SERVES FOUR)

There is nothing like tortillas with fried egg in the center, and a lively green sauce spooned over and grated cheese to finish the dish. Serve for a late breakfast or an early supper with lots of warm tortillas on the side.

1 recipe Salsa Verde (p. 388)	4 eggs
3 tablespoons vegetable oil	1 cup grated Monterey Jack
4 corn tortillas	cheese
2 tablespoons butter	Cilantro sprigs, for garnish

Warm the salsa in a small covered saucepan over medium-low heat for about 5 minutes. Heat the vegetable oil in a skillet over medium-high heat and quick-fry the tortillas one at a time, 3–4 seconds per side, just long enough to soften them. Drain on paper towels, wrap in foil, and keep warm in a low oven. Melt the butter in the skillet over moderate heat and fry the eggs (p. 476) until set, sunny side up. To assemble, place a tortilla on each of four warmed plates. Top each with a fried egg, then spoon some of the salsa over the tortilla and the white of the egg, leaving the yolk exposed. Sprinkle with the grated cheese and garnish with cilantro sprigs. Serve at once.

NOTE
see page 471

HAM TIMBALES   (SERVES FOUR)

A timbale is a cross between a custard and a soufflé, made in individual custard cups, or small molds, or even muffin tins; the timbales are then unmolded and served with a sauce. They may be made of almost any mixture of tasty cooked meat, poultry, fish and shellfish, or vegetables and cheese, so they provide a good way of transforming leftovers into a delicious luncheon dish.

4 tablespoons butter	2 tablespoons minced parsley
½ cup bread crumbs	4 eggs, slightly beaten
1¼ cups milk	Salt to taste
2 cups minced ham	Freshly ground pepper

Preheat the oven to 350°F. Lightly butter eight custard cups or muffin tins. Melt the 4 tablespoons of butter, add the bread crumbs and milk, and cook over medium-low heat 5 minutes, stirring constantly. Add the ham, parsley, and eggs. Season to taste with salt and pepper. Fill the cups—they should be about two-thirds full—and place them in a pan of hot water that comes about two-thirds of the way up the sides. Bake for 20 minutes. Remove and let stand 5 minutes, then unmold by slipping a knife around the inside of each cup and turning onto warm plates or a platter. Surround with *Mushroom Sauce* (p. 386) or *Curry Cream Sauce* (p. 380).

CHICKEN OR TURKEY TIMBALES

Use *2 cups minced cooked chicken* or *turkey* instead of ham and add *½ teaspoon dried* or *2 teaspoons fresh tarragon*. Serve with *Mushroom Sauce* (p. 386) or *Lemon Sauce* (p. 382).

FISH OR SHELLFISH TIMBALES

Use *2 cups minced cooked fish* or *shellfish* instead of ham and add *¼ teaspoon dried dill* or *1 teaspoon fresh chopped dill* and a few drops of *lemon juice*. Surround with *Seafood Velouté Sauce* (p. 381) or *Sauce Mousseline* (p. 389).

(SERVES FOUR)   ❧ **CHEESE SOUFFLÉ**

This is a light fragile soufflé that must be brought to the table as soon as it is ready. Soufflés can be made of many kinds of leftovers—ground meat or poultry that has a good flavor, a bit of fish, finely chopped vegetables that have intense color and taste. Follow the proportions for the Spinach Soufflé variation.

1 cup plus 2 tablespoons grated Cheddar cheese	½ teaspoon salt
4 tablespoons butter	Pinch of cayenne pepper
¼ cup flour	4 egg yolks, slightly beaten
1 cup hot milk	5 egg whites

Preheat the oven to 375°F. Butter a 1½-quart straight-sided soufflé dish and sprinkle 2 tablespoons of the cheese over the bottom and around the sides. Melt the butter in a saucepan, add the flour, and cook gently 2–3 minutes, stirring constantly. Add the milk and continue to cook over low heat 2–3 minutes, stirring, until thick and smooth. Add the salt, cayenne pepper, and the rest of the cheese, blending in the cheese thoroughly; the sauce should be very thick. Beat 3 table-

NOTE
see page 471

spoons of the hot cheese mixture into the egg yolks and then return to the saucepan, stirring 1 minute over low heat. Remove and pour into a large bowl. Beat the egg whites until they are stiff but not dry. Stir a fourth of the whites into the cheese sauce, then fold in the remaining whites. Spoon into the soufflé dish. Bake on the middle rack of the oven for 35 minutes. Serve immediately.

HERB SOUFFLÉ

Omit the cheese and add *1½ tablespoons minced onion, 1 teaspoon basil, crumbled, 1 teaspoon tarragon, crumbled,* and *1 tablespoon minced parsley* to the cream sauce base.

SPINACH SOUFFLÉ

Instead of the 1 cup Cheddar cheese, use *¾ cup well-drained, finely chopped cooked spinach* and *⅓ cup grated Swiss cheese.*

STURDY SOUFFLÉ   ≈   (SERVES THREE OR FOUR)

This light but dense soufflé comes from the oven nicely rounded and shiny. Although it will fall in about 10 minutes, it will not really flatten, unlike the preceding cloudlike soufflé made of separated eggs. Serve hot or at room temperature, and try making it in a colorful ovenproof bowl or casserole instead of a classic soufflé dish.

4 tablespoons butter	Pinch of cayenne pepper
¼ cup flour	½ cup grated Parmesan cheese
1 cup hot milk	4 eggs, well beaten
Pinch of salt	

Preheat the oven to 375°F. Butter a 3-cup or 1-quart ovenproof bowl or baking dish. Place it in the oven in a pan containing 1 inch of hot water. Melt the butter in a saucepan. Stir in the flour and blend until smooth. Cook over low heat for 2–3 minutes. Slowly add the milk and cook, stirring constantly, for 3 minutes, until smooth and thick. Add the salt, cayenne pepper, and cheese. Stir until the cheese is melted and blended into the sauce. Remove from the heat. Beat 3 tablespoons of sauce into the eggs, then return the egg-sauce mixture to the saucepan and beat until smooth. Pour into the baking dish and bake for about 20 minutes, until set.

(SERVES TWO)   ❧ **EGGS À LA SUISSE**

A simple dish to make if you keep the heat very low.

1 tablespoon butter	Pinch of cayenne pepper
4 eggs	2 tablespoons freshly grated
½ cup heavy cream	Gruyère or Swiss cheese
Salt	2 slices toast, buttered

NOTE
see page 471

Melt the butter in a skillet. Break eggs carefully into a bowl. Add the cream to the skillet and gently pour in the eggs. Sprinkle with salt and cayenne pepper. Cook over very low heat, basting with the cream, until the whites are almost firm. Sprinkle the cheese evenly over the top. Place 2 eggs and a spoonful of cream on each piece of buttered toast.

(SERVES THREE OR FOUR)   ❧ **BAKED EGGS IN MORNAY SAUCE**

A good Sunday supper: eggs nestling in a cheese-flavored cream sauce. Spoon each egg with some sauce over toast or English muffins.

2 recipes Mornay Sauce	6 eggs
(p. 380)	

Preheat the oven to 375°F. Butter a shallow gratin dish or baking dish large enough to hold the eggs and the sauce. When the sauce is very hot, pour it into the dish. Break the eggs, one by one, into a saucer, and drop each one gently at evenly spaced intervals over the sauce. Butter a piece of wax paper, cover the baking dish, and bake for 6–7 minutes, just long enough to set the whites and slightly set the yolks. The yolks should remain runny.

NOTE
see page 471

CHEESE

About Cheese

There is no part of the Western world where cheese is not made, whether it be a subtle, well-ripened Brie, the comfortable American cheese we use for toasted cheese sandwiches, or the country Cheddar that makes such a natural partner to autumn's first crisp McIntosh apples.

Cheese, like wine, varies from one season to another and from one location to another. It is highly nutritious, and a good substitute for meat. It developed as a method of preserving surplus milk, and thus is made where there are milk-producing herds, in such places as Switzerland and the American Midwest among others. The milk may be sweet or sour, whole, skim, or mixed with additional cream; it may come from cows, goats, or ewes, or even, in the case of old-fashioned mozzarella and provolone, from water buffaloes.

Kinds of Cheese

Natural Cheese. Natural cheese is made when milk is separated into a firm curd and liquid whey by the action of gentle heat or lactic acid. The whey is drained off, the curd is cut into cubes, and cream is added. We call this simplest natural cheese "fresh" or "unripened," by which we mean that it is unfermented. To this category belong cottage, pot cheese, and farmer cheese, whose names describe their rustic origins; every farmwife used to make her own cottage cheese from milk that otherwise would have gone bad. Some other fresh cheeses are ricotta, feta, fresh cream cheese, and Neufchâtel. They are all quite perishable and, unlike other cheeses, should be served straight from the refrigerator.

Ripened Cheese. Ripened natural cheese is made when the curds are fermented through the action of rennet or various bacteria cultures. The amount of liquid whey left with the curd determines whether the cheese is soft, like Brie and Camembert; semifirm, like Muenster, Cheddar, and Gruyère; or hard, like Parmesan and Romano. The blue cheeses—Roquefort, Stilton, and Danish blue—are considered semifirm. It is not only the amount of whey in the cheese that accounts for the differences in type, however, but rather such mysterious factors as the quality of the milk, the length of the aging process, the humidity and temperature of the place where the cheese is ripened, and the differences in molds from one cave or cellar to another.

Processed Cheese. American technology has tried to standardize the quality of cheese and improve its longevity. The result has been a variety of long-keeping processed cheeses and cheese foods available in American markets.

Processed cheese is natural cheese that has been ground up, pasteurized, reblended, and packaged. Cheese food is a blend of various ground cheeses with whey solids, whey albumins, seasonings, color, and water. Cheese spreads are made by adding gums, fat, and liquid to processed cheese. Processed cheese is lower in butterfat and, therefore, in calories, than natural cheese. It has less food value than natural cheese, however, and lacks its interesting texture and fine flavor.

1. Cheddar; 2. Swiss; 3. Jarlsberg; 4. Edam; 5. Stilton; 6. Roquefort; 7. Parmesan; 8. Romano; 9. Provolone; 10. Liederkranz; 11. Brick; 12. Fontina; 13. Port Salut; 14. Chèvres (goat cheese); 15. Feta (in brine); 16. Brie; 17. Camembert; 18. Boursin.

Buying Cheese

Most supermarkets offer a good variety of cheeses, and local delicatessens carry a large assortment of regional and international varieties. Specialized cheese shops are great fun to explore, and most
owners are happy to let you sample before you buy. The more you
taste good cheeses, the more you will want to serve them and be confi-
dent about your selections. Don't get stuck in the Cheddar rut.

Storing Cheese

The softer a cheese is, the more perishable it will be. Still, even soft
cheese should always be removed from the refrigerator one-half to one
hour (depending on the temperature of your kitchen) before serving to
develop flavor and the proper consistency; then carefully wrap again
in plastic right after using and refrigerate. Only cottage cheese should
be served chilled. Semisoft and medium-firm cheeses should also be
kept in the refrigerator, wrapped tightly in plastic wrap to seal out the
air, and brought to room temperature before serving. Incidentally, if a
cheese develops a little mold on the outside, that doesn't mean it is
spoiled; just scrape the mold away. Very hard cheeses actually need no
refrigeration at all—think of the waxy balls of provolone that hang
from the ceilings of Italian delicatessens—but they should be well
wrapped or kept under a bell in a relatively cool place. Hard and semi-
hard cheeses freeze well; soft cheeses are apt to break down in texture.

Grating Cheese

Try always to grate your own cheese. It will taste so much better and is
more economical. A standard four-sided grater or a small cylindrical
one with a handle works best. You can also use a blender or food
processor if your cheese is not too hard. Softer cheeses such as Cheddar will be easier to grate when ice cold. Hard cheeses like Parmesan,
however, grate more easily at room temperature. Keep a piece of imported Parmesan and another of sharp Cheddar for just this purpose;
well wrapped in the refrigerator they will keep a long time.

Cooking Cheese

Use natural cheeses for cooking and never overheat them, lest they become tough and stringy. Try substituting one cheese for another in recipes: although the taste of the finished dish will be altered, it may be
improved.

Serving Cheese

Serve cheese for breakfast, lunch, or dinner or as a snack any time of day. Mild soft cheeses are suitable for breakfast, served on toast with fruit jams. Most any variety of cheese is welcome for lunch or afternoon snacking with crackers. Cheese may be served before dinner or during the evening with drinks, passed with the salad, or served after as a separate course with or without fruit. In arranging a cheese board, choose varieties that will contrast in flavor and texture with one another. Try buttery Camembert, rich blue-veined Stilton, and sharp Vermont Cheddar, or combine tangy chèvres (French goat cheese), stolid Edam, and pungent Limburger or Liederkranz. And don't forget about bringing the cheeses to room temperature. Pass a basket of plain crackers or some French bread with your cheese platter.

(SERVES SIX)   ₴→ **CHEESE TOAST**

Like a serving of cheese soufflé on toast, these puffs are nice with a cup of soup; they must be eaten as soon as they are prepared.

2 tablespoons butter	Salt
1 tablespoon flour	2 egg yolks, slightly beaten
⅛ teaspoon cayenne pepper	2 egg whites, stiffly beaten
1 cup hot milk	but not dry
¾ cup grated Cheddar cheese	6 slices toast

Melt the butter in a saucepan. Blend in the flour and cayenne pepper, and cook for 2–3 minutes, stirring. Slowly add the milk, stirring constantly until smooth and thickened. Stir in the cheese and cook until it is melted. Add salt to taste. Beat 2 tablespoonfuls of hot cheese mixture into the yolks. Return the yolk-cheese mixture to the saucepan and cook over medium heat, stirring constantly, for 1–2 minutes, until thickened. Remove from the heat, gently fold in the egg whites, and mound on toast.

(SERVES FOUR)   ₴→ **WELSH RABBIT**

Known as both rabbit and rarebit in Wales and Scotland, this melted cheese dish should always be cooked gently or the cheese will seize.

½ pound sharp Cheddar	1 egg, slightly beaten
cheese, in small dice	Salt
1 tablespoon butter	½ cup beer
½ teaspoon dry mustard	4 slices toast
Cayenne pepper to taste	

Combine the cheese, butter, mustard, and cayenne pepper in a heavy-bottomed pan, a chafing dish, or the top of a double boiler. Cook over low heat, stirring constantly, until the cheese has melted. Beat a little of the hot cheese mixture into the egg, and then return the egg-cheese mixture to the pan. Add salt to taste. Add the beer and cook 1–2 minutes more, until very hot but not boiling. Spoon over toast.

MILD RABBIT

Substitute ½ *cup milk* for the beer.

TOMATO RAREBIT ❧   (SERVES SIX)

2 tablespoons butter	2 cups grated Cheddar cheese
2 tablespoons flour	2 eggs, slightly beaten
1 cup light cream, heated	1 teaspoon dry mustard
½ cup finely chopped canned or fresh tomatoes	Cayenne pepper to taste
	Salt
⅛ teaspoon baking soda	6 slices toast

Melt the butter in a saucepan. Stir in the flour and cook for 2–3 minutes, stirring. Slowly pour in the cream, and cook and stir until the mixture thickens. Add the tomatoes mixed with baking soda, cheese, eggs, mustard, and cayenne pepper. Cook over gentle heat, stirring, until the cheese melts. Salt to taste. Do not boil. Spoon over toast.

CHILALY ❧   (SERVES FOUR)

1 tablespoon butter	¼ teaspoon salt
2 tablespoons finely chopped green pepper	⅛ teaspoon cayenne pepper
2 tablespoons finely chopped onion	1½ cups grated Monterey Jack or Cheddar cheese
½ cup finely chopped tomato pulp	2 tablespoons milk
	1 egg, slightly beaten
	4 pieces toast

Melt the butter in a skillet. Add the green pepper and onion and cook, stirring, until soft. Add the tomatoes and stir over low heat for 5 minutes. Add the salt, cayenne pepper, and cheese and cook, stirring constantly, until the cheese melts. Briskly stir in the milk mixed with the egg, cook 1 minute more, and spoon over toast.

(SERVES FOUR) &ev **SWISS FONDUE**

Make the fondue in a chafing dish, a special fondue dish, or in a heavy earthenware casserole placed over very low heat on an asbestos mat. Then sit around and dunk. If it thickens too much as it cools, thin it with a little more warm wine.

1 clove garlic	¼ teaspoon freshly ground
1 cup dry white wine	pepper
1 pound Swiss cheese, grated	3 tablespoons kirsch
or diced small (about 2½	Salt to taste
cups)	1 loaf French bread, in 1-inch
¼ teaspoon nutmeg	cubes

Vigorously rub the inside of the casserole with the garlic clove. Pour the wine into the casserole and heat until it barely simmers. Over low heat, add the cheese a little at a time, stirring with a wooden spoon until it is melted. Stir in the nutmeg, pepper, kirsch, and salt. Give guests long-handled forks, and let them spear cubes of bread to dunk into the creamy fondue.

(SERVES FOUR) &ev **CHEESE-BREAD PUDDING**

5 slices bread, without crusts	1 teaspoon Worcestershire
1½ cups milk	sauce
1 cup grated Cheddar cheese	Salt to taste
3 eggs, slightly beaten	

Preheat the oven to 300°F. Butter a 1-quart casserole. Cut the bread into 1-inch squares. Scald the milk, cool slightly, and beat in the cheese, eggs, Worcestershire sauce, and salt. Pour into the casserole, add the bread squares, and bake 40–50 minutes, or until firm.

(SERVES FOUR) &ev **HOT CHEESE SAVORY**

Two kinds of cheese make the rich flavor of this custard. It puffs up like a soufflé, so serve immediately.

2 eggs, slightly beaten	¼ teaspoon freshly ground
⅔ cup heavy cream	pepper
½ cup finely diced Swiss	Pinch of cayenne pepper
cheese	½ teaspoon salt
½ cup freshly grated	1 teaspoon finely chopped
Parmesan cheese	chives

Preheat the oven to 450°F. Combine all ingredients. Beat well and pour into four ramekins. Bake 15 minutes.

NEW ENGLAND CHEDDAR PIE ?~   (SERVES SIX)

1½ cups grated sharp
   Cheddar cheese
1 recipe Basic Pastry for 9-
   inch pie shell (p. 895)
4 eggs
2 cups heavy cream

2 hearty shakes of the
   Tabasco bottle
Salt to taste
½ cup coarsely chopped
   walnuts (optional)

Preheat the oven to 425°F. Sprinkle the cheese evenly over the bottom of the pie shell. In a bowl, beat the eggs and stir in the cream and Tabasco. Pour over the cheese in the pie shell. Taste and add salt as needed. Bake for 15 minutes, lower the heat to 300°F, and bake 25–30 minutes more, or until a knife inserted in the center comes out clean. Remove from the oven, sprinkle with chopped walnuts, if desired, and let stand for 5 minutes to make it easier to cut and serve.

SOME VEGETARIAN DISHES

Most of us are eating less meat and a greater variety of vegetables and bean and grain dishes. We also find that we have friends and family who are complete vegetarians and we don't always know where to look to find new and interesting dishes to satisfy them. This chapter was born out of that need. I find myself cooking dishes (in this chapter) like the Chili Cheese Supper Dish, Mexican Hot Pot Soup, White Cheese Tart, Capellini with Salsa Cruda (fresh tomato sauce), and Winter Vegetable Cobbler more and more often, and I think you will too, when you've tried them. In addition, you'll find many other meatless dishes throughout the book, and they have been marked with the symbol below. However, there are many other recipes in this book that could be turned into vegetarian recipes simply by substituting vegetable broth (p. 504) for chicken, beef, or fish stock or broth when one of those is called for.   ð❧

(ABOUT ¾ CUP)   **BASIL CHEESE SAUCE**

This sauce is good as a dipping sauce for fresh vegetables.

1 cup lightly packed basil leaves	1 ounce Gorgonzola or other blue cheese
1 teaspoon minced garlic	Salt to taste
¾ cup regular or low-fat cottage cheese, or ricotta	

Wash, dry, and stem basil leaves. Place the basil, garlic, cottage cheese or ricotta, and Gorgonzola in a food processor or blender and process until mixture is completely blended. Taste and add salt as necessary. Refrigerate in a covered container until used; it will keep only 2 days.

BAKED ITALIAN EGGPLANT (SERVES FOUR TO SIX)

Good Italian flavors. Can be a hot supper dish or cold picnic fare.

1 large eggplant, in ½-inch slices
2 tablespoons vegetable oil
2 or 3 tomatoes, sliced
Salt and freshly ground pepper to taste

1 teaspoon basil, crumbled
1 teaspoon oregano, crumbled
6 ounces Fontina cheese, sliced thin
2 tablespoons chopped parsley, for garnish

Preheat the oven to 400°F. Brush the eggplant slices on both sides with the vegetable oil and place in a single layer on a baking sheet. Bake for 15 minutes. Remove from the oven and lay one or two slices of tomato on top of each eggplant slice. Sprinkle each with salt and pepper and the crushed basil and oregano. Top each with some of the thinly sliced Fontina cheese. Return to the oven and bake for another 10 minutes, or until the cheese has melted and the vegetables have heated through. Sprinkle each with some chopped parsley if desired. Serve at once.

SAUTÉED MUSHROOMS ON POLENTA OR BUTTERED TOAST ✳ (SERVES FOUR)

The flavor of our supermarket mushrooms can certainly compete with the fancy varieties, especially when done this way.

6 tablespoons butter
⅓ cup sliced or chopped shallots, or scallions
1½ pounds mushrooms, cleaned, trimmed, and sliced thin

Salt and freshly ground pepper to taste
1 recipe Basic Polenta (p. 432) or 4 slices buttered toast
2 tablespoons minced parsley

Melt 4 tablespoons butter in a large skillet over medium-high heat. Add the shallots and mushrooms and cook, tossing frequently, for 5–8 minutes, until the mushrooms just begin to brown and most of the moisture has evaporated. Add the remaining 2 tablespoons butter and stir until melted. Add salt and pepper. Remove from the heat. Spoon over hot polenta or toast and sprinkle with the parsley. Serve at once.

(20 PIECES) **MUSHROOMS IN TOAST**

These plain ingredients turn rather fancy when done in this way. Best of all, this tastes great as a lunch or supper dish.

¼ pound mushrooms
4 tablespoons butter
1½ tablespoons flour
Salt to taste

⅓ cup milk
1 tablespoon lemon juice
10 slices very fresh white
  bread

Preheat the oven to 400°F. Wash, dry, trim, and finely chop the mushrooms by hand or in a food processor. Heat 2 tablespoons of the butter in a sauté pan and cook the mushrooms over a medium-high heat for about 5 minutes. Add the flour and salt, and stir to blend. Stir in the milk and cook until the mixture thickens. Stir in the lemon juice and remove from the heat and let cool. Remove the crusts from the bread. Flatten each slice with a rolling pin. Spread some of the cooled mushroom mixture on each slice of bread and roll up. Place, seam down, on a baking sheet. Melt the remaining 2 tablespoons of butter. Brush each roll with the melted butter and bake for about 12–15 minutes, until the rolls are golden. Cut each roll in half and serve warm.

(SERVES SIX) **ZUCCHINI PANCAKES**

Creamy on the inside and golden brown on the outside.

1 pound zucchini, washed,
  trimmed, and coarsely
  grated
3 teaspoons minced parsley
½ cup grated Monterey Jack
  or Cheddar cheese
¼ cup flour
Salt and freshly ground
  pepper to taste

2 eggs, slightly beaten
4 tablespoons butter or
  vegetable oil
½ cup freshly grated
  Parmesan cheese
  (optional)

In a large bowl, stir together the zucchini, parsley, cheese, flour, and salt and pepper. Mix in the beaten eggs. Heat the butter or oil in a large skillet over medium-high heat. Drop spoonfuls of the zucchini mixture into the skillet and cook until golden brown. Turn the pancakes over and brown on the other side. Serve at once sprinkled, if you like, with the Parmesan cheese.

VEGETABLE BROTH   (ABOUT 8 CUPS)

The kinds of vegetables used may vary according to what you have available; amounts given are somewhat flexible. What you need are good, fresh, flavorful vegetables for a good and flavorful broth. Use in place of chicken broth as the base for many soups.

2 tablespoons vegetable oil	1 large tomato, seeded and
2 onions, chopped	chopped
1 large potato, peeled and	1 cup diced eggplant
diced	(optional)
3 large carrots, peeled and	8 cups water
sliced	8 sprigs parsley
2 stalks celery, diced	½ bay leaf
1 turnip, peeled and diced	½ teaspoon dried thyme, or to
1 cup sliced green beans or	taste
zucchini	1 teaspoon salt, or to taste

Heat the oil in a large soup pot. Add the onions and cook over medium heat for about 5 minutes, until they are lightly browned. Add the potato, carrots, celery, turnip, green beans or zucchini, tomato, and optional eggplant. Cook the vegetables, stirring occasionally, for about 15 minutes. Add the water, parsley, bay leaf, thyme, and salt, and simmer for 45–50 minutes. Taste the broth for seasonings. Pour the broth and vegetables through a strainer into a large bowl or container, pressing the vegetables with the back of a spoon to extract all the juices. Cool and refrigerate until used.

FARM CHEESE VEGETABLE SOUP   (SERVES SIX)

A true meal in one. Bread and cheese go on top of the soup.

3 tablespoons butter	1 zucchini, trimmed, halved,
1 cup finely chopped onion	and sliced
2 medium-size carrots, peeled	2 cups shredded cabbage
and diced	¼ cup finely chopped red
3 stalks celery, sliced thin	pepper
2 medium-size boiling	¼ cup minced parsley
potatoes, washed and	Salt and freshly ground
diced	pepper to taste
2 cups small cauliflower	6 slices dense white bread,
flowerets	toasted
1½ quarts Vegetable Broth	3 tablespoons butter
(preceding recipe) or	(optional)
water	⅓ pound Gouda cheese, sliced
	thin

In a heavy-bottomed 3-quart saucepan or soup pot, melt the butter over moderate heat. Add the onion, carrots, and celery, and cook for 5–8 minutes, until the onion is soft. Add the potatoes, cauliflower, and broth or water, and simmer for about 15 minutes. Add the zucchini, cabbage, red pepper, parsley, and salt and pepper and simmer another 5 minutes, or until all the vegetables are tender. Trim the corners of the toast to fit six ovenproof soup bowls. Spread the toast pieces with the 3 tablespoons butter if you wish. Lay the cheese slices evenly over each of the six slices of toast so that the cheese extends to the outer edges. Ladle the soup into the bowls and top each with a slice of the toast and cheese. Place the bowls on a cookie sheet or baking pan and put under the broiler for 2–3 minutes, until the cheese has melted and started to brown.

(SERVES FOUR)   ✳   **MEXICAN HOT POT SOUP**

This is a great way to get your soup and salad in one bowl.

2 tablespoons vegetable or olive oil	1½ cups water
1 large onion, chopped	1 teaspoon salt
2 cloves garlic, peeled and minced	½ teaspoon cumin
1 pound tomatoes, peeled and chopped, or 15–16-ounce can tomatoes	½ teaspoon hot chili flakes or chili powder (optional)
	2 cups corn kernels
1½ cups cooked red kidney beans	2 cups finely shredded iceberg lettuce
1½ cups cooked chickpeas or garbanzo beans	2 tablespoons chopped cilantro (Chinese parsley, fresh coriander)

In a large soup pot or kettle, heat the oil and add the onion and garlic. Cook over medium heat until the onion is soft. Add the tomatoes and their juice, the kidney beans, chickpeas, water, salt, cumin, and chili, if using, and stir to blend. Cover and simmer for about 30 minutes. Let cool, then purée in batches in a food processor or put through a food mill or sieve. Return the soup to the pot, add the corn, and reheat. Add more water if the soup is too thick. Serve hot in large warmed soup bowls garnished with the shredded lettuce and cilantro.

MUSTARD GREEN SOUP

(SERVES FOUR)

Creamy beans and bitter greens complement each other. Serve with sliced tomatoes, bread, and Fontina cheese.

¼ cup olive oil
1 tablespoon finely chopped garlic (approximately 3 cloves)
1 cup chopped leeks (or onion)
2 cups cooked, diced turnip

2 cups cooked navy beans
½ pound mustard greens (or any bitter greens)
6 cups Vegetable Broth (p. 504)
Salt and freshly ground pepper to taste

Heat the olive oil in a soup kettle or pot. Add the garlic and leeks and cook over medium-low heat, stirring often, until the garlic and leeks are softened, but not browned. Stir in the turnip, beans, greens, and broth. Simmer, adding salt and pepper, for about 15 minutes. Serve hot.

BEET AND CELERY ROOT SALAD   (SERVES FOUR TO SIX)

This makes a wonderful-looking, flavorful dish, composed on a handsome platter.

4 hard-boiled eggs, 2 with yolk and white separated
¼ cup olive oil
4 anchovy fillets, minced
2 tablespoons Dijon mustard
2 teaspoons soy sauce
1 teaspoon minced sour or dill pickles
Salt and freshly ground pepper to taste
3 tablespoons red wine vinegar

12 leaves butter lettuce
12 leaves red oak leaf or bronze lettuce
2 cups quartered, cooked beets
6 small red potatoes, cooked and sliced
1 celery root, peeled, cooked until just tender, and diced
6 stalks celery, sliced
Celery leaves, for garnish

Make the dressing ahead and refrigerate: Put the yolks from 2 of the eggs and the olive oil in a bowl and blend into a paste. Add the anchovies, mustard, soy sauce, pickles, 2 chopped egg whites, salt and pepper, and vinegar, and mix well. On a large serving platter or individual salad plates arrange a bed of mixed lettuce leaves. Place the beets, potatoes, and celery root in separate groups on the platter or plates. Scatter the sliced celery over the tops of all. Put the remaining 2 eggs through a sieve. Just before serving, spoon the dressing evenly over the vegetables and garnish with the sieved hard-boiled eggs and celery leaves.

SPINACH SALAD WITH
(SERVES FOUR) ✱ **CHUTNEY DRESSING**

This is a sensational salad that I have made many times. Don't change a thing.

⅔ cup vegetable oil
6 tablespoons spicy chutney, homemade or prepared (mango-ginger is best)
1 teaspoon curry powder
1 teaspoon dry mustard
½ teaspoon salt
3 tablespoons lemon juice

2 large bunches spinach, washed, dried, and stems removed
1 large Red Delicious apple, cored
1 cup pecans, toasted
½ cup Muscat raisins
6 scallions, sliced

Make dressing ahead and refrigerate until used; in a bowl, whisk together the oil, chutney, curry powder, dry mustard, salt, and lemon juice until well blended. Tear spinach into bite-size pieces and chill until salad is assembled. Just before serving, thinly slice the apple and place the slices in a large salad bowl with the spinach, pecans, raisins, and scallions. Pour enough of the dressing over the salad, tossing gently, to coat the greens well. Serve at once.

(SERVES SIX) **YAM AND POTATO SALAD**

Yams are more than just a Thanksgiving side dish. This salad proves it.

4 white boiling potatoes, peeled and halved lengthwise
4 yams, peeled and halved lengthwise
1 bunch scallions, sliced
⅓ cup mayonnaise

½ cup sour cream
3 tablespoons lemon juice
2 tablespoons chopped parsley
Salt and freshly ground pepper to taste

Boil the potatoes and yams until just tender when pierced with a fork. Drain, and place in cold water to cool. Drain again, then cut into dice. Place the potatoes and yams in a large bowl and toss with the scallions, mayonnaise, sour cream, lemon juice, parsley, and salt and pepper. If the mixture seems a little dry, add more mayonnaise or sour cream. Refrigerate until served.

BREAD SALAD ✳ (SERVES SIX)

This wonderful Tuscan salad was kept a secret too long. I have loved it from my first bite.

5 ripe (and juicy) tomatoes, peeled (about 3 cups)
2 large cloves garlic, peeled
1 teaspoon salt, or to taste
2 teaspoons balsamic vinegar
3 tablespoons olive oil

3 cups torn French bread, crust removed
1 bunch Italian flat-leaved parsley, washed and trimmed

Put the tomatoes in a large bowl and mash into a coarse purée (I use my hands to squish them). Put the garlic cloves through a garlic press and mix with the tomatoes. Add the salt, vinegar, and olive oil, and mix well. Taste and correct seasonings. Tear the bread into irregular chunks of about 1½ inches. Add the bread to the tomato mixture and mix the tomato purée and juices with the bread until the bread has absorbed lots of the mixture. Tear the parsley into sprigs. Serve each portion of salad with a handful of the parsley.

VEGETABLE BARLEY SALAD (SERVES SIX)

This is bright with taste and color and holds up well for a picnic or barbecue. The vegetables can vary, but stick to the ones with crunch that are good raw.

½ cup pearl barley (about 2 cups cooked)
6 cups salted water
1 recipe Tomato Vinaigrette (on facing page)
1 red, green, or yellow pepper, diced
1 bunch radishes, diced
1 small red onion, chopped fine

1 cup diced celery
1 cup diced carrot, zucchini, or fennel (optional)
¼ cup chopped fresh cilantro or parsley
Salt and freshly ground pepper
6 small iceberg or butter lettuce leaves

Cook the barley in the water for about 40–50 minutes. While the barley is cooking gently, make the Tomato Vinaigrette. Drain barley in a colander and transfer to a large bowl. Add the vinaigrette and toss to mix well. Add the diced pepper, radishes, onion, celery, and other vegetable, if used, and stir to coat. Add the cilantro or parsley and season to taste with salt and pepper. Serve chilled or at room temperature spooned into lettuce-leaf cups.

(ABOUT 1¼ CUPS)   **TOMATO VINAIGRETTE**

1 clove garlic
1 cup seeded tomato, in
   chunks
½ cup olive oil
2 tablespoons white wine
   vinegar

1 teaspoon salt
1 teaspoon cumin
¼ teaspoon freshly ground
   black pepper
⅛ teaspoon cayenne pepper

Place the garlic and tomato in a food processor or blender and process until puréed. Add the olive oil, vinegar, salt, cumin, black pepper, and cayenne, and process until well blended. If made ahead, store in the refrigerator.

BAKED ITALIAN CUSTARD
(4 SANDWICHES)   ✳   **AND CHEESE SANDWICH**

This is a dish to get excited about. Golden custard becomes puffy and light with good flavor mingling.

Custard

6 eggs, beaten
1½ cups milk
½ teaspoon salt
½ teaspoon freshly ground
   pepper

2 tablespoons grated
   Parmesan cheese

Sandwich

3 tablespoons butter
Eight ½-inch-thick slices white
   bread, crusts removed

2 cups grated Fontina cheese

In a large bowl mix the eggs, milk, salt, pepper, and Parmesan cheese until well blended. Set aside. Butter well an 8-inch square baking dish with 1 tablespoon of the butter. Preheat oven to 350°F. Place four of the bread slices in the bottom of the baking dish. Sprinkle the Fontina cheese evenly over the bread. Place the remaining slices of bread on top. Pour the custard batter over the sandwiches. Cover with wax paper or plastic wrap and let stand for at least 15 minutes. Bake uncovered for about 25–30 minutes. Remove from oven and keep warm. Melt 2 tablespoons of butter in a large skillet over medium-high heat, remove the sandwiches from the baking dish with a spatula, and place in the pan. Cook on each side until golden brown. Cut in half and serve hot.

WHITE CHEESE TART (SERVES EIGHT)

The earthy taste of goat cheese in this creamy filling makes it an ideal companion to fresh fruit or crisp green salad. A good breakfast dish with your favorite jam or preserve.

5 ounces goat cheese (chèvres)	½ teaspoon salt, or to taste
1 pound cream cheese	1 prebaked tart shell (9½ inches in diameter and 2 inches deep)
4 eggs	
1 cup sour cream	

Preheat the oven to 350°F. In the bowl of a food processor, blend the goat cheese and cream cheese until well mixed. Add the eggs and process until well mixed. Add the sour cream and salt and process only until just mixed. Pour into a prebaked tart shell and bake for 25–30 minutes, until lightly browned and just set in the center (when a knife inserted in the center comes out clean). Cool about 15 minutes before cutting. Serve warm or cool.

GREEN CHILI PIE (ONE 9-INCH PIE)

This was a winner years ago in a savory pie contest in Los Angeles, California. I still make it.

6 or 7 fresh California or Anaheim chilies, roasted, peeled, split, and seeded (p. 589), or 10 ounces canned roasted whole green chilies	4 eggs
	2 cups light cream, or 1½ cups milk
	½ teaspoon salt
	Freshly ground pepper to taste
1¼ cups grated Fontina or any soft white milk cheese	Cilantro, for garnish

Preheat the oven to 425°F. Butter the bottom of a 9-inch pie pan. Line the pie pan with the split chilies so they cover the bottom and sides of the pan. Sprinkle the cheese evenly over the chilies. In a mixing bowl, beat the eggs until they are blended. Add the cream or milk, salt, and pepper, and mix well. Pour the custard over the cheese. Bake for 15 minutes, then lower the heat to 325°F. Bake for 20–30 minutes more, or until the custard is set. If the center trembles a bit, remove it from the oven, as the custard will continue to cook a little. Don't overcook. A knife inserted halfway from the center should come out clean when the pie is done. Garnish the top with lots of cilantro. Serve hot or cold.

(SERVES SIX) ❋ **WINTER VEGETABLE COBBLER**

This will win any contest. It is as wonderful as the family's favorite stew.

1 turnip, peeled and in bite-size wedges
1 potato (russet or baking), peeled and diced
1 celery root, peeled and diced (about 1½ cups)
1 onion, coarsely chopped
3 carrots, peeled and sliced

½ cup chopped parsley
1 cup Vegetable Broth (p. 504), chilled
2 tablespoons cornstarch
1 teaspoon salt
Freshly ground pepper
4 tablespoons butter

Cobbler Dough

1¾ cups flour
1 tablespoon baking powder
½ teaspoon salt

6 tablespoons butter, chilled and in small pieces
¾ cup cream

Put the turnip, potato, celery root, onion, carrots, and parsley in a 2-inch-deep 8-cup ovenproof baking dish. (You should have about 6 cups of vegetables.) In a small mixing bowl, blend the broth with the cornstarch, pour over the vegetables, and mix well. Add salt and pepper to taste, and mix to blend. Dot the top of the vegetables with the butter. Preheat the oven to 350°F. Make the cobbler dough: Mix flour, baking powder, and salt in a large mixing bowl and stir with a fork to blend. Drop the pieces of chilled butter into the flour mixture and rub quickly with your fingertips until the mixture resembles coarse crumbs. Using a fork, slowly stir in the cream, until roughly mixed. Gather the dough into a shaggy mass and knead five or six times. Roll the dough on a lightly floured board to the size of the top of the baking dish. The dough should be about ¼ inch thick. Place the dough on top of the vegetables. Bake for 45–55 minutes, until vegetables are cooked through and crust is browned. Test vegetables for doneness with a knife tip or skewer.

CHILI CHEESE SUPPER DISH (SERVES SIX)

Moist and golden, this is filled with cheese and chilies—mild but very flavorful. And a big plus—it is easy to make.

6 eggs, beaten
1 cup milk
1 teaspoon salt
1 pound Monterey Jack cheese, grated
1 cup (8 ounces) cottage cheese

3 ounces cream cheese, in small cubes
4 tablespoons butter, melted
1½ teaspoons baking powder
½ cup cornmeal
8-ounce can green chilies, chopped

Preheat the oven to 350°F. Grease a 9-inch square baking dish. In a large mixing bowl combine the eggs, milk, salt, Jack cheese, cottage cheese, cream cheese, butter, baking powder, cornmeal, and green chilies, and mix until well blended. Pour into the prepared pan and bake for about 40 minutes, until the center is set. Serve hot or warm.

BAKED VEGETABLES WITH CHEESE (SERVES FOUR TO SIX)

This recipe is simple to do with the aid of a food processor. Nourishing ingredients are brought together in a simple form that is appealing. The dish is also good served with Egg Sauce, p. 380.

4 cups finely chopped leeks
2 cups finely chopped Swiss chard leaves (red or green)
4 cups finely chopped fresh spinach leaves
3 eggs, beaten
2 tablespoons flour, or 1 tablespoon flour and 1 tablespoon cornmeal

1 teaspoon salt
½ teaspoon freshly ground pepper
¼ pound Fontina cheese, grated
4 tablespoons butter

Preheat the oven to 350°F. Mix together the chopped leeks, chard, and spinach in a large bowl. (You should have about 10 cups, lightly packed, of finely chopped vegetables.) In a separate bowl, combine the beaten eggs with the flour, salt, and pepper, and mix well. Add the egg mixture to the vegetables, then stir in the grated cheese. Butter a 2-quart casserole with 1 tablespoon of the butter. Pour the vegetable mixture into the prepared casserole and dot the top with the remaining 3 tablespoons of butter. Bake for 35–40 minutes, until the center is firm.

(SERVES SIX) **MUSHROOM POTATO CASSEROLE**

These are humble but wholesome ingredients. The potatoes soak up all of the good juices from the mushrooms.

1 cup ricotta cheese
¼ cup finely chopped parsley
2 cloves garlic, minced
1 teaspoon dried thyme
2 cups grated Monterey Jack cheese
1 pound potatoes, peeled or unpeeled and sliced

1 teaspoon salt
Freshly ground pepper to taste
1 pound mushrooms, cleaned, trimmed, and sliced
½ pound onions, peeled and sliced

Preheat oven to 400°F. Lightly grease a 11 × 14-inch baking dish or lasagne dish. Put the ricotta in a large mixing bowl along with the parsley, garlic, thyme, and 1 cup of the Monterey Jack cheese and beat with a spoon until the mixture is smooth. Set aside. Place the potato slices in a layer in the bottom of the baking dish. Sprinkle with some of the salt and pepper. Spread the ricotta mixture over the potato layer. Toss the mushrooms and onions together and layer on top of the ricotta. Sprinkle with the remaining salt and pepper and top with the other cup of Monterey Jack cheese. Bake for about 35–40 minutes, or until the potatoes are tender when pierced with a fork and the top is lightly browned.

BRAISED FRESH SUMMER VEGETABLES

(SERVES SIX)

These mild, sweet vegetables bring out the best tastes of summer when cooked together.

4 tablespoons butter
1 cup fresh peas, shelled
3 cups fresh corn kernels
1 red pepper, in small dice
3 zucchini, in bite-size pieces
3 pattypan squash, in bite-size wedges

⅓ cup water
Salt and freshly ground pepper
1 tablespoon chopped summer savory, or chopped flat-leaved parsley

Melt the butter in a large frying pan. Add the peas, corn, red pepper, zucchini, pattypan squash, water, and salt and pepper, cover, and braise over low heat for about 10 minutes, stirring occasionally until vegetables are crisp-tender. Stir in the chopped savory or parsley at the end. As an alternate cooking method you may melt butter in a large ovenproof casserole, then add the vegetables, water, and salt and pepper, and mix thoroughly. Bake, covered, in a 350°F oven for 40–45 minutes. Sprinkle with savory or parsley before serving.

EGGPLANT PARMIGIANA (SERVES SIX)

This makes a robust supper dish. Preparation may be made in advance of the last baking step. The baked dish will freeze well.

½ cup flour
Salt and freshly ground
    pepper
2 pounds eggplant in ½-inch
    slices, approximately
½ cup olive oil
3 cups tomatoes, broken or
    chopped with juice
1 tablespoon chopped parsley
    (preferably flat-leaved
    Italian)

2 teaspoons finely chopped
    fresh oregano, or 1
    teaspoon dried, crumbled
1½ cups grated and loosely
    packed mozzarella
    cheese
¾ cup grated Parmesan
    cheese

Preheat the oven to 325°F. Put the flour in a shallow dish and season with salt and pepper to taste. Lightly coat each eggplant slice on both sides, and set aside. Heat the olive oil in a skillet until it is very hot. Quickly fry each eggplant slice until browned on both sides. Don't crowd the skillet. Remove each slice as it is browned and place on paper towels to drain, patting tops to collect excess oil. Repeat until all the slices are browned. Spread half the tomatoes and juice over the bottom of a shallow baking dish. Salt and pepper lightly. Place the eggplant slices over the tomatoes so they overlap a little. Sprinkle the parsley and oregano over the slices, saving a little parsley to add just before serving. Spread the remaining tomatoes and juice over the top. Sprinkle the mozzarella and Parmesan cheeses all over the top. Cover the dish with foil and bake 20 minutes. Uncover and bake 10–15 minutes more. Serve hot; though it is very tasty cold, too.

EGGPLANT BAKED WITH WALNUTS

(SERVES FOUR TO SIX)

Walnuts and eggplant bring out the best flavors in each other.

1 large eggplant, in about 12
    slices
4 tablespoons butter,
    softened, approximately
½ cup chopped walnuts
Salt and freshly ground
    pepper to taste

¼ teaspoon mace or nutmeg
¾ cup cream
¾ cup bread crumbs, tossed
    with 2 tablespoons melted
    butter

Preheat the oven to 325°F. Spread each side of the eggplant slices with
½ teaspoon of the butter. In a large skillet, over medium-high heat,
quickly brown the eggplant slices. (Add more butter or vegetable oil to
the pan if necessary.) Place them in a casserole dish in layers, sprinkling each layer with some of the walnuts, salt and pepper, and mace.
Pour the cream over and bake for 20–25 minutes.

SQUASH AND CABBAGE SAUTÉ

(SERVES FOUR)

Quick cooking keeps the color and texture of the vegetables lively.

3 tablespoons butter or
    vegetable oil
1 cup chopped green pepper
2 cups sliced zucchini
2 cups shredded cabbage
Salt and freshly ground
    pepper to taste

1 tablespoon vinegar
¼ teaspoon oregano,
    crumbled
¼ teaspoon thyme, crumbled

Melt the butter or oil in a skillet. Add the green pepper, zucchini, and
cabbage and cook over low heat for about 5–10 minutes, tossing occasionally, or until the zucchini is barely tender. Stir in the salt and pepper, vinegar, oregano, and thyme. Serve at once.

TOMATO CURRY

(SERVES FOUR)

3 tablespoons butter
1 small onion, peeled and
    chopped fine
1 tart apple, peeled and
    chopped
2 cups peeled and chopped
    fresh tomatoes, or canned
    tomatoes, partially
    drained and chopped

2 teaspoons curry powder
1 teaspoon vinegar
¼ teaspoon freshly ground
    pepper
1½ cups cooked rice
Salt

Melt the butter in a large skillet, add the onion, and cook over medium heat, stirring often, until translucent. Add the apple and cook gently for 5 more minutes. Stir in the tomatoes, curry powder, vinegar, and pepper. Cook, stirring often, for 5 more minutes, then add the rice and salt to taste. Heat well before serving.

CURRIED POTATOES

(SERVES FOUR)

4 tablespoons butter
1 small onion, chopped fine
3 cups diced cooked potatoes
    (about 4 potatoes)
½ cup Vegetable Broth (p. 504)

2 teaspoons curry powder
2 teaspoons lemon juice
Salt
Freshly ground pepper

Melt the butter in a skillet. Add the onion and cook, stirring frequently, until the onion is translucent. Add the potatoes and cook over low heat, stirring occasionally, until the potatoes have absorbed the butter. Add the broth, curry powder, and lemon juice. Stir to blend all the ingredients and continue to cook over low heat until all the broth has been absorbed. Season to taste with salt and pepper.

(SERVES FOUR)   **BAKED STUFFED TOMATOES**

About 2 cups of stuffing will fill four large tomatoes nicely.

4 firm large tomatoes	2 tablespoons finely chopped
Salt	onion
1¼ cups dried homemade	2 tablespoons finely chopped
bread crumbs	green pepper
1 teaspoon chopped fresh	1½ tablespoons olive oil
basil, or ½ teaspoon dried,	Freshly ground pepper
crumbled	

Preheat the oven to 400°F. Film a shallow baking pan with oil, using a pan large enough so that eight tomato halves will not be crowded. Carefully cut a slice from the top of each tomato and scoop out most of the pulp, leaving a thick shell so that the tomato will hold its shape. Sprinkle the insides of the tomatoes with salt, invert them on paper towels, and let them drain for about 15 minutes. Squeeze the juice out of the pulp and chop pulp fine. In a bowl, *lightly* toss the bread crumbs, basil, onion, green pepper, and tomato pulp, then add the olive oil and season to taste with salt and pepper. Lightly fill each tomato, without packing. Place on the baking pan and bake for 15–20 minutes.

BAKED TOMATOES WITH MUSHROOM STUFFING

Omit the basil, green pepper, and olive oil and reduce the amount of bread crumbs to ½ cup. Clean and chop *½ pound mushrooms* and sauté them with the onion in *4 tablespoons butter* over moderate heat for about 5 minutes; cool. Lightly toss the bread crumbs, tomato pulp, mushroom and onion mixture, salt, and pepper together and proceed as for Baked Stuffed Tomatoes.

VEGETARIAN STUFFED GREEN PEPPERS

(SERVES SIX)

This vegetarian stuffed pepper is good to look at and has lively flavor. For stuffed pepper using meat in the filling, see p. 589.

3 large green peppers, halved and seeded
3 tablespoons olive oil
1 onion, chopped fine
2 cups cooked corn kernels
2 tomatoes, peeled and coarsely chopped
2 tablespoons minced parsley

1 tablespoon chopped fresh basil, or 1½ teaspoons dried, crumbled
½ teaspoon salt
¼ teaspoon freshly ground pepper
1 cup freshly made bread crumbs

Preheat the oven to 350°F. Oil a shallow baking dish large enough to hold pepper halves in a single layer. Cook the peppers in boiling water for 2 minutes; drain and set aside. Heat the oil in a skillet and add the chopped onion. Cook, stirring, until soft. Put the onion in a bowl, add the corn, tomatoes, parsley, basil, salt, and pepper, and mix very well. Lightly fill each pepper half with some of the mixture. Sprinkle the tops with the bread crumbs. Bake for 30–40 minutes or until crumbs are lightly browned.

RICE-AND-CHEESE–STUFFED GREEN PEPPERS

Substitute 1 cup cooked rice and 1 cup grated Cheddar cheese for the corn. Add ½ teaspoon savory, crumbled, instead of the basil.

MUSHROOM CRÊPES

(SERVES SIX)

1¼ pounds mushrooms
5 tablespoons butter
1/4 cup minced shallots or scallions
5 tablespoons flour
1½ cups hot Vegetable Broth (p. 504)

1½ cups heavy cream
Salt and freshly ground pepper
1 recipe Crêpes or French Pancakes (p. 778)

Preheat the oven to 350°F. Butter a shallow baking dish, approximately 13 × 9 × 2 inches. Slice the mushrooms, including the stems, and sauté them in the butter with the shallots or scallions, for about 4 minutes, until soft. Sprinkle on the flour and cook for 2 minutes. Slowly add the broth, stir until thick and smooth, then add the cream, and season with salt and pepper to taste. Continue cooking, stirring, for 5 minutes to reduce and thicken slightly. Spoon 3 tablespoons of filling in the center of each crêpe. Fold the ends over and place each crêpe, end side down, in the baking dish. Spoon the remaining mushroom filling over the top of the crêpes. Bake for 25 minutes, or until sauce bubbles.

ZUCCHINI RING

(SERVES SIX)

Sweet marjoram tastes good with zucchini. Fill the center of the ring with braised carrots, cut into small matchstick shape.

3 cups cooked zucchini, drained and mashed	2 tablespoons finely grated onion
1 teaspoon salt	3 eggs, well beaten
1 teaspoon chopped fresh marjoram, or ½ teaspoon dried	½ cup buttered bread crumbs

Preheat the oven to 350°F. Butter a 1½-quart ring mold generously. Put the zucchini, salt, marjoram, onion, and eggs together in a bowl and mix thoroughly. Sprinkle the bread crumbs evenly on the inside of the buttered mold. Spoon in the zucchini mixture. Set the mold in a shallow pan of hot water that comes up the side about 2 inches. Bake for 35–45 minutes, or until firm. Turn the zucchini out of the mold onto a platter and fill if desired. Serve hot.

NUT AND POTATO CROQUETTES

(SERVES FOUR)

2 cups mashed potatoes	1 tablespoon minced onion
½ cup heavy cream	2 egg yolks
1 teaspoon salt	1½ cups freshly made bread crumbs
¼ teaspoon freshly ground black pepper	⅓ cup finely chopped pecans
Pinch of cayenne pepper	3 tablespoons shortening

Combine the potatoes, 3 tablespoons of the cream, ½ teaspoon of the salt, the pepper, cayenne pepper, onion, and 1 egg yolk. Beat until well blended; set aside. Cook ⅓ cup of the crumbs with the remaining 5 tablespoons of cream, stirring until a thick paste is formed; let cool. Put the cooled paste in a bowl and add the remaining egg yolk, the pecans, and the remaining ½ teaspoon salt. Mix well. Shape half the potato mixture into small nests, fill with the nut mixture, then cover with the remaining potato mixture. Pat to shape and make firm. Heat the shortening in a skillet. Dip the croquettes in the remaining crumbs, then fry until brown on both sides. Serve hot.

POTATO AND SPINACH CROQUETTES

Add *1 egg yolk* and *¼ cup finely chopped cooked spinach* to the potato mixture. Proceed as directed.

LASAGNE ROLLS   (SERVES SIX)

This is a variation on the traditional layered lasagne and makes an attractive and colorful dish.

2 tablespoons olive or vegetable oil	½ teaspoon salt
1½ cups chopped onions	3 cups grated zucchini
2 cloves garlic, minced	½ pound lasagne noodles, cooked
2 cups ricotta cheese	3 cups Marinara Sauce or Tomato Sauce (p. 387)
1 teaspoon dried basil	½ cup grated Parmesan cheese
1 teaspoon dried oregano	

Heat the oil in a skillet. Add the onions and garlic, and cook, stirring frequently, until the onions are soft and translucent. Set aside to cool. Put the ricotta cheese, basil, oregano, salt, zucchini, and the cooled onion mixture in a large mixing bowl and mix well to blend. Preheat the oven to 375°F. To assemble, lay each strip of cooked lasagne noodles on a work surface and spread about ¼ cup of the cheese mixture evenly along the strip from end to end. Roll up the strip and place it on end in a greased 13½ × 8½ × 1½-inch baking dish. Continue until all noodles are rolled and placed in dish. Pour the tomato sauce around each lasagne roll but not over the tops. Cover the baking dish with aluminum foil and bake for about 20–25 minutes, or until hot and bubbling. Sprinkle on the Parmesan cheese just before serving.

(SERVES FOUR) **CAPELLINI WITH SALSA CRUDA**

The hot pasta "cooks" the sauce. Any very thin pasta can be used.

1½ pounds ripe tomatoes,
    seeded and chopped, and
    juice reserved from
    seeding
2 teaspoons minced garlic
2 tablespoons chopped basil
⅓ cup olive oil

1 tablespoon red wine vinegar
Salt and freshly ground
    pepper to taste
12 ounces dry capellini
4 quarts water, boiling
½ cup grated Parmesan cheese

In a large bowl, combine the chopped tomatoes, tomato juice, garlic, basil, olive oil, vinegar, and salt and pepper. Toss well to mix and set aside. Cook the capellini in the boiling water for about 8–10 minutes, until just tender. When done, drain and immediately pour into the bowl with the tomato sauce. Toss to mix and coat all the pasta. Serve at once on warmed plates with the grated Parmesan cheese.

(SERVES SIX) **MACARONI CUSTARD**

The cinnamon may sound strange, but is amazingly good in this dish. Don't be put off by the spices in this dish. Try it—you'll find the flavors blend like old friends.

1 cup chopped onion
1 teaspoon cinnamon
1 teaspoon salt
½ cup water
4 tablespoons butter
15-ounce can tomatoes,
    chopped
Freshly ground black pepper
    to taste

½ teaspoon nutmeg
½ pound small elbow
    macaroni, cooked and
    drained
3 eggs, beaten
4 ounces Parmesan cheese,
    grated

Custard

1½ tablespoons butter, melted
1 teaspoon cornstarch

2 cups milk
3 eggs, beaten

Topping

1 ounce Parmesan cheese,
    grated (about 4
    tablespoons)

Preheat the oven to 325°F. Put the onion, cinnamon, and salt in a large skillet with the water, and simmer uncovered for about 30 minutes, or until the water has evaporated and the onion is tender. Add the butter to the skillet and let the onion brown over moderate heat. Add the tomatoes with their juice, black pepper, and nutmeg, and continue to cook until all the liquid has evaporated. Add the cooked macaroni, 3 beaten eggs, and the Parmesan cheese to the tomato mixture and mix well. Transfer to a 1-quart baking casserole or baking dish large enough to hold the macaroni mixture plus about ½ inch of custard. For the custard, put ½ tablespoon of the melted butter in a saucepan with the cornstarch and milk and stir to blend. Simmer for a few minutes. While stirring, add the beaten eggs and continue to cook over medium heat until creamy. Pour the remaining 1 tablespoon of melted butter over the macaroni, pour on the custard, and sprinkle with a little more Parmesan cheese. Bake for about 30 minutes, until heated through.

VEGETABLE PAELLA (SERVES SIX TO EIGHT)

A vegetarian version of a Spanish rice dish, paella. This freezes well.

2 tablespoons olive or vegetable oil
2 onions, chopped
2 cloves garlic, minced
1½ pounds tomatoes, peeled, seeded, and chopped
6 medium artichoke hearts, frozen or canned, sliced
2 red or green peppers, sliced
2 cups green beans, in 2-inch pieces
1 cup peas

5½ cups Vegetable Broth (p. 504)
Zest of 1 lemon, in 2–3-inch strips
½ teaspoon paprika
½ teaspoon tumeric
Pinch of saffron (optional)
¼ cup minced parsley
Salt to taste
1 pound medium- or short-grain white rice (Calrose or arborio)

Garnish

½ cup toasted sliced almonds Parsley leaves

In a large, wide, flat-bottomed pan or paella pan, heat the oil. Add the onions and garlic and cook until the onions are soft. Add the tomatoes and cook another 2–3 minutes. Add the artichokes, peppers, green beans, peas, and 2 cups of the vegetable broth, and simmer, covered, for 10 minutes. Add the lemon zest, paprika, tumeric, optional saffron, chopped parsley, salt, rice, and the remainder of the vegetable broth, and mix well. Cook, covered, over medium-high heat, stirring only occasionally, for about 20–25 minutes, or until the rice is done and the liquid has evaporated. Remove lemon zest. Garnish with the toasted almonds and parsley leaves.

(SERVES FOUR TO SIX) **VEGETARIAN BAKED BEANS**

This is a bean and vegetable dish somewhat in the style of a French cassoulet.

8 ounces Great Northern, navy, or white beans	Salt and freshly ground pepper to taste
2 tablespoons olive or vegetable oil	2 cups cooked spinach, squeezed dry and chopped
1 onion, chopped	
2 cloves garlic, minced	1 cup cottage cheese
½ pound mushrooms, sliced	2 cups grated Fontina or Monterey Jack cheese
1 cup tomato sauce	
½ teaspoon dried oregano	½ cup grated Parmesan cheese
½ teaspoon dried thyme	

Soak beans overnight in water to cover. Drain. Put in a large pot, cover with water, and bring to a boil. Reduce heat, cover, and simmer for about 45 minutes, or until beans are tender but not overcooked. Drain and set aside. (This can be done a day ahead.) In a skillet, heat the oil over medium-high heat and add the onion and garlic and cook for about 5 minutes. Add the mushrooms and continue cooking for about 10 minutes, until the onions are soft and the mushrooms have cooked through. Preheat the oven to 375°F. In a large mixing bowl, combine the beans, onion-mushroom mixture, tomato sauce, oregano, thyme, salt and pepper, and spinach, and toss lightly to mix. Add the cottage cheese and Fontina cheese and toss barely to mix. Pour into a 3-quart baking dish or casserole, sprinkle with the Parmesan cheese, and bake, uncovered, for about 1 hour, until golden.

(SERVES FOUR) **TURKISH PILAF**

Fragrant with spices, this pilaf is good with an avocado salad.

6 tablespoons butter	¼ teaspoon cinnamon
1 cup rice	½ cup raisins
1½ cups finely chopped onion	½ cup sliced, toasted almonds
½ teaspoon salt	2 cups vegetable broth
1 bay leaf, crumbled	

Preheat the oven to 375°F. Melt the butter in a skillet. Stir in the rice and cook over low heat until all the grains glisten. Add the onion and cook, stirring, until they are soft. Put the mixture into a 1½-quart casserole. Add the salt, bay leaf, cinnamon, raisins, and almonds. Heat the broth to a boil, mix with all the ingredients, cover, and bake for 45 minutes.

VEGETABLES

The newest trend in vegetable cookery is, of course, the microwave, and there are mixed feelings about the results. So I decided that I should make a comparison test of just about every vegetable in this chapter and give you a forthright appraisal. It is a shame to waste a beautiful, fresh vegetable by microwaving it if it comes out withered-looking and unpleasant-tasting when you could have boiled or steamed it, taking very little more time (and sometimes no more time) for a perfect result.

Testing side by side the microwave and stove-top methods, I used only small amounts of each vegetable (enough for two) to give the microwave the opportunity to perform at its best; microwaving larger amounts would entail lifting off the top or plastic wrap to stir and/or sometimes rotating the dish, and the amount of time saved diminishes greatly with the larger quantity. I used no salt or other seasoning.

NOTE In my early experiments, when I followed manufacturers' directions, many of the green vegetables, such as broccoli, beans, and asparagus, emerged gray, tough, and bitter tasting. But I found that when I almost doubled the amount of water called for in the manufacturers' instructions the cooked vegetables had good color and texture. However, the additional amount of water increased the cooking time.

So throughout this chapter I have given you my observations and recommendations under each vegetable entry. No matter which method you choose, buying good, fresh vegetables makes a great difference. Old, tired vegetables remain old and tired no matter what.

I should add that cooking vegetables in the mi-

crowave oven did not prove appreciably faster than
boiling or steaming them, with the exception of whole
vegetables such as potatoes, beets, artichokes, and
kohlrabi.

ABOUT VEGETABLES

Attitudes toward vegetable cooking have changed dramatically over
the years. Today the emphasis is on preserving the natural goodness of
vegetables, cooking them for the shortest time possible, until just
barely tender with a slight suggestion of crispness or crunchiness.

Those of us who were brought up on soggy, overcooked vegetables
and learned at an early age to dislike them thoroughly have since discovered that the same vegetables, properly cooked to retain color, flavor, shape, and texture, are not only nourishing but very delicious.
And proper cooking is only part of the secret—it is also important to
know *when* to buy fresh vegetables, *what* to look for, and *how* to serve
them.

Buying Vegetables

Careful selection of green groceries is important: if vegetables are
weary when purchased, you will not be able to perk them up by cooking them. It's worth going out of your way to find a special produce
market or to drive to a country farm stand in order to get crisp, firm,
fresh vegetables with bright, natural color. Or try growing them in
your own backyard.

Whenever possible, try to get fresh rather than canned or frozen
vegetables. Buy them when they are in season: they are less expensive
and also at their best when they have been born and nurtured in
rhythm with the earth's master plan. Somehow man's forced system
for producing certain vegetables all year round results in vegetables
that lack character, although they often look glamorously bright and
large.

Storing Vegetables

Try to buy vegetables shortly before you plan to use them, and do not
buy more than you need. Even vegetables like peas and corn, which do
not change in appearance as they get older, will become starchy and
lose their sweetness when they are held for any time.

Most vegetables should be kept in the refrigerator or in a cool place.

FARMERS' MARKETS

Wonderful farmers' markets have continued to proliferate all over the country during the last decade. If you haven't made it a practice to shop at your local farmers' markets, it is well worth your effort. You'll be delighted at the quality and variety of the seasonal fruits and vegetables and other farm products, and you'll enjoy the camaraderie between shoppers and farmers that goes on at the colorful stalls out in the fresh air.

Cooking Vegetables

The taste and tenderness of a vegetable will vary, according to its age, size, and freshness. These recipes give general guidelines for cooking times and seasonings, but the best test of all is your own taste. The general guidelines for cooking times are based on cooking vegetables at room temperature, not cold from the refrigerator. If in doubt, it is always better to undercook vegetables than to let them get limp and lifeless.

A wonderful way to cook many vegetables—such as broccoli, green beans, spinach, cauliflower, Brussels sprouts, cabbage, and carrots—is to give them a brief baptism in boiling water. Fresh natural flavors and bright colors intensify when vegetables are cooked briskly in an uncovered pot. It's easy to tell when the vegetable is done: just pluck one out and taste it. Use lots of water so that it returns quickly to a boil after the vegetables are added to the pot. Cook the vegetables as briefly as possible, just until they are tender-crisp. Drain, add salt and butter, and serve, or drain and set aside until later, reheating them quickly, just before serving, in a little melted butter.

Some vegetables, like broccoli, cauliflower, and green beans, taste very good steamed, although green vegetables lose some of their color. Steam them in a covered steamer basket over briskly boiling water. Steaming will take longer than boiling. There are several kinds of steamer pots available, as well as a collapsible vegetable holder that will adjust to any pot. The new electric steamers are excellent, enabling you to steam more than one vegetable at a time.

Roasting vegetables around meat mingles lovely juices and turns the vegetables a rich brown. Potatoes, turnips, carrots, and onions blossom this way. Parboil potatoes and turnips before they join the roast by peeling them and dropping them into a large pot of boiling water. Let them boil merrily for 10 to 20 minutes until they are barely tender when pierced with a knife. Then place them around the roast about an hour before the meat is done. See White Turnips Roasted with Meat or Fowl (p. 625) for a master recipe.

Crisp, batter-coated, deep-fried vegetables, or fritters, make a light, yet crunchy accompaniment to roasts and broiled meats. Or a whole platter of various combinations when the garden abounds with tender young vegetables is such a treat that one might want little else for supper. Zucchini and eggplant cut in 1-inch pieces, cauliflower and broccoli flowerets, mushrooms and whole green beans take particularly well to the fritter treatment. See p. 533 for Beer Fritter Batter, which has a tangy flavor particularly well suited to vegetables.

Vegetable custards are light suppers in themselves and are also good for lunch. Use Broccoli in Cheese Custard (p. 547) as a basic recipe and vary it with other vegetables.

The food processor, with a flick of the wrist, will purée cooked vegetables in a matter of seconds. Add butter, seasonings, and a bit of cream, perhaps, and try combining several vegetables in a purée. Turnips with potatoes, celeriac with potatoes, and pumpkin with yams are among many happy unions. Use the recipe for Mashed or Puréed Parsnips (p. 585) and try it with other vegetables as well. You can also use a blender to purée, but you're apt to have to add more liquid to get it going—more cream or a little of the vegetable cooking juice.

Vegetables can be cooked in many other interesting ways, as the recipes in this chapter indicate: sautéed or stir-fried in butter or oil, braised in broth or wine, baked with buttered crumbs, broiled, glazed or candied, or stuffed with tangy fillings.

You can also cook vegetables in a pressure cooker, which is time-saving with certain vegetables and a good way to preserve healthful vegetable juices. Pressure cooking has its disadvantages, however: since you cannot remove the cover to taste a sample bean or pea, you can't test for doneness and adjust the cooking time accordingly.

If you use a pressure cooker, be sure to follow the manufacturer's directions carefully (on p. 530 there is a general guide to timing pressure-cooked vegetables).

As noted in the introduction to this chapter, a microwave oven is often an acceptable alternative to stove-top cooking; see notes under individual vegetable entries. The microwave is especially useful and time-saving for small amounts of vegetables.

Serving Vegetables

Vegetables are used in soups, stews, and salads. They are also good combined with rice, beans, or pasta or served with a variety of sauces, both hot and cold. Make them the appetizer to a meal, use them as side dishes to a main meat course, or plan an all-vegetable meal or a country corn boil with vegetables as the main attraction.

You'll want to use the same vegetable frequently while it's in season. This can be made less repetitious with a few small innovations—a light blanket of cream or olive oil, some buttered crumbs, a little lemon juice or, perhaps, a sprinkling of a friendly herb.

Use restraint, however, in adding sauces, garnishes, and herbs to vegetables. Think of the total meal and adorn the vegetable only when the other dishes are very plain. Many times a light salting and a dollop of butter over a spanking-fresh vegetable are just enough.

Think also of color, texture, and taste when you select a vegetable, so that it will balance and enhance the other dishes you are serving. It is dreadful to face a dinner plate on which everything is pale and white or of a uniformly soft consistency. It is even worse to eat a combination of highly seasoned dishes that compete with or cancel out one another's tastes.

Leftover Vegetables

Soups and stocks are good catch-alls for vegetable juices and for leftover vegetables, whether raw or cooked, in large quantities or just a few scraps. Use leftover vegetables in custards, in soufflés, or in omelets and frittatas. You can also purée leftover vegetables in a blender or food processor and heat them with a little butter, salt, and cream. Or add puréed vegetables to soups, soufflés, or custards.

Leftover cooked vegetables are seldom very good when simply reheated the next day. It's better to serve them cold in French Dressing or Basic Vinaigrette (p. 703) or to cut them up and add them to a tossed salad. If the vegetables have been buttered, you can wash off the congealed butter with a little hot water before adding them to a salad.

If you must reheat vegetables, do so in a microwave oven on medium power or in a double boiler, and do not heat them any longer than necessary. Try serving them with White Sauce (p. 379) or Cheese Sauce (p. 380).

Frozen or Canned Vegetables

Frozen or canned vegetables, always second best to fresh, may be used in some of these recipes. Check under the individual vegetable listings to see if such substitutions are advisable.

Frozen vegetables are generally preferable to canned and usually work best when combined with sauces or other vegetables. When cooking frozen vegetables, it's often best to disregard the package directions, allowing the vegetable to defrost enough so that it can be broken up easily; then cook as quickly as possible in a very small amount of water.

For canning vegetables, see p. 1110.

For freezing vegetables, see p. 1125.

Pressure Cooking Chart for Fresh Vegetables

This chart provides a general guide to pressure cooking vegetables. It is geared to average-size vegetables bought in the market. If your vegetables have been picked very young and are garden fresh, you'll want to cook them a shorter time. You may also find that you like your vegetables slightly less or more done than recommended here. In any case, make notes of your results and keep a record for future use.

It is possible to cook more than one vegetable at once provided both vegetables require the same amount of cooking time. It is better to season vegetables after cooking because you can judge better what is needed; pressure-cooked vegetables retain more of their own natural mineral salts and their flavor is apt to be more intense, so you may need less seasoning. Always make sure that the vent of your pressure cooker is open. Put it up to the light to see if the hole is clear; if not, clean it out with a pipe cleaner. Place vegetables on the rack and do not have the pressure cooker more than two-thirds full.

VEGETABLE	PREPARATION	AMOUNT OF WATER	TIME
Artichokes	Wash and trim (p. 534). Leave whole.	1 cup	10 minutes
Asparagus	Break off stems, wash, and peel. Leave whole.	½ cup	2 minutes
Beans (green, wax, and pole)	Wash. Remove ends and strings, if any. Leave whole, unless very thick—then French or cut into 1-inch pieces.	½ cup	2 minutes
Beans (lima, shell, and fava)	Shell.	½ cup	2 minutes
Beets	Wash. Cut off all but 1 inch of the top; leave roots on. After cooking, cool and slip off skins.	1½ cups	15 minutes
Broccoli	Wash and prepare (p. 545). After cooking, cut flowerets diagonally, peeled stems together.	½ cup	2 minutes
Broccoli Rabe	Wash and cut into 2-inch pieces.	½ cup	2 minutes
Brussels Sprouts	Wash. Remove wilted outer leaves and cut a cross in the root ends.	½ cup	3 minutes

VEGETABLE	PREPARATION	AMOUNT OF WATER	TIME
Cabbage (green and red)	Remove wilted outside leaves, cut away inner core, and cut into 2-inch wedges.	½ cup	3 minutes
Carrots	Wash and peel. Leave small carrots whole or slice ¼ inch thick.	1 cup ½ cup	5 minutes 2 minutes
Cauliflower	Remove outer leaves and stalk. Break into flowerets and wash.	½ cup	2 minutes
Celery	Separate stalks. Remove strings and wash. Leave whole or cut into pieces.	½ cup	2 minutes
Celery Root or Celeriac	Peel, wash, and cut into ½-inch slices.	½ cup	3 minutes
Corn (on the cob)	Remove husk and silk.	½ cup	3 minutes
Fennel	Wash, trim away tough outer part, slice ½ inch thick.	½ cup	2 minutes
Greens (collards, beet greens, Swiss chard, and turnip greens)	Remove wilted leaves and tough root ends. Wash thoroughly in several changes of water.	½ cup	3 minutes
Jerusalem Artichokes	Scrub and peel. Leave whole.	1 cup	3 minutes
Kohlrabi	Wash, peel, and cut into ½-inch cubes.	1 cup	2 minutes
Onions	Wash and peel. Leave whole— up to 2-inch diameter; larger than that, cut in halves or quarters.	1 cup	5 minutes
Parsnips	Wash and peel or scrape. Trim root ends and leave whole.	1 cup	8 minutes
Peas (green)	Shell.	½ cup	2 minutes
Potatoes	Wash and scrub. Don't peel new potatoes. Leave whole unless very large; if so, cut into pieces 1½ inches thick.	1 cup	10 minutes

VEGETABLE	PREPARATION	AMOUNT OF WATER	TIME
Spinach	Wash thoroughly in several changes of water. Remove tough stems.	½ cup	1 minute
Squash (winter) and Pumpkin	Wash and cut into 1½–2-inch chunks. Scrape out meat when cooked.	1½ cups	12 minutes
Sweet Potatoes	Wash and scrub. Leave whole.	1 cup	10 minutes
White Turnips and Rutabagas	Wash, peel, and cut into 1-inch cubes or slices.	½ cup	3 minutes

MICROWAVING VEGETABLES

Cooking most vegetables in the microwave is not significantly quicker than cooking them on top of the stove. See specific vegetables for more details. The exceptions are whole beets, whole potatoes, whole artichokes, yams, and kohlrabi. Using sufficient water when cooking vegetables in the microwave (½–¾ cup per ½ pound of vegetable) may add a minute or two to the cooking time, but it will give you unblemished vegetables. High-water-content vegetables such as tomatoes and mushrooms do not need as much water to achieve good results.

For a comparison of vegetables cooked on top of the stove and in the microwave, I prepared ½ pound of vegetables in the same way as for the basic method for cooking and microwaved them in ¾ cup water (unless noted otherwise), in a glass dish with a lid, on high power, in a full-size microwave (600–700 watts). In similar tests, using a minimal amount of water (2–4 tablespoons per ½ pound), which is the amount that most microwave cooking instructions indicate, many of the vegetables cooked in the microwave tended to look shriveled and dehydrated and were tough and stringy.

Some vegetables microwaved successfully; some fared less well (see notes on individual vegetables). Age and quality are all-important. Longer cooking of an old, mature vegetable in the microwave did not make it more tender and moist.

(1½ CUPS)   ৯**   BEER FRITTER BATTER**

This is good not only for vegetables but for seafood and chicken, as
well as for fruit fritters, such as banana, pineapple, and apple.

1 cup flour	Salt
1 egg	½ cup beer, approximately
1 tablespoon butter, melted	

Combine the flour, egg, butter, salt, and beer in a blender, or processor,
or a bowl. Beat until the batter is smooth. Let the batter stand, covered,
for 4 hours before using. Have vegetables well drained and patted dry
if they have been washed. Cut into 1-inch pieces or use whole flowerets; leaving green beans and mushrooms whole. Dip in batter and fry
in about 1½ inches of deep fat, 365°F, about 5–7 minutes, until golden.
Remove quickly and drain on paper towels. (See Fry. Deep-fat frying,
p. 57.)

(1 CUP)   **BUTTERED BREAD CRUMBS**

1 cup fresh bread crumbs   2 tablespoons butter, melted

Put the bread crumbs into a small bowl, pour the melted butter
over, and, using a fork, toss until the crumbs are coated. These
may be frozen for later use.

About Globe Artichokes

Height of Season: April and May.

What to Look For: Green stems and firm, unblemished leaves. Size
does not affect taste.

Uses: *Cooked*, as a first or separate course; bottoms or hearts in salads.

Amount: One per person.

Alternatives to Fresh: Both frozen and canned hearts and bottoms are
available and good. Rinse brine from canned hearts.

Cooking in the Microwave: 1 medium whole artichoke in ½ cup water
    in a glass dish with a lid, about 5 minutes on high power
  M≋ (in a 600–700-watt oven). Results: color and taste compara-
    ble to cooking on top of the stove; texture not quite as good; cook-
ing time faster for 1 artichoke.

Globe artichokes, sometimes called French or Italian artichokes,
resemble a flower bud with a fascinating, complex construction.

If you've never eaten an artichoke, here's how you proceed. Start with the outer leaves and work toward the center, taking off each leaf with your fingers and dipping it in melted butter or a special sauce. Scrape off the edible bottom part of the leaf with your teeth and discard what remains. In the center of the artichoke is a light green cone of tiny leaves which can be removed in one piece. Under this cone is the prickly center, or "choke," which is inedible and should be scraped off. (See illustration of cross section, below.)

The tender, delicious artichoke bottom, sometimes erroneously called the "heart," is just below the choke. It is slightly cuplike in shape and captures the intense, delicious flavor of the artichoke.

The heart is actually the whole tender center of an artichoke, including the bottom and some of the most tender leaves; the bristly choke is removed. The hearts of tiny artichokes are sold frozen and in jars.

BASIC METHOD FOR
COOKING ARTICHOKES ❧ (ALLOW ONE PER PERSON)

Cooked artichoke stems are delicious. Do not detach them until after cooking, and use them in salads or as an appetizer.

To prepare for cooking, peel the coarse fibers from the artichoke stem. Remove the tough bottom leaves, then slice off about an inch from the leaves at the top. With scissors, snip off the prickly tops of the remaining side leaves. Plunge the artichokes into a very large pot filled with boiling water and boil them gently until done. Allow 25–40 minutes: they are done when an outer leaf pulls off easily and the bottom is tender when pierced with a fork. Drain them upside down. Serve them hot or warm, with *melted butter* or *Hollandaise Sauce* (p. 388) on the side, or cold with *French Dressing* (p. 703) or *mayonnaise seasoned with lemon juice and a drop of prepared mustard.*

(SERVES FOUR)   ₴❧   **SAUTÉED ARTICHOKE HEARTS**

Two 8½-ounce packages   6 tablespoons butter
   frozen artichoke hearts, or   Salt to taste
   two 9-ounce cans drained,   2 tablespoons minced parsley
   rinsed hearts

If you are using frozen, thaw them enough to break apart. Then cook them in ¼ cup water, covered, for 5 minutes. Melt the butter in a skillet and add the drained artichoke hearts. Stir often so they are well coated with butter, sprinkle with salt and parsley, and serve when thoroughly hot.

About Jerusalem Artichokes

Height of Season: Winter months.
What to Look For: Firm, hard tubers.
Uses: *Raw*, peeled, then sliced or grated, as an hors d'oeuvre or in salads. *Cooked*, in soups (see p. 128). *As a vegetable accompaniment*, particularly good with red meat.
Amount: One pound serves four.
Cooking in the Microwave: ½ pound Jerusalem artichokes peeled and
    M≋ sliced in ¾ cup water in a glass dish with a lid, about 5
        minutes on high power (in a 600–700-watt oven). Results:
color and taste comparable to cooking on top of the stove, texture uneven.

Jerusalem artichokes, often called sunchokes, are not related to globe artichokes. They are tubers and look something like ginger root, with a knobby, irregular shape, a mild sweetness in taste, and a crunchy, slightly watery consistency. They are very easy to grow in backyard gardens and will return and multiply year after year.

___

BASIC METHOD FOR COOKING
(SERVES THREE OR FOUR)   ₴❧   **JERUSALEM ARTICHOKES**

Peel Jerusalem artichokes with a vegetable peeler. If you remove the bumps, the artichokes will cook more evenly. Don't be a perfectionist—a little of the skin tastes fine.

1 pound Jerusalem artichokes   3 tablespoons butter
1 teaspoon lemon juice   Salt to taste
2 tablespoons finely chopped   Freshly ground pepper
   parsley

Scrub the artichokes with a brush, peel, and drop into cold water with a teaspoon of lemon juice. Then boil in water to cover for 10–20 minutes, depending on their size. Test often by piercing them with the point of a knife; they should be a bit resistant in the center, but not hard. Remove from the heat and drain. Slice, toss with the parsley and butter, and sprinkle with salt and pepper. Serve hot.

CREAMED JERUSALEM ARTICHOKES

Just before serving, stir in *1 cup White Sauce* (p. 379) and sprinkle a little more *finely chopped parsley* on top. Serve hot.

About Asparagus

Height of Season: April and May.

What to Look For: Round, firm, fresh-looking spears, very green with smooth, tight tips. Thickness does not affect tenderness.

Uses: *Cooked*, plain or with sauces, boiled, steamed, stir-fried, as an appetizer, in soups, in salads, in vegetable custards, or in quiches. *As a vegetable accompaniment*, particularly good with beef, veal, and salmon.

Amount: Six to eight per person.

Alternatives to Fresh: Frozen retain the taste of asparagus better than canned, but the texture suffers in both cases.

Cooking in the Microwave: ½ pound unpeeled asparagus in ½ cup water, in a glass dish with a lid, about 5 minutes on high power (in a 600–700-watt oven). Results: color brighter green; taste and texture not quite as good; cooking time comparable to cooking on top of the stove.

The asparagus is a perennial vegetable, well worth growing at home. Its fern makes a beautiful addition to any backyard, and asparagus cooked straight from the garden is a great spring feast. It may take a few years to get an asparagus patch established, but then it will provide succulent green spears for as long as thirty-five or forty years.

BASIC METHOD FOR COOKING ASPARAGUS

(SERVES ABOUT FOUR)

The shorter the cooking time, the fresher and greener the color.

24 large asparagus

Wash the asparagus and cut or break off the tough, colorless, woody bottom of each stalk. Peel with a vegetable peeler, lightly near the top and more deeply toward the bottom to make more of the stalks edible. Plunge the spears into a large pot of boiling water and boil gently until the bottoms are just tender when pierced with a knife. Begin testing after 5–8 minutes, depending on the thickness of the stalks. Drain well and serve with *melted butter*, *Hollandaise Sauce* (p. 388), *Cheese Sauce* (p. 380), or with mayonnaise mixed with a few drops of Oriental sesame oil.

ASPARAGUS VINAIGRETTE

Spoon ½ *cup French Dressing* (p. 703) over hot or cold asparagus, either ahead of time or just before serving.

(SERVES TWO OR THREE)   ≈   ## STIR-FRIED ASPARAGUS

Asparagus cooked in the Chinese way will be crisp and very green.

1 pound thin asparagus	Salt
2–3 tablespoons cooking oil	Freshly ground pepper

Wash the asparagus and trim the bottoms. Cut asparagus in ½-inch slices, slanted at the ends. Heat the oil in a wok or a skillet, add the asparagus, and sauté quickly, tossing frequently, until all the pieces are coated, about 2 minutes. Add 2 tablespoons water and cover. Cook over medium heat for about 3 minutes, until just tender. Season to taste, and serve immediately.

DRIED BEANS

See p. 445.

About Green Beans

Availability: Year round, especially in spring and summer.
What to Look For: Crisp, firm beans, with good, fresh color; should snap when broken.
Uses: *Hot or cold*, boiled or steamed, as an appetizer, salad, or vegetable; add leftovers to soups or salads, or purée. *As a vegetable accompaniment*, good with just about everything.
Amount: One pound serves three or four.
Alternatives to Fresh: Frozen preferable to canned, but will be limp.

Cooking in the Microwave: ½ pound whole green beans in ¾ cup water in a glass dish with a lid, about 6 minutes on high power (in a 600–700-watt oven). Results: color brighter; taste fresh, texture and cooking time comparable to cooking on top of the stove.

Green beans were once called string beans. Today they are stringless; just break off the ends as you wash them. Green beans, wax beans, and pole beans may all be cooked the same way, until just tender but crunchy. Try them fried whole in a beer batter for a change sometimes (see p. 533).

BASIC METHOD FOR COOKING
GREEN BEANS ॐ   (SERVES THREE OR FOUR)

If you leave the beans whole, they will be less watery and more flavorful. If they are very thick, however, you may wish to slice them diagonally or "French" them.

    1 pound green beans   Salt
    Butter   Freshly ground pepper

Wash the beans and remove the ends and strings, if there are any. Leave them whole or cut them in diagonal strips. Drop them into a large pot of boiling water and boil them gently until just done, allowing about 5–10 minutes, depending on the size and age of the beans. Taste one to see if it is done; it should still be very crunchy. Drain the beans and rinse them thoroughly in cold water to stop the cooking. Reheat them in lots of butter, salt, and pepper just before serving.

GREEN BEANS WITH HERBS

As you reheat the beans in the butter, add 1 teaspoon fresh (or ½ teaspoon dried) thyme, rosemary, or savory, and a generous squeeze of lemon juice.

GREEN BEANS WITH ALMONDS

Cook ⅓ cup slivered, blanched almonds in the butter until lightly browned, then reheat the beans with the nuts and the browned butter, adding salt and pepper to taste.

GREEN BEANS VINAIGRETTE

Toss the beans with ½ *cup French Dressing* (p. 703) and let them sit at room temperature for at least 1 hour before serving.

GREEN BEANS AU GRATIN

Let the beans boil for only 2 or 3 minutes; they should be very crisp and underdone. Drain and combine them with 1½ *cups Cheese Sauce* (p. 380). Arrange in buttered casserole, sprinkle with *Buttered Bread Crumbs*, and bake, uncovered, in a preheated 400°F oven just until bubbly and brown, about 20 minutes. Serve immediately. Frozen green beans, defrosted but uncooked, will work in this recipe.

(SERVES THREE OR FOUR) &ะ STEAMED GREEN BEANS

Steaming is a perfectly acceptable alternative to cooking beans in lots of boiling water, although the color will not be as vivid. The method of cooking is less important than the timing: be sure that the beans are crunchy and not overcooked.

1 pound green beans	Salt
Butter	Freshly ground pepper

Wash the beans and remove the ends and strings, if there are any. Leave them whole or cut them in diagonal strips. Steam them, covered, in a steamer basket over an inch or so of rapidly boiling water until just tender, but still crunchy, about 10–15 minutes. Drain, toss with butter, season to taste, and serve, or see variations in the preceding recipe.

About Fresh Shell Beans

Availability: Varies according to variety and region; check in farmers' markets or grow them yourself.

What to Look For: Fresh, firm beans with good color and pliable, velvety pods.

Uses: *Cold*, as a salad. *Hot*, in soups and casserole dishes. *As a vegetable accompaniment*, particularly good with ham.

Amount: One pound shelled (about 3 pounds unshelled) serves four or five.

Alternatives to Fresh: Frozen and canned are acceptable.

Cooking in the Microwave: ½ pound raw, shelled beans in ¾ cup water in a glass dish with a lid, about 8–10 minutes on high power (in a 600–700-watt oven). Results: color, taste, and texture comparable to cooking on top of the stove. Some time savings for small amounts.

Competition from the frozen product has made fresh shell beans scarce in our markets. The best-known shell beans—lima beans, green soy beans, fava beans, and kidney beans—usually used in their dried form, are especially good when cooked fresh (for information about dried beans, see p. 443). If you can't get them, it's well worth the trouble of growing them yourself.

Most shell beans are shelled by breaking or cutting the pods open and squeezing the beans out. To shell green soy beans, drop them into boiling water, cover, and let stand for 5 minutes; then drain and press out the beans.

FRESH LIMA BEANS ❧   (SERVES FOUR)

Slivers of cooked ham or a sprinkling of sage are nice additions.

2½ pounds unshelled green lima beans	½ cup heavy cream
	Salt
3 tablespoons butter	Freshly ground pepper

Prepare the limas by snapping open the pods or use a knife to cut them open; remove the beans. Put the beans and 2 quarts water in a large pan. Cover and cook for about 20 minutes or until tender; drain. Melt the butter in the pan, then add the beans, cream, and salt and pepper to taste. Shake the pan to keep the beans from sticking or burning and to coat them evenly. Serve when hot.

FAVA BEANS ❧   (SERVES FOUR)

Fava beans are large, shiny green beans, often called broad beans. They are found in the market in April, May, and June.

3 pounds unshelled fava beans	1 teaspoon marjoram, crumbled
4 tablespoons butter	Salt
1 onion, chopped	Freshly ground pepper

Shell the beans. Melt the butter in a pan, add the onion, and stir until soft. Add the beans and just enough water to cover. Add the marjoram,

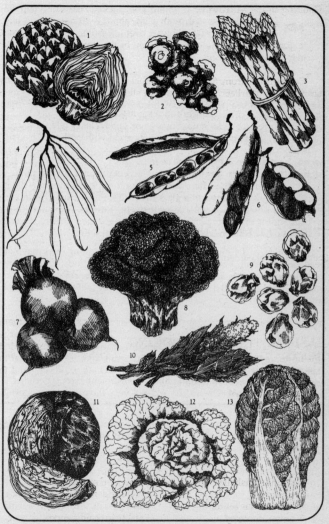

1. *artichokes with cross section showing choke and heart; 2. Jerusalem artichoke; 3. asparagus; 4. green beans; 5. shell beans; 6. lima beans; 7. beets; 8. broccoli; 9. Brussels sprouts; 10. broccoli rabe; 11. red cabbage; 12. Savoy cabbage; 13. Chinese cabbage.*

cover, and cook for about 10–15 minutes or until the beans are tender. Drain, saving the liquid, and put the beans in a warm oven. Return the liquid to the pan, turn the heat on high, and reduce the liquid to about ½ cup. Season to taste. Pour over the beans and serve.

About Beets

Availability: Year round, especially from June to October.

What to Look For: Smooth, firm, round beets—small or medium size— with deep red color and fresh-looking leaves.

Uses: *Cold*, pickled, as an hors d'oeuvre or salad. *Hot or cold*, in soups. *As a vegetable accompaniment*, especially good with pork and ground beef.

Amount: One pound serves three or four.

Alternatives to Fresh: Canned beets are acceptable in many recipes.

ME **Cooking in the Microwave:** ½ pound unpeeled medium beets in ¼ cup water in a glass dish with a lid, about 11 minutes on high power (in a 600–700-watt oven). Results: color and taste comparable to cooking on top of the stove; texture a little too moist; and cooking time much faster for this small amount.

Beets are usually peeled after boiling, but very young ones may not need peeling at all. Young beets are tender and delicious; if you grow them in your garden, let them grow to the size of marbles before you thin the rows. Cook the beets you pull out with their delicate leaves still attached.

BASIC METHOD FOR COOKING
BEETS ?? (SERVES THREE OR FOUR)

Young boiled beets need nothing for embellishment except, perhaps, a little butter. If your beets are old and not very flavorful, try sugaring them or pickling them (see opposite).

1 pound beets	Freshly ground pepper
Butter	Chopped parsley
Salt	

Cut off all but 1 inch of the beet tops; do not pare or remove the roots. Drop the beets into enough boiling water to cover them, and cook them, uncovered, until they are tender, allowing 30 minutes to 1 hour, depending on the age of the beets. Drain the beets, drop them in cold water for a minute or two to cool them slightly, then slip off the skins. Leave them whole or quarter them, or slice them with an egg slicer. Toss them with butter, salt and pepper to taste, and some chopped parsley, and reheat them, if necessary, before serving.

SUGARED BEETS

Toss each pound (about 2 cups) of sliced, cooked beets with *2 tablespoons butter*, *1 teaspoon sugar*, and *½ teaspoon salt*. Reheat, if necessary, before serving.

PICKLED BEETS

Mix *½ cup vinegar* with *¼ cup sugar* and boil for 5 minutes. Add *1 teaspoon caraway seeds* and *¼ teaspoon salt*. Pour over 1 pound (about 2 cups) of sliced, cooked beets and serve cold or at room temperature.

(SERVES FOUR)   ≈ **BAKED BEETS**

Sweetly tender with a nice taste. Leftovers are particularly good in salad.

1 pound beets	2 tablespoons butter
Salt	

Preheat the oven to 375°F. Butter a baking dish that will hold the beets in a single layer. Wash and trim the beets. Put them into the baking dish and sprinkle salt and bits of butter on top. Cover and bake for 1–1½ hours. If the skins are tough or unattractive, slip them off before serving.

(SERVES SIX)   ≈ ✳ **HARVARD BEETS**

½ cup sugar	3 cups sliced or cubed cooked
1½ teaspoons cornstarch	beets
¼ cup cider vinegar	2 tablespoons butter
¼ cup water	

Mix the sugar, cornstarch, vinegar, and water in a pot and boil for 5 minutes. Add the beets, toss well, and let stand for 30 minutes or more. Just before serving, add the butter and reheat to the boiling point.

BEETS AND GREENS ❧ (SERVES TWO)

Use very young beets, the size of marbles, and cook them with their tender leaves. To cook mature beet greens, see About Collards and Other Greens (p. 561).

About 12–15 tiny beets and leaves	Salt
Butter	Freshly ground pepper

Wash the beets and leaves thoroughly and cut off the roots. Cut the leaves coarsely. Bring about ½ inch of water to a boil in a pot or skillet. Add the beets and greens, cover, and boil gently for 20–30 minutes, taking care that they do not burn. When the beets can be pierced easily with a fork, they are done. Drain. Toss with lots of butter, season to taste, and serve immediately.

SHREDDED BEETS ❧ (SERVES THREE OR FOUR)

1 pound young beets	Salt
3 tablespoons butter	Freshly ground pepper
1 tablespoon lemon juice	

Shred the beets by rubbing them against the large holes of a grater or in a food processor. Heat the butter in a skillet. Add the shredded beets, toss, then add the lemon juice and 1 tablespoon of water. Cover and cook over moderate heat, stirring frequently, for 5 minutes or until tender. Season to taste and serve hot.

About Bok Choy

Availability: Year round.

What to Look For: Sometimes called Chinese chard or Pak choy. Very green leaves with firm, thick white stalks. May be small, 4 to 5 inches long; or, mature, the size of a head of celery.

Uses: May be steamed, sautéed, braised, or used with other vegetables in Chinese-style stir-fry dishes.

Amount: One pound serves three or four.

Cooking in the Microwave: ½ pound bok choy, washed and cut in half or quartered if large, in ¾ cup water in a glass dish with a lid, about 5–6 minutes on high power (in a 600–700-watt oven). Results: color, taste, texture, and cooking time comparable to cooking on top of the stove.

(SERVES SIX)

❋ BRAISED BOK CHOY

1 cup chicken broth
1½-inch piece ginger root, in
  quarters
2 pounds bok choy
Salt to taste
3–4 tablespoons rice wine
  vinegar

Few drops hot pepper oil
  (optional)
¼ pound cooked ham, in
  small strips (optional)

Pour broth into a large sauté pan and add the pieces of ginger root. Cut the bok choy into halves or quarters and add to the sauté pan with the salt. Cover and simmer on low heat for about 10–12 minutes. Test for doneness by piercing the bulb end with a knife tip. When done, discard the ginger root and place bok choy on a serving dish. Sprinkle with the vinegar (and the hot pepper oil if desired), and garnish, if you wish, with the cooked ham.

About Broccoli

Availability: Year round, especially from October to May.

What to Look For: Tight, compact deep green or purple-green flowerets. Avoid wilted or yellowish flowerets and stems that are very thick.

Uses: *Raw*, with a dip, or as a first course or in salads. *Cooked*, boiled or steamed, in soups, purées, custards, and quiches; also, dipped in batter and fried. *Good warm as a vegetable accompaniment* and cold with vinaigrette.

Amount: One pound serves two or three.

Alternatives to Fresh: Frozen best when puréed or combined with a sauce.

Cooking in the Microwave: ½ pound broccoli stems and flowerets in ¾ cup water in a glass dish with a lid, about 4 minutes on high power (in a 600–700-watt oven). Results: color bright; taste and texture not as good as cooking on top of the stove.

Broccoli belongs to the cabbage family. It is a very satisfactory vegetable to grow at home, for the more it is cut, the more it produces.

(SERVES TWO OR THREE)

BASIC METHOD FOR COOKING ❧ BROCCOLI

It's true for many vegetables, but especially true with broccoli: Don't overcook!

1 pound broccoli   Salt
Melted butter

Cut off and discard the tough end of the stems and coarse outer leaves
of the broccoli. Cut the broccoli into flowerets with short stems and
peel the stems lightly with a vegetable peeler. Peel more deeply the
thick stems cut from the flowerets, and slice them diagonally, so that
they will cook quickly. Drop the stems into a large pot of boiling,
salted water and boil 3 or 4 minutes, then add the flowerets. Boil for
another 3–5 minutes, until the stems are just tender when pierced with
a sharp knife. Drain. Toss with melted butter and salt or serve with
Hollandaise Sauce (p. 388).

PURÉED BROCCOLI

Put the cooked broccoli through a vegetable mill or purée it in a food
processor. Reheat, seasoning to taste with lots of butter, salt, and
pepper.

STEAMED BROCCOLI   ஜ   (SERVES TWO OR THREE)

An alternative to the Basic Method, steamed broccoli will have a fine
texture and taste, but the color fades. Take care that the broccoli is not
overcooked.

1 pound broccoli   Lemon juice (optional)
Melted butter

Clean and cut up the broccoli as directed in the preceding Basic
Method for Cooking Broccoli. Steam it, covered, in a steamer basket
over boiling water until the thickest stems are just tender when pierced
with a sharp knife, about 6–10 minutes. Drain. Toss with melted butter
and lemon juice or *Hollandaise Sauce* (p. 388).

BROCCOLI WITH GARLIC AND OLIVE OIL

Instead of butter, toss the cooked broccoli with *2 tablespoons olive oil*
and *1 or 2 cloves of minced garlic*, and a little *lemon juice*.

(SERVES SIX) 🠴 **BROCCOLI IN CHEESE CUSTARD**

This custard recipe may also be used with other cooked vegetables such as cauliflower, corn kernels, onions, spinach, and cabbage.

2 cups chopped cooked broccoli
¼ cup grated Cheddar cheese
3 eggs
1½ cups milk or light cream
¾ teaspoon salt
¼ teaspoon freshly ground pepper

Preheat the oven to 350°F. Butter a 1½-quart baking dish, put the chopped broccoli into it, and sprinkle with the cheese. Beat the eggs lightly in a bowl and stir in the milk or cream, salt, and pepper. Stir into the broccoli-cheese mixture. Put the baking dish in a shallow pan with hot water halfway up its sides. Bake for 45–60 minutes, or until the custard is set.

About Broccoli Rabe (Cima di Rabe)

Availability: Late summer and fall, especially in Italian markets.
What to Look For: Thin, firm stems, and small, open, yellowish flowerets.
Uses: *Cooked, cold* in salads, or *hot*, boiled or blanched and then sautéed. *As a vegetable accompaniment*, especially suitable with meat and pasta dishes.
Amount: One pound serves two or three.

Broccoli rabe has a strong, slightly bitter flavor. It profits from special treatment, like the addition of a little garlic and oil.

(SERVES TWO OR THREE) 🠴 **SAUTÉED BROCCOLI RABE**

1 pound broccoli rabe
2 cloves garlic, minced
3 tablespoons cooking oil
Salt
Freshly ground pepper

Wash the broccoli rabe and cut it into 2- or 3-inch pieces. Drop them into a large pot of boiling water and boil for about 5 minutes, or until not quite tender; drain. Sauté the garlic in the oil for a minute or two without browning, then add the broccoli rabe and cook over medium heat, stirring frequently, until tender but still firm. Season to taste and serve immediately.

About Brussels Sprouts

Height of Season: Late fall and winter.

What to Look For: Unblemished, tightly closed sprouts, bright green in color. Avoid soft, wilted, or yellowing sprouts.

Uses: *Cooked*, with chestnuts or in casserole dishes. *As a vegetable accompaniment*, good with pork and ham, not with delicate meats or fish.

Amount: One pound serves four.

Alternatives to Fresh: Frozen are good.

Cooking in the Microwave: ½ pound whole Brussels sprouts in ¾ cup water in a glass dish with a lid, about 6 minutes on high power (in a 600–700-watt oven). Results: color bright; taste, texture, and cooking time comparable to cooking on top of the stove.

Brussels sprouts look like tiny cabbages. They grow close together on a long, single stem which can reach as high as 3 feet. The plants are not much affected by cold weather and you can often harvest them right through the winter.

BASIC METHOD FOR COOKING BRUSSELS SPROUTS ও   (SERVES FOUR)

Properly cooked Brussels sprouts should be bright green and never overcooked.

1 pound Brussels sprouts	Salt
Melted butter	Caraway seeds

Wash the sprouts in cold water, removing any wilted leaves and cutting off the stems. Pierce the stem end with a knife tip for more even cooking. If they are large, cut in half. Drop them into a large pot of boiling, salted water for 6–8 minutes, or until just tender. Taste one to see if it's done; it should still be slightly crunchy. Drain. Toss with melted butter and salt to taste or sprinkle with caraway seeds.

BRUSSELS SPROUTS WITH CHESTNUTS ও   (SERVES SIX)

Use the leftover broth to make a soup.

1 pound Brussels sprouts, trimmed	1 cup cooked (p. 560) or canned chestnuts
1½ cups beef broth	Salt
3 tablespoons butter	Freshly ground pepper
1 teaspoon sugar	

Put the Brussels sprouts in a pan with the beef broth. Simmer for about 8–10 minutes or until tender; drain. Melt the butter and sugar together in a pan, stirring until golden. Add the chestnuts and cook until they are slightly brown. Add the sprouts and cook over low heat, stirring occasionally, for about 5 minutes more. Season lightly and serve.

About Cabbage

Availability: Year round.

What to Look For: Crisp, firm, heavy heads with good color. Avoid those with blemishes or too many loose outer leaves.

Uses: *Raw,* for dipping or in salads, cole slaw. *Cooked,* boiled, steamed, braised, baked, sautéed, pickled, shredded, stuffed, in soups and stews. *As a vegetable accompaniment,* especially good with corned beef, game, pork, or smoked meats.

Amount: One pound serves three.

Cooking in the Microwave: ½ pound cabbage, in wedges, in ¾ cup water in a glass dish with a lid, about 7 minutes on high power (in a 600–700-watt oven). Results: color, taste, texture, and cooking time comparable to cooking on top of the stove.

Cabbage has been cultivated as a vegetable since ancient times, when it was valued for its health-giving and healing properties. It comes in many varieties, the most common of which are smooth green cabbage, crinkly green Savoy cabbage, red cabbage, and Chinese cabbage.

A lot of people hate cabbage because it's usually cooked to lifelessness and served without texture or taste. It also has an unpleasant odor when it's been boiling for a long time. Except when it's being braised, cabbage should actually be cooked quickly until just tender and should retain its color and crispness.

BASIC METHOD FOR COOKING ❧ CABBAGE

(SERVES THREE)

1 pound cabbage

Cut the cabbage in half; cut away and discard the hard, whitish core. Slice into wedges. Drop them into a large pot filled with boiling, salted water and boil until the cabbage is just tender, about 5–7 minutes. The cabbage should be crisp-tender and retain its color. Drain well.

BLANCHED, BUTTERED CABBAGE *   (SERVES SIX)

Beautiful color, mild taste, this is a marvelous method for those who are dubious about cabbage.

2 pounds cabbage, cored
4 slices bacon (optional)
4 tablespoons butter, melted

Salt to taste
½ teaspoon freshly ground
   pepper

Bring a big pot of water to boil. Tear the cabbage leaves into large pieces. If you use the bacon, fry it until crisp; drain, crumble, and set aside. Plunge cabbage into the boiling water for only 30 seconds; drain immediately. Return to the pot and toss with the melted butter, salt, and pepper. Serve hot.

BUTTERED CABBAGE WITH PINE NUTS

Add *2 tablespoons lemon juice* and *⅔ cup toasted pine nuts* when tossing the cabbage with the melted butter.

COLCANNON ૐ   (SERVES SIX)

This is a wonderful and much-overlooked dish of Irish origin, made of cabbage and mashed potatoes.

2 pounds boiling potatoes,
   peeled and quartered
1½ pounds cabbage, quartered
   and cored
4 tablespoons butter

1 cup light cream or milk
1 teaspoon salt, or to taste
Freshly ground pepper
6 scallions, sliced thin

Put the potatoes in a pan and just cover them with cold water. Bring to a boil and boil gently for a total of 15–20 minutes, or until tender when pierced with a fork. Halfway through the cooking, add the cabbage quarters to the pot. When done, drain very well. Remove the cabbage, slice into thin strips, and set aside. Add the butter, ½ cup of the cream or milk, salt, and pepper to the pot with the potatoes and mash with a potato masher, fork, or electric mixer, smoothing out all the lumps. Add the remaining cream or milk, blending until you have a thick purée. Add the shredded cabbage and mix until well blended. Taste and correct seasonings. Return the pot to low heat, stirring frequently until hot. Serve in a heated serving bowl garnished with the sliced scallions.

BRAISED RED CABBAGE AND APPLES

This is exceptionally good: moist and faintly sweet. A roasted loin of pork would be a splendid companion.

4 tablespoons bacon fat
2 tablespoons sugar
1 onion, chopped
2 pounds red cabbage, shredded
2 tart apples, peeled, cored, and sliced thin

2 tablespoons cider vinegar
⅛ teaspoon cayenne pepper
½ cup dry red wine
½ cup water
Salt

Melt the bacon fat in a skillet, add the sugar and cook, stirring, for 2 minutes. Add the onion and cook slowly until lightly colored. Stir in the cabbage, apples, vinegar, cayenne, and red wine. Cook over low heat, covered, for 10 minutes, then add the water and cook, with cover askew, stirring occasionally, for 30–40 minutes more. Add salt to taste. Serve hot or cold.

SAUERKRAUT

Sauerkraut, German in origin, is shredded cabbage preserved in a salt-water brine. It is not necessary to wash the brine from the sauerkraut unless a milder taste is desired. Sauerkraut, with its assertive flavor, is very compatible with goose and with pork sausages.

1 pound sauerkraut
1 large tart apple, peeled, cored, and diced
1 cup beef bouillon

1 teaspoon caraway seeds
¼ teaspoon freshly ground pepper
Salt

Wash the sauerkraut in several changes of cold water if desired; drain thoroughly. Combine the sauerkraut, apple, bouillon, caraway seeds, and pepper. Cook over low heat, stirring occasionally, for about 30–35 minutes. Add salt to taste. Serve hot.

BRAISED CHINESE CABBAGE   (SERVES FOUR)

8 strips bacon
1 head Chinese cabbage,
    shredded
Salt

Freshly ground pepper
Soy sauce or rice wine
    vinegar

Cook the bacon in a skillet until crisp; remove and drain. Pour off all
but 2 tablespoons of bacon fat. Heat the remaining fat, then add the
cabbage. Cover and cook slowly, stirring occasionally, until just tender,
about 3 minutes. Crumble the bacon and stir it into the cabbage. Season to taste with salt and pepper and serve with soy sauce, or toss with
a sprinkling of rice vinegar.

HOT SLAW ⮞   (SERVES FOUR)

A tart, vinegary dressing that is a good foil for shredded cabbage. This
would be nice with pork or ham.

1 pound cabbage
2 egg yolks
¼ cup cold water

1 tablespoon butter
¼ cup cider vinegar
Salt

Shred the cabbage and have it ready in a bowl. Mix the egg yolks, water, butter, and vinegar in a heavy-bottomed pan. Cook, stirring constantly, over low heat until thickened. Add the cabbage and stir briskly
to coat. Add salt to taste. Heat through and serve.

About Carrots

Availability: Year round.
What to Look For: Fairly small, firm, smooth carrots with good color
and no cracks or green areas at the top.
Uses: Whole, diced, sliced, or grated. *Raw*, for dipping, in juice, salads.
Cooked, boiled, braised, baked, as a seasoning, in stocks, soups,
casserole dishes, cakes, breads, cookies. *As a vegetable accompani-
ment*, good with just about anything.
Amount: One pound serves three or four.
Alternatives to Fresh: Frozen preferable to canned, but texture is poor.
Cooking in the Microwave: ½ pound peeled carrots in 1-inch pieces, in
           ¾ cup water in a glass dish with a lid, about 5 minutes on
    M≋   high power (in a 600–700-watt oven). Results: color good
but taste and texture less mellow than cooking on top of the stove;
time comparable.

Carrots are rich in vitamin A. When small and new, they may not need peeling. To peel, use a vegetable scraper and keep them in cold water until ready to use.

Cooked carrots, even old carrots, may be very sweet; use them with discretion or you may overpower the flavor of a soup, sauce, or stew.

If you plan to grow carrots yourself, choose one of the shorter varieties: it's hard to grow straight, long, tapered carrots unless you have specially prepared, rock-free soil.

BASIC METHOD FOR COOKING ᨹ CARROTS

(SERVES THREE OR FOUR)

Cooking times vary greatly with carrots, depending on their size and age.

1 pound carrots, trimmed and peeled	Salt
2 tablespoons butter	Freshly ground pepper

Slice or cube the carrots, or leave them whole if they are small. Cook them, covered, in about 2 inches of boiling water until they are tender, about 10–12 minutes if they are sliced, longer if they are whole. Drain. Coat with the butter, season to taste, and reheat, if necessary, before serving.

CANDIED CARROTS

Melt *5 tablespoons butter* in a heavy skillet, stir in ¼ *cup brown sugar*, and heat, stirring, until melted. Add the cooked, seasoned carrots and cook slowly until they are well glazed.

CARROTS AND PEAS

Add *cooked green peas* to diced cooked carrots, dot with butter, season to taste with salt and freshly ground pepper, and reheat slowly.

MASHED OR PURÉED CARROTS

Mash the cooked carrots, put them through a food mill, or purée them in a food processor. Season to taste with butter, salt, freshly ground pepper, and a whisper of *nutmeg* or *chopped dill*. Reheat slowly, preferably in the top of a double boiler.

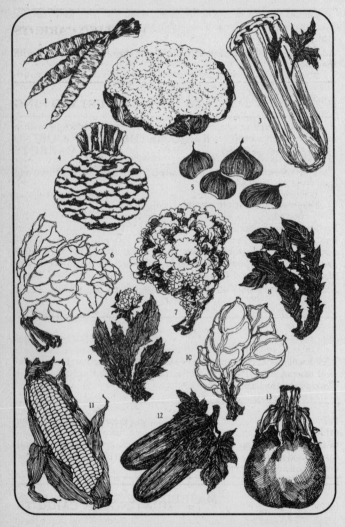

1. *carrots;* 2. *cauliflower;* 3. *celery;* 4. *celeriac;* 5. *chestnuts;* 6. *collards;* 7. *kale;*
8. *dandelion greens;* 9. *turnip greens;* 10. *beet greens;* 11. *corn;* 12. *cucumbers;*
13. *eggplant.*

PARSLIED CARROTS

Add 2 *tablespoons finely chopped parsley* to the carrots when coating with the butter.

(1-QUART RING) ɞ **CARROT CUSTARD RING**

A custard of puréed carrots baked in a ring mold—delicious with a mound of fresh cooked green peas in the center.

2½ cups mashed cooked carrots (1 pound)	1 tablespoon flour
1 teaspoon thyme, crumbled	1 cup milk or light cream
3 tablespoons butter, melted	½ teaspoon salt
2 eggs, well beaten	¼ teaspoon freshly ground pepper

Preheat the oven to 350°F. Amply butter a 1-quart ring mold and lightly dust it with flour. Mix all ingredients in a bowl, stirring vigorously. Spoon into the mold. Set the mold in a shallow pan of hot water and bake until firm, about 45 minutes. Unmold, fill the center, if you like, with peas or another green vegetable, and serve.

(SERVES THREE OR FOUR) **BAKED CARROTS**

1 pound carrots	Salt
3 tablespoons butter	Freshly ground pepper
1 small onion, chopped	½ cup broth or stock
1 teaspoon sugar	
1 sprig fresh thyme, or ½ teaspoon dried	

Preheat the oven to 350°F. Peel and grate the carrots and set them aside. Melt the butter in a small casserole, add the onion, and cook until soft and transparent. Stir in the carrots, season with the sugar and thyme, and add salt and pepper to taste. Add the broth or stock, cover, and bake until tender, about 30–40 minutes.

(SERVES THREE OR FOUR) ɞ **HUNTINGTON CARROTS**

1 pound carrots, preferably small	Salt
¼ pound butter	½ teaspoon sugar
	½ cup heavy cream

Clean and peel the carrots. Leave them whole if they are small, or cut them into 1½-inch strips. Melt the butter in a heavy pan, add the carrots, and turn them over and over in the butter until they are well coated. Season them with salt to taste and sugar, cover, and cook very slowly until the carrots are tender, about 25–35 minutes. Turn them occasionally and be sure that they do not burn. Before serving, adjust the seasonings, add the cream, and reheat.

About Cauliflower

Height of Season: Fall or winter.

What to Look For: Firm, white, compact flowerets without spots or bruises; crisp, green leaves.

Uses: *Raw*, in flowerets, for dipping or in salads. *Cooked*, whole or in flowerets, boiled, steamed, deep-fried in batter, and pickled. *As a vegetable accompaniment*, especially good with steak or chops.

Amount: One medium head, about two pounds, serves four or five.

Alternatives to Fresh: Frozen acceptable.

Cooking in the Microwave: ½ pound cauliflower flowerets and stems in ¾ cup water in a glass dish with a lid, about 7 minutes on high power (in a 600–700-watt oven). Results: color, taste, texture, and cooking time comparable to cooking on top of the stove.

Cauliflower, like broccoli, is grown for its clusters of unopened flower buds, called curds. If you grow it yourself, the flowerets will most likely be tinged with purple (unless they are well shielded from the light) but will taste just fine.

BASIC METHOD FOR COOKING CAULIFLOWER ⁓

(SERVES FOUR OR FIVE)

1 medium cauliflower (about 2 pounds)	Salt
Melted butter	Freshly ground pepper

Remove the leaves from the cauliflower. Wash it well, leaving it whole or separating it into flowerets. Steam, covered, in a steamer basket over boiling water until tender, allowing about 6–8 minutes for flowerets, 15–20 minutes for the whole head. Drain. Pour melted butter over it and season to taste.

CAULIFLOWER WITH CHOPPED WALNUTS

Before serving, sprinkle with ½ cup coarsely chopped walnuts.

CAULIFLOWER AU GRATIN

Leave the cauliflower whole and put it on a shallow, ovenproof dish. Sprinkle with ¾ *cup freshly grated Parmesan cheese* and ½ *cup buttered bread crumbs*. Bake in a preheated 400°F oven until brown on top, about 15 minutes.

CREAMED CAULIFLOWER AU GRATIN

Arrange cooked cauliflower flowerets in a baking dish, season with salt and freshly ground pepper, and cover with 1½ *cups White Sauce* (p. 379). Sprinkle ½ *cup grated Cheddar or Parmesan* over the top. Bake in a preheated 400°F oven until hot and bubbly throughout and golden on top, 15–20 minutes.

CAULIFLOWER WITH SCALLIONS

Before serving, toss with ½ *cup chopped scallions*.

CURRIED CAULIFLOWER

While cauliflower is cooking, make 1 *recipe Curry Cream Sauce* (p. 380). Before serving, toss with the hot Curry Cream Sauce in place of the melted butter.

About Celery

Availability: Year round.
What to Look For: Fresh, firm, unwilted stalks, preferably with leaves.
Uses: *Raw,* with a dip or in salads. *Cooked,* steamed, sautéed, braised, as a seasoning, in stocks, soups, stews, and casserole dishes. Leaves also used for seasoning. *As a vegetable accompaniment,* it's good with everything.
Amount: One pound serves two or three.
Cooking in the Microwave: ½ pound celery in 3-inch pieces in ¾ cup water in a glass dish with a lid, about 7 minutes on high power (in a 600–700-watt oven). Results: color, taste, texture, and cooking time comparable to cooking on top of the stove.

The pale celery that we find in the markets is intentionally "blanched" while it is being grown. Many home gardeners do the same, planting celery in trenches which they gradually fill with soil as the celery grows. This keeps the light from the celery stalks, making them white and their flavor mild. Some people, however, prefer the strong flavor of unblanched green celery.

BRAISED CELERY   (SERVES TWO OR THREE)

Braising celery this way brings out its rich flavor.

1 pound celery	Salt
2 tablespoons butter	Freshly ground pepper
Chicken broth	

Wash the celery and cut off the leaves and any discolored parts. Cut the stalks in even lengths, about 3 inches long. Sauté in the butter for about 5 minutes, then add about ½ inch of broth, just enough to keep the celery from burning. Season with salt and pepper, unless the stock is already well seasoned. Cover and cook over low heat until the celery is just tender, about 8–12 minutes. Put the celery in a serving dish. Rapidly boil the liquid in the pan until it is reduced to just a few tablespoons. Pour over the celery and serve.

BRAISED CELERY AU GRATIN

Arrange the braised celery in a shallow baking dish and add a little of the cooking liquid. Sprinkle with ½ cup freshly grated Parmesan cheese and put under the broiler until the cheese has melted.

CREAMY CELERY   (SERVES FOUR TO SIX)

1 pound celery, sliced (about 4 cups)	¼ cup milk
	Salt
2 tablespoons butter	½ cup sliced blanched almonds, toasted
3 tablespoons flour	
¾ cup chicken broth	

Bring a large pot of salted water to a boil. Add the celery and cook for about 6–8 minutes, or until tender but firm. Drain and set aside. Melt the butter in a saucepan and stir in the flour. Cook over medium heat for about 2 minutes, stirring constantly. Slowly stir in the chicken broth and continue to cook and stir until the sauce has thickened. Add the milk and salt to taste and cook until smooth and well blended. Stir the sauce and ¼ cup of the almonds into the celery. Serve at once or pour into a buttered casserole dish and heat in a 375°F oven for about 20 minutes, or until heated through before serving. Sprinkle the top with the remaining almonds just before serving.

About Celery Root or Celeriac

Height of Season: October through April; not all markets sell it.
What to Look For: Firm, unwilted root.
Uses: *Raw*, grated, as a first course or salad. *As a vegetable accompaniment*, especially good with veal and beef when braised.
Amount: One pound serves four.
Cooking in the Microwave: ½ pound celery root, peeled and in ¼-inch slices, in ¾ cup water in a glass dish with a lid, about 7 minutes on high power (in a 600–700-watt oven). Results: color, taste, texture, and cooking time comparable to cooking on top of the stove.

Celery root or celeriac is also known as celeri-rave or celery knob. It is large, brown, and lumpy in appearance. It has a slightly mealy texture when cooked and an earthy, concentrated celery flavor with a slightly sweet overtone that is unusual and utterly delicious. Try it also in the Scalloped Potatoes with Celery Root or Celeriac, p. 597.

BRAISED CELERY ROOT OR CELERIAC

(SERVES FOUR)

1 pound celery root	About 2 cups beef bouillon
2 tablespoons butter	2 tablespoons minced parsley

Peel the celery root and cut into ¼-inch slices. Arrange in a skillet—preferably not iron because it is apt to discolor the celery root—dot with butter, add the bouillon, and cook over medium high heat with cover askew until tender, but not mushy, about 8–12 minutes. Then remove the celery root with a slotted spoon to a serving dish and keep warm while you boil down the remaining liquid until it is almost syrupy. Pour over the celery root and sprinkle with parsley.

SAUTÉED CELERY ROOT OR CELERIAC ҂ (SERVES FOUR)

A combination of faintly sweet grapes and a fine, sharp celery flavor, this is a particularly nice dish to serve with fish.

1 pound celery root	2 teaspoons minced parsley
1 cup water	¾ cup green seedless grapes
Juice of 1 lemon	Salt
3 tablespoons butter	

Peel the celery root and cut it into eighths. Put into a pot with the water, lemon juice, and 1 tablespoon of the butter. Cover and simmer about 10–15 minutes, or until tender. Drain off the liquid and add the remaining 2 tablespoons of butter, the parsley, the grapes, and salt to taste. Turn up the heat and shake the pan to coat the ingredients with the butter and to prevent sticking. Heat through and serve.

About Chestnuts

Height of Season: Winter, especially around Thanksgiving and Christmas.

What to Look For: It is hard to tell how fresh chestnuts are when they're in the shell. Feel them and be sure that the nut seems firm and has not drawn away from the shell.

Uses: *Cooked*, in stuffings or combined with other vegetables, such as Brussels sprouts or red cabbage. *As a vegetable accompaniment*, especially good with fowl or pork. Cooked in syrup and put through a ricer, chestnuts also make an elegant dessert, served with whipped cream.

Amount: One pound serves three or four.

Alternatives to Fresh: Canned (unsweetened).

Technically nuts, chestnuts are primarily used as a vegetable.

There's no substitute for their unique flavor. It's worth the bother of shelling them and removing the inner skin.

To shell, cut slits or crisscross gashes in the flat sides of the chestnuts and drop them into boiling water for a minute or two. While the chestnuts are still warm, remove the shells and inner skins, using a sharp knife. If any of the skins are especially difficult to peel, reboil the chestnuts for a few seconds.

(SERVES FOUR) **BRAISED CHESTNUTS**

1 pound chestnuts, shelled (above)
1 cup beef broth
¼ teaspoon salt

⅛ teaspoon freshly ground pepper
2 tablespoons butter

Put the chestnuts into a pan with the beef broth, salt, and pepper. Cover and simmer for about 15–20 minutes; drain. Add the butter, turn the heat up, and shake the pan so the chestnuts are well anointed with the butter. Serve hot.

CREAMED CHESTNUTS

Add ¼ *cup heavy cream* with the butter.

PURÉED CHESTNUTS

Put the buttered chestnuts through a food mill or purée them in a blender or food processor, beating in a little *hot heavy cream* if too thick.

About Collards and Other Greens

Availability: Year round, especially summer and fall.

What to Look For: Crisp, green leaves without blemishes or discoloration.

Uses: *As a vegetable accompaniment*, especially good with ham or pork chops.

Amount: One pound serves two.

Blanching in the Microwave: ½ pound greens, tough ribs removed, leaves in small pieces, in ¾ cup water in a glass dish with a lid, about 7 minutes on high power (in a 600–700-watt oven). Results: for blanching only, comparable to stove-top method. Longer cooking in the microwave toughens greens. Recommend cooking on top of the stove.

Beet greens, kale, turnip and mustard greens may all be cooked in the same fashion as collards. In fact, these greens often taste better in combination, cooked with a ham bone. If the stems are thick, remove them and cook them separately.

BRAISED COLLARDS   ⭕   (SERVES TWO)

It's fine to cook other greens by this method, although the cooking time
may need adjusting.

1 pound collards or other greens	1–2 cloves garlic, minced
¼ cup olive oil	Salt
	Freshly ground pepper

Wash the greens well, removing all sand, in several changes of cold
water. Remove any tough ribs, then cut or tear into small pieces. Drop
the greens into a large pot of boiling water and blanch them for about
10 minutes; remove and drain well. Put the olive oil and garlic in a
pan, add the blanched, drained greens, cover, and cook over low heat
for 20–30 minutes. Season with a little salt and pepper, if necessary.

MIXED GREENS SOUTHERN STYLE   (SERVES SIX)

Save a ham bone (with a little meat clinging to it) to make this. The
greens can vary, but there should be a good proportion of collards.
Southerners would serve in soup plates with hot corn bread to mop up
what they call the pot liquor.

1 ham bone	Salt
¼ pound salt pork, cubed	Freshly ground pepper
6 cups water	
3 pounds collards, kale, turnip greens, mustard greens, and/or dandelion greens	

Boil the ham bone and salt pork in the water for 45 minutes. Wash the
greens carefully, remove tough ends of the stalks, and chop up the rest
along with the greens. Add to the pot and cook until tender, about 45
minutes. At that point the water should almost have disappeared and
the salt pork will have melted away. Remove the ham bone and scrape
any bits of meat back into the pot. Add salt and pepper to taste.

About Corn

Height of Season: Spring or summer, depending on region.
What to Look For: Moist, plump, juicy-looking yellow or white kernels, not too large; green, fresh-looking husks.

Uses: *Cooked,* boiled, roasted, pickled, on the cob or off, in succotash, soup, salads, puddings, and fritters. *As a vegetable accompaniment,* good with everything.

Amount: Two or more ears per person.

Alternatives to Fresh: Frozen better than canned.

Cooking in the Microwave: 1 ear of corn in husk with silk removed about 2–3 minutes on high power (in a 600–700-watt oven). Results: color, taste, texture, and cooking time comparable to cooking on top of the stove.

½ pound fresh corn kernels (about 1½ cups), in ½ cup water in a glass dish with a lid, about 2–3 minutes on high power (in a 600–700-watt oven). Results: color and cooking time comparable to cooking on top of the stove; taste and texture slightly altered.

The sugar in corn turns to starch very rapidly after it is picked. How lucky are those who can rush fresh ears from the field, husk them quickly, and plunge them into a pot of boiling water!

If you must hold corn for any length of time, keep it unhusked in the refrigerator until you are ready to cook it.

Cut the kernels from any leftover cooked, fresh corn and freeze them in a plastic container. Reheated quickly in a little boiling water, drained, and tossed with butter, home-frozen corn kernels make a delicious midwinter vegetable.

BASIC METHOD FOR COOKING
(SERVES FOUR)   ❧   CORN ON THE COB

There is nothing like fresh corn on the cob, quickly boiled, spread with lots of sweet butter, and sprinkled with salt. Two ears per person may seem like a proper serving, but appetites often run high when corn is in season and freshly picked.

8 ears of corn	Salt
Butter, softened	

Just before cooking, husk the corn, pull off the silky threads, and cut out any blemishes with a pointed knife. Drop the corn into a large pot filled with boiling salted water. Cover the pot and let the water return to a boil again, then turn off the heat and keep the pot covered. After about 5 minutes, remove enough ears for a first serving. You can keep the remaining corn warm in the water for another 10 minutes without its becoming tough. Serve with lots of butter and salt.

FOIL-ROASTED CORN ON THE COB ɛ❧ (SERVES FOUR TO SIX)

12 ears of corn   Salt
Butter

Preheat the oven to 400°F. Husk the corn and wrap each ear in foil, adding 2 teaspoons of butter to each packet. Bake for about 25 minutes. Or roast the foil-wrapped corn over hot coals, turning once during the cooking. Serve with more butter and salt.

SAUTÉED FRESH CORN ɛ❧ (SERVES FOUR)

2 tablespoons butter   Salt and freshly ground
4 ears of fresh corn, kernels   pepper to taste
   removed

Melt the butter in a large skillet. Add the corn kernels and salt and pepper and cook over medium heat, stirring often, about 6 minutes, or until the rawness disappears.

SUCCOTASH ɛ❧ (SERVES THREE)

1 cup cooked corn kernels   Cream
1 cup cooked lima beans or   Salt
   other shell beans   Freshly ground pepper
Butter

Heat the corn and lima beans in butter and a little cream in a saucepan. Season to taste.

SOUTHERN CORN PUDDING ɛ❧ (SERVES FOUR)

Fresh corn kernels extracted from the cob give this a special quality.

2 cups fresh grated or   2 cups hot milk
   chopped corn kernels   ½ teaspoon salt
2 eggs, slightly beaten   ⅛ teaspoon freshly ground
2 tablespoons butter, melted   pepper

Preheat the oven to 350°F. Butter a 1½-quart casserole. Mix all ingredients together in a bowl. Pour into the casserole and place in a pan of hot water. Bake until firm, about 45 minutes.

(SERVES SIX) &ex; **CORN SOUFFLÉ**

1 tablespoon butter	1 teaspoon salt
2 tablespoons flour	¼ teaspoon freshly ground
1 cup milk	pepper
2 eggs, separated	
2 cups cooked, canned, or	
frozen and thawed corn	
kernels	

Preheat the oven to 350°F. Generously butter a 1½-quart casserole. Melt the butter in a pan, slowly stir in the flour, and cook over moderate heat for 2 minutes, stirring constantly. Slowly add the milk and continue stirring constantly until thickened; continue to cook for 2 or 3 more minutes. Stir the egg yolks in a small bowl, then add a little of the hot milk mixture, stirring briskly. Add the yolk mixture to the milk mixture in the pan, stir for 1 minute, then remove from the heat and add the corn, salt, and pepper; set aside. Beat the egg whites until stiff but not dry. Fold a fourth of the whites into the corn mixture and blend, then gently fold in the remaining whites. Spoon into the baking dish and bake for about 30–35 minutes.

(SERVES SIX) &ex; **SCALLOPED CORN**

3 tablespoons flour	½ onion, chopped fine
1 teaspoon salt	1 cup milk
¼ teaspoon paprika	2 cups fresh or canned,
¼ teaspoon dry mustard	drained corn kernels
Pinch of cayenne pepper	1 egg yolk, slightly beaten
3 tablespoons butter	⅔ cup buttered bread crumbs
1 small green pepper,	
chopped fine	

Preheat the oven to 400°F. Generously butter a 1½-quart baking dish. Mix the flour, salt, paprika, mustard, and cayenne pepper together; set aside. Melt the butter in a skillet, add the green pepper and onion, and cook until soft. Stir in the flour mixture and cook, stirring and smoothing, for 2 or 3 minutes. Add the milk, stirring constantly, and bring it to the boiling point. Stir in the corn and egg yolk. Spoon into the baking dish and sprinkle with the crumbs. Bake for 25 minutes until the crumbs are brown.

CORN OYSTERS ॐ

(TEN 2½-INCH OYSTERS;
SERVES FOUR OR FIVE)

Lightly browned, with a chewy texture, simple flavor, and fresh corn taste. Serve these with ham, perhaps with a few drops of maple syrup over them.

1 cup grated or chopped fresh corn kernels	¼ teaspoon salt
1 egg, well beaten	⅛ teaspoon freshly ground pepper
¼ cup flour	4 tablespoons butter

Combine the corn with the egg, flour, salt, and pepper and mix well. Shape into patties (or "oysters") about 2½ inches in diameter. Heat the butter in a skillet until foaming, then add the corn oysters. Cook over medium heat for 3–4 minutes. Turn when golden brown, and brown the other side. Keep warm in a low oven until ready to serve.

About Cucumbers

Availability: Year round, especially good at farmers' markets in summer.

What to Look For: Firm, slender, well-shaped, dark-green cucumbers, preferably fresh, not waxed.

Uses: *Raw*, with dips or in soups, salads, or sandwiches. *Cooked*, in soups, stuffed, or pickled. *As a vegetable accompaniment*, good with fish or veal.

Amount: One large cucumber serves two.

Cooking in the Microwave: ½ pound cucumbers, peeled, seeded, and in ½-inch slices, in ¾ cup water in a glass dish with a lid, about 6 minutes on high power (in a 600–700-watt oven). Results: color, taste, texture, and cooking time comparable to cooking on top of the stove.

Store cucumbers in the refrigerator and do not keep them too long. They contain a lot of water and are cooling and thirst-quenching. Salting draws the water out of cucumber slices, as does blanching. More often used raw, cucumbers are also delicious cooked or stewed as on facing page.

(SERVES FOUR) 🐦 **BUTTER BRAISED CUCUMBERS**

Pale, delicate green, and faintly piquant; good with fish or lamb.

2 large cucumbers
6 tablespoons butter

½ teaspoon chervil, crumbled
Salt

Peel the cucumbers, slice lengthwise, scoop out the seeds, and cut into ½-inch slices. Put in a heavy-bottomed pan with a lid; add 1 cup water, 4 tablespoons of the butter, and the chervil. Cover and gently simmer for 8–10 minutes. Drain, then add salt to taste and the remaining 2 tablespoons of butter. Serve hot.

CUCUMBERS WITH SCALLIONS

Substitute *⅓ cup finely chopped scallions* for the ½ teaspoon chervil.

CUCUMBERS WITH DILL

Substitute *½ teaspoon dry dillweed* or *1 tablespoon chopped fresh dill* for the ½ teaspoon chervil.

About Eggplant

Availability: Year round, especially in August and September.

What to Look For: Heavy, smooth, firm vegetables with shiny, unscarred skins.

Uses: *Cooked*, with or without skin, pan-fried, batter-fried, sautéed, baked, chopped, stuffed, marinated. *Cold*, in salads. *Hot*, in stews and casserole dishes or as a main course. *As a vegetable accompaniment*, good with lamb and pork.

Amount: One medium eggplant, about 1½ pounds, serves four.

Cooking in the Microwave: ½ pound peeled eggplant, in ½-inch cubes, in ¾ cup water in a glass dish with a lid, about 5 minutes on high power (in a 600–700-watt oven). Results: color, taste, texture, and cooking time comparable to cooking on top of the stove.

Eggplant is known as *aubergine* in France and England and *melanzana* in Italy. There are several varieties, including white eggplant and tiny purple eggplants only 3–4 inches long, but the large, tapered, purple vegetable is the one we usually see here.

Keep eggplants in the refrigerator and use them as soon as possible. Eggplant has a great capacity for absorbing oil, but if the slices are salted to drain them of excess water, then dried and fried in well-heated butter or oil, they will absorb less.

BAKED STUFFED EGGPLANT ✳ ≈   (SERVES FOUR TO SIX)

1½ pounds eggplant
3 tablespoons olive or
   vegetable oil
3 cloves garlic, minced
½ cup chopped onion
2 cups mushrooms, chopped

Salt and freshly ground
   pepper to taste
2 tablespoons minced parsley
½ cup pitted black olives,
   quartered

Preheat the oven to 375°F. Cut the top off the eggplant and cut in half lengthwise. Run a knife around the edge of each half, about ¼ inch in from the skin, to cut the pulp free, leaving a shell. Cut the removed eggplant pulp into cubes (you will have about 4 cups). Place 2 tablespoons of the oil in a large skillet over medium heat, add the garlic, onion, and eggplant pulp, and sauté for about 5 minutes. Add the mushrooms, salt, and pepper, and continue to cook about 5–7 more minutes, or until the mushrooms and eggplant are soft and cooked through. Remove from the heat and stir in the parsley and black olives. Film the skin of the eggplant shells with the remaining oil and place in a greased casserole. Spoon some of the eggplant mixture into each half. Cover and bake for about 1 hour.

BAKED EGGPLANT ≈   (SERVES FOUR)

1 eggplant (about 1½ pounds)
1 cup soft fresh bread crumbs
2 tomatoes, seeded and
   chopped
4 tablespoons butter
1 small onion, chopped fine

¼ teaspoon oregano,
   crumbled
Salt
Freshly ground pepper
1 egg, well beaten

Preheat the oven to 375°F. Put the eggplant in a large pot filled with boiling, salted water and cook for 12–15 minutes. Drain, then cut in half lengthwise. Cube the eggplant, including the seeds, and stir in the bread crumbs and tomatoes; set aside. Melt the butter in a skillet. Add the onion and cook until soft; add to the eggplant mixture. Add the oregano and salt and pepper to taste. Stir in the beaten egg and toss to mix well. Spoon the eggplant mixture into a buttered baking dish and bake for 35–40 minutes. Serve hot or cold.

(SERVES FOUR)   ૐ **SCALLOPED EGGPLANT**

1 eggplant (about 1½ pounds)	Salt
2 tablespoons butter	Freshly ground pepper
1 small onion, chopped fine	Buttered bread crumbs
2 cloves garlic, chopped fine	Freshly grated Parmesan
1 tablespoon finely chopped parsley	cheese

Preheat the oven to 375°F. Peel the eggplant and cut it into ½-inch cubes. Put the eggplant in a pot with an inch of boiling water, cover, and cook gently until tender, about 5–10 minutes. Drain. Melt the butter in a skillet, add the onion and garlic, and cook over low heat until soft but not brown. Stir in the eggplant and parsley, season with salt and pepper, and combine gently. Spoon into a buttered baking dish, cover with lots of bread crumbs and grated cheese, and bake about 20–25 minutes, until the eggplant is heated through and the crumbs are brown.

(SERVES FOUR)   ૐ **GARLIC FRIED EGGPLANT**

A simple preparation, good for eggplant lovers.

1 medium eggplant (about 1½ pounds)	6 tablespoons olive oil
Salt	2 cloves garlic, chopped fine
Freshly ground pepper	3 tablespoons finely chopped parsley

Cut the eggplant into slices ¼–½ inch thick. Sprinkle lightly with salt and pepper and let drain on paper towels for 30 minutes; pat dry. Heat the olive oil in a large skillet. Add the garlic to the skillet, then the eggplant slices, and cook over moderate heat, turning once or twice until they are golden. Serve hot, sprinkled with the parsley.

About Belgian Endive

Availability: Most of the year; usually quite expensive.

What to Look For: Fresh, crisp, tender stalks, without discoloration or signs of insect damage.

Uses: *Raw*, in salads. *Cooked*, braised, baked, sautéed. *As a hot vegetable accompaniment*, especially good with ham.

Amount: One or two stalks per serving.
Cooking in the Microwave: ½ pound endive, halved lengthwise, in ¾
  cup water in a glass dish with a lid, about 5 minutes on
  high power (in a 600–700-watt oven). Results: color dull,
taste and texture poor. Microwaving not recommended.

Belgian endive, also known as witloof chicory, is a compact vegetable, budlike in form, which is grown in the dark to give it its creamy
white color. It has a slightly bitter flavor, especially when cooked.

BRAISED ENDIVE   (SERVES FOUR)

Don't use an iron skillet, or the endive will turn black.

8 small endive	Chicken broth
3 tablespoons butter	Salt

Wash the endive and cut off any discolored spots. Split them lengthwise if they are large; leave them whole if they are small. Sauté them in
the butter for about 5 minutes, then add about ½ inch of broth. Cover
and cook slowly until just tender when pierced with the tip of a sharp
knife, about 20 minutes. Arrange the endive in a serving dish. Boil the
cooking liquid rapidly until it is reduced to just a few tablespoons.
Add salt to taste. Pour over the endive and serve.

About Florentine Fennel

Availability: Most of the year, especially in Italian markets.
What to Look For: Firm, fresh stalks and leaves.
Uses: *Raw,* like celery, or in salads. *Cooked,* in soups, stews, casserole
dishes, stuffings. *As a vegetable accompaniment,* especially good with
chicken, veal, or fish.
Amount: One pound serves three.
Cooking in the Microwave: ½ pound trimmed fennel, in ½-inch slices,
  in ¾ cup water in a glass dish with a lid, about 6 minutes
  on high power (in a 600–700-watt oven). Results: color,
taste, texture, and cooking time comparable to cooking on top of
the stove.

Florentine fennel, also called *finocchio,* has celerylike stalks that
broaden to a bulb shape, with feather leaves at the stem end, and the
licorice flavor of anise. It is not to be confused with common fennel,
which is used as a seasoning but not as a vegetable.

(SERVES THREE)   **BRAISED FENNEL**

1 pound fennel	Salt
2 tablespoons butter	Freshly ground pepper
Chicken broth	

Wash the fennel and remove any tough or discolored outer parts. Slice the bulb into ½-inch pieces, the tender part of the stems into smaller. Sauté in the butter in a skillet for about 5 minutes, then add about ½ inch of broth, enough so that the fennel does not burn. Cover and simmer over low heat until tender, about 15–20 minutes. Arrange the fennel in a serving dish. Boil the cooking liquid down to just a few tablespoons, and season to taste. Pour over the fennel and serve.

BRAISED FENNEL AU GRATIN

Arrange the cooked fennel in a shallow baking dish and pour a little of the pan juices over it. Sprinkle generously with *freshly grated Parmesan cheese* and put under the broiler until the cheese has melted.

About Fiddleheads

Availability: Found wild in the spring, or in specialty markets.
What to Look For: Young, curled, unopened fern shoots.
Uses: *As an unusual vegetable accompaniment,* good with ham.
Alternatives to Fresh: Frozen or canned, best with a sauce, like Hollandaise Sauce (p. 388).

Fiddleheads are feathery and a little crisp. If you pick them yourself, you must know what you are looking for—otherwise you may pick varieties that are quite bitter.

❧ BASIC METHOD FOR COOKING FIDDLEHEADS

Fresh or frozen fiddleheads	Salt
Butter	Freshly ground pepper

Wash fresh fiddleheads, drain them, and rub off their woolly skins. If you are using frozen fiddleheads, let them defrost partially. Melt a tablespoon or two of butter in ½ inch of boiling water in a skillet, lay the fiddleheads flat in the pan, cover, and simmer for about 10 minutes. Season to taste with salt and pepper.

About Garlic

Availability: Year round, especially late summer and fall.

What to Look For: Firm bulbs in white papery skin, heavy to the touch with no soft spots.

Uses: Mainly as a seasoner (see Garlic, p. 15) but can be eaten baked as an appetizer or vegetable (see below). Flavor is strong and pronounced when

raw but pleasant and mild when cooked. If cooked until browned, it develops a strong, acrid taste that some people like. Boiling or baking garlic gives the cloves a mild, faintly sweet flavor. Sautéing without browning lends a stronger garlic flavor than boiling or baking.

Alternatives to Fresh: Powdered, dehydrated flakes can be acceptable in some recipes.

BAKED WHOLE GARLIC ✳ ౭ଓ   (SERVES FOUR)

This is good served with a soft white cheese or cream cheese and French bread. The garlic mellows and turns creamy as it bakes. To eat, squeeze one clove at a time out of the skins onto bread.

4 whole heads of garlic	Salt and pepper to taste
¼ cup olive oil, approximately	1 teaspoon thyme leaves

Preheat the oven to 275°F. Slice the top ¼ inch from the heads of garlic and rub to remove some of the papery skin from the outside, taking care not to separate the cloves. Put the heads in a baking dish that will just hold them. Pour the olive oil over each, add the salt, pepper, and thyme, cover, and bake for 30 minutes. Remove the cover and continue to bake for about 1–1½ hours longer. The garlic should be very tender. Serve whole heads warm, one per person, with the oil poured over them.

Kale

See About Collards and Other Greens, p. 561.

About Kohlrabi

Availability: June and July are height of season.

What to Look For: Small, young, tender globes.

Uses: *Raw*, with salt, as a snack or salad. *Cooked*, in soups or stews. *As a vegetable accompaniment*, especially good with pot roast.

Amount: Two or three small kohlrabi per person.
Cooking in the Microwave: ½ pound peeled kohlrabi, in ¼-inch slices, in ¾ cup water in a glass dish with a lid, about 7 minutes on high power (in a 600–700-watt oven). Results: color, taste, and texture comparable to cooking on top of the stove, and for this small amount cooking time is faster.

Kohlrabi is a strange-looking light-green and purple vegetable. It's in the cabbage family, as its leaves indicate. Its globe, however, resembles a turnip and tastes like one, too, though milder. The globe grows above ground, unlike a turnip, and is part of the stem, not the root.

BASIC METHOD FOR COOKING ಳಿ KOHLRABI

(SERVES FOUR)

If the kohlrabi tops are young and tender, cook them separately in boiling salted water, drain and chop them, and add them to the cooked kohlrabi globe.

1 pound kohlrabi	Salt
Melted butter	Freshly ground pepper

Cut off the tops of the kohlrabi and peel and slice the globes. Cook, uncovered, in boiling, salted water until tender, about 20–30 minutes (cook less if the kohlrabi are very small). Or steam on a rack, over boiling water, covered for about 15 minutes until tender. Drain. Toss with melted butter and season to taste.

KOHLRABI AU GRATIN

Put the cooked, seasoned kohlrabi in a shallow, buttered baking dish. Sprinkle with ½ *cup freshly grated Parmesan cheese* and put under the broiler until the cheese has melted.

KOHLRABI WITH BUTTERED BREAD CRUMBS

Sprinkle with *Buttered Bread Crumbs* (p. 533) just before serving.

About Leeks

Availability: Year round, especially in the fall.
What to Look For: Young, fresh-looking leeks, supple not stiff; avoid discolored tops.

Uses: *Cooked*, braised, served hot or cold, as a first course, or in soups and stews. *As a vegetable accompaniment*, especially good with a roast of beef.

Amount: One pound serves three.

Cooking in the Microwave: ½ pound trimmed leeks, halved lengthwise, in ¾ cup water in a glass dish with a lid, about 6 minutes on high power (in a 600–700-watt oven). Results: color, taste, texture, and cooking time comparable to cooking on top of the stove.

Although leeks are in the onion family, their sweet, delicate flavor is distinctively their own. Often quite expensive in stores, they are exceedingly easy to grow at home and an infinitely useful vegetable to have in a home garden. They are very hardy and may be dug until the ground has frozen.

Because the bottoms of leeks are grown underground, sand often gets inside the leaves and works its way down within them. Leeks thus require a good deal of washing. To clean them, cut off the soft tops, leaving 1–2 inches of green. Slice them lengthwise to within ½ inch of the bottom, spread the leaves, and wash well in cold water. Use the cut-off tops in soups and stocks.

BRAISED LEEKS

(SERVES THREE)

2 large bunches (about 1 pound) leeks	Salt
2 tablespoons butter	Freshly ground pepper
Chicken broth	2 tablespoons chopped parsley

Wash the leeks thoroughly (see preceding discussion) and trim them, leaving about 1½ inches of the green tops. Sauté them in butter in a skillet for about 5 minutes, then add about ½ inch of broth, enough so that the leeks will not burn. Cover, and simmer slowly until the leeks are tender, about 15–20 minutes. Arrange the leeks on a serving platter. Boil the cooking liquid down to a few tablespoons, season to taste, pour over the leeks, and serve, sprinkled with the parsley.

BRAISED LEEKS AU GRATIN

Arrange the cooked leeks in a shallow baking dish, spoon a little of the cooking liquid over them, and sprinkle with *½ cup freshly grated Parmesan cheese*. Put under the broiler until the cheese melts.

About Mushrooms

For many years the only mushroom that we could buy was the white or rather creamy colored commercial mushroom (*Agaricus bisporus*) in the supermarket. In the last few years occasionally some exciting new varieties appear in our markets, such as the *shiitake, enoki, chanterelle,* and *oyster.* The shiitake has a pleasing mild taste, the enoki is very mild and often used decoratively in salads, the chanterelle is generally cooked and has a captivating delicate flavor, and the oyster or tree oyster is good sautéed or used in stuffings.

Height of Season: It used to be fall and winter, but thanks to commercial growers, today we have availability all year round.

What to Look For: The *common* is a firm, white, fresh-looking mushroom, caps closed around stems with no pleats or gills showing; avoid discoloration or soft spots.

   The *shiitake* has a large, light brown flat cap and is often used in Oriental cooking.

   The *enoki* is white, with a very thin, long stem and a tiny ball-like cap. It requires little cooking or can be eaten raw.

   The *chanterelle* is yellow or black and trumpet-shaped. When fresh it smells like an apricot and has a delicate taste.

   The *oyster* or *tree oyster* grows in clusters with stems fused together and small caps on top. It generally has a creamy white color.

Uses: Whole or sliced, cold or hot. *Raw or cooked,* as an hors d'oeuvre, with a dip, as a salad or first course. *Cooked,* sautéed, broiled, baked, coated in batter and fried, stuffed, in soups, stews, casserole dishes, quiches, duxelles. *As a vegetable accompaniment,* especially good with steak or chops.

Amount: One pound serves four.

Alternatives to Fresh: Canned or frozen will not have the flavor but may be used in a pinch. Dried varieties are delicious but have a different texture so cannot be used as substitutes in the recipes that follow. However, they are excellent to use in soups, sauces, and stews and can add a stronger mushroom accent, sometimes complementing blander fresh mushrooms. Dried mushrooms must be soaked for 30 minutes; save the soaking liquid to add to a soup or sauce.

Cooking in the Microwave: ½ pound mushrooms, sliced, in ½ cup water in a glass dish with a lid, about 4 minutes on high power (in a 600–700-watt oven). Results: color all right but taste and texture not as good as when sautéed in butter or oil on top of the stove.

   Unless you're expert, don't eat wild mushrooms picked in the woods.

It's best not to wash mushrooms, since they will absorb too much water. Just wipe them clean, using a damp towel or cloth, and cut off ¼ inch from the bottoms of the stems.

SAUTÉED MUSHROOMS (SERVES FOUR)

1 pound mushrooms
6 tablespoons butter
2 tablespoons minced shallots
 or scallions

2 teaspoons minced parsley
Salt
Freshly ground pepper

Wipe the mushrooms clean and slice them. Melt the butter in a pan, add the shallots or scallions, and cook for 3 minutes, stirring often. Add the mushrooms and continue to cook over low heat for 10 minutes. Add the parsley, season to taste, and mix well.

BAKED STUFFED MUSHROOMS (SERVES FOUR)

12 large mushroom caps
¼ pound butter
½ cup dry homemade bread
 crumbs
1 tablespoon finely chopped
 parsley
1 tablespoon finely chopped
 onion

½ teaspoon salt
½ teaspoon pepper
1 egg, lightly beaten
½ cup freshly grated
 Parmesan cheese

Preheat oven to 350°F. Generously butter a shallow baking dish. Wipe the mushroom caps clean. Melt 4 tablespoons of the butter in a small pan and let it cool a bit. Using the palms of your hands, thoroughly coat mushroom caps with butter and put them in the baking dish. Mix the bread crumbs, parsley, onion, salt, pepper, and egg together. Fill each mushroom cap with the mixture. Melt the remaining 4 tablespoons of butter. Sprinkle a little Parmesan cheese over each cap, drizzle a little melted butter on top, and bake for 15–20 minutes.

CREAMED MUSHROOMS ✳ (SERVES FOUR)

Cream and mushrooms complement each other—in a luscious way. They are also very good served on toast.

1½ pounds mushrooms
¼ pound butter
4 tablespoons Madeira wine

¾ cup heavy cream
Salt
Freshly ground pepper

1. *endive;* 2. *fennel;* 3. *fiddleheads;* 4. *kohlrabi;* 5. *leeks;* 6. *mushrooms;* 7. *okra;*
8. *onions;* 9. *garlic;* 10. *shallots;* 11. *scallions.*

Wipe the mushrooms clean and cut caps in half with the stems attached. Melt the butter over medium heat until it foams, stir in the mushrooms, and turn the heat to low. Simmer for 5 minutes, then add the Madeira and cream. Continue to cook over low heat for about 10 minutes, stirring once in a while. Season to taste. Serve hot.

MUSHROOM DUXELLES ❧ (1½ CUPS)

A French method of preserving mushrooms for use in fillings, soups, and sauces. Duxelles should be cooked until all moisture is absorbed.

4 tablespoons butter	Salt
½ onion, chopped fine	Freshly ground pepper
1 pound mushrooms, chopped fine	

Melt the butter in a very large skillet over medium heat, add the onion, and cook, stirring, for 2 minutes. Add the mushrooms and continue to cook over low heat, stirring occasionally, until all the moisture has evaporated—about 20 minutes. Season to taste. Cool, then put in a container and close tightly. Refrigerate up to a week or freeze until needed.

MUSHROOM CRÊPES (SERVES SIX)

1¼ pounds mushrooms	1½ cups heavy cream
5 tablespoons butter	Salt
4 tablespoons minced shallots or scallions	Freshly ground pepper
5 tablespoons flour	1 recipe Crêpes or French Pancakes (p. 778)
1½ cups hot chicken broth	

Preheat the oven to 350°F. Butter a shallow baking dish, approximately 13 × 9 × 2 inches. Slice the mushrooms, including the stems, and sauté them in the butter with the shallots or scallions, for about 4 minutes, until soft. Sprinkle on the flour and cook for 2 minutes. Slowly add the broth, stir until thick and smooth, then add the cream, and season with salt and pepper to taste. Continue cooking, stirring, for 5 minutes to reduce and thicken slightly. Spoon 3 tablespoons of filling in the center of each crêpe. Fold the ends over and place each crêpe end side down in the baking dish. Spoon the remaining mushroom filling over the top of the crêpes. Bake for 25 minutes or until sauce bubbles.

About Okra

Availability: May to October height of season.

What to Look For: Small, green, tender, flexible pods, about 2–4 inches long.

Uses: *Cooked,* steamed, boiled, sautéed, in soups or stews, with other vegetables, in casserole dishes. *As a vegetable accompaniment,* especially good with chicken or fish.

Amount: One pound serves four.

Alternatives to Fresh: Frozen or canned acceptable.

Cooking in the Microwave: ½ pound trimmed, whole okra in ¾ cup water in a glass dish with a lid, about 4 minutes on high power (in a 600–700-watt oven). Results: color, taste, texture, and cooking time comparable to cooking on top of the stove.

Okra, actually the immature seed pod of the okra plant, is used a great deal in the southern United States. Its gummy texture provides a good thickening base for gumbos: indeed, okra is sometimes incorrectly called "gumbo," although "gumbo" really describes the dishes in which it appears.

(SERVES FOUR) &ev; **SAUTÉED OKRA**

When okra is blanched and sautéed in butter, it has good flavor, a velvety outside, and a chewy texture.

1 pound okra	Salt
6 tablespoons butter	Freshly ground pepper

Start a large pot of water boiling. Wash the okra and snap or cut off the stems. Drop it in the boiling water for 1 minute; drain. Melt the butter over medium heat. Add the okra and cook for 3 minutes, shaking the pan often to coat the okra with butter. Season lightly with salt and pepper. Serve hot.

SAUTÉED OKRA WITH BROWNED CRUMBS

Drop the okra into boiling water and let cook 3 minutes. Drain. Sauté ¼ *cup freshly made bread crumbs* in the butter until browned. Add the okra, season, and toss together.

OKRA, TOMATOES, AND CORN ?❧   (SERVES SIX)

2 tablespoons butter
1 small onion, chopped fine
1 small green pepper,
    chopped fine
1 pound okra, in ½-inch slices
2 large fresh tomatoes, peeled,
    seeded, and chopped

1 cup corn kernels
½ teaspoon oregano, crumbled
Salt
Freshly ground pepper

Melt the butter in a pan, add the onion and green pepper, and cook over medium heat for 3–4 minutes, stirring often. Add the okra slices and cook, stirring often, for 2 minutes. Add the tomatoes, corn, and oregano. Cover and simmer over low heat for 10 minutes. Season to taste. Serve hot.

About Onions

Availability: Year round.
What to Look For: Firm, well-shaped onions with dry skins and no sprouts.
Uses: Sliced, chopped, or whole. *Raw*, in salads, sandwiches, as a garnish. *Cooked*, boiled, baked, sautéed, fried, stuffed, pickled, braised, or roasted, in soups, stews, casserole dishes, sauces, and just about everything else.
Amount: One pound serves four.
Alternatives to Fresh: Canned or frozen in a pinch.
Cooking in the Microwave: ½ pound onions, peeled and sliced, in ¾ cup water in a glass dish with a lid, about 7 minutes on high power (in a 600–700-watt oven). Results: color, taste, texture, and cooking time comparable to cooking on top of the stove.

It's hard to imagine what food would be like without onions! Fortunately, they are readily available and in many varieties. Most familiar are the yellow cooking onions which have a strong flavor and often make your eyes water when you slice them. Long, slow cooking will change the character of a strong onion and turn it mild and sweet. There are also sweet, mild Spanish or Italian onions; large, delicately flavored Bermudas; small white onions to glaze or cream or put in stews, and the scallions or green onions and shallots described on facing page.

Keep onions in a cool, dry, dark place. Once you've peeled or sliced them, it's best to keep them in the refrigerator.

About Scallions or Green Onions

Availability: Year round.
What to Look For: Crisp, tender scallions with firm, white bottoms and
   fresh green tops.
Uses: Whole, sliced, or chopped. *Raw*, with a dip, in salads, sandwiches, as a garnish. *Cooked*, sautéed or braised, in sauces, soups,
   stews, as a flavoring. *As a vegetable accompaniment*, good with
   chopped beef or just about anything.
Cooking in the Microwave: ½ pound trimmed whole scallions, in ¾
   cup water in a glass dish with a lid, microwaved for about
   7 minutes on high power (in a 600–700-watt oven). Results:
   texture tough and longer cooking did not improve tenderness. Recommend cooking on top of the stove.

Green onions, or scallions, are onions that have been harvested
while young. They have a milder flavor than mature onions. Keep
them in the refrigerator.

About Shallots

Availability: Year round, mainly in specialty stores.
What to Look For: Clusters of crisp, tender, plump bulbs, with dry
   rust-colored skins and no sprouts.
Uses: *Raw* (used sparingly) or *cooked*, as a flavoring for sauces and an
   aromatic base for braising.

Shallots have a delicate, somewhat sweet flavor. They add a fine,
subtle touch to sauces.

(SERVES FOUR)   ❧ **BAKED ONIONS**

A little sweet, opaque, moistly tender.

   4 medium onions, peeled   Salt
   2–3 tablespoons butter

Preheat the oven to 350°F. Rub the onions all over with the butter. Put
the onions in a small casserole. Sprinkle with salt and cover with foil.
Bake for 45–60 minutes. Serve hot.

CREAMED ONIONS ᕯ᠍᠍᠍ᴥ   (SERVES FOUR)

1 pound small white boiling
   onions
¾ cup heavy cream

Salt
2 teaspoons minced parsley

NOTE

To make peeling easier, bring a large pot of water to boil, drop
the onions into the boiling water, and cook for 2 minutes; drain
and peel. Put the onions into a pan, pour the cream over, and
simmer, turning often, for 15–20 minutes. Add salt to taste.
Sprinkle with parsley. Serve hot.

CREAMED ONIONS IN WHITE SAUCE

If you prefer a more traditional recipe with a thicker cream sauce,
blanch and peel the onions as in the recipe for Creamed Onions. Then
cook them in 1 cup lightly salted water until tender. Drain and combine them with *1 cup White Sauce* (p. 379) and reheat.

GLAZED ONIONS ᕯ᠍᠍᠍ᴥ   (SERVES FOUR)

1 pound small white boiling
   onions
5 tablespoons butter

1½ tablespoons honey
Salt

Bring a pot of water to a boil. Add the onions and boil for 5 minutes;
drain and peel. Melt the butter in a skillet and stir in the honey. Add
the onions and cook over medium heat, stirring often, for about 10
minutes or until the onions are slightly browned. Sprinkle with salt
and serve.

BRAISED SMALL WHITE BOILING
ONIONS ᕯ᠍᠍᠍ᴥ   (SERVES FOUR)

Silky texture and a mildly sweet onion taste.

1 pound small white boiling
   onions

4 tablespoons butter
Salt

Bring a large pot of water to boil. Drop the onions into the boiling water and cook for 3 minutes; drain and remove the outer skin. Melt the

butter in a skillet with a lid. Add the onions, cover, and cook over low heat for 20 minutes. Shake the skillet often. Uncover and cook 5 minutes more. Add salt to taste.

SCALLOPED ONIONS

Boil the onions for 10 minutes before peeling. Drain and put the onions into a buttered baking dish. Add *1 cup White Sauce* (p. 379) and sprinkle *1 cup grated Cheddar cheese* on top. Bake in a 350°F oven for 20 minutes.

(SERVES SIX)   ?❧   ## ONIONS, CORN, AND PEPPERS

A most agreeable mixture.

5 tablespoons butter	1½ cups cooked corn kernels
1 pound onions, in ¼-inch slices	Salt
2 green, red, or yellow peppers, seeds removed, in ¼-inch strips	

Melt the butter in a pan, add the onions, and cook, stirring, until they are limp. Add the peppers and continue to cook until they turn a little dull in color, about 5 minutes. Stir in the corn, add salt to taste, and cook for 2–3 minutes more.

(SERVES EIGHT)   ?❧   ## FRENCH-FRIED ONION RINGS

Golden and good. Soaking the onions first in milk takes away some of their sharpness.

4 large Bermuda onions, in ¼-inch slices	½ cup flour
2 cups milk	Salt
	Oil for deep frying

Separate the onion slices into rings. Put them in a shallow dish and pour the milk over them. Soak for 30 minutes, turning once or twice. Mix the flour with a sprinkle of salt, and dip the rings into this mixture, coating them all over. Heat oil to 370°F and deep-fry the rings several at a time until golden on both sides. Pat free of oil, keep warm while frying the rest, and sprinkle with more salt, if desired, before serving.

BRAISED SCALLIONS (OR GREEN ONIONS) ঙ

(SERVES FOUR)

4 bunches scallions, about 2 dozen

3 tablespoons butter

Trim the coarse or discolored green from the scallion tops, and trim off the bottom roots; rinse scallions. Melt the butter in a skillet with a lid. Add the scallions, sprinkle 2 tablespoons of water over them, cover, and turn the heat to low. Simmer for 4–6 minutes. Serve hot.

About Parsnips

Availability: Year round, especially late winter.

What to Look For: Small, well-shaped parsnips, smooth and firm.

Uses: *Raw,* with dips. *Cooked,* in soups, stews, fritters. *As a vegetable accompaniment,* good with beef or lamb.

Amount: One pound serves three or four.

Cooking in the Microwave: ½ pound peeled parsnips, in ½-inch sticks about 2 inches long, in ¾ cup water in a glass dish with a lid, about 5 minutes on high power (in a 600–700-watt oven). Results: color, taste, and texture comparable to cooking on top of the stove. Smaller amounts cook faster.

Parsnips are a creamy pale color—a member of the carrot family, whose shape they resemble. Their flavor becomes sweeter after they have been held for a while at temperatures below 40°F. Use them in moderation, or their sweetness may overpower other ingredients in a dish.

BASIC METHOD FOR COOKING PARSNIPS ঙ

(SERVES FOUR)

1 pound parsnips
2 tablespoons butter

Salt
Freshly ground pepper

Scrape the parsnips and cut them in ½-inch sticks, about 2 inches long. Cook them, covered, in about 2 inches of boiling water until tender, about 10 minutes; drain. Coat them with the butter, season to taste, and reheat them, if necessary, before serving.

CANDIED PARSNIPS

Melt 4 *tablespoons butter* in a skillet, stir in 2 *teaspoons sugar*, and cook, stirring, until the sugar dissolves. Add the parsnips, ½ *teaspoon salt*, and ¼ *teaspoon freshly ground pepper*, and cook over medium-low heat, stirring often, for 10–15 minutes or until the parsnips are golden. Serve hot.

MASHED OR PURÉED PARSNIPS

Mash the cooked, drained parsnips or purée them through a food mill or in a food processor. Stir in 1 *tablespoon butter*, 1–2 *tablespoons heavy cream*, and season to taste with salt and freshly ground pepper. Reheat slowly, preferably in the top of a double boiler.

(SERVES FOUR)   ₰ **PARSNIP FRITTERS**

 1 pound parsnips, cooked   ½ teaspoon salt
 4 tablespoons butter   ½ teaspoon ginger

Mash the parsnips with 2 tablespoons of the butter and the salt and ginger, beating until smooth. Flour your hands and shape into balls about 1¼ inches in diameter, then flatten into patties. Melt the remaining 2 tablespoons of butter in a skillet and fry the patties on each side until brown. Serve hot.

About Green Peas

Availability: Most of the year, especially spring.
What to Look For: Fresh-looking, bright green pods. To test, crack open and taste; the peas should be sweet and tender.
Uses: *Cooked*, braised or boiled, in cold salads, or in soups, stews, casserole dishes, with other vegetables. *As a vegetable accompaniment*, good with everything.
Amount: One pound shelled peas serves four. Two pounds of unshelled peas yield about 1 pound of shelled peas.
Alternatives to Fresh: Frozen are good, better than canned.
Cooking in the Microwave: 1 cup shelled peas in ¾ cup water in a glass dish with a lid, about 4 minutes on high power (in a 600–700-watt oven). Results: color, taste, texture, and cooking time comparable to cooking on top of the stove.

About Snap Peas

Snap peas are bred from the snow pea and the result is a fatter, sweeter pea. They are about 2½–3 inches long, bright green, plump with mature peas, and eaten whole, pod and peas together. Just pinch off the ends and remove the strings before eating. They are good raw or can be cooked like snow peas.

Cooking in the Microwave: ½ pound snap peas, ends and strings removed, in ¾ cup water in a glass dish with a lid, about 2–3 minutes on high power (in a 600–700-watt oven). Results: color bright, taste watery and dull, and texture uneven. Recommend cooking on top of stove.

About Snow Peas

Snow peas, also called sugar peas, Chinese peas, pea pods, or *mangetouts*, are eaten crisp, barely cooked, in their flat, edible pods—and you eat the whole pod. They are generally available in food stores. They are also easy to grow and they yield enormously.

Cooking in the Microwave: ½ pound snow peas, ends and strings removed, in ¾ cup water in a glass dish with a lid, about 3–4 minutes on high power (in a 600–700-watt oven). Results: color bright, taste watery and dull, and texture uneven. Recommend cooking on top of the stove.

BASIC METHOD FOR COOKING
GREEN PEAS ૐ (SERVES FOUR)

Reserve a few of the pea pods and add them to the cooking water; this will impart more pea flavor.

2 pounds fresh peas (1 pound shelled)	3 tablespoons butter
	Salt

Put the shelled peas, 1 cup water, and 1 tablespoon of the butter in a pan, cover, and cook over medium heat. After 6 minutes, check for doneness by pressing or tasting one or two; they should be tender but firm, which may take only a few minutes if young, or up to 20 minutes for older peas. Drain, coat with the remaining 2 tablespoons of butter, and lightly sprinkle salt over all.

MINT-FLAVORED PEAS

Add *1 tablespoon finely chopped mint* with the remaining 2 tablespoons of butter.

PURÉE OF GREEN PEAS

Add *1 slice onion* to the water. Add *½ cup heavy cream* with the remaining 2 tablespoons of butter. Put through a food mill or purée in a blender or food processor. Serve hot.

(SERVES FOUR)   ❧ **BRAISED PEAS**

6 large lettuce leaves	4 tablespoons butter, melted
2 pounds fresh peas (1 pound shelled)	Salt
	Freshly ground pepper

Rinse the lettuce leaves, leaving the drops of water on them. Use 3 of the leaves to line a heavy-bottomed pan with a lid. Put the shelled peas on the leaves and distribute the butter over them. Sprinkle with salt and pepper and cover with the remaining lettuce leaves. Cover the pan and simmer gently for 15–20 minutes or until the peas are tender. Usually one discards the lettuce leaves before serving the peas, but they taste good, so serve them if you wish.

BASIC METHOD FOR COOKING
(SERVES FOUR)   ❧ **SNAP PEAS**

These little wonders are sugar sweet and you can eat the whole pea, pod and all. Only the matured peas need shelling.

1 teaspoon salt	3 tablespoons butter
1 pound young snap peas, left whole	

Bring a large pot of water to a boil with the salt. Add the pea pods and cook over medium heat, until tender but crunchy—1–2 minutes. Toss with butter and serve.

BASIC METHOD FOR COOKING
SNOW PEAS ?⁓   (SERVES FOUR)

1 pound snow peas   Salt
3 tablespoons butter

Wash the snow peas and remove any strings. Bring a large pot of water
to boil and drop the snow peas in; boil for 1 minute. Drain and quickly
glisten with the butter, sprinkle with salt, and serve.

STIR-FRIED SNOW PEAS

Using a wok or a skillet, stir fry whole snow peas as you would sliced
asparagus in Stir-fried Asparagus (p. 537), cooking only 2 minutes under cover.

About Peppers

Availability: Year round, especially in the summer.
What to Look For: Good color and sheen; smooth, firm sides.
Uses: *Raw,* with dips, in salads, stuffed. *Cooked,* in soups, sauces, stews,
   stuffed, with other vegetables, in casserole dishes. *As a vegetable ac-
   companiment,* good with sausages and beef.
Amount: One per serving.
Cooking in the Microwave: ½ pound green and/or red sweet peppers,
          in ¼-inch strips, in ¾ cup water in a glass dish with a lid,
   M⋐ about 8 minutes on high power (in a 600–700-watt oven).
   Results: color and taste all right but texture soggy compared to
   cooking in butter or oil on top of the stove.
Peppers vary greatly in both appearance and taste. Sweet bell peppers,
both red and green, are the most common. Red bell peppers are actually green peppers that have
been allowed to mature fully;
they are a bit sweeter than the
green. Pimientos are more heart-
shaped with a thicker flesh but
taste much like a red bell pepper.
There are yellow or golden and
purple sweet bell peppers available. All have a sweet mild flavor.

   Tapered, light-green Italian
peppers are found in stores more

frequently these days. They have thinner skins and a sweeter, more delicate flavor than bell peppers.

Hot red and green chili peppers come in several varieties; they should be handled carefully—use gloves and don't touch your eyes—and should be used sparingly, as a seasoning in dishes that call for them. Chili powder and cayenne are made from hot peppers.

The membranes or ribs and seeds of sweet peppers are bitter and should be removed before the peppers are eaten or cooked.

Roasting and Peeling Hot or Sweet Peppers

Arrange peppers in a single layer on a baking sheet. Place them in the oven under the broiler. Broil, turning them until they are blistered and charred on all sides. Then place them in a heavy plastic or paper bag, close the end, and let them steam for about 20 minutes. Remove peppers and peel; the peel will come off easily by scraping and pinching the charred skins and wiping with paper towels. If a few charred spots remain, don't worry—they'll add good flavor.

An alternate way to roast chilies: Place peppers in a single layer on a baking sheet and place in a 325°F oven for about an hour, or until skin of peppers has shriveled. Turn off oven and open door to cool oven down to about 150°F. Place a towel over the peppers, close the door, and leave several hours or overnight. In the morning the peppers will be ready to peel and seed.

(SERVES SIX)   **STUFFED GREEN PEPPERS**

A good way to serve leftover meats in a fresh way.

3 large green peppers, halved and seeded
3 tablespoons olive oil
1 onion, chopped fine
1 pound ground cooked or uncooked beef, pork, veal, or lamb
2 tomatoes, peeled and coarsely chopped
2 tablespoons minced parsley
1 tablespoon chopped fresh basil, or 1½ teaspoons dried, crumbled
Salt
¼ teaspoon freshly ground pepper
1 cup freshly made bread crumbs

Preheat the oven to 350°F. Oil a shallow baking dish. Cook the peppers in boiling water for 2 minutes; drain and set aside. Heat the oil in a skillet and add the chopped onion. Cook, stirring, until soft. If using uncooked meat, add it and cook lightly for 5–10 minutes. Otherwise, mix the onion and meat together, then add the tomatoes, parsley, basil, salt to taste, and pepper, combining thoroughly. Lightly fill each pepper half with some of the meat mixture. Sprinkle the tops with bread crumbs. Bake for 30–40 minutes.

SAUTÉED SWEET RED, GREEN, AND YELLOW PEPPERS ॐ (SERVES SIX)

Sweet red, green, and yellow bell peppers, slightly different in taste, are very compatible cooked together.

¼ cup vegetable oil	2 yellow peppers, in ¼-inch
2 sweet red peppers, in ¼-inch	strips
strips	Salt
2 green peppers, in ¼-inch	Freshly ground pepper
strips	

Heat the oil in a skillet. Put the peppers in the skillet and cook for 5–7 minutes, stirring to coat with the oil. Sprinkle with salt and pepper to taste.

About Potatoes

Availability: Year round.

What to Look For: Firm, well-shaped potatoes without sprouts, cracks, or discolored spots.

Uses: Whole, sliced, cubed, grated, mashed, or puréed. *Cold*, in salads, soup. *Hot*, baked, boiled, fried, in soups, stews, casseroles, around a roast, with other vegetables, in pancakes. *As a vegetable accompaniment*, good with just about everything.

Amount: Allow one medium potato per person or a pound to serve about three.

Alternatives to Fresh: Canned potatoes are not very good, although sweet potatoes take to canning more successfully and their texture is better preserved. There are, of course, frozen French-fried potatoes, but once you've made your own—and it is a relatively simple task—you'll never settle for less. Instant mashed potatoes can be used in a pinch quite successfully, with lots of butter or a little cream but, again, aren't as good as the real thing.

Cooking in the Microwave: ½ pound peeled, sliced potatoes, in ¾ cup
water in a glass dish with a lid, about 5 minutes on high
power (in a 600–700-watt oven). Results: color, taste, texture, and cooking time comparable to cooking on top of the stove.

1 whole unpeeled potato (about ½ pound), about 6–7 minutes on
high power (in a 600–700-watt oven); turn over once halfway
through cooking. Results: color, taste, and texture comparable to
baking in an oven except skin did not crisp and cooking time much
less for this small amount.

½ pound peeled and sliced sweet potato or yam, in ¾ cup water
in a glass dish with a lid, about 6 minutes on high power (in a
600–700-watt oven). Results: color, taste, texture, and cooking time
comparable to cooking on top of the stove.

The potato has fallen into disfavor in many American households,
owing to the mistaken belief that it is fattening. Actually, a baked
potato has 90 calories, 27 less than an apple. Nor is it always necessary
to douse potatoes with lots of butter or cream. Prepare them simply
and use them like any other vegetable accompaniment: they are wonderful for sopping up good juices and sauces.

There are many different kinds of potatoes. Most common are "all-
purpose" potatoes which are used for boiling, baking, French frying,
mashing, or just about any other kind of potato dish. Idaho and russet
potatoes are very flaky and are best for baking. Red or white "new"
potatoes are young potatoes which have not been kept in storage; they
are ideal for salads, or you can boil or steam them in their skins until
they are just tender, then toss them with a bit of butter, salt, and some
chopped parsley.

Commercially frozen potatoes have been partially dehydrated so
that they keep their texture after defrosting. Don't freeze potato dishes
yourself, for they lose their consistency. Always store potatoes in a
cool, dry, dark place and use them before they start to sprout. Do not
refrigerate.

If they are not cooked immediately, peeled potatoes will discolor
unless you cover them with cold water.

About Sweet Potatoes

There are two kinds of sweet potatoes: a light-colored, dry sweet
potato and the sweeter, more common, deep-orange, moist type, generally referred to as a yam. Choose medium or small yams that are
smooth and tapered at each end. Sweet potatoes or yams don't keep
more than two weeks; store them in a very cool, dark place.

BAKED POTATOES ↝   (ALLOW ONE PER SERVING)

If you can, use Idaho or russet potatoes for baking; "all-purpose" will do fine but you won't get the same lovely, mealy texture. Incidentally, russets are very often packed in 5-pound bags in supermarkets, so read the labeling carefully when you are looking for them. Don't wrap potatoes for baking in foil—contrary to current fashion; foil steams them so that the jackets will be limp and the insides will taste steamed rather than having that good dry, baked taste and texture.

Preheat the oven to 450°F. Scrub potatoes with a brush and water to remove all dirt. Place them slightly apart from each other on the oven rack and bake for 1 hour for large potatoes; 50 minutes for medium; 40–45 for small, children-size potatoes. Test for doneness by piercing the potatoes with the point of a knife or by squeezing to see if the potato feels soft. Break baked potatoes apart with a fork while they are still very hot and add *butter* and *salt* to taste.

CRUSTY BAKED POTATOES

If you want a marvelous, thick, crackly potato skin—for those who love to eat them—let them bake 1½ hours for medium, 2 hours for large.

STUFFED BAKED POTATOES

Cut the baked potato in half lengthwise and scoop out the pulp, leaving the skins intact. Beat until fluffy, adding *2–4 tablespoons milk or cream* per potato, *1–2 tablespoons butter*, and *salt* and *freshly ground pepper* to taste. Refill the shells and sprinkle *2 tablespoons grated cheese* over the top, if desired. If the potatoes are at room temperature, reheat them in a 400°F oven for 20 minutes before serving. If chilled, reheat them for 30–40 minutes.

STEAMED NEW POTATOES ↝   (SERVES SIX)

Steaming is a lovely way to treat very fresh potatoes, particularly very tiny ones. No butter is necessary, just a light sprinkling of salt.

   2 pounds tiny new unpeeled   Salt
      potatoes

Wash the potatoes well and place them in a steamer basket in a pot filled with a few inches of water. Cover, bring to a boil, and steam until the potatoes are just tender, about 30 minutes. Sprinkle lightly with salt and eat at once.

(SERVES SIX) ?✍ **PARSLIED NEW POTATOES, BOILED**

12 or more small new potatoes	6 tablespoons butter
	Salt
2 tablespoons finely chopped parsley	Freshly ground pepper

Scrub the potatoes—peeling is not necessary unless you prefer to for aesthetic reasons. Cover with cold water in a saucepan, bring to a boil, and boil gently for 15–20 minutes, or until tender when pierced with a knife; drain. Add the parsley and butter, season to taste, and shake the pan to coat the potatoes. Serve hot.

PAN-ROASTED POTATOES

Use either all-purpose or new potatoes. Peel them and cover them with cold water. Bring to a boil and boil 10–15 minutes or until barely tender. Drain well and place in a pan with roasting meat, at least 1 hour before the meat is done. Turn the potatoes all over in the meat drippings, then sprinkle with salt and freshly ground pepper. Baste with drippings and turn once or twice during roasting. They will be done in 1 hour, but more time won't hurt them.

(SERVES FOUR OR FIVE)   ?✍ **CHANTILLY POTATOES**

3 cups mashed potatoes (following recipe)	Salt
	Freshly ground pepper
½ cup heavy cream	
½ cup grated Swiss or Gruyère cheese	

Preheat the oven to 350°F. Butter a shallow 1½-quart baking dish. Spread the mashed potatoes in the baking dish. Whip the cream until stiff, fold in the cheese, and add salt and pepper to taste. Spread over the potatoes. Bake for 25–30 minutes or until the top is delicately brown.

MASHED POTATOES ❧   (4 CUPS)

Don't try beating potatoes in a food processor: the fast spinning motion
will develop the gluten in the potatoes and turn them into a gray,
sticky mass. You can use an electric beater if your potatoes are mealy—
russet or Idahos.

6 medium all-purpose potatoes	4 tablespoons butter
½–¾ cup hot milk	Salt
	Freshly ground pepper

Peel the potatoes and cut them into quarters. Put them in a pan and
just cover them with cold water. Bring to a boil and boil gently for
15–20 minutes or until tender when pierced with a fork. Drain very
well and return to very low heat. Add ½ cup hot milk and the butter
and start mashing with a potato masher or a fork (or put them through
a potato ricer), smoothing out all the lumps. When you have worked
the potatoes free of the lumps, transfer to a warm bowl and whip with
a fork or whisk until light and fluffy, adding the remaining milk, if
necessary, and salt and pepper to taste. Serve immediately, or keep
hot, uncovered, in a double boiler.

POTATO CAKES

Using leftover mashed potatoes, shape into small flat cakes. Dip lightly
in *flour*, shake off any excess, and brown each side in hot *bacon fat* or
butter over medium heat.

POTATO CROQUETTES ❧   (SERVES FOUR)

2 cups mashed potatoes (above)	1 cup freshly made bread crumbs
2 eggs	½ cup vegetable oil
4 tablespoons flour	

Put the potatoes into a bowl and lightly beat one of the eggs. Add the
egg to the potatoes and mix well. Shape the potato mixture into 8 balls,
cover, and chill. Beat the remaining egg lightly. Dip the potato balls
into the flour, shake off any excess, dip into the egg, and then into the
crumbs. Place on a piece of wax paper. Heat the oil in a skillet over
medium-high heat. Add the balls and let them heat and brown for several minutes, turning the heat down if they brown too quickly. Turn

the balls and brown on all sides. Keep the croquettes warm in a 300°F oven until all are ready, then serve immediately.

FRENCH-FRIED
?~ POTATOES

It's water that makes hot fat sputter and spray, so be sure to dry the potatoes well and stand back when adding them to the hot fat. If you haven't had a lot of experience with deep-fat frying, you'll find a frying thermometer necessary. A frying basket that fits inside a pan is also very handy; if you don't have one, you can use a slotted spoon to extract the potatoes, but it takes longer and once your potatoes are fried to a turn, you want to get them out quickly. Be sure there's enough fat in the pan so that the potatoes will be completely submerged. You can fry just a few at a time, if necessary.

Wash and peel firm, mature potatoes and cut them into long strips about ¼ inch wide. Place in a bowl, cover with cold water, and let stand for at least 30 minutes. Drain and dry thoroughly with paper towels. Heat several inches of fat or oil in a pan until a frying thermometer reads 360°F. Add the potatoes without crowding and fry, moving them about with a fork or spoon until they are golden brown. Lift out and drain on paper towels. Keep hot in a warm oven until all are done.

OVEN-FRIED POTATOES

Peel and slice potatoes as directed in the recipe for French-fried Potatoes. Dip the sliced potatoes in melted butter. Spread in a shallow pan and bake in a 400°F oven for about 45 minutes or until brown and tender.

POTATO CHIPS

Peel potatoes and slice them very thin. Soak them in cold water for about 1 hour, then pat them as dry as possible with paper towels. Fry as in the recipe for French-fried Potatoes, using oil that has been heated to 390°F. Salt before serving.

GERMAN FRIED POTATOES ⧉ (SERVES FOUR)

6 tablespoons vegetable oil   Salt
4 cups sliced cooked potatoes

Pour the oil into a large sauté pan and heat. Add the potatoes and turn the heat down to medium low. Cook, frequently turning, until well browned. Quickly remove to paper towels, lightly pat free of excess oil, and sprinkle with salt. Serve hot.

POTATO PANCAKES ✳ ⧉ (NINE 3½-INCH PANCAKES)

Crisp and brown, good with applesauce and roast pork. Peel and grate the potatoes immediately before cooking, or they will discolor: while this doesn't affect the taste of the pancakes, they will not look as appetizing. If you put grated potatoes in a bowl of cold water, they will not discolor, but you will then have to be especially careful to squeeze out the excess moisture before cooking.

3 medium potatoes   1 egg, beaten
1 tablespoon flour   Salt to taste
1 tablespoon heavy or light   4 tablespoons bacon fat or oil
  cream

Peel and grate the potatoes. Place them on a double thickness of paper towels, fold the towels around them, and twist and squeeze until most of the moisture is extracted. Put the potatoes in a bowl, add the flour, cream, egg, and salt, and toss until well mixed. Heat the fat or oil in a large skillet. Put about 2 tablespoons of the potato mixture in the pan and press and shape with a spatula into a flat, 3½-inch pancake; repeat until the pan is full but not crowded. Cook each pancake about 5 minutes over medium-low heat until the bottom is crisp and brown; turn and cook the other side 5 minutes more. Keep warm in a 300°F oven until all are ready, then serve immediately.

SIMPLE POTATO PANCAKES

Omit the flour, cream, and eggs. Toss well with salt. Use about ⅓ cup *potatoes for each pancake* in place of the potato mixture and cook following directions above.

COTTAGE-FRIED OR HASHED BROWN POTATOES

(SERVES FOUR)

6 tablespoons bacon fat or oil
4 cups finely diced potatoes, raw or cooked
1 tablespoon finely chopped onion

Salt to taste
1½ teaspoons coarsely ground pepper

Heat the fat or oil in a large skillet. Spread the potatoes evenly over the bottom and sprinkle the onion, salt, and pepper on top. Cook over low heat, pressing down on the potatoes firmly with a spatula several times. Cook until the bottom side is golden brown, allowing more time if the potatoes are raw; in fact, if you use raw potatoes, cover the pan and cook over a low heat to cook them through; then turn up the heat for a final browning. With the spatula cut down the middle of the potatoes and turn each side over. Cook until golden, again pressing down with a spatula several times. Serve hot.

❧ SCALLOPED POTATOES

(SERVES FOUR)

Little rivers of buttery milk, lots of pepper, and creamy potatoes.

4 medium potatoes, peeled and sliced ¼ inch thick
Salt
Freshly ground pepper

3 tablespoons flour
4 tablespoons butter
About 1½ cups milk

Preheat the oven to 350°F. Butter a 1½-quart casserole. Cover the bottom of the casserole with a single layer of potatoes. Sprinkle generously with salt, pepper, flour, and a few dots of butter. Repeat until all the potato slices are used. Pour milk over the potato slices until the top is almost covered. Dot with the remaining butter. Bake for 1 hour or until the potatoes are soft.

SCALLOPED POTATOES WITH CELERY ROOT OR CELERIAC

Alternate each layer of potatoes with a layer of *peeled, thinly sliced celery root*.

POTATOES HASHED IN
CREAM ๖   (SERVES FOUR OR FIVE)

  4 medium baking potatoes   1 cup heavy cream
  2 tablespoons butter   Salt
  1 tablespoon flour   Freshly ground pepper

Preheat oven to 350°F. Butter a 2-quart baking dish. Scrub the potatoes
and bake them for about 1 hour or until barely tender; let cool, then
peel and dice. Melt the butter in a skillet and stir in the flour. Blend
and stir for a couple of minutes, then slowly add the cream. Cook, continuing to stir, until the sauce bubbles and thickens. Add the potatoes,
season to taste, mix well, and spoon into the baking dish. Bake uncovered for about 30 minutes or until lightly browned on top. Serve hot.

SKILLET POTATOES   ๖   (SERVES FOUR)

  8 new potatoes (about 1½   ½ cup milk
      pounds)   2 tablespoons finely chopped
  Salt   parsley

Peel and dice the potatoes, put them in a pan, and cover with ½ cup
boiling water and a sprinkle of salt. Cook, covered, for 6–8 minutes.
Uncover and continue to cook until the water has evaporated. Add the
milk and more salt, if needed. Cook over low heat, stirring gently with
a fork until well blended and slightly thickened. Add the parsley.
Serve hot.

LYONNAISE POTATOES   (SERVES FOUR)

  3 tablespoons butter   4 tablespoons beef stock or
  1 small onion, chopped fine   broth
  3 cups potatoes in small cubes   Salt
      (3–4 potatoes)   Freshly ground pepper

Melt the butter in a skillet. Add the onion and cook until transparent.
Add the potatoes, and mix well. Stir in the stock or broth, lower the
heat, and simmer, covered, until the potatoes are tender and lightly
browned on the bottom. Season to taste. Serve hot.

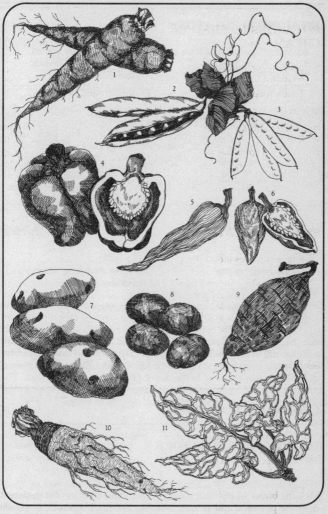

1. parsnip; 2. peas; 3. snow peas; 4. green pepper; 5. hot pepper; 6. Italian pepper and cross section; 7. potato; 8. new potato; 9. sweet potato; 10. salsify; 11. spinach.

DELMONICO POTATOES ‏ঌ   (SERVES SIX)

6 potatoes, peeled and boiled
1½ cups White Sauce (p. 379)
Pinch of cayenne pepper
Salt to taste

2 egg yolks, slightly beaten
½ cup grated mild Cheddar
  cheese
1 cup Buttered Bread Crumbs

Preheat the oven to 375°F. Butter a 2-quart casserole. Slice the potatoes
¼ inch thick. Make the white sauce and stir in the cayenne pepper, salt,
egg yolks, and cheese. Stir over medium heat until the cheese melts.
Spoon a film of sauce over the bottom of the casserole and place a layer
of potatoes over it. Continue alternating sauce and potatoes, finishing
with sauce. Sprinkle the buttered crumbs on top and place in the oven.
Bake for 20–25 minutes or until the sauce is bubbling.

CURRIED POTATOES   (SERVES FOUR)

Nice with chicken or lamb.

4 tablespoons butter
1 small onion, chopped fine
3 cups diced, cooked potatoes
  (about 4 potatoes)
½ cup chicken stock or broth

2 teaspoons curry powder
2 teaspoons lemon juice
Salt
Freshly ground pepper

Melt the butter in a skillet. Add the onion and cook, stirring frequently,
until the onion is transparent. Add the potatoes and cook over low
heat, stirring occasionally, until the potatoes have absorbed the butter.
Add the chicken stock or broth, curry powder, and lemon juice. Stir
and blend all the ingredients and continue to cook over low heat until
all the stock or broth has been absorbed. Season to taste.

BAKED SWEET POTATOES   (ALLOW ONE MEDIUM POTATO
OR YAMS ‏ঌ   PER SERVING)

Preheat the oven to 375°F. Scrub the potatoes and cut a small piece off
one end so the potato won't burst during baking. Place the potatoes,
slightly apart, on the oven rack. Bake for about 1 hour or until tender
when pierced with a knife. Fork open and put a pat of butter inside to
serve.

(ALLOW ONE MEDIUM POTATO   **BOILED SWEET POTATOES**
PER SERVING)   **ð✷   OR YAMS**

Scrub the potatoes, put them into boiling water, cover, and boil gently
for 20–30 minutes or until tender when pierced with a knife. Drain,
peel, and add *butter, salt*, and *freshly ground pepper*.

(ALLOW ONE MEDIUM POTATO   **FRIED SWEET POTATOES**
PER SERVING)   **ð✷   OR YAMS**

Scrub the potatoes, put them into boiling water, and boil for 10 minutes. Drain, peel, and cut into ⅛-inch slices. Put enough oil in a pan to
completely cover the slices. Heat to 375°F. Add the potatoes without
crowding and fry until lightly browned. Remove and drain on paper
towels. Keep hot in a warm oven until all the slices are fried. Add salt
and serve.

SWEET POTATO AND APPLE
(SERVES FOUR)   **ð✷   SCALLOP**

    2 cups thinly sliced boiled   ½ cup brown sugar
       sweet potatoes or yams   4 tablespoons butter
       (about 2 medium   Salt
       potatoes)
    1½ cups peeled, thinly sliced
       tart apples

Preheat the oven to 350°F. Butter a 1½-quart baking dish. Put half the
potatoes in the baking dish. Cover with half the apples, sprinkle with
half the sugar, dot with half the butter, and sprinkle with salt. Repeat.
Cover and bake for 30 minutes. Uncover and bake about 30 minutes
more or until the apples are soft.

CANDIED SWEET POTATOES
(SERVES FOUR)   **ð✷   OR YAMS**

    4 medium sweet potatoes or   ⅓ cup brown sugar
       yams   ¼ cup water
    4 tablespoons butter

Boil the potatoes until tender; drain. Peel and cut in half lengthwise. Put the butter and sugar in a heavy skillet and heat, stirring occasionally, until melted. Add the potatoes and turn until lightly browned. Add the water, cover, and simmer over low heat for about 10–15 minutes.

BAKED CANDIED SWEET POTATOES OR YAMS

After the butter and sugar have melted, put the potatoes in a buttered baking dish, pour the butter-sugar mixture on top, cover, and bake in a preheated 350°F oven for 45 minutes to 1 hour.

MASHED SWEET POTATOES
OR YAMS ﻬ   (SERVES FOUR)

Add spices—nutmeg, allspice, cinnamon, or ginger—according to taste, but in small quantities, about ⅛ teaspoon per potato.

4 medium sweet potatoes or yams	Spices (see above)
Butter	Orange juice or milk
Salt	(optional)

Wash and peel the potatoes, put in a pot, and cover with cold water. Bring to a boil and cook gently until tender, about 30 minutes; drain. Mash with a potato masher, put through a ricer, or whip in an electric mixer, adding butter, salt, and spices to taste. Add a few tablespoons of orange juice or milk, if you wish, especially if you are using light, dry sweet potatoes. Beat until smooth.

MASHED SWEET POTATOES OR YAMS WITH PINEAPPLE AND PECANS

Add ¼ cup crushed, drained pineapple and ¼ cup chopped pecans to the finished mashed potatoes. (This may be done in advance.) Put the potato mixture into a 1-quart buttered baking dish. Bake in a 375°F oven for 30–35 minutes or until hot.

SWEET POTATOES GEORGIAN

Put the mashed potatoes in a 1-quart buttered baking dish. Combine *2 tablespoons molasses* and *1 teaspoon butter* in a small pan and boil for 1 minute. Pour over the potatoes and bake in a preheated 400°F oven until slightly brown on top.

About Pumpkin

Height of Season: Fall.

What to Look For: Hard rind, bright orange color, firm stem. The size does not seem to affect the taste and a good-size pumpkin is always a good buy.

Uses: As a soup, a vegetable, in bread, and primarily as a filling for the all-American pie.

Amount: One pound serves two.

Alternatives to Fresh: Canned and frozen both good. In buying canned, be sure not to purchase the kind that has been sweetened and spiced; it can only be used for pie and it is better to do your own flavoring.

Cooking in the Microwave: ½ pound pumpkin, skin on, in a glass dish, uncovered, about 5 minutes on high power (in a 600–700-watt oven). Results: color, taste, and texture comparable to cooking in the oven and cooking time much less for this small amount.

Technically a member of the squash family, pumpkin can be prepared in the same ways as winter squash; it is particularly good cut into fair-size pieces and baked with a little maple syrup and butter.

Pumpkin Seeds: Long popular in Mexican cooking, pumpkin seeds are relished today by the health-minded; they make a nourishing, chewy nibble and an interesting garnish for a pumpkin soup. When you are opening a pumpkin, scoop out the seeds, wash them under running water, then spread on paper towels to dry. Scatter them over an oiled cookie sheet and bake in a slow 250°F oven to dry out completely for at least 1 hour, shaking them a few times and turning up the heat for about 5 minutes at the end of cooking to brown slightly. Remove, store in an airtight tin, salted or not, as you wish.

BASIC METHOD FOR COOKING PUMPKIN

(SERVES FOUR TO SIX, ABOUT 2½ CUPS)

Steaming is more successful than boiling because the cooked pulp is less watery and seems to retain both color and flavor better.

2 pounds pumpkin, in
    large chunks with the skin
    left on

Place the pumpkin pieces on a steamer rack over boiling water in a
large pan, cover, and steam for about 30–45 minutes. Check after 30
minutes of vigorous steaming. Remove when the interior is soft, and
cut, spoon, or scrape the pulp from the skin.

PURÉED PUMPKIN

Either whip with a hand or electric beater or purée in a food processor.
Use as is in savories, soups, casseroles, pies, and desserts; or, for an accompaniment to meats and poultry, beat in a little *butter* and *cream*,
and add a sprinkling of *nutmeg*, and *salt* and *pepper* to taste. Puréed
pumpkin keeps well frozen.

VERMONT PUMPKIN CASSEROLE   (SERVES FOUR)

Good with wedges of warm corn bread.

4 cups mashed or puréed pumpkin	1⅓ cups coarsely grated sharp Cheddar cheese
1 cup Thick Cream Sauce (p. 380)	2 hard-boiled eggs, sliced
2 cups diced ham	½ cup broken soda crackers
	2 tablespoons butter

Preheat the oven to 350°F. Mix together thoroughly the pumpkin,
cream sauce, ham, and 1 cup of the cheese. Place half of this mixture in
a 2-quart casserole, then cover with the sliced hard-boiled eggs, and
top with the remaining pumpkin mixture. Sprinkle over the top the
coarsely crumbled soda crackers, the remaining cheese, and dot with
butter. Bake for 30 minutes.

About Salsify (Oyster Plant)

Height of Season: Fall or winter; look in specialty stores.
What to Look For: Firm roots with either black or white skin.
Uses: A good accent in stews or chicken and meat pies. *As a vegetable
    accompaniment*, especially good with roast beef, roast chicken,
    chops, and meat loaf.
Amount: One pound serves two or three.
    Salsify is a root vegetable, long and tapering, of a grayish-white

cast. It is sometimes called "oyster plant" because its delicate flavor is a little like that of oysters.

BASIC METHOD FOR COOKING ❧ SALSIFY

(SERVES TWO OR THREE)

1 pound salsify
Butter
Salt

Freshly ground pepper
Chopped parsley or chives

Have ready a bowl of cold water to which a little lemon juice or vinegar has been added. Cut off the tops of the salsify root, peel with a vegetable scraper, and drop immediately into the cold acidulated water to prevent discoloration. Cut into ½-inch-wide strips about 2 inches long. Drop them into a large pot filled with boiling water and cook, covered, until tender, about 20 minutes; taste to check doneness—the flesh should not become mushy. Drain. Add some butter, salt, pepper, and a sprinkling of parsley or chives and toss well before serving.

MASHED OR PURÉED SALSIFY

Mash the cooked, drained salsify or purée it through a food mill or in a food processor. Stir in some *butter, salt, freshly ground pepper,* and a little *cream.* Reheat, if necessary, preferably in the top of a double boiler. Or put in a shallow baking dish and sprinkle some *bread crumbs* dotted with butter on top and put under the broiler to brown.

❧ SALSIFY FRITTERS

(SERVES THREE)

1 pound salsify, cooked
4 tablespoons butter
Salt

1–2 tablespoons chopped
chives

Mash the cooked salsify with 2 tablespoons of the butter, adding salt and chives to taste. Beat until smooth. Shape into balls about 1¼ inches in diameter, then flatten into patties. Melt the remaining 2 tablespoons of butter in a skillet and fry the patties on each side until brown. Serve hot.

About Spinach

Availability: Year round.
What to Look For: Fresh, dark-green leaves.
Uses: *Raw*, in salads. *Cooked*, as a bed for eggs, fish, or meat (dishes that are usually described as Florentine), in custards, quiches, soufflés, stuffings, soups. *As a vegetable accompaniment*, good with almost everything, especially with fish.
Amount: One pound serves two or three.
Alternatives to Fresh: Frozen perfectly acceptable but flavor not as good.
Cooking in the Microwave: ½ pound spinach leaves in ¾ cup water in a glass dish with a lid, about 5 minutes on high power (in a 600–700-watt oven). Results: taste less bitter; color, texture, and cooking time comparable to cooking on top of the stove.

Loose, bulk spinach is far preferable to the spinach that comes pre-washed in a package. If using the latter, be sure that it is fresh and not slimy.

BASIC METHOD FOR COOKING SPINACH ?

(SERVES TWO OR THREE)

1 pound spinach   Salt
Melted butter   Freshly ground pepper

Wash the spinach leaves well in several changes of water and remove tougher stems and ribs. Bring a large pot of water to a fast boil, plunge the spinach into the boiling water, cook for 3–6 minutes, depending on how young it is, and drain it in a colander. Leave the cooked spinach whole or chop it, toss it with melted butter, season with salt and pepper, and serve at once.

PURÉED SPINACH

Purée the cooked spinach in a blender or food processor. Reheat it with some butter, season with salt and freshly ground pepper, and add a little *heavy cream*, if you wish.

(SERVES TWO OR THREE) ➢ **BRAISED YOUNG SPINACH**

This method works well with tender, young spinach leaves.

1 pound young spinach   Salt
Melted butter   Freshly ground pepper

Wash spinach leaves well. Put them in a pot or skillet with the water
still clinging to them. Cover and cook over low heat until the spinach is
tender, about 2 minutes. Toss with melted butter, season with salt and
pepper, and serve at once.

SPINACH AND ZUCCHINI
(SERVES SIX) ➢ **CASSEROLE**

2 pounds fresh spinach,   Salt and freshly ground
  trimmed and washed   pepper
1½ pounds zucchini, trimmed   ¼ cup olive oil
  and sliced   Grated Parmesan cheese
2 onions, sliced   (optional)
2 teaspoons chopped basil

Preheat the oven to 350°F. Combine the spinach, zucchini, onions, and
basil in a casserole. Add salt and pepper to taste. Mix the ingredients
so the basil and seasonings are distributed. Drizzle the olive oil over
the top. Cover and bake about 40 minutes. Remove cover and sprinkle
with the cheese if desired. Serve hot or cold.

ABOUT SQUASH

Squash, a true American vegetable, is somewhat bland and very versatile, conducive to good seasonings and a natural partner to a number
of vegetables and meats.

There are two main categories of squash: summer squash and winter squash. Summer squash have soft skins and a tender, more watery
interior, while winter squash are hard-shelled and mealier inside.

About Summer Squash

Availability: Most of the year, especially summer.
What to Look For: Small, young, firm squash with good color and
  smooth, shiny green or yellow skins.

Uses: *Raw,* with a dip or in salad. *Cooked,* in soups, stews, stuffed (p. 611), baked, in casserole dishes, with other vegetables. *As a vegetable accompaniment,* good with fish, meat, and chicken.

Amount: One pound serves four.

Cooking in the Microwave: ½ pound summer squash, in ½-inch slices, in ¾ cup water in a glass dish with a lid, about 5 minutes on high power (in a 600–700-watt oven). Results: color, taste, texture, and cooking time comparable to cooking on top of the stove.

Squash blossoms have become available in produce markets and make a wonderful carrier for good fillings. Or they can be steamed or sautéed in a little butter or oil.

Summer squash should be picked while still immature, about 6–9 inches long, and before the skins harden. If you grow squash yourself, you will soon learn how quickly the vegetables grow; picking them at the correct, early stage often involves split-second timing. Do not peel summer squash; the skins provide good taste and texture. Large summer squash are best scooped out and stuffed.

The larger summer squash are known outside the United States as vegetable marrows, the smaller as courgettes. There are many varieties available, among them smooth, yellow squash, both crooknecks and straightnecks; thin, dark-green zucchini; and scalloped, pale-green pattypan squash, also called cymlings. The various kinds of summer squash are interchangeable in recipes.

Unlike winter squash, summer squash is quite perishable: it should be kept refrigerated and used promptly.

About Winter Squash

Height of Season: Fall and winter.

What to Look For: Firm, hard squash without blemishes: often rough and bumpy.

Uses: *Cooked,* baked, puréed, in soups and in pie. *As a vegetable accompaniment,* excellent with all kinds of meats, particularly country ham.

Amount: One pound serves two.

Alternatives to Fresh: Frozen mashed winter squash is very good.

Cooking in the Microwave: ½-pound piece of winter squash with the skin left on, in a glass dish uncovered, about 5 minutes on high power (in a 600–700-watt oven). Results: color, taste, and texture comparable to cooking in the oven and cooking time much less for this small amount.

Winter squash are picked in the fall when they are mature and their skins have hardened. If you grow them yourself and plan to store them for future use, be sure to leave part of the stems attached or they will not keep very well.

Among the more common forms of winter squash are acorn squash, green hubbard squash, tan butternut squash, buttercup or turban squash, green and gold delicious squash, banana squash, and pumpkins. Another variety is the spaghetti squash, about the size of a football, so called because when it has been cooked and the flesh is scraped out, it forms spaghettilike ribbons. Squash vary greatly in size, from the small, 1-pound acorn squash to the 5- or 6-pound, or more, hubbard.

BASIC METHOD FOR COOKING
(SERVES FOUR) &ep; **SUMMER SQUASH**

1½ cups water
1 pound summer squash, in
 ½-inch slices

3 tablespoons butter
Salt
Freshly ground pepper

Bring the water to a boil, add the squash, and simmer over medium heat, covered, for 3–5 minutes or until just tender; drain. Add the butter, season to taste, and toss to coat. Serve hot.

SUMMER SQUASH AND ONION

Add *1 onion, coarsely chopped*, and cook with the squash.

SUMMER SQUASH AND TOMATOES

Two minutes before the squash is done, add *2 tomatoes, peeled, seeded, and chopped*, with some of the liquid gently squeezed out.

SUMMER SQUASH WITH HORSERADISH CREAM

Mix *½ cup sour cream* with *1 tablespoon prepared horseradish*, add to the cooked squash, and reheat briefly before serving.

SAUTÉED SUMMER SQUASH ह≫ (SERVES FOUR)

This is another way to cook summer squash, equally basic and good with all sorts of variations. Any of the variations for the preceding recipe may be used with this sauté, too.

> 3–4 tablespoons butter
> 1 pound summer squash, in ½-inch slices
>
> Salt
> Freshly ground pepper

Melt the butter in a skillet, add the squash, and cook over low heat, stirring and tossing from time to time, until the squash is tender, about 8–10 minutes. Season to taste.

VARIATIONS

> Combine both *zucchini* and *yellow squash.*
> Add *2 or more thinly sliced scallions* as you sauté the squash.
> Sprinkle with herbs—*parsley, chives, basil, summer savory*—before serving.
> Toss in ¼ *cup Buttered Bread Crumbs* during the last minute of cooking.

SAUTÉED ZUCCHINI ह≫ (SERVES FOUR)

> 2 tablespoons olive or other oil
> 2 cloves garlic, minced
> 1 pound zucchini, in ½-inch slices
>
> Salt
> Freshly ground pepper

Heat the oil in a skillet, add the minced garlic, and cook for a few minutes without letting the garlic brown. Add the zucchini and cook over low heat, stirring occasionally, until the squash is tender, about 10 minutes. Season to taste.

STUFFED ZUCCHINI

These are also good served cold.

4 medium zucchini
¼ cup olive oil
½ cup finely chopped onion
1 clove garlic, minced
¼ pound ground beef, or 1
    cup leftover cooked beef
    or pork, ground
2 tomatoes, peeled, seeded,
    and chopped

½ cup freshly made dry bread
    crumbs
1 tablespoon minced parsley
Salt
Freshly ground pepper
¼ teaspoon basil, crumbled

Preheat the oven to 350°F. Oil a shallow baking dish large enough to
hold the eight halves of zucchini in one layer. Trim the ends off the
zucchini and cook in a large pot of boiling salted water for 3 minutes.
Drain, cut in half lengthwise. Scoop out the pulp, leaving a sturdy
shell; chop and reserve the pulp. Sauté the onion slowly in the oil for 5
minutes, then add the garlic and meat. Cook, stirring constantly, until
the meat loses its color. Remove from the skillet and set aside. Pour off
all but 2 tablespoons of oil from the skillet, heat again, and add the
chopped zucchini pulp and tomatoes. Sauté for 1 minute and add to
the meat mixture. Add the bread crumbs, parsley, salt, pepper, and
basil. Toss together lightly until mixed. Fill the zucchini shells, without
packing down, and place on baking dish. Bake for 30 minutes.

❧ **ZUCCHINI RING**

Sweet marjoram tastes good with zucchini. Fill the center of the ring
with braised carrots, cut into small matchstick shape.

3 cups cooked zucchini,
    drained and mashed
1 teaspoon salt
1 teaspoon chopped fresh
    marjoram, or ½ teaspoon
    dried

2 tablespoons finely grated
    onion
3 eggs, well beaten
½ cup Buttered Bread Crumbs

Preheat the oven to 350°F. Butter a 1½-quart ring mold generously. Put
the zucchini, salt, marjoram, onion, and eggs together in a bowl and
mix thoroughly. Sprinkle the bread crumbs evenly on the inside of the
buttered mold. Spoon in the zucchini mixture. Set the mold in a shallow pan of hot water that comes up the side about 2 inches. Bake for

35–45 minutes or until firm. Turn the zucchini out of the mold onto a platter and fill if desired. Serve hot.

STUFFED SQUASH BLOSSOMS   ✷

3 chicken livers or 2 ounces ham, chopped
4 tablespoons butter
2 minced shallots or 3–4 scallion bulbs
1 cup fresh bread crumbs
2 tablespoons chopped parsley

Salt and freshly ground pepper to taste
1 egg, lightly beaten
16 squash blossoms
¼ cup chicken broth

Sauté the livers in 2 tablespoons of the butter with the shallots or scallions for 2 to 3 minutes, turning, until just done; they should be slightly pink inside. Chop fine. If you are using ham, sauté 1 minute only. Mix the livers or ham and pan juices with the bread crumbs, parsley, salt, pepper, and egg. Spoon a little of this stuffing into each blossom, leaving enough room to fold the tips of the petals over to enclose the stuffing. Melt the remaining butter in a skillet, add the broth, and cook until syrupy. Lay the stuffed blossoms in the pan and cook gently, turning them once carefully, for a minute or so. Serve and pour any remaining pan juices on top.

FRIED STUFFED SQUASH BLOSSOMS

Instead of sautéing the stuffed blossoms in butter and broth, dip them into *Beer Fritter Batter* (p. 533), and deep-fry them.

(SERVES FOUR) ॐ **BAKED WINTER SQUASH**

2 small acorn or butternut	2 tablespoons butter
squash	3 tablespoons maple syrup
Salt	

Preheat the oven to 400°F. Split the squash and remove the seeds. Sprinkle the cut sides with salt. Place cut side down in a baking dish and bake for about 40–50 minutes or until the squash is easily pierced with a fork. Turn and make indentations with a fork across the cut side of the squash. Spread with the butter, drizzle with the maple syrup, and return to the oven for a minute or two. Serve hot.

QUICK COOKED
(SERVES FOUR TO SIX) ॐ **BUTTERNUT SQUASH**

This is a quick way to oven bake a winter squash. I have used the butternut here because it is the easiest to peel raw.

| 2½–3 pounds butternut | About 4 tablespoons butter, |
| squash | melted |

Preheat the oven to 400°F. Peel squash with a vegetable peeler and cut off both ends. Cut into rings about ¼ inch thick starting at the neck. When you get to the base of the squash, remove the seeds and stringy material with a spoon. Then continue to cut the base into rings. Lay the rings in a single layer on a buttered baking sheet and brush with melted butter. Bake for 10 to 12 minutes, or until just soft when pierced with a fork.

(SERVES FOUR) ॐ **WHIPPED WINTER SQUASH**

This can be prepared ahead and reheated in the oven.

2 pounds winter squash	½ cup heavy cream
4 tablespoons butter	Salt
¼ teaspoon nutmeg	

Preheat the oven to 350°F. Cut the squash in half and remove the fibers and seeds. Place cut side down in a baking pan. Bake for 40–50 minutes or until tender. Or cut in large chunks and boil in salted water until tender, then drain well. Scoop out the pulp and put into a mixing bowl with the butter, nutmeg, and cream. Beat with an electric beater or by hand until smooth and well blended. Add salt to taste. Serve hot.

BASIC METHOD FOR COOKING SPAGHETTI SQUASH ✳ ટ્ર

(SERVES SIX)

 1 spaghetti squash (about 2 to   Salt and freshly ground
    3 pounds)   pepper
 4 tablespoons butter

Preheat the oven to 350°. . Pierce the shell of the spaghetti squash with a skewer and place whole on a baking dish or sheet with sides. Bake uncovered for 45 minutes; turn squash over and continue to bake for about 15 to 30 minutes more, until the shell has softened and gives to the touch. Let rest until cool enough to handle. Cut in half lengthwise and remove the seeds. Using a fork, scrape out the spaghettilike strands into a saucepan. Add the butter and salt and pepper to taste, and reheat over low heat.

MICROWAVE METHOD

Cut the spaghetti squash in half lengthwise and remove seeds. Place halves side by side in a microwave-safe baking dish and spread cut surfaces with 2 tablespoons of the butter. Microwave on high for 12–15 minutes. Let stand 5 minutes, then prepare as above.

About Swiss Chard

Availability: Summer and fall height of season.

What to Look For: Crisp, crinkly leaves, deep-green color.

Uses: *Raw*, in salads. *Cooked*, like spinach, in stuffings, quiches, and soups. *As a vegetable accompaniment*, especially good with meat, eggs, and fish.

Amount: One pound serves two.

Cooking in the Microwave: ½ pound Swiss chard leaves, large stems
Mℰ removed, in ¾ cup water in a glass dish with a lid, about 7
minutes on high power (in a 600–700-watt oven). Results:
color, taste, texture, and cooking time comparable to cooking on
top of the stove.

Swiss chard looks like spinach, but has a coarser texture and a stronger taste with a sharp bite to it.

Young Swiss chard can be cooked like most greens. Cook the stems first, then when they are almost tender add the leaves. Older chard has thick stems which are good braised separately from the leaves. Red Swiss chard, sometimes called rhubarb chard, has thick, reddish stems that are also good cooked separately.

BASIC METHOD FOR COOKING
(SERVES SIX)   ❧ SWISS CHARD

Swiss chard is most delicious when you cook the stems and the leaves separately following this method.

3 pounds Swiss chard	2 tablespoons lemon juice
3 tablespoons flour	Salt
3 cups water	2 tablespoons butter

Separate the leaves from the stalks, pulling away the rib from the leaf along with the stem. Wash both thoroughly. Chop the stems into ½-inch pieces. Whisk the flour into the water, then bring to a boil, and drop the chopped stems in along with the lemon juice and ½ teaspoon salt. Simmer gently for 20–30 minutes, depending on the tenderness of the stalks. Meanwhile bring a large pot of salted water to a boil and drop the leaves in. Boil rapidly for 10–15 minutes, depending on their tenderness. Drain and chop roughly; toss with butter and salt to taste. Place the cooked stems and their juice, which will have thickened to the consistency of cream sauce, in the center of a hot platter and surround with the greens.

GRATIN OF SWISS CHARD

After preparing the Swiss chard as on p. 615 (or use any leftover cooked Swiss chard), place both stems and greens in a shallow casserole, mix *2–3 tablespoons heavy cream* in with the chard sauce, correct seasoning, and top with *¼–½ cup bread crumbs* and *an equal amount of grated cheese.* Bake in a 425°F oven for 15 minutes.

About Tomatillos

Availability: Summer and fall, almost year round in some locations.

What to Look For: Firm, round tomatillos in a paper-like husk, which is peeled away and discarded. Peeled, the tomatillo is shiny green and slightly sticky until washed.

Uses: Use without peeling or seeding, after removing husk, *raw* in salads or sauces, or cooked in many Mexican or southwestern dishes.

Alternatives to Fresh: Canned can be acceptable in some recipes, but they tend to be pale and watery.

Cooking in the Microwave: ½ pound tomatillos, husks removed and halved, in ¼ cup water in a glass dish with a lid, about 5 minutes on high power (in a 600–700-watt oven). Results: color, taste, and cooking time comparable to cooking on top of the stove, but skins toughen and are unpleasant in a sauce unless strained. Recommend stove-top cooking.

About Tomatoes

Availability: Almost year round but August and September height of season for fresh.

What to Look For: Firm, smooth, ripe but not overripe tomatoes, without bruises or soft spots.

Uses: *Raw,* like fruit, in salads, sandwiches, as a first course. *Cooked,* broiled, sautéed, stewed, and baked, in soups, stews, casserole dishes, and, of course, as the foundation of an indispensable sauce (see p. 387). Also used for juice, tomato paste, catsup, chili sauce, and in relishes and pickles.

Amount: One per person.

Alternatives to Fresh: Canned plum tomatoes for sauces, stews, and casserole dishes.

Cooking in the Microwave: ½ pound tomatoes, in chunks, in ½ cup water in a glass dish with a lid, about 5 minutes on high power (in a 600–700-watt oven). Results: color brighter, taste and cooking time comparable to cooking on top of the stove, but skins toughen.

The pale, hard-skinned hothouse tomatoes that most markets stock during the winter months lack flavor and have a mealy texture, having been grown mainly for their durability during shipping and handling. Tiny round cherry tomatoes or small pear-shaped or egg-shaped tomatoes, available most of the year, though also grown in hothouses, seem to have more flavor during the out-of-season months.

If tomatoes are not quite ripe, keep them at room temperature until they ripen. Do not refrigerate them: once they've been refrigerated, they will not ripen. Tomatoes actually taste best when they've not been refrigerated at all.

To peel a tomato, submerge it in boiling water for about 15–30 seconds, then let it cool a bit, or plunge into cold water. The skin can then be pulled off easily with a sharp knife. *To seed a tomato,* cut it in half and gently squeeze out the excess juice and seeds, scraping off those that adhere.

Green tomatoes, which are unripened tomatoes, are excellent fried, sautéed, or cooked in sauces or stews. Use small green tomatoes for pickling. Large, unblemished green tomatoes will ripen on a sunny windowsill, or you can wrap them in newspaper and let them ripen slowly in a cool, dark place.

(SERVES SIX)   ₰ **SAUTÉED TOMATOES**

The secret of this recipe is to cook the tomatoes only slightly, browning them quickly in hot butter. They are firm and flavorful with the basil and cream.

6 large tomatoes	2 tablespoons chopped fresh
½ cup flour	basil, or 1 tablespoon
½ teaspoon freshly ground	dried, crumbled
pepper	¾ cup heavy cream
¼ pound butter	Salt

Slice the tomatoes ½ inch thick. Mix the flour and pepper together. Heat the butter over medium-high heat. Dip the tomato slices into the flour mixture and coat on each side; shake free of excess flour. Put the slices into the hot butter and cook just a minute on each side or until

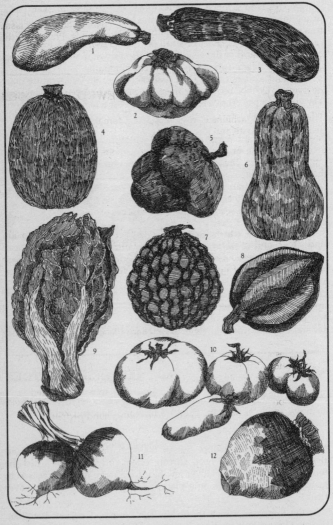

1. *yellow or crookneck squash;* 2. *pattypan squash;* 3. *zucchini;* 4. *spaghetti squash;* 5. *turban squash;* 6. *butternut squash;* 7. *hubbard squash;* 8. *acorn squash;* 9. *Swiss chard;* 10. *tomatoes;* 11. *turnip;* 12. *rutabaga.*

lightly golden. Remove and keep in warm oven. Pour off all but 1 tablespoon of the butter, then stir in the basil, cream, and salt to taste. Bring to a boil and boil rapidly about 3 or 4 minutes. Pour over the tomato slices and serve.

(SERVES SIX)   &✖ **STEWED TOMATOES**

This is the old-fashioned way of stewing tomatoes. If it seems too sweet for your taste, use less sugar.

6 large tomatoes, peeled (above), or 2½ cups canned tomatoes	2 teaspoons sugar
	⅛ teaspoon cloves
	Salt
1 tablespoon butter	Freshly ground pepper
2 tablespoons finely chopped onion	1 slice fresh bread, torn in pieces (optional)

Cut the tomatoes into eighths. Melt the butter in a pan, add the onion and sugar, and cook for 3 or 4 minutes, stirring, over medium heat. Add the tomatoes and cloves. Cover and simmer for 15 minutes. Season to taste. If a thicker stew is desired, add the bread and cook another 10 minutes.

(SERVES FOUR)   &✖ **BRAISED HERB TOMATOES**

4 tablespoons butter	2 teaspoons chopped fresh thyme, or 1 teaspoon dried, crumbled
4 scallions, chopped	
1 tablespoon finely chopped parsley	8 medium tomatoes, peeled
	Salt
4 teaspoons chopped fresh basil, or 2 teaspoons dried, crumbled	Freshly ground pepper

Melt the butter in a skillet. Stir in the scallions, parsley, basil, and thyme. Cook over low heat, stirring often, for 5 minutes. Add the tomatoes, cover, and cook over low heat for 5 more minutes. Season to taste. Place the tomatoes on a platter and spoon the herb juices over them.

BROILED TOMATOES ≈ (SERVES FOUR)

Delicious with chops and roasts, particularly lamb.

4 large tomatoes	1 teaspoon salt
2 teaspoons chopped fresh oregano or marjoram, or 1 teaspoon dried, crumbled	1 cup buttered bread crumbs ¼ teaspoon freshly ground pepper

Cut the tomatoes in half and arrange them cut side up in a shallow, buttered baking dish. Mix the oregano or marjoram, salt, bread crumbs, and pepper together and sprinkle evenly over tomatoes. Place under the broiler, watching carefully, until the crumbs brown and the tomatoes heat slightly. Be careful not to overcook or you will ruin the texture and the shape. Serve hot or cold.

BROILED TOMATOES WITH CHEESE

Add ½ cup freshly grated Parmesan cheese and ½ clove garlic, minced, to the seasoned crumbs.

BROILED TOMATOES WITH MUSTARD CREAM

Omit the oregano or marjoram. Combine 1 cup heavy cream and 1½ tablespoons prepared mustard in a small pan and heat, stirring. Pour the mustard cream around the tomatoes just before serving.

BAKED STUFFED TOMATOES ≈ (SERVES FOUR)

About 2 cups of stuffing will fill four large tomatoes nicely.

4 firm large tomatoes	2 tablespoons finely chopped onion
Salt	
1¼ cups dried homemade bread crumbs	2 tablespoons finely chopped green pepper
1 teaspoon chopped fresh basil, or ½ teaspoon dried, crumbled	1½ tablespoons olive oil Freshly ground pepper

Preheat the oven to 400°F. Film a shallow baking pan with oil, using a pan large enough so that 8 tomato halves will not be crowded. Carefully cut a slice from the top of each tomato and scoop out most of the pulp, leaving a thick shell so that the tomato will hold its shape. Sprinkle the insides of the tomatoes with salt, invert them on paper towels, and let them drain for about 15 minutes. Squeeze the juice out of the pulp and chop pulp fine. In a bowl, *lightly* toss the bread crumbs, basil, onion, green pepper, and tomato pulp, then add the olive oil and season to taste with salt and pepper. Lightly fill each tomato, without packing. Place on the baking pan and bake for 15–20 minutes.

BAKED TOMATOES WITH MUSHROOM STUFFING

Omit the basil, green pepper, and olive oil and reduce the amount of bread crumbs to ½ cup. Clean and chop *½ pound mushrooms* and sauté them with the onion in *4 tablespoons butter* over moderate heat for about 5 minutes; cool. Lightly toss the bread crumbs, tomato pulp, mushroom and onion mixture, salt, and pepper together and proceed as for Baked Stuffed Tomatoes.

BAKED TOMATOES WITH TUNA STUFFING

Omit the basil and reduce the amount of bread crumbs to ½ cup and the onion and green pepper to 1 tablespoon each. Add *½ teaspoon chopped fresh tarragon or ¼ teaspoon dried tarragon, crumbled*, and *a 6½-ounce can tuna*, well drained and broken into small pieces. Lightly mix the bread crumbs, tomato pulp, tarragon, tuna, onion, and green pepper, then add the olive oil, salt, and pepper. Proceed as for Baked Stuffed Tomatoes.

BAKED TOMATOES WITH MEAT, FISH, OR
CHICKEN STUFFING

Omit the basil, green pepper, and olive oil and reduce the amount of bread crumbs to ½ cup. Add *1 teaspoon chopped fresh thyme or ½ teaspoon dried thyme, crumbled*, *2 tablespoons melted butter*, and *1 cup minced cooked meat, fish,* or *chicken*. Proceed as for Baked Stuffed Tomatoes.

BAKED TOMATOES WITH SPINACH AND WATER CHESTNUT STUFFING

Omit the green pepper and reduce the amount of bread crumbs to ½ cup. Add 1 cup *well-drained chopped cooked spinach* and ¼ cup *sliced canned water chestnuts*. Proceed as for Baked Stuffed Tomatoes.

CREOLE TOMATOES ತ‌

(SERVES SIX)

3 tablespoons butter
1 large green pepper, chopped
1 onion, chopped
6–7 medium tomatoes, quartered
⅛ teaspoon cayenne pepper

1 tablespoon chopped fresh thyme, or 1½ teaspoons dried, crumbled
Salt
2 tablespoons finely chopped parsley

Melt the butter in a large skillet, add the green pepper and onion, and cook slowly over medium-low heat, stirring occasionally, for about 10 minutes or until the onions are lightly colored. Add the tomatoes, cayenne pepper, and thyme. Cook for 5–6 minutes, stirring frequently. Add salt to taste, sprinkle with parsley, and serve.

FRIED GREEN TOMATOES * ತ‌

(SERVES SIX)

This is one of the most overlooked, good treats I know of.

1 cup cornmeal
5 medium green tomatoes, in ¼- to ⅜-inch slices
½ cup vegetable oil or bacon fat

Salt and freshly ground pepper
6 sprigs cilantro or Chinese parsley (optional)

Sprinkle cornmeal on a piece of wax paper or a large flat plate. Dip each tomato slice into cornmeal and pat gently until cornmeal covers the surface; turn slice over and coat the other side. Heat the oil in a large skillet over medium heat. Add tomato slices, and fry in one layer, without crowding, for 2–3 minutes on each side, until golden brown. Season with salt and pepper to taste. Serve hot, garnished with sprigs of cilantro.

(SERVES FOUR) &~ **CURRIED GREEN TOMATOES**

This is good hot or cold. The tomatoes should be barely cooked.

2 tablespoons butter
½ onion, chopped fine
1½ teaspoons curry powder
Pinch cayenne pepper

2 cups coarsely chopped
green tomatoes
Salt

Melt the butter in a skillet, add the onion, and cook slowly until onion is transparent. Add the curry powder and blend well. Stir in the cayenne pepper and green tomatoes. Cook, stirring, for 3–4 minutes. Add salt to taste.

About Turnips and Rutabagas

Availability: White turnips, year round; rutabagas or yellow turnips, mainly fall and winter.

What to Look For: Firm, smooth, round, unblemished turnips.

Uses: Whole when small, or sliced or grated. *Raw*, julienned or sliced thin, salted, with dips. *Cooked*, in stews, casserole dishes, braised, puréed, creamed, around a roast, with other vegetables. *As a vegetable accompaniment*, especially good with pork and duck; yellow turnips or rutabagas puréed are excellent with beef, lamb, and a roast turkey.

Amount: One pound serves three.

Cooking in the Microwave: ½ pound turnips, peeled and quartered, in ¼ cup water in a glass dish with a lid, about 8 minutes on high power (in a 600–700-watt oven). Results: color, taste, texture, and cooking time comparable to cooking on top of the stove.

½ pound rutabaga, peeled and quartered, in ¼ cup water in a glass dish with a lid, about 10 minutes on high power (in a 600–700-watt oven). Results: color, taste, texture, and cooking time comparable to cooking on top of the stove.

White turnips, particularly the small ones, are somewhat milder than rutabagas and cook more quickly. Turnips are easy to grow and will thrive in about any kind of soil. The greens can be cooked like collards and other field greens (p. 561).

BASIC METHOD FOR COOKING
WHITE TURNIPS 🍃 (SERVES FOUR)

1½ pounds white turnips
3 tablespoons butter
Salt to taste

1 tablespoon finely chopped
parsley

If the turnips are old, peel them; small young turnips need only be scrubbed. If large, cut them into quarters; if small, cut in half. Drop turnips into a large pot of boiling water and boil for 8–10 minutes or until tender when pierced with a knife or skewer; drain. Add the butter, sprinkle with salt and parsley, and toss until coated.

WHIPPED TURNIPS

After boiling, mash with a fork, then add *½ cup heavy cream, heated, 2 ta-blespoons softened butter, 1 teaspoon grated lemon rind,* and *½ teaspoon salt.* Beat by hand or with an electric mixer until smooth.

CREAMED TURNIPS

After boiling, drain and dice. Melt *2 tablespoons butter* in a skillet, add the turnips, pour *1 cup heavy cream* over them, and stir in *¼ teaspoon ginger* and *salt to taste.* Stir until well blended and hot. If a thicker sauce is desired, boil, drain, and dice the turnips, then toss them in *1 cup White Sauce* (p. 379).

BRAISED TURNIPS (SERVES FOUR)

Either white or yellow turnips can be done this way. Usually rutabagas are larger and will take longer to cook.

3 tablespoons butter
1 cup beef broth
1 pound small young turnips,
    peeled and halved

Salt
Freshly ground pepper

Melt the butter in a heavy-bottomed pan with a lid. Add the beef broth and bring it to a simmer. Add the turnips, cover, and simmer for 10–15 minutes or until tender. Remove from the heat, add salt and pepper to taste, and serve hot.

WHITE TURNIPS ROASTED WITH MEAT OR FOWL

(SERVES FOUR)

Turnips taste wonderful roasted with a pork or beef roast or with turkey or duck: the rich pan drippings blend nicely with the sweet tangy character of the turnips.

1½ pounds medium white
    turnips

Peel the turnips, drop them into boiling water, and let them boil for 10 or more minutes until they are barely tender. If they are quite large, halve or quarter them; otherwise place them whole around roast meat or fowl during the last hour of roasting. Turn them and baste them every 20–30 minutes with the pan juices.

BASIC METHOD FOR COOKING ಒ RUTABAGAS

(SERVES FOUR)

1½ pounds rutabagas or   Melted butter
    yellow turnips   Lemon juice
Salt

Peel the rutabagas and cut them up or dice them. Drop them into boiling water to cover and cook briskly about 7–10 minutes or until soft. Drain well, season with salt, toss with melted butter, and add a squeeze or so of lemon juice to taste.

MASHED OR PURÉED RUTABAGAS

Drain and mash the cooked rutabagas with a fork or potato masher or purée them in a food processor. Add a little *butter, salt, freshly ground pepper,* and *cream* to taste. A *dash of cinnamon or freshly grated nutmeg* is also a good accent.

MICROWAVE COOKING

Learning to use a microwave oven entails learning a new language. It is entirely different from using a traditional stove top or oven, where we are guided in the cooking process by the sounds of bubbling liquids, sizzling fat, and all the savory aromas that direct heat produces. The microwave oven gives no sensory tips; it is speedy, clean, and silent, and because it works so quickly, we must learn new cooking rhythms. Microwaving a dish 30 seconds is vastly different from cooking it for 5 minutes in the traditional way.

Cooking in a microwave oven lacks the personal involvement that is the pleasure of cooking the conventional way. I don't think using a microwave oven encourages people to enjoy cooking and to expand their abilities by trying new recipes and techniques. But microwave ovens, along with answering machines, word processors, and faxes, are part of today's need for efficiency. Surveys report that 80 percent of all the nation's households have a microwave oven and the majority of owners use their microwave ovens only to heat, reheat, thaw, and melt foods. Obviously the microwave has more capabilities than that, and it is important to learn what they are and to utilize the appliance's potential. There is a lot of good basic information available, but there is also some overly optimistic writing on the subject that promises cooking results that the microwave cannot deliver. Therefore, it is helpful to learn about what makes a microwave a totally different breed of cat.

The microwave oven does not cook with flames or red-hot electric coils that can be fine-tuned by turning a dial from simmer to boil or from warm to broiling hot. The microwave oven is controlled only by limiting the number of waves released per second, and those waves have one fixed degree of energy. Full power on a microwave oven means that the maximum number of microwaves are being produced per second. Half-power produces the same intensity of wave, but only releases half as many waves in the same amount of time. You cannot control the intensity of energy of the waves, only the number emitted. The microwaves are generated by a magnetron tube and are distributed by a fan or rotating antenna. Microwaves don't penetrate everything that comes within their radius; they are attracted only to molecules in water, fat, and sugar. The waves create the intense energy that causes the molecules to vibrate, and it is this friction among the moving molecules that cooks the food while the cookware remains relatively cool. When it does get hot, it is because the very hot food has conducted the heat to the cookware. Microwaves cook food from the outside in and penetrate the food only to a depth of 1½ to 2 inches.

Microwave ovens vary in size and wattage. Most people don't know the wattage of their ovens; it is enough to know that 500 watts and up is high, 400 watts and under is low. Each microwave has its little quirks, hot spots, and cold spots, just as our conventional ovens do, but because cooking takes place with such speed it is particularly important to learn your microwave oven's peculiarities.

I found that learning to use my microwave efficiently and easily took lots more practice and experience than most kitchen equipment. I cooked many rubbery chicken breasts in the beginning before I finally learned that a nicely cooked chicken breast took 4 minutes in my microwave, plus 3 minutes of standing time for the heat of the food to finish the cooking. It will probably take a different amount of time in yours. In other words, you have to work out the timing in accordance with the idiosyncrasies of each oven. It is a process of trial and error; you can't go by the book. Start by following your manufacturer's instructions, then make your own notes and adjust your timing accordingly.

For this thirteenth edition I tested hundreds of recipes from the twelfth in order to determine what really works in the microwave oven and what doesn't. I invariably made the same recipe on the top of the stove or in the conventional oven to compare the results, and you will find in this chapter several boxes on my observations, tips, and findings, in addition to my comments throughout the book. Obviously my conclusions come down to a matter of taste but my judgment is based on a lifetime of experience in the kitchen and teaching good cooking. The final criterion for me is always how something tastes. If taste and texture don't mean anything to you and only speed counts, then ignore my comments.

It is in the nature of American business to want to make a new product do everything, with its promoters blindly optimistic about what it can accomplish. The same goes for books that are devoted exclusively to cooking with one particular piece of equipment.

In the process of testing I have come up with more than fifty recipes that work well in the microwave oven and should please most people. They are collected here in this chapter.

MICROWAVE OBSERVATIONS

One of the daunting factors about learning to use a microwave oven is the numerous variables you have to take into account for good results—the size, amount, and composition of your ingredients, the container they must be cooked in, the position of the food in the cooking dish, and the fact that there is no standardization of microwave ovens. Resting time—that is, letting a microwaved dish stand outside the oven to allow the heat of the food to finish the cooking—is important in some cases, not in others.

Cooking on low power, turning, rotating, and stirring do give the cook some control, but often it is awkward—lifting off the plastic wrap or cover (and risking steam burn), and poking the food to determine which pieces are done and which need to be moved to the edge.

MICROWAVE TIPS

- Do not try to cook foods in the microwave that you want browned, crisp, or baked.
- The smaller the portion of food, the quicker it will cook in the microwave.
- Don't operate a microwave oven when it is empty.
- Don't use metal in the microwave, such as twists for bags, metal dishes, or even dishes and cartons that have metal trim. The metal causes arcing, which will damage the oven. It is best to use microwave-safe dishes.
- Use only plastic wrap, bags, and paper towels that are labeled safe for microwave use. Wax paper is also acceptable. Do not let plastic wrap touch the food.
- Pierce foods such as eggs, sausages, chicken livers, whole baking potatoes, etc., that can explode in the oven.
- Foods cook more quickly around the outer edge of the dish, so place thick pieces around the outside and thinner ones on the inside of the dish to help achieve even cooking.
- Steaming or moist-heat cooking is what the microwave does best, so to retain the moisture, cover the dish snugly with plastic wrap, venting with a hole or two, or cover it with the microwave dish lid if it has one.
- Because food cooks from the outer edge of the dish toward the center, casseroles or stews should be stirred once or twice during cooking for more even cooking.

MICROWAVE FINDINGS

- Microwave cooking does not integrate and blend flavors successfully.
- Fish cooks nicely in the microwave but, to remind you again, the thickest part should be placed on the outside of the baking dish and the thinner part toward the center. Also, because microwaves cook unevenly, leaving hot spots and cold spots, there is some concern today that not all bacteria are killed in microwave cooking.
- Meat does not respond well to microwave cooking. The juices leach out quickly and form puddles, and the cooked meat tastes and looks steamed, which it is. The texture is apt to be tough and dry.
- White meat poultry does well if the timing is carefully monitored. Dark meat on the bone has a slightly unpleasant taste and the skin is not pleasing to eat.

- Sauces in small amounts can be made successfully in the microwave.
- Beans, rice, and pasta take too long in the microwave, and the hot and cold spots make them cook unevenly. It is essential to stir and rotate to even out the cooking and if you are preparing amounts to serve four or more, it is not worth the trouble.
- Eggs are difficult to cook in the microwave without overcooking. In a flash they toughen and become coarse. They cook so quickly and easily on top of the stove that you are better off doing them that way and being in control.
- Most vegetables and fruits do well, but not all. I have found that they require more water than most microwave cooking instructions call for. See notes on the individual entries in those chapters.
- The microwave oven cannot bake successfully because it produces moist cooking, not the dry heat required for baking.
- Candy can be made surprisingly successfully in the microwave. The sugar does not tend to turn granular or to crystallize as readily as it does cooked on top of the stove.
- The microwave can be a great helper in preparing a dish, such as cooking onions or aromatic vegetables to be used in a casserole, defrosting frozen stock, and melting or softening butter and chocolate for baking.

BASIC WHITE SAUCE ès   (1 CUP)

This all-purpose sauce is quick to make in the microwave.

2 tablespoons butter	Salt and freshly ground
2 tablespoons flour	pepper to taste
1 cup milk	

Put the butter in a microwave-safe 1-quart bowl and melt on high for 15–30 seconds. (This may take longer if the butter is ice cold.) Stir in the flour until smooth and blended. Stir in the milk and salt and pepper and microwave on high for about 2 minutes. Stir and microwave on high for another 1–2 minutes until thickened.

CHEDDAR CHEESE SAUCE

Stir *½–1 cup grated Cheddar cheese* into the finished sauce. Reheat for a few seconds if necessary.

WHITE CHEESE SAUCE

Stir *¼ cup grated Parmesan cheese* and *¼ cup grated Fontina* or *Swiss cheese* into finished sauce. Reheat for a few seconds if necessary.

(ABOUT 2 CUPS) &❧ **CHUNKY TOMATO SAUCE**

This quick sauce comes out tasting fresh and lively.

1 tablespoon olive oil	3 cups coarsely chopped fresh
2 cloves garlic, minced	ripe tomatoes
1 small onion, chopped	2 tablespoons tomato paste
(about 1 cup)	½ teaspoon salt, or to taste

Put the oil, garlic, and onion in a 2- to 3-quart microwave-safe casserole, cover, and microwave on high for 3 minutes. Stir in the tomatoes, tomato paste, and salt and microwave uncovered on high for 5 minutes. Stir and microwave on high for another 5 minutes. If you wish a thicker sauce, continue to microwave for 5–10 minutes more.

ITALIAN TOMATO SAUCE

Add *½ teaspoon dried basil, ½ teaspoon dried oregano,* and *1 tablespoon chopped parsley* before the last 5 minutes of cooking.

(½ CUP) &❧ **HOLLANDAISE SAUCE**

Be sure and let the butter cool down before adding the egg yolks.

4 tablespoons butter	2 egg yolks
1 tablespoon lemon juice	½ teaspoon salt
2 tablespoons water, or more	

Put the butter, lemon juice, and 2 tablespoons water in a 1–2-cup microwave-safe bowl (I use a Pyrex 1-cup measuring cup with handle). Microwave on high for about 50 seconds or until butter has melted. Remove from the oven and whisk to blend. Let cool to the touch about 3–4 minutes, whisking occasionally. Add the egg yolks and salt and whisk to blend. Cover with plastic wrap, poke a hole to vent, and microwave on medium for 15 seconds. Remove plastic wrap and whisk to blend. Re-cover and microwave on medium for another 15 seconds. Remove cover and whisk to blend. The sauce will thicken as it sits. If you wish a very thick sauce, microwave again for 5 seconds or so. If you wish a thinner sauce, add warm water 1 tablespoon at a time and whisk to blend.

NOTE
see page 471

APPLESAUCE ≷ (ABOUT 1 CUP)

This is good served warm or cold with roast pork or turkey.

1 pound tart green apples, peeled, cored, and in large dice (about 3 cups)	⅛ teaspoon cinnamon
	⅛ teaspoon allspice
3 tablespoons sugar, or to taste	

In a 1½–2-quart microwave-safe casserole, toss the apples with the sugar. Cover and microwave on high for 5 minutes. Uncover, stir in the cinnamon and allspice, and microwave on high for 2–3 minutes until thickened. Mash apples with a fork to a chunky-sauce consistency.

RASPBERRY SAUCE ≷ (1½ CUPS)

2 cups raspberries   ⅓ cup sugar

Put the raspberries and sugar into a 2-quart container. Cover with plastic wrap and cook for 3 minutes, uncover, stir, cook on high for 1 minute more. Force the raspberry sauce through a sieve to remove seeds. Keep refrigerated in a covered jar until needed.

SHREDDED VEGETABLE SOUP (4 CUPS)

This makes a perfect first course. It is light and colorful.

1 tablespoon butter
½ cup grated onion
½ cup grated potato
½ cup grated carrot

1 cup grated zucchini
3 cups chicken broth
Salt and freshly ground
  pepper to taste

In a 3-quart microwave-safe bowl or deep casserole melt the butter for 30 seconds. Add the onion, potato, and carrot, stir, cover, and microwave on high for 3–4 minutes. Add the salt and pepper. Add the zucchini, cover, and microwave on high for 2–3 minutes. Add the chicken broth, re-cover, and microwave on high for 4–6 minutes or until hot.

(SERVES FOUR) **PARSNIP SOUP**

A hearty soup with a sweet parsnip flavor.

1 pound parsnips, peeled and
  diced (about 4 cups)
¼ cup water
2 cups chicken broth
1 cup milk

Salt and freshly ground
  pepper to taste
¼ cup sliced scallions, for
  garnish

In a 2½–3-quart microwave-safe casserole, put the parsnips and water. Cover and microwave on high for 7–8 minutes or until the parsnips are soft. Transfer to a food processor or blender, add 1 cup of the broth, and process until puréed. Return the mixture to the casserole and stir in the remaining broth, milk, and salt and pepper. Thin with more milk or broth if desired. Re-cover and microwave on high for 5–7 minutes or until the soup is hot. Sprinkle about a tablespoon of the scallions over the top of each serving.

(4 CUPS) **ZUCCHINI SOUP**

The lemon juice and sour cream make this a good cold soup too.

1 tablespoon butter or olive
  oil
1 cup chopped onion
½ cup diced potato
½ pound zucchini, sliced or in
  large dice
3 cups beef broth

1 tablespoon lemon juice
Salt and freshly ground
  pepper to taste
¼ cup sour cream
½ teaspoon dried dillweed, or
  1–2 teaspoons fresh

Put the butter or oil, onion, and potato into a 2–3-quart microwave-safe casserole or 8-cup glass measure with handle, cover, and microwave on high for 3 minutes. Add the zucchini, re-cover, and microwave on high for 4–5 minutes or until the zucchini is tender. Purée the vegetables with about ½ cup of the broth in a food processor or blender and return to the casserole. Add the remaining broth, lemon juice, and salt and pepper. Cover and microwave on high for 4–6 minutes until hot. In a small bowl, mix together the sour cream and dillweed. Float a spoonful of the dill-cream in each bowl of soup as served.

CREAM OF MUSHROOM SOUP (4 CUPS)

Light, delicate, and creamy but almost fat-free.

1 tablespoon butter	1 cup chicken stock
¼ cup finely chopped onion	1 teaspoon lemon juice
2 cups sliced mushrooms	¾ teaspoon salt
2 cups milk	Freshly ground pepper to
1 tablespoon cornstarch	taste

Melt the butter in a 2–3-quart casserole on high for 30–40 seconds. Add the onion and microwave on high for 1 minute. Add mushrooms, cover, and microwave 5 minutes on high. Purée mushroom mixture with 1 cup of the milk in a food processor or blender. Return mixture to casserole. Stir cornstarch into the cold chicken stock until dissolved. Add the stock, the remaining cup of milk, lemon juice, salt, and pepper and microwave on high 6–8 minutes, stirring at 4 minutes, or until hot and slightly thickened.

CARROT SOUP ❧ (SERVES FOUR)

Buy young firm carrots. They are sweeter and their flavor is better.

2 tablespoons butter	3 cups half-and-half or milk
1 onion, chopped	Salt and freshly ground
6–8 carrots, peeled and in 1-inch slices (about 3 cups)	pepper to taste
	Chopped parsley
¼ cup water	

Put the butter, onion, carrots, and water in a large microwave-safe bowl, and microwave on high for 6–8 minutes, until carrots are soft when pierced with a fork. Purée the carrot mixture with 1 cup of the half-and-half or milk in a food processor. Return the carrot mixture to the bowl, stir in the remaining half-and-half or milk and microwave on high for 4–6 minutes, stirring once, until hot. Add the salt and pepper. Garnish with the parsley.

(8 CUPS) **FISH CHOWDER**

This delicious chowder can be made with a combination of fish, such as bass, red snapper, cod, halibut, or salmon.

2 tablespoons butter
1 cup diced onion
2 cups peeled and diced
  potatoes
4 cups milk

2 cups corn kernels
¾ pound white-fleshed fish
  fillets, in bite-size chunks
Salt and freshly ground
  pepper

Put the butter and onion in a 3-quart microwave-safe bowl, cover, and microwave on high for 3–4 minutes. Add the potatoes and milk, re-cover, and microwave on high for 4–5 minutes. Stir in the corn and fish, cover, and microwave on high for 8–10 minutes, or until the fish is tender and flakes with a fork and the soup is hot. Add salt and pepper to taste.

(7 CUPS) **BEET SOUP**

A hearty soup which becomes a whole meal by adding cooked beef. Top with sour cream if you like.

2 cups diced fresh beets
  (about 1 pound)
1 cup diced potato
½ cup chopped onion

2 cups shredded cabbage
4 cups beef broth
Freshly ground pepper
Salt

Put beets, potato, and onion in a 3-quart microwave-safe bowl. Cover and microwave on high for 8–10 minutes. Add the cabbage, broth, and pepper and microwave on high for 8–10 minutes or until hot. Salt to taste.

POTATO AND CABBAGE SOUP (SERVES FOUR)

The microwave is very kind to cabbage. It retains the good flavors.

4 slices bacon, in 1-inch pieces	½ cup chopped scallions
1 cup chopped onion	2 cups chicken broth
2 cups diced potatoes	Salt and freshly ground
2 cups shredded cabbage	pepper to taste

Put the bacon and onion in a 3–4-quart microwave-safe bowl and microwave on high for 5 minutes. Add the potatoes, cabbage, and scallions, cover, and microwave 5–6 minutes. Add the chicken broth and salt and pepper, re-cover, and microwave on high 4–6 minutes or until hot.

CREAMED POTATOES AND TURNIPS (SERVES FOUR)

This is a home-style side dish which goes well with duck, chicken, or lamb.

¾ cup milk	1 pound turnips, peeled and
2 tablespoons cornstarch	sliced thin
½ cup cream	1 pound potatoes, peeled and
2 tablespoons minced parsley	sliced thin
Salt	

In a small bowl, stir together ¼ cup of the milk and the cornstarch until dissolved. Pour into a 3–4-quart microwave-safe casserole. Add the remaining ½ cup milk, cream, and parsley and stir to blend. Salt the slices of turnip and potato and add to the casserole. Mix well with a spoon to coat the slices with the milk mixture. Cover with plastic wrap and microwave on high for 4 minutes. Stir, re-cover, and microwave on high for 4 more minutes.

ZUCCHINI AND TOMATOES (SERVES FOUR)

A flavorful side dish to serve with a simple meat. It is also good as a quick sauce for cooked pasta.

1 tablespoon olive oil
1 clove garlic, chopped fine
1 medium onion, chopped
2 large zucchini, in strips
    about 3 inches long or
    ¼-inch slices

2 tomatoes, coarsely chopped
½ teaspoon salt, or to taste
Freshly ground pepper to
    taste
½ teaspoon dried basil

Put the olive oil, garlic, and onion into a microwave-safe casserole, cover, and microwave on high for 2–3 minutes. Add the zucchini and toss, re-cover, and microwave on high for 2 minutes. Add the tomatoes, salt, pepper, and basil, toss and re-cover, and microwave on high for 2–3 minutes.

(SERVES FOUR) ટે **STEWED RHUBARB**

1 pound rhubarb, cut into
    ½-inch pieces

⅔ cup sugar
3 tablespoons water

Put the rhubarb, sugar, and water into a 2-quart microwave-safe casserole and stir to mix well. Cover with plastic wrap and cook on high for 4 minutes, uncover and stir. Check for doneness; the rhubarb should be very tender. If not, cook on high for another 2 minutes.

(SERVES FOUR) ટે **ROOT VEGETABLES**

An earthy winter vegetable dish.

1 potato
1 yellow or red onion
1 turnip
1 rutabaga
1 large carrot

1 tablespoon butter
2 tablespoons water
Salt and freshly ground
    pepper

Peel and cut into cubes the potato, onion, turnip, rutabaga, and carrot. You should have about 1½ pounds of vegetables. Put the vegetables in a microwave-safe casserole with the butter and water. Cover and microwave on high for 8–11 minutes, stirring once halfway through the cooking time. Add salt and pepper to taste and serve hot.

SPAGHETTI SQUASH
WITH MARINARA SAUCE ⋟   (SERVES FOUR)

Spaghetti squash is magic. It looks like a squash on the outside and
spaghetti strands on the inside.

2½-pound spaghetti squash   ½ cup tomato sauce
   (3½ cups cooked squash)   2 tablespoons tomato paste
1 teaspoon salt, or to taste   ¼ cup water
1 tablespoon olive oil   ¾ cup grated Fontina cheese

Cut squash in half lengthwise. Place cut side down in a shallow
microwave-safe baking dish. Microwave on high for 9–10 minutes, or
until outside gives a little when pressed. Remove from oven and cool
slightly. Remove the seeds from the squash and, using a fork, rake and
separate the strands of squash from the rind and place in a 2-quart
microwave-safe casserole. Add salt to taste. In a small bowl, combine
the olive oil, tomato sauce, tomato paste, and water, stir until blended,
and microwave on high for 1 minute or until hot. Spoon the sauce over
the squash. Sprinkle the cheese over the top and microwave on high
for about 1 minute, or until the cheese is melted.

SCHOOLTEACHER SQUASH ⋟   (SERVES FOUR)

An old-fashioned vegetable casserole that a schoolteacher of mine used
to make. It adapted well to the microwave and is just as good today as
ever.

1 pound zucchini, sliced   ¼ cup olive oil
¼ cup water   ½ cup grated sharp Cheddar
Salt to taste   cheese
⅓ cup chopped onion   1 egg, slightly beaten
⅓ cup chopped green pepper

Put the zucchini, water, and salt in a 2-quart microwave-safe casserole,
and microwave on high for 6 minutes, or until soft. Drain off the excess
water and mash the zucchini. In a separate small dish, microwave the
onion and pepper with 2 tablespoons of the olive oil on high for 1
minute. Add the onion mixture to the zucchini along with the cheese
and egg and stir to blend. Drizzle remaining 2 tablespoons olive oil
over top. Microwave, uncovered, on high for 4 minutes, then turn the
dish and microwave on high for 3 more minutes.

(SERVES FOUR)   &ᴥ   **CABBAGE AND APPLES**

You can use red or green cabbage and red or green apples.

2 tablespoons butter
1 tablespoon lemon juice
1 tablespoon water
1 tablespoon brown sugar
½ teaspoon caraway seed

½ teaspoon salt, or to taste
4 cups shredded green or red
   cabbage (about ½ pound)
1 large apple, peeled and
   sliced or in bite-size pieces

In a 2–3-quart casserole melt butter on high for 30–50 seconds. Add the lemon juice, water, sugar, caraway, and salt, and stir until blended. Add cabbage and apple and toss to blend. Cover and microwave on high 2–3 minutes. Let stand about 2 minutes.

(SERVES FOUR)   &ᴥ   **CELERY WITH TOMATO**

Too often celery is forgotten as a vegetable. This will remind you how good it can be.

3 cups sliced celery (about ½
   pound)
½ cup chopped tomato
2 tablespoons water or
   chicken broth

Salt and freshly ground
   pepper to taste
¼ cup grated Parmesan
   cheese

Put the celery in a 2–3-quart microwave-safe casserole, and scatter the tomato over the top. Add the water or broth and salt and pepper, and cover. Microwave on high for 6–8 minutes, or until the celery is tender when pierced with a fork. Sprinkle with the Parmesan cheese and serve.

(SERVES FOUR)   &ᴥ   **ORANGE BEETS**

Fresh beets are wonderful and sweet but they can stain. Salt will remove beet stains from clothing; soap and water will remove most of the stain from your fingers. This is good cold as a salad tossed with a vinaigrette.

1 pound fresh beets, peeled
   and in large dice
¼ cup orange juice
1 teaspoon grated orange zest

Sections from 1 orange,
   optional (see p. 1028)
1 teaspoon sugar (optional)
Salt to taste

Put the beets, orange juice, orange zest, the optional orange sections and sugar, and salt in a 2–3-quart microwave-safe casserole. Cover and microwave for 10–12 minutes. Let stand for 2–3 minutes. Test for doneness. Cook 1–2 minutes longer if you like soft beets.

QUICK POLENTA ⧀⧐   (SERVES FOUR)

This is good for breakfast, lunch, or dinner.

¾ cup cornmeal or polenta   ½ teaspoon salt
3 cups water

In a 3-quart Pyrex bowl, mix the cornmeal, water, and salt. Cover and microwave on high for 8 minutes. Remove and stir briskly until well blended. Microwave for another 2–3 minutes for thicker polenta. The polenta may be eaten as soft polenta at this point or you may spoon it into a buttered baking dish and let it cool and get firm. When firm, cut in pieces and reheat in the microwave for 1–2 minutes, or pan fry in a nonstick pan in a little butter or oil.

POLENTA WITH ZUCCHINI
AND TOMATO ⧀⧐   (SERVES FOUR)

This makes a good side dish with a simple roast chicken or roasted meat.

¾ cup cornmeal or polenta   ½ cup chopped onion
3 cups water   1 cup corn kernels
1 teaspoon salt, or to taste   3-ounce package cream
1½ cups diced or shredded   cheese
    zucchini   1 cup chopped tomato

In a 3–4-quart microwave-safe bowl, mix the cornmeal or polenta and the water. Cover and microwave on high for 7 minutes. Stir well until blended. Add the salt, zucchini, onion, and corn, re-cover, and microwave on high for 4–5 minutes. Place dabs of the cream cheese over the top and stir in with the tomato until blended. Recover and microwave on high for 2–3 minutes until heated through.

(SERVES FOUR) **SPINACH AND RICE**

This is similar to a risotto (see p. 439). As a side dish with lamb or chicken, it serves four; alternatively, it makes a luncheon dish for two.

1 bunch spinach, washed and
  trimmed (about 1 cup
  cooked)
2 tablespoons olive oil
½ cup chopped onion
½ cup medium-grain white
  rice (Calrose or Arborio)

2 cups chicken broth
Salt to taste
Freshly ground pepper
¼ cup Parmesan cheese

Put the spinach with the water that clings to it from washing into a 2–3-quart microwave-safe casserole, cover, and microwave on high for 4–5 minutes. Remove from the casserole and set aside. Add the oil and the onion to the casserole, cover, and microwave on high for 3 minutes. Stir in the rice and 1 cup of chicken broth, re-cover, and microwave on high for 3–4 minutes. Stir in another ½ cup of broth and microwave for 7–8 minutes uncovered. Stir in the remaining ½ cup of broth and the chopped spinach, and microwave on high 4–5 minutes, or until the broth is absorbed but the rice is still creamy. Add salt and freshly ground pepper to taste. Sprinkle on the Parmesan cheese before serving.

(SERVES FOUR) **COZY CHICKEN**

Like chicken pot pie without the crust, this dish is familiar and satisfying. Serve over buttered toast or with baking powder biscuits.

1 cup finely diced carrots
1 cup finely diced celery
1 cup finely diced onion
1 cup finely diced potato
¼ cup chicken stock
¼ teaspoon salt
⅛ teaspoon pepper

4 chicken breast halves,
  skinned and boned (about
  1½ pounds)
2 tablespoons butter
2 tablespoons flour
1 cup milk
2 teaspoons lemon juice
1 cup frozen peas

Put the carrots, celery, onion, and potato in a 2–3-quart microwave-safe casserole. Stir in the chicken stock and salt and pepper to taste. Cover and microwave on high for 7–9 minutes, until vegetables are tender. Cut the chicken into large chunks, add to the vegetable mixture, and stir to evenly distribute. Cover and microwave on high for

4–5 minutes. Remove from the microwave and stir to redistribute the chicken pieces. Re-cover and set aside while making the sauce. In a 4-cup microwave-safe measure or bowl, melt the butter on high for about 45 seconds. Mix the flour, salt, pepper, and milk together until smooth and add to the butter. Microwave on high 2 minutes. Whisk until smooth and microwave on high 1 additional minute or until sauce has thickened. Add lemon juice, whisk the sauce until smooth, and stir into the chicken-vegetable mixture. In a small bowl, microwave peas on high for 3 minutes. Stir into the casserole, cover, and microwave on high 3–4 minutes, or until heated through. Taste and correct seasonings.

ORANGE POACHED CHICKEN BREASTS

(SERVES FOUR)

Grated fresh orange (or lemon) brightens the flavor of the chicken.

1⅓ tablespoons olive oil	4 teaspoons orange zest
1 small onion, sliced thin	½ teaspoon salt, or to taste
1 clove garlic, minced	4 chicken breast halves,
1 teaspoon sugar	skinned and boned (about
1 tablespoon cornstarch	1½ pounds)
¼ cup orange juice	

Put 1 tablespoon of the olive oil in a 2–3-quart microwave-safe casserole along with the onion, garlic, and sugar, and toss. Cover and microwave on high for 3 minutes. Stir cornstarch into the orange juice and pour over onion mixture. Add 3 teaspoons of orange zest and salt, stirring to mix well. Place chicken breasts in a ring on top of the onion mixture. Very lightly coat each chicken breast with olive oil. Cover and microwave on high 4–6 minutes. Check for doneness: to test, make a small cut into the thickest part—the flesh should not be pink; if necessary, microwave for 1 more minute. Let stand 3–4 minutes, covered. Garnish top of each chicken breast with remaining orange zest.

POACHED CHICKEN BREASTS WITH SCALLIONS AND GINGER

(SERVES FOUR)

Ginger root is a must in this dish.

1 bunch scallions, washed and trimmed (about 6 ounces)	1 teaspoon minced ginger root
1 tablespoon water	½ teaspoon salt, or to taste
1 teaspoon rice wine vinegar or lemon juice	4 chicken breast halves, skinned and boned (about 1½ pounds)

Cut the scallions in half and then slice lengthwise. Scatter them evenly over the bottom of a large 2–3-quart microwave-safe casserole. Cover and microwave on high for 2–3 minutes. Add the water, vinegar, ginger root, and salt, and stir to blend. Arrange the chicken breasts in a ring around the edge of the casserole, in a single layer. Cover and microwave on high 4–6 minutes. Let stand for 3–4 minutes. To serve, cut each breast into 5 or 6 slices and arrange over the scallions on a warm platter or on individual serving dishes.

TROPICAL CHICKEN

(SERVES FOUR)

This gets a fresh sweet flavor from the coconut and pineapple. Serve with chilled banana slices.

⅓ cup grated fresh or flaked sweetened coconut	1 teaspoon finely chopped ginger root
⅓ cup milk	Salt to taste
4 chicken breast halves, skinned and boned (about 1½ pounds)	½ cup chopped fresh pineapple
1 tablespoon cornstarch	2 tablespoons chopped parsley
2 tablespoons water	1 lemon, quartered

In a microwave-safe mixing bowl, put the coconut and the milk. Stir, and let stand for about 10 minutes. Put the chicken breasts in a 2–3-quart microwave-safe casserole in a single layer with the thicker parts to the outside of the dish. Mix the cornstarch with the water, pour it into the coconut-milk mixture, and stir to blend. Stir in the ginger root. Sprinkle some salt on the chicken and scatter the pineapple over the top. Pour the coconut-milk mixture over all. Cover and microwave on high for 6–7 minutes. Let stand for 3–4 minutes, then test for doneness. Sprinkle with the chopped parsley and serve with the lemon wedges.

CHICKEN CELERY VICTOR (SERVES FOUR)

This is a wonderful cold dish adapted from the classic Celery Victor.

1 whole bunch celery
1¼ cups chicken broth
Salt and freshly ground
    pepper to taste
4 chicken breast halves,
    skinned and boned (about
    1½ pounds)

¾ cup mayonnaise
1 tablespoon prepared
    mustard
Iceberg or butter lettuce
    leaves

Remove the tough outer stalks of celery and cut about 3–4 inches off the tops of the remaining stalks; reserve for another use. You now have the heart of the celery, weighing about 12–14 ounces. Cut this lengthwise into quarters. Put the celery into a 2–3-quart microwave-safe casserole, add 1 cup of the chicken broth and salt and pepper, cover, and microwave on high for 8–10 minutes, or until tender when pierced with a fork. Allow the celery to cool in the broth. Refrigerate until used. Put the chicken breasts in a microwave-safe casserole dish in a single layer with the thicker parts to the outside of the dish. Add the remaining broth. Cover and microwave on high for 3–5 minutes. Let stand for 4–5 minutes, then test for doneness. Let cool and refrigerate. In a small bowl, mix the mayonnaise and mustard until blended and smooth. Refrigerate. To serve, place lettuce leaves on four serving plates and lay a quarter of the poached celery on each plate. Pull the chicken meat apart into strips and scatter over the lettuce and celery. Spoon some of the dressing over each serving or pass the dressing at the table.

TART CHICKEN SALAD (SERVES FOUR)

Lettuce, tomatoes, and black olives nicely finish this dish.

3 chicken breast halves,
    skinned and boned
2 tablespoons water
1 potato, peeled and
    quartered lengthwise
1 cucumber, peeled, seeded,
    quartered, and sliced
½ cup sliced scallions
½ cup chopped dill pickles

⅓ cup mayonnaise
⅓ cup sour cream
2 tablespoons capers
1 teaspoon dillweed
2 teaspoons vinegar or lemon
    juice
Salt and freshly ground
    pepper to taste

Put the chicken breasts in a single layer in a small, microwave-safe baking dish with the thicker parts to the outside of the dish. Add a tablespoon of the water. Cover and microwave on high for 4–5 minutes. Let stand for 2–3 minutes, then check for doneness. Set aside to cool. Put the potato in a microwave-safe dish, add a tablespoon of water, cover, and microwave on high for 2–3 minutes. Set aside to cool. When the chicken is cool, cut into chunks or shred meat into bite-size pieces. Slice the potato. In a large bowl toss together the chicken, potato, cucumber, scallions, and dill pickles until well mixed. In a small bowl, combine the mayonnaise, sour cream, capers, dillweed, and vinegar, and stir until well blended. Taste and season with salt and pepper. Pour over the chicken mixture and toss until the salad is well coated. Refrigerate until served.

(SERVES FOUR)   **WARM TURKISH TURKEY SALAD**

Toss this while the turkey and dressing are hot.

6–8 cups mixed salad greens (such as iceberg, romaine, butter, or watercress), torn in pieces	3 tablespoons olive oil
	1 clove garlic, minced
	2 tablespoons balsamic or red wine vinegar
1 bunch radishes, sliced thin	¼ teaspoon dried thyme
1 small red onion or 1 bunch scallions, sliced thin	¼ teaspoon freshly ground black pepper
1 pound turkey breast meat, in small bite-size strips or pieces	⅛ teaspoon salt, or to taste

Toss the greens, radishes, and onion or scallions together in a large mixing bowl. Put the turkey pieces and 1 tablespoon of the olive oil in a 1–1½-quart microwave-safe casserole, cover, and microwave on high 2–4 minutes. Break up the pieces with a fork, re-cover, and let stand for about 2 minutes. In a small bowl, combine the remaining olive oil, garlic, vinegar, thyme, pepper, and salt, and microwave on high for 20–30 seconds until just boiling. Put the turkey meat into the bowl with the lettuces, pour the hot vinaigrette over, toss gently to coat well, and arrange on a serving platter or individual serving dishes.

TURKEY BREAST WITH
SAGE STUFFING

(SERVES FOUR)

Now you can have the taste of Thanksgiving dinner any time of year. Serve with cranberry sauce.

2 tablespoons butter
1 cup chopped onion
½ cup chopped celery
6 slices bread, cut in cubes
    and dried (about 4 cups)
½ teaspoon poultry seasoning
½ teaspoon ground sage

1 tablespoon chopped parsley
Salt and freshly ground
    pepper to taste
1¼ pounds turkey breast
    meat, in 4 slices
½ cup chicken broth

In an 8-inch square microwave-safe baking dish put the butter, onion, and celery, cover, and microwave on high for 3 minutes. Add the bread cubes, poultry spice, sage, and parsley and toss until mixed. Season with salt and pepper. Place the turkey slices on the bottom of the dish in a single layer, spooning the dressing over the top of each slice. Pour the chicken broth over the top, cover, and microwave on high for 4–6 minutes. Let stand for 2–3 minutes, then test for doneness by cutting into the meat. It should no longer be pink. Microwave for another minute if necessary. Timing will depend on the thickness of the slices.

POACHED SALMON

(SERVES FOUR)

Serve this hot or cold with Cucumber Relish (p. 1108).

1 tablespoon butter
1 tablespoon water

1½ pounds salmon fillets, in 4
    pieces

Put the butter, water, and fish fillets in a 2-quart microwave-safe baking dish, arranging the fillets with the thicker parts to the outside of the dish. Cover and microwave on high for 3–4 minutes, or until the fish flakes easily with a fork.

SALMON STEAKS WITH
WATERCRESS AND DILL

(SERVES FOUR)

Good hot or cold. Serve with red potatoes.

1 bunch watercress, washed
    and stems removed
4 salmon steaks (about 1¾
    pounds)
1 tablespoon lemon juice

1 tablespoon olive oil or
    butter
1 teaspoon dillweed
¼ teaspoon salt

Put the watercress in the bottom of a 2-quart microwave-safe baking dish and lay the salmon steaks on top. In a small bowl, mix together the lemon juice, oil or butter, dill, and salt and pour over the fish. Cover and microwave on high for 5–7 minutes, or until fish flakes easily with a fork.

SIMPLE SALMON STEAKS WITH CREAMED POTATOES

(SERVES TWO OR THREE)

½ pound red new potatoes
Salt and freshly ground
    pepper to taste
2 tablespoons cream
1 tablespoon butter

½ cup finely chopped red or
    yellow onion
¼ cup chopped parsley
3 salmon steaks (about 1¼
    pounds)

Cut the unpeeled potatoes in half and then slice. Sprinkle with the salt and pepper and toss. Put the potatoes in a 1-quart microwave-safe baking dish, add the cream, cover, and microwave on high for 4–6 minutes. Set aside and keep warm. Put the butter and onion in a 1½-quart microwave-safe baking dish, cover, and microwave on high for 1 minute. Stir in the parsley. Add the fish steaks and spoon the onion mixture over each steak. Cover and microwave on high for 3–5 minutes. Serve with the creamed potatoes on the side.

POACHED TROUT

(SERVES FOUR)

Trout is a delicious inexpensive fish.

4 whole trout, cleaned and
    heads removed (about 2
    pounds, total weight)

¼ cup water

Put trout in a 12 × 7-inch microwave-safe baking dish. Add the water, cover, and microwave on high for 6–8 minutes, or until fish flakes easily with a fork.

SEA BASS WITH CELERY ROOT (SERVES FOUR)

½ pound celery root, peeled
   and in 4 thin slices
1¼ pounds sea bass or other
   whitefish fillets
¼ cup cream

2 teaspoons Dijon mustard
2 tablespoons chopped
   parsley
Salt to taste

Put the celery root slices in a single layer in the bottom of a 2-quart microwave-safe baking dish, cover, and microwave on high for 3 minutes. Cut the fish fillets into 4 pieces and place on the celery root slices. In a small bowl, mix together the cream and the mustard and pour over the fish. Sprinkle with the chopped parsley and a little salt, cover, and microwave on high for 6–8 minutes, or until the fish is opaque and flakes when a fork goes in.

FISH FILLETS WITH ASPARAGUS (SERVES FOUR)

1 pound asparagus (about
   16–20 spears)
2 tablespoons butter
1 pound white-fleshed fish
   fillets (sole, snapper, or
   cod)

1 tablespoon chopped shallot
2 tablespoons chopped
   parsley
Salt and freshly ground
   pepper
4 lemon wedges

Wash and trim the asparagus and peel the lower part of the stalk with a vegetable peeler. Put 1 tablespoon of the butter in a 2–3-quart microwave-safe casserole or baking dish, lay the asparagus out evenly over the bottom, cover, and microwave on high for 4 minutes. Place the fish on top of the asparagus. If using fillet of sole or a thin fillet, fold each fillet into thirds, with the ends tucked under, then place on the asparagus. Dot with the remaining butter. Sprinkle with the shallot, parsley, and salt and pepper to taste, cover, and microwave on high for 5–7 minutes, or until fish is opaque and flakes easily with a fork. Serve with the lemon wedges.

SHARK WITH A BITE (SERVES FOUR)

Give this a try at least once. Serve with warm tortillas.

½ teaspoon salt, or to taste
1½ pounds shark fillets, in 4
   pieces
3 tablespoons olive oil
1 teaspoon minced garlic
¼–1 teaspoon ground hot red
   chili, or to taste

1 large tomato, seeded and
   chopped fine
10–12 sprigs cilantro
1 tablespoon lime or lemon
   juice

Salt the shark fillets. Put the olive oil, garlic, and chili into a 2–3-quart microwave-safe baking dish, cover, and microwave on high for 1 minute. Add tomato and cilantro, cover, and microwave on high 2 more minutes. Add the shark and lime or lemon juice, re-cover, and microwave on high 4–6 minutes, until the fish is tender and flakes easily with a fork.

(SERVES FOUR)

RED SNAPPER SAN FELIPE

Everyone loves this dish.

2 cloves garlic
2 avocados (about 2 cups of
   pulp)
3 canned green chilies
2 tablespoons lemon juice
½ teaspoon salt, or to taste

2 tablespoons olive oil
¼ cup cilantro leaves, plus
   several cilantro sprigs, for
   garnish
1 pound red snapper fillets, in
   4 pieces

Process the garlic in a blender or food processor until minced. Add the avocado pulp, green chilies, lemon juice, and salt and process until smooth. Add the olive oil and the cilantro leaves and process until well blended. Refrigerate until used. Place the fish fillets on a microwave-safe dish, cover, and microwave on high for 5–7 minutes, or until fish is opaque throughout. Serve the fish topped with some of the sauce and garnished with cilantro sprigs.

FISH FILLETS WITH TOMATO AND ONION

(SERVES FOUR)

This is a good-looking dish. Serve with Basic Polenta (p. 430).

1 tablespoon olive oil
1 cup chopped onion
1 cup chopped tomato
½ teaspoon salt
½ teaspoon dried basil

1 tablespoon water or chicken
   broth
1 pound white-fleshed fish
   fillets (cod, red snapper, or
   orange roughy)

Put the olive oil and onion in a 2–3-quart microwave-safe casserole, and toss to blend. Cover and microwave on high for 3 minutes. Stir in the tomato, salt, basil, and water or broth. Cut the fish fillets in 4 pieces. Put the fish in the casserole and spoon some of the tomato-onion mixture over. Cover and microwave on high for 5–7 minutes, or until fish is opaque throughout.

FISH CAKES

(SERVES FOUR)

A good way to make use of cooked fish.

1 pound cooked fish, bones removed	2 tablespoons mayonnaise
¼ cup fresh bread crumbs	2 tablespoons milk
¼ cup finely chopped scallions	1 egg
¼ cup finely chopped parsley	½ teaspoon salt, or to taste
1 tablespoon lemon juice	Freshly ground pepper to taste
	4 lemon wedges

Put the fish in a large mixing bowl and flake it with a fork. Add the bread crumbs, scallions, 2 tablespoons of the parsley, lemon juice, and mayonnaise, and toss lightly to mix. Beat the milk and egg together and stir into the fish mixture. Add the salt and pepper and mix to blend. Form the fish mixture into four patties about ¼ inch thick and place in a microwave-safe baking dish. Cover and microwave on high for 5–8 minutes or until firm and heated through. Sprinkle with the remaining parsley and serve with the lemon wedges.

BANANAS IN CARAMEL SAUCE

(SERVES FOUR)

Top with chopped pecans and serve with vanilla ice cream and crisp cookies. It is a meal in itself—or should be.

4 tablespoons brown sugar	4 medium ripe bananas, peeled and left whole
2 tablespoons butter	

Put the brown sugar and butter in a microwave-safe bowl or baking dish and microwave on high for 2 minutes. Add the bananas and spoon the sauce over to coat well. Microwave on high for 1 minute, or until the bananas are hot throughout but not mushy. Serve warm.

(SERVES FOUR)   **POACHED APPLES**

A quick version of a family favorite. Serve with vanilla ice cream or lightly whipped cream and crunchy cookies.

2 large cooking apples,   ⅓ cup dark or golden raisins
    peeled, cored, and halved   2 tablespoons butter
¼ cup brown sugar   ¼ cup water

Put the apple halves in a single layer in a small microwave-safe baking dish. Sprinkle the brown sugar and the raisins over the top. Dot each with butter and add the water to the dish. Cover and microwave on high for 4 minutes. Turn the apples one-half turn, spoon some of the juices over each, re-cover, and microwave on high for 2–3 minutes until tender. Serve hot or warm.

POACHED PEARS

Substitute any firm winter *pear* such as Bosc or Anjou for the apple.

(SERVES FOUR)   **BREAD AND BUTTER PUDDING**

Hot or cold, this is very good with a little heavy cream.

4 slices white bread (or   1 egg yolk
    enough to cover bottom of   ⅓ cup granulated sugar
    an 8-inch square pan),   ⅛ teaspoon salt
    lightly toasted and crusts   1½ cups milk
    removed   ½ teaspoon vanilla
2 tablespoons butter, at room   Confectioners' sugar and
    temperature   cinnamon, for sprinkling
2 eggs   (optional)

Butter one side of each slice of bread. Put the bread, buttered side up, in an 8-inch square microwave-safe baking dish and set aside. Put the eggs, yolk, granulated sugar, and salt in a large bowl and beat until thoroughly mixed. Pour the milk into a microwave-safe bowl or glass measure and microwave on high for 3–4 minutes, until scalded (tiny bubbles will form around the edges). Remove and, whisking briskly, slowly add the egg mixture. Stir in the vanilla. Strain the custard into the baking dish (the bread will float to the top). Microwave on high for 3–5 minutes, or until the custard is set but still trembles slightly. Remove and cool a bit. Sprinkle confectioners' sugar and cinnamon on top before serving, if you like.

RAISIN OR CINNAMON BREAD AND BUTTER PUDDING

Substitute *4 slices of raisin bread or cinnamon bread* for the plain white bread on p. 651.

EGG CUSTARD   (SERVES FOUR)

Put this in the microwave as you sit down to dinner and you can have this warm for dessert.

1¼ cups milk	⅛ teaspoon salt
2 teaspoons vanilla	2 tablespoons brown sugar
4 eggs, beaten	(optional)
⅓ cup granulated sugar	

In a 4-cup glass measure, combine the milk and vanilla. Microwave on high for 2 minutes until hot, but not boiling. In a medium bowl, beat the eggs, granulated sugar, and salt until frothy. Slowly add the heated milk to the egg mixture, stirring constantly until blended. Pour into four 5–6-ounce custard cups. Place the cups on a round plate or tray, about 1 inch apart. Microwave uncovered on medium for 6–8 minutes, or until set, rotating the cups once or twice. The center should tremble a little; don't overcook. Serve in custard cups or unmold on dessert plates. To unmold and serve, run a knife around the rim of the cup and invert onto a serving plate. Serve warm or chilled. If desired, sprinkle brown sugar over the top of the warm custard.

FRESH LIME PUDDING   (SERVES SIX)

A variation of cottage pudding from the 1920s. It will separate into two layers as it cooks.

2 tablespoons butter	2 tablespoons flour
¼ cup sugar	⅓ cup lime juice
3 eggs, separated	Grated rind of 1 lime (about 1
1 cup milk	tablespoon)

Beat the butter until soft, then gradually add the sugar, beating until it is all incorporated. Beat in the egg yolks one at a time. Add the milk, flour, lime juice, and rind, and beat until well blended. Beat the egg whites until they form soft peaks, then fold into the batter. Turn into an 8-inch square microwave-safe baking dish and microwave on medium for 8–11 minutes or until barely set. Let cool slightly and serve warm.

BUTTERMILK PRALINES

(ABOUT 40 PIECES)

This is a great praline.

2 cups sugar
1 teaspoon baking soda
1 cup buttermilk
¼ cup butter

1 teaspoon vanilla
40 pecan halves or large
pieces

In a large 3–4-quart microwave-safe bowl, combine the sugar, soda, buttermilk, and butter. Microwave uncovered on medium for 5 minutes. Stir until butter is blended, then microwave on medium for 22–25 minutes, or until a soft ball forms in a cup of cold water. (See p. 1046, Stages for Candy Syrup.) Add the vanilla and beat with an electric mixer until the mixture forms soft peaks. Drop by teaspoonfuls onto wax paper and lightly press a pecan half into the center of each praline. Let cool completely until firm. Store in an airtight container.

ALMOND TOFFEE

(1 POUND)

A super almond toffee in about 10 minutes.

¾ cup butter
1 cup brown sugar
¼ cup chopped almonds

4 ounces semisweet chocolate,
grated fine

Line an 8-inch square baking dish with foil, and oil or butter the foil. Put the butter and sugar in a 2-quart glass measure or microwave-safe bowl. Microwave uncovered on high for 3 minutes. Beat with a whisk until smooth. Microwave uncovered on high for 4 more minutes. Stir in ½ cup of the almonds and microwave uncovered on high for about 2–3 minutes more, or until the mixture thickens and forms a firm ball when tested in cold water. Watch carefully the last 2–3 minutes because the sugar can burn quickly. (See p. 1046, Stages for Candy Syrup.) Whisk for a few seconds, then pour mixture into prepared pan.

Sprinkle with the grated chocolate, cover with plastic wrap, and let chocolate melt for about 5 minutes. Spread the melted chocolate evenly over the toffee and sprinkle with the reserved ¼ cup almonds. Let chocolate harden in a cool place. Remove foil and break into pieces. Store refrigerated in an airtight container.

PEANUT BRITTLE   (1½ POUNDS)

A shining example of microwave candy.

1½ cups sugar	1 teaspoon vanilla
¼ cup light corn syrup	1 teaspoon baking soda
2 tablespoons butter	
2 cups peanuts (Spanish, dry roasted, or regular)	

Grease a jelly-roll pan. In a 2-quart glass measure or microwave-safe bowl, put the sugar and corn syrup, and stir until blended. Microwave uncovered on high for 3 minutes. Stir and microwave for another 4 minutes. Stir in the butter, peanuts, and vanilla and microwave uncovered on high for 5–6 minutes, or until it forms brittle threads (hard-crack stage) when dropped into a cup of cold water. (See p. 1046, Stages for Candy Syrup.) Beat in the baking soda and immediately pour the mixture onto the prepared pan. Using a spatula, quickly spread out as evenly as possible. Let cool for at least an hour, then break into pieces. Store in an airtight container.

CHOCOLATE TRUFFLES   (ABOUT 40 PIECES)

These are ultra-rich. Use a good eating chocolate in making them; the better the chocolate, the better the truffle. They make a good Christmas gift.

8 ounces semisweet chocolate	⅔ cup heavy cream
4 ounces milk chocolate	Cocoa or ground almonds for coating
4 tablespoons butter	

Put the chocolates and butter in a 2-quart glass measure or microwave-safe bowl and microwave uncovered on high for 3–3½ minutes until the chocolate and butter are just melted. Beat to blend thoroughly. Put the cream in a glass measure or microwave-safe bowl and microwave on high for 1½–2 minutes, or until just boiling. Whisk the hot cream into the chocolate mixture until well blended. Refrigerate the chocolate mixture for at least an hour, until it is firm again. Using a very small ice cream scoop, melon-baller, or spoon, dipped in water, scoop up a small amount of the chocolate and very quickly form it into a ball about 1 inch in diameter. Roll each truffle in cocoa or ground almonds until completely coated. Return to the refrigerator and allow to chill again until very firm to the touch. Store in an airtight container in the refrigerator for up to 2 weeks.

BRANDY TRUFFLES

Add *1–2 tablespoons brandy or Cognac* after adding the cream and mix well. Keep in refrigerator.

(1 CUP) ## STRAWBERRY JAM

This is a quick and easy way to have homemade jam on your table often. It is made in a small quantity, and is nonprocessed, so it must be kept refrigerated.

2 cups fresh strawberries
¾ cup sugar

2 teaspoons lemon juice

Wash and hull strawberries, cutting large ones in half. Put them in a large 3–4-quart microwave-safe bowl, add the sugar, stir, and microwave, uncovered, on high for 5 minutes. Stir and microwave for another 5 minutes. Stir and microwave for 2–4 minutes or until thickened. Stir in the lemon juice. Cool and store in a covered container in the refrigerator.

(ABOUT 1½ CUPS) ## PEACH JAM

This jam is best made with good, flavorful, ripe summer peaches.

3 cups peeled peaches (1 pound), in chunks
1 cup sugar

1–2 tablespoons lemon juice, or to taste

Put the peaches and sugar in a 3–4-quart microwave-safe bowl and microwave, uncovered, on high for 5 minutes. Stir and mash the peaches. Microwave on high for another 8 minutes. Stir again, and microwave for 2–4 minutes or until thickened. Stir in 1 tablespoon lemon juice, taste, and add more lemon juice, if necessary. Cool and store in a covered container in the refrigerator.

APPLE CHUTNEY

(ABOUT 2 CUPS)

This is a pleasant, tart-sweet chutney. Serve it with roast chicken or a leg of lamb.

1 tablespoon yellow mustard seeds
1 teaspoon salt
¾ cup brown sugar
⅔ cup cider or white vinegar
3 large apples (1 pound), peeled, cored, and coarsely chopped

1 large clove garlic, chopped fine
1 tablespoon minced or grated ginger root
¼ cup golden raisins
⅛ teaspoon cayenne pepper

Combine seeds, salt, sugar, vinegar, apples, garlic, ginger root, raisins, and pepper in a 3–4-quart microwave-safe bowl. Microwave, uncovered, on high for 10 minutes. Stir and microwave for another 10–13 minutes, or until mixture has cooked down and slightly thickened. Taste and correct seasoning. Ladle into a jar and store in the refrigerator.

PEACH CHUTNEY

(ABOUT 1½ CUPS)

This is too good to save for only curry dishes. Use it with sandwiches and fruit salads.

2 cups peaches, peeled and in large dice
¾ cup brown sugar
⅔ cup cider or white vinegar
½ cup raisins

2 teaspoons ground ginger
¼ teaspoon cinnamon
⅛ teaspoon allspice
⅛ teaspoon clove

Put the peaches, sugar, vinegar, raisins, ginger, cinnamon, allspice, and cloves into a 3–4-quart microwave-safe bowl. Microwave, uncovered, on high for 10 minutes. Stir and microwave for another 10–13 minutes, or until mixture has cooked down and slightly thickened. Taste and correct seasonings. Ladle into a jar and store in the refrigerator.

SALADS

With farmers' markets sprouting up all over the country one can find a greater variety of seasonal salad makings, such as arugola, cress, romaine, and ruffled red lettuce. And if you are a gardener, the seed catalogues are offering all kinds of new varieties to experiment with growing. As well, there are various-colored sweet peppers available now and different varieties of tomatoes, which inspire us to make more salads than ever.

Here you will find some new salad recipes—one in which parsley is the star; one of pure onions, iced and crunchy; one of Brussels sprouts that will make you feel more friendly toward that much-maligned vegetable; and a chicken salad with Chinese accents, among others.

ABOUT SALAD

The Role of Salad

Salads in all their various shapes and forms play a large part in the American diet. A salad can be a whole meal, a starter, an accompaniment to the main course, or a refresher after it. With the abundance of fresh produce available year round and with the growing awareness of the role of healthful raw foods, there is less concentration today, particularly among the young, on jellied salads made from synthetic flavors with overly sweet dressings and more concern for lightness, crispness, color, and balance of flavors.

Types of Salad

Green salad, in keeping with the tendency to serve simpler and fewer dishes at a meal, appears now as often as a first course as the pause between the main course and dessert. (Westerners have always preferred it first anyway.) So there are no rules about *when* it should appear, only *how*. A green salad should sparkle and be made of clean, chill, crisp greens, fresh oil, light tingling vinegar and/or fresh lemon juice, with salt, freshly ground pepper, sometimes mustard, herbs, and aromatics as accents.

The salad course need never be monotonous. There is such a variety of greens to choose from in our markets; in addition to the standby iceberg lettuce, there are leafy heads of Boston, romaine, and sometimes garden varieties, when in season, as well as greens with sharper flavor, such as spinach, chicory, watercress, escarole, and endive. Mustard greens, arugola, dandelion greens, and others that grow easily in home gardens are beginning to find their way into ethnic produce markets in urban areas. In addition, there are many salad "companions" (see p. 662), most of them available year round, to be used judiciously for a touch of contrast. And there are many ways to vary your dressings with herbs, the addition of mustard, garlic, or cheese.

Green salads should be dressed lightly just before serving or even at table. Most greens should be more or less bite size, sometimes with smaller leaves or the heart just pulled apart, the shape left intact. Be subtle with sharp raw onion and garlic; red or sweet onions, scallions, and chives are milder and generally better to use in salads that require an accent. When you want a really garlicky salad, be sure the garlic is fresh and mince the clove very fine, then mash it into the dressing; always make it fresh—garlic, once it's crushed, does not keep well.

A molded salad should have good, intense—preferably natural—flavor. It should be attractive to look at, but not too gussied up, and while it must hold its shape, the jelly should never be overly firm and rubbery.

Vegetables used in salads can be raw or cooked. If raw, they should be young and tender. It is nice to use some of the skin for flavor and color, but avoid tough skins or ones that have been waxed. Cooked vegetables should have a crisp texture and bright color, which is best achieved by brief cooking. Advance-cooked vegetables can be used, but the sooner the better, and if they have been tossed with butter, be sure to scald with boiling water to remove any congealed fat. The same goes for potatoes, macaroni, and rice, which form the basis of so many substantial salads; don't use refrigerator-weary leftovers.

A composed salad means one that has been arranged, the ingredients imaginatively combined and placed on a plate. You can create an attractive first course simply by making a circle of sliced garden tomatoes with chopped fresh parsley and maybe basil sprinkled on the top, or on a bed of watercress by placing a halved hard-boiled egg, dotted with coarse pepper, and a small stack of lightly cooked green beans with a few slivers of anchovy on top. There are further suggestions on p. 665 but use your ingenuity, too. Or you can choose from any of the American favorites like Crab Louis or Ravigote, Chicken or Lobster Salad, or shrimp and artichoke, arranged enticingly on separate plates, waiting at each place as you sit down to the meal.

Washing, Drying, and Storing Greens

Wash greens that are dirty as soon as you get them home, using very cold water, separating the leaves, and soaking in several changes of water if they are gritty. There are some you may not need to wash at all, like iceberg lettuce or endive, and in this case do not separate the leaves until you are ready to use them. The best way to dry greens is in a salad spinner—see p. 35. Lacking that, wrap loosely in a towel and shake. If your refrigerator has a salad crisper drawer, simply store the greens in that. Otherwise fold loosely in a towel. Avoid wrapping washed greens in plastic bags which create too much moisture so that the greens are apt to turn dank more quickly. There is no exact rule about how long they will keep; they're usable as long as they seem fresh and crisp—so much depends on how fresh they were when you bought them. It is a good idea to check and remove any leaves that have turned brown because they can infect the whole lot.

Salad Dressings

The amount of dressing on a salad is critical. Too much dressing drenches and wilts the greens and robs them of taste and texture. Not enough dressing leaves a salad unseasoned, unfinished. Here is a rough guide:

For 2 quarts of mixed greens (2 quarts will serve four): use 5 tablespoons vinaigrette or 6 tablespoons mayonnaise-type dressing.

4 tablespoons mayonnaise will coat 2 cups moist, cooked chicken pieces. If the chicken is dry it will take 1 or 2 more tablespoons.

½ cup mayonnaise will dress and moisten 2 cups well-drained tuna.

Salad Dressing Ingredients

Olive Oil. Money does not always buy the best olive oil. Disregard the labels that say virgin and extra virgin olive oil. Buy an oil that pleases you; taste and compare. Select a more delicate oil for salads of tender greens or fruits and a more robust oil for a garlicky dressing or a salad of lusty ingredients. Do not refrigerate olive oil. A fine-quality olive oil won't turn rancid if kept in your coolest storage place. Buy in smaller quantities if your consumption is small.

Vegetable Oil. Considerably less expensive than olive oil, vegetable oils such as safflower or corn oil are perfectly acceptable for salad dressings, particularly when you are using assertive flavorings. But be sure to taste before using—these oils can become rancid. Peanut oil is too heavy for salads.

Vinegar. There are many varieties of vinegars. Which you should use depends upon the salad ingredients. Soft, tender Bibb lettuce is nice with a mild wine vinegar and oil. Red wine vinegars are lusty and strong; white wine tarragon vinegar is light with an aromatic flavor. Japanese rice vinegars are wonderful on fruits. *Balsamic vinegar* is seen frequently on the grocery shelf now and in specialty food catalogues. It is a special Italian aged vinegar and makes a nice change occasionally from red wine vinegar, but use it sparingly. You'll find that there are mild and subtle balsamic vinegars and there are sharp ones. In this case, the more expensive tends to be better, but since you don't use much of it, it is not an extravagant investment. *Cider vinegar*, which has a slight apple flavor, and distilled white vinegar both are strong and assertive. So if you are substituting them for wine vinegars, use slightly less than is called for. Many people who find vinegar too assertive prefer to use fresh *lemon juice*; or it may be used in combination with vinegar.

Yogurt. Now being used more and more in interesting ways as a base for salad dressing, yogurt is tart and delicious and you don't have to be a weight-watcher to enjoy it.

Mayonnaise. Homemade mayonnaise is delicious and easy to make— a simple sleight of hand. It is worth making if only to NOTE *see page 471* watch the liquids become transformed into a creamy, pale sauce. Such a lovely result for so little effort. And with the advent of the blender and the food processor, it can be even more simply made. There is no reason not to have some always on hand, particularly as you can freeze any excess amount. Mayonnaise is a basic sauce, and a variety of flavors can be added to make it more finished and to complement different ingredients—see the variations that follow the recipe, p. 707.

Avoid sweet dressings on most salads that go with a meal. They are fine with a fruit salad at the end and some people enjoy them with a main-course luncheon salad, but be careful not to overwhelm natural flavors with too much sweetness.

Types of Salad Greens

Iceberg. The all-purpose lettuce that is available year round. The head is large and tight, the leaves crisp, and it keeps well. Don't separate the leaves before storing. Iceberg has a milder flavor than other lettuces, so for a salad it is best mixed with other greens and crunchy salad companions. It is particularly good in sandwiches, makes nice lettuce cups, and a bed of shredded iceberg will hold up well as a base for stuffed eggs, avocados, and other composed salads.

Boston or Butter Lettuce. Generally available, this looser head has large, deep-green, soft leaves and a lighter, tender heart. Its delicate flavor is best enhanced by a light vinaigrette.

Bibb or Limestone Lettuce. The heads are a little smaller and more pointy than Boston and the leaves are somewhat firmer. Some Bibb used to be grown in limestone, hence the alternate name for it. A prized lettuce for green salads, it too is best served by a light vinaigrette, though will hold up to something stronger.

Leaf Lettuce or Garden Lettuce. Fresh and tasty, the curly loose leaves of garden lettuce wilt quickly and should be kept very cold and used as soon as possible. Good by itself with a light vinaigrette, made perhaps with lemon and fresh herbs. The leaves are also an addition to any mixed salad.

Red Leaf Lettuce. Another loose-leaf garden variety with leaves that are tinged in red—the color of oak in autumn. Red leaf looks and tastes lovely in any kind of mixed green salad.

Escarole. A large spready head of longish leaves that splay out at the end with wide ribs at the base, escarole can be a bit tough on the outside, so some of the more mature leaves should be discarded; the heart is always tender. It makes a fine wintry salad that can stand up to a more robust dressing like a Roquefort or a cream dressing or vinaigrette spiked with garlic; walnuts and apples can also be good companions.

Chicory. Sometimes known as curly endive, the spiky, curly-edged leaves have a pleasing bitter taste and make a good foil for milder greens. Again, an assertive dressing holds up best.

Watercress. Deep green, the small flat leaves of watercress have a peppery taste that mixes well with other greens. For salads, trim off some of the stem. Watercress is good with astringent fruits like oranges and grapefruit, makes a handsome garnish for almost anything, and is good in sandwiches.

Belgian Endive. The slender, long, blanched leaves from a head of endive offer contrast of color, texture, and a slightly bitter taste in a mixed salad. It's very expensive, but a little goes a long way and the crisp leaves, which can be left whole or broken in pieces, hold up well. A lovely salad can be made of just endive and beets, a perfect marriage, dressed in vinaigrette.

Spinach. For salad use young, tender, very fresh leaves and trim off the stems. Wash well—spinach can be gritty. A raw spinach salad of chopped hard-boiled eggs, sliced raw mushrooms, and bacon is good as a whole lunch or to balance out a meal, and a few crisp leaves are always welcome in a mixed salad. Young *dandelion leaves, beet greens, kale,* and *chard,* when very fresh, also add to a green salad.

Romaine. A long, sometimes quite fat head of crisp leaves that always give a wonderful crunch to a salad. When very young the tender heart is sometimes served whole, but more often leaves are torn into bite-size pieces; romaine takes well to an assertive dressing.

Chinese Cabbage. A long tight head of Chinese cabbage with its pale green fringed leaves is a more familiar sight in our markets today. The leaves cut in pieces make a lovely-looking salad with a beautiful mild cabbagey flavor, particularly good with Lemon Soy Dressing.

Arugola or Rocket. More likely to be found in Italian neighborhoods, where it is much appreciated. A few arugola leaves add a surprising, pronounced flavor to a green salad. Aficionados will make a whole salad of it with a wine vinegar and olive oil dressing, but if you haven't had the arugola experience, you might be put off.

Mache or Lamb's Lettuce. A small flat-growing head with spoon-shaped pale to dark green leaves. It is a bland-tasting green that can balance bitter greens in a salad.

Radicchio or Wild Chicory. A small compact head with red-purple leaves and white veins and looks like a little cabbage. It has a slightly bitter flavor and is good in salads, or braised or steamed with meat dishes.

Fresh Herbs

Tossed on a green salad or blended in with the dressing, these fresh herbs are particularly pleasing: tarragon; basil (fresh far preferable); chives; Italian (flat-leafed) parsley; dill (particularly with cucumbers); summer savory (particularly with cooked vegetables); chervil.

Salad Companions

Use singly or in combination to give variety—a little contrast in texture, taste, and color—to a mixed green salad. It's up to you how much of anything to use, depending on the place of the salad in your meal; if the salad is simply a refresher after the main course, don't add any of the more substantial salad companions—and what you do include should be just a very light accent.

RAW VEGETABLES

Tomatoes. Peel only if tough-skinned, then slice or cut in wedges. Leave cherry tomatoes whole or halve them.

Cucumbers. Peel if skin is waxed. Leave unpeeled and scored, or semi-peeled, if young and tender. Slice very thin or dice.

Radishes. Scrub and slice or grate.

Scallions or Green or Spring Onions. Chop, using most of the green if tender.

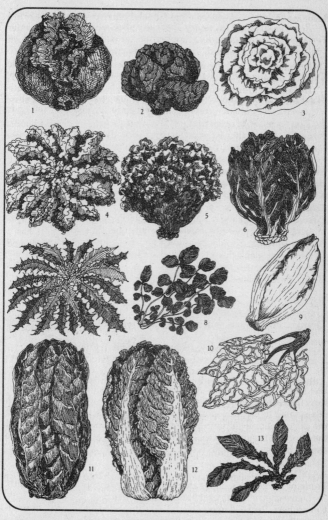

1. *iceberg lettuce;* 2. *Bibb lettuce;* 3. *Boston lettuce;* 4. *loose-leaf lettuce;* 5. *red leaf lettuce;* 6. *escarole;* 7. *chicory;* 8. *watercress;* 9. *endive;* 10. *spinach;* 11. *romaine;* 12. *Chinese cabbage;* 13. *arugola.*

Celery. Use tender stalks (leaves are a bit dominant for a mixed salad). Remove strings if necessary, then slice, dice, or julienne.

Fennel. Use bulb primarily, chopped or julienned, and a little of the feathery green, if liked. The flavor is assertive, so don't overpower with it.

Carrots. Scrape, then julienne or grate. Or make carrot curls for garnish.

Mushrooms. They should be very fresh to use raw. Wipe clean with a damp cloth, remove stems if at all woody, or just trim the ends. Don't peel. Slice or quarter.

Avocado. Peel at the last moment, then slice, dice, or chunk. If storing an unused portion, rub cut sides with lemon juice, keep the pit in the center, wrap tightly with plastic wrap, and refrigerate.

Young Zucchini. Just scrub, don't peel, and cut in thin slivers.

Jicama. Peel, then dice, cut in slivers, or julienne.

Kohlrabi. Same as jicama.

Jerusalem Artichokes. Same as jicama.

Green, Yellow, Orange, Red, and Purple Peppers. Scrape out seeds and remove inner ribs, then dice or julienne.

Alfalfa Sprouts. Should be plump and fresh-looking. Rinse and remove any dank threads. Unused sprouts should be stored in water and refrigerated for up to a week.

Bean Sprouts. Same as alfalfa sprouts.

RAW FRUIT

Grapefruit. Peel while whole and separate into segments.

Orange. Peel whole and separate into segments or cut across into slices.

Apple. Peel or not as you wish and dice or cut in thin slices.

Pear. Same as apple. A little pear is good in a winter salad with slightly bitter greens.

Other Suggestions. Pineapple, banana, grapes, nectarine, peach, kiwi.

PRESERVED THINGS

Olives. Green, stuffed, ripe, or black Mediterranean. Pit and slice. Use sparingly in a green salad; more appropriate for a mixed concoction or a composed salad (in which case leave whole).

Pimiento. Again, more appropriate for a composed salad, sliced or chopped.

Anchovies. Use sparingly in tiny pieces or mash into the dressing—the flavor is very robust. More appropriate in special salads.

Capers. Drain and rinse if very briny. Same kind of use as anchovies.

OTHER THINGS

Hard-boiled Eggs. Chopped or quartered eggs are more suitable to a substantial salad, but grated they can give an attractive mimosa effect to a green salad.

Walnuts, Pecans, or Almonds. Roughly chopped, they can be particularly good as an accent in a winter salad of tart greens.

Beets. An exception to the raw vegetable practice, beets are usually added cooked to a green salad, either diced or julienned. Particularly good with endive and chicory.

Cottage Cheese. Better for a luncheon salad, placed on top in attractive mounds and sprinkled with chives or chopped scallions.

Cream Cheese. Same as cottage cheese.

Wheat Berries. Cooked until just tender, a scattering of wheat berries in a salad adds a nice chewy texture and a lot of nutrition.

Croutons. They give a pleasing contrast in texture. Be sure they taste fresh. Rubbing them with garlic is a good way of imparting that flavor to a salad.

Chickpeas or Garbanzo Beans. Cooked, just a few tablespoons scattered in a big salad are good.

Composed Salads

The exact amounts for a composed salad really depend upon the eye and appetite of the maker. For a rough guide, ⅓ cup of each of three basic ingredients per serving seems reasonable. This would be about 1 cup per serving. Too much is a greater error than too little. Getting the best out of your salads depends on selecting fruits and vegetables with great care. Good salads start with good ingredients.

SOME IDEAS FOR COMPOSED SALADS

Belgian endive, Red Delicious apple pieces, walnuts, soft cream cheese.

Raw snow peas, cooked chicken pieces, salted cashews, cilantro (Chinese parsley).

Cooked leeks, diced cooked potatoes, slices of sausage, hard-boiled eggs.

Cold cooked fish, sliced red onions, cucumber, cold cooked brown rice.

Grapefruit sections, asparagus, papaya slices, prosciutto, water chestnuts.

Artichoke hearts, mushrooms, black olives, marinated cold beef, capers.

TOSSED AND COMPOSED SALADS

CHEF'S SALAD   (SERVES FOUR)

This is a main dish for a summer evening or a lunch.

1 head iceberg lettuce
12 radishes, trimmed and
sliced
2 stalks celery, julienned
1½ cups French Dressing (p.
703), Cream French
Dressing (p. 704), or
Russian Dressing (p. 708)
4 tomatoes, peeled and each
in 6 wedges
¾ cup Swiss cheese strips, ⅛
inch wide, 1½ inches long

1 cup cooked ham or tongue
(or both) strips, ⅛ inch
wide, 1½ inches long
1 cup cooked chicken or
turkey strips, ⅛ inch wide,
1½ inches long
4 hard-boiled eggs, quartered
Salt
Freshly ground pepper

Core the iceberg lettuce and save four outside leaves for the bed in which to put the salad. Place them around the edges of a large salad bowl. Cut or tear the remaining lettuce into bite-size pieces, place in the bowl, and toss with the radishes, celery, and half of the dressing. Arrange the tomato wedges around the inside edges of the lettuce. Combine the cheese, ham or tongue, and chicken or turkey, toss, and spread it over the lettuce and vegetables. Place the hard-boiled eggs between the tomato wedges. Sprinkle salt and pepper lightly over the salad. Spoon the rest of the dressing over the salad.

CUCUMBER SALAD ࢯ   (SERVES SIX)

This is a sharp cucumber salad, maybe too much so for some tastes—if so add a little sugar.

3 medium cucumbers
Salt
4 tablespoons sour cream or
mayonnaise
3 tablespoons minced
scallions

1 teaspoon lemon juice
2 tablespoons vinegar
½ teaspoon dry mustard
1 tablespoon minced dill or
parsley

Peel the cucumbers and slice thin. Spread them over the bottom of a colander and sprinkle salt on top. Let them drain for 30 minutes, press gently to remove excess liquid, then chill. Blend the sour cream or mayonnaise, scallions, lemon juice, vinegar, and dry mustard together. Add salt to taste. Toss the dressing with the cucumbers. Sprinkle the dill or parsley on top and serve cold.

(SERVES FOUR) 〰 **WILTED CUCUMBER SALAD**

3 cucumbers, peeled and
  sliced thin
1 clove garlic, peeled
Salt

¼ cup vinegar
2 tablespoons sugar
Watercress

Cover the cucumbers with water. Add the garlic and sprinkle well with salt, stirring to dissolve the salt. Let stand 1 hour. Drain, pressing gently to rid of excess liquid, and discard garlic. Stir the vinegar, sugar, and 2 tablespoons water together until the sugar is dissolved. Pour over the cucumbers and stir. Add salt to taste. Chill well and serve on a bed of watercress.

RAW GREEN BEANS, TOMATOES, OLIVES,
(7 CUPS) 〰 **SCALLIONS, AND CELERY SALAD**

Pick vegetables with care: look for bright color and firm texture.

4 cups tiny tender green
  beans; if larger blanch 2
  minutes
1 cup small cherry tomatoes
¾ cup Greek olives
½ cup chopped scallions
1 cup matchstick-size celery
  pieces

½ cup French Dressing (p.
  703)
Salt to taste
2 tablespoons chopped dill
2 tablespoons minced parsley

Wash and trim the green beans; cut them in 1½-inch lengths. Wash and dry the tomatoes. Arrange the green beans, tomatoes, olives, scallions, and celery in a shallow bowl, pour the dressing over, and sprinkle with salt, dill, and parsley.

CAESAR SALAD (SERVES FOUR)

Caesar salad was created in Tijuana in 1924, and like a true classic its popularity is as great as ever. This is our variation that retains the basic taste but is simpler to make and does not use raw egg.

½ cup olive oil
2–3 cloves garlic
2 tablespoons lemon juice, approximately, or to taste
Pinch of salt
4–5 anchovy fillets, or to taste
1 head romaine lettuce, leaves separated, washed, dried, and any but the freshest, unblemished leaves discarded

2 cups fresh, dried croutons
⅓ cup Parmesan cheese, freshly grated or shredded into paper-thin bits

Combine the olive oil and garlic in a blender and blend until smooth and creamy. Add the lemon juice and the pinch of salt. Pour the dressing into the bottom of a large salad bowl. Add the anchovy and mash it into the dressing until well blended. Add the romaine, and toss together until the leaves are all coated and shiny. Add the croutons and toss lightly to mix. Sprinkle the cheese over just before serving.

RED ONION, SPINACH, AND TOMATO WITH HORSERADISH DRESSING ≥ (SERVES FOUR)

4 cups fresh spinach leaves, washed, dried, trimmed of stems
4 tomatoes, trimmed and sliced ¼ inch thick
2 red onions, sliced thin in rings

Salt to taste
¼ cup olive oil
1½ tablespoons vinegar
½ teaspoon freshly ground pepper
1 tablespoon prepared horseradish

Arrange a bed of spinach leaves on a platter. Place the slices of tomato over it, and the onion rings over the tomatoes. Sprinkle salt evenly over all. Combine the oil, vinegar, pepper, and horseradish in a small bowl and beat until blended. Pour the dressing over the vegetables and serve.

(SERVES FOUR)   ટેન **COLE SLAW**

    1 medium head cabbage   1 teaspoon celery seed
    1 cup Boiled Dressing (p. 706)   Salt

Cut the head of cabbage in half, place in a bowl of cold water, and refrigerate for 1 hour. Drain well. Shred finely, and add the dressing and
celery seed. Toss to mix well and add salt to taste.

COLE SLAW WITH CHINESE CABBAGE
(SERVES FOUR)   ✳ ટેન **AND WATERCRESS**

    2 cups shredded cabbage   3 tablespoons lemon juice
    2 cups shredded Chinese   Salt to taste
      cabbage   ½ teaspoon celery seed
    1½ cups thinly sliced celery   ½ teaspoon mustard seed
    ¼ cup mayonnaise   1 bunch watercress, washed,
    ¼ cup heavy cream   dried, and chopped
    1 tablespoon honey

Put both cabbages and the celery in a bowl of ice water and let stand 30
minutes in the refrigerator. Combine the mayonnaise, cream, honey,
lemon juice, salt, celery seed, and mustard seed in a bowl and blend
until well mixed. Drain the cabbages and celery, and thoroughly toss
with the dressing. Just before serving sprinkle the watercress over the
salad and around the edges.

(SERVES SIX)   ટેન **CARROT SLAW**

A great favorite with children.

    6 medium carrots   ½ cup diced apple
    ¾ cup diced celery   ½ cup mayonnaise
    ¼ cup diced onion   Salt
    ⅓ cup raisins   Freshly ground pepper

Grate the carrots by hand or in a food processor. Toss with the celery,
onion, raisins, and apple. Mix in the mayonnaise, season well with salt
and pepper, and chill thoroughly.

TURNIP SLAW ⮞   (SERVES FOUR)

This keeps just a couple of days and then it turns bitter, so don't make
tons of it.

5 medium white turnips,
   peeled
½ cup mayonnaise
3 tablespoons sour cream
2 teaspoons tarragon vinegar
1 teaspoon prepared mustard
1 teaspoon sugar

Pinch of salt
¼ teaspoon celery seed
¼ teaspoon freshly ground
   pepper
½ teaspoon dried dillweed, or
   1 teaspoon chopped fresh

Slice the turnips into very thin matchstick strips (julienne) and place in
a large bowl. Add the mayonnaise, sour cream, vinegar, mustard,
sugar, salt, celery seed, pepper, and dill, and stir well until the dressing
is mixed and has coated the turnips. Refrigerate until served.

SPINACH, MUSHROOM,
AND BACON SALAD   (SERVES FOUR)

1 pound fresh young spinach
¼ pound raw mushrooms,
   sliced thin
2 hard-boiled eggs, coarsely
   chopped
½ cup vegetable oil
½ teaspoon dark sesame oil
   (optional)

1 teaspoon sugar
3 tablespoons lemon juice
½ teaspoon Dijon mustard
Freshly ground pepper
Salt to taste
5 strips bacon, fried crisp,
   crumbled

Wash and dry the spinach and discard the stems. If leaves are small,
leave whole; if large, cut or tear into bite-size pieces. Toss the spinach,
mushrooms, and eggs together in a salad bowl. Mix in a separate bowl
the vegetable oil, sesame oil, if you want to use it, sugar, lemon juice,
mustard, pepper, and salt. Beat well, then pour over the salad and toss
until all leaves are coated. Serve on individual plates and sprinkle the
bacon over each serving.

(SERVES FOUR)   ॐ **BULGUR WHEAT SALAD**

Known as "tabbouli" in the Middle East, this cold salad is fresh and
light with lemon juice, parsley, and mint. Serve it on crisp lettuce
leaves.

1 cup bulgur	½ cup finely chopped parsley
5 tablespoons oil	3 tablespoons finely chopped
½ cup lemon juice	mint
About 1½ teaspoons salt	1 bunch scallions, chopped
1 teaspoon freshly ground	fine
pepper	2 tomatoes, diced

Put the bulgur in a bowl with 2 cups cold water and let stand for 1
hour; drain well and squeeze in a towel. Toss in the salad bowl with
the remaining ingredients. Taste and correct the seasoning. Chill before
serving.

(SERVES SIX)   ॐ **RAW VEGETABLE SALAD**

1 cup grated carrots	1½ cups raw cauliflower
½ cup grated young raw beets	flowerets
1 cup grated zucchini	2 cups cherry tomatoes
1 cup grated cucumber	1 recipe Yogurt Dressing (p.
4 tablespoons finely chopped	709)
red onion	1 cup alfalfa sprouts
Salt	
2 bunches watercress, washed	
and dried	

Combine the carrots, beets, zucchini, cucumber, and onion in a bowl.
Toss and gently mix. Salt to taste. Make a bed of the watercress. Pile
the mixed grated vegetables in the center, and arrange the cauliflower
flowerets and cherry tomatoes around them. Spoon some of the dressing over the top and pass the remainder. Sprinkle the alfalfa sprouts on
top.

WATERCRESS, SLICED ORANGE, AND AVOCADO SALAD ✻ ❧   (SERVES FOUR)

2 bunches watercress,
   washed, dried, and stems
   trimmed
4 large oranges, peeled and
   sliced
1 large ripe avocado

¼ cup vegetable oil
¼ cup orange juice
1 tablespoon white vinegar
½ teaspoon celery seed
Salt
4 radishes, grated

Arrange the watercress on a large plate or individual salad plates. Distribute the orange slices over each plate. Peel and dice the avocado and scatter the pieces among the orange slices. Combine the oil, orange juice, vinegar, and celery seed in a jar or small bowl. Shake or whisk to blend the ingredients until smooth and well mixed. Add salt to taste. Pour the dressing over the salad and sprinkle the grated radishes over the top.

FENNEL, RADISH, AND PARSLEY SALAD WITH HAM   (SERVES FOUR)

1 medium to large bulb
   fennel, sliced thin
1 bunch radishes, stems
   removed and sliced thin
1 cup flat-leaved parsley,
   leaves whole but removed
   from stems
2–4 ounces ham (prosciutto,
   Black Forest, Westphalian,
   or good-quality dry-cured
   ham), sliced thin and torn
   in pieces

Juice of 1 lemon
¼ cup olive oil
Salt and freshly ground
   pepper to taste
2 ounces Parmesan cheese,
   sliced thin and broken
   into about-2-inch pieces

In a large bowl put the fennel, radishes, parsley, and ham. Add the lemon juice, olive oil, and salt and pepper, and toss until well blended. Add the cheese and toss lightly to mix, being careful not to break up the cheese too much.

(SERVES FOUR)   **DANDELION SALAD WITH BACON**

¼ cup vinegar
1½ teaspoons sugar
1 clove garlic, minced
½ teaspoon freshly ground
    pepper
6 slices bacon

1 pound dandelion greens,
    trimmed, washed, and
    dried
2 large ripe tomatoes, each in
    4 thick slices
½ cup thinly sliced scallions

Mix the vinegar, sugar, garlic, and pepper in a small bowl. Let stand at least 30 minutes. Fry the bacon in a large skillet until crisp. Place on paper towels to free of excess fat. Remove the skillet from the heat and add the greens to the hot bacon fat in the skillet, gently stir for a minute or until the greens wilt a little. Add the vinegar mixture and mix well. Arrange the tomato slices on a large plate or individual salad plates, mound a portion of dandelion greens on each slice, and sprinkle the scallions on top.

SUMMER RED AND GREEN
(SERVES FOUR)   ❧   **TOMATO SALAD**

Make sure the red tomatoes are very ripe.

2 large red-ripe tomatoes
2 large green tomatoes
1 small red onion

1 recipe French Dressing (p.
703)

Slice the tomatoes and place in a large salad bowl. Very thinly slice the red onion and add to the tomatoes. Pour the French Dressing over and chill before serving.

PICKLED BEETS AND
(SERVES FOUR TO SIX)   ✳   ❧   **RED EGGS**

6 medium-small beets
2 teaspoons pickling spice
6 eggs
1 bunch young greens such
    as dandelion, mustard, or
    spinach

2 tablespoons cider vinegar
Salt
Freshly ground pepper

Cut off all but 1 inch of the beet tops; do not pare or remove the roots. In a large pot, bring enough water to boil to cover the beets. Add the beets and the pickling spice to the boiling water and cook them uncovered until they are tender, about 30–50 minutes depending on the size and the age of the beets. When tender, remove and cool the beets, reserving the liquid. In a separate pot, hard-boil the eggs. Set aside to cool. When the eggs are cool, shell them and place them into the reserved beet liquid. Let them marinate for several hours. Meanwhile, wilt the greens by pouring boiling water over them. Let sit 5 minutes, then drain and toss with the cider vinegar and salt and pepper to taste. To serve, peel the beets, cut in half, and place them on a bed of the wilted greens and garnish with the red eggs.

ENDIVE AND PROSCIUTTO SALAD   (SERVES FOUR)

The bitterness of the endive is matched nicely with the sweet-saltiness of the ham and the fruity oil.

- 4 Belgian endives, cleaned and trimmed
- 4 ounces prosciutto or Smithfield ham, in thin strips
- 2 tablespoons olive oil

Slice the endive horizontally into ⅛-inch rings. Put the endive and prosciutto or Smithfield ham into a large bowl and toss with the olive oil.

PARSLEY SALAD   ✳   ಶಿ   (SERVES FOUR TO SIX)

This salad should be served in small portions, about ½ to ¾ cup per person. It keeps well for a week and is good with all kinds of barbecued food.

- 6 tablespoons olive oil
- 2 cloves garlic, peeled
- 1½ tablespoons red wine vinegar
- Salt and freshly ground pepper to taste
- 4 cups parsley, stems removed, torn into pieces
- ⅓ cup freshly grated Parmesan cheese

Combine the oil and garlic in a blender or food processor and blend until garlic is smoothly incorporated into the oil. Add the vinegar and salt and pepper, and blend. When ready to serve, place the parsley and Parmesan cheese in a bowl and toss with the garlic oil and vinegar.

WHEAT BERRIES, BEAN SPROUTS, TOMATO, AND AVOCADO SALAD

(SERVES FOUR)

1½ cups cooked wheat berries
1½ cups bean sprouts
2 tomatoes, chopped
1 large avocado, peeled and diced
8–12 spinach leaves, trimmed, washed, and dried
½ teaspoon freshly ground pepper

6 tablespoons olive oil
½ teaspoon dry mustard
2 tablespoons lemon juice
2 teaspoons grated lemon rind
Salt to taste

Just before serving, combine the wheat berries, bean sprouts, tomatoes, and avocado in a bowl. Arrange spinach leaves on a plate. Mix remaining ingredients briskly until well blended, pour over the wheat berry mixture, and toss to mix. Spoon onto the spinach leaves and serve.

✳ ❧ ICED ONION RINGS

(SERVES FOUR)

These are cool and crisp, perfect in the summer as a salad with grilled meat. These must be eaten icy cold.

2 yellow onions, in ¼-inch rings

1 red onion, in ¼-inch rings

Put the onion rings in a large bowl of ice cubes and water. Be sure all the rings are submerged. If necessary place a dish on top of the rings to hold them down. Chill in the refrigerator for at least 1 hour before serving. Drain and serve immediately.

COOKED VEGETABLE SALADS

About Cooked Vegetable Salads

What makes a good mixed cooked vegetable salad? A combination of vegetables, cooked until barely tender (sometimes less than a minute), well drained, and chilled. You want to have contrast in color and in texture, so it is nice to have one raw ingredient that will provide a crunchier foil. Use only enough dressing to coat and flavor the vegetables. And don't select a vegetable that is so overpowering that it smothers the flavor of its companions.

What makes a poor cooked vegetable salad? Too many vegetables, cooked until limp, inadequately drained, and overdressed so that they are swimming in oil or cream dressing. Don't use a heavy hand with onion or garlic, and don't abuse herbs (too much dried tarragon, for instance, has ruined many a fine salad). An all-too-common mixture is peas, diced carrots, and potatoes—a poor balance because two of the vegetables tend to be sweetish in taste and there is too much mealiness in texture.

In addition to the recipes that follow, some good combinations might be:

> Whole green beans, sliced beets, and new potatoes.
> Sliced yellow squash and zucchini, just blanched, diced cucumber, and strips of green pepper and celery.
> Flowers of broccoli and of cauliflower, and strips of red pepper.
> Eggplant and zucchini, sautéed in oil, and fresh tomato wedges.
> Blanched Chinese cabbage and red pepper and cucumber strips (with Lemon Soy Dressing).

Single cooked vegetables, such as asparagus, green beans, beets, broccoli flowerets, are also good by themselves, tossed with vinaigrette, French Dressing, Boiled Dressing, mayonnaise, or perhaps Avocado Mayonnaise and a little chopped scallions or chives and parsley, served on a bed of lettuce.

ZUCCHINI, NEW POTATO, AND TOMATO SALAD ᐤ (SERVES FOUR)

Cook the vegetables only until tender: about 5 to 8 minutes for the zucchini, about 20 minutes for the potatoes (but check—potatoes vary). And remove the salad from the refrigerator half an hour before serving: it tastes better at room temperature.

3 medium zucchini, cooked whole 8 minutes	1 recipe French Dressing (p. 703)
4 new potatoes, cooked	Salt to taste
2 ripe, fresh tomatoes, peeled and chopped	¼ teaspoon freshly ground pepper
2 tablespoons finely chopped onion	

Trim away the ends of the zucchini and slice about ¼ inch thick. Peel and dice the potatoes. Combine the zucchini, potatoes, tomatoes, and onion in a bowl. Add the dressing and toss to coat well. Add salt and pepper. Mix well and chill.

(SERVES SIX)   **CELERY VICTOR**

This is a time-saver if you can find celery hearts in your market.

3 bunches celery
1½ cups chicken broth, or
   enough to barely cover
   celery
Herb bouquet of (tied
   together): 1 bay leaf, 4
   sprigs parsley, and celery
   leaves

Salt and freshly ground
   pepper to taste
3 tablespoons tarragon
   vinegar
½ cup olive oil
Celery leaves, for garnish

Trim the celery bunches, cutting off outer stalks (save them for soup), and cut each bunch in half lengthwise. Arrange in a pan and pour the chicken broth over. Add the herb bouquet and salt and pepper, and cook until barely tender, about 6 minutes. Let the celery cool in the broth. Beat the vinegar into the olive oil. Drain the celery, pour the vinegar and oil mixture over, and chill. Serve garnished with the celery leaves.

CELERY VICTOR WITH MUSTARD MAYONNAISE

Omit the vinegar and olive oil. Mix *2 teaspoons Dijon mustard* into *½ cup mayonnaise* and stir until well blended. Spoon about 1½ tablespoons of dressing on each serving.

MARINATED BRUSSELS SPROUTS
(SERVES FOUR)   ❧ SALAD

¾ pound Brussels sprouts,
   washed and trimmed
1 tablespoon minced shallot
   or scallion
6 tablespoons olive oil
2 tablespoons fresh lemon
   juice

1 tablespoon finely chopped
   parsley
Salt and freshly ground
   pepper to taste

Pierce the stem end of the Brussels sprouts and cook in boiling salted water for 8–10 minutes. Plunge into ice water to stop cooking. When cool, drain. In a large bowl, mix the shallot or scallion, olive oil, and lemon juice. Add the Brussels sprouts and toss to blend. Let stand for at least 30 minutes. Before serving, add the parsley and salt and pepper and mix well.

ARTICHOKE HEARTS, PEAS, AND JERUSALEM ARTICHOKE SALAD ৯ (SERVES FOUR)

1 package frozen artichoke
   hearts, cooked and
   drained
1 cup small peas, cooked and
   shelled

¾ cup thinly sliced Jerusalem
   artichokes
1 bunch watercress, washed
¾ cup French Dressing (p.
   703)

Cut the artichoke hearts in half lengthwise and mix with the peas and sliced Jerusalem artichokes. Arrange the watercress on a platter and place the vegetables on top. Toss with the French Dressing. Serve chilled.

CAULIFLOWER, BEET, AND GREEN BEAN SALAD ৯ (SERVES FOUR)

2 cups cauliflower flowerets,
   cooked 5 minutes
2 cups green beans, cooked 5
   minutes, in 1-inch pieces
2 beets, cooked and sliced

1 cup sliced mushrooms
1 recipe French Dressing (p.
   703)
2 teaspoons Dijon mustard
Salt

Combine the cauliflower, green beans, beets, and mushrooms. Mix the dressing and mustard together until well blended, then stir into the combined vegetables and toss to mix well. Salt to taste. Serve chilled or at room temperature.

VARIATIONS

Omit the cauliflower and add 2 *cups cooked corn kernels* or 2 *cups cooked lima beans.*

SUBSTANTIAL SALADS

(SERVES SIX)   ई**MACARONI SALAD**

One-half pound uncooked macaroni makes 4 cups cooked.

4 cups cooked macaroni	2 tablespoons finely chopped
1 cup sliced celery	parsley
½ cup sliced scallions	1 cup mayonnaise
4 tablespoons coarsely	2 tablespoons vinegar
chopped green pepper	½ teaspoon freshly ground
2 tablespoons chopped red	black pepper
pepper	Salt
4 tablespoons pitted, chopped	
black olives	

Combine macaroni, celery, scallions, green pepper, red pepper, olives, and parsley in a large bowl; toss to mix. In a small bowl mix the mayonnaise and vinegar together until smooth. Add to the macaroni mixture. Add pepper and salt to taste. Toss and mix well. Refrigerate several hours before serving.

PASTA SALAD WITH PARMESAN
(SERVES FOUR)   ई**AND CAPERS**

1 recipe French Dressing or	1½ teaspoons capers, slightly
Basic Vinaigrette (p. 703)	mashed into the dressing
1 tablespoon finely chopped	4 cups cooked pasta, thin
onion	spaghetti, or capellini (8
2 tablespoons grated	ounces dry)
Parmesan cheese	

Combine the vinaigrette, onion, Parmesan cheese, and capers in a large bowl. Add the cold, cooked pasta and toss to mix.

SPICY ASIAN PASTA SALAD ટે   (SERVES FOUR TO SIX)

1 tablespoon chopped ginger
    root
1 tablespoon chopped garlic
1 teaspoon soy sauce
1 teaspoon rice vinegar
1 teaspoon sugar
½ teaspoon freshly ground
    white pepper
⅓ cup vegetable oil (not olive
    oil)

2 tablespoons sesame oil
1 teaspoon chili oil (optional)
4 cups cooked pasta, thin
    spaghetti, or capellini (8
    ounces dry)
¼ cup sliced scallions
½ cup cilantro leaves
1 cup chopped cucumber
6 cups shredded iceberg
    lettuce

In a small bowl mix together the ginger root, garlic, soy sauce, vinegar, sugar, pepper, vegetable oil, sesame oil, and optional chili oil until well blended. In a large bowl combine the pasta, scallions, cilantro, and cucumber; toss to mix. Add the dressing and toss to coat. Then add lettuce, toss, and serve.

PASTA SALAD WITH FRESH BASIL ટે   (SERVES FOUR)

If you break the dry pasta in half or thirds, it will be more manageable.

1 recipe French Dressing or
    Basic Vinaigrette (p. 703)
1½ teaspoons finely chopped
    garlic
1 tablespoon finely chopped
    fresh basil

4 cups cooked pasta, thin
    spaghetti, or capellini (8
    ounces dry)

In a large bowl combine the vinaigrette, garlic, and basil. Add the cold, cooked pasta and toss to mix.

(SERVES FOUR)   **RICE SALAD**

This is a salad that has so many possibilities for variations that a list of suggestions follows the basic recipe. So use your ingenuity.

3 cups cooked rice
1 cup thin strips cooked ham
1 cup baby frozen peas, defrosted, or fresh young peas, blanched 1 minute
¼ cup chopped red pepper
2 tablespoons finely chopped chives or scallions

1 tablespoon finely chopped parsley
1 recipe French Dressing (p. 703)
1½ teaspoons Dijon mustard
Salt
Freshly ground pepper

Combine the rice, ham, peas, red pepper, chives or scallions, and parsley in a large bowl. In a small bowl mix the dressing and mustard until blended. Combine with the rice mixture, seasoning to taste.

VARIATIONS AND ADDITIONS

1 cup rare roast beef instead of the ham
1 cup vegetables cut in dice, such as tomatoes, green and red peppers, young raw zucchini, cucumbers, in addition to, or in place of, the meat
½ cup black olives, cut in half
1 cup cooked shrimp and/or other seafood such as crabmeat, mussels, lobster, baby clams

(SERVES FOUR)   **SALADE NIÇOISE**

Full of the flavors of the Mediterranean.

1 small head lettuce
1 cup lightly cooked green beans
1½ cups cubed cooked new potatoes
1 can tuna fish
1 recipe French Dressing (p. 703), made with 1 teaspoon minced garlic

4 anchovy fillets
8 black olives
½ green pepper, in thin strips
2 hard-boiled eggs, quartered

Tear up the lettuce and mix with the green beans and new potatoes. Drain and break up the tuna fish, and add it with all but a couple of tablespoons of the dressing. Toss in a salad bowl. Over the top arrange the anchovy fillets, olives, green pepper strips, and eggs decoratively, and drizzle the remaining dressing over.

CHICKPEA SALAD &\~ (SERVES FOUR)

2 cups cooked or canned
   chickpeas
2 cloves garlic, minced
3 tablespoons oil
1 tablespoon vinegar
¼ teaspoon chili powder
Salt to taste
Freshly ground pepper to
   taste

4 large radishes, sliced
3 tablespoons chopped
   parsley
3–4 leaves fresh basil,
   chopped, or ½ teaspoon
   dried

Drain the chickpeas, reserving 1 tablespoon of their cooking or canning liquid. Add liquid to the garlic, oil, vinegar, chili powder, salt, and pepper, and stir to blend. Pour over the chickpeas, toss with the radishes, and sprinkle parsley and basil over the top.

CHICKPEA SALAD WITH SAUSAGE

Add *½ cup sliced sausage* (salami, pepperoni, or cooked sausages), *½ cup chopped pimiento or red pepper*, and toss.

CHICKPEA SALAD WITH TUNA

Add *1 can drained tuna fish, a dozen black olives, halved,* and toss. Lay *4 anchovy fillets* over the top.

LENTIL SALAD &\~ (SERVES SIX)

1 cup lentils
Salt
3 tablespoons oil
1 tablespoon vinegar

1 medium onion, minced
Freshly ground pepper
¼ teaspoon dry mustard
2 tablespoons minced parsley

Simmer the lentils in 3 cups water with 1 teaspoon salt for 30–40 minutes, until tender. Drain. In a small bowl, mix the oil, vinegar, onion, pepper, and mustard. Toss with the lentils while they are hot. Refrigerate and, when cool, mix in the parsley and salt to taste.

(SERVES FOUR) **WHITE BEAN AND SAUSAGE SALAD**

Serve with sour pickles, mustard, and a hearty rustic bread.

2½ cups white beans, cooked (Great Northern or cannellini)
½ onion, chopped fine
½ cup olive oil
3 sweet or mild Italian sausages, grilled or pan-fried

Salt and freshly ground pepper to taste
Fresh parsley or basil, chopped (optional, for garnish)

In a large bowl combine the beans, onion, and olive oil. Cut the sausage into ¼-inch slices and add to the bean mixture. Add salt and pepper and mix thoroughly. Serve at room temperature. Garnish with fresh chopped parsley or basil if desired.

(SERVES TWO) ❧ **KIDNEY AND GREEN BEAN SALAD**

A fine way of using up cooked green beans. Cut them up after rather than before cooking—they'll taste better.

1 cup red kidney beans
1 cup cooked green beans
3 finely sliced scallions, or ½ small red onion, sliced fine

¼ cup mustardy French Dressing (p. 704)

Drain the kidney beans and rinse them. Dry thoroughly. Cut the green beans about the same size as the kidney beans. Toss together with the scallions or red onion and the dressing. Refrigerate for several hours before serving.

TUSCAN BEAN AND TUNA SALAD   *   (SERVES SIX)

I love this salad sprinkled with coarse black pepper and some ice cold
sliced tomatoes on the side.

6 cups cooked cannellini
    beans or any white beans
2 tablespoons wine vinegar
6 tablespoons olive oil
Salt and freshly ground
    pepper to taste
2 tablespoons chopped fresh
    basil

½ cup chopped parsley
    (Italian flat-leaved if
    available)
1 cup finely chopped onion
14 ounces canned tuna,
    drained and flaked

Drain the beans and put in a large mixing bowl. Combine the vinegar,
olive oil, and salt and pepper in a small bowl and whisk until well
blended. Pour the dressing over the beans, add 1 tablespoon of the
basil and half of the parsley, and gently toss to coat. Arrange the beans
on a platter or serving dish, sprinkle with the onion, and top with the
tuna. Garnish with the remaining basil and parsley. You may drizzle a
little more olive oil and vinegar over all if you wish.

POTATO SALAD   *   ⤾   (SERVES SIX)

8 medium new potatoes
¼ cup lemon juice
¼ cup vegetable oil
Salt
½ teaspoon freshly ground
    pepper

2 celery stalks, chopped fine
4 hard-boiled eggs, coarsely
    chopped
1–1¼ cups mayonnaise
3 tablespoons cider vinegar
Six large leaves lettuce

Boil the potatoes just until tender when pierced with a fork. Drain, and
as soon as you can handle them, peel and dice. Toss with the lemon
juice, oil, and salt to taste (the flavor is better when they have this preliminary dressing while very warm, and the potatoes, thus coated,
won't absorb as much mayonnaise later). Cool. Add the pepper, celery,
and chopped eggs. Blend 1 cup mayonnaise with vinegar, then toss
over the potato salad, gently folding until all pieces are coated. If the
potatoes seem a little dry, add more mayonnaise. Line a bowl or a platter with lettuce leaves and pile the potato salad in the middle.

VARIATIONS AND ADDITIONS

3 tablespoons finely chopped onion
2 tablespoons dry mustard mixed into the mayonnaise
3 tablespoons sweet pickle relish
2 tablespoons minced parsley

(SERVES SIX)   **HOT OR GERMAN POTATO SALAD**

8 medium new potatoes
6 slices bacon
2½ tablespoons flour
6 tablespoons cider vinegar
1½ tablespoons sugar
1 teaspoon dry mustard

Salt to taste
½ teaspoon freshly ground
    pepper
10 romaine lettuce leaves
3 large ripe tomatoes

Boil the potatoes in their jackets until just tender. Meanwhile, fry the
bacon until crisp. Reserving ¼ cup bacon fat, drain the bacon well and
crumble; set aside. Heat the bacon fat and stir in the flour. Cook
slowly, continuing to stir for a minute. Off heat add 1½ cups hot water
and the vinegar, mix well, return to low heat, and cook, stirring, until
smooth and thickened. Add sugar, mustard, salt, and pepper, and cook
2 minutes. Drain the potatoes, peel and slice them warm. Toss with the
dressing until well coated. Arrange lettuce leaves in a large bowl and
mound the hot salad in the center. Cut the tomatoes in wedges and
arrange around edge. Sprinkle the crumbled bacon on top and serve
warm.

CELERY ROOT SALAD WITH
(SERVES SIX)   ❧ **WATERCRESS DRESSING**

2–3 celery roots, peeled,
    trimmed, and in ½-inch
    slices (about 6 cups
    loosely packed)
½ cup olive oil
3 tablespoons white wine
    vinegar

½ cup minced watercress
2 large shallots, minced
Salt and freshly ground
    pepper
6 large leaves butter lettuce

Put the celery root slices in a pot of boiling water and cook for about
15–20 minutes or until just tender. Drain and chill. In a large bowl, mix

together the olive oil and vinegar. Add the watercress, shallots, and salt and pepper to taste. Cut the celery root into dice or julienne, add to the bowl with the dressing, and toss to coat. Spoon some of the salad into the center of each lettuce leaf and serve.

AVOCADO WITH CHICKEN STUFFING   (SERVES FOUR)

½ cup mayonnaise
2 tablespoons lemon juice
1½ cups diced cooked chicken
¼ cup finely chopped celery
Salt

⅓ cup coarsely chopped
    blanched almonds
2 ripe, firm avocados
8 leaves Bibb lettuce

Blend the mayonnaise and lemon juice together. Mix with the diced chicken and celery. Salt to taste and stir in the almonds. Peel the avocados and cut in half lengthwise. On each salad plate, place two lettuce leaves with one avocado half on top. Spoon one-fourth of the chicken salad into the hollow of each avocado half, letting some spill over onto the lettuce.

AVOCADO WITH SEAFOOD STUFFING

Substitute 1¾ cups cooked shellfish or fish, or a combination thereof, for the chicken. Eliminate the almonds and sprinkle ½ dozen or so capers on top of each serving.

STUFFED TOMATO SALAD   (SERVES FOUR)

4 firm ripe tomatoes
¾ cup cooked corn kernels
⅓ cup chopped cucumber
½ cup finely diced ham
2 teaspoons minced chives
¼ cup cooked peas

¼ teaspoon freshly ground
    pepper
⅓ cup mayonnaise
1½ teaspoons prepared
    horseradish
8 leaves butter lettuce

Bring a large pot of water to a boil and drop in the tomatoes. Boil for about 20 seconds, remove, and slide the tomato skin off, trimming the little stubborn pieces away with a paring knife. Cut the core of the tomato out, and with a teaspoon, gently scoop out the inside of the tomato, leaving a good sturdy shell. Turn the tomatoes upside down on a rack to drain. Combine the corn, cucumber, ham, chives, peas, and pepper in a bowl. Mix the mayonnaise and horseradish together until well blended, then gently toss mixture with the vegetables to thoroughly coat. Spoon the vegetable filling into the hollowed tomatoes. Place the tomatoes on the lettuce leaves and serve cold.

STUFFED TOMATO SALAD WITH BACON

Use 4 *slices bacon* cooked until crisp, drained, and crumbled in place of the ham.

STUFFED TOMATO SALAD WITH TUNA

Eliminate the corn, ham, and peas and use instead *1 can tuna*, *¼ cup chopped green pepper*, and *⅓ cup chopped celery*. Instead of the horseradish, use *a few drops of lemon juice* for flavoring.

(SERVES FOUR)   ❧ **EGG SALAD**

Have all the ingredients chilled.

⅔ cup mayonnaise	Salt
2 tablespoons lemon juice	⅓ cup finely chopped green
2 teaspoons vinegar	pepper
1 tablespoon finely chopped	8 hard-boiled eggs, diced
chives	4 crisp outer leaves iceberg
1 tablespoon chopped fresh	lettuce and 2 cups
dill, or 1½ teaspoons dried,	shredded iceberg lettuce,
crumbled	or 1 head Boston or Bibb
⅛ teaspoon freshly ground	lettuce and several sprigs
pepper	watercress

Combine the mayonnaise, lemon juice, vinegar, chives, dill, and pepper. Mix until well blended, and add salt to taste. Add the green pepper and eggs; gently toss to mix. Arrange one lettuce leaf on each salad plate and put ½ cup shredded lettuce on top. Or make a bed of lettuce leaves and watercress (reserving a few leaves for the top). Put a portion of egg salad on each lettuce bed. Serve.

TUNA SALAD   (SERVES FOUR)

Canned salmon or crab may be used instead of tuna, but omit the
sweet pickle relish (some may not like it even with tuna). Add a teaspoon of capers to the salmon or crab. Chill all the ingredients.

1½ cups canned tuna, well drained, flaked	½ cup mayonnaise
½ cup finely chopped celery	4 outer crisp leaves iceberg lettuce and 2 cups shredded iceberg lettuce, or 1 head Boston lettuce
2 tablespoons sweet pickle relish (optional)	
3 tablespoons lemon juice	1 tablespoon minced parsley

Combine the tuna, celery, pickle relish (if you wish), lemon juice, and
mayonnaise. Toss until well mixed. Put the lettuce leaves on four salad
plates with ½ cup shredded lettuce on top of each, or make a bed of
loose lettuce leaves. Put a fourth of the tuna salad on each lettuce bed.
Sprinkle with parsley and serve.

CHICKEN SALAD   (SERVES FOUR)

4 cups bite-size pieces cooked chicken	¼ cup heavy cream
2 teaspoons grated onion or chopped scallions (optional)	2 tablespoons vinegar
	⅛ teaspoon freshly ground pepper
1 cup sliced celery	Salt to taste
⅔ cup mayonnaise	1 head Bibb lettuce, washed and dried

Put chicken in a bowl and add the onion or scallions (if you like) and
celery. Combine the mayonnaise, cream, and vinegar and blend well.
Add pepper and salt, and toss with chicken, until well mixed. Make a
bed of the lettuce leaves and spoon the chicken salad over.

VARIATIONS AND ADDITIONS

Sprinkle *1 cup chopped almonds* over salad.
Instead of the celery add *1 cup seedless grapes* to chicken
  mixture.
Add *2 teaspoons curry powder* to the mayonnaise.

Omit the celery and add ½ *cup peeled, seeded, diced cucumber* and
½ *cup pineapple bits.*
Add 1 *cup diced, unpeeled red apple* and ½ *cup chopped walnuts.*

(SERVES SIX) ## CHINESE-STYLE CHICKEN SALAD

1 teaspoon Chinese "5 Spice"
¾ cup vegetable or olive oil
1 whole chicken, poached or
  roasted, meat removed
  and in strips
2 tablespoons dry mustard
  mixed with 2–3
  tablespoons water
1–2 teaspoons sesame oil
1 cup chopped cilantro or
  parsley

1 cup chopped scallions, most
  of the green removed
3 cups shredded iceberg
  lettuce
1½ cups coarsely chopped
  dry-roasted peanuts
1 tablespoon sesame seeds,
  toasted
Salt and freshly ground
  pepper to taste

In a large bowl, mix the "5 Spice" and oil. Add the chicken, toss, and
let stand for a while. Then add the mustard mixture and sesame oil
and mix well. Add the cilantro, scallions, lettuce, peanuts, sesame
seeds, and salt and pepper. Serve immediately.

(SERVES FOUR) ## SHRIMP AND PAPAYA SALAD

1½ pounds medium-size raw
  shrimp
1 tablespoon minced parsley
1 recipe Handmade Basic
  Mayonnaise (p. 707)

1 papaya, peeled and seeded
Salt
1 head Bibb lettuce, washed
  and dried

Bring a pot with enough water to cover the shrimp to boil. Add the
shrimp and cook only until pink (about 5 minutes). Drain, rinse with
cold water, peel, shell, and remove any black vein, then chill in the refrigerator. Mix the parsley into the mayonnaise. Cut papaya in slices
or large cubes. Toss the shrimp and papaya in the mayonnaise until
well coated. Add salt to taste. Arrange the shrimp mixture on lettuce
leaves.

CRAB RAVIGOTE

(SERVES FOUR)

1 tablespoon olive oil
3 tablespoons vinegar
⅛ teaspoon cayenne pepper
1 teaspoon prepared mustard
1 hard-boiled egg, chopped
fine

1 teaspoon minced parsley
2 cups cooked crabmeat
Salt to taste
1 cup Green Mayonnaise (p. 708)

Combine the oil, vinegar, cayenne pepper, mustard, egg, and parsley in a mixing bowl. Mix until well blended. Add the crab and salt. Spoon the crab mixture into scallop shells or small dishes, and cover with the mayonnaise.

CRAB LOUIS

(SERVES FOUR)

½ large head iceberg lettuce, shredded
3 cups cooked crabmeat
1 cup mayonnaise

⅓ cup whipped cream
¼ cup chili sauce
2 teaspoons grated onion
Pinch of cayenne pepper

Arrange the lettuce on four salad plates. Divide crabmeat and place on top. Combine remaining ingredients and mix until well blended. Spoon over each serving of crabmeat.

LOBSTER SALAD

(SERVES FOUR)

Lobster salad is at its best when made very simply with lobster meat, a little crunchy celery, and adequately dressed with a creamy, mild homemade mayonnaise. Have all the ingredients chilled.

3 cups cooked lobster meat
½ cup finely chopped celery
½ cup mayonnaise

1½ tablespoons heavy cream
Salt to taste
1 head Bibb lettuce

Cut the lobster meat into large bite-size pieces, place them in a bowl, and add the celery. Blend the mayonnaise and cream in a small bowl, then gently combine with the lobster, toss to mix, and add salt. Arrange a bed of lettuce leaves and put the lobster salad on top.

FRUIT SALADS

About Fruit Salads

What makes a good fruit salad? Luscious, ripe, fresh fruit that is sweet and firm with its own distinct flavor. Use fruits that mingle well. The pieces of fruit should be uniform in size and easy to eat. Each of the fruits should retain its own characteristic taste. Make and serve fruit salad fresh whenever possible and strive for good contrast in color and texture.

What makes a bad fruit salad? Unripe or overripe fruit with spoiled spots that go untrimmed. Don't mix fruits that aren't compatible—for instance, the acidity of grapefruit will overwhelm the delicate taste of melon. Fruit should be neatly cut and in not-too-large pieces. Don't prepare too far ahead or the fruits become limp and drained of their vitality. Avoid dullness in color and texture.

FRUIT SALAD COMBINATIONS

Use crisp lettuce or watercress as a bed for some of these salads or one or two sprigs of mint on top of the fruit. The following proportions are for one serving; multiply for the number to be served.

½ cup sliced peaches, ¼ cup diced pears, ¼ cup seedless grapes, dressed with 2 teaspoons mayonnaise thinned with 1 teaspoon cream, or Nut Dressing.

½ cup grapefruit sections, ½ cup banana slices, 1 tablespoon pomegranate seeds, if available, dressed with 1 tablespoon French Dressing, or if you prefer a sweeter dressing, Cleveland.

⅓ cup papaya cubes, ⅓ cup kiwi slices, ¼ sliced avocado, dressed with 1 teaspoon vegetable oil, 1 teaspoon lime juice, and 1 teaspoon honey blended together, or Lime Dressing.

⅓ cup pineapple cubes, ⅓ cup cantaloupe balls, 5 strawberries, no dressing.

¾ cup orange sections, ¼ cup thin red onion rings, dressed with 1 tablespoon French Dressing.

⅓ cup pineapple cubes, ½ cup avocado slices, ⅓ cup mango slivers, 2 tablespoons grated coconut, dressed with 1 teaspoon lime juice blended with 2 teaspoons mayonnaise, or Pineapple-Honey Dressing.

¾ cup honeydew melon balls, ¼ cup blueberries, dressed with 1 teaspoon lemon juice, 1 teaspoon vegetable oil, pinch of salt, ½ teaspoon sugar blended.

⅓ cup cantaloupe balls, ⅓ cup honeydew melon balls, ⅓ cup
   watermelon balls, served with mint sprig and lime wedge.
1 orange, sectioned, ½ banana, thinly sliced, dressed with 1
   teaspoon lemon juice blended with 1 teaspoon honey.
⅓ cup chopped apples, ⅓ cup orange sections, ½ cup sliced
   bananas, dressed with 2 teaspoons Poppy-Seed Dressing.

Mixed Combinations

Prunes stuffed with cream cheese and walnut halves.
Pear halves, pitted cherries, watercress.
Cantaloupe rings with small mound of raspberries in the center.

Fruit Salad Additions

Sliced kumquats, raisins, nuts, cottage cheese, celery, cucumber,
chopped dates.

WALDORF SALAD ✽ ଧ⦆   (SERVES FOUR)

Sometimes it's pleasing to have two different kinds of apples in a Wal-
dorf salad, if the season is right and you can get different varieties like
a sweet Delicious and a tart greening. In any case, be sure the apples
you use are crisp.

2 firm ripe green apples	½ cup mayonnaise
1 firm ripe red apple	1½ teaspoons honey (optional)
1 tablespoon lemon juice	Iceberg or Bibb lettuce leaves
1 cup sliced celery	
½ cup coarsely chopped walnuts	

Core and quarter the apples (leave the skin on unless it is tough) and
slice thin. Put in a bowl and toss with the lemon juice to coat. Add the
celery and walnuts. Cover and chill. Mix the mayonnaise and honey (if
you like a little sweetness in the dressing) together until smooth, add
to the apple mixture, and toss. Serve on a bed of lettuce.

CRANBERRY WALDORF SALAD

Reduce mayonnaise to about ¼ cup and mix with ½ cup *whole-berry
cranberry sauce*. Omit the honey. Add to the apple mixture and toss.

(SERVES SIX)   ❧ **APPLE AND TANGERINE SALAD**

This salad is an interesting combination of tart/sweet and textures and makes a good party or holiday treat.

1 tablespoon zest from tangerine peel
¼ cup tangerine juice (from 1 large tangerine)
⅓ cup olive oil
1 tablespoon lemon juice (optional)
Salt and freshly ground pepper to taste
4–5 Belgian endives
1 Red Delicious apple, core removed and sliced thin

1 tart green apple (pippin or Granny Smith), core removed and sliced thin
4 tangerines, seedless if possible, peeled, halved, and sliced
½ cup dates, seeded and in thin lengthwise strips
½ cup walnuts, broken in large pieces

Combine the tangerine zest, tangerine juice, olive oil, optional lemon juice, and salt and pepper, and mix until well blended. Set aside. Wipe endives with damp paper towel, trim stem end, and break off and separate leaves. Place endive, apples, tangerines, dates, and walnuts in a salad bowl and toss together lightly. Add the tangerine vinaigrette and toss to coat and mix.

MOLDED SALADS

About Aspics

Too many poorly conceived molded salads have, alas, graced (or disgraced) the American table. But a really fine-tasting fruit or vegetable jelly—not overly jellied—with combinations that are compatible, or a beautiful clear aspic studded with colorful morsels can be a credit to any good cook and looks so tempting on a buffet or a summer lunch table that it is worth mastering this very simple art.

An aspic is as good as the flavor and quality of the liquid that you set to jell. It follows that a good homemade broth—made of chicken or other poultry, beef, or fish, well seasoned—will provide the base for the most delicious aspics. There is no reason why you can't use a canned broth; however, it will taste better if you simmer it with aromatic vegetables. To 4 cups of canned broth add ½ cup minced carrots, onion, and some celery, plus 3 or 4 sprigs of parsley, ½ bay leaf, and a pinch of thyme. About ½ cup red wine plus a couple of teaspoons of tomato paste, if you like a strong flavor, is good with beef broth, and dry white wine enhances a chicken broth. Simmer the mixture gently for 30 minutes, then strain.

The best substitute for fish stock is bottled clam juice, but it must be cut in half with water, preferably mixed with a little dry white wine or vermouth, simmered for a few minutes with chopped onion and a few sprigs of parsley.

In using either a canned stock or your own homemade, you should determine first how much jelling power the broth has naturally. Test by refrigerating. If the broth is firmly jelled, to make the aspic you will need only 1 teaspoon gelatin to 2 cups liquid, but if it barely holds together, use the usual formula of 1 envelope (1 tablespoon) gelatin to 2 cups liquid. This will be firm enough to hold up to 2 cups of solids, unless you are including uncooked vegetables in your mold; they tend to give off some water, so 1 envelope gelatin to 2 cups liquid to 1 cup solids would be a safer rule. Never attempt to hold an aspic containing uncooked vegetables for more than a day or two, or they will release their water.

An aspic that is too firm is rubbery and unappealing. If you are serving an unmolded aspic that may have to sit around in warm weather, it is better to place your platter on a bed of ice than to try to increase its holding power by adding extra gelatin when you make it.

For a decorative transparent mold with attractively arranged shapes and colors, you want to be sure to have your aspic crystal clear, so it is necessary to clarify the stock. It's a fussy procedure, but if you follow the directions on p. 107 carefully, you should have no trouble, and other faster methods are just not as foolproof.

To insure that the solids stay in place and don't all float to the top, you have to partially set a bottom layer of aspic in the mold by chilling, then arrange a decorative pattern on that, spoon in more aspic, which should be cool just to the point of being syrupy, about the consistency of lightly beaten egg white, and let that set before you proceed. Sometimes you may want to build several layers in this manner, but it is the bottom one that counts most, because when you unmold, you want the design to look attractive and orderly—the way you have arranged it. Jelling time varies; to be safe, for a large aspic with solids, allow 6 hours before unmolding.

If you're uneasy at first about making your own aspics, to get the feel of working with jelly try some of the simple jellied salads first, made with commercial flavored gelatins. And they're fine to fall back on if your family enjoys them. But they do tend to be sweet—more a dessert—and they haven't the pure essence of good flavor that your own delicious homemade aspics will have.

SIMPLE JELLIED SALADS

Dissolve 1 package flavored gelatin in 1 cup boiling water. Add 1 cup cold liquid—this can be plain water or a fruit juice that is compatible with the flavor, or water or juice flavored with a little wine (sherry, dry white wine, or Port). Season to taste and chill.

When the jelly begins to thicken to about the consistency of lightly beaten egg white, fold in 1½ cups prepared fruits or vegetables; cooked meat or fish would not taste good in these sweetened jellies. Chill until firm—about 4 hours.

SOME IDEAS FOR COMBINATIONS

Lemon or lime gelatin with small diced cucumber and radishes plus 3 tablespoons chopped chives.

Apple gelatin with finely cut celery and ¼ cup chopped walnuts.

Lemon gelatin with 1 cup finely diced beets, 2 tablespoons minced red onion, 1 tablespoon prepared horseradish, and ¾ cup finely diced celery. Use ¾ cup beet juice and 3 tablespoons vinegar for the 1 cup cold liquid required.

Lemon, lime, or apple gelatin with 1 cup chopped nuts and ½ cup plumped raisins.

Raspberry gelatin with 1 cup canned black cherries poured into a mold lined with cream cheese balls (from a 4-ounce package). Use ¾ cup cherry juice and 3 tablespoons dry white wine, 1 tablespoon fresh lemon juice, and 2 tablespoons water for the 1 cup cold liquid required.

(SERVES FOUR) ✳ **CUCUMBER ASPIC**

This is wonderful with cold salmon or chicken and deviled eggs.

1 envelope plus 1 teaspoon gelatin	¼ cup grated onion
½ cup cold water	3 cucumbers, peeled, seeded, and grated
2½ cups chicken broth	Juice of 1 lemon

In a small bowl, stir the gelatin into the water and let stand 5 minutes to soften. Heat the chicken broth to a simmer, remove from the heat, and stir in the gelatin until it has completely dissolved. Let the gelatin mixture cool. Stir in the onion, cucumbers, and lemon juice. Refrigerate for at least 4 hours, until set. Cut into squares to serve.

BING CHERRY MOLD ᨠ   (SERVES SIX)

Heightened by the fresh astringent flavor of cranberry juice, this tart
mold is particularly good with cold chicken, or turkey, or duck. Serve
garnished with watercress and cream cheese.

18-ounce jar or can Bing cherries	1 cup cranberry juice
	1 envelope gelatin

Drain cherries, add the juice to the cold cranberry juice and sprinkle
the gelatin over. Heat until almost simmering. Remove from heat, and
stir until gelatin is thoroughly dissolved. Pour into a 4-cup mold and
cool. Pit the cherries, if necessary. When the liquid is about the consistency of egg whites, spoon in the cherries and chill until set.

GRAPEFRUIT JELLY SALAD ᨠ   (SERVES FOUR TO SIX)

Made with fresh juicy grapefruit at the peak of season, this tart and
cleansing aspic needs no additional sugar and looks attractive unmolded with slices of grapefruit and avocado (or other fruit) interspersed. Decorate the serving platter with watercress and cream cheese
balls.

1 envelope gelatin	1 small avocado
1½ cups freshly squeezed grapefruit juice, or canned or bottled unsweetened	Segments from 1 fresh grapefruit, or 1 cup canned
1 or more teaspoons sugar (optional)	

Sprinkle the gelatin over the cold grapefruit juice, add sugar, if desired,
then heat it to a simmer and stir well to make sure the gelatin is dissolved. Pour enough of the hot liquid into a 3- or 4-cup mold to cover
the bottom ½ inch. Chill until almost firm. Peel the avocado and cut
into the same number of slices as you have grapefruit segments. Place
alternating pieces of grapefruit and avocado on the slightly firm jelly,
chill again, and then pour the last of the juice over. Refrigerate until
firm. Unmold to serve.

VARIATIONS

Alternate *segments of orange* and grapefruit.
Alternate *strips of peeled and seeded cucumber* and grapefruit.

Use *1½ cups cubed apples and seedless grapes* and distribute evenly through the gelatin-thickened grapefruit juice after chilling until it is about the consistency of egg whites.

(SERVES SIX) → **TOMATO ASPIC**

Tomato aspic is good with so many things—seafood, chicken, and other cold meats, or just by itself on a bed of lettuce with a dollop of good homemade mayonnaise on top. Try this as a luncheon dish served with deviled eggs, black olives, and homemade crackers.

2 envelopes gelatin	2½ teaspoons sugar
⅓ cup water	1 teaspoon salt
4 cups tomato juice	½ teaspoon freshly ground
1 onion, sliced thin	pepper
4 tablespoons chopped celery	1 tablespoon pickling spice
leaves	¼ cup lemon juice

Sprinkle the gelatin into a small bowl, add the water, stir, and let stand. Combine the tomato juice, onion, celery leaves, sugar, salt, pepper, and pickling spice in a pan. Bring to a boil, lower the heat to simmer, cook for 5 minutes, remove from the heat, strain, stir in the softened gelatin, and stir until the liquid clears. Add the lemon juice. Pour into a 1-quart mold and chill until set.

TOMATO ASPIC WITH VEGETABLES

Fill the bottom ½ inch of a 1-quart mold with the liquid; chill until just set. Distribute *1½ cups finely diced raw vegetables such as celery, zucchini, cucumber, red and green peppers* with the lemon juice, and add remaining liquid.

TOMATO ASPIC WITH SHRIMP

Fill the bottom ½ inch of a 1-quart mold with the liquid. After the ½ inch of aspic has chilled until barely set, distribute *small cooked shrimp* in a decorative pattern over the jelly, then spoon more liquid aspic over and around the shrimp and chill. When set, add remaining liquid and refrigerate until ready to unmold and serve.

FRESH TOMATO ASPIC ε⧹   (SERVES FOUR)

If you are lucky to have a garden or have an abundance of vine-ripened tomatoes from a farmers' market, it is worth making a fresh tomato aspic. Be sure to taste the tomatoes, however, because even though they may look bursting with ripeness, they can have a lot of acidity and you may need to use a little sugar; lemon juice will help to bring up the flavor. The preceding Tomato Aspic with Vegetables and the other variation, with shrimp, will both taste delicious made this way.

2 pounds ripe tomatoes, about 5 cups, chopped	Salt
1 cup water	Up to 1 teaspoon sugar (optional)
1 envelope gelatin	1 tablespoon lemon juice (optional)
1 teaspoon grated onion	
¼ cup minced celery and leaves	

Boil the tomatoes with ¾ cup of the water over medium-high heat, stirring often, for 15 minutes. Dissolve the gelatin in remaining ¼ cup cold water. Put the tomatoes through a vegetable mill or strainer, then return the purée to the pan and add onion and celery. Add salt generously to taste, and sugar and lemon, if needed. Cook 5 minutes, stirring briskly. Remove from the fire and add the gelatin, stirring until thoroughly dissolved. Turn into a 1-quart ring mold and chill until firm.

JELLIED VEGETABLE RING ε⧹   (SERVES SIX)

Vegetables should be varied according to what is in season. Young zucchini, yellow squash, and tender green beans, blanched for only 2 minutes and then chopped, are good, for instance, with pimientos for contrast. All ingredients should be cut in small cubes so that the mold can be cut neatly. Serve on a bed of lettuce or watercress with mayonnaise or Boiled Dressing (p. 706).

1 cup cold water	⅓ cup chopped cabbage
1 envelope gelatin	2 tablespoons peeled, seeded, and cubed cucumber
¼ cup sugar	
¼ cup cider vinegar	¼ cup fresh peas, blanched 1 minute, or defrosted frozen baby peas
3 tablespoons lemon juice	
1 teaspoon salt	
½ cup chopped celery	¼ cup cubed cooked beets

Mix the water, gelatin, and sugar in a saucepan; stir over low heat until dissolved. Add the vinegar, lemon juice, and salt, and chill until as thick as an unbeaten egg white. Stir in the vegetables, pour into a 4-cup ring mold, and chill.

(SERVES FOUR) **SEAFOOD ASPIC**

This may be varied with whatever combinations of seafood and fish are available, but it is interesting to have the crystal-clear aspic studded with contrasting shapes and colors.

2 cups clarified well-seasoned fish stock (p. 112)	Freshly ground pepper
1 envelope gelatin	8 medium shrimp, cooked
2 tablespoons dry white wine	8 mussels, cooked
2 tablespoons water	8 scallops or chunks of whitefish, cooked
Salt	

Heat the fish stock. Soften the gelatin in the wine and water. Add to the hot stock and mix until thoroughly dissolved. Taste, and season well with salt and pepper. Pour ½ inch of liquid into a 1-quart mold—a ring mold or a fish shape if you have one—and chill until just set. Distribute the seafood in a decorative contrasting pattern, then gently pour in the rest of the gelatin and chill until set.

(SERVES FOUR TO SIX) ✱ **CHICKEN IN LEMON ASPIC**

This is a luncheon or summer supper dish with lots of flavor of fresh lemon.

¼ cup vegetable oil	½ cup sliced celery
3-pound chicken, in 8 pieces	1 bay leaf
Salt and freshly ground pepper	½ teaspoon dried thyme
1 cup dry white wine	1½ lemons, sliced thin
1 cup white wine vinegar	2 envelopes gelatin
2½ cups chicken broth	1 bunch watercress, washed, stemmed, and dried
½ cup sliced carrots	Mustard Mayonnaise (p. 707), for garnish
½ cup sliced onion	

Heat the oil in a Dutch oven over medium heat. Add the chicken pieces, season to taste with salt and pepper, and sauté until lightly browned. Reduce the heat to low, add the wine, vinegar, 2 cups of the chicken broth, carrots, onion, celery, bay leaf, and thyme. Cut half of the lemon slices into eighths and add them to the pot. Bring to a boil, turn heat to low, cover, and simmer for 20 minutes. Meanwhile, stir the gelatin into the remaining chicken broth to soften. Set aside. When the chicken is done, remove it from the broth. Strain the broth, then add the gelatin, stirring to dissolve. Set aside to cool, then skim off the fat. Skin and bone the chicken and cut in bite-size pieces. Arrange the chicken in a shallow rectangular pan and pour the broth over; cover with plastic wrap and refrigerate for 1½ hours. Decorate the top with the reserved lemon slices; cover, and return to refrigerator until completely set, 3–4 hours. Cut in squares and serve on a bed of watercress. Garnish each portion with a dollop of Mustard Mayonnaise.

PARSLIED HAM IN ASPIC   (SERVES SIX)

Serve this pretty aspic unmolded with a bowl of Mustard Mayonnaise (p. 707) on the side.

2 envelopes gelatin	3 cups chopped ham (½-inch
¼ cup Madeira wine	dice)
2 tablespoons cold water	¾ cup chopped parsley
3½ cups hot chicken broth, clarified (p. 110)	

Soak the gelatin in the Madeira and water. Dissolve thoroughly in the hot chicken stock. Pour ½ inch of the aspic into a 2-quart mold and chill until just set. Also refrigerate the rest of the aspic. When it is the consistency of lightly beaten egg whites, fold in the ham and the parsley. Fill the mold gently with this mixture and chill until very firm.

ASPIC OF COLD BEEF
AND VEGETABLES   (SERVES EIGHT)

No one would suspect that this handsome dish was made from leftover beef; the pieces should be tender and free of fat. It requires some patience to put together while layers of aspic set, but you can be doing other kitchen tasks.

8 cups clarified beef stock (p. 108)	16 tiny cooked onions
	1 cooked beet
4 envelopes gelatin	10 slices cold cooked beef
5 whole cooked carrots, halved lengthwise	

Pour 2 cups cold stock into a small bowl, sprinkle the gelatin over, and let stand a few minutes. Heat the rest of the stock to simmering, add the gelatin mixture, and stir until completely dissolved. Remove from the heat and refrigerate until it has become syrupy. Line the bottom of a large bowl with about ¼ inch of thickened aspic, chill until firm, then add another shallow layer of aspic. Place carrots, as many as you need to fit, in rows 1½ inches apart on the bottom of the bowl. Put tiny onions in between. Cut the beet in decorative slices and place along the sides. Cover the vegetables with a thin layer of aspic and chill until firm. Place the slices of beef upright through the center of the bowl, using remaining carrot cut in small pieces to hold them evenly apart. Pour in the remaining syrupy aspic to fill the bowl. Refrigerate until firm, at least 6 hours—better overnight. Unmold and serve with a mustardy mayonnaise.

About Cream Molds and Mousses

Cream molds or mousses are made with the addition of mayonnaise and/or cream, which adds richness and greater fullness to the dish. The molds should always be lightly oiled before the mixture is poured in. They make enticing first courses, done in small shapes and turned out on a bed of watercress or shredded lettuce and garnished with something appropriate and colorful, such as black olives, a few strips of pimiento, a shrimp, if it is a fish mousse. A large mold can be served as a main course at lunch or as an important feature of a buffet table, presented on a platter surrounded by watercress or other greens. If it is a ring mold, spoon dressing inside, or serve the dressing separately in a glass dish.

Remember in making any kind of aspic that cold tends to dull flavors, and thus you want to make the seasoning a little more intense than you would for a warm dish. Taste critically before you chill, and heighten the flavors if necessary.

LEMON CHICKEN AND ASPARAGUS CREAM MOLD

(SERVES FOUR TO SIX)

1 envelope gelatin
2 tablespoons cold water
2 teaspoons lemon juice
¾ cup chicken broth
¼ pound asparagus
½ cup sour cream
½ teaspoon salt
⅛ teaspoon freshly ground pepper

Grated rind of 1 small lemon
2 scallions, finely chopped, including green part
1¼ cups finely chopped cooked chicken
¾ cup heavy cream, whipped
Watercress sprigs

Soften the gelatin in the water and lemon juice. Heat the broth, then stir in gelatin until thoroughly dissolved. Cool. Meanwhile blanch the asparagus in boiling, salted water to cover for 5 minutes. Cut off an inch of the tips and reserve for garnish. Slice the stems in thin diagonals, then quarter the slices if the stems are thick. Add to the cooled broth along with the sour cream, salt, pepper, lemon rind, scallions, and chicken, mix well, and correct seasoning. Fold in the whipped cream and pour into a lightly oiled 4-cup ring mold. Chill until set. Unmold and garnish with asparagus tips and watercress. Serve with Yogurt Dressing (p. 709).

CHICKEN AND ALMOND MOUSSE   (SERVES SIX)

A delicate summer dish that calls for Parker House Rolls (p. 738).

1 envelope gelatin	Dash of cayenne pepper
1 cup cold chicken broth	1 teaspoon chopped fresh
3 egg yolks, lightly beaten	tarragon, or ½ teaspoon
1 cup ground cooked white	dried, crumbled
chicken	Salt
½ cup ground blanched	1 cup heavy cream, beaten
almonds	stiff
Few drops fresh lemon juice	

Sprinkle the gelatin over the broth, then heat just until the gelatin has dissolved. Pour the hot liquid over the egg yolks in a steady stream, stirring vigorously, return the mixture to the saucepan, and heat gently, stirring constantly until it thickens slightly. Add the ground chicken and almonds (they may be ground very successfully in a food processor), lemon juice, cayenne pepper, and tarragon. Season liberally with salt, as chilled foods always become more bland. Chill until the mixture thickens to the consistency of an unbeaten egg white, then fold in the whipped cream. Pour into a 4-cup mold and chill.

FISH MOUSSE   (SERVES SIX)

If you have a fish-shaped mold, this delicate mousse will look very pretty when it is turned out on a platter garnished with black olives, sprigs of parsley, and lemon slices.

1 pound lean turbot or
flounder fillets, fresh or
frozen
2 cups chicken broth or fish
stock (p. 110), chilled
2 egg yolks, lighty beaten
2 envelopes gelatin
⅓ cup dry white wine
¾ pound cooked shrimp, or
1¼ cups small, canned
2 tablespoons chopped
parsley

1 tablespoon chopped scallion
greens or chives
1 tablespoon chopped fresh
basil, or ½ teaspoon dried,
crumbled
Few drops fresh lemon juice
Salt
Freshly ground pepper
Several dashes of cayenne
pepper
¾ cup heavy cream, whipped

Cover the fish fillets with cold chicken broth or fish stock and bring
slowly to a boil. Simmer about 8 minutes, until fish is opaque
through. Remove the fish and purée in a blender or in a food processor with a little of the stock. Temper the egg yolks by gradually
adding the hot stock, then return to the pan and cook gently, stirring,
until the liquid thickens enough to just coat the spoon. Remove from
the heat. Soften the gelatin in the wine and mix into the hot stock until completely dissolved. Reserving 6 shrimp for garnish, cut the remaining into ½-inch pieces and toss with the chopped herbs and
lemon juice. Combine the puréed fish, the shrimp mixture, and the
stock, and season liberally with salt, pepper, and a little cayenne pepper. Refrigerate until the mixture is somewhat thickened—about the
consistency of egg whites. Then fold in the whipped cream and pour
into a lightly oiled 3-cup mold. Refrigerate until set. Turn out and
decorate the platter with the remaining shrimp and other suggested
garnishes.

SALAD DRESSINGS

FRENCH DRESSING OR BASIC VINAIGRETTE

(SERVES FOUR)

2 tablespoons vinegar
½ teaspoon salt
¼ teaspoon freshly ground
pepper

½ cup olive or vegetable oil

In a small bowl mix the vinegar and salt and let stand a few minutes.
Add the pepper and slowly stir or whisk in the oil. Taste for acid and

salt and add more if too bland. Stir to blend before using, or store in a jar with a tight lid and shake well before using.

MUSTARDY FRENCH DRESSING

Add *1–1½ teaspoons Dijon mustard*. Blend well. Include onion and garlic, if desired.

ONION OR GARLIC FRENCH DRESSING

Add *1–2 tablespoons minced onion, scallions, or shallots* or *½–1 teaspoon minced garlic*.

FRENCH DRESSING WITH FRESH HERBS

Add *2 teaspoons fresh chopped herbs,* such as basil, chervil, or tarragon.

CURRIED FRENCH DRESSING

Add *1 teaspoon curry powder* and blend well.

CREAM FRENCH DRESSING

Add *3 tablespoons heavy cream* or *sour cream* and blend well.

FRUIT SALAD FRENCH DRESSING

Use *lemon juice* instead of vinegar and add *⅓ cup honey*. Blend well.

BLUE CHEESE DRESSING

Add *3 tablespoons crumbled blue cheese*. Blend well.

CUMBERLAND DRESSING

Add 1 tablespoon heavy cream, 1 tablespoon currant jelly, and ¼ teaspoon grated lemon rind. Mix until well blended.

CHIFFONADE DRESSING

Add 1 tablespoon minced parsley, 2 tablespoons minced red pepper, 1 tablespoon minced onion, and *2 hard-boiled eggs, chopped fine.* Blend all ingredients well.

(¾ CUP)   ₴❥ **PINEAPPLE-HONEY DRESSING**

For fruit salads.

½ cup honey	¼ cup lemon juice
3 tablespoons crushed pineapple	Salt

Put the honey, pineapple, and lemon juice in a blender or food processor and process about 15 seconds or until well blended. Add salt to taste.

(⅓ CUP)   ₴❥ **LIME DRESSING**

For fruit salads.

¼ cup vegetable oil	¼ teaspoon freshly ground
2 tablespoons lime juice	pepper
¼ teaspoon Tabasco	Salt to taste
2 teaspoons sugar	

Combine all ingredients in a jar with a snug-fitting lid. Shake until blended.

BOILED DRESSING ‏ﻪﺑ (1¼ CUPS)

Best made a day in advance. This dressing also makes a good sauce for ham.

1½ tablespoons flour	1½ tablespoons butter, melted
1 teaspoon dry mustard	¾ cup milk
1 tablespoon sugar	¼ cup vinegar
2 egg yolks, lightly beaten	Salt
Pinch of cayenne pepper	

Combine the flour, mustard, and sugar in a heavy-bottomed pan. Slowly add the yolks, cayenne pepper, melted butter, milk, and vinegar. Heat, stirring constantly, over low heat until thickened and smooth. Add salt to taste. Remove and store covered in the refrigerator until needed.

NUT DRESSING ‏ﻪﺑ (½ CUP)

For fruit salad.

5 pecan halves, blanched	¼ teaspoon sugar
10 almonds, blanched	1 tablespoon vinegar
¼ teaspoon dry mustard	⅓ cup vegetable oil
¼ teaspoon paprika	Salt
½ teaspoon catsup	

Grind the nuts or whirl in blender to pulverize. Add the mustard, paprika, catsup, sugar, and vinegar. Blend. Slowly add the oil, then salt to taste.

THOUSAND ISLAND DRESSING ‏ﻪﺑ (1¾ CUPS)

I have reworked this and it's better than ever.

1 cup mayonnaise	½ teaspoon chopped fresh
½ cup chili sauce	tarragon, or ½ teaspoon
¼ cup catsup	dried
½ tablespoon tarragon vinegar	½ tablespoon minced parsley

In a bowl, put the mayonnaise, chili sauce, catsup, vinegar, tarragon, and parsley and mix well until smooth. Store covered in the refrigerator until needed.

(1 CUP)   ?? **HANDMADE BASIC MAYONNAISE**

Have your eggs at room temperature. Always add the oil drop by drop when first incorporating it with the egg and seasonings. After emulsion has begun, the oil may be added in a slow thin stream. Be patient! If you follow these rules, you should have no trouble.

1 egg yolk	Pinch of cayenne pepper
½ teaspoon Dijon mustard or dry mustard	1 tablespoon vinegar
½ teaspoon salt	¾ cup olive or vegetable oil, or a combination of both

NOTE
see page 471

Put the yolk, mustard, salt, cayenne pepper, and vinegar in a clean bowl, put the bowl on a towel so it will remain stationary, and whisk until blended. Beat in the oil, drop by drop. As the sauce thickens, increase the flow of oil, but be slow and patient. If it should separate, follow the suggestions on p. 388 for restoring "broken" mayonnaise. The sauce, when finished, should be very thick. Taste critically and adjust the seasoning, adding a little more vinegar or salt, if necessary.

CREAM MAYONNAISE

Fold into the finished mayonnaise *½ cup heavy cream, whipped*. Serve with fruit salads, cold fish, or cold chicken.

MUSTARD MAYONNAISE

Blend *1 additional tablespoon Dijon mustard* thoroughly into the finished mayonnaise.

APPLESAUCE MAYONNAISE

Add *1 cup unsweetened applesauce* and *1 tablespoon prepared horseradish* to the finished mayonnaise and mix well. Serve with cold ham or pork.

RUSSIAN DRESSING

Add to the finished mayonnaise *1 cup chili sauce, 2 tablespoons minced celery, 2 tablespoons minced red pepper, 2 tablespoons minced green pepper,* and add more salt to taste. Blend well.

BLENDER MAYONNAISE ಌ   (1½ CUPS)

A whole egg is needed when making mayonnaise in a blender. For a food processor 1 whole egg plus 1 yolk will give you the right consistency.

1 egg
¼ teaspoon salt
½ teaspoon dry mustard, or 1 teaspoon Dijon mustard
1 cup olive, peanut, or vegetable oil (or a combination)

1½ tablespoons vinegar or lemon juice
1 tablespoon boiling water
Salt to taste

NOTE
see page 471

Place the egg, salt, mustard, and ¼ cup of the oil in the electric blender. Turn on the motor and add the remaining ¾ cup oil in a slow, thin stream. Add the vinegar or lemon juice, and water. Taste, correct the seasoning, and refrigerate until needed.

FOOD PROCESSOR MAYONNAISE

Use 1 egg *plus 1 egg yolk* and process. Add up to ½ *cup more oil* and adjust the amount of vinegar or lemon juice. Omit the water.

GREEN MAYONNAISE
(MACHINE-MADE) ಌ   (1¾ CUPS)

This must be used within a few days; after that the greens tend to turn sour. If you plan to keep it longer, blanch the greens for a minute in boiling water, then squeeze dry before using.

¾ cup fresh mixed greens:
    parsley, watercress, young
    spinach leaves
¼ cup fresh basil, tarragon, or
    dill
1 egg
1 egg yolk
Freshly ground pepper to
    taste

1 cup olive, peanut, or
    vegetable oil (or a
    combination)
1½ tablespoons mild vinegar
    or lemon juice or a
    combination
Salt to taste

NOTE
see page 471
Place the greens and the herb with the egg, egg yolk, and pepper in an electric blender or food processor and blend until the greens are puréed. Start adding the oil in a slow, thin stream until the mixture becomes too thick, then add the vinegar and/or lemon juice and continue until all the oil is used up. If too thick, add a small amount of boiling water. Taste, add salt, and refrigerate in a covered jar or bowl until needed.

HERMINE JACOB'S
✳ GREEN GODDESS DRESSING

(2 CUPS)

2-ounce can anchovy fillets
½ cup chopped parsley
3 tablespoons chopped chives
1 cup mayonnaise
1 cup sour cream

2 tablespoons tarragon
    vinegar
½ teaspoon salt
Dash of freshly ground
    pepper

Put all ingredients in a blender or food processor and blend for about 20 seconds. Cover and refrigerate until needed.

❧ YOGURT DRESSING

(1¼ CUPS)

1 cup yogurt
2 tablespoons white vinegar
1½ tablespoons lemon juice
⅛ teaspoon freshly ground
    pepper

2 tablespoons finely chopped
    chives
2 tablespoons finely chopped
    parsley
Salt to taste

Combine all ingredients in a bowl and blend until well mixed. Refrigerate and use as needed.

HONEY YOGURT DRESSING

Add 2 *tablespoons honey* and omit the chives and parsley.

YOGURT, GARLIC, AND BLUE CHEESE DRESSING

Add ¼ *cup crumbled blue cheese* and 2 *cloves garlic, chopped fine*.

YOGURT AND MAYONNAISE DRESSING

Add up to 1 *cup mayonnaise* and mix well.

ROQUEFORT OR BLUE CHEESE DRESSING ɞ   (1 CUP)

This is good on cold, crisp greens.

2 ounces Roquefort or blue cheese	1 teaspoon vinegar
¼ cup mayonnaise	1 tablespoon milk
½ cup sour cream	¼ teaspoon salt

Crumble the cheese into a small mixing bowl. Add the mayonnaise and sour cream and mix well with a fork. Add the vinegar, milk, and salt and stir to blend. Use more milk for a thinner dressing. Refrigerate until used.

LEMON SOY DRESSING ɞ   (1 CUP)

2 tablespoons soy sauce	¼ cup vegetable oil
⅓ cup fresh lemon juice	¼ cup water

Mix together well or shake in a bottle all ingredients.

TARRAGON-MUSTARD ❧ VINAIGRETTE

(ABOUT ⅓ CUP)

This is a good sauce for cooked broccoli or cauliflower.

1 tablespoon tarragon vinegar   ½ teaspoon salt
2 teaspoons Dijon mustard   ¼ cup vegetable oil

In a small bowl, whisk together the ingredients until well blended.

❧ SOUR-CREAM DRESSING

(1¼ CUPS)

For fruit salads and vegetable salads.

1 cup sour cream   1 teaspoon dry mustard
¼ cup vinegar   ⅛ teaspoon cayenne pepper
2 teaspoons sugar (for fruit   (optional)
    salad), or 1 teaspoon sugar   Salt to taste
    (for vegetable salad)

Combine all ingredients in a bowl and whisk until well blended.

❧ CLEVELAND DRESSING

(1¾ CUPS)

A very sweet dressing, for those who like them on fruit salads. You must make this 24 hours in advance of use. The fruit should be tart and include some grapefruit segments.

1 teaspoon dry mustard   ¼ cup vinegar
½ cup sugar   1 cup vegetable oil
1 teaspoon paprika   Salt

Combine the mustard, sugar, paprika, and vinegar in a bowl and chill in the refrigerator. With an electric or hand beater, slowly add the vegetable oil, beating constantly. Beat until thickened. Add salt to taste.

POPPY-SEED DRESSING

Substitute *lemon juice* for the vinegar and add *1 tablespoon poppy seeds*. Mix well.

(1 CUP)   ɜ❧ **AVOCADO MAYONNAISE**

Serve on tomatoes with salad greens, or use as a dip for tacos.

1 ripe avocado	1 teaspoon Dijon mustard
2 tablespoons milk	⅛ teaspoon Tabasco
1 tablespoon lemon juice	Salt

Peel and remove pit from avocado. Put avocado in a bowl and mash it until smooth, slowly add the milk, lemon juice, mustard, and Tabasco. Beat until smooth and blended. Add salt to taste.

YEAST BREADS

All the good bread recipes from the last edition are still here. In addition, I am giving you a formula for a crustier French bread, a method for baking doughnuts, and I have revived a recipe, which had almost been lost, for Dutch Crunch Topping that adds a flaky texture to the top of a loaf.

Don't try to bake breads in the microwave oven. It won't work. Even reheating bread in the microwave is precarious; a second too long and you can use that slice to resole your shoe.

ABOUT BREADMAKING

Baking bread at home is uniquely satisfying. It is an art involving patience, creativity, and an intuitive feeling for the constantly changing texture of the dough. It is a lovely feeling to sink your hands into the dough to mix and knead it; it's hard work but, like the best of physical exercise, thoroughly relaxing. There is a sense of mystery in watching basic ingredients like flour, water, sugar, and salt respond to the almost magical power of the yeast to lift and expand; that yeast matures according to its own timetable and cannot be hurried along to fit our crowded daily schedules commands our respect. When the yeasty smell of baking bread fills your home as it did the homes of earlier generations, when you cut thick slices of crusty, chewy, oven-warm bread baked expressly for your family and your friends, you cannot help but feel a special kind of pride and elation in your achievement.

Many families have begun to bake their own bread these days because they appreciate the wholesomeness and incomparable taste of their own product. They find that baking bread at home is no longer the time-consuming, uncertain process it once was. Modern calibrated ovens, stable, dependable yeasts, and the large variety of wholesome flours now easily available make bread baking infinitely easier today. Furthermore, there are machines that can aid you in the kneading.

Many of the bread and roll recipes in this section can be traced back to the nineteenth century, but they have all been adapted for contemporary use. Each recipe is self-contained, but we urge you to look at the general notes about ingredients and breadmaking before proceeding to the recipes. They explain basic procedures to the novice and will also refresh the memories of those who do not bake bread regularly.

Ingredients

Yeast. Yeast is what releases the gases that make the dough rise, thus lightening the bread. It is really a tiny living fungus that thrives on sweetness, warmth, and moisture. Yeast should not be rushed in its activity: given sufficient time, it will not only make dough rise but will work on the gluten in the flour to develop good flavor and texture.

Yeast comes in compressed cakes or in dry, granular form, both equally satisfactory. The compressed cakes must be stored in the refrigerator and will keep from one to two weeks; they may also be frozen but must be used immediately after defrosting. Dry yeast usually comes in ¼-ounce packages, each containing one tablespoon, but you can get it in larger amounts and measure out your own. Manufacturers tell us that one package of dry yeast is the equivalent of one ⅗-ounce cake of compressed yeast, but many home breadmakers work out their own formulas, using somewhat less dry yeast to fresh proportionately.

There is also a new variety of faster-rising yeast called rapid-rise or quick-rise. It is not dissolved first but mixed into the flour and other dry ingredients and then very hot liquid is stirred in. I find it trickier for a beginner to use because you have to watch the temperature carefully. Also, the assurance you get from dissolving the yeast and watching it become active is missing with this new method, and the time saved is really not that impressive. So these recipes call for regular dry yeast, which is available everywhere and keeps longer than yeast cakes. It should be stored in a cool, dry place; note the expiration date on each package. Should you buy your granular yeast in bulk, then be sure to proof it to make sure it is still alive and well. If you do decide to use the new fast variety, carefully follow the directions on the package.

To Proof: Yeast is usually stirred into a small amount of warm water and allowed to stand for about 5 minutes to dissolve. If you have any doubt about freshness, "proof" the yeast by dissolving it in ¼ cup of warm water and adding a teaspoon sugar and 2 tablespoons flour; if the yeast is active it will be spurred on by the sugar to feed on the flour, and within 10 minutes you will see it begin to expand and foam.

The temperature of the liquid in which yeast is dissolved is important. Yeast will not grow in a solution that is too cold, while one that is too hot will kill it. Compressed yeast should be dissolved in lukewarm water at about 100–105°F; dry yeast will tolerate somewhat warmer temperatures—about 100–115°F. It's not necessary to use a thermometer: test the water with your fingers or on your wrist and you will soon have a good feel for it.

Flour. Yeast bread depends upon wheat flour, rich in a protein called "gluten," which makes dough strong and elastic. It is capable of expanding greatly, forming a network of hundreds of little pockets to trap the yeast-produced gases which would otherwise escape from the dough. True whole-wheat flour contains all of the wheat kernel including the bran and the germ. All-purpose white flour is made from the inner part of the wheat kernel, known as the endosperm.

Bread recipes that use yeast must contain at least some white or whole-wheat flour for the gluten they provide. Bread made with gluten-rich wheat flour is a perfect food except for a slight deficiency in fat, which is probably why the custom arose of spreading bread with butter.

The hard-wheat flour used by professional bakers is richest in gluten and best for baking bread. When white flour is called for in a bread recipe, you may use either bread flour or all-purpose flour (bleached or unbleached). Bread flour will make your loaves rise a little higher, but the bread will not taste different. All-purpose flour is readily available, is widely used, and produces a highly satisfactory loaf. The unbleached variety contains none of the chemicals used for bleaching the flour, so it is less white.

Flours vary considerably and react in different ways, making it hard to specify an exact amount of flour in a bread recipe. That is one reason we suggest holding back the final cup, kneading it in only as necessary. With a little experience you will know when dough has reached the proper consistency.

There are special flours, such as rye, corn, barley, graham, soy bean, rice, and buckwheat, and meals, such as oat, corn, barley, and rye; they have good flavor and texture but *must* be used with white or whole-wheat flour in yeast-bread recipes, since they do not react to yeast. Bran, wheat germ, whole-wheat kernels, and wheat berries will add both texture and nutrients to your bread. Stoneground flours have a good, coarse texture and are generally considered to be more nutritious as well. The list of special flours and grains is lengthy: as you become more experienced, you will want to seek them out and try them in these recipes.

Liquid. It is the liquid in the dough which, during baking, turns to steam and helps create the texture of the bread. As a general rule, about 2 cups of liquid are used for 1 package of yeast and 6 cups of flour, but this proportion will vary considerably from recipe to rec-

1. oats; 2. barley; 3. rice; 4. durum wheat (hard); 5. rye; 6. buckwheat; 7. soft wheat; 8. magnified cross section of wheat kernel; 9. corn.

ipe, affecting the speed with which the dough will rise and the texture of the loaf itself.

Water, potato water, milk, or even beer can be used as the liquid. Milk produces a richer bread with a more tender crumb and a less grainy taste. Bread made with milk or potato water will keep longer than bread made with water.

Sweeteners. Sugar, used sparingly, makes the dough rise more quickly and helps brown the crust, but follow the recipe carefully, for too much sugar will inhibit the action of the yeast. Also, as an accompaniment to dinner, it is preferable not to serve a sweet bread.

Honey, molasses, corn syrup, or brown sugar can be used to sweeten bread, as can raisins and dates.

Salt. Salt is used primarily for flavor.

Shortening. Shortening is often added to enrich bread, give it flavor, and make it tender. It is not essential to any recipe, though it does make bread keep longer and better. Sometimes, when a dough is especially rich with fat, the yeast may act more slowly.

You can use butter, margarine, vegetable shortening, lard, or oil wherever shortening is called for. Vegetable shortening gives a good, crisp texture to nonsweet breads. Butter is best in rich, sweet doughs.

Breadmaking Machines

Recently there have come on the market automatic breadmaking machines that produce one loaf. You simply put the ingredients in, set the timer, and out comes a finished loaf. If you can afford one (and the machines are expensive), this provides a wonderful way of recapturing the smell and flavor of homemade baking with no effort on your part. But you miss a lot of the fun.

Mixing Dough

It is important to mix all the ingredients thoroughly and vigorously at the start so that the yeast is evenly distributed. Dough that is not well mixed at the beginning may result in a loaf with rough, coarse grain. You can use an electric beater or a wooden spoon to beat in the flour at first; once the dough becomes stiff, you'll find it easiest to use the spoon or your hands to complete the mixing. Hold back a cup of the designated amount of flour and mixing will be easier; then knead in later only what you need to keep the dough from being too sticky to handle. As the dough is mixed it will form a ball that comes away from the sides of the bowl.

Some of the recipes in this book use a "sponge" method to start: the yeast is mixed with the full amount of liquid but only part of the flour and set to rise before the remaining flour is added. We use this speedy first rising in recipes for certain rolls and buns in which an airy texture is desirable.

Kneading Dough

Kneading serves to blend all the ingredients thoroughly, to distribute the yeast evenly, and to give the dough elasticity and a smooth, even texture.

After the dough is mixed, turn it out onto a lightly floured board for kneading. If you knead it for a minute or two and then let it rest for

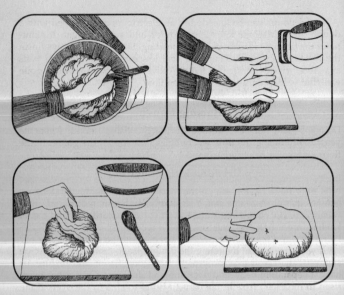

10 minutes, it will be easier to work, although it still may be a bit sticky at first.

Sprinkle the dough with a little flour and flour your hands generously. Push the dough quickly away from you, using the heels of your hands. Pull the far end of the dough toward you with your fingertips, folding it over. Give the dough a quarter-turn and repeat these two motions, using not just your arms but your whole body and setting a vigorous rhythm as you work. Knead for about 10 minutes, until the dough holds together, becomes smooth and satiny, and is no longer sticky but elastic to the touch. Depress the dough with your fingers: if it springs back, it has been kneaded enough. Don't worry about kneading too much—it can never hurt. If dough is not well kneaded, the resulting loaf may be heavy.

If you must interrupt the kneading process for more than 10 or 15 minutes, turn a bowl over the dough so that it does not dry out.

Occasionally dough will become "bucky" and develop folds that remain while you are kneading. If that should happen, slam the dough down on a hard surface several times to make it pliable.

Bread dough can be kneaded in an electric mixer equipped with a dough hook. Machine kneading is quick and very efficient. It eliminates the unique pleasure of hand kneading, but you can always finish the kneading by hand. There are also less expensive kneading pails available, which you turn by hand. And a food processor works quite well, but will do only a single loaf at a time.

Raising Dough

Dough should not be disturbed during the rising period, when the yeast is producing the little gas bubbles that stretch the gluten in the flour and make the dough expand.

The time required for dough to rise will vary considerably, depending on a number of uncontrollable factors. Thus, these recipes describe how *much* the dough should rise, rather than how *long* it will take. As a general guideline, a first rising should take two or more hours in a warm place (longer if the dough contains no sugar and is in a cool kitchen under 70°F), a second rising (if there is one) about one and one-half hours, and the final phase, in the pans, about an hour or less.

If you "overproof" by letting the dough rise to more than the recipe suggests, the bread may be yeasty, lack good flavor and texture, or have a separation between the crumb and the crust. Or if it has over-risen in the final phase in the pans, it is apt to sink in the oven. If the dough is not given sufficient time to rise, it may be too moist and heavy. If you wish to extend the rising time for your own convenience, put the bowl in the refrigerator and cover it with a plate to retard the action of the yeast.

Prepare the dough for rising by greasing a large mixing bowl and placing the ball of kneaded dough in it. Turn the dough so that it is coated on all sides, then cover the bowl with a clean towel and set it aside to rise. If you put it in a warm place (75–85°F), the dough will rise more rapidly, but if your kitchen is cool, just be patient: it will rise in time. Let the dough rise to the desired bulk. Depress the raised dough with your fingers: if the indentations remain, the dough has fully risen.

Punch the dough down with your fist to let the trapped gases escape, and knead it if the recipe suggests; usually it isn't necessary. Some recipes call for a second rising, which produces a finer-textured bread and a more developed flavor. Others proceed directly to the final rising—after the dough has been shaped and put in a loaf pan or on a baking sheet. The loaves are covered with a towel and set in a

warm place until the dough has risen the required amount. Remember
to preheat the oven when the dough is almost ready to bake.

If the dough should rise too much in the pan, punch it down, knead
it for a minute or two, reshape it, and let it rise again in the pan.

Forming Loaves

Once you have tried a few of the techniques we suggest for shaping
loaves, you will find the way that seems most natural to you and will
probably stick to it. Remember that part of the charm of homemade
bread is in its appearance: seams and little imperfections keep it from
being factory-perfect and make each loaf original.

Begin by cutting the dough with a knife into two or more parts, ac-

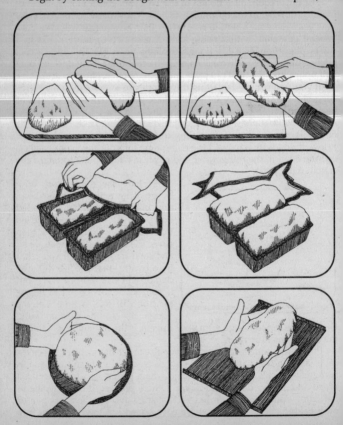

cording to the number of loaves the recipe makes. Pat each piece into a ball and let it rest while you grease the bread pans.

There are many ways of shaping a loaf, but this procedure is so easy and satisfactory that there really is no need to master more complicated techniques, unless you wish to play around with them. Simply pat the dough into an oval approximately the length of your bread pan. Then plump it up by drawing your hand down the sides, gently stretching the dough toward the bottom to make a smooth shape. If there is a fold on the bottom, pinch it together, but this is not absolutely necessary. Place the dough in the pan, with the seams or creases on the bottom. The ends should touch the sides of

---

IMPORTANT POINTS ABOUT YEAST BREAD

1. If you buy yeast in bulk, a scant tablespoon equals 1 package dry active yeast.
2. Do not have the water too hot when adding it to the yeast or it will kill it. It should be approximately 115°F. (For advice about fast-rising yeast, see p. 714.)
3. Plain warm water or potato water works the fastest for dissolving. Don't drown the yeast; ½ cup is sufficient to dissolve 1 tablespoon.
4. The proportion of flour to liquid can be given only as a close but not exact amount. Use only enough flour to make the dough manageable. "Manageable" means you should be able to knead the dough without constantly flouring your hands or the work surface.
5. Wheat flour is the only flour that has gluten, which is essential for the bread to rise. Gluten makes the dough strong and elastic.
6. Too much grain or flour that does not have gluten in it will make a very crumbly loaf that is hard to keep intact when slicing it.
7. Sugar, used sparingly, makes the dough rise more quickly and gives balanced flavor to the loaf.
8. Salt is for balanced flavor.
9. The addition of shortening or fat in bread helps keep it from getting stale.
10. Kneaded yeast bread doesn't get stale as fast as a yeast batter bread or quick bread.
11. Loaf pans should be filled one-half to two-thirds full. They come in two standard sizes: 9 × 5 × 3 inches and 8½ × 4½ × 2½ inches. Either size can be used in these recipes; the smaller size is preferable, as it produces a higher loaf.

the pan; if they don't or if the shape seems uneven, just pat it to even out.

You can also make free-form shapes by plumping the dough into a round or oval loaf. To make the round shape, draw your hands down the sides, stretching the dough and turning it, until you have a perfect round; pinch the bottom where the dough comes together. An oval is shaped very much like the simple forming of the loaf for the bread pan above; simply taper the ends so that the loaf swells more in the center. Let these loaves rise on a greased cookie sheet, which will then go straight into the oven for baking.

Baking Bread

Baking kills the action of the yeast. When bread is baked properly, it will be well browned and will pull away from the sides of the pan and slip out easily.

Loaf pans should be filled one-half to two-thirds full. They come in two standard sizes: $9 \times 5 \times 3$ inches and $8\frac{1}{2} \times 4\frac{1}{2} \times 2\frac{1}{2}$ inches. Either size can be used in these recipes; the smaller size is preferable, as it produces a higher loaf. You can also get high, domed loaves by doubling a two-loaf recipe and baking three loaves in $9 \times 5 \times 3$-inch pans.

The standard test to see if bread is done is to tap the bottom and listen for a hollow sound, but bread often sounds hollow when it is not yet done, so it is best to bake it for the full recommended time. A standard loaf needs 40–55 minutes in a 375°F oven, depending on the flours and meal used. If you have any question, you can put a bread back in the hot pan and bake it a little longer. Sometimes a loaf is removed from the pan when it's done and put back on the oven rack for a final crisping.

For a hard, crisp crust, brush the bread with cold water several times during baking. If you prefer a soft crust, brush the bread with milk or melted butter. Or mix an egg yolk with a tablespoon of milk for a glaze which will make the crust golden and shiny.

If you wish, you can make a few diagonal slashes, about ½ inch deep, across the top of the bread, using a sharp knife. The slashes are decorative and they will prevent cracking.

Cooling and Storing Bread

Remove the loaf from the pan immediately after taking it from the oven and let it cool on a rack. Cover it with a dishtowel while it is cooling if you want a soft crust.

Do not wrap bread until it is thoroughly cool. Store it in a plastic bag or wrapped in foil, in or out of the refrigerator. Most breads taste best the first or second day after baking, although some will keep longer, especially those that are very moist or are made from dough that is rich in butter and milk.

Bread freezes well. You can often save both time and money by doubling a recipe and freezing what you do not immediately need. You can even freeze half a loaf, if you wish. To defrost, reheat the bread, wrapped in foil and still frozen, in a 350°F oven for about 30 minutes. Or simply let the bread defrost at room temperature for about 3 hours and crisp it in a hot oven for a few minutes before serving.

Stale bread can be used for toast, stuffing, bread pudding, or croutons, or you can use a rolling pin, a blender, or a food processor to make it into bread crumbs.

LOAF BREADS (KNEADED)

(2 LOAVES)   **WHITE BREAD**

A pure, tender loaf, exactly what a basic white bread should be.

2 tablespoons shortening or vegetable oil	1 cup hot water
2 teaspoons salt	1 package dry yeast
2 tablespoons sugar	¼ cup warm water
1 cup hot milk	6 cups white flour, approximately

Mix the shortening, salt, and sugar in a large bowl, add the hot milk and hot water, and let cool to lukewarm. In a small bowl or cup mix the yeast with the warm water and let it stand for 5 minutes to dissolve. Add the dissolved yeast and 3 cups of the flour to the first mixture and beat until well blended. Add 2 more cups of flour, mix, and turn out onto a lightly floured board. Knead for a minute or two and then let rest for 10 minutes. Adding just enough of the remaining flour so that the dough is not sticky, resume kneading until the dough is smooth and elastic. Put the dough in a large, greased bowl, cover, and let rise in a warm spot until double in bulk. Punch down and shape into two loaves. Place in greased loaf pans, cover, and let double in bulk again. Preheat oven to 425°F. Bake bread for 15 minutes, reduce heat to 375°F, and bake for 30 minutes more. Remove from pans and cool on racks.

CHEESE BREAD

Mix *1½ cups grated Cheddar or other sharp cheese* with the last flour added.

ITALIAN HERB AND CHEESE BREAD

Mix 2 *cloves garlic, minced*, 1 *cup grated Parmesan cheese*, and ¼ *cup chopped fresh basil or 2 tablespoons dried basil, crumbled*, and add with the last batch of flour.

CINNAMON SWIRL BREAD

After the dough has been punched down, divide the dough in half and pat each half into a piece about 8 inches square. Combine ½ cup sugar with 5 teaspoons cinnamon and sprinkle the sugar mixture over each square of dough. Roll each piece and place in a greased loaf pan. Bake as directed above.

WHOLE-WHEAT BREAD (2 LOAVES)

You'll get fine-textured wheat slices with a whole-grain flavor from these loaves.

½ cup water
1 cup milk
¼ cup sugar
2 teaspoons salt
½ cup warm water

1 package dry yeast
2 cups whole-wheat flour
4 cups white flour,
   approximately

Bring ½ cup water to a boil, mix it with the milk, sugar, and salt in a large bowl, and let cool to lukewarm. In a separate container, measure ½ cup warm water, stir in the yeast, and let it stand for 5 minutes to dissolve. Add the dissolved yeast, the whole-wheat flour, and 2 cups of the white flour to the first mixture. Beat thoroughly, then turn out onto a lightly floured board, adding enough flour so that the dough handles easily. Knead for a few minutes and let rest for 10 minutes. Add as much of the remaining flour as necessary to keep the dough from being sticky. Resume kneading for 10 minutes or until the dough is smooth and elastic. Place in a greased bowl, cover, and let rise in a warm spot until double in bulk. Punch down and shape into two loaves. Place in greased loaf pans, cover, and let rise again until almost double. Preheat oven to 375°F. Bake bread for about 45 minutes. Remove from pans and cool on racks.

WHOLE-WHEAT BREAD WITH WHEAT BERRIES

Simmer ½–¾ cup dry wheat berries in water to cover for several hours or until soft. Drain and knead them into the Whole-Wheat Bread dough after the first rising.

WHOLE-WHEAT BREAD WITH WHEAT GERM

Mix ½ cup wheat germ in with the flour.

WHOLE-WHEAT OATMEAL BREAD

Knead in 1 cup uncooked rolled oats with the whole-wheat flour. You will need ½–1 cup less of the white flour if you add the oats.

WHOLE-WHEAT OAT BRAN BREAD

Knead 1 cup oat bran with the whole-wheat flour. You will need a little less white flour.

(2 LOAVES)   **CRACKED-WHEAT BREAD**

A good brown crust, nice tender crumb, and bits of cracked wheat make this a perfect loaf to balance a supper salad.

½ cup water	1 package dry yeast
1 cup milk	1 cup cracked wheat
¼ cup molasses	1 cup whole-wheat flour
2 teaspoons salt	4 cups white flour,
½ cup warm water	approximately

Bring ½ cup water to a boil, mix it with the milk, molasses, and salt in a large bowl, and let cool to lukewarm. In a separate container, measure ½ cup warm water, stir in the yeast, and let it stand for 5 minutes to dissolve. Add the dissolved yeast, cracked wheat, whole-wheat flour, and 1 cup of the white flour to the first mixture and beat thoroughly. Add most of the remaining 3 cups of flour and beat well. Turn out onto a lightly floured board, knead for a minute or two, and let rest for 10 minutes. Resume kneading until the dough is smooth and elastic, adding the remaining flour only if necessary. Place in a greased bowl, cover, and let rise in a warm place until double in bulk. Punch down and form into two loaves. Place in greased loaf pans, cover and let rise until almost double in bulk. Preheat the oven to 375°F. Bake bread for 45–50 minutes. Remove from pans and cool on racks.

WATER BREAD AND ROLLS   (1 LOAF AND 8 ROLLS)

Light and tender, good with delicate, subtle dishes.

1 tablespoon butter	¼ cup warm water
1 tablespoon shortening	1 package dry yeast
1 tablespoon sugar	6 cups white flour,
1½ teaspoons salt	approximately
2 cups water	

Mix the butter, shortening, sugar, and salt in a large bowl. Bring 2 cups water to a boil, add it to mixture, and let cool to lukewarm. Measure ¼ cup warm water in a separate container, add the yeast, and let it stand for 5 minutes to dissolve. Add the dissolved yeast and 5 cups of the flour to the first mixture and mix thoroughly. Turn out onto a lightly floured board and let rest for about 10 minutes. Adding as much of the remaining flour as necessary, knead until smooth and elastic. Place the dough in a large, buttered bowl, cover, and let rise in a warm place until double in bulk. Punch the dough down and knead it once or twice. Half-fill a buttered loaf pan; break the remaining dough into pieces the size of small lemons and arrange them, sides touching, on a buttered 9-inch pie plate. Cover the pan and the pie plate and let the dough double in bulk once again. Preheat the oven to 375°F. Bake bread, allowing about 25 minutes for the rolls and about 45 minutes for the loaf. Remove from pans and cool on racks.

OATMEAL BREAD ✳   (2 LOAVES)

Honey-colored, chewy, and moist with a distinct molasses flavor.

1 cup instant oats	2 teaspoons salt
2 cups water	1 tablespoon butter or
1 package dry yeast	vegetable oil
¼ cup warm water	5½ cups white flour,
½ cup molasses	approximately

Put the oats in a large bowl. Bring 2 cups water to a boil, pour it over oats, and let stand for at least 15 minutes. Stir the yeast into ¼ cup warm water and let it stand for 5 minutes to dissolve. Feel the oats at the bottom of the bowl to be sure they're lukewarm, then add the molasses, salt, butter, and dissolved yeast. Work in enough of the flour so that the dough is easy to handle. Turn out onto a lightly floured board, knead for a minute or two, and let rest for 10 minutes. Resume kneading until the dough is smooth and elastic, adding more flour as necessary. Place in a greased bowl, cover, and let rise in a warm spot until double in bulk. Punch down and shape into two loaves. Place in buttered loaf pans, cover, and let rise again until double in bulk. Preheat oven to 375°F. Bake bread for 45 minutes. Remove from pans and cool on racks.

OATMEAL BREAD WITH HONEY

Use ⅓ *cup honey* instead of molasses.

(2 LOAVES)   ## RYE BREAD

Rye flour will remain a bit sticky, even when it has been thoroughly kneaded. This recipe makes a light, moist loaf.

1 cup water	½ cup warm water
1 cup milk	2 packages dry yeast
2 tablespoons shortening or vegetable oil	3 cups rye flour, approximately
2 tablespoons dark-brown sugar	3 cups white flour, approximately
1 tablespoon salt	

Bring 1 cup water to a boil, mix it with the milk, shortening, sugar, and salt in a large bowl, and let cool to lukewarm. Measure ½ cup warm water in a separate container, stir in yeast, and let it stand for 5 minutes to dissolve. Add the dissolved yeast and the rye flour to the first mixture and combine thoroughly. Add enough of the white flour so that you can handle the dough. Turn out onto a lightly floured board, knead for a minute or two, then let rest for 10 minutes. Resume kneading for about 10 minutes, adding the remaining flour as necessary. Put the dough in a greased bowl, cover, and let rise in a warm place until almost double in bulk. Punch down and shape into two loaves. Place in greased loaf pans, cover, and let rise again until double in bulk. Preheat oven to 375°F. Bake bread for 45–50 minutes. Remove from pans and cool on racks.

CRUSTY FRENCH BREAD

(4 LOAVES,
ABOUT 14 × 2½ INCHES)

This recipe makes long, crusty, slender loaves with a soft, chewy center. The bread goes stale in a day, so freeze any extra wrapped tightly in foil or plastic wrap.

1 package dry yeast
2½ cups warm water
1 tablespoon salt
6½–7½ cups all-purpose flour,
    approximately

2 tablespoons cornmeal (for
    the baking sheets)
1 egg white, lightly beaten
    with 1 tablespoon cold
    water

Dissolve the yeast in ¼ cup of the warm water in a large mixing bowl, and let it stand a minute or so to dissolve. Add the remaining 2¼ cups water, the salt, and 5 cups of the flour, and beat vigorously until well mixed. Add enough additional flour to make a manageable dough, then turn out onto a lightly floured surface and knead for a minute or two. Let rest for 10 minutes. Resume kneading, adding just enough additional flour to keep the dough from being sticky, and knead for about 8–10 minutes, until smooth and elastic. Place in a large greased bowl, cover with plastic wrap, and let rise until double in bulk. (This first rise might take 2 or more hours, because of the small amount of yeast in proportion to the flour.) Punch the dough down and divide into four equal parts. On a lightly floured surface, use the palms of your hands to roll each piece into a rope about 14 inches long and 1¾–2 inches across; don't worry if it is slightly irregular. Place the formed loaves in greased French bread pans, or about 3 inches apart on large baking sheets that have been generously sprinkled with cornmeal. Spray a fine mist of water over each, cover lightly with plastic wrap, and let rise in a warm spot for 40 minutes. Carefully remove the plastic wrap, and brush each risen loaf with the egg-white glaze. Using a sharp knife or razor blade, slash each loaf at an angle lengthwise three times. Place in a preheated 450°F oven and bake for 15 minutes, then spray with a fine mist of water and lower the oven temperature to 375°F. Bake for 15 minutes more, then spray the loaves again. Bake for 10–15 minutes more, until the crust is dark golden. Remove the loaves and cool on racks.

GARLIC BREAD

Smash 2 *cloves garlic*, remove peel, and finely chop. Mix together with *6 tablespoons softened butter*, blending thoroughly. Cut 1 loaf French Bread in diagonal slices without cutting all the way through. Spread the garlic butter between the slices, wrap the bread in foil, and heat in a preheated 400°F oven until very hot, about 20 minutes.

(2 LOAVES) **GERMAN CARAWAY BREAD**

A dense, chewy loaf distinctly flavored with rye and caraway. Rye flour makes a sticky dough; if you flour your hands well, it will be easier to handle.

1 cup water	¼ cup warm water
1 cup milk	2 packages dry yeast
2 tablespoons shortening	2 cups white flour,
2 teaspoons salt	approximately
1 tablespoon sugar	4 cups rye flour,
1 tablespoon caraway seeds	approximately

Bring 1 cup water to a boil, mix it with the milk, shortening, salt, sugar, and caraway seeds in a large bowl, and let cool to lukewarm. In a separate container, measure ¼ cup warm water, stir in the yeast, and let it stand for 5 minutes to dissolve. Add the dissolved yeast and the white flour to the first mixture and combine well. Beat in about 3 cups of the rye flour, or enough to make a moderately stiff dough. Turn out onto a lightly floured board, knead for a few minutes, and then let rest for 10 minutes. Resume kneading for about 10 minutes, adding the remaining rye flour as necessary; the dough will be a bit sticky even when thoroughly kneaded. Put the dough in a greased bowl, cover, and let rise in a warm spot until double in bulk. Punch down and form into two loaves. Place in greased loaf pans, cover, and let rise again until almost double in bulk. Or shape into two rounds or ovals and place on a greased cookie sheet, cover, and let rise. Preheat oven to 375°F. Bake bread for about 45 minutes. Remove from pans or cookie sheet and cool on racks.

(1 LOAF AND 6 ROLLS) **BRIOCHE BREAD AND ROLLS**

Bread and rolls with a mildly sweet, pale yellow crumb and the gentle flavor of lemons and butter.

2 packages dry yeast	½ cup sugar
1 cup warm milk	1½ teaspoons salt
⅔ cup butter	Grated rind of 1 lemon
1 egg	5½ cups white flour,
4 egg yolks	approximately

Stir the yeast into the milk in a large mixing bowl and let it stand for 5 minutes to dissolve. Add the butter, egg, egg yolks, sugar, salt, lemon rind, and about 2½ cups of the flour. Beat thoroughly, then add as much of the remaining flour as is necessary for a dough that handles easily. Turn out onto a lightly floured board. Knead for a minute or two and let rest for 10 minutes. Continue to knead until smooth and elastic. Put the dough in a large, buttered bowl, cover, and let rise in a warm spot until double in bulk. Punch down and let it rise again until slightly less than double in bulk, for at least 4 hours or in a covered bowl in the refrigerator overnight. Butter a loaf pan and a 6-cup muffin pan and fill them one-third full. Cover and let double once again. Preheat oven to 375°F. Bake bread, allowing about 20 minutes for the rolls and 45 minutes for the bread. Remove from pans and cool on racks.

MEXICAN BREAD ✳   (2 LARGE LOAVES)

This bread is full of the snappy flavors of peppers and cheese and the cornmeal gives it a slightly coarse texture.

½ cup warm water	½ cup vegetable oil
2 packages dry yeast	1 cup creamed corn
1 cup yellow cornmeal	5 cups all-purpose flour,
2 teaspoons salt	approximately
1 tablespoon sugar	1½ cups grated Cheddar
½ teaspoon baking soda	cheese
2 eggs	¼ cup chopped mild green
1 cup buttermilk	chilies, fresh or canned

Put the warm water in a large mixing bowl and stir in the yeast. Let stand to dissolve for 5 minutes. Add the cornmeal, salt, sugar, and baking soda and beat until well mixed. Add the eggs, buttermilk, oil, corn, and 2 cups of flour. Beat vigorously until well blended. Add the cheese and chilies and stir in enough flour to make the dough manageable. Turn out and knead until the cheese and chilies are well distributed. Let the dough rest 10 minutes. Resume kneading until the dough becomes smooth and elastic. Put the dough into a greased bowl, cover with plastic wrap, and let stand until the dough doubles in bulk. Punch down the dough. Divide the dough in half and form into two loaves. Place in two greased 9 × 5 × 3-inch loaf pans, cover lightly, and let rise to the tops of the pans. Bake in a preheated 350°F oven for 50–60 minutes. Remove from pans and cool on racks.

COLONIAL BREAD   (2 LOAVES)

A honey-colored bread, dotted with pieces of pecan and candied orange peel.

½ cup water
1 cup milk
¼ cup honey
2 teaspoons salt
1 package dry yeast
½ cup warm water

4 cups white flour
2 cups whole-wheat flour,
    approximately
½ cup finely chopped candied
    orange peel
1 cup pecans, in coarse pieces

Bring ½ cup water to a boil, mix it with the milk, honey, and salt in a large bowl, and let cool to lukewarm. In a separate container, stir the yeast into ½ cup warm water and let it stand for 5 minutes to dissolve. Add the dissolved yeast and 3 cups of the white flour to the first mixture and beat vigorously. Add the remaining cup of white flour and 1 cup of the whole-wheat flour and mix well. Turn it out onto a lightly floured board, knead for a minute or two, and let rest for 10 minutes. Using the remaining flour only if the dough is too sticky to handle, resume kneading until smooth and elastic. Place the dough in a greased bowl, cover, and let rise in a warm place until double in bulk. Punch down and knead in the candied orange peel and the pecans. Shape into two loaves, place in greased loaf pans, cover, and let rise until almost double in bulk. Preheat oven to 375°F. Bake bread for 45–55 minutes. Remove from pans and cool on racks.

(2 LOAVES)   **CORNELL BREAD**

This high-protein bread was developed for use in public institutions and has been acclaimed for providing excellent nutritional value at low cost. A creamy, light-textured loaf laced with tiny flecks of wheat germ, it is not only health-giving but appealing in looks and taste.

1 cup water
1 cup milk
2 tablespoons shortening
1 tablespoon salt
2 tablespoons brown sugar
½ cup warm water

1 package dry yeast
6 tablespoons soy flour
6 tablespoons nonfat dry milk
2 tablespoons wheat germ
5 cups white flour,
    approximately

Bring 1 cup water to a boil, mix it with the milk, shortening, salt, and sugar in a large bowl, and let cool to lukewarm. In a separate container, measure ½ cup warm water, stir in the yeast, and let it stand for 5 minutes to dissolve. Add the dissolved yeast, soy flour, dry milk, wheat germ, and 2 cups of the white flour to the first mixture and beat until well blended. Add 2 more cups of the white flour, mix, and turn out onto a lightly floured board. Knead for a minute or two and then let rest for 10 minutes. Adding just enough of the remaining flour so that the dough is not sticky, resume kneading until smooth and elastic. Put the dough in a large greased bowl, cover, and let rise in a warm spot until double in bulk. Punch down and shape into two loaves. Place in greased loaf pans, cover, and let rise again until double in bulk. Preheat oven to 375°F. Bake bread for 45–50 minutes. Remove from pans and cool on racks.

BRAN AND HONEY BREAD   (2 LOAVES)

Sweet, light, and wholesome.

1 cup water	1 package dry yeast
1 tablespoon butter	¼ cup warm water
¼ cup honey	1 cup bran
2½ teaspoons salt	5 cups white flour,
1 cup milk	approximately

Bring 1 cup water to a boil, mix it with the butter, honey, salt, and milk in a large bowl, and let cool to lukewarm. In a separate container, stir the yeast into ¼ cup warm water and let it stand for 5 minutes to dissolve. Add the dissolved yeast, the bran, and 2 cups of the white flour to the first mixture and stir vigorously. Add 2 more cups of white flour and mix well. Turn out onto a lightly floured board and let rest for 10 minutes. Adding as much of the remaining flour as necessary to keep the dough from sticking, knead until smooth and elastic—about 10 minutes. Put the dough in a greased bowl, cover, and let rise in a warm place until double in bulk. Punch down and shape into two loaves. Place in greased loaf pans, cover, and let rise again until double in bulk. Preheat oven to 425°F. Bake bread for 10 minutes, reduce heat to 375°F, and continue to bake for 30–35 minutes more. Remove from pans and cool on racks.

RAISIN AND NUT BREAD   (2 LOAVES)

A soft-crumbed, tender loaf. It's good toasted, too—with honey.

1 cup water	1 package dry yeast
1 cup milk	6 cups white flour,
4 tablespoons butter	approximately
¼ cup sugar	¾ cup raisins
1 tablespoon salt	¾ cup chopped nuts
½ cup warm water	

Bring 1 cup water to a boil, mix it with the milk, butter, sugar, and salt in a large bowl, and let cool to lukewarm. In a separate container, measure ½ cup warm water, stir in the yeast, and let it stand for 5 minutes to dissolve. Add the dissolved yeast and 3 cups of the flour to the first mixture and combine thoroughly. Add the raisins and nuts. Work in enough of the remaining flour so that the dough is easy to handle. Turn out onto a lightly floured board, knead for a few minutes, and let rest for 10 minutes. Resume kneading until the dough is smooth and elastic. Put the dough in a buttered bowl, cover, and let rise in a warm spot until double in bulk. Punch down and shape into two loaves. Place in buttered loaf pans, cover, and let rise again until almost double in bulk. Preheat oven to 375°F. Bake bread for 45–55 minutes. Remove from pans and cool on racks.

(2 LOAVES)   ✳ **DUTCH CRUNCH TOPPING**

Bakeries used to make their breads look and taste terrific with this topping. The secret had all but disappeared years ago. The idea originally came from an old *Sunset* magazine recipe, and as a guide I have made some variations and adapted their recipe. Here is my version with some changes. Dutch Crunch splits and cracks as it bakes and forms a golden, crusty top to loaves, rolls, or buns.

2½ teaspoons sugar
2 packages dry yeast
¼ teaspoon salt
6 tablespoons rice flour (do not use the Oriental or sweet rice flour)

1 teaspoon vegetable oil
⅓ cup warm water, approximately (about 110°F)

When your dough is in a bowl for its first rise, make the topping. In a 4-cup bowl, stir together the sugar, yeast, salt, and rice flour. Add the vegetable oil and warm water and stir to blend well. Some rice flours will thicken more than others so add liquid until the mixture resembles a thick paste. Cover and let rise in a warm place until very bubbly and at least doubled in size; this will take about 30 minutes. When the dough is shaped, stir down and spread half of the mixture evenly over the top of each loaf. (If you have to delay the shaping of the loaves, stir down the topping and set aside.) Let rise again as directed in the basic bread recipe, then bake.

LOAF BREADS (BATTER)

Batter breads are much quicker to make because they require no kneading. After the yeast is dissolved, all the ingredients are combined and beaten well, preferably with an electric beater. The dough is then set to rise. Batter breads are the easiest kind of yeast breads to make, and people who are afraid of kneading or lack the arm power seem more secure making them. Since the gluten in the flour is not developed through kneading, they usually have a coarser, more porous texture than kneaded breads and will get stale more quickly.

ANADAMA BREAD (2 LOAVES)

Brown and crusty with a chewy, springy texture, this old-fashioned batter bread, quick and easy to make, is an American classic.

½ cup yellow cornmeal	½ cup molasses
2 cups water	2 teaspoons salt
1 package dry yeast	1 tablespoon butter
½ cup warm water	4½ cups white flour

Put the cornmeal in a large mixing bowl. Bring 2 cups water to a boil and pour it over the cornmeal. Stir until smooth, making sure that the cornmeal does not lump. Let stand for 30 minutes. Stir the yeast into ½ cup warm water and let it stand for 5 minutes to dissolve. Add the molasses, salt, butter, and dissolved yeast to the cornmeal mixture. Stir in the flour and beat thoroughly. Spoon into 2 buttered loaf pans, cover, and let rise in a warm spot until double in bulk. Preheat oven to 350°F. Bake bread for 45–50 minutes. Remove from pans and cool on racks.

ENTIRE WHEAT BREAD (1 LOAF)

The original recipe for this batter bread called for "entire wheat flour"—made from whole kernels of wheat with only the outer husk removed before grinding—which was probably not very different from the excellent, finely milled whole-wheat flours available in supermarkets today. Unusually tender and refined, it is a splendid wheat bread and requires no kneading.

2 cups hot milk	1 package dry yeast
⅓ cup molasses	¼ cup warm water
1½ teaspoons salt	4⅓ cups whole-wheat flour

Mix the milk, molasses, and salt in a large bowl and let cool to lukewarm. Stir the yeast into the warm water and let it stand for 5 minutes to dissolve. Add the dissolved yeast and the flour to the first mixture. Beat well, cover, and let rise in a warm place until double in bulk. Beat briefly and turn into a greased loaf pan. Cover and let rise again to not quite double in bulk. Preheat oven to 375°F. Bake bread for about 45 minutes. Remove from pan and cool on a rack.

(1 LOAF) **CINCINNATI COFFEE BREAD**

This bread is reminiscent of coffee cake; good toasted with your morning coffee.

1 cup hot milk
⅓ cup sugar
5 tablespoons butter
1 teaspoon salt

1 package dry yeast
¼ cup warm water
2 eggs, well beaten
4 cups white flour

Filling

1 cup bread crumbs
3 tablespoons sugar

1 tablespoon cinnamon
4 tablespoons butter, melted

Mix the milk, sugar, butter, and salt in a large bowl and let cool to lukewarm. Stir the yeast into the warm water and let stand for 5 minutes to dissolve. Add the dissolved yeast, eggs, and flour to the first mixture and beat very well. Cover and let rise until double in bulk. Stir down with a spoon and beat thoroughly. Spoon into a buttered loaf pan. Mix the filling ingredients together and stir them into the batter, just barely swirling the filling through. Cover the pan, and let rise again until double in bulk. Preheat oven to 350°F. Bake loaf for about 40–50 minutes. Remove from pan and cool on rack.

(2 LOAVES) **THIRD BREAD**

Called "third bread" because of the three types of flours—actually, two flours and one meal—that go into it, this is better balanced and lighter than most loaves made with several flours and requires no kneading.

1 package dry yeast
2 cups warm water
½ cup molasses
1½ teaspoons salt

1 cup rye flour
3 cups white flour
1 cup yellow cornmeal

In a large bowl stir the yeast into 2 cups warm water and let it stand for 5 minutes to dissolve. Add the molasses and salt and stir well. Beat in the rye flour, white flour, and cornmeal. Cover and put in a warm place until the dough doubles in bulk. Beat again briefly and form into two loaves. Place in greased loaf pans, cover, and let double in bulk once again. Preheat oven to 375°F. Bake bread for about 45 minutes. Remove from pans and cool on racks.

GRAHAM BREAD   (2 LOAVES)

Graham flour, a coarsely milled whole-wheat flour that includes the
bran, was developed by the Reverend Sylvester Graham in the nineteenth century. A fat slice of this satisfying, richly flavored batter
bread, some cheese, and a pear make a splendid lunch.

⅓ cup molasses or honey	1 package dry yeast
1½ teaspoons salt	3 cups white flour
2¾ cups warm water	3 cups graham flour

Mix the molasses or honey, salt, and 2½ cups warm water in a large
bowl; let cool to lukewarm. Stir the yeast into the remaining ¼ cup
warm water and let it stand for 5 minutes to dissolve. Add the dissolved yeast, the white flour, and 2½ cups of the graham flour to the
lukewarm molasses mixture and beat well. Slowly add the remaining
graham flour. Cover and let rise in a warm place until double in bulk.
Beat again briefly and divide the dough evenly into two greased loaf
pans. Cover and let rise to the tops of the pans. Preheat oven to 375°F.
Bake bread for about 45 minutes. Remove from pans and cool on racks.

ROLLS, DOUGHNUTS, AND COFFEE CAKES

STANDARD ROLLS   (2½–3 DOZEN ROLLS)

With this basic recipe you can make fine, light rolls and biscuits in a
variety of shapes.

4 tablespoons butter	¼ cup warm water
2 tablespoons sugar	6 cups white flour,
2 teaspoons salt	approximately
2 cups warm milk	Melted butter
1 package dry yeast	

Mix the butter, sugar, salt, and milk in a large bowl and let cool to
lukewarm. Stir the yeast into the warm water and let it stand for 5 minutes to dissolve. Add 3 cups of the flour and the dissolved yeast to the
first mixture and beat vigorously for 2 minutes. Cover and let rise in a
warm place until double in bulk. Stir the dough vigorously and add as
much of the remaining flour as necessary in order to knead the dough.
Turn out onto a lightly floured board, knead for a minute or two, and
let rest for 10 minutes. Resume kneading until smooth. Shape (see following suggestions). Arrange the shaped dough in buttered muffin

tins or close together on buttered cookie sheets, brushing between them with melted butter so that they separate easily after baking. Cover and let rise again until double in bulk. Preheat oven to 425°F. Bake rolls for about 12–15 minutes.

Shaping Rolls

BISCUITS

Using a rolling pin, roll out the dough for Standard Rolls on a lightly floured board until it is ⅓ inch thick; cut with a small, round biscuit cutter. Or shape the dough into a long, thin cylinder and with a floured knife cut off pieces about ⅓ inch thick.

FINGER ROLLS

Cut the dough for Standard Rolls as you would for Biscuits, then roll each piece with one hand on an unfloured board into a long, thin oval.

1. biscuits;   *2. finger rolls;*

CLOVER LEAF ROLLS

Shape the dough for Standard Rolls into 1-inch balls, brush with *melted butter*, and place three balls in each section of a buttered muffin tin.

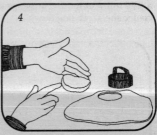

3. clover leaf rolls;   4. Parker House rolls;

PARKER HOUSE ROLLS

Using a rolling pin, roll out the dough for Standard Rolls until it is ⅛ inch thick and cut with a round biscuit cutter or with an oval Parker House roll cutter. Using the dull edge of a knife, make a crease through the center of each piece of dough, brush with *melted butter*, fold in half along the crease, and press edges lightly together. Place 1 inch apart on a buttered cookie sheet.

BOWKNOTS OR TWISTS

Using your hands, roll thin strips of the dough for Standard Rolls into sticks 8–10 inches long. Twist them or tie them loosely in knots.

BUTTER ROLLS

Using a rolling pin, roll the dough for Standard Rolls into a rectangle about 12 × 16 inches. Spread with *softened butter*. Cut lengthwise into four strips and stack them evenly in a pile. Cut into 1-inch pieces and arrange them on their sides in a buttered muffin tin.

PINWHEEL BISCUITS

Using a rolling pin, roll out the dough for Standard Rolls until it is ¼ inch thick and spread it with *softened butter*. Roll from the long side like a jelly roll. Cut in ¾-inch pieces and place close together on a buttered cookie sheet, cut side down.

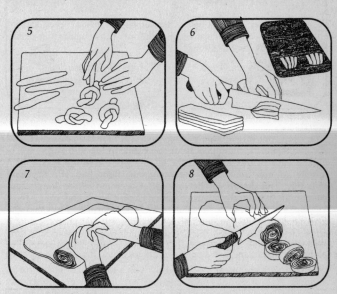

5. bowknots or twists; 6. butter rolls; 7. & 8. pinwheel biscuits.

(12 ROLLS)

FEATHER ROLLS

Feather rolls, as their name indicates, are high and very light.

1 package dry yeast	¾ teaspoon salt
¼ cup warm water	1 egg
4 tablespoons butter, softened	¾ cup warm milk
1 tablespoon sugar	2 cups white flour

Stir the yeast into the warm water and let it stand for 5 minutes to dissolve. Mix the butter, sugar, salt, egg, milk, and dissolved yeast in a large bowl and beat until smooth. Add the flour and beat vigorously until well blended. Cover and let rise in a warm spot for about 1 hour. Stir down and fill buttered muffin tins half full. Cover and let rise for about 30 minutes. Preheat oven to 400°F. Bake rolls for 15–20 minutes.

ENGLISH MUFFINS   (16 MUFFINS)

Pleasantly crusty on the outside, tender on the inside, when toasted and buttered lavishly, these English muffins prove again that everything is best baked at home.

½ cup warm water	3½ cups all-purpose flour
1 package dry yeast	3 tablespoons vegetable oil or
1½ teaspoons salt	melted shortening
1 tablespoon sugar	½ cup cornmeal
1 cup warm milk	

Pour the water into a large mixing bowl, sprinkle the yeast over, and stir. Let stand for 5 minutes to dissolve. Stir in the salt, sugar, warm milk, 2 cups of the flour, and the oil. Stir briskly with a spoon for a minute to mix well. Add the remaining flour and stir to blend smoothly. This dough will be very soft. Cover and let the dough double in bulk (it will take about an hour). Flour a board and your hands. Put the dough on the board, and add a little flour if it is too sticky to manage. Knead the dough three or four times. Pat and push the dough out so it is about ¼ inch thick. Using 3-inch rings (or 6½-ounce tuna cans with the tops and bottoms cut out) as a cutter, cut the dough out and place the muffins 1 inch apart on a baking sheet that has been sprinkled with cornmeal. Cover lightly with a towel, and let rest for 30 minutes. Heat a griddle until medium hot and film it with grease. Grease the inside of the rings and place them on the griddle. Put the muffins in the rings and cook over low–medium heat 10 minutes on one side and 5 minutes on the other. Let cool on racks. Before serving, split the muffins in half with a fork and toast them. Butter generously and serve warm.

HARD ROLLS   (1½ DOZEN ROLLS)

The secret to making hard rolls is to create steam in the oven so that they will develop a good crust as they bake.

1 package dry yeast	3½ cups white flour,
1½ cups warm water	approximately
1½ teaspoons salt	Cornmeal

In a large bowl, mix the yeast in ¼ cup of the warm water and let stand a few minutes until dissolved. Add another 1¼ cups warm water, stir in the salt, and then 3 cups of the flour. Turn out and knead for about 10 minutes, until smooth, adding more flour as necessary. Place in an unbuttered bowl, cover, and let rise in a warm place until double in bulk; it will take longer than other bread doughs because it contains no sugar. Punch down and turn out onto a board. Pull off pieces of dough slightly larger than a golf ball and turn them, cupping your hands over and pulling the dough toward the bottom, until you have perfect rounds. Pinch the seams at the bottoms and place on a cookie sheet, sprinkled with cornmeal, 2 inches apart. Cover lightly with a towel and let rise again until doubled. Preheat the oven to 450°F about halfway through the final rising. Brush the risen rolls with cold water, put in the oven, and immediately throw several ice cubes on the floor of the oven, or put a pan of boiling water there, or spray the oven quickly with a plant atomizer. If you use the latter system, repeat twice during the first five minutes of baking. Check after 15 minutes; when the rolls are browned, they should be done. Cool on racks.

SESAME OR POPPY-SEED ROLLS

Brush the rolls with an *egg white* beaten with 1 tablespoon cold water and sprinkle liberally with *sesame seeds* or *poppy seeds*.

HARD WHOLE-WHEAT ROLLS

Use ½ *cup whole-wheat flour* for white flour to give these rolls a delicious light wheat flavor.

(ABOUT 15 BISCUITS)   ## POTATO BISCUITS

Old-fashioned potato biscuits are light, moist, and golden. And they do taste good!

½ cup hot milk	1 teaspoon salt
2 tablespoons shortening	3¼ cups white flour
2 tablespoons sugar	1 package dry yeast
½ cup warm mashed potatoes	¼ cup warm water

Mix the hot milk, shortening, sugar, potatoes, salt, and ¼ cup of the flour in a large bowl and let cool to lukewarm. Stir the yeast into the warm water and let it stand for 5 minutes to dissolve. Add the dissolved yeast to the first mixture and beat vigorously. Cover and let rise in a warm place until light. Stir, add the remaining 3 cups of flour, and mix well. Cover and let rise again to double in bulk. Turn out onto a lightly floured board. Pat the dough until it is ¼ inch thick and cut into 2-inch rounds. Place the rounds about 1 inch apart on a greased baking sheet, cover, and let rise until almost double. Preheat oven to 425°F. Bake biscuits for about 15 minutes.

BREAD STICKS

(ABOUT 3 DOZEN 6-INCH STICKS)

Serve these crisp, brown bread sticks with an appetizer or with any kind of soup.

1 cup hot milk	3 cups white flour,
4 tablespoons butter	approximately
1½ tablespoons sugar	1 egg white, lightly beaten
2 teaspoons salt	with 1 tablespoon cold
1 package dry yeast	water
¼ cup warm water	

Mix the hot milk, butter, sugar, and salt in a large bowl and let cool to lukewarm. Stir the yeast into the warm water and let it stand for 5 minutes to dissolve. Add the dissolved yeast and 2 cups of the flour to the first mixture, stir vigorously, and add enough of the remaining flour so that the dough pulls away from the sides of the bowl. Turn out onto a lightly floured board, knead for a minute or two, and let rest for 10 minutes. Resume kneading until smooth and elastic. Put in a buttered bowl, cover, and let rise in a warm place until double in bulk. Punch down and roll out with a rolling pin into a rectangle ½ inch thick. Cut into strips about ½ inch wide and of uniform length. Place 1 inch apart on buttered cookie sheets, cover, and let rise a little. Brush with the egg-white glaze before baking. Preheat oven to 300°F. Bake bread sticks for 30 minutes or until lightly browned.

SALT STICKS

Brush Bread Sticks with the glaze and sprinkle them with *coarse salt* before baking.

SESAME OR POPPY-SEED STICKS

A few minutes before the Bread Sticks have finished baking, remove them from the oven, brush them with some more of the glaze, and roll them in *sesame or poppy seeds*. Return them to the oven and bake 5 minutes more.

CHEESE STICKS

Remove the Bread Sticks from the oven a few minutes before they have finished baking, brush them with glaze, and roll them in *freshly grated Parmesan cheese*, seasoned with *salt* and *freshly ground pepper*. Bake 5 minutes more.

(12 FINGERS) **CREAM BREAD FINGERS**

Slender little golden breads, delicate in shape and flavor.

½ cup heavy cream, heated	¼ cup warm water
1 tablespoon sugar	1¼ cups white flour,
½ teaspoon salt	approximately
1 package dry yeast	2 tablespoons milk

Mix the hot cream, sugar, and salt in a large bowl and let cool to luke-warm. Stir the yeast into the warm water and let it stand for 5 minutes to dissolve. Add the dissolved yeast and the flour to the first mixture and beat well. Turn out onto a lightly floured board and, adding a little more flour only if necessary to handle the dough, knead until smooth. Put in a greased bowl, cover, and let rise in a warm place until double in bulk. Roll or pat into a rectangle ¼ inch thick. Cut into strips 1 inch wide and 4 inches long. Cover and let rise until almost double. Brush the tops with milk. Preheat oven to 375°F. Bake bread fingers for 6 minutes, turn, and bake for another 6 minutes or until tops are golden.

(ABOUT 18 ROLLS) **SWEET ROLLS**

These rolls are made from a dependable, basic sweet dough, good for buns and coffee cakes. The texture is fine, rather dense, and rich. Doughs like this, enriched with eggs, milk, butter, and more sugar than usual, do not rise as rapidly as plainer doughs.

¾ cup warm milk	1 package dry yeast
¼ cup sugar	¼ cup warm water
1 teaspoon salt	2½ cups white flour,
4 tablespoons butter, softened	approximately
2 eggs	

Mix the milk, sugar, salt, butter, and eggs in a large bowl and let cool to lukewarm. Stir the yeast into the warm water and let it stand for 5 minutes to dissolve. Add the dissolved yeast to the first mixture, beat thoroughly, and add 1½ cups of the flour, beating well. Cover and let rise in a warm place for about 1 hour. Add the remaining cup of flour and blend in well, adding more flour if necessary to make the dough firm enough to handle. Knead until smooth and elastic. Put the dough in a buttered bowl, cover, and let rise until almost double in bulk. Punch down, shape into rolls (see p. 736 for directions), and let rise for about 1 hour. Preheat oven to 400°F. Bake rolls for 15–20 minutes.

CINNAMON BUNS

Add *1 tablespoon cinnamon* to the dough in the first step.

ORANGE ROLLS

Use *¾ cup orange juice* instead of milk and add *1 tablespoon grated orange peel*. Shape like Parker House Rolls (p. 738). Dip *orange sections* in sugar and put one in the center of each roll before folding and baking.

SALLY LUNN TEA CAKES

(24 TEA CAKES OR
ONE 10-INCH TUBE CAKE)

They say that Sally Lunn lived in Bath, England, and sold this kind of tender, semisweet tea cake—almost weightless with a light yellow crumb, they can also be made as one large cake.

1 cup hot milk	1 package dry yeast
¼ pound butter	¼ cup warm water
⅓ cup sugar	3 eggs
1 teaspoon salt	3½ cups white flour

Mix the hot milk, butter, sugar, and salt in a large bowl and let cool to lukewarm. Stir the yeast into the warm water and let it stand for 5 minutes to dissolve. Add the dissolved yeast and the eggs to the first mixture and beat vigorously. Gradually add the flour. Cover and let rise in a warm place until about double in bulk. Spoon the dough into buttered muffin tins, filling each section about half full, or put it all in a buttered 10-inch tube pan. Preheat oven to 425°F for muffins, 350°F for cake. Bake muffins for 20 minutes, tube cake for about 50 minutes.

(ABOUT 16 ROLLS) **CINNAMON ROLLS**

These rolls rise very high and are mildly sweet with a light cinnamon flavor.

1 package dry yeast	2 eggs
¼ cup warm water	2 tablespoons butter
4½ cups white flour, approximately	½ cup raisins
	Milk
1 cup lukewarm milk	¾ cup confectioners' sugar
¾ cup granulated sugar	1 teaspoon vanilla
1 teaspoon salt	4 teaspoons warm water
1 tablespoon cinnamon	

Stir the yeast into ¼ cup warm water and let it stand for 5 minutes to dissolve. Add the dissolved yeast and 3 cups of the flour to the milk and blend well. Cover and let rise in a warm place until double in bulk. Add the granulated sugar, salt, cinnamon, eggs, butter, and ¾ cup of the flour and blend. Turn out onto a lightly floured board and knead gently, slowly adding the remaining ¾ cup of flour until the dough can be easily handled. Knead in the raisins. Pull off pieces of dough the size of medium lemons, roll each about 8 inches long, and wind it into a coil. Arrange on two buttered 9-inch cake pans, cover, and let rise until double in bulk, then brush tops with milk. Preheat oven to 375°F. Bake rolls for 25 minutes. Mix the confectioners' sugar and vanilla with 4 teaspoons warm water to make a glaze, and spread a thin layer on rolls immediately after removing from the oven.

(ABOUT 2 DOZEN DOUGHNUTS PLUS HOLES) **RAISED DOUGHNUTS**

The temperature of the cooking oil is very important when frying doughnuts: if it is too cool, the doughnuts will absorb it and be greasy; if it is too hot, the doughnuts will burn on the outside or remain uncooked inside. Unless you have had a great deal of experience with deep frying, a frying (candy) thermometer to establish and maintain the proper heat is essential. (See also Old-fashioned Doughnuts, p. 779.)

1 cup warm milk	1 cup light-brown sugar
1 package dry yeast	2 eggs, well beaten
1 teaspoon salt	½ teaspoon nutmeg
2 tablespoons granulated sugar	Vegetable shortening or oil for frying
3½ cups flour, approximately	Confectioners' sugar
¼ cup melted butter	

Put the milk, yeast, salt, granulated sugar, and 2 cups of the flour in a bowl and beat thoroughly. Cover and let rise until double in bulk. Stir down and add the butter, brown sugar, eggs, nutmeg, and an additional 1 cup flour. Beat well, cover, and let rise again until almost double in bulk. Stir down and turn out onto a lightly floured board, kneading in only enough flour so that the dough handles easily. Let rest for 10 minutes, then roll out about ½ inch thick. Cut with a doughnut cutter or a sharp knife into 3-inch rounds, cut out the centers and save these "holes," which can also be fried. Let rise, uncovered, for about 1 hour. Using a heavy pot and a thermometer, heat about 4 inches of shortening or oil to 360°F. Lower the doughnuts into the hot fat, cooking three or four at a time. Turn them when they are brown on one side, and brown the other side. Drain them on paper towels and sprinkle freely with confectioners' sugar.

CRULLERS   (3 DOZEN)

After the dough has risen for the second time, roll it out ⅛ inch thick. Cut in strips 8 inches long and ¾ inch wide. Let rise, uncovered, for about 1 hour. Twist each strip several times and pinch the ends. Fry, drain, and roll in *granulated sugar*.

JELLY DOUGHNUTS   (ABOUT 15)

Cut the dough in 2½-inch rounds. Place heaping teaspoons of *strawberry or raspberry jelly or jam* on half of them, brush the edges with *slightly beaten egg white*, and cover with the other rounds, pressing the edges firmly together. Let rise, uncovered, for about 1 hour. Fry, drain, and dust with confectioners' sugar.

(ABOUT 2 DOZEN DOUGHNUTS   ✳   **BAKED DOUGHNUTS**
PLUS HOLES)

This is a good alternative to deep frying. Light and tender, from start
to finish these take a little under two hours to make. They freeze well
too.

2 packages dry yeast
⅓ cup warm water
1½ cups milk
⅓ cup vegetable shortening
¼ cup sugar
2 teaspoons salt
2 teaspoons freshly grated
    nutmeg

2 eggs, lightly beaten
4½ cups all-purpose flour,
    approximately
½ cup melted butter
1 cup sugar mixed with 1
    teaspoon cinnamon

Sprinkle the yeast over the warm water in a small bowl and let it dissolve for 5 minutes. Put the milk and shortening in a saucepan and
heat until the shortening is melted. Cool to lukewarm. Pour the yeast
mixture into a large mixing bowl and add the milk mixture. Stir in the
¼ cup sugar, salt, nutmeg, eggs, and 2 cups flour. Beat briskly until
well blended. Add the remaining 2½ cups flour and beat until smooth.
Cover the bowl and let double in bulk, about 1 hour. Dust a board
generously with flour and turn the dough mass onto it. This dough
is soft and needs enough flour on the board to prevent sticking, but
is easy to handle. Pat the dough into a round about ½ inch thick. Use
a 3-inch doughnut cutter and cut out the doughnuts, placing them
(and the doughnut holes) on greased baking sheets, 1 inch apart. These
don't spread much; they rise. Preheat the oven to 450°F. Let the doughnuts rest and rise for 20 minutes, uncovered. Bake about 10 minutes,
or a little longer, until they have a touch of golden brown. Remove
from the oven. Have ready the melted butter and a brush. On a sheet
of wax paper spread the cinnamon sugar. Brush each doughnut
and doughnut hole with butter and roll in the cinnamon sugar. Serve
hot.

(ONE 14-INCH STOLLEN)   **CHRISTMAS STOLLEN**

Christmas Stollen are made from a sweet dough, rich in butter and
eggs, with lemon rind, almonds, and candied fruit added for festive
trimmings.

1 package dry yeast
¼ cup warm water
¾ cup warm milk
¼ cup granulated sugar
1 teaspoon salt
4 tablespoons butter, softened
2 eggs

3 cups white flour,
   approximately
1 tablespoon grated lemon
   rind
½ cup chopped almonds
¾ cup candied fruit

Glaze

1 cup confectioners' sugar
2 tablespoons lemon juice

1–2 tablespoons water

Garnish

Candied fruit and nuts

Stir the yeast into the warm water and let it stand for 5 minutes to dissolve. Mix the milk, granulated sugar, salt, butter, and eggs in a large mixing bowl. Add the dissolved yeast, beat thoroughly, and add 1½ cups of the flour, beating until well blended. Cover the bowl and let rise in a warm place for about 1 hour. Add enough of the remaining flour so that the dough is easy to handle. Cover and chill in the refrigerator for about 30 minutes. Turn out onto a lightly floured board and knead with the lemon rind, almonds, and candied fruit for a few minutes. Pat dough into an oval ¼ inch thick. Fold the dough in half lengthwise bringing the upper half not quite to the edge of the lower half and press down along the edge to secure. Place on buttered cookie sheets, cover, and let double in bulk. Preheat oven to 375°F. Bake stollen for 35 minutes. Mix the sugar, lemon juice, and water and glaze the cake while it is still warm. Decorate with garnish of candied fruit and nuts.

(ONE 10-INCH TUBE CAKE)

RUTH'S COFFEE CAKE

Prepare the dough for Christmas Stollen, omitting the lemon rind, almonds, and candied fruit. Roll it into a long cylinder about 1 inch in diameter. Cut off 1-inch pieces and form them into balls. Dip each ball into *melted butter* and then into a mixture of *cinnamon* and *sugar*, using 1 tablespoon cinnamon to ½ cup sugar. Arrange the balls in two layers in a buttered 10-inch tube pan, sprinkling each layer with *chopped nuts and/or raisins*. Bake in a preheated 350°F oven for 50–60 minutes.

(2 LOAVES)

SWEDISH BREAD

What could be better than warm Swedish bread with sweet butter to go with freshly ground coffee on a cold Sunday morning? Try shaping the dough into a lovely braid or tea ring to serve when you have guests for brunch.

½ cup melted butter	¼ cup warm water
⅔ cup sugar	1 egg, well beaten
1 teaspoon salt	1 teaspoon almond extract
2¼ cups hot milk	7 cups white flour,
1 package dry yeast	approximately

Mix the butter, sugar, salt, and hot milk in a large bowl and let cool to lukewarm. Stir the yeast into the warm water and let it stand for 5 minutes to dissolve. Add the dissolved yeast, egg, almond extract, and 3 cups of the flour to the first mixture and mix vigorously. Add 3 more cups of the flour and mix well. Turn out onto a lightly floured board, knead for a minute or two, and let rest for 10 minutes. Adding the remaining flour only if the dough is too sticky, resume kneading until smooth and elastic. Put the dough in a large, buttered bowl, cover, and let rise in a warm place until double in bulk. Punch down, knead for a minute or two, and shape into two loaves. Place in buttered loaf pans, cover, and let rise until double in bulk once again. Preheat oven to 375°F. Bake bread for 40–50 minutes. Remove from pans and cool on racks.

SWEDISH BRAIDED BREAD   (TWO BRAIDS)

After the dough has risen for the first time, punch it down, knead it for
a minute or two and divide it into six equal pieces. Stretch and roll
each piece with your hands until you have six long rolls of uniform

size. Make two braids with them, pinching the three pieces of dough
firmly together when you start the braiding and again when you finish. Leave as is or form each braid into a ring if you wish. Place them
on buttered cookie sheets, cover, and let rise to about double in bulk.
Brush with *1 egg yolk*, lightly beaten with 1 teaspoon cold water, and
sprinkle with *blanched, chopped almonds*. Bake for only 25–30 minutes.

SWEDISH TEA RING (ONE TEA RING AND ONE STANDARD LOAF)

After the dough has risen for the first time, punch it down, knead it for
a minute or two, and divide it in half. Roll and shape the first piece
with your hands into a long, thin roll. Using a rolling pin and an unfloured board, roll it into a thin rectangle, about 7 × 16 inches; it will
stick to the board but may easily be lifted with a knife. Spread with

melted butter and sprinkle with *sugar, cinnamon, ¾ cup candied fruit or raisins,* and *½ cup chopped walnuts or almonds.* Starting with the long side, roll like a jelly roll. Trim, if necessary, and join the ends to form a ring. Place on a buttered cookie sheet, make perpendicular cuts, as illustrated, with a scissors, about 1 inch apart and then spread open, so that one side falls flat. Repeat with the other piece of dough, if you wish, or use the remaining dough to make one standard loaf of Swedish Bread. Cover and let rise to almost double in bulk. Bake for 25–30 minutes.

QUICK BREADS

There are a number of new quick-bread recipes here, among them one that I worked out for the Bridge Creek restaurant in Berkeley, where it became a favorite—Custard-filled Corn Bread. I have also included two recipes for making crackers that lift the humble cracker to heights you can't imagine—and they keep well, too.

Like cakes, quick breads won't bake in the microwave oven (see the Cakes chapter for further explanation).

ABOUT QUICK BREADS

Quick breads are made without yeast from batters which require no kneading and do not have to rise before going into the oven. These breads are valued for the ease and speed with which they can be turned out, as well as for their light, cakelike crumb, which is frequently embellished with fruits, nuts, and other seasonings. They rise quickly once they are in the oven, leavened by steam, air, and carbon dioxide gases created by baking powder, baking soda, beaten eggs and egg whites, and other combinations of leavening agents.

Quick-Bread Tips

Replace your baking powder every six months. It has a short shelf life and loses its leavening power rapidly.

No-stick cooking sprays do a good job on loaf pans and muffin tins.

Quick breads can be made into muffins. Simply fill greased or paper-lined muffin pans two-thirds full with batter and bake in a 375°F oven for about 15–20 minutes.

Paper muffin cups or liners or Teflon or nonstick muffin pans make removing muffins easier. But be sure to lightly grease the nonstick pans to insure easy removal.

Quick breads are apt to crack in baking. There's no way to prevent this; the cracks are simply characteristic of this kind of bread.

Very fresh bread crumbles easily. If you make these quick loaves several hours ahead and let them cool thoroughly, you will find them easier to slice.

LOAF BREADS

(8½ × 4½ × 2½-INCH LOAF)   **NUT BREAD**

2 cups flour
½ cup dark-brown sugar
2 teaspoons baking powder
1 teaspoon salt

1 egg
1 cup milk
2 tablespoons butter, melted
½ cup chopped nuts

Preheat the oven to 350°F. Butter a loaf pan. Mix the flour, brown sugar, baking powder, and salt in a large bowl, add the egg, milk, and butter, and stir until well blended. Add the nuts. Spoon into the pan and bake for 45 minutes. Remove from the pan and cool on a rack.

(9 × 5 × 3-INCH LOAF)   **QUICK WHOLE-WHEAT BREAD**

Brown as a chestnut, moist, and honest in taste.

½ cup white flour
1 teaspoon baking powder
1 teaspoon baking soda
1 teaspoon salt

2 cups whole-wheat flour
¼ cup shortening, melted
1½ cups sour milk (p. 17)
½ cup molasses

Preheat the oven to 375°F. Grease a loaf pan. Mix the white flour, baking powder, baking soda, salt, and whole-wheat flour in a large bowl, add the shortening, sour milk, and molasses, and stir until well blended. Spoon into the pan and bake for about 50 minutes. Remove from the pan and cool on a rack.

APPLE LEMON BREAD   (9 × 5 × 3-INCH LOAF)

Light and moist, flavored with apple and lemon zest, this bread freezes well, if there is any left.

¼ cup butter	1 teaspoon salt
¾ cup sugar	2 green apples, peeled, cored, and grated (about 2 cups)
2 eggs, beaten	
2 cups flour	Zest or peel from 2 lemons, minced (approximately 1½ tablespoons)
1 teaspoon baking powder	
1 teaspoon baking soda	

Preheat the oven to 350°F. Butter or grease a loaf pan. In a large bowl, cream together the butter and sugar until light and fluffy. Beat in the eggs until blended. Mix the flour, baking powder, baking soda, and salt together and add to the creamed mixture alternately with the grated apple. Add the lemon zest and mix until well blended. Spoon into the loaf pan and bake for 50–55 minutes. Remove from the pan and cool on a rack.

WINCHESTER NUT BREAD   (TWO 8½ × 4½ × 2½-INCH LOAVES)

A dark, sweet, moist, and nourishing whole-wheat bread.

½ cup dark-brown sugar	1 teaspoon salt
¾ cup cold water	2½ teaspoons baking powder
½ cup molasses	¾ teaspoon baking soda
¾ cup milk	1 cup coarsely chopped walnuts
1 cup white flour	
2 cups whole-wheat flour	

Preheat the oven to 275°F. Grease two loaf pans. Put the brown sugar in a large bowl, add the cold water, and stir until the sugar dissolves. Stir in the molasses and milk. Add the white flour, whole-wheat flour, salt, baking powder, and baking soda, and mix well. Stir in the walnuts. Spoon into the pans and bake for 2 hours. Remove from the pans and cool on racks.

(8½ × 4½ × 2½-INCH LOAF)   **HONEY BREAD**

Honey bread has a fine, silky texture and the sweet, mild flavor of spice. Very long beating is the secret of its tender grain.

2 cups white flour
1 teaspoon baking powder
1 teaspoon baking soda
1 teaspoon salt
½ teaspoon cinnamon

1 teaspoon ginger
½ cup honey
1 egg, slightly beaten
1 cup milk

Preheat the oven to 350°F. Butter a loaf pan. Put the flour, baking powder, baking soda, salt, cinnamon, and ginger in a large bowl, add the honey, egg, and milk, and beat thoroughly with an electric mixer for about 20 minutes. Spoon into the pan and bake for about 50 minutes. Remove from the pan and cool on a rack.

(8½ × 4½ × 2½-INCH LOAF)   **APPLESAUCE NUT BREAD**

Serve this wonderful spicy-apple bread with butter or honey.

½ cup shortening
¾ cup sugar
2 eggs
1 teaspoon vanilla
2 cups white flour
1 teaspoon salt
1 teaspoon baking powder

1 teaspoon baking soda
1 teaspoon cinnamon
½ teaspoon nutmeg
1 cup applesauce, preferably
  chunky
¾ cup chopped walnuts

Preheat the oven to 350°F. Butter or grease a loaf pan. In a large mixing bowl, cream together the shortening and sugar. Add the eggs and vanilla to the sugar mixture and mix well. Sift together the flour, salt, baking powder, baking soda, cinnamon, and nutmeg and add to the egg and sugar mixture. Stir well to blend. Stir the applesauce and walnuts into the batter. Spread the batter into the greased loaf pan and bake for 50–55 minutes. Remove from the pan and cool on a rack.

DATE NUT BREAD   *   (8½ × 4½ × 2½-INCH LOAF)

This is delicious served with a soft farmer cheese.

1 cup pitted dates, chopped	¾ cup boiling water
1 cup walnuts, coarsely chopped	2 eggs
	¾ cup sugar
1½ teaspoons baking soda	½ cup whole-wheat flour
½ teaspoon salt	1 cup all-purpose flour
3 tablespoons vegetable shortening	

Preheat the oven to 350°F. Grease a loaf pan. Put the dates, walnuts, baking soda, salt, and shortening in a bowl. Pour the boiling water over and stir. Let the mixture stand for 15 minutes. Using a fork, beat the eggs and sugar together in a bowl. Add the flours and stir (the dough will be too stiff to mix well at this point). Add the date mixture and mix briskly until the batter is well blended. Spoon into the loaf pan and bake for about 1 hour, or until a straw comes out clean when inserted into the center. Remove and cool on a rack.

PRUNE BREAD

Omit the dates and walnuts. Substitute *1½ cups pitted, chopped prunes.* Proceed as directed above.

APRICOT ALMOND BREAD   (9 × 5 × 3-INCH LOAF)

Brown and crusty on the outside, with bits of tart apricot and white almonds scattered throughout.

1½ cups coarsely chopped dried apricots	1½ cups white flour
	1 cup whole-wheat flour
1½ cups boiling water	1 teaspoon baking soda
2 tablespoons butter	1 cup chopped almonds
1 cup sugar	1 egg, well beaten
1 teaspoon salt	1 teaspoon orange extract

Preheat the oven to 350°F. Butter a loaf pan. Put the apricots in a bowl and pour the boiling water over them. Add the butter, sugar, and salt and let cool to lukewarm. Stir in remaining ingredients and mix very well. Spoon into the pan and bake for 1¼ hours. Remove from the pan and cool on a rack.

(TWO 8½ × 4½ × 2½-INCH   **✳ ORANGE PEEL BREAD**
LOAVES)

The flavor of orange is just right with the moist, slightly coarse texture of this outstanding bread.

5–6 oranges	2 cups milk
1½ cups sugar	4 cups white flour
1 tablespoon butter	4 teaspoons baking powder
1 egg	½ teaspoon salt

Preheat the oven to 325°F. Butter two loaf pans. Peel outer skins of the oranges with a vegetable parer until you have enough to fill 1 cup loosely. Chop into small pieces and put in a small pan with just enough water to cover. Cook over medium-low heat, adding more water if necessary, for 15–20 minutes or until tender. Add 1 cup of the sugar and boil about 10 minutes, until thick and syrupy. Cream the butter with the remaining sugar, and add the egg and milk. Mix the flour, baking powder, and salt, and add to the batter, beating well. Add the cooked orange peel and syrup. Put in the pans and bake for 40–50 minutes. Remove from the pans and cool on racks.

(9 × 5 × 3-INCH LOAF)   **PUMPKIN BREAD**

Nicely sweet and lightly spiced, Pumpkin Bread keeps well wrapped in the refrigerator. Serve slices spread with chopped walnuts in cream cheese and a fruit salad.

1½ cups flour	2 eggs, beaten
½ teaspoon salt	¼ cup water
1 cup sugar	¼ teaspoon nutmeg
1 teaspoon baking soda	¼ teaspoon cinnamon
1 cup pumpkin purée	¼ teaspoon allspice
½ cup vegetable oil	½ cup chopped nuts

Preheat the oven to 350°F. Sift together the flour, salt, sugar, and baking soda. Mix the pumpkin, oil, eggs, water, and spices together, then combine with the dry ingredients, but do not mix too thoroughly. Stir in the nuts. Pour into a well-buttered loaf pan. Bake 50–60 minutes until a straw comes out clean. Turn out of the pan and cool on a rack.

CRANBERRY NUT BREAD   (8½ × 4½ × 2½-INCH LOAF)

Chopped red cranberries make this loaf look good. Warm slices taste tart with roast chicken or duck. Cranberries are sold seasonally in the market, packed in cellophane bags; buy some and freeze for use during the year.

1 orange	½ cup chopped walnuts
Boiling water	2 cups white flour
2 tablespoons butter	½ teaspoon salt
1 egg	1½ teaspoons baking powder
1 cup sugar	½ teaspoon baking soda
1 cup cranberries, chopped	

Preheat the oven to 325°F. Butter a loaf pan. Grate the rind of the orange, and squeeze out all the juice into a measuring cup and add enough boiling water to make ¾ cup. Add the orange rind and the butter and stir to melt the butter. Beat the egg in another bowl and gradually add the sugar, beating well. Add remaining ingredients and orange mixture, and blend well. Spoon into the pan and bake for 1 hour. Remove from the pan and cool on a rack.

PEANUT BUTTER BREAD   (8½ × 4½ × 2½-INCH LOAF)

Tan, moist, and close-textured, peanut butter bread is slightly sweet with a distinct peanut flavor. If you use "chunky" peanut butter, there will be bits of peanut in the bread.

2 cups white flour	¾ cup peanut butter
⅓ cup sugar	1 cup milk
2 teaspoons baking powder	1 egg, well beaten
¼ teaspoon salt	

Preheat the oven to 350°F. Grease a loaf pan. Put the flour, sugar, baking powder, and salt in a large bowl. Add the peanut butter, milk, and egg, and mix until well blended. Spoon into the pan and bake for about 50–55 minutes. Remove from the pan and cool on a rack.

(8½ × 4½ × 2½-INCH LOAF)   **BANANA NUT BREAD**

This is pure and simple banana bread, heavy, moist, and dark.

3 ripe bananas, well mashed
2 eggs, well beaten
2 cups flour
¾ cup sugar

1 teaspoon salt
1 teaspoon baking soda
½ cup coarsely chopped
    walnuts

Preheat the oven to 350°F. Grease a loaf pan. Mix the bananas and eggs together in a large bowl. Stir in the flour, sugar, salt, and baking soda. Add the walnuts and blend. Put the batter in the pan and bake for 1 hour. Remove from the pan to a rack. Serve still warm or cooled, as you like it.

(TWO 8½ × 4½ × 2½-INCH LOAVES)   **PRUNE BREAD**

A dark and nourishing breakfast bread, good with spicy sausages and coffee.

1 cup sugar
1 cup whole-wheat flour
2 cups white flour
1 teaspoon baking soda
¼ teaspoon baking powder
½ teaspoon salt

2 tablespoons melted butter
1 egg, well beaten
1 cup cooked, pitted prunes,
    in small pieces
½ cup prune juice
1 cup sour milk or buttermilk

Preheat the oven to 350°F. Butter two loaf pans. Put the sugar, whole-wheat flour, white flour, baking soda, baking powder, and salt in a large bowl. Stir in remaining ingredients and mix very well. Spoon into the pans and bake for 1 hour. Remove from the pans and cool on racks.

MUFFINS, TOAST, BREAKFAST BREADS, AND TEA BREADS

(12 MUFFINS)   **BASIC MUFFINS**

What could be nicer than warm muffins wrapped in a napkin on the morning breakfast table? And they are so quick and easy to make, particularly since the ingredients are only lightly mixed, not beaten smooth.

2 cups white flour
1 tablespoon baking powder
½ teaspoon salt
2 tablespoons sugar

1 egg, slightly beaten
1 cup milk
¼ cup melted butter

Preheat the oven to 375°F. Butter muffin pans. Mix the flour, baking powder, salt, and sugar in a large bowl. Add the egg, milk, and butter, stirring only enough to dampen the flour; the batter should *not* be smooth. Spoon into the muffin pans, filling each cup about two-thirds full. Bake for about 20–25 minutes.

BLUEBERRY MUFFINS

Use *½ cup sugar*. Reserve ¼ cup of the flour, sprinkle it over *1 cup blueberries*, and stir them into the batter last.

PECAN MUFFINS

Use ¼ cup sugar. Add *½ cup chopped pecans* to the batter. After filling the cups, sprinkle with *sugar*, *cinnamon*, and more *chopped nuts*.

WHOLE-WHEAT MUFFINS

Use *¾ cup whole-wheat flour* and *1 cup white flour*.

DATE OR RAISIN MUFFINS

Add *½ cup chopped pitted dates* or *⅓ cup raisins* to the batter.

BACON MUFFINS

Add 3 *strips bacon, fried crisp and crumbled,* to the batter.

(12 MUFFINS) ## OATMEAL MUFFINS

These are the next best things to a bowl of hot oatmeal.

1½ cups flour	½ cup milk
2 tablespoons sugar	1 egg, well beaten
4 teaspoons baking powder	2 tablespoons butter, melted
½ teaspoon salt	1 cup cooked oatmeal

Preheat the oven to 400°F. Butter the muffin pans. Combine flour, sugar, baking powder, and salt. In a separate bowl stir the milk, egg, and butter into the oatmeal. Stir until well blended. Combine the two mixtures and mix well. Spoon each muffin cup two-thirds full of batter. Bake for about 20 minutes, or until a broomstraw comes out dry when inserted in center.

(24 MUFFINS) ## IRISH OATMEAL MUFFINS

The Irish cook their oatmeal all night long for a rich and creamy effect. These muffins take on that same flavor from soaking the oatmeal overnight in buttermilk.

2 cups buttermilk	1⅔ cups whole-wheat flour
1 cup rolled oats	1 teaspoon baking soda
2 eggs	1 teaspoon salt
¾ cup dark-brown sugar	2 tablespoons vegetable oil

Combine the buttermilk and the oats in a bowl, stir well, cover, and refrigerate. Let stand for at least 6 hours, preferably overnight, before mixing and baking the muffins. Preheat the oven to 400°F. Grease muffin pans. Put the eggs in a mixing bowl and beat just until blended. Add the sugar and beat until smooth and well blended. Stir in the buttermilk-oatmeal mixture. Add the flour, baking soda, salt, and oil, and beat until the batter is well blended. Fill the muffin tins about three-quarters full with batter and bake for about 20 minutes. Start testing for doneness after 15 minutes. Remove the muffins from the cups and cool on racks or serve hot from the pan.

(12 MUFFINS) ## APPLE OAT BRAN MUFFINS

If you're looking for a strong dose of fiber, this is a way of getting it. And the muffins taste good.

2 cups oat bran
½ cup brown sugar
2 teaspoons baking powder
1 teaspoon cinnamon
½ teaspoon salt
1 cup milk (lowfat milk
  acceptable)

2 egg whites
2 tablespoons vegetable oil
1 cup grated apple or 1 cup
  apple in small dice

Preheat the oven to 425°F. Grease muffin pans. Put the oat bran, brown sugar, baking powder, cinnamon, and salt in a mixing bowl and stir to blend. In a separate bowl, combine the milk, egg whites, vegetable oil, and grated apple. Pour the apple mixture into the dry ingredients and stir just to mix. Spoon into the muffin pans, filling each cup about two-thirds full. Bake for 15–17 minutes, until golden brown.

VARIATIONS

Omit the apple and add one of the following:

½ cup raisins, either black or golden
½ cup mashed banana
½ cup applesauce
¾ cup chopped prunes
½ cup chopped dried apricots
½ cup chopped walnuts or pecans (may also be added with any
  of the ingredients above)

MOLASSES OAT BRAN MUFFINS

Substitute ¼ cup molasses for half of the brown sugar and ½ cup raisins for the apple. Omit the cinnamon and add ¼ teaspoon ground ginger, if desired.

BRAN MUFFINS

(12 MUFFINS)

Split, toasted, and lightly spread with butter, these are earthy and good.

1 egg, slightly beaten
1 cup milk
2 tablespoons butter, melted
1 cup bran

1 cup white flour
1 tablespoon baking powder
¼ cup sugar
½ teaspoon salt

Preheat the oven to 375°F. Butter muffin pans. Put the egg, milk, butter, and bran in a mixing bowl and let stand for 10 minutes. Add the flour, baking powder, sugar, and salt and stir just enough to dampen. Spoon into the muffin pans, filling each cup about two-thirds full. Bake for about 20 minutes.

(12 MUFFINS)

BANANA RICE BRAN MUFFINS

As of this writing, rice bran threatens to overtake oat bran in the nineties.

1½ cups rice bran	1 cup milk (lowfat milk acceptable)
1 cup flour	2 egg whites
½ cup brown sugar	2 tablespoons vegetable oil
2 teaspoons baking powder	½ cup mashed banana
1 teaspoon cinnamon	½ cup pecan pieces (optional)
½ teaspoon salt	

Preheat the oven to 425°F. Grease muffin pans. Put the rice bran, flour, brown sugar, baking powder, cinnamon, and salt in a mixing bowl and stir to blend. In a separate bowl, combine the milk, egg whites, vegetable oil, banana, and pecans. Pour the banana mixture into the dry ingredients and stir just to mix. Spoon into the muffin pans, filling each cup about two-thirds full. Bake for 15–17 minutes, until golden brown.

(12 SMALL MUFFINS)

BERKSHIRE MUFFINS

A bit of leftover rice and some cornmeal give these muffins a rustic texture and taste.

⅔ cup milk	3 teaspoons baking powder
½ cup cornmeal	½ teaspoon salt
½ cup cooked rice	1 egg yolk, well beaten
½ cup white flour	1 tablespoon butter, melted
2 tablespoons sugar	1 egg white, beaten stiff

Preheat the oven to 375°F. Butter muffin pans. Scald the milk, slowly pour it on the cornmeal, and let stand 5 minutes. Stir in the rice, flour, sugar, baking powder, and salt. Add the egg yolk and butter, and blend well. Gently fold in the egg white and spoon into the muffin pans, filling each cup about one-half full. Bake for about 20 minutes.

STICKY ORANGE MUFFINS   *   (12 MUFFINS)

A morning muffin, delicately flavored with orange and honey. A glazed orange slice on the bottom of each muffin makes it as nice to look at as it is to eat.

2 oranges	1 teaspoon salt
¼ cup honey	½ cup sugar
2 cups flour	2 eggs, lightly beaten
½ cup uncooked oatmeal or oat bran (not instant)	⅔ cup milk
1 tablespoon baking powder	5 tablespoons butter, melted (about ⅓ cup)

Preheat the oven to 400°F. Grease muffin pans. Using the small side of a grater, grate the rind from the oranges, removing only the bright orange part; set aside. With a sharp knife remove all the remaining peel and, if necessary, trim the oranges all around so that the slices will fit in the bottoms of your muffin cups. Cut the oranges into slices about ¼ inch thick, remove any seeds, and set the slices aside. Put about 1 teaspoon of honey in the bottom of each muffin cup and place an orange slice on top. In a mixing bowl, combine the flour, oatmeal or oat bran, baking powder, salt, and sugar, and stir to mix. Add the reserved orange rind, eggs, milk, and melted butter, and stir just until mixed. Spoon the batter over the orange slices, filling each cup about two-thirds full. Bake for 15–20 minutes, or until a broomstraw or toothpick inserted in the center comes out clean. Serve warm.

BAKING POWDER BISCUITS   (16 BISCUITS)

Light-gold and crusty outside, moist and fine-textured inside.

2 cups flour	1 tablespoon sugar
½ teaspoon salt	½ cup vegetable shortening
4 teaspoons baking powder	⅔ cup milk

Preheat the oven to 425°F. Grease two 8-inch cake pans. Put the flour, salt, baking powder, and sugar in a bowl. Cut the shortening into the flour with two knives or a pastry blender until the mixture resembles coarse meal. Add the milk all at once and stir just until the dough forms a ball around the fork. Turn the dough onto a lightly floured board and knead 14 times. Pat until ½ inch thick. Cut into rounds with a 2-inch cookie cutter. Place touching each other in the cake pans and bake for 15–20 minutes.

CRUSTY BAKING POWDER BISCUITS

Roll biscuits to ¼ inch thick and place 1 inch apart. Bake in a 450°F oven for 12 minutes. This will yield almost twice as many biscuits.

BUTTERMILK BISCUITS

Use ⅔ cup buttermilk instead of sweet milk and ½ teaspoon baking soda, cutting the amount of baking powder in half, to 2 teaspoons.

CHEESE BISCUITS

Add ½ cup grated sharp Cheddar cheese to the dry ingredients.

DROP BISCUITS

Add an additional ⅓ cup milk and drop by teaspoonfuls onto a buttered baking sheet.

(12 BISCUITS)

✳ CREAM BISCUITS

In the summer cooking classes James Beard conducted for many years in Seaside, Oregon, this is the biscuit we often made to go with either the marvelous fresh berries or the chicken dishes. Light, buttery, and so simple to make, they were loved by everyone.

2 cups flour
1 teaspoon salt
1 tablespoon baking powder
2 teaspoons sugar

1–1½ cups heavy cream
6 tablespoons butter, melted
(about ⅓ cup)

Preheat the oven to 425°F. Use an ungreased baking sheet. Combine the flour, salt, baking powder, and sugar in a mixing bowl. Stir the dry ingredients with a fork to blend and lighten. Slowly add 1 cup of the cream to the mixture, stirring constantly. Gather the dough together; when it holds together and feels tender, it is ready to knead. But if it seems shaggy and pieces are dry and falling away, then slowly add enough additional cream to make the dough hold together. Place the dough on a lightly floured board and knead the dough for 1 minute.

Pat the dough into a square about ½ inch thick. Cut into twelve squares and dip each into the melted butter so all sides are coated. Place the biscuits 2 inches apart on the baking sheet. Bake for about 15 minutes, or until they are lightly browned. Serve hot.

HOMINY GEMS (12 MUFFINS)

To make these old-fashioned gems, use the cereal hominy that comes in a box, also known as grits.

¼ cup hominy
½ teaspoon salt
½ cup boiling water
1 cup scalded milk
1 cup cornmeal

3 tablespoons sugar
3 tablespoons butter
3 teaspoons baking powder
2 eggs, separated

Preheat the oven to 400°F. Line muffin pans with cupcake papers or grease each cup. Put the hominy and salt in a bowl and pour the boiling water over. Let stand for a few minutes, until the hominy has absorbed the water. In a separate bowl, thoroughly mix the scalded milk, cornmeal, sugar, and butter. Combine the two mixtures, stir, and cool slightly. Add the baking powder. Beat the egg yolks and add to the mixture. Beat the egg whites until stiff but not dry. Stir a third of the whites into the batter and gently fold in the rest. Spoon the batter into the muffin cups. Bake 15–20 minutes, or until a broomstraw comes out dry when inserted in the center of a muffin. You may bake these in miniature muffin tins or "gem" pans. If so, reduce the baking time to about 12–15 minutes. The yield will increase to about 24 miniature muffins.

FRENCH TOAST (6 SLICES)

French toast is always better if your bread is a little dry—a day or two old, or leave the slices out overnight. Serve these crusty slices with bacon and warmed maple syrup, jam, or marmalade, or sprinkle them with a mixture of cinnamon and sugar.

3 eggs, slightly beaten
½ teaspoon salt
2 tablespoons sugar

1 cup milk
6 slices bread

Mix the eggs, salt, sugar, and milk in a shallow dish or pie pan. Soak the bread in the mixture until soft, turning once. Cook on a hot, well-greased skillet or frying pan, turning to brown each side.

(SERVES TWO)

FILLED FRENCH TOAST

½ cup apple or apricot purée
4 slices white bread, not more
    than ½ inch thick
2 eggs
½ cup milk or half-and-half
4 tablespoons butter

Confectioners' sugar, for
    dusting
2 tablespoons sour cream,
    approximately
Maple syrup

Spread the purée on two of the bread slices and top each with the remaining slices. In a bowl or pie pan, mix the eggs and milk or half-and-half until blended. Dip, but don't soak, each sandwich in the egg mixture quickly on both sides. Put the butter in a skillet over medium heat. When the butter is hot and just foaming, add the sandwiches and fry on both sides until golden. Remove to warm plates and dust with confectioners' sugar. Put a small scoop of sour cream in the middle of each and pour a little maple syrup over.

CINNAMON TOAST

Warm, crisp, buttery, spicy, and sweet; this never goes out of style. Use a good white bread.

Bread for toasting
Butter

Sugar
Cinnamon

Toast the bread. Butter one side generously and sprinkle it with a mixture of sugar and cinnamon, using 1 part cinnamon to 3 parts sugar. Toast again under the broiler, sugared side up, or place in a hot oven until sugar melts.

(SERVES TWO)

MILK TOAST

The image of Caspar Milquetoast—the "Timid Soul"—may have contributed to the fading reputation of this bland dish. Today it is mainly a curiosity, although sometimes comforting to the ill or convalescent.

Butter
4 slices white or wheat toast
2 cups milk

¼ cup raisins
¼ teaspoon salt

Butter the toast generously and place it in two soupbowls. Heat the milk with the raisins and salt, and simmer for a minute or two so that the raisins plump up. Pour half the milk mixture over each serving.

CROUTONS

For soups and salads—a good way to use stale or slightly stale bread.

SAUTÉED CROUTONS

Cut slices of *bread* in even cubes, removing the crusts. Sauté in hot *butter*, turning to brown all sides. Drain on paper towels.

BAKED CROUTONS

Lightly *butter* slices of *bread* on both sides, then cut in cubes, removing the crusts. Bake on a cookie sheet in a preheated 350°F oven, turning a few times until evenly brown.

GARLIC OR HERB CROUTONS

Add a *minced clove garlic* or some *minced fresh herbs* to the butter when you sauté or butter the bread.

POPOVERS ✳ (ABOUT 10 POPOVERS)

Forget what you've read elsewhere. The secret in making good popovers is to start them in a cold oven.

2 eggs	1 cup white flour
1 cup milk	¼ teaspoon salt
1 tablespoon butter, melted	

Put all ingredients in a large bowl and mix thoroughly, without overbeating. Half-fill buttered muffin pans or custard cups. Put them in a cold oven and set the heat for 450°F. Bake for 15 minutes, then reduce heat to 350°F and bake for another 15–20 minutes. Test one to be sure it's done by removing it from the pan: it should be crisp outside and moist and tender inside.

WHOLE-WHEAT POPOVERS

Use ⅔ *cup whole-wheat flour* and ⅓ *cup white flour* instead of all white flour. (Whole-wheat popovers will not rise as high as regular popovers.)

(SERVES SIX)

YORKSHIRE PUDDING

First cousin to the popover, this crisp, golden-brown puff is a glorious accompaniment to Roast Beef (p. 215). Remove the roast from the oven 25 minutes before it is to be served. It's essential that it be cooked in the roast beef fat and drippings, which flavor it so beautifully. The Yorkshire pudding will cook while the roast "rests" and can be brought to the table after you have carved the meat.

¼ cup roast beef pan
    drippings
2 eggs

1 cup milk
1 cup flour
¾ teaspoon salt

Turn the oven up to 450°F and pour the pan drippings into a 9 × 9-inch pan or an 11 × 7-inch pan. Put the pan in the oven to keep sizzling while you prepare the batter. Combine the eggs, milk, flour, and salt and beat until well blended. Pour batter into the prepared pan and bake 25–30 minutes. Serve piping hot from the baking pan, a generous square with each helping of roast beef.

(SIXTEEN 2-INCH SQUARES)

CORN BREAD

Sturdy, solid, slightly dry—a direct legacy from our American past.

¾ cup yellow cornmeal
1 cup flour
⅓ cup sugar
3 teaspoons baking powder
½ teaspoon salt

1 cup milk
1 egg, well beaten
2 tablespoons melted
    shortening or bacon fat

Preheat the oven to 425°F. Grease an 8-inch square cake pan. Mix the cornmeal, flour, sugar, baking powder, and salt in a large bowl. Add the milk, egg, and shortening or bacon fat, and blend well. Spoon into the pan and bake for about 20 minutes. Cool and cut in squares.

MEXICAN CORN BREAD

Add 2 *tablespoons diced green chilies, 1 cup cooked or canned corn kernels (or canned cream-style corn),* and *½ cup grated Cheddar or Jack cheese* to the batter and mix well.

CORN MUFFINS

Thoroughly grease muffin pans and pour the batter into the cups about three-quarters full. You should have 12 muffins. For a richer version use the recipe for Rich Corn Cake that follows.

RICH CORN CAKE   (SIXTEEN 2¼-INCH SQUARES)

1 cup yellow cornmeal	¾ teaspoon salt
1 cup flour	1 cup sour cream
4 tablespoons sugar	¼ cup milk
1 teaspoon baking soda	2 eggs, well beaten
2 teaspoons cream of tartar	4 tablespoons butter, melted

Preheat the oven to 425°F. Butter a 9 × 9 × 2-inch pan. Combine the cornmeal, flour, sugar, baking soda, cream of tartar, and salt and mix well. Quickly add the sour cream, milk, eggs, and butter. Stir just to mix. Spoon into pan and bake for about 20 minutes. Cool and cut in squares.

CORNSTICKS

Heavily grease cornstick pans and place them in the oven empty to get them smoking hot. Then fill them two-thirds full of corn cake batter. Bake for about 15 minutes or until a broomstraw inserted comes out dry.

WHITE CORN CAKE   (SIXTEEN 1-INCH SQUARES)

The soft, coarse crumb of this corn cake is fine with fried chicken and pan gravy.

4 tablespoons butter
½ cup sugar
1¼ cups white cornmeal
1¼ cups flour

4 teaspoons baking powder
1 teaspoon salt
1⅓ cups milk
3 egg whites, beaten stiff

Preheat the oven to 425°F. Butter an 8-inch square cake pan. Cream the butter in a mixing bowl, slowly add the sugar, and beat until light. Mix together the cornmeal, flour, baking powder, and salt. Add the milk to the butter mixture, alternating it with the mixed dry ingredients, and beat thoroughly. Stir a third of the beaten egg whites into the batter, then fold in the remaining whites. Spoon into the pan and bake for about 30 minutes. Cool and cut in squares.

(SERVES EIGHT)   **CUSTARD-FILLED CORN BREAD**

Like magic, when the corn bread is done, a creamy, barely set custard will have formed inside. Serve with maple syrup and a good country ham.

2 eggs
3 tablespoons butter, melted
3 tablespoons sugar
½ teaspoon salt
2 cups milk
1½ tablespoons white vinegar

1 cup all-purpose flour
¾ cup yellow cornmeal
1 teaspoon baking powder
½ teaspoon baking soda
1 cup heavy cream

Preheat the oven to 350°F. Butter an 8-inch square baking dish or pan that is about 2 inches deep. Put the buttered dish or pan in the oven and let it get hot while you mix the batter. Put the eggs in a mixing bowl and add the melted butter. Beat until the mixture is well blended. Add the sugar, salt, milk, and vinegar and beat well. Sift into a bowl or stir together in a bowl the flour, cornmeal, baking powder, and baking soda, and add to the egg mixture. Mix just until the batter is smooth and no lumps appear. Pour the batter into the heated dish, then pour the cream into the center of the batter—don't stir. Bake for 1 hour, or until lightly browned. Serve warm.

(2 DOZEN 3-INCH PANCAKES)   ✳   **THIN YELLOW CORNMEAL PANCAKES**

½ cup yellow cornmeal
½ cup boiling water
½ cup all-purpose flour
½ teaspoon salt
1 tablespoon sugar

1 tablespoon baking powder
1 egg, well beaten
1¼ cup melted butter
½ cup milk

Put the cornmeal in a mixing bowl and pour the boiling water over, stirring briskly until well blended. Add the flour, salt, sugar, baking powder, beaten egg, melted butter, and milk. Beat the batter until it is thoroughly mixed.

Heat the griddle over medium-high heat (don't cook these pancakes over as high a heat as you would normally use). Film the griddle with grease when it is hot. Use 2 tablespoons of batter for each pancake. Cook until bubbles break on top of the pancakes and turn them over. Cook another few minutes, or until the bottoms of the pancakes are lightly browned and set. Serve hot.

IRISH SODA BREAD   (8-INCH ROUND LOAF)

This is an authentic Irish soda bread, which contains no baking powder and is leavened solely by the acid and alkaline combination of the buttermilk and baking soda. The loaf is tender, compact, slightly moist, and has a rough crust with the characteristic **X** slashed on top.

4 cups flour	1 teaspoon baking soda
1½ teaspoons salt	2 cups buttermilk

Preheat the oven to 375°F. Grease a baking sheet or an 8-inch round cake pan. In a large mixing bowl, stir and toss together the flour, salt, and baking soda. Add the buttermilk and stir briskly with a fork until the dough holds together in a rough mass. Knead on a lightly floured surface for about 30 seconds, then pat into an 8-inch round about 1½ inches thick. With a sharp knife, slash a large ¼-inch-deep **X** across the top. Place the formed dough on the prepared baking sheet or cake pan and bake for about 45–50 minutes, until it is nicely browned and the **X** has spread open. Transfer to a rack to cool, then wrap in a slightly damp towel and let rest, on the rack, for at least 8 hours. Soda bread should always be completely cooled before serving.

BOSTON BROWN BREAD   (10 OR MORE SLICES)

This bread is traditionally served with baked beans. Use a 1-pound coffee tin if you do not have a pudding mold, and cover it with aluminum foil tied tight with string.

½ cup rye flour	½ teaspoon salt
½ cup cornmeal	⅓ cup molasses
½ cup whole-wheat flour	1 cup sour milk (p. 17)
1 teaspoon baking soda	

Mix the rye flour, cornmeal, whole-wheat flour, baking soda, and salt in a large bowl. Stir in the molasses and milk and blend well. Butter a 1-quart pudding mold or a 1-pound coffee tin and fill no more than two-thirds full. Cover tightly and place in a deep kettle. Add boiling water halfway up the mold. Cover the kettle and steam over moderate heat for 2 hours, replacing the water if necessary. Remove from mold. Cut slices with a string while hot by drawing the string around the bread, crossing, and pulling the ends. Or reheat, if necessary, in a 300°F oven.

RAISIN BROWN BREAD

Add ½ cup seedless raisins to the batter.

CREAM SCONES

(12 WEDGES)

Wedge-shaped with lightly browned sides and tops, cream scones and English tea are traditional partners. Serve with a plump mound of butter and some marmalade or jam.

2 cups flour	4 tablespoons butter
2 teaspoons baking powder	2 eggs, well beaten
1 tablespoon sugar	½ cup cream
½ teaspoon salt	

Preheat the oven to 425°F. Lightly butter a cookie sheet. Mix the flour, baking powder, sugar, and salt in a large bowl. Work in the butter with your fingers or a pastry blender until the mixture resembles coarse meal. Add the eggs and cream and stir until blended. Turn out onto a lightly floured board and knead for about a minute. Pat or roll the dough about ¾ inch thick and cut into wedges. Place on the cookie sheet and bake for about 15 minutes.

SHARON'S BUTTERMILK
* CURRANT SCONES

(16 WEDGES)

These scones have a fine, dense crumb with a little orange and cinnamon—a delicious combination of texture and flavor.

3 cups flour
⅓ cup plus 2 tablespoons
   sugar
2½ teaspoons baking powder
½ teaspoon baking soda
¾ teaspoon salt
¾ cup butter

1 cup buttermilk
¾ cup currants
1 teaspoon grated orange rind
   (orange part, or zest, only)
1 tablespoon heavy cream
¼ teaspoon cinnamon

Preheat the oven to 400°F. Use an ungreased baking sheet. Combine the flour, ⅓ cup of the sugar, baking powder, baking soda, and salt in a mixing bowl. Stir with a fork to mix well and aerate. Cut the butter into the flour mixture, using a pastry blender or two knives or working in with your fingertips, until the mixture looks like fresh crumbs. Add the buttermilk, currants, and orange rind. Mix only until the dry ingredients are moistened. Gather the dough into a ball and press so it holds together. Turn the dough out onto a lightly floured surface. Knead lightly twelve times. Divide the dough in two and pat each half into a circle ½ to ¾ inch thick. In a small bowl combine the cream, cinnamon, and remaining 2 tablespoons sugar, stirring to blend. Brush the dough with the glaze. Cut each circle into eight pie-shaped pieces. Place the scones slightly apart on the baking sheet. Bake for about 12–15 minutes, or until the tops are browned. Serve hot.

QUICK COFFEE CAKE   (8-INCH SQUARE CAKE)

Simple to make, good to eat.

1 cup sugar
1¼ cups white flour
2 teaspoons baking powder
4 tablespoons butter
1 egg, lightly beaten

½ cup milk
1 tablespoon sugar mixed
   with 1½ teaspoons
   cinnamon

Preheat the oven to 375°F. Butter an 8-inch square cake pan. Mix the 1 cup sugar, the flour, and the baking powder in a large bowl. Work in the butter with your fingers or a pastry blender until the mixture resembles coarse meal. Add the egg and milk and blend. Spoon into the pan. Sprinkle the sugar-cinnamon mixture evenly over the top. Bake for 20 minutes.

GRIDDLECAKES, WAFFLES, AND DOUGHNUTS

(16 GRIDDLECAKES) ## GRIDDLECAKES

The amount of milk you use will determine how thick these griddle-cakes or pancakes are. Start with the smaller amount suggested and add more if the batter seems too thick. Try to have the milk at room temperature before mixing and take care not to overbeat: a few lumps in the batter will do no harm. You can make lighter, fluffier griddle-cakes by separating the egg, beating the white, and folding it in last. Serve with maple syrup or honey.

½–¾ cup milk
2 tablespoons butter, melted
1 egg
1 cup white flour

2 teaspoons baking powder
2 tablespoons sugar
½ teaspoon salt

Beat the milk, butter, and egg lightly in a mixing bowl. Mix the flour, baking powder, sugar, and salt and add them all at once to the first mixture, stirring just enough to dampen the flour. Lightly butter or grease a griddle or frying pan and set over moderate heat until a few drops of cold water sprinkled on the pan form rapidly moving glob-ules. If you wish small pancakes, drop about 2 tablespoons of the bat-ter onto the pan, or pour about ¼ cup from a measuring cup if larger pancakes are desired. Bake on the griddle until the cakes are full of bubbles on the top and the undersides are lightly browned. Turn with a spatula and brown the other sides. Place finished griddlecakes on a warm plate in a 200°F oven until you have enough to begin serving.

BUTTERMILK GRIDDLECAKES

Use *buttermilk, sour milk, or yogurt* instead of milk and substitute *½ tea-spoon baking soda* for the 2 teaspoons baking powder.

WHOLE-WHEAT GRIDDLECAKES

Use *⅓ cup whole-wheat flour* and *⅔ cup white flour*. If you wish, sweeten the batter with 2 *tablespoons molasses or honey* instead of sugar.

OATMEAL GRIDDLECAKES

Heat the ½ cup of milk, stir in *½ cup quick-cooking oatmeal,* and let stand for 10 minutes. Add the remaining ingredients, reducing the flour to 2 tablespoons.

BUCKWHEAT CAKES

Use *½ cup buckwheat flour* and *½ cup white flour.*

APPLE GRIDDLECAKES

Peel *1 tart, juicy apple,* cut it in thin slices, and stir it in. Optional: toss apple slices with ½ teaspoon cinnamon or allspice.

BLUEBERRY GRIDDLECAKES

Add *½ cup blueberries.* If you use canned blueberries, strain them before adding.

ANY FRESH FRUIT GRIDDLECAKES

After the griddlecake is cooking on the first side, sprinkle it with *1–2 tablespoons diced fresh fruit.* When cakes are full of bubbles on top, turn and continue cooking as directed.

BUTTERMILK WAFFLES   (6–8 WAFFLES)

These waffles are appealing because of their slightly tart buttermilk taste, perfect with warm honey.

1½ cups all-purpose flour	3 eggs
2 teaspoons baking powder	1½ cups buttermilk
¾ teaspoon baking soda	¼ cup melted butter
½ teaspoon salt	¼ cup milk, if needed
2 tablespoons sugar	

Put the flour into a mixing bowl and add the baking powder, soda, salt, and sugar. Stir with a fork to blend. In another mixing bowl, beat the eggs until well blended. Stir in the buttermilk and the melted butter (cooled off a little). Add the flour mixture and stir until well mixed. If the batter seems rather thick, add the milk to thin it. The batter should flow from the spoon, not plop. Bake in a hot waffle iron until crisp and golden. Serve hot.

WHOLE-WHEAT BUTTERMILK WAFFLES

Replace ¾ cup of all-purpose flour with ¾ cup of whole-wheat flour and proceed as directed above.

COTTAGE CHEESE GRIDDLECAKES

(12 GRIDDLECAKES)

Turn these tender pancakes gently, and let them cook a little longer than you would a traditional pancake.

1 cup large-curd cottage cheese	2 tablespoons butter, melted
3 eggs	¼ cup white flour
	¼ teaspoon salt

Dry the cottage cheese in a sieve, pressing it down firmly and letting it stand and drip for an hour or so. Beat the eggs well in a mixing bowl. Add the cottage cheese, butter, flour, and salt, and mix only enough to blend. Drop by large spoonfuls onto a buttered, moderately hot griddle or frying pan. Turn gently with a spatula when lightly browned on the underside and bake on the other side until light brown. Keep warm in a 200°F oven until you have enough to serve.

BAKED PANCAKES (GERMAN OR DUTCH BABIES)

(12-INCH BAKED PANCAKE, OR FOUR 6-INCH DUTCH BABIES)

This is not a griddled pancake at all, but an eggy batter baked in the oven like Yorkshire pudding or popovers. You'll be surprised at what three eggs can do when beaten with milk and flour. This mixture billows up to unbelievable heights and turns golden.

3 eggs, room temperature	2 tablespoons butter, melted
½ cup milk	2 tablespoons lemon juice
½ cup all-purpose flour	Confectioners' sugar
½ teaspoon salt	

Preheat the oven to 450°F. Butter a 12-inch skillet or four small skillets (with ovenproof handles) or pans (you can use small pie pans or cake pans). Break the eggs into a mixing bowl and beat until thoroughly mixed. Add the milk and blend well. Sift the flour and salt onto a square of wax paper. Lift the wax paper up by two corners and let the flour slowly drift into the egg and milk, whisking steadily. (Or slowly sift the flour and salt directly into the egg mixture, while whisking to blend and smooth.) Add the melted butter and mix briskly so the batter is smooth. Pour the batter into the pan or pans and bake for 15 minutes. If you are baking small pancakes, they will be done after 15 minutes. If you are baking just one big pancake, reduce the heat to 350°F and bake for another 10 minutes. Sprinkle the lemon juice over the pancake (or pancakes) and dust the top(s) with confectioners' sugar. Serve at once while hot and high and mighty.

CRÊPES OR FRENCH PANCAKES

(ABOUT TWELVE 7-INCH PANCAKES OR SIXTEEN 5-INCH PANCAKES)

This crêpe recipe first appeared in the *Fannie Farmer Cook Book* in 1930, although the thin French pancakes that it produces seem always to have had a place in American cookery. Simple to make and extraordinarily versatile, they are good plain, stuffed and rolled, or sweetened. Like a velvet cape wrapped around a simple dress, they transform good leftovers (see index for crêpes with savory fillings and sweet fillings).

2 eggs	1 cup flour
1 cup milk	2 tablespoons butter, melted
½ teaspoon salt	

Beat the eggs well, then beat in the milk, salt, flour, and butter. (Or mix all the ingredients in a blender until smooth.) Cover and let stand for at least 30 minutes. Heat a 7-inch or 5-inch skillet or crêpe pan until moderately hot, then film it with butter or shortening, using a brush or a folded paper towel. Using a ladle or small cup, pour in several tablespoons of batter, then quickly tilt the pan so that the batter spreads evenly in the thinnest possible layer. (If there is too much batter in the pan, pour it back into the bowl of batter and use less for the next pancake.) Cook for a few more minutes, until the bottom is lightly browned and the edges lift easily from the pan. The pancake should then slide loosely about in the pan. Turn it with a spatula or by catching an edge with your fingers and flipping it over. Cook the second side for a few minutes; it will brown in spots, not as evenly as the first side, but it doesn't matter because this side should be used inside when the crêpes are rolled. Remove to a plate and film the pan again lightly with butter or shortening before cooking the next pancake. If the batter seems to be getting too thick as you get toward the end of it, add a little milk. Crêpes freeze very well simply stacked and wrapped in foil or plastic with the edges tightly sealed. Defrost at room temperature before separating them.

(ENOUGH FOR TWELVE 7-INCH PANCAKES OR SIXTEEN 5-INCH PANCAKES)

Cheese Filling

Make 2 *cups White Sauce* (p. 379). Stir in 1½ *cups grated Swiss or Cheddar cheese* and heat until melted. Spoon about 4 tablespoons of filling onto the bottom third of each pancake; the mixture will be enough to fill the number of pancakes the preceding recipe yields. Roll up the pancakes and arrange side by side in a shallow, buttered baking dish. Sprinkle with ½ *cup grated cheese*. Heat in the upper part of a preheated 350°F oven until lightly browned. Or heat thoroughly and then brown quickly under the broiler.

(ABOUT 18 DOUGHNUTS) **OLD-FASHIONED DOUGHNUTS**

Easier to make and more cakelike than yeast-leavened doughnuts (p. 745), these doughnuts have a fine, creamy crumb. The temperature of the cooking oil is crucial, so use a frying (candy) thermometer.

½ cup milk
½ cup granulated sugar
2 teaspoons baking powder
¼ teaspoon nutmeg
½ teaspoon salt
1 egg, beaten
1 tablespoon butter, melted

1¾ cups white flour, approximately
Vegetable shortening or oil, for frying
Confectioners' or granulated sugar, for dusting

Mix the milk, granulated sugar, baking powder, nutmeg, salt, egg, and butter in a large bowl. Add the flour gradually, using just enough so that the dough is firm enough to handle yet as soft as possible. Cover the dough and chill for about 1 hour. Turn out onto a lightly floured board and knead for a few minutes. Roll out about ½ inch thick. Cut with a doughnut cutter or sharp knife into 3-inch rounds, cutting out and saving the centers (which can also be fried). Place on a lightly floured piece of wax paper and let rest for about 5 minutes. Using a heavy pan and a thermometer, heat about 4 inches of shortening or oil to 360°F. Fry three or four doughnuts at a time, turning them with a fork or tongs when one side is browned and continuing to fry until brown all over. Drain on paper towels and dust with sugar.

CRULLERS
(THREE DOZEN)

Prepare the batter for Doughnuts. Roll it out ⅓ inch thick. Cut it in strips 8 inches long and ¾ inch wide. Let rest for 10 minutes, then twist each strip several times and pinch the ends. Fry, drain, and roll in sugar.

CHOCOLATE DOUGHNUTS

Mix ½ cup *unsweetened cocoa* with the flour. Dust the drained doughnuts with sugar or spread with *Creamy Chocolate Frosting* (p. 839).

WAFFLES
(8 WAFFLES)

Many automatic waffle irons have thermostats that indicate when to add the batter. To test one that doesn't, put 1 teaspoon of water inside, close it, and turn it on; when the steaming stops, the iron is ready for the batter. Modern waffle irons do not need greasing. If the first waffle sticks, as it is often inclined to do, bake it a little longer and expect no problem with the others. Remember that a thin batter makes tender waffles. Serve them with melted butter and warmed maple syrup.

2 eggs, well beaten
1 cup milk
3 tablespoons vegetable oil
1½ cups flour

3 teaspoons baking powder
2 teaspoons sugar
½ teaspoon salt

Mix the eggs, milk, and oil in a large bowl or pitcher. Stir in the flour, baking powder, sugar, and salt and mix until blended. Heat the waffle iron, brush it with melted shortening or oil if necessary, pour in enough batter to just fill. Close and bake until the steaming stops and the waffles are crisp, tender, and brown.

(6 STANDARD-SIZE WAFFLES) **SPECIAL WAFFLES**

This method makes waffles extra-light.

2 cups flour
3 teaspoons baking powder
½ teaspoon salt
3 eggs, separated

1¾ cups milk
4 tablespoons butter, melted
3 tablespoons sugar

Combine the flour, baking powder, and salt in a bowl. In a separate bowl beat the egg yolks well, and add the milk and butter. Combine the flour and yolk mixture and beat until smooth. Beat the egg whites until stiff, but not dry. Slowly add the sugar, beating constantly. Mix a third of the beaten whites gently into the batter, then fold in the remaining whites very carefully. Spread ½ cup of waffle batter in the hot waffle iron. Bake until golden.

(8 WAFFLES) **CORNMEAL WAFFLES**

1¾ cups white flour
1 cup yellow cornmeal
2½ teaspoons baking powder
½ teaspoon baking soda
1 teaspoon salt

3 eggs, separated
2½ cups buttermilk
4 tablespoons butter, melted
3 tablespoons sugar

Mix well together the flour, cornmeal, baking powder, baking soda, and salt. In a separate bowl, beat the egg yolks. Add the buttermilk and butter, and stir to blend. Combine with the flour mixture and mix well. Beat the egg whites until stiff but not dry, and slowly add the sugar, beating until it is absorbed. Stir a third of the whites into the flour mixture and gently fold the remaining whites in. Spoon ½ cup of waffle batter in a greased hot waffle iron. Bake until golden.

RAISED WAFFLES *   (ABOUT 8 WAFFLES)

This is the best waffle I know. The mixing is done the night before and
all you have to do in the morning is add a couple of eggs and some
baking soda. They are crisp on the outside and delicate on the inside.

½ cup warm water
1 package dry yeast
2 cups warm milk
½ cup melted butter
1 teaspoon salt

1 teaspoon sugar
2 cups all-purpose flour
2 eggs
¼ teaspoon baking soda

Use a rather large mixing bowl—the batter will rise to double its original volume. Put the water in the mixing bowl and sprinkle in the yeast.
Let stand to dissolve for 5 minutes. Add the milk, butter, salt, sugar,
and flour to the yeast mixture and beat until smooth and blended. (I often use a hand rotary beater to get rid of the lumps.) Cover the bowl
with plastic wrap and let stand overnight at room temperature. Just before cooking the waffles, beat in the eggs, add the baking soda, and stir
until well mixed. The batter will be very thin. Pour about ½–¾ cup batter into a very hot waffle iron. Bake the waffles until they are golden
and crisp. This batter will keep well for several days in the refrigerator.

WHITE CRACKERS   (5 DOZEN 2-INCH CRACKERS)

Is it really worth making crackers? Yes, indeed. These are terrific just
buttered or with cheese or some of the spreads in the appetizer chapter. Stored in a sealed container, they keep indefinitely.

2 cups flour
1 tablespoon sugar
2 teaspoons salt,
    approximately

2 tablespoons butter, chilled
⅔ cup milk, plus droplets
    more if needed

Preheat oven to 425°F. Use ungreased cookie sheets. Combine the
flour, sugar, and ½ teaspoon of the salt in a mixing bowl. Stir the dry
ingredients to blend well. Cut the butter into small pieces and add to
the dry mixture. Using either your fingertips or a pastry cutter, cut the
bits of butter into the dry mixture until it looks like fine crumbs.
Slowly stir in the milk, adding enough so the dough pulls away from
the sides of the bowl. Add a few drops more if the dough seems dry—
it should be soft and pliable, not wet and sticky. Divide the dough in
half. Lightly dust a surface with flour. Roll each half out to a square approximately 13 × 13 inches and thinner than ⅛ inch. Trim the uneven

edges and lift the dough onto the cookie sheet, or roll over a rolling pin and unroll onto the cookie sheet. Use a sharp knife to score the dough into 2-inch squares, cutting *almost* through the dough. Sprinkle the top with the remaining salt and press down onto the dough. Bake for 6–8 minutes, or until the edges are slightly golden. Remove from the oven and with a large spatula loosen the squares and turn them over (often I do this gently by hand). Return to the oven and bake for another 5–6 minutes, or until the edges are well browned. Remove from oven and slide the sheet onto racks to cool. Break the crackers apart when cool and store in an airtight container. These will keep for weeks and taste fresh.

(3 DOZEN 1½-INCH SQUARES)   ✳ **OATMEAL CRACKERS**

Crisp and very coarse with a nutlike taste.

2½ cups old-fashioned rolled oats	½ cup cold water
	Salt to taste

Preheat the oven to 275°F. Stir 2 cups of the oatmeal together with the water in a bowl until the dough holds together in a mass. Sprinkle your work surface with ¼ cup oatmeal and turn the dough out on top of it. With a rolling pin, roll the dough to ⅛-inch thickness, moving and lifting it as necessary to prevent sticking and sprinkling on more oatmeal so that the top and bottom are amply coated. If the dough cracks while you are rolling it, push it together with your fingers to seal the cracks. Trim the edges and cut the dough in half. Lift the dough with a spatula, and place each half on an ungreased cookie sheet. Lightly sprinkle salt over the top, and with a knife score the dough, without cutting through, into 1½-inch squares. Bake for 30 minutes, turn each rectangle over with a spatula, and bake for 15–20 minutes longer. To prevent the rectangles from curling a little around the edges, press the edges down with a spatula while they bake. Remove from the oven and cool on racks. Break into individual square crackers and serve. Store in an airtight container.

CAKES

Don't be timid about baking a cake. If it does not turn out perfect in appearance, there are ways to remedy slight flaws (see Box on the following page). I have worked out all of these cake recipes specifically for the home baker and you shouldn't have trouble with them. However, I have found that readers are somewhat daunted by having too many cake recipes to choose from and they often ask how to select the right cake for a particular occasion. So I have selected below some of my favorites, including some new ones that are dandies, and matched each one to the occasion.

One word about sugar. It is essential to the balance of flavor in a good cake. If you begin to reduce the sugar you lose some of the essential texture and the result is bound to disappoint anyone who loves cake. There are plenty of other choices for dessert that contain little sugar. But if you are going to bake a cake, make it a good one.

Don't try to bake a cake in the microwave. True, there are some mousselike or puddinglike cakes that respond well to the steaming effect of the microwave but they are not true cakes. Because the microwave oven remains cool with only the irregular distribution of waves doing the cooking, you can't get the steady, even dry heat required for baking.

The Right Cake for the Right Occasion

BIRTHDAY CAKES:
Chocolate Cake, p. 793, very silky with a fine texture.
Lady Baltimore Cake, p. 799, fine-textured, lightly flavored—a drift of pure white.
Birthday Cake, p. 802, an old-fashioned birthday cake flavored with fruits and nuts.

DESSERT CAKES:
German Sweet Chocolate Cake, p. 796, a classic, new to this

edition, rich with a seductive blend of chocolate, caramel, and coconut.

Raised Cheese Cake, p. 824, another new entry, a fluffy and moist cheese cake.

GOOD TRAVELING CAKES:

Lazy Daisy Cake, p. 823, easy-to-make one-layer sponge cake with a caramel topping, easy to move in its pan.

Sweet Almond Cake, p. 823, a one-layer, moist cake.

Rabbit's Carrot Cake, p. 819, filling and satisfying for a picnic.

BETWEEN-MEALS CAKES:

Walnut Mocha Cake, p. 798, a good-looking, delicious cake with a penuche frosting.

Daffodil Cake, p. 812, a pretty cake for the tea table that looks magical.

WEDDING CAKE:

Making an oversize wedding cake at home demands special equipment and a certain amount of skill (for a detailed recipe see *The Fannie Farmer Baking Book*), so I recommend making several 8- or 9-inch layer cakes and arranging them around a fresh bouquet of flowers. My favorite is *Fresh Coconut Cake*, beautiful, light, tender, and lofty in height.

ABOUT CAKEMAKING

Baking is not any more difficult than other kinds of cooking, but it *is* very different. That is why it sometimes seems a bit intimidating, even to those with lots of kitchen experience. When you're making a cake, you can't rely merely on good taste, instinct, and ingenuity, which mean so much in other kinds of cooking. Baking requires skill and accuracy: there are special techniques, like folding and whipping, to master, and there are basic rules of chemistry to obey. It is important to follow a recipe exactly, to measure accurately, and to use a well-regulated oven and properly prepared pans of the right size.

NOTE

Once you accept these facts, however, you'll find that it does not take long to acquire a feeling for baking procedures and a respect for the wondrous process by which butter, sugar, eggs, flour, and a few other simple ingredients are transformed into the sweet, light, tempting array of confections that we call "cake." Using good, well-tested recipes like the ones in this chapter, you'll find that it's easy to make perfect cakes—cakes that are light, fine, and tender with an even-textured, slightly moist crumb. And your feeling of pride will be heightened by the pleasure that comes from knowing that your cakes are made with fresh, wholesome ingredients.

Tips on Cakes

- If cakes have trouble baking evenly it is because the heat in your oven is uneven. Sometimes it is necessary to turn the cake during baking.
- If you are uncertain about whether your oven is properly calibrated, hang a mercury thermometer from the rung in the center and adjust the heat accordingly.
- Begin to test a cake 5–10 minutes before it is supposed to be done by inserting a toothpick or broomstraw near the center: if it comes out clean the cake is done.
- If cakes are left in the oven even a few minutes too long they may be dry.
- To fix a lopsided baked cake, shave off with a sharp knife a thin horizontal slice to even up the surface.
- If you have a sunken cake, simply add more filling in the center.
- If you have a badly misshapen cake, don't throw it away. Cut it up into squares and frost them.

Kinds of Cakes

There are two basic kinds of cakes: those made with butter or some other kind of shortening and those made without any shortening.

Cakes Made with Shortening. Many of the cakes with which we are most familiar—standard white, gold, and chocolate cakes, spice cakes, pound cakes, fruit cakes, and gingerbreads—fall into this category and are frequently referred to as "butter" cakes. These cakes usually use baking powder or baking soda for leavening. More finely grained than those made without shortening, they are easy to fill and frost and make excellent layer cakes.

Sometimes the eggs in butter cakes are added whole; sometimes they are separated and the beaten egg whites are folded in just before baking. Butter cakes made with separately beaten egg whites are lighter and fluffier than cakes made with whole eggs.

Cakes Made Without Shortening. Sponge cakes and angel food cakes are made without butter or shortening. Sponge cakes use separately beaten egg yolks and whites; angel food cakes are made only with beaten egg whites.

Cakes in this category usually do not use chemical leavening but depend exclusively on the air beaten into eggs or egg whites instead. These cakes are delicate and need to be assembled with special care.

Tortes. Tortes are European in origin. They are usually made with separated eggs; ground nuts or crumbs are often used instead of flour, although many tortes do contain some flour. Tortes are very rich and require no more finishing than a dusting of confectioners' sugar or a little whipped cream. They will stay fresh longer than other cakes.

Ingredients

Shortening. Butter, margarine, vegetable shortening, vegetable oil, or a combination of several of these may be used as shortening in cakes.

Vegetable shortening is cheaper than butter and somewhat easier to use because of its soft, spreadable consistency. It keeps indefinitely and requires no refrigeration. We use it in those cakes where the *flavor* of butter is not important, either because there is very little shortening in the cake or because the flavor of the spices and seasonings in the cake is stronger than the taste of butter. Because so many people are purists when it comes to using butter in baking, we've compared carefully the same cake made with butter and with shortening. The texture of the cake with vegetable shortening seemed a bit springier and the color was lighter, but we all found it hard to distinguish a noticeable difference in taste.

Butter, nevertheless, is generally favored by cooks and bakers. It should be fresh and, preferably, sweet (unsalted). Let it become slightly soft, not mushy, at room temperature before you use it.

Vegetable oil is used most often in chiffon cakes or in "quick" cakes that can be easily beaten without an electric beater.

Sugar. Sugar adds sweetness and tenderness to cakes. If your sugar is lumpy, be sure to sift it before using. Do not use lumpy brown sugar when baking; the hard lumps will *not* dissolve in baking. For storing brown sugar and keeping it soft, see p. 20.

Eggs. Eggs make a cake rich and give it good taste and texture. As elsewhere in this book use eggs that are officially graded "large." To substitute eggs of a different size in these recipes, follow the proportions outlined on p. 473.

Some cakes that call for separated eggs depend on beaten egg whites exclusively for leavening, so in these instances it is especially important that the whites be beaten properly. Always have the eggs at room temperature and follow the directions for beating and folding on pp. 473–74.

Cutting corners in cakemaking doesn't pay. It would, of course, be easier to beat the egg whites when you first begin to mix a cake, while the beaters are clean and dry and have not yet been used to combine the other ingredients. Indeed, many cookbooks do recommend this method for that very reason. But we have found that egg whites have a tendency to deflate when they stand around for any length of time. And since their volume is so important to the success of a cake, we recommend that they be beaten last, just before they are folded into the batter.

Tip on Overbeaten Egg Whites

If you have overbeaten your egg whites and they are very dry, stiff, and break apart, they cannot be successfully folded into a batter. To correct the problem, add 1 unbeaten egg white to your overbeaten whites and beat for a few seconds or until they are the proper consistency. If this doesn't occur within 1 minute, beat in another egg white.

Flour. All flour should be stored in airtight containers. The recipes in this chapter call either for all-purpose flour or for cake flour, a soft-wheat flour that contains more starch and less gluten than hard-wheat bread flour or all-purpose flour.

Cake flour makes a cake lighter and more delicate. It can compensate for the drying and coarsening qualities of baking powder. It can be used in any cake recipe, but since it is more expensive than all-purpose flour, we call for it only in recipes where we feel it will make a significant difference. It is even a bit difficult to find in some supermarkets today.

All-purpose flour produces fine cakes, and you can substitute it for cake flour whenever necessary.

Instant-blending all-purpose flour, milled so fine it will pass right through a sifter, is not a substitute for cake flour. Since it will dissolve instantly in cold (but not hot) liquids, use it, if you wish, in sauces, fillings, and gravies, but not in cakes.

Do not use self-rising flour in these cake recipes; it is premixed with salt and leavening and requires adjustment of the recipe.

Sifting is a way of lightening flour and thoroughly mixing it with the other dry ingredients. In the past it was considered absolutely essential to sift flour in any cake recipe, and most cake recipes still call for sifted flour. Flour today, however, is sifted many times during milling before it is packaged and sent to the stores. We find that many cakes are just as good when made with unsifted flour, and this certainly makes them easier to prepare. At least one major flour company, after extensive research, has arrived at similar conclusions. Thus, you will find that we have eliminated the direction to sift in many of these recipes and suggest simply mixing the flour with the other dry ingredients, blending them well with a fork.

To measure flour without sifting, scoop it up in a dry-measure cup or spoon it lightly into the measuring cup. Level it off with a straight knife. Do not tap or bang the cup or the flour will settle. Better a little *less* flour in a cake than a little more.

We continue to recommend sifting in recipes for refined cakes like sponge or angel food cakes, where the lightness of sifted flour will make it easier to fold it into the beaten egg whites. When sifting, sift onto wax paper, from which the dry ingredients can then be added directly to the measuring cup or mixing bowl. It is better not to wash the sifter, since the flour residue may make cake. Tap out as much of the remaining flour as possible and wrap the sifter in a plastic bag before putting it away.

Leavening. Use double-acting baking powder in these recipes. To make sure it is always fresh, replace it every six months. For information about baking powder, baking soda, and other leaveners, see p. 17.

Chocolate. Chocolate burns easily. It is best to melt it over simmering water, rather than over a direct flame. For information about kinds of chocolate, storing chocolate, melting chocolate, and substituting cocoa for chocolate, see p. 12.

Dried Fruit and Nuts. Dried fruit and nuts, when added to cake batters, often sink to the bottom. In thin batters, chop the fruit and nuts finely and gently stir in batter just before popping cake into the oven. This sometimes holds them evenly throughout the batter.

Dried fruit that is old and hard will not soften during baking. Soften it by boiling it in water for about 10 minutes, then drain it thoroughly and pat it dry before adding it to the batter. Fruit prepared specifically for use in fruit cakes is available in stores, especially at holiday time.

Nuts keep best when stored in the refrigerator or freezer. When grinding nuts for tortes, keep them light and fluffy and take care not to overgrind. If using a blender, do only ½ cup at a time and turn the motor on and off. Very finely ground or pulverized nuts will become oily and make a heavy, sodden cake.

Preparing Cake Pans

Make sure that you use the size pan that is called for in the recipe. For most cakes the pans should be greased and lightly floured so that the cakes do not stick. Pans and molds with designs in them need especially heavy greasing so that cakes will come out easily.

Prepare the pans for butter cakes before you begin to mix the ingredients so that the pans will be ready when you need them. First, grease them. Using your fingers, scoop up about a teaspoon of soft butter or vegetable shortening and smear it around the bottom and sides of the cake pan. Then sprinkle it liberally all over with flour, and shake out the excess.

Angel food cakes and sponge cakes do not call for greased pans: the beaten egg whites that leaven them will rise better and higher on an ungreased surface. Bake angel food cakes in clean, dry tube pans; sponge cakes in ungreased pans that have been fitted with a round of wax paper on the bottom. You can butter the bottom of the tube pan to keep the wax paper in place, if you wish. Some tube pans come with removable bottoms (in which case don't use a paper liner).

Jelly-roll pans are traditionally lined with wax paper: simply grease the bottom of the pan, then cover it with wax paper, leaving about 2 inches overlap at each of the short ends of the pan; the paper will peel off easily when the cake is turned out to cool.

Tip for Easy Cake Removal

Lining any cake pan with aluminum foil cut to size, placed in the pan shiny side up, then greased and floured, will insure easy cake removal. Just peel off the foil after the cake is turned out to cool.

Vegetable cooking spray is a great boon to preparing muffin tins and cake pans for batters, instead of greasing by hand. The pure vegetable cooking spray works better than the combination spray with oil and flour.

Mixing Cake Batters

Have the ingredients at room temperature and measure them all out first before you begin to mix them. Try to get in the habit of turning on the oven to preheat while you assemble and mix the ingredients, so that it will be hot and ready when you need it.

It is almost impossible to give the exact amount of time that it will take to mix a cake batter—the time will vary, according to the recipe and the type of beater that you use. These recipes assume that you are using some form of electric beater which will combine the ingredients quickly and efficiently. Needless to say, if you are beating a cake by hand it will take more time and the ingredients should be added more gradually. In general, cake batters should be beaten just long enough to combine all the ingredients thoroughly.

The procedure for mixing the batter for a butter cake differs considerably from that used for sponge cakes. With butter cakes the shortening is usually softened, or "creamed," first, so that it blends more readily with the other ingredients. This can be done by beating it with a wooden spoon or at low speed with an electric beater. The sugar should then be added gradually and beaten in well. Shortening and sugar, when properly creamed together, will get light in color and creamy in consistency. Eggs or egg yolks are usually added next, along with vanilla or other flavorings. Add them all at once if you're using an electric mixer; if you're beating by hand or with a less efficient beater, add the eggs one at a time, beating each one in well before adding the next. The mixed dry ingredients and the liquid are added next, again all at once if an electric mixer is used. When mixing by hand, it's best to add the dry and liquid ingredients alternately, beginning and ending with the dry ones, for this is the fastest way to incorporate them without overbeating the cake (that is why so many old recipes detail this method). If the butter cake recipe calls for separated eggs, the egg whites should be beaten separately at the end and folded in just before baking.

Sponge cakes are very delicate, and their ingredients must be combined carefully. The egg yolks are generally beaten first, and then the sugar and other flavorings are added. The whites, which do the leavening, should be carefully beaten, but not overbeaten, just before they are to be folded in. We suggest beating a little sugar into the beaten egg whites to help them hold the air. Stir a little of the beaten whites into the egg yolk mixture to lighten it before folding in the remaining whites and the sifted flour very gently and with a light hand.

Filling Cake Pans

Most cake pans should be filled no more than two-thirds full to allow room for the cake to rise. Spread the batter up against the sides of the pan a bit and well into the corners.

You can substitute square, rectangular, or irregularly shaped pans for round layer pans. Measure the volume of the layer pan by filling it with water, then pour the water into the pan you wish to use to judge its volume. Adjust the amount of batter you prepare accordingly. Remember, when you substitute pans that are different from those called for in the recipe, the baking time may also vary.

Baking Cakes

Always bake cakes in a preheated oven unless the recipe says otherwise: many a cake has been ruined by a slow start in a cool oven. Make sure that your oven temperature is accurate. You can use an oven thermometer to check it out, but the best test is your own experience: if your cakes bake unevenly or consistently take more or less time than the recipe suggests, it's worth having the oven regulator checked by a reliable service company.

Glass or dark-colored pans will retain more heat than shiny ones. When using them, bake the same amount of time but reduce the oven temperature by 25 degrees.

Bake cakes on the center rack of the oven, or as near the center as possible to allow room for the heat to circulate. Do not overcrowd the oven or let pans touch each other. If using two racks, stagger the pans so that they are not right on top of each other. If the cake is baking unevenly, turn the pan several times during baking.

Begin to test a cake, 5–10 minutes before it is supposed to be done, by inserting a toothpick or a broomstraw near the center: if it comes out clean the cake is done. Use a long piece of straw or a long wooden skewer to test a high tube cake; do not use metal cake testers, for they do not work well. You can also test a cake by pressing it lightly with your fingertip: most cakes, unless they are very rich, will spring back, leaving no depression, when they are done. Remember also that a cake that is done will shrink a bit away from the sides of the pan.

High-Altitude Baking

At altitudes of 3,500 feet or higher, the amount of leavening in a cake must be reduced and the oven temperature raised, or the cake will be dry, coarse, and crumbly. Decrease the amount of baking powder or baking soda by one-third at 3,500 feet, by one-half at 5,000 feet, and by two-thirds above 5,000 feet. Raise the oven temperature by 25 degrees, and do not beat the eggs or egg whites quite as much as usual.

The agriculture departments in many states issue books of recipes especially adapted for baking at high altitudes.

Cooling Cakes

Let butter cakes cool and shrink in their pans for about 5 minutes, then turn them out on a wire rack to cool completely. If the cake should stick to the pan, use a spatula to loosen it gently.

Sponge cakes, angel food cakes, and chiffon cakes should be allowed to cool upside down by inverting the tube pans in which they were baked. If the pan does not have little "feet" to raise it above the surface on which it rests, set the pan over the neck of a bottle so that air can circulate around the cake while it is cooling. When completely cool, loosen with a spatula or a knife, if necessary, and turn out.

Frosting Cakes

For information about frosting and filling cakes, see p. 833.

Storing Cakes

Most cakes taste best when they are fresh, no more than a day or two old. If you plan to keep a cake for several days, wrap it well in foil or plastic wrap. Store it in a cake box, cover it with a deep bowl, or keep it in the refrigerator. Some cakes—those with perishable fillings or frostings—must be refrigerated. An iced cake will keep better than unfrosted layers.

All cakes freeze well. They should be wrapped tight before freezing to prevent the "freezer burn" that results when air gets into the wrappings.

Defrost cakes at room temperature for 1–2 hours. Let them thaw completely before you unwrap them.

Cakes can be frozen with or without frosting, though it's easier to freeze them without. To wrap and freeze a frosted cake, set it on a piece of foil on a plate in the freezer; *after* it is frozen, remove it from the plate, wrap it well, and return it to the freezer.

CAKES MADE WITH SHORTENING
(BUTTER CAKES)

(TWO 8-INCH ROUND LAYERS)   ✳   **CHOCOLATE CAKE**

A fine-grained, tender cake—ice water is its secret. If you wanted a chocolate cake for a birthday, this would be the one to pick.

2 ounces unsweetened
  chocolate
¼ pound butter
1½ cups sugar
2 eggs

2 teaspoons vanilla
2 cups cake flour
1½ teaspoons baking soda
½ teaspoon salt
1 cup ice water

Preheat the oven to 350°F. Butter and lightly flour two 8-inch round cake pans. Melt the chocolate in a small pot or bowl over simmering water; set aside to cool. Cream the butter, slowly beat in the sugar, and beat until light. Add the eggs and the vanilla, mixing well. Add the chocolate and combine thoroughly. Mix the flour, baking soda, and salt together, add to the first mixture, and blend. Add the water and beat until smooth. Pour the batter into the pans and bake for 25–30 minutes, until a toothpick comes out clean. Cool in the pans for 5 minutes before turning out onto racks. Frost with *Portsmouth* (p. 837) or *Creamy Chocolate Frosting* (p. 839).

HUNTINGTON CHOCOLATE CAKE (TWO 9-INCH ROUND LAYERS)

This plain, satisfying chocolate cake can be made very quickly and easily.

4 ounces unsweetened
  chocolate
1 cup shortening, or ½ pound
  butter
1 teaspoon vanilla
2 cups cake flour

2 cups sugar
1½ teaspoons baking powder
1 teaspoon baking soda
1 teaspoon salt
1 cup milk
4 eggs

Preheat the oven to 350°F. Butter and lightly flour two 9-inch round cake pans. Melt the chocolate and shortening or butter together in a bowl or pot over simmering water; stir in the vanilla. Mix the flour, sugar, baking powder, baking soda, and salt together in a large bowl. Add the chocolate mixture, the milk, and the eggs and beat until smooth. Spread in the pan and bake for about 30–35 minutes. Cool in the pans for 5 minutes before turning out onto racks. Frost with *Confectioners' Frosting I* (p. 837) or any other you wish.

CHOCOLATE BUTTERMILK CAKE

This eggless cake with its deep chocolate flavor can be made very quickly.

1⅔ cups flour
1 cup sugar
½ cup unsweetened cocoa
1 teaspoon baking soda
½ teaspoon salt

1 cup buttermilk or sour milk (see pp. 17–18)
½ cup vegetable oil
2 teaspoons vanilla

Preheat the oven to 350°F. Butter and lightly flour two 8-inch round cake pans or one 9 × 13-inch pan. Mix the flour, sugar, cocoa, baking soda, and salt in a bowl. Add the buttermilk or sour milk, vegetable oil, and vanilla, beating until smooth. Spread in the pans or pan and bake, about 20–25 minutes for the small pans, 35–45 minutes for the large one. Test to see if a toothpick comes out clean. Cool for 5 minutes in the pan before turning out onto a rack. Frost with *Creamy Chocolate Frosting* (p. 839) or *Seven-Minute Coconut Frosting* (p. 844).

DEVIL'S FOOD CAKE

¼ cup unsweetened cocoa
1 cup plus 3 tablespoons sugar
3 tablespoons water
½ cup milk
¼ pound butter, or ½ cup shortening

1 teaspoon vanilla
2 eggs, separated
1 cup flour
½ teaspoon cream of tartar
½ teaspoon salt
½ teaspoon baking soda

Preheat the oven to 350°F. Butter and lightly flour two 8-inch round cake pans. Put the cocoa, 3 tablespoons of the sugar, and 3 tablespoons water in a small pan and cook over low heat until smooth and blended. Remove from the heat and stir in the milk; set aside. Cream the butter or shortening, add the vanilla and ½ cup of the remaining sugar, and beat until light. Beat in the egg yolks, and then add the cocoa mixture, beating well. Mix the flour, cream of tartar, salt, and baking soda together, add to the first mixture, and blend until smooth. Beat the egg whites separately until they are foamy, slowly add the remaining ½ cup of sugar, and continue to beat until the whites are stiff but not dry. Fold the whites into the batter. Spread in the pans and bake for 25–30 minutes; test with a toothpick until it comes out clean. Cool in the pans for 5 minutes before turning out onto racks. Frost with *Confectioners' Frosting II* (p. 838) or *Fudge Frosting* (p. 840).

FUDGE LAYER CAKE   (TWO 9-INCH ROUND LAYERS)

A delicious, tender cake, dark with chocolate frosting. The cake is named after the fudge frosting.

4 ounces unsweetened chocolate	3 eggs
6 tablespoons water	2 cups cake flour
1½ cups sugar	1 teaspoon baking soda
½ cup shortening	¼ teaspoon salt
1 teaspoon vanilla	⅔ cup milk

Preheat the oven to 350°F. Butter and lightly flour two 9-inch cake pans. Put the chocolate, water, and ½ of the sugar in a heavy-bottomed small pan over low heat, stirring often. As the chocolate melts, stir vigorously to blend. Cook until the chocolate has completely melted and mixture is smooth. Set aside. Cream the shortening and remaining 1 cup sugar together until light. Add the vanilla and beat until well blended. Add the eggs, one at a time, beating thoroughly after each addition. Sift the flour, baking soda, and salt together on a piece of wax paper. Add the dry ingredients alternately with the milk in three parts. Add the chocolate mixture and beat until well blended. Pour the batter into the pans. Bake for 35–40 minutes, or until a straw comes out dry when inserted in center of cake. Cool in the pans for 10 minutes, then turn cakes out on racks. Frost with *Fudge Frosting* (p. 840).

GERMAN SWEET CHOCOLATE CAKE *   (THREE 9-INCH ROUND LAYERS)

4 ounces Baker's German's Sweet Chocolate	2¼ cups all-purpose or cake flour
½ cup boiling water	1 teaspoon baking soda
1 cup butter or margarine	½ teaspoon salt
2 cups sugar	1 cup buttermilk
4 eggs, separated	1 recipe Coconut-Pecan Frosting (p. 841)
1 teaspoon vanilla	

Preheat the oven to 350°F. Butter and flour three 9-inch round cake pans. Line the bottom of the pans with buttered parchment, wax paper, or aluminum foil, shiny side up. Melt chocolate in boiling water. Cool. In a mixing bowl, cream butter and sugar until fluffy. Add yolks, 1 at a time, beating well after each addition. Blend in vanilla and chocolate. Mix the flour with the soda and salt, then add alternately with butter-

milk to chocolate mixture, beating after each addition until smooth.
Fold in beaten egg whites. Pour into the three prepared pans. Bake for
30–35 minutes. Cool in the pans for 5 minutes before turning out onto a
rack to cool. Frost only the tops with *Coconut-Pecan Frosting*.

SAUCEPAN
CHOCOLATE CAKE

(TWO 8½ × 4½ × 2½-INCH LOAVES)

It is a rich, dark, moist loaf cake—great for beginning bakers because it
is quickly and easily mixed, right in a saucepan. It needs no icing, just
a spoonful of unsweetened whipped cream.

7 ounces unsweetened chocolate	1 teaspoon vanilla
¾ cup butter	2 cups cake flour
1¾ cups coffee	1½ cups sugar
2 eggs	1 teaspoon baking soda
	¼ teaspoon salt

Topping

2 cups heavy cream	2 teaspoons vanilla

Preheat the oven to 275°F. Grease and lightly flour two 8½ × 4½ × 2½-
inch loaf pans. Put the chocolate, butter, and coffee in a heavy-
bottomed pan of about 4-quart capacity. Place over low heat and stir
almost constantly until the chocolate melts, then stir vigorously to
blend and smooth the mixture completely. Set aside to cool for about
10 minutes, then beat in the eggs and vanilla. Sift the flour, sugar, baking soda, and salt together. Add the dry ingredients to the chocolate
mixture, and beat with a wooden spoon or wire whisk until the batter
is well blended and perfectly smooth. Divide the batter evenly between the two prepared pans, and bake for about 45–55 minutes, or
until a broomstraw inserted in the center of a loaf comes out clean. Remove from the oven and cool the cakes in the pans for about 15 minutes, then turn them out onto racks to finish cooling completely. Before
serving the cake, place the cream and vanilla in a large mixing bowl
and whip until the cream just barely stands in peaks. It should be
fluffy but thin enough to run down the sides of the cake when you
place a spoonful on each serving.

WALNUT MOCHA CAKE

(TWO 8-INCH ROUND LAYERS
OR ONE 8-INCH SQUARE CAKE)

¾ cup milk
3 tablespoons instant coffee
2 teaspoons vanilla
¼ pound butter
1½ cups sugar

3 eggs
2¼ cups cake flour
¾ teaspoon salt
3 teaspoons baking powder
1 cup chopped walnuts

Preheat the oven to 350°F. Butter and lightly flour two 8-inch round cake pans or one 8-inch square pan. Heat the milk and stir in the instant coffee until it dissolves. Add the vanilla and let cool. Cream the butter and gradually add the sugar, beating until light. Add the eggs and beat well. Stir in the coffee mixture. Combine the flour, salt, and baking powder, and add them to the first mixture, mixing well. Stir in the walnuts. Spread batter in the pans and bake, about 30 minutes for the round layers, 40–50 minutes for the square cake. Test to see if a toothpick comes out clean. Cool in the pans for 5 minutes before turning out onto racks. Frost with *Penuche Frosting* (p. 841).

VELVET CAKE

(TWO 8-INCH ROUND LAYERS)

This simple cake with its fine flavor and smooth, velvet texture is an old classic. It would be a good simple cake to fill and frost for a child's birthday.

¼ pound butter
1 cup sugar
4 eggs, separated
½ cup cold water

1½ cups cake flour
½ cup cornstarch
½ teaspoon salt
4 teaspoons baking powder

Preheat the oven to 350°F. Butter and lightly flour two 8-inch round cake pans. Cream the butter and slowly add the sugar, beating until light. Beat in the egg yolks and cold water and combine well. Combine the flour, cornstarch, salt, and baking powder, add to the first mixture, and mix thoroughly. Beat the egg whites separately until stiff but not dry. Gently stir a third of the whites into the first mixture, then fold in the remaining whites. Spread the batter in the pans and bake for about 25 minutes, until a toothpick comes out clean. Cool in the pans for 5 minutes before turning out onto racks. Frost with *Chocolate Butter Frosting* (p. 843) or *Mocha Rum Butter Frosting* (p. 843).

(TWO 8-INCH ROUND LAYERS) **LORD BALTIMORE CAKE**

This classic gold cake can be made with a variety of fillings and frostings. It becomes "Lord Baltimore Cake" when you use Lord Baltimore filling and frosting.

¼ pound butter	1 cup milk
1 cup sugar	2 cups cake flour
5 egg yolks	2½ teaspoons baking powder
1 whole egg	¼ teaspoon salt
2 teaspoons vanilla	

Preheat the oven to 350°F. Butter and lightly flour two 8-inch round cake pans. Cream the butter and slowly add the sugar, beating until light. Add the egg yolks and beat well. Add the whole egg, vanilla, and milk and beat well. Combine the flour, baking powder, and salt, and add to the first mixture, beating until smooth. Spread in the pans and bake for about 20–25 minutes, until a toothpick comes out clean. Cool in the pans for 5 minutes before turning out onto racks. Fill with *Lord Baltimore Filling* (p. 849) and frost with *Seven-Minute Frosting* (p. 844).

(TWO 8-INCH ROUND LAYERS) **LADY BALTIMORE CAKE**

There was a Lady Baltimore Tea Room in late-nineteenth-century Charleston, South Carolina, where this cake undoubtedly was served. It is light and delicate—ideal for birthdays and baby showers—and is nice accompanied by vanilla ice cream. Fill the pure white layers with the traditional *Lady Baltimore Filling* of nuts and dried fruit, and cover the cake with billows of *Seven-Minute Frosting*.

1¾ cups cake flour	1¼ cups sugar
2 teaspoons baking powder	1 teaspoon vanilla
¼ teaspoon salt	¾ cup milk
8 tablespoons (½ cup) butter, softened	3 egg whites (about ½ cup)

Preheat the oven to 350°F. Grease and flour two 8-inch round cake pans. Combine the flour, baking powder, and salt, and sift them together onto a piece of wax paper. Put the butter and sugar in a mixing bowl, and beat until smooth and well blended. Stir the vanilla and the milk together and add to the butter-sugar mixture in two stages alternately with the flour mixture, beating until the batter is well blended and smooth after each addition. In a separate mixing bowl, beat the egg whites until they are stiff but moist. Gently stir one-third of the beaten whites into the batter, then scoop up the remaining beaten whites, drop them onto the batter, and fold them in. Divide between the prepared cake pans. Bake for 20–25 minutes, or until a toothpick or straw inserted in the center of a cake comes out clean. Remove from the oven and let cool in their pans for 5 minutes, then turn them out of the pans onto a rack to cool completely. Fill with *Lady Baltimore Filling* (p. 850) and frost with *Seven-Minute Frosting* (p. 844).

FRESH COCONUT CAKE *   (TWO 9-INCH ROUND LAYERS)

Light, tender, and moist—the fresh coconut adds a good texture.

1 coconut	2¼ cups cake flour
¾ cup shortening	2 teaspoons baking powder
1½ cups sugar	½ teaspoon salt
3 eggs, separated	1 cup milk
½ teaspoon coconut extract	

Preheat the oven to 350°F. Butter and lightly flour two 9-inch round cake pans. Remove the meat from the coconut (see p. 12), and grate it in a hand grater or the food processor. You should have about 3 cups. Cream the shortening and slowly add the sugar. Beat until light and smooth. Add the egg yolks, one at a time, beating well after each addition. Stir in the coconut extract. Sift the flour, baking powder, and salt together on a piece of wax paper. Add the dry ingredients alternately in three parts with the milk, beating until well blended. Stir in 1 cup of grated coconut. Beat the egg whites until stiff but not dry, stir a third of the whites into the batter, and gently fold in the remainder. Spoon the batter into the cake pans. Bake for 25 minutes, or until a straw inserted in the center of the cake comes out dry. Let the cakes cool for 10 minutes in the pans, then turn onto a cake rack. Cool. Frost with *Seven-Minute Coconut Frosting* (p. 844). Cover the top and sides of the cake with the remaining freshly grated coconut.

POUND CAKE *   (9 × 5-INCH LOAF)

Everyone likes a good old-fashioned pound cake, and it keeps well. Serve with fresh fruit, ice cream, or a sauce.

½ pound butter	½ teaspoon salt
1⅔ cups sugar	1 teaspoon vanilla, or ½
5 eggs	teaspoon mace
2 cups cake flour	

Preheat the oven to 325°F. Butter and lightly flour a 9 × 5-inch loaf pan. Cream the butter, slowly add the sugar, and beat until light. Add the eggs, one at a time, beating each in well. Stir in the flour, salt, and vanilla or mace, and combine well. Spoon into the pan and bake for 1¼–1½ hours, or until a toothpick comes out clean. Cool in the pan for 5 minutes before turning out onto a rack. Serve very thin slices.

(TWO 8-INCH ROUND LAYERS)   **BOSTON FAVORITE CAKE**

This is an excellent basic butter cake. It can also be made as cupcakes or one 7 × 11-inch rectangular.

6 tablespoons butter	1¾ cups cake flour
1 cup sugar	2 teaspoons baking powder
2 eggs, separated	½ teaspoon salt
1½ teaspoons vanilla	⅔ cup milk

Preheat the oven to 350°F. Butter and lightly flour two 8-inch round cake pans. Cream the butter until softened and slowly add the sugar, beating until light. Add the egg yolks and vanilla and beat to blend well. Sift the flour, baking powder, and salt onto a piece of wax paper. Alternately blend the dry ingredients and the milk into the butter mixture in three stages. Beat until smooth. In a separate bowl, beat the egg whites until stiff but not dry. Stir a third of the whites into the cake batter and gently fold in the remaining. Spoon into the cake pans. Bake for 30–35 minutes, or until a straw inserted in the center of the cake comes out dry. Cool in pans for 5 minutes before turning out onto racks. Fill and frost with *Creamy Chocolate Frosting* (p. 839) or *Maple Frosting* (p. 841).

MARBLE CAKE

Divide the batter in half. Melt *1 ounce unsweetened chocolate* over simmering water and add it to half the batter. Fill the pans using large spoonfuls and alternating between the plain and the chocolate batters.

PRISCILLA CAKE

For a richer cake use 1⅓ cups sugar and 3 eggs.

BIRTHDAY CAKE   (TWO 8-INCH ROUND LAYERS)

This is a charming, old-fashioned birthday cake, orange-flavored with pieces of candied orange peel, raisins, and walnuts.

¼ pound butter, or ½ cup shortening	3 teaspoons baking powder
	½ teaspoon salt
1¼ cups dark-brown sugar, firmly packed	⅔ cup milk
	½ cup raisins
2 teaspoons orange extract	½ cup chopped walnuts
2 eggs	2 tablespoons minced candied orange peel
2 cups flour	

Preheat the oven to 325°F. Butter and lightly flour two 8-inch round cake pans. Cream the butter or shortening with the brown sugar until light. Add the orange extract and the eggs and beat well. Mix the flour, baking powder, and salt and stir into the first mixture. Add the milk and beat until smooth. Fold in the raisins, walnuts, and orange peel. Spoon into the pans and bake for 25–30 minutes, or until a toothpick comes out clean. Cool in the pans for 5 minutes before turning out onto racks. Fill with *Lemon Coconut Cream Filling* (p. 850), frost with *Seven-Minute Frosting* (p. 844), and decorate with *Confectioners' Frosting II* (p. 838), tinted with a few drops of vegetable coloring.

WAR CAKE   (8 × 4-INCH LOAF OR 8-INCH SQUARE CAKE)

An eggless, almost fatless, milkless cake, very aptly named—it was popular during wartime shortages. It is dense and delicious uniced. For those who yearn for a good cake, but must resist fat, this will do it.

1 cup brown sugar	1½ cups flour
1 cup water	½ teaspoon salt
1 cup raisins	½ teaspoon baking powder
2 tablespoons margarine	½ teaspoon baking soda
1 teaspoon ground cinnamon	½ cup chopped walnuts
½ teaspoon ground cloves	

Preheat the oven to 350°F. Grease and flour an 8 × 4-inch baking pan. Place the brown sugar, water, raisins, margarine, cinnamon, and cloves in a heavy-bottomed saucepan and bring to a boil. Cook gently for 5 minutes, then remove from heat and let cool until the mixture is comfortably warm to your finger. Sift together the flour, salt, baking powder, and baking soda. Add them to the cooled sugar mixture, beating until no drifts of flour are visible and the batter is smooth. Stir in the walnuts. Spread evenly in the baking pan and bake for 25–30 minutes, or until a broomstraw inserted in the center of the cake comes out clean. Let cool in the pan for 10 minutes, then turn onto a rack to cool completely.

(TWO 8-INCH ROUND LAYERS) **BOSTON CREAM PIE**

A simple cake filled with rich cream custard, its top thinly glazed with chocolate, this variation of Boston Favorite Cake has become a great American favorite. If you are in a hurry, prepare the custard while the cake is in the oven, but do not fill the cake until it is completely cool. You may dust with confectioners' sugar in place of the chocolate.

1 cup milk
½ cup granulated sugar
3 tablespoons flour
⅛ teaspoon salt
2 egg yolks

1½ teaspoons vanilla
Two 8-inch layers Boston
   Favorite Cake (p. 801)
1½ recipes Chocolate Frosting
   for Cream Puffs (p. 839)

Heat the milk in a pan until very hot, then briskly stir in the granulated sugar, flour, and salt. Cook over moderate heat, stirring constantly, until very thick. Add the egg yolks and cook, continuing to stir, for another 4–5 minutes. Remove from the heat, add the vanilla, and cool, stirring occasionally. Cover well and refrigerate until ready to use. Spread the custard between the cake layers and spoon frosting over the top of the cake, letting it drip down the sides. Keep refrigerated.

(9-INCH SQUARE CAKE) **GINGERBREAD**

Moist, spicy, and sweet. Gingerbread is good served warm with sweetened whipped cream. You may serve it with applesauce, if you wish, or spread it with Butter Frosting II (p. 843).

¼ pound butter
1 cup sugar
2 eggs
¾ cup boiling water
¾ cup molasses

2½ cups flour
2 teaspoons baking soda
½ teaspoon salt
2 teaspoons powdered ginger

Preheat the oven to 350°F. Butter and lightly flour a 9-inch square cake pan. Cream the butter, add the sugar, and beat until light. Add the eggs and beat well. Add the boiling water and molasses and blend. Mix together the flour, baking soda, salt, and ginger, add to the first mixture, and combine thoroughly. Pour into the pan and bake for 35–45 minutes, until a toothpick comes out clean. Cool in the pan for about 5 minutes before turning out onto a plate.

SOUR CREAM GINGERBREAD ✳ (9-INCH SQUARE CAKE)

More cakelike than plain gingerbread, with a light texture and a creamy crumb.

¼ pound butter	1½ cups flour
1 cup sugar	1 teaspoon baking powder
½ cup molasses	½ teaspoon baking soda
½ cup sour cream	½ teaspoon salt
2 eggs	1½ teaspoons ground ginger

Preheat the oven to 350°F. Butter and lightly flour a 9-inch square pan. Cream the butter and slowly add the sugar, beating until light. Add the molasses and sour cream and blend well. Add the eggs, continuing to beat until well mixed. Mix together the flour, baking powder, baking soda, salt, and ginger, add to the first mixture, and beat until smooth. Pour into the pan and bake for 30–40 minutes, until a toothpick comes out clean. Cool in the pan for 5 minutes before turning out onto a rack.

APPLESAUCE CAKE (TWO 8-INCH ROUND LAYERS OR ONE 9 × 13-INCH CAKE)

This cake keeps well and will stay fresh for picnics or trips. Add a teaspoon of ground ginger if you want it more spicy.

¼ pound butter, or ½ cup shortening	1½ teaspoons baking soda
	½ teaspoon salt
1½ cups sugar	2 teaspoons cinnamon
1 cup applesauce	½ teaspoon nutmeg
2 eggs	½ cup raisins
2 cups flour	½ cup chopped walnuts

Preheat the oven to 350°F. Butter and lightly flour two 8-inch round cake pans or one 9 × 13-inch cake pan. Cream the butter or shortening, add the sugar gradually, and beat well. Add the applesauce and blend. Beat in the eggs and mix thoroughly. Mix together the flour, baking soda, salt, cinnamon, and nutmeg, add to the first mixture, and beat just until mixed. Stir in the raisins and nuts. Spread in the pans or pan and bake, 25–30 minutes for the layers, 35–40 minutes for the rectangle. Test to see if a toothpick comes out clean. Cool in the pans for 5 minutes before turning out onto racks. Spread with *Cream-Cheese Frosting* (p. 842) before serving, if you wish.

(TWO 8-INCH ROUND LAYERS OR   **✱ SPICE CAKE**
ONE 8-INCH SQUARE CAKE)

Cinnamon, cloves, nutmeg, and cayenne make this a lively cake.

¼ pound butter, or ½ cup shortening	2¼ cups flour
1 cup granulated sugar	1 teaspoon salt
½ cup dark-brown sugar	½ teaspoon baking soda
4 eggs	2 teaspoons cinnamon
½ cup milk	¼ teaspoon cloves
½ cup molasses	¼ teaspoon nutmeg
	⅛ teaspoon cayenne pepper

Preheat the oven to 350°F. Butter and lightly flour two 8-inch round cake pans or one 8-inch square pan. Cream the butter or shortening and slowly add the two sugars, beating until light. Beat in the eggs, then add the milk and molasses, beating thoroughly. Mix together the remaining ingredients and add to the first mixture, beating until well blended. Pour the batter into the pans or pan and bake, about 30 minutes for the round layers, 45–50 minutes for the square cake. Test to see if a toothpick comes out clean. Cool in the pans for 5 minutes before turning out onto racks. Frost with *Quick Caramel Frosting* (p. 840).

(TWO 8-INCH ROUND LAYERS)   **JAM CAKE**

¼ pound butter, or ½ cup shortening	1 teaspoon nutmeg
1½ cups sugar	½ teaspoon salt
3 eggs	1 teaspoon baking powder
2¼ cups flour	½ teaspoon baking soda
1 teaspoon allspice	1 cup blackberry, raspberry, or strawberry jam
1 teaspoon cinnamon	¼ cup sour milk (p. 17)

Preheat the oven to 350°F. Butter and lightly flour two 8-inch round cake pans. Cream the butter or shortening, add the sugar, and beat until light. Add the eggs and beat very well. Mix together the flour, allspice, cinnamon, nutmeg, salt, baking powder, and baking soda; add to the first mixture and beat until well mixed. Stir in the jam and sour milk and blend thoroughly. Spread in the pans and bake for 25 minutes, or until a toothpick comes out clean. Cool in the pans for 5 minutes before turning out on a rack. Frost with *Portsmouth Frosting* (p. 837).

FRESH BANANA CAKE ✳ (9-INCH SQUARE CAKE)

Moist and banana-sweet, with dark banana flecks throughout.

¼ pound butter, or ½ cup
   shortening
1½ cups sugar
1 cup mashed banana (about
   2 medium bananas)
2 eggs

1 teaspoon vanilla
2 cups cake flour
1 teaspoon baking soda
½ teaspoon salt
½ cup sour milk (p. 17) or
   sour cream

Preheat the oven to 350°F. Butter and lightly flour a 9-inch square cake
pan. Cream the butter or shortening, slowly add the sugar, and beat
until light. Add the banana, eggs, and vanilla and beat well. Mix the
flour, baking soda, and salt, add to the first mixture, and blend. Slowly
add the sour milk or sour cream and beat until well blended. Spread in
the pan and bake for about 45 minutes, or until a toothpick comes out
clean. Cool in the pan for 5 minutes before turning out onto a rack.
Split the cake and fill with *Banana Cream Filling* (p. 848) and frost with
Portsmouth Frosting (p. 837).

FRESH ORANGE CAKE ✳ (TWO 8-INCH ROUND LAYERS OR
ONE 9 × 5 × 3-INCH LOAF)

Be sure to use the entire orange, skin and all. And be sure to beat the
eggs and sugar a minimum of 5 minutes. This recipe does not work
well when doubled.

1 large bright-skinned orange
3 eggs
2 egg whites
1 cup granulated sugar
¼ cup cornstarch

1 cup flour
¼ teaspoon salt
Confectioners' sugar
   (optional)

Preheat the oven to 350°F. Grease and lightly flour the baking pan(s).
Quarter the orange and remove any seeds, then finely chop the orange,
skin and all, in a food processor or by hand. Put the eggs and whites in
a mixing bowl and beat with an electric mixer, using a whisk attachment if available, until well blended and foamy. Continue beating and
slowly add the granulated sugar. Beat until thick and light-colored, a
minimum of 5 minutes. Fold in the cornstarch, flour, and salt, using the
lowest speed on the electric mixer, for the briefest second or two. Remove the bowl from the mixer and gently fold in any remaining drifts
of the flour mixture. Fold in the chopped orange. Don't overfold.
Spread the batter in the baking pan or pans. If baking in a loaf pan,

bake for about 45 minutes and start checking for doneness at about 35 minutes. In layer cake pans, bake about 20–25 minutes, or until a broomstraw comes out clean when inserted in the center of the cake. Turn onto a rack to cool. Dust with confectioners' sugar, if desired, and serve.

(TWO 9-INCH ROUND LAYERS)   **PRINCETON ORANGE CAKE**

This orange-flavored velvet cake is fresh and bright with a delicate texture and keen orange taste.

1 large orange	1½ cups cake flour
¼ pound butter	½ cup cornstarch
1 cup sugar	½ teaspoon salt
4 eggs, separated	4 teaspoons baking powder
½ cup orange juice	

Preheat the oven to 350°F. Butter and lightly flour two round cake pans. Grate the rind of the orange, cream the butter and slowly add the sugar, beating until light. Add the egg yolks, orange juice, and orange rind, and beat well. Mix the flour, cornstarch, salt, and baking powder, stir into the first mixture, and blend until smooth. Beat the egg whites in a separate bowl until stiff but not dry. Gently stir a third of the egg whites into the first mixture, then fold in the remaining whites. Spread the batter in the pans and bake for 30–40 minutes, or until a toothpick comes out clean. Cool in the pans for 5 minutes before turning out onto racks. Frost with *White Mountain Cream* (p. 845) and sprinkle with ¾ *cup grated coconut*, if you wish.

(TWO 9 × 5-INCH LOAVES)   **DARK FRUIT CAKE**

Every kitchen file should have a recipe for a distinguished dark fruit cake. This is as good as any to be found.

¼ pound butter, or ½ cup shortening	½ teaspoon mace
	¼ teaspoon cloves
1 cup dark-brown sugar, firmly packed	½ teaspoon salt
	½ cup milk
1 teaspoon lemon extract	2 cups small pieces mixed candied fruit
2 eggs	
½ cup molasses	½ cup small pieces candied citron
2 cups flour	
½ teaspoon baking soda	1 cup raisins
1 teaspoon cinnamon	1 cup chopped pecans
½ teaspoon allspice	

Preheat the oven to 325°F. Butter two 9 × 5-inch loaf pans, line them with foil, then butter the foil. Cream the butter or shortening, add the brown sugar, and beat until light. Add the lemon extract and eggs and beat well. Stir in the molasses and blend. Mix together the flour, baking soda, cinnamon, allspice, mace, cloves, and salt; beat into the first mixture. Add the milk and beat until smooth. Stir in the candied fruit, citron, raisins, and pecans, and mix well. Spoon into the pans and bake for 1–1¼ hours, or until a toothpick comes out clean. Turn out onto racks to cool. When completely cool, wrap well and store in an airtight container.

BRANDIED FRUIT CAKE

Soak two large pieces of cheesecloth in *brandy*. Wrap each fruit cake in the cheesecloth, covering all sides, then wrap well in foil. Moisten the cheesecloth with additional brandy every few days for about a week. The brandy will flavor the cake and help preserve it too.

LIGHT FRUIT CAKE   (TWO 9 × 5-INCH LOAVES)

This is exceptionally good. Any combination of candied fruits and nuts will do, but the stuffed dates, which you want to prepare before you start, are particularly good. Simply fill each date with a piece of nut and roll it in sugar. You'll need about 1 pound of dates and a dozen or so extra nuts for this.

½ pound butter	2 cups seedless white raisins
2 cups sugar	2 cups pecans in large pieces
1 tablespoon vanilla	1 cup candied cherries
7 eggs, separated	1 cup candied pineapple in
2¾ cups flour	large pieces
1 teaspoon salt	2 cups dates, stuffed with
2 teaspoons baking powder	nuts and rolled in sugar
1 cup milk	

Preheat the oven to 325°F. Butter and lightly flour two 9 × 5-inch loaf pans. Cream the butter and slowly add the sugar, beating until light. Add the vanilla and the egg yolks and beat well. Mix the flour, salt, and baking powder, and stir them and ½ cup of the milk into the first mixture. Add the remaining ½ cup of milk and beat well. Stir in the raisins and the pecans. Beat the egg whites separately until they are stiff but not dry. Gently stir a third of the whites into the batter, then fold in the remaining whites carefully. Spoon a layer of batter into each loaf pan. Arrange several rows of candied cherries and pineapple and the dates on top of the batter, then cover with the remaining batter, filling each pan one-half to two-thirds full. Bake for about 1 hour or until a toothpick comes out clean. Cool in the pans for 5 minutes before turning out onto racks. When completely cool, wrap well and store in an airtight container up to two months.

(TWO 8-INCH ROUND LAYERS) **CHOCOLATE FRUIT CAKE**

This combination of chocolate, cinnamon, and brandy is unusual and good. The raisins should be soaked in brandy for at least several hours before using, preferably overnight.

⅓ cup raisins	1 teaspoon vanilla
2 tablespoons brandy	1 cup milk
2 ounces unsweetened chocolate	2 cups cake flour
	2 teaspoons baking powder
¼ pound butter, or ½ cup shortening	½ teaspoon salt
	2 teaspoons cinnamon
1¼ cups sugar	⅓ cup candied cherries
2 eggs	½ cup chopped walnuts

Preheat the oven to 350°F. Butter and lightly flour two 8-inch round cake pans. Soak the raisins in the brandy for at least 2 hours, or overnight if possible. Melt the chocolate in a pot or bowl over simmering water; set aside to cool. Cream the butter or shortening in a large mixing bowl, gradually add the sugar, and beat until light. Add the eggs and beat well. Beat in the chocolate and the vanilla, then add the milk and beat well. Mix the flour, baking powder, salt, and cinnamon together and add to the batter, beating thoroughly. Stir in the raisins and brandy, cherries, and walnuts. Spread the batter in the pans and bake for about 35 minutes, testing until a toothpick comes out clean. Cool in the pans for 5 minutes before turning out onto a rack.

CAKES MADE WITHOUT SHORTENING (SPONGE CAKES)

(9-INCH TUBE CAKE OR   **TRUE SPONGE CAKE**
TWO 8-INCH ROUND LAYERS)

This is a classic sponge cake, made without any baking powder, leavened by air held within well-beaten eggs.

5 eggs, separated
1 tablespoon lemon juice
1 cup sugar

¼ teaspoon salt
1 cup cake flour

Preheat the oven to 325°F. Line the bottom of a 9-inch tube pan or of two 8-inch round cake pans with wax paper, cut to fit. Beat the egg yolks with the lemon juice until pale and thick. Gradually add ¾ cup of the sugar and beat thoroughly. Beat the egg whites until foamy, add the salt, and continue beating until the whites hold soft peaks, then slowly add the remaining ¼ cup of sugar and beat until stiff but not dry. Stir a fourth of the beaten whites into the egg yolk mixture. Spoon the remaining whites over the yolk mixture and sift the flour on top. Gently fold until blended. Spoon into the pan or pans. Bake for 45–55 minutes in the tube pan, 25–30 minutes in the layer pans, or until a toothpick or straw comes out clean. Invert the pan or pans on a rack and let the cake cool completely before removing from the pan. Dust with *confectioners' sugar*, sifted through a strainer, or frost with lemon-flavored *Confectioners' Frosting II* (p. 838) or any other light frosting you wish.

HOT-WATER SPONGE CAKE   (9-INCH SQUARE CAKE OR 12 CUPCAKES)

Hot-water sponge cake is made with baking powder, which insures its lightness. It's an easy sponge cake for those new to baking.

2 eggs, separated
¼ cup hot water
1 teaspoon vanilla
¾ cup sugar

⅛ teaspoon salt
1 cup cake flour
1¼ teaspoons baking powder

Preheat the oven to 325°F. Line the bottom of a 9-inch square cake pan with wax paper or place 12 fluted paper liners in a 12-cup muffin pan. Beat the egg yolks, hot water, and vanilla together until very thick and pale. Slowly beat in ½ cup of the sugar; set aside. Beat the egg whites until foamy, add the salt, and continue beating until they hold soft peaks. Gradually beat in the remaining ¼ cup sugar and beat until stiff but not dry. Stir a fourth of the whites into the yolk mixture and sift the flour and baking powder over them. Gently fold in remaining egg whites until blended. Spoon into the pan and bake, 25–30 minutes for the cake, 20 minutes for the cupcakes, or until a toothpick comes out clean. Invert the pan on a rack and let the cake or cupcakes cool completely before removing from the pan. Frost with *Quick Caramel Frosting* (p. 840).

(9-INCH TUBE CAKE) ## CHOCOLATE SPONGE CAKE

This very delicate chocolate sponge cake is exceptionally good.

6 ounces semisweet chocolate	1 teaspoon vanilla
4 eggs	⅛ teaspoon salt
¾ cup sugar	½ cup cake flour

Preheat the oven to 350°F. Line the bottom of a 9-inch tube pan with wax paper, cut to fit. Melt the chocolate in a small pan or bowl over simmering water; set aside to cool. Beat the eggs until light, then gradually add the sugar, vanilla, and salt. Stir in the melted chocolate. Sift the flour over the batter and fold in just until blended. Spoon into the pan and bake for 40–50 minutes, until a straw comes out clean. Invert the pan on a rack and let the cake cool completely before removing from the pan. Frost with *Portsmouth Frosting* (p. 837) or *Coffee Butter Frosting* (p. 843).

(8-INCH TUBE CAKE OR
TWO 8-INCH ROUND LAYERS) ## CREAM SPONGE CAKE

4 eggs, separated	1 cup sugar
1 tablespoon lemon juice	¼ teaspoon salt
1½ tablespoons cold water	1 cup cake flour
1 teaspoon vanilla	1¼ teaspoons baking powder

Preheat the oven to 325°F. Line the bottom of an 8-inch tube pan or of two 8-inch round cake pans with wax paper, cut to fit. Beat the egg yolks with the lemon juice, cold water, and vanilla until thick and pale. Gradually add ¾ cup of the sugar and blend well; set aside. Beat the egg whites separately until foamy, add the salt, and continue beating until the whites form soft peaks. Gradually add the remaining ¼ cup of sugar and beat until stiff but not dry. Gently stir a fourth of the whites into the yolk mixture. Spoon the remaining whites onto the yolk mixture and sift the flour and baking powder on top. Carefully fold until blended. Spoon into the pan or pans and bake, allowing 40–50 minutes for the tube cake, about 25 minutes for the layers. Test to see if a straw or toothpick comes out clean. Invert each pan on a rack and let the cake cool completely before removing the pan. If you have used a tube pan, split the cake horizontally to make two even layers. Fill and frost with *Chocolate Whipped Cream Filling* (p. 852).

DAFFODIL CAKE

Called daffodil because the bursts of yellow throughout the white cake look like flowers. As good to eat as it is to look at. Don't expect the cake to rise more than halfway up the pan.

¼ teaspoon salt	4 egg yolks
2 teaspoons vanilla	2 teaspoons grated orange
9 egg whites (1¼ cups)	rind
1¼ cups sugar	
1 cup plus 1 tablespoon sifted flour	

Preheat the oven to 375°F. In a large mixing bowl, sprinkle the salt and vanilla over the egg whites. Beat until the whites hold a soft peak, and slowly add 1 cup of the sugar. Beat just until the sugar is blended into the whites. Add the flour in four parts, folding in each time gently with a rubber spatula, until all the flour is incorporated. In another bowl, beat the egg yolks and orange rind until thick, slowly adding the remaining 4 tablespoons of sugar. Beat until thick and pale yellow. Fold a third of the egg white mixture into the yolk mixture, fold gently until blended. Fill an ungreased 10-inch tube pan, using large spoonfuls and alternating the yellow batter with the white batter until all is used. Bake about 35 minutes, or until a broomstraw comes out dry when inserted into the cake. Frost with *Fluffy Butter Frosting* (p. 843) to which 2 *teaspoons grated orange rind* plus ½–1 *teaspoon orange extract* are added (taste to determine how much is needed for a light orange flavor).

SUNSHINE CAKE

An airy yellow cake; light in texture, sweet in taste.

8 eggs, separated	1 teaspoon cream of tartar
2 teaspoons grated lemon zest	1 cup cake flour
1½ cups confectioners' sugar	¼ teaspoon salt

Preheat the oven to 325°F. Line the bottom of a 10-inch tube pan with wax paper, cut to fit. Beat the egg yolks, add the lemon zest and 1 cup of the confectioners' sugar, and beat until thick and pale; set aside. Beat the whites until foamy, add the cream of tartar, and beat until the whites form soft peaks. Gradually add the remaining ½ cup confectioners' sugar and beat until stiff. Stir a fourth of the whites into the yolk mixture. Spoon the remaining whites on top of the yolk mixture and sift the flour and salt over them. Carefully fold until blended. Spoon into the pan and bake for 50–60 minutes, until a straw comes out clean. Invert the pan on a rack and let the cake cool completely before removing from the pan. Frost with *Confectioners' Frosting I* (p. 837).

(10-INCH TUBE CAKE)   ❋   **ANGEL FOOD CAKE**

Save your egg whites and freeze them until you have enough to make this cake. With no egg yolks or fat, this is a no-cholesterol cake. Try it sliced and toasted—butter the slices only if you dare.

12–13 egg whites (2 cups)	1 teaspoon vanilla
¼ teaspoon salt	1¼ cups sugar
1½ teaspoons cream of tartar	1 cup cake flour
1 teaspoon almond extract (optional)	

Preheat the oven to 325°F. Beat the egg whites until foamy, add the salt and cream of tartar, and beat until soft peaks form. Add the almond extract and the vanilla, then gradually add the sugar, beating until stiff. Sift the flour over the whites and gently fold it in. Bake in an ungreased 10-inch tube pan for 50–60 minutes, until a straw comes out clean. Invert the pan on a rack and let the cake cool completely before removing from the pan. Frost with *Chocolate Frosting* (p. 839).

(TWO 9 × 5 × 3-INCH LOAVES)   **ELECTION CAKE**

Loaf cakes made with yeast were popular in New England, especially around holiday time and at church suppers and family feasts, as far back as the early 1800s. Election Cake (also known as Dough Cake and March Meeting Cake) often was baked on election days and allegedly sold and served only to those who voted a straight ticket. The loaf is deliciously moist and spicy.

⅔ cup warm water	2 teaspoons cinnamon
2 packages dry yeast	½ teaspoon cloves
3⅔ cups flour	½ teaspoon mace
½ pound (1 cup) butter, softened	½ teaspoon nutmeg
2 eggs, beaten	2 teaspoons salt
2 cups brown sugar	1⅓ cups raisins
1 cup sour milk (see p. 17) or buttermilk	2 cups chopped dried figs
1 teaspoon baking soda	1 cup chopped walnuts or pecans
	1 tablespoon flour

Grease two 9 × 5 × 3-inch loaf pans. Pour the water into a large mixing bowl and sprinkle the yeast over. Stir, and let stand for 5 minutes to dissolve. Add 1 cup of the flour and beat until well blended: the mixture will be quite stiff. Add the butter and beat until smooth, then add the eggs, brown sugar, sour milk or buttermilk, 2⅔ cups flour, the baking soda, cinnamon, cloves, mace, nutmeg, and salt, and beat for 3 minutes. Toss the raisins, figs, and walnuts in the tablespoon of flour to coat them, then add them to the batter, and stir to mix throughout. Divide the batter evenly between the prepared pans. Cover loosely with a towel and let rest for 1½ hours. Preheat the oven to 350°F near the end of the resting time. Bake the cakes for about 55–65 minutes, or until a broomstraw inserted in the center of a loaf comes out clean. Start testing for doneness at 45 minutes. Remove from the oven and let cool in the pans for 5 minutes, then turn out onto racks to cool completely.

TORTES, JELLY ROLLS, AND OTHER SPECIAL CAKES

NUT TORTE   (TWO 8-INCH ROUND CAKES)

5 eggs, separated	1 teaspoon baking powder
1 cup sugar	1 teaspoon vanilla
2 cups ground walnuts	⅛ teaspoon salt
1 cup bread crumbs	

Preheat the oven to 325°F. Butter and lightly flour two 8-inch round cake pans. Line pans with wax paper or foil shiny side up, and grease and flour the paper or foil. Beat the egg yolks until pale and thick. Slowly add the sugar and continue to beat until well blended. Stir in the walnuts, crumbs, baking powder, and vanilla, and mix well. Beat the egg whites separately until foamy, add the salt, and continue to beat until stiff but not dry. Gently stir a third of the whites into the batter, then fold in the remaining whites. Spread in the pans and bake for about 30 minutes, or until a toothpick comes out clean. Let cool in the pans for 5 minutes before turning out onto racks. Serve spread with *sweetened whipped cream* between the layers and dust the top with sifted *confectioners' sugar*.

(9-INCH ROUND CAKE)   **ALMOND TORTE**

Moist, delicate, and mildly sweet, just right with sweetened whipped cream.

4 eggs, separated	2 ounces unsweetened
1½ cups confectioners' sugar	chocolate, grated fine
½ cup fine cracker crumbs	1 teaspoon baking powder
½ cup chopped almonds	½ teaspoon salt

Preheat the oven to 325°F. Butter and lightly flour a springform pan. Beat the egg yolks until thick and pale. Slowly add 1 cup of the sugar and continue to beat until blended. Stir in the crumbs, almonds, chocolate, baking powder, and salt, and mix well. Beat the egg whites separately until they hold soft peaks, then slowly beat in the remaining ½ cup of sugar, continuing to beat until stiff but not dry. Gently stir a third of the whites into the batter, then fold in the remaining whites. Spread lightly in the pan and bake for about 30 minutes, or until a toothpick comes out clean. Run a knife around the edge, remove the rim, and let cool. Serve with *sweetened whipped cream*.

(15-INCH JELLY ROLL)   **✱ JELLY ROLL**

This is the best sponge-cake jelly roll we've found. The cornstarch gives it a fine, springy texture. Fill it with jelly or jam, whipped cream, ice cream, or any other filling you wish.

5 eggs, separated	⅓ cup cornstarch
1 teaspoon vanilla	⅓ cup flour
½ teaspoon salt	Confectioners' sugar
⅓ cup granulated sugar	Jelly or jam

Preheat the oven to 375°F. Grease a 10½ × 15½-inch jelly-roll pan and cover it with wax paper or foil shiny side up. Grease and lightly flour the paper or foil. Beat the egg yolks and add the vanilla; set aside. Beat the egg whites until foamy, add the salt, and continue beating until the whites form soft peaks. Slowly add the granulated sugar and beat until stiff but not dry. Spoon the whites over the yolks and sprinkle the cornstarch and flour on top. Fold gently until blended. Spread in the pan and bake for about 12 minutes, until a toothpick comes out clean. Meanwhile, liberally dust a kitchen towel with confectioners' sugar. Turn the jelly roll out onto the towel, carefully remove the wax paper or foil, and trim off any crisp edges. Roll the cake up in the towel from the long side and let it rest for a minute, unroll it and let it rest for a

few minutes, then roll it up in the towel again and let it cool completely. Unroll, spread all over with jelly or jam right to the edges, roll up—this time *without* the towel inside—and sprinkle with confectioners' sugar.

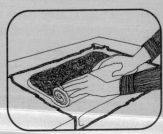

Jelly-Roll Fillings

WHIPPED CREAM FILLING

Whip *1½ cups heavy cream*, flavoring it with *sugar to taste* and *2 teaspoons vanilla* or *1 tablespoon instant coffee*. Spread on the jelly roll instead of the jelly or jam and roll up.

ICE CREAM FILLING

Omit the jelly or jam and spread the roll with *1 quart softened chocolate ice cream*, or another flavor, if you wish. Roll up and keep in the freezer until ready to serve.

LEMON FILLING

Omit the jelly or jam and spread the roll with *1 recipe Lemon Filling* (p. 850).

(9- OR 10-INCH ROUND CAKE)　　　　　　**CARROT TORTE**

4 eggs, separated	½ cup flour
1 cup granulated sugar	1 teaspoon baking powder
1 cup grated raw carrots	⅛ teaspoon salt
Grated rind of 1 lemon	Confectioners' sugar
1 tablespoon lemon juice	

Preheat the oven to 325°F. Butter and lightly flour a 9- or 10-inch springform pan. Beat the egg yolks until they are pale and thick. Slowly add the granulated sugar and continue to beat until smooth and blended. Stir in the carrots, lemon rind, lemon juice, flour, and baking powder and mix thoroughly. Beat the egg whites separately until foamy, add the salt, and continue to beat until stiff but not dry. Gently stir a third of the whites into the batter, then fold in the remaining whites. Spread in the pan and bake for 30–40 minutes, or until a toothpick comes out clean. Run a knife around the edge, remove the rim, and let cool. Sprinkle the top with confectioners' sugar, sifted through a strainer.

(15-INCH ROLL)　　　　　　**NUT ROLL**

This sophisticated version of the classic jelly roll is made with chopped nuts instead of flour. This cake keeps well.

6 eggs, separated	⅛ teaspoon salt
¾ cup granulated sugar	1½ cups heavy cream
1½ cups finely chopped walnuts	¼ cup confectioners' sugar
	2 tablespoons rum
1 teaspoon baking powder	

Preheat the oven to 350°F. Butter a 10½ × 15½-inch jelly-roll pan, line it with wax paper or foil shiny side up. Grease and lightly flour the paper or foil. Beat the egg yolks until they are pale and thick. Slowly add the granulated sugar and continue to beat until blended. Stir in the walnuts and baking powder; set aside. Beat the egg whites until foamy, then add the salt and continue to beat until stiff but not dry. Gently stir a third of the whites into the batter, then fold in the remaining whites. Spread lightly in the pan and bake for 12–15 minutes, until a toothpick comes out clean. Turn out onto a clean kitchen towel. Remove the wax paper or foil and trim off any crisp edges. Roll the cake up in the towel, starting from the long side like a jelly roll, and let it rest for a minute. Unroll the cake, let it rest for a few minutes, then roll it up in the towel again and let it cool completely. Whip the cream, adding the confectioners' sugar and the rum. Spread it over the cake and roll up gently without the towel. Cover and refrigerate until ready to serve.

CHOCOLATE ROLL   (15-INCH ROLL)

> 5 eggs, separated
> 1¼ cups confectioners' sugar
> ¼ cup cocoa
> ¼ teaspoon salt
>
> 1½ cups sweetened heavy cream, whipped, or 1 quart vanilla ice cream, softened

Preheat the oven to 350°F. Butter a 10½ × 15½-inch jelly-roll pan and line it with wax paper or foil. Grease and lightly flour the paper or foil. Beat the egg yolks until they are pale and thick; set aside. Sift the sugar and cocoa together onto a piece of wax paper. Beat the egg whites until they are foamy, add the salt, and continue to beat until they hold soft peaks. Fold the sugar and cocoa into the whites. Gently fold a third of the egg white mixture into the yolks, then lightly fold in the remaining whites. Spread evenly in the pan and bake for about 20 minutes, until a toothpick comes out clean. Turn the cake out onto a clean kitchen towel. Remove the wax paper or foil and trim off any crisp edges. Roll the cake up with the towel from the long side, like a jelly roll (see p. 815), and let it rest for a minute. Unroll it and let it rest for a few minutes, then roll it up in the towel again and let it cool completely. Unroll and spread with sweetened whipped cream or softened ice cream. Roll up again without the towel. Dust the top of the roll with more confectioners' sugar sifted through a strainer. Refrigerate the whipped cream roll until ready to serve; keep the ice cream roll in the freezer.

COTTAGE PUDDING CAKE   (8-INCH SQUARE CAKE)

This is a good basic recipe with the pleasing flavor of butter. A similar batter is used in the recipes for pineapple and gingerbread upside-down cakes.

> 1½ cups flour
> 2 teaspoons baking powder
> ½ teaspoon salt
> ½ cup sugar
>
> ¼ pound butter
> ½ cup milk
> 1 egg

Preheat the oven to 400°F. Butter and lightly flour an 8-inch square cake pan. Mix the flour, baking powder, salt, and sugar together in a large bowl. Melt the butter in a small pan, remove from the heat, and stir in the milk and the egg, beating well. Add to the flour mixture and blend. Pour into the pan and bake for about 25 minutes, until a toothpick comes out clean. Cool in the pan for 5 minutes before turning out onto a rack. Serve warm with *Lemon Sauce* (p. 992). Or frost with *Creamy Chocolate Frosting* (p. 839) or *Sultana Nut Frosting* (p. 842).

CHOCOLATE CHIP CAKE

Add *1 cup (6 ounces) chocolate chips* to the batter before pouring it into the pan.

DUTCH APPLE CAKE

Spread the batter ¾ inch thick in a 10 × 6 × 2-inch baking dish. Pare and core *5 tart apples*, cut into wedges of eighths, and press them in uniform rows into the batter. Mix *½ cup sugar* with *½ teaspoon cinnamon* and *2 tablespoons raisins*. Sprinkle evenly over the top. Bake as directed. Serve with *heavy cream*.

(TWO 8½ × 4½ × 2½-INCH LOAVES) **RABBIT'S CARROT CAKE**

A traditional moist, crumbly carrot cake, made with vegetable oil and baked in a loaf pan. It is a snap to make in the food processor, and with two loaves you can put one in the freezer for later.

1½ cups finely grated raw carrots (3 medium-size carrots)	1 teaspoon cinnamon
	½ teaspoon cloves
	½ teaspoon nutmeg
2 tablespoons lemon juice	½ teaspoon allspice
½ cup canned crushed pineapple, well drained	¾ cup vegetable oil
	3 eggs
1½ cups all-purpose flour	1 cup golden raisins
1¼ cups sugar	1 cup walnuts, in large pieces
1 teaspoon baking powder	8 tablespoons butter, softened
1 teaspoon baking soda	6 tablespoons honey
1 teaspoon salt	

Preheat the oven to 350°F. Grease and flour two 8½ × 4½ × 2½-inch loaf pans. If you are mixing in the food processor, cut each cleaned and scrubbed carrot into about four pieces, and grate them fine in the processor. Transfer to a bowl, and stir in the lemon juice and pineapple; set aside. Put the flour, sugar, baking powder, baking soda, salt, cinnamon, cloves, nutmeg, and allspice into the processor and process for a few seconds, until combined. Add the oil and process until well mixed, then add the eggs, one at a time. Add the raisins, walnuts, and the carrot mixture, and flick off and on a few times, just until mixed—you don't want to chop the walnuts too much. If you are mixing by hand, shred the carrots on the fine side of the grater and mix them with the lemon juice and pineapple; set aside. In another bowl, combine the flour, sugar, baking powder, baking soda, salt, cinnamon, cloves, nutmeg, and allspice, and mix well. Add the oil and beat until blended, then add the eggs, one at a time, beating well after each addition. Add the raisins, walnuts, and the carrot mixture, and beat until thoroughly combined. Divide the batter evenly between the two prepared loaf pans and bake for about 45 minutes, or until a broomstraw inserted in the center of a cake comes out clean. Remove from the oven and turn each cake out onto a rack to cool. Beat the butter with the honey until smooth, and spread across the top of the cake.

PINEAPPLE UPSIDE-DOWN CAKE ✳   (8- OR 9-INCH ROUND CAKE)

Sweet butter syrup over pineapple and fresh cake; you can make this in an old-fashioned black iron skillet, or "spider."

12 tablespoons butter	1 egg
1 cup dark-brown sugar	1½ cups flour
¼ cup pineapple juice	2 teaspoons baking powder
5 whole pineapple rings	½ teaspoon salt
5 Maraschino cherries	½ cup granulated sugar
½ cup milk	Whipped cream (optional)

Preheat the oven to 400°F. Melt 4 tablespoons of the butter in an ovenproof skillet or an 8- or 9-inch cake pan. Stir in the brown sugar and continue to stir over low heat until it dissolves. Remove from the heat and add the pineapple juice. Arrange the pineapple rings in one layer in the pan and place a cherry in the center of each; set aside. Melt the remaining 8 tablespoons butter in a small pan. Remove from the heat and stir in the milk and egg, beating well. Mix the flour, baking powder, salt, and granulated sugar in a bowl, then add the milk-egg mixture and beat until smooth. Pour over the pineapple slices and bake for about 35 minutes, or until a toothpick comes out clean. Let cool in the pan for 10 minutes, then turn out onto a plate, fruit side up. Serve with whipped cream, if you wish.

GINGERBREAD UPSIDE-DOWN
(8-INCH SQUARE CAKE)   ✳ CAKE

12 tablespoons butter	2 teaspoons powdered ginger
⅓ cup dark-brown sugar	½ teaspoon salt
3 ripe pears, peeled, cored, and halved, or 6 canned pear halves	½ cup granulated sugar
	½ cup milk
	1 egg
1½ cups flour	Whipped cream (optional)
2 teaspoons baking powder	

Preheat the oven to 375°F. Melt 4 tablespoons of the butter in a small pan, add the brown sugar, and stir over low heat until blended. Pour into a square cake pan and arrange the pear halves round side down in the pan; set aside. The pear halves may also be sliced and spread evenly over the bottom of the pan. Mix the flour, baking powder, ginger, salt, and granulated sugar in a bowl. Melt the remaining 8 tablespoons of butter in a small pan. Remove from the heat, add the milk and the egg, and beat well. Add to the flour mixture and beat until smooth. Pour over the pears and bake for about 25 minutes, or until a toothpick comes out clean. Cool in the pan for about 10 minutes, then turn out onto a serving plate, fruit side up. Serve with whipped cream, if you wish.

(10-INCH TUBE CAKE)   **CHIFFON CAKE**

2¼ cups cake flour	¾ cup cold water
1 tablespoon baking powder	2 teaspoons vanilla
1½ cups sugar	8 egg whites
1 teaspoon salt	½ teaspoon cream of tartar
½ cup vegetable oil	Seven-Minute Lemon or
6 egg yolks	Orange Frosting (p. 844)

Preheat oven to 325°F. Line the bottom of a 10-inch tube pan with wax paper, cut to fit. Sift the flour, baking powder, sugar, and salt into a large bowl. Pour in the oil, egg yolks, the cold water, and vanilla, and beat until smooth and shiny; set aside. Beat the egg whites separately until foamy, add the cream of tartar, and continue beating until stiff but not dry. Blend a fourth of the whites into the batter, then fold in the remaining whites. Spoon the batter into the tube pan and bake for

50–60 minutes, until a straw comes out clean. Invert the pan on a rack and let the cake cool completely before removing from the pan. Frost with the *Seven-Minute Lemon or Orange Frosting*.

BABA CAKES   (TWELVE 2½-INCH CUPCAKES)

1 package dry yeast	¼ cup sugar
½ cup warm water	¼ teaspoon salt
1¾ cups flour	¼ pound butter, softened
4 eggs, at room temperature	

Stir the yeast into the warm water and let it stand for 5 minutes to dissolve. Add ½ cup of the flour and mix well with an electric beater. Beat in the eggs, one at a time, then add the sugar, salt, and remaining flour. Mix until the dough is smooth. Cover and let rise until double in bulk. Beat the softened butter into the dough, bit by bit, until smooth. Butter the muffin pans. Put 2 tablespoons of dough in each opening, cover, and let rest 45 minutes. Preheat oven to 400°F. Bake for about 20 minutes or until lightly golden on top. Remove from the pans and cool on a rack.

Rum Sauce

1 cup sugar	½ cup rum
1 cup water	

Mix the sugar with the water in a small pot and boil 10 minutes. Cool to lukewarm, then add the rum. Dip the baba cakes in this sauce and spoon some over the top of each cake.

SAVARIN   (TWO RINGS)

Prepare 1 recipe of Baba Cake dough. Preheat the oven to 400°F. Butter two 8- or 9-inch ring molds and divide dough between them. Bake for 20 minutes, or until golden brown. Turn each Savarin ring onto a rack placed over a shallow bowl. While still warm, spoon Rum Sauce (see above) over the ring several times until the cake is moist and well flavored. Before serving, fill the center with *sugared strawberries, ice cream,* or *sweetened whipped cream.*

(8-INCH ROUND CAKE)   *** SWEET ALMOND CAKE**

This is a single-layer, dense, heavy, moist cake, full of almond flavor.

7 ounces almond paste	1 teaspoon baking powder
¼ pound butter	2 cups berries, fresh or frozen,
¾ cup granulated sugar	for sauce
3 eggs	Confectioners' sugar, to
¼ cup flour	sprinkle on top of cake

Preheat the oven to 350°F. Combine the almond paste, butter, and granulated sugar in the bowl of a food processor and process until well blended. Add the eggs and process until well blended and smooth. Add the flour and baking powder and process only until the flour is incorporated. Spoon into an 8-inch greased springform pan and bake for 35–40 minutes. Cool slightly before removing from pan. Purée or mash the berries. Sprinkle confectioners' sugar over the top of the cake and serve with some of the berry purée spooned over or alongside each slice.

(8-INCH SQUARE CAKE)   *** LAZY DAISY CAKE**

This small cake, made with hot milk, is high, light, delicate, and very easy to make. Once the hot milk has been stirred into the batter, quickly pour it into the prepared pan and pop it into the oven, because as soon as the baking powder is combined with a hot liquid it begins its work of leavening and you want that to happen only when it gets into the heat of the oven. (This is not the case with cool or cold liquids.) You can omit the broiled topping, if you wish, and frost the cake instead, once it has cooled. But the traditional Lazy Daisy topping is very, very good.

2 eggs	4 tablespoons butter
1 teaspoon vanilla	3 tablespoons dark-brown
1 cup granulated sugar	sugar
1 cup flour	2 tablespoons cream
1 teaspoon baking powder	½ cup grated coconut or
¼ teaspoon salt	chopped nuts
½ cup milk	

Preheat the oven to 350°F. Butter and lightly flour an 8-inch square cake pan. Beat the eggs with the vanilla until they have thickened slightly. Gradually add the granulated sugar and beat thoroughly. Mix the flour, baking powder, and salt together and add to the first mixture, blending until smooth. Heat the milk and 1 tablespoon of the butter together in a small pan. When the butter has melted, stir the milk and melted butter into the batter and mix well; the batter will be very liquid. Work quickly now as noted above. Pour into the pan and bake for about 25 minutes, until a toothpick comes out clean. Remove the cake from the oven. Mix the 3 remaining tablespoons of butter, the brown sugar, the cream, and the coconut or nuts together in a small pan over low heat until melted and well blended. Spread over the hot cake and brown lightly under the broiler for a minute or two, taking care that it does not burn.

CHEESE CAKE
(9-INCH ROUND CAKE)

1 cup zwieback or graham cracker crumbs	1 cup sour cream
4 tablespoons butter, melted	2 tablespoons flour
¼ teaspoon cinnamon	¼ teaspoon salt
¼ teaspoon nutmeg	1 teaspoon vanilla
1¼ cups sugar	1 pound cream cheese, at room temperature
4 eggs, separated	

Combine the crumbs, melted butter, cinnamon, nutmeg, and ¼ cup of the sugar in a bowl and mix well. Butter a 9-inch springform pan and pat the crumb mixture over the bottom and 1 inch up the sides. Chill. Preheat the oven to 325°F. Beat the egg yolks with an electric beater until they are thick and pale. Add the sour cream, flour, salt, ¾ cup of the sugar, and the vanilla, and beat until well blended. Add the cream cheese and beat until smooth. Beat the egg whites until foamy, then gradually beat in the remaining ¼ cup of sugar, beating until the whites are stiff and shiny. Fold into the cream cheese mixture. Spoon into the crumb crust. Bake about 1 hour, or until the center does not tremble when the cake is gently shaken. Cool, then chill in the refrigerator.

RAISED CHEESE CAKE ✳
(9-INCH ROUND CAKE)

Pastry

1 cup flour	1 egg yolk
¼ pound butter, softened	2 tablespoons sugar

Filling

1 pound cream cheese	¼ cup heavy cream
1 tablespoon flour	¼ cup sour cream
½ cup sugar	2 teaspoons vanilla
4 eggs, separated	¼ teaspoon salt

Preheat the oven to 400°F. Make the pastry first. Mix the flour and butter until well blended. Add the egg yolk and sugar and blend well. Take apart a 9-inch springform pan with a removable bottom and press about half of the pastry into the bottom. Bake for about 8 minutes and cool. Fit the rim of the pan onto the bottom, then press the remaining pastry all around the inside of the rim about halfway up. Don't worry if it is not even. Lower the oven temperature to 350°F. Set aside and make the filling. In a mixing bowl, cream the cheese until soft. Add the flour and sugar and mix well. Add the egg yolks, heavy cream, sour cream, and vanilla, and beat well. Beat the egg whites with the salt until they hold stiff peaks but are not dry. Fold the egg whites into the cheese mixture and pour into the pan. Bake for about 45 minutes. Let cool and serve at room temperature.

(9-INCH ROUND CAKE)   **CHOCOLATE MOUSSE CAKE**

This flourless cake has a light mousselike texture unlike other more moist, dense mousse cakes. It is very easy to make.

8 ounces semisweet chocolate	⅓ cup granulated sugar
7 tablespoons butter	Confectioners' sugar
7 eggs, separated	

Preheat the oven to 250°F. Grease and flour a 9-inch springform pan. Melt the chocolate and butter in the top of a double boiler over hot water or use a heavy-bottomed saucepan. Set the mixture aside and let it cool to room temperature. Beat the egg whites until foamy. Add the granulated sugar and continue beating until stiff. Stir the egg yolks into the cooled chocolate mixture, then fold in the egg whites. Pour the batter into the prepared pan and smooth the top evenly. Bake for 1 hour and 15 minutes. Cool the cake in the pan for 15 minutes. Remove the sides of the pan and sprinkle the top with confectioners' sugar.

QUICK GOLD CAKE

(TWO 8-INCH ROUND LAYERS)

2¼ cups cake flour
3 teaspoons baking powder
1 teaspoon salt
1¼ cups sugar

½ cup vegetable oil
1 cup milk
2 eggs
2 teaspoons vanilla

Preheat the oven to 350°F. Butter and lightly flour two 8-inch round cake pans. Mix the flour, baking powder, salt, and sugar in a bowl. Stir in the oil and milk, and beat for 2 minutes. Add the eggs and vanilla, and beat for another 2 minutes. Pour into the pans and bake for 25–30 minutes, or until a toothpick comes out clean. Cool in the pans for 5 minutes before turning out onto racks. Frost with *Fluffy Butter Frosting* (p. 843) or *Mocha Rum Butter Frosting* (p. 843).

QUICK DATE CAKE

(9-INCH SQUARE CAKE)

5 tablespoons butter, softened
1 cup dark-brown sugar
2 eggs
½ cup milk
1¾ cups flour

2 teaspoons baking powder
½ teaspoon cinnamon
½ teaspoon nutmeg
½ pound dates, in pieces
Confectioners' sugar

Preheat the oven to 350°F. Butter and lightly flour a 9-inch square cake pan. Combine all the ingredients in a mixing bowl and beat for 3 minutes with a wooden spoon. Pour into the pan and bake for 35–40 minutes, until a toothpick comes out clean. Cool in the pan for 5 minutes before turning out onto a rack. While still warm, dust with confectioners' sugar sifted through a strainer.

CUPCAKES

About Cupcakes

Just about any plain white, butter, or chocolate cake recipe can be used for cupcakes. Bake them in muffin pans, greased or lined with fluted paper cups. Fill each cup halfway. Cupcakes will bake in less time than layer cakes, usually about 15 minutes in a preheated 350°F oven, or until a straw inserted in the center comes out clean. Let cupcakes cool in the pan for about 5 minutes before turning them out onto a rack to cool thoroughly. The five recipes that follow make particularly nice cupcakes.

(12 MEDIUM CUPCAKES) **BOSTON CUPCAKES**

There's more than a little hint of mace to give these a true New England quality.

5 tablespoons butter	2 teaspoons baking powder
1 cup sugar	¼ teaspoon mace
2 eggs	¼ teaspoon salt
1¼ cups cake flour	½ cup milk

Preheat the oven to 350°F. Butter muffin pans for 12 cupcakes or line them with fluted paper cups. Cream the butter, gradually add the sugar, and beat until light. Stir in the eggs and beat well. Mix the flour, baking powder, mace, and salt together. Add to the first mixture, then stir in the milk and beat until well combined. Spoon into the pans, filling each cup about two-thirds full. Bake for 15 minutes, until a straw or toothpick comes out clean. Cool in the pan for 5 minutes before turning out onto a rack. Frost with *Creamy Chocolate Frosting* (p. 839) or *Coffee Butter Frosting* (p. 843).

CHEWY BROWN-SUGAR
(ABOUT 16 CUPCAKES) *** WALNUT CUPCAKES**

Dark, chewy, sweet, and nutty, these are best served warm from the oven. If you don't want to frost them, they are equally delicious buttered.

4 eggs	1 cup chopped walnuts, in
2 cups dark-brown sugar	large pieces
2 tablespoons butter	2 teaspoons vanilla
1½ cups all-purpose flour	Quick Caramel Frosting (p.
½ teaspoon salt	840)
1½ teaspoons baking powder	

Preheat the oven to 350°F. Grease the muffin pans, line them with fluted paper baking cups, or spray them with no-stick coating. Put a large pan of water on the stove and bring to a simmer. Crack the eggs into a mixing bowl (one that will fit into the pan of water) and beat with a fork to blend. Stir in the brown sugar and butter. Set the bowl in the simmering water, and stir constantly until the mixture is very warm, about 150°F. Remove from the water and add the flour, salt, and baking powder, and beat until the batter is well blended and smooth. Stir in the walnuts and vanilla. Spoon into the muffin pans, filling each cup about half full. Bake for about 18–20 minutes, or until a toothpick or broomstraw inserted in the center of a cake comes out clean. Remove from the oven and let cool for a moment, then turn the cupcakes out onto a rack. Split, butter, and serve warm, or cool completely and frost with Quick Caramel Frosting.

ALMOND TEA CAKES   (8 CAKES)

These are moistly delicate, lovely for afternoon tea or with a dish of vanilla ice cream with caramel sauce.

¼ pound butter	¼ teaspoon salt
¾ cup sugar	⅓ cup milk
2 eggs, well beaten	1 cup blanched almonds, in
1½ cups cake flour	pieces
2 teaspoons baking powder	

Preheat the oven to 375°F. Line a muffin pan with cupcake papers or grease well. Cream together the butter and sugar until light and fluffy. Add the eggs, beating thoroughly. Stir in the flour, baking powder, and salt; beat, and add the milk. Mix well and stir in the almonds. Spoon the batter into the muffin tins two-thirds full. Bake for 15–20 minutes or until center is dry when a straw is inserted.

DATE NUT CAKES   (12 CAKES)

Easy to make; even non–date lovers like these. A delicious dessert crowned with a generous amount of whipped cream.

1 cup boiling water	½ teaspoon salt
1 teaspoon baking soda	2 eggs, well beaten
8 ounces pitted chopped	1 cup flour
dates, approximately 1	1 cup coarsely chopped
cup	walnuts
1 tablespoon butter, softened	Softly whipped cream
1 cup sugar	

Preheat the oven to 325°F. Line a 12-cup muffin pan with cupcake liners or grease well. Mix the boiling water with the soda, then add the dates. Set aside to cool. Combine the butter, sugar, salt, eggs, and flour.

Mix well. Add the date mixture and walnuts. Beat until well blended. Spoon into each cup until almost full. Bake 40–50 minutes, or until a toothpick comes out clean when inserted. Serve with softly whipped cream.

LITTLE LIGHT CHOCOLATE CAKES

(ABOUT 16 CUPCAKES)

I've been making these for thirty-five years and they still taste wonderful to me. They get stale quickly, so freeze them if you're not going to eat them all the first day.

¼ cup vegetable shortening	½ teaspoon baking powder
1 cup sugar	½ teaspoon baking soda
¼ cup unsweetened cocoa	1 egg, slightly beaten
½ cup boiling water	1 teaspoon vanilla
1½ cups all-purpose flour	½ cup sour cream
½ teaspoon salt	

Preheat the oven to 350°F. Either line muffin pans with fluted paper baking cups, grease them well, or spray with no-stick coating. Put the shortening, sugar, and cocoa in a mixing bowl, pour in the boiling water, and beat until smooth. Combine the flour, salt, baking powder, and baking soda, and sift them into the bowl over the shortening mixture. Beat until well blended. Add the egg, vanilla, and sour cream, and beat until smooth and creamy. Spoon the batter into the prepared pans, filling each cup about three-quarters full. Bake for about 20 minutes, or until a toothpick inserted in the center of a cake comes out clean. Remove from the oven and let cool in the pan for a moment, then gently remove them to a rack to cool completely. Spread the top of each cake with a very thin coating of *Chocolate Butter Frosting* (p. 843.)

YESTERDAY'S CAKES

Yesterday's cake can return, in a different disguise, sometimes reaching new heights with such simple, good additions as Chocolate Cream Filling (p. 848), Lemon Filling (p. 850), or just softly whipped sweetened cream flavored with rum. When cake loses its appeal or becomes dry, take what is left and cut into bite-size cubes, place in a bowl, add a flavored cream or custard, and gently mix with the cake pieces. Cover and refrigerate at least 4 hours. A lovely change takes place: textures and taste are fresh and new. The remains of a spice cake or a light cake can be cut into strips, spread with a little jam or jelly, rolled up, enclosed in plastic wrap, refrigerated for several hours, and served with coffee or as dessert. Some other suggested additions for re-creating cake are: flavored whipped creams, custards, fresh sliced fruit, berries, ice cream, nuts, liqueurs.

RUM CAKE

Use the equivalent of one layer of plain (not chocolate or spice) cake. Cut into serving pieces, or smaller, then sprinkle ⅓–½ cup rum over the pieces. Place them in a 1½-quart serving dish—glass, if possible. Whip 1½ cups heavy cream, sweeten with 3–4 tablespoons sugar, and flavor with ½ cup (or more) apricot preserves or raspberry jam. Spread over and around the cake. Press gently, so the cake settles down. Cover and chill for at least 4 hours. Serve from its dish.

ICEBOX CAKE   (SERVES SIX)

Line a mold or large bowl with strips of leftover sponge cake, angel food cake, pound cake, or other plain cake. If there is enough cake, have the pieces overlap at the edges. Fill with one of the following fillings:

Butter Filling

| ¼ pound unsalted butter, softened | 4 eggs, separated |
| 1 cup confectioners' sugar | 2 teaspoons vanilla, or 3 tablespoons rum |

NOTE
see page 471

Beat the butter, slowly adding the sugar. Continue to beat until light and fluffy. Add the egg yolks, one at a time, beating well after each addition. Add vanilla or rum. In a separate bowl beat the egg whites until stiff but not dry. Gently fold the whites into the butter mixture, then spoon into the cake-lined mold. Cover and chill overnight. Unmold and serve with *whipped cream*.

CHOCOLATE FILLING

Melt *1 ounce unsweetened chocolate* with *2 tablespoons water*. Cool and add to the butter mixture before folding in the egg whites. Continue as directed.

LEMON FILLING

Add the *grated rind and juice of 1 lemon* to the butter mixture before folding in the egg whites.

COFFEE FILLING

Add *3 tablespoons instant coffee* to the butter mixture before folding in the egg whites.

TIPSY PUDDING

(SERVES SIX)

½ cup sherry
3 cups unfrosted cake cut in
   1-inch cubes
1 recipe Soft Custard (p. 939)

1 cup heavy cream, whipped
1 cup macaroon crumbs
   (optional)

Put the sherry in a bowl, add the cake cubes, and lightly toss to get some sherry on each piece. Cover with Soft Custard, spoon whipped cream on top, and sprinkle with crumbs, if you wish. Cover and refrigerate at least 2 hours.

ENGLISH TRIFLE

Add *a cup or so of fresh diced fruit*—peaches, bananas, plums, berries—or *canned fruit* to the cake cubes when you toss them.

TIPSY PUDDING WITH LADYFINGERS

Instead of using cake, line the bowl with 1 *dozen or so ladyfingers*, then pour soft custard, flavored with sherry, over.

FROSTINGS & FILLINGS

ABOUT FROSTINGS AND FILLINGS

You can add a complex blend of flavors and textures to a plain cake by using a special filling between the layers and a contrasting frosting on the sides and top of the cake. Most frequently, however, layer cakes are filled and frosted with the same frosting. In general, 1½–2 cups of frosting will fill and cover two 8- or 9-inch layers. Since this varies, depending on the thickness of the frosting, we indicate with the recipe how much cake each frosting will cover. As a general rule, ½–¾ cup of filling will fill a two-layer cake.

If you are short of time, you can always fill a cake with jam or jelly or with sliced soft fruits or berries, then dust the top with confectioners' sugar. Whipped cream or softened ice cream (spread on the cake only just before serving) are also good alternatives.

How Much Frosting?

The amounts of frosting are variable. If you are using a whipped cream or fluffy frosting it takes more to cover and fill a cake than when using the thin glaze variety. Some people like lots of frosting; some like just a little. It is often a good idea to increase these recipes by a third so there is an ample amount and some to spare. You can always use extra frosting on graham crackers or melt it to use as a dessert sauce. Extra frosting will keep well in the refrigerator.

CAKE SIZE	FROSTING NEEDED
One 8-inch two-layer cake, top and sides	1½ cups
One 8-inch two-layer cake, top, sides, and filling	2 cups
One 9-inch two-layer cake, top and sides	2 cups
One 9-inch two-layer cake, top, sides, and filling	2½ cups
One 8-inch square cake, top only	¾ cup
One 8-inch square cake, top and sides	1½ cups
One 13 × 9-inch cake, top only	2 cups
One 13 × 9-inch cake, top and sides	2½ cups
One 9- or 10-inch tube cake	3 to 4 cups
One 9 × 5 × 3-inch loaf cake, top and sides	1½ cups
12 cupcakes	¾ to 1 cup

Whenever possible, spread *uncooked* frostings on cakes that are still slightly warm. *Cooked* frostings, on the other hand, should be used after the cake has cooled completely.

Correcting a Frosting

It's easy to make frostings come out the way you want. If a cooked egg-white frosting isn't stiff enough, just put it in the top of a double boiler and beat it a little over simmering water; to stiffen cooked butter creams, refrigerate for several minutes, beat over ice, or beat in a little more butter. To thin a frosting that's too thick to spread easily, beat in a few drops of hot water or milk.

Frostings made with eggs or butter should be refrigerated if you are not serving the cake until the next day. Frostings will keep a long time refrigerated; there's no need to freeze them.

If a cake is lopsided or uneven, do not hesitate to reshape it before you frost it. Use a sharp knife and slice off whatever is necessary to make a cake regular or cake layers uniform. If you are making a three-layer cake and the middle layer has a rounded top, slice off the raised portion so that the layers fit together evenly. You can also slice through cake layers horizontally to make a cake with lots of filling and four or more thin layers. Before you slice through horizontally, as illustrated, first make a shallow vertical cut to mark the place where you'll need to fit the layers together later.

Frosting Cakes

Place the bottom layer upside down on a serving plate. Tuck strips of wax paper or foil around to catch any icing that may drip down.

Spread filling on the bottom layer and then set the top layer over it, right side up, so that the two level surfaces are face to face. (If you are doing several layers, align the vertical cuts you made before slicing the layers in half.) Using a wide knife or a spatula, cover the sides first, then pile the remaining frosting on the top and swirl it to the edges. This progression seems to work best. (If you dip the knife or spatula in warm water from time to time, the frosting will be shiny and spread more easily.) If you are not going to decorate, you can make a simple cross hatching with the tines of a fork on the top.

After the cake is completely frosted and the frosting has had time to set, remove the strips of paper or foil protecting the serving plate.

Decorating Cakes

You can decorate a cake very simply, using chopped or whole nuts, coconut, tiny candies, colored sugar, or candied fruit or flowers. Arrange them in patterns or sprinkle them at random over the cake. Candles are, of course, essential for birthday cakes; they should be in holders, which you can buy—or even make yourself, if you are inventive.

If you wish to do something elaborate, decorate your cake with icing pushed through a pastry bag. A pastry bag is a worthwhile investment, and far easier and more satisfactory to use than metal cake decorators. Pastry bags come with a set of tips; each is cut in a special way to make specific patterns.

If you don't have a pastry bag, or if you are using a number of different colors and need a different bag for each, try making your own pastry bags out of sheets of heavy typing paper or baking parchment. Fold each sheet into a tight cornucopia with a sharp point, and fasten it firmly with cellophane tape. Pinch the point flat and cut it according to the design you want: straight across to make a ribbon design, in two points to make leaves, or in three points to make stars. Or drop metal decorating tips into the bags.

Confectioners' Frosting II (p. 838), *Royal Icing* (p. 838), or any butter frosting will work well in a pastry bag. Before filling the bag, fold one-third of the top back. Also, push the fabric down into the large end of the metal tube to block the opening. Fill the bag half full—about to the

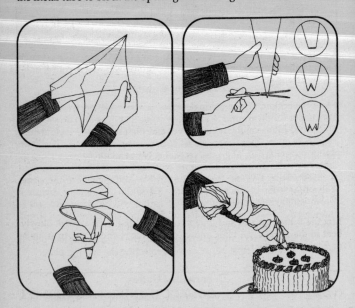

level where you have folded the top down; then unfold and twist the top of the pastry bag firmly around the filling.

Spread out a piece of wax paper near the cake. Push a little frosting out onto the paper to make sure there are no air bubbles in the cone and practice a little before you tackle the cake. Then decorate the cake itself; one hand should be near the nozzle guiding the tip and squeezing the bag slightly while the other hand holds the twisted end and exerts a little downward pressure.

FROSTINGS

(FROSTS 8-INCH SQUARE CAKE) **BROILED FROSTING**

This simple frosting, also used as lazy daisy topping, is to be spread on a warm, freshly baked one-layer cake which is then set under the broiler to brown. Watch carefully to be sure that the topping browns lightly and evenly.

3 tablespoons butter, melted	2 tablespoons cream
3 tablespoons dark-brown sugar	½ cup shredded coconut or chopped nuts

Mix all the ingredients together and spread over a warm cake while it is still in the pan. Set the pan under the broiler until the frosting bubbles and turns golden.

(ABOUT 1¾ CUPS) **PORTSMOUTH FROSTING**

This tastes of butter and cream, and what could be nicer?

¼ cup butter, melted	About 3 cups confectioners' sugar
¼ cup cream	
1 teaspoon vanilla or rum	

Mix the butter, cream, and vanilla or rum together in a bowl. Slowly beat in the sugar until thick and creamy. This is enough to frost an 8- or 9-inch two-layer cake.

(1 CUP) **CONFECTIONERS' FROSTING I**

You can give this sweet frosting different flavors by substituting the same amount of hot coffee, lemon juice, or orange juice for the hot water. Or substitute 1 teaspoon of vanilla for the hot water. For a fine creamy consistency, be sure to beat the frosting very well.

3 tablespoons hot water
About 2½ cups confectioners'
    sugar

Put the hot water in a small bowl and beat in the confectioners' sugar until the frosting is thick enough to spread. Continue to beat for several minutes until very creamy. This will be enough frosting for an 8-inch two-layer cake.

CONFECTIONERS' FROSTING II   (ABOUT 1 CUP)

This pure-white, creamy frosting is excellent for decorating cakes; the shortening will keep it from becoming dry and it can be tinted with vegetable coloring, if you wish.

⅓ cup vegetable shortening   2 tablespoons cream or milk,
⅛ teaspoon salt   approximately
2 cups confectioners' sugar,
    approximately

Cream the shortening and the salt together, then add the sugar and stir briskly. Stir in the cream or milk and beat well, adding more sugar or more milk if necessary to get an easily spreadable consistency. This is enough to frost an 8-inch two-layer cake.

ROYAL ICING   (ABOUT 2 CUPS)

A fine basic frosting that is very light and airy rather than creamy. Use on chocolate cakes, for decorating cookies, or any time you want a firm frosting that holds up well.

2 egg whites (¼ cup)   1 tablespoon lemon juice
3 cups confectioners' sugar   ¼ teaspoon salt

NOTE
see page 471

Combine the egg whites, sugar, lemon juice, and salt in a mixing bowl. Beat at high speed (or very fast with a rotary beater) for several minutes, until the mixture holds soft peaks. You will have enough to fill and frost an 8-inch two-layer cake.

CHOCOLATE FROSTING

(ABOUT 1 CUP)

Thick but spreadable with a mild chocolate flavor.

2 ounces unsweetened
    chocolate
1 tablespoon butter
⅓ cup milk (more if
    necessary)

2 cups confectioners' sugar
1 teaspoon vanilla

Melt the chocolate, butter, and milk together in a small bowl or pot over simmering water or in a heavy-bottomed saucepan. Cool to luke-warm, then stir in the sugar and vanilla. Beat until thick enough to spread. This will be enough to frost an 8-inch two-layer cake.

CREAMY CHOCOLATE FROSTING

(ABOUT 2 CUPS)

Smooth, shiny, sweet, and thick.

2 ounces unsweetened
    chocolate, grated
1 cup sugar
3 tablespoons cornstarch

1 cup boiling water
1 tablespoon butter
1 teaspoon vanilla
⅛ teaspoon salt

Combine the chocolate, sugar, and cornstarch in a heavy-bottomed pan. Stir in the boiling water, and cook over moderate heat about 2–3 minutes, stirring constantly, until thick and smooth. Remove from the heat and add the butter, vanilla, and salt. Beat well. You will have enough to fill and frost an 8- or 9-inch two-layer cake.

CHOCOLATE FROSTING FOR CREAM PUFFS
* AND ÉCLAIRS

For recipes for Cream Puffs and Éclairs, see p. 926.

3 ounces semisweet chocolate

2 tablespoons butter

Melt the chocolate and the butter in a heavy-bottomed small pan over moderate heat, stirring constantly until smooth. Spoon over filled cream puffs or éclairs and let drip down the sides.

FUDGE FROSTING

(ABOUT 2 CUPS)

This is like a spreadable fudge.

2 ounces unsweetened
   chocolate, in bits
1½ cups sugar
½ cup milk

4 tablespoons butter
1 tablespoon corn syrup
¼ teaspoon salt
1 teaspoon vanilla

Stir together all the ingredients except the vanilla in a heavy-bottomed pan. Bring to a rolling boil and cook, stirring vigorously, for just 1 minute; cool. Add the vanilla and beat until thick. This will fill and frost an 8- or 9-inch two-layer cake.

VANILLA FUDGE FROSTING

(ABOUT 1½ CUPS)

1 tablespoon butter
1½ cups sugar
½ cup milk

⅛ teaspoon salt
1 teaspoon vanilla

Mix the butter, sugar, milk, and salt in a heavy-bottomed pan. Bring to the boiling point over moderate heat, then boil without stirring until the mixture reaches 234°F, or the "soft-ball stage" (see p. 1046). Let cool, then beat until thick enough to spread. Add the vanilla. You will have enough to fill and frost an 8- or 9-inch two-layer cake.

QUICK CARAMEL FROSTING

(ABOUT 1½ CUPS)

¼ pound butter
½ cup dark-brown sugar

¼ cup milk
2 cups confectioners' sugar

Melt the butter and brown sugar in a heavy-bottomed pan, stirring over moderate heat until the sugar is dissolved. Add the milk and blend. Cool, then beat in the confectioners' sugar until thick enough to spread. You will have enough to fill and frost an 8- or 9-inch two-layer cake.

(ABOUT 2 CUPS)   **PENUCHE FROSTING**

Excellent caramel flavor.

1½ cups dark-brown sugar
¾ cup granulated sugar
⅛ teaspoon salt
½ cup milk

3 tablespoons butter
1½ tablespoons corn syrup
1½ teaspoons vanilla

Mix all the ingredients except the vanilla in a heavy-bottomed pan. Bring slowly to the boiling point, stirring constantly, and boil for just 1 minute. Cool to lukewarm, add the vanilla, and beat until thick enough to spread. You will have enough to fill and frost an 8- or 9-inch two-layer cake.

(ABOUT 2½ CUPS)   **MAPLE FROSTING**

1½ cups maple syrup
⅛ teaspoon salt
¼ teaspoon cream of tartar

¼ cup sugar
2 egg whites

Combine all the ingredients in the top of a double boiler or in a bowl. Beat the mixture over simmering water until it stands in stiff peaks, about 5–7 minutes, no longer. You will have enough to fill and frost an 8- or 9-inch two-layer cake.

(2½ CUPS)   ✳ **COCONUT-PECAN FROSTING**

This is the traditional frosting for the German Sweet Chocolate Cake (p. 796).

1 cup evaporated milk
1 cup sugar
2 egg yolks, slightly beaten
½ cup butter

1 teaspoon vanilla
1⅓ cups Baker's Angel Flake
    Coconut
1 cup chopped pecans

In a saucepan, mix the evaporated milk, sugar, egg yolks, butter, and vanilla. Cook and stir over medium heat until thickened, about 12 minutes. Stir in the coconut and pecans. Cool until thick enough to spread, beating occasionally. You will have enough to fill and frost a 9-inch three-layer cake.

CREAM-CHEESE FROSTING   (2 CUPS)

Very good on spice cakes, gingerbreads, carrot cakes, and fruit cakes.

8 ounces cream cheese, at   2 cups confectioners' sugar,
    room temperature   sifted if lumpy
¼ cup butter   1 teaspoon vanilla

Combine the cream cheese, butter, confectioners' sugar, and vanilla in
a mixing bowl or the bowl of a food processor. Beat well or process until perfectly smooth and spreadable. You will have enough to fill and
frost an 8-inch two-layer cake.

SULTANA NUT FROSTING   (ABOUT 2¼ CUPS)

Creamy and good, with a praline taste.

2 cups dark-brown sugar   ¼ cup seedless raisins
¾ cup heavy cream   ¼ cup finely chopped walnuts

Mix the brown sugar and cream in a heavy-bottomed pan and boil
without stirring until the mixture reaches 234°F, or the "soft-ball stage"
(see p. 1046). Pour onto a large platter and let cool. Work with a spatula until creamy, then stir in the raisins and walnuts. You will have
enough to fill and frost an 8- or 9-inch two-layer cake.

BUTTER FROSTING I   (ABOUT ¾ CUP)

If you want more frosting, double the butter and the sugar, but use
only the one yolk.

4 tablespoons butter   1 cup confectioners' sugar
1 egg yolk

NOTE
see page 471

Beat the butter until light and creamy. Stir in the egg yolk
and continue to beat, adding the sugar, 2 tablespoons at a
time. Beat until all the sugar is added and the frosting is
fluffy. You will have enough to frost an 8-inch two-layer
cake.

(ABOUT 1 CUP)   **BUTTER FROSTING II**

½ cup sugar   1 egg yolk
¼ cup water   ¼ pound butter, chilled

NOTE
see page 471 Boil the sugar and water without stirring in a heavy-bottomed pan until the mixture reaches 240°F, or the "medium soft-ball stage" (see p. 1046). While the sugar syrup is cooking, beat the egg yolk well. Slowly pour the 240° syrup over the beaten yolk, beating constantly. Beat in bits of the cold butter until it is all incorporated. Continue to beat until the frosting is of spreading consistency. You will have enough to frost a 9-inch two-layer cake.

CHOCOLATE BUTTER FROSTING

Melt *4 ounces semisweet chocolate* and add to the frosting after the butter has been incorporated.

COFFEE BUTTER FROSTING

Add *2 teaspoons instant coffee* to the frosting after the butter has been incorporated.

MOCHA RUM BUTTER FROSTING

Add *1½ tablespoons rum* and *2 teaspoons instant coffee* after the butter has been incorporated.

(ABOUT 1½ CUPS)   **FLUFFY BUTTER FROSTING**

Light and airy.

4 tablespoons butter   2 egg whites
1½ cups confectioners' sugar

NOTE
see page 471 Cream the butter until light. Gradually add ½ cup of the sugar; set aside. Beat the egg whites until foamy, slowly add the remaining cup of sugar and continue to beat until stiff. Combine the two mixtures and blend. Add more

sugar if necessary to make the frosting thick enough to spread. You will have enough to fill and frost an 8- or 9-inch two-layer cake.

SEVEN-MINUTE FROSTING   (ABOUT 3–4 CUPS)

A light, billowy frosting with a sheen, very much like a "boiled" frosting. Seven-minute frosting dries out quickly, so keep it refrigerated if you're not using it within a few hours.

1½ cups sugar	2 egg whites
¼ teaspoon cream of tartar	¼ cup water
⅛ teaspoon salt	2 teaspoons vanilla

Mix sugar, cream of tartar, salt, egg whites, and water in a pot or bowl over simmering water. Beat steadily over low heat with a rotary or electric hand beater until the frosting stands in peaks, about 5–7 minutes, no more. Remove from the heat and continue to beat until thick enough to spread. Add the vanilla before spreading. You will have enough to fill and frost an 8- or 9-inch two-layer cake.

CARAMEL FROSTING

Omit the vanilla and substitute *1 cup dark-brown sugar* for 1 cup of the white sugar.

COCONUT FROSTING

Omit the vanilla and stir in *½ cup grated coconut* (p. 13) before spreading.

COFFEE FROSTING

Omit the vanilla and add *1 tablespoon instant coffee* before spreading.

LEMON OR ORANGE FROSTING

Omit the vanilla and substitute *¼ cup lemon or orange juice* for the water. Add *1 teaspoon grated lemon or orange rind* before spreading.

PEPPERMINT FROSTING

Omit the vanilla. Add ½ *teaspoon oil of peppermint* and a few drops of *green food coloring* before spreading.

(ABOUT 5 CUPS)   **ITALIAN MERINGUE**

This light, fluffy frosting should be applied very generously to the cake. Cooking procedures are important here to prevent the syrup from crystallizing or becoming grainy.

3 egg whites	½ cup water
Pinch of salt	1½ teaspoons vanilla
1 cup sugar	

Combine the egg whites and salt in a bowl and beat until the whites are stiff but not dry; set aside. Combine the sugar and water in a small, heavy-bottomed pan. Heat, without stirring, until the mixture begins to boil. Cover for 3 minutes to dissolve any sugar crystals on the sides of the pan. Remove the lid and let the syrup boil without stirring for about 10–15 minutes until it "spins a thread" (see p. 1046) or reaches 230–232°F on a candy thermometer. Very slowly pour the syrup over the beaten whites, beating constantly all the while; continue to beat until the meringue has cooled to room temperature. Beat in the vanilla. You will have frosting enough to fill and frost an 8- or 9-inch two- or even three-layer cake.

(ABOUT 2 CUPS)   **✳ WHITE MOUNTAIN CREAM**

This is the classic "boiled" frosting, fluffy with a marshmallowlike consistency. A hot sugar syrup cooks the egg whites as it thickens them.

1 cup sugar	⅛ teaspoon salt
⅓ cup water	2 egg whites
⅛ teaspoon cream of tartar	1 teaspoon vanilla

Mix the sugar, water, cream of tartar, and salt in a heavy-bottomed pan. Boil without stirring until the mixture reaches 240°F, or the "medium soft-ball stage" (see p. 1046). Beat the egg whites until stiff, then pour the 240° sugar syrup over them in a slow, thin stream, beating constantly until thick enough to spread. Stir in the vanilla. You will have enough to fill and frost an 8- or 9-inch two-layer cake.

PETITS FOURS FROSTING (FROSTING FOR 80 PETITS FOURS)

Use this on any cake or to cover Petits Fours (p. 887).

    2 cups granulated sugar   1½ cups or more
    ⅛ teaspoon cream of tartar   confectioners' sugar
    1 cup water

Combine the granulated sugar, cream of tartar, and water in a sauce-pan. Bring to a boil and boil without stirring until the mixture becomes a thin syrup, 226°F on a candy thermometer. Cool until slightly above lukewarm (100°F). Gradually stir in confectioners' sugar until the syrup is just thick enough to coat a spoon. Test it by pouring a little over a cake to see if it's the proper consistency. Use while warm or re-heat over simmering water.

COLORED PETITS FOURS FROSTING

Divide Petits Fours Frosting into separate bowls and tint each with a different shade of vegetable coloring. Or tint the frosting delicately, frost one row of petits fours, then add more coloring, making each row of cakes a bit deeper in color. White, pink, rose, and red make a good series, as do white, yellow, pale orange, and deep orange.

CHOCOLATE PETITS FOURS FROSTING

Melt *3 ounces unsweetened chocolate* over simmering water and stir it into warm Petits Fours Frosting. Use less chocolate if you are flavoring only part of the frosting.

BASIC GLAZE

Use hot orange juice, lemon juice, strong coffee, or another liquid of your choice instead of the hot water, if you wish to change the flavor of this basic glaze.

    Hot water   Confectioners' sugar

Add hot water *very gradually* to the confectioners' sugar, a few drops at a time, and beat constantly until the glaze is thin enough to pour. Pour it over cake and let it dribble down the sides.

CHOCOLATE GLAZE

This is a decorative "finishing" glaze, usually used over another frosting.

    Unsweetened chocolate
    Butter

Melt the chocolate with the butter over simmering water, using 1 tablespoon of butter for each ounce of chocolate. Let the glaze cool slightly, then dribble it over white frosting after it has set. Use the tines of a fork to create a lined or crisscrossed effect in the chocolate.

APRICOT GLAZE

    1 small jar apricot preserves

Melt the apricot preserves over low heat until liquid. Strain and spread on the cake.

FILLINGS

(ABOUT 1½ CUPS)   ## BASIC CREAM FILLING

Also known as *crème patissière*, this basic custard is good by itself or used in cream puffs, pies, and other pastries.

    1 cup milk   ⅛ teaspoon salt
    ½ cup sugar   2 egg yolks, slightly beaten
    3 tablespoons flour   2 teaspoons vanilla

Heat the milk in a heavy-bottomed pan until very hot but not boiling. Mix the sugar, flour, and salt together in a bowl, stir in the hot milk, and beat until well blended. Pour back into the pan and continue to stir vigorously over low heat for 4–5 minutes, until very thick and smooth. Add the egg yolks and cook for a few more minutes. Cool, stirring from time to time, then add the vanilla. You will have about enough filling for an 8- or 9-inch three-layer cake.

BANANA CREAM FILLING

Omit the vanilla. Mash *1 large banana* and beat it until smooth, add *2 tablespoons lemon juice,* and stir the mixture into the cooled filling.

CHOCOLATE CREAM FILLING

Melt *2 ounces unsweetened chocolate* in the milk and use *1 cup sugar* instead of ½ cup.

COOKED BUTTER CREAM FILLING   (ABOUT 1½ CUPS)

Silken and rich—the most refined of all butter creams.

½ cup milk
2 egg yolks
¼ cup confectioners' sugar,
   sifted if lumpy

2 teaspoons vanilla
1 cup butter, at room
   temperature

Scald the milk in a heavy-bottomed saucepan. While the milk is heating, combine the egg yolks and sugar in a mixing bowl, and beat vigorously until blended and smooth. Slowly pour the hot milk over the yolk mixture, stirring constantly with a spoon. (Don't stir with a whisk or rotary beater, which would create a foamy layer on top of the sauce and prevent you from seeing the consistency underneath.) Pour the mixture into the saucepan, and cook over medium heat, stirring constantly, until slightly thickened, about 4–5 minutes. Do not boil. You can test by putting your finger in—it should feel very hot, and you will also see wisps of steam rising. Remove from heat and add the vanilla, then beat until the sauce is cool; you can hasten this step by beating with the pan in a bowl of ice, if you wish.

When cool, begin beating in the butter by tablespoon bits, beating after each addition until smooth. If it begins to separate or has a curdled look, beat well with an electric mixer or put in a food processor and it will smooth out. Cover and refrigerate until needed. You will have enough to fill a 9-inch three-layer cake. Halve the recipe if you wish to fill a 9-inch two-layer cake.

COOKED CITRUS BUTTER CREAM FILLING

Add 2 *teaspoons finely grated lemon rind* or 2 *teaspoons finely grated orange rind* when you add the vanilla.

COOKED COFFEE BUTTER CREAM FILLING

Add 1½ *tablespoons powdered instant coffee* when you add the vanilla.

COOKED CHOCOLATE BUTTER CREAM FILLING

Beat 2 *ounces unsweetened chocolate, melted and cooled,* into the finished butter cream.

COOKED LIQUEUR BUTTER CREAM FILLING

Beat 2 *tablespoons Grand Marnier, Cointreau, Amaretto, rum, bourbon, brandy*—or any liqueur of your choice—into the finished butter cream.

(ABOUT 3½ CUPS)   ## LORD BALTIMORE FILLING

Use this with Lord Baltimore Cake (p. 799). It is what makes the cake.

1 recipe Seven-Minute
    Frosting (p. 844)
½ cup dry macaroon crumbs
¼ cup chopped pecans

¼ cup chopped almonds
12 candied cherries, in
    quarters
2 teaspoons lemon juice

Divide the frosting in half. Fold all of the remaining ingredients into half the frosting and use as a filling between two yellow 8-inch cake layers. Use the remaining plain frosting to cover the sides and the top of the cake.

LADY BALTIMORE FILLING

(ABOUT 3 CUPS)

Use this with Lady Baltimore Cake (p. 799).

1 recipe Seven-Minute
    Frosting (p. 844)
⅓ cup chopped pecans
⅓ cup dried figs or dates, in
    bits

½ cup raisins
½ teaspoon almond extract

Divide the frosting in half. Fold the pecans, figs, raisins, and almond extract into half the frosting and use it as a filling between two white 8-inch cake layers. Use the remaining plain frosting to cover the sides and the top of the cake.

LEMON COCONUT CREAM FILLING

(ABOUT 2 CUPS)

Juice and grated rind of 1
    lemon
1 cup sugar

2 egg yolks, slightly beaten
1 cup shredded coconut

Mix the lemon juice and rind, sugar, and egg yolks in a heavy-bottomed pan and cook over moderate heat, stirring constantly, until smooth and thickened. Remove from the heat, stir in the coconut, and cool. You will have enough filling for an 8- or 9-inch three-layer cake.

LEMON FILLING

(ABOUT 2 CUPS)

This is a clear filling with the zippy taste of fresh lemon. Make this ahead because it thickens when chilled. Lemon filling also makes a delightful dessert topped with fresh berries, oranges, or bananas.

1 cup sugar
3 tablespoons cornstarch
½ teaspoon salt
1 cup water

2 tablespoons grated lemon
    rind
½ cup lemon juice
2 tablespoons butter

In a saucepan, stir together the sugar, cornstarch, salt, water, lemon rind, lemon juice, and butter, and bring to a boil. Reduce the heat and boil for 1 minute, stirring constantly. Let cool, then refrigerate until well chilled and thick. You will have enough filling for an 8- or 9-inch three-layer cake.

(ABOUT 2 CUPS)   **ORANGE FILLING**

Make this ahead because it thickens when chilled. Orange filling also makes a pretty and unusual dessert topped with fresh orange sections.

¾ cup sugar
3 tablespoons cornstarch
½ teaspoon salt
¾ cup water
2 tablespoons grated orange
   rind

¾ cup orange juice
1 tablespoon lemon juice
2 tablespoons butter
   (optional)

In a saucepan, stir together the sugar, cornstarch, salt, water, orange rind, orange juice, lemon juice, and butter, and bring to a boil. Reduce the heat and boil for 1 minute, stirring constantly. Let cool, then refrigerate until well chilled and thick. You will have enough filling for an 8- or 9-inch three-layer cake.

(ABOUT 1¾ CUPS)   **BUTTERSCOTCH FILLING**

Good, also, with sliced bananas or some softened vanilla ice cream.

½ cup dark-brown sugar
2 tablespoons butter
1 cup milk
3 tablespoons flour

½ teaspoon salt
2 eggs, slightly beaten
½ teaspoon vanilla

Mix the sugar and butter in a heavy-bottomed pot. Cook over low heat, stirring constantly, until the sugar has melted and blended with the butter. Add ½ cup of the milk and continue cooking until well blended. Mix the flour and salt with the remaining ½ cup of milk, add to the first mixture, and cook, stirring constantly, until thickened. Add the eggs and cook for another 2 minutes. Cool, then stir in the vanilla. You will have enough filling for an 8- or 9-inch three-layer cake.

(ABOUT 3 CUPS)   **FRENCH CREAM FILLING**

1 egg white
⅛ teaspoon salt
1 cup heavy cream

¼ cup confectioners' sugar
1 teaspoon vanilla

NOTE
see page 471
Beat the egg white until foamy, then add the salt and continue beating until stiff but not dry. Beat the cream separately until it forms soft peaks, then slowly beat in the sugar and the vanilla. Fold the two mixtures together. You will have enough filling for an 8- or 9-inch three-layer cake.

FRENCH COFFEE FILLING

Add 2 *teaspoons instant coffee* instead of the vanilla.

FRENCH STRAWBERRY FILLING

Use ⅓ *cup confectioners' sugar* instead of ¼ cup and fold in ½ *cup mashed strawberries* at the end.

CHOCOLATE WHIPPED
CREAM FILLING   (ABOUT 2½ CUPS)

Try this as a filling for Chocolate Roll (p. 818).

4 ounces unsweetened
  chocolate
2 tablespoons butter
1 cup heavy cream

2 cups confectioners' sugar
⅛ teaspoon salt

Melt the chocolate and butter together in a small pan or bowl over simmering water. Combine the cream, 1 cup of the confectioners' sugar, and the salt in a bowl; add the melted chocolate and butter mixture. Beat, slowly adding the remaining cup of sugar, for about 10 minutes, until the filling is light and fluffy. You will have enough filling for an 8- or 9-inch three-layer cake.

COOKIES, CAKE SQUARES & BARS

It's been eleven years since I last revised the cookie chapter and as I've worked on it I have become more and more devoted to the satisfying virtues of a good cookie. Next to dogs, cookies are a man's best friend. They fill in the little chinks in the day when one is hungry for something sweet and rewarding. Neat and tidy, cookies can be eaten without plates, forks, or napkins; they can be enjoyed when you're seated quietly by a window or they can be taken on a stroll; they appease one's appetite when traveling, and with a little milk they can induce sleep on a restless night. But to perform its duty properly, a cookie must be first-rate, and this chapter has been enhanced by my collecting some new recipes (some using oat bran, a wonderful chewy walnut brownie, and a double-baked orange biscotti) and reworking some of the old ones over the years, so that I have the best example of each cookie that I could find.

Cookies are not demanding; they can be made in a few easy steps. In fact, it is hard to ruin a good cookie if you are following a recipe that has been well tested. The critical points are:

1. Make the cookies the shape and the thickness that the recipe calls for. Too thick or too thin can spoil the result.
2. Watch the timing carefully. Cookies bake in minutes; two or three minutes too long can make them a little drier or crisper than desirable. You will learn that cookies continue to bake when removed

from the oven for a few minutes, so remove them just a minute before done.

It doesn't take that long to bake cookies so why fool around with the microwave oven when you aren't going to get good results. The cookies won't brown, and you can't get a crisp cookie when you want one.

ABOUT MAKING COOKIES, CAKE SQUARES, AND BARS

See About Cakemaking (p. 785).

Cookies and cake squares, so good to eat and so easy to make, are often the enticements that first lure youngsters into the mysterious ways of the kitchen. Many accomplished adult cooks recall childhood "apprenticeships" in the family kitchen, mixing doughs and batters, buttering pans, and shaping cookies.

Ingredients

As with cakes, it's best to have all the ingredients for cookies and cake squares at room temperature before you mix them.

Use all-purpose white flour, unless otherwise indicated. It is not necessary to sift flour when making cookies or cake squares.

As elsewhere, use "large" eggs in these recipes, or make the correct adjustment (see p. 473).

Preparing Pans for Cookies, Cake Squares, and Bars

Use sturdy cookie sheets that are the right size for your oven, allowing room for the heat to circulate freely around them. Do not use pans with high sides for cookie baking: they will deflect the heat and the cookies will not bake properly.

Greasing cookie sheets is unnecessary when the cookie dough contains a lot of fat, but you can always put a light film of butter or shortening on the pans if you have any question. Use your fingers or a piece of crumpled paper towel to grease the pans, dipping it into soft butter or vegetable shortening and running it lightly over the pans. Cookie sheets don't need washing or regreasing between batches; just wipe off any crumbs.

Cake squares are usually baked in greased and lightly floured pans, 1½–2 inches deep. Be sure to use the pan size called for in the recipe if you want the cake to turn out right.

DOUBLE-PANNING. Here's a wonderful tip for handling one of baking's oldest, most irritating problems. When baking on metal, especially at high temperature, cookies and pastries have a tendency to brown on the bottoms before the centers are done. A simple technique called "double-panning" moderates this tendency so things come out an even color all around, with no dark bottoms. By stacking two baking sheets or baking pans together (they need not sit completely flush), you put an extra layer of metal or insulation under the pastries as well as a thin cushion of air. The effect is to slow the heat and allow more even baking.

Mixing Cookie Doughs and Cake-Square and Bar Batters

Preheat the oven, prepare the pans, and measure out the ingredients before you begin to combine them.

Many cookie doughs and cake-square batters can easily be blended together with a wooden spoon, or you can use an electric beater if you find it more convenient.

Cookie doughs can be made quickly and successfully in the food processor, because unlike cake batters they don't have air incorporated into the batter.

Filling Cookie, Cake-Square, and Bar Pans

Dropped Cookies. To make dropped cookies, take a spoonful or less of the dough and drop or push it off onto a cookie sheet. Leave 1–2

inches of space between the cookies, for they will spread, thin doughs more than thick ones.

Thicker doughs can be placed on the cookie sheets and then pressed flat with the back of a floured spoon or the bottom of a glass. Or spread them flat with a knife that has been dipped in cold water.

Or shape dropped cookies by forming them into balls with your fingers and arranging them on a cookie sheet, flattening them if you wish.

If cookies are flattened before baking, they will be more uniform in shape than if they are allowed to spread naturally.

Rolled Cookies. Chill the dough for rolled cookies so that it will not stick when you roll it out on a board. If the dough still seems sticky, sprinkle the rolling pin and the board lightly with flour or confectioners' sugar.

Roll the dough until it is ⅛–¼ inch thick and then cut it into shapes, using cookie cutters or the rim of a glass. Or cut the rolled dough into squares or diamonds, using a sharp knife.

After the shaped cookies have been cut out, gather up all the scraps of dough, put them together, and roll or pat them out again to make more cookies.

Refrigerator Cookies. Shape the dough for refrigerator cookies by hand into rolls about 2 inches in diameter, then wrap the rolls with foil or plastic wrap. Or use a cookie mold designed for this purpose. Well-wrapped cookie dough will keep in the refrigerator for at least a week and can also be frozen.

Use a sharp knife to slice off each cookie, making the slices as thin or as thick as you wish. Bake them on ungreased pans. Refrigerator cookies are practical, especially for small families, because you can bake only as many as you need at a particular time.

Any cookie recipe that uses at least ¼ cup of butter or shortening for each cup of flour may be used for refrigerator cookies; doughs that use less shortening, however, may dry out or crumble.

Pressed Cookies. If you use a cookie press, you can make cookies in a variety of professional-looking shapes to suit a number of occasions. The doughs for Norwegian Butter Cookies (p. 879) and Refrigerator Cookies (p. 878) work particularly well in a cookie press. Select disks with the shapes you want, pack the dough into the press, and push the cookies out onto cookie sheets. Electric cookie presses are also available; follow the manufacturer's directions when using them.

Holiday and Christmas Cookies. Christmas cookies and cookies shaped for other occasions can be made with a cookie press or with molds or be shaped by hand—stars, Santas, bells, Christmas trees, or whatever you like. It's fun to assemble an assortment of different sizes, shapes, and flavors.

For holiday giving select cookies that keep well so you can make them a week or two ahead. Store them in airtight containers. You can also make gift cookies ahead of time and freeze them. Cookies tend to take on each other's flavors if stored together for even a few days: pack different kinds of cookies separately until you are ready to combine them in gift boxes, or wrap them in separate boxes if they are very strongly flavored.

Cookies can also be ornaments to hang on the Christmas tree. To create a loop for hanging them, cut string in 3-inch pieces, fold each piece in half, and press the cut ends into the underside of unbaked cookies. The finished cookies will have loops baked right into them.

Cookie Bars and Cake Squares. Bars and squares are the easiest small confections to make. The dough or batter is mixed, spooned into a greased pan of the right size, spread evenly with a spatula, baked, and cut into bars or squares.

Baking Cookies, Cake Squares, and Bars

Always bake cookies in a preheated oven unless the recipe says not to and do only one sheet at a time, unless your oven is wide enough to accommodate two sheets on the same rack. The cookie sheet should be on the center rack, allowing room for heat to circulate around it, and turn it if the cookies are baking unevenly.

Cake squares should also be baked in the center of the oven. Check them to see if they're done about 5 minutes before the suggested baking time is over. If you like them very chewy, shorten the baking time a little.

Cooling Cookies, Cake Squares, and Bars

Remove cookies from the hot pans as soon as they are firm enough to handle, or they will continue to bake. Use a spatula and be careful that they do not crumble. Let very delicate cookies cool slightly before trying to remove them. If the cookies should harden and stick to the

WHEN ARE COOKIES DONE? Check cookies for doneness about 2 minutes before the suggested minimum baking time. This can make the difference between an OK cookie and a wonderful cookie.

Watch cookies carefully while they are baking: many thin cookies require 5 minutes or less to brown, and the baking time may vary a bit each time you bake, depending on the heat of the oven and the placement of the pan.

If some bake more quickly, remove them with a spatula when they are done and continue baking the rest. If you like cookies chewy and slightly soft, keep them in the oven for a shorter time than called for; leave them in longer if you want them to be firm or crisp. Let the pans cool off a bit before putting new cookies on them, or the next batch may not hold their shapes.

pan, put them back in the hot oven for a few minutes to soften them again.

Let warm cookies cool on a plate without touching one another. Do not stack or store them until they have cooled completely or they will not be crisp.

Cake squares are usually left to cool in the pan for about 10–15 minutes before they are cut and removed. If they seem very crumbly, cut them but let them cool thoroughly in the pan before removing them.

Storing Cookies, Cake Squares, and Bars

Store cookies and cake squares in a tightly covered jar or airtight box to keep them crisp. If they should become soggy, you can freshen them by heating them for a few minutes in a 300°F oven.

If you are storing soft cookies, and you wish them to remain that way, a small slice of apple in the cookie jar will keep them from drying out. Put sheets of wax paper between layers if the cookies or cake squares are very delicate.

All cookies and cake squares freeze well, wrapped in foil or freezer paper or packed in plastic containers or clean coffee tins. Frozen cookies will defrost quickly; indeed, many taste just fine while they are still partially frozen.

Decorating Cookies, Cake Squares, and Bars

You can decorate cookies and cake squares before they are baked by sprinkling them with plain or colored sugar, or by pressing into them lightly a few nuts, raisins, or bits of citron, coconut, angelica, dates, figs, or candied fruit or fruit peel. Or make a depression in the center of each cookie and fill it with chocolate chips, jam or jelly, candied ginger, or candied orange or lemon peel.

Cookies or cake squares can be dipped in confectioners' sugar while they are still warm, or frosted with tinted frostings, such as Confectioners' Frosting II (p. 838) or Portsmouth Frosting (p. 837). See also Decorating Cakes, p. 835.

COOKIES

(ABOUT 40 COOKIES)   ## SUGAR COOKIES

Old-fashioned sugar cookies are sweet, rich, and delectable, the essence of what a "plain" cookie should be.

¼ pound butter	1 tablespoon cream or milk
¾ cup sugar	1¼ cups flour
1 egg	⅛ teaspoon salt
½ teaspoon vanilla	¼ teaspoon baking powder

Preheat the oven to 350°F. Cream the butter, then gradually add the sugar, beating until light. Add the egg, vanilla, and cream or milk, and beat thoroughly. Mix the flour, salt, and baking powder together, add to the first mixture, and blend well. Arrange by teaspoonfuls on cookie sheets, 1 inch apart. Bake for 8–10 minutes or until lightly browned.

ALMOND SPICE COOKIES

Fold *⅓ cup finely chopped, blanched almonds, ½ teaspoon cinnamon, ½ teaspoon ground cloves, ½ teaspoon nutmeg, and the grated rind of ½ lemon* into the cookie dough.

COCONUT COOKIES

Add *½ cup finely chopped coconut* to the dough.

LEMON SUGAR COOKIES

Omit the vanilla and add ½ *teaspoon lemon extract* and 2 *teaspoons grated lemon rind* to the dough.

NUT COOKIES

Add ½ *cup chopped nuts* to the dough.

RAISIN COOKIES

Add ½ *cup chopped raisins* to the dough.

FILLED SUGAR COOKIES

Add *about ¼ cup flour* to the dough, just enough so that it can be rolled out. Roll ¼ inch thick and cut into 3-inch circles. Spread half the circles with *jam, jelly, mincemeat,* or the *Fruit and Nut Filling* that follows. Cover with the remaining circles and press the edges together with a fork. Prick well. Bake on buttered cookie sheets in a preheated 325°F oven until lightly browned, about 12 minutes.

FRUIT AND NUT FILLING FOR FILLED SUGAR COOKIES

In a saucepan mix ½ *cup chopped raisins,* ½ *cup finely cut dates,* ¼ *cup chopped walnuts,* ½ *cup water,* ½ *cup sugar,* and 1 *teaspoon flour.* Cook slowly until thick. Use as recommended above.

RICH BUTTER COOKIES　✳　　　(ABOUT 60 COOKIES)

½ pound butter	2 eggs
1 teaspoon vanilla	1½ cups flour
⅔ cup sugar	½ teaspoon salt

Preheat the oven to 375°F. Cream the butter and the vanilla. Gradually add the sugar and the eggs and beat well. Mix the flour and salt together, add to the first mixture, and blend thoroughly. Arrange by half-teaspoonfuls on cookie sheets, leaving 2 inches between the cookies—they will spread during baking. Flatten them with a knife dipped in cold water. Bake for about 8 minutes or until lightly browned.

SOUR CREAM COOKIES

(ABOUT 60 COOKIES)

2 eggs
1 cup sugar, white or light brown
½ cup sour cream
5 tablespoons butter, melted

½ teaspoon vanilla
2 cups flour
½ teaspoon baking soda
¼ teaspoon nutmeg

Preheat the oven to 375°F and butter some cookie sheets. Beat the eggs well, then add the sugar, sour cream, butter, and vanilla, beating until well incorporated. Mix the flour, baking soda, and nutmeg together and add to the first mixture, beating well. Arrange by teaspoonfuls, 1 inch apart, on the cookie sheets and bake for about 10 minutes or until lightly browned.

CREAMY CHOCOLATE COOKIES

(ABOUT 4 DOZEN COOKIES)

This is the perfect chocolate cookie—creamy and moist with a brownielike texture. It is a batter rather than a dough cookie. The batter must chill in the refrigerator for at least an hour before baking.

6 ounces unsweetened chocolate
2 tablespoons butter
¼ cup flour
½ teaspoon baking powder

½ teaspoon salt
3 eggs
1¼ cups sugar
6 ounces semisweet chocolate chips (1 cup)

Melt the chocolate with the butter in a heavy-bottomed saucepan over very low heat. Mix together the flour, baking powder, and salt. In a mixing bowl, beat the eggs, then add the sugar, and continue beating until light and well blended. Add the chocolate mixture to the egg mixture and beat well. Add the flour mixture and mix until well blended. Stir in the chocolate chips and then chill the mixture in the refrigerator for at least 1 hour. Preheat the oven to 350°F. Grease a cookie sheet. Drop by teaspoonfuls onto the cookie sheet and bake for 5–6 minutes. Do not overbake; these cookies are best if slightly underbaked. Remove to a rack to cool.

BOSTON COOKIES

(ABOUT 30 COOKIES)

Chewy, wholesome, full of good tastes and textures.

4 tablespoons butter	Few grains of salt
½ cup sugar	½ teaspoon cinnamon
1 egg, well beaten	½ cup chopped nuts
1 cup flour	½ cup raisins
¼ teaspoon baking soda	

Preheat the oven to 350°F and butter some cookie sheets. Cream the butter, then gradually add the sugar, mixing well. Beat in the egg. Mix together the flour, baking soda, salt, and cinnamon and add to the first mixture, blending thoroughly. Add the nuts and raisins and mix well. Arrange by spoonfuls, 1 inch apart, on the cookie sheets and bake about 10–12 minutes or until delicately brown.

MOLASSES COOKIES

(ABOUT 40 COOKIES)

Some like these plain—some spicy.

¼ cup molasses	1 cup flour
½ cup shortening	½ teaspoon salt
¾ cup dark-brown sugar	½ teaspoon baking soda
1 egg	

Preheat the oven to 350°F. Mix the molasses, shortening, brown sugar, and egg in a bowl, combining well. Mix the flour, salt, and baking soda together, add to the first mixture, and blend thoroughly. Arrange by teaspoonfuls on ungreased cookie sheets, about 1 inch apart, and bake for 6–8 minutes or until crisp and lightly browned.

SPICED MOLASSES COOKIES

Add ¼ teaspoon ground ginger, ¼ teaspoon ground cloves, ¼ teaspoon cinnamon, and ¼ teaspoon nutmeg to the flour mixture.

(ABOUT 70 COOKIES)   **CAPE COD OATMEAL COOKIES**

A fine, chewy oatmeal cookie, wholesome and nourishing.

1½ cups flour
½ teaspoon baking soda
1 teaspoon cinnamon
½ teaspoon salt
1 egg, lightly beaten
1 cup sugar
½ cup melted shortening, or ½
     cup melted butter

1 tablespoon molasses
¼ cup milk
1¾ cups uncooked oatmeal
½ cup raisins
½ cup chopped nuts

Preheat the oven to 350°F. Mix the flour, baking soda, cinnamon, and salt together in a large bowl. Stir in the remaining ingredients. Arrange by teaspoonfuls on unbuttered cookie sheets and bake until the edges are brown, about 10–12 minutes.

(ABOUT 60 COOKIES)   **✳   CRISP OATMEAL COOKIES**

Lightly spiced oatmeal cookies with raisins—crunchier than those in the preceding recipe.

1 cup vegetable shortening
¾ cup granulated sugar
¾ cup brown sugar
2 eggs
1 teaspoon vanilla
3 tablespoons water
1½ cups flour

½ teaspoon salt
1 teaspoon baking soda
1 teaspoon cinnamon
3 cups uncooked oatmeal (not
     instant)
½ cup chopped walnuts
½ cup raisins

Preheat the oven to 350°F and grease some cookie sheets. Combine the shortening and sugars and beat until thoroughly blended. Add the eggs, vanilla, and water, and beat until light and fluffy. Stir together the flour, salt, baking soda, and cinnamon. Add to the first mixture and beat until completely mixed. Add the oatmeal, walnuts, and raisins, and stir until thoroughly blended. Arrange by rounded teaspoonfuls on the greased cookie sheets, placing them about 2 inches apart. Flatten cookies slightly with your wet fingertips into rounds about 1½ inches across and ⅓ inch thick. Bake for 10–12 minutes, or until the cookies have spread a little and are lightly browned all over.

OAT BRAN OATMEAL COOKIES   (2 DOZEN COOKIES)

These are lacy-crisp and flavorful flourless cookies and a good source of oat bran and oats, not at all like "health-food" cookies. They break easily, so handle them carefully.

¼ cup margarine, softened	½ cup rolled oats
¼ cup dark-brown sugar	¼ teaspoon baking soda
¼ cup granulated sugar	¼ teaspoon salt
1 egg white	¼ teaspoon cinnamon
1 cup oat bran	

Preheat the oven to 350°F. Lightly grease some cookie sheets. In a mixing bowl, combine the margarine and sugars, and stir until well blended. Add the egg white and beat well. Mix together the oat bran, rolled oats, baking soda, salt, and cinnamon, add to the margarine mixture, and mix until blended. Drop by teaspoonfuls onto cookie sheets and flatten with your fingertips (dip your fingers into cold water to prevent stickiness). Bake for approximately 7 minutes, or until the cookies are just lightly browned. Remove from the oven and let cookies rest on the cookie sheet for about 2–3 minutes, until they are easy to remove gently with a spatula. If the cookies become too hard to remove easily, put the cookies back in the oven for about a minute to soften enough to remove. These freeze well; gently stack and place in a plastic bag to store.

OAT BRAN OATMEAL COOKIES II

Substitute ½ *cup flour* for ½ cup oat bran. These cookies can be removed from the cookie sheet right away because the flour helps hold the dough together and produces a more solid cookie.

APPLESAUCE COOKIES   (ABOUT 40 COOKIES)

¼ pound butter	½ teaspoon salt
½ cup brown sugar	1 teaspoon cinnamon
½ cup granulated sugar	1 teaspoon nutmeg
1 egg	½ teaspoon cloves
1 cup applesauce	1 cup raisins
2 cups flour	½ cup chopped nuts
1 teaspoon baking soda	

Preheat the oven to 375°F and grease some cookie sheets. Cream the butter and add the two sugars, beating until light. Stir in the egg and the applesauce. Mix together the flour, baking soda, salt, cinnamon, nutmeg, and cloves, and add to the first mixture, beating until smooth. Add the raisins and nuts. Arrange by spoonfuls on the cookie sheets and bake for 5–7 minutes or until lightly browned.

(ABOUT 40 COOKIES)   **CHOCOLATE COCONUT COOKIES**

Almost a candy, these are chewy, not too sweet, but very chocolaty.

14-ounce can sweetened condensed milk	2 cups shredded coconut
3 ounces unsweetened chocolate	1 cup pecan pieces
	1 teaspoon vanilla
	Dash of salt

Preheat the oven to 300°F. Grease some cookie sheets very well. Heat the sweetened condensed milk and the chocolate together in a small pot over simmering water until the chocolate has melted. Remove from the heat and stir in the remaining ingredients. Arrange by teaspoonfuls on the cookie sheets and bake for about 15 minutes, taking care that the bottoms do not burn.

(ABOUT 50 COOKIES)   ✳ **CHOCOLATE CHIP COOKIES**

Is there anyone in America who does not know and love these cookies? They were, incidentally, created by a Massachusetts housewife in 1929. The cookies should have crisp edges and chewy centers.

¼ pound butter	½ teaspoon salt
½ cup dark-brown sugar	½ teaspoon baking soda
½ cup granulated sugar	½ cup chopped nuts
1 egg	6 ounces semisweet chocolate
¾ teaspoon vanilla	chips (1 cup)
1⅛ cups flour	

Preheat the oven to 375°F and grease some cookie sheets. Cream the butter, then gradually add the two sugars, beating until light and smooth. Beat in the egg and the vanilla. Mix the flour, salt, and baking soda together and add it to the first mixture, blending well. Stir in the nuts and the chocolate chips. Drop by teaspoonfuls onto the cookie sheets about 1 inch apart and bake for 8–10 minutes or until lightly browned.

CHOCOLATE CHIP OATMEAL COOKIES

Use ½ cup *uncooked oatmeal* instead of the chopped nuts.

NUT COOKIES   (ABOUT 50 COOKIES)

2 eggs, separated	Dash of salt
1 cup brown sugar	⅓ cup flour
1 cup chopped nuts	

Preheat the oven to 350°F. Beat the egg yolks until they are pale and thick. Gradually beat in the sugar, then add the nuts and salt. Beat the egg whites separately until stiff but not dry. Fold them into the first mixture, then stir in the flour. Drop by teaspoonfuls onto ungreased cookie sheets, leaving about 2 inches between cookies for them to spread. Bake for 4–7 minutes or until firm.

PEANUT BUTTER COOKIES   ✳   (MAKES 50–60 COOKIES)

These are one of our household favorites and have been for over thirty-five years. My husband ate thousands of these over the years.

1 cup shortening	1 cup peanut butter
1 teaspoon vanilla	3 cups flour
1 cup granulated sugar	⅛ teaspoon salt
1 cup brown sugar	2 teaspoons baking soda
2 eggs, beaten	

Preheat the oven to 350°F and grease some cookie sheets. In a mixing bowl, thoroughly cream the shortening, vanilla, and sugars. Add the eggs and beat well. Stir in the peanut butter. Mix together the flour, salt, and baking soda, and add to the peanut butter mixture, combining thoroughly. Form into tiny balls with the palm of your hands and place on the cookie sheets. Press each cookie twice with the back of a fork to make a crisscross design. Bake about 8–10 minutes or until firm.

CHOCOLATE WALNUT WAFERS   (ABOUT 50 COOKIES)

Take care not to overbake this chewy, brownielike cookie.

2 ounces unsweetened chocolate	1 cup chopped walnuts
	⅔ cup flour
¼ pound butter	¼ teaspoon salt
1 cup sugar	¼ teaspoon vanilla
2 eggs	

Preheat the oven to 350°F and grease some cookie sheets well. Melt the chocolate in a bowl or pot over simmering water; set aside to cool.

Cream the butter and gradually beat in the sugar and the eggs, blending well. Add the chocolate and the walnuts and combine thoroughly. Mix the flour and salt together and add to the first mixture, along with the vanilla. Mix well. Arrange by teaspoonfuls on the cookie sheets and bake for 10–12 minutes or until firm but chewy.

(ABOUT 75 COOKIES)   **SWEDISH NUT WAFERS**

Thin, crisp, and nut-flavored, these are exceptionally good—and thrifty as well: a little bit of batter goes a long way.

4 tablespoons butter	1⅓ cups flour
¾ cup sugar	1 teaspoon baking powder
1 egg, well beaten	½ teaspoon salt
2 tablespoons milk	⅓ cup chopped nut meats
1 teaspoon vanilla	

Preheat the oven to 325°F. Lightly butter a cookie sheet or jelly-roll pan. Cream the butter, then gradually beat in the sugar, until well blended. Add the egg, milk, and vanilla and beat well. Mix together the flour, baking powder, and salt and beat into the first mixture. Spread the dough on the cookie sheet as thin as possible, just enough to cover the bottom. Sprinkle with the chopped nuts and press them gently into the dough. Mark with a sharp knife into cookie-sized rectangles and bake about 12 minutes or until delicately browned. Cut while still warm.

(ABOUT 50 COOKIES)   **SWEDISH ALMOND WAFERS**

These buttery, lacelike cookies are so delicate they must be handled with extreme care. They are exceptionally easy to prepare, but they really spread in baking, so use scant teaspoonfuls of batter and space them far apart on the cookie sheet.

¾ cup finely ground, unblanched almonds	½ cup sugar
¼ pound butter	1 tablespoon flour
	2 tablespoons light cream

Preheat the oven to 350°F. Mix all the ingredients in a heavy saucepan and cook, stirring, over moderate heat until the butter has melted. Arrange by scant teaspoonfuls, 3 inches apart, on a lightly buttered cookie sheet and bake for 3–5 minutes, watching carefully, until delicately brown at the edges but still bubbling slightly in the center. As soon as the edge is firm enough to lift the cookies with a spatula, remove them to a plate and let them cool. Do not stack the cookies until cool, and handle them with care.

LACE COOKIES   (ABOUT 60 COOKIES)

Thin, crisp, and almost transparent, these splendid cookies are simple to make. The little lumps of dough that you put on the baking sheet will spread, melt, and bubble as the cookies bake.

1½ cups uncooked oatmeal
1½ cups light-brown sugar
2 tablespoons flour
½ teaspoon salt

⅔ cup melted butter
1 egg, lightly beaten
½ teaspoon vanilla

Preheat the oven to 350°F. Mix the oatmeal, brown sugar, flour, and salt in a bowl. Stir in the melted butter, then add the egg and vanilla and combine well. Arrange the batter by half-teaspoonfuls, about 2 inches apart, on ungreased cookie sheets. Bake until lightly browned, about 5 minutes. Cool slightly, removing the cookies from the cookie sheet with a spatula as soon as they are firm. If they become too hard, return to the oven for a few minutes to soften.

BRANDY SNAPS *   (ABOUT 70 COOKIES)

These cookies are heavenly. But expect the first few tries not to be perfect, until you get the hang of shaping them.

⅓ cup dark corn syrup
¼ pound butter, in pieces
½ cup plus 1½–2 tablespoons
   sugar, or to taste

½ cup flour
1 cup heavy cream
2 teaspoons brandy

Preheat the oven to 350°F. Grease a cookie sheet. Put the syrup, butter, and ½ cup sugar in a heavy-bottomed saucepan. Heat over low heat, stirring, until the butter has melted and the syrup is smooth. Don't let the mixture get very hot. Remove from the heat and stir in the flour vigorously, beating until smooth. Drop by teaspoonfuls onto the cookie sheet. These spread, so space them far apart. Bake only five cookies at a time. Bake for about 5–7 minutes, or until the cookies are spread, golden, and bubbling. You will have to try a few to see when they are done; they should not be pale. Remove from the oven and let stand (but do not walk away), testing how firm they are becoming by lifting the edge of a cookie with a spatula. When cool enough to hold together but still warm enough to be flexible, form each into a fat tube. Work quickly, forming all five cookies and placing them on a piece of wax paper. Whip the cream and add the brandy and sugar to taste. When the cookies are cool and ready to serve, pipe the whipped cream into the center of each Brandy Snap. Handle these cookies carefully as they break easily. Unfilled, these keep indefinitely in a cookie tin or an airtight container.

(60 COOKIES)   **SAND TARTS**

¼ pound butter	¼ teaspoon salt
1½ cups sugar	1 egg white, slightly beaten
1 egg	1 teaspoon cinnamon
2 cups flour	

Preheat the oven to 400°F. Beat the butter until softened, then slowly add 1¼ cups of the sugar, continuing to beat until creamy and smooth. Add the egg and mix well. Add the flour and salt and beat until well blended. Chill the dough for 30 minutes. Sprinkle a surface lightly with flour and roll out the dough *very* thin, then brush it with beaten egg white. Mix the remaining ¼ cup of sugar with the cinnamon and sprinkle over the dough. Cut into desired cookie shapes and place on ungreased cookie sheets. Bake for about 6 minutes or until the edges of the cookies turn slightly golden. Remove from oven; let cool a minute or two before removing to racks to cool. Store in airtight container.

(30 COOKIES)   **MACAROONS**

True macaroons are made of egg whites, sugar, and almond paste.

½ pound almond paste	⅓ cup confectioners' sugar
1 cup granulated sugar	2 tablespoons cake flour
3 egg whites	⅛ teaspoon salt

Preheat the oven to 300°F. Cover cookie sheets with parchment paper or brown paper. Using your hands or the food processor, soften the almond paste. Gradually blend in the granulated sugar and egg whites; then mix in the confectioners' sugar, flour, and salt. Force through a cookie press or drop by teaspoonfuls onto the paper-covered cookie sheets. Cover and let stand 30 minutes. Bake 25 minutes; lay the paper linings on a damp cloth, let cool, and peel off the macaroons.

CHERRY MACAROONS

Add 2 *tablespoons chopped candied cherries* to the dough.

ALMOND MACAROONS

Sprinkle before baking with 2 *tablespoons chopped blanched almonds*.

COCONUT MACAROONS   ✯   (ABOUT 25 COOKIES)

Soft and chewy with a good coconut flavor.

2 egg whites	1 teaspoon vanilla
⅔ cup sugar	½ teaspoon coconut extract
2 tablespoons flour	1½ cups shredded coconut
Pinch of salt	

Preheat the oven to 325°F and grease some cookie sheets. Beat the egg whites until they stand in stiff peaks, then continue beating as you add the sugar gradually (the sugar will not dissolve completely). Beat in the flour, salt, and vanilla and coconut extracts. Stir in the coconut. Drop mounds of the mixture from a teaspoon onto the prepared cookie sheets, and bake for about 15 minutes. Remove from the oven and let the cookies cool on the sheets.

CHOCOLATE COCONUT MACAROONS

Add 1 *ounce melted unsweetened chocolate* to the mixture when you add the coconut.

(18 COOKIES)   ## CORNFLAKE "MACAROONS"

1 egg white
½ cup sugar
½ cup shredded coconut
1 cup cornflakes

¼ teaspoon almond extract
¼ teaspoon vanilla
Dash of salt

Preheat the oven to 350°F and grease some cookie sheets. Beat the egg white until stiff, then stir in the remaining ingredients. Place by teaspoonfuls on the cookie sheets and bake for about 10 minutes or until lightly browned.

(ABOUT 40 COOKIES)   ## JUBILEES

Use jams of various colors to fill the centers of these crisp, chewy cookies.

¼ pound butter
1 cup sugar
2 eggs
1 teaspoon vanilla
1½ cups flour
1 teaspoon baking powder

¼ teaspoon baking soda
½ teaspoon salt
2 cups cornflakes,
   approximately, slightly
   crumbled
Jam or jelly

Preheat the oven to 350°F and grease some cookie sheets. Cream the butter, then add the sugar gradually, combining well. Add the eggs and vanilla and mix well. Mix together the flour, baking powder, baking soda, and salt. Add to the first mixture and combine thoroughly. Chill until firm enough to handle, then shape with your fingers into 1-inch balls. Roll in cornflakes and place on the cookie sheets, about 2 inches apart. Indent each in the center with your finger and fill with a little jam or jelly. Bake for 15–20 minutes or until firm.

(ABOUT 36 COOKIES)   ## CHARLESTON BENNE WAFERS

Crisp and sweet with good sesame flavor. Bake a few of these for practice to test the baking time and removal from the cookie sheet.

½ cup sesame seeds
1 tablespoon butter
1 cup light-brown sugar
3 tablespoons flour

1 egg, beaten
1 teaspoon vanilla
¼ teaspoon salt

Preheat the oven to 350°F. Butter and lightly flour some cookie sheets. Put the sesame seeds in a small pan and stir or shake them over moderate heat until they are slightly brown. Remove from the heat, stir in the remaining ingredients, and mix well. Drop by teaspoonfuls onto the cookie sheets, leaving 2 inches between them for the cookies to spread. Bake until just slightly brown, 4–6 minutes. Remove from the cookie sheets very carefully while still warm. If they stiffen and are hard to remove, put the cookie sheets back in the oven for 1 minute.

MINCEMEAT COOKIES

(ABOUT 85 COOKIES)

Mincemeat flavors will vary. You may add ½ cup more mincemeat or a teaspoon of cinnamon or a pinch of other spices to pick up the flavor in these cookies.

1 cup shortening	1 teaspoon salt
½ teaspoon vanilla	1 teaspoon baking soda
1 cup honey, or 1½ cups sugar	1 cup chopped nuts
3 eggs	1½ cups mincemeat, drained if
3¼ cups flour	necessary

Preheat the oven to 350°F. Lightly grease some cookie sheets. Cream the shortening, then beat in the vanilla, honey or sugar, and eggs. Mix the flour, salt, and baking soda together and add to the first mixture, blending well. Stir in the nuts and the mincemeat. Arrange by teaspoonfuls on the cookie sheets. Bake until light brown, about 8–10 minutes.

WASPS' NESTS ✳

(ABOUT 50 COOKIES)

3 egg whites	¼ cup water
¼ teaspoon salt	½ pound almonds, chopped
1¼ cups confectioners' sugar	6 ounces semisweet chocolate,
½ cup granulated sugar	grated fine

Preheat the oven to 300°F. Butter and flour cookie sheets. Beat the egg whites with the salt until barely stiff, adding the confectioners' sugar by spoonfuls until the mixture is stiff and shiny. Set aside. In a heavy-bottomed saucepan, cook the granulated sugar in the water until the syrup "spins a thread." (This takes about 3 minutes. Test for thread by dipping a teaspoon into syrup and holding it over the pan so the syrup runs off the tip of the spoon. It is done when a fine thread forms from the tip of the spoon or when a candy thermometer registers 240°F.) Quickly stir in the almonds. Remove from the heat. Stir the almond mixture and the grated chocolate into the egg whites. Drop by tea-spoonfuls onto the cookie sheets, leaving 1 inch between the cookies. Bake for about 11–12 minutes, until the cookies are mostly dry. Let stand 5 minutes, gently remove from the pan with a spatula, and place on a rack to cool completely.

(ABOUT 40 COOKIES)   **GINGERSNAPS**

A thin, crisp, spicy, crinkly-topped gingersnap, easily made by hand or in the food processor.

¾ cup vegetable shortening	2 cups flour
1 cup sugar, plus extra to roll the cookies in	2 teaspoons baking soda
	½ teaspoon salt
1 egg	1 tablespoon ground ginger
¼ cup molasses	1 teaspoon cinnamon

Preheat the oven to 350°F and grease some cookie sheets. Beat together the shortening and 1 cup of the sugar. Add the egg, and beat until light and fluffy, then add the molasses. Stir and toss together the flour, baking soda, salt, ginger, and cinnamon, and add to the first mixture, beating until smooth and blended. Gather up bits of the dough and roll them between the palms of your hands into 1-inch balls, then roll each ball in sugar. Place about 2 inches apart on the prepared cookie sheets and bake for 10–12 minutes, until the cookies have spread and the tops have cracked. Remove from the sheets and cool on a rack.

(ABOUT 12 SMALL MERINGUES)   **MERINGUES**

Make these sweet confections, sometimes known as "kisses," anytime you have a few extra egg whites. Be sure the whites are at room temperature before you begin to beat them, and add the sugar very gradually so that the beaten whites do not lose any volume. Meringues are baked in a very slow oven and then left in the turned-off oven for a long time to crisp.

2 egg whites	1 teaspoon vanilla
8 tablespoons sugar, preferably superfine	

Preheat the oven to 250°F. Cover a cookie sheet with brown paper or parchment. Beat the egg whites until stiff but not dry, and add 6 table-spoons of the sugar, a spoonful at a time, beating well between each addition. Add the vanilla, and fold in the remaining 2 tablespoons of sugar. Shape the meringues on the cookie sheet with a pastry bag and tube or a spoon. Bake for 1 hour. Turn off the oven and let the meringues remain in the oven for 6 more hours. Don't open the oven door—they must dry out to be nice and crisp.

MERINGUE SHELLS

Using a spoon or a pastry bag, shape the egg-white mixture into 3-inch rings. Bake at 250°F until completely dry but not colored. Fill with *whipped cream* or *ice cream* and top with *crushed strawberries, blueberries,* or *chocolate sauce.*

NUT MERINGUES

Add about *½ cup chopped nuts.*

CHOCOLATE MERINGUES

Add 4 *tablespoons unsweetened cocoa* to the egg whites after you have beaten in the sugar.

LADYFINGERS   (ABOUT TWENTY-FOUR 4-INCH COOKIES)

Delicate, soft, and fine-textured, ladyfingers are lovely with fruit and ice cream or sherbet. They also are used to line molds for icebox cakes, Bavarian creams, and custards. Gather and make ready all the equipment and ingredients you'll need and organize the steps of preparation, because once air is beaten into the eggs, you will want to work quickly so that the ladyfingers will be light and plump when baked. Attach a ½-inch plain nozzle to a 14- or 16-inch pastry bag unless you plan to spread the batter by spoon into finger shapes, and have a sifter or sieve standing ready with some (about ½ cup) confectioners' sugar in it to quickly dust the ladyfingers before baking.

3 eggs	⅓ cup flour
⅓ cup granulated sugar	¼ teaspoon salt
1 teaspoon vanilla	Confectioners' sugar

Preheat the oven to 325°F. Grease and lightly flour two cookie sheets or baking sheets. Separate the eggs. (I put the egg yolks into the electric mixer bowl and the egg whites into a smaller bowl with the rotary beater nearby so that I can hand-beat the whites with the rotary during the last minute the yolk mixture is beating.) Combine the egg yolks, granulated sugar, and vanilla in the mixing bowl. Beat for 4 minutes, until the mixture is pale and thickened. It is important to beat long enough. Add the flour and beat until blended; the mixture will be very thick and stiff. Add the salt to the egg whites. Beat until the whites are stiff but not dry and no longer slide around in the bowl. Gently stir half of the whites into the yolk mixture—don't overblend—then fold the remaining whites into the yolk mixture. With a grease pencil, if you have one, mark a 4-inch length on the baking sheet to serve as a guide for the first ladyfinger—or simply lay a ruler alongside. Ladyfingers will not spread much during baking, so you can place them ½ inch apart or a little less. Spoon the batter into the pastry bag and pipe 4-inch finger shapes onto the two prepared sheets. Or dribble the batter from a spoon. Bake for 15–18 minutes; they should be light and golden all over. Remove from the oven and lift gently with a spatula to a rack and cool. Ladyfingers freeze well.

(ABOUT 3 DOZEN COOKIES)　　　　　**ORANGE BISCOTTI**

These biscotti are good for breakfast with a cup of hot coffee or tea. They are double-baked cookies that are nice and dry and will keep forever.

¾ cup almonds (3½ ounces), whole and unblanched	2 tablespoons orange-flavor liqueur
¼ pound butter	1½ teaspoons cinnamon
¾ cup sugar	2¼ cups flour
2 eggs	1½ teaspoons baking powder
Zest from 1 orange, grated or minced	¼ teaspoon salt

Preheat the oven to 350°. Toast the almonds for a few minutes until they are light golden. Let cool, then chop by hand into ¼-inch chunks. Reduce the oven to 325°F. Cream the butter until light. Add the sugar and beat until smooth and creamy. Beat in the eggs until the mixture is smooth. Beat in the orange zest, orange-flavor liqueur, and cinnamon. Mix in the flour, baking powder, and salt, and beat just until mixed. Stir in the chopped almonds. On a lightly floured board, divide the dough in half and form each half into a long roll, about 1½ inches in diameter and about 10 inches long. Set the rolls on the baking sheet about 2 inches apart and bake in the top third of the oven for about 25 minutes, or until they are set and lightly browned on top. Cool the rolls for 5 minutes or so; then slice them diagonally about ½ inch thick. Lay the slices back flat on the baking sheet and return to the oven for another 10 minutes to dry them. Turn the slices over and return to the oven to dry again for another 10 minutes. If you want the biscotti very hard for dunking, turn off the oven and leave them for another 20 minutes. Cool on a rack and store in a tightly covered container. They will keep for months. Serve with coffee or tea.

ANISE BISCOTTI

Omit the orange, orange liqueur, and cinnamon. Replace with *1–2 teaspoons crushed anise seeds*.

CRESCENTS

(24 COOKIES)

½ pound almond paste
½ cup confectioners' sugar
1 egg white
½ cup chopped blanched
   almonds

1 recipe Confectioners'
   Frosting I made with
   lemon juice (p. 837) using
   2–4 tablespoons lemon
   juice

Preheat the oven to 300°F. Cover cookie sheets with aluminum foil, parchment paper, or brown paper. Using your hands or a food processor, soften the almond paste. Add the sugar and egg white and blend thoroughly. Shape the mixture into a long roll. Cut in ¾-inch pieces, roll each piece in chopped almonds, and shape into crescents. Put on the

cookie sheets, cover, and let stand 20 minutes. Bake for 20 minutes; lay the paper linings on a damp cloth, let cool, and peel off the cookies. When they are cool, paint them with frosting.

(ABOUT 50 SMALL COOKIES)   **✻   VIENNESE CRESCENTS**

The meltingly light taste of these rich, buttery confections makes them disappear almost as quickly as you can make them. Almonds are traditional in this recipe.

½ pound butter
¾ cup confectioners' sugar,
    plus more for coating
2 cups flour

1 cup ground almonds or
    walnuts
1 teaspoon vanilla

Preheat the oven to 300°F. Cream the butter, then add the confectioners' sugar, flour, nuts, and vanilla and mix thoroughly. Shape with your fingers into delicate crescents, about 2 inches long and ¼ inch wide and thick. Roll in confectioners' sugar and bake on ungreased cookie sheets for about 12–15 minutes, until just faintly browned. Cool, then roll in more confectioners' sugar before serving.

                                  SCOTCH
(ABOUT TWENTY-FOUR 1 × 2-INCH BARS)   **SHORTBREADS**

Sandy and crumbly, as the perfect shortbread should be.

½ pound butter
½ cup confectioners' sugar

2 cups flour
¼ teaspoon salt

Preheat the oven to 350°F. Cream the butter, then gradually add the sugar, beating well. Mix the flour and salt together and add to the first mixture, combining thoroughly. Roll out the dough with a rolling pin until it is ¼ inch thick, then cut into rectangles or any other shape desired. Put them on ungreased cookie sheets, prick each cookie with a fork, and bake for 20–25 minutes or until lightly browned around the edges.

GINGERBREAD MEN

(ABOUT EIGHT 5 × 3½-INCH MEN OR
TWENTY-FOUR 2 × 1½-INCH MEN)

½ cup molasses
¼ cup sugar
3 tablespoons butter or
　shortening
1 tablespoon milk
2 cups flour
½ teaspoon baking soda

½ teaspoon salt
½ teaspoon nutmeg
½ teaspoon cinnamon
½ teaspoon cloves
½ teaspoon ground ginger
2–3 tablespoons water, if
　needed

Preheat the oven to 350°F and butter some cookie sheets. Heat the molasses to the boiling point, then add the sugar, butter or shortening, and milk. Mix the flour with the baking soda, salt, nutmeg, cinnamon, cloves, and ginger. Add to the first mixture and blend well. Add water if necessary, enough so that the dough holds together and handles easily. On a very lightly floured surface, roll or pat out the dough about ¼ inch thick. Cut into large or small gingerbread men, using special cookie cutters or a very sharp knife. Bake for 5–7 minutes. When cool, frost with *Confectioners' Frosting I* (p. 837) and decorate with *candies, raisins, or bits of citron.*

REFRIGERATOR COOKIES

(ABOUT 60 COOKIES)

A basic refrigerator cookie—sweet, crisp, and chewy.

¼ pound butter
1 teaspoon vanilla
⅔ cup brown sugar
⅓ cup granulated sugar

1 egg
1½ cups flour
¼ teaspoon cream of tartar
¼ teaspoon salt

Cream the butter and vanilla together, then beat in both sugars and the egg. Mix the flour, cream of tartar, and salt together, add to the first mixture, and combine well. Shape in a roll or rolls about 2 inches in diameter. Wrap in foil and store in the refrigerator until ready to bake; the dough will keep well for at least a week and may also be frozen. Before baking, preheat the oven to 400°F. Using a sharp knife, slice in rounds ⅛ to ¼ inch thick. Bake on ungreased cookie sheets for about 8 minutes, until crisp and lightly browned.

CINNAMON OR NUTMEG REFRIGERATOR COOKIES

Add *⅓ teaspoon cinnamon or nutmeg* to the flour mixture.

CHOCOLATE REFRIGERATOR COOKIES

Add *2 ounces unsweetened chocolate, melted,* with the egg.

RAISIN, NUT, OR COCONUT REFRIGERATOR COOKIES

Add *½ cup chopped nuts, raisins,* or *shredded coconut* to the cookie dough before shaping it into a roll.

(ABOUT 30 COOKIES)   ## NORWEGIAN BUTTER COOKIES

These are excellent cookie-press cookies.

¼ pound butter
2 hard-boiled egg yolks
¼ cup sugar

1 cup flour
½ teaspoon vanilla or lemon
    extract

Preheat the oven to 375°F. Cream the butter, then add the egg yolks, and beat well. Beat in the sugar. Add the flour and the vanilla or lemon extract and combine thoroughly. Put through a cookie press or arrange by teaspoonfuls on ungreased cookie sheets. Bake for 10–12 minutes or until lightly browned.

(ABOUT 24 COOKIES)   ## DATE-FILLED OATMEAL COOKIES

1 cup pitted dates, chopped
½ cup granulated sugar
¾ cup water, approximately
¼ pound butter
½ cup brown sugar

1½ cups flour
¼ teaspoon baking soda
½ teaspoon salt
1¼ cups oatmeal

Preheat the oven to 350°F. Put the dates, granulated sugar, and ½ cup of the water in a small pot and cook slowly until thick and smooth, about 15 minutes; set aside. Cream the butter, then add the brown sugar, and mix well. Mix together the flour, baking soda, and salt and add to the butter and brown sugar, beating well. Combine with the oatmeal, mixing thoroughly. Add about 2–4 tablespoons water, enough to form the dough into a ball so that it can be rolled. Refrigerate for about 15 minutes to facilitate rolling. Roll ⅛ inch thick. Cut into 2-inch rounds. Put them together in pairs with the date mixture as a filling and press the edges firmly together. Bake about 15 minutes, until browned.

CHOCOLATE COOKIES

(ABOUT 50 COOKIES)

These work well in a cookie press.

2 ounces unsweetened chocolate	½ teaspoon vanilla
	¼ teaspoon salt
¾ cup shortening	2 tablespoons milk
1 cup sugar	2 cups flour
1 egg	

Preheat the oven to 375°F. Melt the chocolate in a small pot or bowl over simmering water; set aside. Cream the shortening, then gradually add the sugar, creaming well. Add the egg, vanilla, salt, chocolate, and milk and beat well. Gently stir in the flour and combine thoroughly. Put through a cookie press or arrange by teaspoonfuls on ungreased cookie sheets. Bake for 8–10 minutes or until crisp.

CAKE SQUARES AND BARS

THE BEST BROWNIES

(ABOUT TWENTY-EIGHT
2 × 2-INCH BROWNIES)

6 ounces unsweetened chocolate	½ teaspoon salt
	2¾ cups sugar
¾ cup butter (1½ sticks)	1½ cups all-purpose flour
4 eggs	1½ cups chopped walnuts
2 tablespoons vanilla	

Preheat the oven to 375°F. Butter and lightly flour a 9 × 13 × 2-inch baking pan or dish. (If you are using a Pyrex glass dish, place it on a baking sheet during baking.) In a heavy-bottomed pan melt the chocolate and butter over low heat, watching and stirring often. When melted, remove from the heat and cool. In a mixing bowl, put the eggs, vanilla, salt, and sugar, and beat well using an electric mixer for 8–10 minutes. Stir in the chocolate mixture gently, then add the flour, stirring only until blended. Stir in the walnuts. Spread evenly in the pan and bake for 25 minutes. When done, the center should be moist. Remove from the oven and let cool. Let settle for a few hours, then cut into squares.

(16 BROWNIES)   **❋   PARKER BROWNIES**

These are especially rich and chewy.

2 ounces unsweetened chocolate	½ cup flour
	½ cup chopped walnuts
¼ cup butter or margarine	1 teaspoon vanilla
1 cup sugar	Confectioners' sugar, for
1 egg	dusting (optional)
⅛ teaspoon salt	

Preheat the oven to 300°F. Butter an 8-inch square pan. Line the bottom of the pan with wax paper, then butter and flour the paper. In a saucepan over low heat, melt the chocolate with the butter, stirring to blend. Remove from the heat and stir in the sugar, egg, salt, flour, walnuts, and vanilla. Spread in the prepared pan and bake for about 30 minutes. Cool for about 5 minutes, then turn out onto a rack and peel the wax paper from the bottom. Transfer to a cutting board and cut in squares. Dust brownies with confectioners' sugar if desired.

(16 BROWNIES)   **CHEWY PEANUT BUTTER BROWNIES**

A definite peanut flavor in a chewy brownie.

½ cup peanut butter	⅔ cup flour
4 tablespoons butter, softened	1 teaspoon baking powder
1 cup brown sugar	¼ teaspoon salt
1 teaspoon vanilla	½ cup chopped salted peanuts
2 eggs	

Preheat the oven to 350°F. Grease an 8-inch square baking pan. Combine the peanut butter and butter in a mixing bowl, and beat until smooth and well blended. Add the brown sugar and vanilla and beat well, then add the eggs, and beat until the mixture is light and fluffy. Combine the flour, baking powder, and salt, then stir and toss them together. Add to the first mixture and beat until completely mixed. Stir in the peanuts. Spread the batter evenly in the prepared pan and bake for 25–30 minutes, or until the top appears dry and a toothpick inserted in the center comes out barely clean. Remove from the oven and cool on a rack. Cut in 2-inch squares.

BUTTERSCOTCH BROWNIES ✳ (36 BROWNIES)

½ cup melted butter
2 cups dark-brown sugar
2 eggs
½ teaspoon salt

1½ cups flour
2 teaspoons baking powder
1 teaspoon vanilla
1 cup chopped nuts

Preheat the oven to 350°F. Butter a 9 × 13-inch cake pan. Mix all the ingredients together, combining them well. Spread in the pan and bake for 25–30 minutes, or until dry on top and almost firm to the touch. Let cool for 10–15 minutes, then cut in small squares.

CHEWY WALNUT BROWNIES (SIXTEEN 2 × 2-INCH BROWNIES)

These are first-rate chewy brownies—and better for you than the usual rich brownie.

¼ cup melted margarine
6 tablespoons carob powder
1 cup sugar
2 egg whites

¼ teaspoon salt
½ cup flour
2 teaspoons vanilla
1 cup chopped walnuts

Preheat the oven to 300°F. Grease an 8-inch square pan. Put the margarine, carob, sugar, egg whites, salt, flour, and vanilla in a mixing bowl and stir briskly until blended. Add the walnuts and stir. Spread the dough evenly in the baking pan. Bake 30–35 minutes. Remove from the oven and let cool 10 minutes. Cut into 2-inch squares, remove from the pan and place on a rack to cool completely.

(16 SQUARES)   **COCONUT SQUARES**

Coconut and nuts give these good texture. They are chewy, moist, and sweet.

2 eggs

2 cups light-brown sugar

⅛ teaspoon salt

½ teaspoon vanilla

2 cups shredded coconut (p. 12)

¼ cup chopped walnuts

6 tablespoons flour

Preheat the oven to 350°F. Butter a 9-inch square cake pan. Using a whisk or an electric beater, beat the eggs until they are foamy, then beat in the brown sugar, salt, and vanilla. Stir in the coconut and walnuts, then sprinkle the flour over the batter and stir in lightly. Spread in the pan and bake for about 30 minutes. Cool in the pan for 10–15 minutes, then cut in squares.

(36 SQUARES OR ABOUT 60 COOKIES)   **HERMITS**

¼ cup raisins or currants

¼ cup chopped nuts

2 cups flour

4 tablespoons butter

½ cup sugar

½ teaspoon salt

2 eggs

½ cup molasses

1 teaspoon baking soda

½ teaspoon cream of tartar

1 teaspoon cinnamon

½ teaspoon cloves

¼ teaspoon mace

¼ teaspoon nutmeg

Preheat the oven to 350°F. Grease a 9 × 13-inch cake pan or some cookie sheets. Toss the raisins or currants and the chopped nuts in ¼ cup of the flour; set aside. Cream the butter, then add the sugar and blend well. Add the salt, eggs, and molasses and beat well. Mix together the remaining 1¾ cups flour, the baking soda, cream of tartar, cinnamon, cloves, mace, and nutmeg, add to the butter-sugar-egg mixture, and beat thoroughly. Stir in the raisins and nuts. Spread in the pan or drop by teaspoonfuls onto the cookie sheets. Bake only until the top is firm and the center chewy, about 15–20 minutes for the squares, 8–10 minutes for the cookies.

CONCORD HERMITS

Substitute *1 cup dark-brown sugar* for the white sugar and molasses and add *½ cup sour cream*. You may also add *3 tablespoons chopped citron or candied orange peel*, if you wish.

COCONUT BARS

(16 BARS)

Rich and sweet as candy, this delicious confection has a pastry base with a chewy coconut topping.

¼ pound butter
2 tablespoons confectioners' sugar
1 cup plus 2 tablespoons flour
2 eggs
1¼ cups light-brown sugar
1 teaspoon vanilla

¼ teaspoon salt
1 teaspoon baking powder
1 cup coarsely chopped nut meats
1–1½ cups moist grated coconut (p. 12)

Preheat the oven to 350°F. Butter and flour an 8 × 8-inch square pan. Cream the butter, then add the confectioners' sugar and the cup of flour and blend. Pat evenly into the pan and bake for 15 minutes. While the pastry is baking, beat the eggs, then add the brown sugar and vanilla, beating until thick. Mix the remaining 2 tablespoons of flour, salt, and baking powder together and add to the egg mixture, incorporating well. Beat in the nuts and coconut. Spread evenly over the pastry and bake for 25–30 minutes. Cool in the pan, then cut in 1 × 4-inch bars.

PECAN SQUARES

(36 SQUARES)

These have a good butter and pecan taste, and a nice short texture.

½ pound butter
1 cup sugar
1 egg, separated

1 teaspoon vanilla
2 cups flour
1 cup chopped pecans

Preheat the oven to 375°F. Grease a jelly-roll pan about 9 × 15 inches. Cream the butter and sugar together until smooth and light. Beat in the egg yolk, vanilla, and flour until well mixed. Pat evenly into pan. Beat the egg white slightly and brush over the dough. Sprinkle the pecans evenly on top and press them in the dough slightly. Bake 16–18 minutes or until golden brown. Cool in the pan and cut in small squares.

(80 SQUARES)   **DATE LEBKUCHEN**

Dense, moist, with a fine flavor, this makes a good picnic sweet.

Grated rind and juice of 1
    lemon
Grated rind and juice of 1
    orange
1 pound dates, pitted and cut
    small
4 eggs
1 pound dark-brown sugar
2 cups flour

¼ teaspoon salt
1 teaspoon instant coffee
2 teaspoons baking powder
2 teaspoons cinnamon
1 cup chopped walnuts
3 tablespoons orange juice
1 teaspoon butter, melted
1 cup or more confectioners'
    sugar

Preheat oven to 375°F. Butter a 12 × 15-inch pan. Combine the rind and juice of the lemon and orange in a bowl, add the dates, and let marinate for 1 hour, turning them in the juices often. Beat the eggs until light. Gradually add the brown sugar, flour, salt, coffee, baking powder, and cinnamon. Beat until well blended. Stir in the dates and walnuts. Spread in the pan and bake for 30 minutes. Cool in pan. In a small bowl combine the 3 tablespoons orange juice and the melted butter, and add confectioners' sugar until you have the consistency of softened butter. Spread over the lebkuchen and cut into 1½-inch squares.

(40 COOKIES)   **LINZER SCHNITTEN**

A very good, rather heavy, spicy cookie.

3 eggs
2¼ cups sugar
¾ cup butter, melted
3½ cups flour
1 teaspoon baking powder
2 teaspoons cinnamon

1 teaspoon cloves
¼ teaspoon salt
Grated rind and juice of 1
    lemon
1 cup apricot preserves

Preheat oven to 375°F. Beat 2 of the eggs until light. Gradually add 1½ cups of the sugar and the butter, blending well. Sift the flour, baking powder, cinnamon, cloves, and salt together, then stir into the egg mixture and mix well. Add the lemon rind and juice. Mix well. Turn dough onto a floured board and knead until smooth. Cover with a bowl and let stand 1 hour. Roll out to ½ inch thick. Cut in strips 1½ × 10 inches. Mark a groove down the center of each strip with the handle of a wooden spoon. Fill the grooves with apricot preserves. Place on ungreased cookie sheet and bake 20 minutes or until lightly browned.

Beat the remaining 1 egg and ¾ cup sugar together, brush over the baked strips while they are still hot, and cut immediately into diagonal pieces.

NOELS

(16 SQUARES)

Very rich and very chewy.

2 eggs	¼ teaspoon salt
1 teaspoon vanilla	1 cup coarsely chopped
1 cup dark-brown sugar	walnuts or pecans
⅓ cup flour	2 tablespoons butter
¼ teaspoon baking soda	Confectioners' sugar

Preheat the oven to 350°F. Beat the eggs and vanilla together lightly. Mix together the brown sugar, flour, baking soda, salt, and nuts. Add to the eggs and mix well. Melt the butter in a 9-inch square pan. Pour the batter into the pan and bake for about 20–25 minutes, until firm to the touch. While hot, loosen with a spatula and turn out onto wax paper, buttered side up. Dust lightly with confectioners' sugar while still warm, then cut in squares.

HONEY DATE AND NUT BARS

(16 BARS)

2 tablespoons melted butter	Dash of salt
½ cup honey	½ cup dates, cut fine
2 eggs, well beaten	½ cup chopped nuts
¾ cup flour	Confectioners' sugar
½ teaspoon baking powder	

Preheat the oven to 350°F. Butter an 8-inch square cake pan. Mix all the ingredients except confectioners' sugar together in the order given. Spread in the pan and bake for about 25 minutes or until firm and delicately brown. Cool for 5–10 minutes, then cut in bars 1 × 4 inches and roll in confectioners' sugar while still warm.

WALNUT MERINGUE BARS

(24 BARS)

¼ pound butter	2 eggs, separated
2 cups light-brown sugar	1¼ cups flour
½ teaspoon salt	1½ teaspoons baking powder
2 teaspoons vanilla	1 cup chopped walnuts

Preheat the oven to 300°F. Butter a pan about 8 × 12 inches. Cream the butter and 1 cup of the sugar together until light and smooth. Beat in the salt, 1 teaspoon vanilla, and egg yolks. Add the flour and baking powder. Beat well. Spread evenly in the pan. Beat the egg whites until soft peaks are reached, then slowly beat in the remaining 1 cup brown sugar until all is incorporated. Gently stir in the walnuts and remaining teaspoon of vanilla. Spread over the cookie dough. Bake 35 minutes. Cool. Cut in bars 4 × 1 inch.

(16 BARS)   **JAM OR MARMALADE BARS**

½ cup shortening	1 teaspoon baking powder
½ cup sugar	½ teaspoon cinnamon
½ teaspoon vanilla	¼ teaspoon cloves
½ teaspoon almond extract	½ teaspoon salt
1 egg	Raspberry jam or marmalade
1½ cups flour	

Preheat the oven to 400°F. Grease an 8-inch square pan. Cream the shortening with the sugar, vanilla, and almond extract. Stir in the egg and blend well. Mix together the flour, baking powder, cinnamon, cloves, and salt, add to the first mixture, and combine thoroughly. Spread half the dough in the pan. Cover with a layer of jam or marmalade. Pat the remaining dough on top and bake for about 25 minutes. Cool, then cut in bars 4 × 1 inch.

(ABOUT 80 SMALL CAKES)   **PETITS FOURS**

These pretty, small cakes are lovely for parties and buffets.

2 eggs	½ cup milk
2 egg yolks	5 tablespoons melted butter
1 cup sugar	1 recipe Petit Fours Frosting
2 cups flour	(p. 846)
2 teaspoons baking powder	

Preheat the oven to 350°F. Butter and lightly flour a 10½ × 15½-inch jelly-roll pan. Beat the eggs and egg yolks until they are blended, gradually add the sugar, and beat until very pale and fluffy, about 10 minutes with an electric beater. Sift the flour and baking powder over the egg mixture, add the milk, and fold together lightly until the batter is well mixed. Add the melted butter and combine thoroughly. Spread the batter in the pan and bake for 12–15 minutes, until a toothpick comes out clean. Turn the cake out onto a sheet of wax paper and cool completely. Cut into small squares, rectangles, or triangles and arrange them in rows on a fine-mesh cake rack with plenty of space between the rows. Set the cake rack over a shallow pan or raised over a piece of wax paper. Heat *Petits Fours Frosting* in a pan over simmering water until it is thin enough to pour; you can thin it with water or thicken it with confectioners' sugar if the consistency is not right when the icing is heated. Pour the frosting over the cakes, moving slowly down each row and back again and letting the icing spread over the cakes and drip down through the cake rack. Lift the cake rack and move it gently back and forth to loosen any icing that is clinging to the underside. Scrape up the drippings and reuse them, heating them again over simmering water. When the cakes are dry, lift them from the rack with a spatula and trim the bottom edges with a sharp knife. Decorate each little cake with *a whole nut, some candied fruit, tiny candies, sprinkles,* or *coconut.*

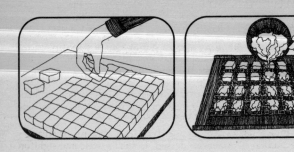

PIES & PASTRIES

I have added a Stirred Dough recipe to this chapter, which is a foolproof way for beginners of making a pie dough—and, incidentally, doesn't use shortening or butter. There is a wonderful Shaker Lemon Pie, a Best-of-All Pecan Pie, and in response to a request from several readers, I have added a luscious Chess Pie.

Need I say it? Don't try to bake pies in a microwave oven.

ABOUT MAKING PIES

A light-brown flaky crust holding fresh fruit, custard, or cream—pie, the traditional American dessert, is such a welcome sight on the table.

Learn to make your own piecrusts; it's not hard, and the results are so much better than commercial products. Each of the piecrusts we offer here differs from the others in taste, texture, and structure. Try them all; you will soon develop your own favorites.

Kinds of Pie Pastry

Basic Pastry is flaky and tender and at its best when freshly baked. It should be made with vegetable shortening for the lightest, flakiest results.

Tart Pastry is buttery, crisp, and strong, with a crumbly, rather than a flaky, consistency. It includes an egg, which gives it extra firmness, enough to hold a filling without a pan to support the sides. The butter in tart pastry adds strength as well as good taste.

Hot-Water Pastry and **Stirred Pastry** are interchangeable with basic

pastry and somewhat easier to make. Hot-water pastry calls for
melted shortening and stirred pastry uses vegetable oil, both of
which are *stirred*, rather than *cut*, into the flour. The ease of blending these doughs makes them less intimidating to beginners. Once
you've got the knack of it, however, you'll find that basic pastry is
also easy to assemble and, we believe, the lightest and flakiest of
the three.

Catherine's Pastry is a sturdy pastry using both lard and butter and is
especially good with meat and other savory fillings. It will be particularly delicious if you live on or near a farm and have access to
pure, unadulterated lard.

Crumb Crusts, made with cracker crumbs, are not true pastry. They
are the simplest pie shells to make and are especially good with
chiffon and other cold fillings.

Special pastry flour may be used in these piecrusts, but all-
purpose white flour is just fine for any crust.

Rolling and Shaping Pie Doughs

Do not chill *basic pastry* before you roll it out; line the pie pan with it
first and then refrigerate it. Pastry made with butter, such as *tart pastry*,
will, however, be easier to handle if you chill it for 30 minutes or so *before* you roll it out (see p. 897).

No matter what piecrust you use, let the bottom crust chill in the
pie pan in the refrigerator while you prepare the filling and the top
crust.

Bottom Crust. Divide the dough in half, if you have made enough for a
two-crust pie, and pat each piece into a ball. Flatten one of the balls
with the heel of your hand, keeping it round. Place it on a lightly
floured board or on a pastry cloth and sprinkle the top with a little
flour. Using a rolling pin, start in the center and roll lightly in all directions, lifting and turning the dough frequently to make sure it is
not sticking to the board. Do not roll quite to the edge of the dough
until the last few turns.

If the dough seems to be sticking, dust the board with more flour. Roll the dough until you have a round piece about ⅛ inch thick and 2 inches greater in diameter than the pie pan you plan to use. Fold the dough in half and lift it gently into the pan with the fold in the center. Unfold it and fit it to the pan, easing it in loosely without stretching it. Pat it into all the edges, then trim the extra dough hanging over the edge so that it is ¾ inch larger than the pan.

Refrigerate the bottom crust until you are ready to fill and bake it.

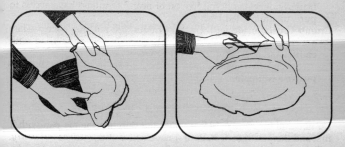

Pie Shell. If you are making a pie shell for a single-crust, open-face pie, fold the extra ¾ inch under along the rim of the pan so that it is double in thickness, then crimp using one of the following methods: 1) press the tines of a fork all around the rim (below left). 2) Using your thumb and forefinger, press and pinch the dough together at even intervals around the rim (as has been done on the crust, below). 3) Build the dough up around the rim about ¾ inch; then using your two forefingers press and pleat at intervals to make a stand-up, scalloped edge (below right).

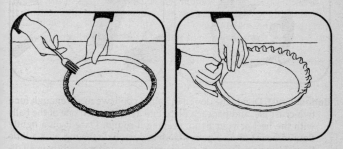

Instead of using a rolling pin when making a pie shell, you can pat the dough into a pie pan or springform pan with your fingers. This method works especially well with tart pastry, for which a slightly thick bottom crust is desirable and the dough is not harmed by handling.

Top Crust. For a two-crust pie, roll out the second piece of dough just like the first. Fill the bottom crust generously with the pie filling, then fold the dough for the top crust in half and gently lift it onto the filling with the fold in the center. Unfold it and trim it so that the dough for both crusts extends over the rim of the pan by about ¾ inch. Press the edges of the top and bottom crusts together, tucking the top one over the bottom one to make a thick edge. Crimp the edges with the tines of a fork or flute them with your fingers.

Prick the top with a fork in several places or cut vents or a small design or two so that steam can escape while the pie is baking.

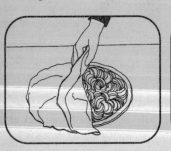
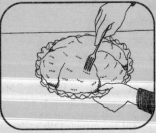

Lattice Crust. Lattice crusts make beautiful finishes, especially for shiny berry pies. To make one, roll out the dough as for a top crust and then cut it in strips ½–¾ inch wide. Place the strips on the filled pie, weaving them in and out of each other, or, if you prefer, just laying them across each other at right angles. When all the strips are loosely arranged on the pie, trim them so that they are even with the overhanging bottom crust. Fold the edge of the bottom crust up over the ends of the strips and press together. Crimp or flute the edge all around.

Lattice strips may also be twisted to give a spiral effect.

Using a Food Processor to Make Pastry

The food processor does not prepare good *basic pastry:* it blends the flour and shortening into a paste, instead of keeping bits of shortening separate from the flour to create a flaky texture when baked.

The food processor will, however, blend *tart pastry* most satisfactorily. Be sure to have the butter very chilled. Use the metal blade and follow the directions on p. 897. Process just until a ball of dough forms on the blade; do *not* overblend.

The food processor will make perfect crumbs for crumb crusts. You can also use the slicing blade to prepare many fruits for pie fillings.

Glazing Pies

We sometimes like to sprinkle granulated sugar over lattice tops or top crusts before we bake a pie.

Melted currant jelly makes a nice glaze for an open fruit tart (p. 901). You can also put a sugar glaze on a two-crust pie right after it comes out of the oven (p. 901).

Baking Pies and Pie Shells

For a crisp bottom crust, be sure to bake pies on the lowest rack of a thoroughly preheated oven.

Use heavy-gauge steel or aluminum pans for the best results. Glass and ceramic pans also work well, and glass has the added advantage of letting you see how brown the bottom crust is getting. However, pies baked in glass or ceramic pans should be baked at about 25 degrees less oven heat than the recipe calls for.

Foil pans are often not strong enough to hold certain fillings firmly in place. They also overheat because they are so thin. But they are very welcome in emergencies.

Beware of some of the newer finishes in bakeware: predarkened tin-oxide pans brown pies and breads too quickly and you have to compensate by shortening the baking time. White Teflon-finished pans, on the other hand, often produce pastries and breads that are pale and colorless.

Unfilled Pie Shells. Unfilled pie shells should be baked at 425°F for 12 minutes for a tart shell, 18–20 minutes for the Basic Pastry—or until lightly browned. Let them cool before filling them.

If the dough has been fitted to the pan loosely without stretching, the pie shell is less likely to buckle up during baking. Many books recommend that unfilled pie shells be covered with foil and then weighted down with beans or rice to prevent the pastry from puffing up in spots while it is baking. We have found, however, that this method often creates an undesirable moist bottom. We prefer to prick the bottom all over with a fork before baking and then, after the pie shell has been in the oven for about 5 minutes, to open the door to see if any spots have begun to swell; if so, push them down gently. Repeat this again, if necessary, after 5 minutes and you will have a dry, flaky pie shell.

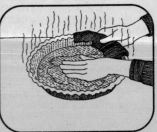

Filled Pies and Filled Pie Shells. Filled pies are generally baked at 425°F for the first 10 minutes and then at 350°F for the remainder of the baking time. The higher baking temperature at the beginning helps produce a crisp crust. Baking temperatures vary, of course, with specific pies, so follow the instructions given with the recipe.

If the tops or edges of a piecrust begin to brown too quickly, cover the pie lightly with a piece of foil and continue baking.

Storing and Freezing Pie Dough and Pies

Unbaked Pie Dough. Unbaked pie dough will keep in the refrigerator, tightly wrapped, for about 4 days. Pat the dough into a ball and wrap it well with foil or plastic wrap. Let it soften a bit at room temperature before you roll it out. Unbaked pie dough can also be frozen for at least 3 months. Save bits and scraps each time you make pastry and you will soon have enough for a complete pie. Or line small tart shells with unbaked pastry scraps and keep them in the freezer; filled with savories or sweets, they make delightful appetizers or desserts.

When you are preparing a pie ahead of time, roll the dough out, line the pan with it, wrap well with foil or plastic, and put it in the refrigerator. If you are making a two-crust pie, roll the top out, too, and place it on a piece of wax paper over the lined pan. Cover it all securely and keep refrigerated until you are ready to fill and bake the pie. Wrapped this way, unbaked piecrusts will keep in the refrigerator for about 4 days or in the freezer for at least 3 months. You can make several pies at the same time, following this procedure; stack the rolled-out crusts carefully, one on top of another, with wax paper separating the layers.

Unfilled Pie Shells. Unfilled pie shells may be frozen either baked or unbaked, but unbaked is preferable by far. Wrapped well in foil or freezer paper, an unbaked pie shell will keep in the freezer for at least 3 months. Unbaked shells should be unwrapped and baked while still frozen in a 450°F oven for 15–20 minutes (less for a tart shell, longer for a basic piecrust) or until browned. Allow approximately 3 minutes more than usual baking time for frozen dough.

Baked pie shells should not be held in the freezer for more than 6 weeks. Their texture may lose some crispness in the freezing-defrosting process; try crisping in a preheated 450°F oven for 10 minutes. They are great to have in an emergency, since they will defrost in less than 2 hours and may be filled with a variety of cold fillings for a quick, delicious dessert.

Filled Pies and Filled Pie Shells. Although you should not freeze pies with custard or cream fillings, pies and pie shells filled with fruit and other mixtures will keep well in the freezer for at least 3 months. We find that unbaked pies remain crisper and more tender and pleasing after freezing than baked pies. Do not defrost them before baking them: bake them unwrapped, directly from the freezer, in a preheated 425°F oven for 15–20 minutes and then in a 350°F oven for the remainder of the baking time. The total baking time for a frozen pie will be about 20 minutes longer than for an unfrozen one.

Baked pies should be frozen only when necessary: if you are left with an uneaten pie on your hands, for example, or are preparing large quantities of pies in advance for the town fair. Let baked frozen pies defrost unwrapped at room temperature for about 3 hours, then crisp them in a preheated 450°F oven for about 20 minutes.

PIE PASTRY

BASIC PASTRY

Don't handle this pastry dough any more than necessary or it will be tough: treat it firmly, not timidly, but don't fuss with it. The flour and shortening should not be blended too well: it is the bits of shortening left in the dough that puff and expand during baking and give the pastry its flaky identity. For that reason, the dough cannot be mixed as successfully in a food processor. Follow illustrated details pp. 890–92.

(8-INCH PIE SHELL)

1 cup plus 2 tablespoons flour	⅓ cup shortening
¼ teaspoon salt	2–3 tablespoons cold water

(8-INCH TWO-CRUST PIE)

2 cups flour	⅔ cup shortening
½ teaspoon salt	⅓ cup cold water

(9-INCH PIE SHELL)

1½ cups flour	½ cup shortening
¼ teaspoon salt	3–4 tablespoons cold water

(9-INCH TWO-CRUST PIE)

2½ cups flour	¾ cup shortening
½ teaspoon salt	6–7 tablespoons cold water

Mix the flour and salt. Cut in the shortening with a pastry blender or two knives (see illustration p. 890). Combine lightly only until the mixture resembles coarse meal or very tiny peas: its texture will not be uniform but will contain crumbs and small bits and pieces. Sprinkle water over the flour mixture, a tablespoon at a time, and mix lightly with a fork, using only enough water so that the pastry will hold together when pressed gently into a ball.

Pie Shell
Roll the dough out 2 inches larger than the pie pan, then fit it loosely but firmly into the pan. Crimp or flute the edges. For a *baked pie shell* (sometimes known, incidentally, as baking blind) prick the bottom dough all over with a fork and bake the shell for 16–18 minutes in a preheated 425°F oven (for a partially baked shell, bake 10 minutes). Open the oven door once or twice during the baking and see if the shell again has begun to swell up in spots; if it has, push it down gently. Or fill the *unbaked pie shell* with pie filling and then bake the pie as directed in the recipe.

Two-Crust Pie
Divide the dough into two balls. Roll the bottom crust out 2 inches larger than the pie pan. Ease it into the pan, fitting it loosely but firmly. Roll out the top crust. Fill the pie generously, then put on the top crust and prick in several places with a fork or cut vents. Or cover with lattice strips. Crimp or flute the edges. Bake as indicated in the recipe.

(ONE 9-INCH TART) **TART PASTRY**

This well-balanced, basic recipe produces a firm, crisp crust with the taste of butter. You can sweeten it slightly, if you wish, by adding 1½ tablespoons of sugar to the flour. Unlike the preceding Basic Pastry, Tart Pastry will not get tough if you handle it a lot and you can mix it in a food processor.

1 cup flour	1 egg yolk
¼ teaspoon salt	2 tablespoons ice water
¼ pound cold butter, in small pieces	

Mix the flour and salt in a bowl. Cut in the butter with your fingers or a pastry blender until the mixture resembles coarse meal or tiny peas. Whisk the egg yolk and water together in another bowl, add to the flour mixture, and blend until the pastry is smooth and holds together in a ball. It can be mixed in a food processor; process first the flour, salt, and butter quickly together, then add the egg yolk and water through the funnel and process until the dough balls up around the blade. Wrap in foil or plastic and refrigerate it for at least 20 minutes. You can roll this dough out with a rolling pin, but you would have to chill it, wrapped in plastic, for at least 20 minutes. We find it easier to pat it into a pie pan or springform with our hands. Pull pieces of dough from the ball and press them over the bottom and sides of the pan, using the heel of your hand. The dough should be thick enough to hold the filling, but be careful that it is not too thick around the bottom edge or the finished tart will seem coarse. If there's time, cover the lined pan snugly with foil and refrigerate it before filling and baking it. Bake as directed in the filling recipe. Or prick the bottom with a fork and bake it unfilled for 12 minutes in a preheated 425°F oven. If you use a springform pan, do not remove the sides until you are ready to serve the tart.

(8- OR 9-INCH PIE SHELL) **HOT-WATER PASTRY**

This is a good recipe for beginners. Somewhat less flaky and tender than the Basic Pastry, it is still very acceptable.

½ cup shortening	½ teaspoon salt
⅓ cup boiling water	¼ teaspoon baking powder
1½ cups flour	

Put the shortening in a bowl, add the boiling water, and stir until the shortening melts. Add the flour, salt, and baking powder, and mix with a fork until blended. Form the dough into a ball. Roll it out 2 inches larger than the pie pan. Ease the dough into the pan and fit it loosely, but firmly. Cover the pan and let the dough chill in the refrigerator for at least 4 hours before baking. Bake for 15 minutes in a preheated 425°F oven. Or fill first and bake as directed in the filling recipe.

STIRRED DOUGH   (8-INCH PIE SHELL)

This easy-to-make dough produces a dandy, softly crisp crust similar to a cracker. Oil is used instead of shortening, making it a good choice for a low-fat, low-cholesterol diet.

1 cup flour	1 tablespoon milk
¼ teaspoon salt	
½ teaspoon sugar	
4–5 tablespoons oil (either peanut, corn, or other vegetable, in that order of preference)	

Preheat the oven to 425°F if you are baking the pie shell. Combine the flour, salt, and sugar in a bowl and stir with a fork to mix. Stir together 3 tablespoons of the oil and the milk, sprinkle them evenly over the flour mixture, and stir again. Add another tablespoon of oil, still stirring. Gently pat the dough into a ball, and if it holds together and feels moist (it will have a rather translucent, oily look to it), it is ready to roll out. If it crumbles rather than forms a ball, stir in the remaining tablespoon of oil. Place a sheet of wax paper approximately 16 inches long on your rolling surface. Pat the dough into a cake about 5 inches in diameter, place it on the wax paper, and place another sheet of wax paper on top. Roll the dough out between the sheets of wax paper to a circle about ⅛ inch thick and at least 2 inches larger in diameter than your pie pan. Gently peel off the top sheet of wax paper. Invert the dough over the pie plate and gently ease it into the pan, peeling away the paper as you go. This dough breaks easily, so patch or piece wherever necessary. Trim the edges and make a decorative design with the tines of a fork. The pie shell may now be filled and baked, or left unfilled and may be partially or fully baked. To bake the unfilled pie shell: prick the dough with a fork all over at ½-inch intervals, and press a 12-inch square of heavy-duty foil firmly into the pie shell. Bake for 6 minutes. Remove the foil and continue baking for another 4 minutes for a partially baked shell. For a fully baked shell, bake for an additional 8–10 minutes after removing the foil, or until the crust seems dry, crisp, and lightly browned. If the dough swells during baking, press it down gently with a fork.

(8-INCH TWO-CRUST PIE   **CATHERINE'S PASTRY DOUGH**
OR 9-INCH LATTICE-TOP PIE)

This flaky crust is very durable. Try it if you can get some good fresh lard. It is fine for meat or other main-dish pies.

2 cups flour	⅓ cup ice water,
1 teaspoon salt	approximately
½ teaspoon baking powder	⅓ cup butter
⅓ cup lard	

Mix the flour, salt, and baking powder in a bowl. Work in the lard until it resembles coarse meal or very small peas. Sprinkle in up to ⅓ cup ice water, drop by drop, stirring lightly with a fork and using only enough water to hold the dough together. Roll out the dough into a rectangle. Dot with a third of the butter, then roll up the dough like a jelly roll. Roll out again until ¼ inch thick and dot with a third of the butter. Roll up the dough and repeat once more. Chill 30 minutes. Roll the bottom crust out 2 inches larger than the pie pan. Fit the dough in the pan. Roll out the top crust. Fill the pie, then put on the top crust and cut vents in it. Or cover the top with lattice strips. Crimp or flute the edges. Bake as indicated in the filling recipe.

(8- OR 9-INCH PIE SHELL)   **CHOCOLATE COCONUT CRUST**

Fill this with ice cream for a quick, delectable dessert.

2 ounces unsweetened	1 cup confectioners' sugar
chocolate	3 tablespoons hot water
2 tablespoons butter	1½ cups flaked coconut

Melt the chocolate and butter in a small pan over low heat. Mix the sugar and hot water together in a small bowl. Add the chocolate and butter to the sugar, then stir in the coconut. Press the mixture firmly into a pie pan and chill.

(8- OR 9-INCH PIE SHELL)   **CRUMB CRUST**

1½ cups fine crumbs (graham	⅓ cup sugar
cracker, gingersnap, rusk,	⅓ cup melted butter
zwieback, or vanilla or	
chocolate wafers)	

Mix the crumbs, sugar, and butter together in a bowl. Press and pat the crumb mixture into the pie pan. Bake 8–10 minutes in a preheated 350°F oven or fill unbaked as directed in the filling recipe.

PIE TOPPINGS

MERINGUE TOPPING

Meringue toppings for pies often "weep," shrink, or turn rubbery. Follow this somewhat unconventional method and yours will hold up well and stay light for several days. Be sure to refrigerate a meringue pie if it isn't served within a few hours of making it.

(FOR 8-INCH PIE)

4 egg whites, at room temperature	6 tablespoons sugar
	⅛ teaspoon salt

(FOR 9-INCH PIE)

NOTE
see page 471

5 egg whites, at room temperature	½ cup sugar
	¼ teaspoon salt

Put the egg whites and sugar in a mixing bowl and place the bowl in a pan of hot water. Stir constantly until the whites feel warm, then add the salt. Remove the bowl from the hot water and beat with an electric beater until the meringue is stiff and shiny. Spread the meringue over a filled and baked pie shell. Be sure that the meringue touches the inner edges of the crust; this will keep it from shrinking. Put the pie under the broiler and let the meringue peaks brown a little. Watch carefully, as this will take only a minute or two.

JACOBSON'S MERINGUE   (FOR 8- OR 9-INCH PIE)

Several generations of New Englanders swear by this. It produces great volume and stability. Use it on any pie calling for a meringue topping.

3 tablespoons ice water	½ cup sugar
3 egg whites, at room temperature	¾ teaspoon baking powder

Add the ice water to the egg whites; whip to froth. Mix the sugar with the baking powder and add very gradually to the egg whites, whipping until glossy and stiff. Spread the meringue over a filled and baked pie shell. Be sure that the meringue touches the inner edges of the crust; this will keep it from shrinking. Bake about 20 minutes at 325°F.

(ABOUT 2 CUPS) **CRUMB OR STREUSEL TOPPING**

Make lots of this and store in the freezer. Then use what you need. It is wonderful to have on hand. Use as a topping on fruit pies instead of a top crust or on a Crisp or Brown Betty (p. 1007), or on muffins to give them a crunchy finish.

½ cup light- or dark-brown sugar	1 cup flour
	¼ pound butter, chilled

In a bowl, mix the sugar and flour until blended. Rub the butter into the flour mixture with your fingers, or cut in with a pastry blender until the mixture resembles coarse bread crumbs. Use 1 recipe or about 2 cups of the topping for an 8-inch square baking dish or an 8- or 9-inch pie. Spread the crumbs evenly over the prepared fruit in the pan. (Sweeten the fruit lightly if it is tart.) This topping should be baked in a moderate oven (350–375°F). Too hot an oven will burn the crumbs.

(FOR 10-INCH TART) **GLAZE FOR FRUIT TARTS**

1 cup red currant jelly or 1½ cups apricot or strawberry preserves

Melt the jelly or preserves in a small saucepan over low heat, stirring. If you are using preserves, strain. Let cool a bit, then spread over the fruit-filled tart.

(FOR 9-INCH PIE) **SUGAR GLAZE FOR PIECRUSTS**

½ cup confectioners' sugar   1 tablespoon water

Mix the sugar with the water and brush it on a hot baked pie immediately after it is removed from the oven.

PIES

APPLE PIE

Apple pie is a symbol of the many good things in the American home. You will not be disappointed with this one. It is especially good served warm with a wedge of sharp Cheddar cheese or a spoonful of whipped cream.

Basic Pastry dough for 9-inch
two-crust pie (p. 895)
¾–1 cup sugar
½ teaspoon salt
1 teaspoon cinnamon
(optional)

½ teaspoon nutmeg (optional)
1½ tablespoons flour
6–8 large, firm, tart apples
(about 10 cups)
2 tablespoons butter

Preheat the oven to 425°F. Line a pie pan with half the pastry dough. Mix the sugar, salt, cinnamon, nutmeg, and flour in a large bowl. Peel, core, and slice the apples and toss them in the sugar mixture, coating them well. Pile them into the lined pan and dot with the butter. Roll out the top crust and drape it over the pie. Crimp the edges and cut several vents in the top. Bake 10 minutes, then lower the heat to 350°F and bake 30–40 minutes more or until the apples are tender when pierced with a skewer and the crust is browned.

FRESH PEACH PIE

If you submerge peaches in boiling water for a minute or two, then plunge them into cold water, their skins will be easier to peel.

Basic Pastry dough for 9-inch
two-crust pie (p. 895)
1 cup sugar
4 tablespoons flour

4 cups peeled and sliced fresh
peaches
1 tablespoon lemon juice

Preheat the oven to 425°F. Line a pie pan with half the pastry dough. Mix the sugar and flour in a large bowl. Add the peaches and lemon juice and toss well. Pile the fruit into the lined pie pan. Roll out the top crust and drape it over the pie. Crimp or flute the edges and cut several vents in the top. Bake for 10 minutes, then lower the heat to 350°F and bake 30–40 minutes more, until the top is browned.

(9-INCH PIE)   **APRICOT PIE**

Basic Pastry dough for 9-inch
    two-crust pie (p. 895)
4 cups pitted, halved apricots
1 cup sugar

2 tablespoons tapioca
1½ tablespoons lemon juice
2 tablespoons butter

Preheat the oven to 425°F. Line a pie pan with half the pastry dough.
Spread half the apricots in the lined pan and sprinkle half the sugar
over them. Spread the remaining apricots on top and sprinkle with the
remaining sugar and the tapioca and lemon juice. Dot with the butter.
Roll out the top crust and drape it over the pie. Crimp or flute the
edges and cut several vents in the top. Bake for 10 minutes, then lower
the heat to 350°F and bake 30–40 minutes, until the top is browned.

(9-INCH PIE)   **BLUEBERRY PIE**

Basic Pastry dough for 9-inch
    two-crust pie (p. 895)
4 cups fresh or frozen
    blueberries
3 tablespoons flour

1 cup sugar
⅛ teaspoon salt
1 tablespoon lemon juice
1 tablespoon butter

Preheat the oven to 425°F. Line the pie pan with half the pastry dough.
Wash and pick over the blueberries if you are using fresh ones; if you
are using frozen berries, it is not necessary to defrost them completely.
Mix the flour, sugar, and salt in a large bowl. Add the blueberries and
lemon juice and toss well. Pile the mixture into the lined pie pan and
dot with the butter. Roll out the top crust and drape it over the pie.
Crimp or flute the edges and cut several vents in the top. Bake for 10
minutes, then lower the heat to 350°F and bake for 30–40 minutes or
until the top is browned.

(9-INCH OPEN PIE)   **OPEN BLUEBERRY PIE**

Blueberries and cream in a crisp, prebaked pie shell.

Tart Pastry dough for 9-inch
    tart (p. 895)
1 cup sugar
3 tablespoons cornstarch
1 cup water
⅛ teaspoon salt

1 tablespoon butter
4 cups fresh or frozen
    blueberries
1 cup heavy cream
Sugar

Preheat the oven to 425°F. Line a pie pan with the pastry dough, prick the dough all over, and bake for 10–15 minutes, until lightly browned. Mix the sugar, cornstarch, salt, and water in a pan. Cook over low heat, stirring constantly, until thickened. Add the butter, stir until melted, and let cool. Fold in the blueberries and pile into the baked pie shell. Before serving, whip the cream, adding sugar to taste, and spread it over the blueberry filling.

SOUR CHERRY PIE (8-INCH LATTICE PIE)

There's nothing like the flavor of sour cherries wrapped in flaky pastry. Serve slightly warm for the best flavor.

Basic Pastry dough for 8-inch
two-crust pie (p. 895)
1 cup sugar
1½ tablespoons flour

⅛ teaspoon salt
4 cups fresh or canned sour
cherries, pitted

Preheat the oven to 425°F. Line a pie pan with half the pastry dough. Mix the sugar, flour, and salt in a large bowl, add the cherries (if canned, drain them; use only ¼ cup sugar and add ½ cup of the juice to the sugar mixture), and toss until well coated. Pile into the lined pie pan. Use the remaining dough to make a lattice top. Crimp the edges. Bake for 10 minutes, then reduce the heat to 350°F and bake for 30–40 minutes more or until the crust is browned.

SWEET CHERRY PIE (8-INCH PIE)

Basic Pastry dough for 8-inch
two-crust pie (p. 895)
3 cups fresh or canned sweet
cherries, pitted

¼ cup sugar
2½ tablespoons quick-cooking
tapioca
2 teaspoons butter

Preheat the oven to 425°F. Line a pie pan with half the pastry dough. Drain the cherries, saving ½ cup of the juice. (If you are using fresh cherries, the natural juices which bubble up during baking are sufficient.) Mix the juice, sugar, and tapioca in a bowl, add the cherries, and toss well. Pile into the lined pan and dot with the butter. Roll out the top crust and drape it over the pie. Crimp the edges and cut several vents in the top. Bake for 10 minutes, reduce the heat to 350°F, continue to bake for 30–40 minutes more, until the crust is lightly browned.

(9-INCH TART) **GLAZED FRESH STRAWBERRY TART**

Wait until the spring when strawberries are plump and juicy, then fill a buttery prebaked tart shell with glazed berries topped with clouds of lightly sweetened whipped cream. Other fresh berry tarts can be made the same way—substituting blueberries, raspberries, blackberries for the quart of strawberries.

Tart Pastry dough for 9-inch
tart (p. 897)
1 cup granulated sugar
3 tablespoons cornstarch
¼ teaspoon salt
¾ cup orange juice

1 tablespoon lemon juice
1 quart strawberries, hulled
and sliced
1 cup heavy cream
Confectioners' sugar

Preheat the oven to 425°F. Line a pie pan or springform with the tart dough, prick the dough all over, and bake for 12 minutes or until lightly browned. Combine the granulated sugar, cornstarch, salt, orange juice, and lemon juice in a saucepan. Cook over low heat, stirring constantly, until thickened, then continue to cook for about 10 minutes. Spoon into a bowl to cool. Fill the baked tart shell with the strawberries and cover them with the cornstarch mixture. Before serving, whip the cream, sweetening it to taste with confectioners' sugar. Spread over the strawberry filling.

(9-INCH LATTICE PIE) **RHUBARB PIE**

Rhubarb is sometimes called "pie plant." Use only the stalks: the leaves are poisonous. Flatter this pie, if you wish, by adding a cup of crushed, drained strawberries or pineapple to the rhubarb filling.

Basic Pastry dough for 9-inch
two-crust pie (p. 895)
1¼ cups sugar
4 tablespoons flour

⅛ teaspoon salt
4 cups ¼-inch pieces rhubarb
stalks
2 tablespoons butter

Preheat the oven to 425°F. Line a pie pan with half the pastry dough. Combine the sugar, flour, and salt in a bowl. Add the rhubarb and toss well. Pile the rhubarb filling into the lined pie pan and dot with the butter. Roll out the remaining dough and make a lattice top. Crimp the edges. Bake for 10 minutes, then reduce the heat to 350°F and bake for 30–40 minutes more, until the filling is tender when pierced with a skewer and the crust is browned.

DEEP-DISH PEACH PIE

(SERVES EIGHT)

1½ recipes Basic Pastry dough
    for 8-inch pie shell (p. 895)
2 tablespoons lemon juice
6 cups peeled, pitted, sliced
    peaches
1¼ cups plus 2 tablespoons
    sugar

⅛ teaspoon salt
¼ teaspoon nutmeg
¼ teaspoon cinnamon
3 tablespoons flour
4 tablespoons butter
1 cup heavy cream, whipped

Preheat the oven to 450°F. Prepare the pastry dough and set it aside.
Sprinkle the lemon juice over the peaches in a large bowl. Mix 1¼ cups
of the sugar with the salt, nutmeg, cinnamon, and flour, then add to the
peaches and toss until they are evenly coated. Spread the peaches
in a 1½- to 2-quart baking dish and dot all over with the butter. Roll out
the pastry dough to cover the top of the dish with a 1½-inch overhang.
Press the pastry to the edge of the dish and flute it. Cut two or three
vents on top for steam to escape. Sprinkle the top with the remaining
2 tablespoons of sugar. Bake for 10 minutes, then reduce heat to
350°F and continue to bake for 30 minutes more. Serve with whipped
cream.

DEEP-DISH APPLE PIE

Substitute 6 cups peeled, cored, sliced apples for the peaches and use 2 teaspoons cinnamon.

DEEP-DISH BLUEBERRY PIE

Substitute 6 cups blueberries for the peaches and use ½ teaspoon cinnamon.

PRUNE PIE

(9-INCH LATTICE PIE)

1 pound dried prunes
Basic Pastry dough for 9-inch
    two-crust pie (p. 895)
½ cup sugar

1 tablespoon flour
Grated rind of 1 lemon
2 tablespoons lemon juice
2 tablespoons butter

Cook the prunes slowly in water to cover until they are tender, about 30 minutes. Drain them, reserving ½ cup of the juice. Preheat the oven to 425°F. Line a pie pan with half the pastry dough. Pit the prunes and cut them in quarters. Mix the reserved prune juice, sugar, flour, lemon rind, and lemon juice in a small bowl. Spoon the prunes into the lined pie pan and pour the juice evenly on top. Dot with the butter. Roll out the remaining dough and make a lattice top. Crimp or flute the edges. Bake for 10 minutes, then lower the heat to 350°F and continue baking for about 35 minutes or until the crust is browned.

(9-INCH PIE)   ✳   **BEST-OF-ALL PECAN PIE**

A wickedly rich pecan pie. The nuts float to the surface of the filling during baking, and my family loves the sight of whole, perfect pecan halves atop the pie. Chopped nuts do make the pie easier to cut, and possibly give you a little more pecan in each bite—just because the pieces of nut are smaller and more numerous. All of these things considered, I'd rather have beautiful pecan halves, but the choice is up to you.

Basic Pastry dough for a 9-inch pie shell (p. 895)	4 tablespoons butter, melted
3 eggs	1 teaspoon vanilla
1 cup dark corn syrup	1¼ cups pecan halves or
½ cup dark-brown sugar	coarsely chopped pecans

Topping

1 cup heavy cream, chilled

Preheat the oven to 425°F. Line a pie pan with the rolled-out dough and set aside. Beat the eggs in a bowl with a fork or wire whisk until the yolks and whites are blended. Add the corn syrup, brown sugar, melted butter, and vanilla, and blend well. Stir in the pecans, then pour the mixture into the pie shell. Bake the pie for 15 minutes, then reduce the heat to 350°F and continue baking for another 15–20 minutes, or until the edges are set and the center quivers slightly. Don't overbake! Let the pie cool a bit, and just before serving whip the cream, then spread it over the pie or pass separately.

CHESS PIE   *

The top is golden and almost crisp—a beautiful cover for the buttery filling.

Basic Pastry dough for an 8- or 9-inch pie shell (p. 895)	1 tablespoon cider vinegar
3 eggs	½ cup melted butter
1 cup sugar	1 tablespoon vanilla
2 tablespoons yellow cornmeal	Heavy cream, whipped

Preheat the oven to 425°F. Line a pie pan with the rolled-out dough, then prick all over with a fork and press a piece of heavy-duty foil snugly into the shell. Bake for 6 minutes, then remove the foil and bake for 4 minutes more, until the shell is just beginning to color. Remove from the oven and prepare the filling. Reduce the heat to 350°F. Put the eggs in a bowl and beat with a fork until the yolks and whites are blended. Add the sugar, cornmeal, and vinegar, and stir only enough to incorporate them. Stir in the butter and vanilla. Pour the mixture into the pie shell and bake at 350°F for about 45 minutes, until the top has browned and the filling has set. The pie will puff during baking, but will sink as it cools. Serve slightly warm (or at room temperature, but not chilled!), with a dollop of unsweetened whipped cream.

RAISIN PIE

Fill a child's hands with raisins or, better still, put the raisins in a pie faintly flavored with lemon and orange. This old-fashioned recipe will please grownups, too.

1 cup orange juice	1½ cups sugar
1 cup water	4 tablespoons flour
2 cups raisins	3 tablespoons lemon juice
Basic Pastry dough for 9-inch two-crust pie (p. 895)	⅛ teaspoon salt

Put the orange juice and water in a pan and bring to a boil. Remove from the heat and stir in the raisins. Let stand for 2 hours. Preheat the oven to 425°F. Line a pie pan with half the pastry dough. Add the sugar, flour, lemon juice, and salt to the raisin mixture. Cook over low heat, stirring frequently, for about 10 minutes or until well thickened. Pile the filling into the lined pie pan. Roll out the remaining dough and make a lattice top. Crimp the edges. Bake for 10 minutes, then lower the heat to 350°F and bake about 35 minutes longer, until the top is browned.

(9-INCH PIE)   **APPLE-CRANBERRY-RAISIN PIE**

Basic Pastry dough for 9-inch   1 cup cranberries
   two-crust pie (p. 895)   ½ cup raisins
1 cup sugar ·   Grated rind of 1 lemon
½ teaspoon salt   5 large tart apples
3 tablespoons flour   2 tablespoons butter

Preheat the oven to 425°F. Line a pie pan with half the pastry dough. Stir the sugar, salt, and flour together in a large bowl. Add the cranberries, raisins, and lemon rind. Peel, core, and slice the apples and toss them in the sugar mixture. Pile the filling into the lined pie pan and dot with the butter. Roll out the top crust and drape it over the pie. Crimp the edges together and cut several small vents in the top. Bake for 10 minutes, then lower the heat to 350°F and continue baking for 30–40 minutes or until the apples are tender when pierced with a skewer and the crust is browned.

(9-INCH PIE)   ✳ **CRANBERRY-RAISIN PIE**

Not just another cranberry and raisin pie; this one has been a favorite of mine for many years.

2 cups raisins   1 cup sugar
Basic Pastry dough for 9-inch   ¼ cup Grand Marnier or
   two-crust pie (p. 895)   cream sherry
4 cups fresh cranberries   2 teaspoons orange zest
2 tablespoons flour

Soak the raisins for at least 2 hours in a bowl in water to cover. Drain. Preheat the oven to 400°F. Line a 9-inch pie pan with half the pastry dough. Put the raisins and cranberries in a mixing bowl. Stir the flour into the sugar, mixing well, and sprinkle over the raisin mixture. Add the Grand Marnier or sherry and orange zest and toss all together to mix and coat the fruit thoroughly. Put the filling into the lined pie pan and spread evenly. Roll out the top crust and drape it over the pie. Crimp the edges and cut several vents in the top. Bake at 400°F for 15 minutes, then reduce the heat to 350°F and continue to bake for another 45 minutes, or until the juices bubble and the top is browned.

MINCE PIE

In the first edition Fannie Farmer recommended puff paste for special
Thanksgiving or Christmas mincemeat pies. Try using puff pastry, if
you wish, but Basic Pastry dough makes a splendid mince pie.

Basic Pastry dough for 9-inch   1 pint Mincemeat (following
    two-crust pie (p. 895)   recipes)

Preheat the oven to 425°F. Line a pie pan with half the pastry dough.
Fill the lined pan with the prepared mincemeat. Roll out the remaining
dough and make a top crust or lattice crust. Crimp the edges. Cut
vents if a top crust is used. Bake 10 minutes, then lower the heat to
350°F and bake about 40 minutes more, until the top is lightly
browned. Serve with softly *whipped cream* or *Hard Sauce* (p. 989), if you
wish.

MINCEMEAT I

Mincemeat developed as a way of preserving meat without salting or
smoking it. Traditionally, the minced beef and suet are combined with
fruits, spices, and spirits, packed in jars, and sealed with wax. Make it
well ahead of time: it keeps indefinitely, mellows with age, and is
grand to have on hand as the holiday season approaches.

This is enough mincemeat for ten pies. You can make it in smaller
quantities, if you wish, but before you reduce the recipe, consider the
fine, old-fashioned holiday gifts that jars of homemade mincemeat
make!

4 pounds chopped lean beef   1 quart brandy
2 pounds chopped beef suet   1 tablespoon cinnamon
3 pounds dark-brown sugar   1 tablespoon mace
2 cups molasses   1 tablespoon cloves
2 quarts cider   1 teaspoon nutmeg
3 pounds dried currants   1 teaspoon allspice
4 pounds raisins   2 teaspoons salt
½ pound citron, chopped
3 pounds apples, peeled,
    cored, and sliced

Put the beef, suet, brown sugar, molasses, cider, currants, raisins, and
citron in a large pot. Cook slowly, stirring occasionally, until the sugar
and citron melt. Add the apples and cook until tender. Add the remaining ingredients and cook 15 minutes more, stirring frequently.
Spoon into clean, hot jars, leaving 1-inch headspace. Close the jars and

process at 10 pounds pressure for 20 minutes. You can then store the mincemeat indefinitely. If you do not want to process it, it is safer to refrigerate.

(4 PINTS)   **MINCEMEAT II**

This recipe for meatless mincemeat will provide enough filling for four 8- or 9-inch pies.

1 pound suet, ground	4 ounces citron, diced
1½ pounds apples, peeled, cored, and chopped	Grated rind of 2 lemons
	Juice of 3 lemons
1½ cups dark-brown sugar	1 teaspoon cinnamon
1 pound dried currants	½ teaspoon nutmeg
1 pound golden raisins	½ teaspoon mace
1 pound raisins	1 teaspoon allspice
4 ounces candied lemon peel, diced	1 cup brandy
4 ounces candied orange peel, diced	

Put all the ingredients in a large bowl and mix with your hands until well blended. Pack into sterilized jars and seal. Store in a cool place. It is not necessary to process this mincemeat because it doesn't contain fresh meat, but if you feel more comfortable about it, follow the directions for processing in the preceding recipe.

(9-INCH TART)   **MINCEMEAT TART**

Fill a prebaked tart shell with this simple, meatless "mincemeat" mixture for a quick, easy, delicious version of mincemeat pie.

Tart Pastry dough for 9-inch tart (p. 897)	½ cup cider vinegar
1½ cups raisins	1½ cups dark-brown sugar
4 tart apples, peeled and cored	½ teaspoon salt
½ orange, including rind	½ teaspoon cinnamon
½ lemon, including rind	½ teaspoon nutmeg
	½ teaspoon cloves

Topping

1½ cups heavy cream
3 tablespoons confectioners' sugar

Preheat the oven to 425°F. Line a pie pan or springform pan with the pastry dough. Prick the dough all over and bake for 10–15 minutes, until lightly browned. Chop the raisins, apples, orange, and lemon coarsely. Add the vinegar and heat to the boiling point, then reduce the heat and simmer for 10 minutes. Add the sugar, salt, cinnamon, nutmeg, and cloves and simmer 15 minutes more. Let cool. Before serving, fill the tart with the cooled mincemeat. Whip the cream, sweetening it with the sugar, and spread over the mincemeat filling.

PUMPKIN PIE   (9-INCH OPEN PIE)

A really good pumpkin pie that deservedly goes with Thanksgiving.

Basic Pastry dough for 9-inch pie shell (p. 895)	1½ cups cooked (p. 604) or canned (unseasoned) pumpkin, mashed or puréed
1 cup sugar	
½ teaspoon salt	
1½ teaspoons cinnamon	1½ cups evaporated milk
½ teaspoon ground ginger	½ cup milk
½ teaspoon cloves	2 eggs, slightly beaten

Preheat the oven to 425°F. Line a pie pan with the pastry dough. Combine the remaining ingredients in a large bowl and beat until smooth. Pour into the lined pie pan. Bake for 10 minutes, then lower the heat to 300°F and bake for about 45 minutes or until the filling is firm.

SWEET POTATO PIE   (9-INCH OPEN PIE)

Long ago the sweet potato was called a "long potato" or "Virginia potato." Southern states take pride in this very American pie.

Tart Pastry dough for 9-inch tart (p. 897)	¾ cup sugar
	½ teaspoon salt
2 cups mashed cooked sweet potatoes	½ teaspoon cinnamon
	½ teaspoon nutmeg
2 eggs, well beaten	2 tablespoons rum
1¼ cups milk	4 tablespoons butter, melted

Preheat the oven to 425°F. Line a 9-inch pie pan with the pastry dough. Combine the remaining ingredients in a large bowl and beat until smooth and well blended. Pour into the lined pan. Bake for 10 minutes, then reduce the heat to 300°F and bake for about 50 minutes more or until the filling is firm.

(9-INCH OPEN PIE)   **RICH SQUASH PIE**

Basic Pastry dough for 9-inch   3 tablespoons brandy
   pie shell (p. 895)   1 teaspoon cinnamon
1 cup puréed cooked winter   1 teaspoon nutmeg
   squash   ½ teaspoon ground ginger
1 cup heavy cream   ½ teaspoon salt
1 cup sugar   ¼ teaspoon mace
3 eggs, slightly beaten

Preheat the oven to 425°F. Line a pie pan with the pastry dough. Combine the remaining ingredients in a large bowl and beat until smooth and well blended. Pour into the lined pie pan. Bake for 10 minutes, then reduce the heat to 300°F and bake for 45–60 minutes more or until the filling is firm.

(10-INCH OPEN PIE)   **PARSNIP PIE**

Even if you've been prejudiced about parsnips since childhood, you should try this surprisingly delicious pie with a tantalizing flavor that most people are hard put to identify. Proportions are large because it is worth serving at a dinner party or a holiday feast.

1 recipe Basic Pastry using 2   2 tablespoons orange rind
   cups flour (p. 895)   2 eggs, lightly beaten
3 cups puréed plain parsnips,   ½ teaspoon cinnamon
   unseasoned (p. 585)   ½ teaspoon mace
2 tablespoons butter, softened   ¼ teaspoon allspice
½ cup plus 2 tablespoons   ¼ teaspoon cloves
   honey   1 teaspoon fresh lemon juice

Preheat the oven to 425°F. Line a pie pan with the pastry dough. Beat all the other ingredients together until smooth, reserving the 2 additional tablespoons of honey. Prick the bottom of the pastry dough all over and bake for 5 minutes. Pour the parsnip filling into the partially baked shell and drizzle the remaining honey over the top. Lower the heat to 375°F. Bake 50–60 minutes or until the filling is firm in the center. Serve with a pitcher of *heavy cream* or a bowl of *lightly whipped cream* after the pie has cooled to room temperature.

LEMON CRUMB PIE   (9-INCH OPEN PIE)

Crumb Crust for 9-inch pie
  shell (p. 899), using vanilla
  wafers
3 eggs, separated
Grated rind and juice of 2
  lemons

14-ounce can sweetened
  condensed milk
⅛ teaspoon salt

Preheat the oven to 325°F. Line a pie pan with the crumb crust mixture, reserving ¼ cup of the crumbs for the top. Refrigerate. Beat the egg yolks until they are thick and pale. Stir in the grated lemon rind, juice, milk, and salt. Beat the egg whites until stiff but not dry and fold them into the yolk mixture. Pour into the lined pie pan. Sprinkle the reserved crumbs on top and bake for 40 minutes.

LEMON MERINGUE PIE   (9-INCH OPEN PIE)

A classic filling for a prebaked pie shell.

Basic Pastry dough for 9-inch
  pie shell (p. 895)
4 tablespoons cornstarch
4 tablespoons flour
¼ teaspoon salt
1¼ cups sugar
1½ cups water

Grated rind of 1 lemon
½ cup lemon juice
2 tablespoons butter
4 egg yolks, slightly beaten
Meringue Topping for 9-inch
  pie (p. 900)

Preheat the oven to 425°F. Line a pie pan with the pastry dough, prick the dough all over, and bake for 16–18 minutes, until lightly browned. Mix the cornstarch, flour, salt, sugar, and water in a saucepan. Cook over medium-high heat, stirring constantly, until thickened, about 3 minutes. Remove from the heat. Stir in the lemon rind, lemon juice, and butter. Stir ½ cup of the hot mixture into the egg yolks, then stir the yolks into the remaining hot mixture and cook, stirring, for another 3 minutes. Let cool a bit. Spread the lemon mixture in the baked pie shell and cover with the meringue. Run under the broiler until the meringue peaks are delicately browned, taking care not to burn them. This particular meringue will hold up as long as two days without weeping and shrinking. Refrigerate for storage, but serve at room temperature.

NOTE
see page 471

(8-INCH PIE)   **❋ SHAKER LEMON PIE**

2 large lemons   4 eggs, well beaten
2 cups sugar
Basic Pastry dough for 8-inch
    two-crust pie (p. 895)

Slice the lemons very thin, leaving the rind on, and remove seeds. In a
bowl, mix together thoroughly the lemon slices and sugar. Let stand
for at least 3 hours, stirring occasionally. Overnight is best; the longer
the mixture stands the softer the rind becomes. Preheat the oven to
450°F. Line a pie pan with half of the pastry dough. Stir the beaten
eggs into the lemon mixture and pour into the pie shell. Roll out the
top crust and drape it over the pie. Crimp the edges together and cut
several vents in the top. Bake for 15 minutes at 450°F, then reduce the
heat to 375°F and bake for about 20 minutes more, or until a knife
comes out clean when inserted in the center.

(8-INCH OPEN PIE)   **BUTTERSCOTCH PIE**

A butterscotch custard, covered with soft whipped cream—most children love this pie.

Tart Pastry for 8-inch tart (p.   5 tablespoons flour
    897)   ¼ teaspoon salt
4 tablespoons butter   2 eggs, slightly beaten
¾ cup dark-brown sugar   ¼ teaspoon vanilla
2 cups milk

Topping

1 cup heavy cream   Sugar

Preheat the oven to 425°F. Line a pie pan with the pastry dough, prick
the dough all over, and bake for 12 minutes, until lightly browned. Put
the butter and brown sugar in a sturdy pan and cook over medium
heat for 2 minutes or until the mixture is brown and syrupy. Add 1⅔
cups of the milk, stir, and cook until very hot. Blend the flour, salt, and
the remaining ⅓ cup of milk together in a small bowl until smooth.
Add to the hot mixture and cook, stirring frequently, for 15 minutes.
Stir some of the hot mixture into the beaten eggs, then return egg mixture to the pan. Cook, stirring, for 2 minutes. Cool. Add the vanilla,
spread in the baked pie shell, and chill. Before serving, whip the
cream, sweetening slightly, and spread it over the pie filling.

KEY LIME PIE   (9-INCH OPEN PIE)

Florida produces our key limes, which are Mexican in origin. They are smaller, rounder, and more acid than the common Persian lime we find in most of our markets. Either variety works well.

Basic Pastry dough for 9-inch
  pie shell (p. 895)
5 egg yolks
14-ounce can sweetened
  condensed milk
6–8 tablespoons lime juice, or
  more

1 cup heavy cream
3 tablespoons confectioners'
  sugar
Grated rind of 1 lime (green
  part, or zest, only)

Preheat the oven to 425°F. Line a pie pan with the pastry dough, prick it all over with a fork, then press a piece of heavy-duty foil snugly into the pie shell. Bake for 6 minutes, remove the foil, and bake for about 4 minutes more, until just beginning to color. Remove the pie shell from the oven. Reduce the heat to 350°F. Put the yolks in a large bowl and beat them with a whisk, just breaking them and mixing them well. Slowly stir in the sweetened condensed milk. Mixing well, stir in the lime juice. The filling should be tart; if it isn't pleasantly tangy, add more lime juice. Pour the filling into the pie shell. Bake at 350°F for 12–15 minutes. Remove and cool. Whip the cream, slowly adding the confectioners' sugar. Spread over the pie and sprinkle the lime rind over. Serve at room temperature, but refrigerate if not serving within 3 hours.

ORANGE MERINGUE PIE   (8-INCH OPEN PIE)

This pie has a thin layer of filling much like a tart.

Basic Pastry dough for 8-inch
  pie shell (p. 895)
4 eggs, separated
½ cup plus 1 tablespoon sugar
3 tablespoons flour
1 cup orange juice

1 tablespoon grated orange
  rind
Juice of 1 lemon
2 tablespoons butter
Meringue Topping for 8-inch
  pie (p. 900)

Preheat the oven to 425°F. Line a pie pan with the pastry dough, prick the dough all over, and bake for 16–18 minutes, until lightly browned. Beat the egg yolks until they are thick and pale. Mix the sugar, flour, orange juice, orange rind, lemon juice, and butter together in a small pot. Add the egg yolks and cook over moderate heat, stirring constantly, until thick, about 5 minutes. Let cool. Spread the cooled mixture in the baked pie shell. Cover with meringue topping and run under the broiler until the meringue peaks are delicately browned, taking care not to burn them. Try not to do the meringue too far ahead.

PINEAPPLE WITH LEMON PIE

(ONE 9-INCH LATTICE-TOP PIE)

A not-too-sweet pie, combining pineapple with the keen tartness of lemon. It is not entirely open-face; a lattice top finishes it off nicely.

Basic Pastry dough for a 9-inch two-crust pie (p. 895)	2 teaspoons grated lemon rind (yellow part, or zest, only)
2 eggs	
6 tablespoons sugar	1-pound 4-ounce can unsweetened pineapple chunks, drained and in small pieces
2 tablespoons flour	
⅛ teaspoon salt	
2 tablespoons lemon juice	

Preheat the oven to 375°F. Line a pie pan with half the rolled-out dough, then roll out the remaining dough as for a top crust and cut strips for the lattice top. Combine the eggs, sugar, flour, salt, lemon juice, and lemon rind in a mixing bowl, and beat until the mixture is well blended. Stir in the pineapple. Spread the filling in the unbaked pie shell. Make a lattice top (p. 892); trim and crimp the edges. Bake for about 40 minutes or until the filling is set and the crust is lightly browned.

BANANA CUSTARD PIE

(9-INCH OPEN PIE)

Nourishing, wholesome, and very pleasant to eat. The crisp, prebaked tart shell may be prepared in advance.

Tart Pastry dough for 9-inch tart (p. 897)	2 cups milk
⅔ cup sugar	2 teaspoons vanilla
3 tablespoons flour	1½ tablespoons butter, melted
¼ teaspoon salt	2 bananas, sliced
4 eggs, separated	Meringue Topping for 9-inch pie (p. 900)

Preheat the oven to 425°F. Line a pie pan with the pastry dough, prick the dough all over, and bake for 16–18 minutes, until lightly browned. Combine the sugar, flour, salt, and lightly beaten egg yolks in a bowl. (Reserve the whites for the Meringue Topping.) Scald the milk in a pan and slowly add it to the egg mixture, stirring constantly. Pour back into the pan and cook over moderate heat, stirring constantly, until thickened. Remove from the heat and pour into a bowl. Stir in the vanilla. Spread melted butter with a knife over the top of the custard to prevent a skin from forming. Cover and chill. Shortly before serving, cover the bottom of the baked pie shell with the sliced bananas. Add the chilled custard, spreading it evenly with a spatula. Cover with the meringue and run under the broiler until the meringue peaks are delicately browned, taking care not to burn them.

SLIPPED CUSTARD PIE (9-INCH OPEN PIE)

This pie is a dandy, sitting smugly on its crisp prebaked crust. An easy, old-fashioned method keeps the piecrust flaky and the custard silken: they meet just before they are served.

Basic Pastry dough for 9-inch pie shell (p. 895)	2½ cups milk, scalded
½ cup sugar	1½ teaspoons vanilla
¼ teaspoon salt	4 eggs, slightly beaten

Preheat the oven to 425°F. Line a pie pan with the pastry dough, prick the dough all over, and bake for 16–18 minutes, until lightly browned. Set aside. Reduce the oven heat to 350°F. Combine the sugar, salt, milk, and vanilla, add the eggs, and mix well. Pour into a buttered 9-inch pie pan the *same size and shape* as the baked pie shell. Set the pan in a larger pan filled with ½ inch hot water. Bake about 35 minutes or until the custard is barely set; overbaking will make it watery. Remove from the oven and cool; refrigerate if the custard is not to be served within a couple of hours. Assemble the pie as close to serving time as possible: loosen the edge of the custard with a sharp knife, shaking gently to free the bottom; hold over the pie shell and ease the filling gently into the shell, shaking it a bit if necessary to make it settle into place.

COCONUT CUSTARD PIE

Add 1 *cup grated coconut* to the custard before baking.

CREAM PIE (9-INCH OPEN PIE)

Fill prebaked pie shells with cream filling as close to serving time as possible so that they do not get soggy.

Tart Pastry dough for 9-inch
    tart (p. 897)
¾ cup sugar
½ cup flour
¼ teaspoon salt

3 cups milk
3 egg yolks, slightly beaten
2 tablespoons butter
1 teaspoon vanilla

Preheat the oven to 425°F. Line a pie pan with the pastry dough, prick
the dough all over, and bake for 12 minutes until lightly browned. Set
aside. Combine the sugar, flour, and salt in a saucepan. Stir in the milk
and cook over low heat, stirring constantly, until thick. Add the egg
yolks and continue to cook, stirring, for about 3 minutes. Remove from
the heat and blend in the butter and vanilla. Let the custard cool for
about 15 minutes, then pour it into the pie shell and refrigerate until
ready to serve.

CHOCOLATE CREAM PIE

Before adding the milk, heat it with *2 ounces unsweetened chocolate*, stirring until the milk and chocolate are smoothly blended.

COCONUT CREAM PIE

Add *½ cup shredded coconut* together with the butter and vanilla. Sprinkle the top of the pie with *5 tablespoons shredded coconut*.

BANANA CREAM PIE

Peel and slice *2 ripe bananas* and arrange over the top of the finished pie
shortly before serving.

(9-INCH OPEN PIE)   ## CHOCOLATE CHIFFON PIE

Crumb Crust (p. 899) or
    Chocolate Coconut Crust
    (p. 899)
1½ cups cold milk
1 envelope gelatin

½ cup sugar
⅛ teaspoon salt
4 eggs, separated
6 tablespoons unsweetened
    cocoa

Preheat the oven to 350°F. Pat the crumb mixture into a pie pan and bake for 8–10 minutes; set aside. Put the milk in a saucepan, sprinkle the gelatin over it, and let it soften for about 3 minutes. Stir in the sugar, salt, and egg yolks and beat thoroughly. Cook, stirring, over moderate heat until thickened; do not boil. Add the cocoa and stir until dissolved. Chill just until the mixture mounds when dropped from a spoon. Beat the egg whites until they are stiff but not dry. Fold them into the gelatin mixture. Spoon into the pie shell and chill until ready to serve.

COFFEE CHIFFON PIE

Substitute 2 *tablespoons instant coffee* for the cocoa.

EGGNOG CHIFFON PIE

Substitute 3 *tablespoons rum* for the cocoa. Top the finished pie with a thin layer of *whipped cream* and sprinkle with *nutmeg*.

STRAWBERRY CHIFFON PIE   (9-INCH OPEN PIE)

Crumb Crust for 9-inch pie
  shell (p. 899)
1 pint strawberries
¾ cup sugar
1 envelope gelatin

¾ cup cold water
1 tablespoon lemon juice
⅛ teaspoon salt
2 egg whites

Preheat the oven to 350°F. Pat the crumb mixture into a pie pan and bake for 8–10 minutes; set aside. Reserve 6 whole strawberries for a garnish, then slice the rest and toss them in ½ cup of the sugar. Sprinkle the gelatin over the water and let it soften for about 3 minutes. Add the lemon juice, salt, and remaining ¼ cup sugar. Cook over moderate heat, stirring, until the gelatin dissolves; do not let the mixture boil. Cool a little, then stir in the sliced strawberries. Chill until the mixture mounds when dropped from a spoon. Beat the egg whites until stiff but not dry and fold them into the strawberry mixture. Spoon into the baked pie shell, garnish with the whole strawberries, and chill until ready to serve.

(9-INCH OPEN PIE)   **✳ LEMON CHIFFON PIE**

Crumb Crust for 9-inch pie   1 cup sugar
   shell (p. 899), using   ⅛ teaspoon salt
   graham crackers   1 teaspoon grated lemon rind
¼ cup cold water   ½ cup lemon juice
1 envelope gelatin   4 eggs, separated

Preheat the oven to 350°F. Pat the crumb mixture into a pie pan and
bake for 8–10 minutes; set aside. Put the cold water in a saucepan,
sprinkle the gelatin on top, and let it soften for about 3 minutes. Stir in
½ cup of the sugar and the salt, lemon rind, and lemon juice. Add the

NOTE
see page 471

egg yolks and stir vigorously until well blended. Cook,
stirring, over moderate heat until the gelatin has dissolved; do not allow to boil. Chill until the mixture
mounds when dropped from a spoon. Beat the egg whites
until they are foamy, then gradually add the remaining ½ cup of sugar,
continuing to beat until smooth and shiny. Fold the whites into
the lemon mixture, spread in the pie shell, and chill until ready to
serve.

LIME CHIFFON PIE

Using gingersnap crumbs in the crust substitute *1 teaspoon grated lime
rind* and *½ cup lime juice* for the lemon rind and juice.

ORANGE CHIFFON PIE

Using vanilla wafers in the crust substitute *1 teaspoon grated orange rind*
and *½ cup orange juice plus 2 tablespoons lemon juice* for the lemon rind
and juice.

BLACK-BOTTOM PIE   (9-INCH OPEN PIE)

Crumb Crust for 9-inch pie
   shell (p. 899), using
   chocolate wafers
1½ cups cold milk
1 envelope gelatin
½ cup sugar
⅛ teaspoon salt

4 eggs, separated
1½ ounces unsweetened
   chocolate, melted
1 teaspoon vanilla
1 tablespoon rum
½ cup heavy cream

NOTE
see page 471

Preheat the oven to 350°F. Pat the crumb mixture into a pie pan and bake for 8–10 minutes; set aside. Put the milk in a saucepan, sprinkle in the gelatin, and let it soften for about 3 minutes. Stir in the sugar, salt, and egg yolks and beat to blend thoroughly. Cook over moderate heat, stirring, until thickened; do not let the mixture boil. Remove from the heat and divide in half. Add the melted chocolate and the vanilla to one half and the rum to the other. Chill until the mixtures mound when dropped from a spoon. Beat the egg whites until stiff but not dry. Divide the beaten whites in half. Fold half into the chocolate mixture and the other half into the rum mixture. Spread the chocolate mixture over the crumb crust, then spread the rum mixture over the chocolate mixture. Whip the cream and spread that over all. Refrigerate until ready to serve.

ANGEL PIE *   (9-INCH OPEN PIE)

This angel pie has a crunchy, light-golden meringue crust filled with lemon custard, covered with clouds of sweetened whipped cream, and garnished with fresh strawberries. Meringues are temperamental: it's better to make them on a cool, dry day than a warm, humid one. Don't be alarmed when the crust collapses a bit and cracks as it cools. This is as it should be—the cracks won't show once it's filled.

4 eggs, separated and at room
   temperature
⅛ teaspoon salt
¼ teaspoon cream of tartar
1½ cups granulated sugar

¼ cup lemon juice
1½ cups heavy cream
⅓ cup confectioners' sugar
8 whole strawberries

Preheat the oven to 275°F. Butter a pie pan. Combine the egg whites, salt, and cream of tartar in a large mixing bowl. Beat with an electric beater until soft peaks form. Slowly add 1 cup of the granulated sugar and beat until shiny peaks form. Spread the mixture over the bottom of the pie pan and build it up around the rim about 1 inch higher than the edge of the pan. Bake for about 1 hour or until lightly brown and firm to the touch. Turn off the heat and let cool in the oven with the door open. While the crust is cooling, beat the egg yolks until they are thick and pale. Slowly beat in the remaining ½ cup of the granulated sugar. Add the lemon juice. Cook over moderate heat, stirring constantly, until the mixture thickens. Cool. Spread in the meringue shell. Shortly before serving, whip the cream, slowly adding the confectioners' sugar until it holds soft peaks. Spoon the cream over the top and decorate with the strawberries. Refrigerate until ready to serve.

SMALL TARTS

Tarts are open pies—filled pastry shells without a top crust. Made with strong, buttery tart pastry, both small and large tarts are often freestanding, needing no pans to support their crisp, golden sides after they are baked. Small tarts are easy to serve and tidy to eat, conveniences you'll appreciate when you have a large group of guests. And they look so enchanting, filled with a variety of different sweets and set out on a large platter.

Making small tarts is a fine way to use up leftover pie dough or tart pastry. Even if you have only a little bit of leftover dough, it's often nice to have a few tarts on hand. Or wrap and freeze bits and scraps of leftover dough until you have enough for a big batch of tarts. If you have tart tins, line them with the dough and then freeze them; it's very handy to have some small tarts in the freezer, ready to bake at a moment's notice.

The most common small tart tin is 4 inches in diameter and 1 inch deep, holding ½ cup of filling. If you don't have small tart tins, invert a muffin tin and pat the pastry dough over the bottoms of the inverted cups and about an inch up the sides. Bake, then let the pastry cool a bit before easing the baked tarts from the tins.

LEMON TARTS   (6 SMALL TARTS)

Tart Pastry dough for 9-inch   Grated rind of 2 lemons
   tart (p. 897)   Juice of 3 lemons
¼ pound butter   6 eggs, slightly beaten
1½ cups sugar

Topping

1 cup heavy cream, whipped

Preheat the oven to 375°F. Line six 4-inch tart tins with the pastry
dough, prick the bottoms, and bake for about 10 minutes or until the
pastry is golden. Cool and remove from the tins. Mix the butter, sugar,
lemon rind, lemon juice, and eggs together in a heavy-bottomed pan or
double boiler. Cook over moderate heat, stirring constantly, until thick.
Cool in the refrigerator. Before serving, fill the tart shells with lemon
filling and top with whipped cream.

FRUIT OR BERRY TARTS   (6 SMALL TARTS)

Tart Pastry dough for 9-inch   1½ cups currant jelly, or 1 cup
   tart (p. 897)   heavy cream, whipped
3 cups drained cooked fruit or   with some sugar
   fresh berries, sugared

Preheat the oven to 375°F. Line six 4-inch tart tins with the pastry
dough, prick the bottoms, and bake for about 10 minutes, or until the
pastry is golden. Cool and remove from the tins. Just before serving,
fill each baked tart shell with ½ cup fruit or berries. Melt the currant
jelly in a pan over low heat and pour it over the fruit to glaze. Or top
each tart with sweetened whipped cream.

PECAN TARTS   (6 SMALL TARTS)

dough for 9-inch   1 cup dark corn syrup
                        ½ teaspoon vanilla
                        2 tablespoons butter, melted
                        1 cup pecan pieces

Topping

1 cup heavy cream, whipped   Sugar

Preheat the oven to 375°F. Line six 4-inch tart tins with the pastry dough; set aside. Beat the eggs in a bowl for a minute or less, then add the brown sugar, salt, corn syrup, vanilla, and melted butter. Stir vigorously, then add the pecans. Pour filling into tarts. Bake for 25 minutes or until the filling is set. Before serving, top with whipped cream lightly sweetened with sugar.

(24 SMALL TARTS)   **RAISIN TARTS**

Basic Pastry dough for 8-inch   2 tablespoons butter, melted
  two-crust pie (p. 895)   1 tablespoon grated orange
¾ cup raisins   peel
2 tablespoons chopped citron   ¼ cup dark-brown sugar
3 tablespoons honey   Milk

Preheat the oven to 450°F. Roll the pastry dough very thin. Cut 2½-inch rounds, 48 in all. Mix the raisins, citron, honey, butter, orange peel, and brown sugar in a bowl. Place a rounded teaspoonful in the center of half the pastry rounds. Moisten the edges with milk and place an unfilled round on top of each filled one. Seal the edges with the tines of a fork and prick the top. Bake 10–15 minutes or until golden.

(12 SMALL TARTS)   **BANBURY TARTS**

Banbury tarts come from Banbury, England, where street vendors sold them steaming hot from flannel-lined baskets.

Basic Pastry dough for 8-inch   1 egg, slightly beaten
  two-crust pie (p. 895)   1 tablespoon cracker crumbs
1 cup raisins   Grated rind and juice of 1
1 cup sugar   lemon

Preheat the oven to 350°F. Roll the dough out ⅛ inch thick and cut it in 3 × 3½-inch pieces. Mix the raisins, sugar, egg, cracker crumbs, lemon rind and juice together in a bowl and toss until well mixed. Put about 2 teaspoonfuls on one half of each piece of pastry. Moisten the edges with cold water, fold in half into little triangles, and press the edges together with a fork dipped in flour. Prick the tops. Bake on an ungreased cookie sheet for about 20 minutes.

CREAM PUFFS   (FOURTEEN 2-INCH PUFFS)

Cream puffs are versatile. In addition to the charming sweet described below, the puffs may be filled with cold mixed seafood, flavored cream cheese, or chicken salad. You can make tiny puffs, fill them with a variety of fillings, and use them as appetizers.

It is best to assemble cream puffs as close to serving time as possible, since the pastry will remain crisper if it is not refrigerated. Make the filling ahead and keep it refrigerated until you are ready to assemble the puffs.

½ cup water	½ cup flour
4 tablespoons butter	2 eggs, at room temperature

Preheat the oven to 375°F. Combine the water and butter in a saucepan and bring to a boil. Remove from the heat and add the flour all at once, stirring vigorously with a wooden spoon. Return to moderate heat and stir constantly until the dough leaves the sides of the pan and forms a ball. Remove from the heat and let cool for about 5 minutes. Add the eggs, one at a time, beating hard until the dough is smooth. Place large, rounded tablespoons of dough on an ungreased cookie sheet, 2 inches apart. Bake for 30 minutes or until the puffs are golden. Carefully slice the tops off the puffs and scoop out the centers. Cool on a rack. Fill with *Basic Cream Filling* (p. 847). Replace the tops and cover them with *Chocolate Frosting for Cream Puffs and Éclairs* (p. 839).

ÉCLAIRS   (8 ÉCLAIRS)

Prepare 1 recipe Cream Puff dough. Put the dough in a pastry bag and pipe onto an ungreased cookie sheet in strips about 4½ inches long and 1 inch wide. Bake as above. Carefully split the éclairs lengthwise and cool them on a rack. Scoop out the insides and fill with *Basic Cream*

Filling (p. 847) or with *sweetened whipped cream*. Replace the top halves and ice with *Chocolate Frosting for Cream Puffs and Éclairs* (p. 839).

PUFF PASTRY

Puff pastry, basic to French cuisine, has been popular in this country for a long time. The first edition of this book gave instructions for making it, cautioning the novice baker to "work rapidly and with a light touch"—there were no refrigerators then to chill the dough and let it rest between rollings-out.

Sometimes referred to as the "pastry of a thousand leaves," its many buttery, crisp layers, light enough to be all but airborne, are a flaky miracle of levitation. It is often used to make small patty shells which can lift meat, fish, or cheese mixtures to glorious heights or present delectable frames for custards, creams, and fruits. It is well worth learning to make puff pastry, if only for the confidence it inspires.

Puff pastry, like many marriages, unites separate identities in a compatible relationship, in this case between the butter and the dough. Both should have approximately the same consistency and temperature: adding a small amount of butter to the dough and a small amount of flour to the butter helps to achieve this.

The process of rolling, folding, and turning creates hundreds of alternating sheets of butter and dough. The heat of the oven melts the butter and creates steam which puffs the dough into light, flaky layers. Keeping this in mind will encourage you to roll it out lightly: you do not want to smear the butter into the flour.

Don't try to make puff pastry when the temperature in your kitchen is over 75°F. The dough must be somewhat chilled before you begin rolling it out—but don't let it get too cold. By the same token the butter shouldn't get too cold or you won't be able to pat it into the dough.

While rolling the dough, lift and move it constantly so it doesn't stick to the surface. Dust the working surface lightly with flour as needed. Brush off any excess flour before folding the dough. If it sticks or some butter shows through, lightly dust the spot with flour.

It is important to let the dough relax and cool in the refrigerator between each rolling-out, so that it will lose some of its elasticity and firm up. Moreover, while you are rolling it out, if it ever becomes too warm and smeary, stop right away and just fold it up in thirds, envelope-fashion, wrap it in foil or plastic, and return it to the refrigerator. If it is ever too cold when you take it out, leave it at room temperature a few minutes and, if necessary, give it a few whacks with the rolling pin in different places to loosen up the chilled butter inside.

All this sounds very complicated but as soon as you actually make the puff pastry, adhering carefully to the directions in the recipe that follows, you will find it surprisingly easy.

BASIC PUFF PASTRY

2 cups all-purpose white flour   ½ teaspoon salt
½ pound unsalted butter   ½ cup water

Put 1¾ cups of the flour, 4 tablespoons of the butter, salt, and water into a bowl—the bowl of your electric mixer, if you have one. Beat with an electric hand-held beater or your mixer for 4 minutes at medium speed. Shape the dough into a ball, wrap in foil or wax paper, and refrigerate for 15 minutes. Put the remaining butter in the mixer bowl with the remaining ¼ cup of flour and beat until the butter and flour are blended and smooth. If the butter feels too soft and smeary, refrigerate it for about 5 minutes: the dough and the butter must be at about the same temperature. Roll the dough into a 12-inch circle. Pat the butter into a 4-inch square in the center of the dough. Fold the dough over the butter making a plump, square package. Place, folded sides down, on a lightly floured board. Roll out into a rectangle about 6–8 inches wide and 14–18 inches long, then fold the dough into thirds like an envelope. This rolling out and folding is known as the first "turn." With the narrow end of the "envelope" facing you, roll the dough into another rectangle the same size as the first and then fold that rectangle into thirds once again—the second "turn." Make two indentations in

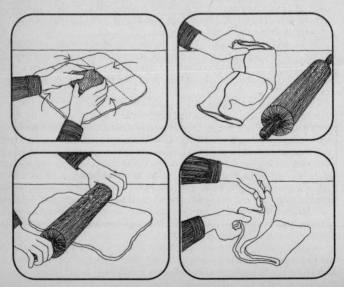

the dough with your fingers to remind you it has had two "turns." Let the dough chill in the refrigerator for about 45 minutes. Take it out of the refrigerator and give it two more "turns," then refrigerate again for 45 minutes. Altogether the dough should have six "turns." After the sixth, fold it again in an envelope form, wrap it in foil or plastic, and refrigerate for at least 1 hour before preparing it for baking. If you want to freeze puff pastry dough for use at another time, wrap it well and freeze it after the fourth "turn." Let it defrost in the refrigerator, then give it the final two "turns" before preparing it for baking.

(6–8 PATTY SHELLS)   **PATTY SHELLS**

Fill these crisp, airy shells with creamed seafood or poultry for a main course, or with glazed fruit, custard, or whipped cream for dessert.

    Basic Puff Pastry (preceding
       recipe)

Preheat the oven to 425°F. Roll the puff pastry dough into a rectangle ¼ inch thick or a little less. Cut it into circles 3 inches in diameter; you will need two circles to make each patty shell. Remove the centers from half the rounds with a small round cutter 2 inches in diameter. Sprinkle a cookie sheet with water and shake off the excess. Place the whole rounds on the cookie sheet and brush the edges of the rounds with water. Place a cut-out ring on top of each round and press gently to seal evenly. Prick the bottom of each unbaked shell in several places with a fork. Bake for 20–25 minutes. Remove from the oven and cool on a rack. Carefully remove uncooked pastry from the center, using a knife or a teaspoon.

NAPOLEONS

(8–10 NAPOLEONS)

Basic Puff Pastry (p. 928)
Basic Cream Filling (p. 847)
Confectioners' Frosting I (p. 837)

1 ounce semisweet chocolate (optional)

Divide the prepared puff pastry dough in half, returning one half to the refrigerator. Preheat the oven to 425°F. Roll out the unrefrigerated half of the dough about ⅛ inch thick into a 6 × 16-inch rectangle. Sprinkle a cookie sheet with water and shake off the excess. Place the dough on the sheet and prick it all over with a fork. Bake for 20–25 minutes. Cool on a rack. Roll and bake the other half of the dough in the same fashion. Carefully cut each pastry rectangle into three long strips, 2 inches wide, and slice each strip in half lengthwise. Spread three of the strips with the cream filling. Make two stacks of strips, two strips high,

with cream filling between each layer and unfrosted strip on top. Frost the top strip with the confectioners' frosting and drizzle warm melted chocolate over the top, making a pattern as indicated in the illustration. Cut into serving portions.

(12 HORNS)   **CREAM HORNS**

Basic Puff Pastry (p. 928)   About 3 cups sweetened
1 egg white   whipped cream
1 teaspoon water

Preheat the oven to 450°F. Roll puff paste into a rectangle about 8 × 10 inches. Cut into twelve 10-inch strips. Roll each strip over a special cone-shaped form, having the edges overlap. Chill 20 minutes. Beat the egg white with the water and brush the mixture over the horns. Place horns on cookie sheet and bake for 8 minutes, then reduce heat to 350°F and bake until lightly golden. Remove from oven, and slip the forms out of the pastry. When cool, fill with *sweetened whipped cream flavored with rum* or *Basic Cream Filling* (p. 847).

PALM COOKIES

A full recipe of Basic Puff Pastry (p. 928) will make 60 cookies, but chances are you'll be making these with leftover pieces of dough, instead. It's a great way to use up the sometimes considerable amounts of puff pastry dough that are left after special shapes are cut.

Puff pastry dough   Sugar

Fit leftover pieces of dough together as best you can, overlapping the edges slightly and then roll out with a rolling pin on a lightly floured board into a rectangle about ⅛ inch thick. Sprinkle the dough heavily with sugar. Fold the long edges of the dough lengthwise to the center. Fold the folded edges lengthwise to meet in the center. Flatten slightly with a rolling pin, then close the halves together as if shutting a book; you will have a long roll. Slice the roll into cookies ⅛ inch thick.

Arrange each cookie on a heavily sugared baking sheet. Chill for 30 minutes. Preheat the oven to 450°F. Bake for about 6 minutes, removing when the sugar has begun to melt and caramelize; turn cookies over and bake another few minutes, taking care that they do not burn. Remove and cool. Palm cookies will keep in an airtight container for about 3 days. They also freeze well.

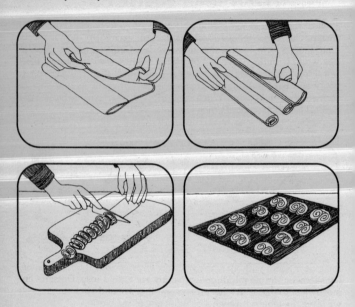

DESSERTS &
DESSERT SAUCES

You'll find all your favorite old-fashioned desserts
here, including a Semolina Pudding that I have redis-
covered, and a fine Steamed Persimmon Pudding that
I consider the best of the steamed puddings. However
did we lose sight of Lemon Curd in the older editions
of *Fannie Farmer*? It's a kitchen treasure with many
uses, and you'll be glad now to have it in your reper-
toire. And there are lots of new ideas for making ice
creams and sorbets plus new sauces to go with them.

ABOUT DESSERTS

Imagine a world without creamy custards, sweet soufflés, rich creams,
icy sherbets, simple puddings—what joy we would lose. Desserts are
mostly just to please. It's not an accident that sweet dishes end a meal;
we leave the table with such a benign view of the world.

It is like unearthing a collection of old treasures to discover the
goodness of the simple desserts that families loved in the last century.
An egg or two, milk, bread, rice or somesuch, a bit of sugar, flavor—
simple combinations of these good things become splendid, wholesome dishes, easy to prepare and more economical and delicious than
commercially packaged desserts.

If you are young and new to cooking, some of these lovely old
dessert names may sound only vaguely familiar to you. Try them anyway, starting with Baked Rice Pudding or Chocolate Bread Pudding—
you will be impressed.

Custards and Puddings

Custards. A custard is a cooked, egg-thickened dessert with eggs, milk, and sugar as its basic ingredients. Baked Custard in simple brown custard cups is one of the most familiar, homy American desserts. Soft Custard, also called "boiled custard," is a thinner, almost runny, custard, often used like a sauce with fruits or other desserts. It is made with whole eggs and usually cooked over very low heat or in the top of a double boiler. English Custard, or Crème Anglaise, is a richer, creamier soft custard, made with egg yolks, rather than whole eggs. It is also used as a sauce and as the base for other desserts, such as Bavarian Cream.

Blancmange. Blancmange is a starch-thickened dessert. Its name comes from the French and means "white food."

Puddings. "Pudding" used to be the general name for most desserts. It now usually refers to a cooked or steamed dessert that has been thickened.

Steamed Puddings

Steamed puddings are cooked by steam slowly. They are sometimes served cold, but we like them best served warm, and usually with a sauce. They make fine winter desserts.

Some steamed puddings are made with ground suet (beef fat), which gives them a rich, distinctive flavor. The suet dissolves during the steaming and moistens the pudding. You can have your own suet on hand if you collect and freeze the fat from various cuts of beef as you use them. When you have enough fat for a pudding, defrost it and grind it, leaving it at room temperature so that it can be creamed and blended with the other ingredients.

Steamed puddings should be made in a well-buttered mold or container. Fill the container no more than two-thirds full to allow room for expansion.

The pudding mold or container must be tightly covered. Use a standard pudding mold with a lid that clamps snugly, or cover a can with a double thickness of foil and tie the foil down securely with string.

Choose a large pot with a cover in which·the pudding mold or container will fit when the pot is tightly covered. Set a canning rack or other rack in the pot to raise the mold so that water can circulate all around it. Or put a Mason jar ring or a hollowed-out ring from a small tuna fish can under the mold to raise it. Add enough water to the pot so that the mold will be covered halfway up its sides. Bring the water to a boil, then place the covered mold on the rack and cover the pot. Lower the heat so that the water boils gently, and cook as directed in the recipe, adding more water if necessary.

Dessert Soufflés

If you want to do a little spellbinding during a meal, include a soufflé in the menu. Simple as they are to prepare, soufflés demand attention. When a soufflé is served, everyone feels that you have done something special.

A true dessert soufflé has a cream-sauce base to which sugar, flavoring, and egg yolks are usually added. This flavored base can be prepared well in advance of serving, even several days ahead if necessary. All that remains to be done before baking is to fold beaten egg whites into the base. A soufflé made with a cream-sauce base will bake in just about the time it takes to eat the main course. Put it in the oven right before you sit down to dinner.

"Fruit soufflés," made with fruit purée, sugar, and egg whites, are really "whips" (see p. 998). The ingredients are folded together and baked into a fluffy froth. More fragile than soufflés with a cream-sauce base, they take only about 20 minutes to bake. To have them ready for dessert, you may have to be absent from the table for a few minutes during the meal.

Follow the same rules about beating and folding egg whites (pp. 473–74) carefully as you would for a savory soufflé.

Butter the soufflé dish amply and sprinkle sugar all over the bottom and the sides. Fill the dish almost to the top.

You can help a soufflé to rise well above the top of the dish by forming a collar as follows: cut a piece of wax paper or foil long enough to encircle the soufflé dish. Fold it in half lengthwise to give it extra strength. Butter the inside of the paper, then wrap it around the dish extending above the top rim, and tie a string around, fastening the top part with Scotch tape or a paper clip. Fill the dish to the top, and the soufflé mixture will rise up inside the collar. When it is done, remove the collar carefully and serve immediately.

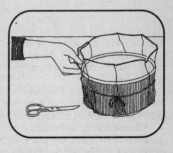

Always bake a soufflé in the oven on a cookie sheet so that the heat is evenly distributed. For our basic two-quart soufflés, bake in a preheated 375°F oven, allowing 25–30 minutes if you wish a moist center, 35–45 minutes if you prefer it somewhat drier.

It is often nice to dust the top of a dessert soufflé with confectioners' sugar before presenting it.

Gelatin Desserts

For instructions on using unflavored gelatin, see Gelatin, p. 17.

Jellies. Lightest of all desserts are the jellies. Unfortunately, they have been replaced in many recipe files by the artificially flavored and colored commercial gelatins that have abounded in the past fifty years or so. Try wine jelly or orange jelly made with freshly squeezed fruit at your next Sunday dinner and you'll see why it's time to bring such old-fashioned jellies back.

Creams. Bavarian cream is English custard with gelatin and whipped cream added. Charlotte Russe is Bavarian cream made in a plain, cylindrical mold which has been lined with sponge cake or ladyfingers.

Using Molds for Chilled or Frozen Desserts. A chilled or frozen dessert often looks nicer when turned out from a nicely shaped mold, rather than being served from a simple bowl. But for many the struggle to remove the dessert from its molded prison is so irritating and the results so likely to be a mess that they avoid it. Unmolding a dessert is really not difficult, however, if you have patience and do not allow yourself to get flustered. Begin by using a sharp knife to loosen the edges of the chilled dessert. Select a pot or pan into which the mold can easily be set, and figure out how much water must be added to cover the mold right up to its rim. Heat the water until it is very hot. Dip the mold in the water for a few seconds, then cover it with a serving platter and turn it over until the dessert loosens. If it doesn't loosen immediately, let it sit for a while. If necessary, you can help it along by covering the mold for a few seconds with a hot, damp towel.

There is a pure-vegetable spray-on coating available now in most supermarkets which is guaranteed to make unmolding easy. Spray the inside of the mold with it generously before you put in the dessert. After the dessert has chilled, turn the mold over onto a serving platter; it should slide out easily and unscarred.

The exception to the unmolding rule comes when you make a chilled "soufflé." Fortified by gelatin and well-beaten egg whites and whipped cream, the soufflé mixture, usually with a puréed fruit or berry base, is poured into a slightly too-small soufflé mold with a collar around it so that when the collar is removed, it stands proudly a couple of inches above the mold just like a beautifully risen soufflé.

Frozen Desserts

Mousses. The word "mousse" is used to describe a variety of desserts, both chilled and frozen, made with any one of a number of combinations of egg yolks, egg whites, cream, gelatin, sugar, and flavorings. Their one consistent feature is a light, airy texture. Early in this century mousses in most cookbooks were all frozen. We give them here, together with an unfrozen, egg-white-lightened chocolate mousse which appears with the custards and puddings.

Parfaits. A parfait is a whipped, frozen dessert, made with Italian meringue, a flavoring, and whipped cream. The flavoring may be vanilla, coffee, maple, a liqueur, or a purée of berries or fruit. Actually, anything served in a parfait glass can be called a "parfait," and in this country we often find a frozen ice cream parfait in tall glasses, made with several flavors of ice cream, sauces, crushed fruit, and other embellishments.

Frozen Soufflés. A frozen soufflé is made of the same mixture of ingredients as a parfait except that it is poured into a soufflé mold with a collar around it, just like the previously mentioned chilled soufflé. It makes a handsome presentation when it comes to the table "risen" above the rim of the mold, particularly if you decorate the top with rosettes of whipped cream, fresh fruit, and maybe even candied violets.

Ice Creams, Sherbets, and Ices

Although ice cream was much in favor among the European nobility of the eighteenth century and was known in this country before President Madison's time, it was Dolley Madison who first made it popular in the United States when she served it to her guests at the White House. Today America produces and consumes more ice cream than any other country in the world; half of it is vanilla.

Making ice cream at home can be an event—an exciting one if everyone participates. You can choose your own flavorings and fresh, wholesome ingredients and the results will be so much better than anything you can buy. Although ice cream will taste the same whether it's made in an electric ice cream maker or a hand-cranked machine, the hand-cranked machine is certainly more fun to use. Even the youngest member of the family can take a turn at cranking, and, of course, in getting that first taste when the dripping dasher is passed around for everyone to lick.

Ice cream is made with cream, sugar, and flavoring; ices with water, sugar, and flavoring, and sherbet with egg white, milk or water, sugar, and flavoring. Gelatin is sometimes used as a stabilizer in ice creams and sherbets.

Making Ice Creams, Sherbets, and Ices. The familiar old-fashioned two-quart ice cream freezer that is hand-cranked and sits inside a wooden pail of ice and rock salt has long been a fixture in many American households, and it is still a splendid way to produce the very best ice cream, particularly if you have those young hands available to help crack the ice and turn the crank. In addition to the electric models in different sizes that work on the same principle as the hand-cranked kind, there is a very simple ice cream maker, called Donvier, with a canister that must go into the freezer for 24 hours; there the ice cream mixer is put in the ice-cold canister and you need turn the paddle only a few times; see manufacturer's directions. With this kind of machine you don't need to pack it in ice and salt; its yield is usually only one quart and the ice cream is good. Try any kind of equipment that will encourage making your own good ice cream! You may have to reduce the proportions in some of the recipes in this chapter, if you have a model that yields only a small amount, but that is a matter of simple arithmetic.

For the old-fashioned ice-packed method, you will need lots of ice—about 20 pounds for the 2-quart model; get it already crushed, if you can. Rock salt is usually recommended at the ratio of 1 part salt to 8 parts ice. But at least one of the new machines we have tried calls for much less ice and recommends that you use cubes straight from the refrigerator, as well as ordinary table salt—and it works beautifully. So be sure to read the manufacturer's instructions. The more salt you use, the faster the ice cream will freeze, but it is *slow* freezing that gives ice cream its velvety texture.

Have the ice cream mixture cold (prepare it a day ahead, if you wish) before pouring it into the freezer can. Fill the container two-thirds to three-quarters full to allow for expansion during freezing. Place the container in the tub or pail. Fit the dasher in place with the crank secure on top.

Fill the tub or pail one-third of the way up with crushed ice, then add the remaining ice and salt in layers until it is slightly above the level of the mixture in the can. Pack the ice down firmly and let it stand for 5 minutes. Or some manufacturers will recommend pouring a glass of ice water over the ice. If you are hand-cranking, slowly begin turning the crank, gradually increasing the speed and replenishing the ice and salt as it melts. When the ice cream is frozen the crank will turn with difficulty; an electric ice cream maker will shut off automatically.

Finished ice cream should be allowed to mellow or ripen for a few hours, if possible, either in the ice cream maker or in the refrigerator freezer. Drain off the water, wipe the lid of the can, remove it, and lift out the dasher. Pack the ice cream down with a spoon, cover the container with a double layer of foil, plug the hole, and replace the lid. Repack the tub or pail with ice and salt, cover with newspapers, and let stand for a few hours. Or simply store the ice cream in a home freezer, if convenient.

Freezing in Refrigerator Trays. Some ice cream, sherbets, and ices can be made and frozen in ice cube trays in the home freezer. A standard ice cube tray will hold one pint of ice cream. You can also freeze ice cream in metal bowls or other metal containers.

If you plan to freeze ice cream in a refrigerator tray, it is better to use only recipes that have been specially adapted to this method, but if you want to modify recipes for refrigerator freezing, keep the proportion of sugar low—not more than one to four—or substitute corn syrup for one-third of the sugar. Beaten egg whites help lighten the mixture.

Dessert Sauces

Dessert sauces, known as "pudding sauces" at the turn of the century, do good things to simple puddings, cooked fruits, and ice creams. It's like a prince marrying a peasant—the peasant becomes royal.

Use a heavy-bottomed pan to cook sauces: it will hold and diffuse the heat evenly and help prevent the scorching and burning that sugar is so inclined to do.

CUSTARDS, PUDDINGS, AND SWEET OMELETS

(2½ CUPS) **SOFT CUSTARD OR BOILED CUSTARD**

Cook this custard over low heat in a heavy-bottomed saucepan or in the top of a double boiler over hot water. Either method requires constant stirring. As thick as whipped cream but heavier, this plain custard is good used like a sauce with fruits and other desserts.

3 eggs	2 cups scalded milk
6 tablespoons sugar	1 teaspoon vanilla
⅛ teaspoon salt	

Put the eggs in a heavy-bottomed pan and whisk just enough to blend. Add the sugar and salt and slowly pour in the hot milk, stirring constantly. Cook over medium heat until the custard coats the spoon, in 7–10 minutes. As soon as you see small bubbles forming around the edge of the pan, remove from the heat quickly; if it boils, the eggs will curdle. Stir in the vanilla, and strain into a bowl or pitcher. Cover and chill. The custard will thicken as it cools.

FLOATING ISLAND

(SERVES SIX)

An ingenious mind conceived this simple, wonderful dessert. All the pieces fit together perfectly, like a puzzle.

2¼ cups milk	5 egg yolks
3 egg whites	2 teaspoons vanilla
1 cup sugar	

Put the milk in a skillet and bring to a simmer over moderately low heat. While the milk is heating, beat the egg whites in a large bowl, slowly adding ⅓ cup of the sugar and beating until shiny and stiff. Using two soupspoons, shape the "islands" by scooping the meringue onto one spoon and placing the other spoon gently on top to shape. Slide the meringues into the barely simmering milk, only three or four at a time. Poach them 1 or 2 minutes on each side, just until they feel firm to the touch, then remove them to paper towels to drain. Continue to poach the remaining "islands" until all the meringue is used. You will have about 12 meringues, measuring 1½ × 2½ inches. Put the egg yolks in a bowl and beat them until they are well blended, slowly adding the remaining ⅔ cup of sugar. Gradually add the simmering milk in which the meringues were poached, stirring well. Transfer to a

heavy-bottomed pan and cook over low heat, stirring constantly, until the mixture thickens; do *not* boil. Pour into a bowl, stir in the vanilla, and let cool. Put the custard in a shallow bowl and arrange the "islands" on top. Chill well before serving.

BAKED CUSTARD

(SERVES EIGHT)

This kindly old dessert still nourishes and comforts. Traditionally served in familiar brown custard cups, it can also be made in one large baking dish.

2 egg yolks
3 eggs
½ cup sugar
⅛ teaspoon salt

3 cups very hot milk
1½ teaspoons vanilla
Nutmeg

Preheat the oven to 325°F. Butter a 1-quart baking dish or 8 ramekins. Set a shallow pan large enough to hold the baking dish or ramekins in the oven, and fill it with 1 inch of hot water. Beat the yolks and eggs together just enough to blend. Stir in the sugar and salt and slowly add the hot milk, stirring constantly. Add the vanilla. Strain into the baking dish or dishes and sprinkle with some nutmeg. Put in the pan and bake for about 45 minutes; the custard is set when a knife inserted in the center comes out clean.

COCONUT CUSTARD

Add ½ *cup flaked coconut* to the custard mixture before putting it into the baking dishes.

CHOCOLATE CUSTARD

Melt 1½ *ounces unsweetened chocolate* in the milk while it is being heated to make the custard.

CARAMEL CUSTARD

NOTE Melt ½ *cup sugar* in a heavy-bottomed skillet and cook without stirring, swirling the pan so that the sugar moves about as it melts. When the sugar becomes caramel-colored, pour about 1 tablespoon of the caramelized sugar into each custard cup and swirl around to coat the bottom and sides. (Or if you are using a large baking dish, pour all the caramelized sugar into it and swirl quickly to coat the bottom and sides.) The caramel will harden at first, but don't worry, the next step takes care of that. Pour the custard on top of the caramel-lined cups (or dish) and bake as above.

COFFEE CUSTARD

Add *2 tablespoons instant coffee* to the milk before it is heated to make the custard.

CRÈME BRÛLÉE   ✳   (SERVES SIX TO EIGHT)

Crème brûlée, or "burnt cream," is a simple and sublime custard dessert. Its brown-sugar topping is melted under the broiler, forming a very thin candied sheet.

2 egg yolks, slightly beaten
2 eggs, slightly beaten
¼ cup granulated sugar
⅛ teaspoon salt

2 cups very hot heavy cream
¾ cup dark-brown sugar,
   sifted or sieved

Mix the egg yolks, eggs, granulated sugar, and salt together in a mixing bowl. Add the hot cream slowly, beating constantly. Pour into a 10 × 6-inch baking dish about 2 inches deep. Bake in a preheated 300°F oven, in a water bath, for 25–30 minutes, or until a knife inserted in the center comes out clean. Cool, cover, and refrigerate. Just before serving, preheat the broiler. Sprinkle the brown sugar *evenly* all over the top of the cream, no more than ¼ inch thick. Run the dish under the broiler and, watching carefully, heat just until the brown sugar melts and turns shiny. Remove and serve immediately.

BLANCMANGE   (SERVES FIVE)

Blancmange, a cornstarch pudding, once seemed so romantic: it is the dessert that Jo of *Little Women* often carried to Laurie, her frail neighbor, to help restore his health. When you want a basic vanilla or chocolate pudding, this is the recipe to use.

3 tablespoons cornstarch
4 tablespoons sugar
⅛ teaspoon salt

2 cups milk
1 teaspoon vanilla

Mix the cornstarch, sugar, and salt with ¼ cup of the milk. Heat the remaining milk, then slowly add it to the cornstarch mixture, stirring constantly. Cook until thickened, stirring constantly, in a heavy-bottomed pan over moderately low heat or in a double boiler over simmering water. Continue to cook for about 15 minutes so that the raw taste of the cornstarch disappears. Let cool, then add the vanilla. Cover and chill.

CHOCOLATE BLANCMANGE

When you heat the milk, add *2 ounces unsweetened chocolate* and stir until smooth.

(SERVES SIX TO EIGHT)   ## CHOCOLATE MOUSSE

Lighter than many mousses, this has no cream. Serve small portions and you will leave the table feeling almost guiltless.

    6-ounce package semisweet   1 teaspoon vanilla, or 1
        chocolate chips   tablespoon rum
    4 eggs, separated

NOTE
see page 471

Melt the chocolate bits in a heavy-bottomed pan over very low heat, stirring often to prevent burning; set aside. Beat the egg yolks until pale and lemon-colored. Slowly stir in the chocolate and blend well. Beat the egg whites until stiff but not dry. Add a third of the whites to the yolks and chocolate, add the vanilla or rum, mix well, then carefully fold in the remaining whites. Spoon into individual serving dishes or a serving bowl. Cover and chill at least 8 hours before serving. .

(SERVES SIX)   ## SEMOLINA PUDDING

This is wonderful with fresh strawberries, lightly sweetened and flavored with a little Grand Marnier.

    1 envelope gelatin   ½ cup sugar
    ¼ cup cold water   1 tablespoon Grand Marnier
    2 cups milk   (or any orange-flavored
    ¼ teaspoon salt   liqueur) or 1 tablespoon
    ½ cup semolina (Cream of   orange zest
        Wheat)   1 cup heavy cream

Stir the gelatin into the cold water and let soften for 5 minutes. Put the milk in a saucepan with the salt, heat to boiling, and then slowly stir in the semolina. Cook, stirring constantly, for about 5 minutes, or until the mixture is thick. Remove from the heat and stir in the softened gelatin and the sugar. Add the Grand Marnier or zest and beat until smooth and blended. Stir occasionally, then let cool. Beat the cream until soft peaks hold (do not beat until stiff or the pudding will not have a soft delicate texture). Fold in the whipped cream. Cover and chill until set.

RICE CREAM (SERVES EIGHT TO TEN)

Snowy white, creamy, and faintly sweet, good with a little maple syrup on top. Don't use imitation maple syrup here!

1½ envelopes (3 teaspoons) gelatin	1½ tablespoons sugar
	⅛ teaspoon salt
3 tablespoons cold water	1 cup heavy cream
3 cups milk	1 teaspoon vanilla
3 tablespoons rice	½ cup maple syrup

Soak the gelatin in the water. Put 2 cups of the milk in a heavy-bottomed saucepan, add the rice, and cook, stirring often to prevent scorching, until the rice is tender, about 20 minutes. Add the gelatin and stir to dissolve, then add the remaining cup of milk, sugar, and salt. Let cool. Whip the cream until soft peaks form, add the vanilla, and fold into the rice mixture. Cover and chill. Serve with maple syrup poured over each portion.

BAKED RICE PUDDING ✳ (SERVES SIX TO EIGHT)

This bears no resemblance to the standard cafeteria version. Long, slow baking gives the rice a golden color and a thick creamy texture. The little bit of rice to a quart of milk is correct. Don't use instant or converted rice. Serve warm or cold, with heavy cream.

4 cups milk	½ teaspoon nutmeg (optional)
½ teaspoon salt	3 tablespoons rice
⅓ cup sugar or to taste	

Preheat the oven to 300°F. Put all the ingredients in a buttered baking dish and stir to blend. If you don't like your rice pudding too sweet, start with only ¼ cup sugar, then taste. Bake for 3½ hours, stirring three times during the first hour of baking so the rice doesn't settle.

RAISIN RICE PUDDING

Add ½ *cup raisins* to the ingredients.

CHOCOLATE RICE PUDDING

Add 2 *ounces unsweetened chocolate, melted,* to the ingredients.

(SERVES FOUR TO SIX) **TAPIOCA CREAM**

Don't be deterred by the children who used to call pearl tapioca "fish eyes." It is time that this almost-forgotten dessert be revived—it tastes wonderful.

3 tablespoons quick-cooking tapioca	2 cups milk
	2 eggs, separated
⅛ teaspoon salt	1 teaspoon vanilla
5 tablespoons sugar	

Mix the tapioca, salt, 3 tablespoons of the sugar, milk, and slightly beaten egg yolks in a heavy-bottomed pot. Let stand for 5 minutes. Cook over medium heat, stirring constantly, for about 6 minutes until the mixture comes to a full boil; remove from the heat. Beat the egg whites until foamy, then slowly add the remaining 2 tablespoons of sugar and continue beating until stiff but not dry. Slowly stir the whites into the hot tapioca mixture, then add the vanilla and blend. Serve warm or cold.

(SERVES FOUR TO SIX) **BUTTERSCOTCH TAPIOCA**

3 tablespoons quick-cooking tapioca	1 tablespoon butter
	½ cup dark-brown sugar
⅛ teaspoon salt	¼ cup finely chopped pecans
2 cups milk	

Mix the tapioca, salt, and milk in a heavy-bottomed pan and let stand for 5 minutes. Cook over moderate heat, stirring constantly, for about 6 minutes, until the mixture comes to a full boil; remove from the heat. Melt the butter in a small skillet and stir in the brown sugar. Cook over moderate heat, stirring, until the sugar melts and bubbles for 1 minute. Stir into the tapioca mixture and add the pecans. Serve warm or cold.

CHOCOLATE BREAD PUDDING (SERVES EIGHT)

Soft as a pillow with a full, light, chocolate-pudding taste. Serve with whipped cream.

2 ounces unsweetened chocolate	⅓ cup sugar
1 quart scalded milk	¼ cup melted butter
2 cups homemade bread crumbs	2 eggs, slightly beaten
	¼ teaspoon salt
	1 teaspoon vanilla

Preheat the oven to 325°F. Butter a 1½- or 2-quart baking dish. Break the chocolate into bits and melt in the milk, stirring until smooth. Add the bread crumbs and set aside to cool. When lukewarm, add remaining ingredients. Mix well, pour into the buttered dish, and bake for about 50 minutes or until set.

LEMON PUDDING (SERVES SIX)

An old favorite, a delicious dessert with its soft lemony custard on the bottom and sponge cake texture on top. Don't let it get too brown.

2 tablespoons butter	1½ tablespoons flour
⅞ cup sugar	⅓ cup lemon juice
3 eggs, separated	Grated rind of 1 lemon
1 cup milk	Heavy cream

Preheat oven to 350°F. Beat the butter until soft, then gradually add the sugar, beating until it is all incorporated. Beat in the egg yolks one by one. Add the milk, flour, lemon juice, and rind, and beat to mix well, although the mixture will have a curdled look. Beat the egg whites until they form soft peaks, then fold into the batter. Turn into a 1½-quart baking dish and set it in a pan of hot water that comes halfway up the sides of the dish. Bake for 50–60 minutes. Let cool and serve either tepid or chilled, with a pitcher of heavy cream.

(ABOUT 2 CUPS) **✳ LEMON CURD**

This is good as a tart filling or spooned into parfait glasses alternately with whipped cream. It is also good just on toast.

Grated zest of 2 large lemons	¼ pound butter
6–7 tablespoons of lemon juice	1 cup sugar
	4 eggs

Put the zest, lemon juice, butter, and sugar in the top of a double boiler or in a bowl over simmering water. Don't let the water boil. Stir occasionally, until the butter melts and the sugar dissolves. In a mixing bowl, beat the eggs until thoroughly blended. Stirring constantly, spoon a little of the hot lemon mixture into the eggs. Pour the egg mixture into the lemon mixture, still stirring constantly, and continue to cook until the curd is thick. This may take up to 20 minutes. Remove from the heat, let cool and store in the refrigerator. It will keep for 2 weeks.

(SERVES FOUR) **LEMON MOUSSE PARFAIT**

A light dessert. Serve with fresh berries and crisp butter cookies.

2 cups Lemon Curd (preceding recipe)	Fresh mint sprigs, for garnish (optional)
2 cups heavy cream, whipped	

Using approximately ½ cup lemon curd and ½ cup whipped cream for each serving, spoon alternate layers of lemon, then cream, into tall stemmed glasses. Garnish with a sprig of fresh mint, if desired. Serve cold.

(SERVES EIGHT TO TEN) **✳ INDIAN PUDDING**

Spicy, coarse, and dark brown, an old-fashioned dessert that celebrates the Indians' gift of corn. Serve with *heavy cream* or *vanilla ice cream*.

4 cups milk	1 teaspoon salt
½ cup yellow cornmeal	4 tablespoons butter
⅓ cup dark-brown sugar	½ teaspoon ground ginger
⅓ cup granulated sugar	½ teaspoon cinnamon
⅓ cup molasses	

Preheat the oven to 275°F. Heat 2 cups of the milk until very hot and pour it slowly over the cornmeal, stirring constantly. Cook in a double boiler over simmering water for 10–15 minutes, until the cornmeal mixture is creamy. Add the remaining ingredients and mix well. Spoon into a buttered 1½-quart baking dish, pour the remaining 2 cups of milk on top, set into a pan of hot water, and bake for 2½–3 hours or until set. The pudding will become firmer as it cools.

BREAD-AND-BUTTER PUDDING (SERVES SIX)

A delectable old-fashioned dessert that emerges puffy from the oven, then falls slowly; golden and slightly crusty on top, it's soft and spoonable inside. Some purists don't even care to flavor this pudding with vanilla and cinnamon, preferring just the good buttery flavor. The important thing is to use a good textured white bread, preferably homemade, which can be a few days old; an equivalent amount of Italian or French bread will do, too, and it's a good way to use up pieces that turn stale so quickly.

Butter, softened	¼ teaspoon salt
7 slices good-quality white bread	½ cup raisins
	1 teaspoon vanilla (optional)
1 quart milk	½ teaspoon cinnamon
3 eggs, slightly beaten	(optional)
½ cup sugar	

Preheat the oven to 325°F. Butter a 2-quart baking dish. Spread a generous amount of butter on one side of each slice of bread and line the bottom and sides of the baking dish. Mix together the milk, eggs, sugar, salt, raisins, and vanilla and cinnamon, if you are using them, and pour over the bread. Place any extra pieces of bread on top and press down so they are submerged. Let stand about 10 minutes, a little longer if the bread is particularly dry. Bake covered for 30 minutes, then uncover and bake for 30 minutes more. If you like a crustier brown top, slip the dish under a hot broiler a few minutes until deep golden. Serve warm with a pitcher of *heavy cream*.

SWEET OMELET (SERVES ONE)

A sweet omelet is a satisfying way to end a meal.

2 eggs	½ teaspoon vanilla
⅛ teaspoon salt	1 tablespoon butter
1½ tablespoons granulated sugar	2 tablespoons confectioners' sugar

Combine the eggs, salt, granulated sugar, and vanilla and beat only long enough to blend. Put a 7-inch nonstick skillet over the heat. When the pan is hot, add the butter and as soon as it foams, tilt the pan so the butter coats the bottom. Pour in the eggs. Shake the pan forward and backward, pulling the eggs with a fork and letting the uncooked part run out to the edges, until the whole is creamy (see illustration p. 482). Fold it in half and roll it out onto a warm plate. Sprinkle with confectioners' sugar.

SWEET OMELET WITH RUM

Add 2 *tablespoons rum* to the eggs when mixing.

SWEET OMELET WITH JAM

Spread ¼ *cup jam or preserves* across the omelet before folding it.

SWEET OMELET WITH BERRIES AND CREAM

Garnish the finished omelet with 2 *tablespoons sour cream* and ¼ *cup sweetened strawberries*, or *other berries*.

DESSERT CRÊPES OR FRENCH PANCAKES
(SIXTEEN 5-INCH PANCAKES)

Follow the recipe for Crêpes (p. 778), adding 2 *tablespoons sugar* to the batter.

JELLY CRÊPES

Spread warm crêpes with *jelly, jam,* or *fruit preserves* (*apricot* is particularly good). Roll them and dust them with *confectioners' sugar*.

WHIPPED-CREAM CRÊPES

Whip *1 cup heavy cream*, sweetening it with *2 tablespoons confectioners' sugar*. Fold in *1 cup chopped toasted almonds*. Spread on the pancakes and roll them up. Dust with confectioners' sugar and a sprinkling of additional *chopped almonds*.

CRÊPES SUZETTE

Cream *1 cup butter* and add *1 cup confectioners' sugar*, mixing together until light. Add the *grated rind of 3 oranges*, the *juice of 1½ oranges*, and *5 tablespoons Grand Marnier or other brandy*. Melt over low heat in a skillet or chafing dish until hot. Fold the pancakes in quarters and add a few at a time to the pan. Heat very slowly, spooning the sauce over them until well saturated. Remove to a heatproof platter and keep warm until all are ready to serve. Pour the sauce in the pan over them and serve. If you wish to flambé, warm *¼ cup brandy*, ignite, and pour flaming over the crêpes.

STRAWBERRY (OR OTHER FRESH BERRY) CRÊPES

Fill each crêpe with about *2 tablespoons crushed strawberries* (or other berries) that have been tossed first with a little sugar and left to stand a short while. Frozen berries, drained of some of the juice, are also good. Roll the crêpe up, top with *confectioners' sugar* and a dollop of *sour cream* or *whipped cream*.

COEUR À LA CRÈME   (SERVES FOUR)

A dense, faintly sweet dessert cheese, traditionally made in a heart-shaped mold. When it is served, a little cream is poured over the cheese, and strawberries or raspberries are spooned around it.

1 cup cream cheese, or 1 cup
  cottage cheese that has
  been rubbed through a
  sieve or puréed in a food
  processor

1½ cups heavy cream
2 tablespoons sugar
2 egg whites, stiffly beaten
2 cups berries

NOTE
see page 471 Blend the cheese with 1 cup of the heavy cream until smooth. Fold in the sugar and egg whites. Line a heart-shaped basket or mold with holes in it, using several layers of cheesecloth. Spoon the mixture into the mold, place it in a shallow bowl, and allow to drain overnight in the refrigerator. Unmold, pour on the remaining ½ cup cream, and garnish with the fruit.

STEAMED PUDDINGS

(SERVES EIGHT)   **STEAMED CHOCOLATE PUDDING**

Dark, moist, and chocolate, not quite as sweet as chocolate cake, just right served with Foamy Sauce.

3 ounces unsweetened	⅔ cup milk
chocolate	2 teaspoons vanilla
6 tablespoons butter	2 cups flour
1 cup sugar	3 teaspoons baking powder
2 eggs	½ teaspoon salt

Butter a 2-quart mold; if it doesn't have a tight lid, see p. 934. Heat water in a pot large enough to hold the mold. Melt the chocolate and butter in a small, heavy-bottomed pan. Remove from the heat and pour into a mixing bowl. Stir in the sugar and eggs, beat until smooth, then add the milk and vanilla. Stir in the flour, baking powder, and salt, and beat until smooth and creamy. Spoon into the mold and cover. Put in the large pot and steam (see p. 934) for 1½ hours. Remove and let cool for 10 minutes before unmolding. Serve warm with *Foamy Sauce* (p. 988).

(SERVES EIGHT)   **OHIO PUDDING**

Mixing this steamed carrot pudding takes a little patience—the moisture from the carrots and potatoes makes blending a slow process, unless you have an electric mixer.

1 cup sugar	1 cup currants
1 cup flour	1 cup raisins
2 teaspoons baking powder	1 cup finely grated raw potato
1 teaspoon salt	1 cup finely grated raw carrot
1 teaspoon baking soda	

Butter a 2-quart mold; if it doesn't have a tight lid, see p. 934. Heat water in a pot large enough to hold the mold. Mix the sugar, flour, baking powder, salt, and baking soda together in a large bowl. Add the currants, raisins, potato, and carrot and mix very thoroughly with your hands. Spoon into the mold and cover. Put in the large pot and steam (see p. 934) for about 3 hours. Remove and cool for 10 minutes before unmolding. Serve warm.

STEAMED FIG PUDDING (SERVES SIX)

3 tablespoons butter, melted	½ teaspoon salt
¾ cup dark-brown sugar	¼ teaspoon allspice
½ cup milk	1 cup dried figs, chopped fine
2 cups flour	1 tart apple, peeled, cored,
½ teaspoon baking soda	and chopped fine

Butter a 2-quart mold; if it doesn't have a tight lid, see p. 934. Heat water in a pot large enough to hold the mold. Put the melted butter in a large bowl and stir in the sugar and milk. Add the flour, baking soda, salt, and allspice and beat until smooth. Stir in the figs and apple. Spoon into the mold and cover. Put in the large pot and steam (see p. 934) for 2½ hours. Remove and cool for 10 minutes before unmolding. Serve warm with *Foamy Sauce* (p. 988).

STEAMED PERSIMMON PUDDING ✻ (SERVES EIGHT)

If you've been searching for a great persimmon pudding, search no more—this one is the best. The color is dark, the texture moist, and the flavor full and spicy. The pudding can be made ahead and reheated or it can be frozen.

1 cup puréed persimmons (about 3 persimmons with skins removed)	2 tablespoons rum
	1 cup all-purpose flour
	1 teaspoon cinnamon
2 teaspoons baking soda	½ teaspoon salt
¼ pound butter, at room temperature	1 cup broken walnuts or pecans
1½ cups sugar	1 cup raisins
2 eggs	Heavy cream, whipped, for garnish
1 tablespoon lemon juice	

Fill a kettle that is large enough to hold a 2-quart pudding mold with enough water to come halfway up the sides of the mold. Let the water come to a boil over medium heat while you are mixing the pudding batter. The mold must have a lid or be snugly covered with foil while steaming (a coffee can with a plastic lid works well). Also there must be a rack of Mason jar rings on the bottom under the mold in the kettle to allow the water to circulate freely while the pudding is steaming. Grease the mold. Put the persimmon purée in a small bowl and stir in the baking soda. Set aside while mixing the other ingredients (the persimmon mixture will become quite stiff). Cream the butter and sugar. Add the eggs, lemon juice, and rum, and beat well. Add the flour, cinnamon, and salt, and stir to blend. Add the persimmon mixture and beat until well mixed. Stir in the nuts and raisins. Spoon the batter into the mold, cover, and steam for 2 hours. Remove from the kettle, and let rest for 5 minutes. Turn onto a rack to cool, or cool just a little and serve warm, with unsweetened whipped cream.

(SERVES EIGHT)   **STERLING PUDDING**

½ cup finely chopped beef
   suet, or ¼ pound butter
2⅔ cups dry bread crumbs
1 cup grated carrots
4 eggs, separated
1⅓ cups dark-brown sugar
Grated rind of 1 lemon
1 tablespoon vinegar

2 tablespoons flour
1 teaspoon salt
1 teaspoon cinnamon
½ teaspoon nutmeg
¼ teaspoon cloves
1 cup raisins
¾ cup currants

Butter a 2-quart mold; if it doesn't have a tight lid, see p. 934. Heat water in a pot large enough to hold the mold. Using an electric mixer or a spoon, beat the suet or butter in a bowl until it is creamy. Add the bread crumbs and carrots and mix well. Beat the egg yolks in a separate bowl until light, add the brown sugar, continue to beat until smooth, and add to the suet mixture. Stir in the lemon rind and vinegar. Add the flour, salt, cinnamon, nutmeg, cloves, raisins, and currants and stir briskly until well blended. Beat the egg whites until they are stiff but not dry. Stir a third of the whites into the pudding mixture, then fold the remaining whites in gently, until no white shows. Spoon pudding batter into the mold and cover. Put in the large pot and steam (see p. 934) for 3½ hours. Remove and cool for 10 minutes before unmolding. Serve warm with *Hard Sauce* (p. 989).

THANKSGIVING PUDDING (SERVES EIGHT)

2½ cups homemade dry bread
  crumbs
¾ cup milk
4 eggs, well beaten
1 cup dark-brown sugar
¾ teaspoon salt
2 teaspoons baking powder
½ teaspoon cinnamon
¼ teaspoon nutmeg

⅓ cup ground suet or butter
1 cup finely chopped dried
  figs
½ cup coarsely chopped
  walnuts
½ cup raisins
¾ cup currants
2 tablespoons flour

Butter a 2-quart mold; if it doesn't have a tight lid, see p. 934. Heat water in a pot large enough to hold the mold. Soak the bread crumbs in the milk, then add the eggs, sugar, salt, baking powder, cinnamon, and nutmeg and combine thoroughly. Work the suet or butter in another bowl until it is creamy, then add the figs. Combine with the bread and milk mixture. Dredge the walnuts, raisins, and currants with the flour. Add to the mixture and beat very well to blend thoroughly. Spoon into the mold and cover. Put in the large pot and steam (see p. 934) for 3 hours. Remove and let cool for 10 minutes before unmolding. Serve warm with *Brandy Hard Sauce* (p. 990).

ENGLISH PLUM PUDDING (SERVES SIX)

English plum pudding makes a lovely Christmas gift. Wrapped well in a brandy-dampened towel, it will keep in the refrigerator for several months. Reheat in the top of a double boiler before serving.

10 slices white bread
1 cup scalded milk
½ cup sugar
4 eggs, separated
1⅓ cups raisins, lightly
  floured
½ cup finely chopped dried
  figs
3 tablespoons finely chopped
  citron

¾ cup finely chopped suet
3 tablespoons brandy
1 teaspoon nutmeg
½ teaspoon cinnamon
¼ teaspoon cloves
¼ teaspoon mace
1 teaspoon salt

Butter a 2-quart mold; if it doesn't have a tight lid, see p. 934. Heat water in a pot large enough to hold the mold. Crumb the bread, and soak it in the hot milk. Cool and add the sugar, the well-beaten egg yolks, raisins, figs, and citron. Break the suet up with a fork and mash until it is creamy or use a food processor. Add to the crumb mixture, then stir in the brandy, nutmeg, cinnamon, cloves, mace, and salt. Beat until well blended. Beat the egg whites until they are stiff but not dry. Stir a third of the whites into the pudding mixture, then gently fold in the remaining whites. Spoon the mixture into the mold and cover. Put in the large pot and steam (see p. 934) for 6 hours. Remove and let cool for 10 minutes before unmolding. Serve warm with *Hard Sauce* (p. 989).

(SERVES EIGHT)   **❊   STEAMED CRANBERRY PUDDING**

⅓ cup butter, softened	⅓ cup milk
1 cup sugar	1½ cups cranberries
2 eggs, well beaten	½ cup chopped walnuts
2⅓ cups flour	1 tablespoon grated orange
¼ teaspoon salt	rind
2½ teaspoons baking powder	

Butter a 2-quart mold; if it doesn't have a tight lid, see p. 934. Heat water in a pot large enough to hold the mold. Cream the butter in a bowl and slowly add the sugar. Stir in the eggs. Mix the flour, salt, and baking powder together and add with the milk to the butter mixture, beating until well blended. Add the cranberries, walnuts, and grated orange rind and mix well. Pour into the buttered mold and cover. Put in the large pot and steam (see p. 934) for 2½ hours. Remove and let cool for 10 minutes before unmolding. Serve warm with *sweetened whipped cream*.

DESSERT SOUFFLÉS

(SERVES SIX TO EIGHT)   **BASIC DESSERT SOUFFLÉ**

Serve a soufflé the moment it leaves the oven. A dessert soufflé must be delicate, so it cannot stand without falling.

4 egg yolks	⅛ teaspoon salt
½ cup sugar	1 cup milk
3 tablespoons butter	5 egg whites
3 tablespoons flour	2 teaspoons vanilla

Preheat the oven to 375°F. Butter a 2-quart soufflé dish or baking dish and sprinkle it with sugar. Beat the yolks and slowly add ¼ cup of the sugar, beating until thick and blended; set aside. Melt the butter in a skillet and stir in the flour and salt. Cook for several minutes over low heat, stirring, then slowly stir in the milk. Cook over medium heat, stirring, until the sauce reaches the boiling point and becomes smooth and thick. Remove from the heat, pour a little of the hot sauce into the yolk-sugar mixture, and stir well. Add the remaining yolk mixture to the sauce, stirring constantly, then return to the heat and cook for another minute; remove and let cool. Put the 5 egg whites in a large bowl and beat until foamy. Slowly add the remaining ¼ cup of sugar and beat until the whites are stiff but not dry. Whisk a fourth of the whites into the sauce to lighten it, then fold in the remaining whites. Stir in the vanilla. Pour into the soufflé dish. Bake for 35 minutes if a slightly runny center is desired and 45–50 minutes for a dry soufflé.

COFFEE SOUFFLÉ

Add 2 *tablespoons instant coffee* to the milk and heat until the coffee is dissolved.

SOUFFLÉ GRAND MARNIER

Use 2 *tablespoons Grand Marnier* instead of the vanilla. Sprinkle *ladyfingers or dry sponge-cake slices* with *Grand Marnier* until dampened and line the soufflé dish with them before adding the soufflé mixture.

CHOCOLATE SOUFFLÉ   ✱   (SERVES SIX)

This is a first-rate chocolate soufflé, light and yet very chocolaty. Most chocolate soufflés are so dense with flavor that their essential lightness is lost.

1½ ounces unsweetened chocolate	⅛ teaspoon salt
5 tablespoons sugar	¾ cup milk
2 tablespoons hot water	3 eggs, separated
2 tablespoons butter	1 teaspoon vanilla
2 tablespoons flour	Whipped cream

Preheat the oven to 325°F. Butter a 1½-quart soufflé dish and sprinkle it with sugar. Put the chocolate, 2 tablespoons of the sugar, and the hot water in a small pan and heat slowly, stirring occasionally, until the chocolate is melted and smooth; remove from the heat and set aside.

Melt the butter in a skillet, then add the flour and salt. Cook over low heat, stirring, for several minutes, then gradually stir in the milk. Cook to the boiling point, stirring; the sauce will become smooth and thick. Blend in the chocolate mixture. Beat the egg yolks well. Stir a little of the hot sauce into the yolks, then add the yolks to the remaining sauce. Stir well, then set aside to cool. Beat the egg whites until foamy, slowly add the remaining 3 tablespoons of sugar, and continue beating until stiff but not dry. Stir a fourth of the whites into the chocolate mixture, then fold in the remaining whites. Stir in the vanilla. Spoon into the soufflé dish and bake for 35–40 minutes. Serve with whipped cream.

(SERVES FOUR OR FIVE) **FRUIT SOUFFLÉ**

This fruit soufflé, made without a cream-sauce base, is as light as a cloud, a delicate reminder of summer during the long, cold winter months. Use canned applesauce, apricots, sour cherries, or pineapple or fresh berries, apricots, pears, or peaches. None of these fruits need cooking, but they should be well drained. The hot fruit purée will set and stabilize the egg whites.

¾ cup fresh or canned fruit   Pinch of salt
    purée   Sugar to taste
1 tablespoon freshly squeezed   5 egg whites
    lemon juice

Preheat the oven to 375°F. Butter a 1-quart soufflé dish and sprinkle it with sugar. Heat the fruit purée in a small pan. Add the lemon juice, salt, and sugar, and stir to blend; remove from the heat. Beat the egg whites until stiff but not dry and stir them into the hot purée until evenly blended. Spoon into the soufflé dish and bake for 20–25 minutes.

(SERVES FOUR) **LEMON SOUFFLÉ**

4 eggs, separated   2 tablespoons lemon juice
⅔ cup sugar   Grated rind of 1 lemon

Preheat the oven to 325°F. Butter a 1½-quart soufflé dish and sprinkle it with sugar. Beat the yolks, slowly adding ⅓ cup of the sugar and continuing to beat until thick and lemon-colored. In a large bowl beat the egg whites until they are foamy, then slowly add the remaining ⅓ cup of sugar and beat until stiff but not dry. Gently stir in the lemon juice and grated rind. Stir a fourth of the whites into the yolk mixture, then fold in the remaining whites. Spoon into the soufflé dish and bake for 35–40 minutes.

MARMALADE SOUFFLÉ   (SERVES FOUR TO SIX)

This dish graced many tables during the servantless days of the late 1930s and '40s and was considered a "ritzy" addition to any dinner. A splendid solution for the cook who is also the host, it will hold for much longer than the hour of cooking time and will not collapse if a draft nips it.

    3 egg whites   Grated rind of 1 orange
    3 tablespoons sugar
    3 tablespoons orange
      marmalade

Start some water simmering in the bottom of a double boiler; butter the top part of the double boiler. Beat the egg whites in a large bowl until foamy, then slowly add the sugar and continue beating until the whites are stiff but not dry. Gently fold in the marmalade and orange rind. Spoon into the buttered pot. Cover and cook over barely simmering water for 1 hour. Serve with *whipped cream* flavored with a touch of sherry.

ORANGE MARMALADE SOUFFLÉ WITH
GRAND MARNIER SAUCE ✳   (SERVES FOUR)

This is a great recipe for the soufflé-timid. Timing is not critical and it does not "fall" dramatically. It is delicious, too.

    ⅔ cup egg whites (about 4   2 tablespoons orange
      "extra-large" eggs)   marmalade
    ½ teaspoon salt   2 teaspoons freshly grated
    ¼ cup granulated sugar   orange zest

Sauce
    1 egg yolk   ¾ cup heavy cream, whipped
    1¼ cups confectioners' sugar   to soft peaks
    ¼ cup Grand Marnier

Use a 2-quart double boiler or a 2-quart bowl which will fit into a saucepan. (It must be raised above the water in the pan or only slightly submerged in the simmering water during the steaming.) The container must have a lid or be snugly covered with aluminum foil. Butter

NOTE
see page 471

the saucepan or bowl and start the water heating to simmer. Put the egg whites and salt in a large mixing bowl and beat until foamy. Slowly add the sugar, a tablespoon at a time, beating constantly, until soft peaks begin to form. Add the marmalade, one tablespoon at a time, and beat just a second more. Gently fold in the orange zest. Spoon the soufflé into the prepared saucepan, cover, and steam for 1 hour or more. Be sure that the water is barely simmering. This soufflé can cook as long as 2 hours without harm. For the sauce, put the egg yolk into a 1-quart mixing bowl and whip with a fork. Stir in the confectioners' sugar and the Grand Marnier and whisk until it is smooth and blended. Fold in the whipped cream. Refrigerate until used. Spoon sauce over each serving.

GELATIN DESSERTS (JELLIES AND CREAMS)

(SERVES EIGHT)   **LEMON JELLY**

Fruit jellies, made with unflavored gelatin and fresh fruit juices, have true, unadulterated flavor. They bear no resemblance to commercially packaged, flavored gelatin mixes. Serve with Gingersnaps (p. 873).

2 envelopes gelatin
2½ cups cold water
1 cup sugar

1 cup freshly squeezed lemon juice

Sprinkle the gelatin over ½ cup cold water and let it soften for 5 minutes. Bring 2 cups water to a boil, add the sugar, lemon juice, and gelatin, and cook over low heat, stirring constantly, for about 3 minutes, until the gelatin dissolves and the liquid is clear. Remove from the heat and pour into individual glasses or a bowl. Chill until firm.

(SERVES EIGHT)   **APRICOT AND WINE JELLY**

2 envelopes gelatin
1 cup sugar
1½ cups water
1 cup apricot juice

1 tablespoon freshly squeezed lemon juice
1 cup sherry

Mix the gelatin and sugar in a small pan. Add the water, stir, and let stand for 5 minutes to soften. Cook over low heat, stirring constantly, until the gelatin dissolves and the liquid is clear. Remove from the heat and add the apricot juice, lemon juice, and sherry. Pour into individual dishes or a bowl and chill until firm.

ORANGE JELLY (SERVES SIX)

2 envelopes gelatin
½ cup cold water
1¾ cups boiling water
1½ cups freshly squeezed
    orange juice

¾ cup sugar
Juice of 1 lemon
Softly whipped cream

Sprinkle the gelatin over the cold water and let it soften, then pour on the boiling water. Mix well to dissolve. Add the orange juice, sugar, and lemon juice. Pour into a 1-quart mold and chill until firm. Serve with lightly whipped cream.

ORANGE JELLY WITH GRAPES

Spread 1½ cups peeled seedless grapes around the mold before adding the liquid and chilling.

COFFEE JELLY * (SERVES SIX)

1 envelope gelatin
6 tablespoons sugar
½ cup cold water

2 cups very strong coffee
Heavy cream

Mix the gelatin, sugar, and cold water together in a small pan and let soften for 5 minutes. Add the coffee and cook over low heat, stirring constantly, until the gelatin dissolves and the liquid is clear. Pour into individual dishes or a bowl and chill until firm. Serve with heavy cream.

(SERVES SIX TO EIGHT)   **WINE JELLY**

2 envelopes gelatin
1 cup sugar
½ cup cold water
1½ cups boiling water
⅓ cup freshly squeezed
   orange juice

3 tablespoons freshly
   squeezed lemon juice
1 cup sherry or Madeira wine

Mix the gelatin and sugar together in a small bowl, stir in the cold water, and let soften for 5 minutes. Pour the boiling water over and mix
well to dissolve. Add the orange juice, lemon juice, and wine. Pour into
individual dishes or a bowl and chill until firm.

(SERVES SIX)   **COFFEE SPONGE**

Make the coffee very strong or the flavor will be lost when the sponge
is chilled. Instant coffee will work fine: use 1 rounded teaspoon per
cup.

1 envelope gelatin
¼ cup cold water
⅔ cup sugar

2 cups strong hot coffee
2 egg whites
Whipped cream

Sprinkle the gelatin over the cold water and let it soften for 5 minutes.
Put the sugar and coffee in a small pan with the gelatin and heat, stirring, until the gelatin dissolves. Remove from the heat and chill until
the mixture is as thick as unbeaten egg white. Add the egg whites and
beat until the mixture is thick enough to hold its shape.

NOTE
see page 471

This will take at least 5 minutes or longer with an electric
mixer. Spoon into a dish or individual dessert dishes and
chill. Serve with whipped cream. You will have about 4
cups.

(SERVES SIX)   **❋ BAVARIAN CREAM**

Bavarian cream is basically English custard made with beaten egg
whites, gelatin, and freshly whipped cream. It should be chilled until
firm.

1 envelope gelatin
¼ cup cold water
2 eggs, separated
1¼ cups milk

½ cup sugar
Pinch of salt
1½ teaspoons vanilla
1 cup heavy cream

NOTE
see page 471

Sprinkle the gelatin over the cold water and let it soften for 5 minutes. Beat the egg yolks slightly. Heat the milk in a heavy-bottomed pan until very hot, then stir a little into the beaten yolks. Return the yolks to the remaining milk in the pan and add the sugar, salt, and gelatin. Stir constantly over medium heat until slightly thickened; do not overcook or boil or the egg yolks will curdle. Remove from the heat and refrigerate for about 15 minutes or until cool. Add the vanilla. Beat the egg whites until they are stiff but not dry and fold them into the custard. Beat the cream until it barely holds soft peaks and fold it into the custard. Spoon into a 2-quart mold, cover, and chill until firm. Unmold before serving.

APRICOT BAVARIAN CREAM (6 CUPS)

1 envelope gelatin	1 teaspoon vanilla
¼ cup cold water	1 cup milk
4 egg yolks	1½ cups apricot preserves
½ cup sugar	1 cup heavy cream, whipped

Dissolve gelatin in the cold water. Beat the yolks and slowly add the sugar, beating until the mixture is thick and creamy; add the vanilla. Heat the milk to the boiling point, then, stirring constantly, pour it slowly over the egg mixture. Blend well, return to the saucepan, and cook over medium heat, stirring constantly, until slightly thickened. Remove from the heat and stir in the gelatin until completely dissolved. Cool. Melt the apricot preserves over low heat, then strain through a sieve (you should have 1 cup purée). Cool and mix with the custard. Fold in the whipped cream. Spoon into a mold. Chill at least six hours.

VANILLA CREAM (SERVES SIX)

Serve this with Rich Butterscotch Sauce (p. 985) or surrounded with fresh berries.

1 envelope gelatin	1 cup milk, scalded
¼ cup water	2 teaspoons vanilla
4 egg yolks	1 cup heavy cream, whipped
1 cup sugar	softly

Soften the gelatin in the water. Beat the egg yolks only until blended. Slowly add the sugar and mix well. Slowly pour the scalded milk over the yolk mixture, stirring constantly until well blended. Pour into a heavy-bottomed saucepan. Add the gelatin and cook over moderate heat, stirring constantly, until the sauce thickens a very little. To test, tilt the pan so you can see the edge of the bottom of the pan, and if there is a little coating that won't run, it is ready. Don't boil. Remove from the heat and add the vanilla. Let cool. Be sure not to whip the cream too stiff, just until it barely holds a soft peak. When cool, gently fold in the whipped cream. Spoon into a mold and chill until set.

(SERVES EIGHT)   **✳ SPANISH CREAM**

    1 envelope gelatin   3 eggs, separated
    ½ cup cold water   ¼ teaspoon salt
    3 cups milk   ¼ cup sherry
    ½ cup sugar

NOTE
see page 471

Sprinkle the gelatin over the cold water and let it soften for 5 minutes. Heat the milk, sugar, and gelatin in a heavy-bottomed pan until the milk is barely scalded, stirring often; do not boil. Beat the egg yolks slightly and pour some of the hot milk mixture over them, stirring constantly. Pour back into the pan and cook over medium heat, stirring, until the custard begins to thicken; be careful not to overcook or boil or the yolks will curdle. Remove from the heat and add the salt and sherry. Beat the egg whites until stiff but not dry and fold them in. Spoon into a 2-quart mold or individual dessert dishes and chill until firm. You will have about 6½ cups.

(SERVES EIGHT)   **MACAROON CREAM**

Crunchy, creamy, and very good.

    1 envelope gelatin   ⅛ teaspoon salt
    ¼ cup cold water   1 cup coarsely crushed
    2 cups milk   macaroons
    3 eggs, separated   2 teaspoons vanilla
    ⅓ cup sugar

NOTE
see page 471

Sprinkle the gelatin over the cold water and let it soften for 5 minutes. Heat the milk to almost boiling and stir a little into the slightly beaten egg yolks. Stir the remainder of the yolks and the sugar into the milk, add the gelatin and salt, and cook over medium heat, stirring constantly, just until the custard begins to thicken; do not overcook or boil or the yolks will curdle. Remove from the heat and add the macaroons and vanilla. Beat the egg whites until they are stiff but not dry and fold them into the custard. Spoon into a 1½-quart mold or individual dessert dishes and chill until firm. You will have about 6 cups.

CHARLOTTE RUSSE (SERVES FOUR)

This fine dish, considered the invention of the great French chef Antonin Carême, became very popular in this country during the nineteenth century. It is made in a cylindrical mold lined with a thin layer of sponge cake and filled with Bavarian cream.

1 envelope gelatin	1½ teaspoons vanilla
¼ cup cold water	1 cup heavy cream
⅓ cup sugar	Sponge cake
½ cup milk	

Sprinkle the gelatin over the cold water and let it soften for 5 minutes. Mix the sugar and milk in a pan, add the gelatin, and cook over medium heat, stirring constantly, until the sugar and gelatin dissolve. Remove from the heat and add the vanilla. Chill until thick and syrupy, then beat until fluffy. Whip the cream to soft peaks and fold in the gelatin mixture. Line individual molds or a 1½-quart mold with ½-inch-thick slices of sponge cake. Spoon in the filling and chill until firm. Unmold before serving.

CARAMEL CHARLOTTE

After softening the gelatin, melt the sugar slowly in a small skillet until it turns golden, then add it to the milk, stirring, and heat until blended. Add the gelatin and cook a minute or two more until the gelatin is dissolved. Remove from the heat, add the vanilla, and proceed as directed.

BURNT ALMOND CHARLOTTE

Fold in ½ cup finely chopped, blanched, toasted almonds with the cream.

CHOCOLATE CHARLOTTE

Melt 1 ounce unsweetened chocolate with 3 tablespoons hot water and ⅓ cup confectioners' sugar and add these with the vanilla to the hot gelatin mixture.

(SERVES EIGHT TO TEN) ## ORANGE CHARLOTTE

Sections of orange, placed around the mold before the charlotte is spooned in, offer good contrast in taste and texture.

1 envelope gelatin	1 cup orange juice
1 cup cold water	3 egg whites
1 cup sugar	1 cup heavy cream
¼ cup lemon juice	Orange sections (see p. 1028)

Sprinkle the gelatin over ¼ cup cold water and let it soften for 5 minutes. Mix the sugar, ¾ cup water, lemon juice, and orange juice together in a pan, add the gelatin, and heat, stirring, until the gelatin dissolves. Chill until as thick as unbeaten egg white, then beat until frothy. Beat the egg whites stiff but not dry and fold them in. Whip the cream to soft peaks and fold it in. Line a 2-quart mold with orange sections, spoon in the charlotte, and chill. Unmold before serving.

NOTE
see page 471

(SERVES SIX) ## COLD RHUBARB SOUFFLÉ

4 cups chopped rhubarb	4 egg whites
6 tablespoons cold water	1 teaspoon vanilla
2¼ cups sugar	12 fresh strawberries
1 envelope gelatin	Additional whipped cream
1 cup heavy cream	

NOTE
see page 471

Cook the rhubarb with ¼ cup water and 1¾ cups of the sugar in a heavy-bottomed saucepan for about 10 minutes until soft. Strain and cook down the juice to ½ cup. Purée the rhubarb in a food mill or a blender, or put through a vegetable mill. Soften the gelatin in 2 tablespoons cold water, then add to the hot rhubarb juice and stir until completely dissolved. Add the purée. Beat the cream until stiff. Beat the egg whites until they begin to stiffen, then add the remaining ½ cup sugar and the vanilla, continuing to beat until stiff peaks form. Fold first the egg-white mixture into the rhubarb, then the whipped cream. Make a collar of wax paper (see illustration p. 935) and fit it around a 1½-quart soufflé mold. Chill for at least six hours. Remove the collar and decorate the top with fresh strawberries and rosettes of whipped cream piped from a pastry tube.

COLD APRICOT SOUFFLÉ

Use 3 *cups sweetened puréed apricots* instead of the rhubarb-and-sugar purée and use ½ *cup warm apricot juice* to dissolve the softened gelatin. Decorate the top with *fresh apricots*, if available, or *walnuts* and whipped-cream rosettes.

COLD STRAWBERRY OR RASPBERRY SOUFFLÉ

Use 3 *cups sweetened purée of strawberries or raspberries* and save about ½ cup strawberry or raspberry juice to heat and dissolve the softened gelatin. Decorate the top with *whole strawberries* or *raspberries* and whipped cream.

FROZEN DESSERTS (MOUSSES AND PARFAITS)

FROZEN VANILLA MOUSSE   (SERVES SIX)

Light and icy cold, plumped up with rich cream, frozen vanilla mousse provides a gentle end to a hot and spicy meal.

2 egg whites	2 cups heavy cream
½ cup confectioners' sugar	2 teaspoons vanilla

NOTE
see page 471

Beat the egg whites until foamy, slowly add ¼ cup of the sugar, and continue beating until the whites hold stiff peaks. Whip the cream, slowly adding the remaining ¼ cup sugar, until the cream barely holds soft peaks. Stir in the vanilla, then fold in the egg whites. Spoon into a mold and freeze. Unmold before serving.

FROZEN APRICOT MOUSSE

Gently add *1 cup apricot purée* after the egg whites and cream have been folded together.

FROZEN COFFEE MOUSSE

Dissolve *3 tablespoons instant coffee* in *¼ cup hot water*. Follow the recipe for Frozen Vanilla Mousse, gently stirring in the coffee after the egg whites and cream have been folded together.

FROZEN CHOCOLATE MOUSSE

(SERVES SIX)

1 cup cold milk
1 envelope gelatin
2 ounces unsweetened
   chocolate

¾ cup sugar
2 teaspoons vanilla
2 cups heavy cream, plus
   additional, for garnish

Put the milk in a heavy-bottomed pan, sprinkle the gelatin over it, and let soften for 5 minutes. Add the chocolate and sugar and cook over moderate heat, stirring constantly, until the chocolate melts and is well blended. Chill until lukewarm. Add the vanilla. Whip the cream until it holds soft peaks, then fold it into the chocolate mixture. Spoon into a mold and freeze. Unmold and serve with whipped cream.

FROZEN PINEAPPLE MOUSSE

(SERVES SIX)

1¼ cups syrup from canned
   pineapple
1 envelope gelatin
½ cup sugar

Pinch of salt
2 tablespoons freshly
   squeezed lemon juice
2 cups heavy cream

Put the pineapple syrup in a heavy-bottomed pan; sprinkle the gelatin over it and let it soften for 5 minutes. Add the sugar and salt and cook over low heat, stirring, until the sugar and gelatin dissolve. Remove from the heat and add the lemon juice. Chill until thick but not set, then beat until light. Whip the heavy cream and fold it into the pineapple mixture. Spoon into a mold or into ice cube trays and freeze.

STRAWBERRY PARFAIT   (SERVES EIGHT TO TEN)

Try this during the summer when strawberries are abundant. It is wonderful.

1 quart strawberries, washed and hulled	Pinch of salt
1¼ cups sugar	½ cup water
3 egg whites	2 cups heavy cream

NOTE
see page 471

Combine the strawberries and ¾ cup sugar. Purée in a blender or food processor and refrigerate. Beat the egg whites and salt until stiff but not dry; set aside. Put the remaining cup of sugar and the water in a heavy-bottomed pan and bring to a boil *without stirring*. Cover to steam the sugar crystals down the sides and boil for 3 minutes. Uncover and continue boiling without stirring until the syrup registers 230–232°F or "spins a thread" (see p. 1046). Slowly pour the syrup over the beaten egg whites, beating constantly until meringue is room temperature. Whip the cream to soft peaks and gently fold it in. Fold in the cold strawberry mixture. Spoon into a mold, dish, or parfait glasses, cover, and freeze until ready to serve. Makes about 7 cups.

ANGEL PARFAIT   (SERVES SIX TO EIGHT)

This whipped cream dessert has a sugar-syrup foundation. The syrup is poured over stiffly beaten egg whites, and whipped cream and vanilla are folded in. When you taste it you will understand its name: it is truly angelic.

3 egg whites	½ cup water
Pinch of salt	2 teaspoons vanilla
1 cup sugar	2 cups heavy cream

NOTE
see page 471

Combine the egg whites and salt in a bowl and beat until stiff but not dry; set aside. Combine the sugar and water in a small, heavy-bottomed pan. Heat *without stirring* until the syrup boils. Cover with a lid to steam the sugar crystals down the sides and continue to boil for 3 minutes. Remove the lid and boil without stirring for 10–15 minutes more until the syrup registers 230–232°F on a candy thermometer or "spins a thread" (see p. 1046). Slowly pour the syrup over the beaten egg whites and beat constantly until the meringue is almost at room temperature. Add the vanilla and blend. Whip the cream to soft peaks and fold it in. Spoon into a mold, bowl, or parfait glasses, cover, and freeze until ready to serve. You will have about 5 cups.

(MAKES 1 QUART)   **✳ ENGLISH TOFFEE BISQUE**

2 cups milk
3 egg yolks
⅓ cup sugar
2 teaspoons vanilla

¼ pound English toffee
1 cup heavy cream
Pinch of salt

Heat the milk in a heavy-bottomed saucepan to the boiling point. Beat the egg yolks and sugar together, then add the hot milk in a slow, steady stream. Return the mixture to the saucepan and cook over medium heat, stirring constantly, until slightly thickened, or until the custard coats the spoon. Cool. Stir in the vanilla. Chop the toffee up into small bits, or put through a food processor. Add to the custard and stir in the cream and the salt. Pour into a 1-quart mold and freeze.

NUT BRITTLE BISQUE

Instead of the toffee, add *1 cup nut brittle, preferably walnut*, broken into small pieces.

(SERVES EIGHT)   **FROZEN RASPBERRY SOUFFLÉ**

By freezing this in a straight-sided dish with a collar around it, the final presentation will look like a soufflé rising above the dish. Pipe extra whipped cream on top and decorate with a few extra raspberries, if you want it to look particularly elegant.

5 egg whites
¾ cup sugar

3 cups raspberries
2 cups heavy cream, whipped

NOTE
see page 471

Combine the egg whites and sugar in a metal bowl and place over hot water until the mixture is tepid (warm to the touch). Remove from the heat and beat with an electric beater until stiff. Set aside. Purée the raspberries and remove the seeds by forcing the purée through a strainer. Fold the raspberry purée into the egg-white mixture and fold in the whipped cream. Make a collar around a 1½-quart soufflé dish. Spoon the raspberry mousse into the dish and freeze at least six hours. Remove the collar to serve.

FROZEN STRAWBERRY SOUFFLÉ

Use *3 cups strawberries* instead of the raspberries.

FROZEN APRICOT SOUFFLÉ

Use *3 cups mashed apricots* (dried apricots that have been stewed in a little water until soft are fine) instead of the raspberries.

FROZEN LEMON YOGURT SOUFFLÉ   (SERVES SIX)

1 cup sugar
4 cups yogurt
1 teaspoon vanilla
Juice and grated rind of 2
   lemons

2 egg whites
½ cup heavy cream

NOTE
see page 471

Beat ⅔ cup of the sugar into the yogurt, then add the vanilla and lemon juice and rind, mixing well. Beat the egg whites until they begin to thicken, then add the remaining ⅓ cup sugar, and continue to beat until stiff peaks are formed. In a separate chilled bowl whip the cream until stiff. Fold first the egg whites, then the whipped cream into the yogurt mixture. Turn into a 1½-quart soufflé dish with a collar around it and freeze at least 8 hours. Remove the collar and serve, decorated, if you like, with additional whipped cream.

MAPLE MOUSSE   (SERVES SIX)

Although this rich and pure maply-tasting mousse should be put in the freezer for 4 hours or more, it will have a more pleasing texture if you remove it from the refrigerator an hour before serving.

1 egg white
¾ cup hot maple syrup
1 cup heavy cream

1 dozen or so pecans or
   walnuts (optional)

NOTE
see page 471

Beat the egg white until it begins to thicken. Slowly add the hot maple syrup and continue beating until it is all absorbed and you have a thick meringuelike mixture. Beat the cream in a chilled bowl until stiff, incorporating as much air as possible into the whipped cream. Fold into the maple mixture. Pour into a 1-quart mold and freeze. Decorate the top, if you like, with pecans or walnuts.

(SERVES SIX TO EIGHT)   **FRUIT AND YOGURT MOUSSE**

This is a very pleasing light dessert. It is less sweet and has fewer calories than most mousses. Serve garnished with fresh fruit if desired.

2 cups puréed ripe fruit
¼ cup lemon juice
¼ cup sugar or honey, or to taste, depending on sweetness of fruit and sweetness desired

2 envelopes gelatin
½ cup water or fruit juice
½ cup lowfat ricotta
1 cup yogurt
½ teaspoon salt, or to taste
4 egg whites

NOTE
see page 471

In a large bowl or food processor combine the puréed fruit, lemon juice, and sugar or honey, and mix until well blended. Mix the gelatin and water or fruit juice and heat, stirring, until dissolved. Add the ricotta, yogurt, and salt to the puréed fruit mixture and mix well. Add the gelatin mixture and stir to blend. Place the bowl in the refrigerator and allow to chill until the mixture just begins to set. Beat the egg whites into soft peaks and gently fold them into the fruit mixture. Spoon into a large soufflé dish or into individual serving dishes and chill for several hours until set.

(SERVES EIGHT)   **BISCUIT TORTONI**

1½ cups dry macaroon crumbs
2 cups light cream

½ cup sugar
⅓ cup sherry
2 cups heavy cream

Put 1 cup of the macaroon crumbs in a bowl, pour the light cream over them, and let soak for 1 hour. Stir in the sugar and sherry. Pour into a metal bowl or 2 ice cube trays and freeze until "mushy." Whip the heavy cream until stiff, fold the crumb mixture in, and blend gently. Spoon into individual cups, small fluted paper cups, or cupcake papers. Sprinkle the remaining ½ cup macaroon crumbs over the tops. Freeze until firm.

BAKED ALASKA ✻

(SERVES EIGHT TO TEN)

The wonder of a baked Alaska: its cold, frozen filling comes right from the hot oven where its topping has just been browned. In this true American dessert, invented by a physicist around 1800, ice cream rests on sponge cake and is covered by meringue which is browned in the oven so quickly that the ice cream doesn't have time to melt. Any kind of ice cream that appeals to you can be used.

Hot-Water Sponge Cake (p. 810), or Lazy Daisy Cake (p. 823)	⅛ teaspoon cream of tartar
	½ cup sugar
	1 quart ice cream, frozen hard
4 egg whites	

NOTE
see page 471

Preheat the oven to 450°F. Choose a board that will fit into your oven, wet it on both sides, then shake off the excess water. Put a piece of brown paper on top of the board. Place the cake on it. Put the egg whites and cream of tartar in a bowl and beat until foamy. Slowly add the sugar and continue to beat until stiff but not dry. Cut the ice cream in slices to cover the cake, leaving a ½-inch rim all around. Cover completely with the meringue. Lightly brown in the oven for about 5 minutes. Serve at once.

ICE CREAMS, SHERBETS, AND ICES

FRENCH VANILLA ICE CREAM

(1½ QUARTS)

Excellent, creamy, and smooth, this French ice cream takes a little more trouble to make than the recipe that follows. Use vanilla bean for real French vanilla flavor; vanilla extract is best in the variations. Either this or the Philadelphia Ice Cream that follows lends itself to the many variations in flavor (opposite page).

½ cup sugar	1 teaspoon finely grated or minced vanilla bean, or 1 tablespoon vanilla
⅛ teaspoon salt	
4 egg yolks, slightly beaten	
2 cups very hot milk	2 cups heavy cream

Mix the sugar, salt, and egg yolks together in a heavy-bottomed pan. Slowly stir in the hot milk and the grated vanilla bean if used. Cook, continuing to stir, until slightly thickened; remove and cool. Strain, then add the cream. Add the vanilla extract, if you are not using vanilla bean. Chill. Freeze in a hand-cranked or electric ice cream freezer (see p. 937).

(1½ QUARTS)   **PHILADELPHIA ICE CREAM**

Deep in flavor, light in texture, easy to make—Philadelphia ice cream is richer and creamier than French vanilla ice cream. If it is too rich for your taste, use one part light cream to one part heavy—a better proportion for some of the rich variations that follow.

    4 cups heavy cream, or 2 cups   Pinch of salt
        heavy cream and 2 cups   1 teaspoon minced vanilla
        light cream   bean, or 2 teaspoons
    ¾ cup sugar   vanilla

Mix everything together and stir until the sugar is dissolved. Freeze in a hand-cranked or electric ice cream freezer (see p. 937).

FLAVORED ICE CREAMS

Using either one of the preceding recipes for French Vanilla Ice Cream or Philadelphia Ice Cream, vary the flavorings as follows:

BUTTERSCOTCH ICE CREAM

First cook the sugar with *2 tablespoons butter* until melted and well browned. Then heat the milk or cream and dissolve the sugar-butter in it. Add the rest of the ingredients and cool before freezing.

CARAMEL ICE CREAM

First caramelize half the sugar (see p. 21). Then heat the milk or cream and dissolve the caramelized sugar in it. Proceed with the rest of the recipe and be sure to cool the mixture before freezing.

TOASTED ALMOND ICE CREAM

Add, along with the vanilla, *1 cup finely chopped almonds* that have been *blanched and toasted* until golden.

COFFEE ICE CREAM

Add *2 tablespoons instant coffee* at the same time as you add the vanilla.

GINGER ICE CREAM

Add *½ cup finely chopped preserved ginger* and *3 tablespoons ginger syrup* when adding the vanilla.

MAPLE AND MAPLE WALNUT ICE CREAM

Use *½ cup maple syrup* instead of the sugar. Add *1 cup chopped walnuts*, if desired.

MINT ICE CREAM

Use *1 teaspoon oil of peppermint* instead of vanilla. Color lightly with *green vegetable coloring*.

PISTACHIO ICE CREAM

Omit the vanilla and add *1 teaspoon almond extract* and *½ cup pistachio nuts, chopped fine*. Color lightly with *green vegetable coloring*.

CHOCOLATE CHIP ICE CREAM

Use only ½ teaspoon vanilla and add *1 cup chocolate chips* to the mixture before freezing.

CHESTNUT ICE CREAM

Add 1 *cup chopped preserved chestnuts and their syrup* and use only half the amount of sugar called for.

PEANUT BRITTLE ICE CREAM

Omit the sugar. Crush ½ *pound peanut brittle* or pulverize in the blender, then sift into the ice cream mixture. Taste and add sugar if necessary.

PEPPERMINT CANDY ICE CREAM

Omit the sugar. Crush ½ *pound peppermint-stick candy* and add to heated milk or cream. Cool before freezing.

PRALINE ICE CREAM

Add 1 *cup finely chopped almonds* that have been *blanched and toasted* until golden. Caramelize half the sugar, heat the milk or cream, and then add the caramelized sugar slowly. Cool before freezing.

OLD-FASHIONED CUSTARD ICE CREAM

(1½ QUARTS)

Good and substantial, with a dense, full texture.

2 cups milk	2 cups heavy cream
1 tablespoon flour	1 tablespoon vanilla
¼ cup sugar	¼ teaspoon salt
2 egg yolks, slightly beaten	

Heat 1½ cups of the milk until very hot. Mix the flour, sugar, and remaining ½ cup milk in a bowl, add the hot milk slowly, and stir until smooth. Return to the pan and cook over moderate heat, stirring constantly, for about 8 minutes. Pour a little of the milk mixture over the yolks, then stir the yolks into the pan. Cook for another minute, then strain and cool. Add the cream, vanilla, and salt. Chill. Freeze in a hand-cranked or electric ice cream freezer (see p. 937).

FRESH FRUIT ICE CREAM (ABOUT 1½ QUARTS)

Using light cream or milk makes this a fresh fruit sherbet; heavy cream makes a rich ice cream.

2 cups milk
2 cups heavy cream
1¼ cups sugar (depending on how sweet the fruit)

1½ cups fresh puréed peeled peaches, apricots, strawberries, or raspberries
Pinch of salt

Put the milk and cream in a pan and heat to the boiling point. Remove from the heat and add half the sugar; stir to dissolve. Cool. Sprinkle the remaining half of sugar over the puréed fruit, taste for sweetness and add more sugar, if needed, after adding the sweetened milk and cream. Stir in the salt and blend well. Freeze in a hand-cranked or electric ice cream freezer (see p. 937).

CHOCOLATE ICE CREAM ❋ (1½ QUARTS)

A rich chocolate ice cream that is very smooth in texture—and easy to make.

½ pound semisweet chocolate, in pieces
2 cups milk
3 eggs

1 cup sugar
2 cups light cream
1 tablespoon vanilla
⅛ teaspoon salt

NOTE
see page 471

Put the chocolate and milk in a pan and cook over low heat, stirring frequently, until melted, about 20 minutes. Beat the eggs in a bowl, slowly adding the sugar. Add the cream, vanilla, and salt and mix well. Stir in the chocolate mixture and chill. Freeze in a hand-cranked or electric ice cream freezer (see p. 937).

OLD-FASHIONED CHOCOLATE ICE CREAM

(1½ QUARTS)

There is even more richness and depth to this lovely ice cream—a must for chocolate ice cream lovers.

1¼ cups sugar	2 cups milk
1 tablespoon flour	2 squares bitter chocolate
Dash of salt	2 cups heavy cream
2 eggs, slightly beaten	1 tablespoon vanilla

Mix the sugar, flour, and salt together, and add the eggs. Heat the milk and melt the chocolate in it. Combine the mixtures and cook over medium heat in a heavy-bottomed saucepan, stirring constantly, until lightly thickened. Cool, then add the cream and the vanilla. Strain and freeze in a hand-cranked or electric ice cream freezer (see p. 937).

FRESH FRUIT OR BERRY ICE CREAM

(1 QUART)

A basic, creamy ice cream that lets the flavor of the fresh fruit dominate. Taste the fruit pulp for flavor and to determine how much sugar is needed; if the fruit is too bland, adjust with lemon juice to bring up its flavor. This ice cream can be made with peaches, pears, apricots, mangoes, or berries.

4 cups fresh fruit or berries, crushed	Up to ¼ cup fresh lemon juice
Pinch of salt	1 cup heavy cream
¾ cup sugar or more, as needed	1 cup light cream

Sprinkle the crushed fruit or berries with salt and half the sugar. Taste and add more sugar and lemon juice, if needed. Put the cream and remaining sugar into the freezer container of a hand-cranked or electric freezer and chill until slightly firm (see p. 937). Then add the sweetened fruit or berries and finish freezing.

FROZEN YOGURT

(1½ QUARTS)

So very simple and good—and so much less caloric than the usual ice cream—no wonder frozen yogurt has become so popular in America.

And, particularly if you make your own yogurt (see p. 18), this can be a very inexpensive treat to have available in the family freezer.

6 cups yogurt   Sugar (optional)
1½ teaspoons vanilla

Mix the yogurt and vanilla and, if you wish, as much sugar as desired. Freeze in a hand-cranked or electric ice cream freezer (see p. 937).

FROZEN FRUIT YOGURT

Use 5 cups yogurt and add *1 cup sugar* and *1 cup mashed fruit* or *berries*, fresh, frozen, or canned. If using fresh, let stand with a tablespoon or so of sugar, depending on the sweetness of the fruit or berries, for about 20 minutes to develop flavor before adding to the yogurt and freezing.

COFFEE ICE CREAM   (1½ PINTS)

1 cup heavy cream   3 eggs
1 cup milk   1 teaspoon vanilla
⅓ cup instant coffee   Pinch of salt
1 cup sugar

Combine the cream and milk in a heavy-bottomed saucepan and heat to boiling. Add the instant coffee and blend. In a small bowl, beat the sugar and eggs together until pale and thick. Add a little of the hot milk mixture to the egg mixture, stirring constantly. Pour this back into the saucepan and cook over moderate heat until slightly thickened. Be careful not to boil. Remove from the heat and add the vanilla and salt. Cool. Freeze in a hand-cranked or electric ice cream freezer (see p. 937).

ABBY'S STRAWBERRY SHERBET   (ABOUT 1 QUART)

You use a food processor for this in place of an ice cream machine. You can use most any berry here but they must be frozen hard. Strawberries make the best sherbet done this way.

3 cups strawberries   1 or 2 "large" egg whites
¼–½ cup sugar, depending on
   sweetness of berries

Hull the berries and cut them in half or in quarters if they are very large. Arrange them on a baking sheet lined with wax paper and freeze them until solid. (Once frozen they can be used right away or stored in the freezer in plastic bags.) Put the frozen berries and the sugar in a food processor. Pulse the machine several times to chop the fruit. Then process continuously until the berries are minced into tiny chips. Scrape down the sides of the bowl several times during the processing.

NOTE
see page 471

With the machine running, pour in the egg white and continue to process until the mixture is completely smooth and fluffy. (Use a second white if the ice fruit is still stiff and not moving in the processor.) This will take several minutes. The mixture must turn a lighter pink: don't be afraid to process longer. The sherbet can be served immediately or stored in the freezer. If it is frozen for more than 12 hours, let it soften just to the point where it can be spooned back into the food processor and processed again until smooth, to eliminate ice crystals.

(1 QUART) **GRAPE ICE CREAM**

A simple and surprisingly delicious ice cream, the color of lilacs.

1 pint heavy cream	⅓ cup sugar
1¼ cups unsweetened grape juice	Few drops fresh lemon or lime juice

Mix the cream, grape juice, and sugar together and stir until the sugar is dissolved. Add fresh lemon or lime juice to taste. Freeze in a hand-cranked or electric ice cream freezer (see p. 937).

(ABOUT 3 CUPS) **LEMON ICE CREAM**

Grated rind of 1 lemon	1 cup sugar
⅓ cup lemon juice	2 cups heavy cream

Put the lemon rind into an 8-inch square baking dish. Add the lemon juice and sugar and stir for 1–2 minutes, or until the mixture is well blended and the sugar has dissolved. Stir in the cream and continue to stir until it is completely smooth. Cover with plastic wrap or foil. Freeze for 4 hours or longer until the mixture is set. Do not stir; spoon into serving dishes.

ORANGE ICE CREAM   (2 QUARTS)

Light ice-milk texture and a fine, sharp orange flavor.

1½ cups sugar
1 cup water
2 cups freshly squeezed
  orange juice

2 cups very hot light cream
2 egg yolks, slightly beaten
2 cups heavy cream

Combine the sugar and water in a pan and boil for 5 minutes. Stir in the orange juice and the hot light cream. Whisk in the egg yolks and cook over low heat, stirring constantly, until thick. Cool. Whip the cream and fold it in. Freeze in a hand-cranked or electric ice cream freezer (see p. 937).

LEMON MILK SHERBET   (1½ QUARTS)

Pleasingly acid, light, and creamy. The unchilled mixture may look curdled, but it will be smooth after freezing.

1 cup freshly squeezed lemon
  juice
1½ cups sugar

Pinch of salt
1 quart milk

Mix all the ingredients together in a bowl. Freeze in metal bowls or three ice cube trays in the refrigerator freezer.

ORANGE CREAM SHERBET   (1½ QUARTS)

Keen flavor and light texture.

1 cup sugar
2 cups freshly squeezed
  orange juice

Pinch of salt
2 cups milk
1 cup heavy cream

Mix all the ingredients in a bowl and stir until blended. Freeze in a hand-cranked or electric ice cream freezer (see p. 937).

(1 QUART)   **CRANBERRY SHERBET**

Icy crisp, light, and fresh—a touch tart, a touch sweet.

> 1½ cups cranberry jelly   Juice of 1 orange
> Grated rind and juice of 1   2 egg whites
>   lemon

Beat the cranberry jelly, lemon rind and juice, and orange juice together until well blended. Freeze to a mush in two ice cube trays. Beat the egg whites until stiff but not dry and whisk them in. Freeze in the ice cube trays or in a metal bowl in the refrigerator freezer.

(1 QUART)   **FRUIT SHERBET**

A clean, light taste, refreshing and nice.

> 1 envelope gelatin   Pinch of salt
> 1 cup cold water   Sugar
> ¼ cup sugar   2 tablespoons freshly
> 2 cups puréed fresh (see p.   squeezed lemon juice
>   1001), cooked, or canned
>   fruit

Sprinkle the gelatin over ¼ cup water and let it soften for 5 minutes. Put the sugar and ¾ cup water in a pan, stir in the gelatin, and cook over low heat until it dissolves. Add the fruit purée, salt, and sugar to taste and cook, stirring, until the sugar has dissolved. Remove and add the lemon juice. Freeze in two ice cube trays or a metal bowl in the refrigerator freezer.

(1½ QUARTS)   **GINGER SHERBET**

Such a clean, tingling taste at the end of a good meal.

> 1 cup sugar   ½ cup freshly squeezed
> 4 cups water   orange juice
> ¼ pound preserved Canton   ⅓ cup freshly squeezed lemon
>   ginger   juice

Bring the sugar and water to a boil. Cut the ginger into small pieces and drop into the boiling syrup. Boil 5 minutes. Add the fruit juices and cool. Strain, mashing the ginger to extract all its flavor. Freeze in a hand-cranked or electric ice cream freezer (see p. 937).

PINEAPPLE ICE

(3 PINTS)

Simple and very good.

2 cups water
¾ cup sugar
2 cups fresh or canned
 crushed unsweetened
 pineapple

½ cup lemon juice
Pinch of salt

Boil the water with the sugar in a pan for 5 minutes. Remove from the heat and stir in the pineapple, lemon juice, and salt. Cool. Pour into three ice cube trays and freeze in the refrigerator freezer.

LEMON ICE

(3 PINTS)

Lovely, fresh, and sharp.

3 cups water
1¼ cups sugar
1 tablespoon grated lemon
 rind

¾ cup lemon juice

Bring the water to a boil, and stir in the sugar until dissolved. Cool, then add the lemon rind and juice. Freeze in a hand-cranked or electric ice cream freezer (see p. 937) or in the refrigerator freezer, using three ice cube trays or a metal bowl.

ORANGE ICE

Omit the lemon rind and juice and substitute *3 cups orange juice, ½ cup lemon juice,* and the *grated rind of 2 oranges.*

GRAPE ICE

Omit the lemon rind and juice and substitute *2 cups grape juice, ⅔ cup orange juice,* and *¼ cup lemon juice.*

RASPBERRY ICE

Omit the lemon rind and juice and substitute *2 cups raspberry juice*.

(1 QUART)   ## GRAPEFRUIT JUICE ICE

Delicious and refreshing.

2⅔ cups unsweetened grapefruit juice	1⅓ cups heavy sugar syrup (p. 1110)

Mix the grapefruit juice and sugar syrup together. Pour into a hand-cranked or electric ice cream freezer, and freeze (see p. 937).

(1 PINT)   ## FRUIT SHERBET OR ICE

Here is a basic formula to use in the new Donvier ice cream maker described on p. 937.

1 egg	¼ teaspoon vanilla
⅓ cup sugar	1 cup cream
1 cup mashed fresh berries or fresh, ripe peaches, or banana or pineapple	

NOTE
see page 471

Beat the egg and sugar until thick and cream-colored. Add berries or fruit to the egg mixture, then add the vanilla and cream and mix until well blended. Chill. Pour into the chilled cylinder and follow manufacturer's directions.

Bombes and Molds

Chill a melon mold or another decoratively shaped mold. Spoon in whatever ice cream or ice you are using for the outside coating; it will help if this ice cream is slightly soft. Spread it all around to make a lining about ¾ inch thick, using the back of a spoon to smooth it in. Fill to overflowing with the contrasting ice cream, ice, or other filling that you have chosen. Put on the cover and press down; the object is to have the mold so well filled that when you press down, the mixture is forced into all the corners and crevices. If you do not have a cover for the mold, use heavy foil and a plate. Freeze either by packing in salt and ice, using 4 parts ice to 1 part salt, or, if you have space, put in the freezer for 4 hours. To serve: invert the mold on a serving dish. Wipe with a cloth that has been soaked in very hot water and then wrung out; repeat if the mold does not lift easily from the ice cream. Decorate with a border of whipped cream, fresh-cut fruit or berries, nuts, flowers—whatever seems attractive.

Suggested combinations for the bombes or molds are:

COATING	CENTER
Ice cream of any flavor	Ice cream of contrasting flavor that is compatible
Raspberry Ice	Vanilla Ice Cream or Vanilla Mousse
Chocolate Ice Cream	Chocolate Chip, Mint, Pistachio Ice Cream, Orange Ice, or Apricot Mousse
Coffee Ice Cream	Italian Meringue, English Toffee or Burnt Walnut Bisque, or Pistachio Ice Cream
Vanilla Ice Cream	Maple Walnut or Burnt Almond Ice Cream, Peanut or Walnut Brittle folded into Italian Meringue

Other Suggestions for Using Ice Cream

The cool creaminess of ice cream makes a delicious filling, providing just the right contrast for certain baked textures. Try spreading a Chocolate Roll with softened vanilla ice cream instead of whipped cream; or fill Éclairs or Cream Puffs with vanilla ice cream and drizzle some Chocolate or Butterscotch Sauce over the top. The crunchy, slightly chewy texture of meringues is marvelously enhanced by a scoop of ice cream, any flavor you like, topped by whipped cream, crushed fruit or berries, or perhaps Chocolate Sauce. All of these concoctions should be served immediately, before the ice cream melts. A rum cake can be made with layers of leftover sponge cake, sprinkled generously with rum, interspersed with layers of vanilla, coffee, or chocolate ice cream, then firmed in the refrigerator; serve this with Rum Sauce (p. 822). And fruits and ice cream, of course, invariably make for a fine marriage. Peach or Pear Melba is simply made by filling poached peach or pear halves, hollow sides up, with scoops of vanilla ice cream and topping with Melba (raspberry) Sauce (p. 990); a dessert of black cherries flamed over ice cream becomes Cherries Jubilee (p. 1015); and for Strawberries Romanoff (p. 1041) the berries are folded into softened vanilla ice cream and whipped cream. Experiment with your own combinations, but use the best of ingredients and aim for a delicate balance of textures and flavors that seem really compatible.

DESSERT SAUCES

(1 CUP)   **BUTTERSCOTCH SAUCE**

A thick, translucent sauce, perfect over ice cream or frozen desserts.

½ cup dark-brown sugar	2 tablespoons butter
½ cup light corn syrup	1 teaspoon vanilla
¼ teaspoon salt	

Stir the brown sugar and corn syrup together in a small, heavy-bottomed pan. Cook over low heat, stirring occasionally, for about 6 minutes. Remove from heat, stir in the salt, butter, and vanilla, and blend well.

(ABOUT 2 CUPS)   **✳ RICH BUTTERSCOTCH SAUCE**

| 1 cup light-brown sugar | ½ cup heavy cream |
| ¼ pound butter | |

Combine the sugar, butter, and cream in a small, heavy-bottomed saucepan. Cook over moderate heat, stirring constantly, about 5 minutes, until the sugar dissolves. Remove from the heat and whisk a little to blend thoroughly.

(1 CUP)   **CARAMEL SAUCE**

A thin caramel syrup, clear and deep gold, this is just right over egg custards or vanilla pudding. It will keep indefinitely.

| 1 cup sugar | 1 cup boiling water |

Put the sugar in a small, heavy-bottomed pan and swirl it over very low heat *without stirring*; it will slowly melt and turn golden. When completely melted, stir in the boiling water. Cook for 3–4 minutes.

CHOCOLATE SAUCE (1 CUP)

A good, shiny, all-purpose sauce, not very thick and not overly rich.

2 tablespoons butter
2 ounces unsweetened
    chocolate
1 cup sugar

Pinch of salt
½ cup water
1½ teaspoons vanilla

Put the butter and chocolate in a heavy-bottomed saucepan and stir over low heat until the chocolate is melted. Remove from the heat and stir in the sugar, salt, and water. Beat until smooth, return to moderate heat, and cook, stirring often, for about 5 minutes. Remove and cool a little, then add the vanilla.

QUICK EASY CHOCOLATE SAUCE (ABOUT 1 CUP)

The secret here is to use a very good chocolate. Some of the dark chocolate "eating" bars work well.

8 ounces semisweet,
    bittersweet, or milk
    chocolate

1 cup heavy cream

Break the chocolate into a heavy-bottomed saucepan and melt over low heat, stirring frequently. While stirring, slowly add the cream and continue to stir until it is well blended. Remove from the heat and serve hot, or let cool to room temperature before serving.

CHOCOLATE FUDGE SAUCE ❋ (ABOUT 3 CUPS)

Very thick, rich, and shiny perfect for ice cream sundaes. This does not get hard when spooned over ice cream. If too thick put the sauce in a pan and warm over low heat.

14-ounce can sweetened
    condensed milk
12 ounces chocolate chips

⅔ cup water
½ teaspoon salt
1 tablespoon vanilla

Combine the milk, chocolate chips, water, and salt in a heavy-bottomed saucepan. Stir over low heat until the mixture is smooth and blended. Remove from the heat and stir in the vanilla. Serve hot or cold.

(SERVES FIVE)

ENGLISH CUSTARD (CRÈME ANGLAISE)

A pale yellow softly flavored vanilla sauce, one of the best of all the dessert sauces and basic to many Bavarian creams and mousses.

2 cups milk	½ cup sugar
4 egg yolks	1½ teaspoons vanilla

Heat the milk in a heavy-bottomed pan until it is very hot. Beat the egg yolks for about 3 minutes while slowly adding the sugar until mixture is a pale lemon color and thick. Very slowly pour in the hot milk, stirring constantly, until blended. Return the mixture to the pan and cook over medium-low heat to just below the boiling point, stirring constantly, until slightly thickened and the froth has disappeared. Do not boil or the sauce will "curdle." Remove from the heat, quickly pour into a bowl, and stir for a minute or two to cool. When completely cool add the vanilla and blend. Cover and chill until needed. You will have about 2½ cups of custard.

RICH CUSTARD

For a thicker, even richer sauce, add *1 more egg yolk* and substitute *½ cup heavy cream* for ½ cup of the milk.

(1½ CUPS)

SEA-FOAM SAUCE

Creamy, but not heavy; beaten egg white is added just before serving. Try this over Steamed Chocolate Pudding (p. 951) or Chocolate Bread Pudding (p. 946).

2 tablespoons butter	1 egg, separated
2 tablespoons flour	½ cup water
½ cup sugar	1 teaspoon vanilla

Cream the butter, flour, and sugar together in a small saucepan. Beat the egg yolk with the water, then add to the creamed mixture. Cook over low heat, stirring constantly, until thickened. Cool. Just before serving, add the vanilla. Beat the egg white until stiff but not dry and fold it in.

FOAMY SAUCE

(1½ CUPS)

This sauce holds well and is wonderful with Steamed Chocolate Pudding (p. 951). Flavored with sherry, it is also very good with Christmas cakes.

1 cup confectioners' sugar	Pinch of salt
¼ pound butter, softened	1 teaspoon vanilla, or 2
1 egg, well beaten	tablespoons sherry

Beat the sugar into the softened butter in the top of a double boiler. Blend in the egg and salt. Beat over simmering water until light, about 5 minutes. Stir in the vanilla or sherry.

ORANGE SAUCE

(1½ CUPS)

NOTE
see page 471

This sauce has a sweet, sharp citrus taste that is grand over Rice Cream (p. 944), Blancmange (p. 942), or Marmalade Soufflé (p. 958). Make it just before using—it thins out after an hour.

3 egg whites	Juice of 1 lemon
1 cup confectioners' sugar	
Grated rind and juice of 2	
oranges	

Beat the egg whites until they are stiff but not dry. Gradually beat in the sugar. Stir in the orange rind and juice and lemon juice and blend well.

COFFEE CUSTARD SAUCE

(2 CUPS)

Splendid over Caramel Custard (p. 941), cake, or vanilla pudding.

3 egg yolks, slightly beaten	1 cup hot strong coffee
¼ cup sugar	⅓ cup heavy cream
⅛ teaspoon salt	

Put the yolks, sugar, and salt in a heavy-bottomed pan and cook over moderate heat, stirring and slowly adding the hot coffee. Cook, stirring constantly, until thickened. Remove from the heat and cool. Whip the cream to soft peaks and fold it in. Refrigerate until needed.

(1 CUP)   **HONEY CREAM SAUCE**

This honey-colored sauce is good over spice cake or puddings. Taste it
by itself; you'll find it sweet, with a bit of tang.

    ½ cup heavy cream   1 teaspoon lemon juice
    ½ cup honey

Whip the cream until it holds soft peaks. Stir in the honey and lemon
juice and whip well. Refrigerate until needed; it will keep for 5–7 days
if made with regular cream and for at least a month if sterilized cream
is used.

(1½ CUPS)   **SABAYON SAUCE**

This sauce is especially good over fruit. It is also sometimes served by
itself in small glasses as a very light whipped-custard dessert. It must
be served at once or it will slowly fall.

    Grated rind and juice of ½   ⅓ cup sugar
        lemon   2 eggs, separated
    ¼ cup sherry or Madeira wine

Put the lemon rind, lemon juice, wine, sugar, and egg yolks into the
top of a double boiler. Beat with a whisk over simmering water until
thick; remove from the heat. Beat the egg whites until stiff but not dry
and fold them in. Serve at once.

(1 CUP)   **HARD SAUCE**

Traditionally served with English Plum Pudding (p. 954), hard sauce is
very sweet and good with many other steamed puddings. Serve it cool,
but not chilled.

    5 tablespoons butter   ½ teaspoon vanilla
    1 cup confectioners' sugar

Cream the butter, then slowly add the sugar, beating well with an electric beater or by hand until creamy and pale yellow. Add the vanilla
and blend. Cover and refrigerate until needed.

BRANDY OR WINE HARD SAUCE

Use *2 tablespoons brandy* or *3 tablespoons sherry* or *Madeira wine* instead of the vanilla.

LEMON HARD SAUCE

Use *1 tablespoon freshly squeezed lemon juice* and *1 tablespoon grated lemon rind* in place of the vanilla.

MOCHA HARD SAUCE

Omit the vanilla and add *2 teaspoons instant coffee* and *2 teaspoons powdered cocoa*.

RASPBERRY HARD SAUCE

Omit the vanilla and add *3 tablespoons raspberry juice* or *4 tablespoons raspberry jam*.

MELBA SAUCE I (1 CUP)

Nothing more than sweetened raspberry juice, but very good over peaches, ice cream, or vanilla mousse.

    1 cup fresh or frozen   ¼ cup sugar
        raspberries

Purée the raspberries in a blender or food processor. Strain the purée to remove the seeds, put it in a small pan, and stir in the sugar. Cook over medium heat, stirring frequently, until the sugar dissolves; remove and cool. Cover and refrigerate.

(1½ CUPS)   **MELBA SAUCE II**

This is thicker and finer than the preceding Melba Sauce I. The currant jelly adds a nice tartness, so don't sweeten the raspberries too much.

2 cups fresh or frozen raspberries	Sugar
½ cup currant jelly	1 teaspoon cornstarch
	1 tablespoon cold water

Crush the raspberries, then strain them to remove the seeds. Put them into a small pan, add the currant jelly, and bring to the boiling point. Stir in sugar to taste and simmer for 2 minutes. Mix the cornstarch with the cold water in a small bowl until smooth. Slowly stir the cornstarch mixture into the raspberry sauce, then cook, stirring, until thick and clear. Cool and store in a covered container until needed.

(1 CUP)   **STRAWBERRY SAUCE I**

This sauce has the consistency of a creamy frosting. Use it on a plain white or yellow cake or over pancakes or waffles.

5 tablespoons butter, softened	⅔ cup strawberries
1 cup confectioners' sugar	

Cream the butter, then add the sugar gradually, beating well. Crush the strawberries and add them a little at a time, beating after each addition until the sauce is smooth. Cover and refrigerate until needed.

(1½ CUPS)   **STRAWBERRY SAUCE II**

The addition of an egg white makes this lighter than Strawberry Sauce I. It is very nice over delicate desserts such as poached pears, vanilla mousse, or fresh, sliced strawberries.

5 tablespoons butter, softened	⅔ cup strawberries
1 cup confectioners' sugar	1 egg white

Cream the butter, then slowly add the sugar, blending well. Crush the strawberries and add them a little at a time, beating until smooth. Add the egg white and beat until the sauce is light and barely holds soft peaks. Cover and refrigerate.

STERLING SAUCE   (1 CUP)

The brown-sugar version of Hard Sauce (p. 989).

5 tablespoons butter, softened	2 tablespoons sherry
¾ cup light-brown sugar	1 tablespoon brandy
2 tablespoons heavy cream	

Cream the butter in a mixing bowl and slowly add the sugar, beating
well with an electric beater or by hand until smooth and creamy.
Slowly add the cream and blend well, then add the sherry and brandy
and mix thoroughly. Cover and refrigerate until needed.

LEMON SAUCE   (ABOUT 1 CUP)

A good old-fashioned sauce for Cottage Pudding Cake (p. 818) and for
steamed puddings.

½ cup sugar	Grated rind of 1 lemon
1 tablespoon cornstarch	Few gratings nutmeg
1 cup boiling water	(optional)
2 tablespoons butter	Pinch of salt
¼ cup lemon juice	

Mix the sugar and cornstarch together in a small saucepan. Add the
boiling water, stirring constantly. Boil 5 minutes. Remove from the
heat and swirl in the butter, lemon juice and rind, optional nutmeg,
and pinch of salt. Serve warm.

CAMBRIDGE SAUCE   (1 CUP)

A rather thin sauce with a smooth texture and a light butter-vanilla flavor. Very good over a rich, robust pudding.

½ cup plus 2 tablespoons cold	5 tablespoons butter
water	1 cup confectioners' sugar
2 teaspoons flour	2 teaspoons vanilla

Put ½ cup water in a small saucepan and bring to a boil. Stir the remaining 2 tablespoons water into the flour and mix until smooth.
Gradually stir the flour mixture into the boiling water, lower the heat,
and simmer, stirring, for 5 minutes; remove from the heat and cool.
Cream the butter, then add the confectioners' sugar and beat until

smooth. Add the flour mixture and the vanilla and blend well. Cover and refrigerate until needed.

(1½–2 CUPS)   **WHIPPED CREAM**

Heavy cream and whipping cream are the same. There are two kinds of heavy cream available today: "old-fashioned" pasteurized heavy cream which will remain fresh for five to seven days, and "sterilized" or "ultrapasteurized" cream that keeps for five to six weeks, having been heated to a high temperature to protect it from bacteria. Use whipped cream as a cake frosting or as a topping for desserts. Sweeten it or not, flavor it or not, depending on how sweet the dessert is and whether you want an additional flavor. Incidentally, sweetened whipped cream with a little vanilla is also known as Chantilly Cream.

1 cup heavy cream	2 teaspoons vanilla, or 1½–2
1–2 tablespoons confectioners'	tablespoons sweet liqueur
sugar (optional)	(optional)

Using a whisk or an electric beater, whip the cream until soft peaks form. With an electric beater the cream can turn buttery very suddenly after it has thickened, so watch it carefully. The more air you can incorporate, the greater the volume of the whipped cream will be; ideally you should double the volume. This is easier to accomplish with a balloon whisk, and if you beat the cream over another bowl of ice, the whipping will go very quickly. Add the sugar and vanilla or liqueur any time after you have started to beat. If you are using a sweet liqueur, you will need very little sugar. Whipped cream will keep in the refrigerator for several hours, but it is better to store it in a strainer set over a bowl so that the liquid that accumulates will drain off. To stabilize whipped cream for use as a frosting or to hold for later use on desserts, add 2 tablespoons nonfat dry milk to each cup of cream before whipping.

WHIPPED EVAPORATED MILK

Canned evaporated milk will whip nicely if it is chilled well.

WHIPPED LIGHT CREAM, HALF-AND-HALF, OR COFFEE CREAM

Sprinkle *1 teaspoon gelatin* over *1 tablespoon cold water* in a small metal bowl and let it soften for 5 minutes. Dissolve it by putting the bowl into a pan of simmering water and stirring until clear. Add the gelatin and *1 egg white* to *1 cup light cream*. Beat until soft peaks form.

MOCK DEVONSHIRE CREAM

Beat *3 ounces cream cheese, softened,* then slowly add *½ cup heavy cream* and beat until smooth.

FRUITS & FRUIT DESSERTS

There are some nice new additions here—a date pudding, a winter fruit dish, a green mango fool, iced oranges—and at the beginning of the chapter a generic recipe for a cobbler and for a crisp that can be made with just about any kind of fruit or berry. As well, you'll find those old-fashioned desserts using biscuit dough in some way or with a crumble topping appearing under the fruit entry associated with it. I have included from my *Fannie Farmer Baking Book* recipes for an apple dumpling and a peach turnover, both of which can be made with other fruits as well. For some reason these two New England classics were missing from the pages of earlier editions.

The microwave oven can be useful for stewing small amounts of fruits and berries and cooking a whole fruit. You'll find notes throughout the chapter on what works well.

ABOUT FRUIT

Whether it is served squeezed for breakfast or cut up over cereal, tucked into a lunch box or munched as an afternoon snack, arranged on a salad plate or in tall sherbet glasses to begin dinner, fruit is one food we can eat with unabashed pleasure, never feeling guilty. As children we learn how good it is for us, and most of us never get over the joy of anticipating the first strawberries and the tart freshness of an apple just shaken from the tree. Today with modern transportation more fruits are available year round and less familiar kinds like papaya and kumquats and mangoes are seen more in our markets. But both these exotic varieties and out-of-season fruits are expensive, and for daily use the sensible cook will try to concentrate on seasonal fruits, which offer not only better value but also much better flavor.

In addition to enjoying fruits whole and raw and cut up in fresh compotes, we have a rich heritage of delectable fruit desserts—pies, shortcakes, whips, soufflés, fritters, and puddings (some with charming names like Brown Betty and Rolypoly and Grunt) that have come down to us from our forebears, who clearly enjoyed making the most of each harvest and of adding variety to their diets during the lean, cold months. If you grew up on these delicious, old-fashioned desserts, you will want to share such treasures with your family; if they weren't part of your past, you'll soon discover why they are held in such affection.

STEWING FRUIT AND BERRIES IN THE MICROWAVE

For a comparison of fruits and berries cooked on top of the stove and in the microwave, I used ½ pound (1 cup) sliced fruit or berries and cooked them in a syrup of ½ cup sugar and ½ cup water (unless otherwise noted). The syrup was simmered for 3 minutes either on top of the stove or in the microwave before the fruit was added (timing is based on room-temperature fruit cooked in hot syrup).

In every instance the fruit cooked on top of the stove tasted slightly sweeter than the microwaved—probably because the direct heat caused more evaporation—and the syrup took on more of the color of the fruit. In most cases the cooking times were the same or very close and there was not much discernible difference between the microwaved fruits and berries and those cooked on top of the stove. So using one cooking method over the other would seem to be a matter of preference.

See the various fruit and berry entries in this chapter for specific timing instructions and comments.

Buying and Storing Fruit

The chances are that when you buy fruit, it will not be fully ripened; see individual listings that follow as to what to look for. Leave fruits out at room temperature or, to hasten the ripening process, put them in a paper bag, twist the top so the air is locked in, and leave until they are ready to eat. If fruits are fully ripe, store them in the refrigerator. If there are any bruised or soft spots, cut them out and don't store the fruits too close together.

Frozen Fruits and Juices

Try not to let frozen fruits and juices defrost on their journey home from market, and store them quickly in the freezer. Depending on how well they have been handled by purveyors, frozen fruits and juices can have better flavor than their out-of-season counterparts. Berries are apt to have a softer texture when defrosted but are fine for sauces and purées and, of course, cooked.

For freezing your own fruits, see p. 1122.

Canned Fruits

See the individual listings for recommendations. While sliced or cut-up fruits may be a better value than whole, they are also more permeated with syrup so tend to taste less of their own natural flavors; for compotes and baked fruit dishes whole canned fruits are therefore preferable.

For canning your own fruits, see p. 1110.

A Bowl of Fresh Fruit

Placing a beautiful and bountiful bowl of fruit in the middle of the table, providing each diner with a handy fruit knife, and encouraging all to help themselves is one of the pleasantest ways to end a dinner, particularly a substantial one when the cleansing lightness of fruit is so welcome. The fruits should look inviting and not disappoint when they are bitten into; market well enough ahead so that unripened fruits will have plenty of time to develop. Select different varieties depending on what's in season and look for nice shapes and contrasting colors that will make up an attractive composition. Polish apples and pears until they shine, freshen anything that looks a little weary in ice water, add leaves or sprigs of holly to the bowl, and include a surprising touch like a sprinkling of bright berries or wedges of pineapple with a few spiky leaves left on. The contrast of dried fruits and nuts is nice, too, particularly in winter.

Here are some suggestions for seasonal fruit bowls:

Fall Fruit Bowls. You might have a mixture of local apples of different kinds, some red-brown small Seckel pears as well as large, yellowy Bartletts, small clusters of green seedless grapes and of blue Concords, some tangerines, dried figs, and raisins and mixed nuts.

Winter Fruit Bowls. Include some longer-keeping apples like Red and Golden Delicious and McIntosh, Anjou and russet pears, kumquats, bananas, red winter grapes and purple Malagas, a pineapple cut into wedges (the pieces loosened and speared with toothpicks for easy handling), dates, dried apricots, and nuts.

Spring Fruit Bowls. These could welcome some of the tropical fruits that ripen early—papayas and mangoes cut in slim wedges—along with navel oranges, greening apples, early nectarines, and a sprinkling of the first strawberries, unhulled.

Summer Fruit Bowls. Early summer could include apricots and the first peaches and plums, and cherries. Later, there will be more plums—from tiny sweet sugar-plums to luscious greengage—fresh figs, and cantaloupes, honeydews and watermelons, which can be cut in thin manageable slices to distribute around the fruit bowl. Decorate with berries as they come into season.

Fruit Cups

See also Fruit Salads (p. 691).

Ideally a festive and truly delicious fruit cup should be made up of fresh fruits, pitted, peeled (unless you want to leave a little tender skin for color and flavor), and cut into not-too-small pieces. Follow the same principles of selection you would for a fruit bowl—let the seasons guide you. Use small berries as they appear and cut some fruits into balls with a melon-ball cutter. Sometimes a teaspoon or so of fresh lemon juice will help to heighten flavors of fruits not quite at their peak (and it's a good idea whenever you include peaches, since they discolor after peeling); toss your mixture with sugar and let it chill. Peaches, nectarines, apricots, cherries, plums, citrus fruits, pineapple, and melons do not ripen further after picking. Something chemical happens and they get softer but do not get sweeter or tastier. They don't develop more sugar.

To serve as a first course, cut-up fruits look lovely in sherbet glasses or goblets with a sprig of mint on top, or arrange them attractively in a large glass bowl. For dessert, a small scoop of a fruit ice is nice, too. Sometimes you may want to macerate the fruits in some sweet Sauterne or kirsch or a very small amount of brandy, but go easy—you want to taste the fruit, and strong liquors like brandy and rum tend to overwhelm it. Sour cream, crème fraîche, or whipped cream lightly flavored with a liqueur and sprinkled with brown sugar can make good toppings. Serve with Lace Cookies (p. 868), or Chocolate Walnut Wafers (p. 866), or other delicate cookies.

Fruit Desserts

Whips. A whip is made with stiffly beaten egg whites, lightly sugared, with chopped or puréed fruit folded in. It may be baked or unbaked. Prune whip, which adorned many tables at the turn of the century, was a great American favorite. Cold puréed fruit or berry soufflés (see p. 969) are a variation on the whip with a little gelatin and whipped cream added to make the airy dessert stand up in a soufflé dish.

Snows. Snows are always unbaked. They are made with stiffly beaten egg whites, sugared, sometimes stabilized with gelatin and flavored with fruit purée or fruit juice.

Brown Betty. Brown Betty, an all-time treasure, is a baked fruit dish with spicy buttered crumbs on top. Occasionally the crumbs are strewn throughout as well.

Fruit Cobblers. Fruit Cobblers are baked fruit dishes with a cobbled topping of biscuit dough.

Fruit Crisps. Fruit Crisps are baked fruit dishes with a crisp, crunchy topping.

Fruit and Berry Shortcakes. Fruit and Berry Shortcakes are made of raw fruit or berries sandwiched between warm baked biscuit dough and topped with whipped cream.

Rolypoly. Rolypoly is made of berries or fruit rolled in a biscuit dough and baked or steamed.

Summer Pudding. Sometimes known as Blueberry Bread Pudding, Summer Puddings are made by lining a bowl with very lightly buttered bread, then pouring over hot, sweetened, lightly stewed berries—whatever kind of fresh berry is in season at that point in the summer. The dessert is then weighted and chilled and emerges tasting like the essence of summer.

Fritters. Certain fruits, like apples, bananas, and pineapple, make especially good fritters. Coated in a batter that becomes crisp when deep-fried, the interior bursts with warm, sweet juices. Morning is a grand time to eat fritters, straight from the pan, just dusted with confectioners' sugar. The fritter batter made with beer (p. 533) gives a pleasant tangy taste that goes well with fruit.

(SERVES SIX)   **ANY FRUIT CRISP**

You can use most any ripe fresh fruit in this recipe, such as apples, rhubarb, berries, peaches, plums, apricots, or nectarines. It is delicious served warm with vanilla ice cream or lightly whipped cream.

4 cups ripe berries or fresh fruit, sliced	1 teaspoon baking powder
1 cup flour	1 egg, beaten
1 cup sugar	¼ pound butter, melted

Butter an 8-inch square baking dish. Put the fruit in the bottom of the dish. In a bowl, mix together the flour, sugar, and baking powder. Add the beaten egg and mix well with a fork or your fingertips until the flour is dampened and in small clumps. Scatter the flour mixture over the fruit. Drizzle the melted butter evenly over the top. Using the back of a spoon or your fingers, distribute the butter over all. Bake in a 375°F oven for about 25 minutes. Serve warm.

ANY FRUIT COBBLER ✳   (9 × 13-INCH PAN)

Peaches, nectarines, plums, apricots, and apples are all good under cobbler crusts. Serve plain or with lightly whipped cream.

1¾ cups flour	½ cup sugar
1 tablespoon baking powder	¾ cup cream
½ teaspoon salt	6 cups fresh fruit
6 tablespoons butter, chilled and in pieces	Sugar, for sweetening fruit

Mix flour, baking powder, and salt in a large mixing bowl and stir with a fork to blend. Put the pieces of chilled butter into the flour mixture and rub quickly with your fingertips until the mixture resembles coarse crumbs. Add the sugar and lightly blend. Using a fork, slowly stir in the cream, until roughly mixed. Gather the dough into a shaggy mass and knead 5–6 times. Set aside. Preheat the oven to 375°F. Butter a rectangular or oval baking dish (a 9 × 13-inch or 13-inch oval of at least 3-quart capacity). Sweeten the fruit to taste and put in the prepared pan. Roll the dough on a lightly floured surface, to the size of the top of the baking dish. Place on top of the fruit mixture. Bake for about 40–50 minutes, until lightly browned and a toothpick inserted in the crust comes out clean.

FRUIT FRITTERS   (SERVES EIGHT TO TEN)

Use peeled apples, bananas, or pineapple, cut in pieces no more than ½ inch thick.

2 eggs	1 teaspoon baking powder
2 teaspoons granulated sugar	¼ teaspoon salt
⅔ cup milk	Vegetable oil for frying
1 teaspoon vegetable oil	5 cups fruit, in large, bite-size pieces
1 teaspoon lemon juice	
1 cup flour	Confectioners' sugar

Beat the eggs until light. Add the granulated sugar, milk, vegetable oil, and lemon juice and mix until blended. Add the flour, baking powder, and salt and stir until smooth. If possible, refrigerate for an hour or so before using. Pour about 2 inches of vegetable oil into a heavy skillet and heat to 370°F. Turn the oven on to 250°F. Pat the pieces of fruit as dry as possible. Spear each piece with a fork and dip it into the batter, letting only excess batter drain back into the bowl, then lower it carefully into the hot oil. Don't overcrowd the pan: fry about 6 pieces at a time. Allow about 2 minutes until the first side is golden brown, turn with a slotted spoon, and brown the other side. Drain on paper towels, patting to absorb the excess fat. Keep finished fritters warm in the oven until all are fried. Dust with confectioners' sugar and serve.

Fruit Purées

Fruit purées, particularly made with fresh fruits, are lovely tasting and are also used as a base in soufflés and other dishes.

(¾ CUP)   **FRESH FRUIT PURÉE**

½ pound fresh fruit, peeled   Sugar
and cut in pieces

If the fruit is hard, cook it in a little water until soft. Purée it by forcing it through a food mill or whirling it in a blender or food processor. Taste and add sugar, if necessary.

DRIED FRUIT PURÉE

Cook the dried fruit according to the directions on the package. Or measure the fruit, combine it in a pot with an equal amount of water, cover, and simmer for 10–15 minutes, until soft. Add sugar to taste, stirring to dissolve. Proceed as for Fruit Purée.

CANNED FRUIT PURÉE

Drain canned fruit and proceed as for Fruit Purée.

Cooked Fruits

See individual listings for recipes for each kind of fruit. But here are two fine recipes for canned fruits used in attractive combinations.

(SERVES EIGHT)   **HOT FRUIT COMPOTE**

Hot Fruit Compote is particularly good served with whipped cream flavored with the same flavoring you have used in the fruit.

1 can pears
1 can Bing cherries
1 can whole apricots, pitted
1 tablespoon slivered orange
    peel

1 tablespoon brandy or rum,
    or 1 teaspoon vanilla,
    approximately

Drain the juice from the cans. Add to the juice the slivered orange peel, and simmer gently for 30 minutes. Add the fruit and the brandy, rum, or vanilla, and heat through.

OTHER COMBINATIONS

Peaches, plums, raisins (added to the juice for the last 10
    minutes of simmering), and slivered toasted almonds
    scattered over the cream.
Peaches, pears, apricots, and chestnuts.
Plums, apricots, and cherries.
Pineapple, mandarin orange sections, and black cherries.
Prunes, apricots, and greengage plums.
Cooked apple slices, raisins (simmered as above), and walnut
    halves on top of the cream.

BAKED FRUIT COMPOTE   (SERVES FOUR)

Serve warm or cold with cream.

2 cups canned fruit: peaches,
    apricots, pears, greengage
    plums, cherries
2 tablespoons brown sugar

Grated rind and juice of ½
    lemon
½ cup macaroon or other
    cookie crumbs

Preheat the oven to 350°F. Arrange layers of fruit in a deep baking dish, sprinkling each layer with brown sugar, lemon rind, and lemon juice. Then pour the reserved juice from the can(s) on top, sprinkle on the crumbs, and bake 35 minutes.

WINTER FRUIT DISH   (ABOUT 4 CUPS)

This tantalizing mixture of sweet and tart flavors could be served for breakfast or for dessert. It is also good as a side dish with roast turkey or pork.

1 cup dried pitted prunes, in quarters
1 cup dried apricots, in quarters
1 cup dried peaches, in quarters
3 cups orange juice
2 tablespoons lemon juice
¼ cup brown sugar
2 teaspoons grated orange zest
4 cups fresh pears, peeled, cored, and diced

In a large saucepan, combine the prunes, apricots, peaches, orange juice, lemon juice, brown sugar, and orange zest. Bring to a boil, reduce the heat to a simmer, cover, and let cook for about 7–8 minutes. Add the fresh pears and cook for about 5 minutes more. Remove from the heat and serve warm.

(ABOUT 3 CUPS) **OATMEAL CRUMB TOPPING**

A sweet topping spread over sliced apples, peaches, or most any ripe fresh fruit. Make a lot and store in the freezer until needed.

¼ pound butter
1 cup brown sugar
¾ cup flour
¾ cup regular or quick-cooking oatmeal (not instant)
½ teaspoon cinnamon
¼ teaspoon salt

In a large mixing bowl combine the butter, brown sugar, flour, oatmeal, cinnamon, and salt. Rub the butter into the flour mixture with your fingers or cut in with a pastry blender until the mixture resembles coarse bread crumbs. Spread the crumbs evenly over the prepared fruit in a pan. (Sweeten the fruit lightly if it is tart.) This topping should be baked in a moderate oven (350–375°F). Too hot an oven will burn the crumbs. If the crumbs begin to brown too much during baking, cover loosely with a piece of foil, but remove the foil the last few minutes of baking so the crumbs will crisp.

About Apples

Availability: Height of season is late summer and fall, but many varieties available through winter and spring, even summer.

What to Look For: Firm, unblemished, bright fruit. Green does not necessarily mean sour; varieties like greenings and Granny Smiths are tart, keep well, and are good for both eating and cooking. Crabapples are small, very hard and sour, best for preserves.

Uses: *Raw*, for eating whole, particularly good with both soft and firm cheeses; also in fresh cut-up fruit bowls and salads. *Cooked*, baked, sautéed, stewed, frittered, and fried, especially as an accompaniment to pork, duck, and goose; baked in fruit desserts, pies, pudding, cakes. Also good in stuffings and preserves.

Amount: One per person raw; two when cooked in a compote or applesauce.

Alternatives to Fresh: Dried fruit can be tastier than canned, but some brands of canned applesauce are good. Bottled or canned juice very good if not too full of preservatives; frozen juice is fine; and, of course, freshly pressed cider excellent.

Stewing in the Microwave: ½ pound peeled, cored, and sliced apples (1 cup) in hot syrup (see p. 996), 3 minutes on high power (600–700-watt oven). Results: Color, taste, and texture comparable to stove-top cooking. Apples disintegrate slightly. This amount cooks faster in the microwave.

At the height of the season there is such a variety of apples available that we have an embarrassment of riches in this country. Take advantage of your local varieties and eat them raw—hard, juicy, and tart. Many regional types—like Jonathans, Northern Spys, winesaps, and Newtons—don't seem to keep well through the winter, and the ubiquitous McIntosh, Red and Yellow Delicious apples, and later greenings are what you'll find in the supermarkets most of the winter. For cooking, you need tart apples, but for a baked apple you want one that will keep its shape, so Delicious, Rome Beauty, or Cortland if you can find it, are your best bet.

APPLESAUCE (SERVES FOUR)

Use a food mill for this, if you have one: you won't have to peel or core the apples if you do, and cooking them with their skins adds taste and color. Late summer and fall apples are so flavorful that they don't need spices, but apples that are kept long into winter will need some tarting up and the added smoothness of butter.

8 tart apples	2 tablespoons butter
Sugar	(optional)
½-inch cinnamon stick	Few gratings of nutmeg
(optional)	(optional)
2 cloves (optional)	

Cut the apples in large chunks; pare and core them if you do not have a food mill. Put them in a pan, add a very small amount of water, bout 2 tablespoons sugar, and the cinnamon and cloves, if you wish. Cover and cook slowly until tender, about 15–20 minutes. Put the apples through a food mill to remove the skins, seeds, and spices, or simply remove the spices if you have peeled and cored the apples before cooking them. Stir in the butter, if you like, and add more sugar to taste and nutmeg if desired.

(SERVES SIX)   **CAPE COD APPLE PUDDING**

Serve with heavy cream, if you like.

4 cups peeled and sliced apples	½ teaspoon cinnamon
¾ cup sugar	¼ cup water
¼ teaspoon salt	Baking Powder Biscuits (p. 764)

Put the apples, sugar, salt, cinnamon, and water in a 2-quart saucepan. Stir occasionally and cook until the apples are tender. Meanwhile, prepare the dough for the biscuits. Roll out and spread over the cooked apples in the pan. Cover tight and cook over moderate heat for 15 minutes. Turn into a shallow bowl.

(8-INCH SQUARE CAKE)   **✳ APPLE COBBLER**

Cobblers got their name from the "cobbled" look the crust gets because the batter is dropped on top in clumps rather than poured on or rolled out and placed on top. This recipe follows the traditional method. Serve with cream or vanilla ice cream, if you wish.

12 tablespoons butter, melted	½ cup milk
3 cups peeled and thinly sliced tart apples	1 egg
½ teaspoon salt	1½ cups flour
⅔ cup sugar	2 teaspoons baking powder

Preheat the oven to 375°F. Pour 4 tablespoons of the butter into a cake pan. Spread it evenly and arrange the apples over it. Mix ¼ teaspoon of the salt with ¼ cup of the sugar and sprinkle evenly over the apples; set aside. Pour the remaining 8 tablespoons of the butter into a bowl, add the milk and egg, and beat well. Mix the flour, baking powder, the remaining 6 tablespoons sugar, and the remaining ¼ teaspoon salt in a bowl. Stir in the milk and egg mixture and beat until smooth. Plop about 12 clumps of biscuit batter (¼ cup each) over the apples and bake for about 35–45 minutes, or until a toothpick comes out clean. (Cover loosely with foil if the top gets too brown.) Serve from the pan in squares, fruit side up.

PEACH COBBLER

Use 3 cups *peeled, sliced peaches* in place of apples.

BERRY COBBLER

Use 3 cups *blueberries, blackberries*, or *raspberries*.

CHERRY COBBLER

Use 3 cups *pitted cherries* (if sour, increase sugar to 1¼ cups).

APPLE CRISP ✳   (SERVES SIX)

Sweet soft apples, mildly spiced, with cinnamony crisp brown crumbs on top. It's good served with heavy cream.

5 cups peeled and sliced apples	½ teaspoon cinnamon
⅓ cup water	¼ teaspoon salt
¾ cup flour	¼ pound butter, in small pieces
1 cup sugar	

Preheat the oven to 350°F. Butter a 1½-quart baking dish, spread the apples in it, and sprinkle the water on top. Combine the flour, sugar, cinnamon, and salt in a bowl, and rub in the butter with your fingers until it resembles coarse crumbs. Spread evenly over the apples. Bake for about 30 minutes or until the crust is browned.

APPLE BROWN BETTY   (SERVES SIX)

If your apples are full of flavor, you won't need the lemon. Serve with heavy cream.

5 tablespoons melted butter
2 cups homemade dry bread
    crumbs
5 cups (about 1½ pounds)
    peeled, sliced tart apples
½ cup brown sugar

½ teaspoon cinnamon
Grated rind and juice of ½
    lemon (optional)
⅓ cup hot water
Heavy cream

Preheat the oven to 350°F. Butter a 1½-quart casserole or baking dish, preferably one with a lid. Toss the melted butter and crumbs together lightly in a bowl. Spread about a third of the crumbs in the baking dish. Toss the apples, sugar, cinnamon, and optional lemon rind and lemon juice together in a bowl. Spread half the apple mixture over the crumbs, add another layer of crumbs, a layer of the remaining apples, and a final layer of crumbs on top. Add the hot water. Cover with a lid or with foil and bake for 25 minutes. Uncover and bake 20 minutes more. Serve with the cream.

PEACH BROWN BETTY

Omit the cinnamon, and optional lemon juice and rind, and substitute *5 cups sliced peaches* for the apples.

APRICOT BROWN BETTY

Substitute *3 cups fresh apricots* or *stewed and drained dried apricots* for the apples and use *⅓ cup stewing liquid* instead of the water.

BAKED APPLES

(4 APPLES)

Use firm apples that will hold their shape, such as Delicious, Rome Beauty, Cortland, pippins, Granny Smith, greening, or other hard fall apples. To my mind, the humble, homy baked apple, done properly, is equal to, if not better than, the fanciest pastry. Serve warm with cream, if you like.

4 firm, ripe apples
⅓ cup sugar
½ cup water

⅛ teaspoon salt
Zest of 1 lemon, cut into large
    strips, optional

Preheat the oven to 350°F. Peel the top third of the apples and core. Put the sugar, water, salt, and lemon zest in a small pan, bring to a boil, stir, and remove from the heat. Set the apples upright in a baking dish and pour the syrup over. Cover (use foil if there is no lid that fits) and bake for about 30 minutes, or until the apples are easily pierced with the tip of a knife. Spoon some of the syrup over the apples and sprinkle a little sugar over the top. You may put them under the broiler for 2 to 3 minutes to brown.

APPLE COMPOTE
(SERVES FOUR)

1 cup sugar
Grated rind of 1 lemon
1 cup water

8 tart apples, pared, cored,
    and quartered

Combine the sugar, grated lemon rind, and water in a saucepan and simmer for 5 minutes. Add the apple pieces, a few at a time, and cook until tender enough to pierce with a toothpick. Continue to cook until all the apples are done. Strain the syrup over the apples. Serve cold.

APPLE SNOW
(SERVES FOUR)

This is particularly delicious served with Soft Custard (p. 939) or English Custard (p. 987).

4 tart apples, pared, cored,
    and sliced
¼ cup water

3 egg whites
½–¾ cup sugar
1 tablespoon lemon juice

NOTE
see page 471

Put the apples and water in a saucepan, cover, and cook over low heat for 7–10 minutes or until mushy, stirring occasionally. Mash or beat until smooth. There should be 1 cup or a bit more of thick applesauce. Beat the egg whites until foamy, then gradually add the sugar and lemon juice, beating until stiff but not dry. Fold into the applesauce and chill. Or serve warm by turning the apple snow into a buttered double-boiler top, covering, and cooking over simmering water for 30 minutes.

CINNAMON APPLES
(6 APPLES)

Cinnamon apples are a fine dessert. Try them also as a relish with roast pork.

1 cup sugar	1½ cups water
2 tablespoons tiny red cinnamon candies	12 cloves
	6 apples, pared and cored

Combine the sugar, cinnamon candies, and water in a saucepan and simmer for 5 minutes. Stick two cloves in each apple. Put the apples in the saucepan, cover, and cook over low heat, basting every 10 minutes until tender when pierced with a toothpick. Remove the apples from the pan and put in a dish to cool. Remove the cloves. Strain the syrup over the apples and serve warm or chilled.

(4 LARGE DUMPLINGS)   *** APPLE DUMPLINGS**

Each apple is wrapped in dough, baked until golden and tender, and served with a creamy, spicy sauce.

Sauce

¾ cup apple juice	¼ teaspoon nutmeg
½ cup water	3 tablespoons butter
¼ teaspoon cinnamon	

Rich Dumpling Dough

2 cups flour	⅔ cup vegetable shortening
2 teaspoons baking powder	½ cup cold milk
1 teaspoon salt	
4 whole apples (Golden Delicious preferable, but pippins or Rome Beauties will do also), peeled and cored	2 tablespoons sugar
	½ cup cream

Preheat the oven to 375°F. Have ready an 8- or 9-inch square baking pan. Combine the apple juice, water, cinnamon, nutmeg, and butter in a small saucepan. Heat, stirring several times, until the butter melts. Remove from the heat and set aside. To make the dough: Put the flour, baking powder, and salt in a large mixing bowl, and stir them together with a fork or wire whisk. Drop in the shortening and work it into the flour using a pastry blender, two knives, or your fingertips, mixing until the fat is reduced to tiny uneven particles and the mixture resembles fresh bread crumbs. Pour in the milk and stir with a fork just until the dough holds together. Form the dough into a square cake about 1 inch thick, and place it on a lightly floured, smooth surface. With a rolling pin, roll the dough lightly in all directions, lifting it frequently to be sure it is not sticking to the surface, and keeping it as square as you can. Roll until the dough is about 13 inches square and ⅛ inch thick. Cut the dough into four equal (6½-inch) squares. Place an apple in the center of each square and bring the four corners of the dough together at the top, enclosing the apple completely. Give the four attached corners a clockwise twist, which seals the dumpling and adds a decorative topknot. Put the dumplings in the baking dish, about 1 inch apart. Pour the applesauce over the dumplings, and sprinkle each one with ½ tablespoon of the sugar. Bake for about 25 minutes, basting the dumplings with the sauce several times. Pour the cream into the sauce and bake for about 15 minutes more. The dumplings are done when the pastry is golden and the apples are tender when pierced with a skewer. Remove from the oven and serve warm with the sauce from the pan.

PEACH DUMPLINGS

Make more dumplings of a smaller size by substituting *8 peeled peach halves* for the whole apples. You must halve the peaches to remove the pits, but you can make dumplings with whole peaches, too. Just peel them first, and wrap them in the dough unpitted.

About Apricots

Availability: June and July.

What to Look For: Small, plump, juicy, orangy-yellow fruit which should yield to slight pressure when pressed.

Uses: *Raw,* whole for hand-eating; in fresh fruit compotes, salads, jelly, ice cream, sherbet, and mousses. *Cooked,* in compotes, soufflés, baked, puréed, whipped. Excellent preserved in jam and as a glaze.

Amount: Three or four per person.

Alternatives to Fresh: Canned very good. Dried excellent both for cooking and just for munching.

Fresh apricots are rather scarce today unless you live in the heart of rich apricot country, like Oregon and Washington, and the ones that have traveled far are apt to soften quite quickly. But when you can find plump fresh ones, take advantage and eat them raw. *To peel:* dip in boiling water, then plunge in cold, and slip off the skins with your fingers. Dried apricots today seldom need presoaking. Simply cook them gently in water to cover for about 15 minutes until just soft; they are delicious served with a dollop of sour cream or crème fraîche.

Stewing in the Microwave: ½ pound (1 cup) apricots in hot syrup (see p. 996), 2 minutes on high power (600–700-watt oven). Results: Color, taste, texture, and cooking time comparable to stove-top cooking.

BAKED APRICOTS

See Baked Fruit Compote (p. 1002).

APRICOT BROWN BETTY

See variation of Apple Brown Betty (p. 1006).

APRICOT SOUFFLÉ

Hot or cold. See Cold Apricot Soufflé (p. 966) or Frozen Apricot Soufflé (p. 970).

(SERVES FOUR)   ## APRICOT WHIP

    1 cup fresh or dried apricots   ⅛ teaspoon salt
    ¼ cup sugar   3 egg whites
    2 teaspoons lemon juice

To make a purée of apricots, slice the fresh apricots (you do not need to peel them) or, if using dried apricots, cook them in water to cover for about 10 minutes, then drain. Put the apricots through a food mill or purée in a blender or food processor. Preheat the oven to 300°F. Combine the apricot purée and the sugar in a heavy-bottomed saucepan and cook over moderately low heat until thickened, stirring often to prevent sticking or burning. Remove from the heat and add the lemon juice and salt. Taste and add more sugar, if necessary. Let cool to lukewarm. Beat the whites until they are stiff but not dry. Whisk a third of the whites into the purée, then fold the mixture gently into the remaining whites. Spoon into a 1-quart soufflé dish. Set the dish in a pan of hot water and bake for about 45 minutes, or until firm to the touch. Serve warm.

NOTE
see page 471

About Bananas

Availability: Year round.
What to Look For: Ripe fruit should be yellow flecked with brown, firm but not hard. Unripe fruit will be hard and slightly green at

the ends; use for cooking, if not too hard. Red bananas are a uniform brown-red and a little softer.

Uses: *Raw*, eaten whole or cut up with cream, on cereal, in fresh fruit compote. Used as a side dish with curry; also mashed in milk shakes. *Cooked*, sautéed, baked, or frittered.

Amount: One per person.

Alternatives to Fresh: Dried, good for munching.

Highly nutritious, bananas seem to be one of our favorite foods from babyhood on, good for breakfast, lunch, or supper. Cut them up only just before serving because they blacken quickly. They also ripen quickly, so don't worry if you find only unripened ones in the market. Just leave out in a cool spot in the kitchen; refrigerate bananas only when fully ripe, and—be forewarned—the skins will turn black but that won't affect their taste.

BAKED BANANAS ❋ (4 BANANAS)

Serve hot with heavy cream.

4 tablespoons butter	4 firm ripe bananas
1 teaspoon grated lemon rind	4 tablespoons dark-brown
1 tablespoon lemon juice	sugar

Preheat the oven to 350°F. Put the butter, lemon rind, and lemon juice in a baking dish and place it in the oven for 2–3 minutes, just long enough to melt the butter; remove and stir. Peel the bananas and put them in the baking dish, turning so they are coated with the butter mixture. Sprinkle the brown sugar over them and bake for 15 minutes.

BAKED BANANAS FLAMBÉED WITH RUM

Pour ¼ *cup warm rum* over the bananas when baked and set aflame, spooning the burning liquor over the bananas.

SAUTÉED BANANAS (4 BANANAS)

This lovely dessert is also a fine accompaniment to curry or chicken dishes.

4 tablespoons butter	¼ cup confectioners' sugar
4 firm ripe bananas	

Melt the butter in a skillet. Peel the bananas and cut them in half lengthwise. Cook over moderate heat for 5 minutes, turning once. Remove to a dish and spoon the butter from the pan over them. Sift the confectioners' sugar on top.

About Blackberries

Height of Season: Midsummer.

What to Look For: Plump, juicy, dark berries.

Uses: *Raw*, as is with sugar and heavy cream, and in a fresh fruit compote. *Cooked*, in puddings, cobblers, compotes, pies, and tarts. *Preserved*, in jams, jellies, and syrup.

Amount: Raw, ½ cup per person; cooked, ¾ cup.

Alternatives to Fresh: Frozen have good flavor. Canned acceptable in pies and purées.

Stewing in the Microwave: ½ pound (1 cup) blackberries in hot syrup
M≋   (see p. 996), 1 minute on high power (600–700-watt oven).
        Results: Color, taste, texture, and cooking time comparable
to stove-top cooking.

The last of the berries of summer, blackberries can be used in all the recipes that call for raspberries when they have vanished.

For use in a lovely bread-and-butter dessert, see Summer Pudding (p. 1014), or use over shortcake (p. 1041).

(SERVES SIX)   **BLACKBERRY ROLYPOLY**

You may substitute any other berry for the blackberries. Serve, if you like, with heavy cream or whipped cream.

6 cups blackberries	1 recipe Baking Powder
1 cup sugar	Biscuit dough (p. 764)
½ teaspoon salt	2 tablespoons butter, melted

Preheat the oven to 425°F. Butter a 7 × 11-inch pan. Combine the berries, sugar, and salt in a bowl. Toss very gently to mix. Set aside. Roll the biscuit dough into a rectangle ½ inch thick. Brush with the melted butter. Spread half the berries over the dough. Roll up loosely like a jelly roll and put into the pan, fold side down. Put the rest of the berries around the roll. Bake for 30–40 minutes or until top is golden and a skewer comes out clean when inserted in the center. Slice and serve warm or cold.

About Blueberries and Huckleberries

Availability: Midsummer for wild; from spring through fall for cultivated.

What to Look For: Blueberries are bright blue with a slightly frosted
look; they should be firm, dry, well rounded. The cultivated berries
are fatter and fleshier and do not have the same intensity of flavor
that you get in wild berries. Huckleberries are larger and darker
and have bigger seeds.

Uses: *Raw,* as is or with cream and sugar, in fresh fruit compote, particularly nice with melon balls and/or strawberries; good in tarts.
Cooked, in pies, muffins, and other baked goods, pancakes, puddings, cobblers, stewed as a dessert sauce. *Preserved,* in jams.

Amount: Raw, ½ cup per person; cooked, ¾ cup.

Alternatives to Fresh: Canned and frozen acceptable for cooking;
frozen better for use fresh but the berries will have softened somewhat.

Stewing in the Microwave: ½ pound (1 cup) blueberries, in hot syrup
(see p. 996), 1 minute on high power (600–700-watt oven).
Results: Color, taste, texture, and cooking time comparable
to stove-top cooking.

If you are in a part of the country where blueberries grow wild, by all
means get a bucket and go out picking. It may spoil your taste for the
cultivated variety, but the treat is worth it.

SUMMER PUDDING OR
BLUEBERRY BREAD PUDDING ✳   (SERVES SIX)

Summer puddings are made with raspberries or blackberries, too. Just
use the same proportions. Serve with heavy cream, if you wish.

7 thin slices white bread	½–⅔ cup sugar
Butter, softened	⅓ cup water
5 cups blueberries	

Butter 6 slices of bread very, very lightly and line the bottom and sides
of a round 3- to 4-cup bowl with the slices, butter side out. Fill in the
gaps with bread trimmed to fit so the bowl is completely covered, saving one unbuttered slice for the top. Cook the blueberries with the
sugar (adjusting according to how sweet the berries are) and water for
10 minutes, then pour into the bread-lined bowl. Place a slice on top
and fold the edges over to meet. Place a saucer on top and press down.
Pour off excess liquid and reserve to serve with the pudding or use for
a sauce or on ice cream. Chill at least 6 hours before serving.

About Cherries

Availability: June, July, and into August.

What to Look For: Bing cherries should be deep red, large, and plump almost to bursting. Equally good and sweet but not as common are the bright reddish brown Lambert cherries. Sour cherries are smaller, paler red (and only for cooking).

Uses: *Raw*, whole with stems left on, or stemmed and pitted in fresh fruit compotes and in tarts. *Cooked*, in pies, in compotes, and as a sauce. Sour and wild cherries make good jellies and syrups.

Amount: ¼ pound per person.

Alternatives to Fresh: Canned and frozen both acceptable.

Stewing in the Microwave: ½ pound (1 cup) pitted cherries, in hot
≈ syrup (see p. 996), 1–2 minutes on high power (600–700-
watt oven). Results: Color, taste, texture, and cooking time
comparable to stove-top cooking.

(SERVES SIX)   **CHERRIES JUBILEE**

2 cups fresh Bing cherries, or	1 tablespoon cornstarch
1 large can black cherries	¼ cup brandy
Water, as needed	1 quart vanilla ice cream
Sugar, as needed	

If using fresh cherries, stem and pit them, then cook them about 5 minutes in 1 cup water and 3 tablespoons sugar. If using canned cherries, add only 1 tablespoon sugar. Dissolve the cornstarch in 1 tablespoon water, then add 1 cup of the cherry cooking juice or of the canned juice, bring to a boil, and simmer with the cherries for 2 minutes. Heat the brandy, add to the cherries, then light and pour them flaming over the ice cream.

About Coconuts

Availability: Year round in some areas, but primarily September through December.

What to Look For: The outside should be hard, with a brown, fibrous husk. Shake it and listen for the liquid sloshing inside; if you can't hear it, the meat, when you open it, will be dried up. Watch out also for mold around the eyes.

Uses: What is called the "milk" doesn't have much flavor and is at best used with other fruits or alcohol in cool drinks. To make the "milk" that is often used in South American cooking, grated coconut must be steeped in this interior liquid. We use the coconut meat, grated, shredded, or flaked for cakes, cookies, desserts, and with other fruits, particularly oranges.

Alternatives to Fresh: Vacuum-packed in cans or plastic pouches, keeps well and tastes fine, although sweeter than fresh.
Amount: The meat of a coconut varies but an average-size coconut of about 1 pound usually yields about 2½ cups of grated coconut.

It is best to refrigerate a fresh coconut.

To extract the meat from a coconut, crack it open by putting it on the middle rack of a preheated 425°F oven for 15–20 minutes, until the shell has split and cracked in several places.

Using an ice pick and hammer, deeply puncture the three eyes, turn upside down over a bowl, and let the coconut milk drain out. (This liquid can be strained to drink or used in cooking.) Tap the shell with the hammer until it splits open. Or, if it is convenient, just go outside and drop it on the hard ground or on a stone. Dislodge the white meat from the shell with a thin screwdriver or knife, and pare off the brown covering with a vegetable peeler. Grate on a hand grater, or in a blender or food processor. Store in an airtight container in the refrigerator or freezer.

About Cranberries

Availability: September through January.
What to Look For: The test of a good cranberry is its bounce. Good firm ones will bounce like rubber balls.
Uses: *Raw* in a relish. *Cooked* in cranberry sauce, jelly, pudding, bread, pie, punch.
Alternatives to Fresh: Frozen. Bottled juice is good and healthful.
Stewing in the Microwave: ½ pound (1 cup) cranberries, in hot syrup (see p. 996), 4 minutes on high power (600–700-watt oven). (Add an extra 2 tablespoons of sugar to the hot syrup before its initial, 3-minute cooking.) Results: Color, taste, texture, and cooking time comparable to stove-top cooking.

About Currants

Availability: Midsummer.
What to Look For: Small, bright red, almost translucent berries.
Uses: *Raw*, stemmed and generously sugared; delicious with raspberries. *Cooked*, principally used cooked, in jellies and jams.
Alternatives to Fresh: Preserved. Dried currants are not really currants but Corinth grapes; they look like small raisins and are used the same way.

About Dates

Availability: Year round packaged.
What to Look For: Plump, not-too-hard, sticky fruit, preferably pitted.

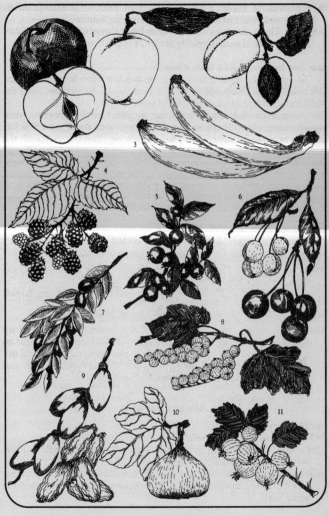

1. apples; 2. apricots; 3. bananas; 4. blackberries; 5. blueberries; 6. cherries;
7. cranberries; 8. currants; 9. dates; 10. figs; 11. gooseberries.

Uses: Plain as a snack or with cream cheese; stuffed with nuts (and sometimes rolled in confectioners' sugar). An addition, chopped, to baked goods, desserts, cakes, cookies. See Date Nut Cakes (p. 828) for a favorite dessert cake.

DATE PUDDING   ✳   (SERVES EIGHT)

This sweet, old-fashioned pudding is good served warm with unsweetened whipped cream. A creamy date pudding layer will form on the bottom as it bakes.

1 cup flour	1 cup walnuts or pecans
1 cup granulated sugar	½ cup milk
½ teaspoon salt	2 cups water
2 teaspoons baking powder	1 cup brown sugar
1 cup chopped dates	2 tablespoons butter

Preheat the oven to 350°F. Use an ungreased 9 × 13-inch baking dish. In a mixing bowl, combine the flour, granulated sugar, salt, and baking powder. If the dates are dry, pour boiling water over them and let stand for 5 minutes, then drain. Add the dates, walnuts, and milk to the flour mixture and beat until blended. Spread the batter in the bottom of the baking dish. In a saucepan, combine the water, brown sugar, and butter, and bring to a boil. Pour this topping over the batter. Bake the pudding for about 20–25 minutes. Serve warm.

About Figs

Availability: Midsummer for fresh figs. Dried available year round.

What to Look For: Fresh figs can be purple or pale green. They should be a little soft and look well filled out and, when cut, pink and juicy inside. There are many varieties of dried figs—those from the Mediterranean and Middle East are particularly plump and good; sometimes they are sold packaged, sometimes in bulk in stores featuring imported foods and spices.

Uses: *Raw,* for eating whole or sliced with a little crème fraîche; delicious served sliced with thin pieces of country ham or prosciutto, as an appetizer. Dried stewed figs, baked goods, puddings (a lovely Steamed Fig Pudding is on p. 952).

Alternatives to Fresh: Dried as noted above, and canned.

(SERVES SIX)   **STEWED FIGS**

> 1 pound dried figs
> 1 cup sour cream or Soft
>   Custard (p. 939)

Cover the figs with cold water and simmer until they are tender, about 15 minutes. Chill. Spoon into goblets with a few tablespoons of their juice and top with sour cream or Soft Custard.

About Gooseberries

Availability: Midsummer.

What to Look For: Round—the size of marbles—green, almost translucent fruit.

Uses: *Cooked*, in puddings and tarts, and as a sauce. *Preserved*, as a relish and in jam. Once abundant in this country, gooseberry shrubs are now subject to stringent laws in many states because of a fungus they harbor which is destructive to pines. We almost never see fully ripened gooseberries in our markets, and the appearance of green ones is fleeting, so grab them while you can if you love their flavor. They can be stewed into a simple sauce to eat with cream or custard on top or, following British tradition, as an accompaniment to fish, particularly mackerel.

About Grapefruit

Availability: Year round, but inferior in quality and more expensive during the summer months.

What to Look For: Firm, heavy, well-filled-out fruits. A coarse, thick-skinned grapefruit, or one that narrows at the stem end, is apt to yield less juice and taste pithy. A few exterior scars don't hurt, but soft skins and dents are not good signs.

Uses: *Raw*, halved and scooped out, peeled and segmented as a breakfast fruit, in fresh fruit salads and compotes, jellies, ices. *Cooked*, baked, or broiled as a first course or dessert. The juice makes an excellent drink.

Amount: Half a grapefruit per person eaten whole. The juice of one grapefruit makes about ⅔ cup, but yield varies considerably.

Alternatives to Fresh: Frozen concentrated juice very good; also canned—unsweetened preferred.

The juicy, almost seedless grapefruit we find today is very much a product of American enterprise of this century. Happily, we have taken to the grapefruit with enthusiasm: since the thirties, grapefruit has become almost as popular as oranges in this country, particularly among dieters.

To prepare a grapefruit half, use a special curved grapefruit knife to cut around each segment and loosen it from the surrounding membrane and skin. Actually a small sharp paring knife works just as well: run it around the whole circumference, then slice between the pulp and membrane on both sides of each segment. If you want to decorate the center with a strawberry or cherry or sprig of mint, cut out the core; otherwise it is not necessary.

To extract whole grapefruit segments, put the fruit on a cutting board. Hold it firmly with your left hand and pare off the skin with a long, very sharp knife. Cut away the white layer beneath the skin as you pare. Remove the pulp by sections, cutting it away from the membrane, first on one side of a section, then the other (see illustration for sectioning an orange, p. 1028). Cut off any white bits that remain, so that you have perfect whole sections of fruit.

GRAPEFRUIT COUPE   (SERVES FOUR)

> Mint sprigs
> 3–4 teaspoons sugar
> 2–3 grapefruit cut in
>   segments, enough to make
>   2 cups

Crush about 6–8 leaves of mint with the sugar and sprinkle it over the grapefruit segments. Macerate in the refrigerator for several hours. Serve in chilled sherbet glasses or goblets with a sprig of mint on top.

GRAPEFRUIT BASKETS

Cut the fruit in half. Remove the pulp and scrape out the white membrane and the core. Scallop the edge with scissors, if you like. Fill with fresh fruit compote, grapefruit segments, and avocado slices or sherbet.

(SERVES FOUR)   **BAKED GRAPEFRUIT**

2 grapefruit   2 tablespoons white or brown
2 tablespoons melted butter   sugar or honey

Preheat the oven to 450°F. Cut each grapefruit in half crosswise. With a
sharp knife, cut each section to loosen the flesh from the membrane
and remove any seeds. Spread the melted butter on each half. Sprinkle
the sugar or honey over the tops. Bake for 15 minutes.

BROILED GRAPEFRUIT

Broil for about 5 minutes, until hot and bubbly.

About Grapes

Availability: Summer and fall for green grapes and local varieties; late
summer, fall, and winter for dark red grapes.

What to Look For: Plump, unblemished fruit of good color, firmly attached to the stems. Check around the stem area for signs of off-
color and deterioration. Unripened grapes will not develop much
flavor after they've been cut.

Uses: *Raw,* for hand-eating; stemmed, pitted, and sometimes even
peeled, in fresh fruit salads and compotes; with fish; in fruit jellies
and other desserts. Bottled grape juice excellent as a refreshing
drink; good, too, as a flavoring in homemade ice cream. Raisins
eaten raw or cooked, in baked goods, desserts, preserves.

Amount: A pound should serve three.

Alternatives to Fresh: Frozen concentrated juice, as well as the bottled,
good. Raisins are dried grapes, available black and yellow; small
seedless sultanas are not to be confused with currants. Both domestic and imported varieties excellent.

Cool grapes are good just by themselves. Fortunately, they have an ex-
tended season—the bright red Tokay and Cardinal grapes, then the
deep red Emperors and almost black Malagas, replace the early pale
green seedless Thompsons on the market. For a quite different flavor,
don't miss the native Northeastern Concords when they mature in the
fall—deep blue with tougher skins that slip easily off the exceptionally
juicy, almost slippery flesh.

For a fancier presentation, pile seedless grapes in sherbet glasses or
goblets and top with whipped cream flavored with a little kirsch, or
crème fraîche with slivered toasted almonds on top.

Frosted grapes are fun at Christmastime. Simply beat an egg white until frothy, then pour over a perfect bunch of Malagas, coating each grape. Dust with granulated sugar and let dry before adding to the fruit bowl.

About Kiwi

Availability: May through December.

What to Look For: Small, brown, oval-shaped fruit with a slightly furry brown skin which is peeled away before eating. The fruit should be firm but give slightly when held in the palm of the hand and squeezed gently. It will ripen at room temperature.

Uses: Raw for eating or in desserts, salads, and occasionally a meat or poultry dish. Cooking brings out the acidity.

About Kumquats

Availability: Late fall and winter.

What to Look For: Small, firm fruit with a bright color (kumquats look like tiny oranges, only more oblong in shape).

Uses: *Raw*, for eating whole (the rind is sweet and flavorful). *Cooked*, in marmalades, jellies, candied as a condiment.

Amount: Three or four per person as dessert.

About Lemons

Availability: Year round.

What to Look For: Heavy, firm (but not hard) fruit, bright yellow color, fairly thin skins; avoid coarse, thick-skinned lemons, which will yield little juice.

Uses: Fresh slices and wedges are a much-used garnish. Lemon juice, used discreetly, is greatly valued as a seasoning to bring out natural flavors; it is useful as an aid in blanching and to prevent discoloration of certain fruits and vegetables; the juice—and often the yellow part of the skin, known as the zest—is an essential flavoring in many savory as well as sweet sauces, in marinades, desserts, baked goods, sherbets, ices, toddies, and cool refreshing drinks.

Alternatives to Fresh: Frozen concentrated juice is acceptable in baking and in drinks, but only fresh will do as a zestful flavoring. Bottled lemon juice should be avoided, as well as the kind that comes in plastic lemon-shaped containers; the taste is disagreeable and would not add real lemon flavor.

Amount: 1 lemon makes about ¼ cup, but yield varies considerably.

No good kitchen should be without a fresh lemon or two, and since they're always available and keep well, there's no reason not to have them on hand. Just a few drops can make such a difference in giving character to a bit of sauce, heightening the flavor of fruits and vegetables, bringing out the essence of fish and shellfish. The more you use lemons, the more they will reveal their secret powers. But they are perverse, too; while their high vitamin C count inhibits cut peaches, pears, bananas, avocados, and apples from turning black and blanches artichoke bottoms, Swiss chard stems, and sweetbreads, at the same time lemon juice can turn certain green vegetables, like beans and broccoli, brownish and red cabbage blue! So get to know your lemons.

One of the most amazing properties of the lemon is its effect on raw flesh, so that when fish is marinated in a lemon bath, the raw fish turns opaque after several hours and is in essence "cooked." In the same way the acidity breaks down tough fibers so that lemons are invaluable in marinades to tenderize meat.

About Limes

Availability: Year round.
What to Look For: Full, heavy fruit with deep, bright green color and glossy skin that isn't too thick.
Uses: Fresh slices and wedges for garnish. The juice, and occasionally the grated rind, is sometimes used with fish and is particularly desirable for chilled desserts and ices, and cool drinks.
Amount: 1 lime produces less than ¼ cup juice, but yield can vary.
Alternatives to Fresh: Frozen concentrated juice is fine for drinks and desserts. Bottled lime juice, used discreetly, has its own special flavor in drinks.
You can use limes in many of the ways you use lemons to blanch and to penetrate fibers because the citric acid content has the same properties. But as a flavoring lime juice does impart a different taste.

About Mangoes

Availability: Midsummer. Increasingly available in our markets.
What to Look For: The skin is sometimes orange, sometimes a deep red with just a little green, and the fruit should be soft to the touch.
Uses: *Raw,* eaten whole; good in ice cream and ices. *Preserved,* in chutneys.
Amount: One mango per person.
A ripe, sweet mango has an indescribably delicious and refreshing taste of ginger and lemon; it should not be puckery—that means it isn't ripe. There is an art to eating a mango. Don't try to remove the seed to which the flesh clings so tenaciously. Simply cut a circle all around the fruit, then peel back the skin, and eat the flesh with a spoon, scraping it away from the pit.

GREEN MANGO FOOL   *   (ABOUT 2½ CUPS)

This is a classic old-fashioned English dessert. Serve with plain Pound Cake (p. 800) or Gingersnaps (p. 873).

2 green, unripe mangoes (very firm and hard)	⅓ cup water
⅓ cup sugar (or more if the fruit is very tart)	1 cup heavy cream
	1½ tablespoons nonfat dry milk

Peel the mangoes. Cut the flesh away from the seed and dice the fruit. Put the diced mangoes in a saucepan and add the sugar and water. Cook over medium heat, stirring often, for about 10 minutes, or until the fruit is soft. Taste and add more sugar if too tart. Remove from heat and mash the mangoes with a fork until you have a coarse purée. If there is extra liquid, drain some away. The purée should have the texture of applesauce. Cool. Put the heavy cream and nonfat dry milk in a bowl and whip until the cream holds firm peaks. (Adding nonfat dry milk will stabilize whipped cream.) Gently stir the cooled mango purée into the whipped cream. Spoon into serving dishes. If you don't use all the mango fool, freeze it. It makes delicious ice cream.

About Melons

Availability: Cantaloupes or muskmelons from May through September; casaba, July to November; Crenshaws, August and September; honeydews, July through October; watermelons, June through August. Expensive, imported varieties in winter months.

What to Look For: Ripe cantaloupes, casabas, Crenshaws, and honeydews should have lost any greenish cast and the flower end should yield slightly to pressure and should give off a pleasant melon smell (except for casabas, which have no aroma). Only a farmer with his trick of plugging a melon can judge accurately the ripeness of a watermelon before it is opened, but most markets will display a cut piece; look for firm, juicy, red-colored flesh and dark seeds.

Uses: *Raw,* halved, quartered, or cut in smaller slices, cut in chunks or balls in salads and fruit bowls; also for sherbets and ices. The rind of watermelon makes a fine pickle.

Individual tastes assert themselves when it comes to eating melons. Some people like to sprinkle sugar on top, some a dash of salt, and sometimes a squirt of lemon or lime will bring out sluggish natural flavor. But a really good melon requires no artful additions. A slice of juicy melon is always a welcome sight at breakfast or lunch, or as a first or last course at dinner.

Melon and ham as an appetizer is simple and delicious. Arrange

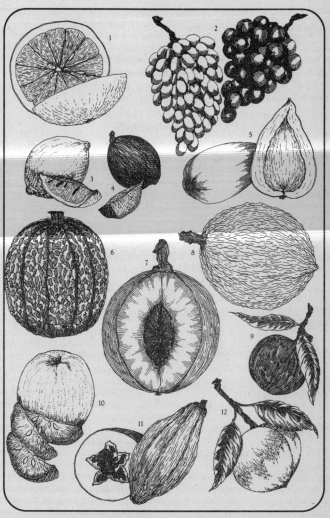

1. grapefruit; 2. grapes; 3. lemon; 4. lime; 5. mangoes; 6. cantaloupe; 7. honeydew melon; 8. Crenshaw melon; 9. nectarine; 10. orange; 11. papaya; 12. peach.

peeled slices of almost any kind of ripe melon (except watermelon) with two or three very thin slices of country ham or Italian prosciutto.

For dessert a scoop of vanilla ice cream or a few tablespoons of raspberries can be nice filling the cavity of a melon. A small half cantaloupe is sometimes very pleasing filled with Port. Combinations of different kinds of melons make lovely dishes, particularly when the fruit is scooped out with a melon baller. Balls of melon are also good with blueberries and a sprinkling of kirsch and sugar.

About Nectarines

Availability: June through September.

What to Look For: Plump fruit of a good color—orangy yellow, deepening to red in areas. When fully ripe, along the seam there will be a little softening.

Uses: *Raw,* whole for hand-eating; cut up in fresh fruit salads, compotes, tarts. *Cooked,* may be used in any of the desserts and preserves that call for peaches.

Stewing in the Microwave: ½ pound sliced nectarines (1 cup), in hot syrup (see p. 996), 3 minutes on high power (600–700-watt oven). Results: Color, taste, texture, and cooking time comparable to stove-top cooking.

NECTARINE AND BLUEBERRY
COBBLER   (SERVES SIX)

Serve plain or, if you wish, with lightly whipped cream.

1¾ cups flour	2 tablespoons cornstarch
1 tablespoon baking powder	¼ cup brown sugar, firmly
½ teaspoon salt	packed
6 tablespoons butter, chilled	¼ cup corn syrup
and in pieces	½ cup water
½ cup granulated sugar	5 cups sliced nectarines,
¾ cup cream	approximately
2 tablespoons butter, melted	1 cup blueberries

Mix flour, baking powder, and salt in a large mixing bowl and stir with a fork to blend. Put the pieces of chilled butter into the flour mixture and rub quickly with your fingertips until the mixture resembles coarse crumbs. Add the granulated sugar and lightly blend. Using a fork, slowly stir in the cream, until roughly mixed. Gather the dough into a shaggy mass and knead 5–6 times. Set aside while making the filling. Preheat the oven to 375°F. Pour melted butter into a rectangular or oval baking dish (9 × 13-inch or 13-inch oval of at least 3-quart capacity) and spread over the bottom and sides. In a saucepan, combine the cornstarch, brown sugar, corn syrup, and water, place over medium heat, and cook until thickened, stirring frequently. Place the nectarines and blueberries in the prepared baking dish and pour the hot syrup evenly over the top. Roll the dough on a lightly floured surface, to the size of the top of the baking dish. Place on top of the fruit mixture. Bake for about 40–50 minutes, until lightly browned and a toothpick inserted in the crust comes out clean.

About Oranges

Availability: Year round, but (except for Valencias) the quality is poor and the fruit expensive during summer months.

What to Look For: Fresh, heavy fruit with bright-looking color and skin that is not too thick and coarse, particularly if you are interested in good juicing oranges. Navel oranges (good for peeling and segmenting) and Valencias should be rich orange, but with other varieties the color is not a guide; for instance, greening is apt to occur late in the season and is not indicative of immaturity. A few scars don't matter, either. Check for discoloration around the stem end—a sign that the fruit is starting to deteriorate, which can affect the taste of the juice.

Uses: *Raw,* peeled and segmented for hand-eating; sliced or segmented in green salads, mixed fruit salads, and compotes, or alone as a dessert; as a flavoring in baked goods; grated peel used in both savory and sweet sauces, frostings, fillings, and dessert; juice in jellies and in sherbets and ices. *Baked,* as a quick relish.

Alternatives to Fresh: Frozen concentrated juice, good; canned not desirable. Freshly squeezed bottled juice acceptable if not kept too long.

The healthy aspect of the average American is often attributed to the amount of orange juice he drinks. Today with the easy availability of frozen concentrated juice, we are drinking even more, but there is nothing like the taste of your own freshly squeezed juice, particularly when oranges are at their peak of flavor. Treat your family to it for breakfast at least sometimes, or add some fresh juice and pulp to the pitcher of frozen to give it a lift. Eating an orange cut in half and sectioned like a grapefruit (see p. 1028) is a very nice way, too, to start the morning. Try desserts like fresh orange jelly—you will revel in their goodness. Or make a coupe out of segments or slices.

To extract segments from an orange, first peel it, by starting at the top with a sharp knife and peeling around and down in a spiral, cutting close to the flesh and removing the white pith at the same time as the peel. Trim away any white bits that you missed. Then remove each section, cutting it away from the membrane, first on one side and then on the other.

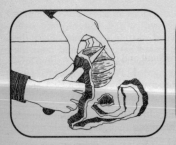 

To make orange slices: Remove the peel in a spiral pattern with a sharp paring knife. Cut away any remaining bits of white. Cut ¼-inch slices, discarding the end pieces. Remove any seeds.

ORANGES AMANDINE (SERVES FOUR)

2 cups orange sections or
    slices
4 teaspoons grated maple
    sugar

4 tablespoons toasted slivered
    almonds

Sprinkle the orange sections or slices with the sugar and almonds and chill thoroughly.

ICED ORANGES ✳ (2½ CUPS)

Sometimes less is more; this is better than most complicated desserts. Be sure to serve it ice-cold.

2 cups fresh orange sections   ½ cup orange marmalade

Stir marmalade into orange sections and chill until very cold.

AMBROSIA (SERVES SIX)

Sliced bananas may be added at the last, but it is not strictly ambrosia then.

3 cups sliced oranges
¾ cup shredded coconut, fresh
    if possible

Sprinkle the orange slices with the coconut and chill well.

About Papayas

Availability: Usually May and June.
What to Look For: Pear-shaped fruit with smooth skin; firm but soft enough to dent slightly with a little pressure of your thumb; not too large, with good orange or yellow color.
Uses: *Raw*, halved and chilled, or cut up in fruit salads and fresh fruit compotes; as papaya juice.

Papaya is a tropical fruit, also known as "pawpaw." In the United States, it is grown mainly in Florida. The ripe, raw fruit has moist, juicy orange flesh and many edible black seeds. Serve it in wedges with most of the seeds removed, accompanied by a slice of lemon or lime. It is cooling on a hot summer day.

About Peaches

Availability: Spring through fall, but especially in the summer months.
What to Look For: Green peaches will *not* ripen well at home: be sure that the peaches you buy are ripe and golden with a well-rounded shape; they should be slightly soft but without any tan or brownish spots.
Uses: *Raw* and whole for hand-eating, or sliced, with or without heavy cream, or in fruit salads. *Broiled or baked*, as a relish, pickled, brandied, spiced. In desserts, such as mousses, pies, cakes, betties, crisps, cobblers, ice cream. *Preserved*, in jellies, jams, and preserves.
Alternatives to Fresh: Frozen taste more like fresh peaches than canned.
Stewing in the Microwave: ½ pound peeled, sliced peaches (1 cup), in
Mɛ hot syrup (see p. 996), 3 minutes on high power (600–700-watt oven). Results: Color, taste, texture, and cooking time comparable to stove-top cooking.

Of the thousands of varieties of peaches, there are two general types: freestone and clingstone. Freestones are more desirable, for the flesh separates easily from the pit. Clingstones are used mainly for canning, since they hold their shape well.

To peel peaches, dip them briefly in boiling water before removing the skin with a sharp knife.

To prevent darkening in sliced peaches, sprinkle them with a little lemon juice.

To serve sliced peaches, arrange in shallow bowls, accompanied by heavy cream or whipped cream, or sprinkle them with blueberries. Or pour a sauce over them, made with sweetened, puréed strawberries and/or raspberries flavored with a few drops of lemon juice.

To bake or broil peaches, slice them in half and remove the stones. Fill the cavities with any one or a combination of the following: butter, sugar, lemon juice, a sprinkle of nutmeg, chopped nuts, raisins, a little brandy. Bake about 15–20 minutes in a 350°F oven, or place at least 6 inches below the broiler and watch carefully.

PEACH BROWN BETTY

See variation of recipe for Apple Brown Betty (p. 1006).

PEACH COBBLER

A cobbler is particularly delicious made with fresh peaches. See p. 1006 for recipe.

FRESH PEACH TURNOVERS (TEN 4½ × 2-INCH TURNOVERS)

You can make turnovers as large or small as you want—from giant ones to tiny ones of only a bite or two each. Just be sure to have plenty of dough to work with—better too much than too little—and don't fill them too full of fruit, or the sides will unseal and the juices leak out. When forming turnovers, seal the edges carefully to prevent leaks. For small turnovers like these, allow two per person for a fair serving. The variations using plums, apricots, and cherries are equally delicious.

1 recipe Basic Pastry Dough (p. 895)	7 tablespoons sugar
1½ cups peaches, peeled, pitted, and in ½-inch-thick pieces	2 tablespoons cream

Preheat the oven to 425°F. Lightly grease and flour a large, flat baking sheet, or cover it with parchment paper. Place the dough on a lightly floured, smooth surface and roll to a thickness of about ⅛ inch—the same thickness you would roll pie dough. With a round cutter (or saucer) approximately 4½ inches in diameter cut out as many pieces of dough as you can—about seven. Gather up the scraps of dough, press them together, and reroll them to cut the remaining three rounds. Place 2 tablespoons of the prepared peaches on each round of dough—or simply divide the fruit equally among the 10 rounds—and sprinkle each mound of fruit with a scant 2 teaspoons sugar. With your fingertips, moisten the edges of the dough with water, and fold each round of dough over to form a half-moon shape. Press the edges gently with your fingers, then press them together with the tines of a fork. Brush the turnovers with cream and sprinkle each one with about ½ teaspoon of the remaining sugar. Place the turnovers on the prepared baking sheet, leaving at least 1 inch between. Bake for about 20 minutes, until the pastry is lightly browned. Remove from the oven and cool on racks. Those not eaten within one day should be carefully wrapped and frozen.

FRESH PLUM TURNOVERS

Substitute *1½ cups sliced pitted plums* for the peaches. Increase the amount of sugar slightly if the plums are tart.

FRESH APRICOT TURNOVERS

Substitute *1½ cups sliced pitted apricots* for the peaches.

CHERRY TURNOVERS

Substitute *1½ cups cherry halves, sweet or sour,* fresh or frozen, for the peaches. If using sour cherries, be sure to increase the amount of sugar.

MIXED FRUIT TURNOVERS

Use two or three of the above fruits in each turnover. Have the prepared fruits in separate bowls until the pastry rounds are ready, then divide the various fruits among the rounds of dough.

About Pears

Availability: Some varieties like Bartlett available in August and fall; others like Anjou, Bosc, and Comice are around through the winter.

What to Look For: Firm fruit with no bad spots; color will vary according to the variety. Most pears you buy will need several days' ripening.

Uses: *Raw*, whole for hand-eating, cut into tart green salads and mixed
with other fruits in salads and compotes. *Cooked*, stewed, baked, in
tarts. *Preserved*, spiced.

Alternatives to Fresh: Canned pears are not as good as fresh, but they
are all right in a pinch.

Stewing in the Microwave: ½ pound peeled, cored, and sliced pears (1
M≋   cup), in hot syrup (see p. 996), 4 minutes on high power
(600–700-watt oven). Results: Color, taste, and texture comparable to stove-top cooking. This amount cooks faster in the microwave.

There are literally thousands of varieties of pears that come in a great
range of colors: yellow, gold, green, brown. Bartlett, Anjou, Bosc, and
Seckel are among the most familiar.

Pears are particularly good with cheese—a firm cheese like aged
Cheddar, a soft cheese like Brie or Camembert, or a good Roquefort;
serve them with one kind or a selection for dessert. They are also good
as a salad peeled, halved, and cored with a ball of cream cheese inside
and on a bed of lettuce.

Pears are good in cobblers and crisps (see p. 999).

PEARS WITH CHOCOLATE SAUCE

Peel pears, cut them in quarters lengthwise, and remove the cores.
Sauté them in butter until tender and golden brown. Serve warm with
Chocolate Sauce (p. 986).

POACHED OR BAKED PEARS   (SERVES FOUR)

4 firm pears	Lemon rind or cinnamon stick
½ cup sugar	Heavy cream or Soft Custard,
½ cup water	optional (p. 939)

Peel the pears, cut them in quarters lengthwise, and remove the cores.
Combine the sugar with the water and some lemon rind or cinnamon
stick; cook rapidly for 5 minutes. Add the pears, cover, and cook
slowly until tender but still firm; or bake in a 300°F oven. Serve warm
or cold with cream or custard, if you wish.

PEARS WITH COINTREAU

When pears are cooked, remove them from the syrup and cook the syrup until it is as thick as honey. Add 1 *tablespoon Cointreau*, pour over the pears, and chill. Serve with cream.

PEARS IN PORT WINE

Pour *Port wine* over the cooked pears, cover, and let sit for at least 1 hour.

PEARS HELENE

When pears are cooked, add *vanilla or brandy* to taste and let cool in the syrup. Serve with *vanilla ice cream* and top with *Chocolate Sauce* (p. 986).

About Persimmons

Availability: October through December.
What to Look For: Deep orange or red color with green cap intact and no signs of damage. Persimmons will ripen at room temperature.

There are two varieties of persimmons commonly found in the markets today. The *Hachiya* variety is shaped like an acorn, and is oval and almost pointed on the bottom. It is very soft when ripe and is most often used for cooking, steamed pudding, or cookies. The second variety, *Fuyu*, is shaped like a squat tomato. It is delicious and usually peeled and eaten raw, although it is good for cooking too. It is ripe when firm but yields a little when pressed. Both varieties make delicious desserts served ripe and raw in a dessert dish with a little heavy cream and maple syrup poured over. Serve icy cold.
Uses: *Raw*, in fruit salads. *Cooked* and puréed, in cakes.

Persimmons are very bitter when not ripe, sweet and delicious when fully ripened. Serve them chilled and cut in half.

About Pineapples

Availability: Year round, especially in the spring.
What to Look For: Large, heavy, sweet-smelling fruit with no soft spots and healthy-looking leaves (leaves pulling out easily is *not* a

sign of ripeness). Moreover, pineapples will *not* ripen further after they've been picked.

Uses: *Raw,* in wedges, chunks, in salad. *Cooked,* in desserts, cakes, cookies, pies, breads; as juice; in sauces; pickled, spiced; as a garnish for ham and other pork dishes.

Amount: A 2-pound pineapple yields 2½ to 3 cups diced fruit.

Alternatives to Fresh: Canned pineapple comes packed in sweet syrup or unsweetened and packed in water.

An interesting fact about pineapple is that if it is used fresh with gelatin, the gelatin will not jell because pineapple contains an enzyme that destroys its jelling power. However, canned pineapple works perfectly well.

For large slices of pineapple, hold the fruit upright and pare with a sharp knife, then dig out the "eyes." Cut in long slices.

To dice a pineapple, cut off the crown. Then cut crosswise in 1- to 2-inch slices. Cut off the rind and the "eyes" and remove the core. Then cut into cubes. Or use the same method, as for Quartered Pineapple, below, simply scooping the fruit out instead of leaving it on the shell; this is by far the easiest method, although you may not get quite as much fruit.

To shred a pineapple, hold upright, pare, and remove the "eyes." Shred the pulp with the tines of a fork.

PINEAPPLE IN THE SHELL. Without paring or removing the top leaves, cut the pineapple lengthwise into halves. Cut the flesh from the rind either in one piece or in chunks. Then remove the core, scraping out any flesh under the core. Slice or chop all the pieces and arrange on the shell. Sprinkle with *sugar, kirsch,* or *white wine* and garnish with *fresh cherries, strawberries, raspberries,* or *sprigs of mint.*

QUARTERED PINEAPPLE ON THE SHELL. Remove the top leaves, unless you want to keep them on for display. Cut the pineapple lengthwise into quarters. Cut out the core, then slice lengthwise

down the center, going through just to the skin. Run the knife under the flesh along the skin to loosen it on both sides. Then cut the loosened strip on each side into bite-size pieces. Serve one quarter per person, or put the quartered shells in a fruit bowl with other fresh fruits, spearing each loosened chunk with a toothpick.

About Plums

Height of Season: July and August.

What to Look For: Plump fruit with good color, slightly soft but with smooth, unshriveled skins. Don't necessarily fall for very large fat plums—their flavor can be bland and watery.

Uses: *Raw* and whole for hand-eating, sliced in salads and fresh fruit compotes, and over ice cream. *Cooked*, in breads, cakes, pies, puddings, jellies, jams, and preserves.

Alternatives to Fresh: Canned, cooked plums are satisfactory in most cooked dishes.

Stewing in the Microwave: ½ pound plums, quartered (1 cup), in hot syrup (see p. 996), 5 minutes on high power (600–700-watt oven). Results: Color, taste, texture, and cooking time comparable to stove-top cooking. **≋**

Plums come in many color combinations—purple, red, blue, yellow, green—and may be round or oval in shape. Familiar varieties are red-skinned Santa Rosas, large purply-blue Presidents, tiny blue Damsons, and sweet small yellowy-red sugarplums, later greengages and Kelseys. See also About Prunes (p. 1036).

To stew plums, cover them with just enough water to keep them from burning and cook gently until soft, about 10 minutes. Add *sugar* to taste and serve with the juices poured over them. If desired, sprinkle with a little *brandy* and serve over *vanilla ice cream.*

About Pomegranates

Height of Season: Fall.

What to Look For: Fruit about the size of an apple, with good color, not too dry looking.

Uses: Cut and eat raw; use seeds as a garnish for salads.

An exotic, refreshing, wonderful-looking fruit. Suck the seed coverings, chew or spit out the seeds, drink the juice, eat the crimson flesh—and wear old clothes: it's a delightfully messy experience.

About Prunes

Availability: Summer and fall.

What to Look For: Slightly soft fruit with deep blue-black color, smooth skin.

Uses: *Raw*, whole, for hand-eating, cut up in salads and fresh fruit compotes, stewed, in compotes; as juice. *Dried and cooked*, in cakes, muffins, cookies, pies, and whips.

Alternatives to Fresh: Canned available, but it is easy to make your own stewed prunes, which will be more tasty and less limp, and dried prunes have so many other delicious uses.

Stewing in the Microwave: ½ pound (1 cup) pitted, dried prunes, in hot syrup (see p. 996), 3 minutes on high power (600–700-watt oven). Results: Color, taste, texture, and cooking time comparable to stove-top cooking.

Prunes are a form of plum that is especially adaptable to drying. In the United States they are grown mainly in California.

To stew dried prunes, put them in a pot with just enough water to cover and simmer gently until they are plump and tender. Serve in their own juices, with *heavy cream*, if desired.

To purée dried prunes, stew them, remove the pits and put the prunes through a food mill, or purée them in a blender or food processor.

PRUNE WHIP   (SERVES FOUR)

Prune whip was a frequent visitor to nineteenth- and early-twentieth-century tables.

1 cup puréed fresh or dried prunes (see above)	1 tablespoon lemon juice
	⅛ teaspoon salt
¼ cup sugar	3 egg whites

Preheat the oven to 300°F. Combine the prune purée and the sugar in a heavy-bottomed saucepan and cook over moderate heat until thickened, stirring frequently. Remove from the heat and add the lemon juice and the salt. Taste and add more sugar, if necessary. Let cool to lukewarm. Beat the whites until they are stiff but not dry. Whisk a third of the whites into the purée mixture and then fold the mixture gently into the remaining whites. Spoon into a 1-quart soufflé dish. Set the dish in a pan of hot water and bake for about 35–40 minutes, or until firm to the touch. Serve warm.

About Quinces

Availability: Occasionally in specialty stores (unless you know someone with a quince tree).

What to Look For: Firm fruit with a deep yellow color. Don't worry if
they are a bit gnarled.

Uses: Mainly in jellies and preserves—quinces have lots of natural
pectin.

BAKED QUINCES

Quinces   Sliced oranges
Sugar

Preheat the oven to 300°F. Peel the quinces, cut them in quarters, and remove the cores. Arrange them in a casserole and sprinkle them with sugar, allowing 2 tablespoons for each quince. Cover with water by ½ inch. Add some sliced oranges, 1 orange for every 4 quinces. Bake about 2 hours, until tender. Serve cold.

About Raspberries

Height of Season: June and July.

What to Look For: Fresh, clean berries with good color, no green spots
or signs of mold or wetness. Stains on the container may indicate
spoilage.

Uses: *Raw*, with heavy cream, with sugar, in fresh fruit salads, and
compotes, in ice cream, mousses, sherbets. *Cooked*, in pies, tarts,
puddings, soufflés, cakes, pancakes; as juice; puréed, in syrups and
sauces; preserved, in jams and jellies.

Amount: One pint serves three.

Stewing in the Microwave: See p. 996.

Alternatives to Fresh: Frozen in dry-pack form is better than frozen in
syrup.

About Rhubarb

Availability: January through June.

What to Look For: Firm, thick, bright reddish stalks, fairly thick and not fibrous.

Uses: *Cooked,* in pies, often with strawberries; as a stewed fruit, sometimes with apples; makes a good cold soufflé (see p. 965).

Amount: One pound produces about 2 cups of cooked rhubarb.

Stewing in the Microwave: ½ pound (1 cup) rhubarb in hot syrup (see p. 996) for 4 minutes. Stir after each minute for more even cooking. Results: Color, taste, texture, and cooking time comparable to stove-top cooking.

Do not eat the leaves of rhubarb: they are poisonous. Though used as a fruit, rhubarb is really a vegetable, belonging to the sorrel family.

BAKED RHUBARB   (SERVES FOUR)

1 pound rhubarb stalks	½ cup sugar

Preheat the oven to 350°F. Wash the rhubarb and cut off the leaves and the stem ends. Don't peel it unless it is very tough. Cut in 1-inch pieces. Put the rhubarb in a casserole and sprinkle the sugar over it. Cover and bake for about 25 minutes, adding more sugar if the rhubarb is too tart.

STEWED RHUBARB   (SERVES FOUR)

1 pound rhubarb stalks	1 teaspoon grated lemon rind
½ cup sugar	¼ cup water

Wash and trim the rhubarb, peeling it if it is tough. Cut into 1-inch pieces and put in a heavy-bottomed saucepan. Add the sugar, lemon rind, and water, cover, and cook gently for 5–7 minutes.

RHUBARB BETTY   (SERVES SIX)

2 pounds trimmed rhubarb stalks, in 2-inch pieces	6 tablespoons butter, melted
¼ cup water	2 cups fresh sliced strawberries, sweetened (optional)
1½ cup sugar	
2 cups homemade dry bread crumbs	Heavy cream or whipped cream (optional)

Preheat the oven to 350°F. Place the rhubarb in a saucepan with the water and sugar, cover, and cook until tender, about 5 minutes. Set aside. Put the bread crumbs in a bowl with the melted butter and toss to coat all the crumbs. Spread the cooked rhubarb in an 8-inch square baking dish. Sprinkle the crumbs evenly over the top and bake for about 30 minutes, or until the crumbs are browned. Just before serving, put a large spoonful of sliced strawberries in a dessert dish, then place a serving of warm Rhubarb Betty beside it. Serve with cream or whipped cream.

About Strawberries

Availability: Hothouse variety most of the year, but peak of the season in May and June.

What to Look For: Bright, red, shiny, well-formed berries, with no signs of mold or wetness. Stains on the container may indicate spoilage.

Uses: *Raw*, dipped in or sprinkled with sugar, or served with heavy cream, whipped cream, sour cream, or yogurt: in fresh fruit salads and compotes; with cereals. *Cooked*, in pies, tarts, shortcakes; puréed, in syrups and sauces, mousses, ice cream; as juice; preserved, in jellies, jams, and preserves.

Amount: One quart serves four to five.

Alternatives to Fresh: Frozen in dry-pack form is better than frozen in syrup, but only for cooking purposes.

Stewing in the Microwave: ½ pound (1 cup) strawberries, cut in half, in hot syrup (see p. 996), 1 minute on high power (600–700-watt oven). Results: Color, taste, texture, and cooking time comparable to stove-top cooking.

Wash strawberries, if necessary, in cold water; hull them after washing so they don't get soggy unless you want to serve them unhulled in a fruit bowl or to dip in sugar. Wash and sugar berries shortly before eating, so they do not soften.

(SERVES EIGHT) **STRAWBERRIES IN SHERRY CREAM**

Sherry cream has a caramel flavor and a slightly golden color. It is exceptionally good with strawberries.

5 egg yolks	1 cup heavy cream
1 cup sugar	6 cups strawberries, washed
1 cup sherry	and hulled

Put the egg yolks in a heavy-bottomed pan over low heat or in a double boiler over hot water. Beat with a whisk or electric mixer until thick

1. pears; 2. persimmon; 3. pineapple; 4. pomegranate; 5. plums; 6. prunes; 7. pumpkin;
8. quince; 9. raspberry; 10. rhubarb; 11. strawberries; 12. tangerine; 13. watermelon.

and pale. Beat in the sugar and sherry. Cook over low heat, stirring constantly, until thickened, about 7–8 minutes. Remove from the heat and let cool. Just before serving, whip the cream and fold it and the strawberries into the cooled egg yolks.

(SERVES EIGHT)   **STRAWBERRIES ROMANOFF**

An old-fashioned dessert which time has not spoiled a bit.

1 pint vanilla ice cream | ¼ cup curaçao or Cointreau
1 cup heavy cream | 2 quarts strawberries, washed
Juice of 1 lemon | and hulled

Put the ice cream in a 2-quart bowl and beat lightly to soften. Whip the cream until soft peaks form. Fold the cream, lemon juice, and liqueur into the ice cream. Add the strawberries and stir gently. Serve immediately.

(SERVES SIX TO EIGHT)   **STRAWBERRY SHORTCAKE**

1 recipe Cream Biscuits, | 1½ cups heavy cream
   p. 765 | About 1 tablespoon
1 quart strawberries | unsweetened butter
Sugar to taste |

Prepare the biscuits, shaping them into rounds, about 3 inches in diameter, or squares, or bake the dough in an 8-inch cake pan. Slice the berries, reserving 6–8 whole ones to decorate the top, and sweeten them to taste. Whip the cream with a little sugar, then fold about one quarter of it into the berries. When baked, split the biscuit(s), spread one half with butter, and top with berries. Cover with the other half biscuit, spread whipped cream on top, and garnish with whole berries.

OTHER BERRY AND FRUIT SHORTCAKES

Use other berries and/or sliced fresh fruits.

About Tangerines

Height of Season: Winter months.
What to Look For: Heavy-feeling fruit with a deep orange color and a
   nice sheen. The skin, which should be unblemished, peels very easily, which is why it seems less firm than an orange skin.

Uses: Peeled and sectioned, with ice cream and other simple desserts; cut up into fruit salads.

About Watermelons

Availability: May through September, but especially in the summer.

What to Look For: A firm, well-shaped melon; one side will be light-colored from resting on the soil. A cut watermelon is easier to judge for quality: it should have juicy, deep-pink flesh with no white streaks, and the seeds should be dark and shiny.

Uses: *Raw*, in wedges or in fresh fruit salads and compotes. The white rind is often pickled and used as a relish.

Amount: Watermelons vary greatly in size and can be bought in sections by the pound. Be generous in serving: watermelon is 92 percent water, to say nothing of all the seeds.

For watermelon cocktail, cut the pink part of the melon into cubes or balls and remove the seeds. Sprinkle with a little lemon juice and chill. Serve alone or combined with other kinds of melon balls.

CANDIES & CONFECTIONS

I have four new candy recipes that work particularly well in the microwave oven because they become less grainy cooked that way. You will find them in the Microwave chapter (p. 626).

ABOUT MAKING CANDY

There is no reason except pure pleasure to make candy. A gift of home-made candy, made from real cream, butter, fresh nuts, and rich chocolate, is a rare and wonderful surprise. A lively family can finish off a batch in a day. Everyone enjoys being offered a small rich sweet; it's a lovely indulgence at the end of a good meal.

Making candy is as exacting as it is fun, as much chemistry as it is cooking. The basic requirements are strict attention and a few good tools. Don't be discouraged by tales of failure. Too many novice candy-makers have been disappointed by inadequate directions.

Kinds of Candy

Candy is simply sugar, liquid, and flavoring that are melted together and heated to a high enough temperature to solidify. The degree to which the syrup is heated dictates the final consistency of the candy; the higher the heat, the harder the candy.

Between certain stages (234° to 240°F) the sugar syrup solidifies but the candy remains creamy. The best example of this category is fudge. (Not necessarily chocolate!—it's a generic term, meaning a soft, creamy candy.) A bit higher up the scale (242° to 268°F), candy becomes firm and chewy; caramels and taffy belong in this group. And at very high heats (270° to 310°F), a great deal of moisture is evaporated with a re-sulting hard and brittle candy, like crunchy toffee or nut brittles.

Then, of course, there are confections, uncooked as well as cooked

1043

little delicacies, usually made of fruit or nuts. These have the added appeal of often being quick to prepare—a bonus for the sweet tooth in a hurry.

Conditions for Candymaking

Since humidity sometimes causes candy to sugar and soften, it's better to make it on a cold clear day. If humidity is a factor, let some of the moisture evaporate by cooking the candy syrup to two degrees higher than specified.

Candy cooks faster at high altitudes; for each 500 feet above sea level cook the syrup one degree less than the recipe specifies.

Equipment

For cooking, a heavy, deep, straight-sided pot helps keep the candy from burning and the cook from being burned. Pots made of copper or enameled cast iron are particularly good. Use a pot that is about four times greater in volume than the dissolved ingredients, because the candy will boil up dramatically as it cooks. A 4-quart saucepan with a cover is a good all-purpose size.

For stirring, use a sturdy wooden spoon with a long handle; a metal-handled spoon can get too hot. A spoon with a flattened tip will pick up all the syrup from the bottom of the pot.

For spading, turning, and spreading, procedures used for fondant, nougat, and brittles respectively, a heavy-duty metal spatula—a pancake turner—is an all-purpose tool.

For testing, an accurate candy thermometer is almost indispensable. At certain stages each degree is crucial, and a thermometer will let you know the exact state of the syrup.

For cooling to the pouring stage, a marble surface will absorb the heat of the cooking pan quickly and evenly, but it is not essential—the pan can be elevated on a cake rack or set on a thick mat.

To become firm, candy should be poured out of the cooking pan onto a cooling surface. This can be any heat-absorbent surface: a cookie sheet, a platter, or a pastry marble. You can use a baking pan, which will give you neat edges and contain the candy, thus making it thicker, if you want it that way. But there is no need to be rigid about sizes, and any flat surface will do. Most candy solidifies quickly when it is poured out to cool, and there is little danger of its spreading too thin. However, if you are uncertain, and fear that the hot candy mixture might spread, play safe and use a pan with sides; that is why we are recommending a jelly-roll pan.

Ingredients

Use only butter for candymaking. It imparts its own good taste. Use mineral oil or flavorless cooking oils for greasing the pan. They won't become rancid if the candy is stored for a long time.

Setting Up

Because everything happens so quickly in candymaking, it is essential to have all equipment immediately at hand. Put a large platter right by the stove to hold the candy spoon, thermometer or testing spoon, cup of cold water, pastry brush, and a small plate for catching drips. Oil the cooling pan in advance. Have a rack or cooling surface nearby and all ingredients prepared and waiting.

Cooking Candy Syrups

Testing. The concentration of the sugar syrup—the degree to which the syrup is heated—can be measured with a thermometer or by eye and hand, using the cold-water test.

Because the temperature may change rapidly, it is important to gauge constantly, watching the candy syrup vigilantly as it cooks. There is some tolerance within each stage, but if the syrup should go a few degrees above the highest point, add 3–4 tablespoons of cold water or more, if needed, to coax the temperature back down again, then let it cook to the proper degree.

Thermometer Test. Buy a heavy-gauge thermometer that registers to 320°F and test its accuracy by immersing it in a pan of water, bringing the water to the boiling point and letting it boil for 10 minutes. It should read 212°F at sea level, one degree less for every 500 feet above sea level.

When using a thermometer for candy testing, warm it up gradually so it doesn't crack: hold it under increasingly hot water, or put it in the candy pan at the very beginning, making sure that the bulb is completely immersed without touching the bottom or sides of the pan. Attach the thermometer by its clip, or prop it at a slight angle on the side of the pan. Stir around it, but don't move it in and out, as this might cause sugaring (see p. 1046). Remove it quickly from the finished syrup, holding it over a small plate so any lingering sugar crystals don't fall back into the pan.

Cold-Water Test. The concentration of the candy syrup can be tested in cold water, although the reading will not be as exact. Remove the pan of cooking syrup from the heat for each test. Spoon out ½ teaspoon of the syrup, drop it into a cup of cold fresh water, and work it with your fingers for a few seconds to determine the stage.

Stages for Candy Syrup

STAGE	ON A THERMOMETER	IN COLD WATER	EXAMPLES
Soft Ball	234°–240°F	Makes a soft ball which does not hold its shape; flattens when held in the fingers.	Fudge Fondant Pralines
Firm Ball	242°–248°F	Makes a firm ball which holds its shape.	Caramels
Hard Ball	250°–268°F	Makes a hard but pliable ball.	Taffy
Soft Crack	270°–288°F	Makes hard separate threads that bend when removed from water.	Butterscotch
Hard Crack	290°–310°F	Makes brittle threads that remain brittle out of water.	Nut Brittles Candy Apples Lollipops

Sugaring. Sugar crystals, the bane of every candy cook, are bits of undissolved sugar which cause candy to "sugar" and become grainy. Even one recalcitrant crystal can turn a velvety mixture into a granular mass. Some recipes call for corn syrup and cream of tartar as partial insurance against sugaring, but careful cooking is the best precaution.

Preventing Sugar Crystals. Before heating, stir all the ingredients together so they dissolve as much as possible.

When the syrup boils, cover the pan and let it boil for 2–3 minutes; the rising steam will wash down the sides of the pan. Uncover and proceed.

Have ready a cup of cold water and a clean pastry brush, preferably one kept specifically for this purpose. As the syrup boils, dip the brush liberally in the water and thoroughly wash down the sides of the pot so that any remaining undissolved crystals go back into the syrup. The extra water will simply boil away.

After the boiling point has been reached, it is ideal not to interrupt the heating syrup by stirring, but this is not always possible. Candies made with milk, butter, and chocolate are sometimes stirred slowly to prevent scorching, and brittles and other highly heated candies must be stirred, albeit briefly, if they start to burn. Always stir slowly and in one continuous direction, and, to avoid picking up sugar crystals, don't touch the sides of the pot with the spoon.

Cooling Candy

If the candy is to be beaten or stirred after it has cooled, let it rest, undisturbed, until it is lukewarm (about 110°F); the bottom of the pot will be cool enough to touch. Be patient! This may take half an hour or longer.

Set the pot on a cooling rack or heat-absorbent surface or, for faster results, immediately set it in a pan of ice water. Don't stir. When the syrup has cooled, beat or stir without stopping until it has thickened and lost its gloss.

When pouring hot syrup from the pot, use only what pours easily, leaving the thick residue in the bottom of the pot. This thick mass may have cooked more than the free-flowing candy and could turn the whole batch granular.

Some candies are better in flavor and texture if they age overnight. Often candies that aren't creamy at first will become so after setting for eight hours or so. Professionals call this the "relaxing" of the sugar syrup.

Cleaning Up

Most pots and implements will wash clean after a preliminary soaking, but any hard brittle can easily be removed by filling the pan with water, putting in the utensils, putting it back on the stove, and letting the water simmer until the residue has dissolved.

Storing Candies

All candy should be stored airtight. For creamy candy this keeps the moisture in; for brittle candy it keeps the moisture out. For special occasions or gifts, pieces of candy can be individually wrapped in foil or plastic wrap, but for everyday storage, candy keeps very well between layers of wax paper in metal, plastic, or glass containers. It's best to use tins for brittle candies; plastic can absorb too much moisture.

In general, the harder the candy the longer it will stay fresh at room temperature. Brittles can be stored for two weeks or longer. Caramels, wrapped individually and stored in a tin, will stay fresh for a week or more. Even creamy candies should not be refrigerated unless the weather is very hot. Humid weather can affect both hard and soft candies, causing them to "melt" or become sticky, and in very hot weather all kinds of candy should be kept in the refrigerator.

Wrapped airtight, candy can be frozen. Although creamy candy, particularly chocolate, will sometimes lose its "bloom," the taste will not be affected. To keep the moisture in, defrost creamy candy still sealed in its package, either in the refrigerator or at room temperature.

BASIC CANDIES

CHOCOLATE FUDGE
(1½ POUNDS)

Old-fashioned basic fudge, smooth and chocolaty.

2 ounces unsweetened chocolate, in small pieces, or 4 tablespoons unsweetened cocoa	¾ cup milk
	2 tablespoons light corn syrup
	2 tablespoons butter, in small pieces
2 cups sugar	2 teaspoons vanilla

Oil a jelly-roll pan or an 8 × 8-inch pan. Combine the chocolate or cocoa, sugar, milk, and corn syrup in a 3-quart heavy pot, stirring to blend all the ingredients. Set over low heat and, stirring slowly, bring to a boil. Cover the pot and let boil for 2–3 minutes. Uncover and wash down the sides of the pot with a pastry brush dipped in cold water, then continue to boil slowly, without stirring, until the syrup reaches the soft-ball stage (234°F). Remove from the heat, add the butter without stirring, and set the pot on a cooling surface or rack. Do not stir until the syrup is lukewarm (110°F), then add the vanilla and stir without stopping until the mixture loses its gloss and thickens. Pour it into the oiled pan and mark into squares. When firm, cut into pieces and store airtight.

CHOCOLATE SOUR-CREAM FUDGE

Substitute ¾ cup plus 2 *tablespoons sour cream* for the milk and butter.

CHOCOLATE NUT FUDGE

Stir in *1 cup chopped nuts* before turning the candy out of the pot.

CHOCOLATE MARSHMALLOW FUDGE

Add *1½ cups small marshmallows* before turning the candy out of the pot.

(1½ POUNDS)   **TWENTY-MINUTE FUDGE**

An uncooked fudge with a deep chocolate taste.

1 egg, well beaten
3 tablespoons heavy cream
2 teaspoons vanilla
1 pound confectioners' sugar, sifted

¼ teaspoon salt
4 ounces unsweetened chocolate
1 tablespoon butter
1 cup chopped walnuts

NOTE
see page 471

Oil a jelly-roll pan or an 8 × 8-inch pan. In a large bowl, combine the egg, cream, vanilla, confectioners' sugar, and salt and mix until well blended. Melt the chocolate and butter together over low heat in a small heavy-bottomed pan. Cool a little, then add to the sugar mixture, stirring vigorously to blend. Stir in the walnuts and spread in the oiled pan. Cut into squares when firm and store airtight.

(2 POUNDS)   **✳ MILLION-DOLLAR FUDGE**

A very fast, very easy method, resulting in a fine, creamy fudge.

12 ounces semisweet chocolate bits, or squares, in small pieces
1 cup marshmallow cream
2 cups sugar

2 tablespoons butter
¾ cup evaporated milk
⅛ teaspoon salt
1 teaspoon vanilla
1 cup chopped nuts

Oil a jelly-roll pan or a 9 × 9-inch pan. Combine the chocolate and the marshmallow cream in a large bowl and set aside. Mix the sugar, butter, and milk in a 3-quart heavy pot, stirring to combine well. Gradually bring to a boil over low heat, stirring until the sugar dissolves. Dip a pastry brush in cold water and wash down the sides of the pot. Continue to boil, stirring constantly without touching the sides of the pot, for 5 minutes, then pour the mixture over the chocolate mixture and add the salt and vanilla. Stir until the chocolate melts and the mixture is smooth, then stir in the nuts. Spread on the cookie sheet or pan and let stand until firm. Cut into squares and store airtight.

PEANUT BUTTER FUDGE   (1 POUND)

A firm fudge, rich in peanut butter flavor.

2 cups sugar	2 tablespoons light corn syrup
⅛ teaspoon salt	¼ cup peanut butter
¾ cup milk or cream	1 teaspoon vanilla

Oil a jelly-roll pan or 8 × 8-inch pan. Combine the sugar, salt, milk or cream, and corn syrup in a 3-quart heavy pot, stirring to mix well. Stir over medium heat until it boils, then cover and let boil for 2–3 minutes. Uncover and wash down the sides of the pot with a pastry brush dipped in cold water. Continue to boil over medium heat, without stirring, to the soft-ball stage (234°F). Put the pot on a cooling surface or rack and, without stirring, let the syrup cool to lukewarm (110°F). Mix in the peanut butter and vanilla, stirring until thickened. Spread in the oiled pan. Cut into squares when firm, and store airtight.

MARSHMALLOW PEANUT BUTTER FUDGE   (2 POUNDS)

The marshmallow cream lightens both the texture and the taste.

2 cups sugar	1 cup peanut butter
⅔ cup milk	2 teaspoons vanilla
1 cup marshmallow cream	

Oil a jelly-roll pan or a 9 × 9-inch pan. Combine the sugar and milk in a 3-quart heavy pot. Stir to mix well and place over moderate heat. Bring to a boil, stirring until the sugar dissolves, then cover and let boil for 2–3 minutes. Uncover and wash down the sides of the pot with a pastry brush dipped in cold water. Continue to boil over medium heat, without stirring, to the soft-ball stage (234°F). Remove from the heat and stir in the marshmallow cream, peanut butter, and vanilla. Mix well and spread in the oiled pan. Cool and cut into squares. Store airtight.

PECAN PENUCHE   (1½ POUNDS)

Penuche is firmer than classic fudge, but because of its deep sweet flavor, it's often called "brown sugar fudge."

2 cups firmly packed dark-brown sugar

¾ cup milk

⅛ teaspoon salt

2½ tablespoons butter, in small pieces

1 teaspoon vanilla

¾ cup chopped pecans

Oil a jelly-roll pan or an 8 × 8-inch pan. Combine the sugar, milk, and salt in a 3-quart heavy pot, stirring to mix well. Place over medium heat and bring to a boil, stirring constantly until the sugar dissolves. Cover and let boil for 2–3 minutes. Uncover, and wash down the sides of the pot with a pastry brush dipped in cold water. Continue to boil over medium heat to the firm-ball stage (244°F), stirring only if it starts to burn. Remove from the heat and immediately place the pot into a larger pan filled with cold water; this will stop the cooking process and bring the temperature down. Drop in the butter and let cool slightly, without stirring. Beat until it starts to thicken, add the vanilla and the pecans, and continue to beat until the candy loses some of its gloss. Spread evenly in the pan and mark into squares. When firm, cut into pieces and store airtight.

(2 POUNDS)   **CHANTILLY CREAM SQUARES**

A creamy candy, soft and delicate.

2 cups sugar

¾ cup heavy cream

1 cup milk

2 tablespoons light corn syrup

⅛ teaspoon salt

1 teaspoon vanilla

1 cup chopped nuts

Oil a jelly-roll pan or an 8 × 8-inch pan. Combine the sugar, cream, milk, corn syrup, and salt in a 4-quart heavy pot, stirring to mix well. Bring to a boil over moderately low heat, stirring slowly. Cover and let boil for 2–3 minutes. Uncover and wash down the sides of the pot with a pastry brush dipped in cold water. Continue to boil slowly, without stirring, to the soft-ball stage (234°F). Remove from the heat, cool slightly, and stir in the vanilla. Beat until it starts to thicken, then stir in the nuts and spread in the oiled pan. When firm, cut into squares and store airtight.

MAPLE PRALINES ✳ (1½ POUNDS)

Pecans are especially good in this candy.

2 cups confectioners' sugar	½ cup heavy cream
1 cup maple sugar or maple syrup	2 cups large pieces of nuts

Combine the confectioners' sugar, maple sugar or syrup, and cream in a 3-quart heavy pot, stirring to blend well. Bring to a boil over medium heat, stirring constantly until the sugar dissolves. Cover and let boil for 2–3 minutes, then uncover and wash down the sides of the pot with a pastry brush dipped in cold water. Without stirring, boil to the soft-ball stage (234°F). Remove from the heat to a cooling surface and let stand, without stirring, until lukewarm (110°F). Beat with a wooden spoon until it starts to thicken and becomes cloudy, then beat in the nuts. Using two metal tablespoons, scoop up the mixture and drop small patties onto a sheet of wax paper. Let stand until firm, then store airtight.

CARAMELS (1 POUND)

Lovely, classic, chewy caramels. Take care that the easily scorched syrup doesn't burn or become granular: stir it continuously over medium-low heat, without touching the sides of the pan. Light cream is called for but you can as easily use half-and-half or ¾ cup milk mixed with ¾ cup heavy cream.

1 cup sugar	1½ cups light cream
⅔ cup corn syrup	1 teaspoon vanilla

Oil a jelly-roll pan or an 8 × 8-inch pan. Put the sugar, corn syrup, and ½ cup of light cream or milk-and-cream combination in a 3-quart heavy pot. Stir until well mixed, then bring to a boil, stirring over medium-low heat until the sugar dissolves. Cover and let boil for 2–3 minutes. Uncover and wash down the sides of the pot with a pastry brush dipped in cold water. Continue to boil over medium-low heat, stirring gently without touching the sides of the pot with the spoon. When the syrup reaches the soft-ball stage (234°F), slowly, without breaking the boil, stir in another ½ cup of light cream. Continue to boil, stirring constantly until the soft-ball stage (234°F) is again reached, then slowly add, without breaking the boil, the remaining ½ cup light cream. Keep it boiling gently, stirring constantly, to the firm-ball stage (244°F). Remove from the heat and stir in the vanilla. Turn into the oiled pan, spreading a layer about ¾ inch deep. Mark into squares and let stand until cool. When firm, cut with a sharp knife into pieces and wrap each piece in plastic wrap or wax paper. Store airtight in a cool place.

(2½ POUNDS) **MR B'S CARAMELS**

Mr. B's secret is the honey.

1¼ cups light corn syrup
½ cup honey
2 cups sugar
1 tablespoon butter

½ teaspoon salt
2 cups heavy cream
1 teaspoon vanilla

Oil a jelly-roll pan or a 9 × 9-inch pan. Combine the syrup, honey, sugar, butter, salt, and 1 cup of the cream in a 4-quart heavy pot. Stir to mix well. Place over medium-low heat and bring to a boil, stirring until the sugar dissolves. Cover and let boil for 2–3 minutes, then uncover and, when the foam subsides, wash down the sides of the pot with a pastry brush dipped in cold water. Continue to boil, stirring without touching the sides of the pot, to the soft-ball stage (234°F). Very slowly, without breaking the boil, add the remaining 1 cup of cream. Then, still stirring, bring up to the firm-ball stage (244°F). Remove from the heat, stir in the vanilla, and pour into the prepared pan. When cool and firm, cut into squares and wrap in pieces of wax paper or plastic wrap. Store in a cool place.

(1 POUND) **DIVINITY**

Divinity is meant to be eaten up in short order: it dries out quickly.

1½ cups firmly packed light-
   brown sugar
½ cup water
1 teaspoon vinegar
1 egg white, at room
   temperature

Pinch of salt
1 teaspoon vanilla
½ cup chopped nuts

Combine the sugar, water, and vinegar in a 3-quart heavy pot, stirring to mix well. Bring to a boil over medium heat, stirring until the sugar is dissolved. Cover and boil for 2–3 minutes, then uncover and wash down the sides of the pot with a pastry brush dipped in cold water. Continue to boil without stirring until the syrup reaches the firm-ball stage (244°F). While it is cooking, beat the egg white and salt in the large bowl of an electric mixer until stiff but not dry. As soon as the syrup is ready, remove it from the heat, turn on the mixer, and pour it slowly onto the beaten egg white, beating until creamy. Stir in the vanilla and nuts and drop by teaspoonfuls onto a sheet of wax paper. Store airtight.

TOFFEE

(1½ POUNDS)

1 pound butter 2 cups sugar

Oil a jelly-roll pan. Put the butter and sugar in a 3–4-quart heavy pot and place over moderate heat, stirring as the sugar dissolves and the mixture comes to a boil. Wash down the sides of the pot with a pastry brush dipped in cold water. Boil slowly over moderate heat until it reaches the hard-crack stage (290°F), stirring gently and touching the sides of the pan only if it starts to scorch. Pour it into the oiled pan and let cool partially, then score the toffee into squares. When completely cool and hard, cut or break into pieces and transfer to an airtight tin.

ALMOND TOFFEE

After the first 5 minutes of cooking, add ¼ *cup chopped almonds* to the mixture and continue as above.

TOFFEE WITH ALMONDS AND CHOCOLATE

Follow the directions for Toffee and Almond Toffee above and, after scoring the toffee, cover the surface with *4 ounces melted semisweet chocolate* and sprinkle with an additional ⅓ *cup chopped almonds*. Let the chocolate harden before cutting or breaking in pieces.

PEANUT BRITTLE ❋

(1 POUND)

A light, clear, crisp brittle.

1 cup skinned salted peanuts ½ cup water
1 cup sugar 1½ tablespoons butter, in
½ cup light corn syrup   pieces

Oil a jelly-roll pan and spread the nuts close together in one layer on the bottom. Grease a sturdy wooden spoon or metal spatula and set aside. Combine the sugar, syrup, and water in a 3-quart heavy pot and bring to a boil over moderate heat, stirring until the sugar dissolves. Cover and let boil for 2–3 minutes, then uncover and wash down the sides of the pot with a pastry brush dipped in cold water. Continue to boil over moderate heat, stirring only if it starts to scorch, until the syrup becomes golden and reaches the hard-crack stage (295°F). Remove from the heat, stir in the butter, and pour the syrup evenly over the nuts. Use the greased spoon or spatula to spread it out slightly. When cool, blot with paper towels, break into irregular pieces, and store in an airtight tin.

WALNUT BRITTLE

Use *1 cup coarsely chopped walnuts* in place of peanuts.

(1½ POUNDS)   OLD-FASHIONED PEANUT BRITTLE

A thick, opaque, golden brittle.

1½ cups skinned salted peanuts	¼ cup water
2 cups sugar	2 tablespoons butter, in pieces
1 cup light corn syrup	2 teaspoons baking soda

Oil two jelly-roll pans and divide the nuts evenly between them, spreading them close together in one layer. Combine the sugar, corn syrup, and water in a heavy 3- or 4-quart pot, stirring to blend well. Stir over moderate heat until the sugar dissolves and comes to a boil. Cover and let boil for 2–3 minutes, then uncover and wash down the sides of the pot with a pastry brush dipped in cold water. Without stirring, continue to boil over moderate heat to the soft-crack stage (280°F). Remove from the heat and drop the butter in, swirling the pan gently so the butter melts; the syrup will turn golden. Return to the heat and cook to the hard-crack stage (295°F). Remove from the heat, thoroughly stir in the baking soda (the syrup will foam up), and pour it evenly over the nuts. When the brittle is cool enough to handle, in just a few minutes, pick it up and pull and stretch it as thin as possible. When cold, blot it with paper towels and break into irregular pieces. Store in an airtight tin.

MOLASSES TAFFY   (1 POUND)

Taffy can be made alone, but it's more fun with two; its unique texture and cylindrical shape are the result of vigorous pulling.

½ cup dark molasses	¼ teaspoon cream of tartar
1½ cups sugar	¼ cup melted butter
½ cup water	⅛ teaspoon baking soda
1½ tablespoons cider vinegar	

Oil a marble slab or large cookie sheet. Combine the molasses, sugar, water, and the vinegar in a 3-quart heavy pot, stirring to blend well. Stirring constantly, bring to a boil over moderately low heat. Stir in the cream of tartar. Cover and let boil for 2–3 minutes. Uncover, and wash down the sides of the pot with a pastry brush dipped in cold water. Without stirring, continue to boil over moderate heat to the hard-ball stage (256°F), adding the melted butter and baking soda right before it is done. Pour it out onto the slab or cookie sheet. As the candy cools around the edges, oil your fingertips and fold it toward the center to form a mass. When it is cool enough to handle, the best method is to find a partner to help pull; both of you should oil or butter your hands and, using your fingertips and thumbs, pull the taffy out about 12 inches. Otherwise, just use your own two hands, well greased. Fold it back on itself, twist, pull again, and repeat until it is porous, light-colored, and almost too hard to pull. Shape into a long rope and cut with a greased knife or scissors into small pieces. Put on wax paper to harden, then store between sheets of wax paper in an airtight tin. Keep it in a cool place so it doesn't get sticky.

BUTTERSCOTCH NUT BRITTLE   (1 POUND)

A dark-brown glossy brittle with a distinct toffee taste.

1 cup chopped salted mixed nuts	¼ pound butter
	1 tablespoon cider vinegar
¼ cup dark molasses	2 tablespoons water
1 cup sugar	

Oil a jelly-roll pan and sprinkle the nuts close together in one layer over the bottom. Grease a sturdy wooden spoon or metal spatula and set aside. Combine the molasses, sugar, butter, vinegar, and water in a 3-quart heavy pot, stirring to mix well. Stir over moderate heat until the sugar dissolves and it comes to a boil. Cover and boil for 2–3 minutes, then uncover and wash down the sides of the pot with a pastry brush dipped in cold water. Continue to cook at a slow boil over moderate heat; stir, without touching the sides of the pan, only if the syrup starts to scorch. Cook to the hard-crack stage (290°F), then pour out over the nuts, using the greased spoon or spatula to spread it evenly. Cool, blot with paper towels, and break into irregular pieces. Store in an airtight tin.

(1 POUND)   **FRENCH NOUGAT**

A light, dry brittle—delicious over ice cream.

   1 cup confectioners' sugar
   1 cup finely chopped toasted
      almonds

Oil a marble slab or large cookie sheet. Oil a heavy wooden spoon or metal spatula and set aside. Put the sugar in a 3-quart heavy pot, set over low heat, and stir now and then as it becomes very hot. Stir continuously as it starts to melt. It may take 10 minutes to begin to melt; as it does it will almost immediately turn to caramel. When completely melted and caramelized, stir in the almonds and turn out onto the slab or cookie sheet. For flat pieces, use the greased spatula or spoon to spread it out until it stops moving, then let it cool and break into pieces. For small rounds, keep it moving at this point; fold it over onto itself with the spatula, keeping it constantly in motion. As soon as it is cool enough to handle, divide into four parts and shape into long rolls about ⅓ inch thick. Keep the rolls moving until they are almost cold. With a sharp knife cut each roll into five sections. Store in an airtight container.

FONDANT

About Fondant

Fondant is a grand thing to learn to make; its uses are so varied it truly could be called the heart of the candy world. Variously flavored, it becomes the center of bonbons and chocolate creams. As a coating it can be used for nuts and dried fruits. Melted with liquid it becomes a smooth shiny glaze for cakes and pastries.

Making fondant is an almost magical process; a simple sugar syrup becomes a creamy white mass literally under the heat of your hands. Once made and stored airtight in the refrigerator, it keeps almost indefinitely, always ready for a spectrum of sophisticated ends.

BASIC FONDANT   (1 POUND)

    2 cups sugar   1 cup water
    ⅛ teaspoon cream of tartar

Wipe a marble slab or large heavy cookie sheet with a damp cloth.
Have ready a heavy metal spatula (a pancake turner). Put the sugar,
cream of tartar, and water in a 3-quart heavy pot, stirring to blend
thoroughly. Place over medium heat and let it come to a boil, stirring
until the sugar is completely dissolved. Cover the pot and let boil for
2–3 minutes. Uncover, dip a pastry brush in cold water, and wash
down the sides of the pot. Boil without stirring until the syrup reaches
the soft-ball stage (238°F). Remove from the heat and, without scraping
the pot, pour out the syrup onto the slab or cookie sheet. Let it cool for
about 10 minutes, until it is just lukewarm. Start to work it with the
spatula, spreading it out and turning it over and over on itself. Professionals call this procedure "spading," and this exactly describes the
motion. As it starts to thicken and whiten, it is easier to knead with
your hands. Continue to knead until it is white, creamy, and too stiff to
knead any more. If it crumbles too much, sprinkle on a little water and
continue to knead; fondant cannot be overkneaded. Cover with a
damp cloth and let it stand for 30 minutes. Knead again for a minute,
then wrap in damp cheesecloth and store in an airtight container in the
refrigerator. Let it mellow for 3–4 days before using.

FONDANT GLAZE

Put the fondant in the top of a double boiler over hot water. Stir in
about a tablespoon of liquid for each cup of fondant and stir gently until it melts into a thick cream. Use immediately, as a glaze for pastries,
cakes, or petits fours. Pour it out evenly, working carefully but quickly;
it hardens fast.

BUTTER FONDANT

Let the fondant come to room temperature. For each cup of fondant,
mix in *2 tablespoons soft butter* and *½ teaspoon vanilla*, kneading thoroughly until mixed.

FLAVORED FONDANT

Any flavoring, liqueur, fruit juice, or powdered ingredient can be kneaded into fondant. Try *cocoa, instant coffee, rum, peppermint extract,* or *vanilla,* adding a bit or a few drops at a time until you reach the desired flavor. A drop or two of vegetable coloring can be kneaded in to visually emphasize a particular taste.

FONDANT CONFECTIONS

BONBONS

Let the fondant come to room temperature, kneading in flavoring if desired. Roll bits into 1-inch balls and set them on a cake rack to dry, then roll them in *finely chopped nuts, shredded coconut,* or *cocoa.* Let dry again before storing.

CHOCOLATE BONBONS

Follow the procedure for Bonbons, dipping the 1-inch balls into *chocolate* that has been melted and cooled to about 85°F. Dip one at a time. Use a fork or improvise a dipper by bending a piece of wire into a circle at one end and bending up the straight piece so it is like a ladle. Let them dry thoroughly on wax paper or a rack.

CREAM MINTS

Melt 1 cup of fondant over hot water, flavoring with 1–2 drops of *oil of peppermint.* Color pale green if desired. Drop from the tip of a spoon onto wax paper and dry thoroughly before using.

FONDANT-COVERED NUTS

Use *whole almonds* or *walnut or pecan halves.* Melt the fondant over hot water. Spear the nuts with a fork, or use tweezers to dip. Dry thoroughly on a rack before storing.

ALMOND PASTE AND MARZIPAN

ALMOND PASTE   (2 POUNDS)

Homemade almond paste will stay fresh for months in the refrigerator. To keep it moist, cover with a piece of dampened cheesecloth and store it in an airtight container.

¼ cup confectioners' sugar	1 pound blanched almonds,
2 cups granulated sugar	ground fine
1 cup water	½ cup orange juice

Dust a marble slab or board with the confectioners' sugar. Put the granulated sugar and water in a 3-quart heavy pot and stir to blend. Bring to a boil over moderate heat, stirring until the sugar is dissolved, cover, and let boil for 2–3 minutes. Uncover and wash down the sides of the pot with a pastry brush dipped in cold water. Cook without stirring to the soft-ball stage (240°F). Remove from the heat and stir in the almonds and orange juice, stirring until creamy. Turn out onto the slab or board and let stand until cool, then knead together. Wrap in a piece of damp cheesecloth and store in an airtight container in the refrigerator. Let it mellow for a week before using, then let it come to room temperature and knead it briefly to soften.

BLENDER ALMOND PASTE   (1½ POUNDS)

An almost instant version.

½ cup orange juice	1 cup sugar
2 cups blanched almonds	

Put the orange juice, 1 cup of the almonds, and the sugar into a blender or food processor and whirl until the nuts are very fine. Add the remaining cup of almonds and whirl again until very fine. Knead together, cover with dampened cheesecloth, and store in an airtight container in the refrigerator.

MARZIPAN   (1¾ CUPS)

Malleable marzipan can be used as a cake filling as well as for a range of beguiling and decorative miniature shapes.

    1 cup or ½ pound almond
        paste (preceding recipes),
        at room temperature

1 cup confectioners' sugar
1½ teaspoons rosewater

Combine the almond paste, sugar, and rosewater, mixing well with your hands. Put it on a marble slab or board and knead for 10–20 minutes, until it is very pliable. Wrap in damp cheesecloth and store in an airtight container. It will keep for months in the refrigerator.

MARZIPAN MINIATURES

Although tiny fruits and vegetables are traditional, any number, letter, or shape that strikes your fancy can be molded from marzipan; think of it as edible modeling clay. Paint the molded shapes with food coloring, using a small brush, or dip them into a small bowl of coloring. Or roll the shapes in confectioners' sugar or spices. (For example, a little potato shape can be covered with a mixture of cocoa and confectioners' sugar.) Use tweezers to apply finishing touches like leaves and stems. They can be made of marzipan too, or use candied fruit or spices; whole cloves as stems, bits of angelica for leaves. The range of possibilities is almost endless. Let the molded shapes dry on a cake rack, then store them in an airtight container in the refrigerator. They can be eaten, of course, or used over and over again to decorate gingerbread houses, desserts, pastries, and birthday cakes.

NUTS AND POPCORN

ROASTED CHESTNUTS

With a sharp paring knife, cut a ½-inch crisscross gash on the flat side of each nut, cutting down to the meat.

To roast in the oven, preheat the oven to 450°F. Spread the nuts out on a cookie sheet and bake, stirring once or twice, for 10–20 minutes, until the shells open and the nuts can easily be dislodged. Peel them while they are still warm.

To roast over a fire, use a perforated-bottom chestnut roasting pan or a popcorn popper, shaking the nuts gently over the fire until the shells open and the nuts become toasty and brown.

SHERRY WALNUTS   (ABOUT 4 CUPS)

Sugared nutmeats with a real sherry flavor. Served with a cup of strong coffee, they're a perfect way to end dinner.

1½ cups sugar   ½ teaspoon cinnamon
½ cup sherry   3 cups walnut halves
Pinch of salt

Lightly oil a cookie sheet. Mix the sugar, sherry, and salt together in a 3-quart heavy pot. Stir over low heat until the sugar has dissolved, bring to a boil, cover, and let boil for 2–3 minutes. Uncover and wash down the sides of the pot with a pastry brush dipped in cold water. Cook without stirring to the soft-ball stage (236°F). Remove from the heat, stir in the cinnamon and walnuts, and stir vigorously until the mixture looks cloudy. Turn out onto the cookie sheet and separate the nuts with two forks. Let cool. Then store in a tin at room temperature.

SPICED NUTS *   (2½ CUPS)

Try these for breakfast with cheese, dried figs, and toast. These crisp sweet nuts go well with many custards, or with fruit and ham.

2½ cups walnut halves or   1 teaspoon cinnamon
    large pieces   1 teaspoon salt
1 cup sugar   1 tablespoon vanilla
½ cup water   (optional)

Preheat the oven to 350°F. Spread the walnuts in one layer on a baking sheet. Roast in the oven for 10–15 minutes (watch carefully—nuts scorch easily), until the nuts become a little toasted, or lightly browned. Put the sugar, water, cinnamon, and salt in a heavy-bottomed saucepan. You will be cooking until the soft-ball (or spin-a-thread) stage (236°F). Let the syrup cook without stirring about 10 minutes. You will notice that the bubbles will become smaller and more compact as the syrup nears the soft-ball stage. Remove from the heat, stir in the vanilla, if using, and add the walnuts. Stir the mixture slowly and gently until it is creamy. Turn onto a buttered platter and separate the walnuts. Allow to cool and serve, or store in an airtight container at room temperature.

POPCORN BALLS

(FIFTEEN 3-INCH BALLS)

An authentic old-fashioned version.

3 quarts popped corn (p. 99), unsalted and unbuttered	1 tablespoon cider vinegar
2 cups light corn syrup	½ teaspoon salt
	2 teaspoons vanilla

Put the popped corn into a large greased bowl and keep warm in a 250°F oven. Oil a large fork and set aside. Combine the corn syrup, vinegar, and salt in a 3-quart heavy pot. Cook over medium heat, stirring occasionally, until the syrup reaches the hard-ball stage (250°F). Remove from the heat and add the vanilla. Slowly pour the syrup over the popcorn, tossing with the fork until it is well distributed. As soon as the mixture is cool enough to handle, quickly and gently shape it into 3-inch balls. Let them stand on wax paper until they are cool and no longer sticky, then wrap each in plastic wrap, a tied plastic bag, or tissue paper, and store at room temperature.

COCONUT

COCONUT CAKES

(20 SMALL BALLS)

These are chewy, toasted, and just sweet enough. A fine complement to fresh fruit desserts.

2 cups coarsely grated fresh coconut (see p. 13)	Pinch of salt
2 tablespoons light corn syrup	1 egg white
½ cup sugar	¼ teaspoon coconut or almond extract

Mix the coconut, corn syrup, sugar, and salt together in a 3-quart heavy pot. Stir over medium heat until the mixture thickens a little, about 5–6 minutes. Stir in the egg white and cook, stirring, for another 5–6 minutes, until the mixture feels sticky; cool a little and feel it with your fingers. Stir in the coconut or almond extract. Remove from the heat. Rinse a shallow pan with cold water, shake out the excess, and spread the mixture over the bottom. Rinse paper towels in cold water, wring them out, and place them over the mixture. Refrigerate until chilled. Preheat oven to 300°F. Lightly grease a cookie sheet. Dip your hands in cold water, then shape the coconut mixture into small balls. Heat the cookie sheet slightly and place the balls on it. Bake for 20 minutes or until golden on top. Store in an airtight container at room temperature.

CANDIED PEEL AND CRYSTALLIZED LEAVES

CANDIED CITRUS PEEL   (2 CUPS)

Refreshing, addictive, and absolutely satisfying at the end of a meal. Candied citrus peel keeps so well that it's a good idea to double the recipe.

2 grapefruit or 3 oranges or 6   3 tablespoons light corn syrup
   lemons   ¾ cup water
2 cups sugar

Peel the fruit in large strips, using only the zest and white peel. If the white is very thick, trim it down a little. Put the peel in a pan, cover with cold water, and simmer for 30 minutes. Drain, cover with cold water, and simmer until tender. Drain and cut the peel into small strips, about ¼ inch wide and 2 inches long. Mix 1 cup of the sugar with the corn syrup and water in a heavy saucepan and stir over low heat until dissolved. Dip a pastry brush in cold water and wash down the sides of the pan, then add the peel and cook very gently over low heat until most of the syrup has been absorbed. Cover and let stand overnight. Reheat and bring to the simmer again, then cool a little and drain. Spread several thicknesses of paper towels with the remaining cup of sugar and roll the peel in it, turning so that all the pieces are well coated. Let them stand until they are dry enough to handle. Stored airtight, they will stay fresh for several months. If they become too dry, put a lemon in the container for a day or two and the peel will soften.

CRYSTALLIZED MINT LEAVES   (36 LEAVES)

Frosted leaves with the pure essence of mint. As enlivening to the palate as they are to the plate. You can treat violets and lemon balm the same way, if you are lucky enough to have them in your garden.

36 fresh mint leaves, without   ¼ teaspoon peppermint
   stems   extract
1 egg white, beaten stiff   ¾ cup superfine sugar

NOTE
see page 471

Preheat the oven to 250°F. Wash the mint leaves, pat dry, and spread on paper towels until thoroughly dry. Brush both sides of each leaf with the beaten egg white. Mix the peppermint extract into the sugar and mix and toss with a fork or your hands until the peppermint is well distributed. Dip each leaf into the flavored sugar. Cover a cake rack or two with wax paper, place the leaves close together on it, and let stand in the oven until dry, about 10–15 minutes. Turn them once so they will dry completely on both sides. Use as both a confection and a decoration. They are very fragile and won't keep long.

UNCOOKED CONFECTIONS

(36 PIECES)   **STUFFED DATES OR PRUNES**

Very nice to have on hand or give as a present.

36 large dates or prunes,   ½–¾ cup sugar
    pitted
36 walnut halves or large
    pieces

If the dates or prunes are very dry, put them in a strainer, cover loosely, and soften them over boiling water for 10–15 minutes. Cool, then fill each one with a walnut piece: use halves for prunes and large pieces for dates. Sprinkle a piece of wax paper with sugar, and roll the dates or prunes in it until coated. Store airtight in the refrigerator; they will keep for several months.

(1½ POUNDS)   **FRUIT LEATHER**

A notable specialty of Charleston, South Carolina—wonderful to take on hikes. Apricots and peaches are traditional, but other dried fruit combinations can be substituted.

1 pound dried apricots   ¼–½ cup sugar
½ pound dried peaches

Put the apricots and peaches through a meat grinder twice or finely chop them together in a food processor. Liberally sprinkle a board with sugar. Pat and roll out the fruit mixture to ⅛ inch thick and cut into 1¼ × 2-inch strips. Roll each strip lengthwise into a tight roll.

Stored in an airtight container, these keep well at room temperature for several months.

DRIED FRUIT AND NUT CANDY (1 POUND)

These dried fruits are naturally sweet so there is little added sugar.

½ cup pitted prunes
½ cup golden or brown raisins
½ cup dried figs
½ cup pitted dates

½–1 tablespoon orange marmalade
½ cup chopped walnuts
Confectioners' sugar

If some of the fruits are very dry or hard, pour boiling water over them and let them soak for about 15 minutes. Drain. Put the prunes, raisins, figs, and dates in a food processor and process until the mixture is "ground" together. Or put the dried fruits through a meat grinder twice. Place the ground fruits in a large bowl and stir in only enough marmalade to bind the mixture. It should resemble a sticky dough. (The mixture will take more marmalade if the fruit is dry, less if it is moist.) Turn the fruit mixture out onto a piece of wax paper and knead in the walnuts until well blended. Pull off walnut-size pieces of the fruit-nut mixture and roll into a ball between the palms of your hands. Then roll each in confectioners' sugar until well coated. Place on a plate or in candy cups to serve. Store in an airtight container.

WALNUT BALLS (½ POUND)

Nut bonbons, with a dusting of confectioners' sugar.

¼ cup light corn syrup
1 teaspoon vanilla
⅛ teaspoon salt
½ cup instant nonfat dry milk

¼ cup finely chopped walnuts, or other nuts
¼ cup confectioners' sugar

Mix the syrup, vanilla, salt, dry milk, and walnuts together in a bowl, using your hands to blend well. Sprinkle a board with a little of the confectioners' sugar and knead the candy on the board until it becomes creamy. Shape into 1-inch balls and dust with the remaining confectioners' sugar. These keep best in the refrigerator.

(1 POUND)   **EASY CHOCOLATE TRUFFLES**

½ pound unsalted butter
2½ cups confectioners' sugar
8 ounces unsweetened
    chocolate, grated fine

2 ounces semisweet or milk
    chocolate, roughly grated

In a large mixing bowl, combine the butter, sugar, and unsweetened chocolate, and mix very well, until you have a paste that is very smooth. You can use your hands to do this or blend in a food processor. Shape into balls about the size of walnuts. Roll them in the roughly grated chocolate and put on a platter to dry. These are best if they are allowed to sit for at least 30 minutes before eating. Store in an airtight container in the refrigerator. The truffles, not being cooked, will keep for only about a week.

(½ POUND)   **PEANUT BUTTER CHEWIES**

A bonanza for peanut lovers: nut-covered nuggets of peanut butter.

½ cup crunchy peanut butter
3 tablespoons honey
1 teaspoon vanilla
¾ cup instant nonfat dry milk
Pinch of salt

3 tablespoons confectioners'
    sugar
½ cup finely chopped
    unsalted peanuts

Mix the peanut butter, honey, vanilla, dry milk, salt, and sugar together in a bowl. Using your hands, blend until very well mixed, then shape the mixture into 1-inch balls and roll them in the peanuts. For longer than a day, store in the refrigerator.

PRESERVES, PICKLES, RELISHES & CANNED FRUITS & VEGETABLES

You will now find fresh relishes in this chapter. It seems the logical place for them as they are served with meals in the same way that pickles are, adding texture and taste to enhance a main dish.

Not many people are willing today to spend hours on a hot summer day doing home canning and preserving, yet they love the sharp taste of a good relish and want to make use of some of the harvest from their gardens or nearby green markets. A quickly made relish, put up in small amounts and refrigerated, provides a good alternative, and you can adapt many of the recipes for preserves, pickles, and condiments to the fast-relish method as explained in the introduction to that section on p. 1102. The microwave oven is also useful for preserving in small quantities and there are some recipes in the Microwave chapter on p. 656. Again, you can adapt any of the other preserving recipes to the microwave method.

ABOUT PRESERVES, PICKLES, RELISHES, AND CANNED FRUITS AND VEGETABLES

Back in the days when our country was more rural and people really lived off their land, the practice of "putting by" summertime produce for winter use was a necessity, not a luxury. Now, of course, with good, commercially canned and frozen products available just about everywhere, it isn't really essential for most of us to do our own preserving, pickling, and canning. Yet many people still do—not just those who are following thrifty, long-established family habits but health-minded young cooks who are wary of chemical preservatives in commercial products.

There's great satisfaction in filling tidy shelves with colorful, glistening jars of home-canned fruits, vegetables, pickles, jams, jellies, and preserves. Set a few aside for giving—they make precious gifts for special friends—and use the others throughout the winter, a source of happy summer memories and of pride in your own well-ordered home.

Whether the foods you process are the extra fruits and vegetables from your own family garden or are purchased at a rural farm stand or a city market, canning is an economical way to use fruits and vegetables when they are abundant. For city dwellers, canning is an especially gratifying way to feel a relationship with the changing seasons.

For Detailed Information

The U.S. Department of Agriculture publishes excellent, up-to-date information about preserving, pickling, and canning. You can get these materials from the U.S. Government Printing Office, Washington, D.C., as well as other information put out by the makers of canning equipment; they provide detailed information, especially useful if you plan to can on a large-scale basis.

Canning versus Freezing

With the advent of the large, freestanding home freezer, those who have the space usually prefer to freeze meats and vegetables rather than to can them. Vegetables, in particular, will have better texture when frozen rather than canned, especially low-acid vegetables which must be processed for a long time and then reboiled before eating.

Pickles, jellies, and preserves, on the other hand, are most appealing in clear jars that let their colors gleam through. They may also be frozen very satisfactorily. If you freeze them, processing will not, of course, be necessary.

A Few Words of Warning

Canned foods must be properly processed to prevent the growth of a toxin that causes botulism poisoning and to prevent other forms of spoilage caused by yeasts, molds, and bacteria. Always use reliable recipes, follow them carefully, and do not take shortcuts.

Botulism. Many people are dissuaded from canning altogether because of an irrational fear of botulism. While botulism *can* be deadly (one tiny bite of contaminated food may be fatal), it is also very rare. Most important, there's no mystery about botulism: if you understand its causes, you can prevent it with self-assurance.

Botulism spores grow naturally in an air-free environment, usually in low-acid foods. They are destroyed by processing at the right temperature and for the designated amount of time.

Since botulism is not readily detectable through sight, smell, or taste, your only safeguard is to be particularly careful when you can your own low-acid foods. Follow the directions in each recipe. If you are in doubt about a home-canned product you have not prepared yourself, empty the contents into a pot and boil for 15 minutes before tasting: high heat and air will destroy the botulism toxin.

Molds, Yeasts, and Bacteria. Molds, yeasts, and bacteria can spoil canned foods if proper processing procedures have not been followed. Molds and yeasts are more likely to be found in acid foods and are easily destroyed by a temperature of 212°F, the maximum reached in a water-bath canner.

Bacteria, on the other hand, thrive in low-acid foods, where they may cause an unpleasant flavor called "flat-sour." They are harder to destroy than molds and yeasts, requiring processing at 240°F in a steam-pressure canner. Signs of possible spoilage include a broken seal, leaky jars, fermented contents, or a heavy layer of mold. Do not use canned foods if any of these signs are present.

Differentiating Between High-Acid and Low-Acid Foods

High-Acid Foods. High-acid foods include fruits, tomatoes, rhubarb, sauerkraut, jellies, jams, preserves, and pickles. Jellies, jams, preserves, and pickles may be prepared by the open-kettle method; some prefer a simmering-water bath at 185°C, but only because it assures a good seal. In the case of pickles, again, processing assures a reliable seal and thus you risk less chance of spoilage, but it *does* destroy some of the crunchiness, so you should weigh the pros and cons and make your own choice. All other high-acid foods require a boiling-water bath at 212°F in a water-bath canner.

Low-Acid Foods. Low-acid foods—most vegetables and all meats, poultry, and seafood—require processing at 240°F in a steam-pressure canner.

Equipment for Preserving, Pickling, and Canning

Canning requires special equipment, some of it used exclusively for that purpose. Check before you get started to be sure you have everything you need.

Jars. Do not use ordinary kitchen jars for canning. Use special canning jars that can be vacuum-sealed so that air does not get in. The best and most commonly used are those with screwbands and flat metal lids edged with a sealing compound.

Canning jars are sealed by vacuum, which creates the pressure that holds the lid down: the red rubber seal at the edge of the metal lid keeps air from getting into the jars. Inspect the jars you plan to use: be sure they have no nicks or cracks and that the lids are not rusty. Make sure you have enough lids and screwbands. You can reuse the screwbands, but you must use a *new* metal lid for each jar that you process.

Jars should be spotlessly clean. Run them through the dishwasher so that they will be clean and hot, or wash or rinse them thoroughly and let them sit in hot water until you are ready to use them. It is not necessary to sterilize jars if they are going to be processed in a water-bath canner or a steam-pressure canner, but you may prefer to boil them anyway. To sterilize jars, boil them gently for 10 minutes and leave them in the hot water until ready to use.

Canners and Pots. Depending on the acidity of the food you intend to can, you will need one or both of the following: a water-bath canner with a rack and a cover or a steam-pressure canner with a well-functioning pressure gauge. You will also need pots of different sizes for cooking the foods you plan to can.

Other Equipment. Jar tongs, a ladle, a long-handled spoon, a slotted spoon, a wide-mouthed funnel, and labels are all useful. You may wish to use paraffin and a candy-jelly thermometer for jellies and jams.

Filling Jars

Fill jars tightly or loosely, according to the recipe instructions. There should be enough juices, water, or syrup to cover the food entirely so that it does not darken. Be sure to leave the specified amount of headspace between the top of the food and the cover of the jar, usually ½–1 inch. Avoid sudden changes of temperature when filling the jars so that they don't crack. To remove air bubbles, run a table knife between the jar and the food.

Open-Kettle Method. In the open-kettle method, food is cooked uncovered, then poured while boiling hot into hot, sterilized jars and
quickly sealed. No processing is necessary.

Raw-Pack Method. In the raw-pack or cold-pack method, clean jars
are filled with raw food and then processed.

Hot-Pack Method. The hot-pack method involves filling clean jars
with hot or cooked food before they are processed.

Processing Jars

After the jars are filled, wipe the rims clean with a hot, damp cloth. If
you are using jars with metal lids and screwbands, place the flat lid on
the jar with the sealing compound next to the glass rim. Screw the
metal band on tight; there will still be space for air to escape during
processing. Do not tighten the screwband after the jar has been
processed.

Water-Bath Method. The water-bath method is required for acid
foods: fruits, tomatoes, rhubarb, sauerkraut, and, if you wish, pickles. The maximum temperature reached in a boiling-water bath is
212°F, enough to destroy any harmful organisms in acid foods; a
simmering-water bath at 185°F is enough for jellies, jams, and preserves, if you choose to process them.

　　The water-bath method requires a water-bath canner—a large
pot with a cover, fitted with a rack or basket to keep the jars from
touching the bottom of the pot. The pot should be deep enough so
that the water will cover the tops of the jars by at least 1 inch. Canners are sold complete with racks, or you can buy the racks separately and fit them into a very large pot. In many households, the
canner doubles as the pot in which corn on the cob is cooked.

　　To use a water-bath canner, fill it with 4–5 inches of water: use
boiling water if the food is "hot-packed" or hot water if the food is
"raw-packed." Jars should be put in the pot slightly apart as soon
as they are filled and closed. They should not touch the bottom or
sides of the pot. When all the jars have been added, cover them
with boiling water by at least 1 inch. Cover the pot and begin timing when the water reaches a boil. Boil gently and steadily (or sim-

mer for jams and preserves), adding more time if you are canning in a high-altitude area (see below).

Steam-Pressure Method. The steam-pressure method is recommended for all low-acid foods—most vegetables and all meats, poultry, and seafood—because food can be processed under 10 pounds of pressure at 240°F, enough to destroy botulism spores and the bacteria that grow in low-acid foods.

A special steam-pressure canner is required, a heavy pot with a cover that can be clamped down tight, equipped with a rack, a safety valve, a pressure gauge, and a petcock (vent). A steam-pressure canner can also be used as a water-bath canner if the cover is left unfastened and the vent wide open.

Before canning, make sure that the canner is clean and functioning properly. Run a heavy string through the petcock and safety valve openings to be sure they are clear.

 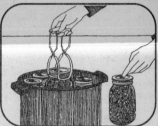

Add about 3 inches of water to the canner, then put in the filled, covered jars. The jars should not touch each other or the bottom or sides of the pot. Clamp down the pot cover, leaving the petcock open until steam has escaped for 10 minutes. Close the petcock and bring the pressure to 10 pounds, following the manufacturer's directions carefully. Start to time after the pressure has reached 10 pounds. Adjust the pressure if processing at a high altitude (see below).

Follow the manufacturer's instructions when opening the canner, being sure to let the pressure return to zero and waiting for a few minutes before slowly opening the petcock.

A pressure cooker may be used to process small jars, but add 20 minutes to the cooking time because the pan heats and cools quickly.

Processing at High Altitudes. When using a water-bath canner at high altitudes, increase the processing time 1 minute for every 1,000 feet above sea level if the total processing time is 20 minutes or less. Increase by 2 minutes for every 1,000 feet above sea level if the total processing time is more than 20 minutes.

When steam-pressure canning at high altitudes, increase the

pressure to 11½ pounds at altitudes between 2,000 and 3,000 feet above sea level. Add ½ pound of pressure for every 1,000 feet thereafter.

Cooling and Storing Jars

Use jar tongs to remove jars from boiling water after the processing time is up. Let the jars cool on a towel, set somewhat apart from each other, in a draft-free place; avoid sudden changes in temperature.

When the jars are cool, check the seal. Press the metal lid to see if it's down tight. You may remove the screwbands after 24 hours and reuse them. If a jar has failed to seal properly, process all over again, using a new lid, or refrigerate and use as you would any cooked food.

Label the jars. Store them in a cool, dry place, out of direct sunlight. Do not, of course, open them until you are ready to use the contents.

Using Home-Canned Foods

Save the liquid left over from home-canned foods: it's a good addition to soups or stocks. Extra pickle juices may be used to make another batch of similar pickles.

Pickles and preserves should stand for a few weeks after canning to develop their full flavor. If jellies are kept *too* long, their bright colors may fade.

PRESERVES

About Preserves

For general information, see About Preserves, Pickles, Relishes, and Canned Fruits and Vegetables (p. 1068).

There is nothing more delicious with breakfast or afternoon tea than a homemade preserve served with freshly baked bread, muffins, or rolls. Homemade jellies and jams are also often used as a condiment with roasts, and homemade preserves, added to ice cream, trifles, cookies, or cakes, will transform them into exceptional desserts. With their concentrated goodness and rich, jewellike colors, homemade preserves make wonderful gifts.

Kinds of Preserves

Jellies. Jellies are made from fruit juices and sugar. They have a firm but spreadable consistency and may be clear or translucent, depending on how the fruit juices are extracted. Jellies differ from other types of jams and preserves because they require two separate cooking processes, one to extract the juice and the other to make the jelly.

Jams. Jams are made with sugar and crushed or chopped fruit. They have a softer consistency than jellies.

Preserves. Preserves are fruits cooked with sugar so that they keep their shape within a jellylike syrup.

Conserves. Conserves are jamlike mixtures of two or more fruits to which nuts or raisins are usually added.

Marmalades. Marmalades are like soft jellies with pieces of fruit or fruit peel in them.

Butters. Butters are thick and smooth for easy spreading. They are made from fruit pulp and sugar which are cooked together, sometimes with spices, and usually strained.

Equipment for Preserving

For general canning equipment, see p. 1070.

Whether you are making jellies, jams, or preserves, you will need a large, heavy-bottomed pot, big enough to hold four times the volume of the ingredients you are using. A jelly or candy thermometer is extremely useful when making jellies, jams, or preserves, especially those without commercial pectin.

When making jelly, a jellmeter is helpful for measuring the natural pectin in fruit juices. You will need a jelly bag and stand for extracting the juices, or some cheesecloth and a colander to improvise one.

You may use either screwtops or paraffin or both to seal jars of preserves made by the open-kettle method. Since paraffin smokes and flames easily, melt it in the top of a double boiler over warm, not boiling, water. Use a single, very thin layer of paraffin, about ⅛ inch thick, and make sure that it touches the glass all around. Prick any air bubbles that form, or they may become holes as the wax hardens. After the paraffin is hard, you may cover the jelly jars with metal lids, if desired, but it's not necessary.

Ingredients

Fruit. Fruit, which gives jellies and jams their flavor and color, also provides at least some of the pectin and acid required for jelling. Fruit that is firm and just barely ripe will be richest in pectin and acid.

The following fruits are rich in pectin: tart apples, crabapples, green barberries, tart blackberries, boysenberries, cranberries, loganberries, red currants, green gooseberries, Concord grapes, sour guavas, fresh prunes, plums, and quinces. Low-pectin fruits, such as strawberries, blueberries, peaches, apricots, cherries, figs, pears, raspberries, and pineapples, should be combined with pectin-rich fruits like apples and quinces, unless you wish to use commercial pectins.

Pectin. Jellies, which must be firm enough to hold their shape, require more pectin than jams or preserves.

The pectin content of fruit juices will determine the amount of sugar needed for a jelly to jell. It can be tested with a jellmeter, a glass tube through which the extracted juice is passed. The rate of flow determines the pectin content of the juice and thus the amount of sugar to be used. Follow the manufacturer's instructions when using a jellmeter.

Another test for pectin content requires mixing 1 teaspoon of grain or ethyl alcohol with 1 teaspoon of extracted fruit juice. If the mixture comes together in one transparent, firm mass when poured into another glass, equal quantities of sugar and juice should be used. If the mixture is soft, use half as much sugar as juice, and if it forms two or three separate masses, use two-thirds as much sugar as juice. Do not taste this mixture.

NOTE Commercial pectins, made from apples or citrus fruits, come in liquid or powdered form. They reduce the cooking times of jellies and jams and eliminate any uncertainty about jelling. They also require a higher proportion of sugar to fruit, and thus many cooks prefer not to use them. None of the recipes in this chapter requires commercial pectins. If you wish to use them, follow the manufacturer's directions carefully.

Acid. Acid is necessary in jellied products, both for flavor and for jelling. Lemon juice is often called for in recipes for jellies and jams using low-acid fruits.

Sugar. Sugar adds sweetness, aids in preserving, and helps make a jelly or jam jell. Either beet or cane sugar may be used. Honey may be substituted for up to one-half the sugar in a recipe.

Testing for the Jellying Point

Since jellies and jams thicken as they cool, it is often difficult to determine when the hot jelly or jam has reached the proper consistency. There are three ways to test the jellying point:

Thermometer Test. A jelly or candy thermometer is probably the most accurate way to test for the jellying point. First it is necessary to know the boiling point of water in your locality, which can be determined by taking the temperature of water with your jelly thermometer. Jelly should register 8 degrees higher than the boiling point of water to assure the proper amount of jell.

Sheet Test. Using a cool metal spoon, scoop up a bit of the boiling jelly mixture. Tip the spoon and let the jelly run off the side. When the jelly separates from the spoon in a sheet, rather than in separate drops, it is done.

Freezer Test. Remove the jelly from the heat while making this test. Put a few drops on a plate and cool it quickly in the freezer to see if it will jell when cool.

Processing Preserves

See Water-Bath Method (p. 1072).

Jellies, jams, preserves, conserves, marmalades, and butters may be made safely by the open-kettle method. The only reason for processing in a simmering-water bath at 185°F for 10–15 minutes is that it does no harm and will assure a better seal.

PRESERVES

BASIC METHOD FOR PREPARING FRUIT JELLY

(ABOUT FOUR 6-OUNCE JARS)

The standard proportion in fruit jellies is about ¾ cup sugar for each cup of fruit juice, but this will vary according to the fruit. You may test the pectin content of the juice (opposite) to adjust the amount of sugar, or follow the general guidelines given in this recipe and its variations, adjusting according to your own experience. Do not peel any fruit except pineapple; fruit skin is rich in pectin. Do not core fruits, except for quinces, which have bitter cores. Old cookbooks will tell you that if you warm the sugar in a moderate oven before adding it to the fruit, it will keep the jelly from clouding, but this is an old wives' tale. In all probability sugar was heated in the old days to get the dampness and consequent lumps out of it, but this is not necessary today with our refined sugar and would simply be a waste of energy. Don't squeeze or press the jelly bag; you will get more jelly but it will not be crystal clear.

3 pounds fruit (to yield about 4 cups juice)   Sugar (about ¾ cup for each cup of juice)

Wash the fruit thoroughly and cut it into pieces. To extract the juice, put the fruit in a large, heavy-bottomed pot. If the fruit is soft, crush it a little and add just enough water to keep it from burning. If the fruit is hard, add water to just below the top layer. Cover and cook over low heat until the juice flows freely, from 3–15 minutes depending on the fruit. Strain through a colander. Pour the juice into a damp jelly bag or through several layers of damp cheesecloth draped over a colander and set over a bowl so the juice will drip freely. Be patient, allowing an hour or more for the juice to drip through. You should have about 4 cups of juice.

To make the extracted juice into jelly, measure no more than 4 cups of juice at a time into a large pot. Boil for 5 minutes, then add the sugar, allowing ¾ cup sugar for each cup of juice. Boil until the mixture jells, from 10–30 minutes depending on the kind of fruit. Test for the jellying point, using a thermometer, the sheet test, or the freezer test (see p. 1077). Skim off the foam and pour the jelly into hot, sterilized jars (see p. 1071). Seal immediately with metal lids or paraffin and cool, label, and store (see p. 1072).

APPLE JELLY

Use 3 *pounds apples* and 3 *cups water* to produce 4 cups extracted juice.

BLUEBERRY APPLE JELLY

Use 2 *cups blueberry juice* and 2 *cups apple juice* and add 2 *tablespoons lemon juice*.

CRABAPPLE JELLY

Use *3 pounds crabapples* and *3 cups water* to produce 4 cups extracted juice. Use *1 cup sugar* for each cup of juice.

MINT JELLY

Use light-colored apples or crabapples or peel the apples if they have very bright skins. After the juice and sugar are combined, add *1 cup chopped mint leaves and stems* for every 4 cups juice. While the jelly is boiling, color lightly with *green vegetable coloring*.

SPICED APPLE JELLY

Use *3 pounds apples, ½ cup mild vinegar, 2½ cups water,* and a spice bag containing *1 teaspoon whole cinnamon, 1 teaspoon whole allspice,* and *½ teaspoon whole cloves*. Extract the juice and proceed as the basic recipe directs.

CURRANT JELLY

Use *2½ quarts currants* (with leaves, but not stems, removed) and *1 cup water* to produce 4 cups extracted juice. Use *up to 1 cup sugar* for each cup of juice.

CURRANT RASPBERRY JELLY

Use *2 cups currant juice* and *2 cups raspberry juice*.

GOOSEBERRY JELLY

Remove the stems and blossom ends from the gooseberries and extract the juice in the same way as for Currant Jelly. Use *4 cups gooseberry juice* instead of currant juice.

GRAPE JELLY

Use Concord or wild grapes, including lots of green, unripened grapes
and removing about half the stems. Crush the grapes in the pot, using
3½ pounds grapes and *½ cup water* to produce 4 cups extracted juice.
Store the juice in the refrigerator overnight so that crystals and sediment will settle. Discard the sediment and proceed according to the basic recipe.

SPICED GRAPE (VENISON) JELLY

Follow the recipe for Grape Jelly, using *½ cup vinegar, 1 tablespoon whole
cloves, a 1-inch stick of cinnamon,* and *4 cups grapes.* Cook slowly for
about 15 minutes. Strain and allow the sediment to settle. To make into
jelly, boil the juice for 20 minutes before adding sugar, and use *up to 1
cup sugar* for each cup of juice.

GUAVA JELLY

Follow the Basic Method for Preparing Fruit Jelly, cooking the fruit for
45 minutes or more to extract the juice and adding the *juice of 1 lime* to
each 4 cups of guava juice.

QUINCE JELLY

Wash the quinces and rub off the fuzz. Remove the stems, cores, and
seeds and slice. Follow the Basic Method for Preparing Fruit Jelly, using *3½ pounds quinces* and *7 cups water* to produce 4 cups juice and
cooking 45 minutes or more to extract the juice. Use *1 cup sugar* for
each cup of juice.

QUINCE APPLE JELLY

Follow the recipe for Quince Jelly, using *2 cups quince juice* and *2 cups
apple juice.*

RASPBERRY OR BLACKBERRY JELLY

Use *4 cups raspberry or blackberry juice.*

(2 PINTS)   **✻   LEMON JELLY**

12 lemons   About 3 cups sugar
4 large tart apples

Slice the lemons, including the rind, seeds and all, thin, and place in a saucepan. Core the apples, but do not peel, and chop coarsely. Add the apples to the pan and pour in enough water to just cover the fruit. Cook over moderate heat, until the fruit becomes mushy. Pour into a jelly bag or a colander lined with several thicknesses of damp cheesecloth and let drip into a bowl for about an hour. Using a spoon, force as much liquid through the cheesecloth as possible. Measure the juice; you should have about 4 cups. For each cup of juice, add ¾ cup sugar. Return to the pan and boil for another 15 minutes or so, until the mixture reaches the jelly stage, about 220–225°F on a candy thermometer. To be absolutely certain, place a tablespoon of the hot mixture on a saucer and set it in the freezer for a few minutes. If it jells, the mixture is ready. Pour the jelly into hot, *sterilized* jars and seal. Process in boiling water bath for 10 minutes. Or it may be stored in a covered container in the refrigerator for several months.

BASIC METHOD FOR PREPARING
(2–3 PINTS)   **FRUIT JAM**

The basic proportions for jam are ¾ cup sugar for each cup of prepared fruit.

4 cups prepared fruit   3 cups sugar

Wash the fruit thoroughly. Peel and remove cores, pits, stems, and seeds. Berries and small fruits may be crushed in the pan. Other fruits should be cut into small pieces. Measure the fruit before putting it into the pan. Cook until tender, adding just enough water to prevent burning. Add the sugar to the fruit, stirring until it dissolves. Boil rapidly until the jam is thick, stirring to prevent sticking. Test for the jellying point, using a thermometer, the sheet test, or the freezer test (p. 1077). Pour into hot, *sterilized* jars and seal.

RASPBERRY JAM   (ABOUT 2 PINTS)

Since it's easy to overcook this jam, it's best to use a jelly thermometer when you make it.

    4 cups raspberries   3 cups warm sugar

Clean the raspberries, put them in a large pot, and crush them with a potato masher. Cook for 15 minutes to reduce the juices. Add the sugar and bring to a boil. Cook, stirring, until the mixture registers 214°F on a jelly thermometer. Skim off the foam and let stand until cool. Pour into hot, *sterilized* jars and seal.

BLACKBERRY JAM

Substitute *4 cups blackberries* for the raspberries. If you prefer to remove the seeds, put the cooked berries through a food mill or coarse sieve.

RASPBERRY CURRANT JAM

Use *3 cups raspberries* and *1 cup currants*.

APRICOT PINEAPPLE JAM   ✳   (ABOUT 4 PINTS)

    1 pound dried apricots   Sugar
    8-ounce can crushed
        pineapple and juice

Put the apricots in a pot, barely cover with cold water, and cook until soft. Drain, reserving the juice. Chop the fruit and return to the juice. Add the canned pineapple with its juices and measure. Put in a large pot and bring to a boil. Measure the sugar, using about two-thirds as much sugar as fruit, and stir in. Boil rapidly, stirring to prevent sticking, until thick. Test for the jellying point, using a thermometer, the sheet test, or the freezer test (p. 1077). Pour into hot, *sterilized* jars and seal.

(ABOUT 6 PINTS) **GOOSEBERRY JAM**

Use currant juice that has been extracted as for jelly; it is not necessary to drip it through a jelly bag; just put it through a mesh strainer. This jam must be processed because it is cooled before it is packed.

4 pounds gooseberries
2 cups red currant juice

3 pounds sugar

Wash and clean the gooseberries and set them aside. Bring the currant juice to a boil in a large pot, then add the sugar and boil together for 5 minutes. Add the gooseberries and boil for 40 minutes, skimming occasionally. Cool and set aside for 24 hours. Drain off the syrup. Pack the gooseberries in clean jars. Boil the syrup until it is as thick as honey, pour it over the berries, and close the jars. Process in a simmering-water bath at 185°F for 10–15 minutes.

BLACK CURRANT JAM

If you are lucky enough to find some wild black currants, wash them well and pick off the stems. Chop them, then put them through a coarse sieve, or purée them briefly in a food processor. Measure, then add an equal amount of sugar. Bring quickly to a boil and cook gently for 20 minutes, stirring. Pour into hot, *sterilized* jars and seal.

(ABOUT 2 PINTS) **STRAWBERRY PRESERVES**

3 cups sugar
1 cup water

1 quart strawberries

Cook the sugar and water together until the mixture reaches 238°F on a jelly thermometer (soft-ball stage, p. 1046). Wash and hull the berries, add to the syrup, cover, and remove from heat. Let stand for 10 minutes. Skim off any foam. Remove the berries and set aside. Cook the syrup to 238°F again, add the berries, and let stand over very low heat for 15 minutes. Skim, remove the berries, and reheat to 238°F. Add the berries once more and cook slowly until the syrup is thick. Let stand for 24 hours before putting into *sterilized* jars and closing them. Refrigerate, freeze, or process in a simmering-water bath at 185°F for 10–15 minutes.

PEACH PRESERVES (ABOUT 7 HALF-PINT JARS)

10 large peaches, peeled, 6 cups sugar
   pitted, and sliced

Combine the peaches and the sugar and let stand in a cool place overnight. Boil gently, stirring frequently, until the fruit is clear and the syrup thick, about 45 minutes. Pour into hot, *sterilized* jars and seal.

RASPBERRY CURRANT PRESERVES (ABOUT SIX 8-OUNCE JARS)

2 quarts raspberries 1½ pounds sugar
Juice from 1½ pounds
   currants (see p. 1077)

Wash the raspberries and set aside. Put the currant juice in a large pot and add the sugar. Heat to the boiling point, then cook slowly for 20 minutes. Add a third of the raspberries. Bring the syrup to the boiling point, then spoon the raspberries into clean, *sterilized* jars. Repeat until all the berries are used. Fill each jar with the boiling syrup and seal.

KUMQUAT PRESERVES (SIX 6-OUNCE JARS)

2 cups sugar 1 quart fresh kumquats
1 cup water

Combine the sugar with the water in a pot and boil for 5 minutes. Add the kumquats and cook gently until tender, about 45 minutes. Pour into hot, *sterilized* jars and seal.

RHUBARB PRESERVES (SIX 6-OUNCE JARS)

2 pounds rhubarb Grated rind and juice of ½
2½ pounds sugar lemon
½ pound raisins
Grated rind and juice of 1
   orange

Wash the rhubarb and cut it into 1-inch pieces. Put in a pot with the remaining ingredients, mix well, cover, and let stand for 30 minutes. Bring to a boil, then simmer for 45 minutes, stirring frequently. Pour into hot, *sterilized* jars and seal.

(ABOUT TEN 6-OUNCE JARS)   **GRAPE CONSERVE**

5 pounds Concord grapes
½ orange, in thin slivers

Sugar
½ cup walnut pieces

Wash the grapes, remove the stems, and separate the pulp from the skins; reserve the skins. Heat the pulp gently to free the seeds, stirring to prevent sticking. Put through a sieve or food mill and discard the seeds. Add the orange to the grape pulp and skins and measure. Add an equal amount of sugar to the grape mixture. Cook slowly in a large, flat skillet, in two batches, if necessary. Use the freezer test (p. 1077) to see if the conserve is thick, then add the walnuts. Spoon into hot, *sterilized* jars and seal.

(ABOUT THREE 6-OUNCE JARS)   **CRANBERRY CONSERVE**

For Cranberry Jelly, see p. 1103.

4 cups cranberries
⅔ cup cold water
⅔ cup apple or pineapple
    juice, boiling
¼ pound raisins

1 orange, sliced, seeded, and
    cut small
1½ pounds sugar
½ pound walnut or filbert
    meats, in pieces

Wash the cranberries and put them in a large pot. Add the cold water and cook until the skins break. Force through a strainer or food mill. Add the apple or pineapple juice, raisins, orange, and sugar. Bring to a boil, then simmer for 20 minutes. Add the nuts and let cool. Spoon into clean jars, close the jars, and process in a simmering-water bath at 185°F for 10–15 minutes.

CRANBERRY GINGER CONSERVE

Add ½ cup *preserved ginger, cut small*, along with the raisins and orange.

ORANGE MARMALADE   (ABOUT 3 PINTS)

6 large oranges
2 lemons

1½ quarts water
Sugar

Peel the oranges and cut the peel into very thin slices. Cut up the orange pulp. Slice the lemons very thin. Combine the fruit in a large pot and add the water. Bring to a boil and simmer for about 10 minutes; then let stand overnight in a cool place. Bring to a boil again and cook rapidly until the peel is tender. Measure the fruit and liquid. For each cup of undrained fruit measure ¾ cup sugar and add it to the fruit. Heat, stirring, until the sugar is dissolved, then cook rapidly until the jellying point is reached (p. 1077), about 30 minutes. Pour into hot, *sterilized* jars and seal.

GINGER MARMALADE

Add 2½ *cups chopped preserved ginger* to each quart of fruit before boiling to the jellying point.

RHUBARB FIG MARMALADE   (ABOUT SIX 6-OUNCE JARS)

1 pound rhubarb, cut fine
1 pound sugar

¼ pound dried figs, cut small
Juice of ½ lemon

Combine the ingredients in a large pot. Cook rapidly, stirring frequently, until the jellying point is reached (p. 1077). Pour into hot, *sterilized* jars and seal.

TOMATO MARMALADE   (ABOUT SIX 6-OUNCE JARS)

3 pounds red or green
    tomatoes, peeled and in
    pieces
1 orange, seeded and sliced
    thin

½ lemon, seeded and sliced
    thin
1½ pounds sugar

Combine all the ingredients in a large pot and cook slowly, stirring frequently, until thick, about 3 hours. Pour into hot, *sterilized* jars and seal.

THREE-FRUIT MARMALADE

(ABOUT TWELVE 6-OUNCE JARS)

1 grapefruit	Water
2 oranges	Sugar
2 lemons	Salt

Scrub the fruit and slice very thin, saving the juice. Discard the seeds and the grapefruit core. Measure the fruit and juice. Put the fruit and juice in a large pot and add three times as much water. Simmer, covered, for 2 hours, then let stand overnight. Measure the fruit and liquid, then add an equal amount of sugar and a sprinkle of salt. Cook rapidly, in two or three batches, until the jellying point is reached (p. 1077), stirring frequently. Pour into hot, *sterilized* jars and seal.

SPICED ORANGE SLICES

(ABOUT EIGHT 6-OUNCE JARS)

Fine with roast duckling.

6 large oranges	1 stick cinnamon
3½ cups sugar	2 teaspoons cloves
1 cup cider vinegar	

Cut the oranges in ¼-inch slices and remove the seeds. Put in a pot, cover with water, simmer for 30 minutes, and drain. In another saucepan, combine the remaining ingredients and boil for 5 minutes. Cook the orange slices in the syrup in batches, so that each batch of slices is completely covered by the syrup. Remove the slices when they are clear, after about 30 minutes. Cover the cooked slices with the syrup and let stand overnight. Drain the slices and cook the syrup separately until it is thick. Add the orange slices and heat to the boiling point. Pour into hot, *sterilized* jars and seal.

✳ APPLE BUTTER

(ABOUT TEN 6-OUNCE JARS)

This recipe works for other fruit butters as well: use fresh apricots, peaches, plums, or the pulp in the jelly bag after the juice has been extracted. When using fruits that are juicier than apples, crush them and add just enough water, not cider or vinegar, to keep the fruit from sticking.

5 pounds tart apples	1 teaspoon cloves,
2 cups cider, or water	approximately
1½ cups sugar, approximately	½ teaspoon allspice,
Salt	approximately
2 teaspoons cinnamon,	Grated rind and juice of 1
approximately	lemon

Cut the apples in pieces without peeling or coring them. Put them in a pot, cover with the cider or water, and cook until soft. Put through a sieve or food mill. Measure. Add the sugar. To the whole mixture, add a dash of salt and the cinnamon, cloves, allspice, and lemon rind and juice. Cook, covered, over low heat until the sugar dissolves, taste, and adjust the seasonings. Uncover and cook quickly, stirring constantly to prevent burning, until thick and smooth when a bit is spooned onto a cold plate. Pour into hot, *sterilized* jars and seal.

BRANDIED PEACHES   (2 OR 3 PINT JARS)

Use perfect peaches for this. If the skins are thin, it is not necessary to peel them: simply rub off the fuzz with a clean cloth and prick each peach twice with a fork. Store these for a month before using.

| 6 peaches | 3 cups water |
| 2 cups sugar | 4–6 tablespoons brandy |

Peel the peaches, if you wish, dipping them quickly in hot water before removing the skins. Combine the sugar with the water and boil for 10 minutes. Cook the peaches, a few at a time, in the sugar syrup until tender when pricked with a toothpick, about 5 minutes. Pack into clean, hot jars, adding 2 tablespoons of brandy to each pint jar. Fill the jars with syrup, close the jars, and process in a simmering-water bath at 185°F for 10–15 minutes.

BRANDIED CHERRIES

Substitute *2 pounds firm cherries* for the peaches.

TUTTI-FRUTTI   (ABOUT 6 QUARTS)

A large stone crock is the traditional container, but a large glass jar or casserole will do. You can put up only half the amount called for here, and jars of tutti-frutti make a perfect holiday gift. It must be made

three months before using, when the summer fruits are available.
Tutti-frutti and ice cream are a splendid combination.

1 quart brandy   Sugar
5–6 quarts assorted fruits:
    berries, cherries, currants,
    apricots, peaches,
    pineapple

Put the brandy in a crock that will hold at least 2 gallons. Add the
fruits, hulling strawberries and raspberries; pitting cherries; pitting,
peeling, and cutting up apricots and peaches; and cutting pineapple in
chunks. Add 2 cups sugar for each 2 cups fruit. Cover tight, or seal in
sterilized jars, and store for 3 months before using.

PICKLES

About Pickles

For general information, see About Preserves, Pickles, Relishes, and
Canned Fruits and Vegetables (p. 1068).

Pickles and relishes, so much a part of our heritage, have given a
lift to many a homely meal. Serve them with snacks and sandwiches,
as an hors d'oeuvre on a relish tray, or as an accompaniment to meats
and poultry. Used in small quantities, they add nice flavor to certain
salads, salad dressings, and sauces, and, like preserves, they make very
special gifts.

Kinds of Pickles

Brined Pickles. Old-fashioned brined pickles are cured in a water and
salt solution over a period of weeks. Dill pickles, sauerkraut, and
green tomatoes are frequently cured that way. Although it is possible to brine pickles at home, the method requires controlled temperatures and conditions as well as patience. Most home cooks
these days use the fresh-pack, or short-brine, method.

Fresh-Pack Pickles. Fresh-pack, or short-brine, pickles are soaked in a
salt solution for several hours or more to extract moisture, then
drained and preserved in vinegar.

Relishes. Relishes usually combine several fruits or vegetables that are
chopped or sliced, cooked and seasoned, then packed in jars and
processed. Some relishes are mild and subtly flavored; others are
spicy and hot. Chutneys, as we know them in this country, are
sweet-spicy fruit relishes, often dotted with raisins.

Fruit Pickles. Fruit pickles are made from whole or sliced fruits that
are simmered in a spicy sweet-sour syrup.

Equipment for Pickling

For general canning equipment, see p. 1070.

Pickles preserved in vinegar are high in acid, which prevents toxic growth. Read the advantage and disadvantage of processing on p. 1069 before you decide which way is for you. If processed do so at 212°F in a boiling-water bath. For this you will need a water-bath canner, equipped with a rack so that the jars do not touch the bottom of the pot (p. 1073).

Do not use copper, brass, or iron utensils, which may react unfavorably to the acid in the pickles.

Ingredients

Vegetables and Fruits. Use fresh, young, tender vegetables and fruits, as free as possible from bruises and blemishes. Wash them very carefully and cut away any bad spots. Slightly underripe vegetables will produce crisper pickles. Do not use waxed cucumbers if you are pickling them whole; the waxed skins will not absorb liquid.

Vinegar. Cider vinegar or any vinegar with a mild flavor is good for pickling. Be sure the label indicates that the vinegar has at least 4 to 6 percent acidity, or your pickled vegetables may spoil. Don't dilute vinegar; if the mixture seems too sour, add sugar to achieve the proper balance. Although cider vinegar may darken pickles slightly, it is desirable for its pleasantly mild flavor. White vinegar has a sharper taste, but should be used when pickling light-colored vegetables like onions.

Water. The water used when pickling should be soft or artificially softened.

Salt. Use pure, granulated salt, if you can get some, or uniodized table salt. Iodized table salt will darken pickles.

Spices. Spices should be fresh, of course. They are usually used whole, and often put in a cloth bag for easy removal. If spices stay in the pickled product too long, they will darken it. You can vary the amount of spices in these recipes to suit your own tastes.

Alum and Lime. Neither alum nor lime is necessary to produce crisp pickles if you use the right ingredients and procedures.

Processing Pickles

See Water-Bath Method (p. 1072).

If you do decide to process pickles, be sure not to overprocess them; you want to retain as much crispness as possible. Begin counting the processing time when the jars are first inserted into the boiling water; do not wait for the water to return to a boil, as you do with other home-canned products.

(ABOUT 4 PINTS)   **BREAD-AND-BUTTER PICKLES**

Use Kirby cucumbers or other small, unwaxed cucumbers, and tiny white onions, if possible.

6 cups thinly sliced cucumbers	½ teaspoon turmeric
1 pound onions	¼ teaspoon cloves
1 green pepper, shredded	1 tablespoon mustard seed
¼ cup salt	1 teaspoon celery seed
2 cups brown sugar	2 cups cider vinegar

Mix the cucumbers, onions (sliced if large), green pepper, and salt. Cover and let stand for 3 hours. Mix the remaining ingredients in a large pot, bring slowly to the boiling point, and boil for 5 minutes. Drain the vegetables in a colander and rinse them well with cold water. Add them to the hot syrup and heat to just below the boiling point. Spoon into hot, *sterilized* jars, fill with the cooking syrup, leaving ⅛-inch headspace, and seal. Or, if you prefer, process in a boiling-water bath for 10 minutes.

(6–8 QUARTS)   **DILL PICKLES**

About 50 unwaxed 3–4-inch cucumbers	2 quarts water
1 quart cider vinegar	Fresh dill sprigs
¾ cup salt	Garlic cloves, peeled

Put the cucumbers in the sink, cover with cold water and let stand overnight. Drain and pack them into hot, *sterilized* jars. Combine the vinegar and salt with the water in a pot and bring to the boiling point. Pour over the cucumbers, leaving ¼-inch headspace. Add a sprig or two of dill and a clove of peeled garlic to each jar and seal. Or close the jars and process in a boiling-water bath for 15 minutes.

(ABOUT 6 PINTS)   **ICICLE PICKLES**

Twenty 6-inch cucumbers, quartered lengthwise	6 cups sugar
6 cups vinegar	2 cups water
	½ cup salt

Cover the cucumbers with ice water and let stand overnight. Drain and pack upright in clean jars. Combine the vinegar and sugar with 2 cups water in a pot, boil for 3 minutes, then add the salt. Pour over the cucumbers, leaving ¼-inch headspace. Close the jars and process in a boiling-water bath for 10 minutes.

MUSTARD PICKLES ✳   (8 PINTS)

Be careful not to overcook so these pickles remain crisp.

3 pounds small cucumbers, sliced	½ cup salt
3 large cucumbers, cubed	4 quarts cold water
2 pounds green tomatoes, diced	1 cup flour
	6 tablespoons dry mustard
1½ pounds small white onions, peeled	1 tablespoon turmeric
	2 quarts cider vinegar
4 green peppers, diced	2 cups sugar
1 large cauliflower, in small pieces	

Put the cucumbers, tomatoes, onions, peppers, and cauliflower in a large bowl. Mix the salt with the cold water, pour over the vegetables, cover, and let stand for 8 hours or overnight. Drain and rinse under cold water. Put the vegetables in a pot, cover them with fresh cold water, bring to the boiling point, and drain in a colander once again. Put the flour, mustard, and turmeric in the pot. Stir in enough vinegar to make a smooth paste, then gradually add the remaining vinegar and the sugar, stirring well. Bring to a boil, stirring constantly, and cook until thick and smooth. Add the vegetables and cook, stirring, until heated through. Spoon into hot, *sterilized* jars, leaving ¼-inch headspace, and seal. Or close the jars and process in a boiling-water bath for 10 minutes.

CURRY PICKLES   (ABOUT 7 PINTS)

8 pounds small cucumbers (2½–3 inches long)	⅓ cup pickling spices
	2 teaspoons turmeric
⅓ cup sugar	1 teaspoon cayenne pepper
⅓ cup kosher or coarse salt	2½ quarts malt or cider vinegar
¼ cup mustard seed	
⅓ cup dry mustard	
⅓ cup curry powder (use ½ cup if you like more flavor)	

Wash and trim the cucumbers. Pour boiling water over them, drain, and wipe dry. Blanch in boiling water for 30 seconds, then drain and pat dry. Pack the cucumbers tightly into hot, *sterilized* jars. In a large pot, combine the sugar, salt, mustard seed, dry mustard, curry powder, pickling spices, turmeric, cayenne pepper, and vinegar, and bring to a boil. Let simmer for about 5 minutes. Ladle enough hot brine into each jar to leave about ⅛-inch headspace. Pop any air bubbles, clean rim, and seal. Process in a boiling-water bath for 10 minutes.

(8–10 PINTS)   **✳ JANICE PIKE'S PERFECT PICKLES**

These are delicious and ready to eat at once.

24 medium cucumbers, sliced thin	2 trays ice cubes
18 small white onions, sliced thin	7½ cups sugar
	2½ teaspoons turmeric
	¾ teaspoon cloves
3 green peppers, in thin strips	3 teaspoons celery seed
3 sweet red peppers, in thin strips	3 tablespoons mustard seed
¾ cup kosher or coarse salt	7½ cups cider vinegar

Place the cucumbers, onions, and peppers in a kettle and pour the salt over. Put the ice cubes over the vegetables, cover, and let stand for 3 hours. Drain, rinse well with cold water, and drain again. Add the sugar, turmeric, cloves, celery seed, mustard seed, and vinegar to the kettle and bring to a boil, stirring, then immediately turn off. Put into hot, *sterilized* jars with the cooking liquid, leaving ⅛-inch headspace, and seal. If you wish, process in a boiling-water bath for 10 minutes.

(ABOUT 8 PINTS)   **PICKLED ONIONS**

4 quarts small white boiling onions, peeled	2 tablespoons prepared horseradish
1 cup salt	White peppercorns
2 quarts white vinegar	Bay leaves
2 cups sugar	Pimiento slices
¼ cup mustard seed	

Sprinkle the onions with the salt. Cover with cold water and let stand 6–8 hours or overnight. Rinse thoroughly with cold water, and drain well. Combine the vinegar, sugar, mustard seed, and horseradish in a pot and simmer for 10 minutes. Spoon the onions into hot, *sterilized* jars, adding a few peppercorns, a bay leaf, and some pimiento slices to each jar. Pour the boiling hot vinegar mixture over the onions, leaving ¼-inch headspace, and seal. Or close the jars and process in a boiling-water bath for 10 minutes.

PICKLED BEETS   (4 PINTS)

4 pounds small beets	½ teaspoon whole allspice
1 quart vinegar	1 stick cinnamon
1½ cups sugar	1 teaspoon cloves

Cook the beets in boiling water until tender when pierced with a fork. Hold them under cold water and slip off the skins. Slice them only if they are large. Mix the remaining ingredients in a large saucepan, add the beets, and bring to a boil. Reduce the heat and simmer for 15 minutes. Spoon into clean, hot, *sterilized* jars, fill with the cooking liquid, leaving ½-inch headspace, and seal. If you wish, process in a boiling-water bath for 30 minutes.

CORN RELISH   (ABOUT 6 PINTS)

Use sweet pimiento or red pepper for a mild relish, hot red pepper for a spicy one. A food processor will be handy here.

18 ears of corn	6 green peppers, chopped fine
1 head green cabbage, chopped fine	2 quarts vinegar
8 white onions, chopped fine	2 cups sugar
½ cup chopped sweet red pepper, pimiento, or 4 small hot red peppers	¼ cup salt
	2 teaspoons celery seed
	2 teaspoons mustard seed

Cut the kernels from the corn ears. Combine them with the remaining ingredients in a large pot, bring to the boiling point, and simmer for 40 minutes. Spoon into hot, *sterilized* jars, leaving ⅛-inch headspace, and seal. If you wish, process in a boiling-water bath for 15 minutes.

CHOW-CHOW *   (8 PINTS)

A beautiful, golden relish with a mustardy tang.

2½ pounds green tomatoes
6 small cucumbers
2 sweet red or green peppers
1 small cauliflower
1 bunch celery
2 pounds small white onions,
  peeled
1 pound green beans, in 1-
  inch lengths
¾ cup salt

2 quarts cider vinegar
2½ cups sugar
2 tablespoons celery seed
3 tablespoons dry mustard
4 tablespoons turmeric
1 tablespoon whole allspice
1 tablespoon freshly ground
  pepper
1 tablespoon cloves

Cut the tomatoes, cucumbers, red or green peppers, cauliflower, and celery in small pieces. Combine with the onions and green beans. Cover with 3 quarts boiling water and the salt and let stand for 1 hour. Drain. Rinse well in cold water and drain again. Mix the remaining ingredients in a large pot and heat to the boiling point. Add the vegetables and cook until tender, stirring frequently. Spoon into hot, *sterilized* jars, fill with the cooking liquid, leaving ⅛-inch headspace, and seal. If you wish, process in a boiling-water bath for 10 minutes.

(6 PINTS)   **PICCALILLI**

Sweet and spicy.

12 green tomatoes
4 green peppers
2 sweet red peppers
6 onions, peeled
1 small cabbage
¼ cup salt
3 cups light-brown sugar

1½ teaspoons celery seed
1 tablespoon mustard seed
1 tablespoon cloves
2-inch stick cinnamon
1 tablespoon whole allspice
2 cups cider vinegar

Chop the tomatoes, peppers, onions, and cabbage coarsely. Sprinkle them with the salt, cover, and let stand overnight. Cover with cold water and then drain. Mix the remaining ingredients in a large pot. Add the vegetables and bring to the boiling point. Reduce the heat and simmer for about 15 minutes. Spoon into hot, *sterilized* jars, fill with the cooking liquid, leaving ⅛-inch headspace, and seal. If you wish, process in a boiling-water bath for 10 minutes.

(6–7 PINTS)   **RED OR GREEN PEPPER RELISH**

You can chop the vegetables for this and other relishes coarse or fine, according to your preference. Use a food processor, if you have one, to save time and effort.

24 sweet red or green peppers
      or a combination
12 onions, peeled
6 stalks celery
1 quart cider vinegar

2 cups sugar
3 tablespoons salt
1 tablespoon mustard or
      celery seed

Chop the peppers, onions, and celery, cover with boiling water, then drain. Put them in a pot, cover with cold water, bring to the boiling point, then drain again. Mix the vinegar, sugar, salt, and mustard or celery seed in a pot, heat to the boiling point, add the vegetables, and simmer for about 10 minutes, adjusting the seasonings if necessary. Spoon into clean, hot jars, fill with the cooking liquid, leaving ⅛-inch headspace, and seal. If you wish, process in a boiling-water bath for 10 minutes.

CELERY RELISH   (3 PINTS)

Sweet and crunchy.

½ cup sugar
2 teaspoons salt
¼ teaspoon dry mustard
¼ teaspoon cloves
¼ teaspoon allspice
¼ teaspoon cinnamon

¼ teaspoon celery seed
1–1½ cups cider vinegar
2 bunches celery, chopped
6 large tomatoes, chopped
1 sweet red pepper, chopped

Mix all the ingredients well in a large pot. Bring to the boiling point, reduce the heat, and simmer until thick, about 1 hour. Spoon into hot, *sterilized* jars, fill with the cooking liquid, leaving ⅛-inch headspace, and seal. If you wish, process in a boiling-water bath for 10 minutes.

GREEN TOMATO RELISH   (4 PINTS)

4 pounds green tomatoes,
      chopped (about 8 cups)
¼ cup salt
1 teaspoon freshly ground
      pepper
1½ teaspoons dry mustard
1½ teaspoons cinnamon
½ teaspoon allspice

1½ teaspoons cloves
¼ cup mustard seed
1 quart cider vinegar
1 cup light-brown sugar
2 sweet red or green peppers,
      chopped
1 onion, chopped

Mix the tomatoes with the salt, cover, and let stand overnight or for 24 hours. Wash in cold water and drain. Mix the remaining ingredients in a pot, add the tomatoes, and bring to a boil. Cook gently for about 15 minutes. Spoon into hot, *sterilized* jars, leaving ⅛-inch headspace, and seal. If you wish, process in a boiling-water bath for 10 minutes.

(2 PINTS)   **TOMATO RELISH**

This is a tart, red tomato relish. Add more sugar if you want it to be sweet.

1 bunch celery	1 tablespoon salt
2 large green peppers	1 tablespoon sugar
1 onion	1¼ cups cider vinegar
6 large tomatoes, peeled and cut in pieces	

Chop the celery, peppers, and onion and mix in a large pot. Add the tomatoes, salt, sugar, and vinegar and simmer, stirring occasionally, until thick, about 1½ hours. Spoon into hot, *sterilized* jars, leaving ⅛-inch headspace, and seal. If you wish, process in a boiling-water bath for 10 minutes.

(3–4 PINTS)   **SWEET CHILI SAUCE**

Good with hamburgers and steak.

3 pounds (about 4 cups) ripe tomatoes, peeled and cut up	1 tablespoon salt
	½ teaspoon freshly ground pepper
2 green peppers, chopped fine	1 teaspoon cinnamon
2 onions, chopped fine	1 teaspoon cloves
2 apples, cored and chopped fine	½ teaspoon allspice
½–1 cup sugar	1 teaspoon nutmeg
	1 cup cider vinegar

Cook the tomatoes slowly for about 30 minutes, until they are soft. Stir in the peppers, onions, and apples and cook 30 minutes more. Add the remaining ingredients, adjusting the amount of sugar to taste. Boil until thick, about 10 minutes, stirring frequently and taking care not to let the mixture burn. Spoon into hot, *sterilized* jars, leaving ⅛-inch headspace, and seal. If you wish, process in a boiling-water bath for 15 minutes.

TOMATO CATSUP

(1 PINT)

A clean, spicy flavor, very different from the commercial product.

10 pounds ripe tomatoes, peeled and cut up	1 teaspoon cloves
3 onions, chopped fine	1 teaspoon whole allspice
2 sweet red or green peppers, seeded and chopped	1 teaspoon celery seed
	¾ cup dark-brown sugar
1 small clove garlic, minced	1 cup cider vinegar
2-inch stick cinnamon	1 tablespoon salt
1 teaspoon peppercorns	2 teaspoons paprika
	¼ teaspoon cayenne pepper

Combine the tomatoes, onions, red or green peppers, and garlic in a pot and cook slowly until soft, at least 30 minutes. Strain through a food mill or a fine sieve. Return to the pot and simmer until the mixture is reduced by one-half, about 30–40 minutes, stirring frequently to be sure that it does not stick or burn. Tie the cinnamon, peppercorns, cloves, allspice, and celery seed in a cheesecloth bag and add them and the remaining ingredients to the tomato mixture. Cook slowly until the catsup is very thick, stirring frequently to prevent burning. This may take several hours. Remove the bag of spices. Spoon into small clean, hot jars, leaving ⅛-inch headspace. Close the jars and process in a boiling-water bath for 10 minutes.

APPLE CHUTNEY

(7 PINTS)

A splendid sweet-and-spicy partner to ham and other pork dishes. Use ripe, red tomatoes, if you wish. You may add ½ cup of finely cut mint leaves, if you have them.

1½ pounds green tomatoes, chopped (about 3 cups)	12 large tart apples, cored and chopped
¼ cup salt	2 Spanish onions, peeled and chopped
1 quart cider vinegar	
1 pound dark-brown sugar	1 pound raisins
½ cup granulated sugar	2 tablespoons ground ginger

Put the tomatoes in a bowl, toss them with 2 tablespoons of the salt, cover, and let stand for about 12 hours. Drain and soak them in cold water for a few minutes, then drain again. Heat the vinegar, the remaining 2 tablespoons of salt, and the sugars in a large pot. Add the drained tomatoes, the apples, onions, raisins, and ginger, and cook over low heat for about 30 minutes, until the apples and onions are tender. Spoon into hot, *sterilized* jars, leaving ¼-inch headspace, and seal. If you wish, process in a boiling-water bath for 10 minutes.

GINGER APPLE CHUTNEY

Omit the ground ginger and substitute *6 ounces preserved ginger, cut small.*

(4 PINTS)   **✳ WIRTABEL'S CHUTNEY**

This is a wonderful chutney recipe from an old friend; it is full of crunch and flavor. She uses firm pears; I like honeydew melon and green apple.

12 cups fruit, peeled, seeded, and diced (leave melon in 1-inch cubes)	4½ cups sugar
	3 cups cider vinegar
	1½ teaspoons whole allspice
2 cups raisins (try 1 cup dark and 1 cup golden)	1½ teaspoons whole cloves
	Two 2-inch pieces cinnamon
1 cup peeled ginger root, in small chunks (approximately 8 ounces)	stick

Combine the fruit, raisins, ginger root, sugar, and vinegar in a large Dutch oven or kettle. Tie the allspice, cloves, and cinnamon sticks in a piece of cheesecloth, smash the spices with a hammer or mallet to break up, and add to the fruit mixture. Bring to a boil, stirring occasionally. Reduce heat to simmer and let mixture cook for about 2 hours, or until thickened and darkened. Remove the spice bag and discard. Pour or spoon into hot, *sterilized* jars, leaving ¼-inch headspace, and seal. Process in boiling-water bath for 10 minutes.

(5–6 PINTS)   **PEACH CHUTNEY**

1 quart cider vinegar	1 teaspoon ground ginger
1 head garlic, cloves separated, peeled, and minced	1 teaspoon allspice
	1 teaspoon cloves
	1 tablespoon pickling spice
2 large onions, peeled and chopped	10 cups raisins
	Salt to taste
2 pounds brown sugar	10 peaches, peeled, seeded, and chopped
1 cup granulated sugar	
1 jar ginger marmalade (approximately 12 ounces)	

In a large pot, combine the vinegar, garlic, onions, sugars, marmalade, ginger, allspice, cloves, pickling spice, raisins, and salt, and bring to a boil, stirring occasionally. Reduce the heat and simmer, stirring occasionally, for about 2 hours. Add the chopped peaches and continue to cook, stirring, until the chutney has thickened and turned dark. Pour or spoon into hot, *sterilized* jars, leaving ¼-inch headspace and seal. Process in boiling-water bath for 10 minutes.

PICKLED CRABAPPLES (ABOUT 3 PINTS)

30 crabapples
1 cup cider vinegar
1 cup brown sugar
1 cup granulated sugar
1 tablespoon cloves
1 stick cinnamon, in pieces
1 cup water

Cut off the blossom end of the crabapples but do not peel. Prick them several times with a fork. Combine the remaining ingredients with the water in a pot and boil for 5 minutes. Add the fruit, in batches if necessary, and simmer until tender. Spoon the crabapples into clean, hot jars. Fill with the hot cooking syrup, leaving ¼-inch headspace. Prepare more syrup, if necessary. Seal and process, if you wish, in a boiling-water bath for 15 minutes.

PICKLED PEARS

Use *Seckel pears*. Peel them, if you wish, or leave the skin on, pricking it well. Use *white vinegar* instead of cider vinegar.

PICKLED WATERMELON RIND ✳ (ABOUT 10 PINTS)

This is well worth doing if you can get slaked lime at a pharmacy. The crunch that these pickles should have cannot be achieved any other way. Don't worry about being exact with the amounts in this recipe; use it as a general guide.

5 pounds prepared
  watermelon rind (from 1
  average-size watermelon)
2 tablespoons slaked lime*
4 cups water
4 cups cider vinegar
14 cups sugar
½ teaspoon oil of cinnamon*
½ teaspoon oil of clove*

Buy these ingredients at the pharmacy.

Prepare the watermelon rind by cutting it into manageable pieces, cutting away all the red melon and removing the green skin with a vegetable peeler. Scrape away any remaining pink flesh and cut the white rind into bite-size cubes. Use one large enamel, plastic, or glass container and mix enough water with the slaked lime to cover the prepared rind. First stir the slaked lime into the water to dissolve, then add the rind and enough water to cover. Let this mixture stand overnight or for at least twelve hours. Drain and return the rind to the container. Make a syrup of the water, vinegar, sugar, and oils of cinnamon and clove. Boil just until the sugar is dissolved and the syrup is clear. Pour the syrup over the rind and weight the rind down with a heavy plate so that the pieces stay under the syrup. Each day for the next four days pour the syrup off the rind and bring it to a boil, then pour the boiling syrup over the rind. The final day, place the rind in hot, *sterilized* jars, bring the syrup to a boil, pour it into the jars, leaving ⅛-inch headspace, and seal. Process in a boiling-water bath for 10 minutes. These pickles are good right away but they do mellow and are at their best after several weeks.

(ABOUT 2 PINTS)   **BEET MARMALADE**

Every time I make this I am amazed at how fast it disappears. It is particularly good with roast chicken or turkey.

4 medium-large beets, cooked and peeled	1 large lemon
1½ cups sugar	2 tablespoons chopped fresh ginger

Put the beets in a food processor and process until coarsely chopped or mash the beets by hand. Transfer the beets to a heavy-bottomed saucepan and stir in the sugar. Put the lemon and ginger into the food processor and process until finely chopped or chop finely by hand. Add the lemon and ginger to the beet mixture and stir to blend. Cook over medium-low heat, stirring often, until the marmalade has thickened a little. This will take about 2 minutes and the marmalade will get thicker when it cools. For keeping not longer than a month, put the hot marmalade into clean jars, cover, and refrigerate. For longer preserving, pour or spoon into hot, *sterilized* jars, leaving ¼-inch headspace, and seal. Process in a boiling-water bath for 15 minutes.

SPICED CRABAPPLES

(SERVES EIGHT TO TEN)

1 cup sugar
24 whole cloves
6 allspice berries
2-inch stick of cinnamon

Salt to taste
1 pound crabapples
2 cups boiling water

Put all the ingredients in a pot and simmer gently until the apples are just tender. Spoon out the fruit and pour a little juice over it. Serve hot or cold.

ABOUT FRUIT RELISHES AND QUICK RELISHES

A long-standing tradition of the American table is to offer an assortment of relishes before or with a meal. They look nice and provide both color and flavor, often perking up a bland dish. The use of relishes and condiments lets everyone at the table add the kinds of flavors each wants with his or her food. Those who have a taste for spicy, sweet, or sour additions can satisfy their yen, and those with more delicate palates can keep it simple. Fruit relishes go especially well with pork, veal, and poultry. Quick relishes resemble pickles but are not so long-keeping. Jams, pickles, relishes, and condiments are usually processed in a boiling-water bath for preserving. They may, however, be made up in smaller quantities ("small-batch") by making one-quarter of a recipe and kept in a covered container, stored in the refrigerator. Refrigeration replaces the traditional boiling-water bath sterilization but does not allow you to store the food for long periods of time. Nonprocessed foods should be used up within a week or so. Most of the preceding recipes can be made fresh, in small batches, and not processed. One of the advantages of quick relishes is that one can use any amount of sugar one desires.

SPICED CARROTS

Substitute *1 pound tiny new scraped carrots* for the crabapples.

SPICED APRICOTS OR PEACHES

Cook the syrup (without the crabapples) for about 10 minutes, then pour it over *peach or apricot halves, cooked and pitted*, and let stand until cool.

HORSERADISH

Horseradish roots	Salt
White vinegar	

Scrape the outside of the horseradish roots until clean and drop them into cold water to prevent discoloration. Drain and chop in a food processor or in a blender with a little vinegar. Spoon into clean pint jars, filling them about two-thirds full. Add 1 teaspoon of salt to each jar, then fill with white vinegar. Close the jars and refrigerate.

(SERVES EIGHT)   ## CRANBERRY SAUCE

12 ounces fresh cranberries	1 cup sugar, or more to taste
1 cup water	

Wash the cranberries. Bring the water to a boil, then add the cranberries and sugar. Cook for 10 minutes or until the skins pop. Skim off the white froth and cool. Refrigerate until ready to serve.

(2½ CUPS)   ## CRANBERRY JELLY

This is a tart, soft-textured jelly, very unlike its canned counterpart.

12 ounces fresh cranberries	1–1½ cups sugar
1 cup water	Salt

Wash the cranberries. Bring the water to a boil, add the cranberries, and boil for 20 minutes, stirring occasionally to keep from burning, especially at the end. Put the berries through a strainer or food mill. Return them to the pot and cook over low heat for 3 minutes, stirring frequently. Add the sugar to taste and a pinch of salt and cook 2 minutes more. Pour into a bowl and chill.

SPICED CRANBERRY JELLY

Add with the cranberries a *2-inch stick of cinnamon, 3 whole cloves,* and *3 allspice berries.*

CRANBERRY AND ORANGE RELISH   (SERVES SIX)

½ pound (2 cups) cranberries   ¾ cup sugar
1 small orange

Wash the cranberries. Cut the orange in pieces and remove the seeds; do not peel. Chop the cranberries and orange with a food chopper or in a food processor. Add the sugar and stir well. Let stand at least 30 minutes before serving.

SUGARED CRANBERRIES   (SERVES SIX TO EIGHT)

4 cups fresh cranberries   ¾–1 cup sugar

Spread the cranberries in a large skillet. Sprinkle with sugar to taste and place over medium heat. Cook, shaking and stirring, for about 8 minutes, or until the sugar has melted and a few of the cranberries have popped. Pour into a serving dish. As the cranberries cool, the sauce thickens.

FRESH FRUIT CHUTNEY   (ABOUT 6–7 CUPS)

This is a fresh condiment, reminiscent of a chutney, but it is not long-cooked or processed. Make up only what you need, as it does not keep well because of the fresh fruit. It is good served warm with cold meat or as a salad with a simple chicken dish.

4 tablespoons butter
½ cup brown sugar
1 teaspoon curry powder
2 tablespoons water, to thin
     sauce if necessary

2 large bananas, sliced
2 cups fresh pineapple, in
     bite-size chunks
2 firm pears, peeled, cored,
     and in pieces

Place the butter and brown sugar in a saucepan and melt over medium-low heat, stirring occasionally. Add the curry powder, stir, and continue to cook for 1–2 minutes. Thin the sauce with the water if necessary. Put the bananas, pineapple, and pears in a large bowl and pour the sauce over. Stir to coat all the fruit.

(SERVES SIX)   **BROILED PEACHES OR APRICOTS**

This relish also makes a delicious and simple dessert.

  6 fresh peaches or apricots   ¼ cup brown sugar
  4 tablespoons butter

Wash peaches or apricots. Cut them in half and remove the stones. Place them in a shallow pan, cut side up. Dot each half with 1 teaspoon butter and sprinkle with 1 teaspoon brown sugar. Broil until the sugar melts.

BROILED PEACHES WITH BLUEBERRIES

Fill each cavity of the peaches or apricots with a spoonful of *blueberries* before dotting with butter and sugar.

BROILED BRANDIED PEACHES

Add ½ *teaspoon brandy* to each cavity before dotting with butter and sugar.

(SERVES FOUR)   **FRIED APPLE RINGS**

Serve these instead of applesauce with ham, pork dishes, or duck.

  2 tart apples   2 tablespoons sugar
  4 tablespoons butter

Core the apples. Peel them only if the skins are very tough. Cut them in ½-inch slices and sauté the slices in butter until just barely tender. Sprinkle with sugar, cover the pan, and cook a few minutes more, until they are glazed and golden.

FRUIT KABOBS

Good with barbecued chicken or spareribs.

Fresh pineapple, cubed	Prunes, pitted and cooked
Spiced Apricots or Peaches (p. 1103)	Butter

Arrange the fruit on skewers, brush with butter, and broil, indoors or out, for 5 minutes.

BAKED ORANGES   (SERVES SIX)

These should be baked alongside a roasting turkey or duck.

6 seedless oranges	2 tablespoons sugar

Cover the oranges with cold water. Bring to the boiling point, simmer 30 minutes, and drain. Cut a slice off the top of each orange and place 1 teaspoon sugar in each. Bake in the roasting pan for about 1 hour.

UNCOOKED TOMATO RELISH   (2 PINTS)

You can keep this uncooked mixture in a cool, dark place for about six months. It lacks the subtlety of cooked relishes, but has a fresh, piquant quality that is decidedly different.

12 large ripe tomatoes, peeled and chopped	2 tablespoons sugar
½ cup chopped celery	1½ tablespoons mustard seed
2 tablespoons chopped sweet red or green pepper	¼ teaspoon nutmeg
	¼ teaspoon cinnamon
2 tablespoons chopped onion	Pinch of cloves
1½ tablespoons salt	½ cup cider vinegar

Drain off the liquid from the tomatoes. Combine the pulp with the remaining ingredients. Put the mixture in a covered crock and let it stand for at least one week before using.

(1½ CUPS)   **CHILI SAUCE**

2 cups canned tomatoes
1 onion, chopped
Dash of cayenne pepper
⅛ teaspoon cloves
⅛ teaspoon cinnamon
1 tablespoon sugar

¼ cup vinegar
2 tablespoons chopped green
    pepper
½ teaspoon salt,
    approximately

In a heavy-bottomed saucepan, combine the tomatoes, onion, cayenne, cloves, cinnamon, sugar, and vinegar. Simmer, uncovered, for 1 hour. Add the green pepper and simmer 30 minutes more. Add salt to taste. Chill before serving.

(3½ PINTS)   **QUICK CHOW-CHOW**

A beautiful golden mustard with a mustardy tang.

4 cups cauliflower flowerets
2 cups coarsely chopped
    cabbage
1 cup coarsely chopped sweet
    red peppers
1 cup chopped onion
1 cup cucumber, cut into
    quarters and then into
    ¼-inch slices

3 teaspoons salt
⅓ cup flour
1 tablespoon dry mustard
1 teaspoon turmeric
1½ cups sugar
3 cups white vinegar (5%
    acidity)

Bring a large pot of salted water to a boil. Using a strainer, individually blanch the cauliflower, cabbage, red pepper, and onion. Put each vegetable in the strainer and lower it into the boiling water, leave for about 5 seconds, remove, and let drain. Put all of the vegetables in a large bowl, add the cucumber, and toss to mix. In a small pan, combine the salt, flour, dry mustard, turmeric, sugar, and 1 cup of the vinegar. Cook over low heat for a few minutes, stirring constantly. Add the remaining 2 cups of vinegar and continue to cook until smooth and thick. Remove from the heat. Fill clean jars with the vegetable mixture, then spoon the mustard-vinegar mixture over until the vegetables are covered. Cover and refrigerate. Use within a month.

CARROT RELISH

(ABOUT 4 PINTS)

Just before serving this relish you can add a small amount of sliced red onion and chunks of green pepper to brighten the color.

2 pounds carrots, peeled
1 medium onion, chopped
1 green pepper, chopped
1 cup tomato sauce

½ cup sugar
⅓ cup vegetable oil
⅓ cup cider vinegar

Steam whole peeled carrots until just done, then plunge them into cold water until cool. Drain, then cut in pieces or dice. In a bowl, combine the carrots, onion, and pepper. In a separate bowl, mix together the tomato sauce, sugar, oil, and vinegar until well blended. Pour over the carrot mixture, cover, and refrigerate 12 hours or longer.

FIRE AND ICE TOMATO RELISH ✳

(ABOUT 3 CUPS)

¼ cup sugar
½ teaspoon salt
⅛ teaspoon freshly ground
   black pepper
1½ teaspoons celery salt
1½ teaspoons mustard seed
¼ teaspoon hot pepper sauce,
   or ⅛ teaspoon cayenne
   pepper

¾ cup white vinegar
¼ cup water
2 large tomatoes, peeled
¼ large onion, diced
½ medium cucumber, peeled,
   sliced thin, and chilled

Combine sugar, salt, black pepper, celery salt, mustard seed, pepper sauce, vinegar, and water in a saucepan and bring to a boil. Turn down heat and simmer for 8–10 minutes. Chill 2–3 hours before using. Slice the tomatoes and let drain. Combine with the onion and marinade, cover, and refrigerate, stirring gently several times while chilling. At serving time add chilled cucumber slices.

CUCUMBER RELISH

(2 PINTS)

3 cucumbers, peeled and
   sliced very thin
1 tablespoon salt
1¼ cups water

¾ cup sugar
⅓ cup white vinegar
1–2 cloves garlic, mashed
   (optional)

Set aside the prepared cucumbers. Mix the salt and water in a large bowl. In a small bowl, combine the sugar, vinegar, and garlic, if using. Pour the sugar mixture into the salted water and stir well. Add the cucumbers and stir well to mix. Refrigerate at least 6 hours before draining and using.

(2½ CUPS) **PHILADELPHIA RELISH**

2 cups finely shredded cabbage
2 green peppers, diced fine
1 teaspoon celery seed

¼ teaspoon mustard seed
2 tablespoons brown sugar
¼ cup vinegar
Salt to taste

Toss together all ingredients. Chill before serving.

(4 CUPS) **FRESH ZUCCHINI RELISH OR PICKLE**

This is quick and requires no cooking. It can be served as a relish with fish or meats, or eat it as you would any pickle.

5–6 medium zucchini
½ green pepper, chopped
½ medium onion, chopped fine

2 tablespoons salt
1 cup sugar
¾ cup white vinegar

Trim the ends off the zucchini and wash thoroughly. Slice the zucchini into very thin slices. In a large bowl, combine the zucchini, green pepper, onion, salt, sugar, and vinegar, mixing well to blend. Refrigerate for 1–2 hours before serving.

(ABOUT 4 CUPS) **ZUCCHINI PICKLES**

This is quick, easy, and produces a small batch of "bread-and-butter" style pickles. It is a great way to use some of the summer garden zucchini.

2 cups cider vinegar
1½ cups sugar
½ teaspoon turmeric
¼ teaspoon cloves
2 teaspoons mustard seed
2 teaspoons celery seed

¼ teaspoon ground ginger
1 teaspoon salt
1 onion, halved and sliced thin
1 pound zucchini, sliced thin (³⁄₁₆–¼ inch thick)

Place the vinegar, sugar, turmeric, cloves, mustard seed, celery seed, ginger, and salt in a large saucepan and bring to a boil. Reduce the heat and simmer for 10 minutes. Bring back to a boil, add the sliced onion, and cook for 1 minute. Add the zucchini slices, bring to a full boil, and cook for just 2 minutes, stirring to push the slices under the liquid. Remove from the heat and let cool. Place in one or several small covered containers and store in the refrigerator. Serve ice cold as you would any bread-and-butter pickle.

CANNED FRUITS AND HIGH-ACID VEGETABLES

About Canned Fruits and High-Acid Vegetables

For general information, see About Preserves, Pickles, Relishes, and Canned Fruits and Vegetables, p. 1068. For freezing fruits, see p. 1122.

Equipment for Canning Fruits and High-Acid Vegetables

All fruits and a few vegetables, such as tomatoes and rhubarb, are high in natural acid. Do not use tomatoes when they are overripe; they are less acid. Fruits and acid vegetables do not require high-heat processing under pressure but should be processed in a boiling-water bath at 212°F. For this you will need a water-bath canner, equipped with a rack so that the jars do not touch the bottom of the pot (p. 1073).

Preparing Fruits and High-Acid Vegetables for Canning

Use firm, fresh produce. Wash fruits and vegetables thoroughly before hulling or removing the skins, pits, cores, or seeds.

To prevent prepared fruit from darkening, drop it into a salt-vinegar-water mixture (2 tablespoons each of salt and vinegar to 1 gallon of water) for no more than 20 minutes. Rinse the fruit before cooking it or packing it into jars. Leave the designated headspace.

Fruits and vegetables may be raw-packed or hot-packed (p. 1072), according to the recipe, in sweetened or unsweetened liquid. Sugar syrup is often used to help preserve the shape, color, and flavor of fruit, but it is not necessary for preserving: fruit juices or plain water will preserve just as well.

Sugar Syrup. Each quart of fruit requires from 1 to 1½ cups of sugar syrup. Sugar syrup is made by cooking sugar in water or fruit juice until it dissolves. Use the following proportions:

LIGHT SYRUP: 2 cups sugar to 4 cups water = 5 cups syrup
MEDIUM SYRUP: 3 cups sugar to 4 cups water = 5½ cups syrup
HEAVY SYRUP: 4¾ cups sugar to 4 cups water = 6½ cups syrup

If you wish, you can replace up to half the sugar with honey or corn syrup. This sugar syrup is also used in freezing fruits (see p. 1122).

Processing Fruits and High-Acid Vegetables

See Water-Bath Method (p. 1072).

(ALLOW 2½–3 POUNDS FOR EACH QUART JAR)   **CANNED APPLES**

Peel, core, and slice the *apples* or cut them into quarters. Boil in *light syrup* (see p. 1110) for 5 minutes. Pack into clean, hot jars and cover with boiling syrup, leaving ½-inch headspace. Close the jars and process in a boiling-water bath for 20 minutes.

APPLESAUCE

Follow instructions for making *Applesauce* (p. 1004). Heat the applesauce until it boils, then spoon it into clean, hot jars, leaving ½-inch headspace. Close the jars and process in a boiling-water bath for 20 minutes.

(ALLOW 2–3 POUNDS FOR EACH QUART JAR)   **CANNED APRICOTS**

Cut the *apricots* in half and remove the pits. Cook gently in *medium* or *heavy syrup* (see p. 1110) until heated through. Pack into clean, hot jars and cover with boiling syrup, leaving ½-inch headspace. Close the jars and process in a boiling-water bath, allowing 20 minutes for pint jars and 25 minutes for quarts.

(ALLOW 1½ QUARTS FOR EACH QUART JAR)   **CANNED BLACKBERRIES AND RASPBERRIES**

Wash the *berries* and remove the caps and stems. Spoon them into clean, hot jars. Cover them with boiling *light* or *medium syrup* (see p. 1110), leaving ½-inch headspace. Close the jars and process in a boiling-water bath, allowing 15 minutes for pint jars and 20 minutes for quarts.

CANNED BLUEBERRIES

(ALLOW 2 QUARTS
FOR 3 PINT JARS)

Wash the *blueberries* and remove the stems. Put them in a square of cheesecloth and gather up the ends to form a bag. Dip the berries into boiling water for about 30 seconds or until spots appear on the bag. Dip into cold water. Pack the berries tightly into jars, leaving ½-inch headspace. Do *not* add sugar or liquid. Close the jars and process in a boiling-water bath, allowing 15 minutes for pint jars and 20 minutes for quarts.

CANNED CHERRIES

(ALLOW 2–2½ POUNDS
FOR EACH QUART JAR)

Stem and pit the *cherries*, or leave the pits in, if desired. Wash them and pack them into jars. Fill with boiling *light syrup* (p. 1110), leaving ½-inch headspace. Close the jars and process in a boiling-water bath, allowing 20 minutes for pint jars and 25 minutes for quarts.

SOUR CHERRIES

Use *medium* or *heavy syrup* (p. 1110).

CANNED PEACHES

(ALLOW 2–3 POUNDS
FOR EACH QUART JAR)

Wash *freestone peaches* and dip them into boiling water, then cold water. Peel them, then cut in half and remove the stones. Slice, if desired. Cook gently in *medium or heavy syrup* (p. 1110) until heated through. Spoon into clean, hot jars, and cover with boiling syrup, leaving ½-inch headspace. Close the jars and process in a boiling-water bath, allowing 20 minutes for pint jars and 25 minutes for quarts.

CANNED PEARS   (ALLOW 2–3 POUNDS FOR EACH QUART JAR)

Wash the *pears* and peel them. Leave them whole or cut them in half and core them. Cook gently in *light syrup* (p. 1110) for 5–6 minutes, about 10 minutes if whole. Pack into clean, hot jars and cover with boiling syrup, leaving ½-inch headspace. Close the jars and process in a boiling-water bath, allowing 20 minutes for pint jars and 25 minutes for quarts.

(ALLOW 2 POUNDS FOR   **CANNED PINEAPPLE**
EACH QUART JAR)

Cut the *pineapple* crosswise in ½-inch slices. Pare the outer shell and cut out the cores. Dice, if desired. Simmer in *light syrup* (p. 1110) until tender. Pack into clean, hot jars and cover with boiling syrup, leaving ½-inch headspace. Close the jars and process in a boiling-water bath, allowing 15 minutes for pint jars and 20 minutes for quarts.

(ALLOW 1½–2½ POUNDS   **CANNED PLUMS**
FOR EACH QUART JAR)

Wash the *plums*, cut them in half, and remove the pits, or prick the skins and use them whole. Heat to the boiling point in *medium or heavy syrup* (p. 1110). Pack in clean, hot jars and cover with boiling syrup, leaving ½-inch headspace. Close the jars and process in a boiling-water bath, allowing 20 minutes for pint jars and 25 minutes for quarts.

(ALLOW 1 POUND FOR EACH PINT JAR)   **CANNED RHUBARB**

Clean the *rhubarb* and cut the stalks into ½-inch pieces. Measure and add ¼ cup sugar for each pint. Mix well and let stand for at least 1 hour, then bring slowly to the boiling point and boil for about 1 minute. Pack into clean, hot jars, leaving ½-inch headspace. Close the jars and process in a boiling-water bath for 10 minutes.

                              CANNED STRAWBERRIES

Strawberries do not can well. It's best to use them in jams and preserves (p. 1083) or to freeze them (p. 1122).

(ALLOW 3 POUNDS   **CANNED TOMATOES**
FOR EACH QUART JAR)

Dip barely ripe *tomatoes* in boiling water for a minute or two and then in cold water. Peel them and cut out the stems and any white cores. Slice them or leave them whole. Pack into clean, hot jars and press down until the jars fill up with liquid, leaving ½-inch headspace. Add 1 *teaspoon salt* for each quart. Close the jars and process in a boiling water bath, allowing 35 minutes for pint jars and 45 minutes for quarts.

CANNED TOMATO PURÉE

Dip barely ripe *tomatoes* in boiling water for a minute or two and then in cold water. Peel them and cut out the stems and any white cores. Slice them and cook over low heat until soft. Press through a food mill or strainer, then return to the pot and continue to cook until thick, stirring constantly to prevent sticking. Season with *salt*, if you wish. Pack in clean, hot jars, leaving ¼-inch headspace. Close the jars and process in a boiling-water bath, allowing 30 minutes for pint jars.

SPICY TOMATO PURÉE

Add to the peeled tomatoes any one or all of the following: *chopped onion, chopped fresh herbs, chopped celery, chopped carrot, chopped green pepper*. Process pint jars for 45 minutes.

CANNED TOMATO JUICE

Wash barely ripe *tomatoes* and cut away the stem ends and any bad spots. Cut in small pieces and simmer over low heat until very soft. Strain through a sieve or a food mill. Reheat the juice to the boiling point, adding *salt*, a touch of *sugar* and *spices to taste*, if you wish. Pour into clean, hot jars, leaving ¼-inch headspace. Close the jars and process in a boiling-water bath, allowing 10 minutes for pint jars and 15 minutes for quarts.

CANNED FRUIT JUICE

Extract the *juice* from fruit as for jelly (p. 1077). Sweeten with *sugar*, if desired. Pour into clean, hot jars, leaving ¼-inch headspace. Close the jars and process in a simmering-water bath at 185°F for 15 minutes.

FROZEN FOODS

ABOUT FREEZING

Freezing is the best way to preserve the fresh, natural colors, textures, flavors, and food values of most foods. It is also easier than canning, requiring less equipment and processing time. No wonder home freezing has replaced or supplemented canning in many parts of our country, even in rural areas where preserving is done on a large scale.

Most homeowners today would find it hard to imagine living without some kind of freezer space. But as freezers become increasingly indispensable to our way of life, they are also being taken for granted, with all the resulting abuses that come with careless handling, packaging, and storing of frozen food. It's important to develop good freezer habits so that you can use your freezer comfortably, productively, and creatively. A good general rule is freeze fast and defrost slowly.

While, in general, freezing arrests the growth of harmful bacteria, molds, and yeasts, it does not destroy them. Use high-quality, fresh foods when freezing, for no matter how carefully foods are packaged and stored, freezing will not transform food into something better than it was when it was first purchased and prepared.

Owning and Maintaining a Freezer

Although freezer-lockers are available in many towns on a rental basis, it may pay to invest in a freezer of your own. You'll save money and reduce shopping time, for you can buy large quantities of foods that are in season or on sale and freeze them for future use. You can also save cooking time by cooking in quantity.

Freezers help you to plan and organize your life. You can prepare weeks ahead for special occasions, and you can always have something on hand for emergencies.

Types of Freezers. A separate, freestanding storage freezer that is opened infrequently provides the most satisfactory storage. Such freezers come in upright and chest styles and in a variety of sizes.

Refrigerator-freezer combinations, with a separate freezer door that is located at the top, bottom, or side, are also very efficient.

Old-style freezer—ice cube compartments that are within the refrigerator itself should be used only for the very short-term storage of commercially frozen products and leftovers.

Temperature. Food should be frozen quickly at 0°F or below. Quick freezing will prevent the formation of large ice crystals between the food fibers which break down the structure of foods and affect their quality.

The best way to check the temperature of your freezer is to use a freezer thermometer. It's good to keep the freezer at −10°F so that when you add unfrozen food the temperature will not rise above 0°F. It is especially important to control the temperature when you are adding a large quantity of unfrozen food at one time.

In Case of Power Failure. During a power failure, a fully loaded freezer will stay cold for one to two days; a partially loaded freezer will hold for a much shorter time. Don't open the freezer door when the power is off.

If the failure threatens to last for more than a day or two, you can buy some dry ice and put it in the freezer. Be sure to handle dry ice carefully, wearing gloves, and place it in the freezer on a piece of cardboard, not directly on the food. A 50-pound cake of dry ice, if added soon after a power failure, will prevent thawing for two or three days.

Defrosting a Freezer. Unless your freezer is the self-defrosting kind, it will need defrosting whenever the ice on the sides is about ¾ inch thick. Transfer frozen foods to the refrigerator during defrosting, or wrap them in layers of newspapers or blankets to keep them insulated. To speed defrosting, set pans of hot water inside the freezer.

Self-defrosting freezers, although they use more electricity than others, are very convenient.

All freezers, including frostless ones, should be thoroughly cleaned while empty once a year. Use a solution of warm water and baking soda, about ¼ cup baking soda to each quart of water.

Unwanted Odors. If you are troubled by off-odors in your freezer, put a few lumps of charcoal in the freezer to absorb them.

Packaging Food for Freezing

Foods should be packed for freezing in quantities geared to your family's needs and your entertaining patterns. If your family is small, for example, use several small containers to pack a stew; you can always defrost an extra package if you have unexpected guests, but a large amount of stew, once defrosted, may leave you with unwanted left-overs that will not benefit from refreezing.

Before you package food for freezing, decide how you will be de-frosting it or if it will need defrosting and proceed with that in mind. If you put soup or other liquid cooked foods in a rigid, heavy plastic or metal container, you'll be able to speed up defrosting by heating the container in a pot of barely simmering water until the contents are soft enough to pour into a pot for slow heating. Casserole dishes should be frozen in the kind of heavy-duty casseroles or foil or glass containers that can go straight from the freezer into a preheated oven. If you are going to need a particular casserole dish and therefore do not want to leave it in the freezer, line it with foil and, once the contents are frozen solid, remove them and wrap and store them; when they are ready to serve, the frozen food will fit neatly into the same casserole for reheat-ing. You can quickly and efficiently defrost in a microwave oven if frozen foods are frozen in or transferred to a microwave-safe con-tainer. Follow the manufacturer's recommendations for defrosting in your particular microwave oven.

Herbed butters and jams can also be frozen the same way by foil-lining crocks in which the butter is packed, then freezing it and remov-ing it, so that it can later be served in the same crocks.

Cakes with frostings should first be frozen and then wrapped in foil, plastic, or other freezer paper; in that way the frosting will not stick to the paper as it freezes. Cooked meat will keep better if frozen unsliced, but if it's more convenient to freeze it in serving portions, slice it and pack it with a little gravy which will help preserve it and make it easy to heat.

Small amounts of stock and concentrated sauces or gravies may be frozen first in ice cube trays and then turned into plastic bags for stor-age. This will reduce thawing time and make it possible to extract just a small amount.

Containers and Wrappings. All freezer wrappings should be mois-ture-proof and vapor-proof. Air is the great enemy of frozen food: exposure to air during freezing may cause an off flavor, the loss of moisture and color, or the development of a tough, dry surface known as "freezer burn."

But although exposure to air is to be avoided, it is important to leave some headspace when packaging soft and liquid food, for many foods expand as they freeze. Leave ½-inch headspace for soft or liquid foods in pint containers and 1-inch headspace for soft or liquid foods in quart containers. Dry-packed fruits and vegetables should have about ½-inch headspace. Headspace is especially im-portant when using glass freezer jars, which might break without room for expansion.

Plastic containers or glass jars with wide mouths are commonly used for freezing foods that have a soft or liquid consistency. An initial investment in good heavy-duty containers is worthwhile, for they can be reused indefinitely. Square or rectangular containers stack well and use space more economically than round ones. There's no reason not to reuse round coffee or nut tins with plastic lids or the extra-heavy plastic containers that come with certain ice cream and dairy products—after all, they're free and work perfectly satisfactorily.

Liquid foods can also be packed in special plastic bags that seal with heat. These freeze-and-cook bags, which come with directions for use, can be submerged in boiling water, an excellent way to re-heat frozen cooked food.

Foods that are not liquid, especially those with bulky shapes, should be wrapped in plastic bags or in flexible wrapping paper suitable for freezing. When using plastic bags, press out all the air, then twist the tops and seal them with the ties that come with the bags.

It's easiest to wrap meat, cakes, pies, and other dry or bulky products in flexible wrappings like foil, plastic wrap, or special freezer wrap. Polycoated freezer wrap is strong and nonporous and will not puncture as easily as foil but it must be folded carefully and secured with tape. Some people find it awkward to use. We find that heavy-duty foil, while expensive, provides splendid pro-tection and is very easy to use, for it can be pressed to fit the shape of the food and does not need to be sealed with tape. Single-weight foil, used in several layers, is also very satisfactory, as is flexible, transparent plastic wrap. Contrary to popular belief, meats and other supermarket products, if they are not to be held more than a few months, may be frozen in the plastic-wrap packages in which they are sold.

Do not use cellophane tape to seal covers or packages: it will not hold. We recommend ordinary masking tape, which is a lot cheaper and just as effective as special freezer tape.

Labeling. Be sure to label foods before you freeze them, indicating the contents, the quantity, and the date. Include other pertinent infor-mation when relevant: "needs seasoning," "thin before using," etc. Use a pencil, a crayon, or a special marking pen for labeling; many ordinary pens and felt-tipped pens will fade or smudge in the freezer and become illegible. Don't write directly on containers you plan to reuse. Make labels with masking tape instead and be sure to put the tape on the package before you freeze it; it will not adhere to a frozen surface.

Loading a Freezer

Don't overtax your freezer by putting in a lot of fresh food at the same time. Add only as much food as will freeze within 24 hours, about 3 pounds for each cubic foot of interior space.

Whenever possible, let newly added food packages touch the

freezer walls or shelves for quick freezing. Set them apart from each other so that cold air can circulate around them. After they are frozen, stack them neatly.

Store foods in groups, keeping meats in one place, soups in another, and so on. Keep foods that have been in the freezer longest near the front so that they will be used in chronological order.

As you fill your freezer, keep an inventory of its contents. Make up a list of all the foods inside, including the dates they were frozen and the quantities in which they were packed. Keep the list taped to the door, crossing off items as you use them and penciling in others as new foods are added. An inventory list will show at a glance just what you have in the right quantity for a particular meal. The dates will enable you to use foods within the proper amount of time. Moreover, if you know what you're looking for before you open the freezer, you won't keep the door open unnecessarily while you rummage around.

Storing Foods

Frozen foods will not turn bad if they are stored too long, but they will gradually lose quality. Cooked foods, cakes, cookies, breads, unbaked pastries, chopped meat, pork products, fish, and liver should be used within a three- to six-month period. Most fruits, vegetables, and meats, frozen under proper conditions, may be kept for about a year.

Defrosting Foods and Refreezing Them

Defrosted food will spoil more rapidly than fresh and should therefore be used promptly.

The best ways to defrost or thaw foods are in the refrigerator (which takes a lot of time), in a microwave (which is much quicker), and under cool running water. Whenever possible, it's best to cook frozen foods directly from a frozen state without defrosting them. When foods require complete defrosting, try to use them while they are still chilled. Prepared and already-cooked dishes that are frozen should go directly from the freezer to the oven or microwave oven for reheating, without first defrosting. The flavors and textures are better preserved than if the dish is allowed to thaw first.

With some meats and poultry, and with fish especially, the texture is preserved better when they defrost slowly in the refrigerator, provided you have the time to do so. Room-temperature defrosting is, of course, much quicker. When using a microwave oven to defrost foods, follow the manufacturer's instructions.

Any defrosted food that is safe to eat may also be safely refrozen. Although the quality, and especially the texture, of food may suffer after refreezing, the only *danger* in refreezing food is that spoilage may have set in before the food was refrozen. Things like bread, butter, and nuts may be defrosted and refrozen several times without noticeable change.

Sometimes, when uncooked foods like meat and poultry have accidentally defrosted, you may find it convenient to cook them and then freeze them in their cooked form. It's a good way to guard against spoilage and to avoid the loss of texture and quality that often comes with refrozen food.

It's good to know when a package has been thawed and refrozen, so that you don't repeat the process over and over again. Be sure to make an appropriate note on the label.

Do not eat thawed foods if you have any question about their taste, smell, or appearance.

WHAT TO FREEZE

Freezing information for specific foods appears throughout this book in the introductions to the individual chapters. This section contains general information about freezing cooked foods and specific information about freezing uncooked meat, fruits, and vegetables.

There are no hard-and-fast rules for what the perfectly planned freezer should contain. The contents of a well-stocked freezer will vary from home to home, depending on individual tastes and eating habits, styles of cooking and entertaining, and, of course, the nature of the household itself. But regardless of whether the food in the freezer is commercially prepared or homemade, whether it's geared toward everyday basics or special indulgences, it is possible for every freezer owner to have good things on hand for all occasions.

Storing Staples in the Freezer

Almost everything freezes well: just look through the frozen food section of any large supermarket. Meat, poultry, fish, hard cheeses, breads, cakes, desserts, pastries, cookies, candies, nuts, dried fruits, and coffee are among the uncooked or commercially prepared unfrozen staples that you can store in your freezer. Some things, like nuts and coffee, are better stored in the freezer than at room temperature. Parsley and fresh herbs, wrapped in foil, will keep their flavor for many months. Milk and cream keep well in the freezer, and it's good to have some on hand for emergencies. If you allow heavy cream to defrost completely, then shake it well, it will whip up just fine. Fruits and vegetables, purchased in season, may be frozen uncooked or partially cooked (see pp. 1122–27).

Foods That Don't Freeze Well

Potatoes, unless mashed, become mushy in the freezer: it's best to freeze soups and stews without them and to add potatoes later. Cream cheese, soft cheeses, chopped liver, cream fillings, custards, egg-thickened sauces, meringue, and many cake frostings (especially those made with brown sugar or egg whites) will not freeze well. Hard-boiled egg whites get rubbery in the freezer, most fried or breaded foods become soggy, and foods made with gelatin do not keep their consistency. Salad greens, radishes, cucumbers, celery, uncooked tomatoes, scallions, and bananas should not be frozen.

Freezing Home-Cooked Foods

The best way to have a very special supply of frozen food at hand is to cook specifically for your freezer. This is doubly useful during harvest times, when low prices tempt you to buy in quantity or when you have a lot of extra produce from your own garden. Cook seasonal vegetables and fruits like tomatoes, squash, and berries; use them in sauces, pies, soups, and casserole dishes and then freeze them for future use.

Stews, casseroles, meat pies, gravies, soups, stocks, and cooked meat and poultry all freeze well. Home-baked breads, pies, cakes, cookies, preserves, pickles, and candies may also be kept in the freezer. Many foods that are to be frozen should be slightly undercooked, since they will cook further when they are reheated. This is especially true for vegetable soups, stews, and pasta dishes.

You may have to readjust the seasonings of frozen cooked foods before you use them. Cool cooked foods thoroughly before freezing them, but do not let them sit around once they have cooled.

It's good to get in the habit of cooking double or even triple amounts of favorite dishes that freeze well, and then putting the extras away for another meal. The additional work is minimal—you're making the dish anyway—and the pleasure of having a meal or two prepared and waiting in the freezer cannot be overestimated.

If your freezer contains a crusty, home-baked bread, some nourishing soup made from last summer's vegetables, a few hard cheeses, and some cookies, ice cream, or sherbet, you'll always be able to put together a quick, impromptu meal.

You can prepare an elegant crêpe dinner if you have some easy-to-defrost crêpes in the freezer, some frozen cooked chicken, and some frozen duxelles. Bind the filling with a velouté sauce, perhaps a very special one made with your own defrosted chicken stock.

Frozen pot roast and gravy are always good to have on hand, as are home-baked cakes and cookies, which defrost readily when you have unexpected guests. Indeed, some cookies are even better when still partially frozen.

If you use your free time every once in a while to make and freeze a supply of special cooking ingredients that take time to prepare—beef stock or puff pastry, for example—you'll find that the creation of "elaborate" dishes at a later date will be a snap.

Freezing Leftovers

The freezer is like a savings bank: use it to collect good things for later use—leftover meat and poultry that can be used in pies, casseroles, and fillings; leftover vegetables, juices, gravies, meat juices, bits, or sauces—no matter how small the amount, it will come in handy to add flavor to soups and sauces. Save bones and giblets for making stock, adding bits of other leftovers as they accumulate. Leftover cooked beans, even rice and noodles, may be frozen and combined with meats and sauces in the future. Save the livers from each chicken you cook until you have enough for a meal. Freeze leftover egg whites, unbeaten, until you have enough for angel cake or meringue. Leftover egg yolks or whole eggs out of the shell will freeze well if you add sugar (1 teaspoon per 6 yolks) or salt (½ teaspoon per 6 yolks). Use the sugared eggs in dessert recipes and the salted ones in sauce and egg dishes.

Freezing Meat and Poultry

Freeze meat in the quantities in which you plan to use it—for example, enough individual hamburger patties or boned chicken breasts for your family or a 2-pound package of chopped meat for a meat loaf. Beef, lamb, veal, and chicken will keep in the freezer for about a year, pork for three to six months, and variety meats for several months. Leftover cooked meat, carefully wrapped, may be frozen for three to six months. Cured frozen meats are more subject to rancidity because they do not freeze as hard due to the salt content; therefore, use them as soon as possible after freezing.

If you should forget to defrost a piece of meat and find yourself with, say, a hard-frozen leg of lamb at three in the afternoon, don't despair. You can cook meat that is still frozen if you allow the amount of time you would if the meat had been at room temperature and then add half as much time again. This is true for all meat except pork which, for safety's sake, should never be cooked frozen.

Freezing Fruits

Uncooked fruit may be packed for freezing in a variety of ways, depending on the fruit and the way in which it will be used. Always select fruit that is ripe and wash it well with cold water, handling it gently to avoid bruising. Most fruits will have good flavor after freezing, but their texture will become softer. Puréed fruit and fruit juices retain their character best after defrosting.

Pack fruits in sugar syrup if you intend to use them as desserts. If you plan to cook the fruit after defrosting it, or to use it in pies, jams, or sauces, pack it dry, with or without sugar. When cooking defrosted fruit, be sure to make allowances for any sugar that was added before freezing.

To Prevent Darkening. An ascorbic acid (vitamin C) solution is recommended to prevent the darkening of certain fruits, especially apricots, cherries, peaches, nectarines, and plums. To make the solution, dissolve ½ teaspoon ascorbic acid crystals in ¼ cup cold water for each quart of sugar syrup or of prepared fruit. There are also commercially prepared ascorbic acid mixtures. When using them, follow the printed directions.

Lemon juice is sometimes substituted for ascorbic acid, but it may change the flavor of the finished product. Steaming is recommended to prevent the darkening of apple and pear slices.

Dry Pack Without Sugar. (See chart, p. 1124.) To pack fruit dry without sugar is very simple: wash the fruit, dry it, sprinkle it with ascorbic acid (if recommended), pack in containers, and freeze.

You can make a loose pack by spreading the fruit out on a tray and freezing it, then packing it in containers and sealing. When fruit is loose-packed, it is easy to use in small quantities.

Dry Pack with Sugar. (See chart, p. 1124.) Wash and dry the fruit, add ascorbic acid (if recommended), then sprinkle with sugar, using ½–¾ cup sugar for each quart of prepared fruit. Toss the fruit gently, then let it stand for about 10 minutes until the sugar dissolves and the juices are drawn out.

Syrup Pack. The sugar syrup used for freezing fruit is the same as that used for canning fruit (p. 1110). Make the syrup, using the strength recommended on the chart on the next page. Cool the syrup thoroughly before adding the fruit. If ascorbic acid is recommended, add it to the syrup just before combining the syrup with the fruit.

You will need ½–¾ cup sugar syrup for each pint package of fruit. Pack the fruit so that it is completely covered with the syrup, leaving the recommended headspace. Cover the top of the fruit with a piece of crumpled foil to hold it under the syrup.

Wet Pack Without Sugar. You can also crush unsweetened fruit and pack it in its own juices, or leave it whole and add water to which ascorbic acid (if recommended) has been added. Leave the proper amount of headspace (p. 1071).

Puréed Fruit. Puréed fruit, of which applesauce is the most familiar example, freezes beautifully. Sugar may be added or not, according to taste. For fruits that work well as purées, see the chart on the next page.

Fruit Juice. To extract fruit juices, see p. 1077. All fruit juices freeze well.

For Freezing Fruits

FRUIT	Preparation	Dry pack without sugar	Dry pack with sugar (amount of sugar per 1-quart package)	Syrup pack (see p. 1123)	Wet pack without sugar	Purée	Use ascorbic acid
Apples	Peel, slice, steam 2–3 minutes over boiling water.	Yes	½ cup	Medium		Yes	Yes
Apricots	Halve and pit; peel and slice, if desired.		½ cup	Medium	Pack in water	Yes	Yes
Berries (except strawberries)	Remove leaves and stems.	Yes	¾ cup	Medium	Pack in berry juice		
Cherries—Sweet and Sour	Pit, if desired.		¾ cup	Heavy			Yes
Cranberries	Remove stems.	Yes		Heavy			
Currants	Remove stems.	Yes	¾ cup	Heavy			
Gooseberries	Remove stems and ends.	Yes	¾ cup	Heavy			
Grapes	Stem; leave whole if seedless; halve and remove seeds if not.	Yes		Medium			
Melons	Peel, remove seeds, cut in cubes or balls.			Light		Yes	
Nectarines	Halve and pit; peel and slice, if desired.		⅔ cup	Medium	Pack in water	Yes	Yes
Oranges and Grapefruit	Peel, section, remove seeds.			Medium			
Peaches	Halve and pit; peel and slice, if desired.		⅔ cup	Medium	Pack in water	Yes	Yes
Pears	Peel, core, slice; heat in boiling, medium syrup 1–2 minutes.			Medium			Yes
Pineapple	Pare; cube or crush.	Yes		Light	Pack in water		

FRUIT	Preparation	Dry pack without sugar	Dry pack with sugar (amount of sugar per 1-quart package)	Syrup pack (see p. 1123)	Wet pack without sugar	Purée	Use ascorbic acid
Plums and Prunes	Halve and pit or leave whole.	Yes	¾ cup	Medium or heavy		Yes	Yes
Rhubarb	Trim, cut in 1-inch pieces; heat 1 minute in boiling water.	Yes	1 cup	Medium			
Strawberries	Hull; leave whole or slice.	Yes	¾ cup	Heavy	Pack in berry juice	Yes	

Freezing Vegetables

Blanching. Most vegetables should be prepared for freezing by a process known as blanching, during which they are scalded in boiling water for a short, designated period of time (see chart, 804). This helps to preserve fresh vegetable flavor, bright color, and vitamin content. Blanching also makes vegetables less bulky and thus easier to pack.

You'll need a large pot. Allow a gallon of water for each pound or quart of vegetables to be blanched. Bring the water to a boil while you are preparing the vegetables.

For best results, use vegetables that are very fresh. Wash them in cold water and prepare them as you would for cooking. When necessary, cut the vegetables into pieces small enough for packaging. Place them in a wire basket or a cheesecloth bag.

Submerge the basket or bag into the boiling water, using a small enough amount of vegetables at one time so that the water will return to a boil within a minute. Cover the pot and begin timing; follow the recommended amount of time in the chart.

When the time is up, plunge the vegetables into a large bowl full of ice water to stop them from cooking further. Leave them there for about as much time as they spent in the boiling water.

Drain the vegetables and pat them dry. Pack them without any liquid in freezer bags or containers and freeze.

You can use the same pot of boiling water for scalding other batches of the same vegetable.

Exceptions to Blanching. To freeze *beets*, cook them until they are tender, then peel them, slice them if you wish, and pack and freeze them.

Potatoes, sweet potatoes, winter squash, and pumpkin should be cooked until soft, then mashed, packed, and frozen. Reheat them in the top of a double boiler, adding butter and seasonings to taste.

To freeze *mushrooms*, sauté them, whole or sliced, in a little butter, then freeze immediately. Or make duxelles (p. 578), which freeze splendidly.

Green pepper should be cleaned, sliced or chopped, wrapped, and frozen without any blanching.

Onions may be parboiled and then frozen, or left raw, chopped and frozen without any blanching.

Cooking Frozen Vegetables. Cook frozen vegetables for a shorter time than you would fresh.

Many frozen vegetables should be cooked directly from a frozen state. Others, like broccoli and greens, are better when they are partially thawed and broken up, then cooked very quickly. Corn on the cob should be thoroughly defrosted, then buttered, wrapped in foil, and reheated in a moderate oven.

For Blanching Vegetables

VEGETABLE	Preparation	Blanching time in minutes	
Asparagus	Cut or break off woody bottom of each stalk.	Thin:	2
	Peel stalks with vegetable peeler.	Thick:	3
Beans, Green, Wax	Wash and trim off ends.		3
Beans, Lima and Other Shell Beans	Remove shells and sort by size.	Small:	1
		Medium:	2
		Large:	3
Beans, Green Soy	Preserve only the newly formed beans in the green stage. Blanch whole pods, cool, then squeeze beans out.		5
Broccoli	Use only the firm young stalks with bright flowerets. Separate the flowerets from the stems, peel stems and slice diagonally, cut into 1½" lengths.		3
Brussels Sprouts	Wash and remove wilted outer leaves. Trim the stems.		3
Carrots	Scrub young carrots but scrape skin off older carrots. Cut the medium size and larger lengthwise and in 2" lengths; younger small carrots in 2" lengths.		2

VEGETABLE	Preparation	Blanching time in minutes	
Cauliflower	Use only firm heads. Trim and break into flowerets, about 1" in diameter, and wash.		2
Corn on the Cob	Remove husks, and silk threads; wash.		6
Corn, Whole-kernel	Remove husks and silk threads. Scrape kernels from cob after blanching.		6
Kohlrabi	Use mature but tender stems. Trim top and bottom, peel away the tough fibers. Cut crosswise ¼" thick—unless very young, then leave whole.		2
Okra	Use young pods. Remove the stem at end.	Small: Large:	3 4
Parsnips	Use firm roots. Remove top, wash, and peel. Slice into ½" pieces.		3
Peas, Black-eyed	Use only young, tender black-eyed peas. Shell.	Small: Large:	1 2
Peas, Green	Use only the young. Shell.		1
Succotash	Blanch whole-kernel corn and lima beans separately as above. Mix equal parts.		2
Turnips and Rutabagas	Remove tops, peel. Slice into ½" pieces.		1

(Add 1 minute to blanching time if you live 5,000 feet or more above sea level.)

APPENDIXES &
INDEX

BEVERAGES

ABOUT COFFEE

Making Good Coffee

A good cup of coffee should have a pleasing, never bitter taste, and it should be full bodied with a rich aroma. Too often the coffee we make misses the mark because the coffee isn't sufficiently fresh and/or we have been careless making it. To brew a good cup of coffee is really a simple procedure, if you bear in mind the following rules:

- Start with fresh coffee. A vacuum-packed can of coffee is fine when just opened, but because the beans are ground, they lose their aroma quickly; aroma is the key to freshness. Keep the tin well sealed and store in a cool place, preferably the refrigerator. If you can buy freshly roasted beans and grind your own each time you make it, you will have much more delicious coffee. Store beans in a tightly sealed jar in the refrigerator or freezer; in the latter case, simply remove what you need and grind the beans still frozen.
- Use 2 level tablespoons of coffee to 1 cup of water. If you want stronger coffee, increase the amount of coffee; don't try to compensate by brewing longer: that only leads to overextraction and consequent bitterness. To make weaker coffee, use the recommended proportions, which preserve the proper balance, and then add boiling water after, rather than reduce the amount of coffee.
- For methods requiring boiling water, ideally the water should be at 205°F—just under boiling. But rather than hover over the kettle to catch the water before it comes to the boil, let the kettle rest a moment after boiling before pouring over the grounds.
- The quality of the water used in brewing can make a difference. If you are a purist about your coffee, and your tap water contains a lot of salts, minerals, or chemicals, try using bottled water.

- Be sure to use the right grind for the particular kind of coffee you are making: Drip for drip method; Regular for percolator, steeped, and boiled coffee; Fine or Vacuum for espresso.
- Glass and porcelain coffee makers are the best. Metal pots tend to make coffee taste bitter; stainless steel has the least ill effect.
- Always be sure that your coffee-making equipment is scrupulously clean, particularly if you are using any kind of metal. Wash after each use with a mild detergent or baking soda; soak any filters.
- Don't leave coffee sitting on the grounds too long.
- Don't repour coffee through the grounds.
- To make *iced coffee*, double the amount of coffee, prepare by one of the methods outlined below, and leave to cool. If you add ice cubes while the coffee is still hot, you may want to make an even stronger brew.
- Try to avoid reheating coffee; it is better to make just what you need.

NOTE
> Coffee that stays too long at a high temperature or is reheated will take on a harsh, burned, and bitter taste. Instead of leaving it on a heating element pour finished hot coffee into a thermos or insulated carafe. This will keep it tasting freshly made and hot for 4–6 hours.

TYPES OF COFFEE

The kind of coffee you like best is a matter of individual taste. Sample different brands until you are satisfied. If you have the opportunity to experiment with freshly roasted beans, try mixing your own blends. The results are more satisfying than using just one individual type, and with a good blend one flavor will enhance another. Many people like to combine one part light-roasted coffee such as Mocha with one part of a full-bodied Brazilian Santos, or Colombian, or Java, and one part of dark-roasted French. Ask questions about the nature of different beans and work out blends that please you.

For those who wish to avoid the stimulating effects of caffeine, decaffeinated coffees are widely available. There are two processes used to decaffeinate coffee, a chemical and a water process. Taste several and choose which you like best.

Usually an after-dinner coffee is stronger than a morning cup, particularly if it is served in demitasses. You can simply double the strength of your usual brew or use French or Italian coffee or combinations thereof.

Steeped Coffee. You can use a clean saucepan or a special glass coffee maker with a plunger (see illustration on p. 1132, the third pot in at top). Measure 2 level tablespoons of regular grind coffee for each cup, then pour barely boiling water over and let steep 5 minutes. If using a saucepan, pour off the coffee through a fine-meshed strainer; for the

special glass model, simply push down the plunger, so the grounds remain at the bottom.

"Boiled" Coffee. This is somewhat of a misnomer because to make coffee successfully using this old-style camping method, you shouldn't boil the coffee; rather let it come just to the boil. Measure 2 level tablespoons of regular grind coffee for each cup desired into the bottom of a clean saucepan or an old-fashioned coffee pot and pour the required number of cups of cold water on top. Add a pinch of salt and cover. Bring the coffee slowly to the boil and just as soon as the bubbles break through the surface crust, stir it and remove from the fire. Sprinkle a little cold water on top and let settle a few minutes before pouring. Some outdoorsmen crack an egg and mix it, crumpled-up shell and all, into the coffee grounds before pouring on the water. It helps the grounds to settle. In either case one is apt to have a slightly muddy but good strong brew. Coffee purists may frown on this method but it can produce a delicious cup.

Percolator Coffee. Be sure that all parts of the percolator are absolutely clean. Fill the basket with the correct amount of regular grind coffee—that is, 2 tablespoons per cup—and pour the measured amount of cold water for the particular percolator into the bottom. Insert the basket and percolate over low heat 6–8 minutes. Electric percolators have the disadvantage of not enabling you to control the timing or the heat so that sometimes overextraction of the beans occurs, causing bitterness.

Drip Coffee. Use 2 level tablespoons drip grind per cup. It's better not to make more than you need, and preheating the pot with boiling water will help to hold the warmth while the coffee is dripping so you needn't reheat. After pouring the first splashes of barely boiling water on the grounds, stir to be sure they are all moistened, then continue. We recommend drip coffee makers of glass or porcelain that use paper filters. Automatic electric drip coffee makers are excellent, provided you don't allow the finished coffee to sit on the warmer too long. Follow the manufacturer's instructions for use, but ignore any suggestions for using less than 2 tablespoons of coffee per cup of water.

Espresso Coffee. One needs a special espresso maker to produce this kind of strong coffee. Use the fine or vacuum grind of French or Italian coffee, 2 tablespoons to 3–4 ounces of water—and follow the manufacturer's instructions. The type of machine that pushes under pressure both steam and hot water through the coffee will give you the true espresso experience, but the two-cylinder pot (facing page, top right) is more familiar for home use and it simulates a fine espresso.

Here are two coffee recipes for special occasions.

(PER SERVING) **IRISH COFFEE**

1 jigger Irish whiskey	2 tablespoons whipped cream
1 teaspoon sugar	
1 cup very hot after-dinner coffee	

Put the Irish whiskey in the bottom of a glass or mug. Stir in the sugar and add piping hot strong coffee. Top with the whipped cream and serve immediately.

(SERVES SIX) **CAFÉ BRÛLOT**

Café Brûlot, which has long been a specialty of New Orleans, can provide a dramatic climax to a fine meal. In New Orleans, it is usually prepared in and served from a special silver brûlot bowl that is warmed over an alcohol flame. A chafing dish will do the job effectively.

1½-inch stick cinnamon	2 lumps sugar
5 cloves	⅓ cup brandy
3 tablespoons slivered orange peel	2 tablespoons curaçao
3 tablespoons slivered lemon peel	3 cups hot after-dinner coffee

Put the cinnamon, cloves, orange and lemon peels, and sugar in a chafing dish or brûlot bowl with a flame under and mash together with the back of a spoon or a pestle. Add the brandy and curaçao, and when hot, ignite. Stir to dissolve the sugar, then gradually add the coffee. Serve in demitasses.

ABOUT TEA

Making Good Tea

To make good tea, the leaves must be steeped in boiling water. Loose tea is the best kind to use, but tea bags are perfectly serviceable as long as they are put in a warm pot, cup, or mug and *boiling* water is used. The way tea is served in most public places—a cup of hot water with a tea bag alongside it—is an insult to anyone who cares about tea and should be protested because it is impossible to produce a decent cup that way.

The important points to remember in making tea are:

- The water you use should always be cold and freshly drawn—no water that has been boiled before or has sat around in a kettle. Bring it to a rolling boil and use immediately.
- Earthenware or china pots are best. Metal is apt to alter the flavor ever so slightly.
- Warm the teapot (mug, or cup) by pouring boiling water in and swirling it around, then discarding water.
- Put 1 scant teaspoon of tea into the steaming pot (or a tea bag into the warm cup or mug) for every cup of water, then gently pour over the leaves water that has just come to a rolling boil. Give a good stir, cover, and let steep 5 minutes. (For the single cup or mug, use a saucer to cover; 3–4 minutes of quiet steeping should be enough; don't dunk the bag.)
- Give a final stir to the pot, let the tea settle, and pour—through a tea strainer or not, depending on whether you mind a few leaves in your cup.
- If the tea is too strong when you pour it out, add boiling water. You may find that for your own taste the proportion of 1 teaspoon per cup for certain strong blends like Irish Breakfast is too strong and that you want to use slightly less tea. But remember that it is easier to weaken tea with boiling water after it is made than to try to add more leaves after it has been brewed.
- Serve with cream or milk, slices of lemon, and sugar on the side for those who want them. Always have available a pot of hot water.
- To make *iced tea*, double the amount of tea per cup, make in the usual way, and then pour off into a pitcher. Add ice when cool; if you are in a hurry and want to add the ice while still hot, triple the

amount of tea used because the ice will weaken it. Refrigerating iced tea will make it cloudy. Add, if you wish, a sprig of mint and a slice of lemon and/or orange, to each glass and let each person sweeten according to his taste. Instant iced tea makes a beverage that tastes little like real tea.

A tea cozy provides a nice way of keeping the pot warm. But don't let tea sit around too long. It is better to make a fresh pot for latecomers. Or you may pour the tea off into another preheated pot and keep warm over a candle.

• Store loose tea and tea bags in airtight tins and keep away from strong light. Tea that is fresh when bought should keep as long as six months this way. Tea bags lose their flavor much more quickly.

Types of Tea

Most of the tea that we buy in tea bags is advertised as Pekoe and Orange Pekoe, which actually refers to the cut and size of the leaf and tells us nothing about the type or origin. If you become interested in tea, as so many Americans have in the past decade or so, you should start sampling some of the various types and blends of imported tea packed in tins and perhaps seek out sources where you can buy your own loose tea. The basic types of tea are the black, fermented teas, which include Ceylon, Darjeeling, Keemun, and Assam, all rich and full-tasting; the green, unfermented teas, which we associate primarily with Japan and China; and the semifermented Oolong teas. Certain teas, like black Lapsang Souchong, have a smoky flavor that comes from the curing process, and others have a perfume because they have been fired with jasmine or other kinds of blossoms.

The most familiar blends are English Breakfast Tea, made up primarily of Keemun; Irish Breakfast, a strong blend of Assam and Ceylon, more often drunk with milk in it; Earl Grey, a delicately scented tea; and Russian, usually a blend of black teas and China green.

Spiced Teas and Herbal Teas. Spiced teas are made from real tea with the addition of such spices as cloves, dried orange or lemon peel, and sometimes with cinnamon, anise, or cardamom. Mint tea can be made of pure mint leaves—usually peppermint or spearmint—or blended with a strong black tea; mint teas are particularly good cold on a hot day.

ABOUT PUNCH

Punches and eggnogs are for celebrations and holidays. They should be served from a large punch bowl, ladled out into small cups or glasses. Here are several to choose from—both with spirits and without. Count on about ¾ cup for each serving.

There are many bottled waters on the market today. Some are carbonated and some are not, and many contain fruit flavors or fruit juices. They make a nice addition to a punch or are good by themselves in a tall glass filled with ice, with maybe the addition of a wedge of lemon or lime. They are convenient to have on hand for guests who prefer not to drink alcohol or drinks containing caffeine.

RUM PUNCH (ABOUT 5 QUARTS)

1 cup sugar	6 cups unsweetened
1 cup water	pineapple juice
1½ cups lemon juice	1 fifth dark Jamaica rum
1½ cups grapefruit juice	2 fifths light West Indian
5 cups orange juice	punch

Make a sugar syrup by boiling the sugar with the water for 5 minutes. Let cool. Mix together with all the other ingredients and let mellow for at least 1 hour. Pour over a large block of ice in a punch bowl and serve when thoroughly chilled.

REGENT PUNCH (5½ QUARTS)

1 quart rye whiskey	1½ cups orange juice
1 quart rum	1 fifth champagne
1 quart strong tea	1 quart soda water
¾ cup lemon juice	

Mix together the rye, rum, tea, and the fruit juices and pour over a large block of ice in a punch bowl. Just before serving add the champagne and soda water.

CHAMPAGNE PUNCH (6 QUARTS)

2 cups sugar	3 cups unsweetened apple
2 cups water	juice
1¼ cups lemon juice	2 cups unsweetened
2 cups apricot nectar	pineapple juice
One 6-ounce can frozen	2 quarts ginger ale
orange juice concentrate	2 fifths champagne

Make a sugar syrup by boiling the sugar with the water for 1 minute. Cool. Add the lemon juice, apricot nectar, and orange, apple, and pineapple juices to the sugar syrup. Chill. Pour over a large block of ice in a punch bowl and just before serving add the ginger ale and champagne.

(8½ QUARTS)   **CREOLE CHAMPAGNE PUNCH**

2 cups sugar
2 fifths dry white wine
1 pint curaçao
1 pineapple

4 quarts soda water
2 fifths champagne
1 quart strawberries

Stir the sugar into the wine and curaçao until completely dissolved. Shred half the pineapple by cutting it into quarters, removing the core, and either putting peeled pieces in a food processor or scraping unpeeled quarters against the large holes of a grater. Peel the other half and cut into slices. Add the grated pineapple to the wine mixture and pour over a large block of ice in a punch bowl. Just before serving, add the soda water and champagne and float the pieces of pineapple and the strawberries, hulled and halved if they are large, on top.

(6½ QUARTS)   **CIDER PUNCH**

1 gallon sweet cider
2 quarts soda water
1¼ cups sherry

1 cup brandy
3 tablespoons lemon juice
Peel of 1 lemon, in strips

Mix all the ingredients together and pour over a block of ice in a punch bowl.

(4 QUARTS)   **FISH HOUSE PUNCH**

Fish House is the informal name of The State in Schuylkill, the oldest men's club in America, and this is the authentic recipe for its much-esteemed and highly potent punch. For a milder version, more suitable for a wedding reception or holiday bowl, try the variation, but if you want the real thing, this is it.

2 cups sugar
1 quart lemon or lime juice, or
    a combination
2 cups water

2 fifths dark rum
1 fifth cognac
2–3 ounces peach brandy

Dissolve the sugar in the citrus juice and water. Mix in the rest of the ingredients and "brew" by letting it sit 2 hours to exchange flavors. Pour over a block of ice in a punch bowl and serve.

MILDER FISH HOUSE PUNCH

Dissolve the sugar in 2 cups water and 2 cups citrus juice. Use only 1 fifth rum and add 3½ *cups tea* and 3 *quarts ginger ale* to the mixture.

BASIC FRUIT PUNCH
(NONALCOHOLIC)   (3½ QUARTS)

1½ cups sugar	1 cup lemon juice
1 quart strong hot tea	1 quart ginger ale
1 quart orange juice	Fresh mint leaves

Dissolve the sugar in the hot tea. Mix together with the citrus juices. Pour over a large block of ice and just before serving add the ginger ale and scatter fresh mint leaves on top.

VARIATIONS

Use ½ *cup fruit syrup* such as raspberry or strawberry instead of the sugar. You may need some additional sugar; taste and add what is needed. Add *fresh fruits,* such as shredded pineapple, strawberries, sliced peaches or mangoes, to the bowl.

SANGRIA   (ABOUT 4½ QUARTS)

1 quart orange juice	1 lemon, washed and sliced
3 quarts dry red wine	Up to ¾ cup confectioners'
2 oranges, washed and sliced	sugar (optional)
4 fresh peaches, peeled and	Soda water (optional)
sliced	

Mix together all except the optional ingredients in several large pitchers and let stand for 4–6 hours. Add ice and taste. If you wish it sweeter, stir in confectioners' sugar to taste. If you like it a little lighter, splash in some soda water. Pour into large wine or old-fashioned glasses, letting a little of the fruit fall into each glass.

(ABOUT 8 QUARTS) **EGGNOG**

Be sure to refrigerate the eggnog and serve ice cold. If any sits out on a buffet table very long, throw it out. Do not save and re-refrigerate.

1 dozen eggs, separated
½ teaspoon salt
2¼ or more cups sugar
2 or more cups bourbon
½ cup rum

1 quart milk
2 tablespoons vanilla
3 pints heavy cream
Nutmeg

NOTE
see page 471

Beat together the egg yolks and salt in a large mixing bowl, slowly adding 1½ cups of the sugar. Continue beating until thick and pale. Stir in the bourbon, rum, milk, and vanilla until well mixed. Beat the egg whites until foamy and slowly add the remaining ¾ cup sugar, continuing to beat until stiff and all the sugar has been incorporated. Whip the cream until stiff. Now fold the egg whites into the yolk mixture and then fold in the whipped cream. Taste and add more bourbon and/or sugar if necessary. Pour into a punch bowl and sprinkle the top with nutmeg.

OTHER DRINKS

(6 CUPS) **HOT COCOA**

¼ cup unsweetened cocoa
2 tablespoons sugar
Pinch of salt
½ cup water

4 cups milk
Few drops vanilla (optional)
Whipped cream (optional)

Mix the cocoa, sugar, and salt with the water in a medium saucepan and boil gently for 2 minutes. Add the milk and heat slowly just to the boiling point. Beat well with a beater or whisk and, if you wish, flavor with a few drops of vanilla. Pour into cups and top with a dollop of whipped cream, if desired.

(SERVES ONE) **BASIC MILK SHAKE**

Vary this shake according to what flavor you want—strawberry ice cream with strawberry syrup, coffee with coffee, maple walnut with maple syrup, etc.

¾ cup milk

2 teaspoons vanilla or 2
tablespoons syrup of your
choice

1–2 scoops ice cream

Beat together all the ingredients or spin quickly in a blender.

BASIC ICE CREAM SODA   (SERVES ONE)

Again, the combination of syrup and ice cream is up to you.

3 tablespoons chocolate,
strawberry, or other fruit,
caramel, or coffee syrup

1 cup soda water
1–2 scoops ice cream

Mix everything in a tall glass, stir a bit, and serve with a straw.

COLD OR HOT LEMONADE   (ONE 10-OUNCE GLASS)

Make a large batch of sugar syrup and keep it in the refrigerator all
summer long. Cold lemonade is just right on those hot summer days,
while hot lemonade has been considered a curative.

2 tablespoons fresh lemon
juice
1½–2 tablespoons sugar
syrup*

1 cup water (carbonated
water is sometimes
refreshing)

For cold lemonade, put the lemon juice, sugar syrup, and water in
a glass and stir. Add ice for the chill. For hot lemonade, add boiling
water to the lemon juice and sugar syrup, stir, and serve.

*To make sugar syrup, bring equal parts of sugar and water to a boil, stir until sugar dis-
solves, and remove from the heat. Cool before using. Store unused syrup in a covered container in the refrigerator.*

MENUS & TABLE SETTINGS

For thoughts about what constitutes a good menu, consult Menu Planning for Family and Friends, p. 1142. The suggestions that follow should serve simply as guidelines. The more you cook, the more you'll want to vary meals your own way and create menus that reflect your particular mood, the occasion, the season, or express some motif that may have meaning for you.

No matter how simple the meal, it's nice to have the table properly set. Knives, then spoons should be on the right side of each place setting, forks on the left. The easiest rule is to place the utensils in the order of their use during the particular meal, starting at the outside. The setting below, at right, would be for a dinner that begins with soup, followed by a main course (large knife and fork), salad (small fork), and dessert; the butter and/or cheese knife goes to the right of the big knife. If you were having salad as a first course, the two forks would be reversed and no soup spoon would be needed, as in left illustration.

All these rules assume that you have plenty of silver. If you haven't, don't worry, and certainly don't hesitate to serve more than just one course because of lack of tableware. You can always slip out between courses and wash up whatever is needed or simply ask guests to keep a knife or a fork. The French use special knife-and-fork rests for just this purpose.

Napkins should go to the left of the forks or under them. Or you can do something fancy, if you're good at that sort of thing, like making the napkin into a fan shape and putting it in the middle of each place setting or stuffing it into a large goblet. Glasses for wine and water are always to the right of the setting. If you are serving both red and white wine, put the smaller glass for white wine on the outside. Butter plates, when used, are to the left.

Most important, whether for guests or when you're just family, remember always to have your plates and serving bowls and platters warm whenever you are serving hot food. It is so unpleasant to have nice hot food congealing on a cold plate after it is served. Warm everything in a low oven or on the back of the stove, if you have room; if not, a radiator, a hot plate, and even the drying cycle of a dishwasher make excellent plate warmers.

FAMILY DINNERS

Here are some suggestions for traditional family dinners. The dishes are relatively simple to make and not too expensive, with many of the main course ingredients providing leftovers that could be used to create another dish for another meal—see Other Suggestions at the end of the Chicken, Beef, Lamb, and Ham recipe sections.

Pan-Fried Chicken	Meat Loaf
Succotash	Hashed Brown Potatoes
Cranberry Jelly	Green Beans
Swiss Chard OR Spinach	Baked Bananas
Lemon Pudding	
Irish Stew	Pot Roast
Crusty French Bread	Potato Pancakes
Green Salad	Brussels Sprouts
Chocolate Bread Pudding	Baked Custard
Picnic Ham	Salmon Loaf
Sweet Potato and Apple Scallop	Rice
OR Spoon Bread	Peas
Blanched, Buttered Cabbage	Baked Pears OR Apples
Gingerbread and Whipped Cream	
New England Boiled Dinner	Smothered Chicken
Cornsticks	Buttered Noodles
Cole Slaw OR Sliced Tomatoes	Sautéed Zucchini
Apple Crisp	Iced Oranges

FAMILY SUPPERS

There are so many good supper dishes to choose from that use little or no meat—an important consideration these days when meat is so expensive and world food supplies so limited. A good pasta, rice, or bean dish, eggs in various guises, stuffed vegetables, a hearty soup with your own homemade bread all make delicious and satisfying main courses for family dinners.

Vegetable Cobbler OR Macaroni and Cheese	Filled Omelets OR Baked Eggs
Mixed Green Salad	Cottage-Fried Potatoes
Hard Rolls	Buttered Peas
Marmalade Soufflé	Pineapple Upside-Down Cake

Baked Spanish Rice	Waffles OR Toast
Watercress, Orange, and Avocado Salad	Creamed Dried Beef
	Braised Spinach
Cottage Pudding Cake	Fruit Salad
	Crackers and Cheese

Baked Beans OR Beans Bretonne	Stuffed Eggplant OR Green Peppers
Boston Brown Bread	
Turnip Slaw	Mixed Green Salad
Floating Island	Boston Cream Pie

Mixed Greens Southern Style OR Chicken Gumbo Soup	Old-Fashioned Fish Chowder, Black Bean, Oxtail, OR Split Pea Soup
Corn Bread	Entire Wheat OR Graham Bread
Brown Betty	Fruit Compote
	Applesauce Cake

LATE SUPPERS

Soups are also good for a late supper after a basketball game or the theater, or at the end of an evening of talk or cards. Here are two attractive possibilities:

Cioppino OR Mulligatawny Soup	Pumpkin OR Onion Soup
Homemade Crackers	Small Biscuits and Ham
Ginger Ice Cream	Meringue Shells with Ice Cream OR Strawberries
Sugar Cookies	

SMALL DINNER PARTIES

Nothing in these menus requires too much last-minute attention, so that the dishes can be prepared ahead as time allows and the host-cook can relax with the guests. Even vegetables can be blanched ahead and heated up in butter between the first and second courses. With everything made at home, the dishes should not be too expensive. Meats are costly, particularly the roast beef and the crown roast of lamb, but these would be for special occasions, or could be replaced with less expensive cuts.

Clear Tomato Soup
Mushroom-Stuffed Chicken Breasts
Buttered Broccoli
Feather Rolls
Deep-Dish Peach OR Apple Pie

Cold Artichokes OR Green Beans
Vinaigrette
Roast Pork
Scalloped Potatoes
Braised Red Cabbage and Apples
Cornsticks
Pears with Chocolate Sauce and
Lace Cookies

Platter of mixed hors d'oeuvre,
such as slices of pâté, olives, celery,
tomatoes, deviled eggs
Sole Baked in Herbed Cream
Parslied New Potatoes, Boiled
Braised Young Spinach
Bread Sticks
Carrot Torte OR Pecan Pie

Watercress, Sliced Orange, and
Avocado Salad
Crown Roast of Lamb
Scalloped Eggplant
Date Nut Cakes with
Whipped Cream

Stuffed Clams OR Oysters
Standing Rib Roast of Beef
Yorkshire Pudding
Puréed Parsnips
Mixed Green Salad
Platter of Cheeses (optional)
Crusty French Bread
Lemon OR Raspberry Ice

Cream of Jerusalem Artichoke
Soup
OR Shrimp and Papaya Salad
Roast Wild Duck
Wild Rice OR a combination of
long-grain and wild rice
Puréed Rutabagas
Strawberry Tart

LUNCH PARTIES

Unless you are a family who sits down together and has dinner in the middle of the day, lunch is apt to be a very informal meal, improvised from what is on hand. The lunch menus that follow are primarily suggestions for small luncheon parties.

Beef Bouillon

Eggplant Quiche with Tomatoes
and Olives

Cold Rhubarb OR Apricot Soufflé

Asparagus OR Artichokes
Vinaigrette

Cheese OR Spinach Soufflé

Rhubarb Pie

Avocados with Chicken or
Seafood Stuffing
Popovers

Lemon, Lime, OR Orange
Chiffon Pie

Corn Chowder

Spinach, Mushroom, and Bacon
Salad

Hominy Gems OR Nut Bread

Dessert Crêpes with Berries
OR Jam

Chicken Crêpes with
Mushroom Filling
Mixed Green Salad

Orange Jelly with Grapes and
Whipped Cream

Baked Eggs in Mornay Sauce

Sautéed Sweet Red, Green,
and Yellow Peppers

Baking Powder Biscuits

Fresh Cut-Up Fruit

Macaroons, Crescents, OR
Other Cookies

TWO MENUS FOR SUMMER

Cold Cucumber Soup

Chicken OR Lobster Salad
Cream Bread Fingers

Summer Pudding

Prosciutto and Melon

Lemon Chicken and Asparagus
Cream Mold

Whole-Wheat Muffins

Bowl of Fresh Fruit

Brownies

BUFFETS

Here are several ideas for a buffet table—some more elaborate than
others.

Smoked Salmon OR Gravlax
OR Cold Fish Mousse
Swedish Meatballs
Buttered Slices of Rye Bread
Wilted Cucumber Salad
Green Beans OR Blanched Asparagus
OR Broccoli Vinaigrette
Strawberry Shortcake OR Nut Roll
with Whipped Cream

Eggplant-Zucchini Appetizer
Stuffed Cherry Tomatoes
New Red Potatoes with
Rosemary
Chicken and Pork Pâté
Buttered Slices of German
Caraway Bread
Savory Tarts
Almond Torte
Fruit Sherbets

Country Terrine
Seafood Aspic
Cheese-Stuffed Manicotti
Crusty French Bread
Parsley Salad OR Rice Salad
Mixed Green Salad

Bowl of Fresh Fruits
Walnut Mocha Cake

Baked Clams
Cannelloni OR Stuffed Manicotti
Mixed Green Salad

Watermelon Filled with
Melon Chunks
Fresh Banana Cake OR
Chocolate Cake

Cold Salmon with Green
Mayonnaise
Baked Ham OR Parslied Ham in Aspic
Water Bread OR Parker House Rolls
Raw Vegetable Salad OR Celery Victor

Frozen Raspberry Soufflé or
Ice Cream Bombe
Daffodil Cake

Chicken and Oysters for
a Chafing Dish
Stuffed Zucchini
Southern Corn Pudding
OR Scalloped Corn
Brioche Rolls OR Corn Bread
Watercress, Sliced Orange,
and Avocado Salad
Pecan AND/OR Squash Pie

BRUNCHES

Brunch is a good way to combine breakfast and lunch for your family
on a lazy weekend morning or to get together with friends for a relaxed midday meal. It's a fine time to enjoy a lot of the old favorites
that used to grace our breakfast tables and to savor some of the wonderful sweet breads that taste so good with a steaming pot of coffee or
tea. If you have a large crowd, combine several of the dishes suggested
in the different menus.

Grapefruit
Goldenrod Eggs
Sausages OR Scrapple
Cinnamon Rolls

Watermelon
Green Chili Pie
Corn Muffins

Fruit Cup
Chicken Sausage Patties
Omelets
Orange Peel Bread

Cut-Up Pineapple
Sautéed Chicken Livers
Scrambled Eggs Bourget
Apricot Almond Bread

Melon
Italian Sausage Meat
Frittata with Cheese and Vegetables
Swedish Braided Bread

Strawberries
Eggs Benedict
Broiled Tomatoes
Quick Coffee Cake

Blueberries
Baked Custard
Baked Ham
Buttermilk Currant Scones

Grapefruit Coupe
Pan-Fried Brook Trout
Cottage-Fried Potatoes
Oatmeal Muffins

CHINESE MENU

Cucumber Sushi
Chinese-Style Chicken Salad
Shrimp with Green Peppers
Coconut Macaroons

ITALIAN MENU

Bread Salad
Capellini with Shrimp, Lemon,
and Parsley
Ossobuco
Orange Biscotti
Coffee Ice Cream

MENU FROM THE GRILL

Marinated Grilled Chicken Halves
Vegetable Brochettes
Garlic Bread
Abby's Strawberry Sherbet

MEXICAN MENU

Fresh Salsa
Chili Con Carne
Tortillas
Pineapple with Lemon Pie

SPANISH MENU

Gazpacho
Paella
Spanish Cream
Almond Spice Cookies

THE MAKE-UP OF OUR FOODS

FOOD	Calories	Cholesterol	Fat	Protein	Carbohydrates (grams)
Almonds (2 oz.)	334	0	30	11	12
Apple:					
1 raw, medium-sized					
(5 oz.)	77	0	0	0	20
baked (p. 1007), 6–7 oz.	196	0	1	0	51
Apple Crisp (p. 1006),					
⅙ of recipe	374	41	16	2	59
Apple juice, 1 cup	117	0	0	0	29
Applesauce:					
sweetened, ¾ cup	145	0	0	0	38
unsweetened, ¾ cup	79	0	0	0	21
Apricots:					
dried stewed,					
sweetened, ½ cup juice	153	0	0	2	39
3 whole fresh	51	0	0	1	12
Artichoke:					
globe, cooked, 1 large	67	0	0	4	16
Jerusalem, 1, 3 oz. raw	65	0	0	2	15
Asparagus, ⅓ lb.	33	0	0	5	6
Avocado, ½ medium-sized	162	0	16	2	7
Bacon, ¼ lb., cooked and					
drained	183	27	16	10	0
Banana:					
1 medium-sized	105	0	1	1	27
baked (p. 1012), ¼ of					
recipe	259	31	12	1	40
Barley, pearled, light,					
uncooked, 1 cup	686	0	2	22	145
Bass, raw, 6 oz.	194	116	6	32	0

FOOD	Calories	Cholesterol	Fat	Protein	Carbohydrates (grams)
Beans:					
green, cooked, ¾ cup	33	0	0	2	7
kidney, cooked, ½ cup	112	0	0	8	20
lima, cooked, ½ cup	105	0	0	6	20
navy, cooked, ½ cup	129	0	1	8	24
Bean soup (p. 126), 1 cup	186	6	6	7	27
Bean sprouts, raw, ¾ cup	23	0	0	2	5
Beef:					
Corned, cooked, 3 oz., 3 slices	213	83	16	15	0
Corned, hash (p. 238), ¼ of recipe	414	126	32	15	17
Creamed dried (p. 226), ¼ of recipe	324	79	26	13	10
Fat, 1 oz.	256	31	28	0	0
Flanksteak, raw, 3½ oz.	194	52	12	19	0
Hamburger, average fat, broiled, 4 oz. raw	219	68	16	18	0
Heart, 3 oz.	100	119	3	15	2
Rib roast, lean, 3 oz.	209	69	12	23	0
Roast, lean tip round, 3 oz.	164	69	7	24	0
Steak, sirloin, lean, broiled, 3 oz.	179	76	8	26	0
Tenderloin, broiled, 3 oz.	176	71	8	24	0
Pot roast (p. 221), ⅛ of recipe	386	126	23	38	4
Beef broth, 1 cup	24	0	1	1	4
Beef Stew, Old-Fashioned (p. 226), ⅙ of recipe	1,023	166	69	45	56
Beef tongue, boiled, 3 oz.	241	91	18	19	0
Beer, 12 oz.	146	0	0	1	13
Beets, ½ cup, cooked	26	0	0	0	6
Biscuit, Baking Powder (p. 764), 1/16 of recipe	123	1	7	2	13
Blackberries, fresh, ¾ cup	56	0	0	1	14
Blueberries, fresh, ¾ cup	61	0	0	1	15
Bluefish, raw, 7 oz.	248	117	8	40	0
Boston Baked Beans (p. 448), ⅛ of recipe	340	12	12	12	47
Bouillon cube, 1 chicken	9	0	0	1	1
Brandy, 1 oz.	73	0	0	0	0
Bread:					
French, 1 slice, 1 oz.	82	1	1	3	16

FOOD	Calories	Cholesterol	Fat	Protein	Carbohydrates (grams)
Rye, 1 slice, 1 oz.	69	0	0	3	15
White, 1 slice, 1 oz.	77	1	1	2	14
Whole wheat, 1 slice, 1 oz.	69	1	1	3	14
Broccoli: cooked, 1 large stalk or ⅔ cup	30	0	0	3	6
Brown Betty (p. 1006), ⅙ of recipe	349	28	11	4	59
Brussels sprouts, ¾ cup, approx. 8	46	0	0	3	10
Butter: 1 tablespoon	102	31	12	0	0
¼ lb.	814	249	92	1	0
Buttermilk, 1 glass, 8 oz.	98	10	2	8	12
Cabbage:					
chopped, raw, ¾ cup	13	0	0	1	3
cooked, ¾ cup	24	0	0	1	5
Cakes (unfrosted):					
Angel Food (p. 813), 1 slice (1/12 of whole cake)	130	0	0	3	29
Cheese (p. 824), 1 slice (1/12 of whole cake)	354	133	24	7	30
Chocolate Layer, Fudge Layer Cake (p. 796), 1 slice (1/10 of whole cake)	383	66	18	5	53
Pound (p. 800), ¾″ (1/11 of whole cake)	378	142	19	5	48
White, Fresh Coconut Cake (p. 800), 1 slice (1/10 of whole cake)	471	56	26	5	56
Yellow, Lord Baltimore (p. 799), 1 slice (1/10 of whole cake)	300	156	13	5	40
See also Frosting					
Cantaloupe, ½ of 5″ melon	93	0	1	2	22
Caramel, 1 medium	37	0	1	0	7
Carrots, cooked, ¾ cup	53	0	0	1	12
Cashew nuts, dry roasted, 2 oz.	325	0	26	9	19
Catsup, 1 tablespoon	18	0	0	0	4
Cauliflower, cooked, 1 cup	30	0	0	2	6
Caviar, 1 tablespoon	40	94	3	4	1

FOOD	Calories	Cholesterol	Fat	Protein	Carbohydrates (grams)
Celeriac, raw, ½ cup shredded	30	0	0	1	7
Celery:					
Braised (p. 558), ½ of recipe	149	31	12	2	10
Raw, 1 rib	6	0	0	0	1
Cheese:					
American, 1 slice, 1 oz.	106	27	9	6	0
Blue, 1″ cube, 1 oz.	100	21	8	6	1
Camembert, one ⅓-oz. wedge	113	27	9	7	0
Cheddar, 1 slice, 1 oz.	114	30	9	7	0
Cottage, creamed, ½ cup	108	16	5	13	3
Cottage, 1% fat, ½ cup	81	5	1	14	3
Cream, one 3-oz. cake	297	94	30	6	2
Parmesan, 1 tablespoon, grated	23	4	2	2	0
Roquefort, 1″ cube, 1 oz.	105	26	9	6	1
Swiss, 1 slice, 1 oz.	107	26	8	8	1
Cheese Soufflé (p. 491), ¼ of recipe	377	286	29	18	10
Cherries, sweet, fresh, ¼ lb.	75	0	1	1	17
Chicken:					
Pan-fried, 2½ lb., ¼ of chicken serving	510	111	31	37	18
Poached, 3 lb., ½ of chicken serving	308	110	18	35	0
Roasted or broiled, 2½ lb., ¼ of chicken serving	349	126	23	34	0
Roasted, dark meat, 3½ oz.	203	92	10	27	0
Roasted, light meat, 3½ oz.	172	84	4	31	0
Chicken broth or stock, 1 cup	45	0	2	1	6
Chicken Salad (p. 688), ¼ of recipe	598	167	45	42	5
Chicory, or curly endive, 15–20 inner leaves, ¼ lb.	26	0	0	2	5
Chili con Carne (p. 233), ¼ of recipe	535	110	46	26	4
Chocolate:					
bitter, 1 oz.	143	0	15	3	8

FOOD	Calories	Cholesterol	Fat	Protein	Carbohydrates (grams)
candy, made with milk, 1 oz.	147	6	9	2	16
semisweet, 1 oz.	144	0	10	1	16
sweet, 1 oz.	143	0	10	1	17
Chocolate fudge, 1" cube	84	0	3	1	16
Chocolate milk shake, made with 1 tablespoon chocolate syrup, 8 oz. milk, and ½ cup ice cream	365	64	16	11	49
Chocolate Mousse, French (p. 943), 1 serving, ⅛ of recipe	196	142	13	5	17
Chocolate syrup, 2 tablespoons	82	0	0	1	22
Cinnamon Roll (p. 745), 1	113	32	4	3	17
Clam Chowder, Manhattan (p. 140), 1 cup	135	30	5	11	12
Clam Chowder, New England (p. 140), 1 cup	215	54	10	15	16
Clams, raw, 3 oz.	63	29	1	11	2
Cocoa, made with whole milk, 1 cup	125	23	6	6	14
Coconut, shredded, dried, loosely packed, 1 cup sweetened	351	0	24	2	35
Codfish:					
Baked or broiled, 8 oz.	238	125	2	52	0
Cakes (p. 205), 1 cake, ⅛ of recipe	219	65	12	20	8
Creamed (p. 204), 1 serving	557	327	21	79	9
Coffee:					
clear, 1 cup	5	0	0	0	1
with 1 lump sugar, 1 cup	24	0	0	0	6
with 1 tablespoon light cream, 1 cup	34	10	3	1	2
Coleslaw (p. 669), ¼ cup	155	99	7	6	19
Cookie:					
Butter (p. 860), 1 cookie (⅟₆₀ of recipe)	50	15	3	1	5
Brownie (p. 880), 1 (⅟₁₆ of recipe)	210	51	12	3	26

FOOD	Calories	Cholesterol	Fat	Protein	Carbohydrates (grams)
Chocolate (p. 861), 1 (⅙₀ of recipe)	69	4	4	1	8
Chocolate Chip (p. 865), 1 (⅙₀ of recipe)	69	9	4	0	8
Gingersnap, 1	29	3	1	0	6
Macaroon (p. 869), 1 (⅙₀ of recipe)	41	0	1	1	7
Nut, Swedish Almond Wafer, (p. 867), 1 (⅙₀ of recipe)	34	5	3	0	2
Spice, Applesauce Cookie (p. 864), 1 (¼₀ of recipe)	91	12	3	1	14
Corn bread, 1 square, 2″ × 2″	24	4	1	1	4
Corn Chowder (p. 131), 1 cup	176	23	10	5	19
Corn on the cob, 1 medium, 7″ long	93	0	1	3	21
Cornmeal, cooked, ⅔ cup	80	0	0	2	17
Corn syrup, 1 tablespoon	59	0	0	0	15
Crab meat:					
canned, 3 oz.	84	76	1	17	0
fresh, ¼ lb.	116	114	2	23	0
Cracker:					
graham, 1, 2½″ square	27	0	1	1	5
saltine, 1, 2″ square	12	0	0	0	2
Cranberry sauce, 2 tablespoons	52	0	0	0	13
Cream:					
half-and-half, 1 tablespoon	20	6	2	0	1
sour, cultured, 1 tablespoon	31	6	3	0	1
whipping, light, 1 tablespoon	44	17	5	0	0
whipping, heavy, 1 tablespoon	51	20	6	0	0
Cream (or white) sauce, ½ cup	204	48	16	5	12
Cream of wheat, cooked, ¾ cup	100	0	0	3	21
Cucumber, medium	31	0	0	1	7
Custard:					
Baked (p. 940), ⅛ of recipe	150	146	6	6	17

FOOD	Calories	Cholesterol	Fat	Protein	Carbohydrates (grams)
Boiled (p. 939), ½ cup	165	141	6	7	20
Date, dried, 4	91	0	0	1	24
Doughnut, yeast, plain (p. 747), 1, 3¾" diameter	178	24	7	3	26
Duck, Roast (p. 337), 3½-oz. serving	334	83	28	19	0
Dumpling, 1 small, ½ of recipe	124	2	5	2	16
Egg:					
boiled or poached, 1	75	213	5	6	1
fried, 1, with 1 teaspoon fat	108	223	9	6	1
scrambled, 2, with 1 tablespoon butter	251	456	22	13	1
Egg white, 1 raw	17	0	0	4	0
Egg yolk, 1 raw	59	213	5	3	0
Fat:					
lard, 1 tablespoon	116	12	13	0	0
vegetable shortening, 1 tablespoon	113	0	13	0	0
Fig:					
dried, 1 large	59	0	0	1	15
fresh, 3 small	89	0	0	1	23
Fish fillets, 6 oz. serving:					
Flounder, raw	155	82	2	32	0
sautéed or baked, with 2 teaspoons butter	223	102	10	32	0
Frankfurter, 1, 10/1-lb.	145	23	13	5	1
(8/1-lb.)	181	28	17	6	1
French Dressing Vinaigrette (p. 703), 1 tablespoon	96	0	11	0	0
French toast, 1 piece	143	113	5	7	18
Frosting:					
Confectioners', II Frosting (p. 838), for 1 slice (⅒ of recipe)	158	2	7	0	24
Cream Cheese (p. 842), for 1 slice (⅒ of recipe)	91	6	2	1	18
Fudge (p. 840), for 1 slice (⅒ of recipe)	200	14	8	1	34
7-Minute (p. 844), for 1 slice (½ of recipe)	102	0	0	58	25
Gelatin, dry, 1 tablespoon	23	0	0	6	0
Gin, 1 oz.	73	0	0	0	0

FOOD	Calories	Cholesterol	Fat	Protein	Carbohydrates (grams)
Gingerbread (p. 803), 1 piece, ¹⁄₁₆ of recipe	213	42	7	3	36
Gooseberries, ½ cup, raw	33	0	0	1	8
Grapefruit, ½ medium	38	0	0	1	10
Grapefruit juice, unsweetened, 1 cup	93	0	0	1	22
Grapes, green seedless, ½ lb.	161	0	1	2	40
Green pepper, 1 whole	19	0	0	1	4
Griddle Cakes (p. 775), 3 (out of 16)	174	56	6	5	24
Grits, Hominy (p. 434), ¼ of recipe	145	0	0	3	31
Halibut steak, raw, 6 oz.	187	54	4	35	0
Ham:					
Baked (p. 277), medium fat, not glazed, 3 oz.	151	50	8	19	0
Boiled, 2 oz.	82	30	3	12	1
Hamburger—see Beef					
Hard sauce, 1 tablespoon	61	10	4	0	8
Herring, fresh, 3 oz., raw	134	51	8	15	0
Hickory nuts, 2 oz.	373	0	37	7	10
Hollandaise Sauce (p. 388), 1 tablespoon	62	55	7	1	0
Honey, 1 tablespoon	64	0	0	0	17
Honeydew melon, 1 wedge, 2" × 7"	45	0	0	1	12
Horseradish, grated, 1 tablespoon	7	0	0	0	2
Ice cream:					
Commercial, plain, ¾ cup	202	45	11	4	24
French Vanilla (p. 972), ¾ cup	326	196	27	5	18
Philadelphia (p. 973), ¾ cup	486	163	44	2	22
Jam, 1 tablespoon	54	0	0	0	14
Jelly, 1 tablespoon	51	0	0	0	13
Kale, boiled, ¾ cup	31	0	0	2	5
Kidneys, veal, broiled (p. 292), ¼ of recipe	272	413	21	18	1
Kiwi, 1	46	0	0	1	11
Kohlrabi, boiled, ¾ cup, USDA	36	0	0	2	8

FOOD	Calories	Cholesterol	Fat	Protein	Carbohydrates (grams)
Kumquats, 3	36	0	0	1	9
Ladyfingers, 1	40	39	0	1	7
Lamb:					
Irish Stew (p. 260), 1					
serving	472	109	37	26	8
loin chop (boneless),					
broiled, 4 oz.	245	108	11	34	0
roast leg, lean, 3½ oz.	190	88	8	28	0
roast shoulder, lean,					
3½ oz.	202	86	11	25	0
Lard, 1 tablespoon	116	12	13	0	0
Lasagna (p. 465), 1 serving	780	140	48	43	42
Leek, 1	31	0	0	1	7
Lemon, 1 medium-sized	22	0	0	1	12
Lemonade, 1 cup	99	0	0	0	26
Lemon ice, ½ cup	116	0	0	0	30
Lemon juice, 1 tablespoon	3	0	0	0	1
Lime juice, 1 tablespoon	3	0	0	0	1
Liver, Calves' (p. 298),					
sautéed, 1 serving of ¼ lb.	280	374	17	21	10
Liverwurst or liver sausage,					
slices, 1 oz.	92	45	8	4	1
Lobster:					
1 cup	142	104	1	30	2
bisque (p. 137), 1 cup	175	45	11	6	12
whole, 1½ lb., baked or					
broiled with 2					
tablespoons butter	350	170	24	31	2
Macaroni and Cheese (p. 464),					
1 serving	669	96	32	25	69
Mackerel, Atlantic, raw,					
6 oz.	349	119	24	32	0
Mango, 1 large	168	0	0	1	44
Maple syrup, 1 tablespoon	50	0	0	0	13
Margarine, 1 tablespoon	102	0	11	0	0
Marmalade, 1 tablespoon	51	0	0	0	14
Marshmallows, 5	115	0	0	1	29
Mayonnaise, 1 tablespoon	99	8	11	0	0
Meat Loaf (p. 229), 1					
serving	301	126	19	22	8
Milk:					
condensed, sweetened,					
½ cup	491	52	13	12	83

FOOD	Calories	Cholesterol	Fat	Protein	Carbohydrates (grams)
dry, nonfat, 2 tablespoons	30	2	0	3	4
evaporated, ½ cup	169	37	10	9	12
half-and-half, ½ cup	156	44	14	4	5
skim, 1 cup	86	5	0	8	12
2%, 1 cup	122	20	5	8	12
whole fresh, 3.3% fat, 1 cup	149	34	8	8	11
Molasses, light, 1 tablespoon	52	0	0	0	13
Muffin:					
Basic (p. 759), 1	137	31	5	3	19
Bran (p. 762), 1	104	26	3	3	16
English, 1 regular size, commercial	130	not available	1	4	26
Mushrooms:					
fresh, ¼ lb.	28	0	0	2	5
sautéed, 6 oz., in 1 tablespoon fat	144	31	12	4	8
Mussels, ½ pound in shell, raw	59	19	2	8	3
Mustard, 1 tablespoon	12	0	1	1	1
Nectarine, 1	67	0	1	1	16
Noodles, egg, cooked, 1 cup	200	50	2	7	37
Oatmeal, cooked, ¾ cup	109	0	2	5	19
Oil:					
olive, 1 tablespoon	119	0	14	0	0
peanut, 1 tablespoon	119	0	14	0	0
vegetable, 1 tablespoon	119	0	14	0	0
Okra, sliced, ½ cup	19	0	0	1	4
Olive:					
green, 2 small or 1 large	5	0	0	0	0
ripe, 2 small or 1 large	8	0	1	0	0
Onions:					
creamed (p. 582), ¼ cup	197	61	17	3	11
green (scallions), 5 medium	11	0	0	1	3
Onion Soup (p. 132), with cheese, 1 cup	396	34	14	10	34
Orange, 1 average-sized, peeled	69	0	0	1	17
Orange ice, ¾ cup	143	0	0	0	37
Orange juice, 1 cup	112	0	0	2	27
Oysters, raw, 1 cup	174	139	6	18	10

FOOD	Calories	Cholesterol	Fat	Protein	Carbohydrates (grams)
Oyster Stew (p. 139), 1 cup	314	126	26	11	10
Papaya, ½ medium	59	0	0	1	15
Parsley, chopped, 2 tablespoons	2	0	0	0	1
Parsnips, boiled, ¾ cup	95	0	0	2	23
Pasta:					
dry, 4 oz.	421	0	2	14	85
dry noodles (egg), 4 oz.	432	108	5	16	81
fresh (egg), 4 oz.	328	83	3	13	62
Peach, fresh, 5 oz.	46	0	0	75	12
Peanut butter, 2 tablespoons	191	0	16	9	5
Peanuts, 2 oz., oil roasted	329	0	28	15	11
Pear, fresh, 6 oz.	92	0	1	1	24
Pea Soup, Cream of (p. 129), 1 cup	154	24	8	6	15
Peas:					
fresh, boiled, ¾ cup	101	0	0	6	19
split dried, cooked, ¾ cup	173	0	1	12	31
Pecans, 2 oz.	378	0	38	4	10
Pepper, green, 1 medium-sized	19	0	0	1	4
Perch, ocean, raw, 6 oz.	160	71	3	32	0
Persimmon, 1, 8 oz.	236	0	1	1	62
Pickles, cucumber:					
1 large dill	15	0	0	1	3
1 sweet-sour	51	0	0	0	13
Pies:					
Apple (p. 902), ⅛ slice of 9″ pie	492	8	23	4	69
Blueberry (p. 903), ⅛ slice of 9″ pie	473	4	21	5	67
Boston Cream Pie (p. 803), 1/12 of 8″ pie	266	91	9	4	43
Deep-Dish Peach (p. 906), 1 serving	562	56	30	5	72
Lemon Meringue (p. 914), ⅛ slice of 9″ pie	452	114	19	6	66
Mince (p. 910), ⅛ slice of 9″ pie	680	27	33	10	89
Pumpkin (p. 912), ⅛ slice of 9″ pie	397	69	18	8	51

FOOD	Calories	Cholesterol	Fat	Protein	Carbohydrates (grams)
Pineapple, fresh, diced, ¾ cup	57	0	0	0	14
Pineapple juice, unsweetened, 1 cup	140	0	0	0	35
Pizza, Cheese (p. 420), ¼ of 12" pie	406	32	16	13	53
Plums, fresh, 4 oz.	59	0	1	1	14
Popover, 1	85	49	3	3	11
Porgy, raw, 6 oz.	179	—	5	32	0
Pork:					
Chop (Skillet-Fried) (p. 268), 4 oz.	332	70	26	19	4
Roast (p. 265), 3½ oz. lean serving	235	90	13	28	0
Tenderloin (p. 265), 3 oz.	174	87	6	27	0
Potato:					
baked, 1 medium-sized	220	0	0	5	51
boiled, 1 small- to medium-sized	116	0	0	2	27
sweet, baked, 1 medium-sized, 4 oz., ½ cup	112	0	0	2	28
sweet, candied (p. 601), 1 serving	306	31	12	2	49
Potatoes:					
French-Fried (p. 595), 8 pieces	126	0	7	2	16
Hash-Browned (p. 597), 1 serving	260	14	16	3	28
Mashed (p. 594), 1 serving of ½ cup	138	18	6	3	18
Potato salad, ¾ cup	268	128	15	5	21
Prunes, Stewed (p. 1036), ½ cup	113	0	0	1	30
Pudding:					
Bread-and-Butter (p. 948), 1 serving	380	151	17	11	48
Indian (p. 947), 1 serving	257	33	10	5	38
Rice (p. 944), 1 serving	177	20	5	5	30
Tapioca (p. 945), 1 serving	201	123	7	7	28
Pumpkin, 1 cup	42	0	0	2	10

FOOD	Calories	Cholesterol	Fat	Protein	Carbohydrates (grams)
Rabbit:					
Braised (p. 300), 1 serving	590	207	28	70	9
Fried (p. 299), 1 serving	583	197	29	70	6
Radishes, 6 medium	5	0	0	0	1
Raisins, seedless, ½ cup	218	0	0	2	57
Raspberries, red, fresh, ¾ cup	45	0	1	1	11
Rhubarb, Stewed, Sweetened (p. 1038), ¼ cup	114	0	0	1	29
Rice:					
brown, cooked, ⅔ cup	156	0	1	3	33
white, cooked, ⅔ cup	150	0	0	3	33
wild, cooked, ⅔ cup	124	0	0	5	27
Roll:					
Hard (p. 740), 1	68	0	0	2	14
Standard (p. 736), 1	125	8	3	3	21
Rum, light or dark, 1 oz.	64	0	0	0	0
Rutabagas, Cooked (p. 625), ¾ cup	52	0	0	2	12
Salad Greens:					
Bibb, 1 serving, ½ cup	5	0	0	0	1
Boston, 1 serving, ½ cup	5	0	0	0	1
Endive, 1 serving, ½ cup	4	0	0	0	1
Iceberg, 1 serving, ½ cup	5	0	0	0	1
Romaine, 1 serving, ½ cup	4	0	0	0	1
Watercress, 1 serving, ½ cup	2	0	0	0	0
Salami, dry, 1 oz.	119	22	10	6	1
Salmon, Atlantic, raw, 6 oz.	242	94	11	34	0
Salmon, smoked, 3½ oz.	116	23	4	18	0
Sardines, canned, in oil, 3 oz.	177	121	10	21	0
Sauerkraut, ⅔ cup	30	0	0	1	7
Sausage, Homemade (p. 286), ¼ of recipe	512	104	48	17	0
Scallops:					
raw, 5 oz.	125	47	1	24	3
sautéed (p. 188), ¼ of recipe	355	118	24	29	4
Sherbet, ¾ cup	203	10	3	2	44
Shortcake with ½ cup berries and cream, 1 medium-sized biscuit	206	18	12	3	18

OOD	Calories	Cholesterol	Fat	Protein	Carbohydrates (grams)
Shrimp:					
boiled, 6 oz.	168	332	2	36	0
fried (p. 193), ⅙ of recipe	413	267	22	34	18
Snapper, all species, 8 oz.	227	84	3	47	0
Sole—see fish fillets					
Soybeans, dried, cooked, ½ cup	149	0	8	14	9
Spaghetti—see pasta					
Spareribs, Barbecued (p. 368), average-sized, ⅙ of recipe	922	214	72	52	15
Spinach, cooked and chopped, ¾ cup	31	0	0	4	5
Split pea soup, 1 cup	183	18	8	8	20
Squash, Hubbard or winter, cooked (p. 613), ¼ of recipe	140	16	6	1	23
Squash, Summer, Cooked (p. 609), ¼ of recipe	112	27	10	1	5
Starch, cornstarch, etc., 1 tablespoon	29	0	0	0	7
Strawberries, fresh, ¾ cup	34	0	—	0	8
Sugar:					
brown, 1 tablespoon	51	0	0	0	13
confectioners', 1 tablespoon	29	0	0	0	7
granulated, 1 tablespoon	48	0	0	0	12
Sweetbreads, Broiled (p. 293), ¼ lb.	216	334	14	21	1
Swordfish, 6 oz., raw	206	66	7	34	0
Syrup, corn, 1 tablespoon	59	0	0	0	15
Tangerine, 1	37	0	0	1	9
Tartare sauce, 1 tablespoon	76	7	8	0	0
Tea, clear, unsweetened, 1 cup	2	0	0	0	1
Thousand Island Dressing (p. 706), 1 tablespoon	84	0	9	0	1
Tomato, fresh, 1, 5 oz.	27	0	0	1	6
Tomato catsup, 1 tablespoon	18	0	0	0	4
Tomato juice, 1 cup	41	0	0	2	10
Tomato purée, 1 tablespoon	6	0	0	0	2
Tomato soup:					
clear (p. 129), 1 cup	57	0	1	3	13
cream of (p. 130), 1 cup	218	44	14	7	18

FOOD	Calories	Cholesterol	Fat	Protein	Carbohydrates (grams)
Trout, broiled, 4 oz.	171	83	5	30	0
Tuna fish, canned:					
in oil, 3 oz.	168	15	7	25	0
water-packed, ½ cup	131	42	0	30	0
Turkey, roast:					
dark meat, 3½ oz.	184	87	7	28	0
light meat, 3½ oz.	153	68	3	30	0
Turnip greens, cooked, ¾ cup	22	0	0	1	5
Turnips, cooked, ¾ cup	21	0	0	1	6
Veal:					
chop, loin, 1 medium-sized, 6 oz.	227	100	15	26	0
cutlet, sautéed (p. 245), ¼ of recipe	311	139	19	32	0
Vegetable shortening, 1 tablespoon	113	0	13	0	0
Venison, broiled (p. 301), 3½ oz.	588	183	27	33	55
Vermouth, dry, 1 oz.	30	0	0	0	0
Vinaigrette (p. 703), 1 tablespoon	96	0	11	0	0
Vodka, 1 oz.	64	0	0	0	0
Waffles (p. 776), ⅛ of recipe	173	57	8	5	21
Waldorf Salad, (p. 692), ¾ cup	360	16	32	3	21
Walnuts, 2 oz.	364	0	35	8	10
Watermelon, 2 cups	102	0	1	2	23
Welsh Rabbit (p. 497), 1 serving	345	121	24	18	14
Wheat germ, 1 tablespoon	27	0	1	2	4
Whiskey, Bourbon or Scotch, 1 oz.	69	0	0	0	0
White sauce—see Cream sauce					
Whitefish, raw, 5 oz.	190	85	8	27	0
Wine:					
dry, red, 4 oz.	85	0	0	0	2
dry, rosé, 4 oz.	84	0	0	0	2
dry, white, 4 oz.	80	0	0	0	1
sweet or fortified, 4 oz.	184	0	0	0	14
Yams—see Potato, sweet					
Yeast:					
brewer's, 2 teaspoons	15	0	0	2	2
compressed, 1 cake	15	0	0	2	2

FOOD	Calories	Cholesterol	Fat	Protein	Carbohydrates (grams)
Yogurt:					
frozen, based on low-fat yogurt (p. 977), ¾ cup	107	10	3	9	12
fruit-flavored, ½ cup, 4 oz.	116	5	1	5	22
low-fat, ½ cup	71	7	2	6	8
non-fat, ½ cup	64	2	0	7	9
whole milk, ½ cup	69	15	4	4	5
Zucchini, cooked, ¾ cup	22	0	0	1	5

MEASUREMENTS & TEMPERATURES

OTHER EQUIVALENTS USEFUL FOR BAKING

Bread crumbs, 4 sandwich slices

fresh	4 ounces (115 g)	=	2 cups, loosely packed
dry	4 ounces (115 g)	=	¾ cup
Brown sugar	1 pound (450 g)	=	2⅓ cups
Confectioners' sugar	1 pound (450 g)	=	4 cups
Egg whites, U.S. large	1	=	2 tablespoons
	8	=	1 cup
Egg yolks, U.S. large	1	=	1 tablespoon
	16	=	1 cup

Fruits, Nuts, and Vegetables

Fruits, dried and pitted

plumped	1 pound (450 g)	=	2⅔ cups
cooked and puréed	1 pound (450 g)	=	2⅛ cups

Fruits, fresh, such as apples and pears (3 medium-small)

raw and sliced	1 pound (450 g)	=	3 cups
cooked and chopped	1 pound (450 g)	=	1⅔ cups
puréed	1 pound (450 g)	=	1¼ cups
Nuts, chopped	4 ounces (115 g)	=	¾ cup
ground	4 ounces (115 g)	=	1 cup, loosely packed

Carrots and other root vegetables (6 medium)

sliced	1 pound (450 g)	=	3 cups
puréed	1 pound (450 g)	=	1⅓ cups

Onions (3 medium)
    sliced or
    chopped —————1 pound (450 g) = 3 cups
Potatoes (3 small-medium)
    raw, sliced or
    chopped _____1 pound (450 g) = 3 cups
Spinach and other leafy greens (destemmed)
    cooked and
    chopped _____1 pound (450 g) = 1½ cups

Always soften gelatin first in cold liquid, then dissolve in hot. Don't really boil it or you'll reduce its jelling power.

The pasteurized milk we get today spoils before it turns sour. To "sour" pasteurized milk, when needed, add 1 tablespoon white vinegar or lemon juice to 1 cup of milk and let stand at room temperature 10–15 minutes.

A brief blanching in boiling water often facilitates peeling: blanch tomatoes and almonds for 1 minute, fruits like peaches less than a minute—and skins will slip off easily.

Yeast should be dissolved in warm, not hot, water—not more than 105 degrees for cake yeast, 115 for dry—about like a baby's bottle. Test on your wrist if you don't want to bother with a thermometer.

LIQUID AND DRY MEASURE EQUIVALENTS

g = grams (dry measure) kg = kilograms dL = deciliters L = liters

The metric amounts represented here are the nearest equivalents.

a pinch = slightly less than ¼ teaspoon
a dash = a few drops
3 teaspoons = 1 tablespoon
2 tablespoons = 1 ounce = ¼ dL (liquid), 30 g (dry)
1 jigger = 3 tablespoons = 1½ ounces
8 tablespoons = ½ cup = 4 ounces = 1 dL
2 cups = 1 pint = ½ quart = 1 pound* = ½ L (liquid), 450g (dry)*
4 cups = 32 ounces = 2 pints = 1 quart = 1 L
4 quarts = 1 gallon = 3¾ L
8 quarts (dry) = 1 peck = 7¼ kg
4 pecks (dry) = 1 bushel

Dry ingredients measured in cups will vary in weight—see p. 1167 for specifics on flour, sugar, etc.

When substituting cornstarch or arrowroot for flour as a thickener, use only half as much.

To correct a curdled or "broken" hollandaise or mayonnaise sauce, whisk in a teaspoon or two of boiling water, a drop at a time. If that doesn't work, put an egg yolk in a bowl and add the "broken" sauce slowly, beating with a whisk, and in time you'll have a smooth sauce.

An egg that is really stale will float or tip upward in a bowl of water. When cracked open, if the white and yolk cling together, the egg is very fresh. The older it gets, the flatter the yolk becomes and the runnier the white.

BASIC PIE DOUGH FORMULA

For an 8-inch shell	1 cup (140 g) plus 2 tablespoons flour ¼ teaspoon salt	⅓ cup (¾ dL) shortening 2–3 tablespoons cold water
For an 8-inch two-crust pie	2 cups (280 g) flour ½ teaspoon salt	⅔ cup (1½ dL) shortening ⅓ cup (¾ dL) cold water
For a 9-inch pie shell	1½ cups (215 g) flour ¼ teaspoon salt	½ cup (1 dL) shortening 3–4 tablespoons cold water
For a 9-inch two-crust pie	2½ cups (350 g) flour ½ teaspoon salt	¾ cup (1¾ dL) shortening 6–7 tablespoons cold water

---

BUTTER, SHORTENING, CHEESE, AND OTHER SOLID FATS

Spoons and cups		Ounces	Grams
1 tablespoon	⅛ stick	½ ounce	15 grams
2 tablespoons	¼ stick	1 ounce	30 grams
4 tablespoons (¼ cup)	½ stick	2 ounces	60 grams
8 tablespoons (½ cup)	1 stick (¼ pound)	4 ounces	115 grams
16 tablespoons (1 cup)	2 sticks (½ pound)	8 ounces	225 grams
32 tablespoons (2 cups)	4 sticks	16 ounces (1 pound)	450 grams (500 grams = ½ kilogram)

To beat egg whites successfully, always have them at room temperature and use a clean, dry bowl and beaters. A single egg white increases its volume to ½ cup, but 3 egg whites will mount to 2⅔ cups, or 9 times their volume.

FLOUR (UNSIFTED)

Spoons and cups	Ounces	Grams
1 tablespoon	¼ ounce	8.75 grams
¼ cup (4 tablespoons)	1¼ ounces	35 grams
⅓ cup (5 tablespoons)	1½ ounces	45 grams
½ cup	2½ ounces	70 grams
⅔ cup	3¼ ounces	90 grams
¾ cup	3½ ounces	105 grams
1 cup	5 ounces	140 grams
1½ cups	7½ ounces	210 grams
2 cups	10 ounces	280 grams
3½ cups	16 ounces (1 pound)	490 grams

Note: 1 cup sifted flour = 1 cup unsifted flour minus 1½ tablespoons.

To measure flour, scoop the amount required into a metal measuring cup exactly that size and level off excess by sweeping a knife or spatula across the top.

GRANULATED SUGAR

Spoons and cups	Ounces	Grams
1 teaspoon	⅙ ounce	5 grams
1 tablespoon	½ ounce	15 grams
¼ cup (4 tablespoons)	1¾ ounces	60 grams
⅓ cup (5 tablespoons)	2¼ ounces	75 grams
½ cup	3½ ounces	100 grams
⅔ cup	4½ ounces	130 grams
¾ cup	5 ounces	150 grams
1 cup	7 ounces (6¾ ounces)	200 grams
1½ cups	9½ ounces	300 grams
2 cups	13½ ounces	400 grams

Egg yolks should always be "tempered" by mixing them with a little hot liquid before incorporating them into a hot sauce. Unless the sauce is bound by flour, don't let it boil again after the egg yolks have been added or they will curdle.

To prevent white sauce from lumping, it's safer to have the milk hot when you add it to the roux (the flour and butter mixture). Always cook your roux a few minutes before adding liquid.

At altitudes above 3000 feet, lower air pressure causes differences in the boiling point of water and syrups and also affects baking time. Consult government bulletins for details.

TEMPERATURE DEFINITIONS

180°F (85°C)	=	simmering point of water
212°F (100°C)	=	boiling point of water
234°–240°F (115°C)	=	soft-ball stage for syrups
290°–310°F (143°–155°C)	=	hard-crack stage for syrups
320°F (160°C)	=	caramel stage for syrups
220°F (108°C)	=	jellying point for jams and jellies

OVEN HEATS

250°F (120°C)	=	very slow
300°F (150°C)	=	slow
325°F (165°C)	=	moderately slow
350°F (180°C)	=	moderate
375°F (190°C)	=	moderately hot
400°F (205°C)	=	hot
450°–500°F (230°–260°C)	=	very hot

Cream should be well chilled before beating. One cup will double in volume when whipped.

ROASTING TEMPERATURES

Temperatures are most accurately determined by using an instant (microwave) thermometer inserted in the meat where indicated and withdrawn to take a reading.

BEEF in the center not touching the bone
  130°F (54°C) rare
  160°F (71°C) medium
  180°F (82°C) well done

LAMB, in the center not touching the bone
140°F (60°C)pink
145°F (63°C) medium-rare
165°F (74°C)well done

PORK AND VEAL, in the center not touching the bone
160°F (71°C)

POULTRY, chicken, in the breast, 170°F (77°C)
chicken, in the thigh, 185°F (85°C)
duck, in the thigh, 180°F (82°C)

INDEX

ABOUT THE AUTHOR

Marion Cunningham was born in southern California and now lives in Walnut Creek. She was responsible for the complete revision of *The Fannie Farmer Cookbook* and is the author of *The Fannie Farmer Baking Book* and *The Breakfast Book*. She travels frequently throughout the country giving cooking demonstrations, has contributed articles to *Bon Appétit*, *Food & Wine*, and *Gourmet* magazines, and writes a column for the *San Francisco Chronicle* and the *Los Angeles Times*. She has also been a consultant to a number of well-known west coast restaurants.